Best Books for Children, Supplement to the Seventh Edition

Best Books for Children, Supplement to the Seventh Edition

Preschool through Grade 6

John T. Gillespie
Catherine Barr

LIBRARIES UNLIMITED

UNLIMITED

A Member of the Greenwood Publishing Group

Westport, Connecticut • London

British Library Cataloguing in Publication Data is available.

ISBN: 1-59158-082-X

First published in 2003

Libraries Unlimited, 88 Post Road West, Westport, CT 06881
A Member of the Greenwood Publishing Group, Inc.
www.lu.com

The paper used in this book complies with the
Permanent Paper Standard issued by the National
Information Standards Organization (Z39.48-1984).

10 9 8 7 6 5 4 3 2 1

Contents

Biography

The Arts and Language

History and Geography

Social Institutions and Issues

Personal Development

Recreation

Major Subjects Arranged Alphabetically

Preface

Since the publication of the first edition of *Best Books for Children* (Bowker, 1978), we have adhered to the same publication schedule — a new edition every four years. Many people have suggested that the book's usefulness would increase if a "between-editions" supplement were published. This publication, a supplement to the seventh edition (2002), is the answer to these suggestions.

This supplement covers a two-year period. Coverage of reviewing journals in the main volume ended with the March 2001 issues; the supplement continues this coverage from April 2001 through March 2003. There are 6,112 titles listed in this supplement; of these, 5,682 are individually numbered entries and 430 are cited within the annotations.

Those familiar with the seventh edition of *Best Books for Children* will notice that an identical topical arrangement has been used in the main body of the supplement and that the same subject headings appear in the subject/grade level index. As well, the same criteria for selecting entries and the same methods of presentation have been used.

A number of sources were used to compile this bibliography, but reviews in five journals were used most extensively. They were: *Booklist* (BL), *Bulletin of the Center for Children's Books* (BCCB), *Horn Book* (HB), *Horn Book Guide* (HBG), and *School Library Journal* (SLJ). Usually at least two recommendations were required from these or other sources for a title to be considered for listing. However, there were exceptions to this rule, particularly with series books where only a single review could be located. If that review was positive, then the book became a candidate for inclusion. To ensure that quality standards were being upheld, particularly with series books, many of the titles were examined and evaluated by the editors using copies supplied by the publisher.

A note or two about the placement of books under various topical headings. The "Imaginative Stories" section in the Books for Younger Readers" area is divided into two categories: "Fantasies" and "Imaginary Animals." The first contains both books that depict humans, usually children, in fanciful, unrealistic situations and books that include mythological beasts. The "Imaginary Animals" category includes stories about anthropomorphized beasts in which animals engage in human activities (such as pigs going to school).

The Books for Younger Readers section ends with a listing of "Books for Beginning Readers." This area contains books of fiction easy enough to be read by beginning readers. Nonfiction beginning readers are integrated into the appropriate subject area with mention in the annotation that the work is suitable for beginning readers. Interactive books, like pop-ups, are integrated into appropriate sections with a mention of their format in the annotation. Beginning chapter books are found in the Fiction for Older Readers area with an indication in their annotations that they are easily read. In the fiction section labeled "Ethnic Groups," only those novels in which ethnicity is the central theme are included. Similarly in the nonfiction Biography section, under "African Americans" for example, only those individuals who have been associated primarily with race-related activities are included. Martin Luther King, Jr., is listed there, but a life story of Magic Johnson would be in sports biographies.

Some types of books have been omitted from this bibliography. These include reference books such as dictionaries and encyclopedias and professional books such as other bibliographies or selection aids. A feature retained from the seventh edition is an introductory listing of "Major Subjects Arranged Alphabetically." This special list provides both the range of entry numbers and page numbers for the largest subject areas covered in the volume.

As in previous editions, titles in the main section of the book are assigned an entry number. The entry contains the following information where applicable: (1) author or editor; (2) title; (3) suitable grade levels; (4) adapter or translator; (5) indication of illustrations or illustrator's name; (6) series title; (7) date of publication; (8) publisher and price of hardbound edition (LB=library binding); (9) ISBN of hardbound edition; (10) paperback publisher (if no publisher is listed, it is the same as the hardbound edition) and price; (11) ISBN of paperback edition; (12) annotation; (13) review citations; (14) Dewey Decimal number.

This supplement contains three indexes: author/illustrator, book title, and subject/grade level. The subject/grade level index includes hundreds of subject headings. Within each subject, entries are listed according to grade-level suitability. The following codes are used to give approximate grade levels:

(P) (Primary) preschool through grade 3
(PI) (Primary-Intermediate) grades 2 through 4
(I) (Intermediate) grades 4 through 6
(IJ) (Intermediate-Junior High) grades 5 through 8 or higher
(All) (All readers) preschool through grade 8 or higher

More exact grade-level suitabilities are given in parenthesis for each book in the main entry.

To facilitate quick reference, all listings in the indexes refer the user to an entry number, not a page number.

It is hoped that this bibliography will be used with the parent volume in four different ways: (1) as a tool to evaluate collections; (2) as a book selection tool; (3) as an aid to giving reading guidance to children; and (4) as a base for the preparation of bibliographies and reading lists.

With this supplement, I am happy to announce a new coauthor/editor, Catherine Barr. Ms. Barr has been involved in the production of previous editions of *Best Books for Children* as well as many, many other publications. We welcome her expertise in the field, as well as her fine organizational and administrative talents. Many other people should be thanked for helping in the preparation of this bibliography. In particular, let me single out our computer genius Julie Miller. Thank you all.

John Gillespie

Literature

Books for Younger Readers

Alphabet, Concept, and Counting Books

Alphabet Books

1 Bunting, Eve. *Girls A to Z* (K–3). Illus. by Suzanne Bloom. 2002, Boyds Mills $15.95 (1-56397-147-X). 32pp. An alphabet book filled with girls pretending to be grown-ups with interesting jobs (such as astronauts and gondoliers). (Rev: BL 9/15/02; HBG 3/03; SLJ 10/02)

2 Capucilli, Alyssa Satin. *Mrs. McTats and Her Houseful of Cats* (PS–1). Illus. by Joan Rankin. 2001, Simon & Schuster $16.00 (0-689-83185-4). 32pp. Mrs. McTats adds alphabetically named stray cats (and one dog) to her household in this nicely illustrated and humorous book that teaches numbers as well. (Rev: BL 9/1/01; HBG 10/01; SLJ 8/01)

3 Catalanotto, Peter. *Matthew A.B.C.* (PS–2). Illus. 2002, Simon & Schuster $14.95 (0-689-84582-0). 32pp. There is a Matthew for every letter of the alphabet in Mrs. Tuttle's class, and each boy has a special characteristic to match his letter. (Rev: BL 7/02; HB 7–8/02; HBG 10/02; SLJ 6/02)

4 Cheney, Lynne. *America: A Patriotic Primer* (2–4). 2002, Simon & Schuster $16.95 (0-689-85192-8). 40pp. The wife of the vice president presents an alphabet book for older children that outlines the virtues of America's democracy. (Rev: BCCB 3/02; BL 6/1–15/02; HBG 3/03; SLJ 7/02) [973]

5 Chesworth, Michael. *Alphaboat* (2–4). Illus. 2002, Farrar $16.00 (0-374-30244-8). 32pp. Spirited rhyming wordplay and cartoon illustrations take the crew of the Alphaboat on a lively journey in search of lost treasure. (Rev: BL 10/15/02; SLJ 9/02)

6 Cline-Ransome, Lesa. *Quilt Alphabet* (PS–1). Illus. by James E. Ransome. 2001, Holiday $17.95 (0-8234-1453-1). 32pp. In this alphabet picture book, the letters are incorporated into quilt squares

and accompanied by riddles. (Rev: BL 9/1/01; HBG 3/02; SLJ 11/01) [811]

7 Dodd, Emma. *Dog's ABC: A Silly Story About the Alphabet* (PS–1). Illus. by author. 2002, Dutton $15.99 (0-525-46837-4). 32pp. Dog's day takes him through the alphabet with a series of events, each of which starts with a different letter. (Rev: BL 2/1/02; HBG 10/02; SLJ 2/02)

8 Edwards, Wallace. *Alphabeasts* (PS–K). Illus. 2002, Kids Can $15.95 (1-55337-386-3). 32pp. Rhyming couplets caption lavish, full-page illustrations of animals from alligator to zebra. (Rev: BL 11/1/02; HBG 3/03; SLJ 12/02)

9 Faulkenberry, Lauren. *What Do Animals Do on the Weekend? Adventures from A to Z* (K–3). Illus. by author. 2002, Novello Festival $17.95 (0-9708972-4-3). An alliterative approach to animal activities, where kangaroos kayak and penguins picnic, that also conveys factual information. (Rev: SLJ 10/02)

10 Fleming, Denise. *Alphabet Under Construction* (PS–2). Illus. 2002, Holt $16.95 (0-8050-6848-1). 32pp. An industrious mouse assembles an alphabet using actions that start with each letter. (Rev: BCCB 10/02; BL 8/02; HB 9–10/02; HBG 3/03; SLJ 9/02)

11 Frampton, David. *My Beastie Book of ABC: Rhymes and Woodcuts* (PS–3). Illus. by author. 2002, HarperCollins LB $15.89 (0-06-028824-8). Animals from A to Z are introduced with a letter, rhyme, and illustration. (Rev: BCCB 9/02; HBG 10/02; SLJ 5/02)

12 Haas, Jessie. *Appaloosa Zebra: A Horse Lover's Alphabet* (PS–3). Illus. by Margot Apple. 2002, HarperCollins LB $15.89 (0-688-17881-2). 40pp. This informative alphabet book for girls who love horses features a different breed for almost every letter. (Rev: BL 1/1–15/02; HBG 10/02; SLJ 2/02)

13 Hopkins, Lee Bennett. *Alphathoughts: Alphabet Poems* (2–6). Illus. by Marla Baggetta. 2003, Boyds Mills $15.95 (1-56397-979-9). An alphabet book that can be used on several levels with brief verses that describe the chosen words. (Rev: SLJ 3/03)

14 Howell, Theresa. *A Is for Airplane / A Es para Avión* (PS–2). Illus. by David Brooks. 2003, Rising Moon $6.95 (0-87358-831-2). A bilingual alphabet book with bright illustrations. (Rev: SLJ 3/03)

15 Howell, Will C. *Zoo Flakes ABC* (PS–2). Illus. 2002, Walker LB $16.85 (0-8027-8827-0). 32pp. Clever cut-paper snowflakes depict the alphabet in animal forms — O is for Octopus, for example — and children will enjoy finding the elusive animals hidden in each flake. Also includes directions on making snowflake cutouts. (Rev: BL 12/1/02; HBG 3/03; SLJ 3/03) [736]

16 Inkpen, Mick. *Kipper's A to Z: An Alphabet Adventure* (PS–2). Illus. 2001, Harcourt $16.95 (0-15-202594-4). 56pp. Arnold the pig and Kipper the dog find animals, sounds, and actions that run from A to Z. (Rev: BL 5/15/01; HBG 10/01; SLJ 6/01*)

17 Kalman, Maira. *What Pete Ate from A to Z* (1–3). Illus. 2001, Putnam $15.99 (0-399-23362-8). 40pp. Pete the dog eats everything in sight — all the way through the alphabet. (Rev: BL 9/1/01; HB 1–2/02; HBG 3/02; SLJ 9/01*)

18 Leopold, Niki Clark. *K Is for Kitten* (PS–2). Illus. by Susan Jeffers. 2002, Putnam $15.99 (0-399-23563-9). 32pp. An alphabet book about a girl and her kitten, with lovely artwork. (Rev: BL 9/15/02; HBG 3/03; SLJ 9/02) [811.6]

19 Marzollo, Jean. *Baby's Alphabet* (PS). Photos by Nancy Sheehan. 2002, Millbrook $9.95 (0-7613-1643-4). Babies from a variety of backgrounds are shown from "All gone!" to "Zzzz." (Rev: HBG 3/03; SLJ 11/02)

20 Melmed, Laura Krauss. *Capital! Washington, D.C. from A to Z* (K–3). Illus. by Frane Lessac. 2003, HarperCollins LB $16.89 (0-688-17562-7). 48pp. Each letter of the alphabet introduces a different monument, museum, or other feature of Washington, D.C., in this book with folk-art-like illustrations. (Rev: BL 2/1/03; SLJ 1/03) [975.3]

21 Milich, Zoran. *The City ABC Book* (PS–2). Illus. 2001, Kids Can $15.95 (1-55074-942-0). 32pp. A Canadian photojournalist cleverly uses pictures of city structures to introduce the letters of the alphabet. (Rev: BCCB 3/01; BL 4/15/01; HB 7–8/01; HBG 10/01; SLJ 6/01)

22 Miranda, Anne. *Alphabet Fiesta: An English/ Spanish Alphabet Story* (PS–2). Illus. 2001, Turtle $18.95 (1-890515-29-9); paper $12.95 (1-890515-30-2). 54pp. The letters of the alphabet are introduced using Spanish and English words in this story of a zebra's birthday party. (Rev: BL 9/15/01; HBG 3/02; SLJ 1/02)

23 Moxley, Sheila. *ABCD: An Alphabet Book of Cats and Dogs* (PS–1). Illus. 2001, Little, Brown $14.95 (0-316-59240-4). 32pp. Inventive illustrations and lots of alliteration are used in this enjoyable alphabet book that features different kinds of dogs and cats. (Rev: BL 4/15/01; HBG 10/01; SLJ 5/01)

24 Murphy, Mary. *The Alphabet Keeper* (1–3). Illus. by author. 2003, Knopf LB $16.99 (0-375-92347-0). The letters escape the Alphabet Keeper and lead her

a merry chase as they rearrange themselves to suit the circumstances. (Rev: BCCB 3/03; SLJ 3/03)

25 *Museum ABC: The Metropolitan Museum of Art* (K–3). Illus. 2002, Little, Brown $16.95 (0-316-07170-6). 60pp. The artwork is stunning in this simple alphabet book from the Metropolitan Museum of Art. (Rev: BL 11/15/02; HBG 3/03; SLJ 9/02) [708.147]

26 Pallotta, Jerry. *The Skull Alphabet Book* (2–5). Illus. by Ralph Masiello. 2002, Charlesbridge $16.95 (0-88106-914-0); paper $7.95 (0-88106-915-9). 32pp. This unusual and challenging book features paintings of animal skulls from anteater to zebra, giving subtle verbal and visual clues to the identity of each animal. (Rev: BL 9/1/02; HBG 3/03; SLJ 7/02) [573.7]

27 Rogers, Jacqueline. *Kindergarten ABC* (PS–K). Illus. 2002, Scholastic $10.95 (0-439-36837-5). 40pp. This alphabet book features a multiracial kindergarten class performing activities and learning words that start with different letters. (Rev: BL 8/02; HBG 3/03; SLJ 10/02)

28 Rumford, James. *There's a Monster in the Alphabet* (1–4). Illus. 2002, Houghton $16.00 (0-618-22140-9). 40pp. An imaginative and complex alphabet book that looks at the origins of the letters, incorporating mythology and the Phoenician alphabet, with attractive Grecian-style illustrations. (Rev: BL 12/1/02; SLJ 10/02) [398.2]

29 Schafer, Kevin. *Penguins ABC* (PS–K). Photos by author. 2002, NorthWord $14.95 (1-55971-831-5). An alphabet book that will please penguin lovers. (Rev: SLJ 1/03)

30 Schnur, Steven. *Winter: An Alphabet Acrostic* (PS–2). Illus. by Leslie Evans. 2002, Clarion $15.00 (0-618-02374-7). 32pp. Poetic acrostics for each letter of the alphabet are included in this beautifully illustrated follow-up to *Autumn* (1997), *Spring* (1999), and *Summer* (2001). (Rev: BCCB 11/02; BL 12/15/02; HBG 3/03; SLJ 11/02) [508.2]

31 Shahan, Sherry. *The Jazzy Alphabet* (K–3). Illus. by Mary Thelen. 2002, Philomel $15.99 (0-399-23453-5). 32pp. A bouncy journey from Abazaba to Zoot that is enhanced by vibrant illustrations. (Rev: BL 6/1–15/02; HBG 10/02; SLJ 7/02)

32 Sneed, Brad. *Picture a Letter* (PS–3). Illus. 2002, Penguin Putnam $15.99 (0-8037-2613-9). 32pp. This imaginative alphabet book with captivating artwork will catch the attention of preschoolers and beginning readers alike. (Rev: BL 8/02; HBG 10/02; SLJ 6/02) [420.1]

33 Teyssedre, Fabienne. *Joseph Wants to Read* (PS–K). Illus. by author. 2001, Dutton $10.99 (0-525-46692-4). 40pp. Little monkey Joseph's friends all band together to help him learn his letters over the summer. (Rev: HBG 3/02; SLJ 9/01)

34 Wisnewski, Andrea. *A Cottage Garden Alphabet* (2–4). Illus. 2003, Godine $18.95 (1-56792-229-5). 64pp. Beautiful cut-paper illustrations of a garden's bounty accompany each letter of the alphabet. (Rev: BL 2/15/03) [635]

35 Wood, Audrey. *Alphabet Adventure* (PS–2). Illus. by Bruce Wood. 2001, Scholastic $15.95 (0-439-

08069-X). 40pp. The 26 letters are on their way to teach a child the alphabet when they encounter some difficulties in this inventive book illustrated with glowing, computer-generated graphics. (Rev: BL 9/1/01; HBG 3/02; SLJ 9/01)

Concept Books

GENERAL

36 Aber, Linda Williams. *Grandma's Button Box* (K–1). Illus. by Page Eastburn O'Rourke. 2002, Kane paper $4.95 (1-57565-110-6). 32pp. When a young girl drops her grandmother's button box, she and her cousins try different ways of sorting them out in this simple concept book. (Rev: BL 4/15/02)

37 Asquith, Ros. *Babies* (PS). Illus. by Sam Williams. 2003, Simon & Schuster $12.95 (0-689-85501-X). 24pp. A book of happy, busy babies, with a mirror on the last page so readers can view the best baby of all. (Rev: BCCB 10/02; BL 2/1/03; SLJ 3/03)

38 Beeke, Tiphanie. *Roar Like a Lion! A First Book About Sounds* (PS). Illus. 2001, Sterling $7.95 (1-86233-143-X). 16pp. This fun-filled book about a mouse trying to find friends will have preschoolers making all kinds of jungle noises. (Rev: BL 3/1/02)

39 Bernhard, Durga. *To and Fro, Fast and Slow* (PS–2). Illus. 2001, Walker LB $16.85 (0-8027-8783-5). 32pp. This clever, well-illustrated concept book uses a girl's visits to her mother's country home and her father's city apartment to show opposites. (Rev: BL 11/1/01; HBG 3/02; SLJ 9/01)

40 Burton, Jane. *My Kitten Friends* (PS). Illus. 2002, Simon & Schuster $5.99 (0-689-84767-X). 14pp. A concept board book that uses delightful pictures of kittens to illustrate behavior. Also use *My Puppy Friends* (2002). (Rev: BL 3/1/02)

41 Cauley, Lorinda Bryan. *What Do You Know!* (PS–3). Illus. 2001, Putnam $15.99 (0-399-23573-6). 32pp. Puzzle pictures test children's understanding of colors, shapes, opposites, numbers, and letters. (Rev: BL 7/01; HBG 10/01; SLJ 6/01)

42 Deegan, Kim. *My First Book of Opposites* (PS). Illus. 2002, Bloomsbury $7.95 (1-58234-756-5). 24pp. A sparkling introduction to opposites for preschoolers. (Rev: BL 8/02; SLJ 11/02) [428.1]

43 Elgar, Rebecca. *Jack and Annie's Story Word Book* (PS–K). Illus. by author. 2002, Kingfisher $12.95 (0-7534-5560-9). Words and concepts are introduced as two animal friends get up and set off for nursery school. (Rev: HBG 3/03; SLJ 2/03)

44 Ellwand, David. *Clap Your Hands: An Action Book* (PS). Photos by author. 2002, Handprint $9.95 (1-929766-50-5). An oversized board book in which teddy bears stamp feet, touch toes, and so forth to the traditional song. (Rev: SLJ 7/02)

45 Falconer, Ian. *Olivia's Opposites* (PS). Illus. 2002, Simon & Schuster $6.99 (0-689-85088-3). 12pp. A simple board book featuring Olivia the pig that demonstrates the concept of opposites. (Rev: BL 7/02; HBG 10/02; SLJ 6/02)

46 Gabriel, Nat. *Sam's Sneaker Squares* (1–2). Illus. by Ron Fritz. 2002, Kane paper $4.95 (1-57565-114-9). 32pp. In this concept book, Sam learns

about measurements to determine the cost of mowing lawns. (Rev: BL 4/15/02)

47 Herman, Gail. *Bad Luck Brad* (1–2). Illus. by Stephanie Roth. Series: Math Matters. 2002, Kane paper $4.95 (1-57565-112-2). 32pp. The concept of probability is explored when a series of misfortunes occur to Brad on a single day. (Rev: BL 5/1/02)

48 Hunter, Tom. *Build It Up and Knock It Down* (PS). Illus. by James Yang. Series: Harper Growing Tree. 2002, HarperCollins $9.95 (0-694-01568-7). 24pp. Children will learn about opposites as they watch two toddlers become friends in this colorful concept book. (Rev: BCCB 5/02; BL 8/02; HBG 10/02)

49 Jocelyn, Marthe. *A Day with Nellie* (PS). Illus. by author. 2002, Tundra $15.95 (0-88776-600-5). 24pp. Numbers, colors, the alphabet, and other concepts are introduced as readers follow preschooler Nellie through the activities of her ordinary day. (Rev: BL 12/1/02; HBG 3/03; SLJ 1/03)

50 Kassirer, Sue. *What's Next, Nina?* (1–3). Illus. by Page Eastburn O'Rourke. Series: Math Matters. 2001, Kane paper $4.95 (1-57565-106-8). 32pp. Nina must reconstruct a broken necklace of beads in this story that subtly but effectively introduces the concept of patterns. (Rev: SLJ 2/02)

51 Kroll, Steven. *That Makes Me Mad!* (PS–1). Illus. by Christine Davenier. 2002, North-South LB $16.50 (1-58717-184-8). A newly illustrated edition of the 1976 story about Nina and everything that makes her mad. (Rev: HBG 3/03; SLJ 8/02)

52 Milgrim, David. *My Friend Lucky* (PS–K). Illus. 2002, Simon & Schuster $12.00 (0-689-84253-8). 32pp. Through the everyday adventures of a boy and his dog, opposites such as wet and dry are explained. (Rev: BL 4/15/02; HBG 10/02; SLJ 2/02)

53 Miller, David. *Just Like You and Me* (PS–1). Illus. 2001, Dial $15.99 (0-8037-2586-8). 32pp. Effective illustrations present animals and humans in shared behaviors — dancing, showing off, racing, blending in. (Rev: BCCB 3/01; BL 5/1/01; HBG 10/01; SLJ 5/01) [156]

54 Minters, Frances. *Too Big, Too Small, Just Right* (PS–1). Illus. by Janie Bynum. 2001, Harcourt $13.00 (0-15-202157-4). 32pp. Opposites are introduced in clear examples and amusing illustrations. (Rev: BL 5/1/01; HBG 10/01; SLJ 4/01)

55 Murphy, Chuck. *Slide 'n Seek: Opposites* (PS–K). Illus. Series: Slide 'n Seek. 2001, Simon & Schuster $5.99 (0-689-84476-X). 12pp. Pull-tabs are used effectively to illustrate opposites in this small board book. (Rev: BL 12/15/01) [513]

56 Parr, Todd. *The Daddy Book* (PS–K). Illus. 2002, Little, Brown $14.95 (0-316-60799-1). 32pp. A bright, simple book that points out the differences, and the similarities, between fathers. Also use the companion volume *The Mommy Book* (2002). (Rev: BL 3/15/02; HBG 10/02; SLJ 5/02)

57 Payne, Nina. *Four in All* (PS–3). Illus. by Adam Payne. 2001, Front Street $15.95 (1-886910-16-2). 32pp. A girl takes an imaginary journey in this richly illustrated, captivating verse for younger readers that uses four-word lines to present items that come in fours (such as north, east, south, and west) and is wonderfully illustrated by the author's son. (Rev: BCCB 12/01; BL 1/1–15/02; HBG 3/02; SLJ 12/01*)

58 Penner, Lucille Recht. *X Marks the Spot!* (1–2). Illus. by Jerry Smath. 2002, Kane paper $4.95 (1-57565-111-4). 32pp. Brothers Leo and Jake learn to read charts to find treasures in their new hometown in this clever concept book. (Rev: BL 4/15/02)

59 Pollard, Nik. *The Tide* (PS–1). Illus. by author. 2002, Millbrook LB $22.90 (0-7613-2467-4). Rhythmic text and brightly colored illustrations convey the rising and falling tide and the sounds of the ocean. (Rev: HBG 10/02; SLJ 5/02)

60 Rotner, Shelley. *Parts* (PS–1). Illus. 2001, Walker LB $17.85 (0-8027-8754-1). 32pp. Close-up shots of parts of everyday objects are accompanied by rhymes that give additional clues to the whole object that is revealed on the next page. (Rev: BCCB 6/01; BL 6/1–15/01; HBG 10/01; SLJ 5/01)

61 Sayre, April Pulley. *Shadows* (PS–1). Illus. by Harvey Stevenson. 2002, Holt $16.95 (0-8050-6059-6). 32pp. In this colorful picture book, a small boy and girl go to the seashore in search of shadows and find that everything has one. (Rev: BL 4/15/02; HBG 10/02; SLJ 6/02)

62 Schaefer, Lola M. *What's Up, What's Down?* (PS–2). Illus. by Barbara Bash. 2002, HarperCollins $15.99 (0-06-029757-3). 32pp. A fascinating and innovative approach that involves turning the book sideways and following arrows up and down to see the world from the point of view of various plants and animals. (Rev: BL 12/1/02; HBG 3/03; SLJ 1/03) [500]

63 Spicer, Maggee, and Richard Thompson. *We'll All Go Flying* (PS–K). Illus. by Kim LaFave. 2002, Fitzhenry & Whiteside $16.95 (1-55041-698-7). Colors, shapes, sounds, and animals are all presented from the platform of a hot-air balloon in this counting book with movable flaps. (Rev: SLJ 12/02)

64 Spurr, Elizabeth. *Farm Life* (PS–1). Illus. by Steve Bjorkman. 2003, Holiday $16.95 (0-8234-1777-8). 32pp. Basic colors and numbers one to 10 are taught by exploring the buildings on a farm. (Rev: BL 3/15/03)

65 Staake, Bob. *My Little Opposites Book* (PS). Illus. 2001, Simon & Schuster $4.99 (0-689-83487-X). 14pp. An appealing board book that uses humans and animals to introduce opposites! (Rev: BL 7/01)

66 Steig, William. *Which Would You Rather Be?* (PS–2). Illus. by Harry Bliss. 2002, HarperCollins LB $15.89 (0-06-029654-2). 32pp. A boy and girl are given a series of choices about what they'd rather be (a dog or a cat; an elbow or a knee?). (Rev: BL 8/02; HBG 10/02; SLJ 6/02)

67 Walsh, Melanie. *My Beak, Your Beak* (PS). Illus. 2002, Houghton $15.00 (0-618-15079-X). 32pp. Bright, simple illustrations complement text that finds differences and similarities between a host of animals in this book for very young readers. Also use *My Nose, Your Nose* (2002), which focuses on children. (Rev: BL 12/15/02; HBG 3/03; SLJ 10/02)

COLORS

68 Brown, Margaret Wise. *My World of Color* (PS–K). Illus. by Loretta Krupinski. 2002, Hyperion LB $15.98 (0-7868-2519-7). 32pp. Two mouse artists introduce the colors of the rainbow plus white, black, brown, pink, and gray in a series of double-page spreads each of which contains a 4-line rhyme. (Rev: BL 5/1/02; HBG 10/02; SLJ 6/02)

69 Crowther, Robert. *Colors* (PS–K). Illus. by author. 2001, Candlewick $12.99 (0-7636-1404-1). Words on movable tabs are paired with bright double-page illustrations to introduce colors. (Rev: SLJ 7/01)

70 Edwards, Pamela Duncan. *Warthogs Paint: A Messy Color Book* (PS–K). Illus. by Henry Cole. 2001, Hyperion $14.99 (0-7868-0470-X). 32pp. When the warthogs decide to paint the kitchen, the primary colors soon get mixed up. (Rev: BL 6/1–15/01; HBG 3/02; SLJ 8/01)

71 Fox, Christyan, and Diane Fox. *What Color Is That, PiggyWiggy?* (PS–K). Illus. 2001, Handprint $5.95 (1-929766-17-3). 20pp. In this book about colors, PiggyWiggy dons articles of clothing of different hues until he becomes a perfect circus clown. (Rev: BL 4/1/01; SLJ 8/01)

72 Gunzi, Christiane. *My Very First Look at Colors* (PS–K). Illus. by Steve Gorton. Series: My Very First Look. 2001, Two-Can $8.95 (1-58728-236-4); paper $5.95 (1-58728-276-3). 24pp. A concept book that uses photographs of everyday objects to teach preschoolers about colors. (Rev: BL 2/15/02; HBG 10/02; SLJ 2/02) [535.6]

73 Harrison, Carlos. *Ruben's Rainbow / El Arco Iris de Ruben* (K–2). Illus. by Grizelle Paz. 2001, Globo Libros $15.95 (0-9706953-0-6). Ruben tumbles from a world of black and white into a world full of color in this bilingual text accompanied by a CD. (Rev: SLJ 1/02)

74 Hissey, Jane. *Old Bear's Surprise Painting* (PS–1). Illus. by author. 2001, Putnam $15.99 (0-399-23709-7). 40pp. In a book that introduces children to colors and patterns, Old Bear and his friends discover that they can create a wonderful painting if they work together. (Rev: BL 11/15/01; HBG 3/02; SLJ 10/01)

75 Holm, Sharon Lane. *Zoe's Hats: A Book of Colors and Patterns* (PS–1). Illus. 2003, Boyds Mills $13.95 (1-59078-042-6). 32pp. Zoe has fun trying on all manner of hats in this simple book for the very young. (Rev: BL 2/1/03; SLJ 2/03)

76 Horacek, Petr. *Strawberries Are Red* (PS). Illus. by author. 2001, Candlewick $4.99 (0-7636-1461-0). Fruit and colors are introduced on brightly illustrated double-page spreads. Also use *What Is Black and White?* (2001). (Rev: SLJ 8/01)

77 Pinkney, Sandra L. *A Rainbow All Around Me* (PS–1). Illus. by Myles C. Pinkney. 2002, Scholastic $14.95 (0-439-30928-X). 40pp. Arresting photographs and simple text introduce colors and convey multicultural awareness. (Rev: BL 2/1/02; HBG 10/02; SLJ 3/02)

78 Priceman, Marjorie. *It's Me, Marva!* (2–4). Illus. 2001, Knopf LB $16.85 (0-679-98993-5). 32pp.

Marva is an enthusiastic young inventor who splashes a lot of color around. (Rev: BL 8/01; HB 7–8/01; HBG 10/01; SLJ 7/01)

79 Rodrigue, George. *Why Is Blue Dog Blue?* (PS–3). Illus. 2002, Stewart, Tabori & Chang $16.95 (1-58479-162-4). 40pp. The artist explains why he paints his dog different colors depending on the situation. (Rev: BL 6/1–15/02; HBG 10/02)

80 Staake, Bob. *My Little Color Book* (PS). Illus. 2001, Simon & Schuster $4.99 (0-689-83486-1). 14pp. An appealing board book that uses animals to introduce colors. (Rev: BL 7/01)

81 Swinburne, Stephen R. *What Color Is Nature?* (PS–K). Illus. 2002, Boyds Mills $15.95 (1-56397-967-5); paper $8.95 (1-59078-008-6). 32pp. Using bright photographs of children, animals, and plants, different colors are introduced. (Rev: BL 6/1–15/02; HBG 10/02; SLJ check)

82 Thompson, Richard, and Maggee Spicer. *We'll All Go Sailing* (PS–1). Illus. by Kim La Fave. 2001, Fitzhenry & Whiteside $16.95 (1-55041-662-6). 48pp. A concept book that introduces colors along with a variety of sea creatures. (Rev: BL 5/15/01; SLJ 7/01) [591.77]

83 Thong, Roseanne. *Red Is a Dragon: A Book of Colors* (PS–2). Illus. by Grace Lin. 2001, Chronicle $18.95 (0-8118-3177-9). 180pp. This concept book, a companion to *A Book of Shapes* (2000), is illustrated with Chinese American images. (Rev: BL 11/15/01; HBG 3/02; SLJ 1/02)

SIZE AND SHAPE

84 Aber, Linda Williams. *Carrie Measures Up* (K–2). Illus. by Joy Allen. Series: Math Matters. 2001, Kane paper $4.95 (1-57565-100-9). 32pp. Carrie gets totally carried away measuring things around the house. (Rev: SLJ 6/01)

85 Fox, Christyan, and Diane Fox. *What Shape Is That, PiggyWiggy?* (PS). Illus. by authors. 2002, Handprint $5.95 (1-929766-44-0). Shapes including squares, circles, arches, triangles, and diamonds are demonstrated as a pig and his teddy bear build a house in this board book. (Rev: SLJ 6/02)

86 Gunzi, Christiane. *My Very First Look at Shapes* (PS–K). Illus. by Steve Gorton. Series: My Very First Look. 2001, Two-Can $8.95 (1-58728-238-0); paper $5.95 (1-58728-278-X). 24pp. Shapes are introduced using colorful photographs of easily recognized objects. Also use *My Very First Look at Sizes* (2001). (Rev: BL 2/15/02; HBG 10/02; SLJ 2/02) [516]

87 Montague-Smith, Ann. *First Shape Book* (PS–1). Illus. by Mandy Stanley. 2002, Kingfisher $12.95 (0-7534-5433-5). 47pp. Cartoon illustrations and a series of questions and games introduce shapes, mirror images, pairs, and size in a way that encourages identification, matching, and counting. (Rev: SLJ 7/02)

88 Murphy, Chuck. *Slide 'n Seek: Shapes* (PS–K). Illus. Series: Slide 'n Seek. 2001, Simon & Schuster $5.99 (0-689-84477-8). 12pp. This small board book introduces shapes using pull-tabs and clear, bright illustrations. (Rev: BL 12/15/01) [513]

89 Pollack, Pam, and Meg Belviso. *Chickens on the Move* (1–2). Illus. by Lynn Adams. 2002, Kane paper $4.95 (1-57565-113-0). 32pp. In this witty concept book, three children use 24 feet of fencing to create coops of different shapes to house their grandfather's three chickens. (Rev: BL 4/15/02)

90 Rau, Dana Meachen. *A Star in My Orange: Looking for Nature's Shapes* (PS–2). Illus. 2002, Millbrook LB $22.90 (0-7613-2414-3). 32pp. Through colorful photographs and simple text, this book explores shapes such as stars and spirals as they occur in nature. (Rev: BL 2/1/02; HBG 10/02; SLJ 5/02) [516]

Counting and Number Books

91 Appelt, Kathi. *Rain Dance* (PS–1). Illus. by Emilie Chollat. 2001, HarperCollins $9.95 (0-694-01291-2). 24pp. A number of different animals enjoy playing in the rain in this simple counting book. (Rev: BL 4/1/01; HBG 3/02; SLJ 12/01)

92 Brown, Ruth. *Ten Seeds* (PS–K). Illus. 2001, Knopf $14.95 (0-375-80697-0). 24pp. Ten seeds are planted at the beginning of this book, but their numbers gradually dwindle as a variety of characters plunder the bed. (Rev: BL 5/15/01; HB 9–10/01*; HBG 3/02; SLJ 7/01)

93 Butler, John. *While You Were Sleeping* (PS). Illus. 2001, Peachtree $6.95 (1-56145-254-8). 12pp. A look at what different animals do at night, in the form of a counting book. (Rev: BL 10/15/01)

94 Chaconas, Dori. *One Little Mouse* (PS–K). Illus. by LeUyen Pham. 2002, Viking $15.99 (0-670-88947-4). 32pp. A little mouse searching for a new house visits other animals' homes before deciding that his own is best of all, in a rhyming text that teaches children to count up to ten and back down again. (Rev: BL 9/1/02; HBG 10/02; SLJ 8/02)

95 Coffelt, Nancy. *What's Cookin'? A Happy Birthday Counting Book* (PS–1). Illus. 2003, Chronicle $14.95 (0-8118-3561-8). 32pp. A counting book featuring ten cooks baking a birthday cake, with a recipe at the end. (Rev: BL 2/15/03; SLJ 3/03)

96 Cotten, Cynthia. *At the Edge of the Woods: A Counting Book* (PS–2). Illus. by Reg Cartwright. 2002, Holt $16.95 (0-8050-6354-4). 32pp. Gentle verse and bright, primitive paintings are used in this incremental tale of a forest day, in which one chipmunk, two young deer, and then more and more animals appear. (Rev: BL 12/1/02; HBG 3/03)

97 Deegan, Kim. *My First Book of Numbers* (PS). Illus. 2002, Bloomsbury $7.95 (1-58234-755-7). 24pp. A sparkling introduction to counting and numbers. (Rev: BL 8/02; SLJ 11/02) [513.2]

98 Demarest, Chris L. *Smokejumpers One to Ten* (PS–1). Illus. 2002, Simon & Schuster $17.00 (0-689-84120-5). 32pp. A counting book featuring courageous and hardworking parachuting fire fighters. (Rev: BCCB 7–8/02; BL 7/02; HBG 10/02; SLJ 7/02) [634.9]

99 Ellwand, David. *Ten in the Bed: A Counting Book* (PS). Photos by author. 2002, Handprint $9.95 (1-929766-49-1). Teddy bears roll off a bed, one by one, and the number on the floor grows as the number on the bed shrinks. (Rev: SLJ 7/02)

100 Falconer, Ian. *Olivia Counts* (PS). Illus. 2002, Simon & Schuster $6.99 (0-689-85087-5). 12pp. A simple board book featuring Olivia the pig with one beach ball, two bows, and so forth up to ten. (Rev: BCCB 6/02; BL 7/02; HBG 10/02; SLJ 6/02)

101 Falwell, Cathryn. *Turtle Splash! Countdown at the Pond* (PS–K). Illus. 2001, Greenwillow LB $15.89 (0-06-029463-9). 32pp. A rhythmic countdown to bedtime as one turtle after another — for a total of ten — splashes into a lake as evening comes closer and animals arrive at the water's edge. (Rev: BL 8/01; HBG 3/02; SLJ 9/01*)

102 Fearrington, Ann. *Who Sees the Lighthouse?* (K–3). Illus. by Giles Laroche. 2002, Putnam $15.99 (0-399-23703-8). 32pp. Lighthouses star in this counting book full of intricate, highly detailed illustrations. (Rev: BL 11/15/02; HBG 3/03; SLJ 10/02)

103 Fleming, Candace. *Who Invited You?* (PS–3). Illus. by George Booth. 2001, Simon & Schuster $16.00 (0-689-83153-6). 32pp. This lively rhyming counting book follows a little girl poling her boat down the river as she is joined by unwanted animal guests. (Rev: BCCB 12/01; BL 10/15/01; HBG 3/02; SLJ 10/01)

104 Fox, Christyan, and Diane Fox. *Count to Ten, PiggyWiggy!* (PS–K). Illus. 2001, Handprint $5.95 (1-929766-18-1). 20pp. A counting book in which PiggyWiggy adds different numbers of ingredients to a mixing bowl to make a wonderful layer cake. (Rev: BL 4/1/01; SLJ 8/01)

105 Gardiner, Lindsey. *Good Night, Poppy and Max: A Bedtime Counting Book* (PS). Illus. by author. 2002, Little, Brown $6.95 (0-316-60122-5). A board book in which Poppy and Max follow their bedtime routine, with one glass of milk, two cookies, and so on up to ten. (Rev: SLJ 3/03)

106 Girnis, Meg. *1, 2, 3 for You and Me* (PS–1). Photos by Shirley Leamon Green. 2001, Albert Whitman LB $14.95 (0-8075-6107-X). Smiling children with Down's syndrome are shown holding toys and everyday objects in this simple counting book. (Rev: HBG 10/01; SLJ 7/01)

107 Gorbachev, Valeri. *One Rainy Day* (PS–2). Illus. 2002, Putnam $15.99 (0-399-23628-7). 40pp. Pig escapes the rain under a tree and is joined by ten other animals also trying to stay dry. (Rev: BL 5/15/02; HBG 10/02; SLJ 8/02)

108 Gunzi, Christiane. *My Very First Look at Numbers* (PS–K). Illus. by Steve Gorton. Series: My Very First Look. 2001, Two-Can $8.95 (1-58728-237-2); paper $5.95 (1-58728-277-1). 24pp. Photographs of everyday objects are used to teach preschoolers about numbers. (Rev: BL 2/15/02; HBG 10/02; SLJ 2/02) [513.2]

109 Helakoski, Leslie. *The Smushy Bus* (K–2). Illus. by Sal Murdocca. 2002, Millbrook LB $22.90 (0-7613-1398-2). 32pp. Mr. Mathers, the clever bus driver, manages to fit 76 kids into a bus with four seats in this adventure combined with an early introduction to mathematical concepts. (Rev: BL 10/15/02; HBG 3/03; SLJ 11/02)

110 Hoberman, Mary Ann. *The Looking Book: A Hide-and-Seek Counting Story* (PS–1). Illus. by Laura Huliska-beith. 2002, Little, Brown $15.95 (0-316-36328-6). 32pp. Readers will find numbers 1 through 28 hidden in the pictures as they search for a lost cat named Pistachio in this newly illustrated edition of the book originally published in 1973. (Rev: BL 7/02; HBG 10/02; SLJ 6/02)

111 Lodge, Bernard. *How Scary!* (PS–K). Illus. 2001, Houghton $15.00 (0-618-11547-1). 32pp. One growling giant, two dreadful dragons, and so on up to ten rattling robots all add up to a satisfying Halloween counting book. (Rev: BL 9/1/01; HBG 3/02; SLJ 9/01)

112 London, Jonathan. *Count the Ways, Little Brown Bear* (PS–1). Illus. by Margie Moore. 2002, Dutton $14.99 (0-525-46097-7). This beautifully illustrated counting book could double as a bedtime story. (Rev: HBG 10/02; SLJ 4/02)

113 McGinty, Alice B. *Ten Little Lambs* (PS–2). Illus. by Melissa Sweet. 2002, Dial $14.99 (0-8037-2596-5). 32pp. Ten little lambs drop off to sleep, one by one, in this illustrated bedtime counting book. (Rev: BCCB 9/02; BL 7/02; HBG 10/02; SLJ 8/02)

114 Mannis, Celeste Davidson. *One Leaf Rides the Wind: Counting in a Japanese Garden* (PS–2). Illus. by Susan Kathleen Hartung. 2002, Viking $15.99 (0-670-03525-4). A Japanese girl counts the plants and objects in a traditional garden in this elegant book that also introduces haiku and the tea ceremony. (Rev: HBG 3/03; SLJ 10/02)

115 Melmed, Laura Krauss. *This First Thanksgiving Day: A Counting Story* (K–3). Illus. by Mark Buehner. 2001, HarperCollins LB $15.89 (0-688-14555-8). 32pp. Pilgrim and Indian children playfully prepare for the Thanksgiving feast in this rhyming counting book. (Rev: BL 9/1/01; HBG 3/02; SLJ 9/01)

116 Miller, Virginia. *Ten Red Apples: A Bartholomew Bear Counting Book* (PS–2). Illus. 2002, Candlewick $13.99 (0-7636-1901-9). 32pp. Bartholomew counts ten apples and ends up with apple pie in this colorful counting book. (Rev: BL 9/15/02; SLJ 11/02) [513.5]

117 Modesitt, Jeanne. *One, Two, Three Valentine's Day* (PS–1). Illus. by Robin Spowart. 2002, Boyds Mills $15.95 (1-56397-868-7). 32pp. A counting book in which Mr. Mouse takes valentine gifts to his friends, to one frog, two pigs, and so forth up to his ten little sons. (Rev: BL 1/1–15/03; HBG 3/03; SLJ 1/03)

118 Murphy, Stuart J. *Double the Ducks* (PS–1). Illus. by Valeria Petrone. Series: MathStart. 2003, HarperCollins LB $16.89 (0-06-028923-6); paper $4.99 (0-06-446249-8). 40pp. Simple addition and multiplication are explained as a young cowboy cares for five little ducks who bring friends and double his work. (Rev: BL 3/15/03) [513.2]

119 Napoli, Donna Jo, and Richard Chen. *How Hungry Are You?* (K–3). Illus. by Amy Walrod. 2001,

Simon & Schuster $16.00 (0-689-83389-X). 32pp. Sharing becomes difficult (and requires some division) when too many friends arrive at an animals' picnic. (Rev: BL 9/15/01; HBG 3/02; SLJ 10/01)

120 Newman, Leslea. *Dogs, Dogs, Dogs!* (PS–1). Illus. by Erika Oller. 2002, Simon & Schuster $16.00 (0-689-84492-1). A boisterous counting book full of appealing dogs that counts from one to ten and down again. (Rev: HBG 10/02; SLJ 8/02)

121 Oborne, Martine. *One Beautiful Baby* (PS–K). Illus. by Ingrid Godon. 2002, Little, Brown $14.95 (0-316-06562-5). 32pp. A simple, sweet counting book about a baby, from "one sweet smile" to "ten sticky fingers." (Rev: BL 9/15/02; HBG 3/03; SLJ 9/02)

122 Ochiltree, Dianne. *Ten Monkey Jamboree* (PS–2). Illus. by Anne-Sophie Lanquetin. 2001, Simon & Schuster $16.00 (0-689-83402-0). A counting book featuring a rambunctious bunch of monkeys, rhythmic and repetitive text that tells a lively story, and rich illustrations that use interesting perspectives. (Rev: HBG 3/02; SLJ 10/01)

123 Paley, Joan. *One More River: A Noah's Ark Counting Song* (PS–1). Illus. 2002, Little, Brown $15.95 (0-316-60702-9). 32pp. Noah and his animals star in this brightly illustrated counting book. (Rev: BL 5/15/02; HBG 10/02; SLJ 4/02) [782.25]

124 Parker, Vic. *Bearum Scarum* (PS–1). Illus. by Emily Bolam. 2002, Viking $14.99 (0-670-03546-7). 32pp. This clever counting book follows a group of hunters in search of a bear, who find themselves being hunted, one by one. (Rev: BL 3/1/02; HBG 10/02; SLJ 2/02)

125 Prelutsky, Jack. *Halloween Countdown* (PS). Illus. by Dan Yaccarino. 2002, HarperFestival $6.99 (0-06-000512-2). Readers count the friendly looking ghosts in a boy's home in this board book. (Rev: BCCB 9/02; SLJ 10/02)

126 Rankin, Laura. *Swan Harbor: A Nature Counting Book* (PS–2). Illus. 2003, Dial $16.99 (0-8037-2561-2). 32pp. A counting book featuring 20 animals, plants, and other natural features of Swan Harbor, Maine. (Rev: BL 2/15/03) [513.2]

127 Schaefer, Carole Lexa. *One Wheel Wobbles: A Homespun Counting Book* (PS–K). Illus. by Pierre Morgan. 2003, Candlewick $15.99 (0-7636-0472-0). 32pp. A country family's various means of transportation serve as the subject of this counting book. (Rev: BL 3/1/03)

128 Schafer, Kevin. *Penguins 123* (PS–K). Photos by author. 2002, NorthWord $14.95 (1-55971-830-7). A counting book that will grab the attention of penguin lovers. (Rev: SLJ 1/03)

129 Schulman, Janet. *Countdown to Spring! An Animal Counting Book* (PS–K). Illus. by Meilo So. 2002, Knopf $9.95 (0-375-81364-0). 24pp. Colorful flora and fauna grace the pages of this counting book for toddlers and preschoolers. (Rev: BL 1/1–15/02; HBG 10/02; SLJ 1/02) [513.2]

130 Singer, Marilyn. *Quiet Night* (PS–K). Illus. by John Manders. 2002, Clarion $15.00 (0-618-12044-0). 32pp. A riotous romp of a counting book in which the quiet of night turns into a symphony of animal noises. (Rev: BCCB 6/02; BL 3/15/02; HBG 10/02; SLJ 3/02)

131 Spanyol, Jessica. *Carlo Likes Counting* (PS–2). Illus. 2002, Candlewick $14.99 (0-7636-1774-1). 32pp. Carlo the giraffe counts from one to ten wherever he goes. (Rev: BL 10/1/02; HBG 3/03; SLJ 1/03)

132 Spowart, Robin. *Ten Little Bunnies* (PS). Illus. by author. 2001, Scholastic $7.95 (0-439-20863-7). A gentle counting book that can double as a bedtime story. (Rev: HBG 10/01; SLJ 8/01)

133 Wadsworth, Olive A. *Over in the Meadow: A Counting Rhyme* (PS–1). Illus. by Anna Vojtech. 2002, North-South $15.95 (0-7358-1596-8). 32pp. This classic nursery counting rhyme is given a fresh look with double-page spreads and stunning watercolors. (Rev: BL 4/15/02; HBG 10/02; SLJ 4/02)

134 Wallace, Nancy Elizabeth. *Count Down to Clean Up!* (PS–2). Illus. 2001, Houghton $14.00 (0-618-10130-6). 32pp. Ten bunnies take a trip to the park, gathering supplies as they go, in this counting book with cut-paper artwork. (Rev: BL 9/15/01; HBG 3/02; SLJ 10/01)

135 Ziefert, Harriet. *A Dozen Ducklings Lost and Found* (K–2). Illus. by Donald Dreifuss. 2003, Houghton $15.00 (0-618-14175-8). 32pp. While proudly parading her dozen ducklings through the barnyard, Mother Duck loses some in newly dug postholes. (Rev: BL 3/15/03; SLJ 3/03)

Bedtime Books and Nursery Rhymes

Bedtime Books

136 Ahlberg, Allan. *Treasure Hunt* (PS–K). Illus. by Gillian Tyler. 2002, Candlewick $14.99 (0-7636-1542-0). 24pp. Little Tilly's family hides everyday "treasures" for her to find in this charming bedtime story. (Rev: BCCB 4/02; BL 3/15/02; HB 5–6/02; HBG 10/02; SLJ 4/02)

137 Appelt, Kathi. *Bubbles, Bubbles* (PS–K). Illus. by Fumi Kosaka. Series: Harper Growing Tree. 2001, HarperCollins $9.95 (0-694-01458-3). 24pp. Realistic illustrations and frothy verse portray a little girl enjoying her bedtime bath. (Rev: BL 10/1/01; HBG 10/02; SLJ 12/01)

138 Apperley, Dawn. *Blossom and Boo Stay Up Late: A Story about Bedtime* (PS–K). Illus. 2002, Little, Brown $14.95 (0-316-05312-0). 32pp. Two friends, a rabbit and a bear, decide to stay in the forest one night and, though frightened, eventually fall asleep in each other's arms. (Rev: BL 5/1/02; HBG 10/02; SLJ 7/02)

139 Apperley, Dawn. *Good Night, Sleep Tight, Little Bunnies* (PS). Illus. by author. 2002, Scholastic $9.95 (0-439-22525-6). A rhyming refrain and cartoon images depict young animals settling down for the night. (Rev: HBG 10/02; SLJ 5/02)

140 Arquette, Kerry. *What Did You Do Today?* (PS–2). Illus. by Nancy Hayashi. 2002, Harcourt $16.00 (0-15-201414-4). 32pp. Many animals and one child describe their busy days in this rhyming picture book. (Rev: BL 5/15/02; HBG 10/02; SLJ 6/02)

141 Arro, Lena. *Good Night, Animals* (PS–1). Trans. by Joan Sandin. Illus. by Catarina Kruusval. 2002, Farrar $15.00 (91-29-65654-0). 28pp. A cumulative bedtime story in which two children who decide to camp out soon find their tent packed with animals. (Rev: BCCB 12/02; BL 12/15/02; HBG 3/03; SLJ 2/03)

142 Ashman, Linda. *Sailing Off to Sleep* (PS–1). Illus. by Susan Winter. 2001, Simon & Schuster $12.95 (0-689-82971-X). 32pp. Watercolor-and-pencil illustrations capture this rhyming bedtime tale of a little girl who imagines she is sailing to the Arctic. (Rev: BL 1/1–15/02; HBG 3/02; SLJ 1/02*)

143 Banks, Kate. *Close Your Eyes* (PS). Illus. by Georg Hallensleben. 2002, Farrar $16.00 (0-374-31382-2). 40pp. A thoroughly enjoyable, dreamily illustrated story about a little tiger who doesn't want to fall asleep, and his mother's patient reassurances. (Rev: BL 10/15/02; HB 9–10/02; HBG 3/03; SLJ 7/02)

144 Bauer, Marion Dane. *Why Do Kittens Purr?* (PS–1). Illus. by Henry Cole. 2003, Simon & Schuster $15.95 (0-689-84179-5). 32pp. Charming rhymes answer a boy's questions about the world about him in a way that will set young ones' minds at ease. (Rev: BL 1/1–15/03; SLJ 3/03)

145 Beck, Andrea. *Elliot's Noisy Night* (PS–1). Illus. 2002, Kids Can $12.95 (1-55337-011-2). 32pp. Elliot the toy moose infects his friends with his fears about the noises at night and they all end up sleeping in Elliot's room. (Rev: BL 1/1–15/03; HBG 3/03)

146 Bergman, Mara. *Musical Beds* (PS–1). Illus. by Marjolein Pottie. 2002, Simon & Schuster $14.95 (0-689-84463-8). 32pp. Three siblings spend the night scuttling from bed to bed, trying to relieve their various fears and discomforts in this appealing bedtime book. (Rev: BCCB 1/03; BL 10/15/02; HBG 3/03; SLJ 12/02)

147 Blomgren, Jennifer. *Where Do I Sleep? A Pacific Northwest Lullaby* (PS–2). Illus. by Andrea Gabriel. 2001, Sasquatch $15.95 (1-57061-258-7). 32pp. A peaceful bedtime book featuring animals native to the Pacific Northwest bedding down for the night. (Rev: BL 11/1/01; HBG 3/02; SLJ 11/01)

148 Bradman, Tony. *Daddy's Lullaby* (PS). Illus. by Jason Cockcroft. 2002, Simon & Schuster $16.95 (0-689-84295-3). 32pp. Late at night, a father tries to soothe his baby to sleep by quietly making his way around the house with the child in his arms. (Rev: BL 4/15/02; HBG 10/02; SLJ 5/02)

149 Branford, Henrietta. *Little Pig Figwort Can't Get to Sleep* (PS–K). Illus. by Claudio Munoz. 2002, Clarion $14.00 (0-618-15968-1). 32pp. When Little Pig Figwort can't sleep he sets out to find other creatures that have the same problem. (Rev: BCCB 5/02; BL 6/1–15/02; HBG 10/02; SLJ 7/02)

150 Brian, Janeen. *Where Does Thursday Go?* (PS–K). Illus. by Stephen M. King. 2002, Clarion $14.00 (0-618-21264-7). 32pp. A little bear and his friend search for Thursday, wondering where the day goes when nighttime comes, in this attractive book that makes a great bedtime story. (Rev: BL 3/1/02; HBG 10/02; SLJ 4/02)

151 Brown, Margaret Wise. *Sheep Don't Count Sheep* (PS). Illus. by Benrei Huang. 2003, Simon & Schuster $14.95 (0-689-83346-6). 32pp. A little lamb can't get to sleep because there's too much going on in the field, so his mother tells him to count butterflies. (Rev: BL 1/1–15/03; SLJ 3/03)

152 Bunting, Eve. *Too Many Monsters* (PS–3). Illus. by James Bernardin. 2001, Troll LB $15.95 (0-8167-7178-2). A mother tells her frightened son that monsters are afraid of ducks, and a great sound of quacking results. (Rev: HBG 3/02; SLJ 2/02)

153 Burningham, John. *Hushabye* (PS). Illus. 2001, Random LB $16.99 (0-375-91414-5). 40pp. Sleepy animals drift off after a hard day to a simple, soothing refrain echoed by calm collages. (Rev: BCCB 11/01; BL 10/1/01; HB 11–12/01*; HBG 3/02; SLJ 12/01*)

154 Butler, John. *Hush, Little Ones* (PS). Illus. 2002, Peachtree $15.95 (1-56145-269-6). 32pp. A very visual bedtime book full of sleeping animals — birds in nests, monkeys up trees, a penguin between his father's feet. (Rev: BL 11/15/02; HBG 3/03; SLJ 10/02)

155 Castle, Caroline. *Naughty!* (PS–K). Illus. by Sam Childs. 2001, Knopf $14.95 (0-375-81359-4). 32pp. Little Zeb the zebra refuses to take a nap and sneaks off to play with Little Hippo until their mothers find them and the young ones agree to settle down together. (Rev: BL 6/1–15/01; HBG 10/01; SLJ 6/01)

156 Charlip, Remy. *Baby Hearts and Baby Flowers* (PS–K). Illus. by author. 2001, Greenwillow LB $15.89 (0-06-029592-9). Babies, puppies, and kittens are found "everywhere" in this gentle bedtime book. (Rev: HBG 10/02; SLJ 1/02)

157 Chorao, Kay. *Shadow Night: A Picture Book with Shadow Play* (PS–1). Illus. by author. 2001, Dutton $15.99 (0-525-46685-1). Readers will learn to make shadow puppets while reading this story about a little boy conquering his fear of the monsters on his wall. (Rev: BCCB 5/01; HBG 10/01; SLJ 5/01)

158 Cohen, Caron Lee. *Martin and the Giant Lion* (PS–K). Illus. by Elizabeth Sayles. 2002, Clarion $15.00 (0-618-04908-8). 32pp. After he is tucked into bed, Martin travels via his purple truck to a land where he plays with a family of lions. (Rev: BL 4/15/02; HBG 10/02; SLJ 7/02)

159 Crum, Shutta. *All on a Sleepy Night* (K–2). Illus. by Sylvie Daigneault. 2002, Stoddart $15.95 (0-7737-3315-9). 24pp. The sounds of his grandparents' house lull a young boy to sleep in this rhyming picture book. (Rev: BL 9/15/02; HBG 3/03; SLJ 5/02)

160 deVries, Maggie. *How Sleep Found Tabitha* (PS–K). Illus. by Sheena Lott. 2002, Orca $16.95 (1-55143-193-9). 32pp. Pastel watercolor illustrations provide an excellent backdrop for this story of a sleepless child. (Rev: BL 8/02; HBG 10/02; SLJ 8/02)

161 Dragonwagon, Crescent. *Is This a Sack of Potatoes?* (PS–1). Illus. by Catherine Stock. 2002, Marshall Cavendish $16.95 (0-7614-5089-0). 32pp. Charlie hides under the covers at bedtime in this lift-the-flap book with charming watercolor illustrations. (Rev: BL 12/15/02; HBG 3/03; SLJ 11/02)

162 Edwards, Pamela Duncan. *Wake-Up Kisses* (PS–1). Illus. by Henry Cole. 2001, HarperCollins LB $15.89 (0-06-623977-X). 24pp. Animal parents wake their babies for nighttime adventures in this soothing bedtime book. (Rev: BL 2/1/02; HBG 3/02)

163 Frampton, David. *The Whole Night Through: A Lullaby* (PS–1). Illus. 2001, HarperCollins LB $15.89 (0-06-028826-4). 32pp. A boisterous little leopard is determined to stay awake. (Rev: BL 5/15/01; HBG 10/01; SLJ 6/01*)

164 Gabriel, Andrea. *My Favorite Bear* (PS–1). Illus. 2003, Charlesbridge $15.95 (1-58089-038-5). 32pp. To get her little bear to sleep, a mother bear sings a song about different kinds of bears. (Rev: BL 2/15/03; SLJ 2/03)

165 Gliori, Debi. *Debi Gliori's Bedtime Stories: Bedtime Tales with a Twist* (PS–2). Illus. 2002, DK $15.99 (0-7894-8861-2). 80pp. Old favorites such as "The Tortoise and the Hare" get surprising revisions in this amusing bedtime book. (Rev: BL 12/15/02; HBG 3/03; SLJ 2/03) [398.2]

166 Gliori, Debi. *Polar Bolero: A Bedtime Dance* (PS–2). Illus. 2001, Harcourt $16.00 (0-15-202436-0). 32pp. When it's too hot to sleep, a young polar bear heads to the place where they dance the Polar Bolero. (Rev: BL 5/1/01; HBG 10/01; SLJ 6/01)

167 Hague, Kathleen. *Good Night, Fairies* (PS–3). Illus. by Michael Hague. 2002, North-South $15.95 (1-58717-134-1). 40pp. This magical bedtime book has a mother explaining to her child all the jobs performed by fairies. (Rev: BL 3/15/02; HBG 10/02)

168 Haines, Mike. *Countdown to Bedtime* (PS). Illus. by David Melling. 2001, Hyperion $12.99 (0-7868-0741-5). 16pp. A lift-the-flap book that accompanies a pair of young animals in their preparations for bed as a 10-minute deadline counts down. (Rev: BL 6/1–15/01; HBG 10/01; SLJ 7/01)

169 Hest, Amy. *Kiss Good Night* (PS–1). Illus. by Anita Jeram. 2001, Candlewick $15.99 (0-7636-0780-0). 32pp. Sam, a little bear, cannot fall asleep without his mother's goodnight kiss. (Rev: BL 10/1/01; HBG 3/02; SLJ 11/01*)

170 Hunter, Sally. *Humphrey's Bedtime* (PS–K). Illus. 2001, Holt $14.95 (0-8050-6903-8). 30pp. Little elephant Lottie watches her baby brother get ready for bed, proud that she's a big girl who can stay up later, but she tires eventually too. (Rev: BL 1/1–15/02; HBG 3/02; SLJ 2/02)

171 McAllister, Angela. *Night-Night, Little One* (PS). Illus. by Maggie Kneen. 2003, Doubleday LB $17.99 (0-385-90861-X). 32pp. A young rabbit is nervous about facing the night until his mother tells him about all the nocturnal animals. (Rev: SLJ 3/03)

172 McBratney, Sam. *In the Light of the Moon and Other Bedtime Stories* (K–2). Illus. by Kady M. Denton. 2001, Kingfisher $18.95 (0-7534-5224-3). 94pp. A compilation of eight low-key tales with appealing illustrations. (Rev: BL 2/1/02; SLJ 1/02)

173 McCourt, Lisa. *Good Night, Princess Pruney Toes* (PS). Illus. by Cyd Moore. 2001, Troll $15.95 (0-8167-5205-2). Sir Daddy helps to get his bouncy daughter, aka Princess Pruney Toes, ready for bed. (Rev: HBG 10/01; SLJ 5/01)

174 McCullough, Sharon Pierce. *Bunbun at Bedtime* (PS). Illus. 2001, Barefoot $14.99 (1-84148-438-5). 24pp. Bunbun dallies while his brother and sister get ready for bed until a scary noise prompts a burst of activity. (Rev: BL 10/1/01; HBG 3/02; SLJ 11/01)

175 Nakamura, Katherine Riley. *Song of Night: It's Time to Go to Bed* (PS). Illus. by Linnea Riley. 2002, Scholastic $15.95 (0-439-26678-5). 40pp. Animal parents help their beloved children get ready for bed in this charming bedtime book. (Rev: BL 2/1/02; HBG 10/02; SLJ 5/02)

176 Nobisso, Josephine. *The Moon's Lullaby* (PS–1). Illus. by Glo Coalson. 2001, Scholastic $15.95 (0-439-29312-X). 32pp. Muted watercolor illustrations complement this quiet tale of a yawn passed from one small baby to people across the world. (Rev: BL 1/1–15/02; HBG 3/02; SLJ 12/01)

177 Roep, Nanda. *Kisses* (PS). Illus. by Marijke Ten Cate. 2002, Front Street $15.95 (1-886910-85-5). Goodnight kisses are the focus of this richly illustrated, gentle story. (Rev: HBG 3/03; SLJ 1/03)

178 Schertle, Alice. *Good Night, Hattie, My Dearie, My Dove* (PS–1). Illus. by Ted Rand. 2002, HarperCollins LB $15.89 (0-688-16023-9). 32pp. A sweet bedtime book about Hattie and the nine stuffed animals she wants to take to bed with her. (Rev: BL 4/1/02; HBG 10/02; SLJ 6/02)

179 Simmons, Jane. *The Dreamtime Fairies* (PS–1). Illus. 2002, Little, Brown $15.95 (0-316-79523-2). 32pp. A magical bedtime story that sends Lucy, her brother, and several of their stuffed animals off to find the Dreamtime Fairies. (Rev: BL 12/15/02; HBG 3/03; SLJ 1/03)

180 Spinelli, Eileen. *Kittycat Lullaby* (PS–K). Illus. by Anne Mortimer. 2001, Hyperion $14.99 (0-7868-0458-0). 32pp. A rambunctious kitten settles down after a long, busy day. (Rev: BL 8/01; HBG 3/02; SLJ 10/01)

181 Sproule, Gail. *Singing the Dark* (PS–2). Illus. by Sheena Lott. 2001, Fitzhenry & Whiteside $16.95 (1-55041-648-0). 40pp. Every night, Kaylie's mother sings a song "calling darkness" to greet the night, and Kaylie chimes in. (Rev: BL 12/15/01)

182 Stickland, Paul. *Bears!* (PS–1). Illus. by author. 2001, Ragged Bear $15.95 (1-929927-34-7). A boy trying to go to sleep is disturbed by bears having a party. (Rev: HBG 10/02; SLJ 2/02)

183 *Twinkle, Twinkle, Little Star* (PS). Illus. by Sylvia Long. 2001, Chronicle $13.95 (0-8118-2854-9). Watercolor illustrations show young animals greeting the first star before going home for the night in this rendition of the traditional lullaby. (Rev: HBG 3/02; SLJ 1/02)

184 Tyger, Rory. *Newton* (PS–1). Illus. by author. 2001, Barron's $13.95 (0-7641-5390-0). Teddy bear Newton investigates the sources of several scary noises before finally settling down to sleep. (Rev: HBG 3/02; SLJ 11/01)

185 Wahl, Jan. *Elf Night* (1–3). Illus. by Peter Weevers. 2002, Carolrhoda $15.95 (1-57505-512-0). 32pp. A young boy spends a magical time with the fairy folk until he goes back to his bed. (Rev: BL 5/1/02; HBG 10/02; SLJ 5/02)

186 *Weave Little Stars into My Sleep: Native American Lullabies* (2–4). Ed. by Neil Philip. Illus. by Edward S. Curtis. 2001, Clarion $16.00 (0-618-08856-3). 48pp. Fifteen Native American lullabies are accompanied by sepia-toned illustrations and background information. (Rev: BL 10/15/01; HBG 3/02; SLJ 11/01) [782.4215]

187 Wells, Philip. *Daddy Island* (PS–K). Illus. by Niki Daly. 2001, Barefoot $15.99 (1-84148-197-1). 24pp. A boy imagines himself as all kinds of things — a crab, a wild storm, a rock — as he completes the mundane task of getting ready for bed. (Rev: BL 11/15/01; HBG 3/02; SLJ 12/01)

188 Weninger, Brigitte. *It's Bedtime!* (PS–2). Trans. by Kathryn Grell. Illus. by Alan Marks. 2002, North-South LB $15.88 (0-7358-1603-4). 32pp. Ben is reluctant to go to sleep until he selects a scary toy to sleep with him and frighten away the monsters. (Rev: BL 7/02; HBG 10/02; SLJ 7/02)

189 Wild, Margaret. *Nighty Night!* (PS–1). Illus. by Kerry Argent. 2001, Peachtree $15.95 (1-56145-246-7). 32pp. Simple, rhythmic text and rich, humorous illustrations describe animal babies resisting their parents' efforts to put them to bed. (Rev: BCCB 9/01; BL 9/1/01; HBG 3/02; SLJ 9/01)

190 Yolen, Jane. *Time for Naps* (PS). Illus. by Hiroe Nakata. 2002, Simon & Schuster $7.99 (0-689-85057-3). This board book tells the story of a little girl putting her stuffed animals to bed. (Rev: SLJ 11/02)

191 Zolotow, Charlotte. *Sleepy Book* (PS–K). Illus. by Stefano Vitale. 2001, HarperCollins LB $15.89 (0-06-027874-9). 40pp. The classic 1958 poem about sleeping animals is newly illustrated. (Rev: BL 11/1/01; HBG 3/02) [591.5]

Nursery Rhymes

192 Alter, Anna. *The Three Little Kittens* (PS–K). Illus. 2001, Holt $15.95 (0-8050-6471-0). 24pp. In this attractive and humorous version of the nursery rhyme, the three kittens recover their mittens from thieving mice. (Rev: BL 10/1/01; HBG 3/02; SLJ 11/01)

193 Beaton, Clare. *Playtime Rhymes for Little People* (PS–K). Illus. 2001, Barefoot $18.99 (1-84148-425-3). 64pp. Forty familiar children's rhymes are accompanied by embroidered collages. (Rev: BCCB 12/01; BL 10/15/01; HBG 3/02; SLJ 11/01) [398.8]

194 *The Blue's Clues Nursery Rhyme Treasury* (PS–2). 2001, Simon & Schuster $15.95 (0-689-84682-7). A collection of classic rhymes with the addition of some Blue's Clues characters and colorful illustrations. (Rev: HBG 3/02; SLJ 1/02) [398.8]

195 Cabrera, Jane. *Old Mother Hubbard* (PS). Illus. 2001, Holiday $15.95 (0-8234-1659-3). 32pp. Old Mother Hubbard's dog is up to some new tricks in this colorful and imaginative rendition of the familiar nursery rhyme. (Rev: BCCB 11/01; BL 9/1/01; HBG 3/02; SLJ 1/02) [821.7]

196 Gliori, Debi. *The Dorling Kindersley Book of Nursery Rhymes* (PS). Illus. 2001, DK $14.94 (0-7894-6678-3). 64pp. This is a collection of 50 familiar nursery rhymes that contains nonsense illustrations and photographs of children. (Rev: BL 4/1/01; HBG 10/01; SLJ 7/01) [398.8]

197 Hague, Michael. *Teddy Bear's Mother Goose* (PS–1). Illus. 2001, Holt $15.95 (0-8050-3821-3). 64pp. Teddy bears substitute for people in this collection of more than 50 rhymes. (Rev: BL 7/01; HBG 10/01; SLJ 7/01) [398.8]

198 Harper, Charise Mericle. *There Was a Bold Lady Who Wanted a Star* (PS–2). Illus. 2002, Little, Brown $15.95 (0-316-14673-0). 32pp. "The Little Old Lady Who Swallowed a Fly" is traded in for a modern lady who tries various modes of transport in her efforts to catch a star. (Rev: BCCB 11/02; BL 11/15/02; HBG 3/03; SLJ 9/02) [782]

199 Hoberman, Mary Ann. *Bill Grogan's Goat* (PS–3). Illus. by Nadine Bernard Westcott. 2002, Little, Brown $14.95 (0-316-36232-8). 32pp. The classic nonsense rhyme about Bill Grogan and the goat that is always in trouble is retold with clever illustrations. (Rev: BL 4/15/02; HBG 10/02; SLJ 4/02)

200 *The House That Jack Built* (K–2). Illus. by Diana Mayo. 2001, Barefoot $15.99 (1-84148-251-X). Double-page illustrations in bold colors bring new life to the classic rhyme. (Rev: HBG 3/02; SLJ 1/02) [398.8]

201 Jackson, Alison. *If the Shoe Fits* (PS–1). Illus. by Karla Firehammer. 2001, Holt $16.95 (0-8050-6466-4). 24pp. The old woman who lives in a shoe visits familiar nursery rhyme locations — Miss Muffet's teacup, a sock hanging from a clock — in search of a new home. (Rev: BCCB 3/02; BL 10/1/01; HBG 3/02; SLJ 12/01)

202 Janovitz, Marilyn. *Three Little Kittens* (PS–2). Illus. 2002, North-South LB $14.50 (0-7358-1643-3). 32pp. The adventures of the three little kittens in search of their mittens are shown in bright, appealing illustrations. (Rev: BL 10/1/02; HBG 3/03; SLJ 8/02) [398.8]

203 Kadair, Deborah Ousley. *There Was an Ol' Cajun* (K–3). Illus. by author. 2002, Pelican $14.95 (1-56554-917-1). Instead of a fly, the ol' Cajun swallows all manner of swamp life before coming across an alligator. (Rev: HBG 10/02; SLJ 12/02) [398.8]

204 Linch, Tanya. *Three Little Kittens* (PS–K). Illus. by author. 2001, Gullane $12.95 (1-86233-204-5).

The kittens' mittens are lost and dirtied, then found and washed, all with mother's forgiveness. (Rev: SLJ 1/02) [398.2]

205 Mayo, Margaret. *Wiggle Waggle Fun: Stories and Rhymes for the Very Young* (PS–1). Illus. 2002, Knopf LB $18.99 (0-375-91529-X). 64pp. Various artists illustrate this rollicking collection of favorite poems, rhymes, and stories for young children. (Rev: BL 2/1/02; HBG 10/02; SLJ 1/02) [808.8]

206 *Michael Foreman's Playtime Rhymes* (PS–K). Illus. by Michael Foreman. 2002, Candlewick $18.99 (0-7636-1812-8). 108pp. An illustrated collection of traditional songs and rhymes, some familiar and some less well-known, that includes some activities. (Rev: HBG 3/03; SLJ 10/02) [398.8]

207 Montgomery, Michael G., and Wayne Montgomery. *Over the Candlestick: Classic Nursery Rhymes and the Real Stories Behind Them* (PS). Illus. by Michael G. Montgomery. 2002, Peachtree $16.95 (1-56145-259-9). 32pp. A large-format collection of classic nursery rhymes and a bit of the history behind them, with full-page illustrations. (Rev: BL 3/15/02; HBG 10/02; SLJ 6/02) [398.8]

208 *Ragged Bear's Nursery Rhymes* (PS–1). Ed. and illus. by Diz Wallis. 2001, Ragged Bear $19.95 (1-929927-36-3). 116pp. This collection of 100 nursery rhymes includes some that may be new to readers. (Rev: BL 2/15/02; HBG 3/02; SLJ 3/02) [398.8]

209 Sierra, Judy. *Monster Goose* (K–3). Illus. by Jack E. Davis. 2001, Harcourt $16.00 (0-15-202034-9). 56pp. Gruesome, gross, and goofy versions of familiar Mother Goose rhymes. (Rev: BCCB 12/01; BL 9/15/01; HBG 3/02; SLJ 9/01) [811]

210 Stevens, Janet, and Susan Stevens Crummel. *And the Dish Ran Away with the Spoon* (K–3). Illus. 2001, Harcourt $17.00 (0-15-202298-8). 48pp. Familiar nursery rhymes are reworked with droll results. (Rev: BL 4/1/01*; HB 7–8/01; HBG 10/01; SLJ 5/01)

211 Taback, Simms. *This Is the House That Jack Built* (PS–2). Illus. 2002, Putnam $15.99 (0-399-23488-8). 32pp. An inventive, spirited take on the traditional nursery rhyme that focuses on the house and its contents. (Rev: BCCB 10/02; BL 10/1/02*; HB 11–12/02; HBG 3/03; SLJ 9/02*) [398.8]

212 Zelinsky, Paul O. *Knick-Knack Paddywhack! A Moving Parts Book* (PS–3). Illus. 2002, Dutton $18.99 (0-525-46908-7). 8pp. This miracle of pull-tabs and flaps is a delicious combination of familiar, bouncy rhyme and counting song full of comedy and small details. (Rev: BCCB 2/03; BL 11/1/02; HB 1–2/03; HBG 3/03; SLJ 12/02) [782.42164]

213 Zemach, Margot. *Some from the Moon, Some from the Sun: Poems and Songs for Everyone* (K–3). Illus. 2001, Farrar $17.00 (0-374-39960-3). 48pp. A collection of traditional children's poems and rhymes illustrated by Caldecott Medal winner Margot Zemach. (Rev: BL 10/1/01; HB 9–10/01*; HBG 3/02; SLJ 8/01*) [398.8]

Stories Without Words

214 Weitzman, Jacqueline Preiss. *You Can't Take a Balloon into the Museum of Fine Arts* (K–3). 2002, Dial $17.99 (0-8037-2570-1). 40pp. In this wordless book, a runaway balloon causes mishaps as it floats around the city of Boston. (Rev: BL 6/1–15/02*; HBG 10/02; SLJ 8/02)

Picture Books

Imaginative Stories

FANTASIES

215 Ada, Alma Flor. *With Love, Little Red Hen* (K–3). Illus. by Leslie Tryon. 2001, Simon & Schuster $16.00 (0-689-82581-1). 40pp. Little Red Hen writes to Hetty Henny about moving to the Hidden Forest, where her neighbors are other characters from children's stories. Third in a series including *Dear Peter Rabbit* (1994) and *Yours Truly, Goldilocks* (1998). (Rev: BL 9/15/01; HB 1–2/02; HBG 3/02; SLJ 10/01)

216 Arro, Lena. *By Geezers and Galoshes* (PS–1). Illus. by Catarina Kruusval. 2001, Farrar $14.00 (91-29-65348-7). 32pp. When two brothers unexpectedly receive a little boy in the mail, he brings with him a kit for a model ship that, when built, grows into full size and carries them off on an adventure. (Rev: BL 7/01; HBG 10/01; SLJ 9/01)

217 Ashforth, Camilla. *Willow by the Sea* (PS–1). Illus. 2002, Candlewick $12.00 (0-7636-1401-7). 32pp. A gentle story about gentle bear Willow having a lovely day with his friends at the seaside. Also use *Willow on the River* (2002). (Rev: BL 7/02; HBG 10/02; SLJ 7/02)

218 Ashman, Linda. *Maxwell's Magic Mix-Up* (PS–3). Illus. by Regan Dunnick. 2001, Simon & Schuster $16.00 (0-689-83178-1). 32pp. A young boy must try to restore the world to rights after his magician uncle messes up. (Rev: BCCB 6/01; BL 7/01; HB 5–6/01; HBG 10/01; SLJ 7/01)

219 Avi. *Things That Sometimes Happen: Very Short Stories for Little Listeners* (PS). Illus. by Marjorie Priceman. 2002, Simon & Schuster $16.95 (0-689-83914-6). 40pp. Lively new illustrations enhance this collection of nine varied stories originally published in 1970. (Rev: BL 10/1/02; SLJ 11/02)

220 Babbitt, Natalie. *Elsie Times Eight* (PS–2). Illus. 2001, Hyperion $15.95 (0-7868-0900-0). 32pp. A hard-of-hearing fairy godmother mistakes "wait" for "eight" and multiplies her young charge, with challenging consequences. (Rev: BCCB 12/01; BL 11/15/01; HB 1–2/02; HBG 3/02; SLJ 11/01)

221 Baker, Lisa. *Harold and the Purple Crayon: Dinosaur Days* (PS–1). Illus. Series: Harold and the Purple Crayon. 2002, HarperCollins $12.99 (0-06-

000541-6). 40pp. Harold uses his crayon to journey to a jungle and play with dinosaurs. (Rev: BL 2/15/03; HBG 3/03; SLJ 1/03)

222 Barrett, Judi. *Which Witch Is Which?* (PS–3). Illus. by Sharleen Collicott. 2001, Simon & Schuster $16.00 (0-689-82940-X). 32pp. Readers must study the illustrations to figure out which witch the rhyme on each spread describes. (Rev: BL 11/1/01; HBG 3/02; SLJ 9/01)

223 Bartels, Alice L. *The Grandmother Doll* (PS–2). Illus. by Dusan Petricic. 2001, Annick LB $17.95 (1-55037-667-5); paper $6.95 (1-55037-666-7). Grandmother, mother, and Katy find ways to communicate their needs across the generations in this fantasy story. (Rev: HBG 10/01; SLJ 8/01)

224 Bateman, Teresa. *Farm Flu* (PS–1). Illus. by Nadine Bernard Westcott. 2001, Albert Whitman $15.95 (0-8075-2274-0). 32pp. In this humorous, rhyming story, a young boy who is in charge of the family farm while his mother is away must cope with a host of sick animals. (Rev: BL 4/1/01*; HBG 10/01; SLJ 4/01)

225 Bateman, Teresa. *The Merbaby* (1–3). Illus. by Patience Brewster. 2001, Holiday $16.95 (0-8234-1531-7). 32pp. A fisherman catches a merbaby and is rewarded when he returns it to the sea. (Rev: BCCB 9/01; BL 9/15/01; HBG 3/02; SLJ 1/02)

226 Bauer, Marion Dane. *If You Had a Nose Like an Elephant's Trunk* (PS–3). Illus. by Susan Winter. 2001, Holiday $16.95 (0-8234-1589-9). 32pp. A girl playfully imagines what she could do if she had the features or attributes of different animals. (Rev: BL 9/15/01; HBG 3/02; SLJ 9/01)

227 Beck, Andrea. *Elliot Digs for Treasure* (PS–2). Illus. 2001, Kids Can $12.95 (1-55074-806-8). 32pp. When stuffed toy Elliot Moose and his friends decide to dig for buried treasure they get stuck in the hole, and only persistence and cooperation can get them out. (Rev: BL 11/1/01; HBG 3/02; SLJ 11/01)

228 Beck, Ian. *Teddy's Snowy Day* (PS–K). Illus. 2002, Scholastic $15.95 (0-439-17520-8). 32pp. The simple story of a teddy bear who gets left out in the snow, has a wonderful time at first, and happily finds a ride home when he tires. (Rev: BL 10/1/02; HBG 3/03; SLJ 10/02)

229 Blackstone, Stella. *An Island in the Sun* (K–3). Illus. by Nicoletta Ceccoli. 2002, Barefoot $15.99 (1-84148-193-9). 24pp. A boy in a small sailboat visits an island where he plays with a polka-dot dog before taking him home at night. (Rev: BL 5/1/02; HBG 10/02; SLJ 7/02)

230 Bloom, Suzanne. *Piggy Monday: A Tale About Manners* (PS–1). Illus. 2001, Albert Whitman $15.95 (0-8075-6529-6). 40pp. Mrs. Hubbub's class has turned into pigs and it's up to the Pig Lady to transform them back into children by teaching them some manners. (Rev: BL 8/01; HBG 3/02; SLJ 1/02)

231 Bradman, Tony. *Midnight in Memphis* (1–2). Illus. by Martin Chatterton. Series: Blue Bananas. 2001, Crabtree LB $14.97 (0-7787-0848-9); paper $4.46 (0-7787-0894-2). 48pp. After a UFO damages their pyramid in Egypt, Mommy Mummy and her mummy family hire some ladies to repair it in this humorous fantasy. (Rev: BL 5/1/02; SLJ 8/02)

232 Brown, Kerry Hannula. *Tupag the Dreamer* (PS–3). Illus. by Linda Saport. 2001, Marshall Cavendish $15.95 (0-7614-5076-9). Banished from his long-ago village at a time when all was dark and cold, lazy Tupag meets Raven the creator and is accorded his one wish, for a season of light. (Rev: HBG 10/01; SLJ 5/01)

233 Brown, Margaret Wise. *Mouse of My Heart: A Treasury of Sense and Nonsense* (PS). Illus. by Loretta Krupinski. 2001, Hyperion LB $20.49 (0-7868-2546-4). 179pp. This handsome book full of lovely illustrations contains more than 50 stories and poems grouped into categories such as Adventure, Nature, and Nonsense. (Rev: HBG 10/01; SLJ 6/01)

234 Buehner, Caralyn. *Snowmen at Night* (PS). Illus. by Mark Buehner. 2002, Penguin Putnam $15.99 (0-8037-2550-7). 32pp. Captivating illustrations and breezy text put snowmen into action (sledding, playing baseball, and drinking iced cocoa), revealing why snowmen look so tuckered out in the mornings. (Rev: BL 10/15/02; HBG 3/03; SLJ 10/02)

235 Burningham, John. *Mr. Grumpy's Outing* (PS–K). Illus. 2001, Holt $6.95 (0-8050-6629-2). 20pp. A board-book version of the tale of Mr. Grumpy and the animals he takes for a trip down the river. (Rev: BL 4/1/01; HBG 3/02)

236 Butterworth, Nick. *Q Pootle 5* (PS–2). Illus. by author. 2001, Simon & Schuster $13.95 (0-689-84243-0). Q Pootle 5 crash-lands on Earth on his way to a party, and finds most earthlings fairly useless until he meets Henry the cat. (Rev: HBG 10/02; SLJ 7/01)

237 Campbell, Ann. *Queenie Farmer Had Fifteen Daughters* (PS–1). Illus. by Holly Meade. 2002, Harcourt $16.00 (0-15-201933-2). 32pp. Preschoolers and early readers will delight in this tale of Queenie Farmer's attempts to please her 15 daughters on their birthday. (Rev: BL 3/1/02; HB 7–8/02; HBG 10/02; SLJ 8/02)

238 Carter, Anne. *From Poppa* (K–3). Illus. by Kasia Charko. 2001, Lobster $16.95 (1-894222-02-4). 32pp. A girl and her grandfather make an enchanted duck decoy. (Rev: BL 10/1/01)

239 Chrismer, Melanie. *Phoebe Clappsaddle and the Tumbleweed Gang* (K–3). Illus. by Virginia M. Roeder. 2002, Pelican $14.95 (1-56554-966-X). Talented young Phoebe gets the best of a gang of mean cowpokes in this tall tale set in the Old West. (Rev: HBG 3/03; SLJ 1/03)

240 Chwast, Seymour. *Harry, I Need You!* (1–3). Illus. by author. 2002, Houghton $15.00 (0-618-17917-8). Harry is an imaginative child who conjures up all sorts of scenarios when his mother calls for him. (Rev: SLJ 9/02)

241 Clark, Emma Chichester. *It Was You, Blue Kangaroo!* (PS). Illus. 2002, Doubleday LB $17.99 (0-385-90846-6). 32pp. Lily blames all her naughtiness on stuffed toy Blue Kangaroo, but when her mother takes him away, it's Blue Kangaroo who comes up with a plan. (Rev: BL 11/1/02; HBG 3/03; SLJ 10/02)

242 Clerk, Jessica. *The Wriggly, Wriggly Baby* (PS). Illus. by Laura Rankin. 2002, Scholastic $16.95 (0-590-96067-9). 32pp. A squirmy baby slithers through a number of fantastic adventures in this rollicking tale. (Rev: BL 10/1/02; HBG 3/03; SLJ 9/02)

243 Cole, Brock. *Larky Mavis* (PS–3). Illus. 2001, Farrar $16.00 (0-374-34365-9). 32pp. Eccentric Larky Mavis finds a baby inside a peanut, which she calls Heart's Delight and cares for despite universal disdain. (Rev: BCCB 9/01; BL 7/01; HB 9–10/01*; HBG 3/02; SLJ 8/01)

244 Collins, Ross. *Busy Night* (PS–2). Illus. 2002, Bloomsbury $15.95 (1-58234-750-6). 32pp. Ben's bedroom gets crowded when the Sandman, the Tooth Fairy, a "thing under the bed," and Santa Claus all come to visit. (Rev: BL 7/02)

245 Corey, Shana. *First Graders from Mars: Episode 3 — Nergal and the Great Space Race* (1–3). Illus. by Mark Teague. 2002, Scholastic paper $4.50 (0-439-42443-2). 32pp. It's Health Week on Mars, and Nergal isn't looking forward to the space race. (Rev: SLJ 1/03)

246 Corey, Shana. *First Graders from Mars: Episode 2 — The Problem with Pelly* (K–2). Illus. by Mark Teague. 2002, Scholastic $14.95 (0-439-26632-7); paper $4.50 (0-439-36784-0). 32pp. This silly book with a serious message tells the story of Pelly, a foreigner to Mars, who is self-conscious because she doesn't look like her Martian classmates. (Rev: BL 2/15/02; HBG 10/02; SLJ 4/02)

247 Cotten, Cynthia. *Snow Ponies* (K–3). Illus. by Jason Cockcroft. 2001, Holt $15.95 (0-8050-6063-4). Snow ponies released by Old Man Winter turn the world white everywhere they roam. (Rev: HBG 3/02; SLJ 12/01)

248 Cowen-Fletcher, Jane. *Farmer Will* (PS). Illus. 2001, Candlewick $14.99 (0-7636-0988-9). 32pp. Young Will's toy animals become real when they get outside, and they all play together until they're tired. (Rev: BL 7/01; HBG 10/01; SLJ 7/01)

249 Crummel, Susan Stevens. *All in One Hour* (PS–1). Illus. by Dorothy Donohue. 2003, Marshall Cavendish $16.95 (0-7614-5129-3). 32pp. Paper-cut collage illustrations tell a "This Is the House That Jack Built" type story featuring a mouse, a cat, a dog, a dogcatcher, a robber, and a police officer. (Rev: BL 3/15/03)

250 Cullen, Catherine Ann. *The Magical, Mystical, Marvelous Coat* (K–3). Illus. by David Christiana. 2001, Little, Brown $15.95 (0-316-16334-1). 32pp. A joyous, rhyming tale for young children about a girl with a magical coat, depicted in mystical watercolors. (Rev: BCCB 9/01; BL 12/15/01; HBG 3/02; SLJ 12/01)

251 Davis, Katie. *Scared Stiff* (PS–3). Illus. by author. 2001, Harcourt $15.00 (0-15-202305-4). Dramatic illustrations show scary everyday objects,

in this story of a little girl who is tired of being afraid and decides to become a witch. (Rev: HBG 3/02; SLJ 9/01)

252 Davol, Marguerite W. *The Snake's Tales* (2–4). Illus. by Yumi Heo. 2002, Scholastic $15.95 (0-439-31769-X). 32pp. In this absorbing and cheerful story inspired by a traditional Seneca tale, the first storyteller is a wily snake who persuades children to swap food for stories. (Rev: BL 1/1–15/03; HBG 3/03; SLJ 9/02)

253 Davol, Marguerite W. *Why Butterflies Go by on Silent Wings* (K–4). Illus. by Robert Roth. 2001, Scholastic $16.95 (0-531-30322-5). Butterflies used to be so noisy (and dull) that they did not see the beauty around them — but a great storm changed their attitude and they became beautiful and peaceful. (Rev: HBG 10/01; SLJ 8/01)

254 Dematons, Charlotte. *Let's Go* (K–3). Illus. 2001, Front Street $15.95 (1-886910-65-0). 32pp. A young boy's trip to the corner store turns into a magical adventure. (Rev: BL 5/15/01; HBG 10/01; SLJ 10/01)

255 Diterlizzi, Tony. *Ted* (PS–1). Illus. by author. 2001, Simon & Schuster $16.00 (0-689-83235-4). A young boy succeeds in getting his father's attention through a lively imaginary friend. (Rev: BCCB 2/01; HBG 10/01; SLJ 4/01)

256 Donaldson, Julia. *Room on the Broom* (K–3). Illus. by Axel Scheffler. 2001, Dial $15.99 (0-8037-2657-0). 32pp. A witch's animal friends cleverly save her from a dragon in this rhyming tale featuring entertaining illustrations. (Rev: BCCB 9/01; BL 9/1/01; HBG 3/02; SLJ 9/01)

257 Donaldson, Julia. *The Spiffiest Giant in Town* (PS–1). Illus. by Axel Scheffler. 2003, Dial $15.99 (0-8037-2848-4). 32pp. George, the giant, buys a new set of clothing but ends up giving it all away to animal friends in need. (Rev: BL 3/1/03; SLJ 3/03)

258 Doyle, Malachy. *The Bold Boy* (PS–K). Illus. by Jane Ray. 2001, Candlewick $15.99 (0-7636-1624-9). 40pp. A modern folktale about a wicked child who claims property as his own until the townspeople rebel . . . but at the end it seems the whole story is ready to repeat in typical circular fashion. (Rev: BL 12/15/01; HB 9–10/01; HBG 3/02; SLJ 1/02)

259 Doyle, Malachy. *Hungry! Hungry! Hungry!* (K–3). Illus. by Paul Hess. 2001, Peachtree $15.95 (1-56145-241-6). A young boy asks a "ghastly goblin" many questions about his size and other scary features. (Rev: BCCB 4/01; HBG 10/01; SLJ 7/01)

260 Dunbar, Joyce. *Magic Lemonade* (1–2). Illus. by Jan McCafferty. Series: Blue Bananas. 2001, Crabtree LB $14.97 (0-7787-0845-4); paper $4.46 (0-7787-0891-8). 48pp. Bossy Zoe proves to be a difficult but imaginative playmate in this amusing fantasy. (Rev: BL 5/1/02)

261 Dyer, Sarah. *Five Little Fiends* (K–3). Illus. 2002, Bloomsbury $15.95 (1-58234-751-4). 32pp. In this unusual picture book, the little fiends of the title emerge from statues to steal parts of the environment, until they realize the error of their ways. (Rev: BL 9/1/02; SLJ 9/02)

262 Eaton, Jason. *The Day My Runny Nose Ran Away* (1–2). Illus. by Ethan Long. 2002, Dutton $15.99 (0-525-47013-1). 32pp. Jason's nose, Montague, slips away in the night — he's fed up with being wiped on Jason's sleeve — leaving a big white space where a nose should be, in this fantasy for younger readers. (Rev: BL 10/15/02; HBG 3/03; SLJ 9/02)

263 Edwards, Julie Andrews, and Emma Walton Hamilton. *Dumpy and the Big Storm* (PS–K). Illus. by Tony Walton. Series: Dumpy the Dump Truck. 2002, Hyperion $15.99 (0-7868-0742-3). 32pp. Dumpy the dump truck comes to the rescue of other trucks and a fishing boat when a big storm hits the lighthouse and the power goes out. (Rev: BL 12/1/02; HBG 3/03)

264 Edwards, Pamela Duncan. *Rude Mule* (K–1). Illus. by Barbara Nascimbeni. 2002, Holt $15.95 (0-8050-7007-9). A young host teaches a rude mule a thing or two about manners. (Rev: HBG 3/03; SLJ 8/02)

265 Esckelson, Laura. *The Copper Braid of Shannon O'Shea* (PS–2). Illus. by Pam Newton. 2003, Dutton $16.99 (0-525-46138-8). 32pp. This is a lively, rhyming tale in which sprites untangle Shannon's 17-mile-long braids only to discover myriad strange things hidden within: a kangaroo, thimbles, a volcano, and even the island of Atlantis, to list only a few. (Rev: BL 1/1–15/03; SLJ 2/03)

266 Fancher, Lou, adapt. *The Velveteen Rabbit* (PS–2). Illus. by Steve Johnson and Lou Fancher. 2002, Simon & Schuster $16.95 (0-689-84134-5). With appealing illustrations and very readable text, Fancher retells the story of a stuffed rabbit that becomes real. (Rev: HBG 3/03; SLJ 12/02)

267 Feiffer, Jules. *The House Across the Street* (PS–2). Illus. 2002, Hyperion $15.95 (0-7868-0910-8). 32pp. Cartoon-style illustrations show the house across the street, where a boy's imaginary self doesn't have to obey his parents and can do whatever he wants — like eating with his elbows on the table and even putting a swimming pool in the bedroom. (Rev: BCCB 1/03; BL 12/1/02; HBG 3/03; SLJ 2/03)

268 Fitzpatrick, Marie-Louise. *I'm a Tiger, Too!* (PS–1). Illus. 2002, Millbrook LB $22.90 (0-7613-2410-0). 32pp. A young boy plays with various animals in different locales but after they each leave him, he makes friends with a boy his own age. (Rev: BL 4/15/02; HBG 10/02; SLJ 6/02)

269 Fox, Frank G. *Jean Laffite and the Big Ol' Whale* (2–3). Illus. by Scott Cook. 2003, Farrar $16.00 (0-374-33669-5). 32pp. A tall tale about the infamous pirate ingeniously dislodging a whale trapped in the Mississippi River. (Rev: BL 2/15/03)

270 Fox, Mem. *The Magic Hat* (PS–1). Illus. by Tricia Tusa. 2002, Harcourt $16.00 (0-15-201025-4). 32pp. A magic hat transforms the people on whose heads it lands into a variety of different animals in this charming fantasy. (Rev: BCCB 7–8/02; BL 4/15/02; HBG 10/02; SLJ 4/02)

271 Freymann, Saxton, and Joost Elffers. *Gus and Button* (PS–3). 2001, Scholastic $15.95 (0-439-11015-7). 32pp. This tale about a bland-colored mushroom boy and his mushroom dog on a quest to find a colorful place that contrasts with their life is artfully illustrated with computer-enhanced photographs of vegetables. (Rev: BL 11/15/01; HBG 3/02; SLJ 12/01)

272 Fuge, Charles. *I Know a Rhino* (PS). Illus. 2002, Sterling $12.95 (1-4027-0137-3). 32pp. This captivating rhyming fantasy about a little girl's imaginary adventures with animals is enriched by amusing illustrations, including a portrayal of a genteel rhino pouring tea. (Rev: BL 12/1/02; SLJ 2/03)

273 Gardiner, Lindsey. *When Poppy and Max Grow Up* (PS–K). Illus. Series: Poppy and Max. 2001, Little, Brown $12.95 (0-316-60342-2). 24pp. Poppy and her dog Max have fun imagining what Poppy may do when she grows up. (Rev: BL 9/1/01; HBG 3/02; SLJ 10/01)

274 Goldfinger, Jennifer P. *A Fish Named Spot* (PS–1). Illus. 2001, Little, Brown $14.95 (0-316-32047-1). 32pp. Simon feeds his fish dog cookies with some surprising results. (Rev: BL 7/01; HBG 10/01; SLJ 6/01)

275 Goode, Diane. *Tiger Trouble!* (PS–2). Illus. 2001, Scholastic $15.95 (0-439-20866-1). 40pp. Lily the tiger's continued residence in Jack's apartment building is at risk until she foils a burglar in this story set in New York in the early 1900s. (Rev: BL 10/1/01; HBG 3/02; SLJ 12/01)

276 Gottfried, Maya. *Last Night I Dreamed a Circus* (PS–3). Illus. by Robert Rahway Zakanitch. 2003, Knopf $15.95 (0-375-82388-3). 32pp. The sights of a dream circus, described in picturesque language. (Rev: BL 2/1/03)

277 Graham, Bob. *Jethro Byrd, Fairy Child* (PS–2). Illus. 2002, Candlewick $15.99 (0-7636-1772-5). 32pp. Young Annabelle becomes friends with a fairy, Jethro Byrd, who is invisible to everyone else. (Rev: BCCB 10/02; BL 5/1/02; HBG 10/02; SLJ 6/02*)

278 Grambling, Lois G. *This Whole Tooth Fairy Thing's Nothing But a Big Rip-off!* (K–2). Illus. by Thomas Payne. 2002, Marshall Cavendish $15.95 (0-7614-5104-8). Little Hippo and the Tooth Fairy come to an agreement when she arrives late for the appropriate exchange. (Rev: HBG 10/02; SLJ 7/02)

279 Grambling, Lois G. *The Witch Who Wanted to Be a Princess* (K–2). Illus. by Judy Love. 2002, Charlesbridge LB $15.95 (1-58089-062-8). Young witch Bella longs to be a princess, but witches are now endangered and are forbidden from transforming themselves. (Rev: HBG 3/03; SLJ 8/02)

280 Greene, Rhonda Gowler. *Eek! Creak! Snicker, Sneak* (PS–1). Illus. by Joseph A. Smith. 2002, Simon & Schuster $16.00 (0-689-83047-5). Two children give monsters Bugbear and Bugaboo a scare of their own. (Rev: BCCB 3/02; HBG 10/02; SLJ 2/02)

281 Grobler, Piet. *Hey, Frog!* (PS–K). Illus. 2002, Front Street $15.95 (1-886910-84-7). 32pp. Humorous illustrations and fast-reading text tell the story of a greedy frog who drinks all the water on the African savannah, leaving the other thirsty animals to plot their revenge, including the tickly eels. (Rev: BL 1/1–15/03; HB 1–2/03; HBG 3/03; SLJ 1/03)

282 Gurney, John Steven. *Dinosaur Train* (PS–1). Illus. 2002, HarperCollins LB $16.89 (0-06-029246-6). 32pp. Dinosaurs and trains: young Jesse combines his two favorite things in a wonderful, fanciful dream. (Rev: BL 11/15/02; HBG 3/03; SLJ 12/02)

283 Hachler, Bruno. *Snow Ravens* (PS–2). Trans. from German by Marianne Martens. Illus. by Birte Muller. 2002, North-South LB $16.50 (0-7358-1690-5). One raven wants to try making a snow angel like the children, while the other two are too busy complaining about winter. (Rev: HBG 3/03; SLJ 2/03)

284 Harker, Lesley. *Annie's Ark* (PS–2). Illus. by author. 2002, Scholastic $15.95 (0-439-36823-5). Noah's granddaughter is so busy looking after the animals on the ark that she can't find time for herself. (Rev: HBG 3/03; SLJ 1/03)

285 Harris, Peter. *Ordinary Audrey* (PS–2). Illus. by David Runert. 2001, ME Media $14.95 (1-58925-014-1). 32pp. When 5-year-old Deadwood Deb, a dangerous cowgirl, isn't around to defend her town against invading outlaws, her timid twin sister Audrey must take her place in this tale set in the Wild West. (Rev: BCCB 2/02; BL 2/15/02)

286 Heap, Sue. *What Shall We Play?* (K–3). Illus. 2002, Candlewick $13.99 (0-7636-1685-0). 32pp. Lily May, who possesses the ability to fly, finally persuades her friends to join her in a game of playing fairies. (Rev: BCCB 7–8/02; BL 6/1–15/02; HBG 10/02; SLJ 4/02)

287 Hindley, Judy. *Rosy's Visitors* (K–3). Illus. by Helen Craig. 2002, Candlewick $14.99 (0-7636-1769-5). 32pp. Rosy finds herself a new home in a hollow of a tree and there she is visited by a number of animals. (Rev: BL 5/1/02; HBG 10/02; SLJ 8/02)

288 Hooper, Patricia. *A Stormy Ride on Noah's Ark* (PS–3). Illus. by Lynn Munsinger. 2001, Putnam $15.99 (0-399-23188-9). 32pp. After a stormy beginning, the animals on the ark gradually learn to trust each other and settle down for the night. (Rev: BL 10/1/01; HB 11–12/01; HBG 3/02; SLJ 12/01)

289 Hort, Lenny. *We're Going on Safari* (PS–2). Illus. by Tom Arma. 2002, Abrams $12.95 (0-8109-0574-4). 32pp. This photographic expedition with rhyming chant pairs costumed babies with real animal equivalents in various habitats. (Rev: BL 11/1/02; HBG 3/03; SLJ 11/02)

290 Howard, Arthur. *Hoodwinked* (PS–1). Illus. 2001, Harcourt $16.00 (0-15-202656-8). 32pp. Mitzi the witch has trouble finding a suitable pet and ends up with an unlikely choice. (Rev: BCCB 9/01; BL 9/1/01; HB 1–2/02; HBG 3/02; SLJ 9/01*)

291 Hubbard, Woodleigh Marx, and Madeleine Houston. *Whoa Jealousy!* (K–3). Illus. by Woodleigh Hubbard. 2002, Putnam $15.99 (0-399-23435-7). Taking animal forms, jealousy, envy, greed, and rivalry turn up and cause all kinds of problems. (Rev: HBG 10/02; SLJ 7/02)

292 Hunter, Jana Novotny. *Little Ones Do!* (PS–K). Illus. by Sally Anne Lambert. 2001, Dutton $14.99 (0-525-46690-8). 32pp. This book aimed at toddlers

and preschoolers follows a busy day in the life of a little dragon. (Rev: BL 11/15/01; HBG 3/02; SLJ 8/01)

293 Huntington, Amy. *One Monday* (PS–1). Illus. 2001, Scholastic $16.95 (0-439-29304-9). 32pp. A blustery wind blows through Annabelle's farm, causing mayhem for the animals who live there. (Rev: BL 2/1/02; HBG 3/02; SLJ 12/01)

294 Hurst, Margaret M. *Grannie and the Jumbie: A Caribbean Tale* (K–3). Illus. by author. 2001, HarperCollins LB $15.89 (0-06-623633-9). A spirited young Caribbean boy ignores his grandmother's warnings about the supernatural, and Jumbie the bogeyman comes to grab him. (Rev: HBG 3/02; SLJ 2/02)

295 Inns, Christopher. *Next! Please* (PS–K). Illus. by author. 2001, Tricycle Pr. $14.95 (1-58246-038-8). A blue rabbit doctor and brown dog nurse spend their days at the toy hospital mending other stuffed animals, healing them with kind words when repairs are not possible. (Rev: HBG 10/01; SLJ 5/01)

296 Jackson, Shelley. *Sophia: The Alchemist's Dog* (1–3). Illus. 2002, Simon & Schuster $17.95 (0-689-84279-1). 48pp. Although the alchemist has failed to turn lead into gold, the king praises his wonderful artwork and neither realizes that the alchemist's dog has got the recipe right. (Rev: BL 10/1/02; HBG 3/03; SLJ 10/02)

297 Jackson, Shirley. *9 Magic Wishes* (K–2). Illus. by Miles Hyman. 2001, Farrar $16.00 (0-374-35525-8). 32pp. The grandson of the author has illustrated in soft-focus pastels this new edition of the story first published in 1963 about a little girl who is offered nine wishes but doesn't need the last one. (Rev: BL 12/15/01; HBG 3/02; SLJ 10/01)

298 Joyce, William. *Big Time Olie* (PS–1). Illus. 2002, HarperCollins LB $17.89 (0-06-008811-7). 40pp. Rolie Polie Olie, the rotund robotlike creature, finds he is sometimes too big and sometimes too small to meet his desires but simply makes things worse by fooling around with the shrink-and-grow-a-lator. (Rev: BL 10/1/02; HBG 3/03; SLJ 11/02)

299 Joyce, William. *Sleepy Time Olie* (PS–K). Illus. 2001, HarperCollins LB $15.89 (0-06-029614-3). 48pp. This brightly colored, rollicking picture book about space-kid Olie (first seen in *Rolie Polie Olie* [1999] and *Snowie Rolie* [2000]) finds him building a laugh-ray to fix his grandfather's broken smile. (Rev: BL 11/15/01; HBG 3/02; SLJ 10/01)

300 Kane, Tracy. *Fairy Houses* (K–3). Illus. by author. 2001, Great White Dog Picture Co. $15.95 (0-9708104-5-8). Kristen builds a fairy house that attracts many animals but will fairies ever come? (Rev: SLJ 1/02)

301 Kastner, Jill. *Princess Dinosaur* (PS–K). Illus. 2001, Greenwillow LB $15.89 (0-688-17046-3). 32pp. An action-filled picture book about the adventures of Princess Dinosaur and her friends Cowboy Tex, a toy, and Bettina, a doll. (Rev: BCCB 5/01; BL 4/15/01; HBG 10/01; SLJ 5/01)

302 Kenah, Katharine. *The Dream Shop* (K–3). Illus. by Peter Catalanotto. 2002, HarperCollins LB

$16.89 (0-688-17901-0). 32pp. A young girl is transported to a shop where dreams are sold in this magical tale. (Rev: BL 2/15/02; HBG 10/02; SLJ 1/02)

303 Kennedy, Kim. *Pirate Pete* (K–3). Illus. by Doug Kennedy. 2002, Abrams $15.95 (0-8109-4356-5). 32pp. Pete and his parrot share a series of swashbuckling adventures after he steals a treasure map from a queen. (Rev: BL 6/1–15/02; HBG 10/02)

304 Khalsa, Dayal Kaur. *Green Cat* (PS–K). Illus. 2002, Tundra $14.95 (0-88776-586-6). 24pp. This posthumous offering tells the tale of a brother and sister who bicker over the space in their room, until a big green cat shows them just how crowded the room can get. (Rev: BL 3/15/02; HBG 10/02; SLJ 5/02)

305 Kimmel, Eric A. *A Cloak for the Moon* (PS–3). Illus. by Katya Krenina. 2001, Holiday $16.95 (0-8234-1493-0). 32pp. A tailor heads for China in search of material for a cloak for the moon, and earns a luminous thread as a reward for a good deed. (Rev: BCCB 4/01; BL 7/01; HBG 10/01; SLJ 5/01)

306 Kimmel, Eric A. *The Erie Canal Pirates* (K–3). Illus. by Andrew Glass. 2002, Holiday $16.95 (0-8234-1657-7). 32pp. A humorous tale about a captain battling pirates on the Erie Canal, using the traditional folk song as a base. (Rev: BCCB 11/02; BL 10/15/02; HBG 3/03; SLJ 11/02)

307 Kimmel, Eric A. *Pumpkinhead* (1–3). Illus. by Steve Haskamp. 2001, Winslow $15.95 (1-890817-33-3). Pumpkinhead sets off on a quest to find out if everyone in the world has a pumpkin head, only to be turned off course by a pair of pesky squirrels. (Rev: HBG 3/02; SLJ 9/01)

308 Kipling, Rudyard. *How the Camel Got His Hump* (K–3). Illus. by Lisbeth Zwerger. 2001, North-South LB $15.88 (0-7358-1483-X). 24pp. The classic Kipling story is complemented by beautiful new, detailed illustrations. (Rev: BL 12/1/01; HBG 3/02; SLJ 12/01)

309 Kleven, Elisa. *The Dancing Deer and the Foolish Hunter* (K–3). Illus. 2002, Dutton $16.99 (0-525-46832-3). 32pp. A hunter captures a dancing deer, but discovers she can't dance without the music of the birds in this tale about nature's reciprocity. (Rev: BL 2/15/02; HBG 10/02; SLJ 4/02)

310 Krulik, Nancy. *Anyone But Me*. Book #1 (2–4). Illus. by John and Wendy. Series: Katie Kazoo, Switcheroo. 2002, Grosset paper $$3.99 (0-448-42653-6). 80pp. Katie, who can change at will, becomes a hamster and transforms a bully who is scared of hamsters into a nice person. In *Out to Lunch* (2002), she becomes a cafeteria worker and improves the food. (Rev: SLJ 5/02)

311 Lawler, Janet. *If Kisses Were Colors* (PS–1). Illus. by Alison Jay. 2003, Dial $15.99 (0-8037-2617-1). 32pp. A fanciful series of characterizations of kisses — as colors, pebbles, comets, flowers, and more — are accompanied by appealing illustrations. (Rev: BL 3/1/03; SLJ 3/03)

312 Lawson, Janet. *Audrey and Barbara* (K–2). Illus. 2002, Simon & Schuster $13.95 (0-689-83896-4). 32pp. A little girl and her reluctant cat take a pretend voyage to India in a bathtub. (Rev: BL 9/15/02; HB 5–6/02; HBG 10/02; SLJ 7/02)

313 Leedy, Loreen. *Follow the Money!* (1–3). Illus. 2002, Holiday $16.95 (0-8234-1587-2). 32pp. George, a newly minted quarter, has a busy day from delivery at the bank through many adventures to his eventual return to the bank. (Rev: BCCB 4/02; BL 4/15/02*; HBG 10/02; SLJ 5/02)

314 Leonard, Marie. *Tibili: The Little Boy Who Didn't Want to Go to School* (K–3). Illus. by Andree Prigent. 2002, Kane $15.95 (1-929132-20-4). 36pp. An African child is reluctant to start school but, when the animals show him how important reading is, he changes his mind. (Rev: BL 6/1–15/02; HBG 10/02; SLJ 4/02)

315 Lerner, Harriet, and Susan Goldhor. *Franny B. Kranny, There's a Bird in Your Hair!* (PS–3). Illus. by Helen Oxenbury. 2001, HarperCollins LB $15.89 (0-06-029503-1). 40pp. A bird settles in Franny's hair when her overabundant locks are put up for a special occasion, and she refuses to dislodge it. (Rev: BCCB 9/01; BL 6/1–15/01; HB 7–8/01; HBG 10/01; SLJ 6/01)

316 Leslie, Amanda. *Who's That Scratching at My Door? A Peekaboo Riddle Book* (PS–K). Illus. by author. 2001, Handprint $12.95 (1-929766-19-X). A young boy is looking for a friend, but the animals that keep showing up at the door (actually, under the flap) are never quite right until a puppy turns up. (Rev: HBG 10/01; SLJ 7/01)

317 Levert, Mireille. *An Island in the Soup* (PS). Illus. 2001, Groundwood $15.95 (0-88899-403-6). 32pp. Victor of the Noodle experiences great danger while traveling through his soup. (Rev: BL 7/01; HBG 10/01; SLJ 6/01)

318 Levine, Gail Carson. *Betsy Who Cried Wolf!* (PS–2). Illus. by Scott Nash. 2002, HarperCollins LB $15.89 (0-06-028764-0). 40pp. A wolf tries to outwit the new shepherd, 8-year-old Betsy, but she manages to make him an ally. (Rev: BCCB 10/02; BL 7/02; HBG 10/02; SLJ 6/02)

319 Levitin, Sonia. *When Elephant Goes to a Party* (PS–3). Illus. by Jeff Seaver. 2001, Rising Moon $15.95 (0-87358-751-0). 32pp. A little girl advises her elephant on proper party behavior. (Rev: BL 5/1/01; HBG 10/01; SLJ 6/01)

320 Lewison, Wendy Cheyette. *Princess Buttercup: A Flower Princess Story* (PS–1). Illus. by Jerry Smath. Series: All Aboard Reading. 2001, Grosset LB $13.89 (0-448-42473-8); paper $3.99 (0-448-42472-X). 32pp. Bright artwork accompanies the simple story of a princess who gets lost in the woods. (Rev: HBG 10/01; SLJ 8/01)

321 Lia, Simone. *Billy Bean's Dream* (PS–3). Illus. by author. 2000, David & Charles $15.95 (1-86233-260-6). Billy, a jelly bean, longs to travel into space and nearly gets his wish in this zany tale with bold illustrations. (Rev: SLJ 4/01)

322 Light, Steve. *The Shoemaker Extraordinaire* (PS–1). Illus. 2003, Abrams $14.95 (0-8109-4236-4). 32pp. The tale of Hans Crispin, who makes magical shoes for a giant named Barefootus. (Rev: BL 3/15/03)

323 Lillegard, Dee. *Tiger, Tiger* (PS–2). Illus. by Susan Guevara. 2002, Putnam $16.99 (0-399-22633-8). 32pp. Dramatic illustrations add to this exciting story, in which lonely Pocu finds a magic feather in the hot jungle and uses it and his imagination to create a tiger — a very hungry tiger. (Rev: BL 1/1–15/03; HBG 3/03; SLJ 12/02)

324 Lindenbaum, Pija. *Bridget and the Gray Wolves* (PS–2). Illus. 2001, Farrar $14.00 (91-29-65395-9). 24pp. Timid little Bridget always expects the worst, but when she becomes surrounded by wolves she surprisingly becomes leader of the pack in this humorous reversal full of funny lupines. (Rev: BCCB 9/01; BL 12/15/01; HBG 3/02; SLJ 11/01)

325 Lindgren, Astrid. *Most Beloved Sister* (2–4). Trans. by Elisabeth Kallick Dyssegaard. Illus. by Hans Arnold. 2002, Farrar $15.00 (91-29-65502-1). 28pp. When her baby brother is born, Barbara's imaginary twin sister, Lalla-Lee, comes to her rescue and the two have a day of magical adventures together in this vividly illustrated story that was originally published a half-century ago. (Rev: BL 7/02; HBG 10/02; SLJ 8/02)

326 Loki. *Jake Greenthumb* (PS–2). Illus. by Jason Gaillard. 2002, Mondo $15.95 (1-59034-186-4). 32pp. Jake's thumb is so green that the plants he is looking after threaten to take over his room. (Rev: HBG 10/02; SLJ 9/02)

327 Lyons, Dana. *The Tree* (PS–2). Illus. by David Danioth. 2002, Illumination Arts $16.95 (0-9701907-1-9). An 800-year-old Douglas fir describes its life in simple verse and worries that its future is threatened. (Rev: SLJ 10/02)

328 McClements, George. *Jake Gander, Storyville Detective: The Case of the Greedy Granny* (1–3). 2002, Hyperion $15.99 (0-7868-0662-1). The humorous story of Jake's efforts to solve a mystery surrounding Red R. Hood's grandmother. (Rev: HBG 3/03; SLJ 9/02)

329 McClintock, Barbara. *Dahlia* (PS–2). Illus. 2002, Farrar $16.00 (0-374-31678-3). 32pp. When Charlotte is given a frilly doll named Dahlia, she includes her in her tomboy adventures in this picture book set in the Victorian age. (Rev: BCCB 10/02; BL 9/1/02; HB 9–10/02*; HBG 3/03; SLJ 11/02*)

330 MacDonald, Amy. *Quentin Fenton Herter III* (K–3). Illus. by Giselle Potter. 2002, Farrar $16.00 (0-374-36170-3). 32pp. Quentin Fenton Herter III is a good boy who's plagued by a not-so-good "shadow," Quentin Fenton Three. (Rev: BCCB 9/02; BL 5/15/02; HB 5–6/02; HBG 10/02; SLJ 5/02)

331 MacDonald, Ross. *Another Perfect Day* (K–2). Illus. 2002, Millbrook LB $22.90 (0-7613-2659-6). 32pp. Jack hits the new day on the run — exercising with alligators, catching the train in his hands — but then his world seems to start changing; his suit is now a tutu, his airplane is now a tricycle . . . and when he wakes up in bed it all becomes clear. (Rev: BL 11/1/02; HBG 3/03; SLJ 9/02)

332 McDonnell, Flora. *Giddy-up! Let's Ride!* (K–3). Illus. 2002, Candlewick $16.99 (0-7636-1778-4). 32pp. Different kinds of horses and other beasts carry a variety of riders — such as a princess, a fairy, a goatherd, and a rajah — in this delightful fantasy. (Rev: BCCB 10/02; BL 5/1/02; HBG 10/02; SLJ 7/02)

333 McMullan, Kate. *I Stink!* (PS–3). Illus. by James McMullan. 2002, HarperCollins LB $15.89 (0-06-029849-9). 40pp. In this boldly illustrated picture book, a garbage truck describes its activities during its nightly rounds. (Rev: BCCB 6/02; BL 6/1–15/02; HB 5–6/02*; HBG 10/02; SLJ 5/02)

334 McPhail, David. *Edward in the Jungle* (PS–3). Illus. 2002, Little, Brown $15.95 (0-316-56391-9). 32pp. While reading about Tarzan, Edward is transported to Africa where he is saved from a menacing crocodile by the Lord of the Jungle. (Rev: BCCB 4/02; BL 4/1/02; HBG 10/02; SLJ 3/02)

335 McQueen, John Troy. *A World Full of Monsters* (PS–3). Illus. by Marc Brown. 2001, HarperCollins LB $15.89 (0-06-029770-0). 32pp. Today, there are few monsters and they mainly do helpful tasks at night, but they used to be plentiful and do much more, according to this amusing picture book. (Rev: BL 9/15/01; HBG 3/02)

336 Many, Paul. *The Great Pancake Escape* (PS–2). Illus. by Scott Goto. 2002, Walker LB $17.85 (0-8027-8796-7). 32pp. When a magician dad mixes up his recipes, he finds that he has replaced every round object in town with a pancake. (Rev: BL 4/1/02; HBG 10/02; SLJ 3/02)

337 Mayhew, James. *Katie and the Sunflowers* (K–3). Illus. 2001, Scholastic $15.95 (0-531-30325-X). 32pp. Katie's museum escapades continue with a romp through Van Gogh, Gauguin, and Cezanne canvases that involves sunflowers, still lifes, and a chase through a cafe. (Rev: BL 6/1–15/01; HBG 10/01; SLJ 7/01)

338 Mayhew, James. *Secret in the Garden: A Peek-Through Book* (K–3). Illus. by author. 2003, Scholastic $15.95 (0-439-40435-5). Sophie finds a number of treasures when a robin gives her the key to a secret garden in this book that uses die-cut holes effectively. (Rev: SLJ 3/03)

339 Meddaugh, Susan. *Harry on the Rocks* (PS–2). Illus. 2003, Houghton $15.00 (0-618-27603-3). 32pp. Stranded on an island, Harry befriends its only other inhabitant, a dragon. (Rev: BL 2/15/03)

340 Melling, David. *The Kiss That Missed* (PS–2). Illus. by author. 2002, Barron's $14.95 (0-7641-5451-6). A royal kiss goes astray and must be retrieved from a spooky forest full of dangers. (Rev: HBG 3/03; SLJ 12/02)

341 Mills, Lauren. *Fia and the Imp* (K–3). Illus. by Dennis Nolan. 2002, Little, Brown $15.95 (0-316-57412-0). 32pp. Fia, a plucky fairy without wings, sets out to rescue her woodkin friends despite the mockery of her kin. (Rev: BL 1/1–15/03; HBG 3/03; SLJ 12/02)

342 Munsch, Robert. *Zoom!* (K–3). Illus. by Michael Martchenko. 2003, Scholastic $13.95 (0-439-18774-5). 32pp. Lauretta's new wheelchair goes so fast she gets a speeding ticket in this playful fantasy. (Rev: BL 2/1/03)

343 Murphy, Jill. *All for One* (PS–1). Illus. 2002, Candlewick $15.99 (0-7636-0785-1). 32pp. Little monster Marlon gives up trying to play with the bigger kids and decides to go off by himself, only to find that he is now the center of attention. (Rev: BL 10/1/02; HBG 3/03; SLJ 12/02)

344 Muth, Jon J. *The Three Questions: Based on a Story by Leo Tolstoy* (PS–3). Illus. 2002, Scholastic $16.95 (0-439-19996-4). 32pp. A conversation-starter about a boy who finds the answers to his philosophical questions in an act of kindness. (Rev: BL 3/15/02; HBG 10/02; SLJ 6/02)

345 Namioka, Lensey. *The Hungriest Boy in the World* (K–3). Illus. by Aki Sogabe. 2001, Holiday $16.95 (0-8234-1542-2). 32pp. A little Japanese boy swallows a hunger monster that causes the boy to eat everything in sight. (Rev: BL 4/1/01; HB 5–6/01; HBG 10/01; SLJ 4/01)

346 Nesbit, E. *The Book of Beasts* (K–3). Illus. by Inga Moore. 2001, Candlewick $16.99 (0-7636-1579-X). When a new young king opens the Book of Beasts and releases the animals therein, a Red Dragon starts to wreak havoc. (Rev: HBG 3/02; SLJ 12/01)

347 Nolan, Dennis. *Shadow of the Dinosaurs* (1–3). Illus. 2001, Simon & Schuster $16.00 (0-689-82974-4). 32pp. Dramatic watercolors complement the magical, exciting adventures of Shadow, a dachshund who digs up a dinosaur bone, and his sleeping master. (Rev: BL 12/15/01; HBG 3/02; SLJ 12/01)

348 Novak, Matt. *No Zombies Allowed* (K–2). Illus. by author. 2002, Simon & Schuster $16.95 (0-689-84130-2). Witch Wizzle and Witch Woddle are busy crossing names off their monster party guest list because of bad behavior the year before. (Rev: BCCB 9/02; HB 9–10/02; HBG 3/03; SLJ 8/02)

349 Noyes, Deborah. *It's Vladimir!* (K–3). Illus. by Christopher Mills. 2001, Marshall Cavendish $15.95 (0-7614-5071-8). 32pp. A young vampire is impatient to learn how to turn into a bat. (Rev: BL 10/15/01; HBG 3/02; SLJ 10/01)

350 Ordal, Stina Langlo. *Princess Aasta* (PS). Illus. 2002, Bloomsbury $16.95 (1-58234-783-2). 32pp. Princess Aasta's polar bear friend, acquired through a letter to the newspaper, takes her on an entertaining trip to the North Pole. (Rev: BCCB 1/03; BL 11/15/02; SLJ 1/03)

351 Ormerod, Jan. *Miss Mouse Takes Off* (PS–K). Illus. 2001, HarperCollins $14.95 (0-688-17870-7). 32pp. Detailed illustrations add to the fun of this story of an airplane ride for Miss Mouse, a stuffed toy. (Rev: BCCB 7–8/01; BL 6/1–15/01; HB 9–10/01; HBG 3/02; SLJ 7/01)

352 Passen, Lisa. *The Incredible Shrinking Teacher* (K–3). 2002, Holt $15.95 (0-8050-6452-4). 32pp. Strict teacher Irma Birnbaum gets her just desserts when she faces a series of indignities after being shrunk. (Rev: BL 6/1–15/02; HBG 10/02; SLJ 5/02)

353 Peake, Mervyn. *Captain Slaughterboard Drops Anchor* (2–4). Illus. 2001, Candlewick $16.99 (0-7636-1625-7). 48pp. A captain and his crew discover an island inhabited by strange creatures in this reprint of a 1939 classic picture book. (Rev: BL 2/1/02; HBG 3/02)

354 Pelletier, Andrew. *Sixteen Miles to Spring* (K–3). Illus. by Katya Krenina. 2002, Albert Whitman $15.95 (0-8075-7388-4). 32pp. A fanciful explanation of spring in which two friends travel from south to north each year, starting at Christmas and spreading seeds as they go. (Rev: BCCB 4/02; BL 5/1/02; HBG 10/02; SLJ 6/02)

355 Pienkowski, Jan. *Pizza! A Yummy Pop-up* (PS). Illus. by author. 2002, Candlewick $12.99 (0-7636-1626-5). Lots of food noises accompany the varied and elaborate pop-ups presented here. (Rev: SLJ 4/02)

356 Plourde, Lynn. *Spring's Sprung* (PS–1). Illus. by Greg Couch. 2002, Simon & Schuster $16.00 (0-689-84229-5). March, April, and May are querulous siblings who test Mother Earth's patience in this ode to spring. (Rev: HBG 10/02; SLJ 3/02)

357 Porto, Tony. *Get Red! An Adventure in Color* (1–3). 2002, Little, Brown $14.95 (0-316-60940-4). A red crayon helps its owners on many assignments but gets crankier as it grows shorter. (Rev: HBG 3/03; SLJ 10/02)

358 Pulver, Robin. *Punctuation Takes a Vacation* (1–3). Illus. by Lynn Rowe Reed. 2003, Holiday $16.95 (0-8234-1687-9). 32pp. Punctuation marks take offense at a teacher's comment and disappear, leaving children unable to write properly. (Rev: BL 3/1/03)

359 Puttock, Simon. *A Ladder to the Stars* (1–4). Illus. by Alison Jay. 2001, Holt $16.95 (0-8050-6783-3). At the age of 107, a woman finally gets her wish to climb up to the stars. (Rev: HBG 3/02; SLJ 1/02)

360 Ray, Mary Lyn. *All Aboard!* (PS–2). Illus. by Amiko Hirao. 2002, Little, Brown $14.95 (0-316-73507-8). 32pp. The rabbit named Mr. Barnes, who appears to be traveling alone, belongs in fact to the little girl on the same train. (Rev: BL 11/1/02; HBG 3/03; SLJ 10/02)

361 Rex, Michael. *My Freight Train* (PS–K). Illus. 2002, Holt $15.95 (0-8050-6682-9). 32pp. A little boy segues from playing with his toy train to a day as engineer of a real freight train, and explains every detail of the train and his duties. (Rev: BL 11/15/02; HBG 3/03; SLJ 11/02)

362 Reynolds, Adrian. *Pete and Polo's Farmyard Adventure* (PS–K). Illus. 2002, Scholastic $16.95 (0-439-30913-1). 32pp. A boy named Pete and his toy polar bear search for missing ducks after they discover the pond has dried up. (Rev: BL 8/02; HBG 10/02; SLJ 7/02)

363 Robledo, Honorio. *Nico Visits the Moon* (PS–2). Illus. 2001, Cinco Puntos $15.95 (0-938317-57-1). 32pp. Baby Nico floats to the moon when he grabs a bunch of balloons intended to hang things out of his reach. (Rev: BL 11/1/01; HBG 3/02; SLJ 12/01)

364 Root, Phyllis. *Soggy Saturday* (PS). Illus. by Helen Craig. 2001, Candlewick $10.99 (0-7636-0778-9). 24pp. In this colorful tale, the tint has washed out of the sky, turning everything blue, and Bonnie Bumble resolves to restore the world to normal. (Rev: BL 12/1/01; HBG 3/02; SLJ 12/01)

365 Roth, Susan L. *Grandpa Blows His Penny Whistle Until the Angels Sing* (PS–3). Illus. 2001, Barefoot $16.99 (1-84148-247-1). 40pp. Using his penny whistle, Grandpa calls on angels to awaken Little Boy James, his grandson, who has fallen from a church roof. (Rev: BL 4/1/01; HBG 10/01; SLJ 5/01*)

366 Ryan, Pam Munoz. *Mice and Beans* (PS–2). Illus. by Joe Cepeda. 2001, Scholastic $15.95 (0-439-18303-0). 32pp. Readers get a mouse's perspective in this story of mice helping Rosa Maria prepare for her grandchild's birthday celebration that interweaves Spanish expressions. (Rev: BCCB 10/01; BL 9/15/01; HBG 3/02; SLJ 10/01)

367 Sage, Angie. *Molly and the Birthday Party* (PS–1). Illus. by author. 2001, Peachtree $9.95 (1-56145-248-3). Fuzzy, green Molly goes to Olly's birthday party but is reluctant to hand over his present. She also appears in *Molly at the Dentist* (2001). (Rev: HBG 3/02; SLJ 11/01)

368 Schachner, Judith Byron. *Yo, Vikings!* (K–3). Illus. 2002, Dutton $16.99 (0-525-46889-7). 32pp. In this fantasy, a girl imagines that she is a Viking and when a Viking ship arrives for her, she takes several of her friends on a high adventure. (Rev: BL 6/1–15/02; HBG 10/02; SLJ 8/02)

369 Schanzer, Rosalyn. *Davy Crockett Saves the World* (K–3). Illus. 2001, HarperCollins LB $16.89 (0-688-16992-9). 32pp. Davy Crockett is called upon to battle Halley's Comet in this tall tale rich with colorful illustrations. (Rev: BCCB 2/02; BL 11/15/01; HBG 10/02; SLJ 8/01)

370 Scheer, Julian. *By the Light of the Captured Moon* (PS–3). Illus. by Ronald Himler. 2001, Holiday $16.95 (0-8234-1624-0). 32pp. Billy captures the moon but soon finds he can't hide it and must let it go again. (Rev: BL 5/1/01; HBG 10/01; SLJ 3/01)

371 Schneider, Christine M. *Horace P. Tuttle, Magician Extraordinaire* (K–3). Illus. 2001, Walker $15.95 (0-8027-8788-6). 32pp. Horace's magic act is in trouble when his animal and human assistants become disgruntled. (Rev: BL 9/15/01; HBG 3/02; SLJ 10/01)

372 Schnitzlein, Danny. *The Monster Who Ate My Peas* (1–4). Illus. by Matt Faulkner. 2001, Peachtree $15.95 (1-56145-216-5). A demanding monster asks for a boy's prize possessions in return for eating his peas. (Rev: HBG 3/02; SLJ 1/02)

373 Schwab, Eva. *Robert and the Robot* (PS–K). Illus. 2001, Front Street $15.95 (1-886910-59-6). 32pp. An alien robot helps Robert clean up his room as a thank you for providing him with batteries. (Rev: BL 7/01; HBG 10/01; SLJ 5/01)

374 Schwarz, Viviane. *The Adventures of a Nose* (PS–3). Illus. by Joel Stewart. 2002, Candlewick

$14.99 (0-7636-1674-5). 32pp. Suitably imaginative artwork accompanies this tale of a nose longing to find a place where he fits in. (Rev: BL 3/15/02; HBG 10/02; SLJ 5/02)

375 Shannon, Margaret. *The Red Wolf* (PS–3). Illus. by author. 2002, Houghton $15.00 (0-618-05544-4). Locked up in her tower, Roseulpin receives a box full of wool for her seventh birthday and knits herself a liberating disguise. (Rev: BCCB 5/02; HBG 10/02; SLJ 5/02)

376 Shields, Carol Diggory. *Food Fight!* (PS–2). Illus. by Doreen Gay-Kassel. 2002, Handprint $15.95 (1-929766-29-7). Pun-filled fun for the contents of the kitchen while the humans are asleep. (Rev: HBG 3/03; SLJ 10/02)

377 Shields, Carol Diggory. *On the Go* (PS–2). Illus. by Svjetlan Junakovic. Series: Animagicals. 2001, Handprint $9.95 (1-929766-14-9). This tall, narrow book uses rhyming riddles, illustrations, and flaps to tickle young imaginations about animal movements. Also use *Patterns* (2001). (Rev: HBG 10/01; SLJ 8/01)

378 Simmons, Steven J. *Alice and Greta's Color Magic* (K–3). Illus. by Cyd Moore. 2001, Knopf $14.95 (0-375-81245-8). 32pp. Greta the bad witch makes all the colors in the world vanish and Alice the good witch fights back but only succeeds in making things worse. (Rev: HBG 3/02; SLJ 10/01)

379 Sis, Peter. *Ballerina!* (PS–K). Illus. 2001, Greenwillow $14.95 (0-688-17944-4). 24pp. In this fantasy, little Terry acts out her dreams of being the "best ballerina of all." (Rev: BCCB 5/01; BL 4/1/01; HBG 10/01; SLJ 4/01)

380 Sis, Peter. *Madlenka's Dog* (PS–2). Illus. 2002, Farrar $17.00 (0-374-34699-2). 40pp. A flap book in which many of Madlenka's friends imagine what her invisible dog looks like. (Rev: BCCB 6/02; BL 4/1/02*; HB 3–4/02*; HBG 10/02; SLJ 4/02*)

381 Smith, Jos. A. *Circus Train* (PS–3). Illus. 2001, Abrams $17.95 (0-8109-4148-1). 38pp. Young Timothy helps a stranded circus train by asking the elephants to fill the railroad cars with air, allowing the train to float to its destination. (Rev: BL 4/1/01; HBG 10/01; SLJ 4/01)

382 Smith, Lane. *Pinocchio the Boy; or, Incognito in Collidi* (K–3). Illus. 2002, Viking $16.99 (0-670-03585-8). 48pp. What happens after Pinocchio is turned into a real boy is the subject of this inventive picture book. (Rev: BL 8/02; HB 9–10/02; HBG 3/03; SLJ 9/02*)

383 Smith, Linda. *Mrs. Biddlebox* (PS–2). Illus. by Marla Frazee. 2002, HarperCollins LB $17.89 (0-06-029782-4). 32pp. Mrs. Biddlebox is having a bad day and decides to cook it away, making a cake of the various components — gloom, fog, sky, and so on — and eating the result before happily greeting the night. (Rev: BCCB 1/03; BL 11/15/02; HB 11–12/02; HBG 3/03; SLJ 10/02)

384 Smith, Linda. *When Moon Fell Down* (PS–K). Illus. by Kathryn Brown. 2001, HarperCollins LB $15.89 (0-06-029497-3). 32pp. In this lighthearted fantasy, the Moon visits the earth, plays in the fields, and gives a ride to a curious cow. (Rev: BL 4/1/01*; HBG 10/01; SLJ 7/01)

385 Spalding, Andrea. *It's Raining, It's Pouring* (PS–3). Illus. by Leslie Elizabeth Watts. 2001, Orca $15.95 (1-55143-186-6). 32pp. A little girl sets out into the clouds on a thundery day to find the old man mentioned in the song and he rewards her kindness by stopping the storm. (Rev: BL 10/1/01; HBG 10/02; SLJ 9/01)

386 Spinelli, Eileen. *Sophie's Masterpiece: A Spider's Tale* (PS–2). Illus. by Jane Dyer. 2001, Simon & Schuster $16.00 (0-689-80112-2). 32pp. As her last project, an unappreciated spider named Sophie weaves a beautiful baby blanket for a pregnant woman. (Rev: BL 4/15/01*; HB 7–8/01; HBG 10/01; SLJ 5/01)

387 Stadler, John. *What's So Scary?* (1–3). Illus. by author. 2001, Scholastic $16.95 (0-531-30301-2). The animals portrayed in a book are upset with the illustrator and decide to take over the story themselves in this humorous and unusual picture book. (Rev: HBG 10/01; SLJ 8/01)

388 Stephens, Helen. *Blue Horse* (PS–K). Illus. 2003, Scholastic $15.95 (0-439-43178-6). 32pp. Shy Tilly is new in town and lonely until her stuffed animal, Blue Horse, advises her to befriend a girl in the park. (Rev: BL 3/15/03; SLJ 3/03)

389 Stern, Ellen. *I Saw a Bullfrog* (PS–2). Illus. 2003, Random LB $16.99 (0-375-92173-7). 32pp. Stern takes names like bullfrog and cowbird literally and creates wonderful images accompanied by humorous verses. (Rev: BL 3/1/03)

390 Suen, Anastasia. *Raise the Roof!* (PS–1). Illus. by Elwood H. Smith. 2003, Viking $15.99 (0-670-89282-3). 32pp. A house is constructed despite a dog's "help" in this picture book with cartoon-like, stylized illustrations. (Rev: BCCB 2/03; BL 2/15/03; HB 3–4/03; SLJ 2/03)

391 Sunami, Kitoba. *How the Fisherman Tricked the Genie* (K–2). Illus. by Amiko Hirao. 2002, Simon & Schuster $16.00 (0-689-83399-7). 40pp. A tale within a tale about a fisherman who releases an angry genie from a bottle. (Rev: BL 8/02; HB 9–10/02; HBG 3/03; SLJ 8/02)

392 Sutherland, Marc. *MacMurtrey's Wall* (1–3). Illus. 2001, Abrams $16.95 (0-8109-4494-4). 28pp. MacMurtrey the giant is accustomed to being the greatest, but discovers he is no match for the sea when he tries to capture it behind a wall. (Rev: BL 11/15/01; HBG 3/02; SLJ 2/02)

393 Taravant, Jacques. *The Little Wing Giver* (2–4). Trans. by Nina Ignatowicz. Illus. by Peter Sis. 2001, Holt LB $14.95 (0-8050-6412-5). 32pp. A little boy sent to Earth by God distributes wings to any creature who wants them, and in the end gets a pair of his own, giving God the idea for angels. (Rev: BL 11/15/01; HBG 3/02; SLJ 11/01)

394 Thomas, Frances. *One Day, Daddy* (PS). Illus. by Ross Collins. 2001, Hyperion $15.99 (0-7868-0732-6). Little Monster weighs the future — will he be an explorer? — but worries that he won't be able to take his parents with him. (Rev: BCCB 10/01; HBG 3/02; SLJ 9/01)

395 Timmers, Leo. *Happy with Me* (K–2). Illus. 2002, Tallfellow/Smallfellow $16.95 (1-931290-08-3). 32pp. After considering the ups and downs of being different animals, a little boy decides he's happy being himself in this colorful picture book. (Rev: BL 7/02)

396 Uribe, Veronica. *Buzz, Buzz, Buzz* (PS–1). Trans. by Veronica Uribe and Elisa Amado. Illus. by Gloria Calderon. 2001, Douglas & McIntyre $15.95 (0-88899-430-3). 32pp. A brother and sister disturbed by an annoying mosquito seek help from the animals in the jungle. (Rev: BL 7/01; HBG 10/01; SLJ 8/01)

397 Van Allsburg, Chris. *Zathura: A Space Adventure* (K–3). Illus. 2002, Houghton $18.00 (0-618-25396-3). 32pp. Twenty years after the publication of *Jumanji*, this sequel rockets Danny and Walter Budwing off to an exciting adventure on the planet Zathura. (Rev: BL 11/15/02; HB 11–12/02; HBG 3/03; SLJ 11/02)

398 Van Laan, Nancy. *Teeny Tiny Tingly Tales* (K–3). Illus. by Victoria Chess. 2001, Simon & Schuster $16.00 (0-689-81875-0). 32pp. Three not-too-scary stories relate odd occurrences and strange creatures, with creepy illustrations. (Rev: BCCB 9/01; BL 10/15/01; HB 9–10/01; HBG 3/02; SLJ 1/02)

399 Vulliamy, Clara. *Small* (PS–K). Illus. 2002, Clarion $15.00 (0-618-19459-2). 32pp. When Tom has an overnight visit with his grandmother, he forgets his stuffed mouse, Small, but Small manages to make his way to Granny's. (Rev: BCCB 4/02; BL 4/15/02; HBG 10/02; SLJ 4/02)

400 Walton, Rick. *That's My Dog* (PS–2). Illus. by Julia Gorton. 2001, Putnam $9.99 (0-399-23352-0). A small boy uses a variety of adjectives to describe his big, red dog. (Rev: HBG 3/02; SLJ 12/01)

401 Walton, Rick, and Ann Walton. *Cars at Play* (PS–1). Illus. by James Lee Croft. 2002, Putnam $15.99 (0-399-23599-X). Cars honk, beep, play games, snack at the pumps, and generally have a wonderful time before growing tired and falling asleep. (Rev: HBG 10/02; SLJ 3/02)

402 Ward, Helen. *The Dragon Machine* (2–3). Illus. by Wayne Anderson. 2003, Dutton $15.99 (0-525-47114-6). 32pp. Dragons that are only visible to George dog his footsteps until he decides to fly them home in a flying machine. (Rev: BL 3/15/03)

403 Ward, Helen. *The Tin Forest* (K–3). Illus. by Wayne Anderson. 2001, Dutton $17.99 (0-525-46787-4). 36pp. A lush, colorful garden blooms from a dreary junkyard of tin, thanks to the efforts of one old man. (Rev: BL 9/15/01; HBG 3/02; SLJ 10/01)

404 Ward, Nick. *Farmer George and the Hungry Guests* (PS–K). Illus. 2001, Pavilion $14.95 (1-86205-436-3). 32pp. Farmer George investigates his missing breakfast ingredients and finds that four hungry foxes have helped themselves. (Rev: BL 4/15/01)

405 Weeks, Sarah. *Angel Face* (PS–1). Illus. by David Diaz. 2002, Simon & Schuster $17.95 (0-689-83302-4). 32pp. When a little boy wanders away, his mother enlists a crow to help find him. (Rev: BL 2/1/02; HBG 10/02; SLJ 3/02)

406 Welling, Peter J. *Andrew McGroundhog and His Shady Shadow* (1–3). Illus. by author. 2001, Pelican $14.95 (1-56554-711-X). Andrew McGroundhog's shadow is cold and wants Andrew to hibernate for the winter. (Rev: HBG 10/01; SLJ 8/01)

407 Whybrow, Ian. *Sammy and the Robots* (PS–1). Illus. by Adrian Reynolds. 2001, Scholastic $15.95 (0-531-30327-6). Sammy's robot is off being mended and when Sammy's grandmother must go into the hospital, Sammy realizes she needs a robot to look after her. (Rev: HBG 10/01; SLJ 7/01)

408 Whybrow, Ian. *Sissy Button Takes Charge!* (PS–2). Illus. by Olivia Villet. 2002, Scholastic $15.95 (0-439-12870-6). 32pp. Sissy isn't good at cleaning up despite her mother's reminders, but when she goes on an imaginary picnic with her teddy bears she finds the mess they make quite frustrating. (Rev: BL 12/1/02; HBG 3/03; SLJ 12/02)

409 Wilcox, Brian, and Lawrence David. *Full Moon* (PS–K). Illus. by Brian Wilcox. 2001, Doubleday $15.95 (0-385-32792-7). 32pp. After hooking the moon with his fishing rod, a boy has a magical adventure that ends with a rewarding birthday party attended by his beloved grandmother. (Rev: BCCB 6/01; BL 12/1/01; HBG 10/01; SLJ 6/01)

410 Williams, Linda. *Horse in the Pigpen* (PS–2). Illus. by Megan Lloyd. 2002, HarperCollins LB $15.89 (0-06-028548-6). 32pp. A farm girl tries to restore order to a very mixed-up farm in this rollicking rhyming story. (Rev: BCCB 5/02; BL 7/02; HBG 10/02; SLJ 6/02)

411 Willis, Jeanne. *The Boy Who Thought He Was a Teddy Bear* (PS–2). Illus. by Susan Varley. 2002, Peachtree $15.95 (1-56145-270-X). Three bears bring up a little boy as if he were their own. (Rev: HBG 3/03; SLJ 12/02)

412 Willis, Jeanne. *Do Little Mermaids Wet Their Beds?* (PS–1). Illus. by Penelope Jossen. 2001, Albert Whitman $15.95 (0-8075-1668-6). 32pp. With a little help from a mermaid, 4-year-old Cecelia stops wetting her bed. (Rev: BL 6/1–15/01; HBG 3/02; SLJ 5/01)

413 Wilson, Gina. *Ignis* (3–5). Illus. by P. J. Lynch. 2001, Candlewick $16.99 (0-7636-1623-0). 40pp. Ignis the dragon who can't shoot flame tries other lifestyles — as hippo, parrot, and child — before he finally finds his spark atop a volcano. (Rev: BL 12/15/01; HBG 3/02; SLJ 12/01)

414 Wilson, Sarah. *George Hogglesberry: Grade School Alien* (K–2). Illus. by Chad Cameron. 2002, Tricycle Pr. $14.95 (1-58246-063-9). 38pp. George comes from planet Frollop II, and he just can't seem to get things right in second grade. (Rev: HBG 3/03; SLJ 12/02)

415 Winnick, Karen B. *Barn Sneeze* (PS–1). Illus. 2002, Boyds Mills $15.95 (1-56397-948-9). 32pp. The animals in Sue's barn are sneezing, so Sue brings them some tea — and sneezes too. (Rev: BL 5/15/02; HBG 10/02; SLJ 6/02)

416 Wisdom, Jude. *Whatever Wanda Wanted* (K–3). Illus. 2002, Penguin Putnam $15.99 (0-8037-2693-7). 32pp. A kite whisks a spoiled little girl off to a deserted island, where she learns to live by her own resources instead of material things. (Rev: BL 3/15/02; HBG 10/02; SLJ 3/02)

417 Wood, Audrey. *When the Root Children Wake Up* (2–4). Illus. by Ned Bittinger. 2002, Scholastic $16.95 (0-590-42517-X). 32pp. Elegant artwork complements this superb retelling of an early 20th-century German tale about the seasons. (Rev: BCCB 7–8/02; BL 2/15/02; HBG 10/02; SLJ 3/02)

418 Yaccarino, Dan. *The Lima Bean Monster* (K–3). Illus. by Adam McCauley. 2001, Walker LB $16.85 (0-8027-8777-0). 32pp. Sammy buries unwanted lima beans in a vacant lot, with monstrous results. (Rev: BL 9/1/01; HBG 3/02; SLJ 9/01)

419 Yorinks, Arthur. *Company's Going* (2–4). Illus. by David Small. 2001, Hyperion $15.99 (0-7868-0415-7). 40pp. In this sequel to *Company's Coming* (2000), the meatball-loving aliens who visited Shirley and Moe on Earth take the elderly couple to their own planet to cater a wedding. (Rev: BCCB 1/02; BL 1/1–15/02; HB 1–2/02*; HBG 3/02; SLJ 2/02)

420 Ziefert, Harriet. *Squarehead* (PS–2). Illus. by Todd McKie. 2001, Houghton $16.00 (0-618-08378-2). Squarehead George is only happy around square shapes until his dreams show him a curving moon and a big, round earth. (Rev: HBG 10/01; SLJ 5/01)

IMAGINARY ANIMALS

421 Adoff, Arnold. *Daring Dog and Captain Cat* (PS–3). Illus. by Joe Cepeda. 2001, Simon & Schuster $16.00 (0-689-82599-4). 32pp. Two pets, known by day as Irving Dog and Ermine Cat, enjoy dramatic nighttime adventures. (Rev: BCCB 10/01; BL 10/1/01; HBG 3/02; SLJ 9/01)

422 Agee, Jon. *Milo's Hat Trick* (PS–2). Illus. 2001, Hyperion $15.95 (0-7868-0902-7). 32pp. Milo isn't much of a magician until he meets a bear who knows hat tricks. (Rev: BL 7/01; HB 5–6/01*; HBG 10/01; SLJ 5/01*)

423 Alborough, Jez. *Fix-It Duck* (PS–K). Illus. 2002, HarperCollins $15.95 (0-06-000699-4). 40pp. A hilarious romp that begins when Duck sets out to fix what he believes is a leaky roof. (Rev: BL 4/1/02; HBG 10/02; SLJ 5/02)

424 Alexander, Martha. *We're in Big Trouble, Blackboard Bear* (PS–1). Illus. 2001, Candlewick $10.99 (0-7636-0670-7). 40pp. Blackboard Bear must confess to stealing and make amends in this charming story presented with minimal text. (Rev: BL 12/15/01; HBG 3/02)

425 Alter, Anna. *Estelle and Lucy* (PS–K). Illus. 2001, Greenwillow LB $14.89 (0-688-17883-9). 24pp. Estelle, a kitten, shows her younger sister, Lucy, a mouse, all the things that older children can do that younger ones are forbidden to do. (Rev: BL 4/1/01*; HBG 10/01; SLJ 7/01)

426 Anderson, Peggy Perry. *Let's Clean Up!* (PS–2). Illus. 2002, Houghton $15.00 (0-618-19602-1). 32pp. Rhyming text tells the story of little frog Joe, who can't resist messing up the room his mother just cleaned. (Rev: BL 3/1/02; HBG 10/02; SLJ 4/02)

427 Anderson, Stephen Axel. *I Know the Moon* (K–4). Illus. by Greg Couch. 2001, Philomel $15.99 (0-399-23425-X). The animals of the forest cannot agree on the nature of the moon, and are not satisfied with the answer they get from the Man of Science. (Rev: BCCB 2/01; HBG 10/01; SLJ 5/01)

428 Andreae, Giles. *Heaven Is Having You* (PS). Illus. by Vanessa Cabban. 2002, Tiger Tales $14.95 (1-58925-016-8). Grandma Bear sees heaven all around her, especially when Little Bear is with her. (Rev: SLJ 7/02)

429 Anholt, Laurence. *Chimp and Zee* (PS–2). Illus. by Catherine Anholt. 2001, Penguin Putnam $16.99 (0-8037-2671-6). Chimp and Zee become separated from Mumkey when they hide in a basket of bananas that is resting on top of an elephant, not a rock. (Rev: HBG 3/02; SLJ 10/01)

430 Anholt, Laurence. *Chimp and Zee and the Big Storm* (K–3). Illus. by Catherine Anholt. 2002, Penguin Putnam $16.99 (0-8037-2700-3). 32pp. Monkey twins Chimp and Zee are swept away by a big wind while folding laundry and must be rescued by Mumkey and Papakey. Also use *Chimp and Zee's Noisy Book* and *Monkey Around with Chimp and Zee* (both 2002). (Rev: BL 10/1/02; HBG 3/03; SLJ 9/02)

431 Appelt, Kathi. *The Alley Cat's Meow* (PS–K). Illus. by Jon Goddell. 2002, Harcourt $16.00 (0-15-201980-4). 32pp. A pair of "hep cats" is depicted in cool verse and flowing acrylics as they meet at the Alley Cat's Meow jazz club, fall in love, and dance their way to fame. (Rev: BL 1/1–15/03; HBG 3/03; SLJ 10/02)

432 Apperley, Dawn. *Don't Wake the Baby* (PS–2). Illus. by author. 2001, Bloomsbury $16.95 (0-7475-5003-4). A young squirrel tries unsuccessfully to keep quiet so as not to disturb her sleeping sibling. (Rev: SLJ 12/01)

433 Apperley, Dawn. *Flip and Flop* (PS–K). Illus. 2001, Scholastic $12.95 (0-439-28892-4). 32pp. Little penguin Flop wants to do everything his big brother Flip does, but must find someone else to play with when big brother goes off with a friend. (Rev: BL 1/1–15/02; HBG 3/02; SLJ 3/02)

434 Araki, Mie. *The Magic Toolbox: Starring Fred and Lulu* (PS–1). Illus. by author. 2003, Chronicle $14.95 (0-8118-3564-2). A magic toolbox comes to the rescue when Fred, a rabbit, can't wield his blocks like Lulu the rhinoceros. (Rev: SLJ 3/03)

435 Arnold, Marsha Diane. *Metro Cat* (PS–3). Illus. by Jack E. Davis. 2001, Golden Books $9.95 (0-307-10213-0). 32pp. A celebrity cat suddenly finds herself in the subway and must learn new skills in this story set in Paris. (Rev: BCCB 7–8/01; BL 6/1–15/01; HBG 10/01)

436 Ashman, Linda. *Can You Make a Piggy Giggle?* (PS–K). Illus. by Henry Cole. 2002, Dutton $12.99 (0-525-46881-1). 32pp. While trying in vain to make a pig laugh, a boy draws giggles from other farm animals in this funny picture book with car-

toon-style illustrations. (Rev: BCCB 4/02; BL 7/02; HBG 10/02; SLJ 6/02)

437 Auch, Mary Jane. *Souperchicken* (K–2). Illus. by Herm Auch. 2003, Holiday $16.95 (0-8234-1704-2). 32pp. Talented hen Henrietta saves her aunts from the "Souper Soup Co." truck on their way to what they think is a free vacation, but is in fact the soup pot. (Rev: BL 3/15/03)

438 Baker, Alan. *Little Rabbits' First Farm Book* (PS). Illus. 2001, Kingfisher $11.95 (0-7534-5352-5). 29pp. Four rabbits complete chores on a farm, introducing children to facts about various animals through illustrations, informational sidebars, and games at the end of the book. (Rev: BL 11/15/01; HBG 10/02; SLJ 2/02)

439 Baker, Keith. *Meet Mr. and Mrs. Green* (PS–2). Illus. by author. 2002, Harcourt $16.00 (0-15-216506-1). Alligator couple Mr. and Mrs. Green enjoy camping, going to the fair, and an agreeable outlook on life. (Rev: HBG 3/03; SLJ 11/02)

440 Baker, Liza. *I Love You Because You're You* (K–3). Illus. by David McPhail. 2001, Scholastic $9.95 (0-439-20638-3). 32pp. In rhyming text, a mother fox reassures her child that her love for him will endure through his many moods and feelings. (Rev: BL 1/1–15/02; HBG 3/02; SLJ 11/01)

441 Banks, Kate. *The Turtle and the Hippopotamus: A Rebus Book* (PS–1). Illus. by Tomek Bogacki. 2002, Farrar $16.50 (0-374-37885-1). 32pp. In this rebus book, a turtle attempts to imitate other animals in his quest to cross a river and avoid a scary-looking hippo. (Rev: BL 8/02; HB 5–6/02; HBG 10/02; SLJ 8/02)

442 Barbero, Maria. *The Bravest Mouse* (K–1). Trans. from French by Sibylle Kazeroid. Illus. by author. 2002, North-South LB $16.50 (0-7358-1709-X). A little mouse who is embarrassed by his birthmark gains self-confidence when he bests a nasty cat. (Rev: HBG 3/03; SLJ 1/03)

443 Barnes, Laura T. *Ernest and the Big Itch* (K–3). Illus. by Carol A. Camburn. 2002, Barnesyard $15.95 (0-9674681-2-4). 32pp. Two birds help Ernest, a donkey, find a new place to scratch his itch. (Rev: BL 5/15/02; SLJ 9/02)

444 Baronian, Jean-Baptiste. *Will You Still Love Me?* (PS–2). Illus. by Noris Kern. 2001, Chronicle $15.95 (0-8118-3319-4). Polar bear cub Polo seeks reassurance that his parents still love him in this beautifully illustrated book. (Rev: HBG 3/02; SLJ 11/01)

445 Bateman, Teresa. *Hunting the Daddyosaurus* (PS–K). Illus. by Benrei Huang. 2002, Albert Whitman $15.95 (0-8075-1433-0). 32pp. A brother and sister dinosaur parade around the house looking for their father and finally find him in his easy chair. (Rev: BL 5/1/02; HBG 10/02; SLJ 3/02)

446 Bauer, Marion Dane. *Frog's Best Friend* (1–2). Illus. by Diane D. Hearn. 2002, Holiday $14.95 (0-8234-1501-5). 32pp. Frog wants Turtle to be his exclusive best friend but Turtle also wants to be friends with Squirrel, Bird, and Otter. (Rev: BL 5/1/02; HBG 10/02; SLJ 6/02)

447 Beaton, Clare. *How Loud Is a Lion?* (PS). Illus. 2002, Barefoot $14.99 (1-84148-896-8). 24pp. Elegant, stylish animals are introduced in this book for toddlers that asks, "How loud is a lion?" (Rev: BL 4/1/02; HBG 10/02; SLJ 6/02)

448 Bechtold, Lisze. *Edna's Tale* (PS–2). Illus. 2001, Houghton $15.00 (0-618-09164-5). 32pp. Edna's tail is her pride and joy and the cat is mortified when she arrives at a party covered in foliage. (Rev: BL 5/1/01; HBG 10/01; SLJ 6/01)

449 Beck, Scott. *A Mud Pie for Mother* (PS–1). Illus. 2003, Dutton $14.99 (0-525-47040-9). 32pp. Little Pig has a hard time finding a gift for his mother, until the farmer's wife, a cow, and a bee help him out. (Rev: BL 2/15/03)

450 Bedford, David. *Big Bears Can!* (K–2). Illus. by Gaby Hansen. 2001, Tiger Tales $14.95 (1-58925-006-0). Big Bear has to babysit his little brother but can't resist his sibling's taunts, with messy results. (Rev: SLJ 8/01)

451 Bedford, David. *Ella's Games* (PS–2). Illus. by Peter Kavanagh. 2002, Barron's $12.95 (0-7641-5583-0). Little mouse Ella's older brothers won't let her play with them until she displays her inventiveness. (Rev: HBG 3/03; SLJ 12/02)

452 Bedford, David. *Shaggy Dog and the Terrible Itch* (PS–2). Illus. by Gwyneth Williamson. 2001, Barron's $12.95 (0-7641-5391-9). Poor Shaggy Dog can't reach his back and needs scratching help from friends, and, it turns out, a good bath. (Rev: HBG 3/02; SLJ 1/02)

453 Bedford, David. *Touch the Sky, My Little Bear* (PS–K). Illus. by Jane Chapman. 2001, Handprint $15.95 (1-929766-20-3). 32pp. A little polar bear wonders what it would be like to be big like his mother. (Rev: BL 4/15/01; HBG 10/01; SLJ 5/01)

454 Benjamin, A. H. *Mouse, Mole, and the Falling Star* (PS–K). Illus. by John Bendall-Brunello. 2002, Dutton $15.99 (0-525-46880-3). Mole and Mouse have a temporary falling-out as they compete to find a falling star. (Rev: HBG 3/03; SLJ 8/02)

455 Bergman, Tamar. *Where Is?* (PS–1). Illus. by Rutu Modan. 2002, Houghton $15.00 (0-618-09539-X). 24pp. A young kitten who is left with his grandparents spends the day wondering where his mother has gone. (Rev: BL 12/15/02; HBG 3/03; SLJ 9/02)

456 Blackaby, Susan. *Rembrandt's Hat* (PS–3). Illus. by Mary N. DePalma. 2002, Houghton $15.00 (0-618-11452-1). Rembrandt the bear has lost his hat and tries many inventive substitutes before finding one that suits him. (Rev: BCCB 5/02; BL 4/15/02; HBG 10/02; SLJ 7/02)

457 Blackstone, Stella. *Bear at Home* (PS–K). Illus. by Debbie Harter. 2001, Barefoot $14.99 (1-84148-436-9). Bear and his cat take readers on a tour of Bear's brightly colored house; a floor plan is provided. (Rev: HBG 3/02; SLJ 10/01)

458 Blackstone, Stella. *Bear in Sunshine* (PS–K). Illus. by Debbie Harter. 2001, Barefoot $14.99 (1-84148-321-4). 24pp. Bear is a cheerful character who makes the best of the weathers. (Rev: BL 5/15/01; HBG 10/01; SLJ 6/01)

459 Blackstone, Stella. *Cleo in the Snow* (PS). Illus. by Caroline Mockford. 2002, Barefoot $14.99 (1-84148-951-4). A kitten sensibly decides that a warm spot in front of the fire is more fun than sledding. (Rev: HBG 3/03; SLJ 11/02)

460 Blackstone, Stella. *Cleo on the Move* (K–2). Illus. by Caroline Mockford. Series: Cleo the Cat. 2002, Barefoot $14.99 (1-84148-898-4). Cleo the cat and Caspar the dog are moving to a new house. (Rev: HBG 3/03; SLJ 10/02)

461 Blackstone, Stella. *There's a Cow in the Cabbage Patch* (PS–1). Illus. by Clare Beaton. 2001, Barefoot $14.99 (1-84148-333-8). 32pp. All the farm animals seem to be in the wrong places until the sound of the dinner bell straightens them out. (Rev: BCCB 4/01; BL 4/15/01; HBG 10/01; SLJ 5/01)

462 Bloom, Becky. *Crackers* (K–2). Illus. by Pascal Biet. 2001, Scholastic $15.95 (0-531-30326-8). Crackers the cat has a good relationship with mice and therefore has trouble finding a job until he finds one that suits him perfectly. (Rev: HBG 10/01; SLJ 8/01)

463 Boelts, Maribeth. *You're a Brother, Little Bunny!* (PS–K). Illus. by Kathy Parkinson. 2001, Albert Whitman $14.95 (0-8075-9446-6). 32pp. Little Bunny's parents help him to adjust when the arrival of his baby brother doesn't quite meet his expectations. (Rev: BL 12/1/01; HBG 3/02; SLJ 1/02)

464 Bohdal, Susi. *Tiger Baby* (K–2). Trans. from German by J. Alison James. Illus. by author. 2001, North-South LB $15.88 (0-7358-1433-3). A young tiger strays from his home, lured by a kingfisher, and has many adventures before he discovers his family out looking for him. (Rev: HBG 10/01; SLJ 7/01)

465 Bond, Michael. *Paddington Bear in the Garden* (PS–2). Illus. by R. W. Alley. 2002, HarperCollins $12.95 (0-06-029696-8). 32pp. When Paddington finds that a pile of concrete has been placed on his garden plot, he decides to create a rock garden. (Rev: BL 4/15/02; HBG 10/02)

466 Bosca, Francesca. *The Apple King* (1–3). Trans. by J. Alison James. Illus. by Giuliano Ferri. 2001, North-South LB $15.88 (0-7358-1398-1). 32pp. The king, a pig, tries many ways to get rid of the worms in the royal apples to no avail. (Rev: BL 4/1/01; HBG 10/01; SLJ 7/01)

467 Boxall, Ed. *Francis the Scaredy Cat* (PS). Illus. 2002, Candlewick $14.99 (0-7636-1767-9). 32pp. A quiet, carrot-loving cat named Francis conquers his secret fears when he believes he must rescue his friend. (Rev: BL 12/15/02; HBG 3/03; SLJ 9/02)

468 Bridges, Margaret Park. *Now What Can I Do?* (PS–K). Illus. by Melissa Sweet. 2001, North-South LB $15.88 (1-58717-047-7). 32pp. A mother raccoon turns her son's chores into pure entertainment. (Rev: BL 7/01; HBG 3/02; SLJ 8/01)

469 Brimner, Larry Dane. *The Littlest Wolf* (PS–2). Illus. by Jose Aruego and Ariane Dewey. 2002, HarperCollins LB $15.89 (0-06-029040-4). His father offers constant comfort as Little Wolf, the runt of the pack, worries that he can't run, jump, roll, and pounce like the other youngsters. (Rev: BCCB 7–8/02; HBG 10/02; SLJ 5/02)

470 Brown, Alan. *Hoot and Holler* (PS–K). Illus. by Rimantas Rolia. 2001, Knopf $15.95 (0-375-81417-5). 32pp. Hoot and Holler, two owl friends, are separated during a storm, and are reunited only when Holler yells his feelings out loud and strong — "Hoo-oot! I love you-hoo!" (Rev: BL 11/1/01; HBG 3/02; SLJ 10/01)

471 Brown, Jo. *Where's My Mommy?* (PS–K). Illus. by author. 2002, Tiger Tales $14.95 (1-58925-019-2). A crocodile baby seeking its mother is humorously persuaded that it's not a monkey, an elephant, a donkey, a tiger, or a zebra. (Rev: SLJ 7/02)

472 Brown, Ken. *What's the Time, Grandma Wolf?* (PS–2). Illus. 2001, Peachtree $15.95 (1-56145-250-5). 32pp. All the animals in the woods are wary of Grandma Wolf, but curiosity keeps pulling them closer in this suspenseful story that turns out well in the end. (Rev: BL 7/01; HBG 3/02; SLJ 9/01)

473 Brown, Marc. *Arthur, It's Only Rock 'n' Roll* (1–3). Illus. 2002, Little, Brown $15.95 (0-316-11854-0). 32pp. Arthur the aardvark's friend Francine starts a band, U Stink, that is invited to play with the successful Backstreet Boys. (Rev: BL 11/1/02; HBG 3/03; SLJ 12/02)

474 Brown, Marc. *D.W.'s Library Card* (PS–2). Illus. by author. 2001, Little, Brown $14.95 (0-316-11013-2). Arthur the aardvark teaches little sister D.W. how to look after — and enjoy — library books. (Rev: HBG 3/02; SLJ 12/01)

475 Brown, Margaret Wise. *Sailor Boy Jig* (PS–K). Illus. by Dan Andreasen. 2002, Simon & Schuster $16.00 (0-689-83348-2). 32pp. A sailor puppy dances the jig, catches his supper, and gets ready for bed in this previously unpublished rhyme. (Rev: BL 3/15/02; HBG 10/02; SLJ 6/02)

476 Bruce, Lisa. *Fran's Friend* (PS–2). Illus. by Rosalind Beardshaw. 2003, Bloomsbury $15.95 (1-58234-777-8). 32pp. Fred the dog tries unsuccessfully to help Fran with her craft project. (Rev: BL 3/1/03)

477 Bruss, Deborah. *Book! Book! Book!* (PS–K). Illus. by Tiphanie Beeke. 2001, Scholastic $15.95 (0-439-13525-7). 40pp. A crew of bored animals head to the library and try to make the librarian understand. (Rev: BCCB 2/01; BL 5/15/01; HBG 10/01; SLJ 5/01)

478 Bunting, Eve. *Little Badger, Terror of the Seven Seas* (PS–K). Illus. by LeUyen Pham. 2001, Harcourt $15.00 (0-15-202395-X). 32pp. Little Badger's pose as a pirate doesn't falter in the face of doubt, as he knows he can be anything he wants. (Rev: BL 6/1–15/01; HBG 10/01; SLJ 5/01)

479 Bunting, Eve. *Little Badger's Just-About Birthday* (PS–2). Illus. by LeUyen Pham. 2002, Harcourt $15.00 (0-15-202609-6). 32pp. Little Badger celebrates his just-about birthday and ends up sharing his presents with all his friends. (Rev: BL 3/15/02; HBG 10/02; SLJ 4/02)

480 Bynum, Janie. *Altoona Up North* (PS–3). Illus. by author. 2001, Harcourt $14.00 (0-15-202313-5).

Altoona Baboona, Raccoon-a, and Loon-a travel to the cold north for an adventurous visit with Auntie. (Rev: HBG 3/02; SLJ 10/01)

481 Cameron, C. C. *One for Me, One for You* (PS–1). Illus. by Grace Lin. 2003, Millbrook LB $22.90 (0-7613-2807-6). 32pp. A young hippo and alligator learn about sharing and fairness. (Rev: BL 3/15/03)

482 Cannon, Janell. *Little Yau* (K–2). Illus. 2002, Harcourt $16.00 (0-15-201791-7). 56pp. Yau, a catlike "Fuzzhead," searches for a cure to help her ailing friend Trupp in this sequel to *Trupp* (1995). (Rev: BL 9/15/02; HBG 3/03)

483 Capucilli, Alyssa Satin. *What Kind of Kiss?* (PS–1). Illus. by Hiroe Nakata. 2001, HarperFestival $6.95 (0-694-01573-3). 12pp. Different kinds of kisses are introduced in this question-and-answer book about a loving bear family that contains foldouts on each double-page spread. (Rev: BL 4/1/02; SLJ 12/01)

484 Carle, Eric. *"Slowly, Slowly, Slowly," Said the Sloth* (K–3). Illus. by author. 2002, Philomel $16.99 (0-399-23954-5). A sloth explains to a variety of jungle animals the reasons why he likes to take things easy in this beautifully illustrated book. (Rev: HBG 3/03; SLJ 9/02)

485 Carle, Eric, and Kazuo Iwamura. *Where Are You Going? To See My Friend!* (K–2). Illus. 2003, Scholastic $19.95 (0-439-41659-0). 40pp. A dog asks various animals to come and meet his friend in this charming and inventive bilingual English-Japanese picture book. (Rev: BL 1/1–15/03; SLJ 3/03)

486 Carlson, Nancy. *How About a Hug?* (PS–K). Illus. 2001, Viking $15.99 (0-670-03506-8). 32pp. A pig family awards hugs in a variety of circumstances. (Rev: BL 7/01; HBG 3/02; SLJ 12/01)

487 Carlson, Nancy. *Smile a Lot!* (PS–2). Illus. 2002, Carolrhoda $15.95 (0-87614-869-0). 32pp. A happy frog greets the challenges of daily life — going to the dentist, spelling tests — with a big smile and a happy attitude. (Rev: BL 9/15/02; HBG 3/03; SLJ 10/02)

488 Carmichael, Clay. *Lonesome Bear* (PS–K). Illus. 2001, North-South $13.95 (1-55858-967-8). 48pp. Bear can't find his owner, but meets two other lonely animals and they try to comfort each other. (Rev: BL 7/01; HBG 10/01; SLJ 8/01)

489 Casanova, Mary. *One-Dog Canoe* (PS–1). Illus. by Ard Hoyt. 2003, Farrar $16.50 (0-374-35638-6). 32pp. A girl and her dog are crowded out when other animals decide to pile into their canoe. (Rev: BL 2/15/03; SLJ 3/03)

490 Catalano, Dominic. *Mr. Basset Plays* (K–3). Illus. 2003, Boyds Mills $15.95 (1-59078-007-8). 32pp. Reginald E. Basset, a hound of means, realizes that money isn't everything. (Rev: BL 3/1/03; SLJ 3/03)

491 Catchpool, Michael. *Where There's a Bear, There's Trouble!* (PS–2). Illus. by Vanessa Cabban. 2002, ME Media $14.95 (1-58925-002-2). 32pp. Geese and mice follow a bouncy bear in search of honey and all goes well until they arrive at a hive full of threatening bees. (Rev: BL 12/1/02)

492 Chataway, Carol. *The Perfect Pet* (PS–2). Illus. by Greg Holfeld. 2002, Kids Can $14.95 (1-55337-178-X). Pigs Hamlet, Pygmalion, and Podge are seeking the perfect pet, and find one through a process of elimination. (Rev: HBG 10/02; SLJ 7/02)

493 Cherry, Lynne. *How Groundhog's Garden Grew* (PS–3). Illus. 2003, Scholastic $15.95 (0-439-32371-1). 40pp. Squirrel shows Groundhog how to plant a garden, with delicious results come harvest time. (Rev: BL 2/1/03; SLJ 2/03)

494 Child, Lauren. *That Pesky Rat* (K–3). Illus. 2002, Candlewick $15.99 (0-7636-1873-X). 32pp. A rat wants to be a pet — like his spoiled cat and rabbit friends — and finally finds a nearsighted owner who thinks he's a cat. (Rev: BL 9/1/02; HBG 3/03; SLJ 8/02)

495 Christelow, Eileen. *The Great Pig Search* (K–3). Illus. 2001, Clarion $15.00 (0-618-04910-X). 32pp. Farmer Bert and his wife Ethel travel to Florida to search in vain for their runaway pigs, who evade them by donning hilarious disguises. (Rev: BL 9/1/01; HB 3–4/02; HBG 10/02; SLJ 9/01*)

496 Churchill, Vicki. *Sometimes I Like to Curl Up in a Ball* (PS). Illus. by Charles Fuge. 2001, Sterling $12.95 (1-86233-253-3). Wombat is a lively preschooler who tackles all kinds of activities with gusto. (Rev: SLJ 1/02)

497 Clark, Emma Chichester. *No More Kissing!* (PS–K). 2002, Doubleday LB $17.99 (0-385-90843-1). 32pp. A little monkey protests all the kissing his family does, until he finds himself kissing his new baby brother. (Rev: BL 1/1–15/02; HB 3–4/02; HBG 10/02; SLJ 1/02)

498 Clements, Andrew. *Big Al and Shrimpy* (PS–2). Illus. by Yoshi. 2002, Simon & Schuster $16.95 (0-689-84247-3). Little Shrimpy gets the chance to reward Big Al's kindness by helping him get his fin free. (Rev: HBG 3/03; SLJ 11/02)

499 Cocca-Leffler, Maryann. *Bravery Soup* (PS–1). Illus. 2002, Albert Whitman $15.95 (0-8075-0870-5). 32pp. Carlin the raccoon is afraid of everything until Bear, who is making bravery soup, helps him conquer his fears. (Rev: BL 4/15/02; HBG 10/02; SLJ 3/02)

500 Cole, Babette. *Lady Lupin's Book of Etiquette* (PS–3). Illus. by author. 2002, Peachtree $14.95 (1-56145-257-2). Lady Lupin sets about teaching her puppies proper behavior (don't bark with your mouth full, and so forth). (Rev: HBG 10/02; SLJ 7/02)

501 Cole, Babette. *Truelove* (PS–3). Illus. 2002, Dial $15.99 (0-8037-2717-8). 40pp. Truelove the dog must work hard to get attention and feel loved when the new baby arrives, in this humorous book illustrated with droll cartoons. (Rev: BL 12/1/01; HBG 10/02; SLJ 1/02)

502 Corey, Shana. *Ballerina Bear* (PS–K). Illus. by Pamela Paparone. 2002, Random LB $16.99 (0-375-91416-1). It turns out that Bernie's clumsy but enthusiastic ballet style combines perfectly with the smooth but soulless skill of her partner. (Rev: HBG 3/03; SLJ 8/02)

503 Costanzo, Charlene. *A Perfect Name* (PS–3). Illus. by LeUyen Pham. 2002, Dial $15.99 (0-8037-2614-7). 32pp. Mama and Papa Potamus struggle over what to name their baby hippopotamus in this sweet picture book. (Rev: BL 5/15/02; HBG 10/02; SLJ 3/02)

504 Cottle, Joan. *Miles Away from Home* (PS–2). Illus. 2001, Harcourt $15.00 (0-15-202212-0). 32pp. Miles is feeling a bit like a dog out of water until he rescues a woman from drowning. (Rev: BL 5/15/01; HBG 10/01; SLJ 6/01)

505 Cousins, Lucy. *Doctor Maisy* (PS). Illus. Series: Maisy. 2001, Candlewick $9.99 (0-7636-1612-5); paper $3.29 (0-7636-1613-3). 24pp. Maisy the mouse plays doctor when Panda is sick. Also use *Maisy's Morning on the Farm* (2001). (Rev: BL 10/1/01; HBG 3/02; SLJ 12/01)

506 Cousins, Lucy. *Jazzy in the Jungle* (PS). Illus. by author. 2002, Candlewick $14.99 (0-7636-1903-5). Flaps and die cuts enhance the excitement as Mama JoJo searches the jungle for her baby, Jazzy. (Rev: SLJ 12/02)

507 Cousins, Lucy. *Maisy Cleans Up* (PS). Illus. by author. 2002, Candlewick $9.99 (0-7636-1711-3); paper $3.29 (0-7636-1712-1). Maisy the mouse gives her friend a cupcake when he helps her clean the house. Also use *Maisy Makes Lemonade* (2002). (Rev: HBG 10/02; SLJ 5/02)

508 Crimi, Carolyn. *Tessa's Tip-Tapping Toes* (PS–2). Illus. by Marsha Gray Carrington. 2002, Scholastic $16.95 (0-439-31768-1). 32pp. A dancing mouse and a singing cat decide they can no longer stifle their talents, and soon have the whole household joining in. (Rev: BL 3/1/02; HBG 10/02)

509 Cronin, Doreen. *Giggle, Giggle, Quack* (PS–1). Illus. by Betsy Lewin. 2002, Simon & Schuster $15.00 (0-689-84506-5). 32pp. A hilarious cartoon story about novice Bob and his attempts to care for some farm animals in spite of the intervention of bossy Duck. (Rev: BCCB 6/02; BL 4/15/02; HB 5–6/02; HBG 10/02; SLJ 6/02)

510 Crum, Shutta. *Fox and Fluff* (PS–1). Illus. by John Bendall-Brunello. 2002, Albert Whitman $15.95 (0-8075-2544-8). 32pp. A chick with an identity crisis thinks a fox is his papa in this amusing tale for young readers. (Rev: BL 10/15/02; HB 1–2/03; HBG 3/03; SLJ 12/02)

511 Crunk, Tony. *Grandpa's Overalls* (PS–1). Illus. by Scott Nash. 2001, Scholastic $15.95 (0-531-30321-7). 32pp. When Grandpa's overalls run away, he is left unable to work; but then Grandma's nightie takes off too, and the whole neighborhood (all dogs) gives chase. (Rev: BCCB 5/01; BL 8/01; HBG 10/01; SLJ 7/01)

512 Cusimano, Maryann K. *You Are My I Love You* (PS–2). Illus. by Satomi Ichikawa. 2001, Putnam $15.99 (0-399-23392-X). 32pp. Rhyming text and warm illustrations celebrate the relationship between mother and baby teddy bears during a day's activities. (Rev: BL 5/1/01; HBG 10/01; SLJ 5/01)

513 Dallas-Conte, Juliet. *Cock-a-Moo-Moo* (PS–1). Illus. by Alison Bartlett. 2002, Little, Brown $15.95 (0-316-60505-0). 32pp. In spite of being mocked by other barnyard animals because of the sounds he makes, Rooster is able to warn them of a fox attack by using his voice. (Rev: BCCB 4/02; BL 6/1–15/02; HBG 10/02; SLJ 5/02)

514 Davies, Gill. *Tiny's Big Wish* (PS–1). Illus. by Rachael O'Neill. 2001, Sterling $12.95 (0-8069-7839-2). In this quiet tale, a little elephant is reassured that he will indeed grow bigger. (Rev: HBG 3/02; SLJ 2/02)

515 Davies, Gill. *Wilbur Waited* (PS–K). Illus. by Rachael O'Neill. 2001, Sterling $12.95 (0-8069-7843-0). 32pp. A little tiger is jealous of the attention his parents give his new baby sister. (Rev: BL 3/15/02; HBG 3/02)

516 Davis, Katie. *Party Animals* (PS–2). Illus. by author. 2002, Harcourt $15.00 (0-15-216675-0). A tiny blue ant feels left out of preparations for a festive party. (Rev: HBG 3/03; SLJ 12/02)

517 Day, Alexandra, and Cooper Edens. *Special Deliveries* (PS–K). Illus. by Alexandra Day. 2001, HarperCollins LB $15.89 (0-06-205152-0). 32pp. Taffy McDonald becomes rural mail carrier and gathers a crew of human and animal helpers, who decide to do something to cheer the people who don't receive mail. (Rev: BL 5/1/01; HBG 10/01; SLJ 5/01)

518 Deacon, Alexis. *Slow Loris* (PS–2). Illus. 2002, Kane $15.95 (0-916291-27-1). 32pp. During the day Loris the lion is lethargic, but at night he leads a secret life. (Rev: BCCB 5/02; BL 6/1–15/02)

519 Deady, Kathleen W. *It's Time!* (PS). Illus. by Jill Newton. 2002, HarperFestival $9.95 (0-694-01565-2). 24pp. Anticipation builds as barnyard animals spread the news of an event that is revealed only on the last pages — three puppies have been born! (Rev: BL 8/02; HBG 10/02; SLJ 10/02)

520 De Beer, Hans. *Little Polar Bear and the Big Balloon* (K–2). Trans. from German by Rosemary Lanning. Illus. by author. 2002, North-South LB $16.50 (0-7358-1533-X). Little polar bear Lars and a puffin friend take a trip in a brightly colored hot-air balloon. (Rev: HBG 3/03; SLJ 11/02)

521 De Groat, Diane. *Good Night, Sleep Tight, Don't Let the Bedbugs Bite!* (PS–K). Illus. 2002, North-South LB $15.88 (1-58717-129-5). 32pp. Gilbert's spooky first night at camp reveals that other campers are just as fearful as he. (Rev: BL 7/02; HB 7–8/02; HBG 10/02; SLJ 8/02)

522 De Groat, Diane. *Liar, Liar, Pants on Fire* (K–2). Illus. 2003, North-South LB $16.50 (1-58717-215-1). 32pp. Gilbert the opossum, playing George Washington in the school play, learns a lesson about being honest. (Rev: BL 2/15/03)

523 Delaney, Michael. *Birdbrain Amos* (3–5). Illus. 2002, Putnam $14.99 (0-399-23614-7). 160pp. Amos the hippopotamus hires a tick bird, Kumba, to rid him of a bug problem but finds only additional irritation when Kumba builds a nest on his head. (Rev: BCCB 4/02; BL 4/1/02*; HB 3–4/02; HBG 10/02; SLJ 4/02)

524 Depalma, Mary Newell. *The Strange Egg* (PS–2). Illus. by author. 2001, Houghton $15.00 (0-618-09507-1). A monkey has to explain to a small bird that it is sitting on an orange. (Rev: HBG 10/01; SLJ 5/01)

525 dePaola, Tomie. *Meet the Barkers: Morgan and Moffat Go to School* (PS–1). Illus. 2001, Putnam $13.99 (0-399-23708-9). 32pp. Terrier siblings Morgie and Moffie have always been different — Moffie is smart, Morgie gregarious — and these characteristics hold true when they start school. (Rev: BL 6/1–15/01; HBG 3/02; SLJ 8/01)

526 dePaola, Tomie. *A New Barker in the House* (PS–2). Illus. Series: The Barkers. 2002, Putnam $13.99 (0-399-23865-4). 32pp. When the Barker family adopts Spanish-speaking Marcos, twins Morgie and Moffie try hard to make him feel comfortable in this book full of Spanish words and charming art. (Rev: BL 7/02; HBG 10/02; SLJ 6/02)

527 dePaola, Tomie. *T-Rex Is Missing!* (1–2). Illus. by author. 2002, Grosset LB $13.89 (0-448-42882-2); paper $3.99 (0-448-42870-9). 32pp. The disappearance of a toy dinosaur causes a major falling out between two animal friends. (Rev: SLJ 2/03)

528 Desimini, Lisa. *Dot the Fire Dog* (PS–3). Illus. 2001, Scholastic $15.95 (0-439-23322-4). 40pp. Dot the Dalmatian rescues a kitten while helping her fire fighter owners put out a fire. (Rev: BL 10/1/01; HB 11–12/01; HBG 3/02; SLJ 12/01)

529 Dewan, Ted. *Crispin and the 3 Little Piglets* (PS–1). Illus. by author. 2003, Doubleday LB $17.99 (0-385-90859-8). Crispin, a privileged young pig, is not pleased when his mother produces three new little pigs. (Rev: SLJ 3/03)

530 Dickson, Louise. *The Vanishing Cat* (PS–2). Illus. by Pat Cupples. 2001, Kids Can $14.95 (1-55337-026-0); paper $6.95 (1-55074-836-X). 39pp. Detective dogs Lu and Clancy suspect that a cruise ship magician, a cat, is up to no good. (Rev: HBG 3/02; SLJ 12/01)

531 Dockray, Tracy. *My Bunny Diary: By Dora Cottontail* (K–3). Illus. 2002, North-South $15.95 (1-58717-118-X). 40pp. Dora, a tomboy bunny, records in her diary the ups and downs of her friendship with Ally. (Rev: BL 4/1/02; HBG 10/02)

532 Dodd, Emma. *Dog's Noisy Day: A Story to Read Aloud* (PS–K). Illus. 2003, Dutton $14.99 (0-525-47015-8). 32pp. Dog tries to imitate the sounds he hears around the farm, from a rooster's crow to a bee's buzz. (Rev: BL 2/15/03; SLJ 3/03)

533 Dodds, Dayle Ann. *The Kettles Get New Clothes* (PS–2). Illus. by Jill McElmurry. 2002, Candlewick $15.99 (0-7636-1091-7). 32pp. A rhyming tale about a family of dogs who make their yearly pilgrimage to town to buy new clothes, only to find the clothes in the shop are now much fancier than they'd like. (Rev: BL 12/15/02; HB 1–2/03; HBG 3/03; SLJ 12/02)

534 Doray, Malika. *One More Wednesday* (PS–3). Trans. by Suzanne Freeman. Illus. 2001, Greenwillow LB $15.89 (0-06-029590-2). 48pp. A young animal misses his grandmother when she dies but comes to realize that his memories of their good

28

times bring comfort. (Rev: BL 6/1–15/01; HBG 10/01; SLJ 7/01)

535 Dorros, Arthur. *City Chicken* (PS–2). Illus. by Henry Cole. 2003, HarperCollins LB $16.89 (0-06-028483-8). 40pp. Adventurous city chicken Henrietta takes a trip to the country, encounters an industrial egg farm, and gladly returns to her quiet city life. (Rev: BCCB 2/03; BL 3/15/03; HB 3–4/03; SLJ 2/03)

536 Dunbar, Joyce. *Tell Me What It's Like to Be Big* (K–3). Illus. by Debi Gliori. 2001, Harcourt $16.00 (0-15-202564-2). 32pp. Detailed, vivid images illustrate the story of Willa the rabbit, who is frustrated because she is too little to reach the food on the table. (Rev: BL 12/15/01; HBG 3/02; SLJ 9/01)

537 Dunrea, Olivier. *Gossie and Gertie* (PS). Illus. 2002, Houghton $9.95 (0-618-17676-4). 32pp. A little gosling named Gossie learns a lesson in individuality when her best friend Gertie no longer wants to do everything she does. Also use *Gossie* (2002). (Rev: BL 8/02; HB 1–2/03*; HBG 3/03; SLJ 9/02*)

538 Dyer, Jane. *Little Brown Bear Won't Take a Nap!* (PS–1). Illus. 2002, Little, Brown $15.95 (0-316-19764-5). 32pp. Little Bear, reluctant to lie down and hibernate, takes a train ride south with a flock of geese, who help him to get back home when he changes his mind. (Rev: BL 9/15/02; HBG 3/03; SLJ 9/02)

539 Edvall, Lilian. *The Rabbit Who Longed for Home* (PS–K). Illus. by Anna-Clara Tidholm. 2001, R&S $14.00 (91-29-65391-6). 28pp. After finally adjusting to day care, a little rabbit is not sure how he feels when told he won't have to go anymore. (Rev: BL 9/15/01; HBG 3/02; SLJ 11/01)

540 Edwards, Pamela Duncan. *Clara Caterpillar* (PS–1). Illus. by Henry Cole. 2001, HarperCollins LB $15.89 (0-06-028996-1). 32pp. In this alliterative story, vain Catisha grows into a beautiful crimson butterfly but her allure makes her vulnerable and she needs help from plain Clara, the cabbage butterfly. (Rev: BL 7/01; HBG 10/01; SLJ 6/01)

541 Edwards, Pamela Duncan. *Little Brown Hen's Shower* (PS–K). Illus. by Darcia LaBrosse. 2002, Hyperion $15.99 (0-7868-0467-X). 32pp. A hilarious tale about Little Brown Hen who opens up a big umbrella for herself and a small one for her egg because she is going to a baby shower. (Rev: BL 4/1/02; SLJ 7/02)

542 Edwards, Pamela Duncan. *Slop Goes the Soup: A Noisy Warthog Word Book* (PS). Illus. by Henry Cole. 2001, Hyperion $14.99 (0-7868-0469-6). 28pp. The warthogs are at it again, this time making dinner and making lots of (onomatopoeic) noise. (Rev: BL 10/15/01; HBG 3/02; SLJ 12/01)

543 Edwards, Richard. *Always Copycub* (PS–1). Illus. by Susan Winter. 2002, HarperCollins $14.95 (0-06-029691-7). Little bear Copycub enjoys hiding from his mother until the time he really does get lost. (Rev: HBG 10/02; SLJ 2/02)

544 Egan, Tim. *A Mile from Ellington Station* (K–3). Illus. 2001, Houghton $15.00 (0-618-00393-2). 32pp. Preston, a bear who is a checkers champion, is beaten by a multitalented dog from France

named Marley, so Preston claims Marley is a sorcerer. (Rev: BL 4/15/01; HBG 10/01; SLJ 5/01)

545 Egielski, Richard. *Slim and Jim* (PS–3). Illus. 2002, HarperCollins LB $15.89 (0-06-028353-X). 40pp. An orphaned rat named Slim is saved from a world of crime through the intervention of Jim, a mouse-boy. (Rev: BCCB 9/02; BL 5/1/02*; HB 7–8/02; HBG 10/02; SLJ 5/02)

546 Eilenberg, Max. *Squeak's Good Idea* (PS–K). Illus. by Patrick Benson. 2001, Candlewick $14.99 (0-7636-1591-9). 48pp. Young elephant Squeak believes in being prepared and takes piles of clothes and a basketful of food when he sets off for a trip into the backyard. (Rev: BL 12/15/01; HB 1–2/02; HBG 3/02; SLJ 12/01)

547 Elliott, Laura Malone. *Hunter's Best Friend at School* (PS–1). Illus. by Lynn Munsinger. 2002, HarperCollins LB $17.89 (0-06-000231-X). 32pp. Hunter's mother offers guidance when Hunter explains that he doesn't really enjoy being naughty but wants to stay friends with mischievous fellow raccoon Stripes. (Rev: BCCB 10/02; BL 10/1/02; HBG 3/03; SLJ 9/02)

548 Elya, Susan Middleton. *Eight Animals Bake a Cake* (2–4). Illus. by Lee Chapman. 2002, Putnam $15.99 (0-399-23468-3). 32pp. Too many animals almost spoil the cake in this appealing picture book that introduces Spanish words and includes a recipe for pineapple upside-down cake. (Rev: BL 7/02; HBG 3/03; SLJ 8/02)

549 Elya, Susan Middleton. *Eight Animals Play Ball* (1–3). Illus. by Lee Chapman. 2003, Putnam $15.99 (0-399-23569-8). The eight animals from Elya's earlier books go to the park and start a baseball game in a charming mix of English and Spanish. (Rev: SLJ 3/03)

550 Emmett, Jonathan. *Bringing Down the Moon* (PS–2). Illus. by Vanessa Cabban. 2001, Candlewick $15.99 (0-7636-1577-3). 24pp. Little Mole tries to capture the moon from the sky. (Rev: BL 2/1/02; HBG 3/02; SLJ 1/02)

551 Emmett, Jonathan. *Dinosaurs After Dark* (PS). Illus. by Curtis Jobling. 2002, HarperCollins $14.99 (0-00-198375-X). Little Bobby investigates a strange noise one night and comes across a herd of lively dinosaurs. (Rev: BCCB 3/02; SLJ 6/02)

552 Falconer, Ian. *Olivia Saves the Circus* (PS–1). Illus. 2001, Simon & Schuster $16.00 (0-689-82954-X). 32pp. Olivia, the little pig full of talented energy, describes how she took over each and every role when the circus was hit by a rash of earaches. (Rev: BCCB 11/01; BL 8/01; HB 11–12/01; HBG 3/02; SLJ 10/01)

553 Fearnley, Jan. *Just Like You* (PS–3). Illus. 2001, Candlewick $15.99 (0-7636-1322-3). 32pp. Little Mouse and his mother hear other animal mothers making extravagant promises to their young ones, and Little Mouse wonders what his mother can do for him. (Rev: BL 7/01; HBG 10/01; SLJ 4/01)

554 Fearnley, Jan. *A Perfect Day for It* (PS–1). Illus. by author. 2002, Harcourt $16.00 (0-15-216634-3). Bear leads a growing parade of animals to the top of the mountain, each following for a different reason. (Rev: HBG 3/03; SLJ 12/02)

555 Fernandes, Eugenie. *Busy Little Mouse* (PS–K). Illus. by Kim Fernandes. 2002, Kids Can $12.95 (1-55074-776-3). 24pp. Joyful, three-dimensional art is used to illustrate this lighthearted tale of various farm animals who play together. (Rev: BL 4/15/02)

556 Fierstein, Harvey. *The Sissy Duckling* (2–4). Illus. by Henry Cole. 2002, Simon & Schuster $16.00 (0-689-83566-3). 40pp. Young Elmer is branded a sissy because of his feminine ways, but he later shows everyone how really special he is. (Rev: BCCB 7–8/02; BL 6/1–15/02*; HBG 10/02; SLJ 5/02)

557 Finn, Isobel. *The Very Lazy Ladybug* (PS–1). Illus. by Jack Tickle. 2001, Tiger Tales $14.95 (1-58925-007-9). This ladybug is so lazy that she can't be bothered to fly and hops rides with a variety of animals instead, until she is finally forced to take to the air. (Rev: BCCB 5/01; SLJ 7/01)

558 Fisher, Carolyn. *A Twisted Tale* (PS–K). Illus. by author. 2002, Knopf LB $17.99 (0-375-91540-0). A tornado whirls the farm animals around until their sounds and actions get all confused (the pig quacks and dives into a pond, for example). (Rev: BCCB 7–8/02; HBG 10/02; SLJ 6/02)

559 Fontes, Justine Korman. *Signs of Spring* (K–2). Illus. by Rob Hefferan. 2002, Mondo $14.95 (1-59034-189-9). 24pp. On their way to school, Lucy, a mouse, and Zack, a chipmunk, gather signs of spring for show-and-tell. (Rev: BL 6/1–15/02; HBG 10/02; SLJ 8/02)

560 Fox, Christyan, and Diane Fox. *Astronaut PiggyWiggy* (PS). Illus. by authors. 2002, Handprint $9.95 (1-929766-41-6). PiggyWiggy looks through his telescope and pictures himself blasting off and visiting distant places. (Rev: HBG 10/02; SLJ 7/02)

561 Fox, Christyan, and Diane Fox. *Bathtime PiggyWiggy* (PS–K). Illus. 2001, Handprint $12.95 (1-929766-32-7). 24pp. PiggyWiggy's imagination takes him on underwater adventures in the bathtub. (Rev: BL 2/1/02; SLJ 1/02)

562 Fox, Christyan, and Diane Fox. *Fire Fighter PiggyWiggy* (PS–K). Illus. 2001, Handprint $9.95 (1-929766-16-5). 24pp. PiggyWiggy has ideas of what he would do as a fire fighter but at the same time he recognizes that a real fire fighter would be needed in an emergency. (Rev: BL 5/1/01; HBG 10/01; SLJ 5/01)

563 Fraser, Mary Ann. *I. Q. Goes to School* (PS–K). Illus. 2002, Walker LB $16.85 (0-8027-8814-9). 32pp. I.Q., the kindergarten pet rat, enjoys learning everything the students do in hopes of being named "student of the week." (Rev: BL 9/15/02; HBG 3/03; SLJ 9/02)

564 Freedman, Claire. *Where's Your Smile, Crocodile?* (PS–K). Illus. by Sean Julian. 2001, Peachtree $16.95 (1-56145-251-3). Kyle the crocodile can't seem to smile, no matter how hard others try to amuse him, until he comes across a sad little lion and tries in turn to cheer him up. (Rev: HBG 3/02; SLJ 11/01)

565 Galloway, Ruth. *Fidgety Fish* (PS–3). Illus. by author. 2001, Tiger Tales $14.95 (1-58925-012-5). A rambunctious little fish is sent out to swim until he's tired, and ignores warnings to stay away from Big Fish. (Rev: SLJ 2/02)

566 Gantos, Jack. *Practice Makes Perfect for Rotten Ralph* (1–3). Illus. by Nicole Rubel. Series: Rotten Ralph Rotten Reader. 2002, Farrar $15.00 (0-374-36356-0). 48pp. In this easy reader, Rotten Ralph the cat gets a few lessons about jealousy and cheating when he visits the carnival with Sarah and his cousin Percy wins all the prizes. (Rev: BL 3/1/02; HB 5–6/02; HBG 10/02; SLJ 3/02)

567 Garelli, Cristina. *Forest Friends' Five Senses* (PS–2). Illus. by Francesca Chessa. 2001, Knopf $14.95 (0-375-81308-X). 32pp. The animals of the forest exchange stories about the different senses — how the rabbit's hearing disappeared when he had wax in his ears, how glasses helped the hawk to see, and so forth. (Rev: BL 12/1/01; HBG 3/02; SLJ 11/01)

568 Garland, Michael. *Last Night at the Zoo* (K–3). Illus. 2001, Boyds Mills $15.95 (1-56397-759-1). 32pp. The animals at the zoo are bored, so they break out and head for a night at Club Boogie. (Rev: BL 7/01; HBG 3/02; SLJ 5/01)

569 Geisert, Arthur. *The Giant Ball of String* (K–3). Illus. 2002, Houghton $16.00 (0-618-13221-X). 32pp. The children (piglets, actually) of Rumpus Ridge, Wisconsin, devise a clever scheme to reclaim their town's giant ball of string, which a nearby town has taken captive. (Rev: BL 9/15/02; HBG 3/03; SLJ 9/02)

570 Geras, Adele. *The Cats of Cuckoo Square: Two Stories* (2–4). Illus. by Tony Ross. 2001, Delacorte $14.95 (0-385-72926-X). 190pp. Pet cats describe their hilarious adventures with their owners. (Rev: BCCB 12/01; BL 9/1/01; HBG 3/02; SLJ 12/01)

571 Geras, Adele. *My Wishes for You* (PS–1). Illus. by Cliff Wright. 2002, Simon & Schuster $15.95 (0-689-85333-5). 32pp. Kindhearted rabbit parents wish good things for their child in this bucolic, beautifully illustrated picture book. (Rev: BL 12/15/02; HBG 3/03; SLJ 12/02)

572 Gershator, David, and Phillis Gershator. *Moon Rooster* (K–3). Illus. by Megan Halsey. 2001, Marshall Cavendish $15.95 (0-7614-5092-0). A young rooster persists in crowing at the moon despite human annoyance. (Rev: HBG 3/02; SLJ 12/01)

573 Gliori, Debi. *Can I Have a Hug?* (PS). Illus. 2002, Scholastic $5.95 (0-439-27602-0). 8pp. In this oversize board book, a bear is so anxious for a hug he's ready to cuddle up to a hive of bees. Also use *Tickly Under There* (2002). (Rev: BL 6/1–15/02)

574 Gliori, Debi. *Flora's Blanket* (PS). Illus. 2001, Scholastic $15.95 (0-531-30305-5). 32pp. Flora, a young bunny, cannot sleep because her favorite blanket has disappeared. (Rev: BL 5/15/01; HBG 10/01; SLJ 7/01*)

575 Gliori, Debi. *Flora's Surprise!* (PS–2). Illus. by author. 2003, Scholastic $15.95 (0-439-45590-1). Flora, a young rabbit, plants a brick in the hope that it will grow into a house. (Rev: BCCB 3/03; SLJ 3/03)

576 Gliori, Debi. *Penguin Post* (PS–2). Illus. 2002, Harcourt $16.00 (0-15-216765-X). 40pp. While his parents take the day off to tend their ready-to-hatch egg, Milo the penguin takes over their mail route and has a variety of amusing adventures. (Rev: BL 12/15/02; HBG 3/03; SLJ 11/02)

577 Godwin, Laura. *The Best Fall of All* (K–1). Illus. by Jane Chapman. 2002, Simon & Schuster $14.95 (0-689-84713-0). 32pp. Honey the cat and Happy the dog learn to have fun in the fallen leaves. (Rev: BL 12/1/02; HBG 3/03; SLJ 10/02)

578 Gollub, Matthew. *Gobble, Quack, Moon* (PS–2). Illus. by Judy Love. 2002, Tortuga $18.95 (1-889910-20-1). 32pp. Katie the cow and her barnyard friends hop on a rocket ship and spend a happy time on the moon. (Rev: BL 6/1–15/02)

579 Goodings, Lennie. *When You Grow Up* (PS–1). Illus. by Jenny Jones. 2001, Penguin Putnam $14.99 (0-8037-2677-5). 32pp. One by one, bear cub Zachary and his mother consider possible careers for him, and after each he says he'll still come back to live with his mother. (Rev: BL 8/01; HBG 10/01; SLJ 6/01)

580 Goodman, Joan Elizabeth. *Bernard Goes to School* (PS–K). Illus. by Dominic Catalano. 2001, Boyds Mills $15.95 (1-56397-958-6). 32pp. Although he feels shy at first, Bernard the elephant eventually is able to say goodbye to his parents on his first day of preschool. (Rev: BCCB 9/01; BL 10/1/01; HBG 3/02; SLJ 8/01)

581 Gorbachev, Valeri. *Chicken Chickens* (PS–K). Illus. 2001, North-South LB $15.88 (0-7358-1542-9). 40pp. The other young animals help two frightened little chickens to try the various offerings of the playground. (Rev: BL 9/1/01; HBG 3/02; SLJ 9/01)

582 Gralley, Jean. *Very Boring Alligator* (PS). Illus. 2001, Holt $15.95 (0-8050-6328-5). 32pp. A boring alligator just won't go away — until a little girl makes up her mind to get rid of him. (Rev: BL 9/15/01; HBG 3/02; SLJ 10/01)

583 Grant, Rose Marie. *Andiamo, Weasel!* (K–3). Illus. by Jon Goodell. 2002, Knopf LB $17.99 (0-375-90607-X). A Tuscan crow gets her revenge against a crafty weasel in this beautifully illustrated, humorous tale full of Italian touches. (Rev: HBG 3/03; SLJ 8/02)

584 Greene, Rhonda Gowler. *Jamboree Day* (PS–2). Illus. by Jason Wolff. 2001, Scholastic $15.95 (0-439-29310-3). A festive, colorful crew of animals enjoys a toe-tapping jamboree. (Rev: HBG 3/02; SLJ 1/02)

585 Gregory, Valiska. *Shirley's Wonderful Baby* (PS–2). Illus. by Bruce Degen. 2002, HarperCollins LB $16.89 (0-06-028574-5). Young hippo Shirley is tired of people saying her baby brother is wonderful until a crafty baby-sitter succeeds in changing her mind. (Rev: BCCB 1/03; HBG 3/03; SLJ 11/02)

586 Grindley, Sally. *No Trouble at All* (PS–1). Illus. by Eleanor Taylor. 2002, Bloomsbury $15.95 (1-58234-757-3). 32pp. As Grandfather ruminates

about the good behavior of his grandcubs, the two little bears are making mischief throughout the house. (Rev: BL 8/02; SLJ 7/02)

587 Grindley, Sally. *Where Are My Chicks?* (PS). Illus. by Jill Newton. 2002, Penguin Putnam $9.99 (0-8037-2497-7). Mother Hen has lost her chicks, and the farm animals pitch in to help her find them in this brightly illustrated book with cartoon figures. (Rev: HBG 10/02; SLJ 1/02)

588 Gugler, Laurel Dee. *There's a Billy Goat in the Garden* (PS–1). Illus. by Clare Beaton. 2003, Barefoot $14.99 (1-84148-089-4). 32pp. A tiny bee chases a billy goat from the garden after the dog, pig, donkey, cow, and horse are unsuccessful. (Rev: BL 3/15/03)

589 Gutman, Anne. *Gaspard and Lisa at the Museum* (PS–1). Illus. by Georg Hallensleben. 2001, Knopf $9.95 (0-375-81117-6). 32pp. Young animals Gaspard and Lisa have an adventure during their class trip to the Museum of Natural History. Also use *Gaspard in the Hospital* (2001). (Rev: BL 11/15/01; HBG 3/02; SLJ 11/01)

590 Gutman, Anne. *Gaspard at the Seashore* (PS). Illus. by Georg Hallensleben. 2002, Knopf $9.95 (0-375-81118-4). 32pp. Little Gaspard dreams of daring water sports at the seashore, but is afraid because he can't swim. (Rev: BL 8/02; HBG 10/02; SLJ 5/02)

591 Gutman, Anne. *Lisa in New York* (PS). Illus. by Georg Hallensleben. 2002, Knopf $9.95 (0-375-81119-2). 32pp. Lisa gets lost while visiting her uncle, who lives in New York City. (Rev: BL 8/02; HBG 10/02; SLJ 5/02)

592 Hafner, Marylin. *Molly and Emmett's Surprise Garden* (K–2). Illus. by author. 2001, McGraw-Hill $12.95 (1-57768-895-3). 30pp. When Molly and Emmett the cat are planting a garden, Emmett opens all the packets at the same time and the seeds get all mixed up. (Rev: HBG 10/01; SLJ 8/01)

593 Hanel, Wolfram. *Little Elephant Runs Away* (PS–2). Trans. from German by J. Alison James. Illus. by Cristina Kadmon. 2001, North-South LB $15.88 (0-7358-1445-7). When Little Elephant runs away to the sea, he's ashamed to admit that he's lost and pretends to be ill instead. (Rev: HBG 10/01; SLJ 4/01)

594 Harvey, Amanda. *Dog Eared* (PS–1). Illus. by author. 2002, Random LB $17.99 (0-385-90845-8). 32pp. Otis the dog takes a bully's taunt of "Big Ears" to heart until he discovers that his owner loves him just the way he is. (Rev: BCCB 2/02; BL 3/1/02; HBG 10/02; SLJ 3/02)

595 Haseley, Dennis. *A Story for Bear* (K–3). Illus. by Jim LaMarche. 2002, Harcourt $16.00 (0-15-200239-1). 32pp. Although he doesn't understand the words she is saying, a young bear responds to the stories a woman reads to him. (Rev: BL 5/1/02; HBG 10/02; SLJ 3/02)

596 Hayes, Geoffrey. *Patrick and the Big Bully* (K–2). Illus. by author. 2001, Hyperion $15.99 (0-7868-0717-2). Little bear Patrick deals with a bully by pretending to be a dragon. (Rev: HBG 3/02; SLJ 1/02)

31

597 Hayes, Geoffrey. *Patrick at the Circus* (PS–2). Illus. by author. Series: The Adventures of Patrick Brown. 2002, Hyperion $15.99 (0-7868-0716-4). Little bear Patrick's father takes the place of the clown at the circus. (Rev: HBG 10/02; SLJ 7/02)

598 Heide, Florence Parry, and Sylvia Van Clief. *That's What Friends Are For* (PS–2). Illus. by Holly Meade. 2003, Candlewick $15.99 (0-7636-1397-5). 40pp. Poor Theodore the elephant has hurt his leg and gets totally useless advice from most of the animals in the forest. (Rev: BL 3/15/03)

599 Hendry, Diana. *The Very Busy Day* (K–2). Illus. by Jane Chapman. 2002, Dutton $15.99 (0-525-46825-0). 32pp. Big Mouse complains when Little Mouse is unwilling to help him in the garden, but Little Mouse has actually been planning a surprise. (Rev: BL 2/15/02; HBG 10/02; SLJ 3/02)

600 Henkes, Kevin. *Owen's Marshmallow Chick* (PS). Illus. 2002, Greenwillow $6.95 (0-06-001012-6). 24pp. Little Owen the mouse loves all the candy in his Easter basket, most especially the marshmallow chick. (Rev: BCCB 2/02; BL 1/1–15/02; HBG 10/02; SLJ 2/02)

601 Henkes, Kevin. *Sheila Rae's Peppermint Stick* (PS). 2001, HarperFestival $6.95 (0-06-029451-5). 24pp. Mouse Sheila Rae is tormenting her sister with tricky challenges when she falls and breaks the prized peppermint stick in half, prompting her to share it forthwith. (Rev: HB 9–10/01*; HBG 3/02; SLJ 12/01*)

602 Henry, Steve. *Nobody Asked Me!* (PS). Illus. by author. 2001, HarperCollins LB $14.89 (0-688-17866-9). Bo the cat soon finds that his new little brother is actually quite useful for playing with. (Rev: HBG 10/01; SLJ 8/01)

603 Hest, Amy. *Don't You Feel Well, Sam?* (PS–2). Illus. by Anita Jeram. 2002, Candlewick $15.99 (0-7636-1009-7). A gentle story about a little bear who doesn't want to take his cough medicine at first. (Rev: BL 11/15/02*; HBG 3/03; SLJ 9/02)

604 Hest, Amy. *Make the Team, Baby Duck!* (PS–1). Illus. by Jill Barton. 2002, Candlewick $16.99 (0-7636-1541-2). 32pp. Baby Duck, afraid to swim but yearning to be part of the swim team, gains confidence through Grandpa's encouragement. (Rev: BL 8/02; HBG 3/03; SLJ 9/02)

605 Hillerman, Tony. *Buster Mesquite's Cowboy Band* (PS–2). Illus. by Ernest Franklin. 2001, Buffalo Medicine $15.95 (0-914001-11-6). 32pp. The artwork is the highlight of this story about a burro who loses his job and starts a band with other musically inclined animals. (Rev: BL 11/1/01)

606 Hindley, Judy. *Do Like a Duck Does!* (PS–K). Illus. by Ivan Bates. 2002, Candlewick $14.99 (0-7636-1668-0). 40pp. A mama duck out-foxes a fox in this charming, brightly illustrated picture book. (Rev: BCCB 4/02; BL 3/1/02; HBG 10/02)

607 Hindley, Judy. *The Perfect Little Monster* (PS–1). Illus. by Jonathan Lycett-Smith. 2001, Candlewick paper $3.29 (0-7636-0903-X). Baby Monster is perfect in all ways, with horrible features and a real knack for bashing and trashing. (Rev: SLJ 6/01)

608 Hines, Anna Grossnickle. *Which Hat Is That?* (PS). Illus. by LeUyen Pham. 2002, Harcourt $15.00 (0-15-216477-4). 36pp. This guessing game challenges readers to name the activity that matches the little mouse's hat, with answers under the flaps. (Rev: BL 11/15/02; HBG 3/03; SLJ 12/02)

609 Hines, Anna Grossnickle. *Whose Shoes?* (PS–1). Illus. by LeUyen Pham. 2001, Harcourt $14.00 (0-15-201773-9). A bouncy story of a young mouse who likes to try on other people's shoes and listen to the different sounds they make. (Rev: HBG 3/02; SLJ 8/01)

610 Hobbie, Holly. *Toot and Puddle: I'll Be Home for Christmas* (PS–2). Illus. by author. 2001, Little, Brown $15.95 (0-316-36623-4). While Puddle the pig has been eagerly preparing for Toot's return from a trip to Scotland, Toot is spared from a disappointing delay when a sleigh mysteriously picks him up and wafts him home to a happy reunion. (Rev: HBG 3/02; SLJ 10/01)

611 Hobbie, Holly. *Toot and Puddle: Top of the World* (PS–2). Illus. by author. 2002, Little, Brown $15.95 (0-316-36513-0). 32pp. Toot and Puddle, the friendly pigs, visit France and Nepal before deciding that home beckons. (Rev: BL 10/1/02; HBG 3/03)

612 Hogrogian, Nonny. *The Tiger of Turkestan* (K–3). Illus. 2002, Hampton Roads $16.95 (1-57174-308-1). 32pp. After his wise grandmother's death, Little Tiger examines his purpose in life and eventually becomes a dancing tiger in this beautifully illustrated picture book. (Rev: BL 1/1–15/03; HBG 3/03)

613 Holabird, Katherine. *Angelina and Henry* (PS–2). Illus. by Helen Craig. 2002, Pleasant $12.95 (1-58485-523-1). 32pp. A scary episode tests the mettle of mouse Angelina Ballerina and her cousin Henry when they get lost in the woods during a storm. (Rev: BL 10/1/02; HBG 3/03; SLJ 10/02)

614 Honigsberg, Peter Jan. *Armful of Memories* (K–2). Illus. by Tony Morse. 2002, RDR $17.95 (1-57143-089-X). 32pp. Newbery Mole sells all of his deceased grandparents' possessions in order to get rich, but soon realizes his memories are worth more than money. (Rev: BL 1/1–15/02; HBG 10/02)

615 Horse, Harry. *Little Rabbit Lost* (PS–2). Illus. 2002, Peachtree $15.95 (1-56145-273-4). 32pp. Detailed watercolors set the scene as Little Rabbit's birthday trip to RabbitWorld is almost ruined when he gets lost. (Rev: BL 12/1/02; HBG 3/03; SLJ 10/02)

616 Howe, James. *Horace and Morris Join the Chorus / But What About Dolores?* (PS–1). Illus. by Amy Walrod. 2002, Simon & Schuster $16.95 (0-689-83939-1). 32pp. Dolores is so miserable at being left out of the chorus that she writes a sad poetic letter to the Moustro, which is then set to music, gaining her a reputation as a songwriter plus a place in the chorus. (Rev: BL 11/15/02; HB 1–2/03; HBG 3/03; SLJ 11/02)

617 Huneck, Stephen. *Sally Goes to the Farm* (PS–2). Illus. 2002, Abrams $17.95 (0-8109-4498-7). 40pp. Sally the dog visits a farm and has a wonderful time with Molly and other animal friends in this picture book with simple text and large, bold pictures that add to the story. (Rev: BL 7/02; HBG 10/02; SLJ 7/02)

618 Hunter, Sally. *Humphrey's Corner* (PS–1). Illus. by author. 2001, Holt $14.95 (0-8050-6786-8). Young elephant Humphrey can't find anywhere in the house to settle down and play, until his mother shows him the cozy kitchen where she will be. (Rev: HBG 3/02; SLJ 10/01)

619 Hutchins, Pat. *We're Going on a Picnic!* (PS–1). Illus. 2002, Greenwillow LB $15.89 (0-688-16800-0). 32pp. Hen, Duck, and Goose set off for a picnic, but find their food has mysteriously disappeared in this terrific tale for young readers. (Rev: BCCB 7–8/02; BL 3/1/02; HBG 10/02; SLJ 3/02)

620 Inkpen, Mick. *Kipper and Roly* (PS–1). Illus. 2001, Harcourt $13.95 (0-15-216344-1). 32pp. Kipper the dog gets to keep the hamster he bought for his friend Pig's birthday. (Rev: BL 9/15/01; HBG 3/02; SLJ 9/01)

621 Inkpen, Mick. *Kipper's Monster* (PS–K). Illus. by author. 2002, Harcourt $13.95 (0-15-216614-9). Kipper the pup and pal Tiger retreat to Tiger's bedroom after scaring themselves in their tent. (Rev: HBG 10/02; SLJ 7/02)

622 Inkpen, Mick. *Kipper's Rainy Day* (PS–K). Illus. by author. 2001, Harcourt paper $5.95 (0-15-216351-4). Kipper the dog enjoys the rain and wonders which of his friends also like it, in this book with flaps that provide answers to questions. Also use *Kipper's Sunny Day* (2001). (Rev: SLJ 10/01)

623 Jackson, Chris. *The Gaggle Sisters River Tour* (PS–2). Illus. 2002, Lobster $16.95 (1-894222-58-X). 32pp. Sadie the duck is the star of the show on the river, until her hat is ruined and sister Dorothy, the behind-the-scenes toiler, saves the day. (Rev: BL 12/15/02; SLJ 1/03)

624 James, Simon. *Little One Step* (PS–2). Illus. 2003, Candlewick $15.99 (0-7636-2070-X). 32pp. When the youngest duck gets tired, his siblings encourage him to persevere. (Rev: BL 3/15/03)

625 Janovitz, Marilyn. *Good Morning, Little Fox* (PS–2). Illus. 2001, North-South LB $15.88 (0-7358-1441-4). 32pp. Little Fox and his father initially reject porridge for breakfast but after a burst of activity stirs up some hunger they find it's really quite good. (Rev: BL 5/1/01; HBG 10/01; SLJ 6/01)

626 Jennings, Sharon. *Priscilla and Rosy* (PS–2). Illus. by Linda Hendry. 2001, Fitzhenry & Whiteside $15.95 (1-55041-676-6). 32pp. Detailed illustrations complement this story of two rat best friends, in which Priscilla deals with competing invitations and finally recognizes that friendship is most important. (Rev: BL 12/15/01; SLJ 1/02)

627 Jennings, Sharon. *Priscilla's Paw de Deux* (K–3). Illus. by Linda Hendry. 2002, Fitzhenry & Whiteside $14.95 (1-55041-718-5). 36pp. Priscilla the rat sneaks into a dance studio after hours to practice ballet, only to meet up with a menacing cat. (Rev: BL 12/15/02; SLJ 2/03)

628 Jeram, Anita. *I Love My Little Storybook* (PS–K). Illus. 2002, Candlewick $12.99 (0-7636-1698-2). 32pp. A little bunny explains how much he loves his story book and all the characters and situations it contains. (Rev: BL 6/1–15/02; HBG 10/02; SLJ 8/02)

629 Johansen, Hanna. *Henrietta and the Golden Eggs* (1–3). Trans. by John S. Barrett. Illus. by Kathi Bhend. 2002, Godine $16.95 (1-56792-210-4). 64pp. The story of Henrietta, a chicken with dreams of freedom, is told with intricate pen-and-ink drawings. (Rev: BL 3/15/03)

630 Johnson, D. B. *Henry Builds a Cabin* (PS–3). Illus. 2002, Houghton $15.00 (0-618-13201-5). 32pp. A sensible bear called Henry convinces his friends that a Thoreau-style cabin, and the great outdoors, is all that he needs to be happy. (Rev: BCCB 5/02; BL 3/15/02*; HB 7–8/02; HBG 10/02; SLJ 3/02)

631 Johnson, Jane. *Are You Ready for Bed?* (PS–K). Illus. by Gaby Hansen. 2002, Tiger Tales $14.95 (1-58925-017-6). Just as exhausted Mrs. Rabbit gets one child off to sleep, another wakes up. (Rev: SLJ 12/02)

632 Johnson, Paul Brett. *The Goose Who Went Off in a Huff* (PS–1). Illus. 2001, Scholastic $15.95 (0-531-30317-9). 40pp. Magnolia the goose starts acting oddly when she is overwhelmed by a maternal urge. (Rev: BL 5/15/01; HBG 10/01; SLJ 7/01)

633 Johnson, Suzanne C. *Fribbity Ribbit!* (PS–2). Illus. by Debbie Tilley. 2001, Knopf LB $17.99 (0-375-91199-5). A frog evades capture while visiting every corner of the house in this comic book with vivid illustrations of the chase. (Rev: HBG 3/02; SLJ 8/01)

634 Jones, Elisabeth. *Sunshine and Storm* (PS–K). Illus. by James Coplestone. 2001, Ragged Bear $14.95 (1-929927-27-4). 32pp. Attention-grabbing, expressive art accompanies a story of a temporary rift in the friendship between a dog and cat. (Rev: BL 6/1–15/01; HBG 10/01; SLJ 8/01)

635 Kaczman, James. *A Bird and His Worm* (PS–2). Illus. 2002, Houghton $15.00 (0-618-09460-1). 32pp. A bird and his friend, a worm, learn a lesson about strangers in their travels south. (Rev: BCCB 12/02; BL 9/15/02; HBG 3/03; SLJ 9/02)

636 Kasza, Keiko. *The Mightiest* (1–3). Illus. 2001, Putnam $15.99 (0-399-23586-8). 32pp. Lion, Bear, and Elephant argue about who among them is the mightiest, but they are all outdone by an old woman. (Rev: BL 9/1/01; HBG 3/02; SLJ 11/01)

637 Keller, Holly. *Cecil's Garden* (PS–3). Illus. 2002, HarperCollins LB $15.89 (0-06-029594-5). 32pp. A little rabbit named Cecil and his friends argue about their garden, until Cecil comes up with the perfect resolution. (Rev: BL 2/1/02; HBG 10/02; SLJ 3/02)

638 Keller, Holly. *Farfallina and Marcel* (PS–K). Illus. 2002, HarperCollins LB $17.89 (0-06-623933-8). 32pp. A gosling and a caterpillar, best friends, need time to find each other again when they become a goose and a butterfly. (Rev: BL 9/15/02; HBG 3/03; SLJ 10/02)

639 Kelley, True. *Blabber Mouse* (1–3). Illus. 2001, Dutton $15.99 (0-525-46742-4). 32pp. Blabber Mouse's classmates finally are forced to devise a solution to stop his chatter when he reminds teacher that she forgot to assign homework. (Rev: BL 12/1/01; HBG 3/02; SLJ 10/01)

640 Kellogg, Steven. *The Mysterious Tadpole: 25th Anniversary Edition* (PS–2). Illus. 2002, Dial $16.99 (0-8037-2788-7). 36pp. This anniversary edition brings a slightly longer text and new illustrations to the story of the tadpole that won't stop growing. (Rev: BL 11/1/02; HBG 3/03)

641 Kellogg, Steven. *A Penguin Pup for Pinkerton* (PS–2). Illus. 2001, Dial $15.99 (0-8037-2536-1). 32pp. Pinkerton the Great Dane fantasizes that a football is an egg with hilarious consequences in this detailed and humorously illustrated story. (Rev: BL 9/1/01; HB 9–10/01; HBG 3/02; SLJ 8/01*)

642 Kennedy, X. J. *Elefantina's Dream* (K–3). Illus. by Graham Percy. 2002, Putnam $16.99 (0-399-23428-4). 48pp. Elefantina the elephant overcomes great obstacles to pursue her dream of becoming an Elympic ice skater. (Rev: BL 2/15/02; HBG 10/02; SLJ 1/02)

643 Kerr, Judith. *The Other Goose* (PS–2). Illus. 2002, HarperCollins LB $15.89 (0-06-008583-5). 32pp. After catching a bank robber, a lonely goose is rewarded with a gift of another goose who will be a friend. (Rev: BL 4/1/02; HB 7–8/02; HBG 10/02; SLJ 6/02)

644 Kirk, David. *Little Pig, Biddle Pig* (PS). Illus. Series: Biddle Books. 2001, Scholastic $9.95 (0-439-30575-6). 32pp. Little Pig's desire to remain clean wins her no friends in the pig pen. (Rev: BL 1/1–15/02; HBG 3/02; SLJ 11/01)

645 Kleven, Elisa. *Sun Bread* (PS–1). Illus. 2001, Dutton $16.99 (0-525-46674-6). 32pp. Longing for sun, the baker makes a sun-shaped loaf so enticing that the animals cheer up and sun breaks through the clouds. (Rev: BL 5/1/01; HBG 10/01; SLJ 6/01)

646 Kolar, Bob. *Racer Dogs* (PS–2). Illus. 2003, Dutton $15.99 (0-525-45939-1). 32pp. Dogs zoom racecars around a track and end up in a jumbled pileup in this funny picture book. (Rev: BL 2/1/03; SLJ 3/03)

647 Koller, Jackie French. *Baby for Sale* (PS–2). Illus. by Janet Pedersen. 2002, Marshall Cavendish $16.95 (0-7614-5106-4). 32pp. Rabbit Peter, fed up with his baby sister, tries to sell her to the neighbors but finally decides to keep her when he realizes that he loves her. (Rev: BL 9/1/02; HBG 3/03; SLJ 9/02)

648 Kopelke, Lisa. *Excuse Me!* (K–2). Illus. 2003, Simon & Schuster $15.95 (0-689-85111-1). 32pp. Frog, a notorious burper, discovers (after living among other belchers) that it's better to be polite. (Rev: BL 2/15/03)

649 Kopper, Lisa. *Good Dog, Daisy!* (PS). Illus. 2001, Dutton $12.99 (0-525-46661-4). 32pp. When Baby gets too bossy with Little Daisy, the puppy's mother intervenes, and then Baby's mother must get involved too. (Rev: BL 5/15/01; HBG 10/01; SLJ 6/01)

650 Kortepeter, Paul. *The Hugs and Kisses Contest* (PS–1). Illus. by Susan Wheeler. 2002, Dutton $14.99 (0-525-46531-6). 28pp. A sweet story about a brother and sister rabbit who compete for the most hugs and kisses from their mother in a single day. (Rev: BL 4/1/02; HBG 10/02; SLJ 3/02)

651 Lakin, Patricia. *Clarence the Copy Cat* (PS–2). Illus. by John Manders. 2002, Doubleday LB $17.99 (0-385-90854-7). 32pp. Clarence the cat is a pacifist and won't catch mice, which makes it difficult for him to find a home until he discovers the library, but even there a mouse finally turns up and causes much hilarity. (Rev: BL 11/1/02; HBG 3/03; SLJ 10/02)

652 Lakin, Patricia. *Snow Day!* (PS–1). Illus. by Scott Nash. 2002, Dial $15.99 (0-8037-2642-2). 32pp. There's a twist to this story of four crocodiles playing in the snow — they're all school principals. (Rev: BL 11/15/02; HBG 3/03; SLJ 11/02)

653 Landstrom, Lena. *Little Hippos' Adventure* (PS–K). Trans. by Joan Sandin. 2002, Farrar $15.00 (91-29-65500-5). 28pp. Three little hippos disobey their mother's rule to swim in their own part of the river and head off to Tall Cliff to dive. (Rev: BL 3/15/02; HBG 10/02; SLJ 4/02)

654 Langdo, Bryan. *The Dog Who Loved the Good Life* (PS–2). Illus. 2001, Holt $15.95 (0-8050-6494-X). 32pp. Comical illustrations add to the tale of Jake the dog, who wants to be treated as a human, eating "people" food at the table, taking over the TV remote, and even borrowing the car. (Rev: BL 12/1/01; HBG 3/02; SLJ 12/01)

655 Lavis, Steve. *Little Mouse Has a Party* (PS). Illus. by author. Series: Ragged Bears Ready Readers. 2000, Ragged Bear $6.95 (1-929927-11-8). Little Mouse spends a week getting ready for his party, which will take place on Sunday, in this simple text with one sentence per page. Also use *Little Mouse Has a Friend* (2000). (Rev: HBG 10/01; SLJ 6/01)

656 Lawrence, John. *This Little Chick* (PS–K). Illus. 2002, Candlewick $15.99 (0-7636-1716-4). 32pp. A little chick learns the many languages of the barnyard as he visits his animal friends. (Rev: BCCB 4/02; BL 2/1/02; HBG 10/02; SLJ 3/02*)

657 LeGuin, Ursula. *Tom Mouse* (K–3). Illus. by Julie Downing. 2002, Millbrook LB $22.90 (0-7613-2663-4). 40pp. A mouse with wanderlust finds a traveling companion in an elderly African American woman when he boards a train bound for the unknown. (Rev: BCCB 5/02; BL 3/15/02; HB 5–6/02; HBG 10/02; SLJ 5/02)

658 Leslie, Amanda. *Alfie and Betty Bug: A Lift-the-Flap Book* (PS). Illus. by author. 2001, Handprint $10.95 (1-929766-33-5). Each lift-the-flap page offers three options in this colorful story of elephant Alfie's day in the park with Betty Bug and other friends. (Rev: HBG 3/02; SLJ 2/02)

659 Lester, Helen. *Score One for the Sloths!* (PS–3). Illus. by Lynn Munsinger. 2001, Houghton $15.00 (0-618-10857-2). 32pp. A school full of sleepy sloths faces closure for its low test scores and it's up to a new student called Sparky to save the day. (Rev: BL 8/01; HB 9–10/01; HBG 3/02; SLJ 10/01)

660 Lester, Helen. *Tackylocks and the Three Bears* (K–2). Illus. by Lynn Munsinger. 2002, Houghton $15.00 (0-618-22490-4). 32pp. Tacky the penguin adds his own personal touches to his role as

Goldilocks, much to the delight of his audience. (Rev: BCCB 12/02; BL 10/1/02; HBG 3/03; SLJ 9/02)

661 Lesynski, Loris. *Night School* (1–3). Illus. 2001, Annick LB $18.95 (1-55037-585-7); paper $5.95 (1-55037-584-9). 32pp. Being a night owl, Eddie likes the idea of Night School until he realizes that many of the students are not like him. (Rev: BL 6/1–15/01; HBG 10/01)

662 Lewis, Kevin. *My Truck Is Stuck!* (PS–K). Illus. by Daniel Kirk. 2002, Hyperion $14.99 (0-7868-0534-X). 40pp. When their dump truck gets stuck, the two dogs hauling a load of bones seek help, in this amusing, brightly illustrated book with a teasing subplot and some basic counting reminders. (Rev: BL 11/1/02; HBG 3/03; SLJ 10/02)

663 Lewis, Paeony. *I'll Always Love You* (PS). Illus. by Penny Ives. 2002, Tiger Tales paper $5.95 (1-58925-360-4). Alex Bear's mother is disappointed when he behaves badly but always forgives him and says she'll love him. (Rev: SLJ 8/02)

664 Lewis, Rob. *Friends* (PS–2). Illus. 2001, Holt $16.95 (0-8050-6691-8). 32pp. Little rabbit Oscar has trouble making new friends until he accepts that everyone is different in this beginning reader with attractive, cartoonlike illustrations. (Rev: BL 11/15/01; HBG 3/02; SLJ 12/01)

665 Leznoff, Glenda. *Pigmalion* (K–2). Illus. by Rachel Berman. 2002, Tradewind $15.95 (1-896580-20-3). Little pig Juliet is a skilled singer, actor, and dancer but so shy that she must rehearse in private when she's chosen for the part of Eliza Piglittle. (Rev: SLJ 8/02)

666 Lies, Brian. *Hamlet and the Magnificent Sandcastle* (K–3). Illus. 2001, Moon Mountain $15.95 (0-9677929-2-4). 32pp. Hamlet the pig and his porcupine friend Quince are stranded on Hamlet's giant sandcastle when the tide comes in. (Rev: BL 1/1–15/02; SLJ 6/01)

667 Lin, Grace. *Olvina Flies* (PS–1). Illus. 2003, Holt $15.95 (0-8050-6711-6). 32pp. Olvina, a hen, is reluctant to take her first airplane ride but finds a friend in a fellow traveler, a penguin. (Rev: BL 2/1/03)

668 Lindenbaum, Pija. *Bridget and the Muttonheads* (PS–2). Trans. by Kjersti Board. Illus. 2002, Farrar $16.00 (91-29-65650-8). 28pp. Little Bridget, on vacation with her parents and bored by the pool, wanders off to find an adventure of her own in this imaginative tale. (Rev: BL 8/02; HB 11–12/02; HBG 3/03; SLJ 1/03)

669 Lionni, Leo. *The Greentail Mouse* (PS–2). Illus. 2003, Knopf $15.95 (0-375-82399-9). 32pp. A reissue of a 1973 picture book that tells the story of field mice who must learn to trust each other again. (Rev: BL 1/1–15/03)

670 Lithgow, John. *Marsupial Sue* (K–3). Illus. by Jack E. Davis. 2001, Simon & Schuster $17.95 (0-689-84394-1). Sue the kangaroo is unhappy with her fate and wishes she were another kind of animal. (Rev: HBG 3/02; SLJ 11/01)

671 Lithgow, John. *Micawber* (PS–2). Illus. by C. F. Payne. 2002, Simon & Schuster LB $17.95 (0-689-

83341-5). An art-loving squirrel spends a summer in the country mastering brushes and colors, and returns triumphantly to New York to open a gallery above the Central Park carousel in this book/CD combination. (Rev: HBG 3/03; SLJ 9/02)

672 London, Jonathan. *Froggy Eats Out* (PS–1). Illus. by Frank Remkiewicz. 2001, Viking $15.99 (0-670-89686-1). 32pp. Froggy's family tries to take him to a real restaurant, but despite his best intentions Froggy fails to behave and they end up eating fast food after all. (Rev: BL 6/1–15/01; HBG 10/01; SLJ 8/01)

673 London, Jonathan. *Froggy Goes to the Doctor* (PS–2). Illus. by Frank Remkiewicz. 2002, Viking $15.99 (0-670-03857-5). 32pp. Froggy's visit (without underwear) to the doctor is amusing for all concerned. (Rev: BL 1/1–15/03)

674 London, Jonathan. *Froggy Plays in the Band* (PS–2). Illus. by Frank Remkiewicz. 2002, Viking $15.99 (0-670-03532-7). The members of Froggy's marching band must remember one thing — not to stop for anything! (Rev: BCCB 4/02; HBG 10/02; SLJ 4/02)

675 Loupy, Christopher. *Hugs and Kisses* (PS–K). Illus. by Eve Tharlet. 2002, North-South LB $15.88 (0-7358-1485-6). 36pp. Hugs the puppy wants to find out what kisses are all about in this charmingly illustrated story for preschoolers. (Rev: BL 2/1/02; HBG 10/02)

676 Lozoff, Bo. *The Wonderful Life of a Fly Who Couldn't Fly* (PS–2). Illus. by Beth Stover. 2002, Hampton Roads $17.95 (1-57174-286-7). A young fly with a wise mother learns to accept life without wings. (Rev: HBG 3/03; SLJ 2/03)

677 McAllister, Angela. *Barkus, Sly and the Golden Egg* (K–2). Illus. by Sally Anne Lambert. 2002, Bloomsbury $15.95 (1-58234-764-6). Three crafty chickens plan a clever escape from two dastardly foxes and alert the townspeople to the foxes' thieving ways. (Rev: SLJ 9/02)

678 McClintock, Barbara. *Molly and the Magic Wishbone* (PS–3). Illus. 2001, Farrar $16.00 (0-374-34999-1). 32pp. Molly the kitten is given a magic wishbone and wisely uses it to make a very important wish for her little sister in this fairy tale whose illustrations reveal its Dickensian origin. (Rev: BL 9/1/01; HB 1–2/02; HBG 3/02; SLJ 10/01)

679 McCullough, Sharon Pierce. *Bunbun at the Fair* (PS). Illus. by author. 2002, Barefoot $14.99 (1-84148-900-X). Bunbun, a mischievous little rabbit, goes missing at the fair and his siblings search for him. (Rev: HBG 3/03; SLJ 12/02)

680 Mcewan, Jamie. *The Heart of Cool* (2–3). Illus. by Sandra Boynton. 2001, Simon & Schuster $15.00 (0-689-82177-8). 48pp. Polar bear Bobby moves to a new school and does his level best to become as cool as his idol, Harry. (Rev: BCCB 4/01; HBG 10/01; SLJ 8/01)

681 McFarland, Lyn Rossiter. *Widget* (PS–1). Illus. by Jim McFarland. 2001, Farrar $16.00 (0-374-38428-2). 32pp. Preschoolers will love the charming illustrations and humorous story about a stray dog who pretends to be a cat in order to fit in at his new home. (Rev: BL 11/1/01; HBG 3/02; SLJ 8/01*)

682 McLaren, Chesley. *Zat Cat: A Haute Couture Tail* (K–3). Illus. 2002, Scholastic $16.95 (0-439-27316-1). 40pp. A cat who shreds the offerings at a Parisian fashion show becomes a designer sensation. (Rev: BL 3/1/02; HBG 10/02; SLJ 4/02)

683 McMullen, Nigel. *Not Me!* (PS–1). Illus. by author. 2001, Dutton $12.99 (0-525-46789-0). A bear cub takes advantage of his baby brother's inability to talk and blames him for everything that goes wrong. (Rev: HB 9–10/01; HBG 3/02; SLJ 1/02)

684 McNaughton, Colin. *Little Oops!* (PS). Illus. by author. 2001, Harcourt $5.95 (0-15-202537-5). Preston Pig and Mr. Wolf make each other's lives difficult in simple, humorous ways. Also use *Little Goal!* (2001). (Rev: SLJ 7/01)

685 McPhail, David. *The Blue Door: A Fox and Rabbit Story* (K–2). Illus. by John O'Connor. 2001, Fitzhenry & Whiteside $15.95 (1-55041-647-2). Fox and Rabbit set off to visit Fox's storytelling uncle in the city, but all they know about his whereabouts is that he has a blue door. (Rev: SLJ 2/02)

686 Mahoney, Daniel J. *The Saturday Escape* (K–2). Illus. 2002, Clarion $14.00 (0-618-13326-7). 32pp. Three friends shirk their chores in order to make it to library story time. (Rev: BL 3/15/02; HB 5–6/02; HBG 10/02; SLJ 3/02)

687 Malkin, Michele. *Pinky's Sweet Tooth* (K–3). Illus. 2003, Dutton $15.99 (0-525-47088-3). 32pp. Pinky the alligator enters a dessert contest in an effort to promote her bakery. (Rev: BL 3/1/03; SLJ 2/03)

688 Mallat, Kathy. *Just Ducky* (PS). Illus. 2002, Walker LB $16.85 (0-8027-8825-4). 24pp. Ducky has no luck convincing Frog, Mouse, or Bee to play with him, so he plays with his own reflection in a pond in this colorful picture book. (Rev: BL 9/1/02; HBG 3/03; SLJ 11/02)

689 Mammano, Julie. *Rhinos Who Play Soccer* (PS–3). Illus. 2001, Chronicle $12.95 (0-8118-2779-8). 32pp. Soccer fans will welcome this jargon-filled story of Rhinos versus All-Stars. (Rev: BL 7/01; HBG 10/01; SLJ 7/01)

690 Marciano, John Bemelmans. *Delilah* (PS–2). Illus. 2002, Viking $15.99 (0-670-03523-8). 40pp. A farmer named Red and his little lamb Delilah are the best of friends until the other sheep make Delilah question that friendship. (Rev: BL 8/02; HBG 10/02; SLJ 8/02)

691 Martin, Bill, Jr., and Michael Sampson. *The Little Squeegy Bug* (K–2). Illus. by Patrick Corrigan. 2001, Winslow $16.95 (1-890817-90-2). 32pp. A little bug becomes a firefly with help and persistence. (Rev: BCCB 1/02; BL 9/1/01; HBG 10/02; SLJ 9/01)

692 Milford, Susan. *Willa the Wonderful* (PS–2). Illus. 2003, Houghton $15.00 (0-618-27522-3). 32pp. When Willa, a little pink pig, chooses a fairy princess as her favorite career, her teacher and classmates are initially unimpressed. (Rev: BL 3/15/03)

693 Miller, Ruth. *The Bear on the Bed* (PS–2). Illus. by Bill Slavin. 2002, Kids Can $15.95 (1-55337-036-8). A boisterous bear takes over a little girl's cabin at camp, with consequences sure to please children if not adults. (Rev: HBG 10/02; SLJ 7/02)

694 Miller, Virginia. *In a Minute!* (PS–K). Illus. 2001, Candlewick $15.99 (0-7636-1270-7). 32pp. Bartholomew the bear wants to play, but George is too busy doing chores. (Rev: BL 5/15/01; HBG 10/01; SLJ 6/01)

695 Milne, A. A. *Pooh Goes Visiting* (K–2). Ed. by Stephen Krensky. Illus. by Ernest H. Shepard. Series: Winnie-the-Pooh Easy Reader. 2002, Dutton $13.99 (0-525-46821-8). 48pp. The story of Pooh getting stuck in the doorway after eating in Rabbit's hole is made accessible for beginning readers and accompanied by the original Shepard illustrations. Also use *Tigger Comes to the Forest* (2002). (Rev: BL 1/1–15/03; HBG 3/03)

696 Mitton, Tony. *Dinosaurumpus!* (PS). Illus. by Guy Parker-Rees. 2003, Scholastic $15.95 (0-439-39514-3). 32pp. Party with the dinosaurs in this joyous, energetic picture book with vivid, comical illustrations showing the dancing dinos in all their scaly glory. (Rev: BL 1/1–15/03; SLJ 3/03)

697 Mitton, Tony. *Down by the Cool of the Pool* (PS–2). Illus. by Guy Parker-Rees. 2002, Scholastic $15.95 (0-439-30915-8). A group of animals dance and leap around the pool until they all fall in — and continue to party in the water. (Rev: HBG 10/02; SLJ 7/02)

698 Montanari, Eva. *The Crocodile's True Colors* (K–3). Illus. 2002, Watson-Guptill $14.95 (0-8230-2435-0). 32pp. Young readers learn about art forms — cubism, expressionism, and so forth — through this story of animals learning to draw. (Rev: BL 12/1/02; HBG 3/03; SLJ 11/02)

699 Montes, Marisa. *Egg-Napped!* (PS–1). Illus. by Marsha Winborn. 2002, HarperCollins LB $15.89 (0-06-028951-1). 32pp. Mr. and Mrs. Gabbler Goose are in a panic when their egg goes missing in this humorous, rhyming adventure. (Rev: BL 2/15/02; HBG 10/02; SLJ 3/02)

700 Moodie, Fiona. *Noko and the Night Monster* (PS–K). Illus. 2001, Marshall Cavendish $15.95 (0-7614-5093-9). 32pp. The friends of Takadu the aardvark band together to rid him of his fear of the Night Monster in this nicely illustrated, appealing story. (Rev: BL 12/1/01; HBG 3/02; SLJ 12/01)

701 Moran, Alex. *Boots for Beth* (PS–1). Illus. by Lisa Campbell Ernst. 2002, Harcourt LB $11.95 (0-15-216558-4); paper $3.95 (0-15-216546-0). 20pp. Farm animals offer their boots to Beth, a little pig, after she finds that her favorite red boots don't fit her any more. (Rev: BCCB 5/02; BL 4/15/02; HBG 10/02; SLJ 4/02)

702 Morrison, Toni, and Slade Morrison. *The Book of Mean People* (PS). Illus. by Pascal Lemaitre. 2002, Hyperion LB $17.49 (0-7868-2471-9). 48pp. Cartoon-style rabbit children learn the different ways in which people can be mean. (Rev: BCCB 1/03; BL 10/15/02; HBG 3/03; SLJ 11/02)

703 Moss, Miriam. *I'll Be Your Friend, Smudge!* (PS–2). Illus. by Lynne Chapman. 2002, Gullane $12.95 (1-86233-207-X). Young mouse Smudge is crying because she has no friends when Hare turns up and befriends her. Also use *Smudge's Grumpy Day, It's My Turn, Smudge!*, and *A New House for Smudge* (all 2002). (Rev: SLJ 8/02)

704 Moss, Miriam. *The Snow Bear* (PS–1). Illus. by Maggie Kneen. 2001, Dutton $15.99 (0-525-46658-4). Winter scenes and spare, poetic text depict a polar bear cub who gets help from other animals in his search for his mother. (Rev: HBG 3/02; SLJ 10/01)

705 Muller, Birte. *Giant Jack* (PS–3). Trans. by J. Alison James. Illus. 2002, North-South LB $15.88 (0-7358-1621-2). 32pp. Jack, a rat, discovers why he feels different from his sisters: He was adopted into a mouse family. (Rev: BL 5/15/02; HBG 10/02; SLJ 7/02)

706 Muller, Robin. *Badger's New House* (PS–2). Illus. 2002, Holt $15.95 (0-8050-6383-8). 32pp. Badger trades his new big house for Grandmother Mouse's cozy old one in this charmingly illustrated story. (Rev: BL 7/02; HBG 10/02; SLJ 8/02)

707 Murphy, Kelly. *The Boll Weevil Ball* (K–2). Illus. by author. 2002, Holt $15.95 (0-8050-6712-4). A little beetle is out of his depth at a dance until he makes friends with a pretty firefly. (Rev: HBG 3/03; SLJ 9/02)

708 Murphy, Mary. *Koala and the Flower* (PS–2). Illus. 2002, Millbrook LB $21.90 (0-7613-2674-X). 32pp. A curious little koala discovers the wonders of the library, with artwork that becomes more exciting as the story progresses. (Rev: BL 8/02; HBG 10/02; SLJ 9/02)

709 Murphy, Patti Beling. *Elinor and Violet: The Story of Two Naughty Chickens* (PS–1). Illus. 2001, Little, Brown $14.95 (0-316-91088-0). 32pp. Elinor, a young chicken, thought she was quite naughty until she met Violet! (Rev: BL 5/15/01; HB 3–4/01; HBG 10/01; SLJ 6/01)

710 Murray, Marjorie Dennis. *Little Wolf and the Moon* (PS–2). Illus. by Stacey Schuett. 2002, Marshall Cavendish $16.95 (0-7614-5100-5). A little wolf asks many thoughtful questions about the nature of the moon. (Rev: HBG 3/03; SLJ 12/02)

711 Napoli, Donna Jo, and Marie Kane. *Rocky, the Cat Who Barks* (PS–1). Illus. by Tamara Petrosino. 2002, Dutton $15.99 (0-525-46544-8). 32pp. An amusing tale about Rocky, a dog adopted by a new family with five cats who all treat him terribly until he comes to their rescue one day. (Rev: BL 3/1/02; HBG 10/02)

712 Newman, Leslea. *Pigs, Pigs, Pigs!* (PS–2). Illus. by Erika Oller. 2003, Simon & Schuster $15.95 (0-689-84979-6). 32pp. A town joyfully welcomes a group of pigs with feasting and dancing in this rhyming picture book. Also use *Dogs, Dogs, Dogs* (2002) and *Cats, Cats, Cats* (2001). (Rev: BL 2/15/03; SLJ 2/03)

713 Newman, Marjorie. *Mole and the Baby Bird* (2–4). Illus. by Patrick Benson. 2002, Bloomsbury $16.95 (1-58234-784-0). 32pp. Little Mole rescues a baby bird and, with a little help from his grandfather, learns that wild things need to be free. (Rev: BCCB 11/02; BL 10/15/02; SLJ 12/02)

714 Newsome, Jill. *Night Walk* (PS–K). Illus. by Claudio Munoz. 2003, Clarion $15.00 (0-618-32458-5). 32pp. Flute, a cat, and Daisy, a dog, take a nighttime walk with their owner and encounter both friends and foes. (Rev: BL 2/15/03)

715 Newton, Jill. *Bored! Bored! Bored!* (PS). Illus. 2002, Bloomsbury $15.95 (1-58234-760-3). 32pp. Claude the shark finds a way to alleviate his boredom with gardening. (Rev: BL 8/02; SLJ 9/02)

716 Nimmo, Jenny. *Something Wonderful* (PS–2). Illus. by Debbie Boon. 2001, Harcourt $16.00 (0-15-216486-3). 32pp. Little Hen feels ordinary in comparison with the others until she proudly becomes a mother. (Rev: BL 9/15/01; HBG 3/02; SLJ 9/01)

717 Nivola, Claire A. *The Forest* (K–3). Illus. 2002, Farrar $16.00 (0-374-32452-2). 32pp. A young mouse conquers his fear of the forest as he leaves his cozy house and sets off to enter this mysterious place. (Rev: BL 4/15/02; HBG 10/02; SLJ 6/02)

718 Nordholm, Gayle. *The Rainbow Tiger* (PS–1). Illus. by Jennifer Frohwerk. 2002, Hara $16.95 (1-883697-52-2). 40pp. After his wish is granted, a tiger regrets that he asked to exchange his stripes for the colors of a peacock. (Rev: BL 5/1/02)

719 Numeroff, Laura. *If You Take a Mouse to School* (PS–1). Illus. by Felicia Bond. 2002, HarperCollins LB $15.89 (0-06-028329-7). The adventurous mouse has a wonderful day at school. (Rev: BCCB 10/02; HBG 3/03; SLJ 9/02)

720 O'Keefe, Susan Heyboer. *Love Me, Love You* (PS). Illus. by Robin Spowart. 2001, Boyds Mills $15.95 (1-56397-837-7). 32pp. A simple but beautifully rendered story about a mother rabbit and baby engaged in everyday activities. (Rev: BL 4/15/01; HBG 10/01; SLJ 4/01)

721 O'Malley, Kevin. *Little Buggy* (PS–2). Illus. 2002, Harcourt $16.00 (0-15-216339-5). 32pp. Two earthbound slugs watch a young ladybug learning to fly, making caustic comments all the while in this cheerful tale of perseverance. (Rev: BL 10/1/02; HBG 3/03; SLJ 9/02)

722 Ormerod, Jan. *If You're Happy and You Know It!* (PS). Illus. by Lindsey Gardiner. 2003, Star Bright $15.95 (1-932065-07-5); paper $5.95 (1-932065-10-5). 32pp. Animals demonstrate ways to show happiness in this update of the classic song. (Rev: BL 3/15/03)

723 Palatini, Margie. *Earthquack!* (PS–1). Illus. by Barry Moser. 2002, Simon & Schuster $15.95 (0-689-84280-5). 32pp. The barnyard becomes alarmed, Henny-Penny-style, when the animals feel what they think is an earthquake in this rhyming tale. (Rev: BCCB 7–8/02; BL 7/02; HBG 10/02; SLJ 6/02)

724 Paraskevas, Betty. *Marvin the Tap-Dancing Horse* (PS–1). Illus. by Michael Paraskevas. 2001, Simon & Schuster $16.00 (0-689-82153-0). 32pp. Marvin's road to fame is bumpy, but when he finally makes it to Broadway he realizes he'd rather be back tap-dancing at the carnival. (Rev: BL 5/1/01; HBG 10/01)

725 Partis, Joanne. *Stripe's Naughty Sister* (PS). Illus. by author. 2002, Carolrhoda LB $15.95 (0-87614-466-0). The tiger cub's baby sister spoils his games with his friends and exhausts him into the bargain. (Rev: HBG 10/02; SLJ 4/02)

726 Paul, Ann Whitford. *Little Monkey Says Good Night* (PS–K). Illus. by David Walker. 2003, Farrar $16.00 (0-374-34609-7). 32pp. Before going to bed, Little Monkey goes into the circus tent to say goodnight to all the performers. (Rev: BL 3/15/03)

727 Pearson, Tracey Campbell. *Bob* (PS–K). Illus. 2002, Farrar $16.00 (0-374-39957-3). 32pp. Bob the rooster's wide-ranging animal vocabulary — he can meow, moo, and ribbet with the best of them — succeeds in scaring off a fox. (Rev: BL 11/15/02; HBG 3/03; SLJ 8/02)

728 Petty, Dini. *The Queen, the Bear, and the Bumblebee* (K–2). Illus. by Rose Cowles. 2001, Beyond Words $15.95 (1-58270-036-2). When given three wishes, the Queen and the Bear are quick with desires but Bumblebee is quite happy as he is. (Rev: HBG 10/01; SLJ 8/01)

729 Pfister, Marcus. *Just the Way You Are* (PS–K). Illus. 2002, North-South LB $15.88 (0-7358-1616-6). 32pp. Animals wishing they looked different are reassured that they are fine just as they are in this picture book with colorful art and die-cut pages that give a glimpse of the desired change. (Rev: BL 7/02; HBG 10/02; SLJ 9/02)

730 Piepmeier, Charlotte. *Lucy's Journey to the Wild West: A True Story* (1–3). Illus. by Sally Blakemore. 2002, Azro $19.95 (1-929115-07-5). 40pp. Lucy the Labrador relates the new sights as her owners move to New Mexico from North Carolina in this story that comes with a map of the trip. (Rev: BL 2/15/03)

731 Pin, Isabel. *The Seed* (PS–3). Illus. 2001, North-South LB $15.88 (0-7358-1408-2). 32pp. Two teams of beetles vie for the prize of a cherry tree, envisioning future orchards. (Rev: BL 5/15/01; HBG 10/01; SLJ 7/01)

732 Pinkwater, Daniel. *Irving and Muktuk: Two Bad Bears* (PS–3). Illus. by Jill Pinkwater. 2001, Houghton $15.00 (0-618-09334-6). 32pp. Two polar bears plot to steal the main attraction from a town's blueberry muffin festival. (Rev: BL 9/15/01; HBG 3/02; SLJ 9/01)

733 Piven, Hanoch. *The Perfect Purple Feather* (K–2). Trans. from Hebrew by Rachel Tzvia Back. Illus. by author. 2002, Little, Brown $15.95 (0-316-76657-7). A varied group of colorful animals suggest all sorts of uses for Jacob's purple feather. (Rev: HBG 3/03; SLJ 11/02)

734 Posthuma, Sieb. *Benny* (PS–1). Illus. 2003, Kane $15.95 (1-929132-43-3). 32pp. A dog's sniffing ability is impaired when he comes down with a cold. (Rev: BCCB 3/03; BL 2/15/03)

735 Potter, Beatrix. *The Tale of Peter Rabbit* (PS–1). Illus. by Michael Hague. 2001, North-South LB $15.88 (1-58717-053-1). 32pp. The classic Potter book is presented in picture-book format with new illustrations. (Rev: BL 7/01; HBG 10/01; SLJ 4/01)

736 Pratt, Pierre. *Car* (PS). Illus. by author. 2001, Candlewick $4.99 (0-7636-1390-8). Cheerful board-book characters Olaf the elephant and Venus the mouse introduce readers to single words in spreads of bold, appealing art. Also use *Park*, *Shopping*, and *Home*. (Rev: SLJ 11/01)

737 Proimos, James. *The Many Adventures of Johnny Mutton* (PS–3). Illus. 2001, Harcourt $16.00 (0-15-202379-8). 48pp. The zany story of a family that takes in an abandoned baby, not recognizing that it is a sheep. (Rev: BCCB 7–8/01; BL 6/1–15/01; HB 9–10/01; HBG 3/02; SLJ 5/01)

738 Provencher, Rose-Marie. *Mouse Cleaning* (PS–2). Illus. by Bernadette Pons. 2001, Holt $15.95 (0-8050-6240-8). Lazy Grandma Twilly, a squirrel, becomes obsessed with house cleaning when she finds a mouse. (Rev: HBG 10/01; SLJ 7/01)

739 Puttock, Simon. *Big Bad Wolf Is Good* (PS–K). Illus. by Lynne Chapman. 2002, Sterling $12.95 (0-8069-0027-X). A sad and lonely wolf who wants to make friends finds that hardly anyone trusts him. (Rev: HBG 3/03; SLJ 8/02)

740 Puttock, Simon. *Squeaky Clean* (PS–1). Illus. by Mary McQuillan. 2002, Little, Brown $13.95 (0-316-78816-3). 32pp. When Mama Pig rounds up her three piglets for a bath, she encounters fierce opposition. (Rev: BL 6/1–15/02; HBG 10/02; SLJ 4/02)

741 Puttock, Simon. *A Story for Hippo: A Book About Loss* (1–4). Illus. by Alison Bartlett. 2001, Scholastic $15.95 (0-439-26219-4). 32pp. When old, wise Hippo dies, Monkey is disconsolate but learns to find comfort in sharing memories of his old friend. (Rev: BL 12/1/01; HBG 3/02; SLJ 11/01)

742 Quackenbush, Robert. *Batbaby Finds a Home* (1–3). Illus. by author. 2001, Random LB $11.99 (0-375-90430-1); paper $3.99 (0-375-80430-7). 48pp. A homeless family of bats is happy to find a ready-made bat box on the side of a house. (Rev: SLJ 2/02)

743 Radunsky, Vladimir. *Ten* (K–2). Illus. 2002, Viking $16.99 (0-670-03563-7). 32pp. Humorous, giddy artwork draws the reader into this story of newlyweds Mr. and Mrs. Armadillo, who love each other and welcome the simultaneous arrival of 10 babies called One, Two, Three, and so forth. (Rev: BL 11/15/02; HBG 3/03; SLJ 9/02)

744 Rankin, Joan. *First Day* (PS). 2002, Simon & Schuster $16.95 (0-689-84563-4). 32pp. A young puppy has many misgivings about starting school but loves it when he gets there. (Rev: BL 6/1–15/02)

745 Reinen, Judy. *Bow Wow: A Day in the Life of Dogs* (PS–2). Photos by author. 2001, Little, Brown $14.95 (0-316-83290-1). A boa-bedecked spaniel describes the daily routine, from being served breakfast, to drives, bubble baths, and a nightcap at bedtime. A companion book is *A Day in the Life of Cats* (2001). (Rev: HBG 3/02; SLJ 10/01)

746 Reynolds, Peter. *Sydney's Star* (PS–1). Illus. 2001, Simon & Schuster $14.00 (0-689-83184-6).

32pp. Humorous illustrations depict a young mouse named Sydney whose initial failure at the science fair turns into a great success and wins her the longed-for prize. (Rev: BL 12/15/01; HBG 3/02; SLJ 12/01)

747 Richardson, John. *Grunt* (PS–K). Illus. by author. 2002, Clarion $15.00 (0-618-15974-6). The runt of the litter of piglets, Wee-skin-and-bones, runs away from the scorn of his siblings and meets a kindly boar who's into positive thinking. (Rev: BCCB 6/02; HBG 10/02; SLJ 5/02)

748 Riddell, Chris. *Platypus* (PS). Illus. 2002, Harcourt $15.00 (0-15-216493-6). 32pp. Clean, simple illustrations and cheerful text tell the story of a platypus who mistakenly adds a shell — with a hermit crab inside — to his collection of special things. (Rev: BL 3/1/02; HBG 10/02; SLJ 6/02)

749 Riddell, Chris. *Platypus and the Lucky Day* (PS–1). Illus. by author. 2002, Harcourt $15.00 (0-15-216723-4). Mishaps are succeeded by happy discoveries in Platypus's lucky day. (Rev: HBG 3/03; SLJ 11/02)

750 Roche, Denis. *Little Pig Is Capable* (PS–2). Illus. 2002, Houghton $15.00 (0-395-91368-3). 32pp. Little Pig's parents treat him like a baby until he saves his scouting troop from a suspiciously hairy new scoutmaster. (Rev: BL 3/1/02; HB 5–6/02; HBG 10/02; SLJ 8/02)

751 Rockwell, Anne. *Morgan Plays Soccer* (PS–1). Illus. by Paul Meisel. 2001, HarperCollins LB $14.89 (0-06-028444-7). 40pp. Morgan's lack of soccer know-how is frustrating until he is placed as goalie, where it's his turn to shine. (Rev: BL 8/01; HBG 3/02; SLJ 8/01)

752 Roddie, Shen. *Sandbear* (PS–2). Illus. by Jenny Jones. 2002, Bloomsbury $15.95 (1-58234-758-1). Hare creates a bear made of sand, and discovers he's made a friend. (Rev: SLJ 10/02)

753 Rogers, Paul. *Ruby's Dinnertime* (PS). Illus. by Emma Rogers. 2002, Dutton $12.99 (0-525-46847-1). A toddler mouse proudly progresses from playing with her food in her high chair to sitting at the table with a real plate and cup. (Rev: SLJ 5/02)

754 Rogers, Paul, and Emma Rogers. *Ruby's Potty* (PS). Illus. 2001, Dutton $12.99 (0-525-46816-1). 24pp. A little mouse named Ruby loves her precious pink potty and puts it to many unintended uses before finally figuring out its real purpose. (Rev: BL 12/15/01; HBG 3/02; SLJ 11/01)

755 Rohmann, Eric. *My Friend Rabbit* (PS–3). Illus. 2002, Millbrook LB $22.90 (0-7613-2420-8). 32pp. Rabbit gets Mouse's airplane stuck in a tree, and their animal friends form a tower to get it down. Caldecott Medal winner, 2003. (Rev: BL 5/15/02; HBG 10/02; SLJ 5/02)

756 Root, Barry. *Gumbrella* (PS–1). Illus. 2002, Putnam $15.99 (0-399-23347-4). 32pp. Gumbrella the elephant efficiently nurses her animal patients back to health, but then refuses to let them go. (Rev: BCCB 12/02; BL 11/15/02; HB 9–10/02; HBG 3/03; SLJ 11/02)

757 Root, Phyllis. *Oliver Finds His Way* (PS–2). Illus. by Christopher Denise. 2002, Candlewick

$14.99 (0-7636-1383-5). 40pp. Oliver, a little bear, chases a leaf until he gets lost but soon figures out how to return to Mama and Papa in this autumn picture book. (Rev: BCCB 12/02; BL 9/15/02; HB 1–2/03; HBG 3/03; SLJ 10/02)

758 Roth, Carol. *The Little School Bus* (2–4). Illus. by Pamela Paparone. 2002, North-South LB $15.50 (0-7358-1647-6). 32pp. This romp of a read-aloud will have kids chanting along as silly animals board a bus and ride around town. (Rev: BCCB 9/02; BL 8/02; HBG 3/03; SLJ 7/02)

759 Roth, Susan L. *It's Still a Dog's New York: A Book of Healing* (K–3). Illus. by author. 2001, National Geographic $12.00 (0-7922-7050-9). In this sequel to *It's a Dog's New York* (2001), New York dogs Pepper and Rover discuss their feelings about September 11, 2001. (Rev: HBG 10/02; SLJ 6/02)

760 Ruelle, Karen Gray. *Mother's Day Mess* (1–2). Illus. 2003, Holiday $14.95 (0-8234-1773-5); paper $4.95 (0-8234-1781-6). 32pp. Kittens Harry and Emily make great plans for Mother's Day, but somehow they don't quite succeed. (Rev: BL 3/1/03; SLJ 3/03)

761 Rusackas, Francisca. *I Love You All Day Long* (PS). Illus. by Priscilla Burris. 2002, HarperCollins LB $13.89 (0-06-050277-0). 32pp. A little pig, upset that he won't be with his mother at school, is reassured when his mother tells him that she loves him "all day long." (Rev: BL 2/1/03; HBG 3/03; SLJ 2/03)

762 Ryder, Joanne. *Big Bear Ball* (PS–K). Illus. by Steven Kellogg. 2002, HarperCollins LB $15.89 (0-06-027956-7). 32pp. The bears throw a big party and soon many of the other forest creatures join in the festivities. (Rev: BCCB 10/02; BL 5/1/02; HBG 10/02; SLJ 6/02)

763 Rylant, Cynthia. *The Lighthouse Family: The Storm* (1–3). Illus. by Preston McDaniels. 2002, Simon & Schuster $14.95 (0-689-84880-3). 80pp. Pandora the lighthouse keeper cat has a lonely life until Seabold the dog arrives in a storm, only to be followed later by three baby mice, who join the happy and growing family. (Rev: BL 11/15/02; HBG 3/03; SLJ 11/02)

764 Rylant, Cynthia. *Little Whistle's Dinner Party* (PS–K). Illus. by Tim Bowers. Series: Little Whistle. 2001, Harcourt $14.00 (0-15-201079-3). 32pp. Little Whistle the guinea pig has a dinner party for his friends in the toy store in this simple story enhanced by detailed, appealing paintings. (Rev: BL 10/1/01; HBG 3/02; SLJ 10/01)

765 Rylant, Cynthia. *Little Whistle's Medicine* (PS–1). Illus. by Tim Bowers. 2002, Harcourt $15.00 (0-15-201086-6). 32pp. Lovable guinea pig Little Whistle searches the toy store where he lives to find a remedy for his friend Soldier's headache. (Rev: BL 3/1/02; HBG 10/02; SLJ 4/02)

766 Salas-Porras, Pipina. *El Ratoncito Pequeno / The Little Mouse* (PS–1). Illus. by Jose Cisneros. 2001, Cinco Puntos $15.95 (0-938317-56-3). 32pp. A bilingual rendering of the story of the little mouse who gets eaten by a crafty cat. (Rev: BL 7/01; HBG 10/01; SLJ 4/01)

767 Salley, Coleen. *Epossumondas* (PS–3). Illus. by Janet Stevens. 2002, Harcourt $16.00 (0-15-216748-X). 40pp. A bumbling little possum can't seem to get anything right in this uproarious adaptation of a classic Louisiana tale. (Rev: BCCB 10/02; BL 8/02; HB 11–12/02; HBG 3/03; SLJ 9/02*)

768 Schubert, Ingrid, and Dieter Schubert. *Beaver's Lodge* (PS). Illus. 2001, Front Street $15.95 (1-886910-68-5). 32pp. While Beaver is ill, Bear and Hedgehog build him a house but forget to give it a door. (Rev: BL 7/01; HBG 10/01; SLJ 5/01)

769 Schubert, Ingrid, and Dieter Schubert. *There's Always Room for One More* (PS–1). Illus. by authors. 2002, Front Street $15.95 (1-886910-77-4). A butterfly adds the final ounce that tips over the raft bearing Beaver, Badger, Bear, Hedgehog, Mole, and Hare. (Rev: HBG 10/02; SLJ 4/02)

770 Schwartz, Roslyn. *The Mole Sisters and the Blue Egg* (PS–K). Illus. 2001, Annick LB $14.95 (1-55037-705-1); paper $4.95 (1-55037-704-3). 32pp. The energetic Mole sisters aren't sure what they're seeking, but they have a great time on their quest and discover their quarry is a beautiful blue eggshell that makes a perfect swing. Also use *The Mole Sisters and the Moonlit Night* (2001). (Rev: BL 12/15/01)

771 Schwartz, Roslyn. *The Mole Sisters and the Cool Breeze* (PS–K). Illus. 2002, Annick LB $14.95 (1-55037-771-X); paper $4.95 (1-55037-770-1). 32pp. The engaging Mole sisters use leaves as fans on a hot day with amusing consequences in this small book. Also use *The Mole Sisters and the Question* (2002). (Rev: BL 1/1–15/03; HBG 3/03; SLJ 1/03)

772 Selkowe, Valrie M. *Happy Birthday to Me!* (PS–K). Illus. by John Sandford. 2001, Harper-Collins LB $15.89 (0-688-16680-6). 32pp. A young rabbit finds a key that leads him to a roomful of characters who sing his favorite song. (Rev: BL 8/01; HBG 10/01; SLJ 6/01)

773 Shannon, David. *Duck on a Bike* (PS–1). Illus. 2002, Scholastic $15.95 (0-439-05023-5). 40pp. A funny tale about a duck who dares to ride a bike, and the reactions of his farm-animal friends. (Rev: BCCB 3/02; BL 2/15/02; HB 3–4/02; HBG 10/02; SLJ 3/02*)

774 Shannon, George. *Tippy-Toe Chick, Go!* (PS–K). Illus. by Laura Dronzek. 2003, HarperCollins LB $16.89 (0-06-029824-3). 32pp. Little Chick is a dreamer, but she saves the day when a dog threatens Mother Hen and her brood. (Rev: BCCB 3/03; BL 1/1–15/03; HB 1–2/03*; SLJ 2/03)

775 Shields, Carol Diggory. *The Bugliest Bug* (PS–2). Illus. by Scott Nash. 2002, Candlewick $15.99 (0-7636-0784-3). On her way to the Bugliest Bug Contest, Damselfly Dilly recognizes that the judges are really spiders in disguise. (Rev: HBG 10/02; SLJ 5/02)

776 Sierra, Judy. *Preschool to the Rescue* (PS–K). Illus. by Will Hillenbrand. 2001, Harcourt $15.00 (0-15-202035-7). 32pp. A group of animal pre-

schoolers come to the rescue of a pizza van and other vehicles that are stuck in a huge mud puddle. (Rev: BCCB 4/01; BL 4/15/01; HB 5–6/01; HBG 10/01; SLJ 5/01)

777 Simmons, Jane. *Daisy Says "Here We Go 'Round the Mulberry Bush"* (PS). Illus. by author. 2002, Little, Brown $7.95 (0-316-79811-8). Duckling Daisy enjoys dancing along to the song until it's time for bed in this board book. Also use *Daisy Says "If You're Happy and You Know It"* (2002). (Rev: SLJ 8/02)

778 Simmons, Jane. *Daisy's Hide-and-Seek: A Lift-the-Flap Book* (PS). Illus. by author. 2001, Little, Brown $9.95 (0-316-79616-6). Daisy the duck searches for Pip, a baby duck, all over the place before finding him tucked under his mother's wing in this book with flaps to lift. (Rev: SLJ 4/01)

779 Simmons, Jane. *Quack, Daisy, QUACK!* (PS–K). Illus. 2002, Little, Brown $13.95 (0-316-79587-9). 32pp. Daisy the duck and her little brother Pip visit their aunt in the country, where Daisy loses her mother in a crowded duck pond. (Rev: BL 3/1/02; HBG 10/02; SLJ 3/02)

780 *Skidamarink: A Silly Love Song to Sing Together* (PS–1). Illus. by G. Brian Karas. 2001, Harper-Festival paper $6.95 (0-694-01595-4). A humorous penguin and polar bear couple enjoy ice-skating to the words of this romantic song, in a presentation that uses fold-out pages. (Rev: SLJ 1/02)

781 Slate, Joseph. *Miss Bindergarten Plans a Circus with Kindergarten* (PS–2). Illus. by Ashley Wolff. 2002, Dutton $16.99 (0-525-46884-6). Miss Bindergarten and her alphabetical charges each have a role to play in the circus. (Rev: HBG 3/03; SLJ 12/02)

782 Smith, Mary Ann, and Katie Smith Milway. *Cappuccina Goes to Town* (PS–2). Illus. by Eugenie Fernandes. 2002, Kids Can $15.95 (1-55074-807-6). Cappuccina goes shopping, and all the shopkeepers seem oblivious to the fact that she's a cow. (Rev: HBG 10/02; SLJ 8/02)

783 Spanyol, Jessica. *Carlo Likes Reading* (PS–K). Illus. 2001, Candlewick $14.95 (0-7636-1550-1). 32pp. The sink, a frog, his toothbrush — everything in Carlo's world has a label, and the bright yellow giraffe loves to read them. (Rev: BL 11/1/01; HBG 3/02; SLJ 10/01)

784 Spelman, Cornelia Maude. *When I Care About Others* (K–2). Illus. by Kathy Parkinson. Series: The Way I Feel. 2002, Albert Whitman LB $14.95 (0-8075-8889-X). 24pp. Readers are encouraged to be kind to others through the simple story of a little bear shown treating others as he likes to be treated. (Rev: BL 7/02; HBG 10/02; SLJ 7/02)

785 Spelman, Cornelia Maude. *When I Feel Sad* (PS–2). Illus. by Kathy Parkinson. Series: The Way I Feel. 2002, Albert Whitman LB $14.95 (0-8075-8891-1). A guinea pig describes what makes her feel sad. (Rev: HBG 3/03; SLJ 1/03)

786 Spelman, Cornelia Maude. *When I Feel Scared* (PS–K). Illus. by Kathy Parkinson. Series: The Way I Feel. 2002, Albert Whitman LB $14.95 (0-8075-8890-3). 24pp. A little bear talks about his fears, how some fears help him survive, and how others are unnecessary. (Rev: BL 4/15/02; HBG 10/02; SLJ 7/02)

787 Spinelli, Eileen. *Bath Time* (PS). Illus. by Janet Pedersen. 2003, Marshall Cavendish $14.95 (0-7614-5117-X). 32pp. A little penguin has lots of fun preparing for and then having his bath. (Rev: BL 3/15/03)

788 Spinelli, Jerry. *My Daddy and Me* (PS–K). Illus. by Seymour Chwast. 2003, Knopf $15.95 (0-375-80606-7). 40pp. A dog son describes all the joys of his life with his father. (Rev: BL 3/1/03)

789 Spires, Elizabeth. *The Big Meow* (PS–2). Illus. by Cynthia Jabar. 2002, Candlewick $15.99 (0-7636-0679-0). Little Cat's loud meow is scorned far and wide until he uses it against a threatening dog. (Rev: HBG 10/02; SLJ 5/02)

790 Spurling, Margaret. *Bilby Moon* (PS–2). Illus. by Danny Snell. 2001, Kane $14.95 (1-929132-06-9). 32pp. Bilby wonders where the moon has gone and is eventually reassured that it will come back. (Rev: BL 5/1/01; HBG 10/01)

791 Spurr, Elizabeth. *A Pig Named Perrier* (K–3). Illus. by Martin Matje. 2002, Hyperion $15.99 (0-7868-0302-9). 32pp. When movie star Marabella discovers that her spoiled pet pig, Perrier, enjoys playing in the mud, she takes him to a spa for mud baths. (Rev: BCCB 9/02; BL 4/15/02; HBG 10/02; SLJ 7/02)

792 Stadler, Alexander. *Beverly Billingsly Borrows a Book* (PS–2). Illus. 2002, Harcourt $16.00 (0-15-202510-3). 32pp. Beverly is thrilled to have her own library card, until she hears some scary rumors about what happens to children with overdue books. (Rev: BL 3/15/02; HBG 3/03; SLJ 4/02)

793 Stadler, John. *Catilda* (PS). Illus. 2003, Simon & Schuster $16.95 (0-689-84728-9). 32pp. Kitten Catilda's parents discuss her lost teddy bear in the text while the illustrations show Catilda on a long and perilous journey to retrieve the lost toy from the torch of the Statue of Liberty. (Rev: BCCB 3/03; BL 1/1–15/03; SLJ 2/03)

794 Stanley, Mandy. *Lettice: The Dancing Rabbit* (PS–K). Illus. 2002, Simon & Schuster $14.95 (0-689-84797-1). 32pp. A little bunny named Lettice longs to be a ballerina like a human child. (Rev: BL 2/1/02; HBG 10/02; SLJ 4/02)

795 Steer, Dugald. *Time for a Tale* (K–2). Illus. by Elizabeth Moseng. 2002, Dutton $15.99 (0-525-46950-8). 16pp. In a successful effort to avoid being eaten, a goose tells a fox a series of stories that are clever variations on familiar tales, such as "Ali Baa Baa and the Forty Sheep." (Rev: BL 12/1/02; HBG 3/03)

796 Steig, William. *Toby, What Are You?* (PS–1). Illus. by Teryl Euvremer. 2001, HarperCollins LB $14.89 (0-06-205170-9). 32pp. Toby spends an evening pantomiming for his parents before heading off to bed. (Rev: BL 5/1/01; HBG 10/01; SLJ 5/01)

797 Stevens, Janet, and Susan Stevens Crummel. *Jackalope* (K–3). Illus. by Janet Stevens. 2003, Harcourt $17.00 (0-15-216736-6). 56pp. A wild and wacky multilayered story of a jackrabbit who wants

to be scary and his fairy godrabbit's humorous efforts to oblige. (Rev: BL 3/15/03)

798 Stevenson, James. *The Castaway* (2–4). Illus. 2002, HarperCollins LB $15.89 (0-688-16966-X). 32pp. Hubie, a young mouse, falls from a dirigible onto a desert island where he meets a fellow castaway, Leo, a porcupine. (Rev: BL 6/1–15/02; HB 7–8/02; HBG 10/02; SLJ 5/02)

799 Stewart, Paul. *Rabbit's Wish* (PS–1). Illus. by Chris Riddell. 2001, HarperCollins $12.95 (0-06-029518-X). 32pp. Rabbit and Hedgehog get a chance to play together — a rare event, since Hedgehog sleeps during the day. (Rev: BL 10/15/01; HBG 10/01; SLJ 7/01)

800 Stoeke, Janet Morgan. *Minerva Louise and the Red Truck* (PS–1). Illus. 2002, Dutton $14.99 (0-525-46909-5). 32pp. The silly hen Minerva Louise gets taken for a ride in the farm truck and, as usual, misinterprets everything she sees. (Rev: BL 12/1/02; HB 11–12/02; HBG 3/03; SLJ 9/02)

801 Sykes, Julie. *Wait for Me, Little Tiger!* (PS–1). Illus. by Tim Warnes. 2001, Tiger Tales $14.95 (1-58925-009-5). Little Tiger reluctantly takes his annoying little sister out to play, and of course she disappears. (Rev: SLJ 7/01)

802 Tafuri, Nancy. *Where Did Bunny Go?* (PS). 2001, Scholastic $15.95 (0-439-16959-3). 32pp. Bunny disappears during a game of hide-and-seek and his friends worry that he is angry until he returns to reassure them of his friendship in this gentle story. (Rev: BL 12/1/01; HBG 3/02; SLJ 12/01)

803 Taylor, Thomas. *The Loudest Roar* (PS–3). Illus. by author. 2003, Scholastic $15.95 (0-439-50130-X). The animals of the jungle decide to teach a noisy young tiger a lesson. (Rev: SLJ 3/03)

804 Teague, Mark. *Dear Mrs. LaRue: Letters from Obedience School* (K–3). Illus. 2002, Scholastic $15.95 (0-439-20663-4). 32pp. Poor Ike LaRue sends pitiful letters home to his owner, complaining about the conditions at doggy school, but the pictures belie his words. (Rev: BL 11/1/02; HBG 3/03; SLJ 9/02)

805 Tekavec, Heather. *Storm Is Coming!* (PS–1). Illus. by Margaret Spengler. 2002, Dial $14.99 (0-8037-2626-0). 32pp. A group of frightened animals bunch together in the barn, anticipating the arrival of Storm and comforted by the fact that the howling wind, flashing light, and rain will scare him away. (Rev: BL 3/1/02; HBG 10/02; SLJ 3/02)

806 Tomlinson, Jill. *The Owl Who Was Afraid of the Dark* (K–2). Illus. by Paul Howard. 2001, Candlewick $15.99 (0-7636-1562-5). A baby barn owl called Plop discovers that all sorts of people and animals like the dark. (Rev: HBG 3/02; SLJ 8/01)

807 Tryon, Leslie. *Patsy Says* (K–3). Illus. 2001, Simon & Schuster $16.00 (0-689-82297-9). 40pp. With parents' night approaching at school, Patsy Pig, a teacher's helper, tries to give her class lessons in etiquette. (Rev: BL 4/15/01; HBG 10/01; SLJ 5/01)

808 Van Laan, Nancy. *Scrubba Dub* (PS–1). Illus. by Bernadette Pons. 2003, Simon & Schuster

$15.95 (0-689-84459-X). 32pp. A baby rabbit has lots of fun in the bath in this rhyming picture book. (Rev: BL 2/15/03)

809 Vaughan, Marcia. *Kissing Coyotes* (K–4). Illus. by Kenneth J. Spengler. 2002, Rising Moon $15.95 (0-87358-814-2). Jack Rabbit's boasting gets out of hand and his animal friends require that he follow through on his claims. (Rev: SLJ 2/03)

810 Voake, Charlotte. *Pizza Kittens* (PS–2). Illus. 2002, Candlewick $15.99 (0-7636-1622-2). 40pp. Three little kittens and their parents try to solve the problem of different eating preferences and behaviors. (Rev: BCCB 6/02; BL 5/1/02; HBG 10/02; SLJ 5/02*)

811 Waber, Bernard. *Fast Food! Gulp! Gulp!* (PS–2). Illus. by author. 2001, Houghton $15.00 (0-618-14189-8). 32pp. Hungry customers gobble food at such a rate that the cook eventually quits, preferring the pace of a health-food restaurant. (Rev: HBG 10/02; SLJ 9/01*)

812 Waddell, Martin. *Hi, Harry! The Moving Story of How One Slow Tortoise Slowly Made a Friend* (PS). Illus. by Barbara Firth. 2003, Candlewick $14.99 (0-7636-1802-0). 56pp. Harry wants to make friends but all the other animals are in too much of a rush until he thinks of Sam Snail. (Rev: BL 3/1/03; HB 3–4/03*)

813 Waddell, Martin. *Webster J. Duck* (PS–1). Illus. by David Parkins. 2001, Candlewick $13.99 (0-7636-1506-4). 32pp. Webster J. Duck has hatched, but has trouble finding his mother. (Rev: BL 11/15/01; HBG 3/02; SLJ 7/01)

814 Wahl, Jan. *Rabbits on Mars* (PS–3). Illus. by Kimberly Schamber. 2003, Lerner $15.95 (1-57505-511-2). 32pp. Three rabbits who are tired of dodging traffic and dogs set off for Mars, which they imagine to be full of carrots. (Rev: BL 3/15/03)

815 Wallace, Nancy Elizabeth. *Baby Day!* (PS). Illus. 2003, Houghton $9.95 (0-618-27576-2). 32pp. A baby rabbit and mother spend a happy day together in this board book with cut-paper illustrations. (Rev: BL 2/15/03; SLJ 3/03)

816 Wallace, Nancy Elizabeth. *Pumpkin Day!* (PS–2). Illus. 2002, Marshall Cavendish $16.95 (0-7614-5128-5). 32pp. A rabbit family visits a pumpkin farm to learn how they grow, before picking some for carving and eating. (Rev: BCCB 10/02; BL 8/02; HBG 3/03; SLJ 11/02)

817 Walsh, Ellen Stoll. *Dot and Jabber and the Great Acorn Mystery* (PS–2). Illus. 2001, Harcourt $15.00 (0-15-202602-9). 40pp. Mouse sleuths Dot and Jabber investigate who moved the acorn that grew into a little oak tree. (Rev: BL 10/1/01; HBG 3/02; SLJ 9/01)

818 Walsh, Ellen Stoll. *Dot and Jabber and the Mystery of the Missing Stream* (K–2). Illus. by author. 2002, Harcourt $15.00 (0-15-216512-6). Readers will learn a little science and logic from this story of two mice investigating why a stream has dried up. (Rev: HBG 3/03; SLJ 11/02)

819 Walton, Rick. *Bertie Was a Watchdog* (PS–1). Illus. by Arthur Robins. 2002, Candlewick $10.99 (0-7636-1385-1). Bertie the dog doesn't look fierce, but he's smart. (Rev: HBG 10/02; SLJ 8/02)

820 Walton, Rick. *Bunnies on the Go: Getting from Place to Place* (PS–2). Illus. by Paige Miglio. 2003, HarperCollins LB $16.89 (0-06-029186-9). 32pp. Rhyming text and illustrations with visual clues make a guessing game out of this story of a bunny family's vacation on boats, trains, bicycles, and other forms of transportation. (Rev: BL 1/1–15/03; SLJ 3/03)

821 Walton, Rick. *Bunny Day: Telling Time from Breakfast to Bedtime* (PS–K). Illus. by Miglio Paige. 2002, HarperCollins LB $15.89 (0-06-029184-2). 32pp. A bunny family's daily activities take them from morning to night in this picture book. (Rev: BL 5/15/02; HBG 10/02; SLJ 4/02)

822 Walton, Rick. *Herd of Cows! Flock of Sheep! Quiet! I'm Tired! I Need My Sleep!* (K–2). Illus. by Julie Olson. 2002, Gibbs Smith $15.95 (1-58685-153-5). Bright illustrations and expressive language follow animals through their elaborate efforts to rescue Farmer Bob from the flood. (Rev: HBG 3/03; SLJ 9/02)

823 Ward, Helen. *The Rooster and the Fox: A Tale from Chaucer* (K–3). Illus. 2003, Millbrook LB $24.90 (0-7613-2920-X). 40pp. "The Nun's Priest's Tale" about the proud rooster and the wily fox is adapted here in an effective tale using elegant, readable text and realistic watercolor art that makes the various animals come to life. (Rev: BCCB 2/03; BL 1/1–15/03)

824 Ward, Nick. *Don't Eat the Teacher!* (K–1). Illus. by author. 2002, Scholastic $9.95 (0-439-37465-0). When Sammy the shark gets overexcited, he can't stop eating. (Rev: HBG 3/03; SLJ 11/02)

825 Wardlaw, Lee. *The Chair Where Bear Sits* (PS–K). Illus. by Russell Benfanti. 2001, Winslow $14.95 (1-890817-85-6). 56pp. Eye-catching illustrations tell the cumulative tale, in the vein of "The House That Jack Built," of a baby bear who delights in the commotion caused by spilled juice. (Rev: BL 11/15/01; SLJ 2/02)

826 Waring, Richard. *Alberto the Dancing Alligator* (PS–3). Illus. by Holly Swain. 2002, Candlewick $15.99 (0-7636-1953-1). A girl accidentally flushes her musical pet alligator down the toilet, starting a train of uproarious events. (Rev: BCCB 11/02; HBG 3/03; SLJ 11/02)

827 Waring, Richard. *Hungry Hen* (PS). Illus. by Caroline Jayne Church. 2002, HarperCollins $14.95 (0-06-623880-3). 32pp. A greedy fox waits for a hen to grow fatter, but gets a surprise when he finally tries to eat her in this suspenseful and beautiful presentation. (Rev: BCCB 3/02; BL 1/1–15/02; HBG 10/02; SLJ 1/02*)

828 Watt, Melanie. *Leon the Chameleon* (PS–K). Illus. 2001, Kids Can $14.95 (1-55074-867-X). 32pp. Leon's color changes clash with the background, leaving him embarrassed and lonely. (Rev: BL 4/1/01; HBG 3/02; SLJ 4/01)

829 Weaver, Tess. *Opera Cat* (2–4). Illus. by Andrea Wesson. 2002, Clarion $15.00 (0-618-09635-3). 32pp. Alma the cat rescues her mistress,

42

the opera diva Madame SoSo, by singing the solos when Madame SoSo comes down with laryngitis in this humorous book with lovely illustrations. (Rev: BL 10/1/02; SLJ 12/02)

830 Weeks, Sarah. *My Somebody Special* (PS–2). Illus. by Ashley Wolff. 2002, Harcourt $16.00 (0-15-202561-8). 40pp. An encouraging story about animal preschoolers who enjoy their class but are happy to be picked up by their loved ones at the end of the day. (Rev: BL 8/02; HBG 10/02; SLJ 5/02)

831 Weigelt, Udo. *Alex Did It!* (K–2). Trans. from German by J. Alison James. Illus. by Cristina Kadmon. 2002, North-South LB $15.88 (0-7358-1579-8). Three young hares are merrily blaming a fictitious Alex for their various misdeeds when they come across a real Alex. (Rev: HBG 10/02; SLJ 7/02)

832 Weigelt, Udo. *Ben and the Buccaneers* (PS–2). Illus. by Julia Gukova. 2001, North-South LB $15.88 (0-7358-1406-6). 32pp. Brave little sparrow Ben, who has been rejected by the swashbuckling Buccaneers, rescues them from a crafty cat and is rewarded for his efforts. (Rev: BL 8/01; HBG 10/01; SLJ 8/01)

833 Weigelt, Udo. *It Wasn't Me!* (1–3). Illus. by Julia Gukova. 2001, North-South LB $15.88 (0-7358-1524-0). 32pp. Mouse jumps to conclusions when he accuses Raven, the confessed thief of *Who Stole the Gold* (2000), of stealing Ferret's raspberries. (Rev: BL 1/1–15/02; HBG 10/02; SLJ 2/02)

834 Weigelt, Udo. *Old Beaver* (PS–2). Trans. from German by Sibylle Kazeroid. Illus. by Bernadette Watts. 2002, North-South LB $15.88 (0-7358-1565-8). When Old Beaver hears that a successor is arriving, he leaves his home, only to be asked to return when it turns out that the newcomer doesn't have his wisdom and expertise. (Rev: HBG 10/02; SLJ 6/02)

835 Weigelt, Udo. *The Wild Wombat* (PS–1). Trans. from German by Kathryn Grell. Illus. by Anne-Katrin Piepenbrink. 2002, North-South LB $16.50 (0-7358-1512-7). As the news of a wombat's arrival is passed from animal to animal at the zoo, the descriptions of him become more and more fearsome. (Rev: HBG 3/03; SLJ 12/02)

836 Wells, Rosemary. *Felix Feels Better* (PS). Illus. 2001, Candlewick $12.99 (0-7636-0639-1). 32pp. Guinea pig Felix feels so ill the day after eating too much that his mother takes him to the doctor. (Rev: BCCB 6/01; BL 5/1/01; HBG 10/01; SLJ 5/01)

837 Wells, Rosemary. *Mama, Don't Go!* (PS–2). Illus. by Jody Wheeler and Rosemary Wells. Series: Yoko and Friends School Days. 2001, Hyperion $9.99 (0-7868-0720-2); paper $3.99 (0-7868-1526-4). 31pp. The characters from *Yoko* return as kitten Yoko starts school and refuses to be without her mother. (Rev: HBG 3/02; SLJ 1/02)

838 Wells, Rosemary. *Read Me a Story* (K–2). Illus. by Jody Wheeler and Rosemary Wells. Series: Yoko and Friends School Days. 2002, Hyperion $9.99 (0-7868-0727-X); paper $3.99 (0-7868-1533-7). 31pp. Little kitten Yoko is afraid to reveal her reading

ability in case her mother stops reading her bedtime stories. (Rev: HBG 3/03; SLJ 12/02)

839 Wells, Rosemary. *Ruby's Beauty Shop* (PS–K). Illus. 2002, Viking $15.99 (0-670-03553-X). 32pp. Max the bunny gets a beauty makeover from his big sister Ruby and her friend Louise — and then Max does his own. (Rev: BCCB 11/02; BL 8/02; HBG 3/03; SLJ 10/02)

840 Wells, Rosemary. *The School Play* (PS–2). Illus. by Jody Wheeler and Rosemary Wells. Series: Yoko and Friends School Days. 2001, Hyperion $9.99 (0-7868-0721-0); paper $3.99 (0-7868-1527-2). 31pp. Yoko isn't pleased to find she's won the role of a cavity in the school play about hygiene. (Rev: HBG 3/02; SLJ 1/02)

841 Wells, Rosemary. *Timothy's Tales from Hilltop School* (PS–1). Illus. by Rosemary Wells and Jody Wheeler. 2002, Viking $16.99 (0-670-03554-8). 64pp. Timothy the raccoon deals with bullies, teasing, a birthday party, and other experiences in this collection of six stories. (Rev: BCCB 10/02; HB 1–2/03; HBG 3/03; SLJ 10/02)

842 Wells, Rosemary. *Yoko's Paper Cranes* (PS–2). Illus. 2001, Hyperion LB $16.49 (0-7868-2602-9). 32pp. Yoko, a kitten who has immigrated to America, folds paper cranes to send to her beloved grandmother in Japan. (Rev: BCCB 12/01; BL 9/15/01; HBG 3/02; SLJ 11/01*)

843 Weninger, Brigitte. *Davy, Help! It's a Ghost!* (K–2). Trans. from German by J. Alison James. Illus. by Eve Tharlet. 2002, North-South LB $16.50 (0-7358-1688-3). Davy and his rabbit siblings create their own monsters to frighten off the ghosts. (Rev: HBG 3/03; SLJ 10/02)

844 Wheeler, Lisa. *Porcupining: A Prickly Love Story* (PS–1). Illus. by Janie Bynum. 2003, Little, Brown $14.95 (0-316-98912-6). A lonely porcupine tries unsuccessfully to woo a succession of animals before finding the right one. (Rev: SLJ 1/03)

845 Wheeler, Lisa. *Sailor Moo: Cow at Sea* (1–3). Illus. by Ponder Goembel. 2002, Simon & Schuster $16.95 (0-689-84219-8). 32pp. A rhyming, humorous picture book about a young cow who longs to have a life at sea and ends up on a cattle barge turned pirate ship. (Rev: BL 5/1/02; HBG 3/03; SLJ 8/02)

846 Whybrow, Ian. *Wish, Change, Friend* (PS–K). Illus. by Tiphanie Beeke. 2002, Simon & Schuster $16.00 (0-689-84930-3). 32pp. Three words — wish, change, and friend — transform Little Pig's life in this gentle story that is an ode to the power of books. (Rev: BCCB 2/02; BL 2/15/02; HBG 10/02; SLJ 1/02)

847 Wild, Margaret. *Fox* (1–3). Illus. by Ron Brooks. 2001, Kane $14.95 (1-929132-16-6). 40pp. A somewhat dark portrayal of the friendship between a one-eyed dog and an injured magpie, this book set in the Australian bush introduces concepts including grief, cruelty, and self-acceptance. (Rev: BL 11/15/01; HBG 3/02; SLJ 12/01)

848 Williams, Barbara. *Albert's Impossible Toothache* (K–2). Illus. by Doug Cushman. 2003, Candlewick $15.99 (0-7636-1723-7). 40pp. Albert the turtle calls his sore toe toothache, causing some confusion. (Rev: BL 3/15/03)

849 Williams, Sue. *Dinnertime!* (PS–K). Illus. by Kerry Argent. 2002, Harcourt $16.00 (0-15-216471-5). 32pp. A fox hunts six fat rabbits in this exciting animal fantasy with a happy ending. (Rev: BCCB 4/02; BL 4/1/02*; HBG 10/02; SLJ 5/02)

850 Willner-Pardo, Gina. *Spider Storch, Rotten Runner* (2–3). Illus. by Nick Sharratt. 2001, Albert Whitman LB $11.95 (0-8075-7594-1). 83pp. In this beginning chapter book, Spider dreads the Third-Grade Olympics because he can't run fast and must take part in the relay race. (Rev: HBG 3/02; SLJ 12/01)

851 Wilson, Karma. *Bear Snores On* (PS–1). Illus. by Jane Chapman. 2002, Simon & Schuster $16.00 (0-689-83187-0). 40pp. On a cold winter night, animals gather in a sleeping bear's cave to share food and warmth in this charming story told in rhyme. (Rev: BL 1/1–15/02; HBG 10/02; SLJ 1/02*)

852 Wilson, Karma. *Bear Wants More* (PS–2). Illus. by Jane Chapman. 2003, Simon & Schuster $16.95 (0-689-84509-X). When spring comes, Bear wakes up and is extremely hungry. (Rev: BCCB 3/03; SLJ 2/03)

853 Wishinsky, Frieda. *Give Maggie a Chance* (K–2). Illus. by Dean Griffiths. 2002, Fitzhenry & Whiteside $15.95 (1-55041-682-0). 32pp. Maggie is an imaginative little cat who is terrified of public speaking and resents Kimberly's self-confidence in front of the class. (Rev: SLJ 12/02)

854 Wisniewski, David. *Sumo Mouse* (PS–3). Illus. 2002, Chronicle $16.95 (0-8118-3492-1). 32pp. Giant slapstick superhero Sumo Mouse comes to the rescue of kidnapped Tokyo mice in a complex plot that combines lots of action, comedy, and drama. (Rev: BCCB 1/03; BL 1/1–15/03; HBG 3/03; SLJ 12/02)

855 Wojtowycz, David. *A Cuddle for Claude* (PS). Illus. by author. 2001, Dutton $14.99 (0-525-46691-6). Claude's mother is too busy to give him a hug, so the little white bear prepares to leave home only to find his cuddly grandmother at the door. (Rev: HBG 10/01; SLJ 10/01)

856 Wollman, Jessica. *Andrew's Bright Blue T-Shirt* (PS–2). Illus. by Ana L. Escriva. 2002, Doubleday $14.95 (0-385-74616-4). 32pp. A young fox named Andrew dreams of playing soccer and wears his brother's hand-me-down soccer T-shirt every day, until he tragically grows out of it — and his brother says he's now old enough to play. (Rev: BL 10/1/02; HBG 3/03; SLJ 10/02)

857 Wood, A. J. *The Little Penguin* (PS–2). Illus. by Stephanie Boey. 2002, Dutton $15.99 (0-525-47023-9). 32pp. A visually appealing, tender book about a young, fuzzy penguin who longs for his father's refined look. (Rev: BL 10/15/02; HBG 3/03; SLJ 12/02)

858 Wood, Douglas. *What Teachers Can't Do* (PS–2). Illus. by Doug Cushman. 2002, Simon & Schuster $14.95 (0-689-84644-5). 32pp. A young dinosaur looks at all the silly and odd things teach-

ers can't do — be late for school, add 2 + 2, for example. (Rev: BL 8/02; HBG 3/03; SLJ 10/02)

859 Wood, Jakki. *Never Say Boo to a Goose!* (PS). Illus. by Clare Beaton. 2002, Barefoot $14.99 (1-84148-255-2). 24pp. Tiger the kitten ignores his mother's warning and sets off to find out what happens when he says "boo!" to a goose, if only he can find one. (Rev: BL 12/1/02; HBG 3/03; SLJ 11/02)

860 Woodworth, Viki. *Daisy the Firecow* (PS–1). Illus. 2001, Boyds Mills $15.95 (1-56397-934-9). 32pp. Daisy the cow is bored on the farm and becomes a fire station's mascot. (Rev: BL 7/01; HBG 10/01)

861 Wormell, Mary. *Bernard the Angry Rooster* (PS–1). Illus. 2001, Farrar $16.00 (0-374-30670-2). 32pp. Bernard the rooster is unhappy about a new weathervane in this nicely illustrated story. (Rev: BCCB 4/01; BL 5/1/01; HBG 10/01; SLJ 7/01)

862 Yaccarino, Dan. *Oswald the Octopus* (PS–2). Illus. 2001, Simon & Schuster $16.95 (0-689-84252-X). 40pp. Oswald is worried about making friends in a new city, but he and his dog Weenie attract lots of attention when their piano gets loose. (Rev: BCCB 6/01; BL 7/01; HBG 10/01; SLJ 7/01)

863 Yaccarino, Dan. *Unlovable* (PS–1). Illus. by author. 2002, Holt $15.95 (0-8050-6321-8). 32pp. A puppy who is teased unmercifully about his funny looks befriends a dog he can't see — and who can't see him — on the other side of the fence. (Rev: BL 11/15/01; HBG 10/02; SLJ 1/02)

864 Yee, Brenda Shannon. *Hide and Seek* (PS–K). Illus. by Debbie Tilley. 2001, Scholastic $15.95 (0-531-30302-0). 32pp. A mouse finds he enjoys playing hide-and-seek with the woman of the house. (Rev: BL 5/15/01; HBG 10/01; SLJ 7/01)

865 Yee, Wong Herbert. *Fireman Small: Fire Down Below!* (K–2). Illus. by Wong H. Yee. 2001, Houghton $15.00 (0-618-00707-5). Children will learn safety tips while reading this charming story of a very small fireman who rescues the occupants of a hotel. (Rev: HB 11–12/01; HBG 3/02; SLJ 10/01)

866 Yolen, Jane. *How Do Dinosaurs Get Well Soon?* (PS–1). Illus. by Mark Teague. 2003, Scholastic $15.95 (0-439-24100-6). 40pp. Humorous, full-color illustrations are coupled with rhyming text to show giant young dinosaurs who must learn how to behave while ill (taking medicine, resting, and so forth). (Rev: BL 1/1–15/03*; HB 3–4/03; SLJ 2/03)

867 Young, Selina. *Big Dog and Little Dog Go Sailing* (1–2). Series: Blue Bananas. 2001, Crabtree LB $14.97 (0-7787-0845-4); paper $4.46 (0-7787-0891-8). 48pp. When they go boating, two individualistic dogs experience some amazing adventures including an encounter with a whale. (Rev: BL 5/1/02)

868 Zalben, Jane Breskin. *Don't Go!* (PS–K). Illus. 2001, Clarion $15.00 (0-618-07250-0). 32pp. A gentle story of a young elephant who is comforted to have his stuffed toy with him on his first day of preschool. (Rev: BL 8/01; HBG 3/02; SLJ 9/01)

869 Ziefert, Harriet. *Egad Alligator!* (PS–3). Illus. by Todd McKie. 2002, Houghton $16.00 (0-618-14171-5). 40pp. Little Gator doesn't understand why people are afraid of him until he experiences fear himself when he sits on a python. (Rev: BCCB 9/02; BL 4/15/02; HBG 10/02; SLJ 4/02)

870 Ziefert, Harriet. *Murphy Meets the Treadmill* (PS–1). Illus. by Emily Bolam. 2001, Houghton $16.00 (0-618-11357-6). 32pp. Murphy the dog must lose weight, and a treadmill does the trick in this funny book with expressive, cartoonlike illustrations. (Rev: BL 9/1/01; HBG 3/02; SLJ 10/01)

871 Ziefert, Harriet. *What Do Ducks Dream?* (PS–2). Illus. by Donald Saaf. 2001, Putnam $15.99 (0-399-23358-X). Sigmund's farm is a lively place at night, with animals and humans having wonderful, colorful dreams. (Rev: HBG 10/01; SLJ 6/01)

Realistic Stories

ADVENTURE STORIES

872 Carter, Anne Laurel. *Under a Prairie Sky* (PS–3). Illus. by Alan Daniel and Lea Daniel. 2002, Orca $16.95 (1-55143-226-9). 32pp. A Canadian boy gets a taste of being a Mountie when he rescues his younger brother from a coming storm. (Rev: BL 5/15/02; HBG 10/02; SLJ 6/02)

873 George, Jean Craighead. *Cliff Hanger* (1–3). Illus. by Wendell Minor. 2002, HarperCollins LB $15.89 (0-06-000261-1). Young Axel must climb a cliff to rescue his dog in this suspenseful story that conveys a lot of information about mountain climbing and the dangers involved. (Rev: BCCB 7–8/02; HBG 10/02; SLJ 12/02)

874 Lamm, C. Drew. *Pirates* (K–3). Illus. by Stacey Schuett. 2001, Hyperion $15.99 (0-7868-0392-4). 30pp. Ellery reads her little brother Max a book about pirates, intending to scare the pants off him, but in the end it's Max who has the last laugh in a story sure to elicit goosebumps. (Rev: BCCB 1/02; BL 11/1/01; HBG 3/02; SLJ 11/01)

875 Zagwyn, Deborah Turney. *The Sea House* (K–3). Illus. 2002, Tricycle Pr. $15.95 (1-58246-030-2). 32pp. Clee and her brother have an adventure on their uncle's boat. (Rev: BL 4/1/02; HBG 10/02; SLJ 6/02)

COMMUNITY AND EVERYDAY LIFE

876 Aliki. *One Little Spoonful* (PS). Illus. Series: Harper Growing Tree. 2001, HarperFestival $9.95 (0-694-01502-4). 24pp. A cheerful rhyme recited by a mother feeding her baby in a highchair. (Rev: BL 7/01; HBG 3/02; SLJ 9/01)

877 Appelt, Kathi. *Incredible Me!* (PS–K). Illus. by G. Brian Karas. 2003, HarperCollins LB $16.89 (0-06-028623-7). 32pp. A little girl dances and plays while proudly listing all the traits that make her special. (Rev: BL 2/15/03; SLJ 2/03)

878 Armstrong-Ellis, Carey. *Prudy's Problem and How She Solved It* (K–2). Illus. 2002, Abrams $14.95 (0-8109-0569-8). 32pp. Unconventional Prudy collects everything until her room is so full that a single gum wrapper causes it to explode. (Rev: BL 12/15/02; HBG 3/03; SLJ 10/02)

879 Arnold, Tedd. *More Parts* (1–4). Illus. by author. 2001, Dial $15.99 (0-8037-1417-3). A young boy is terrified by phrases that seem to threaten survival such as "laugh your head off" and "give him a hand." (Rev: BCCB 9/01; HBG 3/02; SLJ 9/01)

880 Baicker, Karen. *Tumble Me Tumbily* (PS). Illus. by Sam Williams. 2002, Handprint $15.95 (1-929766-61-0). 36pp. Three rhymes — two bouncy ones for waking up and eating, and a quieter one for bedtime — are decorated by illustrations that introduce a vast cast of characters. (Rev: BL 11/1/02; HBG 3/03)

881 Bailey, Linda. *The Best Figure Skater in the Whole Wide World* (PS–2). Illus. by Alan Daniel and Lea Daniel. 2001, Kids Can $15.95 (1-55074-879-3). Lizzy dreams of becoming a world-class figure skater, but has to accept being cast as a tree. (Rev: HBG 3/02; SLJ 12/01)

882 Brandenberg, Alexa. *Ballerina Flying* (PS–2). Illus. 2002, HarperCollins LB $15.89 (0-06-029550-3). 40pp. Mina pretends she is flying during her ballet class in this book that features names, pronunciations, and drawings of ballet steps and positions. (Rev: BL 7/02; HBG 10/02)

883 Brown, Craig. *Barn Raising* (PS). Illus. 2002, HarperCollins LB $17.89 (0-06-029400-0). 32pp. An Amish community comes together for a barn raising in this handsome picture book. (Rev: BL 8/02; HBG 3/03; SLJ 12/02)

884 Brown, Margaret Wise. *Robin's Room* (PS–2). Illus. by Steve Johnson and Lou Fancher. 2002, Hyperion $14.99 (0-7868-0602-8). 32pp. Robin becomes a model child after his wishes about redecorating his room are granted. (Rev: BCCB 9/02; BL 4/15/02; HBG 10/02)

885 Brownlow, Mike. *The Big White Book with Almost Nothing in It* (PS–1). Illus. by author. 2001, Ragged Bear $13.95 (1-929927-24-X). As the reader turns the apparently almost blank pages, flaps, folds, and die-cut holes soon reveal a whole cast of cartoon circus characters. (Rev: SLJ 10/01)

886 Bunting, Eve. *Peepers* (K–3). Illus. by James E. Ransome. 2001, Harcourt $16.00 (0-15-260297-6). 32pp. Two brothers come to appreciate the beauty of the fall colors so admired by the tourists, or "Leaf Peepers," who visit their New England town. (Rev: BL 9/1/01; HBG 3/02; SLJ 10/01)

887 Burleigh, Robert. *Goal* (K–3). Illus. by Stephen T. Johnson. 2001, Harcourt $16.00 (0-15-201789-5). 32pp. A picture book that explains, in a poetic manner, the important aspects of soccer. (Rev: BL 4/15/01; HBG 10/01; SLJ 4/01) [811.54]

888 Burleigh, Robert. *I Love Going Through This Book* (PS–K). Illus. by Dan Yaccarino. 2001, HarperCollins $15.95 (0-06-028805-1). 32pp. This boisterous excursion through a book, courtesy of a young boy and animal friends, introduces young readers to the parts of a book and the fun of reading. (Rev: BCCB 6/01; BL 6/1–15/01; HBG 10/01; SLJ 6/01)

889 Carlson, Nancy. *There's a Big, Beautiful World Out There!* (K–2). Illus. 2002, Viking $15.99 (0-

670-03580-7). 32pp. Written just after September 11, 2001, this book uses cheery illustrations and a chatty approach to potential terrors to reassure children that anxieties are normal and the world is still a good place. (Rev: BL 10/1/02; HBG 3/03; SLJ 11/02)

890 Carman, William. *What's That Noise?* (K–2). Illus. 2002, Random LB $16.99 (0-375-91052-2). 40pp. A little boy, awakened by a strange noise, imagines all sorts of possibilities before finding its true source — his snoring father. (Rev: BL 9/15/02; HBG 3/03; SLJ 8/02)

891 Caseley, Judith. *On the Town: A Community Adventure* (K–3). Illus. 2002, HarperCollins LB $15.89 (0-06-029585-6). 32pp. For a school assignment, Charlie and his mother visit people and places in the neighborhood but, afterward, Charlie realizes that home is best. (Rev: BL 4/15/02; HBG 10/02; SLJ 5/02)

892 Cash, Megan Montague. *I Saw the Sea and the Sea Saw Me* (PS–1). Illus. 2001, Viking $14.99 (0-670-89966-6). 40pp. Vivid illustrations depict a young girl enjoying the sea, with a text of simple rhyming couplets. (Rev: BL 6/1–15/01; HBG 10/01)

893 Catalanotto, Peter. *Emily's Art* (K–3). Illus. 2001, Simon & Schuster $16.00 (0-689-83831-X). 32pp. Emily is so disappointed when her picture doesn't win the art contest that she says she'll never paint again. (Rev: BCCB 9/01; BL 7/01; HBG 10/01; SLJ 6/01*)

894 Cohn, Diana. *¡Sí, Se Puede! / Yes, We Can! Janitor Strike in L.A* (PS–3). Illus. by Francisco Delgado. 2002, Cinco Puntos $15.95 (0-938317-66-0). 32pp. Mexican American boy Carlitos supports his janitor mother in seeking to start a union, in this bilingual picture book based on a Los Angeles strike in 2000. (Rev: BL 10/1/02; HBG 3/03; SLJ 11/02*)

895 Cole, Joanna. *When Mommy and Daddy Go to Work* (PS). Illus. by Maxie Chambliss. 2001, HarperCollins $5.95 (0-688-17044-7). 24pp. In this small-format picture book a young child tells readers all about the routine at day care. (Rev: BL 8/01; HBG 3/02; SLJ 11/01)

896 Cole, Kenneth. *No Bad News* (PS–3). Illus. by John Ruebartsch. 2001, Albert Whitman $15.95 (0-8075-4743-3). 32pp. Marcus, a young African American boy, is nervous when he ventures out to the barbershop alone in this story set in a south-side Chicago clearly depicted in black-and-white photographs. (Rev: BL 5/15/01; HBG 10/01; SLJ 6/01)

897 Crisp, Marty. *Totally Polar* (PS–2). Illus. by Viv Eisner. 2001, Rising Moon LB $15.95 (0-87358-789-8). Peter much prefers winter weather and in a sultry June indulges in dreams of snow, warm fires, and hot chocolate. (Rev: HBG 3/02; SLJ 12/01)

898 Cummins, Julie. *Country Kid, City Kid* (K–2). Illus. by Ted Rand. 2002, Holt $16.95 (0-8050-6467-2). Ben's life on the farm and Jody's life in the city are contrasted on facing pages. (Rev: HBG 3/03; SLJ 11/02)

899 Curtis, Jamie Lee. *I'm Gonna Like Me: Letting Off a Little Self-Esteem* (1–3). Illus. by Laura Cor-

nell. 2002, HarperCollins LB $17.89 (0-06-028762-4). 32pp. Humorous, detailed illustrations and rhyming text show a boy and girl taking turns liking themselves. (Rev: BL 10/1/02; HBG 3/03; SLJ 10/02)

900 Curtis, Marci. *I Was So Silly: Big Kids Remember Being Little* (PS–K). Illus. 2002, Dial $12.99 (0-8037-2691-0). 32pp. Small children featured in artistic photographs fondly (and humorously) remember their babyhoods. (Rev: BL 9/1/02; HBG 10/02; SLJ 6/02) [305.23]

901 De Regniers, Beatrice Schenk. *Was It a Good Trade?* (PS). Illus. by Irene Haas. 2002, HarperCollins LB $15.89 (0-06-029360-8). A newly illustrated version of the story adapted from song about a man who can't stop swapping. (Rev: HBG 10/02; SLJ 7/02)

902 Devine, Monica. *Carry Me, Mama* (PS–1). Illus. by Pauline Paquin. 2002, Stoddart $15.95 (0-7737-3317-5). A beautifully illustrated story of a mother gently persuading her child to walk further and further. (Rev: HB 5–6/02; HBG 10/02; SLJ 7/02)

903 Diouf, Sylviane A. *Bintou's Braids* (PS–2). Illus. by Shane W. Evans. 2001, Chronicle $14.95 (0-8118-2514-0). 40pp. A little girl yearns for long, beautiful braids in this story featuring daily life and customs in a West African village. (Rev: BCCB 11/01; BL 11/15/01; HB 1–2/02; HBG 3/02; SLJ 1/02)

904 DiSalvo, DyAnne. *A Castle on Viola Street* (PS–3). Illus. by author. 2001, HarperCollins LB $16.89 (0-688-17691-7). Andy and his parents finally get their own home by working with a group that restores deserted buildings. (Rev: HBG 3/02; SLJ 10/01)

905 DiSalvo, DyAnne. *Spaghetti Park* (K–2). Illus. 2002, Holiday $16.95 (0-8234-1682-8). 32pp. A haven for down-and-outs is transformed into a popular neighborhood park with a lively bocce court. (Rev: BL 11/15/02; HBG 3/03; SLJ 1/03)

906 Duncan, Lois. *Song of the Circus* (PS–2). Illus. by Meg Cundiff. 2002, Putnam $15.99 (0-399-23397-0). 32pp. A lively book featuring a hungry tiger that echoes in tempo and color a real visit to a circus. (Rev: BCCB 5/02; BL 8/02; HBG 10/02; SLJ 4/02)

907 Dunrea, Olivier. *It's Snowing!* (PS). Illus. 2002, Farrar $16.00 (0-374-39992-1). 32pp. In a remote, cold place, mother and baby venture out into the snowy night, have fun sledding and creating sculptures, and then head back into the warmth. (Rev: BL 11/15/02; HB 9–10/02; HBG 3/03; SLJ 10/02)

908 Edwards, Michelle, and Phyllis Root. *What's That Noise?* (PS). Illus. by Paul Meisel. 2002, Candlewick $15.99 (0-7636-1350-9). Two young boys try to be brave as the spooky sounds and shadows of night surround them. (Rev: HBG 3/03; SLJ 12/02)

909 Flattinger, Hubert. *Stormy Night* (PS–1). Trans. from German by J. Alison James. Illus. by Nathalie Duroussy. 2002, North-South LB $16.50 (0-7358-1667-0). A reassuring story with the message that even if it's dark and stormy, all will be well. (Rev: HBG 3/03; SLJ 2/03)

910 Fletcher, Ralph. *The Circus Surprise* (PS–2). Illus. by Vladimir Vagin. 2001, Clarion $15.00 (0-395-98029-1). 32pp. Despite all his training, Nick panics when he gets lost at the circus. (Rev: HBG 10/01; SLJ 6/01)

911 Flynn, Kitson. *Carrot in My Pocket* (PS). Illus. by Denise Ortakales. 2001, Moon Mountain $15.95 (0-9677929-6-7). A young farm boy describes in verse a day looking for a lost carrot, and names the animals and farm implements he encounters. (Rev: HBG 3/02; SLJ 2/02)

912 Freeman, Mylo. *Potty!* (PS). Illus. by author. 2002, Tricycle Pr. $13.95 (1-58246-070-1). All the animals of the jungle try out a potty, but it's a small child's bottom that fits it properly. (Rev: HBG 10/02; SLJ 4/02)

913 Gammell, Stephen. *Ride* (PS–1). Illus. 2001, Harcourt $16.00 (0-15-202682-7). 32pp. A squabble between siblings in the back seat is taking on momentous proportions when Mom offers sustenance and the hostilities are abandoned . . . temporarily? (Rev: BCCB 3/01; BL 5/1/01; HB 5–6/01; HBG 10/01; SLJ 5/01)

914 Garland, Sarah. *Ellie's Breakfast* (PS). Illus. by author. 2001, Red Fox paper $8.95 (0-09-969261-9). Father and Ellie do their morning chores — feeding the animals and collecting the eggs. (Rev: SLJ 3/02)

915 Gauch, Patricia Lee. *Tanya and the Red Shoes* (PS–2). Illus. by Satomi Ichikawa. 2002, Putnam $16.99 (0-399-23314-8). 40pp. Young ballet dancer Tanya finds out that graduating to toe shoes isn't everything she thought it would be. (Rev: BL 3/1/02; HB 5–6/02; HBG 10/02; SLJ 3/02)

916 Gay, Marie-Louise. *Stella, Fairy of the Forest* (PS–1). Illus. 2002, Groundwood $15.95 (0-88899-448-6). 32pp. The energetic Stella of the signature red hair answers her little brother Sam's many questions about nature. (Rev: BCCB 3/02; BL 3/15/02; HBG 10/02; SLJ 6/02*)

917 George, Kristine O'Connell. *Book!* (PS). Illus. by Maggie Smith. 2001, Clarion $9.95 (0-395-98287-1). 32pp. A toddler finds great joy in his first picture book in this engaging package of friendly text and lively illustrations. (Rev: BL 12/1/01; HBG 3/02; SLJ 10/01) [811]

918 Gerber, Carole. *Blizzard* (PS–K). Illus. by Marty Husted. 2001, Charlesbridge $15.95 (1-58089-064-4). 32pp. A boy describes in verse the delight of being cozy and warm inside while a winter storm rages outside. (Rev: BL 9/15/01; HBG 3/02; SLJ 10/01)

919 Godwin, Laura. *Central Park Serenade* (2–4). Illus. by Barry Root. 2002, HarperCollins LB $15.89 (0-06-025892-6). 32pp. In double-page spreads, the sights and sounds of New York City's Central Park are re-created. (Rev: BL 6/1–15/02; HBG 3/03; SLJ 5/02)

920 Gold, August. *Where Does God Live?* (PS–1). Illus. by Matthew J. Perlman. 2001, Skylight Paths paper $7.95 (1-893361-39-X). 32pp. With help from her parents, a little girl who wonders where God

lives begins to see evidence of him all around her. (Rev: BL 10/1/01)

921 Griffin, Kitty, and Kathy Combs. *Cowboy Sam and Those Confounded Secrets* (PS–2). Illus. by Mike Wohnoutka. 2001, Clarion $15.00 (0-618-08854-7). 32pp. Sam keeps the town's secrets under his 10-gallon hat, but it eventually becomes full. (Rev: HBG 3/02; SLJ 12/01)

922 Grindley, Sally. *A New Room for William* (PS–2). Illus. by Carol Thompson. 2000, Candlewick $15.99 (0-7636-1196-4). Choosing wallpaper for his room helps William feel more comfortable when he and his mother move. (Rev: BCCB 12/00; BL 3/1/03; HBG 3/01; SLJ 11/00)

923 Harper, Charise Mericle. *When I Grow Up* (K–2). Illus. by author. 2001, Chronicle $14.95 (0-8118-2905-7). "Adventurous" and "generous" are only two of the 14 characteristics that children aspire to in this appealing picture book. (Rev: HBG 10/01; SLJ 7/01)

924 Harper, Jessica. *Nora's Room* (PS–1). Illus. by Lindsay Harper duPont. 2001, HarperCollins LB $15.89 (0-06-029137-0). 32pp. Everyone in the family wonders what's making the incredible noise coming from Nora's room. (Rev: BL 7/01; HBG 10/01; SLJ 7/01)

925 Hatkoff, Craig, and Juliana Lee Hatkoff. *Good-Bye, Tonsils* (PS–3). Illus. by Marilyn Mets. 2001, Viking $15.99 (0-670-89775-2). 32pp. In detail, with illustrations, Juliana Hatkoff describes having her tonsils out and how she felt before and after. (Rev: BL 8/01; HBG 10/01; SLJ 8/01)

926 Hegi, Ursula. *Trudi and Pia* (1–3). Illus. by Giselle Potter. 2003, Simon & Schuster $16.95 (0-689-84683-5). 40pp. Trudi, a dwarf, meets another dwarf at the circus and feels less alone. (Rev: BL 3/1/03; SLJ 3/03)

927 Herrera, Juan Felipe. *Grandma and Me at the Flea / Los Meros Meros Remateros* (2–4). Illus. by Anita De Lucio-Brock. 2002, Children's $15.95 (0-89239-171-5). 32pp. A bilingual story about a boy named Juanito who helps his grandmother at a California flea market. (Rev: BL 4/1/02; HBG 10/02)

928 Hershenhorn, Esther. *Chicken Soup by Heart* (K–3). Illus. by Rosanne Litzinger. 2002, Simon & Schuster $16.95 (0-689-82665-6). 32pp. Rudie and his mother make chicken soup with some special additives for Mrs. Gittel, Rudie's elderly neighbor and babysitter. (Rev: BCCB 1/03; BL 9/1/02; HBG 3/03; SLJ 11/02)

929 Hill, Frances. *The Bug Cemetery* (PS–1). Illus. by Vera Rosenberry. 2002, Holt $16.95 (0-8050-6370-6). A bug-cemetery-lemonade-stand-business turns serious when Billy's cat dies. (Rev: HBG 10/02; SLJ 4/02)

930 Hooks, Bell. *Be Boy Buzz* (PS–K). Illus. by Chris Raschka. 2002, Hyperion $16.99 (0-7868-0814-4). 32pp. Spare, rhythmic text and clear, lively images celebrate the energetic joy of being an African American boy. (Rev: BCCB 12/02; BL 11/1/02; HBG 3/03; SLJ 12/02)

931 Hopkinson, Deborah. *Band of Angels: A Story Inspired by the Jubilee Singers* (2–4). Illus. by Raul

Colon. 1999, Simon & Schuster $16.00 (0-689-81062-8); paper $6.99 (0-689-84897-0). The fictionalized story of Ella Sheppard and the Fisk University Jubilee Singers. (Rev: BL 2/15/03; SLJ check)

932 Hubbell, Patricia. *Black All Around!* (PS–2). Illus. by Don Tate. 2003, Lee & Low $16.95 (1-58430-048-5). 32pp. An African American girl looks around to discover that the world is full of lovely things that are black, such as a lake at night and her Momma's cheek. (Rev: BL 2/15/03)

933 Hubbell, Patricia. *Sea, Sand, Me!* (PS). Illus. by Lisa Campbell Ernst. 2001, HarperCollins LB $14.89 (0-688-17379-9). 32pp. A simple story about a day at the beach, in rhyming text and large illustrations. (Rev: BL 5/1/01; HBG 10/01; SLJ 7/01)

934 Isadora, Rachel. *Not Just Tutus* (K–3). Illus. 2003, Putnam $13.99 (0-399-23603-1). 40pp. The author uses her personal knowledge of ballet school to convey the magic and hardships of a young dancer's life in this book that combines rhyming text and watercolor art that will attract young ballet fans. (Rev: BL 1/1–15/03)

935 Isadora, Rachel. *Peekaboo Morning* (PS–K). Illus. 2002, Putnam $15.99 (0-399-23602-3). 32pp. An African American toddler plays peekaboo with friends, relatives, and family pets in this delightful book for preschoolers. (Rev: BCCB 7–8/02; BL 3/1/02; HBG 10/02; SLJ 7/02)

936 Johnston, Tony. *My Best Friend Bear* (PS–K). Illus. by Joy Allen. 2001, Rising Moon $15.95 (0-87358-775-8). 32pp. Poor stuffed toy Bear has been so loved for so long that he's begun to look like a monkey and must be repaired. (Rev: BCCB 5/01; BL 5/15/01; HBG 10/01; SLJ 8/01)

937 *The Jump at the Sun Treasury: An African American Picture Book Collection* (PS–3). Illus. 2001, Hyperion $15.99 (0-7868-0754-7). 205pp. An anthology of seven previously published picture books with African American themes. (Rev: BL 2/15/02; HBG 3/02)

938 Kamish, Daniel, and David Kamish. *Diggy Dan: A Room-Cleaning Adventure* (PS–2). Illus. by authors. 2001, Random LB $15.95 (0-375-90576-6). Dan makes cleaning his room bearable by imagining himself in all sorts of dramatic roles. (Rev: HBG 10/01; SLJ 4/01)

939 Katz, Karen. *Twelve Hats for Lena: A Book of Months* (PS–3). Illus. by author. 2002, Simon & Schuster $16.95 (0-689-84873-0). Lena creates hats that are suitable for each month of the year, and hat-making directions are included. (Rev: HBG 3/03; SLJ 10/02)

940 Killion, Bette. *Just Think!* (PS–K). Illus. by Linda Bronson. Series: Harper Growing Tree. 2001, HarperCollins $9.95 (0-694-01315-3). 24pp. Mom's admonitions to hurry or to slow down prompt vivid images in her daughter's mind. (Rev: BL 12/15/01; HBG 3/02)

941 King, Stephen Michael. *Emily Loves to Bounce* (PS–K). Illus. by author. 2003, Philomel $15.99 (0-399-23886-7). Emily bounces wherever she can, in brief rhyming text and lively illustrations. (Rev: SLJ 3/03)

942 Kinsey-Warnock, Natalie. *A Farm of Her Own* (K–2). Illus. by Kathleen Kolb. 2001, Dutton $15.99 (0-525-46507-3). 32pp. Emma enjoys summer at Sunnyside Farm so much that when she grows up she buys the farm herself. (Rev: BCCB 6/01; BL 7/01; HBG 10/01; SLJ 6/01)

943 Krebs, Laurie. *The Beeman* (PS–2). Illus. by Melissa Iwai. 2002, National Geographic $16.95 (0-7922-7224-2). 32pp. A beekeeper gives his granddaughter a tour of the hives and the process of extracting honey, then the two enjoy muffins and honey. (Rev: BL 10/1/02; HBG 3/03; SLJ 9/02)

944 Kroll, Virginia. *Girl, You're Amazing!* (K–3). Illus. by Melisande Potter. 2001, Albert Whitman $15.95 (0-8075-2930-3). 32pp. This picture book is a pep talk that tells girls they can do anything they want and be anyone they wish. (Rev: BL 4/1/01; HBG 10/01; SLJ 4/01)

945 Larios, Julie. *Have You Ever Done That?* (PS–3). Illus. by Anne Hunter. 2001, Front Street $15.95 (1-886910-49-9). Rhythmic questions stir a child's imagination and reveal his dreamlike views of the world around him. (Rev: HBG 3/02; SLJ 12/01)

946 Lawrence, Mary. *What's That Sound?* (1–3). Illus. by Lynn Adams. Series: Science Solves It! 2002, Kane paper $4.99 (1-57565-118-1). 32pp. Tim's older sister Amy shrugs off every spooky sound he hears, and scientific sidebars explain how each one was made. (Rev: SLJ 10/02)

947 Lewin, Ted. *Big Jimmy's Kum Kau Chinese Take Out* (K–3). Illus. 2001, HarperCollins LB $16.89 (0-688-16027-1). 40pp. This fast-paced, realistically illustrated book shows a typical day at a busy Chinese restaurant in Brooklyn, as told by the proprietors' young son. (Rev: BCCB 1/02; BL 1/1–15/02; HBG 3/02; SLJ 4/02)

948 Lin, Grace. *Dim Sum for Everyone* (PS–K). Illus. 2001, Knopf $14.95 (0-375-81082-x). 32pp. Text and appealing illustrations show an Asian family enjoying a meal at a dim sum restaurant in Chinatown. (Rev: BL 6/1–15/01; HBG 3/02; SLJ 7/01)

949 London, Jonathan. *Sun Dance Water Dance* (K–3). Illus. by Greg Couch. 2001, Dutton $15.99 (0-525-46682-7). 40pp. Poetic text and bright pictures capture the charms of summer. (Rev: BL 8/01; HBG 10/01; SLJ 7/01)

950 London, Jonathan, and Aaron London. *White Water* (K–3). Illus. by Jill Kastner. 2001, Viking $15.99 (0-670-89286-6). 32pp. Text and illustrations combine to give readers a taste of the thrill of white-water rafting and the cozy evenings around the open fire. (Rev: BCCB 5/01; BL 6/1–15/01; HBG 10/01; SLJ 6/01)

951 Lukasewich, Lori. *The Night Fire* (PS–1). Illus. by author. 2001, Stoddart $15.95 (0-7737-3296-9). Rhyming couplets and bright illustrations follow fire fighters through a nighttime blaze. (Rev: SLJ 1/02)

952 McAllister, Angela. *Be Good, Gordon* (PS–2). Illus. by Tim Archbold. 2002, Bloomsbury paper

$8.95 (0-7475-5580-X). Young Gordon is taken aback when his new babysitter wants to do all the things he's forbidden to enjoy. (Rev: SLJ 1/03)

953 McCoy, Glenn. *Penny Lee and Her TV* (PS–3). Illus. by author. 2002, Hyperion $15.99 (0-7868-0661-3). Once separated from her beloved TV, Penny Lee is fascinated by everything that's going on in the world. (Rev: BCCB 6/02; HBG 10/02; SLJ 6/02)

954 McGee, Marni. *Wake Up, Me!* (PS–2). Illus. by Sam Williams. 2002, Simon & Schuster $17.00 (0-689-83163-3). 40pp. As a child goes through his morning rituals, he must continually remind the parts of his body to "wake up." (Rev: BL 6/1–15/02; HBG 10/02; SLJ 5/02)

955 MacLean, Kole. *Even Firefighters Hug Their Moms* (PS–K). Illus. by Mike Reed. 2002, Dutton $15.99 (0-525-46996-6). 32pp. A young boy is so immersed in his elaborate role-playing (as fire fighter, police officer, doctor) that he's too busy to give his mother the requested hug. (Rev: BL 11/15/02; HBG 3/03; SLJ 10/02)

956 McPhail, David. *The Teddy Bear* (PS–2). Illus. 2002, Holt $15.95 (0-8050-6414-1). 32pp. A young boy generously gives his teddy bear to a homeless man who has become attached to it. (Rev: BL 5/1/02*; HBG 10/02; SLJ 6/02)

957 Mathers, Petra. *Dodo Gets Married* (K–3). Illus. 2001, Simon & Schuster $16.00 (0-689-83018-1). 32pp. Captain Vince, who has lost a leg in a helicopter mission, is helped by his helicopter buddies to woo and win neighbor Dodo. (Rev: BL 4/15/01; HBG 10/01; SLJ 5/01)

958 Middleton, Charlotte. *Tabitha's Terrifically Tough Tooth* (PS–2). Illus. 2001, Penguin Putnam $12.99 (0-8037-2583-3). 32pp. Tabitha tries various methods to dislodge a very wobbly tooth so that the tooth fairy can visit her. (Rev: BL 4/15/01; HBG 10/01; SLJ 6/01*)

959 Moore, Lilian. *While You Were Chasing a Hat* (PS–K). Illus. by Rosanne Litzinger. 2001, HarperCollins $9.95 (0-694-01342-0). 24pp. This book explores all the things that the wind can do on a spring day such as causing a flag to furl and trees to bend. (Rev: BL 4/1/01; HBG 10/01; SLJ 1/02)

960 Mora, Pat. *Maria Paints the Hills* (K–3). Illus. by Maria Hesch. 2002, Museum of New Mexico $19.95 (0-89013-401-4); paper $9.95 (0-89013-410-3). 32pp. A simple story and stunning folk-art illustrations capture the life of a little girl in New Mexico. (Rev: BL 12/15/02; HBG 3/03)

961 Moss, Lloyd. *Our Marching Band* (PS–3). Illus. by Diana C. Bluthenthal. 2001, Putnam $15.99 (0-399-23335-0). 32pp. Silly rhyming text and exuberant cartoon watercolors portray a group of children practicing, and then performing, in a marching band. (Rev: BL 8/01; SLJ 8/01)

962 Mould, Wendy. *Ants in My Pants* (PS–K). Illus. 2001, Clarion $15.00 (0-618-09640-X). 32pp. Jacob wants to play with his trains and comes up with inventive ways to delay getting dressed to go shopping. (Rev: BL 8/01; HBG 3/02; SLJ 9/01)

963 Neitzel, Shirley. *I'm Not Feeling Well Today* (PS–2). Illus. by Nancy Winslow Parker. 2001, Greenwillow LB $15.89 (0-688-17381-0). 32pp. A boy declares that he's not feeling well, and collects all the things he will need during the day in this charmer that uses cumulative verses and rebuses to tell its story. (Rev: BL 4/15/01; HB 5–6/01; HBG 10/01; SLJ 7/01)

964 Nikola-Lisa, W. *Summer Sun Risin'* (PS–1). Illus. by Don Tate. 2002, Lee & Low $16.95 (1-58430-034-5). A gentle story of a young African American boy's busy day on the farm — looking after the animals, plowing, picnicking, fishing, and bedtime stories. (Rev: HBG 10/02; SLJ 5/02)

965 O'Garden, Irene. *The Scrubbly-Bubbly Car Wash* (PS–2). Illus. by Cynthia Jabar. 2003, HarperCollins LB $16.89 (0-06-029486-8). A bouncing rhyme takes a father and two children on a ride through the car wash. (Rev: BCCB 3/03; SLJ 3/03)

966 Ohi, Ruth. *Pants Off First!* (PS). Illus. Series: Early Bird Boardbook. 2001, Fitzhenry & Whiteside $6.95 (1-55041-667-7). 16pp. As a little boy undresses, he puts his clothes on his pets in this humorous story that ends with a twist. (Rev: BL 7/01)

967 O'Neill, Alexis. *Estela's Swap* (K–3). Illus. by Enrique O. Sanchez. 2002, Lee & Low $16.95 (1-58430-044-2). 32pp. Colorful illustrations accompany this story of Estela, a Hispanic girl who wants to sell a music box to earn money for dance lessons. (Rev: BL 12/15/02; HBG 3/03; SLJ 10/02)

968 Parr, Todd. *The Feel Good Book* (PS–2). Illus. by author. 2002, Little, Brown $14.95 (0-316-07206-0). A list of things that make you feel good is illustrated with lively art. (Rev: HBG 3/03; SLJ 10/02)

969 Parr, Todd. *It's Okay to Be Different* (PS–2). Illus. by author. 2001, Little, Brown $14.95 (0-316-66603-3). Readers learn that it's OK to be adopted, to wear glasses, to have an unusual nose, to lose a race — and to have a pet worm. (Rev: HBG 3/02; SLJ 10/01)

970 Piumini, Roberto. *Doctor Me Di Cin* (2–4). Illus. by Piet Grobler. 2001, Front Street $15.95 (1-886910-67-7). A crafty Chinese doctor eventually succeeds in luring a pallid prince outside to get some fresh air. (Rev: HBG 3/02; SLJ 10/01)

971 Plourde, Lynn. *Snow Day* (PS–1). Illus. by Hideko Takahashi. 2001, Simon & Schuster $16.00 (0-689-82600-1). There's plenty of onomatopoeia in this celebration of the activities that take place on a snowy day. (Rev: HBG 10/02; SLJ 1/02)

972 Purmell, Ann. *Apple Cider Making Days* (PS–2). Illus. by Joanne Friar. 2002, Millbrook LB $21.90 (0-7613-2364-3). 32pp. Making cider is a family activity in this colorful book with detailed illustrations of the process. (Rev: BL 12/1/02; HBG 3/03; SLJ 1/03)

973 Rau, Dana Meachen. *Ways to Go* (K–1). Illus. by Jane Conteh-Morgan. 2001, Compass Point LB $18.60 (0-7565-0071-0). 24pp. Minimal text and appealing illustrations portray a choice of modes of transport. (Rev: SLJ 10/01) [388]

974 Richmond, Marianne. *Hooray for You! A Celebration of "You-ness."* (PS–2). Illus. by author. 2001, Waldman $15.95 (0-931674-44-1). Differences in cultures, characteristics, and goals are all shown to be of value. (Rev: HBG 3/02; SLJ 1/02)

975 Roberts, Bethany. *The Wind's Garden* (PS–1). Illus. by Melanie Hope Greenberg. 2001, Holt $15.95 (0-8050-6367-6). 32pp. A little girl and the wind each plant their gardens, and they grow in their different ways. (Rev: BL 6/1–15/01; HBG 10/01; SLJ 5/01)

976 Rock, Lois. *I Wonder Why* (PS–2). Illus. by Christopher Corr. 2001, Chronicle $14.95 (0-8118-3169-8). 32pp. A book full of speculative questions, about such topics as nature, life, enjoyment, and change. (Rev: BL 5/15/01; HBG 10/01; SLJ 8/01)

977 Roddie, Shen. *Good-Bye, Hello!* (PS). Illus. by Carol Thompson. 2001, DK $9.95 (0-7894-7861-7). 24pp. A day in the life of a toddler is presented in rhythmic text and appealing watercolors. (Rev: BL 12/15/01; HBG 3/02)

978 Rogers, Paul. *Tiny* (K–3). Illus. by Korky Paul. 2002, Kane paper $7.95 (1-929132-26-3). A twist on the house, street, town, country, continent progression that moves out from a flea to a star. (Rev: SLJ 8/02)

979 Roosa, Karen. *Beach Day* (PS–K). Illus. by Maggie Smith. 2001, Clarion $15.00 (0-618-02923-0). 32pp. Lively art and detailed illustrations depict a day at the beach for a group of multicultural children. (Rev: BL 5/1/01; HBG 10/01; SLJ 4/01)

980 Rosenberg, Liz. *Eli's Night-Light* (PS–1). Illus. by Joanna Yardley. 2001, Scholastic $15.95 (0-531-30316-0). 32pp. When his light burns out, a brave little boy appreciates the glow from the clock, headlights passing, and above all the shining stars. (Rev: BL 6/1–15/01; HBG 10/01; SLJ 8/01)

981 Rosenberry, Vera. *Vera Goes to the Dentist* (PS–3). Illus. 2002, Holt $16.95 (0-8050-6668-3). 32pp. Vera is so frightened by her first trip to the dentist that she runs out of the office, but she is finally caught and becomes calm enough to finish the examination. (Rev: BL 4/1/02; HBG 10/02; SLJ 5/02)

982 Rubel, Nicole. *No More Vegetables!* (K–2). Illus. 2002, Farrar $16.00 (0-374-36362-5). 32pp. Picky eater Ruthie boycotts all vegetables until her mother asks her to help in the garden. (Rev: BL 12/15/02; HBG 3/03; SLJ 8/02)

983 Russell, Joan Plummer. *Aero and Officer Mike: Police Partners* (2–4). Illus. by Kris Turner Sinnenberg. 2001, Boyds Mills $15.95 (1-56397-931-4). 32pp. Aero is Officer Mike's police dog, and the two of them are shown working together in this book of photographs and text. (Rev: BL 9/15/01; HBG 3/02; SLJ 12/01) [363.2]

984 Ruurs, Margriet. *When We Go Camping* (PS–3). Illus. by Andrew Kiss. 2001, Tundra $14.95 (0-88776-476-2). 32pp. The joys of camping are brought to life in this detailed, realistically illustrated story of siblings on a camping trip with their parents. (Rev: BL 12/15/01; HBG 10/01; SLJ 7/01)

985 Ryan, Pam Munoz. *Mud Is Cake* (PS–1). Illus. by David McPhail. 2002, Hyperion $15.99 (0-7868-0501-3). A brother and sister enjoy playful fantasies, such as a stick becoming a wand and a porch becoming a stage. (Rev: BL 6/1–15/02; HBG 10/02; SLJ 5/02)

986 Rylant, Cynthia. *Let's Go Home: The Wonderful Things About a House* (PS–3). Illus. by Wendy A. Halperin. 2002, Simon & Schuster $16.00 (0-689-82326-6). 32pp. A delightful look at different types of houses and their interiors. (Rev: BL 4/15/02*; HBG 10/02; SLJ 6/02) [392.3]

987 Salat, Cristina. *Peanut's Emergency* (K–2). Illus. by Tammie Lyon. 2002, Charlesbridge $16.95 (1-57091-440-0); paper $6.95 (1-57091-441-9). 32pp. Peanut seeks help when her mother is late picking her up from school in this story about what to do in an "emergency." (Rev: BL 9/15/02; HBG 3/03; SLJ check)

988 Santoro, Scott. *The Little Skyscraper* (K–2). Illus. 2001, Price Stern Sloan $12.99 (0-8431-7677-6). 32pp. The handsome Little Skyscraper was young Jack's favorite building, but it loses its luster with age and it is up to the adult Jack, now an architect, to save it from demolition. (Rev: BL 12/1/01; HBG 3/02)

989 Sayre, April Pulley. *It's My City! A Singing Map* (PS–1). Illus. by Denis Roche. 2001, Greenwillow LB $15.89 (0-688-16916-3). A little girl doesn't need directions because she has made up her own onomatopoeic song that describes the route. (Rev: HB 11–12/01; HBG 3/02; SLJ 10/01)

990 Schaap, Martine. *Mop and the Birthday Picnic* (PS–1). Illus. by Alex de Wolf. Series: Mop and Family. 2001, McGraw-Hill $12.95 (1-57768-882-1). 30pp. Mop the dog eats all the hot dogs at the birthday party for twins Julie and Justin. They also have a good time in *Mop's Mountain Adventure* (2000). (Rev: HBG 10/01; SLJ 10/01)

991 Schertle, Alice. *All You Need for a Snowman* (PS–K). Illus. by Barbara Lavallee. 2002, Harcourt $16.00 (0-15-200789-X). 32pp. As the text describes the essentials for making a successful snowman, a group of children are shown building two gigantic examples. (Rev: BCCB 1/03; BL 11/15/02; HB 11–12/02; HBG 3/03; SLJ 12/02)

992 Schick, Eleanor. *I Am: I Am a Dancer* (PS–1). Illus. by author. 2002, Marshall Cavendish $15.95 (0-7614-5097-1). A girl in a leotard imitates animals, clouds, and a dreamer. (Rev: HBG 10/02; SLJ 1/03)

993 Schneider, Christine M. *Saxophone Sam and His Snazzy Jazz Band* (PS–3). Illus. 2002, Walker LB $17.85 (0-8027-8810-6). 32pp. A tuneful tale with a catchy beat and inventive illustrations about siblings who track a jazz tune through their house until they find the source in the attic. (Rev: BL 12/1/02; HBG 3/03; SLJ 11/02)

994 Schotter, Roni. *Captain Bob Takes Flight* (K–2). Illus. by Joe Cepeda. 2003, Simon & Schuster $15.95 (0-689-83388-1). 32pp. Cleaning his room becomes quite enjoyable when Bob pretends he's a pilot and his mother cooperatively acts as the control tower. (Rev: BL 3/15/03)

995 Schwartz, Amy. *What James Likes Best* (PS). Illus. 2003, Simon & Schuster $16.95 (0-689-84059-4). 32pp. This oversize book contains four stories about preschooler James, who likes expeditions. (Rev: BCCB 3/03; BL 3/1/03*; SLJ 3/03)

996 Scrimger, Richard. *Princess Bun Bun* (PS–K). Illus. by Gillian Johnson. 2002, Tundra $12.95 (0-88776-543-2). Winifred and her family are off to visit Uncle Dave in the Castle Apartments, a name that conjures moats and monsters until Uncle Dave sets them right. (Rev: HBG 10/02; SLJ 7/02)

997 Sears, William, et al. *You Can Go to the Potty* (PS). Illus. by Renee W. Andriani. 2002, Little, Brown $12.95 (0-316-78888-0). 32pp. This introduction to toilet training is designed for adults to read with children, combining text for the young with sidebars for the adults. (Rev: BL 11/15/02; HBG 3/03; SLJ 11/02) [649]

998 Shannon, Terry Miller, and Timothy Warner. *Tub Toys* (PS–1). Illus. by Lee Calderon. 2002, Tricycle Pr. $14.95 (1-58246-066-3). A little boy gets ready for bath time by collecting all his toys. (Rev: HBG 3/03; SLJ 2/03)

999 Siddals, Mary McKenna. *Morning Song* (PS). Illus. by Elizabeth Sayles. 2001, Holt $15.95 (0-8050-6369-2). A small boy greets items in his room with a bright "Good morning." (Rev: HBG 3/02; SLJ 12/01)

1000 Simon, Seymour. *Fighting Fires* (PS–2). Illus. Series: SeeMore Readers. 2002, North-South $13.95 (1-58717-168-6); paper $3.95 (1-58717-169-4). 32pp. An eye-catching book for preschoolers and early readers about fire fighters and their equipment. (Rev: BL 8/02; HBG 3/03; SLJ 7/02) [628.9]

1001 Singer, Marilyn. *Boo Hoo Boo-Boo* (PS–1). Illus. by Elivia Savadier. Series: Harper Growing Tree. 2002, HarperFestival $9.95 (0-694-01566-0). 24pp. Three toddlers take a spill and are fixed up by their caregivers who, along with bandages and ointment, also give lots of love. (Rev: BCCB 9/02; BL 8/02; HBG 10/02)

1002 Singer, Marilyn. *Fred's Bed* (PS). Illus. by JoAnn Adinolfi. 2001, HarperFestival $9.95 (0-694-01451-6). Fred wants a new bed and his teasing mother offers him all kinds of choices — an eagle's nest, a rabbit hole, and so forth. (Rev: HBG 10/01; SLJ 12/01)

1003 Slegers, Liesbet. *Kevin Goes to School* (PS). Illus. by author. 2002, Kane $7.95 (1-929132-31-X). A small-format book in which a toddler deals in simple language with his first day at school. Also use *Kevin Goes to the Hospital, Kevin Spends the Night,* and *Kevin Takes a Trip.* (Rev: HBG 3/03; SLJ 3/03)

1004 Snyder, Carol. *We're Painting* (PS–1). Illus. by Lisa Jahn-Clough. 2002, HarperFestival $9.95 (0-694-01445-1). 24pp. Two children discover the joy of painting in this book featuring vibrant illustrations and rhythmic text. (Rev: BL 8/02; HBG 10/02; SLJ 7/02)

1005 Spinelli, Eileen. *Rise the Moon* (PS–2). Illus. by Raul Colon. 2003, Dial $16.99 (0-8037-2601-5). 40pp. Glowing moonlit illustrations and poetic text introduce moonstruck characters — a wolf who calls to the night, a sailor swaying to sleep, an artist painting. (Rev: BL 1/1–15/03*)

1006 Spinelli, Eileen. *A Safe Place Called Home* (K–2). Illus. by Christy Hale. 2001, Marshall Cavendish $15.95 (0-7614-5085-8). 32pp. A boy is glad to know that home is at the end of a scary walk during which dogs bark and a bully looks threatening. (Rev: BCCB 9/01; BL 10/1/01; HBG 3/02; SLJ 2/02)

1007 Stevens, Jan Romero. *Carlos Digs to China / Carlos Excava Hasta la China* (K–2). Trans. by Mario Lamo-Jimenez. Illus. by Jeanne Arnold. 2001, Rising Moon LB $15.95 (0-87358-764-2). A bilingual story in which Carlos decides to dig to China so that he can taste all that wonderful food. (Rev: HBG 10/01; SLJ 6/01)

1008 Swanson, Susan Marie. *The First Thing My Mama Told Me* (K–2). Illus. by Christine Davenier. 2002, Harcourt $16.00 (0-15-201075-0). 40pp. Seven-year-old Lucy loves her name, and in this book recalls the ways her name has been special to her throughout her childhood. (Rev: BL 7/02; HBG 10/02; SLJ 8/02)

1009 Tarpley, Natasha Anastasia. *Bippity Bop Barbershop* (PS–1). Illus. by E. B. Lewis. 2002, Little, Brown $15.95 (0-316-52284-8). 32pp. Miles accompanies his father to the local barbershop for his first haircut. (Rev: BCCB 3/02; BL 2/15/02; HBG 10/02; SLJ 2/02)

1010 Terasaki, Todd. *Ghosts for Breakfast* (2–4). Illus. by Shelly Shinjo. 2002, Lee & Low $16.95 (1-58430-046-9). 32pp. The Troublesome Trio informs Farmer Tanaka that there are ghosts in his field, so the farmer investigates, only to find that the ghosts are daikon radishes hanging to dry. (Rev: BL 1/1–15/03; HBG 3/03; SLJ 10/02)

1011 Testa, Fulvio. *Too Much Garbage* (PS–1). Illus. by author. 2001, North-South LB $15.88 (0-7358-1452-X). Tony and Bill are unhappy to see all the garbage that is dumped improperly. (Rev: HBG 10/01; SLJ 5/01)

1012 Testa, Fulvio. *The Visit* (K–2). Trans. from German by Marianne Martens. Illus. by author. 2002, North-South LB $16.50 (0-7358-1685-9). A city boy is introduced to the joys of the countryside. (Rev: HBG 3/03; SLJ 1/03)

1013 Tibo, Gilles. *Shy Guy* (PS–3). Trans. from German by Sibylle Kazeroid. Illus. by Pef. 2002, North-South LB $16.50 (0-7358-1711-1). Shy Greg finds that his goldfish gives him confidence. (Rev: HBG 3/03; SLJ 1/03)

1014 Tildes, Phyllis Limbacher. *Billy's Big-Boy Bed* (PS). Illus. by Phyllis L. Tildes. 2002, Charlesbridge LB $15.95 (1-57091-475-3). Billy gets a new, big bed but prefers to remain in his crib for the time being. (Rev: HBG 10/02; SLJ 3/02)

1015 Tripp, Nathaniel. *Snow Comes to the Farm* (PS–2). Illus. by Kate Kiesler. 2001, Candlewick $15.99 (1-56402-426-1). Nostalgic illustrations enhance a boy's recollection of a trip into the woods at the start of a snowstorm. (Rev: BL 12/15/01; HBG 3/02; SLJ 11/01)

1016 Turner, Ann. *In the Heart* (PS–1). Illus. by Salley Mavor. 2001, HarperCollins LB $14.89 (0-06-023731-7). 32pp. A little girl identifies the heart of each part of her life that is important to her. (Rev: BL 8/01; HBG 10/01; SLJ 7/01)

1017 Van Der Meer, Mara. *Can We Play? A Pop-up, Lift-the-Flap Story About the Days of the Week* (PS–K). Illus. by Mara Van Der Meer and Ron Van Der Meer. 2002, Abrams $14.95 (0-8109-0379-2). A little girl anticipates Sunday, when everyone says they'll be free to play. (Rev: SLJ 10/02)

1018 Van Genechten, Guido. *Potty Time* (PS). Illus. 2001, Simon & Schuster $12.95 (0-689-84698-3). 32pp. Animals with all sorts of bottoms use the potty in this very humorous approach to the topic. (Rev: BL 10/1/01; HBG 3/02; SLJ 12/01)

1019 Walton, Rick. *How Can You Dance?* (PS–K). Illus. by Ana Lopez-Escriva. 2001, Putnam $13.99 (0-399-23229-X). 32pp. A celebration of dance, in which a little boy and his mother swing to the rhythm of the text. (Rev: BCCB 7–8/01; BL 6/1–15/01; HBG 10/01; SLJ 7/01)

1020 Warner, Sunny. *The Moon Quilt* (K–4). Illus. 2001, Houghton $15.00 (0-618-05583-5). 32pp. An old woman and her cat spend happy times together until death claims them both after satisfying lives. (Rev: BL 4/15/01; HBG 10/01; SLJ 4/01)

1021 Weatherford, Carole Boston. *Jazz Baby* (PS). Illus. by Laura Freeman. 2002, Lee & Low $11.95 (1-58430-039-6). A crew of ethnically diverse youngsters dances to the beat of a lively rhyme and jazz instruments. (Rev: HBG 10/02; SLJ 6/02)

1022 Wellington, Monica. *Apple Farmer Annie* (PS–2). Illus. 2001, Dutton $14.99 (0-525-46727-0). 32pp. Annie is busy picking, sorting, selling, and baking her apples in this picture book that includes apple recipes. (Rev: BL 9/1/01; HBG 3/02; SLJ 8/01)

1023 Wellington, Monica. *Firefighter Frank* (PS–1). Illus. by author. 2002, Dutton $14.99 (0-525-47021-2). A day in the life of a fire fighter, from simple tasks like shopping and looking after equipment to responding to an emergency. (Rev: HBG 3/03; SLJ 1/03)

1024 Wilcox, Brad. *Hip, Hip, Hooray for Annie McRae!* (PS–1). Illus. by Julie Hansen Olson. 2001, Gibbs Smith $15.95 (1-58685-058-X). Annie McRae has a healthy self-confidence and when her parents and teachers forget to praise her one day, she simply does it herself. (Rev: HBG 3/02; SLJ 10/01)

1025 Wolfe, Frances. *Where I Live* (PS–1). Illus. 2001, Tundra $14.95 (0-88776-529-7). 32pp. A little girl describes where she lives (the seaside) and her activities there. (Rev: BCCB 5/01; BL 5/1/01; HBG 10/01; SLJ 4/01)

1026 Wood, Douglas. *A Quiet Place* (K–3). Illus. by Dan Andreasen. 2002, Simon & Schuster $16.95 (0-689-81511-5). 32pp. A boy searches for a secluded place to be alone with his thoughts, far from the noise and bustle of the city. (Rev: BL 2/15/02; HBG 10/02; SLJ 7/02)

1027 Young, Amy. *Belinda the Ballerina* (PS–2). Illus. 2003, Viking $15.99 (0-670-03549-1). 32pp. Belinda is rejected by ballet judges because of her huge feet, and she sadly abandons dance until a band arrives at Fred's Fine Food and her feet can't resist. (Rev: BL 3/1/03; SLJ 3/03)

FAMILY STORIES

1028 Ada, Alma Flor. *I Love Saturdays y Domingos* (PS–3). Illus. by Elivia Savadier. 2002, Simon & Schuster $16.95 (0-689-31819-7). 32pp. A little girl visits Grandma and Grandpa on Saturday and Abuelito and Abuelita on Sunday in this multicultural story that incorporates Spanish words and phrases. (Rev: BL 2/1/02; HBG 10/02; SLJ 1/02)

1029 Adoff, Arnold. *Black Is Brown Is Tan* (PS–1). Illus. by Emily Arnold McCully. 2002, HarperCollins LB $15.89 (0-06-028777-2). 40pp. A loving, happy, interracial family is depicted in this newly illustrated version of the 1973 poem. (Rev: BL 4/15/02; HBG 10/02; SLJ 7/02)

1030 Altman, Linda Jacobs. *Singing with Momma Lou* (2–5). Illus. by Larry Johnson. 2002, Lee & Low $16.95 (1-58430-040-X). 32pp. Tamika uses photograph albums to help her grandmother, who suffers from Alzheimer's disease, remember some of her past. (Rev: BL 5/15/02; HBG 10/02; SLJ 6/02)

1031 Anderson, Laurie Halse. *The Big Cheese of Third Street* (PS–2). Illus. by David Gordon. 2002, Simon & Schuster $16.00 (0-689-82464-5). 32pp. Benny is the only tiny member of a giant-sized family but he gets a chance to shine at the annual block party's greased-pole climb. (Rev: BCCB 3/02; BL 12/1/01; HBG 10/02; SLJ 2/02)

1032 Andreae, Giles. *There's a House Inside My Mommy* (PS–1). Illus. by Vanessa Cabban. 2002, Albert Whitman $15.95 (0-8075-7853-3). 32pp. Rhythmic text and simple, affectionate illustrations show a young boy's impressions of the baby growing inside his mother. (Rev: BL 11/1/02; HBG 3/03; SLJ 11/02)

1033 Austin, Heather. *Visiting Aunt Sylvia's: A Maine Adventure* (K–2). Illus. by author. 2002, Down East $15.95 (0-89272-523-0). A young narrator looks back at happy times at Aunt Sylvia's cabin in rural Maine — stacking wood, skiing, roasting marshmallows, swimming in the summer, and other seasonal memories. (Rev: SLJ 2/03)

1034 Axelrod, Amy. *My Last Chance Brother* (2–4). Illus. by Jack E. Davis. 2002, Dutton $15.99 (0-525-46659-2). 32pp. Max is irritated by his big brother Gordon's silly antics, but at the last minute decides to give Gordon one last chance. (Rev: BL 7/02; HBG 3/03; SLJ 9/02)

1035 Ballard, Robin. *I Used to Be the Baby* (PS–K). Illus. 2002, HarperCollins LB $15.89 (0-06-029587-2). 24pp. A little boy helps take care of his toddler brother but still expects to spend time on his mother's lap. (Rev: BL 5/1/02; HBG 10/02; SLJ 5/02)

1036 Barclay, Jane. *Going on a Journey to the Sea* (PS–1). Illus. by Doris Barrette. 2002, Lobster $16.95 (1-894222-34-2). 32pp. A boy and his sister spend a pleasant day at the beach in this rhyming picture book. (Rev: BL 5/15/02; SLJ 8/02)

1037 Bea, Holly. *Bless Your Heart* (PS–K). Illus. by Kim Howard. 2001, H. J. Kramer $15.00 (0-915811-94-4). 32pp. A mother offers many blessings to her children as they enjoy a colorful day by the sea. (Rev: BL 10/1/01; HBG 3/02)

1038 Bertram, Debbie. *The Best Place to Read* (PS–1). Illus. by Michael Garland. 2003, Random $14.95 (0-375-82293-3). 32pp. The poor protagonist searches for a good spot to settle down and read his new book, and eventually finds the perfect place with his mother. (Rev: BL 1/1–15/03)

1039 Biro, Maureen Boyd. *Walking with Maga* (PS–3). Illus. by Joyce Wheeler. 2001, All About Kids $16.95 (0-9700863-4-2). 32pp. A young girl accompanies her beloved grandmother Maga on walks, finding joy in what they see and the people they meet. (Rev: BL 12/15/01; HBG 3/03; SLJ 7/02)

1040 Blumenthal, Deborah. *Aunt Claire's Yellow Beehive Hair* (K–3). Illus. by Mary Grandpre. 2001, Dial $15.99 (0-8037-2509-4). 32pp. Annie and her grandmother create an album full of family history, with some space for the future. (Rev: BCCB 7–8/01; BL 5/1/01; HBG 10/01; SLJ 7/01)

1041 Bourgeois, Paulette. *Oma's Quilt* (PS–3). Illus. by Stephane Jorisch. 2001, Kids Can $15.95 (1-55074-777-0). 32pp. Grumpy Oma hates her new life in a nursing home, so granddaughter Emily and her mother decide to make her a special quilt. (Rev: BCCB 12/01; BL 12/15/01; HBG 3/02; SLJ 11/01)

1042 Bowen, Anne. *I Loved You Before You Were Born* (PS–K). Illus. by Greg Shed. 2001, Harper-Collins LB $15.89 (0-06-028721-7). 32pp. A grandmother tells her new grandchild how much she looked forward to the baby's birth. (Rev: BL 7/01; HBG 10/01; SLJ 7/01)

1043 Boyden, Linda. *The Blue Roses* (K–3). Illus. by Amy Cordova. 2002, Lee & Low $16.95 (1-58430-037-X). 32pp. When her beloved grandfather dies, Rosalie remembers the lessons he taught her in the garden. (Rev: BCCB 9/02; BL 5/15/02; HBG 10/02; SLJ 6/02)

1044 Brisson, Pat. *Hobbledy-Clop* (PS–K). Illus. by Maxie Chambliss. 2003, Boyds Mills $15.95 (1-56397-888-1). In the repetitive style of an old Irish folktale, this is the story of Brendan O'Doyle's visit to his grandmother, accompanied by a growing troop of animals. (Rev: SLJ 2/03)

1045 Brutschy, Jennifer. *Just One More Story* (K–2). Illus. by Cat B. Smith. 2002, Scholastic $16.95 (0-439-31767-3). Austin and his parents travel the country living in a trailer, and every night Austin gets one story, until they spend a night at Uncle Rory's two-story house. (Rev: BCCB 7–8/02; HB 7–8/02; HBG 10/02; SLJ 7/02)

1046 Buehner, Caralyn. *I Want to Say I Love You* (K–2). Illus. by Jacqueline Rogers. 2001, Penguin Putnam $15.99 (0-8037-2547-7). A mother express-

es her love for her child, whether she's good or bad. (Rev: HBG 3/02; SLJ 12/01)

1047 Buzzeo, Toni. *The Sea Chest* (2–4). Illus. by Mary Grandpre. 2002, Dial $16.99 (0-8037-2703-8). 32pp. An elderly aunt tells her niece, who is eagerly awaiting an adopted sister, about the girl her family found in a sea chest and adopted many years ago. (Rev: BL 9/15/02; HBG 3/03; SLJ 8/02)

1048 Campos, Tito. *Muffler Man/El Hombre Mofle* (K–3). Illus. by Lamberto Alvarez and Beto Alvarez. 2001, Arte Publico $14.95 (1-55885-318-9). 32pp. Young Mexican Chuy Garcia and his mother are finally able to follow Chuy's father to the United States, where Chuy persuades his father to indulge his artistic abilities. (Rev: BL 12/15/01; SLJ 1/02)

1049 Carlstrom, Nancy White. *Before You Were Born* (PS–2). Illus. by Linda Saport. 2002, Eerdmans $17.00 (0-8028-5185-1). 32pp. This exceptional story inspired by Psalm 139 celebrates the bond between parents and children. (Rev: BL 2/1/02; HBG 10/02; SLJ 6/02)

1050 Carney, Margaret. *The Biggest Fish in the Lake* (K–3). Illus. by Janet Wilson. 2001, Kids Can $15.95 (1-55074-720-7). 32pp. A young girl describes her happy experiences fishing with her grandfather. (Rev: BL 7/01; HBG 10/01; SLJ 7/01)

1051 Carter, Don. *Heaven's All-Star Jazz Band* (PS–2). Illus. 2002, Knopf LB $17.99 (0-375-91571-0). 40pp. A grandson fondly imagines his grandfather hanging out in heaven with his favorite jazz greats, in this lively account with 3-D art and a jazzy beat. (Rev: BCCB 2/03; BL 11/15/02; HBG 3/03; SLJ 11/02)

1052 Cheng, Andrea. *When the Bees Fly Home* (PS–2). Illus. by Joline McFadden. 2002, Tilbury $16.96 (0-88448-238-3). 32pp. A boy who lacks self-confidence finds he has an unsuspected talent as he works to help his bee-keeping family in this novel that includes plenty of bee facts and lovely watercolors. (Rev: BL 7/02; HBG 3/03)

1053 Cooke, Trish. *Full, Full, Full, of Love* (PS–1). Illus. by Paul Howard. 2003, Candlewick $15.99 (0-7636-1851-9). 32pp. A young boy enjoys a family dinner at his grandmother's house in this happy, cozy picture book. (Rev: BCCB 3/03; BL 2/15/03; SLJ 2/03)

1054 Czech, Jan M. *The Coffee Can Kid* (PS–2). Illus. by Maurie J. Manning. 2002, Child Welfare League of America paper $9.95 (0-87868-821-8). 24pp. Six-year-old Annie asks her father to retell the story of her birth in Asia and her adoption. (Rev: BL 7/02; SLJ 7/02)

1055 Daly, Niki. *Old Bob's Brown Bear* (PS–1). Illus. 2002, Farrar $16.00 (0-374-35612-2). 32pp. Emma feels her grandfather isn't giving his new teddy bear enough attention and takes the toy on a joyous spree, but other interests eventually intervene and Grandpa is pleased to get his teddy back. (Rev: BL 10/1/02; HBG 3/03; SLJ 11/02)

1056 D'Arc, Karen Scourby. *"My Grandmother Is a Singing Yaya"* (PS–2). Illus. by Diane Palmisciano. 2001, Scholastic $15.95 (0-439-29309-X). 32pp. A little girl is afraid she will be embarrassed at a

53

Grandparents' Day picnic by her grandmother, who is given to bursting into song at odd moments. (Rev: BL 1/1–15/02; HBG 3/02; SLJ 11/01)

1057 Doyle, Charlotte. *Twins!* (PS–K). Illus. by Julia Gorton. 2003, Putnam $10.99 (0-399-23718-6). 32pp. Twin girls play, splash, share, and enjoy a day together in this rhyming picture book. (Rev: BL 2/15/03; SLJ 3/03)

1058 Ellis, Sarah. *Big Ben* (PS–1). Illus. by Kim LaFave. 2001, Fitzhenry & Whiteside $15.95 (1-55041-679-0). 32pp. Preschooler Ben feels left out when he doesn't get a report card like his older siblings, until they create one especially for him. (Rev: BL 1/1–15/02; HB 3–4/02; HBG 10/02; SLJ 2/02)

1059 Emmons, Chip. *Sammy Wakes His Dad* (PS–2). Illus. by Shirley Venit Anger. 2002, Star Bright $13.95 (1-887734-87-2). Sammy's father is now wheelchair-bound, but Sammy asks him to come fishing anyway. (Rev: HBG 10/02; SLJ 8/02)

1060 Ericsson, Jennifer A. *She Did It!* (PS). Illus. by Nadine Bernard Westcott. 2002, Farrar $16.00 (0-374-36776-0). 32pp. The artwork is detailed and witty in this story about four sisters who giggle and fight their way through their day, with their mother all the while asking, "Who did it?" (Rev: BL 2/15/02; HBG 10/02; SLJ 3/02)

1061 Finkelstein, Ruth. *Big Like Me! A New Baby Story* (PS–K). Illus. by Esther Touson. 2001, Hachai $9.95 (1-929628-04-8). 32pp. Benny has just learned some basic skills from his older brother when a new baby joins his Orthodox Jewish family. (Rev: BL 8/01; HBG 3/02; SLJ 1/02)

1062 Fisher, Valorie. *My Big Brother* (PS–K). Illus. 2002, Simon & Schuster $14.95 (0-689-84327-5). 40pp. The amazing feats of one big brother, from the point of view of his baby sibling. (Rev: BCCB 7–8/02; BL 9/15/02; HBG 3/03; SLJ 7/02)

1063 Furgang, Kathy. *Flower Girl* (PS–2). Illus. by Harley Jessup. 2003, Viking $15.99 (0-670-88950-4). 40pp. Anna's reluctance to participate in her aunt's wedding is overcome by enchantment with the preparations. (Rev: BCCB 3/03; BL 2/1/03; SLJ 2/03)

1064 Gardner, Sally. *Mama, Don't Go Out Tonight* (PS–K). Illus. 2002, Bloomsbury $16.95 (1-58234-790-5). 32pp. This colorful story, in simple dialogue and vivid drawings, describes a young girl's fears when her mother is going out for the evening and then shows the fine time both mother and daughter have in the end. (Rev: BL 1/1–15/03; SLJ 12/02)

1065 Gay, Marie-Louise. *Good Morning, Sam* (PS–1). Illus. 2003, Douglas & McIntyre $14.95 (0-88899-528-8). 32pp. Preschooler Sam's efforts to dress himself are hindered by his dog and helped by his big sister. (Rev: BL 3/15/03)

1066 Gilles, Almira Astudillo. *Willie Wins* (PS–3). Illus. by Carl Angel. 2001, Lee & Low $16.00 (1-58430-023-X). 32pp. Willie isn't much interested in his father's stories of his youth in the Philippines, but when he needs a money bank for a school project, the coconut alkansiya his father gives him has a surprise in it. (Rev: BL 5/1/01; HBG 10/01; SLJ 6/01)

1067 Gilmore, Rachna. *A Gift for Gita* (2–3). Illus. by Alice Priestley. 2002, Tilbury paper $7.95 (0-88448-239-1). 24pp. When Gita's father is offered a job back in their native India, the immigrant family must make a choice. (Rev: BL 9/15/02)

1068 Grambling, Lois G. *Grandma Tells a Story* (PS–1). Illus. by Fred Willingham. 2001, Charlesbridge LB $15.95 (1-58089-057-1). Two grandparents are overjoyed to learn that a longed-for grandchild is on its way in this gentle story with bright illustrations. (Rev: HBG 10/01; SLJ 7/01)

1069 Greenstein, Elaine. *As Big as You* (PS). Illus. by author. 2002, Knopf LB $16.99 (0-375-91353-X). 32pp. A new baby's growth is followed over a year in this gentle, charming picture book. (Rev: BL 1/1–15/02; HBG 10/02; SLJ 3/02)

1070 Guest, Elissa. *Iris and Walter and Baby Rose* (PS–K). Illus. by Christine Davenier. 2002, Harcourt $14.00 (0-15-202120-5). 44pp. Iris can't wait to be a big sister, until the baby arrives and isn't what Iris expected at all. (Rev: BL 3/15/02; HBG 10/02; SLJ 4/02)

1071 Gurley, Nan. *Twice Yours: A Parable of God's Gift* (K–3). Illus. by Bill Farnsworth. 2002, Zondervan $14.99 (0-310-70194-5). 40pp. A grandfather tells his grandson a story relating to the words of the apostle Peter. (Rev: BL 2/1/02)

1072 Hanson, Mary. *The Difference Between Babies and Cookies* (PS–K). Illus. by Debbie Tilley. 2002, Harcourt $16.00 (0-15-202406-9). 32pp. A new sister finds out that babies aren't quite as sweet as Mom told her. (Rev: BL 3/1/02; HBG 10/02; SLJ 5/02)

1073 Harper, Jessica. *Lizzy's Do's and Don'ts* (1–3). Illus. by Lindsay Harper duPont. 2002, HarperCollins LB $15.89 (0-06-623861-7). 40pp. Cartoon art helps to convey the messages of this book, in which a mother and daughter realize they say "don't" to each other far too often. (Rev: BL 3/15/02; HBG 10/02; SLJ 7/02)

1074 Harris, Robie H. *Hello Benny! What It's Like to Be a Baby* (PS–3). Illus. by Michael Emberley. 2002, Simon & Schuster $16.95 (0-689-83257-5). 40pp. Following a baby's life from birth to first birthday, this book combines a fictional storyline with lots of factual information about babies in general. (Rev: BCCB 11/02; BL 10/15/02; HB 11–12/02; HBG 3/03; SLJ 9/02)

1075 Harshman, Marc. *Roads* (PS–2). Illus. by Mary N. DePalma. 2002, Marshall Cavendish $16.95 (0-7614-5112-9). 32pp. A thoughtful picture book about traveling from a child's perspective. (Rev: BL 10/15/02; HBG 3/03; SLJ 9/02)

1076 Haughton, Emma. *Rainy Day* (PS–1). Illus. by Angelo Rinaldi. 2000, Lerner $15.95 (1-57505-452-3). A boy and his father spend a day together and must find a way to work around the rain. (Rev: BL 3/1/03; HBG 9/00; SLJ 8/00)

1077 Hayles, Marsha. *He Saves the Day* (PS–1). Illus. by Lynne W. Cravath. 2002, Putnam $15.99 (0-399-23363-6). An imaginative little boy plays by himself, emerging victorious from a variety of expeditions until his mother must in turn save the day. (Rev: BCCB 3/02; HBG 10/02; SLJ 4/02)

1078 High, Linda Oatman. *Winter Shoes for Shadow Horse* (PS–3). Illus. by Ted Lewin. 2001, Boyds Mills $15.95 (1-56397-472-X). 32pp. A boy shoes a horse for the very first time under the watchful eye of his blacksmith father. (Rev: BL 9/1/01; HBG 3/02; SLJ 10/01)

1079 Hines, Anna Grossnickle. *My Grandma Is Coming to Town* (PS–K). Illus. by Melissa Sweet. 2003, Candlewick $13.99 (0-7636-1237-5). 24pp. When grandma visits Albert for the first time since he was a baby, he is shy and hides while grandma waits patiently. (Rev: BL 3/15/03)

1080 Hojer, Dan, and Lotta Hojer. *Heart of Mine: A Story of Adoption* (PS–1). Trans. by Elisabeth Kallick Dyssegaard. Illus. 2001, Farrar $14.00 (91-29-65301-0). 28pp. Adoptive parents tell the story of preparing for their new child and traveling to Asia to pick her up. (Rev: BL 8/01; HBG 10/01; SLJ 4/01)

1081 Hooks, Bell. *Homemade Love* (PS). Illus. by Shane W. Evans. 2002, Hyperion $16.99 (0-7868-0643-5). 32pp. An African American girl revels in the love of her supportive parents in this brightly illustrated book. (Rev: BCCB 2/03; BL 2/1/03; HBG 3/03; SLJ 12/02)

1082 Hopkinson, Deborah. *Bluebird Summer* (1–3). Illus. by Bethanne Andersen. 2001, Greenwillow LB $15.89 (0-688-17399-3). 32pp. Two young children and their grieving grandfather start a garden project as a tribute to their grandmother, who has recently died. (Rev: BL 4/15/01; HBG 10/01; SLJ 5/01)

1083 Hru, Dakari. *Tickle Tickle* (PS). Illus. by Ken Wilson-Max. 2002, Millbrook LB $21.90 (0-7613-2468-2). 32pp. A small child tells in rhyme how much he loves to be tickled by Papa. (Rev: BL 5/15/02; HBG 10/02; SLJ 8/02)

1084 Hughes, Shirley. *Annie Rose Is My Little Sister* (PS–1). Illus. 2003, Candlewick $15.99 (0-7636-1959-0). 32pp. Alfie's descriptions of his little sister Annie Rose's daily activities are accompanied by appealingly detailed pastel illustrations. (Rev: BL 3/1/03)

1085 Hume, Stephen Eaton. *Red Moon Follows Truck* (PS–3). Illus. by Leslie Elizabeth Watts. 2001, Orca $16.95 (1-55143-218-8). 32pp. A boy narrates his family's move across the country and their adventures along the way, particularly those of Gypsy the dog. (Rev: BL 1/1–15/02; HBG 3/02; SLJ 2/02)

1086 Hundal, Nancy. *Camping* (PS–3). Illus. by Brian Deines. 2002, Fitzhenry & Whiteside $16.95 (1-55041-668-5). 32pp. Luminous illustrations form the backdrop for a young girl's discovery that camping in the wilderness has its delights after all. (Rev: BL 12/1/02; SLJ 11/02)

1087 Hurwitz, Johanna. *Russell's Secret* (PS–3). Illus. by Heather Maione. 2001, HarperCollins $14.95 (0-688-17574-0). 32pp. Pre-schooler Russell envies his baby sister until his mother agrees to treat him just like a baby for a day. (Rev: BL 1/1–15/02; HBG 10/02; SLJ 1/02)

1088 Hutchins, Hazel. *I'd Know You Anywhere* (PS). Illus. by Ruth Ohi. 2002, Annick LB $19.95 (1-55037-747-7); paper $7.95 (1-55037-746-9). 24pp. A father reassures his son that he'd know him no matter how he was disguised in this book for very young readers. (Rev: BL 12/15/02; HBG 3/03)

1089 Joosse, Barbara M. *Ghost Wings* (PS–3). Illus. by Giselle Potter. 2001, Chronicle $15.95 (0-8118-2164-1). 40pp. A young Mexican girl revisits the spot where she and her now-dead grandmother used to watch migrating monarch butterflies. (Rev: BCCB 7–8/01; BL 4/15/01; HBG 10/01; SLJ 5/01)

1090 Kallok, Emma. *Gem* (K–3). Illus. by Joel Bower. 2001, Tricycle Pr. $14.95 (1-58246-027-2). 32pp. A saxophone-playing neighbor welcomes a new baby into the world with her own special song. (Rev: BL 6/1–15/01; HBG 3/02; SLJ 4/01)

1091 Koutsky, Jan Dale. *My Grandma, My Pen Pal* (2–4). Illus. 2002, Boyds Mills $15.95 (1-56397-118-6). 24pp. The story of a granddaughter's relationship with her grandmother, in the form of a treasured scrapbook. (Rev: BL 5/15/02; HBG 10/02; SLJ 6/02)

1092 Kurtz, Jane. *Rain Romp: Stomping Away a Grouchy Day* (PS–1). Illus. by Dyanna Wolcott. 2002, HarperCollins LB $17.89 (0-06-029806-5). 32pp. A little girl's mood matches the stormy sky outside until she joins her parents in a dance in the rain. (Rev: BL 9/15/02; HBG 3/03; SLJ 9/02)

1093 Langley, Karen. *Shine* (K–2). Illus. by Jonathan Langley. 2002, Marshall Cavendish $15.95 (0-7614-5127-7). Jimmy worries that his busy father won't come to see him as the star of Bethlehem. (Rev: HBG 3/03; SLJ 1/03)

1094 Lasky, Kathryn. *Before I Was Your Mother* (PS–2). Illus. by LeUyen Pham. 2003, Harcourt $16.00 (0-15-201464-0). 40pp. Ruby's mother tells Ruby tales about her own childhood and her friends and activities. (Rev: BL 3/15/03)

1095 Lasky, Kathryn, and Jane Kamine. *Mommy's Hands* (PS–K). Illus. by Darcia LaBrosse. 2002, Hyperion $15.99 (0-7868-0280-4). 32pp. Three children — one Asian, one Caucasian, and one African American — describe what they like about their mothers' hands. (Rev: BL 6/1–15/02; HBG 10/02; SLJ 7/02)

1096 Lears, Laurie. *Becky the Brave: A Story About Epilepsy* (PS–3). Illus. by Gail Piazza. 2002, Albert Whitman LB $14.95 (0-8075-0601-X). Sarah admires her older sister Becky's confidence and composure, but Becky has not been brave enough to tell her classmates about her epilepsy. (Rev: HBG 10/02; SLJ 5/02)

1097 LeBox, Annette. *Wild Bog Tea* (K–3). Illus. by Harvey Chan. 2001, Groundwood $16.95 (0-88899-406-0). 32pp. A man's gentle remembrances of childhood with his grandfather include walks through the bogs and marshes of Labrador. (Rev: BL 12/15/01; HBG 3/02; SLJ 9/01)

1098 Lee, Spike, and Tonya Lewis Lee. *Please, Baby, Please* (K–2). Illus. by Kadir Nelson. 2002,

Simon & Schuster $16.95 (0-689-83233-8). 32pp. An appealing picture book by movie director Spike Lee and his producer wife that shows a mother continually pleading with her toddler to behave, until at bedtime it's the little one who begs for a goodnight kiss. (Rev: BCCB 2/03; BL 12/1/02; HBG 3/03; SLJ 12/02)

1099 Lin, Grace. *Kite Flying* (K–3). 2002, Knopf $14.95 (0-375-81520-1). 32pp. A Chinese girl describes the family ritual of making and flying kites. (Rev: BL 6/1–15/02; HBG 10/02; SLJ 7/02)

1100 Lindbergh, Reeve. *My Hippie Grandmother* (PS–2). Illus. by Abby Carter. 2003, Candlewick $15.99 (0-7636-0671-5). 24pp. A little girl talks about her grandmother, who went to Woodstock and has a flower power poster. (Rev: BL 3/1/03)

1101 Lohans, Alison. *Waiting for the Sun* (K–2). Illus. by Marilyn Mets and Peter Ledwon. 2002, Red Deer $16.95 (0-88995-240-X). After a lot of anticipation, Mollie is disappointed at first by the sight of her new baby brother. (Rev: SLJ 7/02)

1102 Louie, Therese On. *Raymond's Perfect Present* (K–2). Illus. by Suling Wang. 2002, Lee & Low $16.95 (1-58430-055-8). 32pp. A tender story about a boy who can't afford flowers for his sick mother, but instead plants seeds. (Rev: BL 10/15/02; HBG 3/03; SLJ 11/02)

1103 McCaughrean, Geraldine. *My Grandmother's Clock* (K–3). Illus. by Stephen Lambert. 2002, Clarion $15.00 (0-618-21695-2). 32pp. A grandmother explains to her young granddaughter how she tells time: by relying on life's rhythms, rather than on clocks. (Rev: BL 9/15/02; HB 1–2/03; HBG 3/03; SLJ 9/02)

1104 McCully, Emily Arnold. *The Orphan Singer* (PS–3). Illus. 2001, Scholastic $16.95 (0-439-19274-9). 32pp. A poor family leaves a talented daughter at an orphanage where she will receive the best vocal training possible. (Rev: BCCB 2/02; BL 11/15/01; HB 9–10/01; HBG 3/02; SLJ 11/01*)

1105 Maloney, Peter, and Felicia Zekauskas. *His Mother's Nose* (K–3). Illus. 2001, Dial $15.99 (0-8037-2545-0). 40pp. Percival learns that he is special even if many of his traits and features were inherited from family members. (Rev: BL 9/1/01; HBG 3/02; SLJ 10/01)

1106 Masurel, Claire. *Two Homes* (PS–K). Illus. by Kady M. Denton. 2001, Candlewick $14.99 (0-7636-0511-5). 40pp. Young Alex takes a matter-of-fact attitude to his two homes, one with his mother, the other with his father. (Rev: BL 6/1–15/01; HBG 10/01; SLJ 8/01)

1107 Melmed, Laura Krauss. *A Hug Goes Around* (PS–k). Illus. by Betsy Lewin. 2002, HarperCollins LB $15.89 (0-688-14681-8). 32pp. In spite of minor disasters, a family muddles through because they can comfort each other with hugs. (Rev: BL 6/1–15/02)

1108 Michels-Gualtieri, Akaela S. *I Was Born to Be a Sister* (PS–2). Illus. by Marcy Ramsey. 2001, Platypus $16.95 (1-930775-03-2). 32pp. A sixth-grader discovers her new baby brother is not as much fun as she initially thought. (Rev: BL 12/1/01; SLJ 11/01)

1109 Michelson, Rich. *Too Young for Yiddish* (K–4). Illus. by Neil Waldman. 2002, Charlesbridge $15.95 (0-88106-118-2). 32pp. A young boy wants his grandfather to teach him the Yiddish language in this poignant tale that is part history, part family story. (Rev: BL 3/1/02; HBG 10/02; SLJ 3/02)

1110 Moon, Nicola. *My Most Favorite Thing* (PS–1). Illus. by Carol Thompson. 2001, Dutton $15.99 (0-525-46780-7). 32pp. Katie lends her beloved stuffed rabbit to her grandfather while his dog spends the night at the veterinarian's. (Rev: BL 9/1/01; HBG 3/02; SLJ 11/01)

1111 Okimoto, Jean Davies, and Elaine M. Aoki. *The White Swan Express: A Story About Adoption* (K–3). Illus. by Meilo So. 2002, Clarion $16.00 (0-618-16453-7). 32pp. This story alternates between adoptive parents in North America and the children awaiting adoption in China, with information on the legalities of adopting children and on China's policies on childbirth. (Rev: BL 11/1/02; HBG 3/03; SLJ 2/03)

1112 Oram, Hiawyn. *Let's Do That Again!* (PS–K). Illus. by Sam Williams. 2003, Dutton $15.99 (0-525-46997-4). 32pp. Little Brownmouse thinks it's hysterically funny when she sneaks up behind Mom and shouts "boo," especially when Mom "boos" back. (Rev: BL 1/1–15/03; SLJ 3/03)

1113 Palatini, Margie. *Goldie Is Mad* (PS–K). Illus. by author. 2001, Hyperion LB $15.49 (0-7868-2490-5). Goldie doesn't like her baby brother at all, but when she imagines him gone she finds she might miss him. (Rev: HBG 3/02; SLJ 7/01)

1114 Paradis, Susan. *My Mommy* (PS–1). Illus. 2002, Front Street $15.95 (1-886910-73-1). 32pp. Radiant, cheery illustrations that feature sly peeks at wild animals accompany a little girl's simple list of the reasons she loves her mother. (Rev: BL 1/1–15/03; HBG 3/03; SLJ 1/03)

1115 Patrick, Jean L. S. *If I Had a Snowplow* (PS–1). Illus. by Karen M. Dugan. 2001, Boyds Mills $14.95 (1-56397-746-X). A loving boy tells his mother what he would do for her if he had various objects (a truck, a tractor, a bulldozer). (Rev: HBG 3/02; SLJ 12/01)

1116 Perkins, Lynne Rae. *The Broken Cat* (PS–2). Illus. 2002, Greenwillow LB $15.89 (0-06-029264-4). 32pp. While Frank waits with his injured cat at the vet's office, his mother, aunt, and grandmother distract him with a story about the time his mother broke her arm. (Rev: BL 3/15/02; HB 5–6/02*; HBG 10/02; SLJ 6/02)

1117 Plourde, Lynn. *Thank You, Grandpa* (K–3). Illus. by Jason Cockcroft. 2003, Dutton $15.99 (0-525-46992-3). 32pp. When a girl's grandfather dies, she uses what she learned on their nature walks together to say good-bye. (Rev: BL 2/15/03)

1118 Polacco, Patricia. *When Lightning Comes in a Jar* (2–4). Illus. 2002, Putnam $16.99 (0-399-23164-1). 40pp. An autobiographical remembrance of fun, games, and traditions at family reunions. (Rev: BL 8/02; HBG 10/02; SLJ 6/02)

1119 Prigger, Mary Skillings. *Aunt Minnie and the Twister* (PS–2). Illus. by Betsy Lewin. 2002, Clarion $15.00 (0-618-11136-0). 32pp. Aunt Minnie and her nine nieces and nephews run to the root cellar to escape a twister that turns their house completely around. (Rev: BL 2/15/02; HB 5–6/02; HBG 10/02; SLJ 4/02)

1120 Pringle, Laurence. *Bear Hug* (K–3). Illus. by Kate S. Palmer. 2003, Boyds Mills $15.95 (1-56397-876-8). Jesse and Becky go camping with Dad and really hope to see a bear. (Rev: SLJ 2/03)

1121 Rau, Dana Meachen. *Yahoo for You* (K–1). Illus. by Cary Pilo. 2002, Compass Point LB $18.60 (0-7365-0177-6). 32pp. Grandma likes to engage in all sorts of activities with her cute granddaughter but draws the line at going on a roller coaster. (Rev: BL 5/1/02)

1122 Ray, Deborah Kogan. *Lily's Garden* (K–2). Illus. 2002, Millbrook LB $21.90 (0-7613-2653-7). 32pp. Lily's grandparents have moved to California, and as the seasons pass in Maine Lily thinks about them while working in her garden. (Rev: BL 10/1/02; HBG 3/03; SLJ 11/02)

1123 Root, Phyllis. *The Name Quilt* (PS–1). Illus. by Margot Apple. 2003, Farrar $16.00 (0-374-35484-7). 32pp. When Sadie stays at Grandma's, she sleeps under a patchwork quilt embroidered with names and listens to Grandma's stories about these relatives. (Rev: BL 3/15/03)

1124 Rosenberg, Liz. *We Wanted You* (PS–3). Illus. by Peter Catalanotto. 2002, Millbrook LB $23.90 (0-7613-2661-8). An adopted son and his parents look back fondly at their anticipation of his arrival and his early life. (Rev: HBG 10/02; SLJ 4/02)

1125 Rossiter, Nan Parson. *Sugar on Snow* (PS–2). Illus. by author. 2003, Dutton $15.99 (0-525-46910-9). Two boys help their parents collecting sap and making maple syrup on their Vermont farm. (Rev: SLJ 12/02)

1126 Rouss, Sylvia. *My Baby Brother* (K–2). Illus. by Liz Goulet Dubois. 2002, Jonathan David $14.95 (0-8246-0445-8). 24pp. Sarah, a young Jewish girl, initially resists the description of her new baby brother as a "miracle." (Rev: BL 10/1/02)

1127 Russo, Marisabina. *Come Back, Hannah!* (PS). Illus. 2001, HarperCollins LB $15.89 (0-688-17384-5). 32pp. Hannah is an excellent crawler and exhausts her mother as she scoots around the house getting into everything. (Rev: BL 8/01; HBG 10/01; SLJ 7/01)

1128 Santucci, Barbara. *Anna's Corn* (PS–3). Illus. by Lloyd Bloom. 2002, Eerdmans $16.00 (0-8028-5119-3). 32pp. Anna misses her grandfather after his death, especially the times they spent walking together in the cornfield. (Rev: BL 10/1/02; HBG 3/03; SLJ 2/03)

1129 Singer, Marilyn. *Didi and Daddy on the Promenade* (PS–K). Illus. by Marie-Louise Gay. 2001, Clarion $14.00 (0-618-04640-2). 32pp. Didi and her father love to walk and play on Sunday mornings on the Brooklyn Heights Promenade that overlooks the Manhattan skyline. (Rev: BCCB 4/01; BL 4/1/01; HBG 10/01; SLJ 5/01)

1130 Smith, Will. *Just the Two of Us* (PS–1). Illus. by Kadir Nelson. 2001, Scholastic $16.95 (0-439-

08792-9). 32pp. Smith uses his song "Just the Two of Us" as the foundation for this celebration of a father's love for his son. (Rev: BL 7/01; HBG 10/01; SLJ 6/01)

1131 Smothers, Ethel Footman. *Auntee Edna* (K–3). Illus. by Wil Clay. 2001, Eerdmans $16.00 (0-8028-5154-1). Tokee doesn't look forward to staying the night with elderly Auntee Edna but has a wonderful time. (Rev: HBG 10/01; SLJ 8/01)

1132 Soto, Gary. *If the Shoe Fits* (PS–3). Illus. by Terry Widener. 2002, Putnam $15.99 (0-399-23420-9). 32pp. Rigo, who is sick of wearing hand-me-downs, gets a new pair of loafers for his ninth birthday. (Rev: BCCB 3/02; BL 1/1–15/02; HB 7–8/02; HBG 10/02; SLJ 1/02)

1133 Stojic, Manya. *Wet Pebbles Under Our Feet* (PS). Illus. 2002, Knopf $15.95 (0-375-81519-8). 32pp. Striking artwork complements this simple story of a girl visiting her grandparents on the island where they live. (Rev: BL 2/15/02; SLJ 3/02)

1134 Thomas, Joyce Carol. *Joy* (PS–K). Illus. by Pamela Johnson. 2001, Hyperion $6.99 (0-7868-0750-4). An African American woman tells her child of her love in this charming board book. (Rev: SLJ 2/02)

1135 Van Leeuwen, Jean. *Sorry* (K–3). Illus. by Brad Sneed. 2001, Penguin Putnam $15.99 (0-8037-2261-3). 32pp. A row over oatmeal leads to a life-long rift between two neighboring brothers and their descendants until their great-grandchildren discover a very useful word. (Rev: BCCB 9/01; BL 6/1–15/01; HBG 10/01; SLJ 5/01)

1136 Van Leeuwen, Jean. *"Wait for Me!" Said Maggie McGee* (PS–2). Illus. by Jacqueline Rogers. 2001, Penguin Putnam $16.99 (0-8037-2357-1). 32pp. Maggie is the youngest of eight and longs to be included in her older siblings' activities. (Rev: BL 5/15/01; HBG 10/01; SLJ 7/01)

1137 Velasquez, Eric. *Grandma's Records* (K–3). Illus. 2001, Walker LB $17.85 (0-8027-8761-4). 32pp. A young boy enjoys summers full of Latin music with his grandmother in Spanish Harlem in this novel based on the author's own memories. (Rev: BL 5/15/01; HBG 10/01; SLJ 9/01)

1138 Vestergaard, Hope. *Driving Daddy* (PS–1). Illus. by Thierry Courtin. 2003, Dutton $6.99 (0-525-47032-8). 24pp. A small-format book in which a little boy gets to ride on his father's shoulders. (Rev: BL 3/1/03; SLJ 3/03)

1139 Vestergaard, Hope. *Wake Up, Mama!* (PS–1). Illus. by Thierry Courtin. 2003, Dutton $6.99 (0-525-47030-1). 24pp. A young child enjoys waking his mother in this small-format book. (Rev: BL 3/1/03; SLJ 3/03)

1140 Vigil-Pinon, Evangelina. *Marina's Muumuu / El Muumuu de Marina* (2–5). Illus. by Pablo Torrecilla. 2001, Arte Publico $14.95 (1-55885-350-2). 32pp. A bilingual story about a girl named Marina who dreams of wearing a colorful, tropical muumuu like those from her grandmother's home. (Rev: BL 1/1–15/02; SLJ 1/02)

1141 Waldherr, Kris. *Harvest* (PS–1). Illus. 2001, Walker LB $16.85 (0-8027-8793-2). 32pp. A girl and her mother harvest and prepare fruits and vegetables from the garden in order to prepare for winter in this simple yet memorable autumn story. (Rev: BL 11/15/01; HBG 3/02; SLJ 11/01)

1142 Whelan, Gloria. *Jam and Jelly by Holly and Nelly* (K–2). Illus. by Gijsbert van Frankenhuyzen. 2002, Sleeping Bear $17.95 (1-58536-109-7). 48pp. A captivating story of a mother's determination to buy her daughter a coat so she can go to school in the cold. (Rev: BL 12/15/02; SLJ 1/03)

1143 Woodson, Jacqueline. *Visiting Day* (K–2). Illus. by James E. Ransome. 2002, Scholastic $15.95 (0-590-40005-3). 32pp. This is a gentle family story of a little African American girl's visit to her father in prison. (Rev: BCCB 12/02; BL 11/1/02; HB 11–12/02; HBG 3/03; SLJ 9/02)

1144 Ziefert, Harriet. *31 Uses for a Mom* (PS–K). Illus. by Rebecca Doughty. 2003, Putnam $12.99 (0-399-23862-X). 32pp. Moms turn out to be fairly useful things in this list that covers a wide range of attributes. (Rev: BL 1/1–15/03; SLJ 3/03)

1145 Zisk, Mary. *The Best Single Mom in the World: How I Was Adopted* (PS–K). Illus. by author. 2001, Albert Whitman LB $14.95 (0-8075-0666-4). A little girl and her mother tell the tale of her adoption across the sea. (Rev: HBG 3/02; SLJ 1/02)

1146 Zolotow, Charlotte. *The Poodle Who Barked at the Wind* (PS–1). Illus. by Valerie Coursen. 2002, Holt $16.95 (0-8050-6306-4). 32pp. Updated illustrations grace this new edition of the charming book about a father who comes to understand why the family poodle barks. (Rev: BL 1/1–15/03; HBG 3/03; SLJ 11/02)

FRIENDSHIP STORIES

1147 Appelt, Kathi. *Bubba and Beau, Best Friends* (PS–K). Illus. by Arthur Howard. 2002, Harcourt $16.00 (0-15-202060-8). 32pp. Bubba, a little boy, and Beau, his puppy, are unhappy when the smelly blanket they love is washed and now smells of soap. (Rev: BCCB 4/02; BL 4/1/02; HBG 10/02; SLJ 7/02)

1148 Beaumont, Karen. *Being Friends* (PS–2). Illus. by Joy Allen. 2002, Dial $15.99 (0-8037-2529-9). 32pp. Two girls, best friends despite their different personalities, have fun together in this rhyming picture book. (Rev: BL 9/15/02; HBG 10/02; SLJ 7/02)

1149 Blake, Quentin. *Fantastic Daisy Artichoke* (PS–1). Illus. by author. 2001, Red Fox paper $11.00 (0-09-940006-5). Rhythmic text and bright, lively drawings tell the story of the fun two children had when they met their friend Daisy. (Rev: SLJ 10/01)

1150 Carlson, Nancy. *My Best Friend Moved Away* (PS–K). Illus. 2001, Viking $15.99 (0-670-89498-2). 32pp. A little girl is sad as she remembers the good times she shared with the girl next door. (Rev: BL 4/1/01; HBG 10/01; SLJ 6/01)

1151 Carter, Anne Laurel. *Circus Play* (K–2). Illus. by Joanne Fitzgerald. 2002, Orca $16.95 (1-55143-225-0). 32pp. A young boy whose mom is a trapeze artist tries to dampen the other children's dreams about circus life, but eventually realizes it's more fun to join in. (Rev: BL 12/1/02; HBG 3/03)

1152 Edwards, Nancy. *Glenna's Seeds* (K–2). Illus. by Sarah K. Hoctor. 2001, Child & Family $9.95 (0-87868-788-2). Glenna gives away a packet of marigold seeds and thereby starts off a chain of kind events that involves all the people on the block. (Rev: SLJ 4/01)

1153 Havill, Juanita. *Brianna, Jamaica, and the Dance of Spring* (PS–3). Illus. by Anne S. O'Brien. 2002, Houghton $16.00 (0-618-07700-6). 32pp. Asian American Brianna longs to play the role of butterfly in the dance recital. (Rev: BL 3/15/02; HBG 10/02; SLJ 4/02)

1154 Jahn-Clough, Lisa. *Alicia's Best Friends* (PS–1). Illus. 2003, Houghton $15.00 (0-618-23951-0). 32pp. Alicia must find a solution when her four close friends insist she choose one as her best friend. (Rev: BL 3/15/03; SLJ 3/03)

1155 Jahn-Clough, Lisa. *Simon and Molly Plus Hester* (PS–K). Illus. 2001, Houghton $15.00 (0-618-08220-4). 32pp. The relationship between two best friends changes when a third playmate joins them. (Rev: BL 9/1/01; HBG 3/02; SLJ 9/01)

1156 Lachtman, Ofelia Dumas. *Tina and the Scarecrow Skins / Tina y las Pieles de Espantapajaros* (2–5). 2002, Arte Publico $14.95 (1-55885-373-1). 32pp. A story, told in both English and Spanish, of Tina and her friend Little Bell, who dresses oddly and makes up strange words, but ends up saving the day (and the tamales). (Rev: BL 2/15/03; SLJ 3/03)

1157 London, Jonathan. *Where the Big Fish Are* (K–3). Illus. by Adam Gustavson. 2001, Candlewick $16.99 (0-7636-0922-6). 40pp. Two boys build a raft so that they can catch big fish out at sea. (Rev: BL 7/01; HBG 10/01; SLJ 8/01)

1158 McDonald, Megan. *Reptiles Are My Life* (K–2). Illus. by Paul Johnson. 2001, Scholastic $15.95 (0-439-29306-5). 32pp. Emily's arrival spoils the friendship between Maggie and Amanda until Amanda defends the other two and the three become inseparable. (Rev: HBG 3/02; SLJ 8/01)

1159 Okimoto, Jean Davies. *Dear Ichiro* (K–2). Illus. by Doug Keith. 2002, Kumagai $16.95 (1-57061-373-7). 32pp. Grampa's comments about the end of hostile feelings between Americans and Japanese make Henry reconsider his recent rupture with his friend Oliver. (Rev: BL 11/15/02; HBG 3/03; SLJ 3/03)

1160 Reynolds, Marilynn. *A Present for Mrs. Kazinski* (PS–3). Illus. by Lynn Smith-Ary. 2001, Orca $15.95 (1-55143-196-3). 32pp. Frank is thrilled that Mrs. Kazinski likes the gift he chooses for her 80th birthday. (Rev: BL 10/15/01; HBG 3/02)

1161 Rickert, Janet Elizabeth. *Russ and the Almost Perfect Day* (K–3). Photos by Pete McGahan. 2001, Woodbine $14.95 (1-890627-18-6). Russ, who has Down syndrome, takes pleasure in helping a classmate in distress. (Rev: HBG 10/01; SLJ 5/01)

1162 Robberecht, Thierry. *Stolen Smile* (PS–2). Illus. by Philippe Goossens. 2002, Doubleday LB $16.99 (0-385-90850-4). Sophie gets her smile back

58

when she confronts the boy who took it away. (Rev: HBG 3/03; SLJ 1/03)

1163 Shriver, Maria. *What's Wrong with Timmy?* (K–3). Illus. by Sandra Spieled. 2001, Little, Brown $14.95 (0-316-23337-4). 48pp. Eight-year-old Kate makes friends with Timmy, a boy who is mentally retarded, and wonders what it feels like to be Timmy. (Rev: BL 10/1/01; HBG 3/02; SLJ 1/02)

1164 Wallace, Ian. *The Naked Lady* (K–3). Illus. 2002, Millbrook LB $23.90 (0-7613-2660-X). 40pp. A young boy is initially shocked by a statue of a naked lady but through a friendship with the sculptor learns to appreciate it and develops his own artistic ambitions. (Rev: BL 12/1/02; HBG 3/03; SLJ 11/02)

1165 Ziefert, Harriet. *39 Uses for a Friend* (PS–3). Illus. by Rebecca Doughty. 2001, Putnam $11.99 (0-399-23616-3). 32pp. Clever pictures humorously illustrate the roles friends can play — alarm clock, napkin, hairdresser, and so on. (Rev: BL 12/1/01; HBG 3/02; SLJ 12/01)

HUMOROUS STORIES

1166 Addy, Sharon Hart. *When Wishes Were Horses* (PS–3). Illus. by Brad Sneed. 2002, Houghton $15.00 (0-618-13166-3). 32pp. Zeb's wishes for horses spiral out of control as each wish is granted, causing great crowding and confusion in an Old West town. (Rev: BL 12/1/02; SLJ 11/02)

1167 Ahlberg, Allan. *The Adventures of Bert* (PS–2). Illus. by Raymond Briggs. 2001, Farrar $16.00 (0-374-30092-5). 32pp. Five short tales about a silly man named Bert, who always seems to get into trouble. (Rev: BCCB 9/01; BL 9/1/01; HB 7–8/01*; HBG 3/02; SLJ 8/01)

1168 Ahlberg, Allan. *A Bit More Bert* (PS–2). Illus. by Raymond Briggs. 2002, Farrar $16.00 (0-374-32489-1). 32pp. The appealing Bert goes about daily life, meets other Berts, looks for his lost dog Bert, and generally bumbles around in a friendly, funny way. (Rev: BCCB 11/02; BL 11/1/02; HB 9–10/02*; HBG 3/03; SLJ 11/02)

1169 Auch, Mary Jane. *The Princess and the Pizza* (K–2). Illus. by Mary Jane Auch and Herm Auch. 2002, Holiday $16.95 (0-8234-1683-6). In a fractured fairy tale, Paulina easily wins the contest for the prince's hand, but prefers instead to open a Pizza Palace. (Rev: BCCB 3/02; HBG 10/02; SLJ 5/02)

1170 Bartram, Simon. *Man on the Moon: A Day in the Life of Bob* (1–3). Illus. by author. 2002, Candlewick $16.99 (0-7636-1897-7). Bob is custodian of the moon, and his daily tasks include clearing litter, entertaining tourists, and selling souvenirs. (Rev: HBG 3/03; SLJ 10/02)

1171 Broadley, Leo. *Pedro the Brave* (PS–2). Illus. by Holly Swain. 2002, ME Media $14.95 (1-58925-024-9). 32pp. Clever Pedro outwits the wolf that plans to eat him and his animal friends by feeding the wolf Pedro's special (fiery) hot sauce. (Rev: BCCB 2/03; BL 12/1/02)

1172 Brown, Margaret Wise. *The Dirty Little Boy* (K–2). Illus. by Steven Salerno. 2001, Winslow $16.95 (1-890817-52-X). First published in 1939 under a different title, this is the story of a little boy who tries to get clean by imitating animals' baths. (Rev: HBG 10/01; SLJ 5/01)

1173 Brumbeau, Jeff. *Miss Hunnicutt's Hat* (K–3). Illus. by Gail de Marcken. 2003, Scholastic $16.95 (0-439-31895-5). 48pp. Miss Hunnicutt strongly defends her right to wear a chicken on her hat for the visit of the queen. (Rev: BL 1/1–15/03; SLJ 3/03)

1174 Calmenson, Stephanie. *The Frog Principal* (PS–2). Illus. by Denise Brunkus. 2001, Scholastic $15.95 (0-590-37070-7). 32pp. A magician turns a school principal into a frog in this humorous story with colorful illustrations. (Rev: BL 9/15/01; HBG 3/02; SLJ 10/01)

1175 Cates, Karin. *A Far-Fetched Story* (PS–2). Illus. by Nancy Carpenter. 2002, HarperCollins LB $15.89 (0-688-15939-7). 32pp. All the members of Grandmother's family, including the baby, have different far-fetched reasons why they came home with no firewood in this newfangled folktale. (Rev: BL 2/15/02; HBG 10/02; SLJ 1/02)

1176 Child, Lauren. *I Am Not Sleepy and I Will Not Go to Bed* (PS–3). Illus. 2001, Candlewick $16.99 (0-7636-1570-6). 32pp. Charlie tries to get his imaginative little sister to go to bed. (Rev: BL 8/01; HBG 3/02; SLJ 9/01)

1177 Child, Lauren. *What Planet Are You From, Clarice Bean?* (K–3). Illus. 2002, Candlewick $16.99 (0-7636-1696-6). 32pp. The delightful Clarice Bean joins her family in supporting her brother in his efforts to save a neighborhood tree. (Rev: BCCB 3/02; BL 4/15/02; HBG 10/02; SLJ 3/02*)

1178 Collins, Ross. *Alvie Eats Soup* (PS–2). Illus. 2002, Scholastic $15.95 (0-439-27260-2). 32pp. Alvie will only eat soup, and his parents despair when his gourmet chef grandmother arrives for a visit. (Rev: BL 11/1/02; HBG 3/03; SLJ 10/02)

1179 Cuyler, Margery. *Skeleton Hiccups* (2–4). Illus. by S. D. Schindler. 2002, Simon & Schuster $14.95 (0-689-84770-X). 32pp. A skeleton tries to rid himself of a bad case of hiccups and is finally scared out of them by looking in the mirror. (Rev: BCCB 9/02; BL 9/15/02; HB 9–10/02; HBG 3/03; SLJ 10/02)

1180 Cuyler, Margery. *That's Good! That's Bad! In the Grand Canyon* (K–3). Illus. by David Catrow. 2002, Holt $16.95 (0-8050-5975-X). 32pp. A boy visiting the Grand Canyon has some "BAD" (but funny) close calls before he catches up with his grandmother. (Rev: BL 5/15/02; HBG 10/02; SLJ 6/02)

1181 DeFelice, Cynthia. *The Real, True Dulcie Campbell* (PS–2). Illus. by R. W. Alley. 2002, Farrar $16.00 (0-374-36220-3). 32pp. Dulcie lives on a farm but fancies herself a princess, switched at birth. (Rev: BCCB 12/02; BL 8/02; HBG 3/03; SLJ 9/02)

1182 Dodds, Dayle Ann. *Pet Wash* (K–2). Illus. by Tor Freeman. 2001, Candlewick $10.99 (0-7636-0989-7). Wally and Gene tackle the task of washing a large variety of animals with aplomb, but then they are asked to clean up a baby. (Rev: HBG 10/02; SLJ 10/01)

1183 Dorros, Arthur. *When the Pigs Took Over* (PS–3). Illus. by Diane Greenseid. 2002, Dutton $15.99 (0-525-42030-4). 32pp. A pair of New Mexican brothers stars in a comic cumulative tale sprinkled with Spanish phrases. (Rev: BL 2/1/02; HBG 10/02; SLJ 2/02)

1184 Dyer, Heather. *Tina and the Penguin* (K–2). Illus. by Mireille Levert. 2002, Kids Can $14.95 (1-55074-947-1). 32pp. Tina fails in her elaborate efforts to keep her penguin secret in this humorous story with funny illustrations. (Rev: BL 1/1–15/03; HBG 3/03; SLJ 11/02)

1185 Feiffer, Jules. *By the Side of the Road* (2–4). 2002, Hyperion $15.95 (0-7868-0908-6). 64pp. A boy becomes so fed up with being bossed around by his dad that he decides to set out on his own. (Rev: BCCB 9/02; BL 6/1–15/02*; HBG 10/02; SLJ 5/02)

1186 Fleming, Candace. *Muncha! Muncha! Muncha!* (PS–2). Illus. by G. Brian Karas. 2002, Simon & Schuster $16.00 (0-689-83152-8). 32pp. Mr. McGreely goes to great lengths to defend his vegetable garden from a group of clever rabbits in this hilarious story. (Rev: BCCB 3/02; BL 1/1–15/02; HBG 10/02; SLJ 2/02*)

1187 French, Vivian. *Oliver's Milk Shake* (PS–1). Illus. by Alison Bartlett. 2001, Scholastic $15.95 (0-531-30304-7). 32pp. Oliver's aunt sees the picky eater drinking orange soda for breakfast and puts Oliver through a busy day of pro-milk orientation before he explains her mistake. (Rev: BL 8/01; HBG 10/01; SLJ 6/01)

1188 Garland, Michael. *The President and Mom's Apple Pie* (PS–1). Illus. 2002, Dutton $15.99 (0-525-46887-0). 32pp. A funny, lively farce about rotund President William Howard Taft's arrival in a small town, and his subsequent search for a pie that is creating a heavenly aroma. (Rev: BCCB 5/02; BL 3/1/02; HBG 10/02; SLJ 6/02)

1189 Geoghegan, Adrienne. *All Your Own Teeth* (K–2). Illus. by Cathy Gale. 2002, Dial $16.99 (0-8037-2655-4). 32pp. Stewart believes his paintings are perfect but his subjects are lacking, so he heads to the jungle in search of the perfect model. (Rev: BL 3/1/02; HBG 10/02; SLJ 4/02)

1190 Gibbons, Faye. *The Day the Picture Man Came* (K–2). Illus. by Sherry Meidell. 2003, Boyds Mills $16.95 (1-56397-161-5). 32pp. The members of the Howard family prepare to have their picture taken by a traveling photographer in this funny story set in the Georgia mountains. (Rev: BL 2/15/03; SLJ 3/03)

1191 Gibbons, Faye. *Emma Jo's Song* (K–3). Illus. by Sherry Meidell. 2001, Boyds Mills $15.95 (1-56397-935-7). 32pp. Emma Jo is the hit of the family reunion when she sings a duet with a howling dog. (Rev: BL 4/1/01; HBG 10/01; SLJ 5/01)

1192 Gill-Brown, Vanessa. *Rufferella* (K–3). Illus. by Mandy Stanley. 2001, Scholastic $12.95 (0-439-25617-8). 32pp. Diamante transforms her dog into Rufferella, who reaches great heights as a singer

until meeting her downfall, a plateful of sausages. (Rev: BL 8/01; HBG 10/01; SLJ 8/01)

1193 Goode, Diane. *Monkey Mo Goes to Sea* (PS–1). Illus. 2002, Scholastic $15.95 (0-439-26681-5). 40pp. Young Bertie and his monkey, Mo, are invited to dine aboard a 1920s luxury liner, where Mo's attempts to "act like a gentleman" have riotous consequences. (Rev: BL 3/15/02*; HB 3–4/02; HBG 10/02; SLJ 3/02)

1194 Graves, Keith. *Loretta: Ace Pinky Scout* (1–2). Illus. 2002, Scholastic $16.95 (0-439-36831-6). 40pp. Loretta discovers that not everyone can be perfect when she fails to earn her marshmallow toasting badge in this bright and silly spoof about scouting. (Rev: BL 10/15/02; HBG 3/03; SLJ 12/02)

1195 Gulbis, Stephen. *Cowgirl Rosie and Her Five Baby Bison* (PS–2). Illus. 2001, Little, Brown $12.95 (0-316-60230-2). 24pp. Cowgirl Rosie sets out to find the villain who stole her five baby bison on the trip into town. (Rev: BL 5/15/01; SLJ 5/01)

1196 Hartman, Bob. *The Wolf Who Cried Boy* (PS–2). Illus. by Tim Raglin. 2002, Putnam $15.99 (0-399-23578-7). 32pp. The cautionary tale is turned inside-out in this humorous story in which a wolf spots a pack of boy scouts. (Rev: BCCB 7–8/02; BL 7/02; HB 5–6/02; HBG 10/02; SLJ 6/02)

1197 Henderson, Kathy. *Baby Knows Best* (PS–1). Illus. by Brita Granstrom. 2002, Little, Brown $15.95 (0-316-60580-8). 32pp. Baby would rather forgo expensive toys for the simpler things in life in this amusing story. (Rev: BL 8/02; HBG 10/02; SLJ 3/02)

1198 Hoberman, Mary Ann. *There Once Was a Man Named Michael Finnegan* (PS–1). Illus. by Nadine Bernard Westcott. 2001, Little, Brown $14.95 (0-316-36301-4). 32pp. This is a wacky collection of simple nonsense verses about poor Michael Finnegan and his dog. (Rev: BCCB 4/01; BL 4/1/01; HBG 10/01; SLJ 5/01)

1199 Jackson, Alison. *The Ballad of Valentine* (K–3). Illus. by Tricia Tusa. 2002, Dutton $16.99 (0-525-46720-3). 32pp. This parody of "My Darling, Clementine" stars a comic Valentine performing everyday tasks in her cabin while an admirer tries and fails to send her expressions of love. (Rev: BCCB 1/03; BL 11/15/02; SLJ 12/02)

1200 Jackson, Ellen. *Scatterbrain Sam* (K–3). Illus. by Matt Faulkner. 2001, Charlesbridge $15.95 (0-88106-394-0). 32pp. In this tall-tale adaptation of a Welsh story, Scatterbrain Sam seeks a cure for his brain and in the process finds true love. (Rev: BL 8/01; HBG 3/02; SLJ 7/01)

1201 Janowitz, Tama. *Hear That?* (PS). Illus. by Tracy Dockray. 2001, North-South LB $15.88 (1-58717-075-2). A boy gives his mother increasingly unlikely explanations for the noises they hear. (Rev: BCCB 4/01; HBG 10/01; SLJ 6/01)

1202 Krosoczka, Jarrett J. *Baghead* (PS–2). Illus. 2002, Knopf $15.95 (0-375-81566-X). 40pp. Confounding the skeptics, Josh succeeds in spending a day with a paper bag over his head, but his reason for doing so remains hidden until the end. (Rev: BL 11/15/02; HBG 3/03; SLJ 10/02)

1203 Ljungkvist, Laura. *Toni's Topsy-Turvy Telephone Day* (K–3). Illus. 2001, Abrams $15.95 (0-8109-4486-3). 32pp. Telephone interference scrambles Toni's potluck invitations and her friends turn up with extra guests instead of food. (Rev: BL 6/1–15/01; HBG 10/01; SLJ 5/01)

1204 McCarthy, Meghan. *George Upside Down* (PS–2). Illus. 2003, Viking $15.99 (0-670-03608-0). 40pp. George is cured of his need to be upside down when he sees the school principal upside down, too. (Rev: BL 2/15/03; SLJ 3/03)

1205 Manning, Maurie J. *The Aunts Go Marching* (PS–1). Illus. 2003, Boyds Mills $15.95 (1-59078-026-4). 32pp. Aunts (rather than the usual ants) march to town in this version of the familiar children's song. (Rev: BL 2/1/03)

1206 Martin, Bill, Jr., and Michael Sampson. *Little Granny Quarterback* (K–3). Illus. by Michael Chesworth. 2001, Boyds Mills $15.95 (1-56397-930-6). A zany story in which Granny Whiteoak, a star football player in her day, saves her team from defeat. (Rev: HBG 3/02; SLJ 12/01)

1207 Munsch, Robert. *More Pies!* (PS–2). Illus. by Michael Martchenko. 2002, Scholastic $13.95 (0-439-18773-7). 26pp. A very hungry Samuel isn't satisfied with his mother's huge breakfast and enters a pie-eating contest, only to arrive home victorious and find that pies are on the menu for lunch. (Rev: BCCB 1/03; HBG 3/03; SLJ 3/03)

1208 Munsch, Robert. *Up, Up, Down* (PS–3). Illus. by Michael Martchenko. 2001, Scholastic $11.95 (0-439-18770-2). 28pp. Although her parents tell her not to, Anna persists in climbing on things. (Rev: HBG 3/02; SLJ 8/01)

1209 Neitzel, Shirley. *Our Class Took a Trip to the Zoo* (PS–2). Illus. by Nancy Winslow Parker. 2002, HarperCollins LB $15.89 (0-688-15544-8). 32pp. A humorous rebus story about a boy's mishaps on a class trip to the zoo. (Rev: BL 3/15/02; HBG 10/02; SLJ 6/02)

1210 Nolen, Jerdine. *Plantzilla* (1–3). Illus. by David Catrow. 2002, Harcourt $16.00 (0-15-202412-3). 32pp. Third-grader Mortimer takes charge of the classroom plant, nicknamed Plantzilla, for the summer, and peculiar things begin to happen. (Rev: BCCB 11/02; BL 10/15/02; HBG 3/03; SLJ 9/02)

1211 Palatini, Margie. *Tub-Boo-Boo* (PS–1). Illus. by Glin Dibley. 2001, Simon & Schuster $16.00 (0-689-82394-0). 40pp. A cumulative tale in which Lucy's younger brother Henry gets his toe stuck in a tap and successive rescuers suffer much the same fate, until Lucy solves the problem. (Rev: BCCB 10/01; BL 9/1/01; HBG 10/02; SLJ 10/01)

1212 Parkinson, Curtis. *Emily's Eighteen Aunts* (PS–2). Illus. by Andrea Wayne von Koniglsow. 2003, Fitzhenry & Whiteside $15.95 (0-7737-3336-1). 32pp. Feeling neglected with a new baby in the house, Emily advertises for an aunt and ends up with 18. (Rev: BL 2/15/03)

1213 Ransom, Jeanie Franz. *Grandma U* (K–2). Illus. by Lucy Corvino. 2002, Peachtree $15.95 (1-56145-214-9). Molly McCool goes to Grandma University to prepare for an impending arrival in this entertaining tale. (Rev: HBG 3/03; SLJ 12/02)

1214 Reiss, Mike. *The Great Show-and-Tell Disaster* (1–4). Illus. by Mike Cressy. 2001, Price Stern Sloan $13.99 (0-8431-7680-6). All kinds of words are turned into anagrams with unfortunate consequences in this humorous, oversized book. (Rev: HBG 3/02; SLJ 1/02)

1215 Robinson, Bruce. *The Obvious Elephant* (PS–2). Illus. by Sophie Windham. 2002, Bloomsbury $15.95 (1-58234-769-7). 32pp. Townspeople are mystified by the appearance of an elephant, unsure of what it is or does, until a small boy sets them straight. (Rev: BL 9/15/02; SLJ 8/02)

1216 Root, Phyllis. *Rattletrap Car* (PS–K). Illus. by Jill Barton. 2001, Candlewick $15.99 (0-7636-0919-6). 32pp. A hilarious picture book in which a family uses ingenious means to repair their old car, such as using a beach ball for a tire. (Rev: BL 4/1/01; HBG 10/01; SLJ 6/01)

1217 Sage, James. *Farmer Smart's Fat Cat* (PS–2). Illus. by Russell Ayto. 2002, Chronicle $14.95 (0-8118-3502-2). 32pp. When Farmer Boast, Farmer Bluster, and Farmer Smart face a mouse problem, the first two come up with inventive but ineffective strategies, while Farmer Smart quietly gets a cat. (Rev: BL 7/02; HBG 10/02; SLJ 7/02)

1218 SanAngelo, Ryan. *Spaghetti Eddie* (PS–2). Illus. by Jackie Urbanovic. 2002, Boyds Mills $15.95 (1-56397-974-8). 32pp. Eddie uses his favorite food — spaghetti — to help a neighbor with broken shoelaces, to fashion a fishing net, and even to stop a robbery. (Rev: BL 8/02; HBG 3/03; SLJ 9/02)

1219 Sayre, April Pulley. *Noodle Man: The Pasta Superhero* (K–3). Illus. by Stephen Costanza. 2002, Scholastic $16.95 (0-439-29307-3). 40pp. Al Dente saves his family's business when the pasta machine he invents helps him perform heroic feats all over town in this pun-filled tale. (Rev: BL 2/15/02; HBG 10/02; SLJ 3/02)

1220 Schnetzler, Pattie. *Widdermaker* (K–4). Illus. by Rick Sealock. 2002, Carolrhoda LB $15.95 (0-87614-647-7). On their way to capture a pesky longhorn called the Widdermaker, Cowpoke Pete and his steed Desert Rose create the Painted Desert and Monument Valley in this zany tall tale. (Rev: HBG 3/03; SLJ 11/02)

1221 Scieszka, Jon. *Baloney (Henry P.)* (1–4). Illus. by Lane Smith. 2001, Viking $15.99 (0-670-89248-3). 32pp. A small green alien comes up with a humdinger of an excuse for being late to school in this story full of humor. (Rev: BCCB 5/01; BL 5/15/01*; HB 5–6/01; HBG 10/01; SLJ 5/01)

1222 Shannon, David. *David Gets in Trouble* (PS–1). Illus. 2002, Scholastic $15.95 (0-439-05022-7). 32pp. David of *No, David* (1998) and *David Goes to School* (1999) denies any responsibility for the trouble he causes — until bedtime, when he finally apologizes to Mom. (Rev: BL 9/15/02; HB 1–2/03; HBG 3/03; SLJ 9/02*)

1223 Sharratt, Nick. *Shark in the Park!* (PS–1). Illus. 2002, Random $14.95 (0-385-75008-0). 24pp. A boy peering through his telescope at the park thinks he sees sharks everywhere, but each turn of the page shows readers the real object — a black cat's ear or a bird's wing. (Rev: BL 9/1/02; HBG 3/03; SLJ 12/02)

1224 Steig, William. *Potch and Polly* (1–3). Illus. by Jon Agee. 2002, Farrar $16.00 (0-374-36090-1). 32pp. Potch, born under a happy angel, falls in love with Polly Pumpernickel, but a series of unfortunate incidents mar the romance, and the happy angel must intervene to help the lovers unite in this charmingly illustrated book. (Rev: BL 9/1/02; HBG 3/03; SLJ 8/02*)

1225 Thompson, Kay. *Eloise Takes a Bawth* (PS–3). Illus. by Hilary Knight. 2002, Simon & Schuster $17.95 (0-689-84288-0). 80pp. The effervescent Eloise ignores Nanny's warnings about her "bawth" and the resulting flood succeeds in making more realistic the Venetian Masked Ball taking place below. (Rev: BL 12/1/02; HB 1–2/03; HBG 3/03; SLJ 12/02)

1226 Wallace, Ian. *The True Story of Trapper Jack's Left Big Toe* (1–3). Illus. 2002, Millbrook LB $24.90 (0-7613-2405-4). 40pp. In this wild romp set in the Yukon, Josh sets out to find the amputated toe of Trapper Jack that is supposedly preserved in an old tobacco tin. (Rev: BCCB 7–8/02; BL 6/1–15/02; HB 5–6/02; HBG 10/02; SLJ 4/02)

1227 Weeks, Sarah. *Oh My Gosh, Mrs McNosh!* (PS–1). Illus. by Nadine Bernard Westcott. 2002, HarperCollins LB $15.89 (0-06-008858-3). 32pp. Mrs. McNosh suffers a series of misadventures when her dog George breaks free from his leash and she chases him through town. (Rev: BCCB 5/02; BL 5/1/02; HBG 10/02; SLJ 6/02)

1228 Willis, Jeanne. *I Want to Be a Cowgirl* (PS–2). Illus. by Tony Ross. 2002, Holt $14.95 (0-8050-6997-6). 24pp. A city girl dreams of forsaking her dolls and tea parties for life as a cowgirl. (Rev: BL 3/15/02; HBG 10/02; SLJ 7/02)

1229 Winters, Kay. *But Mom, Everybody Else Does* (PS–K). Illus. by Doug Cushman. 2002, Dutton $14.99 (0-525-46903-6). 32pp. Typical parent-child conflicts come alive in humorous, over-the-top text and illustrations. (Rev: BL 12/15/02; HBG 3/03; SLJ 9/02)

1230 Wright, Catherine. *Steamboat Annie and the Thousand-Pound Catfish* (PS–3). Illus. by Howard Fine. 2001, Putnam $15.99 (0-399-23331-8). 32pp. Annie, the mayor of a music-loving town plagued by a mean catfish, sets out to rid her citizens of this pest. (Rev: BCCB 9/01; BL 7/01; HBG 3/02; SLJ 10/01)

NATURE AND SCIENCE

1231 Asch, Frank. *Like a Windy Day* (K–2). Illus. by Frank Asch and Devin Asch. 2002, Harcourt $15.00 (0-15-216376-X). 32pp. A little girl thinks about all the neat things the wind can do and imag-

ines herself playing with the personified wind that floats overhead. (Rev: BL 10/1/02; HBG 3/03; SLJ 10/02)

1232 Baillie, Marilyn. *Nose to Toes* (PS–1). Illus. by Marisol Sarrazin. 2001, Boyds Mills $15.95 (1-56397-319-7). Bright, clean illustrations and simple text show children exploring their similarities to different animals. (Rev: HBG 3/02; SLJ 10/01)

1233 Banks, Kate. *Gift from the Sea* (PS–3). Illus. by Georg Hallensleben. 2001, Farrar $16.00 (0-374-32566-9). 40pp. This book traces the past of an ancient rock that a boy finds on the beach. (Rev: BL 4/15/01; HB 5–6/01; HBG 10/01; SLJ 6/01)

1234 Barack, Marcy. *Season Song* (PS). Illus. by Thierry Courtin. 2002, HarperFestival $9.95 (0-694-01567-9). 24pp. Each of the seasons is celebrated in this board book in lilting prose and delightful illustrations. (Rev: BL 6/1–15/02; HBG 10/02; SLJ 6/02)

1235 Bunting, Eve. *Anna's Table* (K–2). Illus. by Taia Morley. 2003, NorthWord $15.95 (1-55971-841-2). 32pp. Anna collects treasures that she finds — such as mouse bones, dead butterflies — and keeps them on her nature table. (Rev: BL 3/15/03)

1236 Carlstrom, Nancy White. *What Does the Sky Say?* (K–2). Illus. by Tim Ladwig. 2001, Eerdmans $17.00 (0-8028-5208-4). 32pp. A poetic celebration of the sky and all its changing features. (Rev: BCCB 7–8/01; BL 7/01; HBG 10/01; SLJ 12/01)

1237 Carr, Jan. *Dappled Apples* (PS–1). Illus. by Dorothy Donohue. 2001, Holiday $15.95 (0-8234-1583-X). 32pp. Cut-paper collages and rhyming text celebrate autumn as three children and a dog enjoy themselves. (Rev: BL 10/1/01; HBG 3/02; SLJ 9/01)

1238 Carr, Jan. *Splish, Splash, Spring* (PS–1). Illus. by Dorothy Donohue. 2001, Holiday $15.95 (0-8234-1578-3). 32pp. It is spring and young playmates and a dog enjoy all its pleasures — playing in the rain, digging for worms, and flying kites. (Rev: BL 4/1/01; HBG 10/01; SLJ 5/01)

1239 Dixon, Ann. *Winter Is* (PS–2). Illus. by Mindy Dwyer. 2002, Alaska Northwest $15.95 (0-88240-543-8); paper $8.95 (0-88240-554-6). 32pp. Three youngsters' joy in a snowy winter is shown in flowing watercolors and bouncy rhymes as the children make snow angels, watch the northern lights, and view winter wildlife from their dogsled. (Rev: BL 1/1–15/03; HBG 3/03; SLJ check)

1240 Dussling, Jennifer. *Rainbow Mystery* (1–3). Illus. by Barry Gott. Series: Science Solves It. 2002, Kane paper $4.99 (1-57565-119-X). 32pp. Annie and Mike solve a mystery (rainbows on a wall) by discovering a science concept (prisms). (Rev: BL 9/15/02)

1241 Ehlert, Lois. *In My World* (PS–1). Illus. 2002, Harcourt $15.00 (0-15-216269-0). 40pp. Die-cut shapes are used to present various flora and fauna and other phenomena of nature in this impressive picture book. (Rev: BL 5/1/02*; HB 7–8/02; HBG 10/02; SLJ 5/02)

1242 Erdrich, Lise. *Bears Make Rock Soup and Other Stories* (2–4). Illus. by Lisa Fifield. 2002,

Children's $16.95 (0-89239-172-3). 32pp. A collection of short stories and art depicting the Native American connection to animals and the earth. (Rev: BCCB 1/03; BL 8/02; HBG 3/03; SLJ 9/02)

1243 Fitch, Sheree. *No Two Snowflakes* (K–3). Illus. by Janet Wilson. 2001, Orca $16.95 (1-55143-206-4). 32pp. A boy in colder climes describes snow to his pen pal in the tropics. (Rev: BL 3/1/02; HBG 3/02; SLJ 1/02)

1244 Florian, Douglas. *Summersaults* (K–4). Illus. 2002, HarperCollins LB $15.89 (0-06-029268-7). 48pp. The freedom and beauty of summer are evoked in this collection of short, rhymed poems with playful pictures. (Rev: BCCB 5/02; BL 4/1/02; HB 7–8/02; HBG 10/02; SLJ 5/02*)

1245 Glaser, Linda. *It's Spring* (PS–1). Illus. by Susan Swan. Series: Celebrate the Seasons. 2002, Millbrook LB $21.90 (0-7613-1760-0). 32pp. A boy enjoys a spring day and muses on the changing seasons. Also use *It's Fall* (2001) and *It's Winter* (2002). (Rev: BL 5/15/02; HBG 10/02; SLJ 3/02)

1246 Godkin, Celia. *When the Giant Stirred: Legend of a Volcanic Island* (K–3). Illus. 2002, Fitzhenry & Whiteside $17.95 (1-55041-683-9). 40pp. A handsomely illustrated story of a people who must leave a lush island when its volcano erupts, with a clear description of the natural cycle of renewal. (Rev: BL 11/1/02; SLJ 12/02)

1247 Hargrove, Linda. *Wings Across the Moon* (PS). Illus. by Joung Un Kim. Series: Harper Growing Tree. 2001, HarperFestival $9.95 (0-694-01280-7). 24pp. A mother and child watch the moon's passage and the animals that make their appearance at night. (Rev: BL 4/15/01; HBG 10/01; SLJ 1/02)

1248 Hoberman, Mary Ann. *Right Outside My Window* (K–2). Illus. by Nicholas Wilton. 2002, Mondo $15.95 (1-59034-194-5). 24pp. Simple two-line rhymes describe the beautiful changing views through the four seasons. (Rev: BL 8/02; HBG 10/02; SLJ 11/02)

1249 James, Simon. *The Birdwatchers* (PS–1). Illus. 2002, Candlewick $15.99 (0-7636-1676-1). 32pp. A young girl accompanies her grandfather on a birdwatching expedition in this book filled with dramatic watercolor illustrations. (Rev: BCCB 6/02; BL 8/02; HBG 10/02; SLJ 5/02*)

1250 Karas, G. Brian. *Atlantic* (PS–3). Illus. 2002, Putnam $15.99 (0-399-23632-5). 32pp. In this first-person narrative, the Atlantic Ocean tells what and where it is, how people view it, and how it is affected by the moon and sun. (Rev: BCCB 4/02; BL 4/15/02*; HBG 10/02; SLJ 6/02)

1251 Kurtz, Jane, and Christopher Kurtz. *Water Hole Waiting* (PS–3). Illus. by Lee Christiansen. 2002, HarperCollins LB $15.89 (0-06-029851-0). 32pp. A picture book about animals taking turns drinking at an African water hole. (Rev: BCCB 6/02; BL 5/15/02; HBG 10/02; SLJ 5/02*)

1252 Lewis, J. Patrick. *Earth and Me: Our Family Tree* (K–4). Illus. by Christopher Canyon. Series: A Sharing Nature with Children Book. 2002, Dawn $16.95 (1-58469-031-3); paper $7.95 (1-58469-030-5). Rich artwork and lyric text introduce animals of

all kinds — and one boy — appreciating the beauty and bounty of their environment. (Rev: HBG 10/02; SLJ 4/02)

1253 Lewis, Richard. *In the Space of the Sky* (PS–2). Illus. by Debra Frasier. 2002, Harcourt $16.00 (0-15-253150-5). 24pp. A poetic introduction to the universe that covers both the external and internal worlds. (Rev: BL 5/1/02; HBG 10/02; SLJ 5/02)

1254 Locker, Thomas. *Walking with Henry: Based on the Life and Works of Henry David Thoreau* (2–4). Illus. 2002, Fulcrum $17.95 (1-55591-355-5). 32pp. A fictionalized account of Henry David Thoreau as he hikes through the wilderness, describing his beliefs about man's relationship with nature. (Rev: BL 12/1/02; HBG 3/03; SLJ 1/03) [818]

1255 London, Jonathan. *Park Beat: Rhymin' Through the Seasons* (PS–3). Illus. by Woodleigh Hubbard. 2001, HarperCollins LB $15.89 (0-688-13995-7). Snappy verses and detailed illustrations with changing perspectives describe how a park changes with the seasons. (Rev: HBG 10/01; SLJ 5/01)

1256 Luke, Melinda. *Green Dog* (1–3). Illus. by Jane Manning. Series: Science Solves It. 2002, Kane paper $4.99 (1-57565-115-7). 32pp. Teddy investigates the cause of murky water in the goldfish bowl and discovers algae. (Rev: BL 9/15/02)

1257 Ryder, Joanne. *The Waterfall's Gift* (1–3). Illus. by Richard J. Watson. 2001, Sierra Club $15.95 (0-87156-579-X). A young girl visits a waterfall in the woods and marvels at the beauties of nature. (Rev: HBG 3/02; SLJ 8/01)

1258 Seuling, Barbara. *Spring Song* (PS–K). Illus. by Greg Newbold. 2001, Harcourt $16.00 (0-15-202317-8). 32pp. Questions and answers are used in this lovely book that depicts spring and animal activities associated with it. (Rev: BL 4/15/01; HBG 10/01; SLJ 5/01)

1259 Spinelli, Eileen. *Here Comes the Year* (PS–1). Illus. by Keiko Narahashi. 2002, Holt $16.95 (0-8050-6685-3). 32pp. Each of the months is personified in this picture book that explains the changes in nature during a single year. (Rev: BCCB 4/02; BL 5/1/02; HBG 10/02; SLJ 6/02)

1260 Taylor, Joanne. *Full Moon Rising* (1–3). Illus. by Susan Tooke. 2002, Tundra $16.95 (0-88776-548-3). An attractive, poetic introduction to the full moons of the year. (Rev: HBG 3/03; SLJ 12/02) [523.3]

1261 Taylor, Theodore. *Hello, Arctic!* (PS–2). Illus. by Margaret Chodos-Irvine. 2002, Harcourt $16.00 (0-15-201577-9). 40pp. A simple text and dramatic illustrations show the changing Arctic seasons and the animals and plants found there. (Rev: BL 10/1/02; HBG 3/03; SLJ 11/02)

1262 Weninger, Brigitte. *Precious Water: A Book of Thanks* (PS–1). Illus. by Anne Moller. 2002, North-South LB $13.88 (0-7358-1514-3). 32pp. A young girl and her cat explore the uses, sources, and nature of water. (Rev: BL 4/15/02; HBG 10/02; SLJ 5/02)

1263 Yolen, Jane. *Harvest Home* (K–2). Illus. by Greg Shed. 2002, Harcourt $16.00 (0-15-201819-0). 32pp. An earthy ode to harvest time, written in verse and complemented by glowing illustrations. (Rev: BL 10/15/02; HBG 3/03; SLJ 11/02)

OTHER TIMES, OTHER PLACES

1264 Ahvander, Ingmarie. *Pancake Dreams* (PS–2). Trans. by Elizabeth Kallick Dyssegaard. Illus. by Mati Lepp. 2002, Farrar $16.00 (91-29-65652-4). 28pp. Stefan yearns for his Swedish grandmother's pancakes and a motley crew of willing helpers goes to great lengths to deliver a batch to his new home in Jordan. (Rev: BL 11/15/02; HB 1–2/03; HBG 3/03; SLJ 12/02)

1265 Alakija, Polly. *Catch That Goat!* (PS–2). Illus. by author. 2002, Barefoot $16.99 (1-84148-908-5). Young Ayoka's goat runs amok in the market in this beautifully illustrated story set in Nigeria. (Rev: HBG 3/03; SLJ 12/02)

1266 Bania, Michael. *Kumak's House: A Tale of the Far North* (PS–2). Illus. 2002, Alaska Northwest $15.95 (0-88240-540-3); paper $8.95 (0-88240-541-1). 32pp. In this story packed with details about Arctic life, Kumak finds his house really feels quite large when all the animals he has taken in finally leave. (Rev: BL 9/1/02; HBG 10/02; SLJ 1/03)

1267 Bauld, Jane Scoggins. *Journey of the Third Seed* (K–2). Illus. by Cynthia G. Darr. 2001, Eakin $16.95 (1-57168-428-X); paper $9.95 (1-57168-429-8). Three lotus seeds lost at sea a thousand years ago resurface, and the third seed journeys to America where lotus blossoms from the plant now flourish. (Rev: HBG 10/01; SLJ 7/01)

1268 Bildner, Phil. *Shoeless Joe and Black Betsy* (2–4). Illus. by C. F. Payne. 2002, Simon & Schuster $17.00 (0-689-82913-2). 40pp. Mixed-media illustrations complement this tale about Shoeless Joe Jackson and Ol' Charlie, the man who fashioned the bat known as Black Betsy. (Rev: BL 2/15/02; HBG 10/02; SLJ 4/02)

1269 Brett, Jan. *Daisy Comes Home* (K–3). Illus. 2002, Putnam $16.99 (0-399-23618-X). 32pp. Detailed artwork complements this tale, set in China, of a put-upon chicken named Daisy who is washed down the river, and the resolute young owner who rescues her. (Rev: BCCB 3/02; BL 3/15/02*; HBG 10/02; SLJ 3/02)

1270 Bridges, Shirin Yim. *Ruby's Wish* (K–2). Illus. by Sophie Blackall. 2002, Chronicle $15.95 (0-8118-3490-5). 32pp. Ruby is an intelligent girl from a wealthy Chinese family who aspires to go to university at a time when few girls were educated, and to her surprise gets her wish. (Rev: BCCB 10/02; BL 11/15/02; HBG 3/03; SLJ 2/03)

1271 Bunting, Eve. *Gleam and Glow* (1–4). Illus. by Peter Sylvada. 2001, Harcourt $16.00 (0-15-202596-0). 32pp. A Bosnian mother and children flee their home leaving two precious golden fish in the pond and later return from a refugee camp to find their home ruined but the pond full of golden fish. (Rev: BCCB 12/01; BL 12/15/01; HBG 3/02; SLJ 9/01)

1272 Burleigh, Robert. *Lookin' for Bird in the Big City* (2–4). Illus. by Marek Los. 2001, Harcourt $16.00 (0-15-202031-4). A young Miles Davis searches for saxophonist Charlie "Bird" Parker in this fictionalized picture book set in 1940s New York City. (Rev: BL 2/15/03; HBG 10/01; SLJ 6/01)

1273 Burleigh, Robert. *The Secret of the Great Houdini* (2–4). Illus. by Leonid Gore. 2002, Simon & Schuster $16.95 (0-689-83267-2). 40pp. Sam and his uncle watch in suspense as Houdini performs an amazing escape in this fictional account mixed with biography and a message of self-esteem. (Rev: BL 7/02; HBG 3/03; SLJ 7/02)

1274 Compestine, Ying Chang. *The Story of Chopsticks* (K–3). Illus. by Yongsheng Xuan. 2001, Holiday $16.95 (0-8234-1526-0). 32pp. An inventive tale of the origin of chopsticks that includes a lesson in table manners and a simple recipe. (Rev: BL 1/1–15/02; HBG 10/02; SLJ 12/01)

1275 Compestine, Ying Chang. *The Story of Noodles* (1–3). Illus. by Yongsheng Xuan. 2002, Holiday $16.95 (0-8234-1600-3). 32pp. The inventive Kang brothers of *The Story of Chopsticks* return to help their mother in the emperor's cooking contest. (Rev: BCCB 2/03; BL 11/1/02; HBG 3/03; SLJ 11/02)

1276 da Costa, Deborah. *Snow in Jerusalem* (K–3). Illus. by Ying-Hwa Hu and Cornelius Van Wright. 2001, Albert Whitman $15.95 (0-8075-7521-6). 30pp. A Jewish boy and a Muslim boy find a way to peacefully resolve a disagreement about a cat in this picture book set in Jerusalem. (Rev: BL 10/15/01; HBG 3/02; SLJ 12/01)

1277 Daly, Niki. *Once upon a Time* (PS–K). Illus. 2003, Farrar $16.00 (0-374-35633-5). 40pp. Sarie overcomes her fear of reading aloud by reading to her aunt in this picture book set in South Africa. (Rev: BL 2/15/03)

1278 Daly, Niki. *What's Cooking, Jamela?* (PS–2). Illus. 2001, Farrar $16.00 (0-374-35602-5). 32pp. Vibrant illustrations capture the colors of a black South African township in this tale of little Jamela, whose pet chicken is in peril. (Rev: BCCB 1/02; BL 11/1/01; HB 9–10/01; HBG 3/02; SLJ 10/01)

1279 Demas, Corinne. *The Boy Who Was Generous with Salt* (K–3). Illus. by Michael Hays. 2002, Marshall Cavendish $15.95 (0-7614-5099-8). As cook aboard a fishing vessel in 1850, Ned plots to get home in time for his ninth birthday. (Rev: HBG 10/02; SLJ 5/02)

1280 Dillon, Jana. *Sasha's Matrioshka Dolls* (K–3). Illus. by Deborah N. Lattimore. 2003, Farrar $16.00 (0-374-37387-6). 32pp. A story of a box maker in old Moscow, who makes the first nesting Russian dolls for his granddaughter. (Rev: BL 3/15/03)

1281 Drummond, Allan. *Liberty!* (1–4). Illus. 2002, Farrar $17.00 (0-374-34385-3). 40pp. An unnamed boy narrates the story of the unveiling of the Statue of Liberty in 1886, in this tale based on fact. (Rev: BL 3/15/02*; HBG 10/02; SLJ 5/02)

1282 Dunlap, Julie, and Marybeth Lorbiecki. *Louisa May and Mr. Thoreau's Flute* (2–4). Illus. by Mary Azarian. 2002, Dial $16.99 (0-8037-2470-5). 32pp. The story of a young Louisa May Alcott and her tutor Henry David Thoreau, based on actual events and accounts. (Rev: BL 9/1/02; HB 9–10/02; HBG 3/03; SLJ 10/02)

1283 Erdrich, Louise. *The Range Eternal* (K–3). Illus. by Steve Johnson. 2002, Hyperion $15.99 (0-7868-0220-0). 32pp. An adult woman buys an antique Range Eternal woodstove, which brings back warm memories of her childhood in the mountains when the stove was the focal point of the kitchen. (Rev: BCCB 12/02; BL 10/1/02; HBG 3/03; SLJ 10/02)

1284 Farley, Carol. *The King's Secret* (K–3). Illus. by Robert Jew. 2001, HarperCollins LB $15.89 (0-688-12777-0). 32pp. A fictionalized account of the development of the Korean alphabet in the mid-15th century, with elaborate illustrations. (Rev: BL 9/15/01; HBG 3/02; SLJ 12/01)

1285 Fitzpatrick, Marie-Louise. *You, Me and the Big Blue Sea* (PS–2). Illus. 2002, Millbrook LB $22.90 (0-7613-2806-8). 32pp. A little boy and his mother have different memories of a sea voyage they took when he was a toddler, in this richly illustrated book set in the 19th century. (Rev: BL 12/1/02; HBG 3/03; SLJ 11/02)

1286 Francis, David "Panama," and Bob Reiser. *David Gets His Drum* (K–2). Illus. by Eric Velasquez. 2002, Marshall Cavendish $16.95 (0-7614-5088-2). 32pp. African American jazz musician "Panama" Francis loved music from a young age and here tells the sad story of his first drum. (Rev: BL 11/15/02; HBG 3/03; SLJ 10/02)

1287 Garay, Luis. *The Kite* (K–2). Illus. 2002, Tundra $14.95 (0-88776-503-3). 32pp. Francisco, a Latin American boy who must help support his family after his father's death, dreams of having a kite. (Rev: BL 8/02; HBG 10/02; SLJ 12/02)

1288 George, Jean Craighead. *Nutik and Amaroq Play Ball* (K–2). Illus. by Ted Rand. 2001, HarperCollins $15.95 (0-06-028166-9). 40pp. Amaroq, an Eskimo boy, discovers that his wolf Nutik's sense of direction is better when they head home after playing football. (Rev: BL 5/15/01; HBG 10/01; SLJ 7/01)

1289 Goodman, Susan E. *Cora Frear: A True Story* (2–3). Illus. by Doris Ettlinger. Series: Brave Kids. 2002, Simon & Schuster LB $11.89 (0-689-84330-5); paper $3.99 (0-689-84329-1). 51pp. A 10-year-old and her doctor father are surrounded by a prairie fire in the late 19th century. (Rev: HBG 10/02; SLJ 8/02)

1290 Greenwood, Mark. *The Legend of Moondyne Joe* (K–3). Illus. by Frane Lessac. 2002, Cygnet $19.95 (1-876268-70-0). Moondyne Joe, a legendary Australian figure who arrived there as a convict in the mid-1800s, was known for his ability to escape from jail. (Rev: SLJ 1/03)

1291 Hartfield, Claire. *Me and Uncle Romie: A Story Inspired by the Life and Art of Romare Bearden* (K–3). Illus. by Jerome Lagarrigue. 2002, Dial $16.99 (0-8037-2520-5). 40pp. James enjoys spending time with his uncle, the Harlem Renaissance artist Romare Bearden, in this picture book with reproductions of the artist's work. (Rev: BL 2/15/03; HBG 3/03; SLJ 12/02)

1292 Hazen, Barbara Shook. *Katie's Wish* (PS–2). Illus. by Emily Arnold McCully. 2002, Dial $15.99 (0-8037-2478-0). 32pp. Beautiful, impressionistic illustrations and powerful narrative enhance this book about a girl named Katie, who survives the Irish potato famine and travels to America to reunite with her Da. (Rev: BL 10/15/02; HBG 3/03; SLJ 9/02)

1293 High, Linda Oatman. *The Girl on the High-Diving Horse: An Adventure in Atlantic City* (2–4). Illus. by Ted Lewin. 2003, Philomel $16.99 (0-399-23649-X). It's 1936 and young Ivy Cordelia longs to ride one of the horses that dive into a tank of water on the boardwalk in Atlantic City. (Rev: BCCB 2/03; BL 4/15/03; SLJ 2/03)

1294 Hoffman, Mary. *The Color of Home* (PS–3). Illus. by Karin Littlewood. 2002, Penguin Putnam $15.99 (0-8037-2841-7). 32pp. A young Somalian boy who has emigrated to America to escape civil war has trouble adjusting to his new life until he is able to paint pictures of his fears and hopes. (Rev: BCCB 10/02; BL 10/15/02; HBG 3/03; SLJ 9/02)

1295 Homan, Lynn M., and Thomas Reilly. *The Tuskegee Airmen Story* (K–3). Illus. by Rosalie M. Shepherd. 2002, Pelican $14.95 (1-58980-005-2). 32pp. A grandfather tells of his days as a Tuskegee Airman during World War II. (Rev: BL 2/15/03; HBG 3/03)

1296 Hopkinson, Deborah. *Under the Quilt of Night* (K–2). Illus. by James E. Ransome. 2002, Simon & Schuster $16.00 (0-689-82227-8). 40pp. A young slave girl describes her dangerous escape through the Underground Railroad. (Rev: BCCB 2/02; BL 2/15/02; HB 7–8/02; HBG 10/02; SLJ 1/02*)

1297 Howard, Ellen. *The Log Cabin Church* (K–3). Illus. by Ronald Himler. 2002, Holiday $16.95 (0-8234-1740-9). 32pp. Elvirey initially questions her Michigan frontier community's desire to build a church in this sequel to *The Log Cabin Quilt* (1996) and *The Log Cabin Christmas* (2000). (Rev: BL 10/1/02; HBG 3/03; SLJ 10/02)

1298 Hughes, Vi. *Aziz the Storyteller* (K–3). Illus. by Stefan Czernecki. 2002, Crocodile $15.95 (1-56656-456-5). Aziz, a lover of storytelling, trades the family's donkey for a special carpet, which proves worthwhile despite his father's ire. (Rev: HBG 10/02; SLJ 11/02)

1299 Hurst, Carol Otis. *Rocks in His Head* (K–3). Illus. by James Stevenson. 2001, Greenwillow LB $15.89 (0-06-029404-3). 32pp. A man pursues his interest in rock collecting from childhood through raising a family in the Depression until he succeeds in turning a hobby into a career. (Rev: BCCB 12/01; BL 6/1–15/01; HB 7–8/01; HBG 10/01; SLJ 6/01)

1300 Iijima, Geneva Cobb. *The Way We Do It in Japan* (K–3). Illus. by Paige Billin-Frye. 2002, Albert Whitman $14.95 (0-8075-7822-3). 32pp. When Gregory's family moves to Japan, he learns about the differences between Japanese and American culture. (Rev: BCCB 3/02; BL 5/15/02; HBG 10/02; SLJ 4/02)

1301 Isadora, Rachel. *Bring on That Beat* (PS–2). Illus. by author. 2002, Putnam $15.99 (0-399-

23232-X). 32pp. In this rhyming, rhythmic ode to jazz set in 1930s Harlem, a band plays on a street corner and a crowd gathers to listen. (Rev: BCCB 1/02; BL 2/15/02; HBG 10/02; SLJ 1/02)

1302 Johnston, Tony. *Sunsets of the West* (1–3). Illus. by Ted Lewin. 2002, Putnam $16.99 (0-399-22659-1). 32pp. A picture book that describes a family's journey westward by covered wagon and their day-to-day life. (Rev: BL 6/1–15/02; HBG 10/02; SLJ 7/02)

1303 Kahn, Rukhsana. *Ruler of the Courtyard* (K–1). Illus. by R. Gregory Christie. 2003, Viking $15.99 (0-670-03583-1). 32pp. Saba overcomes her fear of chickens after facing up to a snake in this story set in Pakistan. (Rev: BL 2/15/03; HB 3–4/03; SLJ 2/03)

1304 Kay, Verla. *Homespun Sarah* (K–3). Illus. by Ted Rand. 2003, Putnam $15.99 (0-399-23417-9). 32pp. Eighteenth-century Pennsylvania farm life is introduced as readers follow Sarah through a typical day. (Rev: BL 3/1/03)

1305 Kay, Verla. *Tattered Sails* (K–3). Illus. by Dan Andreasen. 2001, Putnam $15.99 (0-399-23345-8). 32pp. A description of the difficult voyage of three Pilgrim children and their parents on their way to America in search of a better life. (Rev: BL 10/15/01; HBG 3/02; SLJ 9/01)

1306 Kinsey-Warnock, Natalie. *From Dawn till Dusk* (K–3). Illus. by Mary Azarian. 2002, Houghton $16.00 (0-618-18655-7). 40pp. The author describes her childhood on a Vermont farm, contrasting the hard work with the resulting benefits as she details the different activities throughout the year. (Rev: BL 11/15/02; HBG 3/03; SLJ 10/02)

1307 Krishnaswami, Uma. *Chachaji's Cup* (K–3). Illus. by Soumya Sitaraman. 2003, Children's $16.95 (0-89239-178-2). 32pp. Neel, an Indian boy living in the United States, listens to his great-uncle Chachaji's Hindu legends and his stories of the hardships and dangers he faced as a child refugee during the partition of India and Pakistan in 1947. (Rev: BL 3/15/03)

1308 Kroll, Virginia. *Especially Heroes* (3–5). Illus. by Tim Ladwig. 2003, Eerdmans $16.00 (0-8028-5221-1). 32pp. The narrator remembers an incident in 1962, when her father reacted to an attack on a black woman in their neighborhood. (Rev: BL 2/1/03)

1309 Lamm, C. Drew. *Gauchada* (2–4). Illus. by Fabian Negrin. 2002, Knopf $15.95 (0-375-81267-9). 32pp. A *gauchada*, or selfless gift, created by an Argentine cowboy is passed on from person to person in this richly illustrated story about sharing. (Rev: BCCB 3/02; BL 2/1/02; HBG 10/02; SLJ 1/02)

1310 Lawlor, Laurie. *Old Crump: The True Story of a Trip West* (1–3). Illus. by John Winch. 2002, Holiday $16.95 (0-8234-1608-9). 32pp. The members of a wagon train and their ox, Old Crump, find themselves lost in Death Valley in 1850. (Rev: BL 3/15/02; HBG 10/02; SLJ 6/02)

1311 Lawson, Julie. *The Klondike Cat* (1–3). Illus. by Paul Mombourquette. 2002, Kids Can $15.95 (1-55337-013-9). 32pp. Noah doesn't get in trouble for bringing his cat on the journey to the Klondike in 1896 because it turns out that mousers are in great demand. (Rev: BL 11/15/02; HBG 3/03; SLJ 1/03)

1312 Lee, Jeanne M. *Bitter Dumplings* (K–3). Illus. 2002, Farrar $16.00 (0-374-39966-2). 32pp. An orphaned girl, an old woman, and an escaped slave come to depend on one another in 15th-century China. (Rev: BCCB 5/02; BL 5/15/02; HB 5–6/02; HBG 10/02; SLJ 5/02)

1313 Leiner, Katherine. *Mama Does the Mambo* (K–3). Illus. by Edel Rodriguez. 2001, Hyperion $15.99 (0-7868-0646-X). 40pp. After Sofia's father dies, Sofia is worried that her mother will never dance again in this story set in Havana, Cuba. (Rev: BCCB 12/01; BL 11/1/01; HB 1–2/02*; HBG 3/02; SLJ 11/01)

1314 Lester, Alison. *Ernie Dances to the Didgeridoo* (PS–2). Illus. 2001, Houghton $15.00 (0-618-10442-9). 32pp. Ernie is away in aborigine territory in northern Australia for a year, and sends each of his six friends a letter about each of the six seasons and his various activities. (Rev: BL 5/15/01; HBG 10/01; SLJ 4/01)

1315 Lipp, Frederick. *The Caged Birds of Phnom Penh* (PS–3). Illus. by Ronald Himler. 2001, Holiday $16.95 (0-8234-1534-1). 32pp. Ary, an 8-year-old girl living in Cambodia, tests the proverb that says "letting a caged bird go free makes wishes come true." (Rev: BCCB 4/01; BL 4/1/01; HBG 3/02; SLJ 5/01)

1316 London, Jonathan. *What the Animals Were Waiting For* (K–3). Illus. by Paul Morin. 2002, Scholastic $16.95 (0-439-33630-9). 32pp. An African boy watches animals wait for rain during the dry "Months of Hunger." (Rev: BCCB 6/02; BL 5/15/02; HBG 10/02; SLJ 5/02)

1317 McCaughrean, Geraldine. *One Bright Penny* (1–3). Illus. by Paul Howard. 2002, Viking $15.99 (0-670-03588-2). 32pp. Three farm children try to equal their father's claim that when he was young he could fill the barn with feed for a single penny. (Rev: BCCB 2/03; BL 11/1/02; HBG 3/03; SLJ 2/03)

1318 McKissack, Patricia. *Goin' Someplace Special* (K–3). Illus. by Jerry Pinkney. 2001, Simon & Schuster $16.00 (0-689-81885-8). 40pp. Young Tricia Ann sets off on her first journey by herself and must navigate the South of the 1950s, working out where an African American is allowed to go. (Rev: BCCB 9/01; BL 8/01; HB 11–12/01; HBG 3/02; SLJ 9/01)

1319 Meisel, Paul. *Zara's Hats* (PS–2). Illus. 2003, Dutton $15.99 (0-525-45465-9). 32pp. When Zara's hat-making father must travel abroad in search of feathers, Zara sells beautiful hats of her own making in this story set in turn-of-the-20th-century New York. (Rev: BL 2/15/03; SLJ 2/03)

1320 Miller, William. *Rent Party Jazz* (1–4). Illus. by Charlotte Riley-Webb. 2001, Lee & Low $16.95 (1-58430-025-6). 32pp. A young African American boy named Sonny and an old jazz musician named Smilin' Jack throw a rent party to help Sonny's mother in 1930s New Orleans. (Rev: BL 11/15/01; HBG 3/02; SLJ 11/01)

1321 Nobisso, Josephine. *The Weight of a Mass: A Tale of Faith* (K–3). Illus. by Katalin Szegedi. 2002, Gingerbread House $17.95 (0-940112-09-4); paper $9.95 (0-940112-10-8). In a land where most people have abandoned their faith, an old woman reveals the power of the Mass. (Rev: HBG 3/03; SLJ 1/03)

1322 Noguchi, Rick, and Deneen Jenks. *Flowers from Mariko* (K–3). Illus. by Michelle Reiko Kumata. 2001, Lee & Low $16.95 (1-58430-032-9). 32pp. When Mariko's Japanese American family is released from an internment camp after World War II, they must work to rebuild the life they lost. (Rev: BL 11/1/01; HBG 3/02; SLJ 11/01)

1323 Olaleye, Isaac. *Bikes for Rent!* (PS–3). Illus. by Chris L. Demarest. 2001, Scholastic $16.95 (0-531-30290-3). 32pp. A hard-working Nigerian boy who loves bicycles must prove that he is responsible enough to take care of a new one. (Rev: BCCB 6/01; BL 8/01; HBG 10/01; SLJ 7/01)

1324 Olofsson, Helena. *The Little Jester* (K–3). Illus. 2002, R&S $16.00 (91-29-65499-8). 28pp. French monks reluctantly open the doors of the monastery to a jester, who then performs a miracle. (Rev: BL 3/15/02; HBG 10/02; SLJ 5/02)

1325 Oppenheim, Shulamith Levey. *Ali and the Magic Stew* (PS–3). Illus. by Winslow Pels. 2002, Boyds Mills $15.95 (1-56397-869-5). 32pp. In this Persian tale, a proud, spoiled merchant's son learns humility when he must beg for coins to save his father's life. (Rev: BCCB 5/02; BL 4/15/02; HBG 10/02; SLJ 4/02)

1326 Osborne, Mary Pope. *New York's Bravest* (K–3). Illus. by Steve Johnson and Lou Fancher. 2002, Knopf LB $17.99 (0-375-92196-6). 32pp. A dramatically illustrated tribute to Mose Humphreys, a brave New York fire fighter who died while saving lives in the 1840s. (Rev: BCCB 9/02; BL 7/02; HB 11–12/02; HBG 3/03; SLJ 9/02*)

1327 Pak, Soyung. *A Place to Grow* (K–2). Illus. by Marcelino Truong. 2002, Scholastic $16.95 (0-439-13015-8). 32pp. An Asian immigrant explains through metaphor his journey from a war-torn homeland to a safe place as he and his daughter plant seeds together in the garden. (Rev: BL 10/15/02; HB 1–2/03; HBG 3/03; SLJ 11/02)

1328 Park, Frances, and Ginger Park. *Good-Bye, 382 Shin Dang Dong* (1–3). Illus. by Yangsook Choi. 2002, National Geographic $16.95 (0-7922-7985-9). 32pp. Jangmi is sad to leave Korea and her friends and move to Massachusetts. (Rev: HBG 3/03; SLJ 10/02)

1329 Park, Frances, and Ginger Park. *Where on Earth Is My Bagel?* (K–3). Illus. by Grace Lin. 2001, Lee & Low $16.00 (1-58430-033-7). A Korean boy hungry for a bagel sends a message to New York by pigeon but only receives a recipe in return, which his local baker is happy to make in this book full of bagel shapes. (Rev: HBG 3/02; SLJ 9/01)

1330 Patz, Nancy. *Who Was the Woman Who Wore the Hat?* (3–6). Illus. 2003, Dutton $14.99 (0-525-46999-0). 48pp. The hat, part of the exhibit in the Jewish Historical Museum in Amsterdam, inspires the author to reflect on what the woman who wore it was like. (Rev: BL 2/15/03; SLJ 3/03)

1331 Pilegard, Virginia Walton. *The Warlord's Beads* (K–3). Illus. by Nicolas Debon. 2001, Pelican $14.95 (1-56554-863-9). 32pp. In this story set in China, a boy invents a primitive abacus to help his father keep track of the warlord's riches. (Rev: BL 2/1/02; HBG 3/02; SLJ 2/02)

1332 Pilegard, Virginia Walton. *The Warlord's Fish* (PS–2). Illus. by Nicolas Debon. 2002, Pelican $14.95 (1-56554-964-3). 32pp. A tale set in ancient China that explores the history of the compass. (Rev: BL 2/1/03; HBG 3/03; SLJ 2/03)

1333 Radunsky, Vladimir. *Manneken Pis: A Simple Story of a Boy Who Peed on a War* (K–2). Illus. 2002, Simon & Schuster $15.95 (0-689-83193-5). 32pp. The statue of Menneken Pis in Brussels is the inspiration for this tale of a frightened little boy who stops a war by relieving himself on the combatants. (Rev: BL 10/15/02; HB 9–10/02; HBG 3/03; SLJ 12/02) [398.249]

1334 Ransom, Candice F. *Rescue on the Outer Banks* (1–3). Illus. by Karen Ritz. 2002, Carolrhoda LB $21.27 (0-87614-460-1); paper $6.95 (0-87614-815-1). 48pp. A 10-year-old boy narrates the true story of an 1896 sea rescue by an African American lifeboat crew, a feat that was officially recognized 100 years later. (Rev: HBG 10/02; SLJ 4/02)

1335 Reynolds, Marilynn. *The Name of the Child* (1–3). Illus. by Don Kilby. 2002, Orca $16.95 (1-55143-221-8). 32pp. Nervous young Lloyd is sent to the country during the 1918 flu epidemic for his safety, but ends up having to take charge in the midst of a storm. (Rev: BL 1/1–15/03; HBG 3/03; SLJ 1/03)

1336 Riggio, Anita. *Smack Dab in the Middle* (PS–1). Illus. 2002, Putnam $15.99 (0-399-23700-3). 32pp. The middle child in a large 1950s family, Rosie often feels neglected until a teacher finds a way to show her family what is happening. (Rev: BL 11/15/02; HBG 3/03; SLJ 9/02)

1337 Ringgold, Faith. *Cassie's Word Quilt* (K–3). Illus. 2002, Knopf $13.95 (0-375-81200-8). 32pp. This simple wordbook uses a quilt pattern of pictures to introduce the daily life of Cassie, a little girl living in New York City in 1939. (Rev: BL 3/1/02; HBG 10/02; SLJ 2/02)

1338 Ruepp, Krista. *Winter Pony* (K–3). Illus. by Ulrike Heyne. 2002, North-South LB $16.50 (0-7358-1692-1). 32pp. Anna worries about her pony, Prince, when he is sent to summer pasture in this story set in northern Iceland. (Rev: BL 1/1–15/03; HBG 3/03; SLJ 12/02)

1339 Schaefer, Carole Lexa. *The Little French Whistle* (PS–2). Illus. by Emilie Chollat. 2002, Knopf LB $18.99 (0-375-91569-9). 40pp. Josette's cousin Louie causes havoc with his little whistle that evokes Paris when he comes for a visit. The text includes French words. (Rev: BCCB 2/02; BL 1/1–15/02; HBG 10/02; SLJ 4/02)

1340 Schaefer, Carole Lexa. *Two Scarlet Songbirds: A Story of Anton Dvorak* (K–3). Illus. by Elizabeth

Rosen. 2001, Knopf LB $18.99 (0-375-91022-0). 32pp. The author interweaves fact and fiction in this charmingly illustrated story about the composer Anton Dvorak's experiences with a scarlet tanager. (Rev: BL 12/15/01; HBG 3/02; SLJ 11/01)

1341 Shafer, Anders C. *The Fantastic Journey of Pieter Bruegel* (5–7). Illus. 2002, Dutton $18.99 (0-525-46986-9). 40pp. A fictional account of the 16th-century painter's trip from Antwerp to Rome, in the form of a diary. (Rev: BL 7/02; HBG 10/02; SLJ 7/02)

1342 Siemiatycki, Jack, and Avi Slodovnick. *The Hockey Card* (1–3). Illus. by Doris Barrette. 2002, Lobster $16.95 (1-894222-65-2). 32pp. Uncle Jack tells his nephew about an exciting game during recess many years ago in which he bet everything on his treasured Maurice "The Rocket" Richard card. (Rev: BL 1/1–15/03)

1343 Silvano, Wendi. *Just One More* (K–3). Illus. by Ricardo Gamboa. 2002, All About Kids $16.95 (0-9700863-7-7). Young Hector protests every time another body is added to the overcrowded bus in this story set in the Andes. (Rev: HBG 3/03; SLJ 9/02)

1344 Slate, Joseph. *The Great Big Wagon That Rang: How the Liberty Bell Was Saved* (PS–2). Illus. by Craig Spearing. 2002, Marshall Cavendish $16.95 (0-7614-5108-0). 32pp. The story of a farmer's role in saving the Liberty Bell from the British. (Rev: BL 11/1/02; HBG 3/03; SLJ 11/02)

1345 Slawson, Michele Benoit. *Signs for Sale* (PS–2). Illus. by Bagram Ibatoulline. 2002, Viking $15.99 (0-670-03568-8). 40pp. A tale set in the 1950s about a girl who accompanies her father on his daily route selling signs. (Rev: BL 8/02; HBG 10/02; SLJ 7/02)

1346 Smalls, Irene. *Don't Say Ain't* (1–3). Illus. by Colin Bootman. 2003, Charlesbridge $15.95 (1-57091-381-1). 32pp. A gifted African American student attending an integrated school in 1957 learns to "speak proper" when appropriate. (Rev: BL 2/15/03; SLJ 3/03)

1347 Spinelli, Eileen. *Summerbath Winterbath* (K–3). Illus. by Elsa Warnick. 2001, Eerdmans $16.00 (0-8028-5179-7). 32pp. Althea enjoys both summer and winter baths, which are very different in this early-1900s setting. (Rev: BL 5/15/01; HBG 10/01; SLJ 7/01)

1348 Stanley, Diane. *Joining the Boston Tea Party* (2–4). Illus. by Holly Berry. 2001, HarperCollins LB $15.89 (0-06-027068-3). 48pp. Twins Liz and Lenny travel back in time to take part in the Boston Tea Party in this picture book that also contains nonfiction historical material. (Rev: BL 9/15/01; HB 11–12/01; HBG 3/02; SLJ 8/01)

1349 Stanley, Sanna. *Monkey for Sale* (PS–K). Illus. 2002, Farrar $17.00 (0-374-35017-5). 32pp. Lively illustrations bring to life the story of two girls in the Congo who decide to buy a captured monkey and set it free in the jungle. (Rev: BCCB 2/03; BL 12/1/02; HBG 3/03; SLJ 12/02)

1350 Stark, Ken. *Oh, Brother!* (1–3). Illus. 2003, Putnam $15.99 (0-399-23766-6). 32pp. The author

fondly recalls his childhood in Illinois through text and pictures. (Rev: BL 2/1/03)

1351 Stewig, John W. *Making Plum Jam* (K–2). Illus. by Kevin O'Malley. 2002, Hyperion $15.99 (0-7868-0460-2). 32pp. A boy visiting his three eccentric aunts regrets the fact that they poach plums from a neighboring farm to make jam. (Rev: BCCB 7–8/02; BL 8/02; HBG 10/02; SLJ 6/02)

1352 Taulbert, Clifton L. *Little Cliff and the Cold Place* (K–2). Illus. by E. B. Lewis. 2002, Dial $16.99 (0-8037-2558-2). 32pp. Little Cliff lives in Mississippi in the 1950s and longs to go to the Arctic, so his great-grandfather comes up with a compromise — a fishing expedition at the icehouse. (Rev: BL 11/1/02; HBG 3/03; SLJ 9/02)

1353 Taulbert, Clifton L. *Little Cliff's First Day of School* (PS–3). Illus. by E. B. Lewis. 2001, Dial $15.99 (0-8037-2557-4). 32pp. Little Cliff, an African American child, is terrified of going to school in this story set in the South of the 1950s. (Rev: BL 5/15/01; HB 7–8/01; HBG 10/01; SLJ 6/01)

1354 Thermes, Jennifer. *When I Was Built* (2–3). Illus. by author. 2001, Holt $16.95 (0-8050-6532-6). 32pp. An 18th-century house serves as the narrator for this book comparing the lives of the colonial family that once lived there with the family of today. (Rev: BL 1/1–15/02; HBG 3/02; SLJ 12/01)

1355 Tompert, Ann. *The Pied Piper of Peru* (K–2). Illus. by Kestutis Kasparavicius. 2002, Boyds Mills $15.95 (1-56397-949-7). 32pp. A 16th-century Peruvian saint tries to rid the priory of a colony of mice in this story about Saint Martin de Porres. (Rev: BCCB 4/02; BL 3/15/02; HBG 10/02) [270.6]

1356 Van Leeuwen, Jean. *The Amazing Air Balloon* (1–3). Illus. by Marco Ventura. 2003, Penguin Putnam $16.99 (0-8037-2258-3). 32pp. Based on a true event, this is a 13-year-old boy's fictionalized first-person account of the first American ascent in a hot-air balloon in 1784. (Rev: BL 1/1–15/03; SLJ 3/03)

1357 Vaughan, Marcia. *The Secret to Freedom* (K–3). Illus. by Larry Johnson. 2001, Lee & Low $16.95 (1-58430-021-3). 32pp. Great Aunt Lucy talks about her days as a slave and the secret quilt code that directed her brother Albert and other slaves on the road to freedom. (Rev: BL 6/1–15/01; HBG 10/01; SLJ 6/01)

1358 Wenberg, Michael. *Elizabeth's Song* (1–4). Illus. by Cornelius Van Wright. 2002, Beyond Words $15.95 (1-58270-069-9). 32pp. The fictionalized story of African American folk singer Elizabeth Cotton, 11-year-old author of "Freight Train Comin'." (Rev: BL 2/15/03)

1359 Wilson, Budge. *A Fiddle for Angus* (K–3). Illus. by Susan Tooke. 2001, Tundra $16.95 (0-88776-500-9). 32pp. Angus decides to learn to play the fiddle in this story set in Nova Scotia. (Rev: BL 10/15/01; HBG 3/02; SLJ 10/01)

1360 Winter, Jeanette. *Niño's Mask* (K–3). Illus. 2003, Dial $15.99 (0-8037-2807-7). 40pp. Niño makes his own mask to wear at a Mexican village fiesta in this picture book sprinkled with Spanish words. (Rev: BCCB 3/03; BL 2/1/03; HB 3–4/03)

1361 Woelfle, Gretchen. *Katje, the Windmill Cat* (PS–1). Illus. by Nicola Bayley. 2001, Candlewick $15.99 (0-7636-1347-9). 32pp. A gentle cat saves a baby when the cradle is washed out to sea in this Dutch tale based on a true story. (Rev: BL 2/1/02; HBG 3/02; SLJ 11/01)

1362 Yezerski, Thomas F. *A Full Hand* (PS–2). Illus. 2002, Farrar $16.00 (0-374-42502-7). 32pp. Nine-year-old Asa accompanies his captain father on a canal boat trip, during which he learns a lot about canals. (Rev: BCCB 12/02; BL 1/1–15/03; HBG 3/03; SLJ 9/02)

PERSONAL PROBLEMS

1363 Adams, Eric J., and Kathleen Adams. *On the Day His Daddy Left* (1–3). Illus. by Layne Johnson. 2000, Albert Whitman $14.95 (0-8075-6072-3). Danny worries that his parents' divorce is his fault. (Rev: BL 3/1/03; HBG 3/01; SLJ 12/00)

1364 Bower, Gary. *Ivy's Icicle: Forgiving Others* (K–4). Illus. by Jan Bower. Series: Thinking of Others. 2002, Tyndale $14.99 (0-8423-7417-5). Ivy's heart becomes like an icicle when Dustin breaks her new doll, but she is gently persuaded that grudges are a bad thing. (Rev: SLJ 3/03)

1365 Bunting, Eve. *The Days of Summer* (PS–3). Illus. by William Low. 2001, Harcourt $16.00 (0-15-201840-9). 32pp. In this moving picture book, a girl and her younger sister are bewildered when their grandparents divorce. (Rev: BL 4/1/01; HBG 10/01; SLJ 5/01)

1366 Clifton, Lucille. *One of the Problems of Everett Anderson* (PS–3). Illus. by Ann Grifalconi. 2001, Holt $16.95 (0-8050-5201-1). 24pp. Everett turns to his mother for advice when he becomes concerned about his classmate Greg, who is often bruised and seems troubled. (Rev: BL 9/15/01; HBG 3/02; SLJ 10/01)

1367 Cooper, Helen. *Tatty Ratty* (PS–K). Illus. 2002, Farrar $16.00 (0-374-37386-8). 32pp. When Molly accidentally leaves her favorite stuffed animal on the bus, she is comforted by thoughts of the grand adventures he is having. (Rev: BL 2/15/02; HBG 10/02; SLJ 4/02)

1368 Ehrlich, H. M. *Gotcha, Louie!* (PS–K). Illus. by Emily Bolam. 2002, Houghton $15.00 (0-618-19549-1). 32pp. Young Louie gets lost in the tall grass close to the beach, but his mother very cleverly finds him. (Rev: BL 4/15/02; HBG 10/02; SLJ 4/02)

1369 Elya, Susan Middleton. *Home at Last* (K–3). Illus. by Felipe Davalos. 2002, Lee & Low $16.95 (1-58430-020-5). 32pp. Ana, who has recently arrived from Mexico with her family, helps persuade her mother to attend English-language classes. (Rev: BCCB 9/02; BL 5/1/02; HBG 10/02; SLJ 7/02)

1370 Friedman, Laurie. *A Big Bed for Jed* (PS–K). Illus. by Lisa Jahn-Clough. 2002, Dial $14.99 (0-8037-2562-0). 32pp. Little Jed is apprehensive about the move from his crib to a big bed until the rest of his family joins him in the new bed. (Rev: BL 1/1–15/02; HBG 10/02; SLJ 7/02)

1371 Harris, Robie H. *Goodbye Mousie* (PS). Illus. by Jan Ormerod. 2001, Simon & Schuster $16.00 (0-689-83217-6). 32pp. With help from his parents, a young boy comes to terms with the death of his pet mouse. (Rev: BCCB 10/01; BL 9/1/01; HBG 3/02; SLJ 9/01)

1372 Hellman, Gary. *The Karate Way* (1–3). Illus. 2001, Doubleday $12.95 (0-385-32742-0). 32pp. A young boy who is full of fears is enrolled in a martial arts class and eventually gains confidence. (Rev: BCCB 3/01; BL 4/15/01; HBG 10/01; SLJ 6/01)

1373 Hoban, Russell. *Jim's Lion* (2–4). Illus. by Ian Andrew. 2001, Candlewick $15.99 (0-7636-1175-1). 40pp. A nurse helps a sick boy, Jim, face his fear of surgery in this oversize book with large illustrations. (Rev: BCCB 1/02; BL 1/1–15/02; HBG 3/02; SLJ 1/02)

1374 Johnston, Tony. *That Summer* (K–3). Illus. by Barry Moser. 2002, Harcourt $16.00 (0-15-201585-X). 32pp. A boy remembers the summer his brother Joey died, when he dealt with his grief by helping his grandmother make a quilt to memorialize Joey's life. (Rev: BCCB 9/02; BL 5/15/02; HBG 10/02; SLJ 5/02)

1375 Jonell, Lynne. *When Mommy Was Mad* (PS–1). Illus. by Petra Mathers. 2002, Putnam $13.99 (0-399-23433-0). 32pp. Robbie is upset because Mommy seems angry in this book with stick-figure illustrations. (Rev: BCCB 9/02; BL 5/15/02; HBG 10/02; SLJ 6/02)

1376 Joosse, Barbara M. *Stars in the Darkness* (K–3). Illus. by R. Gregory Christie. 2002, Chronicle $14.95 (0-8118-2168-4). 28pp. A boy becomes involved in a gang, prompting his mother and brother to join in neighborhood peace walks. (Rev: BCCB 9/02; BL 5/15/02; HBG 10/02; SLJ 8/02)

1377 Koski, Mary. *Impatient Pamela Wants a Bigger Family* (K–2). Illus. by Dan Brown. 2002, Trellis $14.95 (1-930650-04-3). Only-child Pamela is much taken with her friend Sam's eight brothers. (Rev: SLJ 11/02)

1378 Lichtenheld, Tom. *What Are You So Grumpy About?* (K–3). Illus. 2003, Little, Brown $15.95 (0-316-59236-6). 32pp. Humorous double-spread cartoons show situations that could provoke a bad temper. (Rev: BL 3/15/03)

1379 Millman, Isaac. *Moses Goes to the Circus* (PS–2). Illus. by author. 2003, Farrar $16.00 (0-374-35064-7). Moses, who is deaf, and his family go to a circus for vision- and hearing-impaired children. (Rev: SLJ 3/03)

1380 Monnier, Miriam. *Just Right!* (PS–K). Illus. 2001, North-South LB $15.88 (0-7358-1522-4). 32pp. A little girl is told she's too big to do some things and too little to do others. (Rev: BL 11/1/01; HBG 3/02; SLJ 11/01)

1381 Montenegro, Laura Nyman. *A Bird About to Sing* (1–3). Illus. 2003, Houghton $15.00 (0-618-18865-7). 32pp. Natalie overcomes her reluctance to read her poems to others after attending a poetry reading. (Rev: BL 2/15/03)

1382 Napoli, Donna Jo. *Flamingo Dream* (K–3). Illus. by Cathie Felstead. 2002, HarperCollins LB

$15.89 (0-688-17863-4). 32pp. A young narrator suffers the loss of her beloved father to cancer. (Rev: BL 4/15/02; HB 7–8/02; HBG 10/02; SLJ 5/02)

1383 Newsome, Jill. *Dream Dancer* (PS–2). Illus. by Claudio Munoz. 2002, HarperCollins LB $15.89 (0-06-001322-2). 48pp. A ballerina doll given to her by her grandmother helps Lily through her long recovery after an injury leaves her unable to dance. (Rev: BL 1/1–15/02; HBG 10/02; SLJ 3/02)

1384 Numeroff, Laura, and Wendy S. Harpham. *The Hope Tree: Kids Talk About Breast Cancer* (K–4). Illus. by David McPhail. 2001, Simon & Schuster $12.00 (0-689-84526-X). Animal narrators describe their feelings and actions when they discovered their mothers had cancer, and give tips for helping mothers — and children — feel better. (Rev: HBG 3/02; SLJ 10/01)

1385 Raschka, Chris. *Waffle* (PS–2). Illus. 2001, Simon & Schuster $16.00 (0-689-83838-7). 40pp. Waffle, a champion worrier and procrastinator, manages to overcome his failings. (Rev: BCCB 5/01; BL 5/15/01; HB 5–6/01; HBG 10/01; SLJ 5/01)

1386 Recorvits, Helen. *My Name Is Yoon* (K–2). Illus. by Gabi Swiatkowska. 2003, Farrar $16.00 (0-374-35114-7). 32pp. Yoon, a Korean immigrant child, is unhappy in America until she begins to feel at home in her new and different surroundings. (Rev: BL 3/15/03)

1387 Rotner, Shelley, and Sheila Kelly. *Something's Different* (K–3). Illus. 2002, Millbrook LB $22.90 (0-7613-1923-9). 32pp. A boy tries to understand his parents' marital problems. (Rev: BL 3/1/02; HBG 10/02; SLJ 8/02)

1388 Schotter, Roni. *Missing Rabbit* (PS–2). Illus. by Cyd Moore. 2002, Clarion $15.00 (0-618-03432-3). 32pp. After her parents divorce, Kara finds a toy rabbit is an anchor in her movements between two homes. (Rev: BL 5/1/02; HBG 10/02; SLJ 4/02)

1389 Schotter, Roni. *Room for Rabbit* (PS–2). Illus. by Cyd Moore. 2003, Clarion $15.00 (0-618-18183-0). 32pp. Kara finds that her father's new wife is taking up too much space and uses her rabbit as her spokesperson. (Rev: BL 3/1/03)

1390 Senisi, Ellen B. *All Kinds of Friends, Even Green!* (K–4). Photos by author. 2002, Woodbine $14.95 (1-890627-35-6). Wheelchair-bound Zaki chooses a neighbor's iguana for his school assignment, because the plucky animal manages to cope despite missing toes. (Rev: SLJ 11/02)

1391 Spalding, Andrea, and Janet Wilson. *Me and Mr. Mah* (PS–2). Illus. 2000, Orca $14.95 (1-55143-168-8). Ian misses his father after his parents divorce but finds a friend and kindred spirit in Mr. Mah, a neighbor who misses his family in China. (Rev: BL 3/1/03; HBG 9/00; SLJ 3/00)

1392 Spinelli, Eileen. *Wanda's Monster* (K–2). Illus. by Nancy Hayashi. 2002, Albert Whitman $15.95 (0-8075-8656-0). 32pp. Granny is the only one who believes there's a monster in Wanda's closet, but points out that it can't be much fun for the monster. (Rev: BL 12/1/02; HB 1–2/03; HBG 3/03; SLJ 10/02)

1393 Vail, Rachel. *Sometimes I'm Bombaloo* (PS–2). Illus. by Yumi Heo. 2002, Scholastic $15.95 (0-439-08755-4). 32pp. Katie is a mostly-good kid who sometimes turns into an angry "Bombaloo." (Rev: BCCB 4/02; BL 2/1/02; HBG 10/02; SLJ 3/02)

1394 Weiss, Ellen. *The Nose Knows* (1–3). Illus. by Margeaux Lucas. Series: Science Solves It! 2002, Kane paper $4.99 (1-57565-120-3). 32pp. Peter's acute nose is useful when everyone has a cold in this story that interweaves scientific facts. (Rev: SLJ 1/03)

1395 Woodson, Jacqueline. *Our Gracie Aunt* (K–3). Illus. by Jon J. Muth. 2002, Hyperion $15.99 (0-7868-0620-6). 32pp. Johnson and his sister Beebee experience different emotions when they are taken in by their aunt after their mother abandons them. (Rev: BCCB 9/02; BL 9/1/02; HBG 3/03; SLJ 12/02)

REAL AND ALMOST REAL ANIMALS

1396 Abercrombie, Barbara. *Bad Dog, Dodger!* (1–3). Illus. by Adam Gustavson. 2002, Simon & Schuster $14.95 (0-689-83782-8). 40pp. Fearful that he might lose his pup because of the dog's bad behavior, Sam decides to give Dodger some obedience lessons. (Rev: BL 4/1/02; HBG 10/02; SLJ 11/02)

1397 Abley, Mark. *Ghost Cat* (PS–K). Illus. by Karen Reczuch. 2001, Groundwood $16.95 (0-88899-433-8). 32pp. Elderly Miss Wilkinson depends on her cat for companionship and is bereft when he becomes ill and dies, but comforted when the rose bush she plants on his grave blooms. (Rev: HBG 3/02; SLJ 9/01)

1398 Ammon, Richard. *Amish Horses* (K–3). Illus. by Pamela Patrick. 2001, Simon & Schuster $17.00 (0-689-82623-0). An Amish boy describes his days caring for horses on his farm and the auctions where horses are bought and sold. (Rev: HBG 10/01; SLJ 5/01)

1399 Appelt, Kathi. *Where, Where Is Swamp Bear?* (PS–1). Illus. by Megan Halsey. 2002, HarperCollins LB $15.89 (0-688-17103-6). 32pp. A young Louisiana boy called Pierre goes fishing with his Granpere, but the boy's main preoccupation is looking for the elusive Swamp Bear and learning about the bear's life. (Rev: BL 2/15/02; HBG 10/02; SLJ 1/02*)

1400 Arnosky, Jim. *Raccoon on His Own* (PS–2). Illus. by author. 2001, Putnam $15.99 (0-399-22756-3). A curious baby raccoon is carried off in a wooden boat. (Rev: BCCB 7–8/01; HBG 10/01; SLJ 5/01)

1401 Arnosky, Jim. *Turtle in the Sea* (PS–2). Illus. 2002, Putnam $15.99 (0-399-22757-1). 32pp. A sea turtle survives the dangers surrounding her in the ocean. (Rev: BL 9/1/02; HBG 3/03; SLJ 8/02)

1402 Ashman, Linda. *The Tale of Wagmore Gently* (PS–2). Illus. by John Bendall-Brunello. 2002, Dutton $15.99 (0-525-46916-8). 40pp. Wagmore the dog obediently struggles to curb his unruly tail, but his family finally comes to appreciate its usefulness in this humorous tale. (Rev: BL 10/1/02; HBG 3/03; SLJ 11/02)

1403 Austin, Patricia. *The Cat Who Loved Mozart* (1–3). Illus. by Henri Sorenson. 2001, Holiday $16.95 (0-8234-1535-X). 32pp. Nine-year-old Jennifer adopts a stray cat that resists her affection until it hears her practicing for a piano recital. (Rev: BL 5/1/01; HBG 10/01; SLJ 6/01)

1404 Base, Graeme. *The Water Hole* (PS–1). Illus. 2001, Abrams $18.95 (0-8109-4568-1). 30pp. Part counting book, part introduction to animal species, and part overview of the water cycle, this richly illustrated picture book shows various animals — from one rhino to ten kangaroos — gathering at a water hole. (Rev: BL 10/1/01; HBG 3/02; SLJ 12/01)

1405 Berkes, Marianne. *Marsh Morning* (2–4). Illus. by Robert Noreika. 2003, Millbrook LB $22.90 (0-7613-2568-9). 32pp. Watercolor illustrations and short rhymes tell the stories of 15 species of birds and their morning songs. (Rev: BL 3/15/03)

1406 Best, Cari. *Goose's Story* (PS–3). Illus. by Holly Meade. 2002, Farrar $16.00 (0-374-32750-5). 32pp. A young girl witnesses how an injured goose copes with his disability and tries to survive though left behind by the flock. (Rev: BCCB 9/02; BL 5/1/02*; HB 5–6/02; HBG 10/02; SLJ 7/02)

1407 Blades, Ann. *Mary of Mile 18* (K–3). Illus. 2001, Tundra $14.95 (0-88776-581-5). 48pp. This 30th anniversary reissue of the classic story of a Canadian girl who takes in a part-wolf pup has a larger format and slight redesign. (Rev: BL 10/15/01; HBG 10/02)

1408 Blake, Robert J. *Togo* (2–4). Illus. 2002, Putnam $16.99 (0-399-23381-4). 48pp. Blake's brilliantly illustrated story is a gripping tribute to Togo, the dog that should have got credit for the famous serum run during the diphtheria epidemic in Nome in 1925. (Rev: BL 9/15/02; HBG 3/03; SLJ 9/02*)

1409 Bogan, Paulette. *Spike in the Kennel* (PS–1). Illus. 2001, Putnam $12.99 (0-399-23594-9). 32pp. Spike the dog must spend a night at the kennel and hates it at first. (Rev: BL 7/01; HBG 10/01; SLJ 6/01)

1410 Bono, Mary. *Ugh! A Bug* (PS–2). Illus. by author. 2002, Walker $15.95 (0-8027-8799-1). Insects of all kinds are introduced with rhyming couplets and illustrations of children and bugs together. (Rev: HBG 10/02; SLJ 7/02)

1411 Bottner, Barbara. *Be Brown!* (PS–1). Illus. by Barry Gott. 2002, Putnam $10.99 (0-399-23775-5). A little boy keeps giving commands that his bouncy dog totally ignores until the order is simply "Be!" (Rev: HBG 10/02; SLJ 2/02)

1412 Brown, Margaret Wise. *The Good Little Bad Little Pig* (PS–1). Illus. by Dan Yaccarino. 2002, Hyperion LB $16.49 (0-7868-2514-6). A little boy gets the pig he wants in this simple story with charming illustrations. (Rev: HBG 3/03; SLJ 11/02)

1413 Calmenson, Stephanie. *Perfect Puppy* (PS–1). Illus. by Thomas F. Yezerski. 2001, Houghton $15.00 (0-618-01139-0). 32pp. A puppy aspires to be the perfect pet in this charming tale about unconditional love and what it takes to train an animal. (Rev: BL 3/1/02; HBG 3/02; SLJ 3/02)

1414 Carrick, Carol. *The Polar Bears Are Hungry* (PS–2). Illus. by Paul Carrick. 2002, Clarion $15.00 (0-618-15962-2). 32pp. A polar bear mother finds it more and more difficult to feed her cubs as spring and summer arrive, in this fictional presentation that will prompt discussion of human impact on animals. (Rev: BL 10/15/02; HBG 3/03; SLJ 11/02)

1415 Casey, Patricia. *One Day at Wood Green Animal Shelter* (K–3). Illus. 2001, Candlewick $16.99 (0-7636-1210-3). 32pp. Photograph collages and watercolor-and-pencil illustrations enhance this description of a day's events at an animal shelter. (Rev: BCCB 9/01; BL 7/01; HBG 10/01; SLJ 8/01)

1416 Chitwood, Suzanne Tanner. *Wake Up, Big Barn!* (PS–1). Illus. 2002, Scholastic $15.95 (0-439-26627-0). 40pp. Farm animals are introduced in lively collage in this rhythmic book for preschoolers. (Rev: BL 2/1/02; HBG 10/02; SLJ 4/02)

1417 Chorao, Kay. *Grayboy* (PS–2). Illus. 2002, Holt $16.95 (0-8050-6411-7). 32pp. This book about two children who rescue an injured seagull expertly weaves nature facts with fiction. (Rev: BL 8/02; HBG 10/02; SLJ 7/02)

1418 Clement-Davies, David, adapt. *Spirit: Stallion of the Cimarron* (2–4). Illus. by William Maughan. 2002, DreamWorks $15.99 (0-525-46735-1). 40pp. The story of Spirit, leader of the wild mustangs, and his exciting adventures. (Rev: HBG 3/03; SLJ 2/03)

1419 Clements, Andrew. *Tara and Tiree, Fearless Friends: A True Story* (K–2). Illus. by Ellen Beier. Series: Pets to the Rescue. 2002, Simon & Schuster LB $15.00 (0-689-82917-5). 32pp. Jim's dogs work together to rescue him when he falls through the ice. (Rev: HBG 3/03; SLJ 3/03)

1420 Coffey, Maria. *A Cat Adrift* (PS–1). Illus. by Eugenie Fernandes. 2002, Annick LB $18.95 (1-55037-727-2); paper $6.95 (1-55037-726-4). 32pp. Teelo the cat makes friends with a little girl and her grandfather when they rescue him from the ocean. (Rev: BL 7/02; HBG 10/02; SLJ 8/02)

1421 Cohen, Barbara S. *Forever Friends* (PS–2). Illus. by Dorothy Louise Hall. 2002, Tallfellow/Smallfellow $16.95 (1-931290-12-1). 32pp. Petey the dog describes all he does for his owner, Skip, in this playful picture book. (Rev: BL 7/02)

1422 Collard, Sneed B., III. *Butterfly Count* (1–3). Illus. by Paul Kratter. 2002, Holiday $16.95 (0-8234-1607-0). 32pp. Amy's great-great-grandmother gave her prairie land to help restore the regal fritillary butterfly to its rightful home, and now Amy awaits its return. (Rev: BL 4/1/02; HBG 10/02; SLJ 6/02)

1423 Cooper, Susan. *Frog* (K–3). Illus. by Jane Browne. 2002, Simon & Schuster $17.00 (0-689-84302-X). 32pp. Joe learns how to swim by watching a frog that has fallen into the family pool. (Rev: BCCB 7–8/02; BL 6/1–15/02; HB 7–8/02; HBG 10/02; SLJ 6/02)

1424 Davies, Nicola. *Bat Loves the Night* (PS–3). Illus. by Sarah Fox-Davies. 2001, Candlewick $15.99 (0-7636-1202-2). 32pp. All about one bat's busy night, with color illustrations and bat facts throughout. (Rev: BCCB 12/01; BL 9/1/01; HBG 3/02; SLJ 9/01)

1425 Dennard, Deborah. *Bullfrog at Magnolia Circle* (K–4). Illus. by Kristin Kest. Series: Smithsonian Backyard. 2002, Soundprints $15.95 (1-931465-04-5); paper $5.95 (1-931465-39-8). 32pp. A young bullfrog who has reached maturity looks for a stretch of bayou to call his own in this accurate portrayal of a bullfrog's life. (Rev: HBG 3/03; SLJ 12/02)

1426 Derby, Sally. *Taiko on a Windy Night* (1–3). Illus. by Kate Kiesler. 2001, Holt $16.95 (0-8050-6401-X). 32pp. Taiko the cat enjoys the freedom of a walk at night. (Rev: BL 5/15/01; HBG 10/01; SLJ 6/01)

1427 Dewey, Jennifer Owings. *Once I Knew a Spider* (K–2). Illus. by Jean Cassels. 2002, Walker LB $17.85 (0-8027-8701-0). 32pp. A woman — first pregnant, then a new mother — watches a spider's transitions as it weaves a web and lays eggs in this book that features fine close-up illustrations of the spider. (Rev: BL 9/15/02; HBG 10/02; SLJ 10/02)

1428 Doyle, Malachy. *Cow* (PS–3). Illus. by Angelo Rinaldi. 2002, Simon & Schuster $17.00 (0-689-84462-X). 40pp. Realistic paintings and a simple text follow a cow through a typical day beginning with morning milking. (Rev: BL 6/1–15/02; HBG 3/03; SLJ 7/02)

1429 Doyle, Malachy. *Sleepy Pendoodle* (PS–1). Illus. by Julie Vivas. 2002, Candlewick $12.99 (0-7636-1561-7). 32pp. A humorous story based on an Irish folktale about a girl who can't remember the right words to wake up her sleeping puppy. (Rev: BL 4/15/02; HBG 10/02; SLJ 3/02)

1430 Doyle, Malachy. *Storm Cats* (PS–1). Illus. by Stuart Trotter. 2002, Simon & Schuster $15.95 (0-689-84464-6). A storm brings two neighboring children, and their cats, together. (Rev: HBG 3/03; SLJ 10/02)

1431 Edwards, Becky. *My Cat Charlie* (K–3). Illus. by David Armitage. 2001, Bloomsbury $17.95 (0-7475-4465-4). A little girl and her beloved cat must separate when her family moves to an apartment. (Rev: SLJ 12/01)

1432 Edwards, Pamela Duncan. *Muldoon* (PS–K). Illus. by Henry Cole. 2002, Hyperion $14.99 (0-7868-0360-6). 32pp. Muldoon, a dog, is convinced that he "works" for the West family — but he's actually a much-loved pet. (Rev: BL 2/15/03; HBG 3/03; SLJ 12/02)

1433 Foreman, Michael. *Saving Sinbad!* (PS–2). Illus. 2002, Kane $15.95 (1-929132-34-4). 32pp. The story of an exciting boat rescue in a seaside village, told and illustrated from a dog's point of view. (Rev: BL 12/15/02; HBG 3/03)

1434 French, Vivian. *Caribou Journey* (1–3). Illus. by Lisa Flather. Series: Fantastic Journeys. 2001, Zero to Ten $15.95 (1-84089-216-1). 32pp. Animal migration is explored in this story about a pregnant caribou, Ragged Ear, and the herd's annual march to the calving grounds. (Rev: BL 4/1/02; SLJ 12/01)

1435 French, Vivian. *Swallow Journey* (K–3). Illus. by Karin Littlewood. Series: Fantastic Journeys. 2001, Zero to Ten $15.95 (1-84089-215-3). 32pp. Dramatic watercolor illustrations accompany this account of the migration of swallows from England to southern Africa. (Rev: BL 1/1–15/02)

1436 Freymann, Saxton, and Joost Elffers. *Dog Food* (PS–3). Illus. 2002, Scholastic $12.95 (0-439-11016-5). 32pp. Clever canine sculptures made entirely of fruits and vegetables fill the pages of this picture book by the authors of *How Are You Peeling?* (1991). (Rev: BL 10/15/02; HBG 3/03; SLJ 9/02) [736]

1437 Friedman, Mel, and Ellen Weiss. *Kitten Castle* (K–3). Illus. by Lynn Adams. 2001, Kane paper $4.95 (1-57565-103-3). 32pp. Anna and her friend Tom use everyday items to build a castle for four lively kittens in this book that introduces shapes. (Rev: SLJ 9/01)

1438 Galvin, Laura Gates. *River Otter at Autumn Lane* (PS–2). Illus. by Christopher Leeper. 2002, Soundprints $15.95 (1-931465-62-2); paper $6.95 (1-931465-70-3). 32pp. A fictional introduction to the behavior, diet, and habitat of a mother otter and her young, with appealing realistic paintings. (Rev: BL 2/1/03)

1439 George, Jean Craighead. *Frightful's Daughter* (1–3). Illus. by Daniel San Souci. 2002, Dutton $16.99 (0-525-46907-9). 32pp. Sam Gribley (of *My Side of the Mountain* and its sequels) must rescue a chick of the falcon he calls Frightful. (Rev: BL 9/1/02; HBG 3/03; SLJ 9/02)

1440 Geraghty, Paul. *Tortuga* (PS–2). Illus. by author. 2001, Hutchinson $16.95 (0-09-176884-5). A tortoise carried away in a storm lands on a beautiful tropical island, survives various adventures, and happily raises a brood of young. (Rev: SLJ 9/01)

1441 Geras, Adele. *Sleep Tight, Ginger Kitten* (PS–1). Illus. by Catherine Walters. 2001, Dutton $15.99 (0-525-46771-8). A kitten searches for a comfortable place to nap, and eventually finds it on the couch with a young boy. (Rev: HBG 10/01; SLJ 5/01)

1442 Godwin, Laura. *What the Baby Hears* (PS). Illus. by Mary Morgan. 2002, Hyperion $15.99 (0-7868-0560-9). 32pp. A charming story that describes the various sounds that baby animals hear from their parents. (Rev: BL 5/1/02; HBG 10/02; SLJ 6/02)

1443 Graham, Bob. *"Let's Get a Pup!" Said Kate* (PS–K). Illus. 2001, Candlewick $14.99 (0-7636-1452-1). 32pp. A little girl and her parents come home from the shelter with a lovely puppy but then return to get an older dog too. (Rev: BCCB 9/01; BL 7/01; HB 9–10/01; HBG 3/02; SLJ 7/01)

1444 Graham-Yooll, Liz. *Timothy Tib* (PS–2). Illus. 2001, Ragged Bear $15.95 (1-929927-25-8). 32pp. A celebration of a cat's life and the pleasure the cat brings to the narrator. (Rev: BL 5/15/01; HBG 10/01; SLJ 7/01)

1445 Greenberg, David T. *Skunks!* (K–4). Illus. by Lynn Munsinger. 2001, Little, Brown $15.95 (0-

316-32606-2). For those who are not overly sensitive to strong smells, this is a witty account of all sorts of things you definitely do not want to do with a skunk. (Rev: HBG 10/01; SLJ 8/01)

1446 Hachler, Bruno. *Pablo the Pig* (PS–1). Trans. by Alison James. Illus. by Nina Spranger. 2002, North-South LB $15.88 (0-7358-1567-4). 36pp. A girl named Vera helps Pablo the pig find a safe home after his meadow is commandeered for a housing development. (Rev: BL 3/15/02; HBG 10/02; SLJ 7/02)

1447 Harper, Dan. *Sit, Truman!* (PS). Illus. by Cara Moser and Barry Moser. 2001, Harcourt $16.00 (0-15-202616-9). 32pp. Truman, a drooling mastiff, is affectionately chastised for his antics throughout the day in this humorously illustrated volume. (Rev: BL 9/15/01; HBG 3/02; SLJ 10/01)

1448 Harvey, Amanda. *Dog Days: Starring Otis* (PS–1). Illus. 2003, Doubleday $15.95 (0-385-74621-0). 32pp. Poor Otis the dog feels so neglected when a new kitten arrives that he runs away from home, only to find he misses his young mistress. (Rev: BL 1/1–15/03; SLJ 2/03)

1449 Heyman, Anita. *Gretchen the Bicycle Dog* (K–3). Photos by author. Illus. 2003, Dutton $14.99 (0-525-47066-2). Like many dachshunds, Gretchen hurts her back and can no longer run and play, so her loving family gets her a special cart attachment that allows her to carry on with life. (Rev: SLJ 3/03)

1450 Himler, Ronald. *Six Is So Much Less Than Seven* (K–2). Illus. by author. 2002, Star Bright $16.95 (1-887734-91-0). An old man mourns the death of his cat, which leaves him with only six. (Rev: HBG 10/02; SLJ 12/02)

1451 Himmelman, John. *Pipaluk and the Whales* (PS–2). Illus. by author. 2002, National Geographic $16.95 (0-7922-8217-5). The fascinating story, based on reality, of villagers who worked for months to save thousands of beluga whales trapped in winter ice. (Rev: HBG 10/02; SLJ 9/02)

1452 Hindley, Judy. *Does a Cow Say Boo?* (PS–1). Illus. by Brita Granstrom. 2002, Candlewick $15.99 (0-7636-1718-0). 32pp. Animal sounds are explored in this tour around a farm. (Rev: BCCB 10/02; BL 6/1–15/02; HBG 10/02; SLJ 9/02)

1453 Hirsch, Ron. *No, No, Jack* (PS–1). Illus. by Pierre Pratt. 2002, Dial $10.99 (0-8037-2612-0). 32pp. A mischievous dog named Jack makes off with the family's things and hides them in the closet in this charming open-the-flap book. (Rev: BL 1/1–15/02; HBG 10/02; SLJ 7/02)

1454 Hiscock, Bruce. *Coyote and Badger: Desert Hunters of the Southwest* (2–4). Illus. 2001, Boyds Mills $15.95 (1-56397-848-2). 32pp. Coyote and Badger discover that each can use the other's talents to make hunting more efficient. (Rev: BL 4/15/01; HBG 10/01; SLJ 7/01)

1455 Hollenbeck, Kathleen M. *Islands of Ice: The Story of a Harp Seal* (PS–3). Illus. by John Paul Genzo. Series: Smithsonian Backyard. 2001, Smithsonian Institution $15.95 (1-56899-965-8). 32pp. This fictional story about a harp seal focuses on true facts about the animal's life and habitat. (Rev: BL 2/1/02)

1456 Huneck, Stephen. *Sally Goes to the Mountains* (PS–1). Illus. by author. 2001, Abrams $17.95 (0-8109-4485-5). Sally the black Lab has a wonderful dream in which she goes to the mountains and meets all kinds of animals. (Rev: HBG 10/01; SLJ 7/01)

1457 Hutchins, Hazel. *One Dark Night* (PS–2). Illus. by Susan Kathleen Hartung. 2001, Viking $15.99 (0-670-89246-7). 32pp. With help from a little boy, a mother cat brings her kittens into safety during a storm. (Rev: BCCB 7–8/01; BL 5/15/01; HB 7–8/01; HBG 10/01; SLJ 6/01)

1458 Jagtenberg, Yvonne. *Jack's Rabbit* (PS–1). Illus. 2003, Millbrook $15.95 (0-7613-1544-5). 32pp. Jack's rabbit escapes while Jack is trying to draw him and Jack hunts for him all over the place. (Rev: BL 3/1/03)

1459 Johnston, Tony. *Desert Dog* (K–3). Illus. by Robert Weatherford. 2001, Sierra Club $15.95 (0-87156-979-5). 32pp. A goat-herding dog offers a portrait of his life in verse. (Rev: BL 1/1–15/02; HBG 3/02; SLJ 11/01)

1460 Kawata, Ken. *Animal Tails* (PS–K). Illus. by Masayuki Yabuuchi. 2001, Kane $13.95 (1-929132-05-0). Readers guess which animal each colorful tail should be attached to, before turning the page and finding the answer. (Rev: HBG 10/01; SLJ 6/01) [573.998]

1461 Kirk, David. *Little Bird, Biddle Bird* (PS–K). Illus. by author. 2001, Scholastic $9.95 (0-439-26092-2). Little Bird must learn to find his own food, and remembers his mother's advice as he forages. (Rev: HBG 10/01; SLJ 7/01)

1462 Kirk, David. *Little Bunny, Biddle Bunny* (PS). Illus. by author. 2002, Scholastic $9.95 (0-439-33819-0). A gentle story of a little rabbit's adventures in sunny meadows. (Rev: HBG 10/02; SLJ 4/02)

1463 Kotzwinkle, William, and Glenn Murray. *Walter the Farting Dog* (K–3). Illus. by Audrey Colman. 2001, Frog $14.95 (1-58394-053-7). 32pp. Poor Walter's flatulence almost causes his new family to return him to the pound, until he uses his unique "gift" to save them from burglars. (Rev: BL 2/15/02)

1464 Kuiper, Nannie. *Bailey the Bear Cub* (PS–K). Trans. from Dutch by J. Alison James. Illus. by Jeska Verstegen. 2002, North-South LB $15.88 (0-7358-1625-5). A sensible bear mother helps her cub overcome his anxieties and learn to catch his own dinner. (Rev: HBG 10/02; SLJ 5/02)

1465 Lang, Glenna. *Looking Out for Sarah* (PS–3). Illus. 2001, Charlesbridge $15.95 (0-88106-647-8). 32pp. Based on a true story, this book presents a typical day in the life of a blind woman through the eyes of her guide dog, Perry. (Rev: BL 11/1/01; HB 9–10/01; HBG 3/02; SLJ 9/01)

1466 Lange, Willem. *John and Tom* (K–3). Illus. by Burt Dodson. Series: Family Heritage. 2001, Vermont Folklife Center $14.95 (0-916718-17-4). 32pp. A young logger named John is pinned beneath a tree and is rescued by his horse in this based-in-truth tale set in 1950s Vermont. (Rev: BL 11/1/01; SLJ 12/01)

1467 Lee, Chinlun. *The Very Kind Rich Lady and Her One Hundred Dogs* (PS–K). Illus. 2001, Candlewick $15.99 (0-7636-1290-1). 40pp. Readers are gradually introduced to all 100 of the dogs adopted by the rich lady in this story that can be used as a counting book. (Rev: BL 5/15/01; HBG 10/01; SLJ 7/01)

1468 Lewis, Kim. *Little Baa* (PS–K). Illus. 2001, Candlewick $15.99 (0-7636-1447-5). 32pp. When Little Baa disappears, Ma sets off in search and is eventually helped by a young shepherd and his dog. (Rev: BL 5/1/01; HBG 10/01; SLJ 6/01)

1469 Liersch, Anne. *Nell and Fluffy* (PS–2). Trans. by J. Alison James. Illus. by Christa Unzner. 2001, North-South $15.95 (0-7358-1424-4). 32pp. Thinking that she is too old to have a guinea pig as a pet, Nell abandons her beloved Fluffy in an empty lot. (Rev: BL 4/15/01; HBG 10/01; SLJ 4/01)

1470 Livingstone, Star. *Harley* (1–3). Illus. 2001, North-South LB $14.88 (1-58717-049-3). 64pp. This is the story of Harley, a bad-tempered llama whose job is to protect a herd of sheep from coyotes. (Rev: BCCB 6/01; BL 4/1/01; HB 7–8/01*; HBG 10/01; SLJ 6/01)

1471 London, Jonathan. *Crunch Munch* (PS). Illus. by Michael Rex. 2001, Harcourt $13.00 (0-15-202603-7). Simple double-page spreads look at the noises animals make when they eat. (Rev: HBG 10/01; SLJ 4/01)

1472 London, Jonathan. *Mustang Canyon* (PS–2). Illus. by Daniel San Souci. 2002, Candlewick $15.99 (0-7636-1554-4). 40pp. An exciting story about Little Pinto the mustang and his desert herd, followed by a glossary and information on the history of the horse in America. (Rev: BL 12/1/02; HBG 3/03)

1473 Macaulay, David. *Angelo* (K–3). Illus. 2002, Houghton $16.00 (0-618-16826-5). 48pp. An Italian artist and a wounded pigeon share an unlikely friendship in this beautifully illustrated picture book that gives a bird's-eye view of Rome. (Rev: BCCB 6/02; BL 7/02; HB 5–6/02; HBG 10/02; SLJ 5/02)

1474 McCarty, Peter. *Hondo and Fabian* (PS–K). Illus. 2002, Holt $16.95 (0-8050-6352-8). 32pp. Captivating illustrations and simple text portray a day in the life of two family pets, Hondo the dog and Fabian the cat. (Rev: BL 2/15/02; HBG 10/02; SLJ 6/02)

1475 McKelvey, Douglas Kaine. *Locust Pocus! A Book to Bug You* (PS–1). Illus. by Richard Egielski. 2001, Putnam $15.99 (0-399-23452-7). 32pp. Rhythmic rhyming verses and colorful, humorous illustrations describe assorted insects and the things they get into. (Rev: BCCB 6/01; BL 8/01; HBG 10/01; SLJ 7/01)

1476 Mahy, Margaret. *Dashing Dog!* (PS–2). Illus. by Sarah Garland. 2002, HarperCollins LB $15.89 (0-06-000457-6). 32pp. Rhyming verse and lively illustrations present a poodle's day at the beach, during which the rambunctious pup ruins his nice hairdo, chases birds and Frisbees . . . and rescues the baby. (Rev: BL 10/1/02; HBG 3/03; SLJ 9/02)

1477 Mallat, Kathy. *Trouble on the Tracks* (PS–K). Illus. 2001, Walker LB $16.85 (0-8027-8773-8). 24pp. A train is derailed by trouble — then it's revealed that Trouble is a cat, and the train is a toy. (Rev: BL 9/1/01; HBG 3/02; SLJ 9/01)

1478 Masurel, Claire. *A Cat and a Dog* (PS–1). Illus. by Bob Kolar. 2001, North-South $13.95 (1-55858-949-X). 32pp. A warring cat and dog suddenly realize they each have different skills and can help each other. (Rev: BCCB 5/01; BL 6/1–15/01; HBG 10/01; SLJ 7/01)

1479 Meade, Holly. *A Place to Sleep* (PS–2). Illus. 2001, Marshall Cavendish $15.95 (0-7614-5096-3). 32pp. Facts about where and how different animals sleep, playfully conveyed through colorful illustrations and amusing text. (Rev: BCCB 12/01; BL 9/1/01; HBG 3/02; SLJ 9/01)

1480 Minshull, Evelyn. *Eaglet's World* (PS–2). Illus. by Andrea Gabriel. 2002, Albert Whitman $15.95 (0-8075-8929-2). 32pp. An eaglet ventures first from his egg and then from his nest in this story about growth and independence. (Rev: BL 3/1/02; HBG 10/02; SLJ 5/02)

1481 Mockford, Caroline. *Come Here, Cleo!* (PS–1). Illus. by author. 2001, Barefoot $14.99 (1-84148-329-X). A cat has simple adventures such as climbing a tree and chasing a butterfly. (Rev: HBG 10/01; SLJ 4/01)

1482 Nicholls, Judith. *Billywise* (PS–2). Illus. by Jason Cockcroft. 2002, Bloomsbury $16.95 (1-58234-778-6). A mother owl urges her owlet to leave the nest and fly. (Rev: SLJ 10/02)

1483 Ochiltree, Dianne. *Pillow Pup* (PS–1). Illus. by Mireille d'Allance. 2002, Simon & Schuster $14.95 (0-689-83408-X). 32pp. Puppy Maggie and her owner enjoy a friendly pillow fight. (Rev: BL 5/15/02; HBG 10/02)

1484 Parker, Marjorie Blain. *Jasper's Day* (1–3). Illus. by Janet Wilson. 2002, Kids Can $15.95 (1-55074-957-9). 32pp. A touching but realistic story of a family's last day with their pet dog, before he is put to sleep. (Rev: BL 12/15/02; HBG 3/03; SLJ 1/03)

1485 Partridge, Elizabeth. *Moon Glowing* (K–2). Illus. by Joan Paley. 2002, Dutton $16.99 (0-525-46873-0). 32pp. Rich, textured illustrations and simple verses present a simple introduction to hibernation, as animals prepare for the winter, gathering food and finding shelters. (Rev: BL 12/1/02; HBG 3/03; SLJ 11/02*)

1486 Pfeffer, Wendy. *Mallard Duck at Meadow View Pond* (PS–3). Illus. by Taylor Oughton. Series: Smithsonian Backyard. 2001, Smithsonian Institution $15.95 (1-56899-956-9). 32pp. This fictional story about a duck focuses on true facts about the animal's life and habitat. (Rev: BL 2/1/02)

1487 Plowden, Sally Hartmam. *Turtle Tracks* (PS–2). Illus. by Tee Plowden. 2002, PCF $14.95 (0-9679016-6-9). 32pp. At the beach one day, a girl learns all about sea turtles in this book that includes turtle facts and wildlife resources. (Rev: BL 7/02)

1488 Radcliffe, Theresa. *Nanu, Penguin Chick* (K–4). Illus. by John Butler. 2001, Viking $15.99 (0-670-88638-6). Nanu's parents come to her rescue when she gets lots in a blizzard. (Rev: SLJ 8/01)

1489 Raff, Courtney Granet. *Giant of the Sea: A Story of a Sperm Whale* (PS–2). Illus. by Shawn Gould. 2002, Soundprints $15.95 (1-931465-72-X); paper $6.95 (1-931465-80-0). 32pp. A fictional look at the behavior, diet, and habitat of a mother sperm whale and her young, with attractive illustrations that often show the animal's perspective. (Rev: BL 2/1/03)

1490 Rand, Gloria. *Little Flower* (PS–1). Illus. by R. W. Alley. 2002, Holt $16.95 (0-8050-6480-X). 32pp. Miss Pearl takes a fall and is saved in a unique way by her potbellied pig, Little Flower. (Rev: BL 3/15/02; HBG 10/02; SLJ 8/02)

1491 Sampson, Michael, and Bill Martin, Jr. *Caddie the Golf Dog* (PS–3). Illus. by Floyd Cooper. 2002, Walker LB $17.85 (0-8027-8818-1). 32pp. Jennifer's parents finally give permission for a dog too late for her to keep her beloved stray, but in a happy turn of events she ends up with the puppy of that very stray. (Rev: BL 12/1/02; HBG 3/03; SLJ 12/02)

1492 San Souci, Robert D. *Birds of Killingsworth* (K–3). Illus. by Kimberly B. Root. 2002, Dial $16.99 (0-8037-2111-0). 32pp. A retelling of the ecologically correct Longfellow poem about a squire who rids his town of birds and thus causes a plague of insects. (Rev: BL 4/1/02; HBG 10/02; SLJ 8/02)

1493 Sayre, April Pulley. *Crocodile Listens* (PS–3). Illus. by JoEllen M. Stammen. 2001, Greenwillow LB $15.89 (0-688-16505-2). A hungry crocodile mother waits attentively, ignoring all the other animals, for her babies to be ready to hatch in this engaging story that includes information about the Nile crocodile. (Rev: BCCB 10/01; HBG 3/02; SLJ 10/01)

1494 Sayre, April Pulley. *Dig, Wait, Listen* (PS–2). Illus. by Barbara Bash. 2001, Greenwillow LB $15.89 (0-688-16615-6). 32pp. A desert-dwelling spadefoot toad is alert for the sound of rain, and when it comes she emerges from under the surface to mate, lay her eggs, and watch her young hatch and grow. (Rev: BL 6/1–15/01; HB 7–8/01; HBG 10/01; SLJ 6/01)

1495 Scamell, Ragnhild. *Wish Come True Cat* (K–2). Illus. by Gaby Hansen. 2001, Barron's $13.95 (0-7641-5392-7). A little girl comes to love a scruffy cat who turns up after she had wished for a cute kitten. (Rev: HBG 3/02; SLJ 1/02)

1496 Schulman, Janet. *A Bunny for All Seasons* (PS–K). Illus. by Meilo So. 2003, Knopf $9.95 (0-375-82256-9). 32pp. A gentle story of a bunny enjoying a wonderful garden full of food, meeting another rabbit, getting cozy for the winter, and the pair returning to the garden with their young in the spring. (Rev: BL 3/1/03; SLJ 2/03)

1497 Simmie, Lois. *Mister Got To Go and Arnie* (K–3). Illus. by Cynthia Nugent. 2002, Raincoast $15.95 (1-55192-494-3). A competition for territory

between a male terrier and a cat is solved when the dog is distracted by a pretty female terrier. (Rev: SLJ 8/02)

1498 Simmons, Jane. *Ebb and Flo and the Baby Seal* (PS–2). Illus. 2002, Simon & Schuster $16.00 (0-689-84368-2). 32pp. A dog named Ebb helps reunite a baby seal with its mother. (Rev: BL 1/1–15/02; HBG 10/02; SLJ 3/02*)

1499 Smith, Charles R. *Loki and Alex: The Adventures of a Dog and His Best Friend* (K–3). Illus. 2001, Dutton $14.99 (0-525-46700-9). 32pp. The events of a day are narrated from the perspectives of a young African American boy and his dog, using color for the boy's comments and black and white for the dog's. (Rev: BL 6/1–15/01; HBG 10/01; SLJ 7/01)

1500 Stanton, Karen. *Mr. K and Yudi* (PS–2). Illus. 2001, Golden Books $14.99 (0-307-10210-6). 40pp. Yudi the dog comes back from a walk and is shocked to find his master missing but eventually finds him in a nursing home. (Rev: BL 7/01; HBG 10/01)

1501 Stojic, Manya. *Snow* (PS–K). Illus. 2002, Knopf $15.95 (0-375-82348-4). 32pp. Lush acrylics and spare but rhythmic text show animals preparing for the coming of winter. (Rev: BL 12/1/02; HBG 3/03; SLJ 12/02)

1502 Swanson, Diane. *Animals Can Be So Sleepy* (PS–K). Illus. 2001, Sterling $10.95 (1-55054-837-9). 24pp. Each spread in this simple picture book features a sleeping animal on one page and a short poem about it on the other. (Rev: BL 1/1–15/02)

1503 Tafuri, Nancy. *Mama's Little Bears* (PS). Illus. 2002, Scholastic $15.95 (0-439-27311-0). 40pp. Under Mama's watchful eye, three curious little bear cubs explore their surroundings. (Rev: BL 3/1/02; HB 3–4/02; HBG 10/02; SLJ 4/02)

1504 Thompson, Lauren. *Little Quack* (PS–K). Illus. by Derek Anderson. 2003, Simon & Schuster $14.95 (0-689-84723-8). 32pp. Five little ducklings follow their mother — the last very reluctantly — into the pond in this charming picture book. (Rev: BL 2/1/03)

1505 Tildes, Phyllis Limbacher. *Calico's Curious Kittens* (PS). Illus. by author. 2003, Charlesbridge $16.95 (1-57091-511-3); paper $6.95 (1-57091-512-1). 32pp. Calico's kittens are full of mischief, but as cute as can be. (Rev: BL 2/1/03; SLJ 2/03)

1506 Waddell, Martin. *A Kitten Called Moonlight* (PS–1). Illus. by Christian Birmingham. 2001, Candlewick $15.99 (0-7636-1176-X). 32pp. A young girl and her mother recall how they found a stray white kitten and brought it home to be their pet. (Rev: BL 4/1/01; HBG 10/01; SLJ 4/01)

1507 Waddell, Martin. *Snow Bears* (PS–2). Illus. by Sarah Fox-Davies. 2002, Candlewick $14.99 (0-7636-1906-X). 32pp. A cozy, well-illustrated tale about a mother bear and her three cubs at play. (Rev: BCCB 2/03; BL 12/15/02; HB 1–2/03; SLJ 1/03)

1508 Walsh, Alice. *Heroes of the Isle aux Morts* (PS–3). Illus. by Geoff Butler. 2001, Tundra $14.95 (0-88776-501-7). 32pp. Based on truth, this is the story of a dramatic rescue at sea in 1832, in which a Newfoundland dog plays a major role. (Rev: BL 6/1–15/01; HBG 10/01; SLJ 10/01)

1509 Ward, Helen. *Old Shell, New Shell: A Coral Reef Tale* (K–3). Illus. 2002, Millbrook LB $24.90 (0-7613-2708-8). 40pp. A hermit crab seeks a bigger home in this boldly illustrated tale, which also includes a detailed key identifying life on a coral reef. (Rev: BL 1/1–15/02; HBG 10/02; SLJ 2/02)

1510 Warrick, Karen Clemens. *If I Had a Tail* (PS–2). Illus. by Sherry Neidigh. 2001, Rising Moon LB $15.95 (0-87358-781-2). 32pp. An amusing picture book in which the tails of various animals and their uses are explored. (Rev: BL 4/1/01; HBG 10/01; SLJ 6/01)

1511 Wells, Rosemary. *McDuff Goes to School* (PS–K). Illus. by Susan Jeffers. 2001, Hyperion LB $15.49 (0-7868-2432-8). 32pp. McDuff goes to obedience school and picks up on the French commands used by the owner of Marie Antoinette, a terrier who has moved into their neighborhood. (Rev: BL 10/1/01; HB 1–2/02; HBG 3/02; SLJ 12/01)

1512 Wheeler, Lisa. *Sixteen Cows* (PS–2). Illus. by Kurt Cyrus. 2002, Harcourt $16.00 (0-15-202676-2). 32pp. After their herds of cows mingle when a dividing fence is blown down, Cowboy Gene and Cowgirl Sue decide they should also, and so they get married. (Rev: BL 6/1–15/02; HBG 10/02; SLJ 4/02)

1513 White, Amanda. *Rip and Rap* (PS). Illus. by Debbie Harter. 2002, Barefoot $14.99 (1-84148-944-1). Sheepdog puppies Rip and Rap become indistinguishable when Rap gets covered in mud. (Rev: HBG 3/03; SLJ 1/03)

1514 Whybrow, Ian. *Good Night, Monster!* (PS). Illus. by Ken Wilson-Max. 2002, Knopf $12.95 (0-375-81579-1). 24pp. A pull-the-flap book featuring farm animals and mischievous "monsters." (Rev: BL 8/02)

1515 Whybrow, Ian. *Little Farmer Joe* (PS–1). Illus. by Christian Birmingham. 2001, Kingfisher $16.95 (0-7534-5213-8). Joe is new to farm life and finds many of the animals scary, until he helps a sheep with a new baby lamb. (Rev: HBG 3/02; SLJ 11/01)

1516 Willis, Nancy Carol. *Raccoon Moon* (PS–2). Illus. 2002, Birdsong $15.95 (0-9662761-2-4); paper $6.95 (0-9662761-3-2). 32pp. Three raccoon cubs are born and grow up in this wonderfully illustrated introduction to a raccoon's lifecycle. (Rev: BL 12/15/02; SLJ 1/03)

1517 Ziefert, Harriet. *Birdhouse for Rent* (PS–K). Illus. by Donald Dreifuss. 2001, Houghton $15.00 (0-618-04881-2). A birdhouse is used by bees and chipmunks before Mrs. Chickadee moves in, lays her eggs, and sees her chicks hatch. (Rev: HBG 3/02; SLJ 9/01)

SCHOOL STORIES

1518 Best, Cari. *Shrinking Violet* (K–3). Illus. by Giselle Potter. 2001, Farrar $16.00 (0-374-36882-1). 40pp. Shy Violet has her moment in the limelight when she's cast in an offstage speaking role.

(Rev: BCCB 10/01; BL 8/01; HB 9–10/01; HBG 3/02; SLJ 8/01*)

1519 Bogacki, Tomek. *Circus Girl* (K–2). Illus. 2001, Farrar $17.00 (0-374-31291-5). 32pp. When the circus comes to town, a young member attends the local school and surprises the students by befriending an outcast. (Rev: BL 7/01; HBG 3/02; SLJ 10/01)

1520 Caseley, Judith. *Bully* (PS–3). Illus. 2001, Greenwillow LB $15.89 (0-688-17868-5). 32pp. Mickey's parents give him good advice when his friend Jack turns into an unfriendly bully. (Rev: BCCB 6/01; BL 5/15/01; HBG 10/01; SLJ 6/01)

1521 Choi, Yangsook. *The Name Jar* (PS–3). Illus. 2001, Knopf LB $18.99 (0-375-90613-4). 32pp. Unhei's classmates offer ideas for a new American name, but Unhei eventually decides to keep her own. (Rev: BL 12/15/01; HBG 3/02; SLJ 11/01)

1522 Corey, Shana. *First Graders from Mars: Episode 1: Horus's Horrible Day* (K–2). Illus. by Mark Teague. 2001, Scholastic $14.95 (0-439-26220-8); paper $4.50 (0-439-31955-2). 32pp. Horus, a Martian lad, is having a horrible time getting used to first grade until he meets another scared student. (Rev: BL 8/01; HBG 3/02; SLJ 9/01)

1523 Creech, Sharon. *A Fine, Fine School* (K–3). Illus. by Harry Bliss. 2001, HarperCollins LB $15.89 (0-06-027737-8). 32pp. A wonderfully illustrated, very funny story about a school principal who just doesn't know when to quit. (Rev: BL 8/01; HBG 3/02; SLJ 8/01)

1524 Cuyler, Margery. *Stop, Drop, and Roll* (K–3). Illus. by Arthur Howard. 2001, Simon & Schuster $16.00 (0-689-84355-0). 32pp. Jessica agonizes over her role in a play for Fire Prevention Week. (Rev: BCCB 11/01; BL 9/15/01; HBG 3/02; SLJ 10/01)

1525 Danneberg, Julie. *First Year Letters* (K–3). Illus. by Judy Love. 2003, Charlesbridge $16.95 (1-58089-084-9); paper $6.95 (1-58089-085-7). 32pp. Letters exchanged by a fictional new teacher and her students reveal how they learn together during the course of a school year. (Rev: BL 2/1/03)

1526 David, Lawrence. *Superhero Max* (K–2). Illus. by Tara Calahan King. 2002, Doubleday LB $17.99 (0-385-90851-2). 32pp. Lonely second-grader Max is so impressed by the draw of his Captain Crusader costume on Halloween that he wears it every day until his father takes it away. (Rev: BL 11/1/02; HBG 3/03; SLJ 11/02)

1527 Edwards, Becky. *My First Day at Nursery School* (PS–1). Illus. by Anthony Flintoft. 2002, Bloomsbury $15.95 (1-58234-761-1). 32pp. A reassuring tale of a child's first day at nursery school. (Rev: BL 8/02; SLJ 8/02)

1528 Falwell, Cathryn. *David's Drawings* (PS–2). Illus. 2001, Lee & Low $16.00 (1-58430-031-0). 32pp. Collages of cut-paper and fabric illustrate this story of how one boy's drawing of a bare tree becomes a classroom's cooperative masterpiece. (Rev: BL 11/15/01; HBG 10/02; SLJ 10/01)

1529 Finchler, Judy. *You're a Good Sport, Miss Malarkey* (K–3). Illus. by Kevin O'Malley. 2002,

Walker LB $16.85 (0-8027-8816-5). 32pp. When Miss Malarkey takes the job of soccer coach, she finds she must give the parents a lesson in sportsmanship. (Rev: BL 10/15/02; HBG 3/03; SLJ 10/02)

1530 French, Simon. *Guess the Baby* (PS–1). Illus. by Donna Rawlins. 2002, Clarion $14.00 (0-618-25989-9). 32pp. Classmates bring in their baby pictures and try to guess who's who. (Rev: BL 12/15/02; HBG 3/03; SLJ 12/02)

1531 Johnson, Doug. *Substitute Teacher Plans* (1–3). Illus. by Tammy Smith. 2002, Holt $16.95 (0-8050-6520-2). 32pp. An exhausted teacher mixes up the instructions for her substitute with her list of things to do on her day off, sending her students on an adventure. (Rev: BL 9/15/02; HBG 3/03; SLJ 8/02)

1532 Karas, G. Brian. *The Class Artist* (K–3). Illus. 2001, Greenwillow LB $15.89 (0-688-17815-4). 32pp. A boy struggles with an art assignment until his teacher suggests that he draw a picture of how he feels. (Rev: BCCB 9/01; BL 11/15/01; HBG 3/02; SLJ 9/01)

1533 Kirk, Daniel. *Bus Stop, Bus Go!* (K–2). Illus. 2001, Putnam $15.99 (0-399-23333-4). 32pp. The busy activity on the morning school bus becomes even more frenetic when Tommy's hamster escapes. (Rev: BCCB 9/01; BL 6/1–15/01; HBG 3/02; SLJ 9/01)

1534 Kline, Suzy. *Horrible Harry and the Dragon War* (1–3). Illus. by Frank Remkiewicz. 2002, Viking $13.99 (0-670-03559-9). 64pp. Harry and classmate Song Lee quarrel over a school project on dragons but finally become friends again. (Rev: BL 6/1–15/02; HBG 3/03; SLJ 8/02)

1535 Layton, Neal. *The Sunday Blues: A Book for Schoolchildren, Schoolteachers, and Anybody Else Who Dreads Monday Mornings* (K–2). Illus. 2002, Candlewick $15.99 (0-7636-1975-2). 40pp. Steve, who dreads returning to school all day Sunday, finds, come Monday, that it isn't so bad. (Rev: BCCB 10/02; BL 9/15/02; HBG 3/03; SLJ 12/02)

1536 Lovell, Patty. *Stand Tall, Molly Lou Melon* (K–3). Illus. by David Catrow. 2001, Putnam $14.99 (0-399-23416-0). First-grader Molly Lou's grandmother has told her to believe in herself, and Molly Lou puts this successfully into action when she moves to a new school and must deal with the bully. (Rev: BCCB 10/01; HBG 3/02; SLJ 10/01)

1537 McCain, Becky Ray. *Nobody Knew What to Do: A Story About Bullying* (K–3). Illus. by Todd Leonardo. 2001, Albert Whitman $14.95 (0-8075-5711-0). 32pp. When a boy sees bullies bothering one of his classmates, he decides to ask the teacher for help. (Rev: BL 5/15/01; HBG 10/01; SLJ 5/01)

1538 McGhee, Alison. *Countdown to Kindergarten* (PS–K). Illus. by Harry Bliss. 2002, Harcourt $16.00 (0-15-202516-2). 32pp. A soon-to-be kindergartner fears starting school because she's heard that, among other things, you must be able to tie your shoes. (Rev: BCCB 10/02; BL 8/02; HBG 3/03; SLJ 9/02)

1539 Moss, Miriam. *Scritch Scratch* (1–3). Illus. by Delphine Durand. 2002, Scholastic $16.95 (0-439-36835-9). It's the teacher's head that harbors the first louse, and the teacher has nobody to comb it out. (Rev: BCCB 11/02; HBG 3/03; SLJ 10/02)

1540 Moss, Miriam. *Wibble Wobble* (K–2). Illus. by Joanna Mockler. 2001, ME Media $14.95 (1-58925-013-3). 32pp. William is elated to lose his first tooth, and when it goes missing he enlists the help of the class to find it. (Rev: BL 2/1/02; SLJ 11/01)

1541 Nobisso, Josephine. *In English of Course* (2–4). Illus. by Dasha Ziborova. 2002, Gingerbread House $16.95 (0-940112-07-8); paper $8.95 (0-940112-08-6). 32pp. Young Josephine, a new immigrant from Italy, manages to communicate with her New York City classmates despite her limited knowledge of English. (Rev: BL 2/15/03; HBG 3/03; SLJ 2/03)

1542 O'Malley, Kevin. *Humpty Dumpty Egg-Splodes* (2–4). Illus. 2001, Walker LB $16.85 (0-8027-8757-6). 32pp. A father who's reading a story to his son's class changes it to something much more exciting when the teacher leaves the room, elaborating extensively on the Humpty Dumpty story. (Rev: BCCB 5/01; BL 7/01; HBG 10/01; SLJ 6/01)

1543 O'Neill, Alexis. *The Recess Queen* (PS–1). Illus. by Laura Huliska-beith. 2002, Scholastic $15.95 (0-439-20637-5). 32pp. Mean Jean, the recess queen, has a change in attitude when the new girl at school asks her to play in this brightly illustrated, energetic tale. (Rev: BCCB 3/02; BL 3/1/02; HBG 10/02; SLJ 3/02)

1544 Perez, L. King. *First Day in Grapes* (1–3). Illus. by Robert Casilla. 2002, Lee & Low $16.95 (1-58430-045-0). 32pp. Chico, the son of migrant workers, starts third grade in yet another school with trepidation, but his first day goes well despite bullies and a surly bus driver. (Rev: BL 11/15/02; HBG 3/03; SLJ 10/02)

1545 Plourde, Lynn. *School Picture Day* (K–2). Illus. by Thor Wickstrom. 2002, Dutton $16.99 (0-525-46886-2). 40pp. Josephina Caroleena Wattasheena's curious nature causes calamity at her school on picture day. (Rev: BL 8/02; HBG 3/03; SLJ 7/02)

1546 Polacco, Patricia. *Mr. Lincoln's Way* (K–3). Illus. 2001, Putnam $16.99 (0-399-23754-2). 40pp. A school principal uses a bully's interest in birds to teach him about tolerance and kindness. (Rev: BL 9/1/01; HBG 3/02; SLJ 8/01)

1547 Rockwell, Anne. *100 School Days* (K–1). Illus. by Lizzy Rockwell. 2002, HarperCollins LB $14.89 (0-06-029145-1). 40pp. Mrs. Madoff's class celebrates the 100th day of school by bringing in hundreds of snacks and they donate the 100 pennies that have been amassed to a needy town. (Rev: BCCB 10/02; BL 9/15/02; HBG 3/03; SLJ 9/02)

1548 Rockwell, Anne. *Welcome to Kindergarten* (PS–K). Illus. 2001, Walker LB $16.85 (0-8027-8746-0). 32pp. A little boy at a kindergarten open house thinks the building is much too big until he learns about all the interesting things he will be doing there. (Rev: BL 6/1–15/01; HBG 10/01; SLJ 5/01)

1549 Ruhmann, Karl. *Who Will Go to School Today?* (PS–1). Trans. by J. Alison James. Illus. by Miriam Monnier. 2002, North-South LB $15.88 (0-7358-1623-9). 32pp. Sam wants to send his huge stuffed monkey to school in his place, but changes his mind when he thinks of the fun he would be missing. (Rev: BL 5/1/02; HBG 10/02; SLJ 6/02)

1550 Rylant, Cynthia. *The Ticky-Tacky Doll* (PS–1). Illus. by Harvey Stevenson. 2002, Harcourt $16.00 (0-15-201078-5). 32pp. A little girl, sad to leave her doll behind when she goes to school, is cheered when her grandmother makes her a smaller doll to take with her. (Rev: BL 9/1/02; HBG 3/03; SLJ 11/02)

1551 Schwartz, Amy. *The Boys Team* (PS–1). Illus. 2001, Simon & Schuster $16.95 (0-689-84138-8). 40pp. As kindergartners, Jacob and his friends rule the preschool and occasionally let the girls play with them in this winsome book with charming illustrations. (Rev: BL 11/1/01; HB 1–2/02; HBG 3/02; SLJ 1/02)

1552 Shaw, Mary. *Brady Brady and the Great Rink* (1–3). Illus. by Chuck Temple. Series: Brady Brady. 2002, Stoddart paper $4.95 (0-7737-6224-8). Brady Brady builds a skating rink in his backyard that comes in handy when the school's power fails. Also use *Brady Brady and the Runaway Goalie* (2002). (Rev: SLJ 10/02)

1553 Slate, Joseph. *Miss Bindergarten Takes a Field Trip* (PS–K). Illus. by Ashley Wolff. 2001, Dutton $16.99 (0-525-46710-6). 32pp. Miss Bindergarten takes her kindergartners on an interesting field trip that subtly introduces all sorts of shapes. (Rev: BL 10/1/01; HBG 3/02; SLJ 9/01)

1554 Stuve-Bodeen, Stephanie. *Elizabeti's School* (PS–1). Illus. by Christy Hale. 2002, Lee & Low $16.95 (1-58430-043-4). 32pp. Elizabeti tackles her first day at school and comes home to tell her loving family all about it in this story set in Tanzania. (Rev: BCCB 12/02; BL 9/15/02; HB 11–12/02; HBG 3/03; SLJ 9/02)

1555 Veldkamp, Tjibbe. *The School Trip* (PS–3). Illus. by Philip Hopman. 2001, Front Street $15.95 (1-886910-70-7). 32pp. Afraid of attending school, Davy opts to build his own, and when he adds wheels the fun really starts. (Rev: BL 8/01; HBG 10/01; SLJ 7/01)

1556 Wallace, John. *The Twins* (PS–1). Illus. 2001, Golden Books LB $9.95 (0-307-10211-4). 32pp. Twins Lil and Nelly, who are temperamental opposites, win a kindergarten writing contest with a paper by sweet Lil to which Nelly has added tart comments. (Rev: BL 8/01; HBG 3/02)

1557 Weston, Carrie. *Lucky Socks* (K–3). Illus. by Charlotte Middleton. 2002, Putnam $14.99 (0-8037-2741-0). 32pp. Kevin can't find his "lucky" yellow socks to wear to school for field day, but discovers that even when things don't go quite right, the day can still be special. (Rev: BL 2/15/02; HBG 10/02; SLJ 3/02)

1558 Wheatley, Nadia. *Luke's Way of Looking* (K–4). Illus. by Matt Ottley. 2001, Kane $15.95 (1-929132-18-2). Appealing illustrations extend this story of a young boy who doesn't match his art teacher's expectations. (Rev: HBG 3/02; SLJ 6/02)

1559 Whelan, Gloria. *Are There Bears in Starvation Lake?* (3–4). Series: Road to Reading. 2002, Golden Books LB $11.99 (0-307-46515-2); paper $3.99 (0-307-26515-3). Fourth-grader Baylor is nervous about an overnight school trip, but gets a chance to shine. (Rev: BL 3/15/03)

TRANSPORTATION AND MACHINES

1560 Barton, Byron. *My Car* (PS). Illus. 2001, Greenwillow LB $14.89 (0-06-029625-9). 40pp. Sam shows readers his car, describing its features, its many uses, and how he drives it. (Rev: BL 7/01; HB 11–12/01*; HBG 3/02; SLJ 8/01)

1561 Booth, Philip. *Crossing* (1–4). Illus. by Bagram Ibatoulline. 2001, Candlewick $16.99 (0-7636-1420-3). 40pp. Excellent gouache artwork accompanies a rhythmic, lyrical poem featuring townspeople watching a period freight train pass. (Rev: BL 11/15/01; HBG 3/02; SLJ 11/01) [811]

1562 Brown, Margaret Wise. *Two Little Trains* (PS–K). Illus. by Diane Dillon. 2001, HarperCollins $15.95 (0-06-028376-9). 40pp. Using double-page spreads, this book shows two parallel journeys, one by a streamlined diesel train as it travels across the country and the other by a toy train as it moves around a house. (Rev: BL 4/15/01*; HB 5–6/01*; HBG 10/01; SLJ 5/01)

1563 Carter, Don. *Get to Work, Trucks!* (PS). Illus. 2002, Millbrook LB $21.90 (0-7613-2518-2). 24pp. Three-dimensional illustrations and a simple text present a crew of colorful trucks and their multiethnic drivers who spend the day digging, hauling, and building. (Rev: BCCB 5/02; BL 3/1/02; HBG 10/02; SLJ 3/02*)

1564 Collicut, Paul. *This Car* (PS–1). Illus. 2002, Farrar $15.00 (0-374-39965-4). 32pp. All types of cars, from toys to high-performance vehicles, are the subjects of this colorful picture book by the author and illustrator of *This Boat* (2001), *This Plane* (2000), and *This Train* (1999). (Rev: BL 8/02; HBG 3/03; SLJ 8/02)

1565 Gibbons, Faye. *Full Steam Ahead* (K–3). Illus. by Sherry Meidell. 2002, Boyds Mills $15.95 (1-56397-858-X). 32pp. Sammy and his family experience the excitement of seeing the first train to roll through their home town in Georgia. (Rev: BL 4/1/02; HBG 10/02; SLJ 7/02)

1566 Hill, Lee Sullivan. *Earthmovers* (2–3). Illus. Series: Pull Ahead Books. 2002, Lerner LB $22.60 (0-8225-0689-0); paper $5.95 (0-8225-0603-3). 32pp. A small-format book for younger readers about how earthmovers and their drivers accomplish their tasks. Also use *Trains* (2002). (Rev: BL 8/02; HBG 3/03; SLJ 10/02)

1567 Hundal, Nancy. *Number 21* (PS–3). Illus. by Brian Denes. 2001, Fitzhenry & Whiteside $16.95 (1-55041-543-3). 32pp. Three children are excited to see Dad's new dump truck, especially when he fills the dump box with water to make an instant swimming pool. (Rev: BL 8/01; SLJ 4/01)

1568 Lenski, Lois. *The Little Fire Engine* (PS). Illus. 2002, Random $6.99 (0-375-82263-1). 30pp. An abridged, colorful board-book version of the 1940s classic about a fireman and his engine rescuing the inhabitants from a house fire. Also use *The Little Train* (2002). (Rev: BL 12/1/02; HBG 3/03)

1569 Mayo, Margaret. *Emergency!* (PS–1). Illus. by Alex Ayliffe. 2002, Carolrhoda $14.95 (0-87614-922-0). 32pp. Arresting artwork details emergency vehicles and their uses in this exciting, large-format picture book. (Rev: BL 8/02; HBG 3/03; SLJ 10/02)

1570 Richards, Laura E. *Jiggle Joggle Jee!* (PS). Illus. by Sam Williams. 2001, HarperCollins LB $15.89 (0-688-17833-2). 32pp. A newly illustrated version of an early-20th-century fantasy poem about a train. (Rev: BL 7/01; HBG 10/01; SLJ 5/01)

1571 Sturges, Philemon. *I Love Planes!* (PS–1). Illus. by Shari Halpern. 2003, HarperCollins LB $14.89 (0-06-028899-X). 32pp. A little boy imagines taking flight in an airplane, a balloon, a spaceship, and more. Also use *I Love Trains!* (2001). (Rev: BL 2/1/03; SLJ 3/03)

1572 Stutson, Caroline. *Night Train* (PS–2). Illus. by Katherine Tillotson. 2002, Millbrook LB $22.90 (0-7613-2662-6). 32pp. The romance and thrill of an overnight train ride is captured in this picture book about a boy's journey with his dad. (Rev: BL 5/1/02; HBG 10/02; SLJ 5/02)

Stories About Holidays and Holy Days

GENERAL AND MISCELLANEOUS

1573 Bauer, Marion Dane. *My Mother Is Mine* (PS–1). Illus. by Peter Elwell. 2001, Simon & Schuster $13.00 (0-689-82267-7). Soft pastel illustrations and gentle verses celebrate the relationship between mother and child as a little girl works on a card for Mother's Day. (Rev: HBG 10/01; SLJ 4/01)

1574 Bertrand, Diane Gonzales. *Uncle Chente's Picnic / El Picnic de Tio Chente* (K–2). Trans. by Julia Mercedes Castilla. Illus. by Pauline Rodriguez Howard. 2001, Piñata $14.95 (1-55885-337-5). Uncle Chente arrives for a Fourth of July picnic, but plans must be changed when there is a huge storm. (Rev: SLJ 1/02)

1575 Bourgeois, Paulette. *Franklin's Holiday Treasury* (PS–1). Illus. by Brenda Clark. 2002, Kids Can $15.95 (1-55337-045-7). 128pp. Four holiday adventures of Franklin the turtle are gathered here: Halloween, Thanksgiving, Christmas, and Valentine's Day. (Rev: BL 1/1–15/03; HBG 3/03)

1576 French, Vivian. *A Present for Mom* (PS). Illus. by Dana Kubick. 2002, Candlewick $13.99 (0-7636-1587-0). 32pp. Stanley, a young cat, finds that the best gift for Mother's Day is a box of kisses. (Rev: BL 5/1/02; HBG 10/02; SLJ 5/02)

1577 Freschet, Gina. *Beto and the Bone Dance* (K–3). Illus. 2001, Farrar $16.00 (0-374-31720-8). 32pp. The spirit of Beto's grandmother visits him on the Day of the Dead in this picture book set in Mexico. (Rev: BCCB 12/01; BL 10/15/01; HBG 3/02; SLJ 10/01)

1578 Nolan, Janet. *The St. Patrick's Day Shillelagh* (2–4). Illus. by Ben F. Stahl. 2002, Albert Whitman $15.95 (0-8075-7344-2). 32pp. On his trip from Ireland to America during the potato famine, Fergus carved a beautiful shillelagh that is passed from generation to generation. (Rev: BL 1/1–15/03; HBG 3/03; SLJ 12/02)

1579 Shragg, Karen I. *A Solstice Tree for Jenny* (K–3). Illus. by Heidi Schwabacher. 2001, Prometheus paper $12.00 (1-57392-930-1). 50pp. Jenny wants to know why her family doesn't celebrate any religious holidays. (Rev: BL 12/15/01)

1580 Van Nutt, Julia. *Skyrockets and Snickerdoodles* (2–4). Illus. by Robert Van Nutt. 2001, Doubleday $15.95 (0-385-32553-3). 32pp. Cobtown's Fourth of July celebration in 1845 includes a baseball game, fireworks, and a problem with the town name. (Rev: BL 9/1/01; HBG 10/01; SLJ 7/01)

1581 Wong, Janet. *Apple Pie Fourth of July* (PS–2). Illus. by Margaret Chodos-Irvine. 2002, Harcourt $16.00 (0-15-202543-X). 40pp. A young Chinese American girl working in her parents' grocery is convinced no one will want to eat their Chinese food on the Fourth of July. (Rev: BL 8/02; HBG 10/02; SLJ 5/02)

BIRTHDAYS

1582 Bacharach, Burt, and Hal David. *I Say a Little Prayer for You* (PS–1). Illus. by Karin Littlewood. 2002, Scholastic $16.95 (0-439-29658-7). 32pp. The Diane Warwick song is translated into a picture book about an African American mother and her young girl on the child's birthday. (Rev: BL 4/15/02; HBG 10/02; SLJ 7/02)

1583 Bertrand, Diane Gonzales. *The Last Doll / La Ultima Muneca* (PS–3). Illus. by Anthony Accardo. 2001, Arte Publico $14.95 (1-55885-290-5). 32pp. A special doll dressed in white lace is chosen to be a gift for Teresa at her *quinceanera* coming-of-age party. (Rev: BL 10/1/01; SLJ 4/01)

1584 Chavarria-Chairez, Becky. *Magda's Pinata Magic / Magda y el Piñata Magica* (K–3). Trans. by Gabriela Baeza Ventura. Illus. by Anne Vega. 2001, Arte Publico $14.95 (1-55885-320-0). 32pp. Gabriel is upset by the idea of destroying his birthday pinata, so his sister Magda comes up with a solution in this bilingual picture book. (Rev: BL 10/15/01; SLJ 1/02)

1585 Cohen, Caron Lee. *Happy to You!* (PS). Illus. by Rosanne Litzinger. 2001, Clarion $15.00 (0-618-04229-6). 32pp. Little Daniel says "Happy to you!" to everything he sees after hearing the song "Happy Birthday to You" in this rhyming picture book. (Rev: BL 9/15/01; HBG 3/02; SLJ 9/01)

1586 Dominguez, Kelli Kyle. *The Perfect Pinata / La Piñata Perfecta* (PS–2). Trans. by Teresa Mlawer. Illus. by Diane Patterson. 2002, Albert Whitman $14.95 (0-8075-6495-8). 32pp. This bilingual text describes Marisa's reluctance to break her beautiful sixth-birthday pinata and her parents' happy solution. (Rev: BL 4/15/02; HBG 10/02)

1587 Lasky, Kathryn. *Starring Lucille* (PS–K). Illus. by Marylin Hafner. 2001, Knopf LB $22.95 (0-517-

80040-3). 32pp. Piglet Lucille has a special birthday despite her siblings' best efforts. (Rev: BL 10/1/01; HBG 3/02; SLJ 1/02)

1588 Look, Lenore. *Henry's First-Moon Birthday* (PS–3). Illus. by Yumi Heo. 2001, Simon & Schuster $16.00 (0-689-82294-4). 40pp. Young Jen, a Chinese American girl, helps her grandmother in the preparation of her young brother's first-moon birthday party. (Rev: BCCB 3/01; BL 4/1/01*; HBG 10/01; SLJ 6/01*)

1589 Rose, Deborah Lee. *Birthday Zoo* (PS–2). Illus. by Lynn Munsinger. 2002, Albert Whitman $15.95 (0-8075-0776-8). 32pp. A little boy is treated to a rollicking birthday party hosted by the animals at the zoo in this rhyming picture book. (Rev: BL 9/15/02; HB 11–12/02; HBG 3/03; SLJ 10/02)

1590 Scrimger, Richard. *Bun Bun's Birthday* (PS–K). Illus. by Gillian Johnson. 2001, Tundra $12.95 (0-88776-520-3). Winifred doesn't see why her baby sister should have a first birthday party, when it's her own turn. (Rev: BCCB 4/01; HBG 10/01; SLJ 6/01)

1591 Spinelli, Eileen. *In My New Yellow Shirt* (PS). Illus. by Hideko Takahashi. 2001, Holt $15.95 (0-8050-6242-4). 32pp. A birthday boy sees lots of potential in his new yellow shirt, despite his friend's dismissal of the gift. (Rev: BCCB 9/01; BL 6/1–15/01; HBG 3/02; SLJ 8/01)

1592 Starr, Meg. *Alicia's Happy Day* (PS–1). Illus. by Ying-Hwa Hu. 2003, Star Bright $15.95 (1-887724-85-6). 32pp. Alicia's birthday is a happy, special day thanks to her friends, neighbors, and family. (Rev: BL 2/1/03)

CHRISTMAS

1593 Ashforth, Camilla. *Willow at Christmas* (PS–2). Illus. 2002, Candlewick $12.00 (0-7636-1850-0). 32pp. Willow, a little teddy bear, enjoys a beautiful Christmas at snowy Paradise Farm. (Rev: BL 9/15/02; HBG 3/03)

1594 Augustin, Barbara. *Antonella and Her Santa Claus* (PS–1). Illus. by Gerhard Lahr. 2001, Kane $14.95 (1-929132-13-1). 40pp. An Italian girl's Christmas wish is granted when Hungarian children find the balloon she has sent to Santa. (Rev: BL 10/15/01; HBG 3/02; SLJ 10/01)

1595 Autry, Gene, and Oakley Haldeman. *Here Comes Santa Claus* (PS–1). Illus. by Bruce Whatley. 2002, HarperCollins LB $18.89 (0-06-028269-X). 32pp. The 1947 song coauthored by Gene Autry forms the basis of this picture book that follows parallel stories of Santa's preparations and a family readying for his arrival. (Rev: BL 10/1/02; HBG 3/03; SLJ 10/02)

1596 Bartoletti, Susan. *The Christmas Promise* (K–3). Illus. by David Christiana. 2001, Scholastic $15.95 (0-590-98451-9). 40pp. A little girl's father promises to return when he finds work in this story set during the Depression. (Rev: BCCB 11/01; BL 9/15/01; HBG 3/02; SLJ 10/01)

1597 Bodkin, Odds. *The Christmas Cobwebs* (PS–3). Illus. by Terry Widener. 2001, Harcourt $16.00 (0-15-201459-4). 32pp. A poor family must sell the treasured Christmas ornaments brought from Germany, but spiders spin beautiful webs to take their place on the tree. (Rev: BCCB 11/01; BL 9/15/01; HBG 3/02; SLJ 10/01)

1598 Bunting, Eve. *Christmas Cricket* (PS–2). Illus. by Timothy Bush. 2002, Clarion $15.00 (0-618-06554-7). 32pp. A cricket perched among the branches of a Christmas tree is heartened to hear his chirping described as an angel's song. (Rev: BL 9/15/02; HBG 3/03; SLJ 10/02)

1599 Bunting, Eve. *We Were There: A Nativity Story* (PS–3). Illus. by Wendell Minor. 2001, Clarion $16.00 (0-395-82265-3). 32pp. A variety of creatures including the rat, spider, toad, and snake claim they too were present at Jesus' birth. (Rev: BL 9/1/01; HBG 3/02; SLJ 10/01)

1600 Calhoun, Mary. *A Shepherd's Gift* (PS–2). Illus. by Raul Colon. 2001, HarperCollins LB $15.89 (0-688-15177-9). 32pp. An orphan boy and a lamb make a visit to a stable, where they find baby Jesus and his family. (Rev: BCCB 11/01; BL 9/1/01; HBG 3/02; SLJ 10/01)

1601 Carlson, Nancy. *Harriet and George's Christmas Treat* (PS–2). Illus. 2001, Carolrhoda $15.95 (1-57505-506-6). 32pp. Harriet and George try unsuccessfully to avoid eating Mrs. Hoozit's Christmas fruitcake. (Rev: BL 10/1/01; HBG 3/02; SLJ 10/01)

1602 Climo, Shirley. *Cobweb Christmas: The Tradition of Tinsel.* Rev. ed. (PS–1). Illus. by Jane Manning. 2001, HarperCollins LB $15.89 (0-06-029034-X). A revised text, new illustrations, and larger format enhance this new edition of the story in which spiders transform Tante's Christmas tree into a glistening thing of beauty. (Rev: HBG 3/02; SLJ 10/01)

1603 David, Lawrence. *Peter Claus and the Naughty List* (PS–2). Illus. by Delphine Durand. 2001, Doubleday $15.95 (0-385-32654-8). 32pp. Santa Claus's son Peter convinces his father to reconsider the children on the "naughty list." (Rev: BCCB 11/01; BL 9/15/01; HBG 3/02; SLJ 10/01)

1604 Derby, Sally. *Hannah's Bookmobile Christmas* (K–3). Illus. by Gabi Swiatkowska. 2001, Holt $16.95 (0-8050-6420-6). 32pp. Snowed in, Hannah and her librarian aunt spend Christmas Eve in a cozy bookmobile. (Rev: BL 9/15/01; HBG 3/02; SLJ 10/01)

1605 Evans, Richard Paul. *The Light of Christmas* (K–2). Illus. by Daniel Craig. 2002, Simon & Schuster $16.95 (0-689-83468-3). 32pp. A boy called Alexander does a good deed and is rewarded with the special right to light the flame on Christmas Eve. (Rev: BL 10/1/02; HBG 3/03; SLJ 10/02)

1606 Foreman, Michael. *Cat in the Manger* (PS–3). Illus. 2001, Holt $16.95 (0-8050-6677-2). 24pp. A cat is displaced from his bed to make room for a baby in the manger. (Rev: BCCB 11/01; BL 9/15/01; HBG 3/02; SLJ 10/01)

1607 Garland, Michael. *Christmas City* (PS–2). Illus. 2002, Dutton $15.99 (0-525-46904-4). 32pp. A magical flying taxi transports Tommy to the architectural wonder called Christmas City, where hidden treasures lurk on his route searching for Aunt Jeanne. (Rev: BL 10/1/02; HBG 3/03; SLJ 10/02)

1608 Garland, Michael. *Christmas Magic* (PS–3). Illus. 2001, Dutton $16.99 (0-525-46797-1). 32pp. Arresting artwork shows how Emily's Christmas Eve was a night of real enchantment. (Rev: BCCB 11/01; BL 9/1/01; HBG 3/02; SLJ 10/01)

1609 Godwin, Laura. *Happy Christmas, Honey!* (K–1). Illus. by Jane Chapman. 2002, Simon & Schuster $14.95 (0-689-84714-9). 32pp. Honey the kitten makes a mess of all the Christmas preparations, so Happy the dog assigns her to help him wait for Santa to arrive in this beginning reader. (Rev: BL 11/1/02; HBG 3/03; SLJ 10/02)

1610 Gutman, Anne. *Gaspard and Lisa's Christmas Surprise* (PS–K). Illus. by Georg Hallensleben. Series: The Misadventures of Gaspard and Lisa. 2002, Knopf $9.95 (0-375-82229-1). Gaspard and Lisa, young animals, set out to make a raincoat for their teacher. (Rev: HBG 3/03; SLJ 10/02)

1611 Hall, Katy, and Lisa Eisenberg. *Ho Ho Ho, Ha Ha Ha: Holly-arious Christmas Knock-Knock Jokes* (1–3). Illus. by Stephen Carpenter. 2001, Harper-Festival paper $6.95 (0-694-01362-5). A collection of Christmas jokes with punch lines under the flaps. (Rev: SLJ 10/01)

1612 Hayles, Marsha. *The Feathered Crown* (K–2). Illus. by Bernadette Pons. 2002, Holt $16.95 (0-8050-6421-4). 32pp. In this Nativity story told in rhyming text, mother birds fly from near and far to feather baby Jesus' "nest." (Rev: BL 9/1/02; HBG 3/03; SLJ 10/02)

1613 High, Linda Oatman. *The Last Chimney of Christmas Eve* (PS–2). Illus. by Kestutis Kasparavicius. 2001, Boyds Mills $15.95 (1-56397-804-0). 32pp. Nicholas, a chimney sweep, repays a kind stranger by growing up to be Santa Claus. (Rev: BL 9/15/01; HBG 3/02; SLJ 10/01)

1614 Hooper, Maureen Brett. *Silent Night: A Christmas Carol Is Born* (1–3). Illus. by Kasi Kubiak. 2001, Boyds Mills $15.95 (1-56397-782-6). 32pp. The fictionalized story behind the carol "Silent Night." (Rev: BL 9/15/01; HBG 3/02; SLJ 10/01)

1615 Horn, Sandra Ann. *Babushka* (K–3). Illus. by Sophie Fatus. 2002, Barefoot $16.99 (1-84148-353-2). 32pp. In this version of a Russian tale, Babushka travels to visit the newly born Christ child, but gives away the gifts she brought to needy people along the way. (Rev: BL 12/15/02; HBG 3/03; SLJ 10/02)

1616 Ichikawa, Satomi. *What the Little Fir Tree Wore to the Christmas Party* (K–3). Illus. 2001, Putnam $15.99 (0-399-23746-1). 32pp. Two unwanted trees find that nature has decorated them for Christmas. (Rev: BL 9/1/01; HBG 3/02; SLJ 10/01)

1617 Inkpen, Deborah. *Harriet and the Little Fat Fairy* (PS–1). Illus. by author. 2002, Barron's $11.95 (0-7641-5562-8). Emily's hamster disappears inside the Christmas tree, but Santa responds to Emily's request for help. (Rev: HBG 3/03; SLJ 10/02)

1618 Jeffs, Stephanie. *Christopher Bear's First Christmas* (PS–K). Illus. by Jacqui Thomas. Series: Christopher Bear. 2002, Augsburg $5.99 (0-8066-4349-8). 29pp. Joe and his bear participate in the preschool's presentation of the first Christmas. (Rev: SLJ 10/02)

1619 Johnston, Tony. *Clear Moon, Snow Soon* (PS–K). Illus. by Guy Porfirio. 2001, Rising Moon $15.95 (0-87358-785-5). 24pp. On a snowy Christmas Eve a boy waits for Santa to come, sneaking downstairs just in time to catch a glimpse of red disappearing up the chimney. (Rev: BL 11/1/01; HBG 3/02; SLJ 10/01)

1620 Joosse, Barbara M. *A Houseful of Christmas* (PS–2). Illus. by Betsy Lewin. 2001, Holt $14.95 (0-8050-6391-9). 32pp. Granny's pets must adapt when Christmas comes and her house fills up with relatives. (Rev: BL 10/1/01; HBG 3/02; SLJ 10/01)

1621 Kasparavicius, Kestutis. *The Bear Family's World Tour Christmas* (K–2). Illus. by author. 2002, Abrams $14.95 (0-8109-0573-6). The Bear Family sets off by hot-air balloon to visit relatives around the world. (Rev: HBG 3/03; SLJ 10/02)

1622 Kastner, Jill. *Merry Christmas, Princess Dinosaur!* (PS). Illus. 2002, HarperCollins LB $17.89 (0-06-000472-X). 32pp. Princess Dinosaur is so excited by the prospect of Santa's visit that she falls asleep in the Christmas tree. (Rev: BL 9/1/02; HBG 3/03; SLJ 10/02)

1623 Krensky, Stephen. *How Santa Lost His Job* (PS–2). Illus. by S. D. Schindler. 2001, Simon & Schuster $15.00 (0-689-83173-0). 32pp. Santa is nearly replaced by a contraption called the Deliverator in this jolly picture book. (Rev: BCCB 11/01; BL 9/15/01; HBG 3/02; SLJ 10/01*)

1624 Krupinski, Loretta. *Christmas in the City* (PS–2). Illus. 2002, Hyperion $15.99 (0-7868-0834-9). 40pp. This beautifully illustrated book tells the tale of Mr. and Mrs. Mouse and their Christmas trip to New York during which they explore the city and Mrs. Mouse gives birth in a manger. (Rev: BL 9/15/02; HBG 3/03; SLJ 10/02)

1625 Lee, Quinlan B. *Crazy Christmas Chaos: A Tongue Twister Tale* (1–3). Illus. by Clive Scruton. 2002, HarperFestival paper $6.99 (0-694-01683-7). Wordplay and moving flaps add to the fun as elves, snowmen, and Santa scurry about. (Rev: SLJ 10/02)

1626 Leeson, Christine. *The Magic of Christmas* (PS–3). Illus. by Gaby Hansen. 2001, ME Media $14.95 (1-58925-011-7). 30pp. In this charming picture book, Molly Mouse and her brothers and sisters decorate a Christmas tree with help from forest friends usually considered enemies. (Rev: BL 9/15/01; SLJ 10/01)

1627 Lobato, Arcadio. *The Secret of the North Pole* (PS–K). Illus. by author. 2002, McGraw-Hill $15.00 (1-56189-309-9). A polar bear discovers how Santa manages to deliver all the presents on Christmas Eve. (Rev: HBG 3/03; SLJ 10/02)

1628 McCourt, Lisa. *Merry Christmas, Stinky Face* (PS). Illus. by Cyd Moore. 2002, Troll $15.95 (0-8167-7468-4). 32pp. Stinky Face has silly worries about Christmas (Santa's boots might fall off, a reindeer might get stuck), but his mother calms his fears. (Rev: BL 9/15/02; HBG 3/03; SLJ 10/02)

1629 McKay, Hilary. *Was That Christmas?* (PS–2). Illus. by Amanda Harvey. 2002, Simon & Schuster $16.00 (0-689-84765-3). 32pp. Bella is crushed when Santa's visit to her preschool doesn't live up to her expectations, but all is well come Christmas morning. (Rev: BCCB 11/02; BL 9/1/02; HB 11–12/02*; HBG 3/03; SLJ 10/02)

1630 Manuel, Lynn. *The Christmas Thingamajig* (K–2). Illus. by Carol Benioff. 2002, Dutton $16.99 (0-525-46120-5). 32pp. Chloe misses her dead grandmother's Christmas rituals, but her grandfather helps her start a new tradition. (Rev: BL 9/15/02; HBG 3/03; SLJ 10/02)

1631 Mathers, Petra. *Herbie's Secret Santa* (PS–2). Illus. Series: Lottie's World. 2002, Simon & Schuster $15.95 (0-689-83550-7). 32pp. Herbie the duck feels dreadful about stealing a Christmas cookie, so his friend Lottie, a hen, helps him set things right. (Rev: BL 9/1/02; HBG 3/03; SLJ 10/02)

1632 May, Robert L. *Rudolph the Red-Nosed Reindeer: The Original Story of Rudolph* (K–3). Illus. by David Wenzel. 2001, Grosset $9.99 (0-448-42534-3). The original text of Rudolph is presented with new illustrations that convey a warm, nostalgic feeling. (Rev: HBG 3/02; SLJ 10/01)

1633 Menendez, Shirley. *Allie, the Christmas Spider* (PS–2). Illus. by Maggie Kneen. 2002, Dutton $15.99 (0-525-46860-9). 32pp. Allie spins a beautiful web to decorate the Christmas tree of a poor bunny family. (Rev: BL 9/15/02; HBG 3/03; SLJ 10/02)

1634 Moore, Clement Clarke. *The Night Before Christmas* (PS–3). Illus. by Raquel Jaramillo. 2001, Simon & Schuster $18.95 (0-689-84053-5). 40pp. The familiar Christmas rhyme, presented in the style of a family photo album. (Rev: BCCB 11/02; BL 9/1/01; HBG 3/02; SLJ 10/01)

1635 Parker, Toni Trent. *Snowflake Kisses and Gingerbread Smiles* (PS–2). Photos by Earl Anderson. 2002, Scholastic $6.95 (0-439-33872-7). Photographs of seasonal items and African American children emphasize the delights of Christmas. (Rev: HBG 3/03; SLJ 10/02)

1636 Peterson, Melissa. *Hanna's Christmas* (K–3). Illus. by Melissa Iwai. 2001, HarperFestival $14.95 (0-694-01371-4). 32pp. Hanna is homesick for her life in Sweden and the celebrations there when a package arrives containing a magical "tomten" and in her efforts to make her guest feel at home, she begins to adapt. (Rev: BCCB 11/01; HBG 3/02; SLJ 10/01)

1637 Pinkney, Andrea Davis. *Mim's Christmas Jam* (PS–3). Illus. by Brian Pinkney. 2001, Harcourt $16.00 (0-15-201918-9). 32pp. Pap, digging subway tunnels in New York in the early 20th century, can't be home for Christmas, so Mim sends him homemade jam that fills Pap's boss with Christmas spirit. (Rev: BCCB 11/01; BL 9/15/01; HBG 3/02; SLJ 10/01)

1638 Primavera, Elise. *Auntie Claus and the Key to Christmas* (K–2). 2002, Harcourt $16.00 (0-15-202441-7). 40pp. Christopher, trying to get on Santa's "bad" list, journeys to the North Pole and

becomes a believer after meeting the bad boys and girls on the list. (Rev: BCCB 11/02; BL 9/15/02; HBG 3/03; SLJ 10/02)

1639 Quattlebaum, Mary. *The Shine Man: A Christmas Story* (K–4). Illus. by Tim Ladwig. 2001, Eerdmans $17.00 (0-8028-5181-9). 32pp. A hobo receives a heavenly reward when he shines a boy's shoes on Christmas Eve. (Rev: BL 9/1/01; HBG 3/02; SLJ 10/01)

1640 Reiss, Mike. *Santa Claustrophobia* (2–5). Illus. by David Catrow. 2002, Price Stern Sloan $10.99 (0-8431-7756-X). Santa is suffering from claustrophobia and Doc Holiday recommends some time off. (Rev: BCCB 12/02; HBG 3/03; SLJ 10/02)

1641 Rosenberg, Liz. *On Christmas Eve* (PS–K). Illus. by John Clapp. 2002, Millbrook LB $21.90 (0-7613-2707-X). 40pp. A little boy worries that Santa won't be able to find him when his family must spend Christmas Eve at a motel. (Rev: BCCB 10/02; BL 9/15/02; HBG 3/03; SLJ 10/02)

1642 Rowlands, Avril. *The Christmas Sheep and Other Stories* (2–4). Illus. by Rosslyn Moran. 2001, Good Books $16.00 (1-56148-336-2). 48pp. Four stories about the animals that were part of the first Christmas. (Rev: BL 9/15/01; SLJ 10/01)

1643 Rylant, Cynthia. *Christmas in the Country* (K–2). Illus. by Diane Goode. 2002, Scholastic $15.95 (0-439-07334-0). 32pp. A story of a loving family's beautiful white Christmas, full of tradition and celebration. (Rev: BL 9/15/02; HB 11–12/02; HBG 3/03; SLJ 10/02)

1644 Scarry, Richard. *Richard Scarry's Mr. Fixit's Mixed-up Christmas! A Pop-Up Book with Flaps and Pull-Tabs on All Sides!* (PS–K). Illus. by author. 2001, Simon & Schuster $14.95 (0-689-84487-5). Pop-ups, flaps, tabs, and upside-down reading all present Mr. Fixit's hapless efforts to decorate town. (Rev: SLJ 10/01)

1645 Sierra, Judy. *'Twas the Fright Before Christmas* (PS). Illus. by Will Hillenbrand. 2002, Harcourt $16.00 (0-15-201805-0). A humorous cumulative tale of woes affecting the residents of a haunted house. (Rev: HBG 3/03; SLJ 10/02)

1646 Sloat, Teri. *Hark! The Aardvark Angels Sing* (PS–3). Illus. 2001, Putnam $15.99 (0-399-23371-7). 32pp. A rollicking version of the well-known carol in which aardvark angels fly through the sky on all sorts of vehicles to deliver the Christmas mail. (Rev: BL 9/1/01; HBG 3/02; SLJ 10/01)

1647 Snell, Gordon. *Twelve Days: A Christmas Countdown* (K–2). Illus. by Kevin O'Malley. 2002, HarperCollins LB $17.89 (0-06-028955-4). The Christmas tree grows as the gifts of decorations get larger in this update of the traditional song. (Rev: HBG 3/03; SLJ 10/02)

1648 Spang, Gunter. *The Ox and the Donkey: A Christmas Story* (PS–3). Trans. by Marianne Martens. Illus. by Loek Koopmans. 2001, North-South LB $15.88 (0-7358-1516-X). 32pp. Quiet text and subtle watercolors show how an ox and a donkey are forever changed when the Holy Family comes to their stable. (Rev: BL 9/15/01; HBG 3/02; SLJ 10/01)

1649 Speirs, John. *The Little Boy's Christmas Gift* (PS–3). Illus. 2001, Abrams $16.95 (0-8109-4399-9). 32pp. A boy's gift to the Holy Family is a decorated tree in this lavishly illustrated picture book. (Rev: BL 10/15/01; HBG 3/02)

1650 Tafuri, Nancy. *The Donkey's Christmas Song* (PS). Illus. 2002, Scholastic $16.95 (0-439-27313-7). 32pp. A donkey is reluctant to add his braying to the manger lullaby. (Rev: BL 9/15/02; HBG 3/03; SLJ 10/02)

1651 Taylor, Jane. *Twinkle, Twinkle Little Star* (PS). Illus. by Lesley Harker. 2001, Scholastic $15.95 (0-439-29656-0). 24pp. Two children follow a star to the baby Jesus in this unique interpretation of the classic poem. (Rev: BL 11/15/01; HBG 3/02; SLJ 10/01)

1652 Turner, Sandy. *Silent Night* (2–4). Illus. 2001, Simon & Schuster $16.00 (0-689-84156-6). 32pp. An inventive and skillfully illustrated story of a dog that barks madly to alert his owners that Santa has arrived, to no avail. (Rev: BL 10/1/01; HB 11–12/01; HBG 3/02; SLJ 10/01*)

1653 Ward, Helen. *The Animals' Christmas Carol* (PS–3). Illus. 2001, Millbrook LB $23.90 (0-7613-2408-9). 40pp. A beautifully illustrated book based on the Christmas carol "The Friendly Beasts," in which animals bring gifts to baby Jesus in the manger. (Rev: BCCB 11/01; BL 9/15/01; HBG 3/02)

1654 Waterhouse, Stephen. *Get Busy This Christmas!* (PS–1). Illus. by author. 2002, Bloomsbury $6.95 (1-58234-802-2). Mama Penguin and her children are busy preparing for Christmas, engaging in all the traditional activities. (Rev: SLJ 10/02)

1655 Watson, Wendy. *Holly's Christmas Eve* (PS). Illus. 2002, HarperCollins LB $17.89 (0-688-17653-4). 32pp. Holly, a Christmas ornament, suffers a broken arm when a cat pounces on the tree, but she is mended with help from Santa and the other ornaments. (Rev: BL 9/15/02; HBG 3/03; SLJ 10/02)

1656 Weinberg, Larry. *The Forgetful Bears Help Santa* (PS–1). Illus. by Jason Wolff. 2002, Random $19.95 (0-375-82291-7). 34pp. Santa gets stuck in the Forgetful Bears' chimney in this new version of the 1988 story. (Rev: BL 9/15/02; HBG 3/03)

1657 Wilder, Laura Ingalls. *Santa Comes to Little House* (K–3). Illus. by Renee Graef. 2001, HarperCollins LB $15.89 (0-06-025939-6). 32pp. A picture-book version of the Christmas chapter from *Little House on the Prairie*. (Rev: BL 9/15/01; HBG 3/02; SLJ 10/01)

1658 Wolff, Patricia Rae. *A New Improved Santa* (K–3). Illus. by Lynne W. Cravath. 2002, Scholastic $15.95 (0-439-35249-5). Santa spends the year on self-improvement — diet, exercise, new hairstyle — only to find the children prefer him the old way. (Rev: BCCB 11/02; HBG 3/03; SLJ 10/02)

1659 Wood, Audrey. *A Cowboy Christmas: The Miracle at Lone Pine Ridge* (PS–4). Illus. by Robert Florczak. 2001, Simon & Schuster $19.95 (0-689-82190-5). 48pp. Christmas becomes a special time for young Evan after he rescues cowboy Cully, who

then marries his mother. (Rev: BL 9/1/01; HBG 3/02; SLJ 10/01)

1660 Wood, Don, and Audrey Wood. *Merry Christmas, Big Hungry Bear!* (PS–2). Illus. 2002, Scholastic $15.95 (0-439-32092-5). 48pp. Little Mouse decides to share his Christmas with Big Hungry Bear, who never gets any presents. (Rev: BCCB 11/02; BL 9/15/02; HBG 3/03; SLJ 10/02)

1661 Yin. *Dear Santa, Please Come to the 19th Floor* (1–3). Illus. by Chris Soentpiet. 2002, Philomel $16.99 (0-399-23636-8). Willy asks Santa for a special present for his friend Carlos, who is in a wheelchair and living in poverty. (Rev: HBG 3/03; SLJ 10/02)

EASTER

1662 Berlin, Irving. *Easter Parade* (PS–1). Illus. by Lisa McCue. 2003, HarperCollins LB $16.89 (0-06-029126-5). 32pp. Father Rabbit and his behatted young daughter parade down the street with all the other finely dressed animals in this cheerful rendition of the famous Irving Berlin song. (Rev: BL 3/15/03; SLJ 2/03) [782.42164]

1663 Friedrich, Priscilla, and Otto Friedrich. *The Easter Bunny That Overslept* (PS–2). Illus. by Donald Saaf. 2002, HarperCollins LB $14.89 (0-06-029646-1). 32pp. In this bright new version of a 1950s classic, the Easter Bunny oversleeps and discovers that no one wants Easter eggs on the Fourth of July or Halloween. (Rev: BL 2/15/02; HBG 10/02; SLJ 1/02)

1664 Weigelt, Udo. *The Easter Bunny's Baby* (PS–2). Trans. by Alison James. Illus. by Rolf Siegenthaler. 2001, North-South LB $15.88 (0-7358-1443-0). 32pp. Easter Bunny receives an egg that hatches into a baby ostrich. (Rev: BL 4/1/01; HBG 10/01; SLJ 4/01)

1665 Weninger, Brigitte. *Happy Easter, Davy!* (PS–2). Trans. by Rosemary Lanning. Illus. by Eve Tharlet. 2001, North-South LB $15.88 (0-7358-1436-8). 32pp. Davy Rabbit's family has never heard of the Easter Bunny so he sets out to find him. (Rev: BL 4/1/01; HBG 10/01)

HALLOWEEN

1666 Adams, Georgie. *The Three Little Witches Storybook* (PS–3). Illus. by Emily Bolam. 2002, Hyperion $15.99 (0-7868-0824-1). 32pp. Young witches Zara, Ziggy, and Zoe have magical fun in these eight short, brightly illustrated stories that make good Halloween reading. (Rev: BL 9/1/02; HBG 3/03; SLJ 12/02)

1667 Bullard, Lisa. *Trick-or-Treat on Milton Street* (K–2). Illus. by Joni Oeltjenbruns. 2001, Carolrhoda LB $15.95 (1-57505-158-3). Charley gets a big surprise on Halloween that makes him look at his new neighborhood in quite a different way. (Rev: HBG 3/02; SLJ 9/01)

1668 Bunting, Eve. *The Bones of Fred McFee* (K–3). Illus. by Kurt Cyrus. 2002, Harcourt $16.00 (0-15-202004-7). 32pp. A toy skeleton hung in a tree makes Halloween particularly eerie for a brother and sister, and the local animals. (Rev: BCCB 10/02; BL 9/1/02; HBG 3/03; SLJ 9/02)

1669 Druce, Arden. *Halloween Night* (PS–K). Illus. by David Wenzel. 2001, Rising Moon $14.95 (0-87358-797-9); paper $6.95 (0-87358-762-6). 32pp. Rhyming riddles about a spooky Halloween night are accompanied by illustrations that suit the mood and contain clues. (Rev: BCCB 9/01; BL 9/1/01; HBG 3/02; SLJ 9/01)

1670 Egan, Tim. *The Experiments of Doctor Vermin* (K–3). Illus. 2002, Houghton $15.00 (0-618-13224-4). 32pp. Sheldon the pig stumbles into Dr. Vermin's spooky mansion on Halloween night, but finds refuge with the wolves next door in this amusing story. (Rev: BL 9/1/02; HBG 3/03; SLJ 10/02)

1671 Fleming, Denise. *Pumpkin Eye* (1–3). Illus. 2001, Holt $15.95 (0-8050-6681-0). 32pp. Lightly scary Halloween excitement is captured in rhyming text and inventive artwork. (Rev: BCCB 10/01; BL 9/15/01; HBG 3/02; SLJ 9/01)

1672 Glassman, Miriam. *Halloweena* (K–2). Illus. by Victoria Roberts. 2002, Simon & Schuster $15.95 (0-689-82825-X). 40pp. Hepzibah, a witch, has trouble raising Halloweena, a baby girl, in this picture book with detailed and clever illustrations. (Rev: BCCB 10/02; BL 9/1/02; HBG 3/03; SLJ 9/02)

1673 Jane, Pamela. *Monster Mischief* (PS–1). Illus. by Vera Rosenberry. 2001, Simon & Schuster $16.00 (0-689-80471-7). 32pp. Monsters settle for candy when their Halloween stew is ruined. (Rev: BCCB 9/01; BL 9/1/01; HBG 3/02; SLJ 9/01)

1674 Lasky, Kathryn. *Porkenstein* (PS–2). Illus. by David Jarvis. 2002, Scholastic $15.95 (0-590-62380-X). 40pp. Porkenstein, a huge mutant pig created to seek revenge on the Big Bad Wolf, gobbles him up on Halloween. (Rev: BCCB 10/02; BL 9/15/02; HBG 3/03; SLJ 9/02)

1675 McCully, Emily Arnold. *Grandmas Trick-or-Treat* (1–2). Illus. Series: An I Can Read Book. 2001, HarperCollins LB $14.89 (0-06-028731-4). 48pp. Grandma Nan and Grandma Sal turn out to be useful trick-or-treating companions after all in this easy reader. (Rev: BCCB 9/01; BL 9/1/01; HBG 3/02; SLJ 9/01)

1676 Martin, Bill, Jr., and Michael Sampson. *Trick or Treat?* (1–3). Illus. by Paul Meisel. 2002, Simon & Schuster $14.95 (0-689-84968-0). 40pp. Cartoon illustrations give additional humor to a little boy's experiences during a "wackbards" trick-or-treat in his apartment building. (Rev: BL 9/15/02; HBG 3/03; SLJ 10/02)

1677 Mayr, Diane. *Littlebat's Halloween Story* (PS–1). Illus. by Gideon Kendall. 2001, Albert Whitman $14.95 (0-8075-7629-8). 32pp. Littlebat loves story time but his mother tells him he must remain hidden until he can make an appearance without scaring the children. (Rev: BL 9/1/01; HBG 3/02; SLJ 9/01)

1678 Melmed, Laura Krauss. *Fright Night Flight* (PS–2). Illus. by Henry Cole. 2002, HarperCollins LB $17.89 (0-06-029702-6). 32pp. A witch and her friends set off on jet-fueled brooms for a trick-or-

treat spree, warning readers in rhyme that they're the next stop. (Rev: BL 9/1/02; HBG 3/03; SLJ 9/02)

1679 Mills, Claudia. *Gus and Grandpa and the Halloween Costume* (2–3). Illus. by Catherine Stock. Series: Gus and Grandpa. 2002, Farrar $15.00 (0-374-32816-1). 48pp. It's Grandpa who solves Gus's Halloween costume crisis, producing a Mounties uniform that Gus's father wore when he was a boy. (Rev: BL 9/1/02; HBG 3/03)

1680 Poydar, Nancy. *The Perfectly Horrible Halloween* (PS–3). Illus. 2001, Holiday $16.95 (0-8234-1592-9). 32pp. Arnold successfully improvises for the Halloween contest after forgetting his costume. (Rev: BL 9/1/01; HBG 3/02; SLJ 9/01)

1681 Preston, Tim. *Pumpkin Moon* (PS–3). Illus. by Simon Bartram. 2001, Dutton $16.99 (0-525-46713-0). 32pp. Halloween night is full of enchantment, including a jack-o'-lantern moon, in this almost text-free picture book. (Rev: BL 9/15/01; HBG 3/02; SLJ 10/01)

1682 Ruelle, Karen Gray. *Spookier Than a Ghost* (1–2). Illus. 2001, Holiday $14.95 (0-8234-1667-4). 32pp. Kitten Emily's Halloween costume doesn't turn out quite as she had hoped, but she and brother Harry still have fun trick-or-treating in this easy reader. (Rev: BL 9/15/01; HBG 3/02; SLJ 9/01)

1683 Saltzberg, Barney. *The Problem with Pumpkins: A Hip and Hop Story* (PS–1). Illus. 2001, Harcourt $14.00 (0-15-202489-1). 40pp. Hip (a hippo) and her best friend Hop (a rabbit) argue about what they should be for Halloween. (Rev: BL 9/15/01; HBG 3/02; SLJ 9/01)

1684 Serfozo, Mary. *Plumply, Dumply Pumpkin* (PS–1). Illus. by Valeria Petrone. 2001, Simon & Schuster $12.95 (0-689-83834-4). 32pp. Rhyming text and bright illustrations show little tiger Peter's search for the perfect pumpkin to carve into a jack-o'-lantern. (Rev: BL 9/1/01; HBG 3/02; SLJ 9/01)

1685 Tagg, Christine. *Who Will You Meet on Scary Street? Nine Pop-Up Nightmares!* (PS–K). Illus. by Charles Fuge. 2001, Little, Brown $14.95 (0-316-25606-4). 22pp. A lively pop-up book of frightening and pun-filled characters for Halloween. (Rev: BL 9/15/01)

1686 Todd, Mark. *What Will You Be for Halloween?* (PS–2). Illus. 2001, Houghton $9.95 (0-618-08803-2). 32pp. Brief, rhymed text accompanies pictures of children dressed in Halloween costumes. (Rev: BL 9/1/01; HBG 3/02; SLJ 9/01)

1687 Vaughan, Marcia. *We're Going on a Ghost Hunt* (PS–3). Illus. by Ann Schweninger. 2001, Harcourt $15.00 (0-15-202353-4). 32pp. A light-hearted rhyming Halloween story of two children who go out hunting for a ghost, only to become frightened and run home. (Rev: BL 9/15/01; HBG 3/02; SLJ 9/01)

1688 Weston, Martha. *Tuck's Haunted House* (PS–2). Illus. 2002, Clarion $14.00 (0-618-15966-5). 32pp. Tuck the pig stages a haunted house for his friends, and his little sister Bunny adds to the scariness of Halloween. (Rev: BL 9/1/02; HBG 3/03; SLJ 10/02)

1689 Wiencirz, Gerlinde. *Teddy's Halloween Secret* (PS–2). Trans. from German by J. Alison James. Illus. by Giuliano Lunelli. 2001, North-South LB $15.88 (0-7358-1531-3). Paul's animal friends are so successful in creating his Halloween costume that nobody recognizes him. (Rev: HBG 3/02; SLJ 9/01)

1690 Williams, Suzanne. *The Witch Casts a Spell* (PS–2). Illus. by Barbara Olsen. 2002, Dial $14.99 (0-8037-2646-5). 32pp. Spookily costumed children at a Halloween party dance along to this song, sung to the tune of "The Farmer in the Dell." (Rev: BL 9/1/02)

1691 Winthrop, Elizabeth. *Halloween Hats* (1–3). Illus. by Sue Truesdell. 2002, Holt $15.95 (0-8050-6386-2). 32pp. Amusing illustrations add to the fun as children try on all sorts of hats for Halloween trick-or-treating. (Rev: BL 9/15/02; HBG 3/03; SLJ 10/02)

1692 Wolff, Patricia Rae. *Cackle Cook's Monster Stew* (K–2). Illus. by S. D. Schindler. Series: Golden Books Family Storytime. 2001, Golden Books $9.95 (0-307-10682-9). A witch chef sends her assistant shopping for an alphabetical list of ingredients, from ape hair to a zombie's back. (Rev: HBG 3/02; SLJ 11/01)

1693 Ziefert, Harriet. *On Halloween Night* (PS–2). Illus. by Renee W. Andriani. 2001, Puffin paper $5.99 (0-14-056820-4). Emily's costume grows in "The House That Jack Built" fashion as her whole family pitches in to help. (Rev: SLJ 9/01)

JEWISH HOLY DAYS

1694 Biers-Ariel, Matt. *Solomon and the Trees* (K–3). Illus. by Esti Silverberg-Kiss. 2001, UAHC $12.95 (0-8074-0749-6). 32pp. King Solomon rues the day that he inadvertently allowed his forest to be cut down to build the Temple, in the legend said to have inspired the Jewish holiday of Tu Bish'vat. (Rev: BL 8/01)

1695 Bunting, Eve. *One Candle* (2–3). Illus. by K. Wendy Popp. 2002, HarperCollins LB $17.89 (0-06-028116-2). 32pp. Grandma brings a potato to the family Hanukkah celebration in remembrance of her time in a World War II concentration camp. (Rev: BL 9/1/02; HBG 3/03; SLJ 10/02)

1696 Carter, David A. *Chanukah Bugs: A Pop-Up Celebration* (PS–K). Illus. by author. 2002, Simon & Schuster $10.95 (0-689-81860-2). Flaps that resemble gift boxes open to reveal the "Shammash Bug," the "Dizzy Dreidel Bug," and so forth, one for each of the eight nights. (Rev: SLJ 10/02)

1697 Hall, Katy, and Lisa Eisenberg. *Hanukkah Ha-Has: Knock-Knock Jokes That Are a Latke Fun* (1–3). Illus. by Stephen Carpenter. Series: A Lift-the-Flap Knock-Knock Book. 2001, HarperFestival paper $6.95 (0-694-01361-7). Punch lines under the flaps make for groaning suspense in this collection that is illustrated with a family enjoying latkes and dreidel games. (Rev: SLJ 10/01) [818]

1698 Hest, Amy. *The Friday Nights of Nana* (PS–2). Illus. by Claire A. Nivola. 2001, Candlewick $15.99 (0-7636-0658-8). 32pp. A little girl tells how she helps her grandmother prepare for the Sabbath dinner. (Rev: BL 10/1/01; HBG 3/02; SLJ 10/01)

1699 Howland, Naomi. *The Matzah Man: A Passover Story* (PS–1). Illus. 2002, Clarion $15.00 (0-618-11750-4). 32pp. Matzah Man attempts to escape the Passover seder in this version of the story of the gingerbread boy filled with familiar Jewish references. (Rev: BL 2/15/02; HBG 10/02; SLJ 3/02)

1700 Jules, Jacqueline. *Clap and Count! Action Rhymes for the Jewish New Year* (PS). Illus. by Sally Springer. 2001, Kar-Ben $17.95 (1-58013-067-4). 56pp. Nursery rhymes and finger plays with a Jewish twist take children through the holidays and holy days of the Jewish year. (Rev: BL 11/1/01)

1701 Kimmel, Eric A. *Zigazak! A Magical Hanukkah Night* (PS–4). Illus. by Jon Goodell. 2001, Doubleday $15.95 (0-385-32652-1). 32pp. A rabbi outwits two playful devils who are disrupting a small town's Hanukkah celebration. (Rev: BCCB 10/01; BL 10/1/01; HBG 3/02; SLJ 10/01)

1702 Manushkin, Fran. *Hooray for Hanukkah!* (PS–2). Illus. by Carolyn Croll. 2001, Random LB $11.99 (0-375-91043-3). The menorah tells the story in this unusual view of a family celebrating Hanukkah. (Rev: SLJ 10/01)

1703 Medoff, Francine. *The Mouse in the Matzah Factory* (K–3). Illus. by Nicole In den Bosch. 2003, Kar-Ben paper $6.95 (1-58013-048-8). 32pp. A curious mouse follows a harvest of wheat from field to mill to bakery, where it is made into matzohs for Passover. (Rev: BL 3/15/03)

1704 Newman, Leslea. *Runaway Dreidel!* (PS–2). Illus. by Krysten Brooker. 2002, Holt $17.95 (0-8050-6237-8). 32pp. A rhyming fantasy about a dreidel that takes off, zooming into space to become a star. (Rev: BCCB 11/02; BL 9/1/02; HBG 3/03; SLJ 10/02)

1705 Pushker, Gloria Teles. *Toby Belfer and the High Holy Days* (K–3). Illus. by Judith Hierstein. Series: Toby Belfer. 2001, Pelican $14.95 (1-56554-765-9). 32pp. Toby explains the meaning of the Jewish holidays of Rosh Hashanah and Yom Kippur to her friend Donna. (Rev: BL 10/1/01; HBG 3/02; SLJ 1/02)

1706 Rosen, Michael J. *Chanukah Lights Everywhere* (PS–2). Illus. by Melissa Iwai. 2001, Harcourt $16.00 (0-15-202447-6). 32pp. A boy discovers there are lights all over the place as his family proceeds through the nights of Hanukkah. (Rev: BCCB 11/01; BL 9/1/01; HBG 3/02; SLJ 10/01)

1707 Simpson, Lesley. *The Shabbat Box* (PS–1). Illus. by Nicole In den Bosch. 2001, Kar-Ben paper $6.95 (1-58013-027-5). 32pp. Ira must come up with a solution when he loses the treasured class Shabbat box on his way home from school. (Rev: BL 10/1/01; SLJ 12/01)

1708 Vorst, Rochel Groner. *The Sukkah That I Built* (PS–2). Illus. by Elizabeth Victor-Elsby. 2002, Hachai $9.95 (1-929628-07-2). 26pp. A young boy (with help from his family) builds a sukkah — a temporary structure used in the celebration of Sukkot — to the refrain of "The House that Jack Built." (Rev: BL 10/1/02; HBG 3/03)

1709 Zalben, Jane Breskin. *Pearl's Passover: A Family Celebration Through Stories, Recipes, Crafts, and Songs* (K–3). Illus. 2002, Simon & Schuster $16.00 (0-689-81487-9). 48pp. A lamb named Pearl and her family prepare for Passover in this volume that interweaves fictional characters with recipes, crafts, and basic information about the holiday. (Rev: BL 2/15/02; HB 3–4/02; HBG 10/02; SLJ 2/02)

THANKSGIVING

1710 Bateman, Teresa. *A Plump and Perky Turkey* (PS–2). Illus. by Jeff Shelly. 2001, Winslow $15.95 (1-890817-91-0). 40pp. Pete the turkey cleverly escapes hungry townspeople on Thanksgiving. (Rev: BCCB 11/01; BL 9/1/01; HBG 3/02; SLJ 9/01)

1711 Corey, Shana. *Millie and the Macy's Parade* (PS–2). Illus. by Brett Helquist. 2002, Scholastic $16.95 (0-439-29754-0). 40pp. Millie, a Polish American girl whose father works for Mr. Macy, comes up with a great idea: a Thanksgiving Day parade. (Rev: BL 9/1/02; HBG 3/03; SLJ 10/02)

1712 De Groat, Diane. *We Gather Together . . . Now Please Get Lost!* (PS–2). Illus. 2001, North-South LB $15.88 (1-58717-096-5). 32pp. Gilbert and his animal classmates take an entertaining, mishap-filled field trip to Pilgrim Town. (Rev: BL 9/1/01; HBG 3/02; SLJ 8/01)

1713 Geisert, Arthur. *Nursery Crimes* (PS–3). Illus. 2001, Houghton $16.00 (0-618-06487-7). 32pp. Turkey-shaped topiaries have gone missing, and the family of pigs who created them must figure out how to expose the thief. (Rev: BCCB 9/01; BL 11/15/01; HBG 3/02; SLJ 11/01)

1714 Greene, Rhonda Gowler. *The Very First Thanksgiving Day* (PS–2). Illus. by Susan Gaber. 2002, Simon & Schuster $15.95 (0-689-83301-6). 40pp. The story of the first Thanksgiving, told in rhyme and accompanied by lovely paintings. (Rev: BL 9/15/02; HBG 3/03; SLJ 10/02)

1715 Jennings, Sharon. *Franklin's Thanksgiving* (PS–1). Illus. by Brenda Clark. Series: Franklin. 2001, Kids Can $10.95 (1-55074-798-3). 32pp. Franklin the turtle's family Thanksgiving dinner becomes so overcrowded that the feast is moved outdoors. (Rev: BL 9/15/01; HBG 3/02; SLJ 9/01)

1716 Kimmelman, Leslie. *Round the Turkey: A Grateful Thanksgiving* (2–4). Illus. by Nancy Cote. 2002, Albert Whitman $15.95 (0-8075-7131-8). 32pp. The members of a family gathered for Thanksgiving take turns giving thanks, in rhyme. (Rev: BL 9/15/02; HBG 3/03; SLJ 9/02)

1717 Lakin, Patricia. *Fat Chance Thanksgiving* (2–4). Illus. by Stacey Schuett. 2001, Albert Whitman $14.95 (0-8075-2288-0). 32pp. Carla and her mother move to a new building but find it hard to make friends until Carla organizes a potluck Thanksgiving dinner. (Rev: BCCB 10/01; BL 9/1/01; HBG 3/02; SLJ 10/01)

1718 Rael, Elsa Okon. *Rivka's First Thanksgiving* (PS–3). Illus. by Maryann Kovalski. 2001, Simon & Schuster $16.00 (0-689-83901-4). 32pp. Young Rivka challenges a rabbi when he says that Jews should not celebrate Thanksgiving in this story set in early 1900s New York. (Rev: BCCB 11/01; BL 9/15/01; HBG 3/02; SLJ 11/01)

1719 Roberts, Bethany. *Thanksgiving Mice!* (PS–1). Illus. by Doug Cushman. 2001, Clarion $13.00 (0-618-12040-8). 32pp. Mice put on a play about the trials of the Pilgrims and the first Thanksgiving. (Rev: BL 9/1/01; HBG 3/02; SLJ 9/01)

1720 Scheer, Julian. *A Thanksgiving Turkey* (PS–3). Illus. by Ronald Himler. 2001, Holiday $16.95 (0-8234-1674-7). 32pp. A boy learns to know his grandfather and Virginia farm life in a beautifully illustrated and sensitive story that culminates with the capture and release of a wild turkey. (Rev: BCCB 10/01; BL 9/1/01; HBG 3/02; SLJ 9/01)

1721 Wheeler, Lisa. *Turk and Runt* (PS–2). Illus. by Frank Ansley. 2002, Simon & Schuster $15.95 (0-689-84761-0). 32pp. The most attractive turkey on the farm, Turk is a natural for Thanksgiving dinner, but his clever brother Runt saves the day in this funny book. (Rev: BL 9/1/02; HBG 3/03; SLJ 10/02)

VALENTINE'S DAY

1722 Bond, Felicia. *The Day It Rained Hearts* (PS–K). 2001, HarperCollins LB $14.89 (0-06-001078-9). 63pp. When it rains hearts, Cornelia catches them and makes unique, individualized valentines for her friends. (Rev: BL 12/1/01; HBG 3/02)

1723 Carr, Jan. *Sweet Hearts* (PS–2). Illus. by Dorothy Donohue. 2002, Holiday $16.95 (0-8234-1732-8). 32pp. Elaborately constructed collage valentines star in this story in which a little panda creates and decorates paper hearts for his parents. (Rev: BL 12/1/02; HBG 3/03; SLJ 11/02)

1724 McNamara, Margaret. *Too Many Valentines* (K–2). Illus. by Mike Gordon. Series: Robin Hill School. 2003, Simon & Schuster LB $11.89 (0-689-85538-9); paper $3.99 (0-689-85537-0). 32pp. Young Neil says he doesn't like valentines and doesn't want to receive any more in this book suitable for beginning readers. (Rev: BCCB 2/03; SLJ 2/03)

1725 Minarik, Else Holmelund. *Little Bear's Valentine* (PS–K). Illus. by Heather Green. Series: Little Bear. 2002, HarperCollins LB $15.89 (0-060-52244-5). 32pp. An anonymous valentine leads Little Bear to his secret admirer — Mother Bear. (Rev: BL 2/15/03; HBG 3/03; SLJ 12/02)

1726 Poydar, Nancy. *Rhyme Time Valentine* (PS–3). Illus. 2002, Holiday $16.95 (0-8234-1684-4). 32pp. Poor little Ruby is dismayed when the valentines she made are blown away by a strong wind. (Rev: BL 1/1–15/03; HBG 3/03; SLJ 11/02)

1727 Thompson, Lauren. *Mouse's First Valentine* (PS). Illus. by Buket Erdogan. 2002, Simon & Schuster $12.95 (0-689-84724-6). 32pp. A little mouse tries to guess what his big sister is up to in this charming book for preschoolers. (Rev: BL 2/1/02; HBG 10/02; SLJ 3/02)

Books for Beginning Readers

1728 Ada, Alma Flor. *Daniel's Mystery Egg* (1–2). Illus. by G. Brian Karas. 2001, Harcourt $10.95 (0-15-216231-3); paper $3.95 (0-15-216237-2). 24pp. Daniel hopes to get a nice, quiet pet when his mystery egg hatches. (Rev: BL 7/01; HBG 3/02; SLJ 2/02)

1729 Adler, David A. *Young Cam Jansen and the Double Beach Mystery* (K–2). Illus. by Susanna Natti. Series: Viking Easy-to-Read. 2002, Viking $13.99 (0-670-03531-9). 32pp. An easy-to-read mystery involving Cam and her friend Eric and mysterious doings on the beach. (Rev: BL 5/1/02; HBG 10/02; SLJ 6/02)

1730 Adler, David A. *Young Cam Jansen and the Library Mystery* (K–2). Illus. by Susanna Natti. 2001, Viking $13.99 (0-670-89281-5). 32pp. Cam is determined to find her father's missing shopping list. (Rev: BL 5/1/01; HBG 10/01)

1731 Baker, Keith. *Little Green* (PS–1). Illus. 2001, Harcourt $16.00 (0-15-292859-6). 32pp. In this easy reader, a boy is fascinated by the behavior of a hummingbird. (Rev: BCCB 4/01; BL 4/15/01; HBG 10/01; SLJ 4/01)

1732 Bang-Campbell, Monika. *Little Rat Sets Sail* (2–3). Illus. by Molly Bang. 2002, Harcourt $14.00 (0-15-216297-6). 48pp. In this beginning chapter book, Little Rat shows great courage as she takes sailing lessons from Buzzy Bear. (Rev: BCCB 5/02; BL 4/1/02; HB 7–8/02*; HBG 10/02; SLJ 6/02)

1733 Bottner, Barbara, and Gerald Kruglik. *It's Not Marsha's Birthday* (1–2). Illus. by Denise Brunkus. Series: Road to Reading. 2001, Golden Books $11.99 (0-307-46333-8); paper $3.99 (0-307-26333-9). 48pp. Lulu feels she's not getting enough birthday attention until she communes with the birthday gorilla at the zoo. (Rev: BL 7/01)

1734 Bowdish, Lynea. *Thunder Doesn't Scare Me!* (K–1). Illus. by John Wallace. Series: Rookie Readers. 2001, Children's $18.00 (0-516-22151-5). 32pp. A small square book about a little girl and her dog who try to be brave during a thunderstorm. (Rev: BL 7/01)

1735 Bowers, Tim. *A New Home* (K–1). Illus. Series: Green Light Reader. 2002, Harcourt $11.95 (0-15-216564-9); paper $3.95 (0-15-216570-3). 20pp. Lonely in his new neighborhood, Matt the squirrel is happy to meet another squirrel named Pam. (Rev: BL 4/15/02; HBG 10/02; SLJ 6/02)

1736 Bridges, Margaret Park. *Edna Elephant* (PS–1). Illus. by Janie Bynum. Series: Brand New Readers. 2002, Candlewick $12.99 (0-7636-1555-2); paper $5.99 (0-7636-1556-0). 40pp. A collection of four stories for beginning readers that star a little elephant who dances, gets a new coat, eats all the cookie batter, and decorates her hat with flowers. (Rev: HBG 3/03; SLJ 1/03)

1737 Cannon, A. E. *On the Go with Pirate Pete and Pirate Joe* (2–3). Illus. by Elwood H. Smith. Series: Viking Easy-to-Read. 2002, Viking $13.99 (0-670-03550-5). 32pp. Three stories for beginning readers about two gentle pirates with smelly feet who have a dog and a cat and gain a parrot. (Rev: BCCB 9/02; HBG 10/02; SLJ 8/02)

1738 Capucilli, Alyssa Satin. *Biscuit Goes to School* (K–1). Illus. by Pat Schories. Series: My First I Can Read Book. 2002, HarperCollins LB $16.89 (0-06-028683-0). 32pp. Biscuit the puppy follows his girl to school in this book for beginning readers. (Rev: BL 8/02; HBG 3/03)

1739 Capucilli, Alyssa Satin. *Biscuit Wants to Play* (PS–K). Illus. by Pat Schories. Series: My First I Can Read Book. 2001, HarperCollins LB $12.89 (0-06-028070-3). 32pp. Biscuit returns, and this time he wants to make friends with two reluctant kittens. (Rev: BL 11/1/01; HBG 10/01; SLJ 4/01)

1740 Cartier, Wesley. *Marco's Run* (1–2). Illus. by Reynold Ruffins. Series: Green Light Reader. 2001, Harcourt $10.95 (0-15-216243-7); paper $3.95 (0-15-216249-6). 20pp. A young African American boy running in a park imagines that he can move as quickly as many different animals in this easy reader. (Rev: BL 4/15/01; HBG 10/01; SLJ 5/01)

1741 Cazet, Denys. *Minnie and Moo: The Night Before Christmas* (K–2). Illus. Series: An I Can Read Book. 2002, HarperCollins LB $17.89 (0-06-623753-X). 48pp. Cows Minnie and Moo decide to dress up as Santa and Mrs. Claus and, accompanied by chickens and a rooster disguised as reindeer, set off to deliver the farmer's presents in this humorous takeoff of the well-known poem. (Rev: BL 10/1/02; HB 11–12/02; HBG 3/03; SLJ 10/02)

1742 Cazet, Denys. *Minnie and Moo: Will You Be My Valentine?* (PS–2). Illus. Series: An I Can Read Book. 2002, HarperCollins LB $16.89 (0-06-623755-6). 48pp. Some feelings are hurt when Minnie and Moo's valentines end up with the wrong recipients in this humorous easy reader. (Rev: BL 1/1–15/03; HB 1–2/03; HBG 3/03; SLJ 2/03)

1743 Cazet, Denys. *Minnie and Moo Meet Frankenswine* (1–2). Illus. by author. Series: An I Can Read Book. 2001, HarperCollins LB $14.89 (0-06-623749-1). 46pp. Cows Minnie and Moo investigate the monster that is terrifying the farm animals. (Rev: HBG 3/02; SLJ 9/01)

1744 Champion, Joyce. *Emily and Alice Baby-Sit Burton* (2–4). 2001, Harcourt $14.00 (0-15-202184-1). 32pp. Young Emily and Alice turn out to be successes as baby-sitters in this easy chapter book. (Rev: BL 7/01; HBG 10/01; SLJ 6/01)

1745 Charles, Veronika M. *Don't Go into the Forest!* (2–3). Illus. by Leanne Franson. Series: Easy-to-Read Spooky Tales. 2001, Stoddart paper $5.95 (0-7737-6190-X). 56pp. Young boys tell each other scary stories while they contemplate entering a forest at night. (Rev: SLJ 1/02)

1746 Charles, Veronika M. *Don't Open the Door!* (2–3). Illus. by Leanne Franson. 2001, Stoddart paper $5.95 (0-7737-6137-3). 56pp. During a sleepover at the narrator's house, the guests enjoy telling each other scary stories. (Rev: BL 4/15/01; SLJ 9/01)

1747 Chorao, Kay. *Up and Down with Kate* (1–2). Illus. Series: Dutton Easy Reader. 2002, Dutton

$13.99 (0-525-46891-9). 48pp. Kate, a little elephant, stars in four charming short stories. (Rev: BL 5/1/02; HBG 10/02; SLJ 7/02)

1748 Clements, Andrew. *Dolores and the Big Fire: A True Story* (1–2). Illus. by Ellen Beier. Series: Pets to the Rescue. 2002, Simon & Schuster $15.00 (0-689-82916-7). 32pp. Dolores, a cat who is afraid of the dark, manages to save her master when their house catches fire. (Rev: BL 6/1–15/02; HBG 10/02; SLJ 5/02)

1749 Clements, Andrew. *Pets to the Rescue: Brave Norman* (1–2). Illus. by Ellen Beier. Series: Ready-to-Read. 2001, Simon & Schuster $15.00 (0-689-82914-0). 32pp. A blind dog rescues a drowning girl in this book for beginning readers. (Rev: BL 11/1/01; HBG 3/02; SLJ 2/02)

1750 Clements, Andrew. *Ringo Saves the Day! A True Story* (K–3). Illus. by Ellen Beier. 2001, Simon & Schuster $15.00 (0-689-82915-9). 32pp. Ringo the cat — named for his affection for drumming — alerts his owners to a broken gas pipe in their backyard. (Rev: HBG 3/02; SLJ 9/01)

1751 Conford, Ellen. *Annabel the Actress, Starring in Hound of the Barkervilles* (2–4). Illus. by Renee W. Andriani. 2002, Simon & Schuster LB $15.00 (0-689-84734-3). 96pp. Annabel's acting career is almost sabotaged by a slobbering dog, a ruined costume, and other nuisances. (Rev: BCCB 10/02; BL 7/02; HBG 3/03; SLJ 7/02)

1752 Cowley, Joy. *Agapanthus Hum and the Angel Hoot* (PS–2). Illus. by Jennifer Plecas. Series: Agapanthus Hum. 2003, Putnam $13.99 (0-399-23344-X). 48pp. When Agapanthus Hum loses a tooth, she finds she can make a special sound her father calls an "angel hoot." (Rev: BCCB 3/03; BL 2/15/03; SLJ 2/03)

1753 Danziger, Paula. *Get Ready for Second Grade, Amber Brown* (1–3). Illus. by Tony Ross. 2002, Putnam $12.99 (0-399-23607-4). 48pp. Amber's concerns about the new second-grade teacher turn out to be unfounded in this prequel for beginning readers. (Rev: BL 11/1/02; HBG 10/02; SLJ 7/02)

1754 Danziger, Paula. *It's a Fair Day, Amber Brown* (1–3). Illus. by Tony Ross. 2002, Putnam $12.99 (0-399-23606-6). 48pp. Amber and her family spend an enjoyable day at the fair despite some arguments and Amber getting lost. (Rev: BL 11/1/02; HBG 10/02; SLJ 7/02)

1755 Danziger, Paula. *What a Trip, Amber Brown* (K–3). Illus. by Tony Ross. Series: A Is for Amber. 2001, Putnam $12.99 (0-399-23469-1). 48pp. Amber and Justin enjoy an on-again off-again friendship on a vacation in the "Poke a nose." (Rev: HBG 10/01; SLJ 4/01)

1756 Denslow, Sharon Phillips. *Georgie Lee* (2–4). Illus. by Lynne Rae Perkins. 2002, HarperCollins LB $15.89 (0-688-17941-X). 96pp. When J.D. visits his grandmother on her farm, they have great times together and with Grandma's intelligent cow, Georgie Lee. (Rev: BCCB 6/02; BL 7/02; HB 7–8/02; HBG 10/02; SLJ 5/02)

1757 dePaola, Tomie. *Boss for a Day* (1–2). Illus. 2001, Putnam LB $13.89 (0-448-42618-8); paper

$3.99 (0-448-42544-0). 32pp. Doggie twins Moffie and Morgie swap their usual roles when Moffie agrees to let Morgie be the boss for a day. (Rev: BL 2/1/02; HBG 3/02; SLJ 2/02)

1758 dePaola, Tomie. *Hide-and-Seek All Week* (1–2). Illus. Series: The Barkers. 2001, Putnam LB $13.89 (0-448-42617-X); paper $3.99 (0-448-42545-9). 32pp. Moffie and Morgie and friends decide they want to play hide-and-seek during recess, but can't decide on the rules. (Rev: BL 2/1/02; HBG 3/02; SLJ 2/02)

1759 Dewey, Ariane, and Jose Aruego. *Splash!* (K–1). Illus. Series: Green Light Reader. 2001, Harcourt $10.95 (0-15-216256-9); paper $3.95 (0-15-216262-3). 24pp. Two clumsy bears play in the river and have no success catching fish. (Rev: BL 7/01; HBG 10/01; SLJ 5/01)

1760 Driscoll, Laura. *Name That Ed* (K–1). Illus. by Esther Szegedy. Series: All Aboard Reading. 2002, Grosset LB $13.89 (0-448-42834-2); paper $3.99 (0-448-42673-0). 32pp. Plain Ed longs for a proper nickname like the others when a family reunion full of Eds with nicknames gathers. (Rev: HBG 3/03; SLJ 2/03)

1761 Duey, Kathleen. *Moonsilver: The Unicorn's Secret #1* (2–4). Illus. by Omar Rayyan. 2001, Simon & Schuster paper $3.99 (0-689-84269-4). 80pp. This alluring fantasy tale for younger readers introduces a young girl who finds a mysterious white mare with a scar on its forehead. (Rev: BL 1/1–15/02; SLJ 12/01)

1762 Duey, Kathleen. *The Mountains of the Moon* (2–4). Illus. by Omar Rayyan. Series: Ready-for-Chapters Unicorn's Secret. 2002, Simon & Schuster LB $11.89 (0-689-85137-5); paper $3.99 (0-689-84272-4). 80pp. The fourth episode in the continuing magical story of Heart and her unicorns, for beginning readers. Also use the third book in the series, *The Silver Bracelet* (2002). (Rev: BL 9/1/02; HBG 3/03)

1763 Duey, Kathleen. *The Sunset Gates* (2–4). Illus. by Omar Rayyan. Series: Unicorn's Secret. 2002, Simon & Schuster LB $11.89 (0-689-85347-5); paper $3.99 (0-689-85346-7). 80pp. The adventures of Heart Avamir, who is on the run in an effort to save two unicorns, continue in this easy-reader as she travels with gypsies and learns to read. Also use *True Heart* (2003). (Rev: BL 3/1/03)

1764 Ehrlich, Amy. *Bravo, Kazam!* (PS–K). Illus. by Barney Saltzberg. Series: Brand New Readers. 2002, Candlewick $12.99 (0-7636-1315-0); paper $4.99 (0-7636-1316-9). 40pp. In this beginning reader illustrated with cartoons, a rabbit is chased by a pack of magical cards. (Rev: BL 4/15/02)

1765 Ehrlich, Amy. *Kazam's Magic* (PS–1). Illus. by Barney Saltzberg. Series: Brand New Readers. 2001, Candlewick $11.99 (0-7636-1309-6). 40pp. Simple tales for beginning readers about an inept young magician. (Rev: HBG 3/02; SLJ 2/02)

1766 Fine, Anne. *The Jamie and Angus Stories* (2–4). Illus. by Penny Dale. 2002, Candlewick $15.99 (0-7636-1862-4). 112pp. Jamie and toy bull Angus have a variety of gentle adventures in these six stories for beginning chapter book readers. (Rev: BCCB 10/02; BL 11/15/02; HB 1–2/03*; HBG 3/03; SLJ 9/02)

1767 Gantos, Jack. *Rotten Ralph Helps Out: A Rotten Ralph Reader* (1–2). Illus. by Nicole Rubel. 2001, Farrar $14.00 (0-374-36355-2). 48pp. Ralph the rotten cat helps — or rather hinders — Sarah with her project on ancient Egypt. (Rev: BL 7/01; HB 9–10/01; HBG 3/02; SLJ 8/01)

1768 Gibala-Broxholm, Scott. *Scary Fright, Are You All Right?* (K–3). Illus. 2002, Dial $14.99 (0-8037-2588-4). 48pp. Scary Fright, a little monster, alarms her parents by acting too much like a human girl. (Rev: BL 9/15/02; HBG 3/03; SLJ 8/02)

1769 Greene, Stephanie. *Owen Foote, Super Spy* (2–4). Illus. by Martha Weston. 2001, Clarion $14.00 (0-618-11752-0). 90pp. Owen and his friends spy on their elementary-school principal in this funny adventure. (Rev: BL 1/1–15/02; HB 11–12/01; HBG 3/02; SLJ 10/01)

1770 Guest, Elissa Haden. *Iris and Walter: The Sleepover* (K–1). Illus. by Christine Davenier. 2002, Harcourt $14.00 (0-15-216487-1). 44pp. Iris can't wait for the sleepover at Walter's house, but when it arrives she can't sleep and has to be taken home to bed. (Rev: BL 11/1/02; HBG 3/03; SLJ 10/02)

1771 Guest, Elissa Haden. *Iris and Walter, True Friends* (2–4). Illus. 2001, Harcourt $14.00 (0-15-202121-3). 44pp. The first two chapters tell the story of Iris, Walter, and their experiences with a lively horse; the last two are school episodes in which Iris must conquer fears and Walter doesn't want to be known as Walt. (Rev: BCCB 9/01; BL 5/1/01; HBG 10/01; SLJ 5/01)

1772 Hall, Katy, and Lisa Eisenberg. *Ribbit Riddles* (2). Illus. by Robert Bender. 2001, Dial $13.99 (0-8037-2525-6). 40pp. A simple book of funny riddles for beginning readers. Also use *Sheepish Riddles* (1996) and *Kitty Riddles* (2000). (Rev: BL 4/15/01; HBG 10/01; SLJ 7/01)

1773 Harrison, David L. *Johnny Appleseed: My Story* (1–2). Illus. by Mike Wohnoutka. Series: Step Into Reading. 2001, Random LB $11.99 (0-375-91247-9); paper $3.99 (0-375-81247-4). 48pp. Johnny Appleseed tells the story of his life to a pioneer family. (Rev: BL 2/1/02; HBG 3/02) [634]

1774 Hayward, Linda. *Pepe and Papa* (K–1). Illus. by Laura Huliska-beith. 2001, Golden Books $13.99 (0-307-46114-9); paper $3.99 (0-307-26114-X). 32pp. Pepe, his Papa, a basket of chilies, and a burro end up in a pile in this silly tale for new readers. (Rev: BL 11/1/01; HBG 10/01)

1775 Hayward, Linda. *What Homework?* (1–3). Illus. by Page Eastburn O'Rourke. 2002, Kane paper $4.99 (1-57565-116-5). 32pp. Andy succeeds in completing his assignment in the nick of time. (Rev: SLJ 11/02)

1776 Heling, Kathryn, and Deborah Hembrook. *Mouse Makes Magic* (K–1). Illus. by Patrick Joseph. Series: Step into Reading. 2002, Random LB $11.99 (0-375-92184-2); paper $3.99 (0-375-82184-8). 32pp. A mouse magician enjoys changing the mid-

dle vowels in three-letter words. (Rev: HBG 3/03; SLJ 1/03)

1777 Heling, Kathryn, and Deborah Hembrook. *Mouse Makes Words: A Phonics Reader* (1–2). Illus. by Patrick Joseph. Series: Step into Reading. 2002, Random paper $3.99 (0-375-81399-3). 32pp. By changing the first letter in a series of words, new words are formed in this beginning reader. (Rev: BL 4/1/02; HBG 10/02; SLJ 7/02)

1778 Holub, Joan. *The Garden That We Grew* (K–2). Illus. by Hiroe Nakata. Series: Viking Easy-to-Read. 2001, Viking $13.99 (0-670-89799-X). 32pp. Children plant pumpkin seeds, tend the plant, harvest the full-grown pumpkins, eat the resulting pies and cookies, and make Halloween faces. (Rev: BL 7/01; HB 7–8/01*; HBG 3/02; SLJ 8/01)

1779 Holub, Joan. *The Pizza That We Made* (K–1). Illus. by Lynne W. Cravath. Series: Easy-to-Read. 2001, Viking $13.99 (0-670-03520-3); paper $3.99 (0-14-230019-5). 32pp. Short sentences and rhyming text are the perfect recipe for new readers in this book about three friends learning how to make pizza. (Rev: BL 11/1/01; HBG 3/02; SLJ 11/01)

1780 Holub, Joan. *Scat, Cats!* (K–1). Illus. by Rich Davis. 2001, Viking $13.89 (0-670-89279-3); paper $3.99 (0-14-130905-9). 32pp. A beginning reader about a boy and girl who shoo an army of cats out of their house only to find that they miss them. (Rev: BL 4/15/01; HBG 3/02; SLJ 8/01)

1781 Hood, Susan. *Look! I Can Tie My Shoes!* (K–1). Illus. by Amy Wummer. Series: All Aboard Reading. 2002, Grosset LB $13.89 (0-448-42835-0); paper $3.99 (0-448-42676-5). 32pp. A mother shows her daughter how to tie shoe laces, in this book for beginning readers and beginning lace tiers. (Rev: HBG 3/03; SLJ 2/03)

1782 Hood, Susan. *Meet Trouble* (PS–1). Illus. by Kristina Stephenson. Series: First Friends First Readers. 2001, Grosset paper $3.99 (0-448-42455-X). Trouble the cat didn't come by his name by accident, and lives up to it in the first of the two stories in this humorous book. (Rev: SLJ 12/01)

1783 Horowitz, Ruth. *Breakout at the Bug Lab* (1–2). Illus. by Joan Holub. Series: Dial Easy-to-Read. 2001, Dial $13.99 (0-8037-2510-8). 48pp. Two boys try to find Max the cockroach, one of the bugs that their mother studies at a nature lab. (Rev: BCCB 7–8/01; BL 4/15/01; HB 7–8/01; HBG 10/01; SLJ 4/01*)

1784 Howard, Reginald. *The Big, Big Wall* (K–1). Illus. by Ariane Dewey and Jose Aruego. 2001, Harcourt paper $3.95 (0-15-216522-3). An easy-reader version of "Humpty Dumpty" in which a mouse, a rabbit, and a pig save the egg from cracking. (Rev: BCCB 2/02; HBG 3/02; SLJ 11/01)

1785 Hurwitz, Johanna. *Ethan Out and About* (PS–1). Illus. by Brian Floca. Series: Brand New Readers. 2002, Candlewick $12.99 (0-7636-1098-4); paper $5.99 (0-7636-1099-2). 40pp. A collection of four stories that star a little African American boy who befriends a cat, learns to ride a bike, chases squirrels in the bird feeder, and forfeits his lunch. (Rev: HBG 3/03; SLJ 1/03)

1786 Hurwitz, Johanna. *Oh No, Noah!* (2–4). Illus. by Mike Reed. 2002, North-South $14.95 (1-58717-133-3). 128pp. Eight-year-old Noah finds it's not so hard to make friends in his new neighborhood in this beginning chapter book. (Rev: HBG 10/02; SLJ 5/02)

1787 Hutchins, Hazel. *Robyn's Art Attack* (K–3). Illus. by Yvonne Cathcart. Series: First Novels. 2002, Formac paper $3.99. CIP (0-88780-564-7). 59pp. Robyn's classmates expect a boring day when she chooses an art gallery for their field trip. (Rev: SLJ 1/03)

1788 Inches, Alison. *Corduroy Writes a Letter* (K–2). Illus. by Allan Eitzen. Series: Viking Easy-to-Read. 2002, Viking $13.99 (0-670-03548-3). 32pp. Corduroy the teddy bear and Lisa, an African American girl, find out how much they can accomplish by writing letters. Also use *Corduroy's Garden* (2002). (Rev: BL 1/1–15/03; HBG 3/03)

1789 Jacobson, Jennifer Richard. *Winnie Dancing on Her Own* (2–3). Illus. by Alissa Imre Geis. 2001, Houghton $15.00 (0-618-13287-2). 96pp. Her father helps clumsy 8-year-old Winnie when she tries to take up ballet to be with her best friends. (Rev: BCCB 11/01; BL 9/15/01; HBG 3/02; SLJ 12/01)

1790 Jennings, Patrick. *The Tornado Watches: An Ike and Mem Story* (2–5). Illus. by Anna Alter. 2002, Holiday $15.95 (0-8234-1672-0). 64pp. A young boy named Ike fears his family is in danger after a tornado warning causes them to spend the night in their basement. (Rev: BL 8/02; HB 1–2/03; HBG 3/03; SLJ 12/02)

1791 Jennings, Patrick. *The Weeping Willow* (2–4). Illus. by Anna Alter. 2002, Holiday $15.95 (0-8234-1671-2). 56pp. Friends Ike and Buzzy decide to build a tree house, only to find themselves embroiled in arguments. (Rev: BL 12/15/02; HB 1–2/03*; HBG 3/03; SLJ 2/03)

1792 Johnston, Tony. *Alien and Possum: Friends No Matter What* (1–2). Illus. by Tony Diterlizzi. 2001, Simon & Schuster LB $15.00 (0-689-83835-2). 48pp. Three humorous episodes involve new friends Possum and Alien, a creature whose spaceship comes down in the neighborhood. (Rev: BL 7/01; HBG 3/02; SLJ 9/01)

1793 Johnston, Tony. *Alien and Possum Hanging Out* (2–3). Illus. by Tony Diterlizzi. 2002, Simon & Schuster $15.00 (0-689-83836-0). 48pp. Three stories about the continuing unlikely friendship between a robot-like alien and a possum. (Rev: HBG 10/02; SLJ 8/02)

1794 Jordan, Sandra. *Frog Hunt* (PS–1). Illus. 2002, Millbrook LB $22.90 (0-7613-2652-9). 32pp. An easily read book about two boys and the animal life they encounter when they go into a freshwater pond looking for frogs. (Rev: BL 6/1–15/02; HBG 10/02; SLJ 4/02)

1795 Kline, Suzy. *Horrible Harry and the Mud Gremlins* (2–4). Illus. by Frank Remkiewicz. Series: Horrible Harry. 2003, Viking $13.99 (0-670-03617-X). 64pp. Horrible Harry encourages his classmates to break a school rule and go under the playground

fence to see fungi with his mini-microscope. (Rev: BL 3/15/03)

1796 Kline, Suzy. *Horrible Harry Goes to Sea* (2–4). Illus. by Frank Remkiewicz. 2001, Viking $13.99 (0-670-03516-5). 64pp. After hearing a student's story of an ancestor who sailed on the *Titanic*, the teacher arranges a class riverboat trip and many humorous adventures ensue. (Rev: BL 12/1/01; HBG 3/02; SLJ 11/01)

1797 Kliphuis, Christine. *Robbie and Ronnie* (1–3). Illus. by Charlotte Dematons. 2002, North-South LB $13.88 (0-7358-1627-1). 47pp. Best friends Robbie and Ronnie, who are physical opposites, defeat a bully in this beginning chapter book. (Rev: HBG 10/02; SLJ 5/02)

1798 Knudsen, Michelle. *Cat Hat* (K–1). Illus. by Amanda Haley. Series: Road to Reading. 2001, Golden Books $11.99 (0-307-46115-7); paper $3.99 (0-307-26115-8). 32pp. Ralph, a cat, can't find a good place for a nap until he comes across a bald man's head. (Rev: BL 7/01)

1799 Krensky, Stephen. *Arthur and the Seventh-Inning Stretcher* (2–4). Illus. Series: Arthur Good Sports. 2001, Little, Brown $13.95 (0-316-11861-3); paper $3.95 (0-316-12094-4). 64pp. Binky feels left out when he can't play baseball because of an injury. (Rev: BL 5/15/01; HBG 3/02)

1800 Kurt, Kemal. *Mixed-Up Journey to Magic Mountain* (2–4). Trans. from German by Marianne Martens. Illus. by Wolfgang Slawski. 2002, North-South LB $13.88 (0-7358-1633-6). 58pp. Marco the magician's inability to spell causes all sorts of problems. (Rev: HBG 10/02; SLJ 4/02)

1801 Labatt, Mary. *Pizza for Sam* (PS–1). Illus. by Marisol Sarrazin. Series: Kids Can Read. 2003, Kids Can $14.95 (1-55337-329-4); paper $3.95 (1-55337-331-6). 32pp. Sam does not want to eat dog food and greets a pizza with joy. (Rev: BL 3/1/03)

1802 Lachtman, Ofelia Dumas. *Pepita Finds Out / Lo Que Pepita Descubre* (1–3). Trans. by Carolina Villarroel. Illus. by Alex P. DeLange. 2002, Piñata $14.95 (1-55885-375-8). Pepita frets because she can't find a suitable subject for her school report in this novel with the English text above the Spanish. (Rev: SLJ 3/03)

1803 Laurence, Daniel. *Captain and Matey Set Sail* (K–2). Illus. by Claudio Munoz. Series: An I Can Read Book. 2001, HarperCollins LB $14.89 (0-06-028957-0). 64pp. Two pirates bicker constantly about everything — what to call their parrot, what to do with the treasure if they ever find it, which song to sing while scrubbing the deck, and so forth. (Rev: BCCB 9/01; BL 7/01; HB 1–2/02; HBG 3/02; SLJ 11/01)

1804 Levinson, Nancy Smiler. *Prairie Friends* (2–4). Illus. by Stacey Schuett. Series: An I Can Read Book. 2003, HarperCollins LB $16.89 (0-06-028002-6). 64pp. Betsy is thrilled when a girl her age moves into the neighborhood, but the city girl takes time to adapt to her new surroundings in this story that includes lots of interesting facts about prairie life in the middle 1800s. (Rev: BL 1/1–15/03; SLJ 3/03)

1805 Levy, Elizabeth. *A Hare-Raising Tail* (2–5). Illus. by Mordicai Gerstein. Series: Ready-for-Chapters. 2002, Simon & Schuster paper $3.99 (0-689-84626-6). 64pp. Fletcher the basset hound finds a new home with Jill, and all goes well until Jill takes him to school for show-and-tell. (Rev: BL 9/1/02; HBG 10/02; SLJ 1/03)

1806 Levy, Elizabeth. *Take Two, They're Small* (2–4). Illus. by Mark Elliott. 2002, HarperCollins LB $15.89 (0-06-028593-1). 86pp. As she enters fourth grade, Eve isn't pleased to find she'll have to deal with her irritating, younger twin sisters in this sequel to *Big Trouble in Little Twinsville* (2001). (Rev: HBG 3/03; SLJ 1/03)

1807 McDonough, Yona Zeldis. *A Doll Named Dora Anne* (2–3). Illus. by DyAnne Disalvo. Series: All Aboard Reading. 2002, Grosset LB $13.89 (0-448-42836-9); paper $3.99 (0-448-42678-1). 48pp. Nine-year-old Kate's mother doesn't believe Kate is ready for the antique doll her grandmother gave her, but the young girl proves her mother wrong. (Rev: HBG 3/03; SLJ 12/02)

1808 McKenna, Colleen O'Shaughnessy. *Doggone . . . Third Grade!* (2–3). Illus. by Stephanie Roth. 2002, Holiday $15.95 (0-8234-1696-8). 80pp. Third-grader Gordie comes up with a trick for his dog to perform in the class talent show. (Rev: BL 7/02; HBG 10/02; SLJ 7/02)

1809 McKenna, Colleen O'Shaughnessy. *Third Grade Ghouls* (2–4). Illus. by Stephanie Roth. 2001, Holiday $15.95 (0-8234-1652-6). 80pp. This simple beginning chapter book finds third-grader Gordie searching for the perfect costume to wear for the Halloween parade. (Rev: BL 1/1–15/02; HBG 10/02; SLJ 2/02)

1810 McKissack, Patricia. *Tippy Lemmey* (2–4). Illus. by Susan Keeter. Series: Ready-for-Chapters. 2003, Simon & Schuster paper $3.99 (0-689-85019-0). 64pp. Mischievous Tippy the dog is a source of annoyance to Leandra and her friends, but when the pup is kidnapped, they come to his rescue in this story set in Tennessee in 1951. (Rev: BCCB 3/03; BL 1/1–15/03; HB 3–4/03; SLJ 1/03)

1811 McKissack, Patricia, and Fredrick McKissack. *Miami Makes the Play* (2–4). Illus. Series: Road to Reading. 2001, Golden Books paper $3.99 (0-307-26505-6). 92pp. Miami and friends head for baseball camp for a summer of fun and play but must make some decisions, such as whether to support a coed team. (Rev: BL 5/1/01; HBG 10/01)

1812 McPhail, David. *Big Pig and Little Pig* (K–1). Illus. Series: Green Light Reader. 2001, Harcourt $10.95 (0-15-216516-9); paper $3.95 (0-15-216510-X). 32pp. Little Pig and Big Pig, each in his own way, build pools to cool off in during a heat wave. (Rev: BL 4/15/01; HBG 10/01; SLJ 5/01)

1813 McPhail, David. *Jack and Rich* (K–1). Illus. Series: Green Light Reader. 2002, Green Light Readers LB $11.95 (0-15-216552-5); paper $3.95 (0-15-216540-1). 24pp. Rich, a bear, and Jack, a rabbit, learn to cooperate so they can happily play together. (Rev: BL 5/1/02; HBG 10/02; SLJ 6/02)

1814 McPhail, David. *Piggy's Pancake Parlor* (1–3). Illus. 2002, Dutton $15.99 (0-525-45930-8). 48pp. A pig and a fox open a pancake parlor using the farmer's secret recipe in this charming beginning chapter book. (Rev: BCCB 7–8/02; BL 8/02; HBG 10/02; SLJ 6/02)

1815 Maitland, Barbara. *The Bookstore Burglar* (K–1). Illus. by Nadine Bernard Westcott. 2001, Dutton $13.99 (0-525-46684-3). 32pp. A sequel to *The Bookstore Ghost* (1998), this easy-to-read chapter book finds Mr. Brown's cat Cobweb and a few of his mousy friends foiling a burglary in the bookstore. (Rev: BL 11/1/01; HBG 3/02; SLJ 10/01)

1816 Maitland, Barbara. *The Bookstore Valentine* (K–2). Illus. by David LaRochelle. Series: Dutton Easy Reader. 2002, Dutton $13.99 (0-525-46913-3). 32pp. Cobweb the ghost-bookstore cat and the bookstore mice plot to get the shop's owner and his new assistant involved in a romantic relationship. (Rev: BCCB 1/03; BL 1/1–15/03; HBG 3/03; SLJ 12/02)

1817 Marzollo, Jean. *I See a Star* (K–2). Illus. by Suse MacDonald. 2002, Scholastic $7.95 (0-439-26616-5). 32pp. Children prepare for a Christmas pageant in this story told completely through rebuses. (Rev: BL 10/15/02; HBG 3/03; SLJ 10/02)

1818 Masurel, Claire. *That Bad, Bad Cat* (1). Illus. by True Kelley. Series: All Aboard Reading. 2002, Putnam $13.89 (0-448-42665-X); paper $3.99 (0-448-42622-6). 32pp. The family cat is always misbehaving, but when he fails to show up for dinner everyone misses him. (Rev: BL 6/1–15/02; HBG 10/02)

1819 Mayfield, Sue. *Shoot!* (1–2). Illus. by Ken Cox. Series: Blue Bananas. 2001, Crabtree LB $14.97 (0-7787-0847-0); paper $4.46 (0-7787-0893-4). 48pp. Shoot the dog, the team mascot, helps Jamie and his friends win the soccer game. (Rev: SLJ 7/02)

1820 Meister, Cari. *Skinny and Fats, Best Friends* (K–2). Illus. by Steve Bjorkman. Series: Holiday House Reader. 2002, Holiday $14.95 (0-8234-1692-5). 32pp. Skinny, a rabbit, and Fats, a pig, enjoy spending time fishing, making marshmallows, and building rockets. (Rev: HBG 3/03; SLJ 10/02)

1821 Meister, Cari. *Tiny the Snow Dog* (K–1). Illus. by Rich Davis. 2001, Viking $13.99 (0-670-89117-7). Giant Tiny the dog hides in the snow from his young owner, who can't see him despite many visual clues. (Rev: HBG 3/02; SLJ 10/01)

1822 Milgrim, David. *Ride Otto Ride!* (K–1). Illus. 2002, Simon & Schuster $14.95 (0-689-84417-4). 32pp. An easy-to-read book about the adventures of a robot named Otto and his animal friends. Also use *See Otto* (2002). (Rev: BL 9/15/02; HBG 3/03; SLJ 3/03)

1823 Milgrim, David. *See Pip Point* (PS–1). Illus. Series: Ready-to-Read. 2003, Simon & Schuster $14.95 (0-689-85116-2). 32pp. A simple book for beginning readers about a mouse named Pip and his adventures with a balloon. (Rev: BL 2/1/03)

1824 Miller, Sara Swan. *Cat in the Bag* (1). Illus. by Benton Mahan. Series: Rookie Readers. 2001, Children's $18.00 (0-516-22014-4). 32pp. While trying to pack, a little girl must keep chasing her cat out of her suitcase in this easy reader. (Rev: BL 11/1/01)

1825 Miller, Sara Swan. *Three More Stories You Can Read to Your Cat* (1–3). Illus. by True Kelley. 2002, Houghton $15.00 (0-618-11035-6). 48pp. These simple, playful stories are about cats who face such problems as wanting to come inside during a snow storm and finding entertainment on a particularly boring birthday. (Rev: BL 4/15/02; HBG 10/02; SLJ 5/02)

1826 Moore, Lilian. *Little Raccoon* (2–4). Illus. by Doug Cushman. 2002, Holt $15.95 (0-8050-6543-1). 64pp. A beginning reader that contains three stories about a little raccoon who is becoming independent. (Rev: BL 4/1/02; HBG 10/02)

1827 Moran, Alex. *Come Here, Tiger!* (K–1). Illus. by Lisa Campbell Ernst. Series: Green Light Reader. 2001, Harcourt $10.95 (0-15-216218-6); paper $3.95 (0-15-216225-9). 32pp. An amusing tale about a girl who is searching for her cat, Tiger, who has disappeared. (Rev: BL 4/15/01; HBG 10/01; SLJ 5/01)

1828 Murphy, Frank. *Ben Franklin and the Magic Squares* (2–3). Illus. by Richard Walz. Series: Step into Reading + Math. 2001, Random $11.99 (0-375-80621-0); paper $3.99 (0-375-80621-0). 48pp. Ben Franklin is shown entertaining himself during meetings by working with magic squares — squares of numbers that add to the same total in any direction. (Rev: BL 7/01; HBG 10/01)

1829 Murphy, Mary. *How Kind!* (PS–2). Illus. by author. 2002, Candlewick $14.99 (0-7636-1732-6). An easy reader in which animals appreciate each other's kindnesses. (Rev: HBG 10/02; SLJ 7/02)

1830 Nelson, Vaunda Micheaux. *Ready? Set. Raymond!* (K–1). Illus. by Derek Anderson. Series: Step into Reading. 2002, Random LB $11.99 (0-375-91363-7); paper $3.99 (0-375-81363-2). 32pp. Raymond, an appealing African American boy, "does things fast," including making a friend and running a race, in this collection of three short, nicely illustrated stories. (Rev: BL 9/15/02; HBG 3/03; SLJ 12/02)

1831 Nixon, Joan Lowery. *Gus and Gertie and the Lucky Charms* (2–4). Illus. by Diane De Groat. 2002, North-South LB $14.88 (1-58717-100-7). 48pp. Gus and Gertie solve a mystery at the Animals' Winter Olympics in this beginning chapter book. (Rev: BL 1/1–15/02; SLJ 1/02)

1832 Nolen, Jerdine. *Max and Jax in Second Grade* (1–3). Illus. by Karen L. Schmidt. 2002, Harcourt $14.00 (0-15-201668-6). 44pp. In this easily read chapter book, brother and sister crocodile twins, who have different interests, join forces to help each other. (Rev: BL 6/1–15/02; HBG 10/02; SLJ 4/02)

1833 O'Connor, Jane. *Dear Tooth Fairy* (K–2). Illus. by Joy Allen. 2002, Grosset LB $13.89 (0-448-42881-4); paper $3.99 (0-448-42849-0). 47pp. Robby obsesses about the fact that he hasn't lost any teeth and starts a correspondence with the tooth fairy. (Rev: SLJ 3/03)

1834 O'Connor, Jane. *Snail City* (K–1). Illus. by Rick Brown. Series: All Aboard Reading. 2001, Grosset $13.89 (0-448-42471-1); paper $3.99 (0-448-42418-5). 32pp. In Snail City, Gail, a little snail, finds she is different because she likes to do things fast. (Rev: BL 4/15/01; HBG 10/01; SLJ 8/01)

1835 Ogren, Cathy Stefanec. *The Adventures of Archie Featherspoon* (1–3). Illus. by Jack E. Davis. Series: Ready-for-Chapters. 2002, Simon & Schuster LB $11.89 (0-689-84284-8); paper $3.99 (0-689-84359-3). 43pp. A tall tale about a clever farm boy who outwits outlaws in the Wild West. (Rev: HBG 10/02; SLJ 8/02)

1836 Parish, Herman. *Calling Doctor Amelia Bedelia* (PS–2). Illus. by Lynn Sweat. Series: Amelia Bedelia. 2002, HarperCollins LB $17.89 (0-06-001422-9). 64pp. When Amelia Bedelia helps out in a doctor's office for the day, she wreaks such havoc that only ice cream can save the day. (Rev: BL 8/02; HB 11–12/02; HBG 3/03; SLJ 8/02)

1837 Park, Barbara. *Junie B., First Grader (at Last!)* (2–3). Illus. by Denise Brunkus. 2001, Random LB $13.99 (0-375-81516-3). 96pp. When her best friend deserts her and she finds out she needs glasses, Junie B. Jones discovers that first grade is not what she expected. (Rev: BL 11/15/01; HBG 3/02; SLJ 1/02)

1838 Parks, Carmen. *Farmers Market* (1–2). Illus. by Ed Martinez. Series: Green Light Reader. 2002, Harcourt $11.95 (0-15-216680-7); paper $3.95 (0-15-216674-2). 20pp. In this charming easy reader, a young girl who is physically disabled accompanies her parents to market to sell their produce. (Rev: BL 5/1/02; HBG 10/02; SLJ 4/02)

1839 Partridge, Elizabeth. *Annie and Bo and the Big Surprise* (1–2). Illus. by Martha Weston. 2002, Dutton $13.99 (0-525-46728-9). 48pp. Bo surprises his best friend Annie with a cake in this story about friendship and affection for beginning readers. (Rev: BL 11/1/01; HBG 10/02)

1840 Paterson, Katherine. *Marvin One Too Many* (K–2). Illus. by Jane Brown. 2001, HarperCollins LB $14.89 (0-06-028770-5). 48pp. Marvin is finding it hard to learn to read, so his father and older sister decide to help. (Rev: BL 7/01; HBG 3/02; SLJ 9/01)

1841 Pinkwater, Daniel. *Mush's Jazz Adventure* (2–4). Illus. by Jill Pinkwater. Series: Ready-for-Chapters. 2002, Simon & Schuster LB $11.89 (0-689-84576-6); paper $3.99 (0-689-84572-3). 37pp. Mush, an alien dog, tells the story of her arrival on Earth and how she and three other animals saved a dance hall owner from robbers in this entertaining and improbable beginning chapter book. (Rev: HBG 3/03; SLJ 2/03)

1842 Rau, Dana Meachen. *Chilly Charlie* (K–1). Illus. by Martin Lemelman. Series: Rookie Readers. 2001, Children's $15.00 (0-516-22210-4); paper $4.95 (0-516-27288-8). 24pp. Charlie feels that he is getting cold and needs a hug to keep him warm. (Rev: BL 4/15/01)

1843 Rau, Dana Meachen. *In the Yard* (K–1). Illus. by Elizabeth Wolf. Series: Compass Point Early Reader. 2001, Compass Point LB $18.60 (0-7565-0116-4). 24pp. A brief, simple text and bold illustrations depict an African American family enjoying their backyard. (Rev: SLJ 2/02)

1844 Rau, Dana Meachen. *Lots of Balloons* (K–1). Illus. by Jayoung Cho. 2001, Compass Point LB $18.60 (0-7565-0117-2). 24pp. A little girl wants balloons of various colors, comparing each to a familiar item. (Rev: SLJ 2/02)

1845 Rau, Dana Meachen. *Shoo, Crow! Shoo!* (1). Illus. by Mary Galan Rojas. Series: Compass Point Early Reader. 2001, Compass Point LB $18.60 (0-7565-0072-9). 24pp. Two children make a scarecrow from old clothes, hay, and a pumpkin. (Rev: BL 7/01; SLJ 8/01)

1846 Ritchie, Alison. *Horrible Haircut* (1–2). Illus. by Ian Newsham. Series: Blue Bananas. 2001, Crabtree LB $14.97 (0-7787-0844-6); paper $4.46 (0-7787-0890-X). 45pp. Lucy and her mother make a deal — if Lucy doesn't like the cut her mother gives her, she gets to cut her mother's hair — in this book for fluent beginning readers. (Rev: SLJ 7/02)

1847 Rocklin, Joanne. *This Book Is Haunted* (K–2). Illus. by JoAnn Adinolfi. 2002, HarperCollins LB $17.89 (0-06-028457-9). 46pp. A selection of not-very-frightening Halloween stories for beginning readers. (Rev: BCCB 10/02; HBG 3/03; SLJ 9/02)

1848 Root, Phyllis. *Mouse Goes Out* (PS–K). Illus. by James Croft. Series: Brand New Readers. 2002, Candlewick $12.99 (0-7636-1351-7); paper $4.99 (0-7636-1352-5). 40pp. A beginning reader about the adventures of a mouse who plays in puddles and goes fishing. (Rev: BL 4/15/02)

1849 Roy, Ron. *Kidnapped at the Capital* (2–4). Illus. by Liza Woodruff. Series: Capital Mysteries. 2002, Golden Books LB $11.99 (0-307-46514-4); paper $3.99 (0-307-26514-5). 80pp. A mystery takes K.C. Corcoran and Marshall Li on a lively hunt through Washington, D.C. (Rev: BL 9/1/02)

1850 Ruelle, Karen Gray. *April Fool!* (1–2). Series: Holiday House Reader. 2002, Holiday $14.95 (0-8234-1686-0). 32pp. Two little kittens try to come up with April Fool's jokes to play on their parents and each other. (Rev: BL 2/1/02; HBG 10/02; SLJ 6/02)

1851 Ruelle, Karen Gray. *Easy as Apple Pie: A Harry and Emily Adventure* (K–2). Illus. by author. Series: Holiday House Reader. 2002, Holiday $14.95 (0-8234-1759-X). 32pp. Kittens Harry and Emily have different reactions when invited to pick apples with their grandparents. (Rev: BL 8/02; HBG 3/03; SLJ 10/02)

1852 Rylant, Cynthia. *Henry and Mudge and Mrs. Hopper's House* (K–2). Illus. by Carolyn Bracken. Series: Ready-to-Read. 2003, Simon & Schuster $14.95 (0-689-81153-5). 40pp. Henry is apprehensive about spending the evening at his babysitter's dark, gloomy house, but when he arrives with his dog Mudge, he finds the house full of music and clothes to dress up in. (Rev: BL 3/15/03)

1853 Rylant, Cynthia. *Henry and Mudge and the Tall Tree House* (K–2). Illus. by Carolyn Bracken. Series: Ready-to-Read. 2002, Simon & Schuster $14.95 (0-689-81173-X). 40pp. Uncle Jake builds Henry a great tree house but Mudge the dog can't climb up to it so the tree house is eventually moved to Henry's bedroom. (Rev: BL 1/1–15/03; SLJ 2/03)

1854 Rylant, Cynthia. *The High-Rise Private Eyes: The Case of the Sleepy Sloth* (1–2). Illus. by G. Brian Karas. Series: High-Rise Private Eyes. 2002, HarperCollins LB $16.89 (0-06-009099-5). 48pp. Bunny and Jack solve a mystery for their friend Ramon in this fifth installment in the humorous, easy-to-read series with cartoon illustrations. (Rev: BL 9/15/02; HBG 3/03; SLJ 12/02)

1855 Rylant, Cynthia. *The High-Rise Private Eyes: The Case of the Troublesome Turtle* (2–4). Illus. 2001, Greenwillow LB $14.89 (0-688-16311-4). 48pp. Bunny Brown and her partner Jack Jones, a raccoon, investigate the disappearance of some balloons. (Rev: BL 5/15/01; HB 5–6/01; HBG 10/01; SLJ 7/01)

1856 Rylant, Cynthia. *Mr. Putter and Tabby Catch the Cold* (K–2). Illus. by Arthur Howard. 2002, Harcourt $14.00 (0-15-202414-X). 44pp. Tabby tries to help Mr. Putter cope with his cold, but it takes neighbor Mrs. Teaberry and her dog Zeke to provide the necessary comfort. (Rev: BL 11/1/02; HBG 3/03; SLJ 10/02)

1857 Rylant, Cynthia. *Mr. Putter and Tabby Feed the Fish* (2–4). Illus. by Arthur Howard. 2001, Harcourt $14.00 (0-15-202408-5). 44pp. Taking home three goldfish turns out to be a mistake when Tabby the cat develops a "fish problem." (Rev: BL 5/1/01; HBG 10/01; SLJ 5/01*)

1858 Rylant, Cynthia. *Poppleton in Winter* (1–3). Illus. by Mark Teague. 2001, Scholastic paper $3.99 (0-590-84838-0). 48pp. Poppleton the pig worries about icicles, tries his hand at sculpting, and has a surprise birthday party. (Rev: BCCB 12/01; HBG 3/02; SLJ 10/01)

1859 Samton, Sheila White. *Hurray for Rosa!* (PS–1). Illus. by author. Series: Brand New Readers. 2001, Candlewick $11.99 (0-7636-1126-3). 40pp. Simple tales about a young girl who imitates animals, goes to the beach, makes a sandwich, and has a birthday cake. (Rev: HBG 3/02; SLJ 2/02)

1860 Schade, Susan, and Jon Buller. *Cat on Ice* (K–1). Illus. Series: Road to Reading. 2001, Golden Books $13.99 (0-307-46213-7); paper $3.99 (0-307-26213-8). 32pp. Winter has ended and Cat and Rat still haven't used their new ice skates, so they are cheered to discover an indoor rink. (Rev: BL 4/15/01; HBG 10/01)

1861 Schaefer, Carole Lexa. *Beep! Beep! It's Beeper!* (PS–1). Illus. by Julie Lacome. Series: Brand New Readers. 2001, Candlewick $11.99 (0-7636-1203-0). 40pp. Simple tales about an alien who paints a picture of a house, counts things, bakes, and flies in patterns. (Rev: SLJ 2/02)

1862 Sharmat, Marjorie Weinman, and Mitchell Sharmat. *Nate the Great and the Big Sniff* (1–2).

Illus. by Martha Weston. 2001, Delacorte $13.95 (0-385-32604-1). 48pp. Boy detective Nate the Great has lost his faithful sidekick, Sludge, outside a department store in this latest installment of the beginning chapter-book series. (Rev: BL 11/1/01; HBG 3/02; SLJ 10/01)

1863 Spohn, Kate. *Turtle and Snake Fix It* (1–2). Illus. Series: Viking Easy-to-Read. 2002, Viking $13.99 (0-670-03540-8). 32pp. Although Turtle is filled with the best intentions, his attempts to act as handyman in Snake's house come to no good end. (Rev: BL 6/1–15/02; HBG 10/02)

1864 Spohn, Kate. *Turtle and Snake's Spooky Halloween* (PS–1). Illus. by author. 2002, Viking $13.99 (0-670-03560-2). 32pp. Turtle and Snake plan a really good Halloween party and follow their checklist. (Rev: HBG 3/03; SLJ 9/02)

1865 *Sports Stories You'll Have a Ball With* (1–2). Illus. Series: Reading Rainbow. 2001, North-South $14.95 (1-58717-085-X); paper $3.99 (1-58717-086-8). 64pp. Using material published in other beginning readers, this is a collection of five easy sports stories and two poems. (Rev: BL 4/1/01; HBG 10/01)

1866 Stern, Maggie. *Singing Diggety* (1–3). Illus. by Blanche Sims. 2001, Scholastic $14.95 (0-531-30318-7); paper $4.95 (0-531-07179-0). 46pp. George and his naughty dog Diggety have further humorous adventures as they go to dog school, enter costume contests, and perform for show-and-tell. (Rev: BCCB 10/01; HB 9–10/01; HBG 3/02; SLJ 8/01)

1867 Suen, Anastasia. *Hamster Chase* (1–2). Illus. by Allan Eitzen. 2001, Viking $13.99 (0-670-88942-3). Peter, Archie, and Amy — from Ezra Jack Keats's picture books — must catch the class hamster and return him to his cage. (Rev: HBG 10/01; SLJ 4/01)

1868 Suen, Anastasia, and Ezra Jack Keats. *The Clubhouse* (K–2). Illus. by Allan Eitzen. Series: Viking Easy-To-Read. 2002, Viking $13.99 (0-670-03537-8). 32pp. Peter, an African American boy, and his friends find a pile of wood and build a place to play. (Rev: BL 4/15/02; HBG 10/02; SLJ 8/02)

1869 Suen, Anastasia, and Ezra Jack Keats. *Loose Tooth* (K–2). Illus. by Allan Eitzen. 2002, Viking $13.99 (0-670-03536-X). 32pp. Young Peter wants to keep his loose tooth in place at least until after the class photo has been taken. (Rev: BL 4/15/02; HBG 10/02; SLJ 4/02)

1870 Thiesing, Lisa. *The Viper* (K–2). Illus. Series: Dutton Easy Reader. 2002, Dutton $13.99 (0-525-

46892-7). 32pp. In this hilarious mystery, Peggy the Pig gets scared when she gets a phone call from "zee Viper." (Rev: BL 5/1/02; HBG 3/03; SLJ 8/02*)

1871 Thomas, Shelley Moore. *Get Well, Good Knight* (K–2). Illus. by Jennifer Plecas. Series: Dutton Easy Reader. 2002, Dutton $13.99 (0-525-46914-1). 48pp. The Good Knight rides off on a quest to cure three little dragons with horrible colds, in this appealing easy reader. (Rev: BCCB 12/02; BL 1/1–15/03; HB 9–10/02; HBG 3/03; SLJ 11/02)

1872 Torrey, Richard. *Beans Baker, Number Five* (1–2). Illus. Series: Road to Reading. 2001, Golden Books $13.99 (0-307-46335-4); paper $4.99 (0-307-26335-5). 32pp. When Beans leaves baseball practice after being teased by his teammates, they use psychology to get him back. (Rev: BL 4/15/01; HBG 10/01)

1873 Vail, Rachel. *Mama Rex and T: Homework Trouble* (2–4). Illus. by Steve Bjorkman. 2002, Scholastic $14.95 (0-439-40628-5); paper $4.99 (0-439-42616-2). 32pp. Mama Rex and T, a young dinosaur, finish the project he's neglected in this challenging beginning chapter book. Also use *Mama Rex and T: The Horrible Play Date* (2002), about friendship. (Rev: HBG 3/03; SLJ 10/02)

1874 Walsh, Vivian. *Gluey: A Snail Tale* (K–3). Illus. by J. Otto Seibold. 2002, Harcourt $15.00 (0-15-216620-3). 48pp. Celerina the rabbit moves into Gluey the snail's home, believing it to be abandoned, and hosts a disastrous party in this complex tale for beginning readers. (Rev: BL 10/15/02; HBG 3/03; SLJ 12/02)

1875 Weston, Martha. *Jack and Jill and Big Dog Bill: A Phonics Reader*. Illus. Series: Early Step into Reading. 2002, Random LB $11.99 (0-375-91248-7); paper $3.99 (0-375-81248-2). 32pp. Two small children, Jack and Jill, along with their dog, try to slide down a snow-covered hillside on their sled with amusing results in this easy reader. (Rev: BL 4/15/02; HBG 10/02; SLJ 7/02)

1876 Zehler, Antonia. *Two Fine Ladies Have a Tiff* (1–2). Illus. 2001, Random LB $11.99 (0-375-91104-9); paper $3.99 (0-375-81104-4). 32pp. Twin sisters fight all day long, but, in the end, can't stand to be apart in this book for beginning readers. (Rev: BL 2/1/02; HBG 10/02)

1877 Ziefert, Harriet. *Toes Have Wiggles Kids Have Giggles* (K–3). Illus. by Rebecca Doughty. 2002, Putnam $13.99 (0-399-23617-2). 32pp. Clever wordplays and amusing rhymes introduce readers to what words can do. (Rev: BL 6/1–15/02)

Fiction for Older Readers

General

1878 Atinsky, Steve. *Tyler on Prime Time* (5–7). 2002, Delacorte $14.95 (0-385-72917-0). 176pp. Tyler has the time of his life when he auditions for a part in a TV show and learns about show business backstage and the problems involved. (Rev: BCCB 9/02; BL 5/1/02; HBG 10/02; SLJ 8/02)

1879 Bradby, Marie. *Once upon a Farm* (2–5). Illus. by Ted Rand. 2002, Scholastic $16.95 (0-439-31766-5). A farm boy recalls in simple rhyming verse the beauty and pleasures of a rural life before the city started to encroach on the country. (Rev: HBG 10/02; SLJ 3/02)

1880 Clements, Andrew. *The School Story* (4–7). Illus. 2001, Simon & Schuster $16.00 (0-689-82594-3). 160pp. Two 12-year-old girls tackle the task of getting a book by a new author published. (Rev: BCCB 7–8/01; BL 6/1–15/01; HB 7–8/01; HBG 10/01; SLJ 6/01)

1881 Cole, Sheila. *The Canyon* (4–6). 2002, Harper-Collins LB $15.89 (0-06-029496-5). 144pp. A California sixth-grader named Zach fights to preserve the canyon near his home when he discovers it is targeted for development. (Rev: BL 8/02; HBG 10/02; SLJ 6/02)

1882 Eccles, Mary. *By Lizzie* (3–6). 2001, Dial $15.99 (0-8037-2608-2). 128pp. Nine-year-old Lizzie finds an old typewriter and starts writing a journal about her life. (Rev: BCCB 6/01; BL 5/15/01; HBG 10/01; SLJ 6/01)

1883 Graves, Bonnie. *Taking Care of Trouble* (3–5). Illus. by Robin P. Glasser. 2002, Dutton $14.99 (0-525-46830-7). 112pp. In this beginning chapter book, Joel is worried about passing his emergency preparedness drill until he's called on to babysit a kid nicknamed Trouble, and realizes he can handle anything. (Rev: BCCB 6/02; BL 3/15/02; HBG 10/02; SLJ 4/02)

1884 Griffin, Adele. *Witch Twins at Camp Bliss* (2–5). 2002, Hyperion $15.99 (0-7868-0763-6). 128pp. Luna and Claire, twin witches first seen in *Witch Twins* (2001), are off to Camp Bliss, where (in addition to typical camp activities) they search for a "rebel witch." (Rev: BCCB 7–8/02; BL 7/02; HBG 10/02; SLJ 6/02)

1885 Hiaasen, Carl. *Hoot* (5–8). 2002, Knopf $15.95 (0-375-82181-3). 272pp. Roy Eberhart, the new kid in Coconut Cove, finds himself embroiled in a battle to save some owls in this Newbery Award-winning story. Newbery Honor Book, 2003. (Rev: BCCB 11/02; BL 10/15/02; HB 11–12/02; HBG 3/03; SLJ 8/02)

1886 Hirsch, Odo. *Antonio S. and the Mysterious Theodore Guzman* (4–6). Illus. 2001, Hyperion LB $16.49 (0-7868-2605-3). 198pp. Antonio lives with his magician father and doctor mother in an apartment in a large mansion that houses a mysterious resident. (Rev: BL 5/15/01; HBG 10/01; SLJ 4/01)

1887 Holub, Joan. *The Haunted States of America: Haunted Houses and Spooky Places in All 50 States . . . and Canada, Too!* (3–6). Illus. by author. 2001, Simon & Schuster paper $4.99 (0-689-83911-1). 176pp. This ghoulish guidebook introduces readers to haunted houses across North America, tells the spooky stories, and teaches some geography and history along the way. (Rev: SLJ 9/01)

1888 Jennings, Patrick. *The Beastly Arms* (5–7). 2001, Scholastic $16.95 (0-439-16589-X). 288pp. A dreamy sixth-grader who pictures animals in everything he sees, discovers a world of real beasts when he and his mother move to the Beastly Arms. (Rev: BCCB 10/01; BL 5/1/01; HB 7–8/01; HBG 10/01; SLJ 4/01)

1889 Jennings, Richard W. *The Great Whale of Kansas* (5–9). 2001, Houghton $15.00 (0-618-10228-0). 160pp. When a boy finds a prehistoric whale fossil in his backyard, the discovery brings unexpected consequences. (Rev: HB 9–10/01; HBG 3/02; SLJ 8/01)

1890 Johnson, Stephen T. *As the City Sleeps* (4–8). Illus. 2002, Viking $16.99 (0-670-88940-7). 32pp. This picture book for older readers portrays a city at night, with eerie, enigmatic illustrations that include dreamlike creatures. (Rev: BL 12/1/02; HB 1–2/03; HBG 3/03; SLJ 1/03)

1891 Kherdian, David. *The Revelations of Alvin Tolliver* (5–7). 2001, Hampton Roads paper $7.95 (1-57174-255-7). 48pp. Twelve-year-old Alvin is fascinated with nature and the great outdoors, and finds some unusual adult friends who introduce him to nature's charms. (Rev: BL 12/1/01; SLJ 3/02)

1892 McDonnell, Christine. *Ballet Bug* (3–5). Illus. by Martha Doty. 2001, Viking $14.99 (0-670-03508-4). 112pp. Bea develops a passion for ballet and must juggle this interest with her commitment to hockey, while also dealing with a pair of very unpleasant twins. (Rev: BCCB 10/01; HBG 3/02; SLJ 9/01)

1893 McMullan, Kate. *Have a Hot Time, Hades!* (3–6). Illus. by David LaFleur. Series: Myth-O-Mania. 2002, Hyperion $15.99 (0-7868-0857-8); paper $4.99 (0-7868-1664-3). 160pp. Hades, the ruler of the underworld, gets a chance to set things straight here and correct our misconceptions about Greek mythology. (Rev: BCCB 12/02; BL 11/1/02; HBG 3/03; SLJ 1/03)

1894 Moss, Marissa. *Madame Amelia Tells All* (3–6). Illus. 2001, Pleasant paper $5.95 (1-58485-305-0). 112pp. Amelia approaches the role of fortune-teller with her usual, entertaining inventiveness. (Rev: BL 8/01; SLJ 7/01)

1895 Radunsky, Vladimir, and Chris Raschka. *Table Manners* (1–4). Illus. 2001, Candlewick $16.99 (0-7636-1453-X). 32pp. Dudunya and Chester illustrate proper dining etiquette in this merry book of manners for younger readers. (Rev: BCCB 12/01; BL 1/1–15/02; HBG 3/02; SLJ 11/01)

1896 Roberts, Ken. *The Thumb in the Box* (3–5). 2001, Douglas & McIntyre $14.95 (0-88899-421-4). 94pp. This is a humorous and interesting story, narrated by 11-year-old Leon, about a small coastal town in British Columbia that receives an unneeded fire truck and a builder with an intriguing practical joke. (Rev: BL 10/15/01; HB 9–10/01*; HBG 3/02)

1897 Romain, Trevor. *Under the Big Sky* (4–7). Illus. 2001, HarperCollins LB $14.89 (0-06-029495-7). 48pp. Encouraged by his grandfather, a young boy searches far and wide for the secret of life. (Rev: BL 8/01; HBG 10/01; SLJ 8/01)

1898 Schmidt, Gary D. *The Great Stone Face* (2–5). Illus. by Bill Farnsworth. 2002, Eerdmans $16.00 (0-8028-5194-0). 32pp. The Great Stone Face in this beautifully illustrated picture-book retelling of Nathaniel Hawthorne's story may be more familiar as the (now-lost) "Old Man of the Mountains." (Rev: BL 10/1/02; HBG 3/03; SLJ 11/02)

1899 Smallcomb, Pam. *Camp Buccaneer* (2–4). Illus. by Tom Lichtenheld. 2002, Simon & Schuster LB $15.00 (0-689-84383-6); paper $3.99 (0-689-84384-4). 64pp. A beginning chapter book about a girl who learns all about piracy — and herself — from the denizens of Camp Buccaneer. (Rev: BL 6/1–15/02; HBG 10/02; SLJ 6/02)

1900 Stern, Ricki, and Heidi P. Worcester. *Beryl E. Bean: Mighty Adventurer of the Planet* (3–5). Illus.

by Amy Bates. 2002, HarperCollins LB $14.89 (0-06-028771-3); paper $5.95 (0-06-442120-1). 64pp. Soccer-loving 10-year-old Beryl is persuaded to take a trip to the natural history museum and finds it's great fun in this vibrantly designed and entertaining book. (Rev: BL 7/02; HBG 10/02; SLJ 1/03)

1901 Thompson, Lauren. *One Riddle, One Answer* (3–6). Illus. by Linda S. Wingerter. 2001, Scholastic $15.95 (0-590-31335-5). Beautiful illustrations set a Persian mood for this tale of a mathematically inclined sultan's daughter who sets a riddle intended to find the perfect husband. (Rev: BCCB 4/01; HBG 10/01; SLJ 4/01)

1902 Weatherford, Carole Boston. *Princeville: The 500-Year Flood* (3–5). Illus. by Douglas Alvord. 2001, Coastal Carolina LB $14.95 (1-928556-32-9). 32pp. An African American family in North Carolina is forced to leave home as the waters caused by Hurricane Floyd rise. (Rev: BL 2/15/02)

1903 Williams, Marcia. *Charles Dickens and Friends* (3–6). Illus. 2002, Candlewick $17.99 (0-7636-1905-1). 48pp. Williams uses a graphic novel style to retell five works by Dickens, weaving in era-accurate artwork and acute commentary. (Rev: BL 10/15/02; HBG 3/03; SLJ 2/03)

1904 Wojciechowski, Susan. *Beany Goes to Camp* (2–4). Illus. by Susanna Natti. 2002, Candlewick $15.99 (0-7636-1615-X). 110pp. Beany (Bernice) has to go to camp for a week, whether she likes it or not, in this beginning chapter book. (Rev: BCCB 7–8/02; BL 7/02; HBG 10/02; SLJ 5/02)

1905 Yep, Laurence. *Angelfish* (4–6). 2001, Putnam $16.99 (0-399-23041-6). 224pp. Robin has won a starring role in *Beauty and the Beast* and at the same time must start working for a man who seems to treat her just like the Beast. (Rev: BL 5/15/01; HBG 10/01; SLJ 6/01)

Adventure and Mystery

1906 Adams, W. Royce. *Me and Jay* (5–8). 2001, Rairarubia paper $10.99 (1-58832-021-9). 125pp. Two 13-year-olds meet with trouble at every turn when they venture into forbidden territory in search of a hidden pond. (Rev: BL 1/1–15/02)

1907 Adler, David A. *Andy Russell, NOT Wanted by the Police* (3–5). Illus. by Leanne Franson. 2001, Harcourt $14.00 (0-15-216474-X). 128pp. Andy and Tamika solve the mystery of an intruder at a neighbor's house in this beginning chapter book. (Rev: BL 1/1–15/02; HBG 3/02; SLJ 1/02)

1908 Adler, David A. *Cam Jansen and the First Day of School Mystery* (2–4). Illus. by Susanna Natti. 2002, Viking $13.99 (0-670-03575-0). 64pp. Cam's great memory comes into play when her teacher is arrested and taken away on the first day of school. (Rev: BL 12/1/02; HBG 3/03; SLJ 1/03)

1909 Adler, David A. *Cam Jansen and the School Play Mystery* (2–4). Illus. 2001, Viking $13.99 (0-670-89280-7). 64pp. Readers already familiar with Cam's exploits will enjoy this story in which Cam uses her photographic memory to solve the mystery of the missing admission money while her friends act onstage in a play about Honest Abe. (Rev: BL 8/01; HBG 3/02; SLJ 1/02)

1910 Anderson, Janet S. *The Last Treasure* (5–7). 2003, Dutton $16.99 (0-525-46919-2). 256pp. A whole family becomes immersed in a saga of intrigue and suspense that reaches back into the 19th century. (Rev: BL 3/15/03)

1911 Ardagh, Philip. *A House Called Awful End* (4–7). Illus. by David Roberts. 2002, Holt $14.95 (0-8050-6828-7). 144pp. Lemony Snicket fans will enjoy this complex story of 11-year-old Eddie, who winds up in a series of bizarre adventures when he has to leave his sick parents and live with eccentric relatives. (Rev: BCCB 12/02; BL 11/15/02; HBG 3/03; SLJ 9/02)

1912 Armstrong, Jennifer, and Nancy Butcher. *The Kindling* (5–9). Series: Fire-Us. 2002, Harper-Collins LB $15.89 (0-06-029411-6). 224pp. In 2007, after a virus has killed the adults, a small band of children join together in a Florida town and try to carry on with life. (Rev: BCCB 6/02; BL 4/15/02; HBG 10/02; SLJ 10/02)

1913 Bartlett, Susan. *The Seal Island Seven* (2–4). Illus. by Tricia Tusa. 2002, Viking $15.99 (0-670-03533-5). 70pp. In this beginning chapter book, Pru and her friends investigate who is destroying the fairy houses that are a Seal Island tradition. (Rev: BCCB 10/02; HBG 3/03; SLJ 10/02)

1914 Bledsoe, Lucy Jane. *Cougar Canyon* (5–8). 2001, Holiday $16.95 (0-8234-1599-6). 130pp. A family story and environmental tale about a 13-year-old girl named Izzy who fights to save a cougar in the local park. (Rev: BCCB 2/02; BL 2/1/02; HBG 3/02; SLJ 2/02)

1915 Bonners, Susan. *Above and Beyond* (5–7). 2001, Farrar $16.00 (0-374-30018-6). 151pp. Jerry makes a new friend and discovers the truth about an incident that took place many years ago. (Rev: BCCB 12/01; HBG 10/02; SLJ 10/01)

1916 Bruchac, Joseph. *Skeleton Man* (5–9). 2001, HarperCollins LB $14.89 (0-06-029076-5). 128pp. After her parents' disappearance, sixth-grader Molly, a Native American, must escape from the spooky man claiming to be her great-uncle. (Rev: BCCB 9/01; BL 9/1/01; HBG 3/02; SLJ 8/01*)

1917 Conrad, Hy. *Whodunit Crime Puzzles* (4–7). Illus. by Tatjana Mai Wyss. 2002, Sterling paper $6.95 (0-8069-9796-6). 96pp. This collection of 25 mysteries involves Sherman Holmes, a descendant of Sherlock, and his sidekick Sergeant Wilson. (Rev: BL 11/1/02)

1918 Crossman, David A. *The Mystery of the Black Moriah* (5–8). Series: A Bean and Ab Mystery. 2002, Down East $16.95 (0-89272-536-2). 234pp. The ever-curious Bean and Ab become caught up in a mystery adventure involving pirates, kidnappers, and a legendary ghost. (Rev: HBG 3/03; SLJ 12/02)

1919 Dahl, Michael. *The Coral Coffin* (5–8). Series: A Finnegan Zwake Mystery. 2002, Simon & Schuster paper $4.50 (0-7434-1698-8). 166pp. Still in search of his archaeologist parents, 13-year-old Finn

finds himself on a remote island on the Great Barrier Reef with a pirate mystery he must solve within 24 hours. (Rev: SLJ 7/02)

1920 Delaney, Mark. *The Protester's Song* (5–9). Series: Misfits, Inc. 2001, Peachtree paper $5.95 (1-56145-244-0). 214pp. Four teens keep themselves busy investigating an incident that occurred during riots in Ohio in 1970 and, in a subplot, try to stop the new principal from removing books from the library. (Rev: SLJ 8/01)

1921 Ellis, Mary. *Lily Dragon* (3–5). Illus. by Rachael Phillips. 2001, HarperCollins paper $7.50 (0-00-675458-9). 139pp. Lily sets off on a trip to visit her mother's family in China, determined to hunt for the hidden treasure she's heard about so often. (Rev: SLJ 8/01)

1922 Ericson, Helen. *Harriet Spies Again* (4–6). 2002, Delacorte LB $17.99 (0-385-90022-8). 230pp. This well-done continuation of the tales of Louise Fitzhugh's *Harriet the Spy* has the junior sleuth investigating her caretaker's sudden bout of sadness. (Rev: BCCB 4/02; BL 3/15/02; HB 5–6/02; HBG 10/02; SLJ 5/02)

1923 Fama, Elizabeth. *Overboard* (4–8). 2002, Cricket $15.95 (0-8126-2652-4). 176pp. Fourteen-year-old Emily struggles to save her own life and that of a boy named Isman when a ferry sinks off the coast of Sumatra. (Rev: BCCB 6/02; BL 7/02; HBG 10/02; SLJ 7/02)

1924 Fienberg, Anna. *Horrendo's Curse* (3–6). Illus. by Kim Gamble. 2002, Annick $18.95 (1-55037-773-6); paper $6.95 (1-55037-772-8). 160pp. Twelve-year-old Horrendo, whose curse is an inability to say anything cruel although surrounded by rude foul-mouths, manages to persuade his pirate kidnappers that politeness is the best policy. (Rev: BL 12/1/02; SLJ 2/03)

1925 Garland, Michael. *Mystery Mansion: A Look Again Book* (2–4). Illus. by author. 2001, Dutton $15.99 (0-525-46675-4). Aunt Jeanne leaves young Tommy a series of rhyming notes that send him (and the reader) on a detecting tour of her mansion and its abundance of wildlife. (Rev: HBG 3/02; SLJ 9/01)

1926 George, Jean Craighead. *Tree Castle Island* (4–7). Illus. 2002, HarperCollins LB $15.89 (0-06-000255-7). 240pp. A boy tests his survival skills in the Okefenokee Swamp, and meets the twin he never knew he had, in this tale rich in details about the setting. (Rev: BL 3/15/02; HBG 10/02; SLJ 5/02)

1927 Gutman, Dan. *Shoeless Joe and Me* (4–7). Series: Baseball Card Adventure. 2002, Harper-Collins LB $15.89 (0-06-029254-7). 144pp. Thirteen-year-old Joe travels back in time to remedy the 1919 Black Sox scandal and save Shoeless Joe's reputation. (Rev: BL 1/1–15/02; HBG 10/02; SLJ 3/02)

1928 Heyes, Eileen. *O'Dwyer and Grady Starring In: Acting Innocent* (4–6). 2002, Simon & Schuster paper $4.99 (0-689-84911-7). 128pp. Billy and Virginia, child actors in the 1930s, find that their friend

Chubby Muldoon is accused of murdering an actress. (Rev: BL 5/1/02; SLJ 3/02)

1929 Hobbs, Will. *Down the Yukon* (5–8). 2001, HarperCollins LB $15.89 (0-06-029540-6). 208pp. In this sequel to *Jason's Gold*, Jason decides to compete in a race to the new gold fields in Alaska. (Rev: BL 4/1/01; HBG 10/01; SLJ 5/01)

1930 Hobbs, Will. *Wild Man Island* (5–9). 2002, HarperCollins LB $15.89 (0-06-029810-3). 192pp. An adventure story in which 14-year-old Andy becomes stranded on a remote Alaska island, faces many dangers, and tests his dead archaeologist father's theories about the earliest prehistoric immigrants to America. (Rev: BL 4/15/02; HB 7–8/02; HBG 10/02; SLJ 5/02)

1931 Holmes, Barbara Ware. *Following Fake Man* (5–8). 2001, Knopf $15.95 (0-375-81266-0). 160pp. Lonely 12-year-old Homer makes a friend while on holiday in Maine, and the two boys uncover secrets about Homer's dead father. (Rev: BCCB 7–8/01; BL 6/1–15/01; HB 7–8/01; HBG 10/01; SLJ 5/01*)

1932 Honey, Elizabeth. *Fiddleback* (4–6). Illus. 2001, Knopf $14.95 (0-375-80579-6). 176pp. Twelve-year-old Henni and an assorted group of friends go camping in the Australian Outback, where they encounter more than they bargained for. (Rev: BCCB 7–8/01; BL 9/1/01; HB 9–10/01; HBG 3/02; SLJ 8/01)

1933 Honey, Elizabeth. *Remote Man* (5–9). Illus. by author. 2002, Knopf LB $17.99 (0-375-91413-7). 256pp. Young Ned, 13, is a loner whose high-tech savvy and interest in reptiles lead him to a key role in creating an international network that uncovers a ring of wildlife poachers. (Rev: BCCB 10/02; BL 10/15/02; SLJ 8/02)

1934 Horowitz, Anthony. *Stormbreaker* (5–9). 2001, Philomel $16.99 (0-399-23620-1). 208pp. Fourteen-year-old Alex becomes embroiled in dangerous undercover exploits when his MI6 uncle is murdered. (Rev: BCCB 9/01; BL 9/1/01; HBG 10/01; SLJ 6/01)

1935 Jennings, Patrick. *The Bird Shadow: An Ike and Mem Story* (2–4). Illus. by Anna Alter. 2001, Holiday $15.95 (0-8234-1670-4). 55pp. Ike and little sister Mem end up making a new friend when they dare to investigate a spooky old house. (Rev: HBG 10/02; SLJ 3/02)

1936 Johnson, Rodney. *The Secret of Dead Man's Mine* (5–7). Illus. by Jill Thompson. Series: Rinnah Two Feathers Mystery. 2001, Uglytown paper $12.00 (0-9663473-3-1). 241pp. Rinnah Two Feathers and two friends set out to solve the mystery of a suspicious stranger and find themselves in danger. (Rev: SLJ 9/01)

1937 Karr, Kathleen. *Bone Dry* (5–8). 2002, Hyperion $15.99 (0-7868-0776-8). 240pp. Young Matthew assists phrenologist Asa B. Cornwall in a hunt for the skull of Alexander the Great in this action-packed adventure story, a sequel to *Skullduggery* (2000). (Rev: BCCB 10/02; BL 9/15/02; SLJ 8/02)

1938 Kehret, Peg. *The Stranger Next Door* (4–6). 2002, Dutton $15.99 (0-525-46829-3). 160pp. Twelve-year-old Alex discovers who's behind a

spate of vandalism and arson in his new neighborhood, with the help of his feline friend Pete. (Rev: BL 2/1/02; HBG 10/02; SLJ 3/02)

1939 Klise, Kate. *Trial by Jury Journal* (5–8). Illus. by M. Sarah Klise. 2001, HarperCollins LB $15.89 (0-06-029541-4). 256pp. When she is given the opportunity to serve as her state's first juvenile juror, 12-year-old Lily's sleuthing skills solve a murder mystery and save the day. (Rev: BCCB 4/01; BL 5–6/01; HB 5–6/01; HBG 10/01; SLJ 6/01)

1940 Mikaelsen, Ben. *Red Midnight* (5–9). 2002, HarperCollins LB $15.89 (0-06-001228-5). 256pp. After soldiers kill their family, a 12-year-old Guatemalan boy and his sister set off on a perilous journey to Florida in a canoe. (Rev: HBG 10/02; SLJ 5/02)

1941 Mitchell, Marianne. *Finding Zola* (5–8). 2003, Boyds Mills $16.95 (1-59078-070-1). 144pp. A 13-year-old girl in a wheelchair investigates the disappearance of an elderly woman who has been staying with her. (Rev: SLJ 2/03)

1942 Morpurgo, Michael. *Kensuke's Kingdom* (4–7). 2003, Scholastic $16.95 (0-439-38202-5). 176pp. A boy washed onto a seemingly deserted island finds a friend in a Japanese solider who has lived there since World War II. (Rev: BL 2/15/03; SLJ 3/03)

1943 Mundis, Hester. *My Chimp Friday* (4–7). 2002, Simon & Schuster $16.00 (0-689-83837-9). 176pp. Rachel and her family grow to love their new pet, a chimp named Friday, but when kidnappers try to steal Friday, Rachel realizes he is not an ordinary chimp. (Rev: BL 6/1–15/02; HBG 10/02; SLJ 6/02)

1944 Murphy, T. M. *The Secrets of Code Z* (4–8). Series: Belltown Mystery. 2001, J. N. Townsend paper $9.95 (1-880158-33-7). 144pp. Orville Jacques becomes embroiled in a fast-paced mystery involving CIA cover-ups, a death powder, and an evil Russian. (Rev: BL 5/15/01; SLJ 7/01)

1945 Napoli, Donna Jo. *Three Days* (4–6). 2001, Dutton $15.99 (0-525-46790-4). 176pp. A harrowing story full of advice on keeping safe in which 11-year-old Jackie is kidnapped on a trip to Italy after her father dies at the wheel of their car. (Rev: BCCB 11/01; BL 10/1/01; HB 9–10/01; HBG 3/02; SLJ 8/01*)

1946 Naylor, Phyllis Reynolds. *Bernie Magruder and the Bats in the Belfry* (4–7). 2003, Simon & Schuster $16.95 (0-689-85066-2). 144pp. Bernie is investigating a bat with a fatal bite; could it be connected to the fact that the bells in the belfry are annoyingly stuck on the same tune? (Rev: BL 1/1–15/03)

1947 Nickerson, Sara. *How to Disappear Completely and Never Be Found* (4–8). Illus. by Sally Wern Comport. 2002, HarperCollins LB $15.89 (0-06-029772-7). 288pp. Two youngsters with problems, 12-year-old Margaret and her friend Boyd, explore a deserted mansion and solve the mystery of the supernatural terrors it supposedly contains. (Rev: BCCB 5/02; BL 4/1/02; HB 7–8/02; HBG 10/02; SLJ 4/02)

1948 Nixon, Joan Lowery. *The Trap* (5–8). 2002, Delacorte LB $17.99 (0-385-90063-5). 192pp. A gripping mystery in which 16-year-old Julie investigates deaths and missing jewelry, and faces danger herself. (Rev: BL 9/15/02; HBG 3/03; SLJ 9/02)

1949 Sedgwick, Marcus. *Witch Hill* (5–7). 2001, Delacorte $15.95 (0-385-32802-8). 148pp. Jamie is haunted by dreams of a witch and by memories of a deadly fire in this suspense novel that includes a look at a British town's history. (Rev: BCCB 10/01; BL 10/1/01; HBG 3/02; SLJ 9/01)

1950 Shands, Linda. *Blind Fury* (4–6). 2001, Revell paper $5.99 (0-8007-5747-5). 176pp. Wakara, who was introduced in *Wild Fire*, must find her brother and father during a blizzard. (Rev: BL 5/1/01)

1951 Shands, Linda. *Wild Fire* (4–6). 2001, Revell paper $5.99 (0-8007-5746-7). 176pp. Wakara, a 15-year-old of American Indian and Irish parentage, is still mourning her mother's death when she and her brother become trapped by a forest fire. (Rev: BL 5/1/01)

1952 Snicket, Lemony. *The Carnivorous Carnival* (4–8). Illus. by Brett Helquist. Series: A Series of Unfortunate Events. 2002, HarperCollins LB $14.89 (0-06-029640-2). 304pp. The Baudelaire orphans pose as carnival freaks in the ninth volume of this unhappily-ever-after series. (Rev: BL 12/15/02; HBG 3/03; SLJ 1/03)

1953 Snicket, Lemony. *The Ersatz Elevator* (3–6). Illus. Series: A Series of Unfortunate Events. 2001, HarperCollins LB $14.89 (0-06-028889-2). 266pp. Count Olaf soon finds the Baudelaire orphans at their new home, chez Mr. and Mrs. Squalor. (Rev: BL 8/01; HBG 10/01; SLJ 8/01)

1954 Snicket, Lemony. *The Hostile Hospital* (4–6). Illus. by Brett Helquist. Series: A Series of Unfortunate Events. 2001, HarperCollins LB $9.89 (0-06-028891-4). 272pp. The Baudelaire children face danger and intrigue in their quest to find out more about their dead parents. (Rev: BL 10/15/01; HBG 3/02; SLJ 11/01)

1955 Snicket, Lemony. *The Vile Village* (3–6). Illus. Series: A Series of Unfortunate Events. 2001, HarperCollins LB $14.89 (0-06-028890-6). 272pp. Aphorisms abound as a village decides to raise three children and takes on the Baudelaire orphans. (Rev: BL 8/01; HBG 3/02; SLJ 8/01)

1956 Snyder, Zilpha Keatley. *Spyhole Secrets* (4–7). 2001, Delacorte $15.95 (0-385-32764-1). 176pp. When Hallie and her mother move to a new town after her father's death, Hallie finds herself preoccupied with the life of a mysterious neighboring family. (Rev: BCCB 10/01; BL 5/1/01; HBG 10/01; SLJ 6/01)

1957 Springer, Nancy. *Lionclaw* (5–8). 2002, Putnam $16.99 (0-399-23716-X). 128pp. Gentle, music-loving Lionel abandons his timidity when Rowan Hood is captured, but, despite his newfound courage, his father still refuses to accept him in this sequel to *Rowan Hood: Outlaw Girl of Sherwood Forest* (2001). (Rev: BL 10/1/02; SLJ 10/02)

1958 Springer, Nancy. *Rowan Hood: Outlaw Girl of Sherwood Forest* (4–7). 2001, Putnam $16.99 (0-399-23368-7). 208pp. A young girl finds adventure when she journeys to Sherwood Forest to find the father she doesn't know, Robin Hood. (Rev: BL 4/15/01; HBG 10/01; SLJ 7/01)

1959 Stengel, Joyce A. *Mystery of the Island Jewels* (5–8). 2002, Simon & Schuster paper $4.99 (0-689-85049-2). 199pp. On a cruise to Martinique with her father and new stepfamily, 14-year-old Cassie and new friend Charles uncover a mystery. (Rev: SLJ 6/02)

1960 Strickland, Brad. *The Tower at the End of the World* (4–6). Series: Lewis Barnavelt. 2001, Dial $16.99 (0-8037-2620-1). 144pp. Lewis Barnavelt is back, this time solving a spooky mystery (and thereby saving the world) while vacationing in Michigan with his uncle and their friends. (Rev: BL 9/1/01; HBG 3/02; SLJ 9/01)

1961 Torrey, Michele. *The Case of the Gasping Garbage* (3–5). Illus. 2001, Dutton $14.99 (0-525-46657-6). 112pp. Fourth-graders Drake and Nell use intuition, observation, and scientific investigation to solve mysteries and problems that involve a noisy garbage can, endangered frogs, a stuck truck, and a love letter. (Rev: BCCB 6/01; BL 8/01; HBG 3/02; SLJ 8/01)

1962 Torrey, Michele. *The Case of the Graveyard Ghost* (3–6). Illus. by Barbara Johansen Newman. Series: Doyle and Fossey: Science Detectives. 2002, Dutton $14.99 (0-525-46893-5). 80pp. In this third book about the junior detectives, Doyle and Fossey use their scientific skills and knowledge to solve four cases, and there are activities and experiments for readers to try themselves. (Rev: BL 10/15/02; SLJ 8/02)

1963 Torrey, Michele. *The Case of the Mossy Lake Monster and Other Super-Scientific Cases* (3–5). Illus. by Barbara Johansen Newman. Series: Doyle and Fossey: Science Detectives. 2002, Dutton $14.99 (0-525-46815-3). 112pp. Fifth-graders Drake Doyle and Nell Fossey solve a string of mysteries using scientific reasoning in this easy-to-read second book in the series. (Rev: BL 1/1–15/02; HBG 10/02; SLJ 2/02)

1964 Van Draanen, Wendelin. *Sammy Keyes and the Art of Deception* (5–8). Series: Sammy Keyes. 2003, Knopf $15.95 (0-375-81176-1). 272pp. Sammy (with some help from Grams) solves a mystery involving an art thief. (Rev: BL 2/1/03; SLJ 3/03)

1965 Vazquez, Diana. *Lost in Sierra* (4–6). Illus. by German Jaramillo. 2002, Coteau paper $7.95 (1-55050-184-4). 173pp. On a visit to Spain, 13-year-old Ana discovers why her grandmother's brother never came back from Spain's civil war. (Rev: SLJ 8/02)

1966 Weir, Joan. *The Mysterious Visitor* (5–7). Series: Lion and Bobbi. 2002, Raincoast paper $6.99 (1-55192-404-4). 176pp. Two Canadian youngsters, Lion and sister Bobbi, try to solve the mystery of strange events occurring on a friend's land. (Rev: BL 5/1/02)

1967 Wilson, Barbara. *A Clear Spring* (4–6). 2002, Feminist Pr. paper $12.50 (1-55861-277-7). 176pp.

While working at a nature center with her aunt's lesbian partner, Willa teams up with her cousins to track down polluters. (Rev: BL 7/02; HBG 10/02)

1968 Woods, Ron. *The Hero* (5–9). 2002, Knopf LB $17.99 (0-375-90612-6). 192pp. When a boy dies in a rafting incident, 14-year-old Jamie tells a lie intended to show the dead boy as a hero. (Rev: BCCB 3/02; BL 2/1/02; HB 3–4/02; HBG 10/02; SLJ 1/02)

1969 Woodson, Marion. *My Brother's Keeper* (5–7). 2002, Raincoast paper $6.95 (1-55192-488-9). 160pp. On Vancouver Island, 13-year-old Sarah believes she is being haunted by a cult leader who founded a colony there in the 1930s. (Rev: BL 5/1/02)

1970 Wynne-Jones, Tim. *The Boy in the Burning House* (5–9). 2001, Farrar $16.00 (0-374-30930-2). 213pp. Disturbed Ruth Rose and 14-year-old Jim investigate the mystery of his father's disappearance — was he killed by Ruth Rose's pastor stepfather? (Rev: BCCB 11/01; BL 9/1/01; HB 11–12/01; HBG 3/02; SLJ 10/01)

1971 Yolen, Jane, and Heidi Elisabet Yolen. *The Wolf Girls: An Unsolved Mystery from History* (3–5). Illus. Series: Unsolved Mystery from History. 2001, Simon & Schuster $16.00 (0-689-81080-6). 32pp. Readers must consider possible solutions to the mysterious origin of two orphan girls. (Rev: BL 7/01; HBG 3/02; SLJ 8/01)

1972 Zindel, Paul. *The E-mail Murders* (5–8). Series: P.C. Hawke Mysteries. 2001, Hyperion paper $4.99 (0-7868-1579-5). 113pp. P.C. and Mackenzie team up with an inspector's daughter to investigate a murder in Monaco. (Rev: SLJ 1/02)

1973 Zindel, Paul. *The Square Root of Murder* (5–7). 2002, Hyperion paper $4.99 (0-7868-1588-4). 131pp. Amateur detective P.C. Hawke and her sidekick Mackenzie Riggs try to solve the mystery of the murder of a calculus teacher. (Rev: BL 5/1/02; SLJ 4/02)

Animal Stories

1974 Avi. *The Good Dog* (3–6). 2001, Simon & Schuster $16.00 (0-689-83824-7). 256pp. A malamute dog reconsiders his position as a pet when a wolf comes to town. (Rev: BL 9/1/01; HB 1–2/02; HBG 3/02; SLJ 12/01)

1975 Bastedo, Jamie. *Tracking Triple Seven* (5–7). 2001, Red Deer paper $9.95 (0-88995-238-8). 224pp. Benji, a teenage boy grieving his mother's death, becomes involved with biologists tracking grizzly bears near his father's mine in Canada. (Rev: BL 2/1/02)

1976 Bauer, Marion Dane. *Runt* (3–6). 2002, Clarion $15.00 (0-618-21261-2). 144pp. A tale of a wolf born the runt of the litter and his struggle to improve his position in the pack and earn his father's approval. (Rev: BL 10/15/02; SLJ 9/02)

1977 Broome, Errol. *Magnus Maybe* (2–4). Illus. by Ann James. 2002, Simon & Schuster paper $4.99 (0-7434-3796-9). 144pp. A shy pet mouse learns a lesson in courage when he escapes his cage and meets up with a family of wild mice. (Rev: BL 8/02; SLJ 8/02)

1978 Daniels, Lucy. *Keeping Faith* (4–6). 2002, Hyperion paper $4.99 (0-7868-1618-X). 135pp. When 12-year-old Josie must find a new home for her elderly mare, she and her mother interview many potential owners before finding just the right one. (Rev: SLJ 8/02)

1979 Daniels, Lucy. *Last Hope* (4–6). Series: The Horseshoe Trilogies. 2002, Hyperion paper $4.99 (0-7868-1619-8). 134pp. Josie's family looks for a home for a horse with skin problems when they must close their stables. (Rev: SLJ 12/02)

1980 Dennard, Deborah. *Lemur Landing: A Story of a Madagascan Tropical Dry Forest* (3–4). Illus. by Kristin Kest. 2001, Soundprints $15.95 (1-56899-978-X). 32pp. This beautifully illustrated, fictional story about lemurs includes much factual detail. (Rev: BL 3/1/02)

1981 Duey, Kathleen. *Bonita* (4–6). Series: Spirit of the Cimarron. 2002, DreamWorks $15.99 (0-525-46711-4); paper $4.99 (0-14-230095-0). 117pp. A beautiful mare called Bonita joins a herd of wild horses and gives birth to a foal called Esperanza. The sequel, *Esperanza*, continues the story. (Rev: HBG 10/02; SLJ 10/02)

1982 Duey, Kathleen. *Sierra* (4–6). Series: Spirit of the Cimarron. 2002, Dutton $15.99 (0-525-46712-1); paper $4.99 (0-14-230096-9). 128pp. Sierra, a high-spirited filly born into a herd of wild horses, finds a new home after her own colt is born. (Rev: BL 6/1–15/02; HBG 10/02; SLJ check)

1983 Edwards, Julie Andrews. *Little Bo in France: The Further Adventures of Bonnie Boadicea* (2–4). Illus. by Henry Cole. 2002, Hyperion LB $19.49 (0-7868-2540-5). 117pp. Little Bo the cat and her sailor owner travel through France having adventures and looking for work. (Rev: HBG 3/03; SLJ 10/02)

1984 Farley, Terri. *The Wild One* (4–6). 2002, Avon paper $4.99 (0-06-441085-4). 224pp. Sam is determined to find her stallion, Blackie, who ran away after she fell off and hit her head. (Rev: BL 9/1/02; SLJ 12/02)

1985 Haas, Jessie. *Runaway Radish* (2–4). Illus. 2001, Greenwillow LB $15.89 (0-06-029159-1). 56pp. A beginning chapter book about a pony named Radish and how he is cared for, first by Judy and later by Nina. (Rev: BCCB 7–8/01; BL 4/15/01; HB 5–6/01; HBG 10/01; SLJ 5/01)

1986 Hosler, Jay. *Clan Apis* (5–7). Illus. 2001, Active Synapse $15.00 (0-9677255-0-X). 158pp. Nyuki, a honeybee, describes his hive's history and migration to a new location in a text presented in graphic-novel style that includes information about bees and their environment. (Rev: BL 7/01)

1987 Hutchins, Hazel. *T J and the Cats* (2–4). 2002, Orca paper $4.99 (1-55143-205-6). 112pp. A beginning chapter book about a boy who doesn't like cats, but agrees to care for his grandmother's four while she's on vacation and slowly changes his mind. (Rev: BL 12/15/02; SLJ 2/03)

1988 Kehret, Peg. *Saving Lilly* (3–6). 2001, Pocket $16.00 (0-671-03422-7). 160pp. Two sixth-graders boycott a class trip to the circus because of animal cruelty and persuade the class to raise funds to send performer Lilly to an elephant sanctuary. (Rev: BL 12/1/01; HBG 10/02; SLJ 11/01)

1989 King-Smith, Dick. *Funny Frank* (3–5). Illus. by John Eastwood. 2002, Knopf LB $16.99 (0-375-91460-9). 112pp. A chick named Frank learns to swim like a duck with some help from the farmer's daughter in this charming beginning chapter book. (Rev: BL 1/1–15/02; HBG 10/02; SLJ 3/02)

1990 Levin, Betty. *That'll Do, Moss* (4–6). 2002, HarperCollins LB $15.89 (0-06-000532-7). 128pp. Moss the Border collie and a girl named Diane, who works at the farm where Moss lives, rescue one of the farmer's sons who has run away. (Rev: BL 8/02; HBG 10/02; SLJ 10/02)

1991 Lottridge, Celia Barker. *Berta: A Remarkable Dog* (3–5). Illus. by Elso Myotte. 2002, Groundwood $14.95 (0-88899-461-3); paper $4.95 (0-88899-469-9). 104pp. Berta, a dachshund, shows that she is a remarkable dog when she cares for and protects a newborn lamb. (Rev: BL 5/1/02; HB 7–8/02*; HBG 10/02)

1992 Malone, Geoffrey. *Torn Ear* (4–6). 2003, Hodder paper $8.95 (0-340-86057-X). 144pp. Readers follow Torn Ear, a fox, as he grows to adulthood, survives dangers, mates, and has his own cubs. (Rev: BL 3/1/03)

1993 Michaels, Vaughn. *Dodi's Prince* (3–5). Illus. by Jacqueline Rogers. 2003, Dutton $15.99 (0-525-47034-4). 96pp. Life in a trailer park in a remote Texas town is lonely for 8-year-old Dodi until a stray dog appears. (Rev: BL 3/15/03; SLJ 3/03)

1994 Pennac, Daniel. *Eye of the Wolf* (5–8). Illus. by Max Grafe. 2003, Candlewick $15.99 (0-7636-1896-9). 112pp. A boy and a captive wolf, who have both suffered at the hands of humans, form a close connection. (Rev: BCCB 3/03; BL 3/1/03; SLJ 2/03)

1995 Popp, Monika. *Farm Year* (2–4). Illus. by Monika Popp and Regine Frick von Schmuck. 2002, Groundwood $18.95 (0-88899-452-4). A young farm boy takes special interest in a Holstein heifer and shepherds her tenderly through her first year of life. (Rev: HBG 10/02; SLJ 6/02)

1996 Pringle, Laurence. *The Dog of Discovery: A Newfoundland's Adventures with Lewis and Clark* (4–6). Illus. by Meryl Henderson. 2002, Boyds Mills $17.95 (1-56397-028-0). 152pp. A Newfoundland dog named Seaman was a valued member of the Lewis and Clark expedition, and his lightly fictionalized story is told here, based on entries in the explorers' journals and illustrated with drawings and photographs. (Rev: BL 12/1/02)

1997 Sachs, Marilyn. *The Four Ugly Cats in Apartment 3D* (3–5). Illus. by Rosanne Litzinger. 2002, Simon & Schuster $15.00 (0-689-84581-2). 80pp. When her neighbor dies, 10-year-old Lily tries to find homes for his four cats. (Rev: BCCB 7–8/02; BL 5/1/02; HB 3–4/02; HBG 10/02; SLJ 3/02)

1998 Seuling, Barbara. *Robert and the Great Pepperoni* (2–3). Illus. by Paul Brewer. 2001, Cricket $14.95 (0-8126-2825-X). 118pp. Second-grader Robert really wants a dog and he starts a pet-sitting service that eventually but temporarily gives him a chance to look after one. (Rev: HB 1–2/02; HBG 3/02; SLJ 10/01)

1999 Spurr, Elizabeth. *Surfer Dog* (3–6). 2002, Dutton $15.99 (0-525-46898-6). 128pp. Eleven-year-old Pete, who is adjusting to a new home and school, finds a companion to surf with when he is joined by Blackie, a stray black Labrador retriever. (Rev: BCCB 9/02; BL 6/1–15/02; HBG 10/02; SLJ 7/02)

2000 Wallace, Bill. *Goosed!* (2–4). Illus. by Jacqueline Rogers. 2002, Holiday $16.95 (0-8234-1757-3). 128pp. T.P. the dog does not welcome the arrival of a Labrador puppy in his life in this beginning chapter book. (Rev: HBG 3/03; SLJ 12/02)

2001 Woods, Shirley. *Jack: The Story of a Beaver* (3–5). Illus. by Celia Godkin. 2002, Fitzhenry & Whiteside $14.95 (1-55041-733-9). 96pp. Nature lovers will enjoy the story of the first two years of life for Jack the Beaver, who evades predators, learns to avoid traps, and finally finds a mate. (Rev: BL 1/1–15/03; SLJ 3/03)

Ethnic Groups

2002 Banks, Jacqueline Turner. *A Day for Vincent Chin and Me* (3–6). Series: Project Wheels. 2001, Houghton $15.00 (0-618-13199-X). 112pp. When the letters KKK are sprayed on Tommy's house, the sixth-grade Japanese American learns about activism, fitting in, and being proud of who you are. (Rev: BCCB 3/02; BL 11/1/01; HBG 3/02; SLJ 12/01)

2003 Caraballo, Samuel. *Estrellita Says Good-bye to Her Island/Estrellita se despide de su isla* (3–5). Illus. by Pablo Torrecilla. 2002, Arte Publico $14.95 (1-55885-338-3). 32pp. In this bilingual book, a young girl bids good-bye to her island home and all the sights and sounds that are important to her. (Rev: BL 5/1/02)

2004 Johnston, Tony. *Any Small Goodness: A Novel of the Barrio* (4–7). Illus. by Raul Colon. 2001, Scholastic $15.95 (0-439-18936-5). 128pp. Eleven-year-old Arturo Rodriguez, whose Mexican family is new to Los Angeles, describes family life, school, celebrations, and dangers. (Rev: BL 9/15/01; HBG 3/02; SLJ 9/01)

2005 Mak, Kam. *My Chinatown* (2–6). Illus. by author. 2002, HarperCollins LB $16.89 (0-06-029191-5). 32pp. A young boy from Hong Kong describes his old life and his new life in New York's Chinatown, using simple free-verse poems and realistic paintings that focus on individual people rather than the wider setting. (Rev: BL 12/1/01; HBG 3/02; SLJ 5/02)

2006 Perry, Michael. *Daniel's Ride* (2–4). Illus. by Lee Ballard. 2001, Free Will $16.00 (0-9701771-9-4). 32pp. In this colorful glimpse of Latino culture, Daniel enjoys a ride in his big brother Hector's convertible and makes an important promise. (Rev: BL 9/1/01; SLJ 1/02)

2007 Saldana, Rene, Jr. *The Jumping Tree: A Novel* (5–9). 2001, Delacorte $14.95 (0-385-32725-0). 181pp. Rey, a Mexican American boy growing up in a poor family near the Mexican border, describes his life and his longing to become a man. (Rev: BL 5/15/01; HBG 10/01; SLJ 6/01)

2008 Walter, Mildred Pitts. *Ray and the Best Family Reunion Ever* (3–5). 2002, HarperCollins LB $15.89 (0-06-623625-8). 128pp. Eleven-year-old Ray attends his family reunion in Natchitoches, Louisiana, where he meets his estranged grandfather who teaches him about his Creole roots. (Rev: BL 1/1–15/02; HBG 10/02; SLJ 1/02)

Family Stories

2009 Barasch, Lynne. *The Reluctant Flower Girl* (PS–3). Illus. 2001, HarperCollins LB $14.89 (0-06-028810-8). 40pp. April doesn't want to lose her older sister and tries to discourage Annabel's fiance, but when the wedding day arrives it's April who averts catastrophe. (Rev: BL 5/1/01; HBG 10/01; SLJ 6/01)

2010 Barnes, Emma. *Jessica Haggerthwaite: Watch Dispatcher* (3–6). Illus. by Tim Archbold. 2001, Walker $15.95 (0-8027-8794-0). 168pp. Young Jessica and her brother are aghast when their mother decides to make her living at witchcraft and her laid-off husband leaves in protest, in this amusing story set in Britain. (Rev: BL 12/1/01; HBG 10/02; SLJ 3/02)

2011 Becker, Bonnie. *My Brother, the Robot* (4–6). 2001, Dutton $15.99 (0-525-46792-0). 144pp. Underachiever Chip is faced with a new challenge — a "perfect" robot that his parents feel will be an example to him. (Rev: BL 12/15/01; HBG 3/02; SLJ 10/01)

2012 Blume, Judy. *Double Fudge* (4–6). Series: Fudge. 2002, Dutton $15.99 (0-525-46926-5). 160pp. Twelve-year-old Peter Hatcher suffers many trials in this novel, as his younger brother Fudge (Farley) becomes obsessed with money, and a family of long-lost relatives arrives for an extended stay in New York. (Rev: BCCB 11/02; BL 9/15/02; HB 11–12/02; HBG 3/03; SLJ 9/02)

2013 Bonners, Susan. *Making Music* (3–4). 2002, Farrar $15.00 (0-374-34732-8). 96pp. Annie's disappointment with her new home and sadness over the loss of her horse collection begin to fade when she befriends an elderly neighbor. (Rev: BL 11/1/02; HBG 3/03; SLJ 10/02)

2014 Butcher, Kristin. *The Gramma War* (4–6). 2001, Orca paper $6.95 (1-55143-183-1). 170pp. Annie's life isn't enhanced when her difficult grandmother moves in and takes Annie's room, but

an interest in genealogy brings them closer. (Rev: BCCB 1/02; BL 10/1/01; SLJ 9/01)

2015 Chambers, Veronica. *Quinceañera Means Sweet 15* (5–8). 2001, Hyperion LB $16.49 (0-7868-2426-3). 192pp. Fourteen-year-old Brooklyn friends Marisol and Magdalena look ahead to their quinceanera coming-of-age parties with anticipation and some frustration. (Rev: BCCB 5/01; HBG 10/01; SLJ 6/01)

2016 Clavel, Bernard. *Castle of Books* (3–5). Illus. by Yan Nascimbene. 2002, Chronicle $14.95 (0-8118-3501-4). 32pp. A whimsical tale of a boy who builds a castle in his apartment building's courtyard with his poet father's books. (Rev: BL 2/15/02; HBG 10/02; SLJ 4/02)

2017 Cohn, Rachel. *The Steps* (4–7). 2003, Simon & Schuster $16.95 (0-689-84549-9). 144pp. Annabel resents the complexity of her family life as she reluctantly sets out to visit her father and his new wife, baby, and stepchildren in Australia, but she gradually learns to accept the situation in this humorous portrayal. (Rev: BCCB 2/03; BL 1/1–15/03; SLJ 2/03)

2018 Creech, Sharon. *Ruby Holler* (4–7). 2002, HarperCollins LB $16.89 (0-06-027733-5). 320pp. An elderly couple, Tiller and Sairy, invite 13-year-old troublesome twins Dallas and Florida to stay with them. (Rev: BCCB 7–8/02; BL 4/1/02; HB 5–6/02; HBG 10/02; SLJ 4/02)

2019 Cutler, Jane. *Leap, Frog* (3–5). Illus. by Tracey Campbell Pearson. 2002, Farrar $16.00 (0-374-34362-4). 208pp. Third-grader Edward has a busy time participating in a variety of projects, particularly the frog-jumping contest that honors Mark Twain, and dealing with newcomer Charlie, a first-grader who regards Edward with awe. (Rev: BCCB 12/02; BL 11/1/02; HB 9–10/02; HBG 3/03; SLJ 10/02)

2020 Deans, Sis. *Racing the Past* (4–7). 2001, Holt $15.95 (0-8050-6635-7). 152pp. Young Ricky is a long-distance runner in training, who uses his time on his feet to work through his problems at home and at school. (Rev: BCCB 6/01; BL 6/1–15/01; HB 7–8/01; HBG 10/01)

2021 Encinas, Carlos. *The New Engine / La Maquina Nueva* (1–5). Illus. by author. 2001, Kiva $15.95 (1-885772-24-6). A man worried that a computer may replace him remembers his family's fear that the arrival of a diesel locomotive would put his own father out of work. (Rev: SLJ 1/02)

2022 Fleischman, Sid. *Bo and Mzzz Mad* (5–7). 2001, Greenwillow LB $14.89 (0-06-029398-5). 112pp. When his father dies, 12-year-old Bo accepts an invitation from relatives despite a longstanding family feud. (Rev: BL 5/15/01*; HB 5–6/01; HBG 10/01; SLJ 5/01)

2023 Fletcher, Brian. *Uncle Daddy* (4–6). 2001, Holt $15.95 (0-8050-6663-2). 133pp. Nine-year-old Rivers's peaceful life is upset when his long-absent father turns up without warning. (Rev: BCCB 5/01; BL 8/01; HB 7–8/01; HBG 10/01; SLJ 5/01)

2024 Fogelin, Adrian. *My Brother's Hero* (5–8). 2002, Peachtree $14.95 (1-56145-274-2). 224pp.

When Ben and his family travel to Florida for a vacation, Ben meets a girl named Mica, whose life he finds exciting and mysterious. (Rev: BL 2/1/03; SLJ 2/03)

2025 Frank, Lucy. *Just Ask Iris* (5–7). 2001, Simon & Schuster $17.00 (0-689-84406-9). 224pp. In this book packed with memorable characters, a 12-year-old girl brings her stand-offish neighbors together while earning the money she needs to buy a bra. (Rev: BCCB 12/01; BL 11/15/01; HB 1–2/02; HBG 3/02; SLJ 12/01)

2026 Haddix, Margaret Peterson. *Takeoffs and Landings* (5–8). 2001, Simon & Schuster $16.00 (0-689-83299-0). 208pp. Popular 14-year-old Lori and her overweight older brother Chuck go on a lecture tour with their mother, and together the three finally start to talk about the guilt they feel over the death of the children's father. (Rev: BCCB 10/01; BL 11/15/01; HBG 3/02; SLJ 8/01)

2027 Hamilton, Virginia. *Time Pieces: The Book of Times* (5–8). 2002, Scholastic $16.95 (0-590-28881-4). 128pp. A young girl living in rural Ohio hears stories about her great-grandfather's escape via the Underground Railroad in this semi-autobiographical novel. (Rev: BL 12/15/02; SLJ 12/02)

2028 Hanel, Wolfram. *Weekend with Grandmother* (2–4). Trans. by Martina Rasdeuschek-Simmons. Illus. by Christa Unzner. 2002, North-South LB $13.88 (0-7358-1631-X). 64pp. Tony's grandmother wheels into town in her convertible for a weekend that Tony won't soon forget. (Rev: BL 3/15/02; HBG 10/02; SLJ 3/02)

2029 Hausman, Gerald, and Uton Hinds. *The Jacob Ladder* (5–8). 2001, Orchard $15.95 (0-531-30331-4). 119pp. This story of a young Jamaican who struggles valiantly to cope with poverty, a charismatic but neglectful father, and the problems of growing up is based on the youth of coauthor Uton Hinds. (Rev: BL 5/1/01; HBG 3/02; SLJ 4/01)

2030 Hicks, Betty. *I Smell Like Ham* (4–6). 2002, Millbrook LB $22.90 (0-7613-2857-2). 144pp. Sixth-grader Nick tries to adjust to his new stepmother (the source of the clove shampoo that inspires the title) and stepbrother, hopes to make the basketball team, and endures teasing at school. (Rev: BCCB 10/02; BL 9/1/02; HBG 3/03; SLJ 9/02)

2031 Hogeweg, Margriet. *The God of Grandma Forever* (4–6). 2001, Front Street $14.95 (1-886910-69-3). 112pp. Maria has a difficult relationship with her religious grandmother in this story translated from Dutch. (Rev: BCCB 6/01; BL 9/15/01; HBG 10/01; SLJ 7/01)

2032 Jarrett, Clare. *Jamie* (PS–2). Illus. by author. 2002, HarperCollins $13.95 (0-00-198414-4). Jamie and his grandfather care for a needy bird in this quiet tale. (Rev: SLJ 9/02)

2033 Killingsworth, Monte. *Equinox* (5–7). 2001, Holt $16.95 (0-8050-6153-3). 118pp. Fourteen-year-old Autumn has been happy living on her remote island, but changing relations between her parents threaten this idyll. (Rev: BL 8/01; HBG 3/02; SLJ 9/01)

2034 Kirby, Susan E. *Ida Lou's Story* (4–6). Series: American Quilts. 2001, Simon & Schuster paper $4.99 (0-689-80972-7). 170pp. Lacey likes to hear stories of times past and her great-great-aunt Ida Lou who dreamed of becoming a trapeze artist. (Rev: SLJ 12/01)

2035 Koss, Amy Goldman. *Strike Two* (4–6). 2001, Dial $16.99 (0-8037-2607-4). 144pp. Cousins Gwen and Jess play softball on the same team and are best friends until a strike at the newspaper where their fathers both work threatens their friendship and divides the community. (Rev: BCCB 10/01; BL 11/1/01; HBG 10/02; SLJ 9/01)

2036 Kurtz, Jane. *Jakarta Missing* (5–8). 2001, Greenwillow LB $15.89 (0-06-029402-7). 272pp. Although Dakar has longed for her sister Jakarta to come from Kenya to their new home in North Dakota, Dakar's problems continue when Jakarta arrives. (Rev: BCCB 5/01; BL 5/15/01; HB 5–6/01; HBG 10/01; SLJ 5/01)

2037 Levy, Elizabeth. *Big Trouble in Little Twinsville* (3–6). 2001, HarperCollins LB $14.89 (0-06-028591-5). 96pp. Ten-year-old Eve finds her twin younger sisters a source of great annoyance, but her attitude changes when the two do badly in a talent contest. (Rev: BCCB 7–8/01; BL 7/01; HBG 10/01; SLJ 5/01)

2038 Levy, Elizabeth. *Night of the Living Gerbil* (3–5). Illus. by Bill Basso. 2001, HarperCollins LB $14.89 (0-06-028589-3). 96pp. When Robert's hamster dies, he has it stuffed by a taxidermist who puts the hamster in such a frightful pose that Robert and his brother fear he has been turned into a Zombie. (Rev: BL 11/1/01; HBG 3/02; SLJ 11/01)

2039 McDonough, Alison. *Do the Hokey Pokey* (3–5). Illus. 2001, Front Street $14.95 (0-8126-2699-0). 120pp. Shy, friendless Brendan is afraid he will be embarrassed by his boisterous mother when she is chosen to be DJ for the all-school party. (Rev: BCCB 9/01; BL 4/1/01; HBG 10/01; SLJ 5/01)

2040 Machado, Ana María. *Me in the Middle* (4–6). Trans. from Portuguese by David Unger. Illus. by Caroline Merola. 2002, Groundwood $14.95 (0-88899-463-X); paper $5.95 (0-88899-467-2). 110pp. Young Bel feels close to her late great-grandmother and hears in her mind her accounts of life in Brazil at the turn of the 20th century, but finds her admonitions on behavior difficult to accept. (Rev: BCCB 7–8/02; HBG 10/02; SLJ 8/02)

2041 McKay, Hilary. *Saffy's Angel* (4–7). 2002, Simon & Schuster $16.00 (0-689-84933-8). 160pp. Saffron learns she was adopted into her artistic family and travels to Italy in search of her roots. (Rev: BCCB 5/02; BL 5/15/02; HB 7–8/02*; HBG 10/02; SLJ 5/02)

2042 Mansfield, Creina. *Cherokee* (5–8). 2001, O'Brien paper $7.95 (0-86278-368-2). 127pp. Gene's wonderful life with his jazz musician grandfather, Cherokee, comes to an end when his aunt decides he needs a home and an education. (Rev: SLJ 11/01)

2043 Matas, Carol. *Sparks Fly Upward* (4–8). 2002, Clarion $15.00 (0-618-15964-9). 192pp. Set in

Manitoba in the early 20th century, this is the story of 12-year-old Rebecca, a Jewish girl, and her life with a Ukrainian foster family. (Rev: BCCB 7–8/02; BL 4/1/02; HBG 10/02; SLJ 3/02)

2044 Matthews, Kezi. *Flying Lessons* (5–7). 2002, Cricket $16.95 (0-8126-2671-0). 168pp. A girl in a small southern town bonds with an eclectic bunch of adults after the airplane in which her mother was traveling disappears. (Rev: BL 12/15/02; HB 1–2/03; HBG 3/03; SLJ 12/02)

2045 Medearis, Angela Shelf. *What Did I Do to Deserve a Sister Like You?* (3–5). Illus. by Don Tate and Mark Galbreath. 2002, Eakin $12.95 (1-57168-471-9); paper $7.95 (1-57168-642-8). 123pp. Sharie, 10, juggles her dislike of her older sister, her problems with her piano teacher, and a longing to ride on a roller-coaster. (Rev: HBG 10/02; SLJ 5/02)

2046 Modiano, Patrick. *Catherine Certitude* (4–7). Trans. by William Rodarmor. Illus. by Jean-Jacques Sempe. 2001, Godine $17.95 (0-87923-959-X). 64pp. An adult Catherine reminisces about her life as a youngster in Paris — living with her father, puzzling over his job, going to ballet classes, eating in restaurants — in this stylishly illustrated chapter book delivered in picture-book format. (Rev: BL 12/15/01; HBG 3/02; SLJ 2/02)

2047 Muldrow, Diane. *Stirring It Up* (4–6). 2002, Grosset paper $4.99 (0-448-42815-6). 160pp. Eleven-year-old twins Molly and Amanda spend an amusing summer learning to cook, making friends and helping neighbors in this book that includes recipes, activities, and tips. (Rev: BL 7/02; SLJ 8/02)

2048 Naidoo, Beverley. *The Other Side of Truth* (5–8). 2001, HarperCollins LB $15.89 (0-06-029629-1). 272pp. Two Nigerian children face a frightening sequence of events as they find themselves abandoned in London, afraid to trust anyone. (Rev: BCCB 9/01; BL 9/1/01; HB 11–12/01*; HBG 3/02; SLJ 9/01*)

2049 Nelson, Rosemary. *Hubcaps and Puppies* (3–6). 2002, Napoleon paper $8.95 (0-929141-98-9). 184pp. Thirteen-year-old Nikki faces difficult choices, such as whether to allow herself to love a stray puppy so soon after the death of her dog. (Rev: BL 3/1/03)

2050 O'Connor, Barbara. *Moonpie and Ivy* (5–8). 2001, Farrar $16.00 (0-374-35059-0). 160pp. Twelve-year-old Pearl is hurt and confused when her mother leaves her at Aunt Ivy's home and disappears. (Rev: BCCB 5/01; BL 5/1/01*; HB 5–6/01; HBG 10/01; SLJ 5/01)

2051 Perez, Amada Irma. *My Diary from Here to There / Mi Diario de Aqui Hasta Alla* (2–4). Trans. by Consuelo Hernandez. Illus. by Maya Christina Gonzalez. 2002, Children's $16.95 (0-89239-175-8). 32pp. Amada tells her diary her worries about moving from Mexico to California in this bilingual book with appealing illustrations. (Rev: BL 11/1/02; HB 9–10/02; HBG 3/03)

2052 Quattlebaum, Mary. *Grover G. Graham and Me* (4–7). 2001, Delacorte $14.95 (0-385-32277-1).

181pp. Eleven-year-old Ben reluctantly begins to care about the members of his new foster family, particularly baby Grover. (Rev: BCCB 1/02; BL 9/15/01; HB 1–2/02; HBG 3/02; SLJ 10/01)

2053 Roos, Stephen. *Recycling George* (4–6). 2002, Simon & Schuster $16.00 (0-689-83146-3). 144pp. An introspective boy must choose between wealth and family. (Rev: BCCB 4/02; BL 1/1–15/02; HB 3–4/02; HBG 10/02; SLJ 3/02)

2054 Rylant, Cynthia. *Summer Party* (2–4). Illus. Series: Cobble Street Cousins. 2001, Simon & Schuster $15.00 (0-689-83241-9). 64pp. A story of anticipation and parties that will please fans of the series. (Rev: BL 6/1–15/01; HBG 3/02; SLJ 5/01)

2055 Rylant, Cynthia. *Wedding Flowers* (2–4). Illus. by Wendy A. Halperin. Series: Cobble Street Cousins. 2002, Simon & Schuster $15.00 (0-689-83242-7). 80pp. Rosie, Lily, and their cousin Tess are enlisted to help plan their Aunt Lucy's wedding. (Rev: BL 2/15/02; HBG 10/02; SLJ 8/02)

2056 Salisbury, Graham. *Lord of the Deep* (5–8). 2001, Delacorte $15.95 (0-385-72918-9). 182pp. During his time working on his stepfather's deep-sea fishing boat, Mikey, 13, learns about financial problems, lying, unpleasant characters, and romance. (Rev: BCCB 7–8/01; BL 8/01; HB 9–10/01*; HBG 3/02; SLJ 8/01*)

2057 Salmansohn, Karen. *One Puppy, Three Tales* (4–6). Illus. by author. Series: Alexandra Rambles On! 2001, Tricycle Pr. $12.95 (1-58246-044-2). Twelve-year-old Alexandra shares vivid details of her life and her relationships with her mother, father, and friends. (Rev: HBG 10/01; SLJ 6/01)

2058 Salmansohn, Karen. *Wherever I Go, There I Am* (4–7). Illus. by author. Series: Alexandra Rambles On! 2002, Tricycle Pr. $12.95 (1-58246-079-5). Alexandra's journal reveals her angst about issues such as scary movies and becoming a teenager. (Rev: HBG 3/03; SLJ 2/03)

2059 Seidler, Tor. *Brothers Below Zero* (5–8). 2002, HarperCollins LB $14.89 (0-06-029180-X). 137pp. Artistic Tim, overwhelmed by his athletic younger brother, eventually runs away to the place he has felt most valued. (Rev: BCCB 3/02; BL 1/1–15/02; HBG 10/02; SLJ 4/02)

2060 Shearer, Alex. *The Great Blue Yonder* (5–8). 2002, Clarion $15.00 (0-618-21257-4). 192pp. Twelve-year-old Harry, who has died in an accident, experiences afterlife on the Other Side and has the opportunity to review his relations with other family members. (Rev: BCCB 6/02; HBG 10/02; SLJ 4/02)

2061 Smith, Jane Denitz. *Fairy Dust* (4–6). 2002, HarperCollins LB $15.89 (0-06-029280-6). 160pp. Nine-year-old Ruthie has a confusing time when her new baby-sitter blends talk of fairies with shoplifting and theft. (Rev: BCCB 4/02; BL 12/1/01; HBG 10/02; SLJ 1/02)

2062 Smith, Roland. *Zach's Lie* (5–8). 2001, Hyperion $15.99 (0-7868-0617-6). 240pp. Young Jack and Joanne have trouble adapting to their new roles as Zach and Wanda when they are taken into the witness protection program. (Rev: BL 5/15/01; HBG 10/01; SLJ 6/01)

2063 Testa, Maria. *Some Kind of Pride* (3–6). 2001, Delacorte $14.95 (0-385-32782-X). 144pp. Eleven-year-old Ruth is the town's star shortstop, but her father's comment that her talent is wasted on a girl leaves Ruth crushed and evokes memories of her dead mother's struggle to become a fire fighter. (Rev: BCCB 12/01; BL 11/15/01; HBG 3/02; SLJ 4/02)

2064 Weeks, Sarah. *My Guy* (4–7). 2001, Harper-Collins LB $14.89 (0-06-028370-X). 192pp. Guy and Lana agree on only one thing — they don't want to become part of a blended family — and they set out to make sure it won't happen. (Rev: BCCB 6/01; BL 8/01; HB 7–8/01; HBG 10/01; SLJ 5/01)

2065 Wesley, Valerie Wilson. *Willimena and the Cookie Money* (2–4). 2001, Hyperion $15.99 (0-7868-0465-3). 128pp. Young Willimena has spent the Girl Scout cookie money on a good cause, which is revealed after she and her older sister fail to recoup her losses. (Rev: HBG 10/01; SLJ 8/01)

2066 Wiles, Deborah. *Love, Ruby Lavender* (4–6). 2001, Harcourt $16.00 (0-15-202314-3). 128pp. Ruby misses her grandmother terribly when she goes to Hawaii on vacation, but over the course of the summer she finds that life goes on and that diversions arise. (Rev: BCCB 9/01; BL 5/1/01; HBG 10/01; SLJ 4/01*)

2067 Williams, Vera B. *Amber Was Brave, Essie Was Smart* (3–5). Illus. 2001, Greenwillow LB $15.89 (0-06-029461-2). 72pp. Poetic text and black-and-white sketches tell the story of two sisters who cling to each other during hard times. (Rev: BCCB 9/01; BL 9/15/01; HB 9–10/01; HBG 3/02; SLJ 9/01*)

2068 Wilson, Jacqueline. *The Story of Tracy Beaker* (3–6). Illus. 2001, Delacorte $15.95 (0-385-72919-7). 192pp. Ten-year-old Tracy longs for her mother to come and claim her, but will settle for almost any foster parent in the meantime, in this first-person narrative set in Britain. (Rev: BCCB 4/01; BL 6/1–15/01; HB 9–10/01; HBG 3/02; SLJ 7/01)

2069 Wilson, Nancy Hope. *Mountain Pose* (5–7). 2001, Farrar $17.00 (0-374-35078-7). 240pp. Ellie is surprised to inherit her grandmother's farm, but when she reads the diaries left for her she begins to understand more about her family. (Rev: BCCB 6/01; BL 8/01; HB 7–8/01; HBG 10/01; SLJ 4/01*)

Fantasy and the Supernatural

2070 Abbott, Tony. *Trapped in Transylvania: Dracula* (4–6). Series: Cracked Classics. 2002, Hyperion paper $4.99 (0-7868-1324-5). 128pp. Devin and Frankie find themselves in Transylvania, inside a spoof version of *Dracula*. (Rev: SLJ 7/02)

2071 Aiken, Joan. *A Necklace of Raindrops* (4–6). Illus. by Kevin Hawkes. 2001, Knopf LB $17.99 (0-375-90584-7). 88pp. A collection of short stories filled with magic and imagination, illustrated with superb black-and-white drawings. (Rev: BL 11/1/01; HBG 3/02)

2072 Alexander, Lloyd. *The Rope Trick* (4–7). 2002, Dutton $16.99 (0-525-47020-4). 256pp. A young magician sets out on a challenging journey to master the difficult rope trick. (Rev: BCCB 1/03; BL 10/15/02; HB 11–12/02; HBG 3/03; SLJ 9/02)

2073 Alphin, Elaine Marie. *Ghost Soldier* (5–7). 2001, Holt $16.95 (0-8050-6158-4). 216pp. Alex, who has special powers that his father wouldn't understand, meets a Civil War ghost and helps him discover what happened to his family. (Rev: BCCB 7–8/01; BL 8/01; HBG 10/02; SLJ 8/01)

2074 Alton, Steve. *The Malifex* (5–8). 2002, Carolrhoda $14.95 (0-8225-0959-8). 182pp. Sam's vacation in contemporary England is complicated by a Wiccan's daughter, the release of the ghost of Merlin's apprentice, and a battle between good and evil. (Rev: BL 9/1/02; SLJ 11/02)

2075 Asch, Frank. *Class Pets: The Ghost of P.S. 42* (2–4). Illus. by John Kanzler. Series: Class Pets. 2002, Simon & Schuster $14.95 (0-689-84653-3). 112pp. Brother and sister mice Molly and Jake seek a new home in a school, but find more than they bargained for, including a threatening cat and a ghost hamster. (Rev: BL 12/15/02; SLJ 10/02)

2076 Auch, Mary Jane. *I Was a Third Grade Spy* (2–4). Illus. 2001, Holiday $15.95 (0-8234-1576-7). 96pp. Young Josh and Artful the dog who can now speak take turns narrating their entertaining efforts to win the talent show. (Rev: BCCB 7–8/01; BL 5/1/01; HBG 10/01; SLJ 7/01)

2077 Bailey, Linda. *Adventures with the Vikings* (3–5). Illus. by Bill Slavin. Series: Good Times Travel Agency. 2001, Kids Can $14.95 (1-55074-542-5); paper $7.95 (1-55074-544-1). 48pp. The Binkerton children travel back in time to the age of the Vikings in this comic-book-style story that interweaves fiction and nonfiction. (Rev: BL 10/15/01; HBG 3/02; SLJ 11/01)

2078 Baker, E. D. *The Frog Princess* (5–8). 2002, Bloomsbury $15.95 (1-58234-799-9). 220pp. When Princess Esmeralda kisses the frog, she turns into one herself in this humorous twist on the traditional saga. (Rev: BCCB 2/03; BL 11/15/02; SLJ 1/03)

2079 Banks, Lynne Reid. *Harry the Poisonous Centipede's Big Adventure* (3–5). Illus. 2001, Harper-Collins LB $14.89 (0-06-029394-2). 192pp. Young centipede Harry finds himself trapped with many of his friends, and they have great adventures finding their way home after escaping. (Rev: BL 6/1–15/01; HBG 10/01; SLJ 5/01)

2080 Barron, T. A. *Tree Girl* (4–8). 2001, Putnam $14.99 (0-399-23457-8). 128pp. Rowanna, 9, discovers she is descended from tree spirits after she is lured into the woods by a shape-shifting bear cub in this book for middle-graders. (Rev: BCCB 10/01; BL 11/1/01; HBG 3/02; SLJ 10/01)

2081 Beckhorn, Susan Williams. *The Kingfisher's Gift* (4–6). 2002, Putnam $17.99 (0-399-23712-7). 192pp. Franny hopes to help her fairy friends recover a lost treasure in this fantasy set in early 20th-century America. (Rev: BL 4/15/02; HBG 10/02; SLJ 7/02)

2082 Borsky, Mary. *Benny Bensky and the Perogy Palace* (2–4). Illus. by Linda Hendry. 2001, Tundra paper $7.95 (0-88776-523-8). 120pp. Benny the dog plays an important role in solving the mystery of the downturn in the perogy business. (Rev: SLJ 8/01)

2083 Brennan, Michael. *Electric Girl*, Vol. 2 (5–8). Illus. 2002, Mighty Gremlin paper $13.95 (0-970355-51-3). 160pp. In this graphic novel, Virginia, who can release bursts of electricity at will, locks horns with evil gremlin Oogleeoog. (Rev: BL 5/1/02; SLJ 5/02)

2084 Briggs, Anita. *Hobart* (2–4). Illus. by Mary Rayner. 2002, Simon & Schuster $14.00 (0-689-84129-9). 64pp. Four little pigs practice their artistic pursuits and put on a show to help their farmer-owner with his finances. (Rev: BCCB 6/02; BL 5/1/02; HBG 10/02; SLJ 6/02)

2085 Brockmeier, Kevin. *City of Names* (3–6). 2002, Viking $15.99 (0-670-03565-3). 144pp. Through a mysterious book of magic, fifth-grader Howie learns how to transport himself from one place to another. (Rev: BCCB 5/02; BL 6/1–15/02; HBG 10/02; SLJ 7/02)

2086 Brown, Jeff. *Stanley, Flat Again!* (2–4). Illus. by Scott Nash. Series: Flat Stanley. 2003, HarperCollins LB $15.89 (0-06-029826-X). 87pp. Stanley, first seen in *Flat Stanley* (1964), is flat once more and has a series of adventures in this entertaining early chapter book. (Rev: SLJ 3/03)

2087 Buffie, Margaret. *The Seeker* (5–8). 2002, Kids Can $16.95 (1-55337-358-8). 384pp. Emma is involved in a quest to reunite her family and becomes embroiled in interplanetary intrigue and gaming in this sequel to *The Watcher* (2000). (Rev: BL 10/1/02; SLJ 11/02)

2088 Byars, Betsy. *Little Horse* (2–4). Illus. by David McPhail. 2002, Holt $15.95 (0-8050-6413-3). 64pp. A tiny horse gets lost in a land where the flowers are as big as trees in this beginning chapter book. (Rev: BCCB 6/02; BL 3/15/02; HB 5–6/02; HBG 10/02; SLJ 4/02)

2089 Carter, Angela. *Sea-Cat and Dragon King* (2–4). Illus. by Eva Tatcheva. 2002, Bloomsbury $12.95 (1-58234-768-9). 96pp. Dragon King, ruler of the sea, envies Sea-Cat's spectacular outfit of seaweed and jewels. (Rev: BL 8/02; SLJ 11/02)

2090 Chabon, Michael. *Summerland* (5 Up). 2002, Hyperion $22.95 (0-7868-0877-2). 512pp. Little Leaguer Ethan Feld is recruited to save the world from an old enemy in this fantasy adventure. (Rev: BCCB 1/03; HB 11–12/02; HBG 3/03; SLJ 11/02)

2091 Chan, Gillian. *The Carved Box* (5–8). 2001, Kids Can $16.95 (1-55074-895-5). 232pp. The acquisition of a dog and a carved box ease the transition for orphaned Callum, 15, who has moved from Scotland to Canada to live with his uncle, in this novel which has an element of fantasy that comes to the fore in the dramatic ending. (Rev: BL 10/01; HBG 3/02; SLJ 10/01)

2092 Colfer, Eoin. *Artemis Fowl: The Arctic Incident* (5–8). 2002, Hyperion $16.95 (0-7868-0855-

1). 277pp. Artemis and Captain Holly band together to free Artemis's father from the Russian Mafiya in this amusing, lively sequel to *Artemis Fowl* (2001). (Rev: BCCB 7–8/01; HBG 10/02; SLJ 7/02)

2093 Collodi, Carlo. *The Adventures of Pinocchio* (5–7). Illus. by Iassen Ghiuselev. 2002, Simply Read $22.95 (0-9688768-0-3). 160pp. The full text of the original is used here with effective black-and-white illustrations and several full-page watercolors. (Rev: BL 4/1/02)

2094 Cooper, Susan. *Green Boy* (4–8). 2002, Simon & Schuster $16.00 (0-689-84751-3). 208pp. Two young boys discover a futuristic world in which natural resources are depleted and a war to save the environment is being waged. (Rev: BCCB 5/02; BL 3/1/02; HB 5–6/02; HBG 10/02; SLJ 2/02)

2095 Corbett, Sue. *12 Again* (5–8). 2002, Dutton $16.99 (0-525-46899-4). 160pp. Patrick's mother becomes 12 again after drinking a magic potion, and it's up to Patrick to save her. (Rev: BCCB 10/02; BL 9/1/02; HBG 3/03; SLJ 7/02)

2096 Corlett, William. *The Steps up the Chimney* (5–8). 2000, Pocket paper $4.99 (0-7434-1001-7). 272pp. Children stuck in a remote mansion in Wales with an uncle and his pregnant, vegetarian girlfriend discover a secret room that houses a magician. (Rev: SLJ 5/01)

2097 Coville, Bruce. *The Monsters of Morley Manor: A Madcap Adventure* (4–6). 2001, Harcourt $16.00 (0-15-216382-4). 224pp. Supernatural events that threaten the world result when sixth-grader Anthony and his younger sister Sarah release a family of monsters from a spell. (Rev: BL 9/1/01; HBG 3/02; SLJ 1/02)

2098 Coville, Bruce. *The Prince of Butterflies* (3–5). Illus. by John Clapp. 2002, Harcourt $16.00 (0-15-201454-3). 40pp. Migrating monarchs turn a boy into a butterfly so he can help them on their journey in this socially conscious story. (Rev: BL 3/15/02; HBG 10/02; SLJ 5/02)

2099 Crilley, Mark. *Akiko in the Castle of Alia Rellapor* (3–5). Illus. 2001, Delacorte $9.95 (0-385-32728-5). 172pp. Fourth-grader Akiko and her celestial friends finally reach the castle and Prince Frogtoppit in this fourth — and mostly text-based — book in a series with graphic-novel roots. (Rev: BL 1/1–15/02; HBG 3/02; SLJ 11/01)

2100 Crossley-Holland, Kevin. *At the Crossing Places* (5–8). 2002, Scholastic $17.95 (0-439-26598-3). 416pp. Thirteen-year-old Arthur continues the story started in *The Seeing Stone* (2001), now on a quest to find his mother and trying to make peace with his discoveries about his father and his own relationship with Arthur-in-the-stone. (Rev: BL 11/1/02; HB 11–12/02; HBG 3/03; SLJ 11/02)

2101 Crossley-Holland, Kevin. *The Seeing Stone* (4–8). 2001, Scholastic $17.95 (0-439-26326-3). 340pp. In the time of Richard the Lion-Hearted, a 13-year-old boy named Arthur finds that his life mirrors that of the legendary King Arthur. (Rev: BL 10/1/01; HB 11–12/01*; HBG 3/02; SLJ 10/01)

2102 Curry, Jane Louise. *The Egyptian Box* (4–7). 2002, Simon & Schuster $16.00 (0-689-84273-2).

192pp. A suspenseful mystery about a middle-schooler who discovers a magical servant, an Egyptian statue come to life, who will obey her wishes. (Rev: BL 6/1–15/02; HBG 10/02; SLJ 3/02)

2103 Danko, Dan, and Tom Mason. *The Minotaur* (4–8). Series: MythQuest. 2002, Bantam LB $16.95 (0-553-13009-9); paper $4.99 (0-553-48759-0). 138pp. Alex is investigating his archaeologist father's disappearance when he is whisked away to ancient Crete and must do battle with the Minotaur. (Rev: HBG 10/02; SLJ 4/02)

2104 David, Lawrence. *Horace Splattly: The Cup-caked Crusader* (2–4). Illus. by Barry Gott. 2001, Dutton $14.99 (0-525-46763-7); paper $4.99 (0-14-230021-7). 144pp. When pint-sized Horace, 10, eats his sister's cupcakes he becomes a superhero and flies around town having wondrously silly adventures. (Rev: HBG 3/02; SLJ 10/01)

2105 David, Lawrence. *When Second Graders Attack* (2–4). Illus. by Barry Gott. Series: Horace Splattly the Cupcaked Crusader. 2002, Dutton $14.99 (0-525-46866-8); paper $4.99 (0-14-230118-3). 152pp. When Horace's younger sister stops baking the cupcakes that fuel Horace's special powers, he must become the chef. (Rev: HBG 10/02; SLJ 7/02)

2106 DeFelice, Cynthia. *The Ghost and Mrs. Hobbs* (4–6). 2001, Farrar $16.00 (0-374-38046-5). 192pp. A ghost asks 11-year-old Allie for help, but scary and mysterious happenings hamper her efforts. (Rev: BL 9/1/01; HB 11–12/01; HBG 3/02; SLJ 8/01)

2107 Denney, Jim. *Battle Before Time* (3–6). Series: Timebenders. 2002, Thomas Nelson paper $5.99 (1-4003-0039-8). 163pp. A young inventor's time machine transports him and three friends into prehistory and an adventure that involves a fierce battle between good and evil. (Rev: BL 10/1/02)

2108 Denney, Jim. *Doorway to Doom* (3–6). 2002, Thomas Nelson paper $5.99 (1-4003-0040-1). 163pp. This sequel to *Battle Before Time* (2002) takes the four time-travelers to the Middle Ages to face another band of villains. (Rev: BL 10/1/02)

2109 Doyle, Roddy. *Rover Saves Christmas* (2–5). Illus. by Brian Ajhar. 2001, Scholastic $14.95 (0-439-30530-6). 160pp. The lively crew from *The Giggler Treatment* (2000) return in an irreverent romp that takes Rover to the North Pole to sub for Rudolph. (Rev: HBG 3/02; SLJ 10/01)

2110 Drake, Emily. *The Magickers* (5–6). 2001, DAW $19.95 (0-88677-935-9). 344pp. Jason, who is 11, finds that Camp Ravenwyng is really a "magick" training ground and he is plunged into mystery and adventure. (Rev: BL 7/01; SLJ 12/01)

2111 Duey, Kathleen. *The Silver Thread: The Unicorn's Secret #2* (2–4). 2001, Simon & Schuster paper $3.99 (0-689-84270-8). 80pp. A young girl must rescue a unicorn child who has been shot by a hunter's arrow in this second volume of a four-part fantasy. (Rev: BL 3/1/02)

2112 Easton, Patricia Harrison. *Davey's Blue-Eyed Frog* (2–4). Illus. by Mike Wohnoutka. 2003, Clarion $14.00 (0-618-18185-7). 104pp. Davey catches a blue-eyed frog that turns out to be a princess in this illustrated chapter book. (Rev: BL 3/1/03)

2113 Elliott, David. *The Transmogrification of Roscoe Wizzle* (3–5). 2001, Candlewick $12.99 (0-7636-1173-5). 115pp. A zany story in which hamburger eaters turn into bugs and are then kidnapped by the wicked owners of the fast-food joint in an effort to hide their evil deeds. (Rev: BCCB 5/01; HBG 10/01; SLJ 6/01)

2114 Farber, Erica, and J. R. Sansevere. *The Secret in the Stones* (5–9). Series: Tales of the Nine Charms. 2001, Dell paper $4.50 (0-440-41820-8). 260pp. In this second installment in a trilogy with an intricate plot, 13-year-old Zoe's blue trinket proves to be one of the famous Nine Charms, leading her into a fantastic adventure far from her home in California. (Rev: SLJ 9/01)

2115 Fienberg, Anna. *The Witch in the Lake* (5–8). 2002, Annick LB $18.95 (1-55037-723-X); paper $7.95 (1-55037-722-1). 216pp. This story of magic and suspense in 16th-century Italy interweaves fantasy with facts about the time. (Rev: HBG 3/03; SLJ 8/02)

2116 Forrester, Sandra. *The Everyday Witch* (5–7). 2002, Barron's paper $4.95 (0-7641-2220-7). 192pp. To establish her magic rating, 11-year-old witch Beatrice is assigned to rescue a famous sorcerer and his daughters from an evil villain. (Rev: SLJ 10/02)

2117 Freeman, Martha. *The Spy Wore Shades* (4–6). 2001, HarperCollins LB $15.89 (0-06-029270-9). 235pp. Eleven-year-old Dougie helps a girl from an underground civilization to save her family's home from land developers. (Rev: BL 10/1/01; HBG 3/02; SLJ 8/01)

2118 Gaiman, Neil. *Coraline* (5–8). Illus. by Dave McKean. 2002, HarperCollins LB $17.89 (0-06-623744-0). 176pp. An Alice-in-Wonderland type of tale for older readers in which a girl finds an alternate world in the empty apartment next door. (Rev: BCCB 11/02; BL 8/02; HB 11–12/02; HBG 3/03; SLJ 8/02)

2119 Garretson, Jerri. *The Secret of Whispering Springs* (5–8). 2002, Ravenstone paper $6.99 (0-9659712-4-4). 206pp. A ghost and a threatening squatter vie for Cassie's attention in this suspenseful adventure. (Rev: BL 8/02; SLJ 8/02)

2120 Gliori, Debi. *Pure Dead Magic* (4–7). 2001, Knopf LB $17.99 (0-375-91410-2). 182pp. Life at the Strega-Borgia castle is an overwhelming riot of problems — a lost father, a mother at witch school, a new nanny, a dragon with an upset stomach, and a baby in Cyberspace — that only a little magic can solve. (Rev: BCCB 2/02; BL 8/01; HBG 10/02; SLJ 9/01)

2121 Gliori, Debi. *Pure Dead Wicked* (5–8). 2002, Knopf $15.95 (0-375-81411-6). 224pp. Siblings Titus, Pandora, and Damp must leave their castle and move with their creepy extended family into the Auchenlochtermuchy Arms with disastrous but humorous consequences in this sequel to *Pure Dead Magic* (2001). (Rev: BL 9/15/02; SLJ 8/02)

2122 Goto, Hiromi. *The Water of Possibility* (5–7). Illus. by Aries Cheung. Series: In the Same Boat. 2002, Coteau paper $8.95 (1-55050-183-6). 319pp. Sayuri, 12, and her younger brother discover a magical world full of danger in this fantasy that includes many elements of Japanese folklore. (Rev: SLJ 8/02)

2123 Grahame, Kenneth. *The Wind in the Willows* (3–5). Illus. by Mary Jane Begin. 2002, North-South $19.95 (1-58717-204-6). 208pp. This unabridged large-format version of the famous story of Toad, Mole, and their friends is embellished with radiant acrylic and watercolor paintings. (Rev: BL 12/1/02; HBG 3/03; SLJ 1/03)

2124 Grahame, Kenneth. *The Wind in the Willows* (3–5). Illus. by Michael Foreman. 2002, Harcourt $24.00 (0-15-216807-9). 240pp. Lively illustrations ranging from endpaper maps to action-packed two-page watercolors accompany this version of the beloved British animal story. (Rev: BL 12/1/02; HBG 3/03; SLJ 1/03)

2125 Gray, Luli. *Falcon and the Charles Street Witch* (4–7). 2002, Houghton $15.00 (0-618-16410-3). 144pp. In this fantasy follow-up to 1995's *Falcon's Egg,* a 12-year-old girl becomes reacquainted with a dragon she released over New York City and befriends a witch who lives in Greenwich Village. (Rev: BL 3/15/02*; HBG 10/02; SLJ 4/02)

2126 Gray, Luli. *Timespinners* (4–6). 2003, Houghton $15.00 (0-618-16412-X). 160pp. While visiting the dioramas in the American Museum of Natural History, twins Allie and Fig Newton are transported backward in time to 1913 France and then to 35,000 B.C. (Rev: BL 3/1/03)

2127 Griffin, Adele. *Witch Twins* (3–5). 2001, Hyperion $14.99 (0-7868-0739-3). 144pp. Fifth-grade twins Claire and Luna are given many opportunities both at home and at school to use their hidden powers as witches. (Rev: BL 4/15/01; HB 9–10/01; HBG 3/02; SLJ 7/01)

2128 Griffin, Peni R. *The Ghost Sitter* (4–6). 2001, Dutton $14.99 (0-525-46676-2). 128pp. A gentle ghost story in which Charlotte tries to help a girl who died 50 years ago to find peace. (Rev: BL 8/01; HB 5–6/01; HBG 10/01; SLJ 6/01)

2129 Gutman, Dan. *Mickey and Me: A Baseball Card Adventure* (4–6). Series: Baseball Card Adventure. 2003, HarperCollins LB $16.89 (0-06-029248-2). 160pp. In this adventure, Joe is supposed to be heading back to 1951 to warn Mickey Mantle about a forthcoming accident, but instead ends up in 1944 with Girls Professional league player Mickey Maguire. (Rev: BL 1/1–15/03)

2130 Gutman, Dan. *Qwerty Stevens Back in Time with Benjamin Franklin* (4–7). 2002, Simon & Schuster $16.95 (0-689-84553-7). 192pp. Benjamin Franklin is transported through time into Robert "Qwerty" Stevens' bedroom, and Qwerty and a friend accompany Franklin to 1776 to sign the Declaration of Independence. (Rev: BL 9/15/02; HBG 3/03; SLJ 8/02)

2131 Hale, Bruce. *The Big Nap* (2–6). Illus. 2001, Harcourt $14.00 (0-15-202521-9). 112pp. Lizard detective Chet Gecko investigates why his classmates are turning into mindless model fourth-graders. (Rev: BL 12/1/01; HBG 3/02; SLJ 10/01)

2132 Hale, Bruce. *The Hamster of the Baskervilles: A Chet Gecko Mystery* (3–5). Illus. Series: Chet Gecko Mystery. 2002, Harcourt $14.00 (0-15-202503-0). 132pp. Fourth-grader gecko detective Chet and his sidekick Natalie set out to find out who is trashing the classrooms at their school. (Rev: BL 5/1/02; HBG 10/02; SLJ 5/02)

2133 Hale, Bruce. *This Gum for Hire* (3–5). Illus. 2002, Harcourt $14.00 (0-15-202491-3). 132pp. Lizard detective Chet Gecko investigates mysterious goings-on on the school football team. (Rev: BL 10/1/02; HBG 3/03; SLJ 9/02)

2134 Hendry, Diana. *Harvey Angell* (4–7). 2001, Pocket paper $4.99 (0-7434-2828-5). 160pp. A spirited story about an orphan, Henry, who lives in a dismal boarding house that brightens up when a new resident brings excitement and mystery. (Rev: BL 1/1–15/02; SLJ 12/01)

2135 Heneghan, James. *Flood* (5–8). 2002, Farrar $16.00 (0-374-35057-4). 192pp. The Little People save a boy from the flood that kills his parents, and save him from the neglectful father he never knew in this poignant story about loss and acceptance. (Rev: BCCB 4/02; BL 3/15/02; HB 7–8/02; HBG 10/02; SLJ 4/02)

2136 Hickman, Janet. *Ravine* (4–6). 2002, HarperCollins LB $15.89 (0-06-029367-5). 192pp. Jeremy enters a dangerous world of fantasy and adventure through a "time slip" in a ravine. (Rev: BCCB 9/02; BL 7/02; HB 5–6/02; HBG 10/02; SLJ 10/02)

2137 Hoban, Russell. *The Mouse and His Child* (4–8). Illus. by David Small. 2001, Scholastic $16.95 (0-439-09826-2). 246pp. A toy mouse and his child embark on a quest to become "self-winding" and have sometimes scary, sometimes humorous adventures in this enchanting fantasy first published in 1967 and now updated with new illustrations. (Rev: BL 12/1/01; HBG 3/02)

2138 Hoeye, Michael. *The Sands of Time* (5–8). Series: A Hermux Tantamoq Adventure. 2002, Putnam $14.99 (0-399-23879-4). 277pp. In this sequel to *Time Stops for No Mouse* (2002), the mouse watchmaker and a chipmunk friend believe that mice were once the slaves of cats. (Rev: HBG 3/03; SLJ 10/02)

2139 Hoeye, Michael. *Time Stops for No Mouse* (5–8). Series: A Hermux Tantamoq Adventure. 2002, Putnam $14.99 (0-399-23878-6). 250pp. Hermux Tantamoq, a mouse, leads a quiet life as a watchmaker until Linka Perflinger enters his life and Hermux becomes entangled in mystery and suspense. (Rev: BL 3/15/02*; HB 7–8/02; HBG 10/02; SLJ 5/02)

2140 Hoffman, Alice. *Indigo* (4–7). Illus. 2002, Scholastic $16.95 (0-439-25635-6). 112pp. Three outcasts save their town from a terrible flood in this aquatic fantasy. (Rev: BCCB 6/02; BL 8/02; HBG 10/02; SLJ 8/02)

2141 Howe, James. *Invasion of the Mind Swappers from Asteroid 6!* (3–6). Illus. by Brett Helquist.

2002, Simon & Schuster $9.95 (0-689-83949-9). 96pp. Lessons about writing are hidden in the tale of a delightful dachshund named Howie, who keeps a journal detailing his writing experiences as he pens a story about an alien invasion. Also use *It Came from Beneath the Bed!* (2002). (Rev: BL 8/02; HBG 3/03; SLJ 11/02)

2142 Hughes, Carol. *Toots Underground* (3–5). 2001, Random LB $17.99 (0-375-91086-7). 176pp. Toots meets her fairy friend Olive and is once again transported to the Upside Down World, where the inhabitants are battling to defeat the evil Waspgnat and save the garden that Toots and the fairies share. (Rev: HBG 10/02; SLJ 10/01)

2143 Hurst, Carol Otis. *The Wrong One* (3–6). 2003, Houghton $15.00 (0-618-27599-1). 160pp. The Spencer children and their recently widowed mother move to a run-down farmhouse where strange things are happening. (Rev: BL 3/1/03)

2144 Hurwitz, Johanna. *Lexi's Tale* (3–5). Illus. by Patience Brewster. 2001, North-South $14.95 (1-58717-091-4). 112pp. Friends Lexi the squirrel and PeeWee the guinea pig have humorous adventures in New York, including an effort to help a homeless man. (Rev: BL 12/15/01; HBG 3/02; SLJ 10/01)

2145 Hurwitz, Johanna. *PeeWee and Plush* (2–4). Illus. by Patience Brewster. Series: Park Pals Adventure. 2002, North-South $14.95 (1-58717-191-0). 134pp. PeeWee, the talented guinea pig of Central Park, finds a mate and they produce four little ones in this story for beginning chapter-book readers. (Rev: HBG 3/03; SLJ 12/02)

2146 Ibbotson, Eva. *Dial-a-Ghost* (4–6). Illus. by Kevin Hawkes. 2001, Dutton $15.99 (0-525-46693-2). 256pp. A house is haunted by all sorts of ghosts — both funny and frightening — who have been employed to scare orphan Oliver to death. (Rev: BCCB 9/01; BL 10/15/01; HB 9–10/01; HBG 3/02; SLJ 8/01)

2147 Ibbotson, Eva. *The Great Ghost Rescue* (3–6). Illus. by Kevin Hawkes. 2002, Dutton $15.99 (0-525-46769-6). 144pp. A homeless ghost family moves into a boys' school and meets young Rick, who tries to establish a "sanctuary" for displaced ghosts in this humorous, scary, and sometimes gruesome book. (Rev: BCCB 11/02; BL 7/02; HB 9–10/02; HBG 3/03; SLJ 8/02)

2148 Jacques, Brian. *The Angel's Command: A Tale from the Castaways of the Flying Dutchman* (5–9). 2003, Putnam $23.99 (0-399-23999-5). 448pp. This action-packed pirate story, set in the 17th century, is the sequel to *Castaways of the Flying Dutchman*. (Rev: BL 2/1/03; HB 3–4/03; SLJ 3/03)

2149 Jacques, Brian. *A Redwall Winter's Tale* (2–5). Illus. by Christopher Denise. 2001, Putnam $18.99 (0-399-23346-6). 80pp. The animals of Redwall Abbey gather once again to enjoy an end-of-autumn festival in this colorful picture book. (Rev: BL 9/1/01; HBG 3/02; SLJ 9/01)

2150 Jacques, Brian. *Taggerung* (5–8). Illus. 2001, Putnam $23.99 (0-399-23720-8). 448pp. The 14th book in the Redwall series features an otter named Taggerung who was kidnapped from the abbey as a

baby and raised by an outlaw ferret. (Rev: BL 8/01; HB 11–12/01; HBG 3/02; SLJ 10/01)

2151 Jacques, Brian. *Triss* (5–8). 2002, Putnam $23.99 (0-399-23723-2). 432pp. An action-packed installment in the Redwall series in which squirrel Triss, an escaped slave, meets up with the badger Sagax and his friend Scarum. (Rev: BL 9/1/02; HB 1–2/03; HBG 3/03; SLJ 10/02)

2152 Jarvis, Robin. *The Crystal Prison: Book Two of the Deptford Mice Trilogy* (5–8). 2001, North-South $17.95 (1-58717-107-4). 240pp. In this sequel to *The Dark Portal*, city mouse Audrey is adapting to country life when she is accused of committing murder. (Rev: BL 8/01; HBG 3/02; SLJ 11/01)

2153 Jarvis, Robin. *The Final Reckoning: Book Three of the Deptford Mice Trilogy* (5–8). 2002, North-South $17.95 (1-58717-192-9). 304pp. Jupiter returns to wreak havoc on the Deptford mice in this thrilling conclusion to the trilogy. (Rev: BL 8/02; HBG 3/03; SLJ 9/02)

2154 Jarvis, Robin. *Thorn Ogres of Hagwood* (5–8). 2002, Harcourt $16.00 (0-15-216752-8). 256pp. Trouble is spreading through Hagwood, and a young, not-too-confident shape-shifting werling will play a role in a gripping battle between good and evil. (Rev: BCCB 12/02; BL 11/1/02; HBG 3/03; SLJ 11/02)

2155 Jeppson, Ann-Sofie. *You're Growing Up, Pontus!* (K–3). Trans. from Swedish by Frances Corry. Illus. by Catarina Kruusval. 2001, R&S $15.00 (91-29-65393-2). 30pp. In this sequel to *Here Comes Pontus* (2000), Pontus, now a fully grown horse, describes his life in great detail, offering readers lots of information on horses, riding, and equipment. (Rev: HBG 3/02; SLJ 11/01)

2156 Jocelyn, Marthe. *The Invisible Enemy* (4–6). Illus. by Abby Carter. 2002, Dutton $15.99 (0-525-46831-5). 144pp. Billy must take extreme steps when Alyssa, her enemy, steals her backpack containing the magic powder that makes people invisible. (Rev: BL 6/1–15/02; HBG 10/02; SLJ 5/02)

2157 Jones, Diana Wynne. *Mixed Magics* (5–8). 2001, Greenwillow LB $15.89 (0-06-029706-9). 138pp. This fantasy contains four short stories each involving an enchanter named Chrestomanci, who has nine lives and oversees the use of magic in his world. (Rev: BL 4/15/01; HB 5–6/01; HBG 10/01; SLJ 7/01)

2158 Jordan, Sherryl. *The Hunting of the Last Dragon* (5–7). 2002, HarperCollins LB $15.89 (0-06-028903-1). 128pp. In 14th-century England a monk records young peasant Jude's story of his quest, accompanied by a young Chinese woman, to kill a dragon. (Rev: BCCB 9/02; BL 4/15/02; HBG 10/02; SLJ 7/02)

2159 Karr, Kathleen. *Playing with Fire* (5–7). 2001, Farrar $16.00 (0-374-23453-1). 192pp. This story about the occult takes place in New York during the 1920s and involves Greer and her spiritualist mother. (Rev: BCCB 5/01; BL 4/1/01; HBG 10/01; SLJ 5/01)

2160 Kehret, Peg. *Spy Cat* (4–6). 2003, Dutton $15.99 (0-525-47046-8). 192pp. Clever cat Pete, who understands everything but is frustrated by his inability to speak, plays a lead role in tracking down the neighborhood burglars. (Rev: BL 1/1–15/03; SLJ 1/03)

2161 Kimmel, Eric A. *Website of the Cracked Cookies* (4–8). Illus. by Jeff Shelly. 2001, Dutton $15.99 (0-525-46799-8). 80pp. A whirlwind, comic cyberadventure that starts with a click on a Web site that houses an evil grandmother and a cast of familiar characters. (Rev: HBG 3/02; SLJ 9/01)

2162 King-Smith, Dick. *Billy the Bird* (3–5). Illus. 2001, Hyperion $14.99 (0-7868-0586-2). 128pp. Mary Bird, 8, confides in her cat and her guinea pig, telling them about her younger brother's ability to fly when the moon is full. (Rev: BL 7/01; HBG 10/01; SLJ 6/01)

2163 King-Smith, Dick. *Lady Lollipop* (2–4). 2001, Candlewick $14.99 (0-7636-1269-3). 124pp. Spoiled Princess Penelope chooses a pig named Lollipop as her pet, and Lollipop's poor owner moves to the palace as the pig's keeper. (Rev: BCCB 9/01; BL 4/15/01; HB 5–6/01; HBG 10/01; SLJ 6/01*)

2164 Kraft, Jim. *The Vampire Hound* (4–6). 2002, Troll paper $4.95 (0-8167-7315-7). 192pp. Set in Victorian London, this is the story of a good vampire dog called Barksdale who is being tracked by a hunter. (Rev: SLJ 2/03)

2165 Labatt, Mary. *The Mummy Lives!* (3–5). Illus. by Troy Hill-Jackson. Series: Sam, Dog Detective. 2002, Kids Can $12.95 (1-55337-023-6); paper $4.95 (1-55337-042-2). 116pp. Telepathic Sam becomes convinced that she is the dog that an Egyptian mummy is seeking, in this novel suitable for reluctant readers. (Rev: HBG 10/02; SLJ 5/02)

2166 Labatt, Mary. *One Terrible Halloween* (2–5). Illus. by Troy Hill-Jackson. Series: Sam, Dog Detective. 2002, Kids Can $12.95 (1-55337-138-0); paper $4.95 (1-55337-139-9). 107pp. Sam the telepathic dog, with the help of owner Jennie and her friend Beth, investigates the mystery of the missing neighbors. (Rev: HBG 3/03; SLJ 10/02)

2167 Labatt, Mary. *The Secret of Sagawa Lake* (2–5). Series: Sam, Dog Detective. 2001, Kids Can $12.95 (1-55074-887-4); paper $4.95 (1-55074-889-0). 118pp. Ten-year-old Jennie, her telepathic dog Sam, and friend Beth investigate a mystery and become convinced there is a monster in the lake. (Rev: HBG 3/02; SLJ 11/01)

2168 Labatt, Mary. *A Weekend at the Grand Hotel* (3–5). Illus. by Troy Hill-Jackson. Series: Sam, Dog Detective. 2001, Kids Can $12.95 (1-55074-883-1); paper $4.95 (1-55074-885-8). 104pp. Sam, the sheepdog detective, who can put thoughts in young Jennie's head, discovers a mystery on a weekend trip to the Grand Hotel. (Rev: HBG 10/01; SLJ 4/01)

2169 Lafaye, A. *Dad, in Spirit* (4–6). 2001, Simon & Schuster $16.00 (0-689-81514-X). 176pp. Ebon's father is in a coma, and when his spirit materializes at the house Ebon sets out to reunite it with his body. (Rev: BCCB 7–8/01; BL 7/01; HBG 10/01; SLJ 6/01)

2170 Lawrence, Michael. *The Toilet of Doom* (4–6). 2002, Dutton $15.99 (0-525-46983-4). 228pp. Jiggy McCue and his friends hit F (for Flush) on the development version of the computer game Toilet of Life and chaos — and a great deal of bathroom humor — ensue as Jiggy and Angie find they have switched bodies. (Rev: BL 11/1/02; HBG 3/03; SLJ 10/02)

2171 Lee, Tanith. *Wolf Queen* (5–8). Series: Claidi Journals. 2002, Dutton $16.99 (0-525-46895-1). 240pp. After *Wolf Tower* and *Wolf Star*, this concluding volume of the Claidi Journals trilogy tells how the fearless Claidi faces the power of the Raven Tower. (Rev: BCCB 6/02; BL 4/15/02; HBG 10/02; SLJ 6/02)

2172 Lee, Tanith. *Wolf Star* (5–8). 2001, Dutton $16.99 (0-525-46673-8). 217pp. This sequel to *Wolf Tower* finds Claidi trapped in a castle with a strange prince who, in time, helps her find a way home. (Rev: BCCB 10/01; BL 4/15/01; HBG 10/01; SLJ 7/01)

2173 Levine, Gail Carson. *The Two Princesses of Bamarre* (4–7). 2001, HarperCollins LB $15.89 (0-06-029316-0). 256pp. Princess Addie sets out on a quest to find a cure for the Grey Death, a sickness that is destroying her older sister. (Rev: BCCB 10/01; BL 4/15/01; HB 5–6/01; HBG 10/01; SLJ 5/01)

2174 Levinson, Marilyn. *Rufus and Magic Run Amok* (3–5). 2001, Marshall Cavendish $14.95 (0-7614-5102-1). 96pp. Rufus Breckenridge, 10, just wants to be normal but instead inherits magical powers from his parents and grandparents and has to cope with a heap of new problems. (Rev: BCCB 1/02; HBG 3/02; SLJ 10/01)

2175 Levy, Elizabeth. *The Principal's on the Roof* (2–4). Illus. by Mordicai Gerstein. Series: Fletcher Mysteries. 2002, Simon & Schuster LB $11.89 (0-689-84630-4); paper $3.99 (0-689-84627-4). 73pp. Fletcher the dog and Jasper the flea tackle the mystery of the sneezing principal. (Rev: HBG 3/03; SLJ 1/03)

2176 Levy, Elizabeth. *Vampire State Building* (3–6). Illus. by Sally Wern Comport. 2002, HarperCollins LB $16.89 (0-06-000053-8). 112pp. Sam and his siblings wonder if Sam's new online chess partner from Romania could be a vampire. (Rev: BL 8/02; HBG 3/03; SLJ 11/02)

2177 Lichtenheld, Tom. *Everything I Know About Monsters: A Collection of Made-up Facts, Educated Guesses, and Silly Pictures About Creatures of Creepiness* (1–4). Illus. by author. 2002, Simon & Schuster $16.95 (0-689-84381-X). An appealingly silly guide to the kinds of monsters you find in various places (under the bed, in the closet), with practical tips on monster avoidance. (Rev: HBG 3/03; SLJ 9/02)

2178 Lyons, Mary. *Knockabeg: A Famine Tale* (4–7). 2001, Houghton $15.00 (0-618-09283-8). 128pp. In order to protect the people of Knockabeg, faeries battle with the creatures who are causing the blight during the great Irish potato famine. (Rev: BL 11/15/01; HBG 3/02; SLJ 9/01)

2179 McCaffrey, Laura Williams. *Alia Waking* (5–7). 2003, Clarion $15.00 (0-618-19461-4). 224pp. Alia, 12, and her best friend Kay long to become "keenten," or warrior women. (Rev: BL 3/1/03)

2180 McNish, Cliff. *The Doomspell* (4–6). 2002, Penguin Putnam $17.99 (0-8037-2710-0). 224pp. Rachel and her younger brother are taken to the magical world of Ithrea where a wicked witch wants to remake Rachel in her hideous image. (Rev: BCCB 10/02; BL 4/15/02; HBG 10/02; SLJ 6/02)

2181 Manns, Nick. *Operating Codes* (5–8). 2001, Little, Brown $15.95 (0-316-60465-8). 182pp. A suspenseful tale of supernatural presences and espionage in which two young children and their father become embroiled. (Rev: BCCB 2/02; BL 12/15/01; HBG 3/02; SLJ 1/02)

2182 Meddaugh, Susan. *Lulu's Hat* (3–5). Illus. 2002, Houghton $15.00 (0-618-15277-6). 64pp. Lulu's deep interest in magic leads her to follow a dog that has jumped into a top hat that has unusual powers. (Rev: BCCB 5/02; BL 5/1/02; HBG 10/02; SLJ 5/02)

2183 Molloy, Michael. *The Time Witches* (5–8). 2002, Scholastic paper $4.99 (0-439-42090-3). 272pp. The characters from *The Witch Trade* (2002) return in this sequel in which Abby, a Light Witch, and her friends must travel into the past to foil a plot hatched by the nefarious Wolfbane. (Rev: BL 1/1–15/03)

2184 Moranville, Sharelle Byars. *The Purple Ribbon* (2–5). Illus. by Anna Alter. 2003, Holt $17.95 (0-8050-6659-4). 80pp. A field mouse called Spring is raising her babies in an old car, dreaming of returning to live with Gran Dora, who gave her the purple ribbon she treasures. (Rev: BL 3/15/03)

2185 Morris, Gerald. *Parsifal's Page* (5–8). 2001, Houghton $15.00 (0-618-05509-6). 240pp. Piers becomes a page to Parsifal and accompanies the innocent young man on his quest to become a knight. (Rev: BCCB 4/01; BL 4/15/01; HB 5–6/01; HBG 10/01; SLJ 4/01)

2186 Morrissey, Dean. *The Winter King* (3–5). Series: Magic Door. 2002, HarperCollins $15.95 (0-06-028583-4). 64pp. Fifth-grader Sarah stows away in Old Man Winter's wagon and helps save him from the wicked plans of his ambitious assistant, Kudgel. (Rev: BL 4/15/02; HBG 10/02; SLJ 7/02)

2187 Morrissey, Dean, and Stephen Krensky. *The Moon Robber* (3–5). Illus. Series: Magic Door. 2001, HarperCollins LB $14.89 (0-06-028582-6). 64pp. Three children and Captain Luna must find a way to escape when an unhappy giant steals the moon in which they are living. (Rev: BL 4/15/01; HBG 10/01; SLJ 9/01)

2188 Myers, Walter Dean. *Three Swords for Granada* (3–6). Illus. by John Spiers. 2002, Holiday $15.95 (0-8234-1676-3). 80pp. Sword-wielding Spanish cats stand up to the dogs of the Fidorean Guard in this exciting fantasy set in 1420. (Rev: BL 7/02; SLJ 9/02)

2189 Nimmo, Jenny. *Midnight for Charlie Bone* (4–6). 2003, Scholastic paper $9.95 (0-439-47429-9). 416pp. Charlie Bone, who can look at photographs and hear the conversations and thoughts of the subjects, is sent to Bloor's Academy to enhance his skills and is drawn into a magical battle, makes friends, and becomes immersed in a mystery. (Rev: BL 1/1–15/03; SLJ 2/03)

2190 Nix, Garth. *Above the Veil* (5–7). Series: The Seventh Tower. 2001, Scholastic paper $4.99 (0-439-17685-9). 248pp. In episode four in this series, Tal and Milla continue their otherworldly adventures full of action, secrets, and surprising twists and turns. (Rev: SLJ 9/01)

2191 Osterweil, Adam. *The Comic Book Kid* (4–6). Illus. 2001, Front Street $15.95 (1-886910-62-6). 152pp. Brian tries to travel back to 1939 and replace his father's prized Superman #1 comic book. (Rev: BL 5/15/01; HBG 10/01; SLJ 8/01)

2192 Palatini, Margie. *Lab Coat Girl in My Triple-Decker Hero* (3–5). Illus. by author. 2000, Hyperion $14.49 (0-7868-2442-5); paper $4.99 (0-7868-1348-2). 100pp. Fifth-graders Trudie and Ben are suspected of having a romance when they are really trying to keep secret their experiments with Ben's extraordinary powers. (Rev: SLJ 4/01)

2193 Peel, John. *Suddenly Twins!* (4–6). Series: The Magical States of America. 2001, Pocket paper $4.99 (0-7434-1762-3). 162pp. Chrissie Scott finds a magical twin in the mirror and the two work together to fight evil. (Rev: SLJ 12/01)

2194 Pennypacker, Sara. *Stuart's Cape* (2–4). Illus. by Martin Matje. 2002, Scholastic $15.95 (0-439-30180-7). 64pp. When Stuart wears his superhero cape, magical things happen — he flies, his cat drives — and he can handle his misgivings about moving to a new town. (Rev: BL 9/1/02; HBG 3/03; SLJ 11/02)

2195 Pilkey, Dav. *Ricky Ricotta's Giant Robot vs. the Voodoo Vultures from Venus* (2–4). Illus. by Martin Ontiveros. 2001, Scholastic $16.95 (0-439-23624-X). 125pp. Ricky the mouse and his giant robot friend tackle villains from Venus with dastardly plans. (Rev: HBG 10/01; SLJ 5/01)

2196 Pilkey, Dav. *Ricky Ricotta's Mighty Robot vs. the Jurassic Jackrabbits from Jupiter* (2–4). Illus. by Martin Ontiveros. 2002, Scholastic paper $3.99 (0-439-37643-2). 127pp. Ricky, his Mighty Robot, and cousin Lucy defeat General Jackrabbit, an invader from Jupiter with nefarious intent. (Rev: SLJ 12/02)

2197 Pilkey, Dav. *Ricky Ricotta's Mighty Robot vs. the Mecha-Monkeys from Mars* (2–4). Illus. by Martin Ontiveros. 2002, Scholastic paper $3.99 (0-439-25296-2). 143pp. Ricky and his robot friend battle the fiendish forces of an evil Martian monkey. (Rev: HBG 10/02; SLJ 4/02)

2198 Raham, Gary. *The Deep Time Diaries: As Recorded by Neesha and Jon Olifee* (4–6). Illus. by author. 2000, Fulcrum paper $17.95 (1-55591-415-2). 82pp. The author supplements the fictional diaries of a 22nd-century family of time travelers with notes, maps, interesting sites, and related activities. (Rev: SLJ 4/01)

2199 Reiss, Kathryn. *Paint by Magic* (4–6). 2002, Harcourt $17.00 (0-15-216361-1). 288pp. A time-travel mystery about a boy who must be transported back to 1926 to help save his mother from the clutches of an evil 15th-century painter. (Rev: BCCB 9/02; BL 4/15/02; HBG 3/03; SLJ 5/02)

2200 Rinaldi, Ann. *Millicent's Gift* (5–8). 2002, HarperCollins LB $15.89 (0-06-029637-2). 224pp. Millicent finds she has problems being in a family where spells and shape-shifting are learned skills. (Rev: BL 6/1–15/02; HBG 10/02; SLJ 6/02)

2201 Roberts, Katherine. *Crystal Mask* (5–8). Series: The Echorium Sequence. 2002, Scholastic $15.95 (0-439-33864-6). 256pp. The Singers, a group of people who maintain peace in the world through their unusual powers, are confronted by evildoers known as the Frazhin. (Rev: BL 4/15/02; HBG 10/02; SLJ 3/02)

2202 Roberts, Katherine. *Spellfall* (4–6). 2001, Scholastic $15.95 (0-439-29653-6). 250pp. In this fast-moving fantasy, 12-year-old Natalie learns she has inherited magic powers from her long-dead mother, and must use them to save a magical universe from an evil Spell Lord. (Rev: BCCB 2/02; BL 11/15/01; HBG 3/02; SLJ 10/01)

2203 Robertson, Barbara. *Rosemary and the Island Treasure: Back to 1947* (3–6). Illus. Series: The Hourglass Adventures. 2001, Winslow paper $4.95 (1-890817-58-9). 113pp. Rosemary travels back in time to meet her grandmother — another Rosemary — on an island in the Bahamas, where together they search for treasure. Also use *Rosemary at Sea: Back to 1919*, which takes place on the *Mauretania*. (Rev: SLJ 2/02)

2204 Robertson, Barbara. *Rosemary Meets Rosemarie: Berlin in 1870* (4–6). Illus. 2001, Winslow paper $4.95 (1-890817-55-4). 125pp. For her tenth birthday, Rosemary Rita receives a magical hourglass that whisks her back in time to 1870 Berlin where she meets her 10-year-old great-great-great-grandmother and the two solve a mystery. Also use *Rosemary in Paris: Back to 1889* (2001). (Rev: SLJ 10/01)

2205 Rodda, Emily. *The Charm Bracelet* (2–5). Illus. by Raoul Vitale. Series: Fairy Realm. 2003, HarperCollins LB $14.89 (0-06-009558-9). 128pp. Queen Jessica must return from the mortal world to renew the magical powers of the realm; when the wicked Valda tries to stop her, Jessica's granddaughter Jessie uses her cleverness, a few helping hands, and some magic to save the day. (Rev: BL 1/1–15/03)

2206 Rodda, Emily. *Rowan and the Keeper of the Crystal* (3–6). Series: Rowan of Rin. 2002, Harper-Collins LB $15.89 (0-06-029777-8). 208pp. Rowan must take on his mother's duties to choose the next Keeper of the Crystal after she is poisoned in this third book in the series. (Rev: BCCB 4/02; BL 1/1–15/02; HB 3–4/02; HBG 10/02; SLJ 5/02)

2207 Rodda, Emily. *Rowan and the Travelers* (3–6). 2001, HarperCollins LB $14.89 (0-06-029774-3).

176pp. This enthralling, stand-alone sequel to *Rowan of Rin* (2001) follows the diminutive herder on a journey to save his village from a mysterious sleeping sickness. (Rev: BCCB 10/01; BL 11/15/01; HB 9–10/01; HBG 3/02; SLJ 1/02)

2208 Rodda, Emily. *Rowan and the Zebak* (3–6). Series: Rowan of Rin. 2002, HarperCollins LB $15.89 (0-06-029779-4). 208pp. Rowan embarks on a quest to rescue his kidnapped sister in this magical fantasy adventure, the fourth in the series. (Rev: BCCB 7–8/02; BL 3/1/02; HBG 10/02; SLJ 7/02)

2209 Rodda, Emily. *Rowan of Rin* (3–6). 2001, Greenwillow LB $14.89 (0-06-029708-5). 160pp. Young Rowan, who is a little timid, nonetheless joins a daring expedition to investigate why the people of Rin are without water and ends up being the bravest of them all. (Rev: BCCB 6/01; BL 5/1/01*; HB 7–8/01; HBG 10/01; SLJ 6/01)

2210 Rosales, Melodye Benson. *Minnie Saves the Day* (2–4). Illus. Series: Adventures of Minnie. 2001, Little, Brown $12.95 (0-316-75605-9). 96pp. Papa, a Pullman porter during the Depression, gives his daughter a rag doll named Minnie that secretly comes alive at night and plays with the other toys. (Rev: BL 4/15/01; HBG 10/01; SLJ 7/01)

2211 Rowling, J. K. *Fantastic Beasts: And Where to Find Them* (4–7). 2001, Scholastic paper $3.99 (0-439-29501-7). 42pp. This guide to 75 magical beasts and their whereabouts is one of the texts that Harry Potter has studied, complete with his jottings in the margins. Similarly, *Quidditch Through the Ages* (2001) contains the game's history, rules, and league details. (Rev: BL 5/1/01; SLJ 6/01)

2212 Rupp, Rebecca. *The Waterstone* (4–8). 2002, Candlewick $16.99 (0-7636-0726-6). 275pp. Twelve-year-old Tad, who has special powers and memories, must find a crystal that will set the world to rights. (Rev: BCCB 10/02; SLJ 11/02)

2213 Schmidt, Gary D. *Straw into Gold* (5–8). 2001, Clarion $15.00 (0-618-05601-7). 172pp. Two boys set off to find the answer to the king's riddle and thereby save the lives of rebels, only to discover much more than they had expected. (Rev: BCCB 9/01; HBG 10/01; SLJ 8/01)

2214 Scieszka, Jon. *Hey Kid, Want to Buy a Bridge?* (3–6). Illus. by Adam McCauley. 2002, Viking $14.99 (0-670-89916-X). 80pp. The Time Warp Trio is transported back to 1877 in their hometown of Brooklyn and gets to meet Thomas Edison and watch the building of the Brooklyn Bridge. (Rev: BL 2/1/02; HBG 10/02; SLJ 3/02)

2215 Scieszka, Jon. *Sam Samurai* (4–6). Illus. by Adam McCauley. Series: Time Warp Trio. 2001, Viking $14.99 (0-670-89915-1). 80pp. While working on an assignment to write a haiku, the Time Warp Trio is accidentally transported back to 17th-century Japan in this wacky time-travel adventure. (Rev: BL 11/1/01; HBG 3/02; SLJ 11/01)

2216 Scieszka, Jon. *Viking It and Liking It* (2–4). Illus. by Adam McCauley. 2002, Viking $14.99 (0-670-89918-6). 80pp. The Time Warp Trio is thrown into the world of the Vikings and meets challenges including a feisty Leif Erickson and meals of whale blubber. (Rev: BL 12/1/02; HBG 3/03; SLJ 1/03)

2217 Sedgwick, Marcus. *The Dark Horse* (5–8). 2003, Random $15.95 (0-385-73054-3). 160pp. A fantasy in which young Sigurd, part of the ancient Storn tribe, helps his people fight the invading Dark Horse. (Rev: BL 2/1/03; HB 3–4/03; SLJ 3/03)

2218 Seidler, Tor. *The Revenge of Randal Reese-Rat* (4–6). Illus. by Brett Helquist. 2001, Farrar $16.00 (0-374-36257-2). 240pp. Soon after Montague and Isabel are married, a fire destroys their home and the prime suspect is Isabel's old flame Randal in this enjoyable sequel to *A Rat's Tale* (1999). (Rev: BCCB 2/02; BL 11/1/01; HBG 3/02; SLJ 10/01)

2219 Shan, Darren. *Cirque Du Freak: A Living Nightmare* (5–8). 2001, Little, Brown $15.95 (0-316-60340-6). 272pp. A supernatural story about a young boy who visits the Cirque Du Freak and is turned into a vampire. (Rev: BL 4/15/01; HBG 10/01; SLJ 5/01)

2220 Shan, Darren. *Cirque Du Freak: The Vampire's Assistant* (5–8). Series: Cirque Du Freak. 2001, Little, Brown $15.95 (0-316-60610-3). 256pp. The creepy, suspenseful second installment about a boy who is "half vampire" and his efforts to adjust to the world of a traveling freak show. (Rev: BL 10/15/01; HBG 3/02; SLJ 8/01)

2221 Shan, Darren. *Tunnels of Blood* (5–8). Series: Cirque Du Freak. 2002, Little, Brown $15.95 (0-316-60763-0). 240pp. Darren Shan, teenage half-vampire, sets out to investigate a spate of recent killings for which he believes his vampire master might be responsible. (Rev: BL 8/02; HBG 10/02; SLJ 5/02)

2222 Shan, Darren. *Vampire Mountain* (5–8). Series: Cirque Du Freak. 2002, Little, Brown $15.95 (0-316-60806-8). 208pp. Darren Shan, teenage half-vampire, and his mentor travel to Vampire Mountain. (Rev: BL 8/02; HBG 3/03; SLJ 9/02)

2223 Shipton, Paul. *Bug Muldoon: The Garden of Fear* (4–6). Illus. by Elwood H. Smith. 2001, Viking $14.99 (0-670-89687-X). 128pp. In this detective-story satire, beetle private eye Bug Muldoon is on the trail of some treasonous ants. (Rev: BL 9/15/01; HBG 10/01; SLJ 10/01)

2224 Sleator, William. *Marco's Millions* (5–9). 2001, Dutton $16.99 (0-525-46441-7). 160pp. In this prequel to *The Boxes* (1998), 12-year-old Marco travels to an alien world. (Rev: BCCB 7–8/01; HB 5–6/01*; HBG 10/01; SLJ 6/01)

2225 Snyder, Zilpha Keatley. *The Ghosts of Rathburn Park* (5–8). 2002, Delacorte LB $17.99 (0-385-90064-3). 192pp. Eleven-year-old Matthew explores Rathburn Park and comes across a mysterious girl dressed in clothes from a bygone era in this suspenseful, well-crafted tale. (Rev: BCCB 2/03; HBG 3/03; SLJ 9/02)

2226 Spalding, Andres. *The White Horse Talisman* (4–7). 2002, Orca $12.95 (1-55143-187-4). 160pp. Two Canadian children vacationing in England help the magical White Horse fight the forces of the

honey-tongued dragon. (Rev: BL 4/15/02; HBG 10/02; SLJ 11/02)

2227 Stanley, Diane. *The Mysterious Matter of I. M. Fine* (4–6). 2001, HarperCollins LB $15.89 (0-06-029619-4). 208pp. Fran and her friend Beamer must find the woman who writes the fiendish Chiller series of books, which are affecting the health of young readers. (Rev: BCCB 10/01; BL 7/01; HBG 3/02; SLJ 8/01)

2228 Stine, R. L. *The Haunting Hour: Chill in the Dead of Night* (5–8). Illus. 2001, HarperCollins LB $11.89 (0-06-623605-3). 160pp. Ten chilling short stories, each with an introduction by the author. (Rev: BCCB 11/01; BL 1/1–15/02; HBG 3/02)

2229 Taylor, Theodore. *The Boy Who Could Fly Without a Motor* (3–6). 2002, Harcourt $15.00 (0-15-216529-0). 144pp. After Jon learns how to fly from a green-eyed magician, he becomes the center of attraction and even meets the President. (Rev: BL 6/1–15/02; HBG 10/02; SLJ 5/02)

2230 Tolan, Stephanie S. *Flight of the Raven* (5–8). 2001, HarperCollins LB $15.89 (0-06-029620-8). 304pp. Amber, whose father is responsible for a terrorist attack, and Elijah, an African American boy who has mysterious powers, attempt to stop further violence in this novel that blends science fiction and suspense. (Rev: BCCB 12/01; BL 10/15/01; HBG 10/02; SLJ 10/01)

2231 Townley, Roderick. *Into the Labyrinth* (5–7). 2002, Simon & Schuster $16.95 (0-689-84615-0). 272pp. In this sequel to *The Great Good Thing* (2001), Princess Sylvie and the other characters in their novel become exhausted as their popularity grows and they must rush from chapter to chapter; when the book goes digital, things spiral out of control and Sylvie must defeat an evil "bot" that threatens to destroy them. (Rev: BL 11/1/02; SLJ 10/02)

2232 Van Leeuwen, Jean. *The Great Googlestein Museum Mystery* (3–6). Illus. by R. W. Alley. 2003, Putnam $16.99 (0-8037-2765-8). 208pp. Three mice have adventures while spending a week at the Guggenheim Museum in New York City. (Rev: BL 2/1/03)

2233 Venokur, Ross. *The Autobiography of Meatball Finkelstein* (4–8). 2001, Delacorte $14.95 (0-385-32798-6). 152pp. Meatball, a vegetarian, gains magic powers when he eats his first meatball in this funny and absorbing book with many twists and turns. (Rev: BCCB 9/01; HBG 3/02; SLJ 8/01)

2234 Vornholt, John. *The Troll King* (4–6). 2002, Simon & Schuster paper $4.99 (0-7434-2412-3). 240pp. A troll named Rollo escapes enslavement and finds himself embroiled in a revolution in this exciting fantasy. (Rev: BCCB 11/02; BL 8/02; SLJ 8/02)

2235 Warfel, Elizabeth Stuart. *The Blue Pearls* (2–4). Illus. by Veronique Giarrusso. 2001, Barefoot $16.99 (1-902283-78-3). 32pp. In this fantasy, a group of angels are preparing a beautiful blue gown for a young mother who is about to die and be welcomed in heaven. (Rev: BL 4/15/01; HBG 10/01; SLJ 7/01)

2236 Waugh, Sylvia. *Earthborn* (4–6). 2002, Delacorte $15.95 (0-385-72964-2). 240pp. Nesta, 12, runs away so she won't be forced to return to the planet Ormingat with her alien parents in this companion to *Space Race* (2000), set in England. (Rev: BL 9/1/02; HB 9–10/02*; HBG 3/03; SLJ 9/02*)

2237 Whelan, Gerard. *Dream Invader* (5–7). 2002, O'Brien paper $7.95 (0-86278-516-2). 176pp. Only Simon's grandmother can break the spell behind the bad dreams he's been having in this supernatural tale set in Ireland. (Rev: BL 9/1/02)

2238 Williams, Mark London. *Ancient Fire* (5–8). 2001, Tricycle Pr. $16.95 (1-58246-033-7); paper $5.95 (1-58246-032-9). 176pp. A 12-year-old boy from the year 2019, a 13-year-old girl from ancient Alexandria, and an intelligent young dinosaur band together in a time-travel tale that interweaves plagues, action, and historical detail. (Rev: HBG 10/01; SLJ 4/01)

2239 Wood, David. *The Phantom Cat of the Opera* (2–5). Illus. by Peters Day. 2001, Watson-Guptill $16.95 (0-8230-4018-6). The classic story is retold with cats as characters, with sumptuous illustrations. (Rev: HBG 10/01; SLJ 11/01)

2240 Yolen, Jane. *The Bagpiper's Ghost* (3–5). Series: Tartan Magic. 2002, Harcourt $16.00 (0-15-202310-0). 144pp. Twins Jennifer and Peter find adventure and mystery in a graveyard haunted by the ghost of a young woman. (Rev: BL 4/15/02; HBG 10/02; SLJ 3/02)

2241 Yolen, Jane, and Robert J. Harris. *Odysseus in the Serpent Maze* (4–7). 2001, HarperCollins LB $14.89 (0-06-028735-7). 256pp. This adventure story involves Odysseus as a teenager, when he was captured by pirates and experienced perilous obstacles and narrow escapes. (Rev: BCCB 5/01; BL 4/15/01; HBG 10/01; SLJ 7/01)

Friendship Stories

2242 Colfer, Eoin. *Benny and Omar* (5–8). 2001, O'Brien $7.95 (0-86278-567-7). 240pp. Benny, a young Irish lad, has trouble adjusting to his new life in Tunisia until he befriends Omar, a local orphan without a home, and the two have some exciting and amusing adventures. (Rev: BL 8/01; SLJ 12/01)

2243 Cox, Judy. *Butterfly Buddies* (2–4). Illus. by Blanche Sims. 2001, Holiday $15.95 (0-8234-1654-2). 80pp. Third-grader Robin learns about being herself — and about butterflies — from a new friend and a new teacher. (Rev: BCCB 1/02; BL 9/1/01; HBG 3/02; SLJ 10/01)

2244 Donahue, John. *Till Tomorrow* (5–7). 2001, Farrar $16.00 (0-374-37580-1). 176pp. When his family moves to a U.S. Army base in France in the early 1960s, Terry befriends an unpopular boy, with surprising results. (Rev: BCCB 11/01; BL 9/15/01; HBG 3/02; SLJ 9/01)

2245 Dower, Laura. *Only the Lonely: From the Files of Madison Finn* (4–6). Illus. 2001, Hyperion paper $4.99 (0-7868-1553-1). 144pp. Madison Finn spends an unexpectedly lonely summer before entering seventh grade and confides her concerns to her laptop computer. (Rev: BL 6/1–15/01; SLJ 8/01)

2246 Dutton, Sandra. *Capp Street Carnival* (4–6). 2003, Farrar $16.00 (0-374-31065-3). 144pp. Eleven-year-old Mary Mae, a bluegrass fan, organizes a neighborhood carnival featuring country music to raise money for a boy with a heart problem. (Rev: BL 3/15/03; SLJ 3/03)

2247 Elliott, David. *The Cool Crazy Crickets to the Rescue* (2–4). Illus. by Paul Meisel. 2001, Candlewick $13.99 (0-7636-1116-6); paper $4.50 (0-7636-1402-5). 56pp. The members of the Cool Crazy Crickets club spend a summer raising money, then decide to spend it caring for a sick cat in this easy-reading chapter book. (Rev: BL 9/1/01; HBG 10/01; SLJ 7/01)

2248 Farrell, Mame. *And Sometimes Why* (5–8). 2001, Farrar $16.00 (0-374-32289-9). 165pp. Thirteen-year-old Jack develops romantic feelings for long-time friend Chris, but his efforts to get together with her are stymied by misunderstandings and interference by others. (Rev: BCCB 4/01; BL 5/1/01; HB 5–6/01; HBG 10/01; SLJ 7/01)

2249 Fine, Anne. *Up on Cloud Nine* (5–7). 2002, Delacorte LB $17.99 (0-385-90058-9). 144pp. While Stolly lies unconscious in a hospital after an accident, his friend Ian remembers his unusual friend and his many strange but interesting habits. (Rev: BCCB 5/02; BL 6/1–15/02*; HB 7–8/02*; HBG 10/02; SLJ 6/02)

2250 Freeman, Martha. *The Trouble with Babies* (2–4). Illus. by Cat B. Smith. 2002, Holiday $15.95 (0-8234-1698-4). 80pp. Holly must learn to adapt — to her new life in San Francisco with her mother and stepfather, to her new friends, and to the fact that she is going to have a new sibling. (Rev: BCCB 11/02; BL 7/02; HBG 3/03; SLJ 8/02)

2251 Garden, Nancy. *Meeting Melanie* (4–7). 2002, Farrar $16.00 (0-374-34943-6). 208pp. Melanie's mother doesn't want Melanie to get friendly with the "natives" on the Maine island where they're spending the summer, but Melanie and Allie become fast allies nonetheless. (Rev: BCCB 1/03; BL 12/1/02; HBG 3/03; SLJ 9/02)

2252 Gonzalez, Rigoberto. *Soledad Sigh-Sighs / Soledad Suspiros* (1–3). Trans. by Jorge Argueta. Illus. by Rosa Ibarra. 2003, Children's $16.95 (0-89239-180-4). 32pp. Latchkey child Soledad lives a lonely life with an imaginary companion until two neighboring sisters befriend her and even envy her solitude, in this bilingual novel set in Brooklyn. (Rev: SLJ 3/03)

2253 Kinsey-Warnock, Natalie. *Lumber Camp Library* (3–6). Illus. by James Bernardin. 2002, HarperCollins LB $14.89 (0-06-029322-5). 96pp. Young Ruby Sawyer is devastated when her father dies, but finds comfort in a friendship with a blind woman who has a house full of books. (Rev: BL 4/15/02; HBG 10/02; SLJ 5/02)

2254 Kline, Lisa Williams. *The Princesses of Atlantis* (5–7). 2002, Cricket $16.95 (0-8126-2855-1). 184pp. Twelve-year-old Arlene experiences ups and downs in her friendship with Carly, with whom she is writing a novel about two princesses. (Rev: BL 4/15/02; HBG 10/02; SLJ 7/02)

2255 Kvasnosky, Laura McGee. *One Lucky Summer* (3–6). 2002, Dutton $15.99 (0-525-46455-7). 112pp. Ten-year-old Steven, just recently moved to Sacramento, discovers that he and the girl next door have more in common than they thought when they rescue a baby squirrel. (Rev: BCCB 5/02; BL 3/1/02; HBG 10/02; SLJ 4/02)

2256 Matlin, Marlee. *Deaf Child Crossing* (4–6). 2002, Simon & Schuster $15.95 (0-689-82208-1). 208pp. Two 9-year-olds, one deaf and one hearing, become firm friends but face the usual — and some additional — childhood tensions and jealousies. (Rev: BCCB 11/02; BL 11/15/02; HBG 3/03; SLJ 12/02)

2257 Myers, Christopher. *Fly!* (K–4). Illus. by author. 2001, Hyperion $15.99 (0-7868-0652-4). A lonely boy makes friends with a man who teaches him about the sparrows and pigeons they see from the roof of his building. (Rev: BCCB 1/02; HB 3–4/02; HBG 10/02; SLJ 12/01)

2258 Rallison, Janette. *Playing the Field* (5–7). 2002, Walker $16.95 (0-8027-8804-1). 180pp. Thirteen-year-old McKay's friend Tony urges him to pursue pretty Serena, but McKay is more interested in friendship than romance. (Rev: BCCB 7–8/02; BL 5/15/02; HBG 10/02; SLJ 4/02)

2259 Salmansohn, Karen. *Oh, and Another Thing* (4–6). Illus. by author. Series: Alexandra Rambles On! 2001, Tricycle Pr. $12.95 (1-58246-045-0). Twelve-year-old Alexandra gets advice on how to handle boys. (Rev: SLJ 2/02)

2260 Shalant, Phyllis. *When Pirates Came to Brooklyn* (4–7). 2002, Dutton $15.99 (0-525-46920-6). 176pp. When Lee, who is Jewish, befriends Polly, who is Catholic, the two imaginative 11-year-olds learn a harsh lesson about prejudice in this tale set in 1960 Brooklyn. (Rev: BCCB 12/02; BL 10/15/02; HBG 3/03; SLJ 10/02)

2261 Shreve, Susan. *Trout and Me* (5–7). 2002, Knopf LB $17.99 (0-375-91219-3). 144pp. Two friends with ADD have very different family experiences. (Rev: BCCB 11/02; BL 8/02; HBG 3/03; SLJ 9/02)

2262 Van Draanen, Wendelin. *Flipped* (5–8). 2001, Knopf $14.95 (0-375-81174-5). 212pp. In second grade Julianna was infatuated with Bryce, but now, six years later, the situation is reversed in this story told from each viewpoint in alternating chapters. (Rev: BCCB 1/02; BL 12/15/01; HBG 3/02; SLJ 11/01**)

2263 Voigt, Cynthia. *Bad Girls in Love* (5–8). Series: Bad Girls. 2002, Simon & Schuster $15.95 (0-689-82471-8). 240pp. Margalo falls in love with a popular boy and Michelle (Mikey) has a crush on a teacher in this fourth book of the series. (Rev: BCCB 10/02; BL 8/02; HB 9–10/02; HBG 3/03; SLJ 7/02)

2264 Warner, Sally. *Bad Girl Blues* (5–8). 2001, HarperCollins LB $15.89 (0-06-028275-4). 224pp. Sixth-grader Marguerite has been allowed to run

wild, and when she is hurt in an accident, Quinney's parents invite her to stay, forcing Quinney and Marguerite to reassess their flagging friendship. (Rev: BL 7/01; HBG 10/01; SLJ 7/01)

2265 Weeks, Sarah. *Guy Wire* (3–6). Series: Guy Series. 2002, HarperCollins LB $17.89 (0-06-029493-0). 144pp. A biking accident puts Guy Strang's best friend Buzz in the hospital, leaving Guy to look back on their friendship as he awaits news of Buzz's condition. (Rev: BCCB 1/03; BL 8/02; HBG 3/03; SLJ 9/02)

Growing into Maturity

Family Problems

2266 Adler, C. S. *The No Place Cat* (5–8). 2002, Clarion $15.00 (0-618-09644-2). 153pp. Twelve-year-old Tess runs away from home only to find that life with her father and new stepfamily had its good side after all. (Rev: BCCB 4/02; HBG 10/02; SLJ 3/02)

2267 Anderson, Laurie Halse. *Say Good-Bye* (4–6). Series: Wild at Heart. 2001, Pleasant paper $4.95 (1-58485-051-5). 125pp. Zoe finds adjusting to her new life with her grandmother becomes easier as she works with the therapy dogs at the Wild at Heart Animal Clinic and trains her puppy Sneakers. (Rev: SLJ 7/01)

2268 Arrington, Aileen. *Camp of the Angel* (5–8). 2003, Putnam $16.99 (0-399-23882-4). 160pp. Despite the intervention of caring professionals, Jordan and her brother continue to suffer physical abuse from their alcoholic father until ultimately the care and love they give to a stray cat prompts Jordan to stand up to her father. (Rev: BL 3/1/03; SLJ 3/03)

2269 Banks, Kate. *Dillon Dillon* (3–7). 2002, Farrar $16.00 (0-374-31786-0). 160pp. When 10-year-old Dillon learns that he was adopted as a baby, he finds comfort in observing a family of loons. (Rev: BCCB 10/02; BL 9/15/02; HB 11–12/02; HBG 3/03; SLJ 10/02)

2270 Baskin, Nora Raleigh. *What Every Girl (Except Me) Knows* (5–8). 2001, Little, Brown $16.95 (0-316-07021-1). 224pp. Young Gabby realizes that her family still hasn't come to terms with her mother's death. (Rev: BCCB 2/01; BL 6/1–15/01; HBG 10/01; SLJ 4/01)

2271 Bauer, Joan. *Stand Tall* (5–7). 2002, Putnam $16.99 (0-399-23473-X). 192pp. Tree, a tall seventh-grader, has a lot of challenges in this nonetheless humorous novel: his height, his lack of athletic ability, shuffling between his divorced parents' homes, and his veteran grandfather's ailments, to name just a few. (Rev: BCCB 10/02; BL 9/15/02; HB 11–12/02; HBG 3/03; SLJ 8/02)

2272 Bunting, Eve. *The Summer of Riley* (4–6). 2001, HarperCollins LB $15.89 (0-06-029142-7). 176pp. The acquisition of a dog helps William to overcome his distress over his parents' separation and grandfather's death, but then the dog gets in trouble with the law. (Rev: BL 7/01; HBG 10/01; SLJ 6/01)

2273 Carey, Janet Lee. *Wenny Has Wings* (5–7). 2002, Simon & Schuster $15.95 (0-689-84294-5). 240pp. After young Will narrowly escapes death in an accident that killed his sister Wenny, he and his parents must work through their grief. (Rev: BCCB 7–8/02; BL 7/02; HBG 3/03; SLJ 7/02)

2274 Choldenko, Gennifer. *Notes from a Liar and Her Dog* (5–8). 2001, Putnam $18.99 (0-399-23591-4). 244pp. A teacher helps Ant, short for Antonia, get a job in a zoo with her friend Harrison, which boosts Ant's self-confidence somewhat, but she continues to find it difficult to relate to her mother. (Rev: BCCB 7–8/01; BL 4/15/01*; HBG 3/02; SLJ 4/01*)

2275 de Guzman, Michael. *Melonhead* (4–7). 2002, Farrar $17.00 (0-374-34944-4). 224pp. Sidney T. Mellon hops a bus to the East Coast to escape the cruelty of his mother and stepfamily in Seattle and the emotional detachment of his father in Los Angeles in a story rich with characterization and an emotionally satisfying ending. (Rev: BL 10/15/02; SLJ 9/02)

2276 Dhami, Narinder. *Genius Games* (4–6). 2001, Hyperion $15.99 (0-7868-2528-6). 160pp. Sixth-grader Jack's life becomes complicated when his precocious sister Annabel begins kindergarten at his school. (Rev: BL 10/1/01; HB 5–6/01; SLJ 7/01)

2277 Doyle, Eugenie. *Stray Voltage* (5–7). 2002, Front Street $16.95 (1-886910-86-3). 136pp. The electrical problems in Ian's family barn reflect the flickering, unpredictable relationships at home, but a wise teacher helps Ian to cope with his circumstances. (Rev: BCCB 1/03; BL 1/1–15/03*; HBG 3/03; SLJ 10/02)

2278 Dreyer, Ann L. *After Elaine* (4–8). 2002, Cricket $16.95 (0-8126-2651-6). 136pp. When her difficult older sister Elaine is killed in a car accident, Gina's grief manifests itself in destructive ways. (Rev: BCCB 5/02; BL 7/02; HBG 10/02; SLJ 7/02)

2279 English, Karen. *Strawberry Moon* (5–8). Illus. 2001, Farrar $16.00 (0-374-47122-3). 128pp. On the drive to Los Angeles to visit Auntie Dot, Junie tells her children about the time she herself spent as a child with Auntie Dot, a time made difficult by her parents' separation, and her daughter Imani wonders why Dad has stayed in Chicago. (Rev: BCCB 2/02; BL 12/15/01; HBG 3/02; SLJ 10/01)

2280 Fogelin, Adrian. *Anna Casey's Place in the World* (4–6). 2001, Peachtree $14.95 (1-56145-249-1). 207pp. Twelve-year-old orphan Anna must adjust to her new foster home and begin to make friends. (Rev: BL 10/15/01; HBG 3/02; SLJ 12/01)

2281 Foland, Constance M. *Flying High, Pogo!* (4–6). 2002, Pleasant $14.95 (1-58485-624-6); paper $5.95 (1-58485-535-5). 144pp. Fifth-grader Pogo's divorced parents can't afford to pay for gym camp, so Pogo sets out to earn the money herself and in the process gets to know her half-sister in this novel presented in diary entries. (Rev: BL 10/1/02; HBG 3/03; SLJ 11/02)

2282 Giff, Patricia Reilly. *Pictures of Hollis Woods* (5–7). 2002, Random $15.95 (0-385-32655-6). 160pp. Twelve-year-old Hollis Woods has finally found a foster home where she feels safe, but when the artist who takes her in begins to suffer from dementia, Hollis finds herself in the position of caregiver. Newbery Honor Book, 2003. (Rev: BCCB 12/02; BL 10/15/02; HB 1–2/03; HBG 3/03; SLJ 9/02)

2283 Golding, Theresa Martin. *The Secret Within* (5–8). 2002, Boyds Mills $15.95 (1-56397-995-0). 240pp. Eighth-grader Carly's secret is that her father is abusive and a criminal; the neighbors in the family's new town help her and her mother to finally escape his grip. (Rev: BL 9/15/02; HBG 3/03; SLJ 8/02)

2284 Graff, Nancy Price. *A Long Way Home* (4–7). 2001, Clarion $15.00 (0-618-12042-4). 200pp. Twelve-year-old Riley's mother has recently moved them to a small town, where her interest in an old boyfriend who refused to fight in Vietnam causes mixed feelings for the boy about courage, honor, and heroism. (Rev: BCCB 12/01; BL 11/15/01; HBG 3/02; SLJ 10/01)

2285 Greene, Stephanie. *Falling into Place* (3–5). 2002, Clarion $15.00 (0-618-17744-2). 128pp. Eleven-year-old Margaret has a lot to deal with now that her father has remarried, her stepmother is expecting a baby, and her grandmother's beloved husband has died. (Rev: BCCB 1/03; BL 10/15/02; HBG 3/03; SLJ 9/02)

2286 Griffin, Peni R. *The Music Thief* (5–7). 2002, Holt $16.95 (0-8050-7055-9). 160pp. Alma must decide what to do when her brother and his friend burglarize a neighbor's house where she often trespasses to listen to music in this story set in San Antonio. (Rev: BCCB 1/03; BL 9/15/02; HBG 3/03; SLJ 12/02)

2287 Haas, Jessie. *Shaper* (5–7). 2002, HarperCollins LB $16.89 (0-06-000171-2). 192pp. After 14-year-old Chad's dog dies, Chad's new neighbor helps him to train a new dog and to reconnect with his family. (Rev: BCCB 9/02; BL 7/02; HB 5–6/02*; HBG 10/02; SLJ 5/02)

2288 Hansen, Joyce. *One True Friend* (4–7). 2001, Clarion $14.00 (0-395-84983-7). 151pp. Amir's correspondence with his friend Doris comforts him as he tries to fulfill a deathbed promise to his mother to keep his family together. (Rev: BCCB 12/01; BL 12/15/01; HBG 3/02; SLJ 12/01)

2289 Hermes, Patricia. *Sweet By and By* (4–8). 2002, HarperCollins LB $17.89 (0-06-029557-0). 160pp. In this moving story that portrays the stages of grief, 11-year-old orphan Blessing is hit hard by the news that the grandmother with whom she lives is dying, and has difficulty accepting that she must live with another family. (Rev: BL 10/1/02; HBG 3/03; SLJ 10/02)

2290 Johnston, Lindsay Lee. *Soul Moon Soup* (5–7). 2002, Front Street $15.95 (1-886910-87-1). 134pp. When homeless Phoebe and her mother hit bottom, Phoebe goes to live with her grandmother and slowly learns to value her own resources in this story told in verse. (Rev: BCCB 2/03; BL 11/15/02; HB 1–2/03; HBG 3/03; SLJ 11/02)

2291 Koss, Amy Goldman. *Stolen Words* (5–7). 2001, Pleasant $14.95 (1-58485-377-8); paper $5.95 (1-58485-376-X). 145pp. Robyn, 11, uses a diary to record her thoughts during her family's trip to Austria and her feelings about her Aunt Beth's death. (Rev: BL 9/15/01; HBG 3/02)

2292 Lafaye, A. *The Strength of Saints* (5–8). 2002, Simon & Schuster $16.95 (0-689-83200-1). 192pp. Racial tensions and family problems plague 14-year-old Nissa, who is trying to run the local library in this novel set in Harper, Louisiana, in 1936. (Rev: BL 6/1–15/02; HBG 10/02; SLJ 6/02)

2293 Lisle, Janet Taylor. *How I Became a Writer and Oggie Learned to Drive* (4–6). 2002, Putnam $15.99 (0-399-23394-6). 160pp. Eleven-year-old Archie creates wild stories to assuage his younger brother's fears as they shuttle between the homes of their divorced parents. (Rev: BL 2/1/02; HB 3–4/02; HBG 10/02; SLJ 3/02)

2294 Mazer, Norma Fox. *Girlhearts* (5–9). 2001, HarperCollins LB $15.89 (0-688-06866-9). 224pp. Thirteen-year-old Sarabeth faces many challenges and difficult choices when her single mother dies suddenly. (Rev: BCCB 4/01; BL 7/01; HBG 10/01; SLJ 5/01)

2295 Mead, Alice. *Junebug in Trouble* (5–8). 2002, Farrar $16.00 (0-374-33969-4). 144pp. Young Junebug and his mother move out of the housing projects, but Junebug continues to get into the trouble his mother was hoping to avoid. (Rev: BCCB 6/02; BL 4/15/02; HB 5–6/02; HBG 10/02; SLJ 3/02)

2296 Moore, Martha. *Matchit* (4–7). 2002, Delacorte LB $17.99 (0-385-90023-6). 197pp. When his father goes on vacation, 11-year-old Matchit must stay with an eccentric woman who runs a junkyard in this story about a child's hopes, fears, and self-esteem. (Rev: BCCB 6/02; BL 2/15/02; HBG 10/02; SLJ 4/02)

2297 Neufeld, John. *The Handle and the Key* (3–6). 2002, Penguin Putnam $16.99 (0-8037-2721-6). 160pp. The Knox family's birth daughter Mary Kate faces emotional upheaval after her parents adopt a young foster child. (Rev: BL 10/15/02; HBG 3/03; SLJ 10/02)

2298 Paterson, Katherine. *The Same Stuff as Stars* (5–7). 2002, Clarion $15.00 (0-618-24744-0). 256pp. An unhappy 11-year-old Angel and her younger brother Bernie are sent to live with their father's grandmother, where Angel finds comfort in a mysterious man who introduces her to astronomy. (Rev: BCCB 10/02; BL 9/15/02; HB 9–10/02; HBG 3/03)

2299 Pearson, Mary E. *Scribbler of Dreams* (5–8). 2001, Harcourt $17.00 (0-15-202320-8). 240pp. Bram, whose family feuds constantly with the Crutchfield clan, finds she has fallen in love with a Crutchfield boy and must keep her identity a secret from him. (Rev: BCCB 5/01; BL 4/15/01; HBG 10/01; SLJ 5/01)

2300 Rodowsky, Colby. *Clay* (4–7). 2001, Farrar $16.00 (0-374-31338-5). 176pp. Eleven-year-old Elsie and her autistic younger brother have been living a desperate life since her mother kidnapped them from their father four years before. (Rev: BCCB 3/01; BL 5/1/01; HBG 10/01; SLJ 4/01)

2301 Shange, Ntozake. *Daddy Says* (5–9). 2003, Simon & Schuster $16.00 (0-689-83081-5). 192pp. Two sisters on a Texas ranch grapple with family problems at the same time that there is rodeo excitement. (Rev: BCCB 3/03; BL 3/15/03; SLJ 2/03)

2302 Shreve, Susan. *Blister* (4–6). 2001, Scholastic $15.95 (0-439-19313-3). 154pp. A girl who calls herself Blister tries to fit in at a new school after her mother has a stillborn baby and her father moves out. (Rev: BCCB 11/01; BL 9/15/01; HBG 10/02; SLJ 11/01)

2303 Springer, Nancy. *Separate Sisters* (5–7). 2001, Holiday $16.95 (0-8234-1544-9). 84pp. Two teenage girls deal with the divorce of their parents in different ways. (Rev: BCCB 2/02; BL 2/1/02; HB 3–4/02; HBG 10/02; SLJ 2/02)

2304 Warner, Sally. *Sister Split* (4–6). 2001, Pleasant $14.95 (1-58485-373-5); paper $5.95 (1-58485-372-7). 144pp. Two sisters, Ivy and Lacey, take sides against each other during their parents' divorce. (Rev: BL 1/1–15/02; HBG 3/02)

2305 Weatherly, Lee. *Child X* (5–8). 2002, Knopf $15.95 (0-385-75009-9). 208pp. Thirteen-year-old Jules (Juliet) faces many puzzles as her parents go through a high-profile and messy divorce that involves questions about Jules's parentage in this story from Britain. (Rev: BCCB 10/02; BL 7/02; HBG 10/02; SLJ 6/02)

2306 Woodson, Jacqueline. *Hush* (5–9). 2002, Putnam $15.99 (0-399-23114-5). 192pp. A girl and her family are relocated in the witness protection program after her father, a police officer, testifies against fellow cops in a case that involves racial prejudice. (Rev: BCCB 3/02; BL 1/1–15/02; HB 1–2/02; HBG 10/02; SLJ 2/02*)

Personal Problems

2307 Bradley, Kimberly Brubaker. *Halfway to the Sky* (5–8). 2002, Delacorte LB $17.99 (0-385-90029-5). 164pp. To escape her grief at the death of her brother and her parents' divorce, 12-year-old Dani decides to hike the Appalachian Trail from Georgia to Maine. (Rev: BCCB 5/02; BL 4/1/02; HBG 10/02; SLJ 4/02)

2308 Caldwell, V. M. *Tides* (5–7). Illus. 2001, Milkweed $15.95 (1-57131-628-0); paper $6.95 (1-57131-629-9). 311pp. In this sequel to *The Ocean Within*, Elizabeth, age 12, has been adopted for a year but continues to find it difficult to fit into the family's way of life. (Rev: BCCB 7–8/01; BL 4/15/01; HBG 10/01; SLJ 8/01)

2309 Clements, Andrew. *The Jacket* (3–6). Illus. by Dan Gonzalez. 2002, Simon & Schuster $12.95 (0-689-82595-1). 80pp. This story about a sixth-grade boy examining race relations and facing his own prejudices is sure to prompt discussion. (Rev: BCCB 3/02; BL 3/1/02; HBG 10/02; SLJ 3/02)

2310 Cooper, Ilene. *The Annoying Team* (2–4). Illus. by Colin Paine. Series: Road to Reading. 2002, Random LB $11.99 (0-307-46512-8); paper $3.99 (0-307-26512-9). 80pp. In this beginning chapter book, Tim tries a new approach to combat the bullying of Big Jon Ferguson. (Rev: BL 6/1–15/02; HBG 10/02)

2311 Crowe, Carole. *Groover's Heart* (4–6). 2001, Boyds Mills $15.95 (1-56397-953-5). 144pp. Orphan Charlotte, age 11, has trouble adjusting to the ways of her guardian, wealthy Aunt Viola. (Rev: BL 4/15/01; HBG 10/01; SLJ 4/01)

2312 Danziger, Paula. *United Tates of America* (4–6). 2002, Scholastic $15.95 (0-590-69221-6). 144pp. Skate Tate, an 11-year-old with problems adjusting to sixth grade, experiences additional stress when her favorite great-uncle dies. (Rev: BCCB 9/02; BL 4/15/02; HB 3–4/02; HBG 10/02)

2313 Duffey, Betsy. *Fur-Ever Yours, Booker Jones* (4–6). 2001, Viking $14.99 (0-670-89287-4). 128pp. Long-suffering Booker must deal with lightweight and serious problems when his parents leave him and his sister alone with their grandfather. (Rev: BL 6/1–15/01; HBG 10/01; SLJ 7/01)

2314 Easton, Kelly. *Trouble at Betts Pets* (3–6). 2002, Candlewick $14.99 (0-7636-1580-3). 144pp. Fifth-grader Aaron faces problems at his family's pet store, at school, and in his neighborhood — until he takes action. (Rev: BCCB 6/02; BL 9/1/02; HBG 10/02; SLJ 4/02)

2315 Gantos, Jack. *What Would Joey Do?* (5–8). 2002, Farrar $16.00 (0-374-39986-7). 240pp. Hyperactive Joey is nearly overwhelmed by the antics of his parents, his dying grandmother, and the needs of his blind homeschool partner, but manages to cope in his own unusual way in this final installment in the Joey Pigza trilogy. (Rev: BCCB 11/02; BL 10/1/02*; HB 11–12/02; HBG 3/03; SLJ 9/02*)

2316 Giff, Patricia Reilly. *All the Way Home* (4–6). 2001, Delacorte $15.95 (0-385-32209-7). 169pp. Polio survivor Mariel befriends homeless Brick, and they together resolve issues from their pasts in this story set in the 1940s. (Rev: BL 10/15/01; HB 11–12/01; HBG 3/02; SLJ 9/01)

2317 Griffin, Adele. *Hannah, Divided* (4–7). 2002, Hyperion $15.99 (0-7868-0879-9). 208pp. Hannah's amazing mathematic ability and obsessive-compulsive disorder make her different from everyone else, but with the help of her grandfather, a philanthropist, and a new friend, she perseveres in this novel set during the Depression. (Rev: BCCB 12/02; BL 10/1/02*; HB 11–12/02; HBG 3/03; SLJ 12/02)

2318 Hatton, Caroline. *Vero and Philippe* (3–5). Illus. by Preston McDaniels. 2001, Front Street $14.95 (0-8126-2940-X). 120pp. Nine-year-old Vero and her family, Vietnamese immigrants to France, move from the country into the city, an adjustment made more difficult for Vero when her beloved nanny is fired. (Rev: BCCB 3/02; HBG 3/02; SLJ 12/01)

2319 Hill, Janet Muirhead. *Miranda and Starlight* (4–6). Illus. by Pat Lehmkul. 2002, Raven paper $9.95 (0-9714161-0-9). 168pp. Miranda finds life complicated when she moves to her grandparents' farm, and her love for a neighbor's stallion leads her into a tangle of deception. (Rev: BL 8/02; SLJ 8/02)

2320 Jiminez, Francisco. *Breaking Through* (5–8). 2001, Houghton $15.00 (0-618-01173-0). 208pp. In this sequel to *The Circuit: Stories from the Life of a Migrant Child* (2001), 14-year-old Francisco recounts his efforts to improve his life and get a good education, as well as describing his school and romantic experiences. (Rev: BCCB 1/02; BL 9/1/01; HB 11–12/01; HBG 3/02; SLJ 9/01)

2321 Kerr, Dan. *Candy on the Edge* (5–8). 2002, Coteau paper $8.95 (1-55050-189-5). 137pp. Candy, an eighth-grader, finds herself drawn into a world of crime as she makes new friends and falls for Ramon. (Rev: SLJ 5/02)

2322 Lachtman, Ofelia Dumas. *The Summer of El Pintor* (5–8). 2001, Piñata paper $9.95 (1-55885-327-8). 234pp. Sixteen-year-old Monica's father loses his job and the two move from their wealthy neighborhood to the barrio house in which her dead mother grew up, where Monica searches for a missing neighbor and discovers the truth of her past. (Rev: BL 8/01; SLJ 7/01)

2323 Little, Jean. *Birdie for Now* (3–5). Illus. 2002, Orca paper $4.99 (1-55143-203-X). 160pp. Troubled, hyperactive Dickon moves to a new home and finds joy and self-knowledge when he gets the opportunity to train an abused dog. (Rev: BL 11/1/02; SLJ 12/02)

2324 McNamee, Graham. *Sparks* (3–5). 2002, Random LB $17.99 (0-385-90054-6). 144pp. When Todd is moved from his special-needs class to a mainstream fifth-grade class, he is taunted by his classmates, struggles with tough homework, and ditches his special-needs friends in the hope of "fitting in." (Rev: BCCB 7–8/02; BL 10/15/02; HBG 3/03; SLJ 8/02)

2325 Moss, Marissa. *Oh Boy, Amelia!* (2–5). Illus. by author. 2001, Pleasant $12.95 (1-58485-344-1); paper $5.95 (1-58485-330-1). 38pp. Amelia's notebook is filled with humorous entries about her sister's crush on a boy and her own aversion to "feminine" activities such as cooking and sewing. (Rev: BL 1/1–15/02; HBG 3/02; SLJ 10/01)

2326 Olsson, Soren, and Anders Jacobsson. *In Ned's Head* (4–6). Trans. by Kevin Read. Illus. 2001, Simon & Schuster $16.00 (0-689-83870-0). 144pp. In diary format, this book describes the trials and tribulations of growing up as experienced by 11-year-old Ned Floyd, who uses the code name Treb Vladinsky. (Rev: BCCB 3/01; BL 4/1/01; HBG 10/01; SLJ 6/01)

2327 Porter, Tracey. *A Dance of Sisters* (5–8). 2002, HarperCollins LB $17.89 (0-06-029239-3). 288pp. When a young ballet dancer's dreams are dashed, she is comforted by her sister. (Rev: BCCB 1/03; BL 2/15/03; HBG 3/03; SLJ 1/03)

2328 Rodowsky, Colby. *Jason Rat-a-tat* (2–4). Illus. by Beth Peck. 2002, Farrar $15.00 (0-374-33671-7). 80pp. In Jason's family everyone else is engaged in a sport, but Jason's grandfather discovers the boy's true talent in this beginning chapter book. (Rev: BCCB 5/02; BL 6/1–15/02; HBG 10/02; SLJ 4/02)

2329 Russo, Marisabina. *House of Sports* (5–8). 2002, Greenwillow LB $15.89 (0-06-623804-8). 192pp. Twelve-year-old Jim faces many problems, from a fear of public speaking to dealing with a girl on the basketball team. (Rev: BCCB 3/02; BL 3/15/02; HBG 10/02; SLJ 4/02)

2330 Santucci, Barbara. *Loon Summer* (1–4). Illus. by Andrea Shine. 2001, Eerdmans $16.00 (0-8028-5182-7). Rainie has fun at the lake with her newly separated father and, although she wishes her mother were there, she learns to accept that things have changed. (Rev: SLJ 8/01)

2331 Siebold, Jan. *Doing Time Online* (3–5). 2002, Albert Whitman $13.95 (0-8075-5959-8). 96pp. Young Mitch learns an important lesson through his community-service e-mail correspondence with the elderly Wootie. (Rev: BL 5/15/02; HBG 10/02; SLJ 3/02)

2332 Silverman. *Mirror Mirror: Twisted Tales* (5–8). 2002, Scholastic $15.95 (0-439-29593-9). 192pp. Disturbing stories serve as metaphors for the problems of drug use, divorce, homelessness, and other ills. (Rev: BL 9/1/02; HBG 10/02; SLJ 8/02)

2333 Smith, Cynthia Leitich. *Rain Is Not My Indian Name* (5–9). 2001, HarperCollins LB $15.89 (0-06-029504-X). 144pp. Native American girl Rain's love of photography helps her to overcome her terrible grief at the death of a friend. (Rev: BCCB 9/01; HBG 3/02; SLJ 6/01)

2334 Stewart, Jennifer J. *The Bean King's Daughter* (5–7). 2002, Holiday $16.95 (0-8234-1644-5). 138pp. Phoebe, a 12-year-old heiress, reluctantly learns about herself and her young stepmother while at an Arizona ranch. (Rev: BL 9/1/02; HBG 10/02; SLJ 7/02)

2335 Stinson, Kathy. *King of the Castle* (3–4). Illus. by Kasia Charko. 2001, Second Story paper $5.95 (1-896764-35-5). 61pp. Watching his grandson at his studies inspires school custodian Mr. Elliott to learn to read himself. (Rev: SLJ 8/01)

2336 Wallace-Brodeur, Ruth. *Blue Eyes Better* (4–6). 2002, Dutton $15.99 (0-525-46836-6). 128pp. A moving novel about 11-year-old Tessa, her family, and their reactions to the death of Tessa's older brother in a drunk-driving accident. (Rev: BCCB 3/02; BL 4/1/02*; HBG 10/02; SLJ 1/02)

2337 Zinnen, Linda. *The Truth About Rats, Rules, and Seventh Grade* (5–7). 2001, HarperCollins LB $14.89 (0-06-028800-0). 160pp. Larch, who faces multiple problems at home and at school, tries to live her life by a set of unemotional rules, but a friendly stray dog and the discovery of the truth about her father's death make these rules hard to keep. (Rev: BCCB 6/01; BL 4/1/01*; HBG 10/01; SLJ 2/01)

Physical and Emotional Problems

2338 Bang, Molly. *Tiger's Fall* (3–6). 2001, Holt $15.95 (0-8050-6689-6). 110pp. After a fall leaves 11-year-old Lupe paralyzed from the waist down,

she is sent to the village center for disabled people where she learns to cope with her challenges and finds hope for the future. (Rev: BCCB 12/01; BL 11/1/01; HBG 3/02; SLJ 12/01)

2339 Byalick, Marcia. *Quit It* (4–7). 2002, Delacorte $15.95 (0-385-72997-9). 144pp. Tourette's syndrome makes life difficult for seventh-grader Carrie but a lunchtime therapy group offers support, and new challenges. (Rev: BCCB 12/02; BL 10/1/02; HBG 3/03; SLJ 11/02)

2340 Carter, Anne Laurel. *In the Clear* (4–7). 2001, Orca paper $6.95 (1-55143-192-0). 133pp. A 12-year-old Canadian polio survivor in the 1950s works through her fears and struggles to recapture her lost childhood. (Rev: BL 11/15/01; SLJ 1/02)

2341 Christopher, Matt. *Wheel Wizards* (3–7). 2000, Little, Brown $15.95 (0-316-13611-5); paper $4.50 (0-316-13733-2). 120pp. Twelve-year-old Seth's life turns around when he discovers wheelchair basketball. (Rev: HBG 3/01; SLJ 4/01)

2342 Denenberg, Barry. *Mirror, Mirror on the Wall: The Diary of Bess Brennan* (4–8). Series: Dear America. 2002, Scholastic $10.95 (0-439-19446-6). 144pp. When she comes home at weekends, 12-year-old Bess, who has lost her sight, shares her new life and school experiences with her twin sister, in this novel set in the Depression that includes many details of how the blind cope. (Rev: BL 10/1/02; HBG 3/03; SLJ 10/02)

2343 Haddix, Margaret Peterson. *Because of Anya* (3–6). 2002, Simon & Schuster $15.95 (0-689-38298-2). 128pp. Anya's friend Keely rallies round when Anya must wear a wig because of her alopecia. (Rev: SLJ 11/02)

2344 Hoopmann, Kathy. *Blue Bottle Mystery: An Asperger Adventure* (3–5). 2001, Jessica Kingsley paper $11.95 (1-85302-978-5). 93pp. Ben is diagnosed as having Asperger Syndrome, a kind of autism that explains his behavior problems, in this novel in which a blue bottle plays a leading role. (Rev: SLJ 8/01)

2345 McDonald, Megan. *Judy Moody Gets Famous* (2–4). Illus. by Peter Reynolds. 2001, Candlewick $15.99 (0-7636-0849-1). 126pp. In this beginning chapter book, Judy Moody is plagued by jealousy until she manages to become famous anonymously and finds she enjoys it. (Rev: HB 9–10/01; HBG 3/02; SLJ 10/01)

2346 *Period Pieces: Stories for Girls* (4–8). Ed. by Erzsi Deak and Kristin Embry Litchman. 2003, HarperCollins LB $16.89 (0-06-623797-1). 160pp. A collection of 13 stories about girls' experiences with their first periods, featuring a variety of characters and settings. (Rev: BCCB 3/03; BL 3/15/03; SLJ 3/03)

2347 Striegel, Jana. *Homeroom Exercise* (4–7). 2002, Holiday $16.95 (0-8234-1579-1). 192pp. A 12-year-old who dreams of becoming a professional dancer is diagnosed with juvenile rheumatoid arthritis. (Rev: BL 3/1/02; HBG 10/02; SLJ 6/02)

2348 Van Leeuwen, Jean. *Lucy Was There . . .* (4–6). 2002, Penguin Putnam $16.99 (0-8037-2738-0). 176pp. Twelve-year-old Morgan gets comfort from an imagined dog, a friend, and music as she learns to accept the deaths of her mother and brother. (Rev: BCCB 3/02; BL 9/1/02; HBG 10/02; SLJ 5/02)

2349 Warner, Sally. *This Isn't About the Money* (4–6). 2002, Viking $15.99 (0-670-03574-2). 224pp. Fourteen-year-old Janey, disfigured in the car crash that killed her parents, tries to adjust to her new life in Arizona with her grandfather and great-aunt. (Rev: BCCB 12/02; BL 9/1/02; HBG 3/03; SLJ 9/02)

2350 Wilson, Jacqueline. *Vicky Angel* (4–7). Illus. by Nick Sharratt. 2001, Delacorte $15.95 (0-385-72920-0). 172pp. A girl conjures up the angel of her dead best friend in this book that examines loss, guilt, suicidal thoughts, and life after death. (Rev: BCCB 10/01; BL 11/15/01; HBG 3/02; SLJ 10/01)

Historical Fiction and Foreign Lands

General and Miscellaneous

2351 Bruchac, Joseph. *The Winter People* (5–9). 2002, Dial $16.99 (0-8037-2694-5). 176pp. A 14-year-old Abenaki boy searches for his mother and sisters after they are kidnapped by English soldiers in the French and Indian War. (Rev: BL 10/1/02*; HBG 3/03; SLJ 11/02)

2352 Caswell, Maryanne. *Pioneer Girl* (5–8). Illus. by Lindsay Grater. 2001, Tundra $16.95 (0-88776-550-5). 82pp. In letters to her grandmother, a 14-year-old girl describes the hardships and interesting experiences of her journey from Ontario to the prairies in the late 1880s. (Rev: HBG 10/01; SLJ 10/01)

2353 Clinton, Cathryn. *A Stone in My Hand* (5–8). 2002, Candlewick $15.99 (0-7636-1388-6). 191pp. Eleven-year-old Maalak's father is killed in the violence of 1988 Gaza, and she must worry about her brother's future. (Rev: BL 9/15/02; HBG 3/03; SLJ 11/02)

2354 Crook, Connie Brummel. *The Hungry Year* (5–8). 2001, Stoddart paper $7.95 (0-7737-6206-X). 190pp. Twelve-year-old Kate must care for her brothers and handle the household chores during a severe Canadian winter in the late 1700s. (Rev: BL 1/1–15/02; SLJ 11/01)

2355 Downie, Mary Alice, and John Downie. *Danger in Disguise* (5–8). Series: On Time's Wing. 2001, Roussan paper $6.95 (1-896184-72-3). 170pp. Young Jamie, a Scot raised in Normandy in secrecy, is scooped up to serve in the British navy and sent to Quebec to fight the French in this complex tale of adventure and intrigue set in the mid-18th century. (Rev: SLJ 5/01)

2356 Doyle, Brian. *Mary Ann Alice* (4–7). 2002, Groundwood $15.95 (0-88899-453-2). 166pp. It's 1926 and a new dam brings many changes to the Canadian community that is home to Mary Ann Alice, a seventh-grader with a love of rocks. (Rev: BCCB 6/02; HB 5–6/02*; HBG 10/02; SLJ 6/02)

2357 Goldring, Ann. *Spitfire* (4–6). 2002, Raincoast paper $6.95 (1-55192-490-0). 160pp. A Canadian girl is determined to compete in a boys-only soap-box derby in this novel set in 1943. (Rev: BL 5/15/02; SLJ 4/02)

2358 Harrison, Troon. *A Bushel of Light* (5–8). 2001, Stoddart paper $7.95 (0-7737-6140-3). 244pp. Fourteen-year-old orphan Maggie juggles her need to search for her twin sister and her responsibilities for 4-year-old Lizzy, in this novel set in Canada in the early 1900s. (Rev: SLJ 10/01)

2359 Logan, Claudia. *The 5,000-Year-Old Puzzle: Solving a Mystery of Ancient Egypt* (3–5). Illus. by Melissa Sweet. 2002, Farrar $17.00 (0-374-32335-6). 48pp. Part fact and part fiction, this picture book for older children takes readers along on an actual 1924 expedition to uncover tombs from the days of ancient Egypt. (Rev: BL 4/15/02; HBG 10/02; SLJ 6/02)

2360 Rand, Gloria. *Sailing Home: A Story of a Childhood at Sea* (2–4). Illus. by Ted Rand. 2001, North-South LB $15.88 (0-7358-1540-2). 32pp. A fictional account, based on a journal, of what life at sea was like for the children of a ship's captain at the turn of the 20th century. (Rev: BL 11/1/01; HBG 3/02)

2361 Reekie, Jocelyn. *Tess* (5–8). 2003, Raincoast paper $7.95 (1-55192-471-4). 296pp. Thirteen-year-old Tess is a plucky, strong-willed girl who must leave her Scottish home and move to British Columbia in 1857. (Rev: BL 3/1/03)

2362 Schwartz, Virginia Frances. *Messenger* (5–9). 2002, Holiday $17.95 (0-8234-1716-6). 277pp. This story of the hardships and joys of a Croatian family living in Ontario's mining towns in the 1920s and 1930s is based on the lives of the author's mother and grandmother. (Rev: HBG 3/03; SLJ 11/02)

2363 Torrey, Michele. *To the Edge of the World* (5–8). 2003, Knopf LB $17.99 (0-375-92338-1). 240pp. On board one of Magellan's ships as a cabin boy, Mateo encounters danger and excitement. (Rev: BL 2/1/03; SLJ 2/03)

Africa

2364 Asare, Meshack. *Sosu's Call* (1–4). Illus. by author. 2002, Kane $15.95 (1-929132-21-2). 37pp. Sosu, an African boy who is rejected by the villagers because he cannot walk, saves them from a terrible storm with the help of his dog. (Rev: BCCB 5/02; HBG 10/02; SLJ 6/02)

2365 Burns, Khephra. *Mansa Musa: The Lion of Mali* (4–7). Illus. by Diane Dillon and Leo Dillon. 2001, Harcourt $18.00 (0-15-200375-4). 56pp. Lavish illustrations complement this handsome, challenging book about Mali and Mansa Musa's journey from a rural village boyhood to becoming the king of Mali. (Rev: BL 12/1/01; HB 11–12/01; HBG 3/02; SLJ 10/01)

2366 Ferreira, Anton. *Zulu Dog* (5–8). 2002, Farrar $16.00 (0-374-39223-4). 208pp. Modern South Africa is the setting for this story, in which a racist white man has a change of heart when his daughter Shirley is rescued by a black boy's puppy. (Rev:

BCCB 1/03; BL 9/15/02; HB 11–12/02; HBG 3/03; SLJ 9/02)

2367 Grifalconi, Ann. *The Village That Vanished* (2–5). Illus. by Kadir Nelson. 2002, Dial $16.99 (0-8037-2623-6). 40pp. African villagers escape slavers by dismantling their village piece by piece. (Rev: BCCB 11/02; BL 9/15/02; HB 9–10/02; HBG 3/03; SLJ 12/02)

2368 Marston, Elsa. *The Ugly Goddess* (5–8). 2002, Cricket $16.95 (0-8126-2667-2). 224pp. In 523 B.C. Egypt, a 14-year-old Egyptian princess, a young Greek soldier who is in love with her, and an Egyptian boy become embroiled in a mystery adventure that blends fact, fiction, and fantasy. (Rev: BL 1/1–15/03; HBG 3/03; SLJ 12/02)

Asia

2369 Bouchard, David. *Buddha in the Garden* (4–6). Illus. by Shong-Yang Huang. 2001, Raincoast $14.95 (1-55192-452-8). 32pp. An abandoned baby raised in a monastery learns to tend the garden in this quiet introduction to Buddhism illustrated with evocative water colors. (Rev: BL 1/1–15/02; SLJ 12/01)

2370 Divakaruni, Chitra Banerjee. *Neela: Victory Song* (5–8). Series: Girls of Many Lands. 2002, Pleasant $12.95 (1-58485-597-5); paper $7.95 (1-58485-521-5). 196pp. Plucky Neela, 12, plunges into the frightening political fray of India in 1939, determined to help her father and a freedom fighter who are protesting British rule. (Rev: BL 11/15/02; HBG 3/03; SLJ 12/02)

2371 Ellis, Deborah. *Parvana's Journey* (5–8). 2002, Douglas & McIntyre $15.95 (0-88899-514-8). 199pp. This sequel to *The Breadwinner* (2001) shows 13-year-old Parvana, whose father has recently died, making a difficult journey across Taliban-ruled Afghanistan disguised as a boy. (Rev: BL 12/1/02; HBG 3/03; SLJ 12/02)

2372 Hill, Elizabeth Starr. *Chang and the Bamboo Flute* (2–5). Illus. by Lesley Hiu. 2002, Farrar $15.00 (0-374-31238-9). 64pp. Chang, a mute boy who lives with his family on a boat on the Li River, decides to sell his beloved flute — his only means of communication — to replace the wok his mother lost in a flood. (Rev: BL 10/15/02; HBG 3/03)

2373 Holman, Sheri. *Sondok: Princess of the Moon and Stars, Korea, A.D. 595* (3–6). Series: The Royal Diaries. 2002, Scholastic $10.95 (0-439-16586-5). 187pp. In notes placed in an ancestral jar, the young princess and future ruler relates her confusion about religion and her love of astronomy. (Rev: HBG 3/03; SLJ 8/02)

2374 Hoobler, Dorothy, and Thomas Hoobler. *The Demon in the Teahouse* (5–8). 2001, Philomel $17.99 (0-399-23499-3). 208pp. Fourteen-year-old Seikei, who plans to become a samurai, investigates a series of fires and murders that appear to be connected to a popular geisha in this story set in 18th-century Japan. (Rev: BCCB 6/01; BL 5/1/01; HB 7–8/01; HBG 10/01; SLJ 6/01)

2375 Lasky, Kathryn. *Jahanara: Princess of Princesses* (4–8). Series: Royal Diaries. 2002, Scholastic $10.95 (0-439-22350-4). 192pp. Princess Jaharana, the daughter of Shah Jahan (who built the Taj Mahal) writes detailed diary accounts of her 17th-century life, with rich descriptions of her surroundings, palace intrigues, and dealing with her family. (Rev: BL 1/1–15/03; HBG 3/03; SLJ 1/03)

2376 Park, Linda Sue. *A Single Shard* (4–8). 2001, Clarion $15.00 (0-395-97827-0). 152pp. This Newbery Award winner describes a Korean boy's journey through unknown territory to deliver two valuable pots. (Rev: BCCB 3/01; BL 4/1/01*; HBG 10/01; SLJ 5/01*)

2377 Park, Linda Sue. *When My Name Was Keoko* (5–9). 2002, Clarion $16.00 (0-618-13335-6). 208pp. A young brother and sister tell, in first-person accounts, what life was like during the Japanese occupation of Korea. (Rev: BCCB 5/02; BL 3/1/02; HB 5–6/02; HBG 10/02; SLJ 4/02)

2378 Tenzing, Norbu. *Himalaya* (3–5). Trans. from French by Shelley Tanaka. Illus. by author. 2002, Groundwood $16.95 (0-88899-480-X). A gripping saga, beautifully illustrated, about the Dolpo people of Nepal, their grueling treks through the mountains, and the transfer of leadership. (Rev: HBG 3/03; SLJ 1/03)

2379 Yep, Laurence. *Lady of Ch'iao Kuo: Warrior of the South* (5–8). Illus. Series: Royal Diaries. 2001, Scholastic $10.95 (0-439-16483-6). 300pp. In this volume of the Royal Diaries series, the teenage Princess Redbird of the Hsien tribe must use her diplomatic skills to save the lives of both her own people and Chinese colonists in the sixth century A.D. Historical notes add background information. (Rev: BL 11/1/01)

2380 Yep, Laurence. *Spring Pearl: The Last Flower* (4–7). Series: Girls of Many Lands. 2002, Pleasant $12.95 (1-58485-595-9); paper $7.95 (1-58485-519-3). 224pp. An adventurous, intelligent orphan faces a difficult time when she goes to live with her artist father's patron in this novel set in the turmoil of 1857 China. (Rev: BL 12/15/02; HBG 3/03; SLJ 10/02)

Europe

2381 Attema, Martha. *Daughter of Light* (3–5). Illus. 2001, Orca paper $4.99 (1-55143-179-3). 138pp. In this affecting novel, which takes place in the Nazi-occupied Netherlands during World War II, a 9-year-old girl braves German soldiers and risks her freedom to help her pregnant mother. (Rev: BL 2/1/02; SLJ 12/01)

2382 Casanova, Mary. *Cecile: Gates of Gold* (4–7). Illus. Series: Girls of Many Lands. 2002, Pleasant $12.95 (1-58485-594-0); paper $7.95 (1-58485-518-5). 191pp. For 12-year-old Cecile, a peasant in 18th-century France, the chance to work at the Palace of Versailles seems like a dream come true until she faces some of the harsh realities of court life. (Rev: BL 10/15/02; HBG 3/03; SLJ 9/02)

2383 Clements, Bruce. *A Chapel of Thieves* (4–6). 2002, Farrar $16.00 (0-374-37701-4). 224pp. In this sequel to *I Tell a Lie Every So Often* (1974), Henry, an adventurous 15-year-old, journeys across the Atlantic to Paris in 1849 to rescue his older brother from a gang of thieves. (Rev: BCCB 4/02; BL 3/15/02; HBG 10/02; SLJ 5/02)

2384 Debon, Nicolas. *A Brave Soldier* (2–5). Illus. 2002, Groundwood $15.95 (0-88899-481-8). 32pp. This picture book for older children, narrated by a young Canadian soldier, introduces readers to the trenches of World War I. (Rev: BL 11/1/02; HBG 3/03; SLJ 2/03)

2385 Ellis, Deborah. *A Company of Fools* (5–8). 2002, Fitzhenry & Whiteside $15.95 (1-55041-719-3). 180pp. Quiet Henri and free-spirited Micah try to cheer the people of a France devastated by the Black Death of 1348 by singing. (Rev: BCCB 1/03; BL 1/1–15/03; HB 1–2/03; HBG 3/03)

2386 Fagan, Cary. *Daughter of the Great Zandini* (3–5). Illus. by Cybele Young. 2001, Tundra LB $16.95 (0-88776-534-3). 57pp. The Great Zandini's son has been groomed to follow in his father's magician footsteps, but it is Fanny, the neglected daughter, who is the success in this story set in 19th-century Paris. (Rev: HBG 3/02; SLJ 4/02)

2387 Gilson, Jamie. *Stink Alley* (4–7). 2002, Harper-Collins LB $15.89 (0-06-029217-2). 192pp. Twelve-year-old orphan Lizzy Tinker, a Separatist who fled England with her family for Holland in 1608, is befriended by the boy who would one day be known as Rembrandt. (Rev: BCCB 9/02; BL 4/15/02; HB 9–10/02; HBG 3/03; SLJ 7/02)

2388 Gregory, Kristiana. *Eleanor: Crown Jewel of Aquitaine* (3–6). Series: Royal Diaries. 2002, Scholastic $10.95 (0-439-16484-2). 192pp. Eleanor's fictional diary details her daily life in the 12th century — as a child and later as a queen — giving readers a good sense of her times. (Rev: BL 2/1/03; HBG 3/03; SLJ 1/03)

2389 Hautzig, Esther. *A Picture of Grandmother* (3–5). Illus. by Beth Peck. 2002, Farrar $15.00 (0-374-35920-2). 96pp. The lifestyle of a wealthy Jewish family in prewar Poland, portrayed in detail, plays an important role in this story of a girl discovering a family secret. (Rev: BCCB 12/02; BL 10/1/02; HBG 3/03; SLJ 10/02)

2390 Jorgensen, Norman. *In Flanders Fields* (4–7). Illus. by Brian Harrison-Lever. 2002, Fremantle Arts Centre $22.95 (1-86368-369-0). During a Christmas Day ceasefire in the World War I trenches, a soldier rescues a trapped robin. (Rev: SLJ 2/03)

2391 Lasky, Kathryn. *Mary, Queen of Scots: Queen Without a Country* (5–8). Illus. Series: Royal Diaries. 2002, Scholastic $10.95 (0-439-19404-0). 224pp. Part of the Royal Diary series, this is a fictional diary of the year 1553, when Mary was betrothed to the son of King Henry II of France. (Rev: BL 5/15/02; HBG 10/02; SLJ 6/02)

2392 Lawrence, Caroline. *The Secrets of Vesuvius* (4–6). 2002, Millbrook LB $22.90 (0-7613-2603-0).

192pp. Clever teen detective Flavia and her friends continue to solve mysteries in ancient Rome in this sequel to *The Thieves of Ostia* (2002) in which Pliny makes a cameo appearance and Vesuvius erupts. (Rev: BL 11/1/02; HBG 3/03; SLJ 11/02)

2393 Lawrence, Caroline. *The Thieves of Ostia: A Roman Mystery* (5–7). 2002, Millbrook LB $22.90 (0-7613-2602-2). 160pp. This fast-paced mystery set in early Rome finds a young sleuth named Flavia Gemina and her friends searching for an animal killer. (Rev: BL 3/15/02*; HBG 10/02; SLJ 5/02*)

2394 Lewin, Waldtraut. *Freedom Beyond the Sea* (5–9). 2001, Delacorte $15.95 (0-385-32705-6). 265pp. Esther, a Jewish girl, disguises herself as a cabin boy on the *Santa Maria* to escape the Spanish Inquisition in this novel set in 1492. (Rev: BCCB 12/01; BL 9/15/01; HB 11–12/01; HBG 3/02; SLJ 1/02)

2395 Moss, Marissa. *Galen: My Life in Imperial Rome* (3–6). Illus. 2002, Harcourt $15.00 (0-15-216535-5). 48pp. Historically accurate details about life in the house of Roman Emperor Augustus are revealed through the eyes of a fictitious Greek slave in a gripping text accompanied by maps, glossary, and captioned illustrations. (Rev: BL 12/15/02; HBG 3/03; SLJ 10/02)

2396 Weston, Carol. *Melanie Martin Goes Dutch* (3–6). 2002, Knopf LB $17.99 (0-375-92195-8). 224pp. Melanie's diary of her trip to the Netherlands with her family and friend Cecily reveals a gradual growth to maturity. (Rev: BL 6/1–15/02; HBG 10/02; SLJ 5/02)

2397 Whelan, Gloria. *Angel on the Square* (5–9). 2001, HarperCollins LB $15.89 (0-06-029031-5). 304pp. The Russian Revolution, World War, and social upheaval totally change life for privileged young Katya, who learns to adapt in this story that starts in 1913. (Rev: BL 9/15/01; HBG 3/02; SLJ 10/01)

2398 Whelan, Gloria. *The Impossible Journey* (5–8). 2003, HarperCollins LB $16.89 (0-06-623812-9). 256pp. A 13-year-old girl named Marya and her younger brother journey to Siberia to find their exiled mother in this book set in Stalin's Russia that includes lots of historical detail. (Rev: BL 12/15/02; HB 3–4/03; SLJ 1/03)

2399 Zucker, N. F. *Benno's Bear* (4–7). 2001, Dutton $16.99 (0-525-46521-9). 256pp. Benno, a young pickpocket in Central Europe, is taken in by a kind family who help him discover the joys of reading. (Rev: BCCB 12/01; BL 11/15/01; HB 11–12/01; HBG 3/02; SLJ 10/01)

Great Britain and Ireland

2400 Almond, David. *Counting Stars* (5–9). 2002, Delacorte LB $18.99 (0-385-90034-1). 205pp. In a series of vignettes based on personal experience, a man recalls growing up in a poor mining town in northern England. (Rev: BCCB 3/02; BL 1/1/02; HB 3–4/02; HBG 10/02; SLJ 3/02)

2401 Avi. *Crispin: The Cross of Lead* (5–9). 2002, Hyperion LB $16.49 (0-7868-2647-9). 261pp. Thirteen-year-old orphan Crispin seeks protection from a juggler named Bear in this complex novel set in medieval England. Newbery Award winner, 2003. (Rev: BL 5/15/02; HB 9–10/02; HBG 3/03; SLJ 6/02*)

2402 Dalton, Annie. *Isabel: Taking Wing* (3–7). Series: Girls of Many Lands. 2002, Pleasant $12.95 (1-58485-593-2); paper $7.95 (1-58485-517-7). 178pp. A rebellious Isabel, 12, is sent from London to the country to live with an aunt who turns out to be really interesting, with the result that a more mature and capable Isabel returns home to deal with problems there in this novel set in the late 16th century, with lots of details about life at that time. (Rev: BL 11/1/02; HBG 3/03; SLJ 10/02)

2403 Griffin, Margot. *Dancing for Danger: A Meggy Tale* (4–6). Illus. 2001, Stoddart $6.95 (0-7737-6136-5). 112pp. Meggy shows real bravery when her forbidden "hedge school" is under threat in 19th-century Ireland. (Rev: BL 6/1–15/01; SLJ 2/02)

2404 Kirwan, Anna. *Victoria: May Blossom of Britannia* (5–8). Series: Royal Diaries. 2001, Scholastic $10.95 (0-439-21598-6). 224pp. Young Victoria's fictional diary describes her over-regimented life at the ages of 10 and 11; background material adds some historical context to this account of the girl who grew up to rule England. (Rev: BL 12/1/01; HBG 10/02; SLJ 1/02)

2405 Lawrence, Iain. *The Buccaneers* (5–8). 2001, Delacorte $15.95 (0-385-32736-6). 232pp. In this final volume in the trilogy that began with *The Wreckers* and *The Smugglers*, 16-year-old John Spencer and his captain rescue a castaway and appear headed for disaster. (Rev: BCCB 7–8/01; BL 5/15/01; HBG 3/02)

2406 Lawrence, Iain. *Lord of the Nutcracker Men* (5–9). 2001, Delacorte $15.95 (0-385-72924-3). 196pp. Ten-year-old Johnny experiences World War I through the letters and carved soldiers his father sends to him from the front lines. (Rev: BCCB 10/01; BL 11/1/01; HB 11–12/01; HBG 3/02; SLJ 11/01*)

2407 Love, Anne D. *The Puppeteer's Apprentice* (3–6). 2003, Simon & Schuster $16.95 (0-689-84424-7). 192pp. In medieval England, an orphan girl called Mouse runs away to become a puppeteer's apprentice. (Rev: BL 3/15/03)

2408 Masefield, John. *Jim Davis: A High-Sea Adventure* (5–8). 2002, Scholastic $15.95 (0-439-40436-3). 224pp. This story about 12-year-old Jim and his adventures with smugglers is set in early-19th-century England and was originally published in 1911. (Rev: BL 11/15/02; HBG 3/03)

2409 Vogiel, Eva. *Friend or Foe?* (5–8). 2001, Judaica $19.95 (1-880582-66-X). 269pp. In this novel set in London during 1948, the girls of the Migdal Binoh School for Orthodox Jewish girls notice strange happenings when the Campbell family moves next door. (Rev: BL 4/1/01)

Latin America

2410 Cohn, Diana. *Dream Carver* (3–6). Illus. by Amy Cordova. 2002, Chronicle $15.95 (0-8118-1244-8). 32pp. A simple story based on the career of the artist Manuel Jimenez, about a young sculptor who carves small wooden animals but dreams of creating big, colorful animals. (Rev: BCCB 10/02; BL 6/1–15/02; HBG 10/02; SLJ 7/02)

2411 Ibbotson, Eva. *Journey to the River Sea* (5–8). 2002, Dutton $17.99 (0-525-46739-4). 336pp. Orphaned Maia journeys from 1910 London to live with relatives in Brazil in this complex story that involves an unwelcoming family, a beloved governess, a child actor, a runaway, and the wonders of Brazil, all presented with a mix of drama and humor. (Rev: BCCB 4/02; BL 12/15/01; HB 1–2/02; HBG 10/02; SLJ 1/02*)

2412 Zoehfeld, Kathleen Weidner. *Amazon Fever* (2–4). Illus. by Paulette Bogan. 2001, Golden Books LB $11.99 (0-307-46407-5); paper $3.99 (0-307-26407-6). 48pp. When Jeff accompanies his Uncle Roy to the Amazon jungle, he is thrilled by his close encounter with nature. (Rev: BL 10/15/01)

United States

NATIVE AMERICANS

2413 Bruchac, Joseph. *The Journal of Jesse Smoke: The Trail of Tears, 1838* (5–8). Illus. Series: My Name Is America. 2001, Scholastic $10.95 (0-439-12197-3). 206pp. Jesse, a 16-year-old Cherokee, chronicles in his diary the tribe's forced journey to Oklahoma and tries to understand the reasons behind this cruel action. (Rev: BL 7/01; HBG 10/01; SLJ 7/01)

2414 Cooper, James Fenimore. *The Last of the Mohicans* (3–5). Illus. by N. C. Wyeth. 2002, Simon & Schuster $18.95 (0-689-84068-3). 54pp. The classic novel is reissued here in abridged form with the Wyeth illustrations from the 1919 edition newly photographed and reproduced. (Rev: BL 11/1/02; HBG 3/03)

2415 Kittredge, Frances. *Neeluk: An Eskimo Boy in the Days of the Whaling Ships* (3–5). Illus. by Howard Rock. 2001, Alaska Northwest paper $18.95 (0-88240-545-4). 88pp. Illustrations by an Inupiat artist combine with simple stories to present the Inupiat way of life in the late 1800s. (Rev: BL 8/01; HBG 3/02; SLJ 1/02)

2416 Matthaei, Gay, and Jewel Grutman. *The Sketchbook of Thomas Blue Eagle* (4–7). Illus. 2001, Chronicle $16.95 (0-8818-2908-1). 64pp. Through drawings and narration, the Lakota artist Thomas Blue Eagle tells how he joined Buffalo Bill's show, traveled to Europe, and made enough money to marry. (Rev: BCCB 5/01; BL 4/1/01)

2417 Rappaport, Doreen. *No More! Stories and Songs of Slave Resistance* (4–7). Illus. by Shane W. Evans. 2002, Candlewick $17.99 (0-7636-0984-6).

64pp. A collection of narratives, prose, poetry, and songs that describes the African slave experience and the various forms of rebellion that took place. (Rev: BCCB 4/02; BL 2/15/02; HB 3–4/02; HBG 10/02; SLJ 2/02*) [306.3]

2418 Shaw, Janet. *Meet Kaya: An American Girl* (3–5). Illus. by Bill Farnsworth. 2002, Pleasant $12.95 (1-58485-424-3); paper $5.95 (1-58485-423-5). 70pp. Nine-year-old Kaya is distracted from babysitting by a riding challenge and the other children of the Nez Perce tribe won't let her forget it, in this tale that includes many historical details. Also use *Kaya's Escape! A Survival Story* (2002). (Rev: BL 1/1–15/03; HBG 3/03)

2419 Smith, Cynthia Leitich. *Indian Shoes* (3–6). Illus. by Jim Madsen. 2002, HarperCollins LB $15.89 (0-06-029532-5). 80pp. In six inter-related stories, Native Americans Ray and Grandpa Halfmoon recall their lives in Oklahoma and reflect on their present-day situation in Chicago. (Rev: BCCB 9/02; BL 6/1–15/02; HBG 10/02; SLJ 5/02)

2420 Spalding, Andrea. *Solomon's Tree* (2–4). Illus. by Janet Wilson. 2002, Orca $16.95 (1-55143-217-X). 32pp. A Pacific Northwest Native American boy mourns when his beloved maple tree falls in a storm, and his uncle comforts him by teaching him to make a traditional wooden mask that celebrates the tree. (Rev: BL 1/1–15/03; HBG 3/03; SLJ 2/03)

COLONIAL PERIOD

2421 Buckey, Sarah Masters. *Enemy in the Fort* (4–7). Series: History Mysteries. 2001, Pleasant $9.95 (1-58485-307-7); paper $5.95 (1-58485-306-9). 163pp. Ten-year-old Rebecca, whose family has been separated by Abenaki Indians, solves a mystery at her New Hampshire fort. (Rev: BL 10/1/01; HBG 3/02; SLJ 12/01)

2422 Butler, Amy. *Virginia Bound* (4–7). 2003, Clarion $15.00 (0-618-24752-1). 192pp. Thirteen-year-old Rob is kidnapped in London and shipped to Virginia as an indentured servant to work on a tobacco farm in 1627. (Rev: BL 3/1/03)

2423 Couvillon, Alice, and Elizabeth Moore. *Evangeline for Children* (3–5). Illus. by Alison Davis Lyne. 2002, Pelican $14.95 (1-56554-709-8). 32pp. In this picture book for older children, the story of Evangeline and her love for Gabriel in colonial Louisiana is retold. (Rev: BL 6/1–15/02; HBG 10/02; SLJ 7/02)

2424 Hermes, Patricia. *Season of Promise* (3–6). Series: My America, Elizabeth's Jamestown Colony Diary. 2002, Scholastic $10.95 (0-439-38898-8); paper $4.95 (0-439-27206-8). 108pp. In 1611, ten-year-old Elizabeth continues to describe life in Jamestown as her twin brother Caleb returns, her father plans to remarry, and there is food to eat, although the colonial leaders are strict. (Rev: HBG 3/03; SLJ 2/03)

2425 Jaspersohn, William. *The Scrimshaw Ring* (2–4). Illus. by Vernon Thornblad. 2002, Vermont Folklife Center $15.95 (0-916718-19-0). 32pp. In this book set in 1710 New England and based on reality, an amazing thing happens to young William

Bateman — one of the pirates plundering his home gives the boy a ring that is then passed down the generations. (Rev: BL 11/15/02; SLJ 12/02)

2426 Karwoski, Gail Langer. *Surviving Jamestown: The Adventures of Young Sam Collier* (5–7). Illus. by Paul Casale. 2001, Peachtree $14.95 (1-56145-239-4); paper $8.95 (1-56145-245-9). 198pp. Full of facts, this novel tells the story of a 12-year-old English boy who sails in 1606 for the colony of Virginia, with details of the struggles the colonists faced. (Rev: HBG 10/01; SLJ 8/01)

2427 Nixon, Joan Lowery. *Maria's Story: 1773* (3–6). Series: Young Americans Colonial Williamsburg. 2001, Delacorte $9.95 (0-385-32685-8). 144pp. Based on a real colonial Williamsburg family, this story of a girl and her widowed mother who runs a printing press examines everyday life as well as political and social issues of the times. (Rev: BL 1/1–15/02; HBG 3/02; SLJ 12/01)

2428 Nixon, Joan Lowery. *Will's Story: 1771* (4–6). Series: Young Americans Colonial Williamsburg. 2001, Delacorte $9.95 (0-385-32682-3). 144pp. This is the story, based on a real person, of 12-year-old Will Pelham, who is not comfortable living in a house attached to the jail in colonial Williamsburg. (Rev: BL 8/01; HBG 10/01; SLJ 9/01)

2429 Platt, Richard. *Pirate Diary: The Journal of Jake Carpenter* (3–6). Illus. by Chris Riddell. 2001, Candlewick $17.99 (0-7636-0848-3). 64pp. Readers of the entries in 9-year-old Jake's journal for 1716 learn all about his exciting adventures fighting pirates, and will also find good historical information about conditions aboard 18th-century ships and about famous pirates. (Rev: BL 12/15/01; HBG 10/02; SLJ 12/01*)

2430 Rees, Celia. *Witch Child* (5–9). 2001, Candlewick $15.99 (0-7636-1421-1). 261pp. Young Mary Newbury keeps a journal of her voyage to the New World and the way in which the Puritan community rejects her when they mistrust her ability to heal. (Rev: BCCB 7–8/01; BL 10/15/01; HB 9–10/01; HBG 3/02; SLJ 8/01)

2431 Strickland, Brad. *The Guns of Tortuga* (5–8). 2003, Simon & Schuster paper $4.99 (0-689-85297-5). 160pp. Young Davy helps the crew of the *Aurora* defeat a band of pirates in this sequel to *Mutiny!* (Rev: BL 2/1/03; SLJ 3/03)

2432 Strickland, Brad, and Thomas E. Fuller. *Mutiny!* (5–8). 2002, Simon & Schuster paper $4.99 (0-689-85296-7). 208pp. Fourteen-year-old orphan Davy arrives in Jamaica to live with his Uncle Patch, only to find himself embroiled in a daring and complex effort to capture Caribbean pirates in a story embellished with interesting facts about the 1680s. (Rev: BL 12/1/02; SLJ 11/02)

THE REVOLUTION

2433 Alsheimer, Jeanette E., and Patricia J. Friedle. *The Trouble with Tea* (5–8). 2002, Pentland $15.95 (1-57197-299-4). 208pp. When Patience visits her friend Anne in Boston in 1773, she witnesses many of the events that led to the American Revolution. (Rev: BL 6/1–15/02)

2434 Gregory, Kristiana. *We Are Patriots: Hope's Revolutionary War Diary, Book Two* (2–4). Series: My America. 2002, Scholastic $8.95 (0-439-21039-9); paper $4.99 (0-439-36906-1). 108pp. Ten-year-old Hope tells her diary the details of the war raging around Philadelphia in 1777. (Rev: HBG 10/02; SLJ 8/02)

2435 Wisler, G. Clifton. *Kings Mountain* (5–7). 2002, HarperCollins LB $15.89 (0-06-623793-9). 160pp. Fourteen-year-old Francis gets caught up in the intrigue and danger of the Revolutionary War when he is sent to South Carolina to help his grandmother run her tavern. Maps and a chronology add context. (Rev: BL 3/15/02; HBG 10/02; SLJ 7/02)

THE YOUNG NATION, 1789–1861

2436 Armstrong, Jennifer. *Thomas Jefferson: Letters from a Philadelphia Bookworm* (5–8). Illus. Series: Dear Mr. President. 2001, Winslow $8.95 (1-890817-30-9). 128pp. Twelve-year-old Amelia and President Jefferson discuss the events of the times in a continuing exchange of letters. (Rev: BL 5/15/01; HBG 10/01; SLJ 6/01)

2437 Atkins, Jeannine. *Becoming Little Women: Louisa May at Fruitlands* (4–6). Illus. 2001, Putnam $16.99 (0-399-23619-8). 176pp. Based on factual sources such as letters and diaries, this novel explores the life of Louisa May Alcott as an 11-year-old, when her father moved the family to an experimental farm called Fruitlands. (Rev: BL 11/15/01; HB 9–10/01; HBG 3/02; SLJ 10/01)

2438 Ayres, Katherine. *Stealing South: A Story of the Underground Railroad* (5–8). 2001, Delacorte $14.95 (0-385-72912-X). 208pp. In pre-Civil War days, 16-year-old Will pretends to be a peddler in Kentucky to help with the escape of two slaves via the Underground Railroad. (Rev: BL 4/1/01; HBG 10/01; SLJ 6/01)

2439 Crook, Connie Brummel. *Laura Secord's Brave Walk* (2–5). Illus. by June Lawrason. 2001, Second Story $14.95 (1-896764-34-7). During the War of 1812, Laura Secord hears American soldiers' plans to attack at Beavers Dam, and sets off on a dangerous journey to warn the British in this novel with realistic battlefield illustrations. (Rev: SLJ 7/01)

2440 Dahlberg, Maurine F. *The Spirit and Gilly Bucket* (5–8). 2002, Farrar $16.00 (0-374-31677-5). 192pp. Eleven-year-old Gilly longs to join her father in his search for gold, but must stay in Virginia on a plantation where she befriends a young slave and helps her escape via the Underground Railroad in this novel full of suspense and surprises. (Rev: BL 1/1–15/03; HBG 3/03; SLJ 12/02)

2441 Duey, Kathleen. *Zellie Blake: Lowell, Massachusetts, 1834* (4–6). Series: American Diaries. 2002, Simon & Schuster paper $4.99 (0-689-84405-0). 133pp. Twelve-year-old Zellie is an African American orphan who relates through her diary her dislike of her job at a boarding house in the mill town of Lowell and her pleasure when she finds a better situation. (Rev: SLJ 10/02)

2442 Frederick, Heather Vogel. *The Voyage of Patience Goodspeed* (4–6). 2002, Simon & Schuster $16.00 (0-689-84851-X). 224pp. Patience, a 12-year-old girl, and her younger brother experience a number of amazing adventures when they join their widower father on a whaling voyage. (Rev: BL 6/1–15/02; HB 9–10/02; HBG 3/03; SLJ 7/02)

2443 Garland, Sherry. *In the Shadow of the Alamo* (5–8). Series: Great Episodes. 2001, Harcourt $17.00 (0-15-201744-5). 282pp. Fifteen-year-old Lorenzo Bonifacio, a conscript in the Mexican army of Santa Ana, describes the harsh life of the soldiers and the family members who follow them on the trek to Texas and the battle of the Alamo. (Rev: BCCB 1/02; BL 10/15/01; HB 11–12/01; HBG 3/02; SLJ 12/01)

2444 Hausman, Gerald. *Tom Cringle: The Pirate and the Patriot* (4–8). Illus. by Tad Hills. 2001, Simon & Schuster $16.00 (0-689-82811-X). 160pp. Tom Cringle, a 14-year-old lieutenant in the Royal Navy, fights pirates, braves storms, and conquers slave traders in this sequel to *Tom Cringle: Battle on the High Seas* (2000). (Rev: BL 9/15/01; HBG 3/02; SLJ 10/01)

2445 Kimball, K. M. *The Star-Spangled Secret* (4–6). 2001, Simon & Schuster paper $4.99 (0-689-84550-2). 240pp. In this historical mystery set in 1814, 13-year-old Caroline and an indentured servant head to the docks of Baltimore harbor to disprove claims that her brother, a deckhand, drowned. (Rev: BL 11/1/01; SLJ 11/01)

2446 Kroll, Steven. *John Quincy Adams: Letters from a Southern Planter's Son* (4–6). Illus. Series: Dear Mr. President. 2001, Winslow $9.95 (1-890817-93-7). 122pp. A fictional correspondence between a young boy and President John Quincy Adams details historical events and gives insight into Adams's character and concerns. (Rev: BL 1/1–15/02; HBG 3/02; SLJ 12/01)

2447 Lunn, Janet. *Laura Secord: A Story of Courage* (3–6). Illus. by Maxwell Newhouse. 2002, Tundra $16.95 (0-88776-538-6). Lunn's text and the accompanying illustrations give drama to the story of Secord's trek to warn the British during the War of 1812. (Rev: HB 3–4/02; HBG 10/02; SLJ 4/02)

2448 McCully, Emily Arnold. *The Battle for St. Michaels* (2–4). Illus. Series: An I Can Read Chapter Book. 2002, HarperCollins LB $17.89 (0-06-028729-2). 64pp. Nine-year-old Caroline helps save her Maryland town from the British in this story set during the War of 1812. (Rev: BL 9/15/02; HBG 3/03; SLJ 9/02)

2449 Myers, Laurie. *Lewis and Clark and Me: A Dog's Tale* (3–6). Illus. by Michael Dooling. 2002, Holt $16.95 (0-8050-6368-4). 64pp. The Lewis and Clark expedition told from the point of view of Seaman, Lewis's Newfoundland dog, with excerpts from Lewis's journal, illustrations and a map of the route. (Rev: BL 9/1/02; HB 9–10/02; HBG 3/03; SLJ 9/02)

2450 Nordan, Robert. *The Secret Road* (5–9). 2001, Holiday $16.95 (0-8234-1543-0). 144pp. Young Laura helps an escaped slave on a long and suspenseful journey to freedom by posing as her sister. (Rev: BL 9/15/01; HBG 3/02; SLJ 10/01)

2451 Robinet, Harriette Gillem. *Twelve Travelers, Twenty Horses* (4–7). 2003, Simon & Schuster $16.95 (0-689-84561-8). 208pp. Ten slaves band together to foil their master's plan to prevent the delivery of a crucial message as they travel to California in 1860. (Rev: BL 2/15/03; SLJ 2/03)

2452 Schneider, Mical. *Annie Quinn in America* (5–9). 2001, Carolrhoda $15.95 (1-57505-510-4). 252pp. In 1847, young Annie and her brother travel from Ireland, a land ravaged by the potato famine, to America, a land fraught with dangers of its own. (Rev: BL 11/15/01; HBG 3/02; SLJ 9/01)

2453 Trottier, Maxine. *Under a Shooting Star* (5–8). Series: The Circle of Silver Chronicles. 2002, Stoddart paper $7.95 (0-7737-6228-0). 212pp. During the War of 1812, a 15-year-old boy who is half English and half Oneida Indian struggles with conflicting loyalties as he tries to protect the two American girls he is escorting. (Rev: SLJ 5/02)

2454 Wait, Lea. *Seaward Born* (4–7). 2003, Simon & Schuster $16.95 (0-689-84719-X). 160pp. Michael, a young slave, makes a dangerous journey to Canada and freedom in this dramatic historical novel. (Rev: BL 2/15/03; SLJ 1/03)

2455 Wait, Lea. *Stopping to Home* (4–7). 2001, Simon & Schuster $16.00 (0-689-83832-8). 160pp. When 11-year-old Abbie's mother dies of smallpox and her father disappears, Abbie takes a job as a housemaid to provide for herself and her young brother in this story set in early-19th-century Maine. (Rev: BCCB 12/01; BL 11/15/01; HB 1–2/02; HBG 3/02; SLJ 10/01)

2456 Whelan, Gloria. *Fruitlands: Louisa May Alcott Made Perfect* (4–6). 2002, HarperCollins LB $17.89 (0-06-623816-1). 128pp. A young Louisa May Alcott documents the time her family spent at Fruitlands farm, a utopian experiment, in two sets of diaries — one for herself, one for her parents' consumption — that are based on Alcott's original diaries. (Rev: BL 11/1/02; HB 9–10/02; HBG 3/03; SLJ 10/02)

2457 Wood, Frances M. *Daughter of Madrugada* (4–7). 2002, Delacorte $15.95 (0-385-32719-6). 192pp. Thirteen-year-old Cesa describes her privileged life in 1840s California, even as the social landscape is changing with the arrival of gold miners and as she herself faces pressures to abandon her tomboy freedom. (Rev: BCCB 6/02; BL 5/15/02; HBG 10/02; SLJ 5/02)

2458 Wyeth, Sharon Dennis. *Flying Free: Corey's Underground Railroad Diary* (2–4). Illus. Series: My America. 2002, Scholastic $8.95 (0-439-24443-9); paper $4.99 (0-439-36908-8). 112pp. In diary form, this novel traces the travels of Corey, a black boy, and his family to freedom in Canada via the Underground Railroad. (Rev: BL 6/1–15/02; HBG 10/02; SLJ 8/02)

2459 Wyeth, Sharon Dennis. *Freedom's Wings: Corey's Diary, Kentucky to Ohio, 1857* (3–6). Series: My America. 2001, Scholastic $8.95 (0-439-14100-1). 108pp. Wyeth interweaves fact and fic-

tion in this diary of a young slave's daily life in Kentucky and dangerous escape via the Underground Railroad. (Rev: HBG 10/01; SLJ 6/01)

PIONEERS AND WESTWARD EXPANSION

2460 Avi. *Prairie School* (2–4). Illus. by Bill Farnsworth. Series: An I Can Read Chapter Book. 2001, HarperCollins LB $14.89 (0-06-027665-7). 48pp. In Colorado during the 1880s, young Noah learns the value of learning how to read in this easy chapter book. (Rev: BCCB 5/01; BL 4/15/01; HBG 10/01; SLJ 5/01)

2461 Calvert, Patricia. *Betrayed!* (5–8). 2002, Simon & Schuster $16.00 (0-689-83472-1). 224pp. Tyler Bohannon of *Bigger* (1994) and *Sooner* (1998) is back, this time traveling west, where he is taken captive by Sioux Indians. (Rev: BL 7/02; HBG 10/02; SLJ 6/02)

2462 Cannon, A. E. *Charlotte's Rose* (5–8). 2002, Random LB $17.99 (0-385-90057-0). 144pp. Thirteen-year-old Charlotte and her father make a difficult journey from Wales to Utah with a group of Mormons in 1856 in a narrative that presents religion as an integral part of life. (Rev: BCCB 1/03; BL 10/1/02; HB 11–12/02; HBG 3/03; SLJ 9/02)

2463 Collier, James Lincoln. *Wild Boy* (5–8). 2002, Marshall Cavendish $15.95 (0-7614-5126-9). 160pp. After knocking his father out during an argument, 12-year-old Jesse runs away from his frontier home to live in the mountains, where he has many adventures, learns many skills, and reflects on his own characteristics before finally deciding to return home in this story that appears to be set in the 19th century. (Rev: BL 11/1/02; SLJ 11/02)

2464 Cullen, Lynn. *Nelly in the Wilderness* (5–8). 2002, HarperCollins LB $15.89 (0-06-029134-6). 192pp. Set in the Indiana frontier of 1821, 12-year-old Nelly and her brother, Cornelius, must adjust to a new stepmother after their beloved Ma dies. (Rev: BCCB 5/02; BL 4/1/02; HB 7–8/02; HBG 10/02; SLJ 2/02)

2465 Ellsworth, Loretta. *The Shrouding Woman* (4–8). 2002, Holt $16.95 (0-8050-6651-9). 160pp. in this novel set in 19th-century Minnesota, 11-year-old Evie resists the efforts of her Aunt Flo ("the shrouding woman") to take care of her after Evie's mother dies. (Rev: BCCB 9/02; BL 5/15/02; HBG 10/02; SLJ 4/02)

2466 Garland, Sherry. *Valley of the Moon: The Diary of Rosalia de Milagros* (5–8). Illus. 2001, Scholastic $10.95 (0-439-08820-8). 224pp. Rosalia, a 13-year-old orphan, keeps a diary about working on a California ranch in 1846. (Rev: BL 4/1/01; HBG 3/02; SLJ 4/01)

2467 Gregory, Kristiana. *Seeds of Hope: The Gold Rush Diary of Susanna Fairchild* (4–8). 2001, Scholastic $10.95 (0-590-51157-2). 182pp. After Susanna's mother dies in 1849, the 14-year-old takes over her journal and describes the hardships she and her sisters face when their father decides to move the family to California in search of gold. (Rev: BL 9/1/01; HBG 10/01; SLJ 7/01)

2468 Hermes, Patricia. *A Perfect Place: Joshua's Oregon Trail Diary* (3–5). Series: My America. 2002, Scholastic $10.95 (0-439-19999-9); paper $4.99 (0-439-38900-3). 112pp. In this sequel to *Westward to Home* (2000), 9-year-old Joshua records the difficult conditions in the Willamette Valley as winter closes in. (Rev: BL 1/1–15/03; HBG 3/03; SLJ 11/02)

2469 Holm, Jennifer L. *Boston Jane: An Adventure* (5–8). 2001, HarperCollins LB $16.89 (0-06-028739-X). 288pp. A well-bred young woman faces hardships as she searches the 19th-century Washington Territory for her lost fiancé. (Rev: BL 9/1/01; HB 9–10/01; HBG 3/02; SLJ 8/01)

2470 Holm, Jennifer L. *Boston Jane: Wilderness Days* (5–8). 2002, HarperCollins LB $18.89 (0-06-029044-7). 256pp. Jane's continued adventures in 1854 Washington Territory include helping to stop a murderer and adjusting to the hardships of pioneer life. (Rev: BL 9/1/02; HB 9–10/02; HBG 3/03; SLJ 10/02)

2471 Hopkinson, Deborah. *Cabin in the Snow* (2–4). Series: Prairie Skies. 2002, Simon & Schuster LB $11.89 (0-689-84352-6); paper $3.99 (0-689-84351-8). 80pp. Charlie must care for his pregnant mother while his father is away in this story set in Kansas during the free-state movement. (Rev: BL 12/15/02; HBG 3/03; SLJ 1/03)

2472 Hopkinson, Deborah. *Our Kansas Home* (3–5). Illus. by Patrick Faricy. Series: Prairie Skies. 2003, Simon & Schuster paper $3.99 (0-689-84353-4). 80pp. In this final volume in the trilogy, Charlie and his father tangle with pro-slavery ruffians and Charlie helps a runaway slave. (Rev: BL 3/1/03; SLJ 3/03)

2473 Hopkinson, Deborah. *Pioneer Summer* (2–4). Illus. by Patrick Faricy. Series: Prairie Skies. 2002, Simon & Schuster LB $15.00 (0-689-84350-X); paper $3.99 (0-689-84349-6). 64pp. Charlie Keller, his family, and other abolitionists travel to Kansas to prevent it from becoming a slave-holding state in this rich historical novel. (Rev: BL 5/1/02; HBG 10/02; SLJ 10/02)

2474 Hurst, Carol Otis. *In Plain Sight* (4–6). 2002, Houghton $15.00 (0-618-19699-4). 160pp. Sarah's father leaves the family in Massachusetts as he sets off to find gold in the West, and Sarah must take on many responsibilities to help her mother. (Rev: BCCB 3/02; BL 3/1/02; HB 5–6/02; HBG 10/02; SLJ 3/02)

2475 Kimmel, E. Cody. *The Adventures of Young Buffalo Bill: In the Eye of the Storm* (3–7). Series: Adventures of Young Buffalo Bill. 2003, Harper-Collins LB $16.89 (0-06-029116-8). 144pp. At the age of nine, young Bill must look after the Kansas homestead in his father's absence and feels resentment against these heavy duties. (Rev: BL 1/1–15/03; SLJ 2/03)

2476 Kimmel, E. Cody. *One Sky Above Us* (3–6). Series: Adventures of Young Buffalo Bill. 2002, HarperCollins LB $17.89 (0-06-029120-6). 208pp. Young Buffalo Bill learns some hard lessons when his family moves to troubled Kansas Territory in the 1850s. (Rev: BL 9/1/02; SLJ 11/02)

2477 Kimmel, E. Cody. *To the Frontier* (3–6). Series: Adventures of Young Buffalo Bill. 2002, HarperCollins LB $15.89 (0-06-029118-4). 208pp. In 1854, 8-year-old Bill Cody travels with his family from Iowa to Kansas Territory to start a new life. (Rev: BL 6/1–15/02; HBG 10/02; SLJ 9/02)

2478 Kirkpatrick, Katherine. *The Voyage of the Continental* (5–8). 2002, Holiday $16.95 (0-8234-1580-5). 297pp. A 17-year-old girl relates in her diary the events of her journey by ship from New England to Seattle in 1866, which involve her in adventure, mystery, and romance. (Rev: BL 12/15/02; HBG 3/03; SLJ 11/02)

2479 Lawson, Julie. *Destination Gold!* (5–8). 2001, Orca $16.95 (1-55143-155-6). 210pp. Ned, Catherine, and Sarah are all on their way to the Klondike in 1897, spurred by different motivations, but their stories all come together in an exciting climax, made more realistic by the background information and maps provided. (Rev: BCCB 4/01; HBG 10/01; SLJ 7/01)

2480 Levine, Ellen. *The Journal of Jedediah Barstow: An Emigrant on the Oregon Trail* (4–7). Series: My Name Is America. 2002, Scholastic $10.95 (0-439-06310-8). 176pp. Jedediah continues his mother's journal about their experiences on the Oregon Trail after she and the rest of his family are drowned while crossing a river. (Rev: BL 2/15/03; SLJ 11/02)

2481 Levitin, Sonia. *Clem's Chances* (4–7). 2001, Scholastic $17.95 (0-439-29314-6). 200pp. Fourteen-year-old Clem becomes acquainted with the hardships and rewards of frontier life when he travels to California to find his father in 1860. (Rev: BL 9/15/01; HB 11–12/01; HBG 3/02; SLJ 10/01)

2482 McMullan, Kate. *As Far as I Can See: Meg's Prairie Diary* (2–4). Series: My America. 2002, Scholastic $10.95 (0-439-42517-4); paper $4.99 (0-439-40321-9). 112pp. City girl Meg describes her new life in Kansas, where she and her brother have been sent to avoid a cholera epidemic in 1856, and writes about the help she gives to a runaway slave. (Rev: BL 10/1/02; HBG 3/03; SLJ 8/02)

2483 Murphy, Jim. *My Face to the Wind: The Diary of Sarah Jane Price, a Prairie Teacher* (5–8). Series: Dear America. 2001, Scholastic $10.95 (0-590-43810-7). 192pp. To avoid being sent to an orphanage, 12-year-old Jessica pretends to be 16 and takes over her father's job as teacher in a 19th-century Nebraska town. (Rev: BL 12/1/01; HBG 3/02; SLJ 12/01)

2484 Philbrick, Rodman. *The Journal of Douglas Allen Deeds: The Donner Party Expedition* (5–7). Series: My Name Is America. 2001, Scholastic $10.95 (0-439-21600-1). 160pp. A fictional account of the Donner Party's hardships as written in a 15-year-old orphaned boy's journal. (Rev: BL 1/1–15/02; HBG 3/02; SLJ 12/01)

2485 Reichart, George. *A Bag of Lucky Rice* (4–6). Illus. by Mark Mitchell. 2002, Godine $17.95 (1-56792-166-3). 158pp. This humorous Old West mystery about treasure buried in the desert skillfully entwines facts about the times. (Rev: BL 10/15/02; SLJ 2/03)

2486 Reiss, Kathryn. *Riddle of the Prairie Bride* (5–7). Series: History Mysteries. 2001, Pleasant paper $5.95 (1-58485-309-3). 170pp. Ida Kate discovers that her father's mail-order bride is actually an impostor. (Rev: BL 4/1/01; HBG 3/02; SLJ 5/01)

2487 Rylant, Cynthia. *Old Town in the Green Groves: Laura Ingalls Wilder's Last Little House Years* (3–7). Illus. by Jim LaMarche. 2002, HarperCollins $15.95 (0-06-029562-7). 176pp. Using notes left by Wilder, Cynthia Rylant has created a novel that fills the gaps found in the Little House series. (Rev: BL 5/1/02; HBG 10/02; SLJ 4/02)

2488 Schultz, Jan Neubert. *Horse Sense* (5–7). 2001, Carolrhoda $15.95 (1-57505-998-3); paper $6.95 (1-57505-999-1). 180pp. Fourteen-year-old Will and his father do not get along, but they join a posse tracking dangerous outlaws in this adventure based on a true story. (Rev: BL 8/01; HBG 3/02; SLJ check)

2489 Seeley, Debra. *Grasslands* (5–8). 2002, Holiday $16.95 (0-8234-1731-X). 128pp. The hard life on the prairie disappoints a 13-year-old newcomer from Virginia until he has the chance to ride as a cowboy in this novel set in the late 19th century. (Rev: BL 11/1/02; HBG 3/03; SLJ 1/03)

2490 Yep, Laurence. *When the Circus Came to Town* (3–5). Illus. by Suling Wang. 2001, HarperCollins LB $14.89 (0-06-029326-8). 128pp. After her face is scarred by smallpox, 10-year-old Ursula refuses to leave her home at a Montana stagecoach station and intervention by a circus arranged by the family's Chinese cook is required to bring her out of her shell. (Rev: BCCB 2/02; BL 12/15/01; HBG 10/02; SLJ 12/01)

THE CIVIL WAR

2491 Crisp, Marty. *Private Captain: A Story of Gettysburg* (4–8). 2001, Philomel $18.99 (0-399-23577-9). 293pp. Ben, 12, and his dog, Captain, travel to find Ben's brother, who is fighting in the Civil War, and persuade him to come home. (Rev: BCCB 3/01; BL 4/1/01; HBG 10/01; SLJ 4/01)

2492 Harness, Cheryl. *Ghosts of the Civil War* (3–5). Illus. by author. 2002, Simon & Schuster $17.00 (0-689-83135-8). 48pp. Lindsey attends a reenactment with her parents and is transported back in time by the ghost of Willie Lincoln in this excellent and attractive introduction to the Civil War. (Rev: BL 1/1–15/02; HBG 10/02; SLJ 1/02)

2493 Keehn, Sally M. *Anna Sunday* (4–8). 2002, Putnam $18.99 (0-399-23875-1). 272pp. In 1863, 12-year-old Anna travels with her younger brother from Pennsylvania to Virginia to find her wounded father. (Rev: BCCB 9/02; BL 6/1–15/02; HBG 10/02; SLJ 6/02)

2494 Lewin, Ted. *Red Legs: A Drummer Boy in the Civil War* (3–5). Illus. 2001, HarperCollins $15.95 (0-688-16024-7). 32pp. A drummer boy dies in a volley of gunfire in this story that is in reality a modern-day re-enactment of the event. (Rev: BL 4/1/01; HBG 10/01; SLJ 6/01)

2495 Matas, Carol. *The War Within* (5–8). 2001, Simon & Schuster $16.00 (0-689-82935-3). 151pp. The story of a 13-year-old Jewish southern girl and her family during the Civil War is told through diary entries. (Rev: BL 4/1/01; HBG 10/01; SLJ 6/01)

2496 Pinkney, Andrea Davis. *Abraham Lincoln: Letters from a Slave Girl* (4–7). Illus. Series: Dear Mr. President. 2001, Winslow $8.95 (1-890817-60-0). 136pp. Twelve-year-old Lettie Tucker, a slave, exchanges thought-provoking letters with President Abraham Lincoln in this story set in the 1860s packed with interesting illustrations. (Rev: BCCB 2/02; BL 9/1/01; HBG 3/02; SLJ 9/01)

2497 Rinaldi, Ann. *Girl in Blue* (5–8). 2001, Scholastic $15.95 (0-439-07336-7). 320pp. A first-person novel about Sarah, who disguises herself as a boy and joins the Union Army. (Rev: BCCB 6/01; BL 4/1/01; HBG 10/01)

2498 Thomas, Carroll. *Blue Creek Farm* (4–8). 2001, Smith & Kraus paper $9.95 (1-57525-243-0). 185pp. In Kansas of the 1860s, Matty Trescott and her father manage a farm and feel the effects of the Civil War. (Rev: BL 4/1/01)

RECONSTRUCTION TO WORLD WAR II, 1865–1941

2499 Alexander, Lloyd. *The Gawgon and the Boy* (5–7). 2001, Dutton $17.99 (0-525-46677-0). 256pp. Set in 1920s Philadelphia, this is the story of a young boy who is encouraged in his love of art by a fierce aunt, nicknamed "the Gawgon." (Rev: BCCB 6/01; BL 5/15/01; HB 7–8/01; HBG 10/01; SLJ 4/01*)

2500 Atwell, Debby. *Pearl* (K–3). Illus. 2001, Houghton $16.00 (0-395-88416-0). 32pp. Pearl, a woman in her 90s, covers a substantial part of American history in her reminiscences, which stretch from her grandfather's encounter with George Washington through World Wars I and II and her hope that her great-granddaughter might someday go to the moon. (Rev: BCCB 4/01; BL 5/1/01; HBG 10/01; SLJ 6/01)

2501 Avi. *The Secret School* (3–6). 2001, Harcourt $16.00 (0-15-216375-1). 153pp. Rather than risking her future education, 14-year-old Ida Bidson takes over as teacher and runs a secret school when the one-room schoolhouse in their mountain district is suddenly closed in 1925. (Rev: BCCB 10/01; HB 11–12/01; HBG 3/02; SLJ 9/01)

2502 Avi. *Silent Movie* (K–3). Illus. by C. B. Mordan. 2003, Simon & Schuster $16.95 (0-689-84145-0). 48pp. In black-and-white silent-movie format, this is the story of an immigrant mother and son arriving in America in the early 20th century, the difficulties they have finding Papa, and the near-miraculous reunion. (Rev: BL 3/1/03*; HB 3–4/03; SLJ 3/03)

2503 Ayres, Katherine. *Macaroni Boy* (5–8). 2003, Delacorte $15.95 (0-385-73016-0). 176pp. Sixth-grader Mike is living in Pittsburgh during the

Depression and has many worries: lack of money, a bully who calls him "Macaroni Boy," and the possible connection between dying rats and his grandfather's illness. (Rev: BCCB 3/03; BL 1/1–15/03; SLJ 2/03)

2504 Beard, Darleen Bailey. *The Babbs Switch Story* (5–8). 2002, Farrar $16.00 (0-374-30475-0). 176pp. A young girl saves her sister from a fire on Christmas Eve in 1924 in this fictional account of a real event. (Rev: BL 3/15/02; HBG 10/02; SLJ 3/02)

2505 Bornstein, Ruth Lercher. *Butterflies and Lizards, Beryl and Me* (5–7). 2002, Marshall Cavendish $14.95 (0-7614-5118-8). 160pp. Eleven-year-old Charley befriends an odd woman named Beryl while her mother works hard to make it through the Great Depression. (Rev: BL 5/15/02; HBG 10/02; SLJ 5/02)

2506 Buchanan, Jane. *Hank's Story* (3–6). 2001, Farrar $16.00 (0-374-32836-6). 144pp. Orphaned Hank tries to escape his brutal foster parents in this novel set in 1923 Nebraska. (Rev: BCCB 6/01; BL 4/1/01; HBG 10/01; SLJ 5/01)

2507 Burleigh, Robert. *Into the Air: The Story of the Wright Brothers' First Flight* (5–8). Illus. by Bill Wylie. Series: American Heroes. 2002, Harcourt paper $6.00 (0-15-216803-6). A high-interest, comic-book presentation of the first flight with fictionalized dialogue. (Rev: HBG 3/03; SLJ 9/02)

2508 Byars, Betsy. *Keeper of the Doves* (5–8). 2002, Viking $14.99 (0-670-03576-9). 112pp. Young Amie McBee is a thoughtful child who loves to write and — unlike her older twin sisters — has the sensitivity to see the softer side of the mysterious Polish immigrant who lives on their estate and keeps doves in this story set at the turn of the 20th century and presented in 26 short, alphabetical chapters. (Rev: BCCB 1/03; BL 10/1/02*; HB 9–10/02*; HBG 3/03; SLJ 10/02)

2509 Cushman, Karen. *Rodzina* (5–9). 2003, Clarion $16.00 (0-618-13351-8). 224pp. On an orphan train going from Chicago to California in 1881, plucky Rodzina worries about her fate and aims to find a better life than some of the other children on the train. (Rev: BCCB 3/03; BL 3/1/03*)

2510 Dadey, Debbie. *Whistler's Hollow* (4–6). 2002, Bloomsbury $14.95 (1-58234-789-1). 104pp. Eleven-year-old Lillie Mae goes to live with a great-aunt and uncle on a Kentucky farm in 1920 and learns the truth about her father's fate. (Rev: SLJ 7/02)

2511 Duey, Kathleen. *Francesca Vigilucci: Washington, D.C., 1913* (3–6). 2000, Simon & Schuster paper $4.99 (0-689-83556-6). 128pp. Thirteen-year-old Francesca, who lives a privileged life, longs to become a reporter. (Rev: SLJ 4/01)

2512 Durbin, William. *The Journal of C. J. Jackson: A Dust Bowl Migrant, Oklahoma to California, 1935* (4–7). Series: My Name Is America. 2002, Scholastic $10.95 (0-439-15306-9). 169pp. Young C.J. Jackson chronicles his family's journey west from the Dust Bowl, portraying clearly the harsh conditions these travelers faced. (Rev: HBG 10/02; SLJ 9/02)

2513 Durbin, William. *Song of Sampo Lake* (4–7). 2002, Random LB $17.99 (0-385-90055-4). 217pp. This portrayal of a young Finnish immigrant's life in Minnesota in 1900 interweaves typical adolescent problems and joys with information on customs, culture, and geography. (Rev: BL 10/15/02; HBG 3/03; SLJ 11/02)

2514 Easton, Richard. *A Real American* (4–7). 2002, Clarion $15.00 (0-618-03339-9). 160pp. Against his father's wishes, 11-year-old Nathan befriends Arturo, the son of Italian immigrants newly arrived in a Pennsylvania coal-mining town. (Rev: BCCB 9/02; BL 5/15/02; SLJ 3/02)

2515 Erickson, John R. *Moonshiner's Gold* (5–9). 2001, Viking $15.99 (0-670-03502-5). 176pp. Fourteen-year-old Riley becomes embroiled in exciting intrigue involving moonshiners and corruption in this novel set in Texas in the 1920s. (Rev: HBG 3/02; SLJ 8/01)

2516 Fletcher, Susan. *Walk Across the Sea* (5–9). 2001, Simon & Schuster $16.00 (0-689-84133-7). 214pp. In spite of her father's dislike of immigrants, 15-year-old Eliza Jane helps a Chinese boy who rescued her and her goat in this story set in California in the late 19th century. (Rev: BCCB 12/01; BL 11/1/01; HBG 3/02; SLJ 11/01)

2517 Fuqua, Jonathon. *Darby* (4–7). 2002, Candlewick $15.99 (0-7636-1417-3). 256pp. A 9-year-old white girl, Darby, and her family become the target of KKK violence after she protests the killing of a black sharecropper's son in 1926 South Carolina. (Rev: BCCB 7–8/02; BL 3/15/02; HB 3–4/02; HBG 10/02; SLJ 3/02)

2518 Granfield, Linda. *97 Orchard Street, New York: Stories of Immigrant Life* (3–6). Photos by Arlene Alda. 2001, Tundra paper $15.00 (0-88776-580-7). 55pp. A detailed and appealing look at the immigrant experience through the stories of families who lived in the building that is now the Lower East Side Tenement Museum, with black-and-white photographs. (Rev: SLJ 12/01) [305.9]

2519 Gray, Dianne E. *Together Apart* (5–9). 2002, Houghton $16.00 (0-618-18721-9). 208pp. After surviving the blizzard of 1888, Isaac and Hannah discover their love for each other while working for feminist publisher Eliza Moore. (Rev: BCCB 11/02; BL 9/15/02; HB 11–12/02; HBG 3/03; SLJ 12/02)

2520 Gundisch, Karin. *How I Became an American* (4–8). Trans. by James Skofield. 2001, Cricket $15.95 (0-8126-4875-7). 128pp. This is the story of Johann, a young German immigrant, who arrives in an Ohio steel town in the early 20th century. (Rev: BL 11/15/01; HBG 3/02; SLJ 12/01)

2521 Harlow, Joan Hiatt. *Joshua's Song* (5–8). 2001, Simon & Schuster $16.00 (0-689-84119-1). 192pp. Thirteen-year-old Joshua has to adjust to many changes in this story that interweaves history and fiction: his father has died in the 1918 flu epidemic, his mother is taking in boarders, and Joshua has left school and is working as a newsboy and learning a different kind of life. (Rev: BL 12/15/01; HBG 3/02; SLJ 11/01)

2522 Harris, Carol Flynn. *A Place for Joey* (4–8). 2001, Boyds Mills $15.95 (1-56397-108-9). 90pp. Twelve-year-old Joey, an Italian immigrant living in Boston in the early 20th century, learns an important lesson through a heroic act. (Rev: BL 9/1/01; HBG 3/02; SLJ 9/01)

2523 Haseley, Dennis. *The Amazing Thinking Machine* (5–7). 2002, Dial $15.99 (0-8037-2609-0). 128pp. Brothers Patrick and Roy invent an "amazing thinking machine" to amuse themselves while they wait for their father's return from his search for work in this novel set in the Great Depression. (Rev: BCCB 5/02; BL 5/15/02; HB 7–8/02; HBG 10/02; SLJ 5/02)

2524 Hesse, Karen. *Witness* (5–9). 2001, Scholastic $16.95 (0-439-27199-1). 176pp. Hesse uses fictional first-person accounts in free verse to tell about Ku Klux Klan activity in a 1924 Vermont town. (Rev: BCCB 11/01; BL 9/1/01; HB 11–12/01; HBG 3/02; SLJ 9/01*)

2525 Hill, Kirkpatrick. *Minuk: Ashes in the Pathway* (4–6). Series: Girls of Many Lands. 2002, Pleasant $12.95 (1-58485-596-7); paper $7.95 (1-58485-520-7). 198pp. As a young Yup'ik Indian girl grows more mature in the late 19th century, she assesses her life, the culture of the Yup'iks, and the contrasting customs and influence of the missionaries, in an account that includes information on epidemics and historical photographs. (Rev: BL 10/1/02; HB 1–2/03*; HBG 3/03; SLJ 10/02)

2526 Hurwitz, Johanna. *Dear Emma* (3–5). 2002, HarperCollins LB $17.89 (0-06-029841-3). 160pp. Letters from 12-year-old Hadassah "Dossi" Rabinowitz to her friend Emma in Vermont continue the story started in *Faraway Summer* (1998) and give details of Dossi's life in New York in the early 1900s, including a diphtheria epidemic and the Triangle Shirtwaist Factory fire. (Rev: BL 12/1/02; HBG 3/03; SLJ 12/02)

2527 Janke, Katelan. *Survival in the Storm: The Dust Bowl Diary of Grace Edwards* (4–8). Series: Dear America. 2002, Scholastic $10.95 (0-439-21599-4). 192pp. The fictional diary of a girl living in the Texas panhandle during the Dust Bowl years. (Rev: BL 2/15/03; SLJ 12/02)

2528 Kimball, K. M. *The Secret of the Red Flame* (4–7). Illus. by Mark Elliot. 2002, Simon & Schuster paper $4.99 (0-689-85174-X). 224pp. In this complex novel, Jozef, a Polish American boy living in Chicago in 1871, joins a gang in an effort to thwart some local criminals. (Rev: BL 7/02; SLJ 8/02)

2529 Kinsey-Warnock, Natalie. *A Doctor Like Papa* (2–4). Illus. by James Bernardin. 2002, HarperCollins LB $14.89 (0-06-029320-9). 80pp. During World War I in Vermont, Margaret puts her doctor-father's practices to work to protect herself and brother when a deadly flu epidemic strikes. (Rev: BL 4/1/02; HBG 10/02; SLJ 7/02)

2530 Koller, Jackie French. *Someday* (5–8). 2002, Scholastic $16.95 (0-439-29317-0). 224pp. Celie's allegiances are divided when her town is flooded to create a reservoir in Massachusetts during the 1930s. (Rev: BCCB 10/02; BL 6/1–15/02; HBG 10/02; SLJ 7/02)

2531 Lasky, Kathryn. *A Time for Courage: The Suffragette Diary of Kathleen Bowen, Washington, DC, 1917* (4–6). Series: Dear America. 2002, Scholastic $10.95 (0-590-51141-6). 217pp. Thirteen-year-old Kat records her increasing interest in politics and her activities supporting the women's suffrage movement. (Rev: HBG 10/02; SLJ 8/02)

2532 Lawlor, Laurie. *Exploring the Chicago World's Fair, 1893* (4–6). Series: American Sister. 2001, Pocket $9.00 (0-671-03924-5). 212pp. While her father works in Buffalo Bill's Wild West Show, 12-year-old Dora, her younger sisters, and their mother are on their own in Chicago during the World's Columbian Exposition in 1893. (Rev: BL 4/1/01; HBG 10/01; SLJ 8/01)

2533 MacLachlan, Patricia. *Caleb's Story* (3–5). 2001, HarperCollins LB $14.89 (0-06-023606-X). 128pp. In 1918 Caleb helps to mend the years-old rift between his long-lost grandfather and Caleb's father in this third book in the series that began with *Sarah Plain and Tall* (1985). (Rev: BCCB 10/01; BL 9/1/01; HB 9–10/01; HBG 3/02; SLJ 9/01)

2534 Moss, Marissa. *Rose's Journal: The Story of a Girl in the Great Depression* (3–5). Illus. by author. Series: Young American Voices. 2001, Harcourt $15.00 (0-15-202423-9). 56pp. In her pink-lined journal, young Rose records the hardships her family faces during the dust storms of 1935 Kansas and details outside events such as the Hauptmann trial. (Rev: HBG 3/02; SLJ 12/01)

2535 Myers, Anna. *Stolen by the Sea* (5–8). 2001, Walker $16.95 (0-8027-8787-8). 121pp. A 12-year-old girl forgets her resentment toward an orphaned 14-year-old boy as they struggle to rescue themselves and others from the devastating hurricane that hit Galveston in 1900. (Rev: HBG 3/02; SLJ 11/01)

2536 Myers, Anna. *Tulsa Burning* (5–8). 2002, Walker $16.95 (0-8027-8829-7). 184pp. In 1921 Oklahoma, a 15-year-old boy helps a black man who is injured during race riots. (Rev: BCCB 12/02; BL 10/1/02*; HBG 3/03; SLJ 9/02)

2537 Peck, Richard. *Fair Weather* (4–6). 2001, Dial $16.99 (0-8037-2516-7). 160pp. A 13-year-old Illinois farm girl and her family take an exciting trip to the 1893 World's Columbian Exposition in Chicago. (Rev: BCCB 10/01; BL 9/1/01; HB 11–12/01*; HBG 3/02; SLJ 9/01*)

2538 Pfitsch, Patricia Curtis. *Riding the Flume* (5–8). 2002, Simon & Schuster $16.95 (0-689-83823-9). 240pp. This adventure story set in the late 19th century in California features a plucky and environmentally conscious 15-year-old called Francie who faces a dangerous ride on the log flume in her quest to solve a mystery. (Rev: BL 11/15/02; HBG 3/03; SLJ 11/02)

2539 Reiss, Kathryn. *The Strange Case of Baby H* (4–7). Series: History Mysteries. 2002, Pleasant $10.95 (1-58485-534-7); paper $6.95 (1-58485-533-9). 163pp. Twelve-year-old Clara and her family survive the San Francisco earthquake of 1906 only to find an abandoned baby whose identity must be discovered. (Rev: BL 12/1/02; HBG 3/03; SLJ 11/02)

2540 Robinet, Harriette Gillem. *Missing from Haymarket Square* (4–6). 2001, Simon & Schuster $15.00 (0-689-83895-6). 160pp. An African American girl named Dinah Bell faces hardships as a child laborer in 1880s Chicago. (Rev: BCCB 10/01; BL 10/1/01; HBG 10/02; SLJ 7/01)

2541 Rogers, Lisa Waller. *Get Along, Little Dogies: The Chisholm Trail Diary of Hallie Lou Wells: South Texas, 1878* (4–7). 2001, Texas Tech $14.50 (0-89672-446-8); paper $8.95 (0-89672-448-4). 174pp. Feisty 14-year-old Hallie Lou records in her diary the details and dangers of a cattle drive from Texas to Kansas. (Rev: HBG 10/01; SLJ 7/01)

2542 Steiner, Barbara. *Mystery at Chilkoot Pass* (5–8). Series: History Mysteries. 2002, Pleasant $10.95, (1-58485-488-X); paper $6.95 (1-58485-487-1). 164pp. Twelve-year-old Hetty and her father, uncle, and friends join the Klondike Gold Rush, encountering danger, physical hardships, and mysterious happenings along the way. (Rev: BL 9/1/02; HBG 10/02; SLJ 6/02)

2543 Stroud, Bettye. *Dance Y'All* (2–4). Illus. by Cornelius Van Wright and Ying-Hwa Hu. 2001, Marshall Cavendish $15.95 (0-7614-5065-3). With some help, Jack Henry overcomes his fear of the snake in the barn in this novel set at the beginning of the 20th century. (Rev: HBG 3/02; SLJ 11/01)

2544 Tate, Eleanora E. *The Minstrel's Melody* (5–7). Series: History Mysteries. 2001, Pleasant paper $5.95 (1-58485-310-7). 156pp. In Missouri of 1904, Orphelia, an African American girl, runs away from home to begin a stage career during the St. Louis World's Fair. (Rev: BL 4/1/01; HBG 3/02; SLJ 8/01)

2545 Taylor, Theodore. *A Sailor Returns* (4–6). 2001, Scholastic $16.95 (0-439-24879-5). 160pp. Evan is thrilled to meet his long-lost sailor grandfather, who has a secret that is finally revealed in this novel set in 1914. (Rev: BCCB 3/01; BL 5/1/01; HBG 10/01; SLJ 4/01)

2546 Thesman, Jean. *A Sea So Far* (5–8). 2001, Viking $15.99 (0-670-89278-5). 224pp. Fourteen-year-old orphan Kate befriends dying Jolie in a story set during and after the 1906 San Francisco earthquake. (Rev: BCCB 11/01; BL 10/15/01; HBG 3/02; SLJ 10/01)

2547 Tripp, Valerie. *Changes for Kit: A Winter Story* (3–5). Illus. by Walter Rane. Series: American Girl. 2001, Pleasant $12.95 (1-58485-027-2); paper $5.95 (1-58485-026-4). 70pp. A section of historical facts and photographs follows the story of Kit seeking clothing donations for children at the local soup kitchen and learning to cope with her grumpy uncle during the Depression. (Rev: BL 12/1/01; HBG 3/02)

2548 Tripp, Valerie. *Happy Birthday, Kit! A Springtime Story, 1934* (3–5). Illus. Series: American Girl. 2001, Pleasant $12.95 (1-58485-023-X); paper $5.95 (1-58485-022-1). 70pp. Kit greets her Aunt Millie's arrival with mixed emotions. (Rev: BL 8/01; HBG 3/02)

2549 Tripp, Valerie. *Kit Saves the Day: A Summer Story, 1934* (3–5). Illus. Series: American Girl. 2001, Pleasant $12.95 (1-58485-025-6); paper $5.95 (1-58485-024-8). 68pp. Kit discovers that a hobo's life isn't as much fun as she first thought. (Rev: BL 8/01; HBG 3/02)

2550 Waldman, Neil. *They Came from the Bronx: How the Buffalo Were Saved from Extinction* (2–5). Illus. by author. 2001, Boyds Mills $16.95 (1-56397-891-1). A Comanche grandmother and grandson await a small herd of buffalo in a story based on efforts to return bison to the plains in 1907. (Rev: HBG 10/02; SLJ 9/01)

2551 Wallace, Barbara Brooks. *Secret in St. Something* (5–7). 2001, Simon & Schuster $16.00 (0-689-83464-0). 160pp. In late-19th-century New York, 11-year-old Robin takes his baby brother and runs away from their abusive stepfather, but later discovers his stepfather's secret. (Rev: BL 5/15/01; HB 9–10/01; HBG 3/02; SLJ 7/01)

2552 Wells, Rosemary. *Wingwalker* (3–5). Illus. by Brian Selznick. 2002, Hyperion LB $16.49 (0-7868-2347-X). 64pp. A young boy's father takes a carnival job as a wing-walker during the Great Depression in this book with illustrations that evoke the atmosphere of the time. (Rev: BCCB 5/02; BL 3/15/02*; HB 7–8/02; HBG 10/02; SLJ 5/02*)

2553 Wells, Rosemary, and Tom Wells. *The House in the Mail* (2–5). Illus. by Dan Andreasen. 2002, Viking $16.99 (0-670-03545-9). 32pp. A scrapbook-style accounting by a 12-year-old girl of her family's mail-order home in 1927 Kentucky. (Rev: BCCB 2/02; BL 3/1/02; HBG 10/02; SLJ 3/02)

2554 Whelan, Gloria. *The Wanigan: A Life on the River* (4–7). Illus. by Emily Martindale. 2002, Knopf LB $16.99 (0-375-91429-3). 112pp. Eleven-year-old Annabel and her family live and work on a logging boat on a Michigan river in 1878. (Rev: BL 5/15/02; HBG 10/02; SLJ 3/02)

2555 White, Ellen Emerson. *Kaiulani: The People's Princess* (5–8). Series: Royal Diaries. 2001, Scholastic $10.95 (0-439-12909-5). 240pp. This story, told in diary form, begins in 1889, when 13-year-old Princess Kaiulani of Hawaii heads to England to finish her studies. (Rev: BL 4/1/01; HBG 10/01; SLJ 6/01)

2556 Winthrop, Elizabeth. *Franklin Delano Roosevelt: Letters from a Mill Town Girl* (5–7). Illus. Series: Dear Mr. President. 2001, Winslow $9.95 (1-890817-61-9). 128pp. Fictional letters between Franklin Delano Roosevelt and a 12-year-old girl illustrate living conditions and government policy during the Depression. (Rev: BL 2/1/02; HBG 3/02; SLJ 12/01)

2557 Yep, Laurence. *The Traitor* (5–8). Series: Golden Mountain Chronicles. 2003, HarperCollins LB $17.89 (0-06-027523-5). 320pp. Two boys who are outsiders (one because he is of Chinese heritage, the other because he is illegitimate), take turns voicing their versions of the increasingly violent struggle between American miners and Chinese immigrants in 1885 Wyoming Territory. (Rev: BL 1/1–15/03; HB 3–4/03; SLJ 3/03)

World War II and After

2558 Avi. *Don't You Know There's a War On?* (4–7). 2001, HarperCollins LB $15.89 (0-06-029214-8). 208pp. It's 1943 Brooklyn, and 11-year-old Howie Crispers sees war, intrigue, and potential romance on every corner. (Rev: BCCB 5/01; BL 6/1–15/01; HB 5–6/01; HBG 10/01; SLJ 6/01)

2559 Coleman, Evelyn. *Circle of Fire* (3–6). Series: History Mysteries. 2001, Pleasant $9.95 (1-58485-340-9); paper $5.95 (1-58485-339-5). 147pp. An African American girl whose best friend is a white boy faces racial tension in a small southern town in a story of the late 1950s that is based on real events. (Rev: BL 1/1–15/02)

2560 Copeland, Cynthia. *Elin's Island* (5–7). 2003, Millbrook LB $22.90 (0-7613-2522-0). 144pp. Raised since infancy by lighthouse keepers, 13-year-old Elin is left on her own to tend the house and light on an eventful night in 1941. (Rev: BL 3/15/03)

2561 Crum, Shutta. *Spitting Image* (5–8). 2003, Clarion $15.00 (0-618-23477-2). 224pp. Jessie has a busy summer in 1967 in her Kentucky hometown, tackling family problems and dealing with well-meaning volunteers and reporters who view them as "rural poor." (Rev: BL 3/1/03)

2562 Danticat, Edwidge. *Behind the Mountains* (5–9). Series: First Person Fiction. 2002, Scholastic $16.95 (0-439-37299-2). 176pp. Danticat skillfully introduces background information on Haitian history and politics into the journal of young Celiane Esperance, who soon leaves the island and moves to Brooklyn to join her much-missed father, a reunion that isn't as easy as she expected. (Rev: BCCB 2/03; BL 10/1/02; HBG 3/03; SLJ 10/02)

2563 Davies, Jacqueline. *Where the Ground Meets the Sky* (5–8). 2002, Marshall Cavendish $15.95 (0-7614-5105-6). 224pp. During World War II, 12-year-old Hazel lives a lonely life in a compound in the New Mexico desert while her father works on a top secret project, until she makes a friend and uncovers a secret. (Rev: BL 9/1/02; HBG 10/02; SLJ 4/02)

2564 Duey, Kathleen. *Janey G. Blue: Pearl Harbor, 1941* (4–8). 2001, Simon & Schuster paper $4.99 (0-689-84404-2). 128pp. Sixth-grader Janey lives through the terror of the attack on Pearl Harbor and her family helps a neighboring Japanese American girl who is separated from her parents. (Rev: SLJ 10/01)

2565 Evans, Freddi Williams. *A Bus of Our Own* (K–4). Illus. by Shawn Costello. 2001, Albert Whitman $15.95 (0-8075-0970-1). 32pp. Based on a real event in segregated Mississippi, this is the story of an African American community that banded together to get a bus to carry their children to school. (Rev: BL 8/01; HBG 3/02; SLJ 9/01)

2566 Flood, Pansie Hart. *Sylvia and Miz Lula Maye* (3–5). Illus. by Felicia Marshall. 2002, Carolrhoda

$15.95 (0-87614-204-8). 120pp. A 10-year-old African American girl and her 100-year-old neighbor form an unlikely friendship in this novel set in 1970s South Carolina. (Rev: BL 2/15/02; HBG 10/02; SLJ 4/02)

2567 Geisert, Bonnie. *Prairie Summer* (4–6). Illus. by Arthur Geisert. 2002, Houghton $15.00 (0-618-21293-0). 128pp. The story of a fifth-grade farm girl in rural South Dakota in the mid-1950s who shows courage and ingenuity when her mother goes into early labor. (Rev: BL 3/1/02; HBG 10/02; SLJ 5/02)

2568 Griffis, Molly Levite. *The Feester Filibuster* (4–8). 2002, Eakin $17.95 (1-57168-541-3); paper $8.95 (1-57168-694-0). 224pp. It's John Allen Feester's turn in this sequel to *The Rachel Resistance* (2001), which introduced the feuding Oklahoma fifth-graders, and he's happy to continue the quarrel until circumstances bring a new understanding. (Rev: BL 11/1/02; HBG 10/01; SLJ check)

2569 Hamisch, Siegfried. *The Bunker on Edelweiss Mountain* (5–8). 2001, Pentland $16.95 (1-57197-282-X). 128pp. Thirteen-year-old Norman, the son of an Allied sergeant, is caught up in dangerous intrigue when he befriends a local boy in this novel based in post-World War II Germany. (Rev: BL 10/15/01)

2570 Hoobler, Dorothy, and Tom Hoobler. *The 1940s: Secrets* (3–6). Illus. Series: Century Kids. 2001, Millbrook LB $21.90 (0-7613-1604-3). 176pp. The story of various branches of the Aldrich family and their contributions to the home front during World War II. (Rev: BL 4/1/01; HBG 10/01; SLJ 5/01)

2571 Kochenderfer, Lee. *The Victory Garden* (4–6). 2002, Delacorte $14.95 (0-385-32788-9). 166pp. Eleven-year-old Teresa writes to her pilot brother and helps her father tend a victory garden in this tale set in Kansas in 1943. (Rev: BCCB 3/02; BL 3/1/02; HBG 10/02; SLJ 1/02)

2572 Littlesugar, Amy. *Lisette's Angel* (2–4). Illus. by Max Ginsburg. 2002, Dial $15.99 (0-8037-2435-7). 32pp. The angel of the title is an American paratrooper, who helps to liberate Lisette's French town from the Nazis in 1945 in this picture book for older readers. (Rev: BL 9/1/02; HBG 10/02; SLJ 8/02)

2573 Lurie, April. *Dancing in the Streets of Brooklyn* (5–8). 2002, Delacorte LB $17.99 (0-385-90066-X). 192pp. Thirteen-year-old Judy has a lot to deal with in this novel set in a Norwegian-American community in 1944: the discovery that Pa is not her biological father, life on the home front, and a budding romance. (Rev: BCCB 12/02; BL 11/15/02; HBG 3/03; SLJ 9/02)

2574 McGill, Alice. *Here We Go Round* (2–5). Illus. by Shane Evans. 2002, Houghton $15.00 (0-618-16064-7). 128pp. A young African American girl named Roberta is sent to stay with her grandparents on their farm until the impending birth of her sibling in this thoughtful story set in 1946 North Carolina. (Rev: BCCB 7–8/02; BL 2/15/02; HBG 10/02; SLJ 4/02)

2575 Martin, Ann M. *A Corner of the Universe* (5–8). 2002, Scholastic $15.95 (0-439-38880-5).

208pp. Hattie recalls the summer she became 12, when a mentally disabled uncle came to stay with her family. Newbery Honor Book, 2003. (Rev: BCCB 2/03; BL 12/1/02; HB 1–2/03*; HBG 3/03; SLJ 9/02)

2576 Mazer, Harry. *A Boy at War: A Novel of Pearl Harbor* (5–9). 2001, Simon & Schuster $15.00 (0-689-84161-2). 112pp. Young Adam Pelko, new to Honolulu, is pressed into action on the morning of the attack on Pearl Harbor while trying to find his father, in this absorbing novel that also looks at relations with Japanese Americans. (Rev: BL 4/1/01; HB 5–6/01; HBG 10/01; SLJ 5/01)

2577 Moranville, Sharelle Byars. *Over the River* (5–7). 2002, Holt $16.95 (0-8050-7049-4). 240pp. Willa Mae's father finally returns from World War II, and although the 11-year-old is happy to have him home, family tensions and secrets persist. (Rev: BCCB 1/03; BL 11/15/02; HBG 3/03; SLJ 11/02)

2578 Myers, Walter Dean. *Patrol: An American Soldier in Vietnam* (4–8). Illus. by Ann Grifalconi. 2002, HarperCollins LB $16.89 (0-06-028364-5). 40pp. A penetrating picture book for older readers told in narrative verse from the perspective of a teenage soldier in Vietnam. (Rev: BL 3/15/02; HB 7–8/02; HBG 10/02; SLJ 5/02)

2579 Recorvits, Helen. *Where Heroes Hide* (4–6). 2002, Farrar $16.00 (0-374-33057-3). 144pp. Junior slowly comes to understand his gruff father, a World War II veteran, in this novel set in 1956 that deals with issues including polio and bullies. (Rev: BL 5/15/02; HBG 10/02; SLJ 5/02)

2580 Rogers, Kenny, and Donald Davenport. *Christmas in Canaan* (5–8). 2002, HarperCollins $15.99 (0-06-000746-X). 336pp. In 1960s Texas, after a black boy and a white boy fight on the school bus, the adults decree that the two boys must spend time together, and a difficult start ends in the boys becoming fast friends when they help a wounded dog. (Rev: BL 11/1/02; HBG 3/03; SLJ 10/02)

2581 Van Steenwyk, Elizabeth. *Maggie in the Morning* (4–6). 2001, Eerdmans $16.00 (0-8028-5222-X). 144pp. An 11-year-old girl who is staying with her aunt and uncle in the early 1940s discovers she is at the center of a family secret. (Rev: BL 1/1–15/02; HBG 3/02; SLJ 12/01)

2582 Watts, Irene N. *Finding Sophie: A Search for Belonging in Postwar Britain* (5–8). 2002, Tundra paper $6.95 (0-88776-613-7). 144pp. In this sequel to *Remember Me* (2000), World War II has ended and 13-year-old Sophie waits anxiously to hear news of her Jewish family in Germany, at the same time hoping she will not have to leave her happy life in London. (Rev: BL 1/1–15/03; SLJ 3/03)

2583 White, Ellen Emerson. *Where Have All the Flowers Gone? The Diary of Molly MacKenzie Flaherty, Boston, Massachusetts, 1968* (5–9). Series: Dear America. 2002, Scholastic $10.95 (0-439-14889-8). 188pp. Fifteen-year-old Molly's brother is fighting in Vietnam, and she wrestles with pride, anxiety, and the antiwar sentiment around her. (Rev: BL 8/02; HBG 10/02; SLJ 7/02)

2584 White, Ruth. *Tadpole* (5–8). 2003, Farrar $16.00 (0-374-31002-5). 208pp. In this novel set in 1950s Appalachia, uncertain 10-year-old Carolina finds her own strengths when her 13-year-old cousin Tadpole arrives, running away from an abusive uncle. (Rev: SLJ 3/03)

2585 Woods, Brenda. *The Red Rose Box* (5–8). 2002, Putnam $16.99 (0-399-23702-X). 144pp. In 1953, Leah, a southern black girl, and her family travel to Los Angeles where they find a different culture and more progressive attitudes. (Rev: BCCB 7–8/02; BL 6/1–15/02; HBG 10/02; SLJ 6/02)

2586 Ylvisaker, Anne. *Dear Papa* (4–6). 2002, Candlewick $15.99 (0-7636-1618-4). 192pp. A nine-year-old girl, Isabelle, writes letters to her dead father in this touching novel set in Minnesota in 1943. (Rev: BL 8/02; HBG 3/03; SLJ 8/02)

Holidays and Holy Days

2587 Ahlberg, Allan. *The Man Who Wore All His Clothes* (2–4). Illus. by Katherine McEwen. 2001, Candlewick $12.99 (0-7636-1432-7). 77pp. A zany adventure that involves 9-year-old twins Gus and Gloria with bank robbers, chase scenes, and a thin father who is wearing all his clothes. (Rev: HBG 3/02; SLJ 10/01)

2588 Buck, Pearl S. *Christmas Day in the Morning* (3–6). Illus. by Mark Buehner. 2002, HarperCollins LB $18.89 (0-688-16268-1). 40pp. Oil paintings illustrate this reissue of the classic story, originally published in 1955, of a young boy who decides to do his father's farm chores on Christmas Day. (Rev: BL 10/15/02; HBG 3/03; SLJ 10/02)

2589 Chaikin, Miriam. *Alexandra's Scroll: The Story of the First Hanukkah* (4–6). Illus. by Stephen Fieser. 2002, Holt $18.95 (0-8050-6384-6). 113pp. Alexandra and her family are caught up in the tumultuous events that lead to the first Hanukkah in this brightly illustrated historical novel. (Rev: BL 9/1/02; HB 9–10/02; HBG 3/03; SLJ 10/02)

2590 *A Christmas Treasury: Very Merry Stories and Poems* (2–5). Illus. by Kevin Hawkes. 2001, HarperCollins LB $16.89 (0-688-12040-7). 48pp. This combination of Christmas stories, carols, and poems is enhanced by Hawkes's detailed, full-color art. (Rev: BL 9/1/01; HBG 3/02; SLJ 10/01)

2591 Davis, C. L. *The Christmas Barn* (4–6). 2001, Pleasant $12.95 (1-58485-414-6). 184pp. Twelve-year-old Roxie tells how her rural family struggles to celebrate Christmas during the Great Depression. (Rev: BL 9/1/01; HBG 3/02; SLJ 10/01)

2592 Kraft, Eric P. *Lenny and Mel* (2–4). Illus. by author. 2002, Simon & Schuster $15.00 (0-689-84173-6). 64pp. Twins Lenny and Mel suffer through a school-year of holidays in this hilarious chapter book. (Rev: BL 3/1/02; HB 5–6/02; HBG 10/02; SLJ 2/02)

2593 Osborne, Mary Pope. *Christmas in Camelot* (2–5). Series: Magic Tree House. 2001, Random LB $13.99 (0-375-91373.4). 116pp. Stalwart Jack and

Annie time-travel to Camelot and must solve riddles to break the spell of the evil Mordred and save the knights of the Round Table. (Rev: BL 12/15/01; HBG 3/02; SLJ 10/01)

2594 Polacco, Patricia. *Christmas Tapestry* (3–6). Illus. 2002, Putnam $16.99 (0-399-23955-3). 160pp. In this heartwarming Christmas story, a boy and his father use a tapestry to cover a hole in a church wall, only to find that the fabric has special meaning to a Jewish couple. (Rev: BCCB 10/02; BL 9/1/02; HBG 3/03; SLJ 10/02)

2595 Wisniewski, David. *Halloweenies* (3–5). Illus. 2002, HarperCollins LB $16.89 (0-06-000514-9); paper $4.99 (0-06-000515-7). 80pp. Five silly Halloween stories, presented as horror-movie send-ups with titles such as "Frankenstein's Hamster," are illustrated with black-and-white cartoons. (Rev: BL 9/1/02; HBG 3/03; SLJ 10/02)

2596 Zalben, Jane Breskin. *The Magic Menorah: A Modern Chanukah Tale* (3–5). Illus. by Donna Diamond. 2001, Simon & Schuster $15.00 (0-689-82606-0). 56pp. Twelve-year-old Stanley dreads Hanukkah — lots of annoying relatives arrive and his grandfather always looks sad — but this year a strange man appears from a menorah Stanley finds in the attic and grants him three wishes. (Rev: HBG 3/02; SLJ 10/01)

Humorous Stories

2597 Ahlberg, Allan. *The Woman Who Won Things* (2–4). Illus. by Katherine McEwen. 2002, Candlewick $14.99 (0-7636-1721-0). 80pp. Gus and Gloria Gaskitt are enamored with their new substitute teacher, but can't figure out why things are disappearing around the school in this fun-filled beginning chapter book, a sequel to *The Man Who Wore All His Clothes* (2001). (Rev: BCCB 6/02; BL 8/02; HBG 10/02; SLJ 6/02)

2598 Bond, Michael. *Paddington Takes the Test* (3–5). Illus. 2002, Houghton $15.00 (0-618-18384-1). 144pp. This new edition of a 1980 release about the ever-popular bear sports a new jacket illustration and a larger typeface. (Rev: BL 3/15/02; HBG 10/02)

2599 Brennan, Herbie. *Fairy Nuff* (3–5). Illus. by Ross Collins. 2002, Bloomsbury $13.95 (1-58234-770-0). 128pp. In this beginning chapter book, bungling Fairy Nuff burns down his cottage, launching a grenade into the grounds of Widow Buhiss, and the over-the-top antics begin. (Rev: BL 8/02; SLJ 8/02)

2600 Briggs, Raymond. *Ug: Boy Genius of the Stone Age* (3–6). Illus. 2002, Knopf LB $17.99 (0-375-91611-3). 32pp. Ug, an ever-curious and inventive Stone Age boy, wants one thing above all — soft, warm pants — in this humorous and thought-provoking story presented in comic-strip style. (Rev: BL 11/15/02; HBG 3/03; SLJ 10/02)

2601 Cooney, Doug. *The Beloved Dearly* (4–6). Illus. by Tony Diterlizzi. 2002, Simon & Schuster LB $16.00 (0-689-83127-7). 192pp. A 12-year-old goes into the pet funeral business in this humorous and inventive novel aimed at a middle-grade audience. (Rev: BCCB 5/02; BL 1/1–15/02; HBG 10/02; SLJ 1/02)

2602 Fienberg, Anna, and Barbara Fienberg. *Tashi and the Big Stinker* (2–4). Illus. by Kim Gamble. 2001, Allen & Unwin paper $5.95 (1-86508-350-X). 63pp. Line drawings illustrate two tall tales from Australia, one full of raucous humor, the other a variation on the Pied Piper of Hamelin. (Rev: SLJ 7/01)

2603 Frank, Lucy. *The Annoyance Bureau* (5–8). 2002, Simon & Schuster $16.95 (0-689-84903-6). 176pp. Lucas, 12, is already having a very annoying Christmas holiday in New York when he meets a Santa who says he works for the Annoyance Bureau, and the irritations begin to multiply. (Rev: BCCB 12/02; BL 11/1/02; HBG 3/03; SLJ 10/02)

2604 Gorman, Carol. *Dork on the Run* (4–7). 2002, HarperCollins LB $15. (0-06-029410-8). 176pp. Flack, a sixth-grader, doesn't foresee the unusual and often funny situations that will arise when he runs for class president. (Rev: BCCB 9/02; BL 6/1–15/02; HB 9–10/02; HBG 10/02; SLJ 6/02)

2605 Howe, James. *Howie Monroe and the Doghouse of Doom* (3–5). Illus. by Brett Helquist. 2002, Simon & Schuster $9.95 (0-689-83951-0). 96pp. Puppy Howie is self-congratulatory about his literary creation, a funny parody of Harry Potter. (Rev: BL 10/1/02; HBG 3/03)

2606 Ives, David. *Monsieur Eek* (4–7). 2001, HarperCollins LB $15.89 (0-06-029530-9). 192pp. Thirteen-year-old Emmaline defends a monkey against criminal charges in the not-quite-right town of MacOongafoondsen, population 21. (Rev: BL 6/1–15/01; HBG 3/02; SLJ 6/01)

2607 Jennings, Richard W. *My Life of Crime* (4–8). 2002, Houghton $15.00 (0-618-21433-X). 160pp. Nothing goes right when sixth-grader Fowler decides to "rescue" a caged parrot. (Rev: BL 1/1–15/03; HBG 3/03)

2608 King-Smith, Dick. *George Speaks* (3–5). Illus. by Judy Brown. 2002, Millbrook LB $21.90 (0-7613-2519-0). 96pp. Laura is shocked to discover her four-week-old baby brother George can already talk. (Rev: BCCB 6/02; BL 2/15/02; HBG 10/02; SLJ 3/02)

2609 King-Smith, Dick. *Titus Rules!* (2–5). Illus. by John Eastwood. 2003, Knopf $15.95 (0-375-81461-2). 128pp. Life among British royalty is described from the point of view of Titus, a palace corgi. (Rev: BL 2/1/03; SLJ 3/03)

2610 Kitamura, Satoshi. *Comic Adventures of Boots* (2–4). Illus. 2002, Farrar $16.00 (0-374-31455-1). 32pp. Boots the cat has three funny adventures presented in comic-book style. (Rev: BL 10/1/02; SLJ 8/02)

2611 Lawrence, Michael. *The Poltergoose* (4–7). 2002, Dutton $14.99 (0-525-46839-0). 144pp. Jiggy McCue's new house is being haunted by the ghost of a cranky goose in this humorous story set in the

English countryside. (Rev: BL 1/1–15/02; HBG 10/02; SLJ 3/02)

2612 Lewis, J. Patrick. *The Shoe Tree of Chagrin Falls* (3–5). Illus. by Chris Sheban. 2001, Creative Editions $17.95 (1-56846-173-9). 32pp. Old cobbler Susannah, tall as a barn, braves ice and snow to deliver a load of handmade shoes to Chagrin Falls by Christmas. (Rev: BL 12/15/01; HBG 3/02; SLJ 2/02)

2613 Mason, Simon. *The Quigleys* (2–4). Illus. by Helen Stephens. 2002, Knopf $14.95 (0-385-75006-4): 160pp. Each of the four members of the eccentric British Quigley family has his or her own chapter in this amusing book. (Rev: BCCB 9/02; BL 7/02; HB 7–8/02; HBG 10/02; SLJ 6/02)

2614 Myers, Bill. *The Case of the Giggling Geeks* (2–4). Illus. 2002, Thomas Nelson paper $4.99 (1-4003-0094-0). 88pp. Secret Agent Dingledorf (really elementary school student Bernie) tries to stop the giggles virus that is infecting only intelligent people in this humorous adventure full of action. Also use *The Case of the Chewable Worms* (2002). (Rev: BL 11/15/02)

2615 Naylor, Phyllis Reynolds. *The Boys Return* (4–6). 2001, Delacorte $15.95 (0-385-32737-4). 131pp. The Malloy girls and Hatford and Benson boys have a lively spring break as they plot against each other and attempt to capture a marauding cougar, with predictably chaotic results. (Rev: BL 12/15/01; SLJ 10/01)

2616 Naylor, Phyllis Reynolds. *The Girls Take Over* (4–6). 2002, Delacorte $15.95 (0-385-32738-2). 160pp. The latest entertaining competitions between the Malloy girls and the Hatford boys involve a river race, a spelling bee, and baseball. (Rev: BL 9/15/02; HBG 3/03; SLJ 9/02)

2617 Palatini, Margie. *The Web Files* (4–8). Illus. by Richard Egielski. 2001, Hyperion LB $16.49 (0-7868-2366-6). 32pp. A clever and humorous takeoff of "Dragnet" that involves Ducktective Web and his feathered partner Bill, who are working the barnyard shift. (Rev: BCCB 2/01; BL 5/1/01; HB 5–6/01; HBG 10/01; SLJ 11/01*)

2618 Pilkey, Dav. *The Adventures of Super Diaper Baby* (2–5). Illus. by author. 2002, Scholastic paper $4.99 (0-439-37606-8). 125pp. As a penance for bad behavior, Harold and George are ordered to tackle the topic of good citizenship and instead invent a diaper-clad superhero. (Rev: HBG 10/02; SLJ 6/02)

2619 Pilkey, Dav. *Captain Underpants and the Wrath of the Wicked Wedgie Woman* (3–6). Illus. 2001, Scholastic $16.95 (0-439-04999-7); paper $4.99 (0-439-05000-6). 176pp. George and Harold of Captain Underpants fame create a comic book about their teacher, Mrs. Ribble, whom they dub Wicked Wedgie Woman. (Rev: BL 1/1–15/02; HBG 3/02; SLJ check)

2620 Pinkwater, Daniel. *Fat Camp Commandos* (2–4). Illus. 2001, Scholastic $14.95 (0-439-15527-4). 96pp. A very funny chapter book about three children who escape from a "fat camp" and return secretly to their hometown to campaign for the rights of fat people. (Rev: BCCB 6/01; BL 4/15/01; HB 5–6/01; HBG 10/01; SLJ 5/01)

2621 Pinkwater, Daniel. *Fat Camp Commandos Go West* (3–5). Illus. by Andy Rash. 2002, Scholastic $14.95 (0-439-29772-9). 96pp. Sylvia and Ralph, who are attending a fat camp, join forces with friend Mavis to bring two warring groups of locals to a truce. (Rev: BCCB 7–8/02; BL 6/1–15/02; HBG 10/02; SLJ 6/02)

2622 Pinkwater, Daniel. *The Werewolf Club, Book 3: The Werewolf Club Meets Dorkula* (3–5). Illus. by Jill Pinkwater. Series: The Werewolf Club. 2001, Simon & Schuster $15.00 (0-689-83848-4). 80pp. The Watson Elementary School Werewolf Club encounters a "fruitpire" — a vampire who preys on fruits and vegetables — and drama and comedy ensue. (Rev: BL 9/15/01; HBG 3/02)

2623 Scrimger, Richard. *Noses Are Red* (4–7). 2002, Tundra $14.95 (0-88776-610-2); paper $7.95 (0-88776-590-4). 208pp. Norbert, the alien who likes to live in Alan's nose, works to Alan's benefit once again when Alan and a friend meet a variety of perils on a camping trip. (Rev: BL 1/1–15/03; HBG 3/03; SLJ 12/02)

2624 Seuling, Barbara. *Robert and the Weird and Wacky Facts* (2–4). Illus. by Paul Brewer. 2002, Cricket $15.95 (0-8126-2653-2). 120pp. Robert believes that he has developed magical powers and can make his wishes come true in this humorous addition to an appealing series. (Rev: BL 4/1/02; HB 7–8/02; HBG 10/02; SLJ 7/02)

2625 Snicket, Lemony. *Lemony Snicket: The Unauthorized Autobiography* (4–7). Illus. 2002, HarperCollins $11.99 (0-06-000720-6). 240pp. Using fake documents, newspaper articles, and transcripts, the author of the funny Series of Unfortunate Events books reconstructs his life. (Rev: BL 6/1–15/02; HBG 10/02; SLJ 7/02)

2626 Thomas, Frances. *Polly's Really Secret Diary* (3–5). Illus. by Sally Gardner. 2002, Delacorte LB $16.99 (0-385-90049-X). 96pp. A little English girl keeps a diary to chronicle her trials and tribulations, such as the disappearance of her pet hamster. (Rev: BL 6/1–15/02; HBG 10/02; SLJ 8/02)

2627 Tolan, Stephanie S. *Surviving the Applewhites* (5–8). 2002, HarperCollins LB $17.89 (0-06-623603-7). 216pp. The convention-flouting Applewhite family's Creative Academy helps a 13-year-old troublemaker to discover hidden talents. Newbery Honor Book, 2003. (Rev: BCCB 10/02; BL 11/1/02; HBG 3/03; SLJ 9/02)

2628 Uderzo, Albert. *Asterix and Son* (4–8). Trans. by Anthea Bell and Derek Hockridge. Illus. 2002, Orion paper $9.95 (0-75284-775-9). 48pp. In comic-book format, this is the entertaining story of French heroes Asterix and Obelix and how they became guardians of a kidnapped baby. Also use *Asterix and the Black Gold* (2002) and *Asterix and the Great Divide* (2002). (Rev: BL 4/15/02)

2629 Uderzo, Albert. *Asterix and the Actress* (4–7). Trans. by Anthea Bell and Derek Hockridge. Illus. 2001, Sterling $12.95 (0-75284-657-4). 48pp. These pun-filled, graphic-novel exploits of Asterix the

Gaul include a boisterous shared birthday with the rotund Obelix and a daring rescue of prisoners in a Roman jail. (Rev: BL 8/01)

2630 Wisniewski, David. *The Secret Knowledge of Grown-Ups: The Second File* (3–6). Illus. 2001, HarperCollins LB $16.89 (0-688-17855-3). 48pp. The author turns undercover investigator to discover the truth about some mysterious adult notions. (Rev: BL 8/01; HBG 3/02; SLJ 9/01)

2631 Yaccarino, Dan. *The Big Science Fair!* (2–5). Illus. by author. Series: Blast Off Boy and Blorp. 2002, Hyperion $15.99 (0-7868-0580-3); paper $4.99 (0-7868-1430-6). Science fairs test the wit of Blast Off Boy and Blorp in their respective exchange schools, with humorous and unexpected results. (Rev: HBG 3/03; SLJ 12/02)

2632 Yaccarino, Dan. *New Pet* (2–4). Illus. 2001, Hyperion LB $16.49 (0-7868-2500-6). 40pp. Space exchange students Blast Off Boy and Blorp each long for animal companions, with comic results on the planets of Earth and Meep. (Rev: BL 12/1/01; HBG 3/02; SLJ 12/01)

School Stories

2633 Cameron, Ann. *Gloria Rising* (2–4). Illus. by Lis Toft. 2002, Farrar $15.00 (0-374-32675-4). 112pp. A young African American girl named Gloria stars in this easy chapter book involving an inspiring woman astronaut and an intimidating fourth-grade teacher. (Rev: BCCB 4/02; BL 2/15/02; HBG 10/02; SLJ 3/02)

2634 Clements, Andrew. *Jake Drake: Teacher's Pet* (3–5). Illus. by Dolores Avendano. 2001, Simon & Schuster $15.00 (0-689-83919-7). 80pp. In this beginning chapter book, Jake Drake faces the worst day of his life — the day he becomes the teacher's pet. (Rev: BL 1/1–15/02; HBG 10/02; SLJ 4/02)

2635 Clements, Andrew. *Jake Drake, Bully Buster* (2–4). Illus. by Amanda Harvey. 2001, Simon & Schuster paper $3.99 (0-689-83880-8). 73pp. Fourth-grader Jake helps out the bully who has been taunting him mercilessly when the bully turns out to be scared of public speaking. (Rev: SLJ 5/01)

2636 Clements, Andrew. *Jake Drake, Class Clown* (2–5). Illus. by Dolores Avendano. 2002, Simon & Schuster $15.00 (0-689-83921-9). 72pp. Jake is determined to make the new student teacher crack a smile. (Rev: HBG 10/02; SLJ 7/02)

2637 Clements, Andrew. *Jake Drake, Know-It-All* (3–5). Illus. by Dolores Avendano. 2001, Simon & Schuster $15.00 (0-689-83918-9). 96pp. In this beginning chapter book, fourth-grader Jake finds himself turning into a person he doesn't like when he must compete with the class know-it-alls in the school science fair. (Rev: BCCB 2/02; BL 11/1/01; HBG 3/02; SLJ 11/01)

2638 Clements, Andrew. *A Week in the Woods* (4–8). 2002, Simon & Schuster $16.95 (0-689-82596-X). 208pp. Mark, a lonely fifth-grader, and a forceful teacher test each other — and Mark's sur-

vival skills — on a weeklong camping trip. (Rev: BCCB 1/03; BL 10/1/02; HBG 3/03; SLJ 11/02)

2639 Cox, Judy. *Cool Cat, School Cat* (2–4). Illus. by Blanche Sims. 2002, Holiday $15.95 (0-8234-1714-X). 96pp. Young Gus is extremely forgetful and puts a stray cat in danger of being fumigated. (Rev: BCCB 2/03; HBG 3/03; SLJ 9/02)

2640 Creech, Sharon. *Love That Dog* (3–6). 2001, HarperCollins LB $14.89 (0-06-029289-X). 112pp. Despite himself, Jack finds he is drawn to poetry and even starts to write poems of his own. (Rev: BL 8/01; HB 11–12/01; HBG 3/02; SLJ 8/01*)

2641 DeLaCroix, Alice. *The Hero of the Third Grade* (2–4). Illus. by Cynthia Fisher. 2002, Holiday $15.95 (0-8234-1745-X). 96pp. Randall, a third-grader, is miserable — his parents have split up, he's moved with his mom to a new town, the kids don't like him — until he remembers the example of the Scarlet Pimpernel and decides to devote himself to helping others. (Rev: BL 1/1–15/03; HBG 3/03; SLJ 12/02)

2642 Edwards, Michelle. *The Talent Show* (2–4). Illus. Series: Jackson Friends. 2002, Harcourt $14.00 (0-15-216403-0). 64pp. Second-grader Howardina "Howie" Smith suffers a case of stage-fright when she's slated to perform at her school's talent show. (Rev: BL 8/02; HBG 3/03; SLJ 10/02)

2643 Edwards, Michelle. *Zero Grandparents* (2–4). Illus. 2001, Harcourt $14.00 (0-15-202083-7). 64pp. Calliope has no grandparents to bring to school on Grandparents Day but she thinks of a clever way out of her problem. (Rev: BCCB 4/01; BL 4/1/01; HBG 10/01; SLJ 7/01)

2644 Gutman, Dan. *The Million Dollar Kick* (5–8). 2001, Hyperion LB $16.49 (0-7868-2612-6). 202pp. A seventh-grader who hates soccer must face her shortcomings and deal with middle-school cliques when she is chosen to try to kick a $1 million goal. (Rev: BL 11/15/01; HBG 3/02; SLJ 12/01)

2645 Haddad, Charles. *Captain Tweakerbeak's Revenge: A Calliope Day Adventure* (3–6). Illus. by Steve Pica. 2001, Delacorte $14.95 (0-385-32712-9). 192pp. Mischievous Calliope, 9, and her "prissy" friend Noreen bring Noreen's parrot to school, with unintended results. (Rev: HBG 10/01; SLJ 6/01)

2646 Haddix, Margaret Peterson. *The Girl with 500 Middle Names* (2–4). Illus. by Janet Hamlin. 2001, Simon & Schuster $15.00 (0-689-84135-3). 81pp. Third-grader Janie moves to a new school and is dismayed to find the girls there are richer and better dressed. (Rev: BCCB 5/01; HBG 10/01; SLJ 6/01)

2647 Hornik, Laurie Miller. *The Secrets of Ms. Snickle's Class* (2–4). Illus. by Debbie Tilley. 2001, Clarion $15.00 (0-618-03435-8). 135pp. Lacey's zeal to find out everyone's secrets endangers her teacher's job. (Rev: HBG 10/01; SLJ 7/01)

2648 Howe, James. *The Misfits* (5–8). 2001, Simon & Schuster $16.00 (0-689-83955-3). 288pp. A group of seventh-grade social misfits challenge the so-called norms at their school by running for student council and instituting a no-names-calling day.

(Rev: BCCB 1/02; BL 11/15/01; HB 11–12/01; HBG 3/02; SLJ 11/01)

2649 Korman, Gordon. *No More Dead Dogs* (5–7). 2001, Hyperion LB $16.49 (0-7868-2462-X). 180pp. Eighth-grade football player and truth-teller Wallace Wallace decides to add some fun to a boring play about a faithful dog, in this complex and zany story. (Rev: BL 10/1/01; HBG 10/01)

2650 Koss, Amy Goldman. *The Cheat* (5–8). 2003, Dial $16.99 (0-8037-2794-1). 144pp. When three eighth-graders are caught cheating on a geography test, they have to make difficult decisions — do they reveal their source? (Rev: BCCB 2/03; BL 1/1–15/03; SLJ 1/03)

2651 Lowry, Lois. *Gooney Bird Greene* (2–5). Illus. by Middy Thomas. 2002, Houghton $15.00 (0-618-23848-4). 96pp. Gooney Bird is a colorful character: a new second-grader who has a fondness for dressing outrageously and telling fanciful stories. (Rev: BCCB 10/02; BL 9/1/02; HB 9–10/02; HBG 3/03; SLJ 11/02)

2652 Lynch, L. M. *How I Wonder What You Are* (5–7). 2001, Knopf LB $17.99 (0-375-90663-0). 208pp. A strange new family with an intriguing son moves into sixth-grader Laurel's neighborhood. (Rev: BCCB 11/01; BL 8/01; HBG 3/02; SLJ 7/01)

2653 MacDonald, Amy. *No More Nasty* (3–6). Illus. by Cat B. Smith. 2001, Farrar $16.00 (0-374-35529-0). 176pp. Eleven-year-old Simon is put in a difficult situation when his great-aunt becomes his substitute teacher. (Rev: BL 9/1/01; HB 11–12/01; HBG 3/02; SLJ 9/01)

2654 McDonald, Megan. *Judy Moody Saves the World!* (2–5). Illus. by Peter Reynolds. 2002, Candlewick $15.99 (0-7636-1446-7). 160pp. Third-grader Judy is busy saving the world with a recycling project in this third installment in the series in which she stars. (Rev: BL 9/1/02; HBG 3/03)

2655 McKenna, Colleen O'Shaughnessy. *Third Grade Stinks!* (2–4). Illus. by Stephanie Roth. 2001, Holiday $15.95 (0-8234-1595-3). 99pp. Gordie is really disappointed when he learns he has to share his third-grade locker with show-off Lucy and concocts a plan to stink her out. (Rev: BCCB 11/01; BL 12/15/01; HBG 10/02; SLJ 11/01)

2656 Maguire, Gregory. *Three Rotten Eggs* (3–7). Illus. by Elaine Clayton. Series: Hamlet Chronicles. 2002, Clarion $16.00 (0-618-09655-8). 192pp. The boys are in competition with the girls in Miss Earth's annual spring egg hunt until a swaggering bully named Thud Tweed joins their class. (Rev: BL 4/1/02; HBG 10/02; SLJ 3/02)

2657 Marsden, Carolyn. *The Gold-Threaded Dress* (3–5). 2002, Candlewick $13.99 (0-7636-1569-2). 73pp. Fourth-grader Oy is torn between her desire to make friends and her classmates' interest in her precious Thai dress. (Rev: BCCB 6/02; BL 5/1/02*; HBG 3/03; SLJ 4/02)

2658 Martin, Ann M. *Belle Teal* (4–6). 2001, Scholastic $15.95 (0-439-09823-8). 224pp. Fifth-grader Belle befriends the only black student in her class in this story about the early days of desegrega-tion. (Rev: BCCB 2/02; BL 10/1/01; HB 1–2/02; HBG 3/02; SLJ 9/01)

2659 Mills, Claudia. *7 x 9 = Trouble!* (2–4). Illus. by G. Brian Karas. 2002, Farrar $15.00 (0-374-36746-9). 112pp. Third-grader Wilson loves the class pet, a hamster, and his best friend, Josh, but he has terrible problems with math, particularly the 12 times tables. (Rev: BL 4/1/02; HB 3–4/02; HBG 10/02; SLJ 4/02)

2660 Morgenstern, Susie. *A Book of Coupons* (4–6). Illus. 2001, Viking $12.99 (0-670-89970-4). 64pp. An elderly teacher rewards his fifth-grade class with books of coupons that are redeemable for such treats as dancing in class, and not going to the blackboard when summoned. (Rev: BL 4/1/01; HB 5–6/01; HBG 10/01; SLJ 5/01)

2661 Naylor, Phyllis Reynolds. *Starting with Alice* (3–8). 2002, Simon & Schuster $15.95 (0-689-84395-X). 192pp. In this prequel, Alice (first seen in *The Agony of Alice* in 1985) is in third grade in a new school in Maryland, initially has trouble finding friends, and still misses her dead mother. (Rev: BCCB 11/02; BL 11/15/02; HB 9–10/02; HBG 3/03; SLJ 9/02)

2662 O'Dell, Kathleen. *Agnes Parker . . . Girl in Progress* (4–6). Illus. by Charise Mericle Harper. 2003, Dial $16.99 (0-8037-2648-1). 160pp. Sixth-grader Agnes learns a lot about life and herself during sixth grade. (Rev: HB 3–4/03; SLJ 2/03)

2663 Park, Barbara. *Junie B., First Grader: Boss of Lunch* (2–3). Illus. by Denise Brunkus. Series: Junie B. Jones. 2002, Random $11.95 (0-375-81517-1). 80pp. There's a strong focus on food, as Junie B. gets a new lunchbox and debates the merits of brown-bagging it versus bought lunches. (Rev: BL 7/02; HBG 10/02; SLJ 8/02)

2664 Park, Barbara. *Junie B., First Grader: Toothless Wonder* (2–4). Illus. by Denise Brunkus. 2002, Random LB $13.99 (0-375-90295-3). 96pp. Junie B. is losing her first tooth and decides to look into the existence of the tooth fairy, which she rather doubts. (Rev: BL 11/1/02; HBG 3/03; SLJ 12/02)

2665 Peters, Julie Anne. *A Snitch in the Snob Squad* (4–6). 2001, Little, Brown $14.95 (0-316-70287-0). 208pp. The members of the Snob Squad wonder who stole from the teacher — could it be one of them? (Rev: BCCB 3/01; BL 5/15/01; HBG 10/01; SLJ 4/01)

2666 Redeker, Kent. *Angela Anaconda: My Notebook* (3–4). Illus. by Barry Goldberg. 2001, Simon & Schuster paper $5.99 (0-689-83995-2). Angela, a third-grader, very frankly records her thoughts about classmates, teachers, food, and other important aspects of life. (Rev: SLJ 4/01)

2667 Seuling, Barbara. *Robert and the Back-to-School Special* (2–4). Illus. by Paul Brewer. 2002, Cricket $15.95 (0-8126-2662-1). 112pp. Insecure third-grader Robert thinks his classmates are mocking him because of the length of his hair, but his brother's efforts to fix it don't make things any better. (Rev: BL 1/1–15/03; HB 1–2/03; HBG 3/03; SLJ 1/03)

2668 Spinelli, Jerry. *Loser* (3–6). 2002, Harper-Collins LB $15.89 (0-06-000483-5). 224pp. Donald Zinkoff, labeled a "loser" by his classmates, is nonetheless happy and secure, unconcerned about what others think of him. (Rev: BCCB 5/02; BL 5/15/02; HB 7–8/02; HBG 10/02; SLJ 5/02)

2669 Zollman, Pam. *Don't Bug Me!* (4–6). 2001, Holiday $15.95 (0-8234-1584-8). 134pp. Megan, a sixth-grader, aims to complete her bug project despite her pesky, interfering brother and her annoying classmate Charlie. (Rev: BL 7/01; HBG 3/02; SLJ 10/01)

Science Fiction

2670 Brennan, Herbie. *Zartog's Remote* (3–5). Illus. by Neal Layton. 2001, Carolrhoda LB $14.95 (1-57505-507-4). 96pp. A fearful 8-year-old alien named Zartog and a feisty 8-year-old girl named Rachel band together when Zartog loses the remote control for his spaceship. (Rev: HBG 10/01; SLJ 4/01)

2671 Crilley, Mark. *Akiko and the Great Wall of Trudd* (3–5). Illus. by author. 2001, Delacorte $9.95 (0-385-32727-7). Readers of the earlier volumes in this series (*Akiko on the Planet Smoo* and *Akiko in the Sprubly Islands*) will enjoy this continuation of the fantasy. (Rev: HBG 10/01; SLJ 4/01)

2672 DeVita, James. *Blue* (4–7). 2001, Harper-Collins LB $14.89 (0-06-029546-5). 288pp. Morgan follows a marlin that has entered his living room and soon finds he is turning into a fish. (Rev: BCCB 5/01; BL 4/15/01; HBG 10/01; SLJ 5/01)

2673 Gutman, Dan. *The Edison Mystery* (4–8). Series: Qwerty Stevens, Back in Time. 2001, Simon & Schuster $16.00 (0-689-84124-8). 201pp. The time machine he finds in his backyard sends 13-year-old Robert "Qwerty" Stevens to 1879 to Thomas Edison's workshop. (Rev: HBG 3/02; SLJ 8/01)

2674 Haddix, Margaret Peterson. *Among the Betrayed* (5–9). 2002, Simon & Schuster $15.95 (0-689-83905-7). 160pp. In this third novel in the series that started with *Among the Hidden* (1998), illegal third child Nina faces danger and difficult decisions. (Rev: BCCB 10/02; HBG 10/02; SLJ 6/02)

2675 Haddix, Margaret Peterson. *Among the Imposters* (5–7). 2001, Simon & Schuster $16.00 (0-689-83904-9). 172pp. As a third child in a society that allows only two per family, Luke has assumed a new identity and at age 12 enrolls in a nightmarish boarding school. (Rev: BCCB 9/01; BL 4/15/01; HBG 10/01; SLJ 7/01)

2676 Korman, Gordon. *Your Mummy Is a Nose Picker* (3–5). Illus. by Victor Vaccaro. Series: L.A.F. Books. 2000, Hyperion LB $14.49 (0-7868-2587-1); paper $4.99 (0-7868-1446-2). 153pp. In this humorously silly science fiction fantasy, Devin and his friend Stan from the planet Pan travel back to ancient Egypt to find a plant that will save

Earth's tourism by making Pant tourists sneeze (an enjoyable activity). (Rev: SLJ 4/01)

2677 Lowenstein, Sallie. *Focus* (5–9). Illus. 2001, Lion Stone $15.00 (0-9658486-3-9). 284pp. The Haldrans leave their planet and relocate to Miners World, where humans live, in order to save their son from discrimination because of his creative intelligence. (Rev: BL 4/15/01; SLJ 8/01)

2678 MacGrory, Yvonne. *Emma and the Ruby Ring* (4–6). Illus. by Terry Myler. 2002, Milkweed $17.95 (1-57131-635-3); paper $6.95 (1-57131-634-5). 137pp. In this sequel to *The Secret of the Ruby Ring* (1994), 11-year-old Emma is transported to 19th-century Ireland and becomes involved in fulfilling a dying woman's last request. (Rev: HBG 10/02; SLJ 5/02)

2679 Mackel, Kathy. *From the Horse's Mouth* (5–7). 2002, HarperCollins LB $15.89 (0-06-029415-9). 224pp. Nick Thorpe is on another science fiction adventure involving a time warp and evil aliens that plan to destroy his town. (Rev: BL 5/1/02; HBG 10/02; SLJ 7/02)

2680 Meacham, Margaret. *Quiet! You're Invisible* (3–5). 2001, Holiday $15.95 (0-8234-1651-8). 80pp. Fifth-grader Hoby is visited by a boy from the future and must outsmart the middle-school bully to retrieve a stolen part from his new friend's space cruiser. (Rev: BL 1/1–15/02; HBG 3/02; SLJ 11/01)

2681 Pierce, Tamora. *Street Magic* (5–9). Series: Circle Opens. 2001, Scholastic $16.95 (0-590-39628-5). 304pp. Briar, a 14-year-old former gang member, finds he is again caught between warring gangs when he helps a female street urchin in this futuristic novel. (Rev: BL 4/15/01; HB 3–4/01; HBG 10/01; SLJ 7/01)

2682 Rector, Rebecca Kraft. *Tria and the Great Star Rescue* (4–7). 2002, Delacorte $14.95 (0-385-72941-3). 184pp. Tria, who has been unwilling to leave her home planet of Chiron, must use her technological savvy and face untold dangers in her quest to rescue her kidnapped mother and holographic best friend, Star. (Rev: BCCB 9/02; HB 5–6/02; HBG 10/02; SLJ 2/02)

2683 Spinner, Stephanie, and Terry Bisson. *Expiration Date: Never* (3–6). 2001, Delacorte $14.95 (0-385-32690-4). 144pp. In this zany sequel to *Be First in the Universe* (2000), the formerly nasty Gneiss twins become sweet as can be and twins Tessa and Tod rescue a rock star from fans only to cause additional problems. (Rev: BL 8/01; HBG 10/01; SLJ 7/01)

Short Stories and Anthologies

2684 *Beware! R. L. Stine Picks His Favorite Scary Stories* (4–6). Ed. by R. L. Stine. Illus. 2002, HarperCollins LB $14.89 (0-06-623843-9). 224pp. Horror author R. L. Stine provides a short introduction to each tale in this collection of stories and poems by such greats as Ray Bradbury, Alvin

Schwartz, and Edward Gorey. (Rev: BL 8/02; HBG 3/03; SLJ 10/02)

2685 Canfield, Jack, et al., eds. *Chicken Soup for the Preteen Soul: 101 Stories of Changes, Choices and Growing Up for Kids Ages 9–13* (5–7). Illus. 2000, Health Communications $24.00 (1-55874-801-6); paper $12.95 (1-55874-800-8). 386pp. The usual mix of verse and prose written by and for preteens, with the aim of offering inspiration, comfort, and practical advice. (Rev: HBG 10/01; SLJ 4/01) [158.1]

2686 Carus, Marianne, ed. *Fire and Wings: Dragon Tales from East and West* (3–6). Illus. by Nilesh Mistry. 2002, Cricket $17.95 (0-8126-2664-8). 146pp. A collection of 15 stories, most of which have appeared in *Cricket* magazine, about all kinds of dragons, by authors including Jane Yolen, Patricia MacLachlan, Eric A. Kimmel, Vida Chu, and E. Nesbit. (Rev: HBG 3/03; SLJ 12/02)

2687 Gac-Artigas, Alejandro. *Off to Catch the Sun* (5–8). 2001, Ediciones Nuevo Espacio $11.95 (1-930879-28-8). 148pp. Thirteen-year-old author Gac-Artigas explores serious issues through poetry, essays, and short stories. (Rev: BL 1/1–15/02) [808]

2688 Lewis, Naomi, comp. *Rocking Horse Land and Other Classic Tales of Dolls and Toys* (4–6). Illus. by Angela Barrett. 2000, Candlewick $19.99 (0-7636-0897-1). 126pp. A collection of six classic stories — including "The Steadfast Tin Soldier," "The Town in the Library," and "Vasilissa, Baba Yaga, and the Little Doll" — with detailed illustrations that evoke the Victorian era. (Rev: HBG 3/01; SLJ 4/01)

2689 *Little Lit: Strange Stories for Strange Kids* (4 Up). Ed. by Art Spiegelman and Francoise Mouly. Illus. 2001, HarperCollins $19.95 (0-06-028626-1). 64pp. This collection of offbeat, imaginative, graphic stories includes something for everyone, from humor to fantasy to horror, from Maurice Sendak to David Sedaris. (Rev: BL 12/15/01; HB 1–2/02; HBG 3/02; SLJ 3/02) [741.5]

2690 Morpurgo, Michael, comp. *The Kingfisher Book of Great Boy Stories: A Treasury of Classics from Children's Literature* (4–8). Illus. 2000, Kingfisher $19.95 (0-7534-5320-7). 160pp. An attractively illustrated collection of stories from authors including Carlo Collodi, Roald Dahl, Ted Hughes, C. S. Lewis, A. A. Milne, Donald Sobol, and Mark Twain. (Rev: HBG 10/01; SLJ 4/01)

2691 Pearce, Philippa. *Familiar and Haunting: Collected Stories* (5–8). 2002, HarperCollins LB $16.89 (0-06-623965-6). 368pp. Thirty-seven short stories, many of them about ghosts and the supernatural, are included in this intriguing collection. (Rev: BL 5/1/02; HB 5–6/02*; HBG 10/02; SLJ 7/02)

2692 Randol, Susan, ed. *Dead Good Read: Classic Tales of Mystery and Horror* (5 Up). Illus. 2001, Reader's Digest $24.95 (0-7621-0347-7). 223pp. Stories by authors including Robert Louis Stevenson, Bram Stoker, and Elizabeth Gaskell are retold for readers who would find the originals too challenging, with definitions of difficult vocabulary. (Rev: HBG 10/02; SLJ 1/02)

2693 Schulman, Janet, sel. *You Read to Me and I'll Read to You: 20th-Century Stories to Share* (K–3). 2001, Knopf $34.95 (0-375-81083-8). 250pp. A selection of stories for beginning readers by authors including Judy Blume, Roald Dahl, Astrid Lindgren, Louis Sachar, and Wiliam Steig. (Rev: HBG 3/02; SLJ 12/01)

Sports Stories

2694 Bates, Cynthia. *Shooting Star* (4–6). Series: Sports Stories. 2001, Lorimer paper $5.50 (1-55028-726-5). 102pp. Eight-grader Quyen Ha, who was a basketball star at her middle school, has some reservations about her decision to join a bantam team in this novel set in Canada that has information on Vietnamese family life. (Rev: SLJ 1/02)

2695 Bledsoe, Lucy Jane. *Hoop Girlz* (5–7). 2002, Holiday $16.95 (0-8234-1691-7). 128pp. When 11-year-old River is denied a place on the girls' basketball team, she forms her own team, with her brother as the coach. (Rev: BL 9/1/02; SLJ 12/02)

2696 Bowen, Fred. *Winners Take All* (3–7). Illus. by Paul Casale. 2000, Peachtree paper $4.95 (1-56145-229-7). 104pp. Twelve-year-old Kyle eventually confesses to faking a catch in this story that includes discussion of Christy Mathewson, a pro pitcher in the early 1900s who was admired for his sportsmanship. (Rev: SLJ 4/01)

2697 Butcher, Kristin. *Cairo Kelly and the Man* (4–8). 2002, Orca paper $6.95 (1-55143-211-0). 176pp. When Midge discovers that his baseball team's umpire, Hal Mann, is illiterate, Midge and his friend Kelly set out to solve the problem. (Rev: BL 9/1/02)

2698 Forsyth, C. A. *Power Hitter* (4–6). Series: Sports Stories. 2001, Lorimer paper $5.50 (1-55028-732-X). 86pp. A 13-year-old boy goes to visit relatives in Winnipeg for a summer full of baseball, unaware that his parents are divorcing and his mother is ill. (Rev: SLJ 1/02)

2699 Hale, Daniel J., and Matthew LaBrot. *Red Card* (4–7). Series: Zeke Armstrong Mystery. 2002, Top paper $7.95 (1-929976-15-1). 170pp. Someone is trying to kill the soccer coach, and young Zeke sets out to discover who and why. (Rev: SLJ 12/02)

2700 Hirschfeld, Robert. *Goalkeeper in Charge* (5–7). Series: Christopher Sports. 2002, Little, Brown $15.95 (0-316-07552-3); paper $6.50 (0-316-07548-5). 144pp. Seventh-grader Tina works to overcome her shyness on and off the soccer field. (Rev: BL 9/1/02; HBG 3/03)

2701 Kline, Suzy. *Molly Gets Mad* (2–4). Illus. by Diana C. Bluthenthal. Series: Molly. 2001, Putnam $14.99 (0-399-23408-X). 72pp. Third-grader Molly's friend Morty is a good sport, even when Molly is a little too competitive on and off the ice. (Rev: BL 9/1/01; HBG 10/01; SLJ 8/01)

2702 Mills, Claudia. *Gus and Grandpa at Basketball* (2–4). Illus. by Catherine Stock. 2001, Farrar $14.00 (0-374-32818-8). 48pp. In this seventh book in the series, Grandpa helps Gus overcome his anxiety about playing basketball in front of a crowd. (Rev: BL 11/15/01; HB 11–12/01; HBG 3/02; SLJ 9/01)

2703 Telander, Rick. *String Music* (4–6). 2002, Cricket $15.95 (0-8126-2647-5). 144pp. Robbie, a fifth-grader with plenty of problems, runs away to the big city, sneaks into a basketball game, and meets basketball's greatest player. (Rev: BCCB 7–8/02; BL 5/1/02)

2704 Walters, Eric. *Full Court Press* (3–5). 2001, Orca paper $4.50 (1-55143-169-6). 152pp. Though only in the third grade, Nick and Kia decide to try out for the fifth-grade basketball team. (Rev: BL 4/1/01)

2705 Walters, Eric. *Long Shot* (2–5). Illus. by John Mantha. 2002, Orca paper $4.99 (1-55143-216-1). 140pp. The new coach of Nick and Kia's basketball team is so unpleasant that all the players walk out. (Rev: SLJ 7/02)

2706 Wooldridge, Frosty. *Strike Three! Take Your Base* (5–9). Illus. by Pietri Freeman. 2001, Brookfield Reader $16.95 (1-930093-01-2); paper $5.95 (1-930093-07-1). 160pp. Baseball provides the setting as two brothers deal individually with the sudden death of their umpire father. (Rev: SLJ 3/02)

Fairy Tales

2707 Andersen, Hans Christian. *Little Mermaids and Ugly Ducklings: Favorite Fairy Tales by Hans Christian Andersen* (4–6). Illus. by Gennady Spirin. 2001, Chronicle $15.95 (0-8118-3320-8). 59pp. Handsome, imaginative illustrations of differing styles and sizes enhance six well-known tales. (Rev: BL 12/1/01; HBG 3/02) [839.8]

2708 Batt, Tanya Robyn. *The Faerie's Gift* (K–3). Illus. by Nicoletta Ceccoli. 2003, Barefoot $16.99 (1-84148-998-0). 32pp. A fairy offers a woodcutter one wish, and the wish he makes pleases everyone in his family. (Rev: BL 2/15/03) [398.221]

2709 Birdseye, Tom. *Look Out, Jack! The Giant Is Back!* (K–3). Illus. by Will Hillenbrand. 2001, Holiday $16.95 (0-8234-1450-7). 32pp. The giant of "Jack and the Beanstalk" fame has a big brother who wants revenge — and Jack narrowly escapes him in this colorful picture book. (Rev: BCCB 10/01; BL 9/1/01; HBG 3/02; SLJ 10/01)

2710 Boada, Francesc. *Cinderella / Cenicienta* (PS–1). Illus. by Monse Fransoy. Series: Bilingual Editions. 2001, Chronicle $12.95 (0-8118-3090-X); paper $6.95 (0-8118-3090-X). 32pp. A bilingual version full of humor that stays close to the original tale. (Rev: BL 7/01; HBG 10/01) [398.2]

2711 Coxe, Molly, retel. *Bunny and the Beast* (K–3). Illus. by Pamela Silin-Palmer. 2001, Random $15.95 (0-375-80468-4). A handsomely presented retelling of a French tale about a beautiful young rabbit and a bull terrier Beast who she releases from his spell. (Rev: HBG 10/01; SLJ 5/01) [398.2]

2712 Craft, Mahlon F. *Sleeping Beauty* (2–4). Illus. by Kinuko Craft. 2002, North-South LB $16.50 (1-58717-121-X). 32pp. A beautifully illustrated retelling of the traditional fairy tale. (Rev: BCCB 1/03; BL 9/15/02; HBG 3/03; SLJ 10/02) [398.2]

2713 de Hann, Linda, and Stern Nijland. *King and King* (PS–2). Illus. 2002, Tricycle Pr. $14.95 (1-58246-061-2). 32pp. When his mother the queen wants him to marry, a prince falls in love with another prince, and they marry and live happily ever after in this alternative fairy tale. (Rev: BL 7/02; HB 7–8/02; HBG 10/02; SLJ 3/02)

2714 de la Paz, Myrna J. *Abadeha: The Philippine Cinderella* (K–3). Illus. by Youshan Tang. 2001, Shens $16.95 (1-885008-17-1). 32pp. A Philippine version of the Cinderella story in which Abadeha is helped by kindly spirits and wins the prince by removing a ring that is stuck on his finger. (Rev: BL 7/01; HBG 3/02; SLJ 12/01) [398.2]

2715 Delessert, Etienne. *The Seven Dwarfs* (3–4). Illus. 2001, Creative Editions LB $17.95 (1-56846-139-9). 32pp. One of Snow White's dwarfs, Stephane, recounts the princess's story in this imaginative take on the fairy tale. (Rev: BL 1/1–15/02; HB 1–2/02; HBG 3/02) [398.2]

2716 dePaola, Tomie. *Adelita: A Mexican Cinderella Story* (PS–2). Illus. 2002, Putnam $16.99 (0-399-23866-2). 32pp. This Cinderella story features a young Mexican girl named Adelita who wins the heart of her prince through her own resources. (Rev: BL 8/02; HBG 3/03; SLJ 9/02) [398.2]

2717 Doherty, Berlie. *The Famous Adventures of Jack* (3–5). Illus. by Sonja Lamut. 2001, HarperCollins LB $14.89 (0-06-623619-3). 128pp. Doherty skillfully interweaves a bunch of well-known "Jack" stories. (Rev: BCCB 10/01; BL 10/1/01; HB 11–12/01*; HBG 3/02; SLJ 1/02)

2718 Donnelly, Jennifer. *Humble Pie* (PS–2). Illus. by Stephen Gammell. 2002, Simon & Schuster $16.95 (0-689-84435-2). 32pp. Stuffed into a "humble pie" by his grandmother, selfish Theo narrowly escapes being eaten and mends his ways in this colorful picture book set in the past with lively illustrations that enhance the story. (Rev: BCCB 11/02; BL 7/02; HBG 3/03; SLJ 9/02)

2719 Ernst, Lisa Campbell. *The Three Spinning Fairies: A Tale from the Brothers Grimm* (PS–3). Illus. by author. 2002, Dutton $16.99 (0-525-46826-9). 40pp. The Royal Baker's lazy daughter Zelda gets what is coming to her in this stylishly illustrated version of a Grimm fairy tale. (Rev: BL

1/1–15/02; HBG 10/02; SLJ 2/02) [398.2]

2720 Ferris, Jean. *Once upon a Marigold* (5–8). 2002, Harcourt $17.00 (0-15-216791-9). 272pp. Christian falls in love with Princess Marigold and wins her heart through his bravery in this fairy tale full of fun. (Rev: BCCB 2/03; BL 9/15/02; HB 9–10/02; HBG 3/03; SLJ 11/02)

2721 Goodhart, Pippa. *Arthur's Tractor: A Fairy Tale with Mechanical Parts* (PS–2). Illus. by Colin Paine. 2003, Bloomsbury $15.95 (1-58234-847-2). 32pp. While Arthur is busy working on his tractor, he stumbles into a funny fairy tale. (Rev: BL 2/15/03; SLJ 3/03)

2722 Gray, Margaret. *The Ugly Princess and the Wise Fool* (3–6). Illus. by Randy Cecil. 2002, Holt $15.95 (0-8050-6847-3). 176pp. There's a happy ending to this tale despite the fact that the princess is ugly and wisdom has been banned from the land. (Rev: BCCB 12/02; BL 11/15/02; HBG 3/03; SLJ 10/02)

2723 Grimm, Jacob, and Wilhelm Grimm. *Hansel and Gretel* (3–6). Trans. by Anthea Bell. Illus. by Dorothee Duntze. 2001, North-South LB $15.88 (0-7358-1423-6). 32pp. This version of the well-known fairy tale presents the dangers clearly and scarily, with striking illustrations. (Rev: BCCB 10/01; BL 9/15/01; HB 1–2/02; HBG 3/02; SLJ 10/01) [398.2]

2724 Hirsch, Odo. *Bartlett and the Ice Voyage* (4–7). Illus. by Andrew McLean. 2003, Bloomsbury $14.95 (1-58234-797-2). 175pp. When a queen demands a far-off fruit, the intrepid explorer Bartlett is ready to oblige. (Rev: BL 2/1/03; SLJ 1/03)

2725 Keller, Emily. *Sleeping Bunny* (PS–3). Illus. by Pamela Silin-Palmer. 2003, Random $15.95 (0-375-91541-9). 40pp. Sumptuous, detailed illustrations set a medieval scene for a Sleeping Beauty retold with a pig fairy godmother and an evil rat fairy. (Rev: BCCB 3/03; BL 1/1–15/03; SLJ 3/03) [398.2]

2726 Lach, William, ed. *Fairyland: In Art and Poetry* (3–7). Illus. by Richard Doyle. 2002, Holt $17.95 (0-8050-7006-0). 40pp. Illustrations from Richard Doyle's classic *In Fairyland* (1870) are paired with selections from writers including Shakespeare, de la Mare, Langston Hughes, and Laura Ingalls Wilder in a handsome volume suited to browsing. (Rev: HBG 10/02; SLJ 7/02) [398.2]

2727 Levine, Gail Carson. *The Fairy's Return* (3–5). Series: Princess Tales. 2002, HarperCollins LB $14.89 (0-06-623801-3). 112pp. Using bits and pieces of fairy tales and folklore, this book tells the story of a princess who falls in love with a baker's son. Another entry in the series is *For Biddle's Sake* (2002). (Rev: BL 8/02; HBG 3/03; SLJ 9/02)

2728 Lorenz, Albert. *Jack and the Beanstalk: How a Small Fellow Solved a Big Problem* (PS–3). Illus. 2002, Abrams $16.95 (0-8109-1160-4). 40pp. Realistic, highly detailed illustrations emphasize the importance of size and Jack's inventiveness. (Rev: BL 10/1/02; HBG 3/03; SLJ 10/02) [398.2]

2729 Martin, Rafe. *The Storytelling Princess* (PS–3). Illus. by Kimberly B. Root. 2001, Putnam

$15.99 (0-399-22924-8). 32pp. A prince and princess who have both refused arranged marriages find their respective criteria are met in each other. (Rev: BCCB 7–8/01; BL 7/01; HBG 3/02; SLJ 9/01)

2730 Mayer, Marianna. *The Adventures of Tom Thumb* (K–4). Illus. by Kinuko Craft. 2001, North-South LB $15.88 (1-58717-065-5). 32pp. Little Tom cleverly survives being eaten by a cow, a fish, and a giant, and is knighted by King Arthur in this illustrated retelling. (Rev: BL 10/15/01; HB 9–10/01; HBG 3/02; SLJ 12/01) [398.2]

2731 Mills, Lauren. *The Dog Prince* (PS–3). Illus. by Lauren Mills and Dennis Nolan. 2001, Little, Brown $15.95 (0-316-57417-1). 32pp. In classic fairy-tale fashion, when a spell turns an ill-mannered prince into a bloodhound, he is befriended — and transformed — by the goat-girl he once scorned. (Rev: BL 11/15/01; HBG 3/02; SLJ 12/01)

2732 Minters, Frances. *Princess Fishtail* (PS–2). Illus. by G. Brian Karas. 2002, Viking $15.99 (0-670-03529-7). 32pp. This modern version of Hans Christian Andersen's mermaid tale has the underwater princess rescuing a surfer and shopping in Los Angeles. (Rev: BCCB 12/02; BL 10/15/02; HBG 3/03; SLJ 9/02)

2733 Mitchell, Marianne. *Joe Cinders* (PS–3). Illus. by Bryan Langdo. 2002, Holt $16.95 (0-8050-6529-6). 32pp. A hilarious, twisted retelling of the classic Cinderella, in which a put-upon young cowpoke and his cantankerous stepbrothers are invited to Miss Rosalinda's fiesta. (Rev: BL 10/15/02; HBG 3/03; SLJ 12/02) [398.2]

2734 Mitchell, Stephen. *The Nightingale* (2–4). Illus. by Bagram Ibatoulline. 2002, Candlewick $17.99 (0-7636-1521-8). 48pp. Artwork with an Asian influence and a lively contemporary text are used in this version of Andersen's tale. (Rev: BCCB 11/02; BL 11/1/02; HBG 3/03; SLJ 11/02) [398.2]

2735 Morgenstern, Susie. *Princesses Are People, Too: Two Modern Fairy Tales* (2–5). Trans. by Bill May. Illus. by Serge Bloch. 2002, Viking $12.99 (0-670-03567-X). 64pp. Two amusing modern fairy tales about princesses and their problems are presented in this book translated from French. (Rev: BL 5/1/02; HBG 10/02; SLJ 5/02)

2736 Pinkney, Jerry. *The Nightingale* (K–4). Illus. 2002, Penguin Putnam $16.99 (0-8037-2426-0). 40pp. The familiar fairy tale of a king and a nightingale with a magical voice is transplanted to Morocco and accompanied by beautiful illustrations. (Rev: BCCB 11/02; BL 9/1/02)

2737 Sanderson, Ruth. *Cinderella* (PS–3). Illus. 2002, Little, Brown $15.95 (0-316-77965-2). 32pp. An exquisitely produced version of the Cinderella story with detailed illustrations and an elegant text. (Rev: BL 4/15/02*; HBG 10/02; SLJ 6/02)

2738 San Jose, Christine. *The Little Match Girl* (PS–3). Illus. by Kestutis Kasparavicius. 2002, Boyds Mills $15.95 (1-59078-000-0). 32pp. Lovely illustrations accompany this retelling of the sad story in which the little girl dies. (Rev: BL 10/1/02;

HBG 3/03; SLJ 10/02) [398.2]

2739 Vaes, Alain. *The Princess and the Pea* (K–2). Illus. 2001, Little, Brown $15.95 (0-316-89633-0). 32pp. The princess has morphed into a tow-truck-driving, independent young lady who is capable of passing all the marriageability requirements. (Rev: BCCB 10/01; BL 7/01; HBG 3/02; SLJ 9/01) [398.2]

2740 Whipple, Laura. *If the Shoe Fits* (5–8). Illus. by Laura Beingessner. 2002, Simon & Schuster $17.95 (0-689-84070-5). 80pp. A handsome retelling of the Cinderella story using blank verse. (Rev: BCCB 3/02; BL 5/1/02; HBG 10/02; SLJ 8/02) [398.2]

2741 Wilde, Oscar. *The Happy Prince* (3–5). Illus. by Robin Muller. 2002, Stoddart $15.95 (0-7737-3218-3). 24pp. Wilde's unusual fairy tale in which a swallow and a statue make sacrifices for each other is retold with effective illustrations. (Rev: BL 3/15/02)

Folklore

General

2742 Adler, Naomi. *The Barefoot Book of Animal Tales* (2–4). Illus. by Amanda Hall. 2002, Barefoot $19.99 (1-84148-941-7). 80pp. Lovely, vivid illustrations brighten retellings of nine animal tales, including a Native American story and the German classic about the Bremen musicians. (Rev: BL 1/1–15/03; HBG 3/03) [398.2]

2743 Andrews, Jan. *Out of the Everywhere: Tales for a New World* (2–6). Illus. by Simon Ng. 2001, Groundwood $19.95 (0-88899-402-8). 95pp. Andrews retells stories, setting them in the New World and showing their relevance to immigrants or people seeking new situations. (Rev: HB 9–10/01; HBG 3/02; SLJ 9/01) [813]

2744 Batt, Tanya Robyn. *A Child's Book of Faeries* (3–5). Illus. by Gail Newey. 2002, Barefoot $19.99 (1-84148-954-9). 64pp. Four stories, with snippets of poetry and folklore, introduce the magical world of fairies and leprechauns. (Rev: BL 12/15/02; HBG 3/03; SLJ 1/03) [398.21]

2745 Crum, Shutta. *Who Took My Hairy Toe?* (PS–3). Illus. by Katya Krenina. 2001, Albert Whitman $15.95 (0-8075-5972-5). 40pp. A light-fingered old man soon regrets picking up that hairy toe, as its owner was quite attached to it. (Rev: BL 8/01; HBG 3/02; SLJ 10/01) [398.2]

2746 DeSpain, Pleasant. *Tales of Nonsense and Tomfoolery* (3–5). Illus. Series: Books of Nine Lives. 2001, August House paper $3.99 (0-87483-645-X). 80pp. A collection of tales from around the world that specialize in nonsense. (Rev: BL 7/01) [398.2]

2747 DeSpain, Pleasant. *Tales of Tricksters* (3–5). Illus. Series: Books of Nine Lives. 2001, August House paper $3.99 (0-87483-644-1). 80pp. A collection of tales from around the world that specialize in tricksters. (Rev: BL 7/01) [398.2]

2748 DeSpain, Pleasant. *Tales of Wisdom and Justice* (3–5). Illus. Series: Books of Nine Lives. 2001, August House paper $3.99 (0-87483-646-8). 80pp. A collection of tales from around the world that specialize in wise decisions. (Rev: BL 7/01) [398.2]

2749 Helmer, Marilyn. *Three Teeny Tiny Tales* (K–2). Illus. by Veselina Tomova. Series: Once-Upon-a-Time. 2001, Kids Can $10.95 (1-55074-841-6). 32pp. "The Elves and the Shoemaker," "The Gingerbread Man," and "Thumbelina" are retold in picture-book format. (Rev: BL 7/01; HBG 3/02; SLJ 6/01) [398.2]

2750 Lupton, Hugh. *The Story Tree: Tales to Read About* (PS–2). Illus. by Sophie Fatus. 2001, Barefoot $18.99 (1-84148-312-5). 64pp. This volume includes seven folktales from around the world, including favorites such as "The Three Billy Goats Gruff" and "The Magic Porridge Pot." (Rev: BL 10/1/01; HBG 3/02; SLJ 11/01) [398.2]

2751 Matthews, John. *The Barefoot Book of Knights* (4–7). Illus. by Giovanni Manna. 2002, Barefoot $19.99 (1-84148-064-9). 80pp. This book contains retellings of seven tales of knights and chivalry from countries around the world. (Rev: BCCB 9/02; BL 4/15/02; HBG 10/02; SLJ 6/02) [398.2]

2752 *Once upon a Fairy Tale: Four Favorite Stories* (K–5). 2001, Viking $30.00 (0-670-03500-9). 61pp. Celebrities are portrayed as characters in these retellings of four classic folktales with modern twists, with accompanying CD read by the stars. (Rev: HBG 3/02; SLJ 1/02) [398.2]

2753 *The Oxford Nursery Treasury* (PS–K). Ed. by Ian Beck. Illus. 2001, Oxford $19.95 (0-19-278164-2). 94pp. This is a collection of folktales and nursery rhymes, illustrated with charmingly silly pictures. (Rev: BL 8/01; HBG 10/01; SLJ 7/01) [398]

2754 Philip, Neil. *The Little People: Stories of Fairies, Pixies, and Other Small Folk* (4–8). Illus. 2002, Abrams $24.95 (0-8109-0570-1). 128pp. Beautiful illustrations accompany stories about fairies and other "magical beings" from Europe. (Rev: BL 2/15/03; HBG 3/03; SLJ 12/02) [398.21]

2755 Powell, Patricia Hurby. *Blossom Tales: Flower Stories of Many Folk* (1–3). Illus. by Sarah Dillard. 2002, Moon Mountain $15.95 (0-9677929-8-3). 32pp. A charming collection of short folktales about flowers from around the world. (Rev: BL 4/1/02; HBG 10/02; SLJ 7/02) [398.24]

2756 Root, Phyllis. *Big Momma Makes the World* (PS–2). Illus. by Helen Oxenbury. 2003, Candlewick $16.99 (0-7636-1132-8). 48pp. Glowing illustrations depict the take-charge Big Momma, baby on hip, as she creates the world and admires her work, though she does have to keep an eye on the humans to make sure they "straighten up." (Rev: BCCB 2/03; BL 1/1–15/03*; HB 3–4/03*; SLJ 3/03) [398.2]

2757 Shannon, George. *More True Lies: 18 Tales for You to Judge* (4–6). Illus. 2001, Greenwillow LB $14.89 (0-06-029188-5). 64pp. Readers are asked to identify truth from untruth in 18 folktales from around the world. (Rev: BL 5/15/01; HB 7–8/01; HBG 10/01; SLJ 5/01) [398.2]

2758 Sierra, Judy. *Can You Guess My Name? Traditional Tales Around the World* (3–5). Illus. by Stefano Vitale. 2002, Clarion $20.00 (0-618-13328-3). 128pp. In this handsome volume with lengthy endnotes, Sierra has collected 15 folktales from all corners of the world that are variants of five favorite stories. (Rev: BL 11/15/02; HB 1–2/03*; HBG 3/03; SLJ 11/02*) [398.2]

2759 Sierra, Judy. *Silly and Sillier: Read-Aloud Tales from Around the World* (PS–2). Illus. by Valeri Gorbachev. 2002, Knopf $19.95 (0-375-80609-1). 96pp. These 20 folktales from around the world and the wonderful illustrations that accompany them are sure to bring smiles to young readers' faces. (Rev: BL 12/15/02; HBG 3/03; SLJ 11/02) [398.2]

2760 Spencer, Ann. *Song of the Sea: Myths, Tales, and Folklore* (4–6). Illus. 2001, Tundra paper $17.95 (0-88776-487-8). 208pp. A handsome and varied collection of sea-related lore from around the world. (Rev: BL 8/01; HBG 3/02; SLJ 7/01) [398.23]

2761 Van Kampen, Vlasta. *A Drop of Gold* (PS–2). Illus. 2001, Annick LB $18.95 (1-55037-677-2); paper $7.95 (1-55037-676-4). 32pp. Spirited artwork illustrates this pourquoi tale of how Mother Nature and her helpers colored the world's birds. (Rev: BL 2/1/02; HBG 3/02; SLJ 1/02) [813]

2762 Van Kampen, Vlasta. *It Couldn't Be Worse!* (PS–1). Illus. 2003, Annick $18.95 (1-55037-783-3); paper $6.95 (1-55037-782-5). 32pp. A humorous tale that involves making the situation so much worse that getting back to normal brings instant relief. (Rev: BL 3/1/03) [813]

2763 Waldherr, Kris. *Sacred Animals* (3–6). Illus. 2001, HarperCollins LB $16.89 (0-688-16380-7). 48pp. Animal folklore and legends from around the world are organized in four sections — earth, water, fire, and air animals — and surrounded with won-

derful illustrations and borders. (Rev: BL 10/1/01; HBG 3/02; SLJ 11/01) [398.2]

Africa

2764 Badoe, Adwoa. *The Pot of Wisdom: Ananse Stories* (4–8). Illus. by Baba Wague Diakite. 2001, Groundwood $18.95 (0-88899-429-X). 64pp. Ten well-written folktales from Ghana recounting the adventures of Ananse, the clever trickster spider. (Rev: BL 12/1/01; HB 1–2/02; HBG 3/02; SLJ 10/01) [398.266]

2765 Bryan, Ashley. *Beautiful Blackbird* (K–2). Illus. 2003, Simon & Schuster $16.95 (0-689-84731-9). 40pp. Bold collages illustrate the Zambian tale of Blackbird, who is the envy of all the brightly colored birds in Africa and generously agrees to share his blackening potion, so that all the birds can be black and beautiful. (Rev: BCCB 2/03; BL 1/1–15/03; HB 3–4/03*; SLJ 1/03) [398.2]

2766 Cummings, Pat. *Ananse and the Lizard* (PS–3). Illus. 2002, Holt $16.95 (0-8050-6476-1). 40pp. The trickster spider meets his match when a cunning lizard wins the competition for the hand of the chief's daughter. (Rev: BL 11/1/02; HBG 3/03; SLJ 10/02) [398.2]

2767 Diakite, Baba Wague. *The Magic Gourd* (2–4). Illus. 2003, Scholastic $16.95 (0-439-43960-4). 32pp. A retelling of a folktale from Mali about a rabbit who, when his magic gourd is stolen, receives a magic rock to help recover it. (Rev: BCCB 3/03; BL 2/15/03; SLJ 2/03) [398.2]

2768 Eisner, Will. *Sundiata: A Legend of Africa* (5–8). Illus. 2003, NBM $15.95 (1-56163-332-1). 32pp. A retelling, in comic book style, of an African folktale about a lame prince who conquers an evil king. (Rev: BL 2/1/03; SLJ 2/03) [398.2]

2769 Janisch, Heinz. *The Fire: An Ethiopian Folk Tale* (PS–2). Trans. by Shelley Tanaka. Illus. by Fabricio Vandenbroeck. 2002, Groundwood $15.95 (0-88899-450-8). 32pp. A slave must spend the night on a snow-capped mountain peak with no clothes or shelter to win his freedom in this Ethiopian folktale with evocative double-page paintings. (Rev: BL 12/15/02; HBG 3/03; SLJ 2/03) [398.2]

2770 Kimmel, Eric A. *Anansi and the Magic Stick* (PS–2). Illus. by Janet Stevens. 2001, Holiday $16.95 (0-8234-1443-4). 32pp. Things don't go as Anansi the tricky spider plans when he steals a magic stick to do his work for him. (Rev: BCCB 12/01; BL 9/15/01; HBG 3/02; SLJ 9/01) [398.2]

2771 Lester, Julius. *Why Heaven Is Far Away* (K–3). Illus. by Joe Cepeda. 2002, Scholastic $16.95 (0-439-17871-1). 40pp. In this delightfully illustrated sequel to *What a Truly Cool World* (1999), God gives snakes their venom but the snakes are too quick to use this gift and problems ensue. (Rev: BCCB 12/02; BL 10/1/02; HB 11–12/02; HBG 3/03; SLJ 10/02) [398.2]

2772 Lexau, Joan M. *Crocodile and Hen: A Bakongo Folktale* (K). Illus. by Doug Cushman. 2001, HarperCollins LB $14.89 (0-06-028487-0). 48pp. In this easy-to-read tale from the Congo, Crocodile spares the life of Hen because he is persuaded that she is his relative. (Rev: BL 4/15/01; HBG 10/01; SLJ 6/01) [398.2]

2773 MacDonald, Margaret Read. *Mabela the Clever* (PS–3). Illus. by Tim Coffey. 2001, Albert Whitman $15.95 (0-8075-4902-9). 32pp. A clever mouse outwits a crafty cat in this West African tale. (Rev: BCCB 5/01; BL 7/01; HB 9–10/01; HBG 3/02; SLJ 6/01*) [398.2]

2774 McIntosh, Gavin. *Hausaland Tales from the Nigerian Marketplace* (4 Up). Illus. 2002, Linnet LB $22.50 (0-208-02523-5). 98pp. This collection of 12 Nigerian folktales skillfully interweaves details of contemporary Hausa society. (Rev: HBG 3/03; SLJ 11/02) [398.2]

2775 Paye, Won-Ldy, and Margaret H. Lippert. *Head, Body, Legs: A Story from Liberia* (PS–2). Illus. by Julie Paschkis. 2002, Holt $16.95 (0-8050-6570-9). 32pp. This amusing tale from Liberia about disjointed body parts teaches the value of cooperation. (Rev: BL 8/02; HB 5–6/02; HBG 10/02; SLJ 4/02) [398.2]

2776 Seeger, Pete, and Paul DuBois Jacobs. *Abiyoyo Returns* (1–3). Illus. by Michael Hays. 2001, Simon & Schuster $17.00 (0-689-83271-0). 40pp. The giant Abiyoyo returns to help the villagers build a dam in this sequel to Seeger's 1986 retelling of a South African folktale. (Rev: BCCB 11/01; BL 11/15/01; HB 11–12/01; HBG 3/02; SLJ 11/01) [398.2]

2777 Tchana, Katrin. *Sense Pass King: A Story from Cameroon* (PS–2). Illus. by Trina S. Hyman. 2002, Holiday $16.95 (0-8234-1577-5). 32pp. Sense Pass King is the name that a child prodigy acquires when she succeeds in discrediting the stupid king and becomes leader of her people. (Rev: BL 11/1/02; HB 11–12/02; HBG 3/03; SLJ 9/02) [398.2]

2778 Williams, Sheron. *Imani's Music* (PS–4). Illus. by Jude Daly. 2002, Simon & Schuster $17.00 (0-689-82254-5). 32pp. A grasshopper brings music to the people of Africa, and then to America when he is captured and transported with slaves. (Rev: BL 2/15/02; HBG 10/02; SLJ 1/02)

2779 Wolkstein, Diane. *The Day Ocean Came to Visit* (PS–3). Illus. by Steve Johnson and Lou Fancher. 2001, Harcourt $16.00 (0-15-201774-7). 40pp. Sun and Moon are married and live on Earth until Sun invites Ocean home for dinner in this pourquoi tale based on an African creation myth. (Rev: BL 7/01; HBG 3/02; SLJ 8/01) [398.8]

2780 Yohannes, Gebregeorgis. *Silly Mammo: An Ethiopian Tale* (PS). Illus. by Bogale Belachew. 2002, African Sun paper $10.00 (1-883701-04-X). 32pp. A contemporary Ethiopian village is the setting for this traditional tale in which a hapless lad gets everything wrong until he kisses a fair lady. (Rev: BL 10/1/02; SLJ 2/03) [398.2]

Asia

General and Miscellaneous

2781 Berger, Barbara Helen. *All the Way to Lhasa: A Tale from Tibet* (PS–2). Illus. 2002, Putnam $15.99 (0-399-23387-3). 32pp. Courage and perseverance win over headlong speed in this tale of two young men journeying to the holy city of Lhasa, with illustrations that contain many Tibetan Buddhist touches. (Rev: BL 10/1/02; HBG 3/03; SLJ 9/02) [398.2]

2782 Garland, Sherry. *Children of the Dragon: Selected Tales from Vietnam* (3–5). Illus. 2001, Harcourt $18.00 (0-15-224200-7). 64pp. Six tales from Vietnam are introduced by material on the land, its history, and folk traditions. (Rev: BL 7/01; HBG 3/02; SLJ 10/01*) [398.2]

2783 Park, Janie Jaehyun. *The Tiger and the Dried Persimmon* (K–3). Illus. 2002, Groundwood $15.95 (0-88899-485-0). 32pp. Vibrant artwork accompanies this version of a comic Korean folktale about a tiger who misinterprets a woman's words to her child and ends up terrified of persimmons. (Rev: BL 12/15/02; HBG 3/03) [398.2]

2784 San Souci, Daniel, retel. *The Rabbit and the Dragon King: Based on a Korean Folk Tale* (1–4). Illus. by Eujin Kim Neilan. 2002, Boyds Mills $15.95 (1-56397-880-6). San Souci retells with humor and drama the story of the king who rules the ocean, who in this case is convinced that eating a rabbit's heart will cure his ills. (Rev: SLJ 11/02) [398.2]

China

2785 Chen, Debby. *Monkey King Wreaks Havoc in Heaven* (4–6). Illus. by Wenhai Ma. 2001, Pan Asian $16.95 (1-57227-068-3). 36pp. A retelling of a Chinese tale about the sly Monkey King. (Rev: BL 10/15/01) [398.2]

2786 Fu, Shelley, retel. *Ho Yi the Archer and Other Classic Chinese Tales* (4–8). Illus. by Joseph F. Abboreno. 2001, Linnet LB $22.50 (0-208-02487-5). 145pp. This collection of folktales and myths, some of which may be familiar, includes notes, a pronunciation guide, and list of characters. (Rev: HB 9–10/01; HBG 3/02; SLJ 7/01) [398.2]

2787 Jiang, Ji-li. *The Magical Monkey King* (3–5). Illus. by Hui Hui Su-Kennedy. 2002, HarperCollins LB $14.89 (0-06-029544-9); paper $4.25 (0-06-442149-X). 96pp. Monkey, a lively trickster, is finally subdued by Buddha in this collection of tales from China. (Rev: BL 4/15/02; HB 9–10/02; HBG 3/03; SLJ 5/02) [398.2]

2788 Provensen, Alice. *The Master Swordsman and the Magic Doorway* (2–5). Illus. 2001, Simon & Schuster $16.95 (0-689-83232-X). 40pp. Two tales of ancient China — one about Little Chu, who wants to be a swordsman, and another about a painter who uses his art to save his own life. (Rev:

BL 10/15/01; HB 1–2/02; HBG 3/02; SLJ 11/01) [398.2]

2789 Shepard, Aaron. *Lady White Snake: A Tale from Chinese Opera* (4–6). Illus. by Song Nan Zhang. 2001, Pan Asian $16.95 (1-57227-072-1). 30pp. A lavishly illustrated story from Chinese opera about a snake that turns into a beautiful woman. (Rev: BL 10/15/01; SLJ 3/02) [398.2]

2790 Te Loo, Sanne. *Ping-Li's Kite* (PS–1). Illus. 2002, Front Street $15.95 (1-886910-75-8). 32pp. A young Chinese boy angers the Emperor of the Sky when he flies an undecorated kite in this book based on a Chinese folktale. (Rev: BL 8/02; HBG 10/02; SLJ 5/02) [398.2]

India

2791 Bateson-Hill, Margaret. *Chanda and the Mirror of Moonlight* (3–4). Illus. by Karin Littlewood. 2001, Zero to Ten $17.95 (1-84089-217-X). An evil stepmother tries to trick the prince into marrying her daughter instead of Chanda, but the mirror reveals the truth. (Rev: SLJ 5/02) [398.2]

2792 Moseley, James. *The Ninth Jewel of the Mughal Crown: The Birbal Tales from the Oral Traditions of India* (3–6). Illus. 2001, Summerwind $24.95 (0-9704447-1-0). 154pp. A collection of stories from India that involve the 14th-century Emperor Akbar and his clever and amusing adviser Birbal. (Rev: BL 7/01; SLJ 10/01) [398.2]

2793 Thornhill, Jan. *The Rumor: A Jataka Tale from India* (PS–2). Illus. 2002, Maple Tree $17.95 (1-894379-39-X). 32pp. Lush illustrations accompany this tale from India of an anxious hare who believes the world is breaking apart when she hears a mango fall to the ground. (Rev: BL 12/15/02; SLJ 11/02) [398.254]

Japan

2794 Hodges, Margaret, adapt. *The Boy Who Drew Cats* (K–3). Illus. by Aki Sogabe. 2002, Holiday $16.95 (0-8234-1594-5). 32pp. A young boy's obsession with drawing cats everywhere he goes eventually changes his life in this tale of the supernatural. (Rev: BCCB 4/02; BL 6/1–15/02; HB 5–6/02; HBG 10/02; SLJ 3/02) [398.2]

2795 Myers, Tim. *Tanuki's Gift: A Japanese Tale* (K–3). Illus. by Robert Roth. 2003, Marshall Cavendish $16.95 (0-7614-5101-3). 32pp. A Japanese folktale of a fond relationship between a Buddhist priest and a magical creature called a tanuki. (Rev: BL 3/15/03) [398.2]

2796 San Souci, Robert D. *The Silver Charm: A Folktale from Japan* (PS–2). Illus. by Yoriko Ito. 2002, Doubleday LB $17.99 (0-385-90847-4). A little magic comes in handy when young Satsu disobeys two important rules. (Rev: HBG 10/02; SLJ 6/02) [398.2]

Southeast Asia

2797 Day, Nancy Raines. *Piecing Earth and Sky Together* (2–4). Illus. by Genna Panzarella. 2001, Shens $17.95 (1-885008-19-8). 32pp. In this creation story from Laos with beautiful illustrations, two heavenly brothers set out to create the sky and the earth. (Rev: BL 4/1/02; HBG 10/02; SLJ 7/02) [398.2]

2798 Mason, Victor, and Gillian Beal, retels. *Balinese Children's Favorite Stories* (1–4). Illus. by Trina Bohan-Tyrie. 2001, Tuttle $16.95 (962-593-440-5). 96pp. Eleven tales from Bali, many of which are about animals, are paired with varied illustrations including detailed Balinese costumes. (Rev: SLJ 5/02) [398.2]

2799 Weitzman, David. *Rama and Sita: A Tale from Ancient Java* (1–3). Illus. 2002, Godine $19.95 (1-56792-151-5). 32pp. A retelling of the story *The Ramayana*, in the style of Javanese shadow puppetry. (Rev: BL 2/15/03) [398.2]

Australia and the Pacific Islands

2800 Romulo, Liana. *Filipino Children's Favorite Stories* (3–6). Illus. 2001, Periplus $16.95 (962-593-765-X). 96pp. This is an engaging collection of 14 traditional myths and folktales from the Philippines. (Rev: BL 4/1/01; HBG 3/02; SLJ 11/01) [398.2]

Europe

Central and Eastern Europe

2801 Lottridge, Celia Barker. *The Little Rooster and the Diamond Button* (K–3). Illus. by Joanne Fitzgerald. 2001, Douglas & McIntyre $16.95 (0-88899-443-5). 32pp. A retelling of a traditional Hungarian folktale about a rooster whose tenacity earns him a reward. (Rev: BL 9/1/01; HBG 3/02; SLJ 1/02) [398.2]

2802 Marshall, Bonnie C., retel. *Tales from the Heart of the Balkans* (3–5). Illus. Series: World Folklore. 2001, Libraries Unlimited $29.00 (1-56308-870-3). 166pp. Marshall retells folk and fairy tales from the region, preceded by historical and cultural information. (Rev: SLJ 2/02) [398.2]

2803 Molnar, Irma. *One-Time Dog Market at Buda and Other Hungarian Folktales* (5–8). Illus. by Georgeta-Elena Enesel. 2001, Linnet LB $25.00 (0-208-02505-7). 160pp. A collection of 23 clever, thought-provoking Hungarian folktales for older readers. (Rev: BL 1/1–15/02; HBG 3/02; SLJ 2/02) [398.2]

2804 Philip, Neil. *Noah and the Devil* (PS–3). Illus. by Isabelle Brent. 2001, Clarion $16.00 (0-618-11754-7). 32pp. The devil makes trouble aboard the ark in this retelling of the Bible story. (Rev: BL 10/1/01; HBG 3/02; SLJ 8/01) [398.2]

2805 Weber, Ilse. *Mendel Rosenbusch: Tales for Jewish Children* (3–6). Trans. from German by Ruth Fisher and Hans Fisher. 2001, Herodias $14.00 (1-928746-19-5). 102pp. A collection of Czech tales about a poor but wise man who lives behind a synagogue and is visited one night by an angel who gives him a gift — the ability to become invisible. (Rev: HBG 3/02; SLJ 11/01) [398.2]

France

2806 Bonning, Tony. *Fox Tale Soup* (PS–3). Illus. by Sally Hobson. 2002, Simon & Schuster $16.00 (0-689-84900-1). 32pp. An energetic retelling of "Stone Soup" in which a fox tricks farmyard animals into providing him with a meal. (Rev: BCCB 3/02; BL 2/1/02; HBG 10/02; SLJ 3/02) [398.2]

2807 Huling, Jan. *Puss in Cowboy Boots* (PS–2). Illus. by Phil Huling. 2002, Simon & Schuster $16.00 (0-689-83119-6). 40pp. The classic cat tale with a Texas twist. (Rev: BCCB 10/02; BL 8/02; HB 7–8/02; HBG 10/02; SLJ 6/02) [398.2]

2808 Muth, Jon J. *Stone Soup* (K–2). Illus. 2003, Scholastic $16.95 (0-439-33909-X). 32pp. In this version of the traditional tale, Buddhist monks want Chinese villagers to learn the joy of sharing, and as contributions come into the soup pot and the mix richens, so do the colors of the lush illustrations. (Rev: BCCB 3/03; BL 1/1–15/03; HB 3–4/03; SLJ 3/03) [398.2]

2809 Pullman, Philip. *Puss in Boots: The Adventures of That Most Enterprising Feline* (PS–3). Illus. by Ian Beck. 2001, Knopf $16.95 (0-375-81354-3). 32pp. Pullman's version adds a few new characters and a couple of mysteries to be solved. (Rev: BCCB 5/02; BL 7/01; HBG 3/02; SLJ 8/01) [398.2]

2810 Watts, Bernadette. *The Rich Man and the Shoemaker: A Fable by La Fontaine* (2–4). Illus. 2002, North-South LB $16.50 (0-7358-4676-X). 32pp. A Renaissance setting graces this tale of the shoemaker who returns a bribe when the gold causes him anxiety. (Rev: BL 10/1/02; HBG 3/03) [398.2]

Germany

2811 Aiken, Joan. *Snow White and the Seven Dwarfs* (PS–2). Illus. by Belinda Downes. 2002, DK $15.99 (0-7894-8799-3). 48pp. The magic mirror, the dark forest, and the lovely but evil queen are beautifully depicted in embroidered artwork, and the sly, fluid text adds new enjoyment to the classic fairy tale. (Rev: BCCB 1/03; BL 1/1–15/03; HBG 3/03) [398.2]

2812 Artell, Mike. *Petite Rouge: A Cajun Red Riding Hood* (PS–2). Illus. by Jim Harris. 2001, Dial $15.99 (0-8037-2514-0). 32pp. The wolf becomes an alligator and the little girl a duck in this Louisiana version of the classic tale. (Rev: BL 7/01; HBG 10/01; SLJ 6/01) [398.2]

2813 Bateman, Teresa. *The Princesses Have a Ball* (K–3). Illus. by Lynne W. Cravath. 2002, Albert Whitman $15.95 (0-8075-6626-8). 32pp. A suspicious king asks detectives to find out what his girls are up to, but a cobbler finds the answer first and advises the young ladies to reveal their athletic skills in this basketball version of "The Twelve Dancing Princesses." (Rev: BL 11/1/02; HB 1–2/03; HBG 3/03; SLJ 12/02) [398.2]

2814 Hoberman, Mary Ann. *The Marvelous Mouse Man* (1–4). Illus. by Laura Forman. 2002, Harcourt $16.00 (0-15-201715-1). 40pp. The pied piper gets a fresh, American update in entertaining rhyming verse with a new twist at the end. (Rev: BL 3/15/02; HBG 10/02; SLJ 5/02)

2815 Hoffmann, E. T. A. *The Nutcracker* (1–5). Illus. by Julie Paschkis. 2001, Chronicle $19.95 (0-8118-2962-6). Selections on CD, played by the London Symphony Orchestra, accompany this handsome adaptation of the famous tale that includes the "Story of the Hard Nut." (Rev: HBG 3/02; SLJ 10/01) [398.2]

2816 Montresor, Beni. *Hansel and Gretel* (K–3). Illus. 2001, Simon & Schuster $17.00 (0-689-84144-2). 32pp. A dramatic and mystical retelling of the classic tale. (Rev: BCCB 10/01; BL 7/01; HB 11–12/01; HBG 3/02; SLJ 9/01) [398.2]

2817 Norling, Beth. *Sister Night and Sister Day* (PS–2). Illus. 2001, Allen & Unwin $14.95 (1-86448-863-8). 32pp. There are quite different outcomes when twin sisters Ruby and Rose go to work for Mother Earth, in this retelling of a Grimm tale. (Rev: BL 8/01; SLJ 6/01) [398.2]

2818 Osborne, Mary Pope. *The Brave Little Seamstress* (K–3). Illus. by Giselle Potter. 2002, Atheneum $16.00 (0-689-84486-7). 40pp. A clever retelling of "The Brave Little Tailor" folktale using a saucy young girl as its heroine. (Rev: BCCB 5/02; BL 4/1/02; HBG 10/02; SLJ 4/02) [398.2]

2819 Price, Kathy. *The Bourbon Street Musicians* (4–6). Illus. by Andrew Glass. 2002, Clarion $16.00 (0-618-04076-5). 40pp. A retelling of "The Bremen Town Musicians" moved to New Orleans and with a Cajun beat. (Rev: BL 6/1–15/02; HBG 10/02; SLJ 5/02) [398.2]

2820 Stewig, John W. *Mother Holly* (K–3). Illus. by Johanna Westerman. 2001, North-South LB $15.88 (1-55858-925-2). 40pp. A retelling of a Grimm tale of two sisters, one good and the other the typical evil stepsister, that ends with the stepsister reforming. (Rev: BCCB 10/01; BL 7/01; HBG 3/02) [398.2]

Great Britain and Ireland

2821 Christelow, Eileen. *Where's the Big Bad Wolf?* (PS–1). Illus. 2002, Clarion $15.00 (0-618-18194-6). 32pp. This humorous retelling of the classic tale — featuring cartoon illustrations and dialogue balloons — is written as a mystery, featuring Detective Doggedly in search of BBW (Big Bad Wolf). (Rev: BL 10/15/02; HBG 3/03; SLJ 9/02)

2822 Cullen, Lynn. *Godiva* (3–5). Illus. by Kathryn Hewitt. 2001, Golden Books $14.99 (0-307-41175-3). 32pp. The legendary tale of Lady Godiva's selfless ride to aid the poor villagers, in a beautifully illustrated presentation for younger readers. (Rev: BL 1/1–15/02; HBG 10/02; SLJ 11/01) [398.2]

2823 Dahlie, Elizabeth. *Bernelly and Harriet: The Country Mouse and the City Mouse* (PS–2). Illus. 2002, Little, Brown $14.95 (0-316-60811-4). 32pp. A clever, charmingly illustrated version of the classic tale of the contrasts between city and country living, as experienced by two modern mice. (Rev: BL 4/15/02; HBG 10/02; SLJ 3/02) [398.2]

2824 Daly, Ita. *Irish Myths and Legends* (4–6). Illus. 2001, Oxford $19.95 (0-19-274534-4). 96pp. Ten traditional tales are retold in contemporary fashion. (Rev: BL 6/1–15/01; HBG 3/02) [398.2]

2825 Fearnley, Jan. *Mr. Wolf and the Three Bears* (PS–2). Illus. by author. 2002, Harcourt $16.00 (0-15-216423-5). Goldilocks arrives uninvited at Baby Bear's birthday party, but Grandma Wolf knows how to deal with her. (Rev: HBG 10/02; SLJ 6/02) [398.2]

2826 Gantschev, Ivan. *The Three Little Rabbits* (K–2). Illus. 2002, North-South $15.95 (0-7358-1474-0). 32pp. This twist on the three little pigs features three rabbits who must outsmart a fox. (Rev: BL 2/15/02; HBG 10/02) [398.2]

2827 Gorbachev, Valeri. *Goldilocks and the Three Bears* (PS–1). Illus. 2001, North-South LB $15.88 (0-7358-1439-2). 40pp. A nicely illustrated, faithful retelling in a large, square format. (Rev: BL 7/01; HBG 3/02; SLJ 6/01) [398.22]

2828 Hague, Michael. *Kate Culhane: A Ghost Story* (1–3). Illus. 2001, North-South LB $15.88 (1-58717-059-0). 40pp. A retelling of a spooky Irish ghost story about a young woman who cunningly outsmarts a ghoul. (Rev: BL 9/15/01; HBG 3/02; SLJ 9/01) [398.2]

2829 Huck, Charlotte. *The Black Bull of Norroway* (2–4). Illus. by Anita Lobel. 2001, Greenwillow LB $15.89 (0-688-16901-5). 40pp. A Scottish beauty-and-the-beast tale, richly illustrated and accompanied by a discussion of the story's origins and variants. (Rev: BCCB 5/01; BL 9/15/01; HB 5–6/01; HBG 10/01; SLJ 6/01) [398.2]

2830 Johnson, Paul Brett. *Jack Outwits the Giants* (PS–3). Illus. 2002, Simon & Schuster $16.00 (0-689-83902-2). 32pp. "Jack the Giant Killer" set in Appalachia and with a few hilarious new twists. (Rev: BCCB 7–8/02; BL 6/1–15/02; HB 7–8/02; HBG 10/02; SLJ 11/02) [398.2]

2831 Jones, Carol. *The Gingerbread Man* (PS–K). Illus. 2002, Houghton $15.00 (0-618-18822-3). 32pp. In this spirited retelling, it is nursery rhyme characters who chase the gingerbread boy. (Rev: BL 2/15/02; HBG 10/02; SLJ 4/02) [398.2]

2832 Light, Steve. *Puss in Boots* (PS–2). Illus. 2002, Abrams $14.95 (0-8109-4368-9). 24pp. Collages illustrate this faithful version of a favorite folktale. (Rev: BCCB 5/02; BL 4/15/02; HBG 10/02; SLJ 4/02) [398.2]

2833 Lowell, Susan. *Dusty Locks and the Three Bears* (PS–1). Illus. by Randy Cecil. 2001, Holt $15.95 (0-8050-5862-1). 32pp. A western version of Goldilocks starring a bad-tempered, ill-mannered runaway. (Rev: BCCB 7–8/01; BL 7/01; HB 7–8/01; HBG 10/01; SLJ 7/01) [398.2]

2834 Milligan, Bryce. *Brigid's Cloak: An Ancient Irish Story* (1–3). Illus. by Helen Cann. 2002, Eerdmans $16.00 (0-8028-5224-6). 32pp. This book with Celtic and early Christian undertones tells the story of Saint Brigid, who is transported to Jerusalem in a vision and helps care for the baby Jesus. (Rev: BL 10/15/02; HBG 3/03; SLJ 2/03) [398.2]

2835 Milligan, Bryce. *The Prince of Ireland and the Three Magic Stallions* (1–3). Illus. by Preston McDaniels. 2003, Holiday $16.95 (0-8234-1573-2). 32pp. An Irish folktale in which a story saves the lives of the storyteller and his friends. (Rev: BL 3/15/03*) [398.2]

2836 Moser, Barry. *The Three Little Pigs* (PS–1). Illus. 2001, Little, Brown $14.95 (0-316-58544-0). 32pp. A humorous retelling that retains much of the original, with delightful illustrations. (Rev: BCCB 3/01; BL 6/1–15/01; HB 5–6/01; HBG 10/01; SLJ 5/01) [398.24]

2837 Ryan, Patrick. *Shakespeare's Storybook: Folk Tales That Inspired the Bard* (3–5). Illus. by James Mayhew. 2001, Barefoot $19.99 (1-84148-307-9). 80pp. A retelling of seven folk tales that may have served as the inspiration for works by Shakespeare. (Rev: BL 11/15/01; HBG 3/02; SLJ 1/02) [822.3]

2838 Schmidt, Gary. *The Wonders of Donal O'Donnell: A Folktale of Ireland* (4–6). Illus. by Loren Long. 2002, Holt $17.95 (0-8050-6516-4). 40pp. Donal and his wife have permitted no visitors since their son's death, but when three peddlers consecutively appeal for help, they let them in and draw comfort from their traditional Irish tales. (Rev: BL 1/1–15/03; HBG 3/03; SLJ 12/02) [398.2]

2839 Souhami, Jessica. *Mrs. McCool and the Giant Cuhullin: An Irish Tale* (K–3). Illus. 2002, Holt $16.95 (0-8050-6852-X). 32pp. A giant of Irish lore, Cuhullin, goes in search of another, Finn McCool, to see who is strongest, but Finn's wife turns out to be strongest of all. (Rev: BL 2/15/02; HB 5–6/02*; HBG 10/02; SLJ 3/02) [398.2]

2840 Vivian, E. Charles. *Robin Hood: A Classic Illustrated Edition* (4–7). Illus. 2002, Chronicle $19.95 (0-8118-3399-2). 174pp. Illustrations ranging from medieval tapestries to comic book drawings by artists including Howard Pyle and N. C. Wyeth give visual interest to this retelling of the beloved Robin Hood tale. (Rev: BL 12/1/02; HBG 3/03; SLJ 3/03) [398.2]

2841 Whatley, Bruce. *Wait! No Paint!* (K–2). Illus. 2001, HarperCollins LB $15.89 (0-06-028271-1). 32pp. It's the illustrator himself who threatens the fate of the three little pigs and the big bad wolf in this colorful and inventive retelling. (Rev: BL 8/01; HB 9–10/01; HBG 3/02; SLJ 7/01) [398.2]

2842 Wiesner, David. *The Three Pigs* (K–6). Illus. by author. 2001, Clarion $16.00 (0-618-00701-6).

This is a fresh twist on the familiar tale, with excellent and inventive illustrations, that has a bewildered wolf searching for pigs that have been blown into a fantasy universe until they return and set the world to rights. Caldecott Medal winner, 2003. (Rev: BCCB 5/01; BL 5/15/01*; HB 5–6/01*; HBG 10/01; SLJ 4/01*) [398.2]

Greece and Italy

2843 Corwin, Oliver J. *Hare and Tortoise Race to the Moon* (K–3). Illus. 2002, Abrams $14.95 (0-8109-0566-3). 40pp. In this modern twist on Aesop's classic, Tortoise and Hare race to the moon in rocket ships. (Rev: BL 10/15/02; HBG 3/03; SLJ 11/02) [398.2]

2844 Repchuk, Caroline. *The Race* (K–3). Illus. by Alison Jay. 2002, Chronicle $15.95 (0-8118-3500-6). 24pp. This update has the hare and the tortoise racing around the world. (Rev: BL 4/15/02; HBG 10/02; SLJ 7/02) [398.24]

2845 Sykes, Julie. *That's Not Fair, Hare!* (PS–3). Illus. by Tim Warnes. 2001, Barron's $13.95 (0-7641-5347-1). A greedy hare gets his comeuppance in this retelling of the classic race tale with a twist at the end. (Rev: HBG 3/02; SLJ 2/02) [398.2]

Russia

2846 Martin, Rafe. *The Twelve Months* (2–4). Illus. by Vladyana Langer Krykorka. 2001, Stoddart $15.95 (0-7737-3249-7). 32pp. In this Russian variation on the Cinderella story, 12 men, representing the 12 months, help the poor young heroine supply the exotic gifts that her mean aunt and cousin demand. (Rev: BL 4/15/01; SLJ 11/01) [398.2]

2847 Riordan, James. *Russian Folk-Tales* (3–5). Illus. 2001, Oxford $19.95 (0-19-274536-0). 96pp. Ten traditional Russian tales including "The Flying Ship" and "The Firebird" are retold with appealing illustrations. (Rev: BL 4/1/01; HBG 3/02; SLJ 7/01) [398.2]

2848 Sanderson, Ruth. *The Golden Mare, the Firebird, and the Magic Ring* (3–5). Illus. 2001, Little, Brown $15.95 (0-316-76906-1). 32pp. This picture book for older readers includes elements from several Russian tales in a story of adventure and romance. (Rev: BL 4/1/01; HBG 10/01; SLJ 4/01) [398.2]

2849 Spirin, Gennady. *The Tale of the Firebird* (K–3). Trans. by Tatiana Popova. Illus. 2002, Putnam $16.99 (0-399-23584-1). 32pp. The tsar's youngest son survives a number of tests before finding the firebird and winning the love of the beautiful Yelena in this lush picture book that melds three traditional Russian tales. (Rev: BCCB 11/02; BL 11/15/02; HBG 3/03; SLJ 9/02) [398.2]

2850 Tolstoy, Alexei. *The Enormous Turnip* (1–2). Illus. by Scott Goto. 2002, Harcourt paper $3.95 (0-15-204584-8). For beginning readers, this is an appealing retelling. (Rev: HBG 3/03; SLJ 1/03) [398.2]

2851 Yolen, Jane. *The Firebird* (PS–3). Illus. by Vladimir Vagin. 2002, HarperCollins LB $15.89 (0-06-028539-7). 32pp. An effective retelling of the Russian story that combines elements from the original story with the ballet version. (Rev: BCCB 7–8/02; BL 6/1–15/02; HBG 10/02; SLJ 6/02) [398.2]

Scandinavia

2852 Brett, Jan. *Who's That Knocking on Christmas Eve?* (K–2). Illus. 2002, Putnam $16.99 (0-399-23873-5). 32pp. A beautifully illustrated folktale of a Christmas Eve feast nearly ruined by hungry trolls. (Rev: BCCB 10/02; BL 9/1/02; HBG 3/03; SLJ 10/02)

2853 Finch, Mary, retel. *The Three Billy Goats Gruff* (PS). Illus. by Roberta Arenson. 2001, Barefoot LB $15.99 (1-84148-349-4). A gentler version of the tale for this young age group, with colorful goats and a singing troll. (Rev: HBG 3/02; SLJ 11/01) [398.2]

2854 Hassett, John, and Ann Hassett. *The Three Silly Girls Grubb* (PS–1). Illus. 2002, Houghton $16.00 (0-618-14183-9). 32pp. The three Grubb girls must get past Ugly-Boy Bobby in this goofy version of "The Three Billy Goats Gruff." (Rev: BCCB 11/02; BL 9/15/02; HB 9–10/02; HBG 3/03; SLJ 11/02*) [398.2]

2855 Lunge-Larsen, Lise. *The Race of the Birkebeiners* (1–3). Illus. by Mary Azarian. 2001, Houghton $16.00 (0-618-10313-9). 32pp. A tale based on a real event in the early 13th century in which an infant prince is rescued from danger in a dramatic ski journey through a blizzard. (Rev: BCCB 10/01; BL 7/01; HBG 3/02; SLJ 9/01) [398.2]

2856 MacDonald, Margaret Read. *Fat Cat* (PS–3). Illus. by Julie Paschkis. 2001, August House $15.95 (0-87483-616-6). 32pp. Brilliant illustrations and rhythmic prose are featured in this Danish folktale about a cat that gobbles up anyone who calls him fat, and the cunning mouse that saves them all. (Rev: BL 11/15/01; HBG 3/02; SLJ 1/02) [398.2]

2857 Salley, Coleen. *Who's That Tripping over My Bridge?* (K–2). Illus. by Amy Jackson Dixon. 2002, Pelican $14.95 (1-56554-890-6). In this retelling of the Norwegian tale, the three Gruff goats live north of Baton Rouge and must cross a bridge guarded by a troll in order to reach the green grasses on the other side. (Rev: HBG 10/02; SLJ 5/02) [398.2]

2858 Shepard, Aaron. *The Princess Mouse: A Tale of Finland* (K–3). Illus. by Leonid Gore. 2003, Simon & Schuster $16.95 (0-689-82912-4). 32pp. A mouse turns out to be a princess and a bride for a worthy brother in this entertaining folktale. (Rev: BL 2/1/03; SLJ 2/03) [398.2]

2859 Youngquist, Catherine Valente. *The Three Billygoats Gruff and Mean Calypso Joe* (K–3). Illus. by Kristin Sorra. 2002, Simon & Schuster $16.00 (0-689-82824-1). 32pp. The classic story of the three billy goats gets a Caribbean twist, complete with a troll named Calypso Joe. (Rev: BL 8/02; HBG 10/02; SLJ 11/02) [398.2]

Spain and Portugal

2860 Campoy, F. Isabel. *Rosa Raposa* (K–3). Illus. by Jose Aruego and Ariane Dewey. 2002, Harcourt $16.00 (0-15-202161-2). 32pp. Rosa, a wily fox, outwits a jaguar in these three traditional Spanish tales set in the Amazon rain forest. (Rev: BCCB 11/02; BL 9/1/02; HB 1–2/03; HBG 3/03; SLJ 9/02) [398.2]

Jewish Folklore

2861 Demas, Corinne. *The Magic Apple* (1–2). Illus. by Alexi Natchev. Series: Road to Reading. 2002, Golden Books $11.99 (0-307-46334-6); paper $3.99 (0-307-26334-7). 48pp. In this easy-to-read variation on a Jewish tale, three sisters help save a dying prince but only one will be rewarded by marrying him. (Rev: BL 4/15/02; HBG 10/02) [398.2]

2862 Fowles, Shelley. *The Bachelor and the Beam* (PS–2). Illus. 2003, Farrar $16.00 (0-374-30478-5). 32pp. In this Jewish folktale, an old bachelor drops a bean down a well, setting off a series of magical events. (Rev: BL 3/15/03; SLJ 3/03) [398.2]

2863 *Ghosts and Golems: Haunting Tales of the Supernatural* (4–6). Ed. by Malka Penn. Illus. by Theodor Black. 2001, Jewish Publication Soc. $14.95 (0-8276-0733-4). 110pp. Ten supernatural short stories with Jewish themes will send chills down the spines of middle-graders and prompt discussions about values. (Rev: BL 11/1/01; HBG 3/02; SLJ 2/02) [398.2]

2864 Schmidt, Gary. *Mara's Stories: Glimmers in the Darkness* (4–8). 2001, Holt $15.95 (0-8050-6794-9). 150pp. Mara tells stories from Jewish folklore to comfort the women and children in her concentration camp. (Rev: BL 10/1/01; HB 1–2/02*; HBG 3/02; SLJ 12/01) [398.2]

2865 Uhlberg, Myron. *Lemuel the Fool* (PS–3). Illus. by Sonja Lamut. 2001, Peachtree $15.95 (1-56145-220-3). 32pp. In this Yiddish folktale, a dreamer sets out to see the world but, because he is walking in a circle, finds himself back home. (Rev: BL 4/15/01; HBG 10/01; SLJ 8/01) [398.2]

Middle East

2866 Wolfson, Margaret Olivia. *The Patient Stone: A Persian Love Story* (3–7). Illus. by Juan Caneba Clavero. 2001, Barefoot $16.99 (1-84148-085-1). 32pp. This retelling of the story of Fatima, who after many trials earns the love of a prince thanks to a magic stone, is accompanied by beautiful watercolors and handsome borders, as well as an author's note that explains some of the symbolism. (Rev: BL 9/15/01; HBG 3/02; SLJ 2/02) [398.2]

2867 Young, Ed. *What about Me?* (K–3). Illus. 2002, Putnam $16.99 (0-399-23624-4). 40pp. A colorful cumulative tale of Sufi origin about a boy who must provide the grand master with a carpet before he will give the youngster the gift of knowledge. (Rev: BCCB 7–8/02; BL 5/1/02*; HB 7–8/02; HBG 10/02; SLJ 6/02) [398.2]

2868 Zeman, Ludmila. *Sindbad in the Land of Giants* (PS–3). Illus. 2001, Tundra $17.95 (0-88776-461-4). 32pp. Sindbad's cunning and courage are tested in this beautifully illustrated adventure. (Rev: BL 8/01; HBG 10/01; SLJ 8/01) [398.2]

2869 Zeman, Ludmila, retel. *Sindbad's Secret: From The Tales of the Thousand and One Nights* (2–5). Illus. by Ludmila Zeman. 2003, Tundra $17.95 (0-88776-462-2). Sindbad recounts two wondrous escapes and his discovery of the ultimate treasure is this last volume of Zeman's trilogy. (Rev: SLJ 3/03) [813.54]

North America

Canada

2870 Jorisch, Stephane, adapt. *As for the Princess? A Folktale from Quebec* (K–3). Illus. by Stephane Jorisch. 2001, Annick LB $19.95 (1-55037-695-0); paper $7.95 (1-55037-694-2). A not-very-bright young man finally gets his revenge against a beautiful but light-fingered princess. (Rev: HBG 3/02; SLJ 3/02) [398.2]

Inuit

2871 Hall, Amanda. *The Stolen Sun: A Story of Native Alaska* (PS–3). Illus. 2002, Eerdmans $17.00 (0-8028-5225-4). 32pp. A Native Alaskan tale with folkloric flavor about the creation of the world and its inhabitants. (Rev: BL 2/15/02; HBG 10/02; SLJ 9/02) [398.2]

2872 Wolfson, Evelyn. *Inuit Mythology* (5–8). Illus. by William Sauts Bock. 2001, Enslow LB $20.95 (0-7660-1559-9). 128pp. Seven tales from Inuit folklore are accompanied by information on the history and culture of the Inuit peoples. (Rev: BL 4/15/02; HBG 3/02; SLJ 3/02) [398.2]

Native Americans

2873 Bierhorst, John. *Is My Friend at Home? Pueblo Fireside Tales* (2–4). Illus. by Wendy Watson. 2001, Farrar $16.00 (0-374-33550-8). 32pp. Seven Hopi pourquoi tales involve trickster inclinations among the animals. (Rev: BL 7/01; HB 9–10/01; HBG 3/02; SLJ 9/01) [398.2]

2874 Bouchard, David. *Qu'Appelle* (3–6). Illus. by Michael Lonechild. 2002, Raincoast $15.95 (1-55192-475-7). A young Cree woman, heartbroken when her betrothed must go to war, calls out to him while dying. (Rev: SLJ 10/02) [398.2]

2875 Bushyhead, Robert H. *Yonder Mountain: A Cherokee Legend* (PS–3). Illus. by Kristina

151

Rodanas. 2002, Marshall Cavendish $16.95 (0-7614-5113-7). 32pp. In this Cherokee folktale, an old chief tests three young men to determine who will be his successor. (Rev: BL 2/15/03; SLJ 12/02) [398.2]

2876 Charles, Veronika M., retel. *Maiden of the Mist: A Legend of Niagara Falls* (1–3). Illus. by Veronika M. Charles. 2001, Stoddart $13.95 (0-7737-3297-7); paper $6.95 (0-7737-6207-8). A beautifully illustrated story of the maiden who sacrifices herself to the Thunder God in order to save her people from illness. (Rev: SLJ 1/02) [398.2]

2877 Curry, Jane Louise. *The Wonderful Sky Boat* (3–7). Illus. 2001, Simon & Schuster $17.00 (0-689-83595-7). 160pp. A collection of nearly 30 Native American creation, pourquoi, and trickster stories. (Rev: BL 5/15/01; HB 9–10/01; HBG 3/02) [398.2]

2878 Goble, Paul. *Storm Maker's Tipi* (2–5). Illus. 2001, Atheneum $18.00 (0-689-84137-X). 40pp. A retelling of a Blackfoot legend about the origin of tipis (tepees), with drawings, photographs, and instructions for making a paper tipi. (Rev: BCCB 1/02; BL 10/1/01; HBG 3/02; SLJ 10/01) [398.2]

2879 Lind, Michael. *Bluebonnet Girl* (K–3). Illus. by Kate Kiesler. 2003, Holt $16.95 (0-8050-6573-3). 40pp. A Comanche legend telling why bluebonnets bloom in Texas. (Rev: BL 3/15/03) [398.2]

2880 London, Jonathan. *Loon Lake* (PS–2). Illus. by Susan Ford. 2002, Chronicle $15.95 (0-8118-2003-3). 32pp. A little girl's father tells a Native American tale about how the loon got its necklace. (Rev: BL 8/02; HBG 10/02; SLJ 9/02)

2881 Martin, Rafe. *The World Before This One* (5–8). Illus. by Calvin Nichols. 2002, Scholastic $16.95 (0-590-37976-3). 208pp. Crow, a Seneca Indian, comes upon a storytelling stone that tells him about the origins of the earth in this series of stories. (Rev: BL 2/15/03; HBG 3/03; SLJ 12/02) [398.2]

2882 Webster, M. L., retel. *On the Trail Made of Dawn: Native American Creation Stories* (4 Up). 2001, Linnet LB $19.50 (0-208-02497-2). 69pp. The author retells 13 creation stories and places them in cultural context. (Rev: HBG 3/02; SLJ 12/01) [398.2]

United States

2883 Doucet, Sharon Arms. *Lapin Plays Possum: Trickster Tales from the Louisiana Bayou* (4–6). Illus. by Scott Cook. 2002, Farrar $18.10 (0-374-34328-4). 64pp. This is a well-illustrated collection of three tales about the trickster rabbit from Cajun country told with many humorous bayou phrases. (Rev: BL 4/15/02; HB 5–6/02; HBG 10/02; SLJ 4/02) [398.2]

2884 Hayes, Joe. *El Cucuy! A Bogeyman Cuento in English and Spanish* (K–4). Illus. by Honorio Robledo. 2001, Cinco Puntos $15.95 (0-938317-54-7). 32pp. A southwestern bogeyman comes down from his mountain to carry off bad children. (Rev: BL 7/01; HBG 10/01; SLJ 7/01) [398.2]

2885 Hayes, Joe. *Juan Verdades: The Man Who Couldn't Tell a Lie* (2–4). Illus. by Joseph Daniel Fiedler. 2001, Scholastic $16.95 (0-439-29311-1). 32pp. The honesty of Juan Valdez (known as Juan Verdades for his amazing truthfulness) is tested in this romantic and richly illustrated tale set in the early American Southwest. (Rev: BL 12/1/01; HBG 3/02; SLJ 12/01) [398.2]

2886 Hayes, Joe. *Pajaro Verde / The Green Bird* (2–4). Illus. by Antonio Castro L. 2002, Cinco Puntos $16.95 (0-938317-65-2). 40pp. A young woman marries a bird to save him from evil in this New Mexican folktale, told in both Spanish and English, filled with magic and monsters. (Rev: BL 10/15/02; HBG 3/03) [398.2]

2887 Johnson, Paul Brett. *Fearless Jack* (K–3). Illus. 2001, Simon & Schuster $16.00 (0-689-83296-6). 32pp. An Appalachian tale in which Jack amazes people with his prowess, overwhelming "varmints" left and right. (Rev: BCCB 9/01; BL 7/01; HB 9–10/01; HBG 3/02; SLJ 7/01) [398.8]

2888 Martin, Rafe. *The Shark God* (PS–3). Illus. by David Shannon. 2001, Scholastic $15.95 (0-590-39500-9). 32pp. Younger readers will thrill to the dynamic illustrations and this ancient Hawaiian tale of two children who are condemned to death by their king. (Rev: BCCB 1/02; BL 11/1/01; HB 11–12/01; HBG 3/02; SLJ 9/01) [398.2]

2889 Nordenstrom, Michael. *Pele and the Rivers of Fire* (2–4). Illus. 2002, Bess Press $9.95 (1-57306-079-8). 32pp. The power of Pele, the Hawaiian volcano goddess, is brought to life by spectacular, vivid paintings accompanied by a simple retelling of Pele's move to Hawaii from Tahiti and her battles with her sister. (Rev: BL 12/1/02; HBG 3/03; SLJ 1/03) [299]

2890 Willey, Margaret. *Clever Beatrice* (PS–3). Illus. by Heather Solomon. 2001, Simon & Schuster $16.00 (0-689-83254-0). 40pp. A tall tale from the wilds of Michigan in which a little girl named Beatrice outwits a rich giant. (Rev: BL 7/01; HB 11–12/01*; HBG 3/02; SLJ 10/01) [398.2]

South and Central America

Mexico and Other Central American Lands

2891 Gerson, Mary-Joan. *Fiesta Feminina: Celebrating Women in Mexican Folktales* (4–8). Illus. 2001, Barefoot $19.99 (1-84148-365-6). 64pp. This volume includes eight tales from Mexican folklore about strong and magical women, presented with bold illustrations, a pronunciation guide, and a glossary. (Rev: BL 9/15/01; HBG 3/02; SLJ 10/01) [398.2]

2892 Mora, Pat. *The Race of Toad and Deer* (PS–1). Illus. by Domi. 2001, Groundwood $15.95 (0-88899-434-6). 32pp. This is a newly illustrated and rewritten version of the Mayan take on the tortoise and the hare, first published in 1995. (Rev: BCCB 12/01; BL 12/15/01; HBG 3/02) [398.2]

Puerto Rico and Other Caribbean Islands

2893 Hallworth, Grace. *Sing Me a Story: Song and Dance Stories from the Caribbean* (K–3). Illus. by John Clementson. 2002, August House $19.95 (0-87483-672-7). 48pp. Caribbean folktales that involve song are accompanied by music and lyrics as well as lively and evocative collage borders. (Rev: BL 11/1/02; HBG 3/03; SLJ 9/02) [398.2]

2894 MacDonald, Amy. *Please, Malese!* (K–3). Illus. by Emily Lisker. 2002, Farrar $16.00 (0-374-36000-6). 32pp. This variation of a Haitian folktale tells the story of wily Malese, a trickster who can convince the villagers of anything. (Rev: BL 8/02; HB 9–10/02; HBG 3/03; SLJ 9/02) [398.2]

2895 San Souci, Robert D. *The Twins and the Bird of Darkness: A Hero Tale from the Caribbean* (K–4). Illus. by Terry Widener. 2002, Simon & Schuster $16.95 (0-689-83343-1). 40pp. Twin brothers — one nasty, one nice — vie to rescue a princess in this Caribbean tale. (Rev: BL 8/02; SLJ 9/02) [398.297]

South America

2896 McDermott, Gerald. *Jabuti the Tortoise: A Trickster Tale from the Amazon* (K–2). Illus. 2001, Harcourt $16.00 (0-15-200496-3). 32pp. A brilliantly colorful retelling of the story of Jabuti, a tortoise who is tricked by a jealous vulture, who in turn is punished as the other birds gain colors and songs. (Rev: BL 9/15/01; HBG 3/02; SLJ 9/01) [398.2]

2897 Maggi, Maria Elena. *The Great Canoe: A Karina Legend* (PS–3). Illus. by Gloria Calderon. 2001, Douglas & McIntyre $15.95 (0-88899-444-3). 32pp. In a tale similar to that of Noah and his ark, four couples must build a canoe and rescue animals and plants from a great flood. (Rev: BL 11/15/01; HB 1–2/02; HBG 3/02; SLJ 10/01*) [398.2]

2898 Olaondo, Susana. *Julieta, ?Que Plantaste? / Julieta, What Did You Plant?* (K–2). Illus. 2001, Montevideo: Alfaguara/Santillana paper $9.95 (9974-671-00-0). 32pp. This folktale about industrious Julieta the armadillo and the indolent but clever fox who tries to outwit her is sprinkled with Uruguayan phrases and accompanied by cartoonlike illustrations. (Rev: BL 12/15/01) [398.2]

Mythology

General and Miscellaneous

2899 Dalal, Anita. *Myths of Oceania* (5–8). Series: Mythic World. 2002, Raintree Steck-Vaughn LB $17.98 (0-7398-4978-6). 48pp. Information about Oceania and its people is included as well as 10 myths about the sea, fishing, and other unique aspects of island living. (Rev: BL 7/02; HBG 10/02) [398.3]

2900 Dalal, Anita. *Myths of Russia and the Slavs* (5–8). Series: Mythic World. 2002, Raintree Steck-Vaughn LB $17.98 (0-7398-4979-4). 48pp. This lavishly illustrated, oversize volume contains 10 myths from Eastern Europe as well as material on the society that created them. (Rev: BL 7/02; HBG 10/02; SLJ 5/02) [398.2]

2901 Gibbons, Gail. *Behold . . . the Unicorns!* (2–4). Illus. 2001, HarperCollins LB $15.89 (0-688-17958-4). 32pp. This handsomely designed book introduces the unicorn and all the myths and symbolism that surround one-horned beasts. (Rev: BCCB 12/01; BL 12/1/01; HBG 3/02; SLJ 12/01) [398.24]

2902 Green, Jen. *Myths of China and Japan* (5–8). Series: Mythic World. 2002, Raintree Steck-Vaughn LB $17.98 (0-7398-4977-8). 48pp. This handsome, oversize book explores the ancient mythology of China and Japan and, in addition to the retelling of ten myths, contains information on the societies that created them. (Rev: BL 7/02; HBG 10/02) [398.2]

2903 Muten, Burleigh, retel. *The Lady of Ten Thousand Names: Goddess Stories from Many Cultures* (4–7). Illus. by Helen Cann. 2001, Barefoot LB $19.99 (1-84148-048-7). 79pp. Eight myths that feature goddesses from cultures around the world are retold in this appealing volume. (Rev: HBG 3/02; SLJ 11/01) [291.2]

Classical

2904 Burleigh, Robert. *Pandora* (3–6). Illus. by Raul Colon. 2002, Harcourt $16.00 (0-15-202178-7). 32pp. A handsome retelling of the Greek myth about Pandora, her longings to open the box, and the terror it produced when she did. (Rev: BCCB 5/02; BL 6/1–15/02; HBG 10/02; SLJ 5/02) [398.2]

2905 Demi. *King Midas* (2–4). Illus. 2002, Simon & Schuster $19.95 (0-689-83297-4). 48pp. Rich illustrations accompany this retelling of the King Midas tale for younger readers. (Rev: BL 3/15/02; HB 5–6/02; HBG 10/02; SLJ 5/02) [398.2]

2906 Green, Jen. *Myths of Ancient Greece* (5–8). Illus. Series: Mythic World. 2001, Raintree Steck-Vaughn LB $18.98 (0-7398-3191-7). 48pp. This volume for older readers separates myth from reality about ancient Greece. (Rev: BL 3/1/02; HBG 3/02; SLJ 12/01) [398.2]

2907 McCaughrean, Geraldine. *Roman Myths* (4–8). Illus. by Emma C. Clark. 2001, Simon & Schuster $21.00 (0-689-83822-0). 96pp. Fifteen Roman myths are retold here in a lively manner, accompanied by appealing color illustrations. (Rev: BL 9/1/01; HB 7–8/01; HBG 10/01; SLJ 7/01) [398.2]

2908 Osborne, Mary Pope. *The One-Eyed Giant* (4–8). Series: Tales from the Odyssey. 2002, Hyperion $9.99 (0-7868-0770-9). 112pp. Osborne recounts the return from the Trojan War and Odysseus's encounter with the Cyclops, followed by guides to the Greek gods and to pronunciation and information on Homer. Also use *The Land of the Dead* (2002). (Rev: BL 11/15/02; HBG 3/03; SLJ 1/03) [883]

2909 Spires, Elizabeth. *I Am Arachne* (4–7). Illus. 2001, Farrar $16.00 (0-374-33525-7). 160pp. Spires takes a fresh look at some ancient stories, breathing new life and humor into first-person tales of Midas, Pan, Narcissus, and Eurydice. (Rev: BL 6/1–15/01; HB 9–10/01; HBG 3/02; SLJ 5/01) [813]

2910 Yolen, Jane, and Robert J. Harris. *Atalanta and the Arcadian Beast* (4–6). Series: Young Heroes. 2003, HarperCollins LB $16.89 (0-06-029455-8). 256pp. The ancient Greek myth of Atalanta, a girl who, accompanied by a bear, searches for her father's killer and discovers her true heritage. (Rev: BL 2/1/03; SLJ 2/03) [398.2]

2911 Yolen, Jane, and Robert J. Harris. *Hippolyta and the Curse of the Amazons* (4–8). Series: Young Heroes. 2002, HarperCollins LB $15.89 (0-06-028737-3). 256pp. It falls to 13-year-old Hippolyta,

an Amazon princess, to find a way to save her people when her mother refuses to sacrifice her second-born male child. (Rev: BCCB 4/02; HBG 10/02; SLJ 3/02) [398.2]

Scandinavian

2912 Fisher, Leonard Everett. *Gods and Goddesses of the Ancient Norse* (K–4). Illus. 2002, Holiday $16.95 (0-8234-1569-4). 40pp. An introduction to 15 ancient Norse gods and goddesses, with a pronunciation guide and a family tree. (Rev: BCCB 6/02; BL 3/1/02; HBG 10/02; SLJ 3/02) [293]

Poetry

General

2913 Andrews, Sylvia. *Dancing in My Bones* (PS). Illus. by Ellen Mueller. 2001, HarperFestival $9.95 (0-694-01316-1). 24pp. A multicultural cast of kids dance their way through a park, adding lines to a rhyme along the way. (Rev: BL 11/1/01; HBG 3/02; SLJ 12/01) [811]

2914 Argueta, Jorge. *A Movie in My Pillow / Una Pelicula en Mi Almohada* (4–8). Illus. by Elizabeth Gomez. 2001, Children's $15.95 (0-89239-165-0). 32pp. The author remembers in poetry his family's immigration to the United States from El Salvador, with each poem accompanied by the translation and rich illustrations. (Rev: BL 10/1/01; HBG 10/01; SLJ 5/01*) [861]

2915 *Around the Day* (PS–K). Ed. by John Foster. Illus. by Carol Thompson. 2001, Oxford $16.95 (0-19-276227-3). 64pp. An anthology of cheerful poems about a young child's everyday life. (Rev: BL 5/1/01; HBG 10/01; SLJ 6/01) [811]

2916 *Around the World in Eighty Poems* (3–5). Ed. by James Berry. Illus. by Katherine Lucas. 2002, Chronicle $19.95 (0-8118-3506-5). 96pp. A collection of poems from countries around the world, illustrated with paintings. (Rev: BCCB 1/03; BL 7/02; HBG 3/03) [808.81]

2917 Bauer, Marion Dane. *Love Song for a Baby* (PS–K). Illus. by Dan Andreasen. 2002, Simon & Schuster $15.95 (0-689-82268-5). 40pp. A tender poem about parents' love for their growing baby, with excellent oil paintings and rhyming text. (Rev: BL 9/1/02; HBG 3/03; SLJ 8/02) [811]

2918 Becker, Helaine. *Mama Likes to Mambo* (K–2). Illus. by John Beder. 2002, Stoddart $15.95 (0-7737-3316-7). 32pp. A collection of amusing, attractively illustrated poems of differing lengths on varied subjects. (Rev: BL 9/15/02; HBG 10/02; SLJ 5/02) [811]

2919 Benet, Rosemary, and Stephen Vincent Benet. *Johnny Appleseed* (PS–2). Illus. by S. D. Schindler. 2001, Simon & Schuster $16.00 (0-689-82975-2). 40pp. Colored-pencil illustrations accompany the verses of this poem that was first published in 1933. (Rev: BL 6/1–15/01; HBG 3/02; SLJ 8/01) [811]

2920 Borden, Louise. *America Is . . .* (2–4). Illus. by Stacey Schuett. 2002, Simon & Schuster $16.95 (0-689-83900-6). 40pp. This patriotic poem for younger readers examines life in America through many prisms. (Rev: BL 8/02; HBG 10/02; SLJ 6/02) [811]

2921 Brown, Margaret Wise. *Give Yourself to the Rain: Poems for the Very Young* (PS–1). Illus. by Teri L. Weidner. 2002, Simon & Schuster $16.95 (0-689-83344-X). 32pp. A collection of 24 previously unpublished poems for young readers, illustrated in beautiful warm pastels. (Rev: BL 2/15/02; HBG 10/02; SLJ 3/02) [811]

2922 Bunting, Eve. *Sing a Song of Piglets: A Calendar in Verse* (PS–1). Illus. by Emily Arnold McCully. 2002, Clarion $16.00 (0-618-01137-4). 32pp. Readers follow a pair of piglets through the year, with lively watercolors that match the bounciness of the simple rhymes. (Rev: BL 11/15/02; HBG 3/03; SLJ 8/02) [811]

2923 Calmenson, Stephanie. *Good for You! Toddler Rhymes for Toddler Times* (PS). Illus. by Melissa Sweet. 2001, HarperCollins LB $16.89 (0-06-029811-1). 64pp. These poems and riddles feature everyday items, activities, and new experiences in a toddler's life: playing, learning, making friends, and so forth. (Rev: BCCB 11/01; BL 10/15/01; HBG 3/02; SLJ 10/01) [811]

2924 Calmenson, Stephanie. *Welcome, Baby! Baby Rhymes for Baby Times* (PS). Illus. by Melissa Sweet. 2002, HarperCollins LB $18.89 (0-06-000492-4). 64pp. Charmingly illustrated peppy poems about and for toddlers bouncily describe events in a baby's life from birth to about 18 months, finishing up with educational poems about the alphabet and colors. (Rev: BCCB 12/02; BL 12/1/02; HBG 3/03; SLJ 9/02) [811]

2925 Carroll, Lewis. *Jabberwocky* (K–2). Illus. by Joel Stewart. 2003, Candlewick $15.99 (0-7636-2018-1). 32pp. An imaginatively illustrated version of the classic nonsense poem. (Rev: BL 3/15/03*) [811]

2926 *Dirty Laundry Pile* (3–6). Ed. by Paul B. Janeczko. 2001, HarperCollins LB $15.89 (0-688-16252-5). 40pp. An anthology of 27 poems told from the standpoint of an object or an animal such as a seashell, a cat, and a tree. (Rev: BL 4/15/01*; HB 7–8/01*; HBG 10/01; SLJ 8/01) [811]

2927 Dotlich, Rebecca Kai. *In the Spin of Things: Poetry of Motion* (2–5). Illus. by Karen M. Dugan. 2003, Boyds Mills $16.95 (1-56397-145-3). 32pp. Everyday items whirl into motion in this collection of free-form poems. (Rev: SLJ 3/03) [811]

2928 Dotlich, Rebecca Kai. *When Riddles Come Rumbling: Poems to Ponder* (2–5). Illus. 2001, Boyds Mills $15.95 (1-56397-846-6). 32pp. Short, rhythmic poems along with picture clues form riddles about everyday objects. (Rev: BL 11/1/01; HBG 3/02; SLJ 10/01) [811]

2929 *The Drowsy Hours: Poems for Bedtime* (PS–1). Ed. by Susan Pearson. Illus. by Peter Malone. 2002, HarperCollins LB $16.89 (0-06-029421-3). 40pp. This thoughtful anthology captures the bedtime mood perfectly, but will be appreciated any time of the day. (Rev: BL 10/15/02; HBG 10/02; SLJ 6/02) [811.008]

2930 Eastwick, Ivy O. *I Asked a Tiger to Tea* (2–6). Illus. by Melanie Hall. 2002, Boyds Mills $15.95 (1-56397-515-7). 32pp. This is a richly illustrated, lyrical collection of poems about nature and childhood. (Rev: BL 12/15/02; HBG 3/03; SLJ 11/02) [811.54]

2931 Eastwick, Ivy O. *Some Folks Like Cats and Other Poems* (1–3). Ed. by Walter B. Barbe. Illus. by Mary Kurnich Maass. 2002, Boyds Mills $15.95 (1-56397-450-9). 28pp. A collection of 20 of the author's poems that deal with such subjects as sunflowers, leaves, rain, and small animals. (Rev: BL 4/15/02; HBG 10/02; SLJ 7/02) [811.54]

2932 *The Fish Is Me: Bathtime Rhymes* (PS). Ed. by Neil Philip. Illus. by Claire Henley. 2002, Clarion $16.00 (0-618-15939-8). 28pp. These 18 rhymes are drawn from poets from several countries, and will immediately appeal to children, whether they enjoy baths or not. (Rev: BL 11/1/02; HBG 3/03; SLJ 8/02) [811.008]

2933 Fisher, Aileen. *I Heard a Bluebird Sing* (2–5). Illus. by Jennifer Emery. 2002, Boyds Mills $18.95 (1-56397-191-7). 64pp. The 41 poems included in this anthology were selected by children around the United States; they are preceded by excerpts from an article by Fisher and by introductions to the thematically organized sections. (Rev: BL 11/15/02; HBG 3/03; SLJ 10/02) [811.54]

2934 Fletcher, Ralph. *Have You Been to the Beach Lately? Poems* (4–7). Photos by Andrea Sperling. 2001, Scholastic $15.95 (0-531-30330-6). 48pp. More than 30 chatty poems, illustrated with black-and-white photographs, are written from the per-spective of a smart and funny 11-year-old. (Rev: HBG 10/01; SLJ 8/01) [811]

2935 George, Kristine O'Connell. *Swimming Upstream: Middle School Poems* (5–8). Illus. by Debbie Tilley. 2002, Clarion $14.00 (0-618-15250-4). 80pp. Brief poems describe how one girl navigates the rapids of middle school, discussing everything from school lunches and lockers to making friends and relationships with boys. (Rev: BL 1/1–15/03; HB 1–2/03; HBG 3/03; SLJ 9/02) [811]

2936 George, Kristine O'Connell. *Toasting Marshmallows: Camping Poems* (K–4). Illus. by Kate Kiesler. 2001, Clarion $15.00 (0-618-04597-X). 48pp. Thirty simple poems clearly depict a family camping trip, from the details of pitching a tent to the wonders of the natural world, with attractive and varied artwork. (Rev: HBG 10/01; SLJ 7/01*) [811]

2937 *A Grand Celebration: Grandparents in Poetry* (3–7). Ed. by Carol G. Hittleman and Daniel R. Hittleman. Illus. by Kay Life. 2002, Boyds Mills $16.95 (1-56397-901-2). 32pp. This anthology of 26 poems about grandparents represents a variety of cultures, levels of activity, and ages. (Rev: BL 4/1/02; HBG 10/02; SLJ 6/02) [808.819]

2938 Grimes, Nikki. *Stepping Out with Grandma Mac* (4–7). Illus. 2001, Orchard $16.95 (0-531-30320-9). 48pp. A loving 10-year-old girl describes a very independent grandmother. (Rev: BL 5/15/01*; HBG 10/01; SLJ 7/01) [811.54]

2939 Harrison, David L. *The Alligator in the Closet: And Other Poems Around the House* (1–5). Illus. by Jane Kendall. 2003, Boyds Mills $16.95 (1-56397-994-2). 48pp. Everyday items are the focus of this collection of lighthearted poems. (Rev: SLJ 3/03) [811]

2940 Hegley, John. *My Dog Is a Carrot* (3–6). Illus. by author. 2003, Candlewick $12.99 (0-7636-1932-9). 64pp. Nonsense verse about everyday items, family, and nature will please lovers of wordplay. (Rev: SLJ 3/03) [811]

2941 High, Linda Oatman. *A Humble Life: Plain Poems* (2–4). Illus. by Bill Farnsworth. 2001, Eerdmans $17.00 (0-8028-5207-6). 40pp. Graceful poems and evocative paintings depict a year in a Mennonite and Amish county in Pennsylvania. (Rev: BL 12/15/01; HBG 3/02; SLJ 10/01) [811]

2942 Hoberman, Mary Ann. *You Read to Me, I'll Read to You: Very Short Stories to Read Together* (2–3). Illus. by Michael Emberley. 2001, Little, Brown $15.95 (0-316-36350-2). 32pp. A collection of short poems designed to be spoken aloud by two readers. (Rev: BL 8/01; HB 11–12/01; HBG 3/02; SLJ 8/01*) [811.54]

2943 *Home to Me: Poems Across America* (2–5). Ed. by Lee Bennett Hopkins. Illus. by Stephen Alcorn. 2002, Scholastic $17.95 (0-439-34096-9). 48pp. From trailer parks to Indian reservations, from cities to prairies, this expansive anthology features poems about Americans and America. (Rev: BL 10/15/02; HB 1–2/03; HBG 3/03; SLJ 10/02) [811.008]

2944 Hooper, Patricia. *Where Do You Sleep, Little One?* (PS–K). Illus. by John Winch. 2001, Holiday

$16.95 (0-8234-1668-2). 32pp. Animals answer the title's question in verse, and gather around a manger to see a sleeping child in this book that features beautiful collage illustrations. (Rev: BL 9/1/01; HBG 3/02; SLJ 9/01) [811]

2945 Johnson, Angela. *Running Back to Ludie* (5–8). 2001, Scholastic $15.95 (0-439-29316-2). 64pp. A teenage girl's friends and family, including her wayward mother, are introduced through a series of free-verse poems. (Rev: BCCB 1/02; BL 1/1–15/02; HB 11–12/01; HBG 3/02; SLJ 12/01)

2946 Katz, Susan. *Mrs. Brown on Exhibit and Other Museum Poems* (2–4). Illus. by R. W. Alley. 2002, Simon & Schuster $16.95 (0-689-82970-1). 40pp. A collection of poems about Mrs. Brown's class field trips to museums and the many discoveries they find there. (Rev: BL 6/1–15/02; HBG 3/03; SLJ 8/02) [811]

2947 Kuskin, Karla. *Moon, Have You Met My Mother? The Collected Poems of Karla Kuskin* (2–4). Illus. by Sergio Ruzzier. 2003, HarperCollins LB $17.89 (0-06-027174-4). 336pp. Poems written over a period of more than 40 years are collected here and arranged according to themes such as animals, seasons, and human personality. (Rev: SLJ 2/03) [811]

2948 *Leaf by Leaf: Autumn Poems* (5–8). Ed. by Barbara Rogasky. Illus. by Marc Tauss. 2001, Scholastic $15.95 (0-590-25347-6). 40pp. Verses by poets including Shelley, Yeats, and Whitman accompany stunning autumnal photographs. (Rev: BL 7/01; HBG 3/02; SLJ 9/01*) [811.008]

2949 Lee, Claudia M., ed. *Messengers of Rain and Other Poems from Latin America* (2–6). Illus. by Rafael Yockteng. 2002, Groundwood $18.95 (0-88899-470-2). 80pp. An anthology of more than 60 poems on a wide range of topics, translated from Spanish, by well-known and less-familiar writers. (Rev: SLJ 1/03) [811]

2950 Lee, Dennis. *Bubblegum Delicious* (2–4). Illus. by David McPhail. 2001, HarperCollins LB $15.89 (0-06-623709-2). 32pp. A charming collection of poems on varied topics with appeal for young children. (Rev: BL 5/15/01; HB 7–8/01*; HBG 3/02; SLJ 9/01) [811]

2951 *Let's Count the Raindrops* (PS–2). Illus. by Fumi Kosaka. 2001, Viking $15.99 (0-670-89689-6). 32pp. A collection of appealing weather-related poems. (Rev: BCCB 6/01; BL 5/1/01; HBG 10/01; SLJ 5/01) [811.008]

2952 Lewis, J. Patrick. *A World of Wonders: Geographic Travels in Verse and Rhyme* (3–5). Illus. by Alison Jay. 2002, Dial $16.99 (0-8037-2579-5). 40pp. Geographic terminology and facts are skillfully woven into verse in this attractive volume that touches on topics including seas, deserts, the poles, and the equator. (Rev: BL 3/15/02; HB 3–4/02; HBG 10/02; SLJ 4/02) [811]

2953 Lillegard, Dee. *Hello School! A Classroom Full of Poems* (PS–1). Illus. by Don Carter. 2001, Knopf $14.95 (0-375-81020-X). 32pp. Short poems introduce many simple aspects of school. (Rev:

BCCB 6/01; BL 8/01; HBG 3/02; SLJ 7/01) [811.54]

2954 Lindbergh, Reeve. *On Morning Wings* (PS–1). Illus. by Holly Meade. 2002, Candlewick $15.99 (0-7636-1106-9). 32pp. A poem, based on Psalm 139 and illustrated in watercolors, thanking God for His loving care. (Rev: BL 9/15/02; HBG 3/03; SLJ 12/02)

2955 Liu, Siyu, and Orel Protopopescu. *A Thousand Peaks: Poems from China* (5 Up). Illus. by Siyu Liu. 2002, Pacific View $19.95 (1-881896-24-2). 52pp. Thirty-five translations of Chinese poems are accompanied by information giving historical and cultural context, the original in Chinese characters and pinyin transliteration, a literal translation, and black-and-white drawings. (Rev: BL 3/15/02; SLJ 2/02*) [811]

2956 Longfellow, Henry Wadsworth. *The Midnight Ride of Paul Revere* (2–4). Illus. by Christopher Bing. 2001, Handprint $17.95 (1-929766-13-0). 40pp. Bing's design juxtaposes historical objects, watercolors, and scratchboard work to great effect in this rendering of Longfellow's famous poem that also includes maps and notes. (Rev: BCCB 2/02; BL 12/15/01; HB 3–4/02; HBG 10/02; SLJ 12/01*) [811]

2957 Longfellow, Henry Wadsworth. *Paul Revere's Ride* (2–5). Illus. by Monica Vachula. 2003, Boyds Mills $16.95 (1-56397-799-0). 32pp. Longfellow's famous poem, with attractive illustrations that show background scenery. (Rev: BL 2/1/03) [811]

2958 Longfellow, Henry Wadsworth. *Paul Revere's Ride: The Landlord's Tale* (2–5). Illus. by Charles Santore. 2003, HarperCollins LB $17.89 (0-06-623747-5). 40pp. The poem about Revere's famous ride is accompanied here by dramatic illustrations that convey a sense of urgency. (Rev: BL 2/1/03; SLJ 3/03) [811]

2959 *Love to Mama: A Tribute to Mothers* (PS–4). Ed. by Pat Mora. Illus. by Paula S. Barragan M. 2001, Lee & Low $16.95 (1-58430-019-1). 32pp. A celebration of Latina mothers and grandmothers that ends with a glossary and notes about the poets. (Rev: BL 5/1/01; HB 7–8/01; HBG 10/01; SLJ 4/01*) [811]

2960 Medina, Tony. *Love to Langston* (3–6). Illus. by R. Gregory Christie. 2002, Lee & Low $16.95 (1-58430-041-8). A celebration in poetry of the life and work of poet Langston Hughes, with biographical notes appended. (Rev: BCCB 3/02; BL 2/15/02; HBG 10/02; SLJ 3/02) [811]

2961 Moore, Lilian. *I'm Small and Other Verses* (PS–2). Illus. by Jill McElmurry. 2001, Candlewick $13.99 (0-7636-1169-7). The delights and trials of childhood are the focus of these friendly poems. (Rev: HB 5–6/01; HBG 10/01; SLJ 5/01) [811]

2962 Myers, Walter Dean. *Blues Journey* (5–8). Illus. by Christopher Myers. 2003, Holiday $18.95 (0-8234-1613-5). 48pp. Poems reflecting the soulfulness of blues music, accompanied by illustrations. (Rev: BL 2/15/03) [811]

2963 Noda, Takayo. *Dear World* (K–3). Illus. by author. 2003, Dial $16.99 (0-8037-2644-9). Wonderful illustrations enhance this series of brief poems framed as letters from a child. (Rev: SLJ 3/03)

2964 Perdomo, Willie. *Visiting Langston* (2–4). Illus. by Bryan Collier. 2002, Holt $15.95 (0-8050-6744-2). A young girl anticipates in poetry a visit to poet Langston Hughes's house in Harlem. (Rev: BCCB 3/02; BL 2/15/02; HBG 10/02; SLJ 4/02) [811]

2965 *Poetry by Heart: A Child's Book of Poems to Remember* (3–5). Ed. by Liz Attenborough. Illus. 2001, Scholastic $17.95 (0-439-29657-9). 128pp. An eclectic, enchanting collection of poetry for younger readers. (Rev: BL 1/1–15/02; HBG 10/02; SLJ 2/02) [811.54]

2966 Prelutsky, Jack. *The Frogs Wore Red Suspenders* (PS–3). Illus. by Petra Mathers. 2002, Greenwillow LB $16.89 (0-688-16720-9). 64pp. Splendid illustrations accompany whimsical rhymes in this charming book for preschoolers and young readers. (Rev: BCCB 3/02; BL 3/15/02; HB 3–4/02; HBG 10/02; SLJ 2/02*) [811]

2967 Prelutsky, Jack. *Scranimals* (2–4). Illus. by Peter Sis. 2002, HarperCollins LB $18.89 (0-688-17820-0). 48pp. The imaginary animals that inhabit Scranimal Island (the "Bananconda" and the "Orangutangerine," for example) are described in fanciful verse and art. (Rev: BCCB 10/02; BL 9/15/02; HB 1–2/03; HBG 3/03; SLJ 9/02*) [811]

2968 Rylant, Cynthia. *Good Morning, Sweetie Pie* (PS). Illus. by Jane Dyer. 2001, Simon & Schuster $16.00 (0-689-82377-0). 32pp. Eight happy poems about babies are accompanied by charming illustrations. (Rev: BL 9/15/01; HBG 3/02; SLJ 12/01) [811]

2969 Shakespeare, William. *To Sleep, Perchance to Dream: A Child's Book of Rhymes* (PS–1). Illus. by James Mayhew. 2001, Scholastic $16.95 (0-439-29655-2). 32pp. This handsome, large-format picture book introduces young readers to extracts from Shakespeare's works. (Rev: BL 12/1/01; HBG 3/02; SLJ 11/01) [822.3]

2970 Shields, Carol Diggory. *Brain Juice: American History Fresh Squeezed!* (4–8). Illus. by Richard Thompson. 2002, Handprint $14.95 (1-929766-62-9). 80pp. A timeline runs across the tops of these pages of poems about events in American history. (Rev: HBG 3/03; SLJ 1/03) [811]

2971 Sidman, Joyce. *Eureka! Poems About Inventors* (4–6). Illus. by K. Bennett Chavez. 2002, Millbrook LB $24.90 (0-7613-1665-5). 48pp. Sidman celebrates the lives and inventions of people throughout history in a chronological collection of free-verse poetry. (Rev: BL 10/15/02; HBG 3/03; SLJ 1/03) [811.54]

2972 Siebert, Diane. *Motorcycle Song* (K–4). Illus. 2002, HarperCollins LB $16.89 (0-06-028733-0). 32pp. Invigorating poetry and energetic artwork capture the thrill of a motorcycle ride. (Rev: BL 2/1/02; HBG 10/02; SLJ 4/02) [793.73]

2973 Singer, Marilyn. *Monster Museum* (1–5). Illus. by Gris Grimly. 2001, Hyperion $14.99 (0-7868-0520-X). 40pp. A humorous, poetic tour through a museum of monsters. (Rev: BCCB 10/01; HBG 3/02; SLJ 11/01) [811]

2974 Smith, Charles R. *Perfect Harmony: A Musical Journey with the Boys Choir of Harlem* (4–7). Illus. 2002, Hyperion $15.99 (0-7868-0758-X). 32pp. Photos of the Boys Choir of Harlem provide a dynamic backdrop for these upbeat poems about songs and singing. (Rev: BL 8/02; HBG 3/03; SLJ 8/02) [811]

2975 Soto, Gary. *Fearless Fernie: Hanging Out with Fernie and Me* (4–6). Illus. by Regan Dunnick. 2002, Putnam $14.99 (0-399-23615-5). 64pp. Older readers are invited into the mind and life of an unnamed middle-school boy in this exceptional collection of poems. (Rev: BL 3/15/02; HB 7–8/02; HBG 10/02; SLJ 3/02*) [811]

2976 Stevenson, James. *Corn-Fed* (K–4). Illus. 2002, Greenwillow LB $15.89 (0-06-000598-X). 48pp. Lovely watercolor sketches pair with thought-provoking verses to challenge readers' perceptions of everyday scenes. (Rev: BCCB 4/02; BL 3/1/02; HBG 10/02; SLJ 3/02) [811]

2977 Swados, Elizabeth. *Hey You! C'mere: A Poetry Slam* (2–5). Illus. by Joe Cepeda. 2002, Scholastic $15.95 (0-439-09257-4). 47pp. A collection of poems, presented by a group of urban children, that reflect their everyday concerns. (Rev: BL 4/15/02; HBG 10/02; SLJ 4/02) [811]

2978 Testa, Maria. *Becoming Joe DiMaggio* (5–8). Illus. by Scott Hunt. 2002, Candlewick $13.99 (0-7636-1537-4). 64pp. The story of an Italian American boy and his family, told through a series of poems set against a backdrop of radio-broadcast baseball games. (Rev: BCCB 5/02; BL 2/15/02; HBG 3/03; SLJ 5/02) [811]

2979 *This Place I Know: Poems of Comfort* (3–5). Ed. by Georgia Heard. Illus. 2002, Candlewick $16.99 (0-7636-1924-8). 48pp. In a bid to offer comfort to children traumatized by the terrorist attacks of September 11, Heard compiled this collection of 18 works dealing with fear and loss by poets including Langston Hughes, Emily Dickinson, and Walt Whitman, and illustrated by such artists as William Steig, Chris Raschka, and G. Brian Karas. (Rev: BL 7/02; HBG 3/03; SLJ 9/02) [811.008]

2980 Vestergaard, Hope. *Baby Love* (PS–K). Illus. by John Wallace. 2002, Dutton $15.99 (0-525-46902-8). 40pp. This collection of poems is an affectionate celebration of babies that includes the joys of being covered in food or water. (Rev: BL 1/1–15/03; HBG 3/03; SLJ 12/02) [811.6]

2981 *Wachale! Poetry and Prose About Growing Up Latino in America* (5–8). Ed. by Ilan Stavans. 2001, Cricket $16.95 (0-8126-4750-5). 160pp. A bilingual anthology about Latino experiences, both in the past and in the present. (Rev: BCCB 2/02; BL 2/1/02; HBG 10/02; SLJ 2/02) [810.8]

2982 Weatherford, Carole Boston. *Sidewalk Chalk: Poems of the City* (3–6). Illus. by Dimitrea Tokunbo. 2001, Boyds Mills $15.95 (1-56397-084-8). 32pp. Poems about the pleasures of urban life are accompanied by colorful full-page illustrations. (Rev: BL 9/15/01; HBG 3/02; SLJ 1/02) [811]

2983 *Whisper and Shout: Poems to Memorize* (4–6). Ed. by Patrice Vecchione. 2002, Cricket $16.95 (0-8126-2656-7). 144pp. An anthology of 55 accessible poems (many by contemporaries) with a lengthy introduction on poetry and a closing section on resources and biographies. (Rev: BL 4/15/02; HBG 10/02; SLJ 5/02) [811]

2984 Winnick, Karen B. *A Year Goes Round: Poems for the Months* (K–2). Illus. by author. 2001, Boyds Mills $15.95 (1-56397-898-9). A look at the months of the year in short, simple poems about children's activities. (Rev: HBG 3/02; SLJ 11/01) [811]

2985 Winter, Jeanette. *Emily Dickinson's Letters to the World* (4–7). Illus. 2002, Farrar $16.00 (0-374-32147-7). 40pp. Brief biographical information is paired with 21 of Emily Dickinson's poems in this small-format picture book told from her sister's point of view. (Rev: BL 3/1/02; HBG 10/02; SLJ 3/02) [811]

2986 Worth, Valerie. *Peacock and Other Poems* (3–6). Illus. by Natalie Babbitt. 2002, Farrar $15.00 (0-374-35766-8). 48pp. A posthumously published collection of 26 poems in the author's signature style, beautifully illustrated with detailed pencil drawings. (Rev: BCCB 6/02; BL 8/02; HB 7–8/02*; HBG 10/02; SLJ 5/02) [811]

2987 Worthen, Tom, ed. *Broken Hearts . . . Healing: Young Poets Speak Out on Divorce* (5 Up). Illus. by Kyle Hernandez. Series: Young Poets Speak Out. 2001, Poet Tree $26.95 (1-58876-150-9); paper $14.95 (1-58876-151-7). 234pp. This large selection of poems written by their peers about divorce, family breakups, and blended families will resonate with young readers. (Rev: SLJ 9/01) [811]

African American Poetry

2988 Boling, Katharine. *New Year Be Coming! A Gullah Year* (K–3). Illus. by Daniel Minter. 2002, Albert Whitman $15.95 (0-8075-5590-8). 32pp. These twelve poems — one for each month of the year — are written in the unique Gullah dialect of a group of African Americans living on the coast of South Carolina and Georgia. (Rev: BCCB 1/03; BL 11/15/02; HB 11–12/02; HBG 3/03; SLJ 9/02) [811]

2989 Greenfield, Eloise. *Honey, I Love* (PS–2). Illus. by Jan S. Gilchrist. 2003, HarperCollins LB $16.89 (0-06-009124-X). 32pp. An illustrated collection of poems about the loves of a young African American girl (such as her mother, car rides, swimming), first published in 1978. (Rev: BL 2/15/03; SLJ 2/03) [811.54]

2990 Grimes, Nikki. *Danitra Brown Leaves Town* (PS–3). Illus. by Floyd Cooper. 2002, HarperCollins LB $15.89 (0-688-13156-5). 32pp. Best friends Danitra and Zuri describe their very different summer experiences through letters in this book of free-verse poems. (Rev: BCCB 4/02; BL 2/15/02; HBG 10/02; SLJ 2/02) [811]

2991 Grimes, Nikki. *A Pocketful of Poems* (K–4). Illus. by Javaka Steptoe. 2001, Clarion $15.00 (0-395-93868-6). 30pp. A lively collection of verses and haikus that look at city life through the year. (Rev: HBG 10/01; SLJ 5/01) [811]

2992 Grimes, Nikki. *When Daddy Prays* (PS–K). Illus. by Tim Ladwig. 2002, Eerdmans $16.00 (0-8028-5152-5). 32pp. An African American child's impressions of his father's reliance on faith during everyday activities such as gardening, attending a baseball game, and celebrating the New Year. (Rev: BL 3/1/02; HBG 10/02; SLJ 4/02) [811.54]

2993 Medina, Tony. *DeShawn Days* (2–5). Illus. by R. Gregory Christie. 2001, Lee & Low $16.95 (1-58430-022-1). DeShawn is a young African American boy who describes in verse his home in the projects, the constant sound of sirens, the grim news on TV, his friends, and the music they enjoy. (Rev: HBG 10/01; SLJ 7/01*) [811]

2994 Thomas, Joyce Carol. *Crowning Glory* (PS–3). Illus. by Brenda Joysmith. 2002, HarperCollins LB $15.89 (0-06-023474-1). 32pp. A collection of free-verse poems that lovingly describe African American hair and hairstyles, accompanied by illustrations. (Rev: BCCB 10/02; BL 9/15/02; HBG 10/02; SLJ 6/02) [811]

2995 Woodson, Jacqueline. *Locomotion* (3–6). 2003, Putnam $15.99 (0-399-23115-3). 128pp. A young boy whose parents have died and whose sister is in a different foster home expresses his grief through poetry. (Rev: BCCB 3/03; BL 2/15/03; HB 3–4/03*; SLJ 1/03) [811]

Animals

2996 Ackerman, Diane. *Animal Sense* (3–7). Illus. by Peter Sis. 2003, Knopf $14.95 (0-375-82384-0). 40pp. Arresting, thoughtful, and sometimes humorous poems about animals, with accompanying artwork. (Rev: BCCB 3/03; BL 2/15/03*; HB 1–2/03; SLJ 2/03) [811]

2997 *Big, Bad and a Little Bit Scary: Poems That Bite Back* (K–3). Illus. by Wade Zahares. 2001, Viking $16.99 (0-670-03513-0). 32pp. Animals that bite are the subject of this collection of poems by authors including Eve Merriam and Dick King-Smith, with illustrations that focus on the scary parts. (Rev: BL 10/15/01; HBG 3/02; SLJ 10/01) [811.008]

2998 Florian, Douglas. *Bow Wow Meow Meow* (PS–2). Illus. 2003, Harcourt $17.00 (0-15-216395-6). 56pp. A collection of offbeat poems about cats and dogs, accompanied by watercolor illustrations. (Rev: BL 2/1/03*) [811]

2999 Foster, John, comp. *My First Oxford Book of Animal Poems* (K–4). Illus. 2002, Oxford LB $19.95 (0-19-276269-9). 94pp. An anthology of classic and new poems about wild and domestic animals that includes much humor and arresting illustrations. (Rev: HBG 3/03; SLJ 9/02) [811]

160

3000 George, Kristine O'Connell. *Little Dog and Duncan* (PS–2). Illus. by June Otani. 2002, Clarion $12.00 (0-618-11758-X). 38pp. Preschoolers and beginning readers alike will enjoy the gentle poetry and charming watercolors in this story of two dogs having a sleepover. (Rev: BL 3/1/02; HB 7–8/02*; HBG 10/02; SLJ 3/02*) [811]

3001 *Hoofbeats, Claws and Rippled Fins: Creature Poems* (3–7). Ed. by Lee Bennett Hopkins. Illus. by Stephen Alcorn. 2002, HarperCollins LB $15.89 (0-688-17943-6). 32pp. Fourteen poets each contribute a single poem inspired by the outstanding woodcuts by Stephen Alcorn that picture animals including the camel and the iguana. (Rev: BL 5/1/02*; HB 3–4/02; HBG 10/02; SLJ 4/02) [811.008]

3002 Hopkins, Lee Bennett. *A Pet for Me: Poems* (1–3). Illus. by Jane Manning. Series: An I Can Read Book. 2003, HarperCollins LB $16.89 (0-06-029112-5). 48pp. Brief poems by recognized authors, combined with watercolor illustrations featuring happy children, celebrate the joy of pets and will appeal to beginning readers. (Rev: BL 1/1–15/03; SLJ 3/03) [811.008]

3003 Howitt, Mary. *The Spider and the Fly* (2–5). Illus. by Tony Diterlizzi. 2002, Simon & Schuster $16.95 (0-689-85289-4). 40pp. Outstanding monochrome artwork brings new life to the classic poem. (Rev: BCCB 11/02; BL 10/1/02; HBG 3/03; SLJ 9/02*) [811]

3004 Johnston, Tony. *Cat, What Is That?* (1–4). Illus. by Wendell Minor. 2001, HarperCollins LB $15.89 (0-06-027743-2). 32pp. Abstract verses and detailed, realistic illustrations bring to life cats of all kinds in a variety of typical feline activities. (Rev: BL 10/1/01; HBG 3/02; SLJ 9/01)

3005 Johnston, Tony. *Gopher Up Your Sleeve* (PS–3). Illus. by Trip Park. 2002, Rising Moon $15.95 (0-87358-794-4). Humorous poems about animals are accompanied by fanciful illustrations. (Rev: HBG 10/02; SLJ 11/02) [811]

3006 Kiesler, Kate. *Wings on the Wind: Bird Poems* (PS–2). Illus. 2002, Clarion $14.00 (0-618-13333-X). 32pp. Vivid oil paintings are used to illustrate this collection of poems about birds by such writers as Edward Lear, Carl Sandburg, and Margaret Wise Brown. (Rev: BL 4/15/02; HBG 10/02; SLJ 4/02) [811.008]

3007 Ryder, Joanne. *Mouse Tail Moon* (2–4). Illus. by Maggie Kneen. 2002, Holt $16.95 (0-8050-6404-4). 32pp. A white-tail mouse describes his night in brief poems, from praising darkness for its safe haven from predators to dealing with fleas and rain to celebrating the morning sun. (Rev: BL 1/1–15/03; HBG 3/03; SLJ 2/03) [811]

3008 Schwartz, Betty Ann, ed. *My Kingdom for a Horse: An Anthology of Poems About Horses* (1–4). Illus. by Alix Berenzy. 2001, Holt $17.95 (0-8050-6212-2). Impressionistic illustrations enhance this collection of poems about horses of all kinds and in all places by poets including Shakespeare, Walt Whitman, Robert Frost, and Jack Prelutsky. (Rev: HBG 3/02; SLJ 11/01) [811]

3009 Singer, Marilyn. *The Company of Crows: A Book of Poems* (2–4). Illus. by Linda Saport. 2002, Clarion $16.00 (0-618-08340-5). 48pp. The intelligent crow is presented in poems written from the viewpoint of onlookers, including children, a farmer, and other animals. (Rev: BL 11/15/02; HBG 3/03; SLJ 11/02) [811]

3010 Sklansky, Amy E. *From the Doghouse: Poems to Chew On* (1–4). Illus. 2002, Holt $17.95 (0-8050-6673-X). 44pp. A delightful collection of poems from the canine perspective about things dogs like — walks in the park and car rides, for example — and things dogs don't like — such as fleas and baths. (Rev: HBG 3/03; SLJ 8/02) [811]

3011 Yolen, Jane. *Wild Wings: Poems for Young People* (3–6). Illus. by Jason Stemple. 2002, Boyds Mills $17.95 (1-56397-904-7). 32pp. Unusual photographs accompany beautiful poems about birds. (Rev: BL 5/15/02; HBG 10/02; SLJ 6/02) [811.54]

Haiku

3012 Chaikin, Miriam. *Don't Step on the Sky: A Handful of Haiku* (K–4). Illus. by Hiroe Nakata. 2002, Holt $16.95 (0-8050-6474-5). 28pp. A delightful book of haiku for younger readers. (Rev: BL 3/15/02; HBG 10/02; SLJ 5/02) [811]

Holidays

3013 Bronson, Linda, comp. *Sleigh Bells and Snowflakes: A Celebration of Christmas* (1–3). Illus. by Linda Bronson. 2002, Holt $17.95 (0-8050-6755-8). 45pp. A nicely illustrated anthology of poetry and song lyrics that includes many well-known favorites. (Rev: HBG 3/03; SLJ 10/02) [811.008]

3014 Cummings, E. E. *Little Tree* (K–4). Illus. by Chris Raschka. 2001, Hyperion $16.99 (0-7868-0795-4). 32pp. A young evergreen travels a long way as it fulfills its dream of becoming a Christmas tree in this appealing and visually satisfying story inspired by an e. e. cummings poem. (Rev: BCCB 11/01; BL 12/1/01; HBG 3/02; SLJ 10/01*) [811]

3015 Cunningham, Julia. *The Stable Rat and Other Christmas Poems* (3–6). Illus. by Anita Lobel. 2001, Greenwillow LB $15.89 (0-688-17800-6). 24pp. These interconnected poems portray Christmas from the viewpoint of the animal and other observers, with vivid artwork. (Rev: BCCB 11/01; BL 9/15/01; HB 11–12/01; HBG 3/02; SLJ 10/01) [811]

3016 Grimes, Nikki. *Under the Christmas Tree* (PS–2). Illus. by Kadir Nelson. 2002, HarperCollins LB $17.89 (0-688-16000-X). 32pp. An African American family celebrates an urban Christmas in this picture book of 23 poems presented from a child's point of view. (Rev: BL 9/1/02; HBG 3/03; SLJ 10/02*) [811]

3017 Merriam, Eve. *Spooky ABC* (3–6). Illus. by Lane Smith. 2002, Simon & Schuster $16.95 (0-689-85356-4). 32pp. A redesigned and renamed version of the blood-curdling *Halloween ABC* (1987) that includes information on the creation of the original book. (Rev: BL 10/1/02; HBG 3/03) [811]

3018 *'Twas the Night Before Christmas; or, Account of a Visit from St. Nicholas* (PS–2). Illus. by Matt Tavares. 2002, Candlewick $16.00 (0-7636-1585-4). 32pp. The classic, original version of the poem, accompanied by old-fashioned artwork. (Rev: BL 9/1/02; HBG 3/03) [811]

3019 *The Young Oxford Book of Christmas Poems* (5–8). Ed. by Michael Harrison and Christopher Stuart-Clark. Illus. 2001, Oxford $19.95 (0-19-276247-8). 160pp. A richly illustrated collection of poems with Christmas themes by poets including Ted Hughes, Sylvia Plath, and Seamus Heaney. (Rev: BCCB 2/02; BL 12/1/01; HBG 3/02) [821]

Humorous Poetry

3020 Aylesworth, Jim. *The Burger and the Hot Dog* (K–3). Illus. by Stephen Gammell. 2001, Simon & Schuster $16.95 (0-689-83897-2). 32pp. A collection of funny poems about anthropomorphic foods with effective, messy illustrations. (Rev: BCCB 12/01; BL 10/1/01; HBG 3/02; SLJ 1/02) [811]

3021 Bagert, Brod. *Giant Children* (K–3). Illus. by Tedd Arnold. 2002, Dial $15.99 (0-8037-2556-6). 32pp. Side-splitting artwork is the perfect accompaniment to this eclectic collection of poems for young readers. (Rev: BL 8/02; HBG 3/03; SLJ 8/02) [811]

3022 Hirsch, Robin. *FEG: Stupid (Ridiculous) Poems for Intelligent Children* (5–8). Illus. by Ha. 2002, Little, Brown $15.95 (0-316-36344-8). 48pp. A collection of amusing, sometimes hilarious, original poems that rely on playing with words and their meanings. (Rev: BL 6/1–15/02; HBG 10/02; SLJ 4/02) [821.914]

3023 *I Invited a Dragon to Dinner: And Other Poems to Make You Laugh Out Loud* (PS–1). Illus. by Chris L. Demarest. 2002, Putnam $16.99 (0-399-23567-1). 40pp. A collection of silly poetry for preschoolers and young readers. (Rev: BL 3/15/02; HBG 10/02; SLJ 2/02) [811]

3024 Katz, Bobbi. *A Rumpus of Rhymes: A Book of Noisy Poems* (1–3). Illus. by Susan Estelle Kwas. 2001, Dutton $15.99 (0-525-46718-1). 32pp. Alliteration and onomatopoeia make for noisy, humorous poems of varying length and subject matter. (Rev: BL 9/1/01; HBG 3/02; SLJ 11/01) [811]

3025 Koontz, Dean. *The Paper Doorway: Funny Verse and Nothing Worse* (4–8). Illus. by Phil Parks. 2001, HarperCollins LB $17.89 (0-06-029489-2). 159pp. A humorous and imaginative collection of poems that feature clever word play. (Rev: HBG 3/02; SLJ 1/02) [811]

3026 Lear, Edward. *Hilary Knight's "The Owl and the Pussy-Cat"* (PS–3). Illus. by Hilary Knight. 2001, Simon & Schuster $17.00 (0-689-83927-8). 40pp. Otto and Polly become the owl and the pussy-cat during a reading of the poem, in this reissue of a 1984 title. (Rev: BL 8/01; HBG 10/01) [821.914]

3027 Lear, Edward. *Poetry for Young People* (3–5). Ed. by Edward Mendelson. Illus. by Huliska-Beit Laura. 2002, Sterling $14.95 (0-8069-3077-2). 48pp. An introduction to the limericks and poetry of Edward Lear. (Rev: BL 3/1/02; HBG 10/02) [821]

3028 Lesynski, Loris. *Nothing Beats a Pizza* (3–6). Illus. by author. 2001, Annick LB $18.95 (1-55037-701-9); paper $7.95 (1-55037-700-0). 32pp. Lesynski's verses take a humorous approach to the serious topic of pizza. (Rev: HBG 3/02; SLJ 2/02) [811]

3029 McGough, Roger, sel. *The Kingfisher Book of Funny Poems* (4–7). Illus. by Caroline Holden. 2002, Kingfisher $18.95 (0-7534-5480-7). 256pp. An anthology of poems arranged by theme that includes many by familiar names such as Ogden Nash, Lewis Carroll, and Shel Silverstein. (Rev: SLJ 6/02) [811]

3030 Prelutsky, Jack. *Awful Ogre's Awful Day* (PS–3). Illus. by Paul O. Zelinsky. 2001, Greenwillow LB $15.89 (0-688-07779-X). 40pp. Humorous poems look at an ogre's daily routine — from breakfast to bedtime — with amusing illustrations. (Rev: BCCB 9/01; BL 10/15/01; HB 9–10/01; HBG 3/02; SLJ 9/01*) [811.54]

3031 Proimos, James. *If I Were in Charge the Rules Would Be Different* (3–5). Illus. 2002, Scholastic $16.95 (0-439-20864-5). 80pp. Playful poems about childhood, with humorous illustrations. (Rev: BL 5/15/02; HBG 10/02; SLJ 3/02) [811]

3032 Wheeler, Lisa. *Wool Gathering: A Sheep Family Reunion* (PS–3). Illus. by Frank Ansley. 2001, Simon & Schuster $16.00 (0-689-84369-0). 32pp. A fuzzy family reunion provides plenty of characters for this collection of hilarious poems about sheep. (Rev: BL 11/1/01; HBG 3/02; SLJ 10/01) [811]

3033 Whitehead, Jenny. *Lunch Box Mail and Other Poems* (2–4). Illus. 2001, Holt $16.95 (0-8050-6259-9). 48pp. Everyday life and experiences are captured in this collection of poems that emphasizes the humorous side of life. (Rev: BL 4/1/01; HBG 3/02; SLJ 10/01) [811]

Native Americans

3034 Kay, Verla. *Broken Feather* (PS–2). Illus. by Stephen Alcorn. 2002, Putnam $15.99 (0-399-23550-7). 32pp. Short verses and block prints tell the story of relations between settlers, the Army, and the Native Americans with glimpses of the past as seen through the eyes of Broken Feather, a Native American boy, and his father. (Rev: BL 11/1/02; HBG 3/03) [811]

3035 Longfellow, Henry Wadsworth. *Hiawatha and Megissogwon* (4–7). Illus. by Jeffrey Thompson. 2001, National Geographic $16.95 (0-7922-6676-5). 32pp. Artwork with an authentic Native American feel illustrates Hiawatha's exciting adventures in the

"Pearl-Feather" section of Longfellow's epic poem. (Rev: BCCB 3/02; BL 11/15/01; HBG 3/02; SLJ 9/01) [811]

3036 Pollock, Penny. *When the Moon Is Full: A Lunar Year* (K–3). Illus. by Mary Azarian. 2001, Little, Brown $15.95 (0-316-71317-1). 32pp. Native American names for the moon are the subject of this book of graceful poems illustrated by Caldecott winner Mary Azarian. (Rev: BL 11/1/01; HBG 3/02; SLJ 9/01) [811]

Nature and the Seasons

3037 Alarcon, Francisco X. *Iguanas in the Snow and Other Winter Poems / Iguanas en la Nieve y Otros Poemas de Invierno* (1–3). Illus. by Maya Christina Gonzalez. 2001, Children's $15.95 (0-89239-168-5). 32pp. A collection of poems about the beauty of winter in northern California, in Spanish and English. (Rev: BL 10/1/01; HBG 3/02; SLJ 8/01) [811]

3038 Baird, Audrey B. *A Cold Snap! Frosty Poems* (2–5). Illus. by Patrick O'Brien. 2002, Boyds Mills $15.95 (1-56397-633-1). 32pp. Effective poems and illustrations capture winter's chill. (Rev: BL 9/15/02; HBG 3/03; SLJ 12/02) [811.54]

3039 Cameron, Eileen. *Canyon* (3–5). Illus. by Michael Collier. 2002, Mikaya $16.95 (1-931414-03-3). 32pp. Water flows from mountains to rivers to a canyon in this poetic book illustrated with striking photographs of nature. (Rev: BL 5/15/02; HBG 10/02; SLJ 5/02) [811]

3040 Esbensen, Barbara J. *Swing Around the Sun* (K–3). Illus. 2003, Carolrhoda LB $16.95 (0-87614-143-2). 48pp. The seasons are the focus of this collection that is illustrated by four well-known artists. (Rev: SLJ 3/03) [811]

3041 Hubbell, Patricia. *Black Earth, Gold Sun* (2–6). Illus. by Mary N. DePalma. 2001, Marshall Cavendish $15.95 (0-7614-5090-4). 32pp. Watercolor illustrations echo the sentiments of these poems about the delights of a garden. (Rev: BL 9/15/01; HBG 3/02; SLJ 11/01) [811.54]

3042 Levy, Constance. *Splash! Poems of Our Watery World* (3–6). Illus. by David Soman. 2002, Scholastic $16.95 (0-439-29318-9). 48pp. A charming collection of 34 poems about water, its characteristics, and its uses. (Rev: BCCB 6/02; BL 4/1/02; HB 7–8/02; HBG 10/02; SLJ 5/02) [811]

3043 Lewis, J. Patrick. *Earth and Us — Continuous: Nature's Past and Future* (K–3). Illus. by Christo-

pher Canyon. Series: Sharing Nature with Children. 2001, Dawn $16.95 (1-58469-024-0); paper $7.95 (1-58469-023-2). 32pp. A book of attractively illustrated poems about the wonders of the earth and our responsibility to care for it. (Rev: BL 9/1/01; HBG 3/02) [550]

3044 Nicholls, Judith, comp. *The Sun in Me: Poems About the Planet* (1–4). Illus. by Beth Krommes. 2003, Barefoot $16.99 (1-84148-058-4). 40pp. An anthology of poems from different places and times that celebrate nature. (Rev: SLJ 3/03) [811]

3045 *Sea Dream: Poems from Under the Waves* (2–5). Ed. by Nikki Siegen-Smith. Illus. by Joel Stewart. 2002, Barefoot $16.99 (1-84148-905-0). 40pp. An absorbing anthology of 26 poems about sea creatures both real and imagined. (Rev: BL 10/15/02; HBG 3/03; SLJ 12/02) [808.81]

3046 Zolotow, Charlotte. *Seasons* (1–3). Illus. by Erik Blegvad. 2002, HarperCollins LB $14.89 (0-06-026699-6). 64pp. A collection of poems that take children through the four seasons in this alluring book for beginning readers. (Rev: BL 2/1/02; HBG 10/02; SLJ 6/02) [811]

Sports

3047 Burg, Brad. *Outside the Lines: Poetry at Play* (PS–4). Illus. by Rebecca Gibbon. 2002, Putnam $15.99 (0-399-23446-2). 32pp. The words work with the illustrations to create visual movement in this book of verse about children's activities. (Rev: BL 3/15/02; HBG 10/02; SLJ 3/02) [811]

3048 Morrison, Lillian. *Way to Go! Sports Poems* (4–8). Illus. by Susan Spellman. 2001, Boyds Mills $16.95 (1-56397-961-6). 48pp. Sport lovers will appreciate this collection of poems full of rhythm and life, with vibrant illustrations. (Rev: HBG 3/02; SLJ 10/01) [811]

3049 Thayer, Ernest Lawrence. *Casey at the Bat* (2–6). Illus. by LeRoy Neiman. 2002, HarperCollins $19.95 (0-06-009068-5). 96pp. The famous baseball poem, illustrated in a bold, striking manner; with an introduction by Jose Torre. (Rev: BCCB 1/01*; BL 9/1/02) [811]

3050 Thayer, Ernest Lawrence. *Casey at the Bat: A Ballad of the Republic Sung in the Year 1888* (4–8). Illus. by C. F. Payne. 2003, Simon & Schuster $16.95 (0-689-85494-3). 40pp. An impossibly muscular Casey is the star of this version of the classic baseball poem. (Rev: BCCB 1/01*; BL 2/1/03; SLJ 3/03) [811]

Plays

General

3051 Van Steenwyk, Elizabeth. *One Fine Day: A Radio Play* (3–5). Illus. by Bill Farnsworth. 2003, Eerdmans $16.00 (0-8028-5234-3). 32pp. A fictional conversation between Orville and Wilbur Wright during their first flight is presented in the form of a radio play. (Rev: BL 1/1–15/03)

Shakespeare

3052 Birch, Beverley. *Shakespeare's Tales* (5–8). Illus. by Stephen Lambert. 2002, Hodder $22.95 (0-340-79725-8). 126pp. This appealing and accessible large-format book introduces modern teens to the plots and language of four Shakespeare plays — *Hamlet, Othello, Antony and Cleopatra*, and *The Tempest*. (Rev: BL 1/1–15/03) [823.914]

3053 Coville, Bruce. *William Shakespeare's Twelfth Night* (3–6). Illus. by Tim Raglin. 2003, Dial $16.99 (0-8037-2318-0). 40pp. Coville provides an easy-reading version of the humorous play, accompanied by appealing ink drawings. (Rev: BL 1/1–15/03; SLJ 3/03) [822]

Biography

Adventurers and Explorers

Collective

3054 Currie, Stephen. *Polar Explorers* (5–9). Series: History Makers. 2002, Gale LB $27.45 (1-56006-957-0). 112pp. The polar explorers profiled here are Roald Amundsen, John Franklin, Matthew Henson, Robert Peary, and Robert Scott. (Rev: SLJ 7/02) [919.804]

3055 Platt, Richard. *Explorers: Pioneers Who Broke New Boundaries* (4–8). Illus. Series: Secret Worlds. 2001, DK $14.95 (0-7894-7973-7); paper $7.95 (0-7894-7974-5). 96pp. An engaging introduction to explorers — of land, sea, and space — with illustrations and interesting, often wacky, facts. (Rev: BL 10/15/01; HBG 3/02) [910.92]

Individual

ARMSTRONG, NEIL

3056 Zemlicka, Shannon. *Neil Armstrong* (2–5). Illus. Series: History Maker Bios. 2002, Lerner LB $23.93 (0-8225-0395-6). 48pp. A simple, absorbing account of the life of the first man to reach the moon, with helpful sidebars that amplify material in the text. (Rev: HBG 3/03; SLJ 12/02) [921]

BOONE, DANIEL

3057 Calvert, Patricia. *Daniel Boone: Beyond the Mountains* (5–8). Series: Great Explorations. 2001, Marshall Cavendish LB $19.95 (0-7614-1243-3). An attractive biography of the American pioneer who explored the Cumberland Gap region and helped settlers in the Kentucky region. (Rev: BCCB 3/02; BL 4/1/02; HBG 3/02; SLJ 3/02) [921]

3058 Riehecky, Janet. *Daniel Boone* (3–6). Series: Raintree Biographies. 2003, Raintree Steck-Vaughn LB $25.69 (0-7398-5672-3). 32pp. A simple biography of the pioneer's life and achievements, with

sidebar features containing primary and background material. (Rev: BCCB 3/02; HBG 3/03; SLJ 3/03) [921]

CABOT, JOHN

3059 Shields, Charles J. *John Cabot and the Rediscovery of North America* (4–8). Series: Explorers of New Worlds. 2001, Chelsea LB $19.75 (0-7910-6438-7); paper $8.95 (0-7910-6439-5). 63pp. An absorbing biography that focuses on Cabot's expeditions at the end of the 15th century in search of a passage to Asia. (Rev: SLJ 3/02) [921]

CARSON, KIT

3060 Boraas, Tracey. *Kit Carson: Mountain Man* (4–6). Series: Let Freedom Ring. 2002, Capstone LB $22.60 (0-7368-1349-7). 48pp. An absorbing account of the life and exploits of the legendary trapper and scout. (Rev: HBG 3/03; SLJ 2/03) [921]

CARTIER, JACQUES

3061 Blashfield, Jean F. *Cartier: Jacques Cartier in Search of the Northwest Passage* (4–6). Series: Exploring the World. 2001, Compass Point LB $21.26 (0-7565-0122-9). 48pp. The story of Cartier's efforts to find a route to China, with color reproductions of maps, paintings, and prints, and information on his contemporaries. (Rev: SLJ 1/02) [921]

COLEMAN, BESSIE

3062 Grimes, Nikki. *Talkin' About Bessie: The Story of Aviator Elizabeth Coleman* (2–5). Illus. by E. B. Lewis. 2002, Scholastic $16.95 (0-439-35243-6). 48pp. In this unusual biography, Grimes uses the voices of friends and relatives at Coleman's funeral to tell the story of her love of flying and her achievements as the first African American woman flyer. (Rev: BL 11/15/02; HB 1–2/03*; HBG 3/03; SLJ 10/02) [629.13]

3063 Plantz, Connie. *Bessie Coleman: First Black Woman Pilot* (4–8). 2001, Enslow LB $20.95 (0-7660-1545-9). 128pp. This is a readable biography that breathes life into Coleman's childhood, training as a pilot, and tragic death. (Rev: HBG 3/02; SLJ 1/02) [921]

COOK, CAPTAIN JAMES

3064 Meltzer, Milton. *Captain James Cook: Three Times Around the World* (5–8). Series: Great Explorations. 2001, Marshall Cavendish LB $19.95 (0-7614-1240-9). This is a fine biography of the English mariner and explorer who, among other feats, explored the west coast of North America. (Rev: BL 4/1/02; HBG 3/02) [921]

CORONADO, FRANCISCO VASQUEZ DE

3065 Doak, Robin S. *Coronado: Francisco Vásquez de Coronado Explores the Southwest* (4–6). Series: Exploring the World. 2001, Compass Point LB $21.26 (0-7565-0123-7). 48pp. The story of Coronado's quest for gold, with color reproductions of maps, paintings, and prints, and information on his contemporaries. (Rev: SLJ 1/02) [921]

COUSTEAU, JACQUES

3066 Bankston, John. *Jacques-Yves Cousteau: His Story Under the Sea* (4–5). Series: Unlocking the Secrets of Science. 2002, Mitchell Lane LB $17.95 (1-58415-112-9). 48pp. A concise look at the pioneering undersea explorer and inventor of the aqualung that opened up exploration of the ocean. (Rev: BL 8/02; HBG 3/03; SLJ 9/02) [921]

3067 King, Roger. *Jacques Cousteau and the Undersea World* (4–6). Illus. Series: Explorers of New Worlds. 2000, Chelsea LB $17.95 (0-7910-5956-1); paper $8.95 (0-7910-6166-3). 63pp. This account of Cousteau's life starts with his childhood, and covers his creativity in designing equipment for underwater exploration as well as his other important contributions. (Rev: SLJ 4/01) [921]

CROCKETT, DAVY

3068 Alphin, Elaine Marie. *Davy Crockett* (2–4). Illus. Series: History Maker Bios. 2002, Lerner LB $23.93 (0-8225-0393-X). 48pp. Legend and fact are clearly separated in this biography that looks mainly at Crockett's career. (Rev: HBG 3/03; SLJ 12/02)

3069 Feeney, Kathy. *Davy Crockett* (2–4). Series: Photo-Illustrated Biographies. 2002, Capstone LB $13.95 (0-7368-1110-9). 24pp. Crockett's life and contributions to the exploration of the West are presented, with care to distinguish between fact and legend. (Rev: SLJ 7/02) [921]

DE LEON, JUAN PONCE

3070 Whiting, Jim. *Juan Ponce de Leon* (5–7). Series: Latinos in American History. 2002, Mitchell Lane LB $19.95 (1-58415-149-8). 48pp. This is the story of the man who is credited with discovering

Florida in 1513 while searching for the fountain of youth. (Rev: BL 2/15/03) [921]

DE SOTO, HERNANDO

3071 Gibbons, Faye. *Hernando de Soto: A Search for Gold and Glory* (4–6). Illus. by Bruce Dupree. Series: American Stories. 2002, Crane Hill paper $9.95 (1-57587-198-X). 112pp. A balanced introduction to the Spanish explorer's travels. (Rev: BL 2/1/03) [970.1]

3072 Whiting, Jim. *Hernando de Soto* (5–7). Series: Latinos in American History. 2002, Mitchell Lane LB $19.95 (1-58415-147-1). 48pp. A simple biography of the Spanish explorer who discovered the Mississippi River in the 16th century while traveling through what is now the southern United States. (Rev: BL 2/15/03) [921]

DRAKE, SIR FRANCIS

3073 Gallagher, Jim. *Sir Francis Drake and the Foundation of a World Empire* (4–8). Series: Explorers of New Worlds. 2000, Chelsea LB $17.95 (0-7910-5950-2); paper $8.95 (0-7910-6160-4). 63pp. This appealing and readable biography of Sir Francis Drake presents his life from childhood and details his major accomplishments, with photographs, sidebar features, documents, and maps. (Rev: HBG 10/01; SLJ 4/01) [921]

EARHART, AMELIA

3074 Mara, Wil. *Amelia Earhart* (K–2). Series: Rookie Biographies. 2002, Children's LB $19.00 (0-516-22522-7); paper $4.95 (0-516-27338-8). 32pp. For beginning readers, this is a simple introduction to the famed aviatrix. (Rev: SLJ 12/02) [921]

ERIKSSON, LEIF

3075 Klingel, Cynthia, and Robert B. Noyed. *Leif Eriksson: Norwegian Explorer* (3–5). Series: Spirit of America: Our People. 2002, Child's World LB $27.07 (1-56766-163-7). 32pp. Eriksson's story is placed in the context of Viking exploration, settlement, society, and family life. (Rev: SLJ 12/02)

HENSON, MATTHEW

3076 Weidt, Maryann N. *Matthew Henson* (2–4). Illus. Series: History Maker Bios. 2002, Lerner LB $23.93 (0-8225-0397-2). 48pp. Henson's explorations are the main focus of this biography that touches on his youth. (Rev: SLJ 12/02) [921]

HILLARY, SIR EDMUND

3077 Brennan, Kristine. *Sir Edmund Hillary: Modern-Day Explorer* (4–8). Series: Explorers of New Worlds. 2000, Chelsea LB $17.95 (0-7910-5953-7); paper $8.95 (0-7910-6163-9). 63pp. An appealing overview of the life and accomplishments of the mountaineer and explorer, with photographs and maps. (Rev: SLJ 4/01) [796.52]

HUDSON, HENRY

3078 Saffer, Barbara. *Henry Hudson: Ill-fated Explorer of North America's Coast* (4–8). Series: Explorers of New Worlds. 2001, Chelsea LB $19.75 (0-7910-6436-0); paper $8.95 (0-7910-6437-9). 63pp. This absorbing biography focuses on Hudson's early 17th-century expeditions from England in search of a sea route to the Far East. (Rev: HBG 10/02; SLJ 3/02) [921]

JEMISON, MAE

3079 Naden, Corinne J., and Rose Blue. *Mae Jemison: Out of This World* (2–5). Illus. Series: Gateway. 2003, Millbrook LB $23.90 (0-7613-2570-0). 48pp. The life story of the first African American woman in space. (Rev: BL 2/15/03) [629.45]

LA SALLE, CAVELIER DE

3080 Faber, Harold. *La Salle: Down the Mississippi* (5–8). Series: Great Explorations. 2001, Marshall Cavendish LB $19.95 (0-7614-1239-5). The exciting story of the French explorer who traveled down the Mississippi River to the Gulf of Mexico and named the region Louisiana. (Rev: BL 4/1/02; HBG 3/02; SLJ 3/02) [921]

3081 Goodman, Joan Elizabeth. *Despite All Obstacles: La Salle and the Conquest of the Mississippi* (3–6). Illus. by Tom McNeely. Series: Great Explorers. 2001, Mikaya $19.95 (1-931414-01-7). 48pp. Journal entries, excerpts from letters, a map, and attractive illustrations enhance this life of explorer Rene-Robert Cavalier, Sieur de La Salle. (Rev: BL 1/1–15/02; HBG 10/02; SLJ 4/02) [973.2]

LEWIS AND CLARK

3082 Adler, David A. *A Picture Book of Lewis and Clark* (2–4). Illus. by Ronald Himler. Series: Picture Book Biography. 2003, Holiday $16.95 (0-8234-1735-2). 32pp. Biographical information about the two explorers and information on the expedition itself are found in this accessible book. (Rev: BL 2/15/03; SLJ 3/03) [917.804]

MAGELLAN, FERDINAND

3083 Burgan, Michael. *Magellan: Ferdinand Magellan and the First Trip Around the World* (4–6). Series: Exploring the World. 2001, Compass Point LB $21.26 (0-7565-0125-3). 48pp. The story of Magellan's groundbreaking voyage, with color reproductions of maps, paintings, and prints, and information on his contemporaries. (Rev: SLJ 1/02) [921]

3084 Levinson, Nancy Smiler. *Magellan and the First Voyage Around the World* (5–8). Illus. 2001, Clarion $19.00 (0-395-98773-3). 144pp. An encompassing look at Magellan's achievements with excellent illustrations, a timeline, and Web site information. (Rev: BCCB 2/02; BL 2/1/02; HB 1–2/02; HBG 3/02; SLJ 1/02) [910.92]

3085 Meltzer, Milton. *Ferdinand Magellan: First to Sail Around the World* (5–8). Illus. Series: Great Explorations. 2001, Benchmark LB $19.95 (0-7614-1238-7). 80pp. An encompassing look at Magellan's achievements is complemented by excellent illustrations, a timeline, and Web site information. (Rev: BL 1/1–15/02; HBG 3/02; SLJ 3/02) [910]

PEARY, ROBERT E.

3086 Calvert, Patricia. *Robert E. Peary: To the Top of the World* (5–8). Series: Great Explorations. 2001, Marshall Cavendish LB $19.95 (0-7614-1242-5). The exciting story of the Arctic explorer who reached the North Pole in 1909. (Rev: BL 4/1/02; HBG 3/02; SLJ 3/02) [921]

PIKE, ZEBULON

3087 Witteman, Barbara. *Zebulon Pike: Soldier and Explorer* (4–6). Series: Let Freedom Ring. 2002, Capstone LB $22.60 (0-7368-1351-9). 48pp. An absorbing account of the life and exploits of the explorer who discovered Pikes Peak. (Rev: HBG 3/03; SLJ 2/03) [921]

QUIMBY, HARRIET

3088 Moss, Marissa. *Brave Harriet* (2–4). Illus. by C. F. Payne. 2001, Harcourt $16.00 (0-15-202380-1). 32pp. A picture book for older readers telling in first person the story of Harriet Quimby, the first woman to fly solo across the English Channel. (Rev: BL 7/01; HBG 3/02; SLJ 9/01) [629.1]

RALEIGH, SIR WALTER

3089 Korman, Susan. *Sir Walter Raleigh: English Explorer and Author* (4–6). Series: Colonial Leaders. 2001, Chelsea LB $16.95 (0-7910-5969-3); paper $8.95 (0-7910-6126-4). 80pp. Korman gives readers a good overview of the many sides of Raleigh, covering his roles as soldier, scientist, and courtier as well as his efforts to colonize Virginia. (Rev: SLJ 7/01) [942.05]

SHACKLETON, SIR ERNEST

3090 Marcovitz, Hal. *Sir Ernest Shackleton and the Struggle Against Antarctica* (4–6). Illus. Series: Explorers of New Worlds. 2001, Chelsea LB $19.75 (0-7910-6424-7). 63pp. Photographs from Shackleton's last expedition and quotations from his own writings add interest to this exploration of his voyages. (Rev: HBG 10/02; SLJ 4/02)

SLOCUM, JOSHUA

3091 Lasky, Kathryn. *Born in the Breezes: The Seafaring Life of Joshua Slocum* (3–5). Illus. by Walter L. Krudop. 2001, Scholastic $16.95 (0-439-29305-7). 48pp. Joshua Slocum went to sea at 14, married and raised his children on a ship, and eventually became the first man, in 1898, to sail around the world alone. (Rev: BL 11/1/01; HBG 3/02; SLJ 11/01) [387.5]

169

Artists, Composers, Entertainers, and Writers

Collective

3092 Gaines, Ann Graham. *American Photographers: Capturing the Image* (4–7). Series: Collective Biographies. 2002, Enslow LB $20.95 (0-7660-1833-4). 112pp. The lives and contributions of 10 well-known photographers are presented with photographs and a brief history of photography. (Rev: HBG 10/02; SLJ 10/02) [921]

3093 Holme, Merilyn, and Bridget McKenzie. *Expressionists* (5 Up). Series: Artists in Profile. 2002, Heinemann LB $27.86 (1-58810-647-0). 64pp. Introduces the movement and gives biographical information on the major artists and their key works, with reproductions and photographs. Also use *Impressionists* and *Pop Artists* (both 2002). (Rev: HBG 3/03; SLJ 3/03) [759.06]

3094 Lester, Julius. *The Blues Singers: Ten Who Rocked the World* (5–8). Illus. by Lisa Cohen. 2001, Hyperion $15.99 (0-7868-0463-7). 48pp. Profiles of 10 African Americans who sang the blues or were influenced by the blues are accompanied by attention-grabbing illustrations and a good discography. (Rev: BL 6/1–15/01; HBG 10/01; SLJ 6/01*) [781.643]

3095 Rubin, Susan Goldman. *The Yellow House: Vincent van Gogh and Paul Gauguin Side by Side* (K–3). Illus. by Joseph A. Smith. 2001, Abrams $17.95 (0-8109-4588-6). 40pp. Juxtaposed illustrations introduce the works of Vincent van Gogh and Paul Gauguin who, for a short time in 1888, lived and worked together in a studio in the south of France. (Rev: BL 11/15/01; HBG 3/02; SLJ 1/02) [759.4]

3096 Stewart, Gail B. *Great Women Comedians* (5–8). Series: History Makers. 2002, Gale LB $27.45 (1-56006-953-8). 96pp. The comedians Gracie Allen, Lucille Ball, Whoopi Goldberg, Roseanne Barr, and Ellen DeGeneres are profiled in this account that focuses on their groundbreaking achievements. (Rev: SLJ 8/02) [921]

Artists

AUDUBON, JOHN JAMES

3097 Burleigh, Robert. *Into the Woods: John James Audubon Lives His Dream* (2–5). Illus. by Wendell Minor. 2003, Simon & Schuster $16.95 (0-689-83040-8). 40pp. Charming watercolors and selections of Audubon's own detailed drawings combine with simple, poetic text and quotes from Audubon's journals to give a good picture of the bird-lover. (Rev: BL 1/1–15/03; SLJ 2/03) [921]

BERENSTAIN, JAN AND BERENSTAIN, STAN

3098 Berenstain, Stan, and Jan Berenstain. *Down a Sunny Dirt Road: An Autobiography* (5–8). Illus. 2002, Random $20.00 (0-375-81403-5). 208pp. This engrossing joint biography of the co-creators of the Berenstain Bears is filled with photographs, early cartoons, and other fascinating artwork. (Rev: BL 12/15/02; HB 1–2/03; HBG 3/03; SLJ 12/02) [813]

CARR, EMILY

3099 Griek, Susan Vande. *The Art Room* (PS–3). Illus. by Pascal Milelli. 2002, Groundwood $15.95 (0-88899-449-4). 24pp. This biography of the West Coast Canadian artist concentrates on her teaching of young students and the inspiration she gave them. (Rev: BL 4/1/02; HBG 10/02; SLJ 6/02) [921]

DALI, SALVADOR

3100 Anderson, Robert. *Salvador Dali* (5–8). Illus. Series: Artists in Their Time. 2002, Watts LB $22.00 (0-531-12231-X); paper $6.95 (0-531-16624-4). 48pp. This volume presents Dali's life and influence with many illustrations and news clippings. (Rev: BL 10/15/02) [709]

DA VINCI, LEONARDO

3101 O'Connor, Barbara. *Leonardo da Vinci: Renaissance Genius* (5–8). Series: Trailblazers Biographies. 2002, Carolrhoda LB $25.26 (0-87614-467-9). 112pp. An excellent biography that details Leonardo's life from childhood, discusses some of his famous paintings, and looks at his inventions and experiments. (Rev: BL 3/15/03; HBG 3/03; SLJ 11/02) [921]

DEGAS, EDGAR

3102 Cocca-Leffler, Maryann. *Edgar Degas: Paintings That Dance* (2–4). Illus. Series: Smart About Art. 2001, Putnam LB $14.89 (0-448-42520-3); paper $7.50 (0-448-42611-0). 32pp. Introduces the work of Degas, using an elementary school student's report as the framework. (Rev: BL 11/15/01; HBG 3/02; SLJ 11/01) [709]

DE KOONING, WILLEM

3103 Hawes, Louise. *Willem de Kooning: The Life of an Artist* (4–6). Series: Artist Biographies. 2002, Enslow LB $18.95 (0-7660-1884-9). 48pp. Covers de Kooning's life from youth, his artistic techniques and work habits, and the impact of his lifestyle. (Rev: SLJ 3/03) [921]

GIACOMETTI, ALBERTO

3104 Gaff, Jackie. *Alberto Giacometti* (5–8). Series: Artists in Their Time. 2002, Watts LB $22.00 (0-531-12224-7); paper $6.95 (0-531-16617-1). 48pp. The life of this Italian artist noted for his elongated sculptures is re-created with comments on his social period. (Rev: BL 10/15/02) [921]

HOKUSAI, KATSUSHIKA

3105 Ray, Deborah Kogan. *Hokusai* (2–4). Illus. 2001, Farrar $18.00 (0-374-33263-0). 40pp. Introduces Japanese artist Hokusai, with excellent descriptions of life in late 18th- and 19th-century Japan. (Rev: BL 11/1/01; HBG 3/02; SLJ 12/01*) [796.92]

KAHLO, FRIDA

3106 Winter, Jonah. *Frida* (PS–3). Illus. by Ana Juan. 2002, Scholastic $16.95 (0-590-20320-7). 32pp. An inspirational biography of Mexican artist Frida Kahlo. (Rev: BCCB 2/02; BL 3/1/02; HB 3–4/02; HBG 10/02; SLJ 3/02) [759.9]

3107 Woronoff, Kristen. *Frida Kahlo: Mexican Painter* (3–5). Series: Famous Women Juniors. 2002, Gale LB $21.54 (1-56711-594-2). 32pp. This account focuses on Kahlo's youth and the events that led to her life as an artist. (Rev: SLJ 9/02) [921]

KLEE, PAUL

3108 Laidlaw, Jill A. *Paul Klee* (5–8). Series: Artists in Their Time. 2002, Watts LB $22.00 (0-531-12230-1); paper $6.95 (0-531-16623-6). 46pp. Photographs, reproductions, maps, and a timeline that links world events with events in the artist's life make this suitable both for browsing and report writing. (Rev: BL 10/15/02; SLJ 1/03) [921]

LAWRENCE, JACOB

3109 Leach, Deba Foxley. *I See You I See Myself: The Young Life of Jacob Lawrence* (5 Up). Illus. by Jacob Lawrence. 2002, Phillips Collection $19.95 (0-943044-26-X). 64pp. A look at the early life and work of the African American artist, with information on his paintings as a teen. (Rev: SLJ 12/02)

LEWIS, MAUD

3110 Bogart, Jo Ellen. *Capturing Joy: The Story of Maud Lewis* (3–6). Illus. by Mark Lang. 2002, Tundra $16.95 (0-88776-568-8). 32pp. The life and work of the Canadian artist who used a folk-art style. (Rev: BL 6/1–15/02; HBG 10/02; SLJ 7/02) [921]

MATISSE, HENRI

3111 O'Connor, Jane. *Henri Matisse: Drawing with Scissors* (1–3). Illus. by Jessie Hartland. Series: Smart About Art. 2002, Grosset LB $14.89 (0-448-42667-6); paper $5.99 (0-448-42519-X). The life and work of Matisse is presented in the form of a child's report, with examples of Matisse's art and photographs of the artist. (Rev: HBG 10/02; SLJ 7/02) [736]

3112 Welton, Jude. *Henri Matisse* (5–8). Series: Artists in Their Time. 2002, Watts LB $22.00 (0-531-12228-X); paper $6.95 (0-531-16621-X). 48pp. The artistic and social periods during which Matisse worked are re-created along with a biography and several color examples of his work. (Rev: BL 10/15/02; SLJ 1/03) [2.2.2]

MONET, CLAUDE

3113 Hodge, Susie. *Claude Monet* (5–8). Illus. Series: Artists in Their Time. 2002, Watts LB $22.00 (0-531-12226-3); paper $6.95 (0-531-16619-8). 46pp. Photographs, reproductions, maps, and a timeline that links world events with events in the artist's life make this suitable both for browsing and report writing. (Rev: SLJ 1/03) [921]

3114 Kelley, True. *Claude Monet: Sunshine and Waterlilies* (2–4). Illus. Series: Smart About Art. 2001, Putnam LB $14.89 (0-448-42613-7); paper $7.50 (0-448-42522-X). 32pp. An interesting overview of Claude Monet's life and work, presented in school-report format. (Rev: BL 11/1/01; HBG 3/02; SLJ 11/01) [759.4]

O'KEEFFE, GEORGIA

3115 Kucharczyk, Emily Rose. *Georgia O'Keeffe: Desert Painter* (3–5). Series: Famous Women Juniors. 2002, Gale LB $21.54 (1-56711-592-6). 32pp. This account focuses on the artist's youth and the events that led to her life as an artist. (Rev: SLJ 9/02) [921]

PICASSO, PABLO

3116 Kelley, True. *Pablo Picasso* (2–4). Series: Smart About Art. 2002, Grosset LB $14.89 (0-448-42879-2); paper $5.99 (0-448-42862-8). 32pp. For young readers, the life and works of this 20th-century master are covered in an attractive format. (Rev: BL 2/15/03) [921]

3117 Scarborough, Kate. *Pablo Picasso* (5–8). Series: Artists in Their Time. 2002, Watts LB $22.00 (0-531-12229-8); paper $6.95 (0-531-16622-8). 48pp. This biography of the 20th century's most famous artist is accompanied by material on the social conditions of his time. (Rev: BL 10/15/02; SLJ 1/03) [921]

3118 Wallis, Jeremy. *Pablo Picasso* (5–8). Series: Creative Lives. 2001, Heinemann LB $18.95 (1-58810-206-8). 64pp. This look at Picasso's life and work discusses the artist's genius and his faults. (Rev: HBG 10/02; SLJ 3/02) [921]

POLLOCK, JACKSON

3119 Greenberg, Jan, and Sandra Jordan. *Action Jackson* (2–5). Illus. by Robert Andrew Parker. 2002, Millbrook LB $22.90 (0-7613-2770-3). 32pp. An informative, thought-provoking biography that focuses on Pollock's famous painting *Lavender Mist.* (Rev: BCCB 11/02; BL 9/15/02; HB 11–12/02*; HBG 3/03; SLJ 10/02) [759.13]

REMBRANDT VAN RIJN

3120 De Bie, Ceciel, and Martijn Leenen. *Rembrandt: See and Do Children's Book* (3–7). Illus. 2001, Getty $19.95 (0-89236-621-4). 64pp. An effectively organized biography is combined with activities that encourage children to look closely at the art. (Rev: HBG 3/02; SLJ 4/02) [921]

ROCKWELL, NORMAN

3121 Roy, Jennifer Rozines, and Gregory Roy. *Norman Rockwell: The Life of an Artist* (4–6). Series: Artist Biographies. 2002, Enslow LB $18.95 (0-7660-1883-0). 48pp. Rockwell's early interest in art and his popularity are highlighted in this account of his life and work. (Rev: SLJ 3/03) [921]

ROUSSEAU, HENRI

3122 Venezia, Mike. *Henri Rousseau* (2–4). Series: Getting to Know the World's Greatest Artists. 2002, Children's LB $23.00 (0-516-22495-6); paper $6.95 (0-516-26998-4). An easy-to-read text and humorous cartoons are used to introduce this famous French artist and his work. (Rev: BL 4/1/02) [921]

SCHULTZ, CHARLES

3123 Whiting, Jim. *Charles Shultz* (3–4). Series: Real-Life Reader Biographies. 2002, Mitchell Lane LB $15.95 (1-58415-131-5). 32pp. A simple retelling of the life of the talented storyteller and cartoonist who created the comic strip "Peanuts." (Rev: BL 9/15/02) [921]

VAN GOGH, VINCENT

3124 Bucks, Brad, and Joan Holub. *Vincent van Gogh: Sunflowers and Swirly Stars* (2–4). Series: Smart About Art. 2001, Grosset $5.99 (0-448-42521-1). Using lively cartoon drawings and reproductions of the artist's works, the life and output of van Gogh are introduced through the eyes of a young student. (Rev: BL 1/1–15/02; HBG 3/02) [921]

3125 Green, Jen. *Vincent van Gogh* (5–8). Series: Artists in Their Time. 2002, Watts LB $22.00 (0-531-12238-7); paper $6.95 (0-531-16648-1). 48pp. The life and times of this 20th-century artistic genius are covered, plus a number of reproductions of his paintings. (Rev: BL 10/15/02) [921]

3126 Greenberg, Jan, and Sandra Jordan. *Vincent van Gogh: Portrait of an Artist* (5 Up). 2001, Delacorte LB $18.99 (0-385-90005-8). 132pp. This absorbing account of the artist's life and dedication to art at the expense of this health draws on correspondence with his brother. (Rev: BL 8/01; HB 11–12/01; HBG 3/02; SLJ 9/01*) [921]

VERMEER, JOHANNES

3127 Venezia, Mike. *Johannes Vermeer* (2–4). Series: Getting to Know the World's Greatest Artists. 2002, Children's LB $23.00 (0-516-22282-1); paper $6.95 (0-516-26999-2). The life and work of this Dutch master are presented with a simple text and many cartoons. (Rev: BL 4/1/02) [921]

WARHOL, ANDY

3128 Bolton, Linda. *Andy Warhol* (5–8). Series: Artists in Their Time. 2002, Watts LB $22.00 (0-531-12225-5); paper $6.95 (0-531-16618-X). 48pp. This biography includes material on the social period in which Warhol worked. (Rev: BL 10/15/02) [921]

WRIGHT, FRANK LLOYD

3129 Middleton, Haydn. *Frank Lloyd Wright* (5–8). Series: Creative Lives. 2001, Heinemann LB $18.95 (1-58810-203-3). 64pp. An attractive look at the architect's life and career with illustrations and a useful timeline. (Rev: HBG 10/02; SLJ 3/02) [921]

Composers

GUTHRIE, WOODY

3130 Christensen, Bonnie. *Woody Guthrie: Poet of the People* (3–5). Illus. 2001, Knopf LB $18.99 (0-375-91113-8). 32pp. This book for younger readers uses words and woodcut illustrations to tell the story of singer Woody Guthrie, best known for his song "This Land Is Your Land." (Rev: BL 9/1/01; HB 1–2/02*; HBG 3/02; SLJ 10/01) [782.42162]

3131 Coombs, Karen Mueller. *Woody Guthrie: America's Folksinger* (4–6). Series: Trailblazers Biographies. 2002, Carolrhoda LB $25.95 (1-57505-464-7). 120pp. A balanced look at the life of the singer/songwriter who died in 1967. (Rev: HBG 10/02; SLJ 7/02) [921]

HANDEL, GEORGE FRIDERIC

3132 Anderson, M. T. *Handel, Who Knew What He Liked* (3–6). Illus. by Kevin Hawkes. 2001, Candlewick $16.99 (0-7636-1046-1). 48pp. Here's an irreverent large-format account of the interesting life of composer Handel, including lively anecdotes and detailed, dramatic illustrations that give a flavor of the time with a dollop of humor. (Rev: BCCB 1/02; BL 12/15/01; HB 11–12/01*; HBG 3/02; SLJ 12/01*)

HANDY, W. C.

3133 Summer, L. S. *W. C. Handy: Founder of the Blues* (4–6). Series: Journey to Freedom: The African American Library. 2001, Child's World LB $17.95 (1-56766-927-1). 40pp. The life of this African American jazz pioneer is told in a concise text with many sepia-toned illustrations. (Rev: BL 12/15/01; HBG 3/02) [921]

IVES, CHARLES

3134 Gerstein, Mordicai. *What Charlie Heard* (3–5). Illus. 2002, Farrar $17.00 (0-374-38292-1). 40pp. This picture-book biography focuses on the American composer Charles Ives and his childhood influences. (Rev: BCCB 4/02; BL 4/1/02; HB 5–6/02*; HBG 10/02; SLJ 3/02) [921]

Entertainers

ALBA, JESSICA

3135 Rivera, Ursula. *Jessica Alba* (5–8). Series: Celebrity Bios. 2002, Children's LB $19.00 (0-516-23909-0); paper $6.95 (0-516-23482-X). 48pp. A quickly read biography of the young actress who appeared in the Fox TV series "Dark Angel" and such movies as *Idle Hands* and *Paranoid*. (Rev: BL 6/1–15/02) [921]

ANDERSON, MARIAN

3136 Meadows, James. *Marian Anderson: 1897-1993* (4–6). Series: Journey to Freedom: The African American Library. 2001, Child's World LB $17.95 (1-56766-921-2). 40pp. Lavishly illustrated with color and sepia-toned illustrations, this is an attractive biography of the great black singer who broke the color barrier at the Metropolitan Opera. (Rev: BL 12/15/01; SLJ 1/02) [921]

3137 Ryan, Pam Munoz. *When Marian Sang: The True Recital of Marian Anderson* (K–3). Illus. by Brian Selznick. 2002, Scholastic $16.95 (0-439-26967-9). 40pp. This large-format picture-book biography presents Anderson's life in glowing words and pictures and interweaves the spirituals that Anderson sang. (Rev: BL 11/15/02; HB 11–12/02; HBG 3/03; SLJ 11/02*) [782.1]

ARMSTRONG, LOUIS

3138 Fahlenkamp-Merrell, Kindle. *Louis Armstrong: 1901-1971* (4–6). Series: Journey to Freedom: The African American Library. 2001, Child's World LB $17.95 (1-56766-919-0). 40pp. Color and sepia-toned illustrations are used on every page in this attractive, well-organized biography of the jazz great. (Rev: BL 12/15/01) [921]

3139 Orgill, Roxane. *If I Only Had a Horn* (PS–3). Illus. by Leonard Jenkins. 1997, Houghton $16.00 (0-395-75919-6); paper $5.95 (0-618-25076-X). A biography of jazz musician Louis Armstrong, with colorful illustrations. (Rev: BL 2/15/03) [921]

BEATLES (MUSICAL GROUP)

3140 Roberts, Jeremy. *The Beatles* (5–8). Series: Biography. 2001, Lerner LB $25.26 (0-8225-4998-0). This is the story of the Beatles, from Liverpool to international stardom and eventual separation. (Rev: BL 4/1/02; HBG 10/02) [921]

CAREY, MARIAH

3141 Parker, Judy. *Mariah Carey* (5–8). Illus. Series: Celebrity Bios. 2001, Children's LB $19.00 (0-516-23425-0); paper $6.95 (0-516-29600-0). 48pp. An attractive simple introduction that looks at the popular singer's childhood and first breaks. [782.42164]

CHRISTENSEN, HAYDEN

3142 Friedman, Katherine. *Hayden Christensen* (5–8). Series: Celebrity Bios. 2002, Children's LB $19.00 (0-516-23907-4); paper $6.95 (0-516-23481-1). 48pp. A high-interest, simple biography of the young Canadian actor who plays Anakin Skywalker in the *Star Wars* prequels. (Rev: BL 6/1–15/02) [921]

COOK, RACHAEL LEIGH

3143 Rivera, Ursula. *Rachael Leigh Cook* (5–8). Series: Celebrity Bios. 2002, Children's LB $19.00 (0-516-23908-2); paper $6.95 (0-516-23484-6). 48pp. Ms. Cook, a Minnesota native, starred in such movies as *Get Carter* and *Josie and the Pussycats*. (Rev: BL 6/1–15/02) [921]

ELLINGTON, DUKE

3144 Pinkney, Andrea Davis. *Duke Ellington: The Piano Prince and His Orchestra* (K–3). Illus. by Brian Pinkney. 1998, Hyperion $15.95 (0-7868-0178-6). The story of the jazz great and his wonderful music, with vivid illustrations. (Rev: BL 2/15/03; HBG 9/98; SLJ 5/98) [781.65]

FITZGERALD, ELLA

3145 Pinkney, Andrea Davis. *Ella Fitzgerald: The Tale of a Vocal Virtuosa* (3–5). Illus. by Brian Pinkney. 2002, Hyperion $16.99 (0-7868-0568-4). 32pp. A picture-book biography told by Scat Cat Monroe with a lengthy text about the singer's life and the thrill of witnessing one of her performances. (Rev: BL 4/1/02; HBG 10/02; SLJ 5/02) [921]

HART, MELISSA JOAN

3146 Ciacobello, John. *Melissa Joan Hart* (5–8). Series: Celebrity Bios. 2002, Children's LB $19.00 (0-516-23906-6); paper $6.95 (0-516-23483-8). 48pp. An easily read, heavily illustrated biography of the young actress who gained stardom as *Sabrina, the Teenage Witch*. (Rev: BL 6/1–15/02; SLJ 8/02) [921]

HENSON, JIM

3147 Durrett, Deanne. *Jim Henson* (2–5). Illus. Series: Inventors and Creators. 2002, Gale LB $23.70 (0-7377-0996-0). 48pp. This look at the life of the Muppets creator includes lots of details on the puppets. (Rev: BL 11/1/02) [791.5]

HILL, FAITH

3148 Hinman, Bonnie. *Faith Hill* (5–9). 2001, Chelsea LB $19.75 (0-7910-6471-9). 64pp. A look at the life and career of the country music star, with information on Nashville's Grand Ole Opry. (Rev: HBG 10/02; SLJ 4/02) [921]

HOUDINI, HARRY

3149 Cox, Clinton. *Houdini: Master of Illusion* (5–9). Illus. 2001, Scholastic $16.95 (0-590-94960-8). 208pp. A fast-paced account of the life of the world-famous magician from childhood on, with eight pages of photographs and reproductions. (Rev: BL 11/15/01; HB 1–2/02; HBG 3/02; SLJ 12/01) [793.8]

3150 Rau, Dana Meachen. *Harry Houdini: Master Magician* (4–6). Series: Book Report Biographies. 2001, Watts LB $22.00 (0-531-11599-2); paper $6.95 (0-531-15551-X). 28pp. An intriguing portrait of the amazing showman told in lively prose with many black-and-white photographs. (Rev: BL 8/1/01; SLJ 9/01) [921]

JACKSON, MICHAEL

3151 Graves, Karen Marie. *Michael Jackson* (5–8). Series: People in the News. 2001, Lucent LB $27.45 (1-56006-707-1). The unusual life of this show business legend is outlined in text and photographs. (Rev: BL 4/1/02) [921]

LATIFAH, QUEEN

3152 Bloom, Sara R. *Queen Latifah* (4–7). Series: Black Americans of Achievement. 2001, Chelsea LB $21.95 (0-7910-6287-2). Numerous photographs add interest to this biography of the amazing singer-actress and her rise to fame. (Rev: BL 4/1/02; HBG 10/02; SLJ 6/02) [921]

LEE, SPIKE

3153 Shields, Charles J. *Spike Lee* (5–7). Illus. 2002, Chelsea LB $21.95 (0-7910-6715-7). 112pp. This look at Spike Lee's career, working methods, and importance includes both strengths and weaknesses. (Rev: BL 11/1/02; HBG 3/03) [791.43]

LENNON, JOHN

3154 Gogerly, Liz. *John Lennon* (4–6). Series: Famous Lives. 2003, Raintree Steck-Vaughn LB $27.12 (0-7398-5522-0). 48pp. The story of the legendary member of the Beatles and how he influenced young people to cherish peace and love. (Rev: BL 2/15/03) [921]

LUCAS, GEORGE

3155 Shields, Charles J. *George Lucas* (5–7). Illus. Series: Behind the Camera. 2002, Chelsea LB $21.95 (0-7910-6712-2). 112pp. A profile of the famous filmmaker, with information on his strengths and weaknesses, his working methods, and his importance to the American film industry. (Rev: BL 11/1/02; HBG 3/03) [791.43]

MUNIZ, FRANKIE

3156 Beyer, Mark. *Frankie Muniz* (5–8). Series: Celebrity Bios. 2002, Children's LB $19.00 (0-516-23910-4); paper $6.95 (0-516-23480-3). 48pp. Using simple sentences and many color photographs, this is a brief biography of the young actor who scored a big hit in "Malcolm in the Middle." (Rev: BL 6/1–15/02; SLJ 8/02) [921]

OAKLEY, ANNIE

3157 Krensky, Stephen. *Shooting for the Moon: The Amazing Life and Times of Annie Oakley* (1–4). Illus. by Bernie Fuchs. 2001, Farrar $17.00 (0-374-36843-0). 32pp. A combination of simple, concise text and skillful oil paintings convey the life of Annie Oakley, from her childhood to her fame for her shooting skills. (Rev: BL 9/15/01; HBG 3/02; SLJ 9/01) [799.3]

3158 Macy, Sue. *Bull's-Eye: A Photobiography of Annie Oakley* (5–8). Illus. 2001, National Geographic $17.95 (0-7922-7008-8). 64pp. This book separates fact from fiction in the life of Phoebe Ann Moses Butler, who came to be known as Annie Oakley. (Rev: BL 11/15/01; HBG 3/02; SLJ 10/01) [799.3]

PAVLOVA, ANNA

3159 Allman, Barbara. *Dance of the Swan: A Story About Anna Pavlova* (3–6). Illus. by Shelly O. Haas. Series: Creative Minds Biographies. 2001, Carolrhoda LB $21.27 (1-57505-463-9). 64pp. Allman presents Pavlova's life from childhood and discusses her love of nature and of children. (Rev: HBG 10/01; SLJ 7/01) [792.8]

PRESLEY, ELVIS

3160 Denenberg, Barry. *All Shook Up: The Life and Death of Elvis Presley* (5 Up). 2001, Scholastic $16.95 (0-439-09504-2). 176pp. This accessible biography of Elvis places him in historical and musical context and discusses both good and bad sides of his personal life and his mismanaged career. (Rev: BL 10/1/01; HB 1–2/02; HBG 3/02; SLJ 1/02) [921]

ROBESON, PAUL

3161 McKissack, Patricia, and Fredrick McKissack. *Paul Robeson: A Voice to Remember*. Rev. ed. (2–5). Series: Great African Americans. 2001, Enslow LB $14.95 (0-7660-1674-9). 32pp. Presents Robeson's personal and professional life and the hardships he faced because of his race and beliefs. (Rev: HBG 10/01; SLJ 8/01) [921]

ROBINSON, BILL "BOJANGLES"

3162 Dillon, Leo, and Diane Dillon. *Rap a Tap Tap: Here's Bojangles — Think of That!* (PS–2). Illus. 2002, Scholastic $15.95 (0-590-47883-4). 32pp. A brilliantly illustrated picture book about legendary tap artist Bill "Bojangles" Robinson. (Rev: BL 10/15/02; HBG 3/03; SLJ 9/02) [792.7]

ROGERS, WILL

3163 Keating, Frank. *Will Rogers* (K–3). Illus. by Mike Wimmer. 2002, Harcourt $16.00 (0-15-202405-0). 32pp. A beautifully illustrated profile of the humorist and newspaper columnist who lived from 1879 to 1935, written by Oklahoma governor Frank Keating. (Rev: BL 9/15/02; HBG 3/03; SLJ 11/02) [792.7]

SENNETT, MACK

3164 Brown, Don. *Mack Made Movies* (1–4). Illus. 2003, Millbrook LB $23.90 (0-7613-2504-2). 32pp. A picture-book biography of film pioneer Mack Sennett, with sepia illustrations. (Rev: BL 3/1/03*; SLJ 3/03) [791.43]

SPIELBERG, STEVEN

3165 Rubin, Susan Goldman. *Steven Spielberg: Crazy for Movies* (5–8). Illus. 2001, Abrams $19.95 (0-8109-4492-8). 94pp. Director Steven Spielberg's love of photography from his youth, his fascination with storytelling, and his successful movie career are presented in lively text and large photographs. (Rev: BL 12/1/01; HBG 3/02; SLJ 12/01) [791.43]

VAN DER BEEK, JAMES

3166 McCracken, Kristin. *James Van Der Beek* (5–8). Illus. Series: Celebrity Bios. 2001, Children's LB $19.00 (0-516-23429-3); paper $6.95 (0-516-29604-3). 48pp. The combination of easy text, photographs, gossip, and details of Van Der Beek's youth will appeal especially to reluctant readers. (Rev: BL 12/15/01) [791.45]

VON TRAPP, MARIA

3167 Ransom, Candice F. *Maria von Trapp: Beyond the Sound of Music* (4–6). Illus. Series: Trailblazers Biographies. 2002, Carolrhoda LB $25.26 (1-57505-444-2). 112pp. A portrait based on von Trapp's own writings that describes her life in war-torn Austria and move to Vermont. (Rev: BL 3/1/02; HBG 10/02; SLJ 5/02) [782.42]

WINFREY, OPRAH

3168 Krohn, Katherine. *Oprah Winfrey* (5–8). Series: Biography. 2001, Lerner LB $25.26 (0-8225-4999-9). The media genius and talk-show hostess is profiled in an interesting text with many photographs. (Rev: BL 4/1/02; HBG 10/02) [921]

3169 Stone, Tanya Lee. *Oprah Winfrey: Success with an Open Heart* (4–7). Illus. Series: Gateway Biography. 2001, Millbrook $22.90 (0-7613-1814-3). 48pp. Oprah's story, with concise text and excellent photographs, will attract and inspire young readers. (Rev: BL 6/1–15/01; HBG 10/01) [791.45]

Writers

ALCOTT, LOUISA MAY

3170 Silverthorne, Elizabeth. *Louisa May Alcott* (4–7). Illus. Series: Who Wrote That? 2002, Chelsea LB $21.95 (0-7910-6721-1). 112pp. A look at the life and works of author Louisa May Alcott, with particular emphasis on her family. (Rev: BL 10/15/02; HBG 3/03; SLJ 10/02) [813]

AUSTEN, JANE

3171 Ruth, Amy. *Jane Austen* (5–8). Series: A & E Biography. 2001, Lerner LB $25.26 (0-8225-4992-1). This is the intriguing story of Jane Austen, who lived a quiet, obscure life yet produced some of the world's greatest novels. (Rev: BL 6/1–15/01; HBG 10/01; SLJ 11/01) [921]

BRONTË FAMILY

3172 Kenyon, Karen Smith. *The Brontë Family: Passionate Literary Geniuses* (5–9). Series: Lerner Biographies. 2002, Lerner LB $25.26 (0-8225-0071-X). 128pp. An absorbing introduction to the individual members of this literary family, with many illustrations and quotations from letters. (Rev: HBG 3/03; SLJ 1/03) [921]

BUNTING, EVE

3173 McGinty, Alice B. *Meet Eve Bunting* (2–4). Illus. Series: About the Author. 2003, Rosen LB $18.75 (0-8239-6411-6). 24pp. Readers learn about Bunting's youth and later life and how and why she started writing for children, with excerpts from her books, reprints from covers, photographs, and other illustrations. (Rev: SLJ 3/03) [921]

BYARS, BETSY

3174 Cammarano, Rita. *Betsy Byars* (4–7). Series: Who Wrote That? 2002, Chelsea LB $21.95 (0-7910-6720-3). 106pp. A profile in text and pictures of one of America's best loved authors and winner of the Newbery and other prizes. (Rev: BL 10/15/02; HBG 3/03) [921]

CURTIS, CHRISTOPHER PAUL

3175 Gaines, Ann. *Christopher Paul Curtis* (3–6). Series: Real-Life Reader Biographies. 2001, Mitchell Lane LB $15.95 (1-58415-076-9). 32pp. The fascinating story of the determination that took African American Curtis from writing in a journal during breaks on a car assembly line to winning notable awards. (Rev: SLJ 9/01) [813]

DAHL, ROALD

3176 Shields, Charles J. *Roald Dahl* (4–7). Series: Who Wrote That? 2002, Chelsea LB $21.95 (0-7910-6722-X). 106pp. A brief biography of the master of whimsical stories that involve such strange elements as secretive chocolate factories and giant peaches. (Rev: BL 10/15/02; HBG 3/03) [921]

DEPAOLA, TOMIE

3177 dePaola, Tomie. *Things Will Never Be the Same* (2–4). Illus. 2003, Putnam $13.99 (0-399-23982-0). 80pp. DePaola's autobiography, with his own drawings, continues through 1941, when he turned seven, and details his everyday life until the morning of December 7, when everything changed. (Rev: BCCB 3/03; BL 3/1/03) [813.54]

3178 dePaola, Tomie. *What a Year!* (2–4). Illus. 2002, Putnam $13.99 (0-399-23797-6). 80pp. DePaola's memoirs continues here, taking readers into the life of 6-year-old Tomie from the beginning of first grade to New Year's Eve in 1940. (Rev: BCCB 3/02; BL 3/1/02; HB 3–4/02; HBG 10/02; SLJ 3/02) [813.54]

GEISEL, THEODORE

3179 Dean, Tanya. *Theodor Geisel (Dr. Seuss)* (4–7). Illus. Series: Who Wrote That? 2002, Chelsea LB $21.95 (0-7910-6724-6). 112pp. A look at the life and works of the author and illustrator known as Dr. Seuss. (Rev: BL 10/15/02; HBG 3/03) [813]

GRIMM BROTHERS

3180 Hettinga, Donald R. *The Brothers Grimm: Two Lives, One Legacy* (5–8). Illus. 2001, Clarion $22.00 (0-618-05599-1). 192pp. An interesting biography that places the brothers' lives in the context of their time and discusses their skills as lexicographers and scholars. (Rev: BL 7/01; HB 1–2/02; HBG 3/02; SLJ 10/01) [430]

HUGHES, LANGSTON

3181 McKissack, Patricia, and Fredrick McKissack. *Langston Hughes: Great American Poet* (2–4). Series: Great African Americans. 2002, Enslow LB $14.95 (0-7660-1695-1). 32pp. An interesting biography of the African American author noted for both his poetry and fiction and for his role in the Harlem Renaissance. (Rev: BL 7/02; HBG 10/02) [921]

3182 Walker, Alice. *Langston Hughes: American Poet* (2–5). Illus. by Catherine Deeter. 2002, HarperCollins LB $16.89 (0-06-021519-4). 37pp. This revised, larger-format edition of a 1974 publication gives young readers a look at the difficulties of Langston's boyhood. (Rev: HBG 10/02; SLJ 2/02) [921]

HURSTON, ZORA NEALE

3183 McKissack, Patricia, and Fredrick McKissack. *Zora Neale Hurston: Writer and Storyteller* (2–4). Series: Great African Americans. 2002, Enslow LB $14.95 (0-7660-1694-3). 32pp. A simple biography of the African American writer who is currently enjoying a revival of interest because of her excellent novels. (Rev: BL 7/02; HBG 3/03) [921]

KEHRET, PEG

3184 Kehret, Peg. *Five Pages a Day: A Writer's Journey* (4–7). 2002, Albert Whitman $14.95 (0-8075-8650-1). 192pp. Aspiring young writers will particularly enjoy Kehret's account of her writing life, from starting a newspaper about the neighborhood dogs to entering writing contests to her career as an author of children's books. (Rev: BL 12/15/02; HBG 3/03; SLJ 9/02) [813]

MILNE, A. A.

3185 Sibley, Brian. *Three Cheers for Pooh: The Best Bear in All the World* (4–6). Illus. 2001, Dutton $22.99 (0-525-46796-3). 126pp. This ambitious volume features all kinds of facts about Pooh and about A. A. Milne and his family, as well as illustrations from different editions and examples of Pooh-related merchandise over the years. (Rev: BL 2/15/02; HBG 3/02) [823.91]

MONTGOMERY, LUCY MAUD

3186 MacLeod, Elizabeth. *Lucy Maud Montgomery: A Writer's Life* (3–5). Illus. 2001, Kids Can LB $14.95 (1-55074-487-9). 32pp. Both black-and-white and color illustrations are used to enhance this biography of one of Canada's most famous writers. (Rev: BL 4/1/01; HBG 10/01; SLJ 4/01) [921]

MORRISON, TONI

3187 Haskins, Jim. *Toni Morrison: The Magic of Words* (4–6). Illus. Series: Gateway Biography. 2001, Millbrook $21.90 (0-7613-1806-2). 48pp. Young readers may not be familiar with Morrison's work, but will still enjoy this clearly presented photo-essay introducing her life from childhood, her work, and her support for other writers. (Rev: BL 6/1–15/01; HBG 10/01; SLJ 5/01) [813.5]

3188 Jones, Amy Robin. *Toni Morrison: 1931-* (4–6). Series: Journey to Freedom: The African American Library. 2001, Child's World LB $17.95 (1-56766-925-5). 40pp. An oversize, attractive volume that presents the life, accomplishments, and importance of this towering figure in contemporary literature. (Rev: BL 12/15/01) [921]

3189 Rhodes, Lisa R. *Toni Morrison: Great American Writer* (4–6). Series: Book Report Biographies. 2001, Watts LB $22.00 (0-531-11677-8); paper $6.95 (0-531-15555-2). 28pp. The life of the prize-winning novelist is told concisely and illustrated with many black-and-white photographs. (Rev: BL 8/1/01) [921]

NAYLOR, PHYLLIS REYNOLDS

3190 Naylor, Phyllis Reynolds. *How I Came to Be a Writer*. Rev. ed. (4 Up). 2001, Simon & Schuster paper $4.99 (0-689-83887-5). 139pp. Naylor describes the joys and difficulties of life as a writer and includes excerpts of her work in this autobiographical account. (Rev: SLJ 5/01) [921]

PAULSEN, GARY

3191 Gaines, Ann. *Gary Paulsen* (3–6). Series: Real-Life Reader Biographies. 2001, Mitchell Lane LB $15.95 (1-58415-077-7). 32pp. Gaines presents Paulsen's difficult childhood, his love of reading, and his fascination with sled dogs and adventure. (Rev: SLJ 9/01) [813]

3192 Paterra, Elizabeth. *Gary Paulsen* (4–7). Series: Who Wrote That? 2002, Chelsea LB $21.95 (0-7910-6723-8). 106pp. A profile of the prolific author (of almost 200 books) who is best known for his young adult outdoor survival stories. (Rev: BL 10/15/02; HBG 3/03) [921]

3193 Paulsen, Gary. *Caught by the Sea* (5–8). 2001, Delacorte $15.95 (0-385-32645-9). 104pp. The author describes his ongoing love of the sea and the adventures he's had, some funny, some scary. (Rev: BL 9/15/01; HBG 3/02; SLJ 10/01) [818]

PINKWATER, DANIEL

3194 McGinty, Alice B. *Meet Daniel Pinkwater* (2–4). Illus. Series: About the Author. 2003, Rosen LB $18.75 (0-8239-6406-X). 24pp. Readers learn about Pinkwater's youth and later life, his varied interests, how and why he started writing for children, and how he uses his own childhood experiences in his books. (Rev: SLJ 3/03) [921]

POE, EDGAR ALLAN

3195 Kent, Zachary. *Edgar Allan Poe* (5–8). Series: Historical American Biographies. 2001, Enslow LB $20.95 (0-7660-1600-5). An informative, well-presented biography of this writer whose unique stories changed the history of American literature. (Rev: BL 1/1–15/02; HBG 3/02; SLJ 9/01) [921]

3196 Streissguth, Tom. *Edgar Allan Poe* (5–8). Series: A & E Biography. 2001, Lerner LB $25.26 (0-8225-4991-3). The tortured life of this early master of the short story is brought to life in an interesting text and many black-and-white illustrations. (Rev: BL 6/1–15/01; HBG 10/01; SLJ 8/01) [921]

POTTER, BEATRIX

3197 Winter, Jeanette. *Beatrix: Various Episodes from the Life of Beatrix Potter* (PS–2). Illus. 2003, Farrar $15.00 (0-374-30655-9). 64pp. Excerpts from Potter's writings are incorporated in this small-format biography that looks mainly at her life as a child and young woman. (Rev: BL 3/1/03; SLJ 3/03) [823]

RAWLINGS, MARJORIE KINNAN

3198 Cook, Judy, and Laura Lee Smith. *Natural Writer: A Story About Marjorie Kinnan Rawlings* (4–6). Illus. by Laurie Harden. Series: Creative Minds Biographies. 2001, Carolrhoda LB $21.27 (1-57505-468-X). 64pp. This easily read biography with full-page illustrations tells the life story of the author of *The Yearling*. (Rev: HBG 10/01; SLJ 8/01) [921]

REESE, DELLA

3199 Dean, Tanya. *Della Reese* (4–7). Series: Black Americans of Achievement. 2001, Chelsea LB $21.95 (0-7910-6291-0). The life and career of this show business giant are outlined with special coverage on her recent successes in television. (Rev: BL 4/1/02) [921]

ROWLING, J. K.

3200 Gaines, Ann. *J. K. Rowling* (3–6). 2001, Mitchell Lane LB $15.95 (1-58415-078-5). 32pp. Gaines chronicles Rowling's struggles as a single mother seeking a publisher before *Harry*'s success. (Rev: BCCB 2/02; SLJ 9/01) [813]

3201 Steffens, Bradley. *J.K. Rowling* (5–7). Series: People in the News. 2002, Gale LB $21.96 (1-56006-776-4). 112pp. Rowling's early life and education figure prominently in this account of her life that also looks at the plot and setting of her novels and wonders what she will do when the series is finished. (Rev: BCCB 2/02; SLJ 10/02) [921]

SHAKESPEARE, WILLIAM

3202 Dommermuth-Costa, Carol. *William Shakespeare* (5–8). Series: Biography. 2001, Lerner LB $25.26 (0-8225-4996-4). A readable, well-illustrated biography of the Bard of Avon with material on many of his plays. (Rev: BL 4/1/02; HBG 10/02; SLJ 3/02) [921]

3203 Rosen, Michael. *Shakespeare: His Work and His World* (5–9). Illus. by Robert Ingpen. 2001, Candlewick $19.99 (0-7636-1568-4). 104pp. An insightful look at Elizabethan culture and the life of William Shakespeare, as well as several of his plays. (Rev: BL 11/1/01; HBG 3/02; SLJ 11/01*) [822.3]

SILVERSTEIN, SHEL

3204 Ward, S. *Meet Shel Silverstein* (2–3). Series: About the Author. 2001, Rosen LB $18.75 (0-8239-5709-8). 24pp. This introduction to the author of

"The Giving Tree" describes his life and work. (Rev: SLJ 6/01) [921]

SPINELLI, JERRY

3205 McGinty, Alice B. *Meet Jerry Spinelli* (2–4). Illus. Series: About the Author. 2003, Rosen LB $18.75 (0-8239-6408-6). 24pp. Readers learn about Spinelli's youth and later life, his varied interests, how and why he started writing for children, and how he uses his own childhood experiences in his books. (Rev: SLJ 3/03) [921]

STOWE, HARRIET BEECHER

3206 Gelletly, LeeAnne. *Harriet Beecher Stowe: Author of Uncle Tom's Cabin* (3–6). 2001, Chelsea LB $18.95 (0-7910-6009-8). 80pp. Easy-to-read information on Stowe's life and work is accompanied by illustrations and sidebars that profile some of her contemporaries, including Harriet Tubman and William Lloyd Garrison. (Rev: SLJ 10/01) [921]

THOREAU, HENRY DAVID

3207 Thoreau, Henry David. *Henry David's House* (2–4). Ed. by Steven Schnur. Illus. by Peter M. Fiore. 2002, Charlesbridge $16.95 (0-88106-116-6). 32pp. Using Thoreau's words, this picture book describes the construction of his cottage in the woods near Walden Pond. (Rev: BL 4/1/02; HBG 10/02; SLJ 5/02) [921]

TWAIN, MARK

3208 Aller, Susan Bivin. *Mark Twain* (5–8). Series: A & E Biography. 2001, Lerner LB $25.26 (0-8225-4994-8). The colorful life of one of America's favorite authors is re-created in accessible text, black-and-white photographs, and such additions as interesting sidebars and extensive reading lists. (Rev: BL 6/1–15/01; HBG 10/01) [921]

3209 Anderson, William. *River Boy: The Story of Mark Twain* (1–4). Illus. by Dan Andreasen. 2003, HarperCollins LB $16.89 (0-06-028401-3). The importance of the Mississippi in Twain's youth is highlighted in this account that includes coverage of his leaving school at the age of 12, working on a steamboat, searching for gold, and his career as a writer and humorist. (Rev: SLJ 3/03) [921]

VERNE, JULES

3210 Schoell, William. *Remarkable Journeys: The Story of Jules Verne* (4–8). Series: World Writers. 2002, Morgan Reynolds LB $21.95 (1-883846-92-7). 112pp. Writing was not Verne's first love, as Schoell explains in this accessible biography. (Rev: BL 6/1–15/02; HBG 10/02; SLJ 9/02)

WHEATLEY, PHILLIS

3211 Gregson, Susan R. *Phillis Wheatley* (4–6). Illus. Series: Let Freedom Ring. 2001, Capstone LB $22.60 (0-7368-1033-1). 48pp. Wheatley's early life, education, marriage, and writing career are placed in historical context and accompanied by excerpts from her poems. (Rev: HBG 3/02; SLJ 7/02)

3212 Lasky, Kathryn. *A Voice of Her Own: The Story of Phillis Wheatley, Slave Poet* (2–4). Illus. by Paul Lee. 2003, Candlewick $16.99 (0-7636-0252-3). 40pp. A biography of the slave and poet, focusing on her childhood. (Rev: BL 2/15/03; SLJ 1/03) [921]

YOLEN, JANE

3213 McGinty, Alice B. *Meet Jane Yolen* (2–4). Illus. Series: About the Author. 2003, Rosen LB $18.75 (0-8239-6407-8). 24pp. Readers learn about Yolen's youth and later life and how and why she started writing for children, with excerpts from her books and reprints of covers. (Rev: SLJ 3/03) [921]

Collective

3214 Aaseng, Nathan. *Business Builders in Fast Food* (5–8). Series: Business Builders. 2001, Oliver LB $19.95 (1-881508-58-7). 160pp. An interesting look at the creators of fast food empires such as McDonald's and Wendy's. (Rev: BL 9/15/01) [381]

3215 Adams, Simon. *The Presidents of the United States* (3–7). 2001, Two-Can $16.95 (1-58728-093-0); paper $9.95 (1-58728-092-2). 96pp. Double-page spreads give basic information on each president, with interesting anecdotes, timelines, full-color portraits, reproductions, and a carefully chosen quotation. (Rev: SLJ 7/01) [973.0099]

3216 Altman, Susan. *Extraordinary African-Americans: From Colonial to Contemporary Times.* Rev. ed. (5–8). Series: Extraordinary People. 2001, Children's LB $37.50 (0-516-22549-9). 288pp. This revision of a 1989 title adds 36 new profiles and offers a good starting point for research into important African Americans throughout history. (Rev: SLJ 3/02) [921]

3217 Ashby, Ruth. *Extraordinary People* (5–8). Series: Civil War Chronicles. 2002, Smart Apple LB $28.50 (1-58340-182-2). 48pp. Key military and civilian figures from both North and South are profiled. (Rev: HBG 3/03; SLJ 2/03) [973.7]

3218 Barber, James, and Amy Pastan. *Presidents and First Ladies* (4–8). Illus. 2002, DK LB $19.95 (0-7894-8454-4); paper $12.95 (0-7894-8453-6). 96pp. For each president and his First Lady, there are biographies, a list of key events, and a box highlighting an important event during that administration, plus plenty of color illustrations. (Rev: BL 4/1/02; HBG 10/02; SLJ 5/02) [920]

3219 Bruning, John Robert. *Elusive Glory: African-American Heroes of World War II* (5–8). Illus. Series: Avisson Young Adult. 2001, Avisson $19.95 (1-888105-48-8). 144pp. The true stories of African American servicemen, including six Tuskegee Airmen, who served the United States during World War II. (Rev: BL 1/1–15/02; SLJ 4/02) [940.54]

3220 Caravantes, Peggy. *Petticoat Spies: Six Women Spies of the Civil War* (5–8). Illus. 2002, Morgan Reynolds LB $20.95 (1-883846-88-9). 112pp. An exciting volume about six women who spied for the Union and Confederacy during the Civil War, with photographs, source notes, a glossary, and a bibliography. (Rev: BL 3/15/02; HBG 10/02; SLJ 8/02) [973.7]

3221 Davis, Kenneth C. *Don't Know Much About the Presidents* (4–6). Illus. by Pedro Martin. Series: Don't Know Much About. 2002, HarperCollins LB $15.89 (0-06-028616-4). 64pp. A question-and-answer format is used to introduce basic facts and trivia about the presidents, with bright cartoons, portraits, quotations, and timelines. (Rev: HBG 10/02; SLJ 1/02) [973.099]

3222 Furbee, Mary R. *Outrageous Women of Colonial America* (3–6). Illus. Series: Outrageous Women. 2001, Wiley paper $12.95 (0-471-38299-X). 120pp. Fourteen women are profiled here, in sections on New England, the middle colonies, and the South. (Rev: BL 5/15/01) [920]

3223 Greenfield, Eloise. *How They Got Over: African Americans and the Call of the Sea* (4–6). Illus. by Jan S. Gilchrist. 2003, HarperCollins LB $17.89 (0-06-028992-9). 128pp. The biographies of seven African Americans who sailed on, dove in, or studied the sea, with illustrations and a bibliography. (Rev: BL 2/15/03; HB 3–4/03; SLJ 1/03) [920]

3224 Hardy, P. Stephen, and Sheila Jackson Hardy. *Extraordinary People of the Harlem Renaissance* (4–8). Series: Extraordinary People. 2000, Children's LB $37.00 (0-516-21201-X); paper $16.95 (0-516-27170-9). 288pp. Black-and-white photographs, reproductions of sheet music, and interesting artwork enhance the extensive information on the artists, photographers, musicians, writers, and poets of Harlem in the 1920s and 1930s. (Rev: SLJ 6/01) [700]

3225 Harness, Cheryl. *Rabble Rousers: 20 Women Who Made a Difference* (3–6). Illus. 2003, Dutton

$17.99 (0-525-47035-2). 64pp. Girls especially will be drawn to these inspiring two-page accounts of feminists ranging from the famous, such as Susan B. Anthony, to less-known figures, including Ann Lee, founder of the Shaker movement, all presented with handsome sepia portraits, timelines, and addresses of relevant organizations. (Rev: BL 1/1–15/03; SLJ 1/03) [305.42]

3226 Harness, Cheryl. *Remember the Ladies* (4–7). Illus. 2001, HarperCollins $16.95 (0-688-17017-X). 64pp. Brief profiles of 100 important American women are each accompanied by a portrait. (Rev: BL 4/15/01; HBG 10/01; SLJ 2/01) [920]

3227 Hoose, Phillip. *We Were There, Too! Young People in U.S. History* (5–8). Illus. 2001, Farrar $26.00 (0-374-38252-2). 276pp. Hoose tells the stories of dozens of young people who contributed to the making of America — some famous but many who will be new to readers. (Rev: BCCB 10/01; BL 8/01; HB 9–10/01*; HBG 3/02; SLJ 8/01*) [973]

3228 Hudson, Wade. *Book of Black Heroes: Scientists, Healers and Inventors* (5–8). Illus. 2002, Just Us paper $9.95 (0-940975-97-1). 70pp. One historic or present-day African American figure is presented on each page of this collective biography of doctors, engineers, and inventors. (Rev: BL 2/15/03) [925]

3229 Kramer, S. A. *The Look-It-Up Book of First Ladies* (4–8). 2000, Random LB $11.99 (0-679-99347-9); paper $9.95 (0-679-89347-4). 128pp. A companion to *The Look-It-Up Book of Presidents* that provides concise biographies of first ladies and discusses their level of participation in the administration and influence on their husbands. (Rev: HBG 10/01; SLJ 6/01) [920]

3230 McLean, Jacqueline. *Women with Wings* (4–7). Illus. Series: Profiles. 2001, Oliver $19.95 (1-881508-70-6). 160pp. An absorbing account of the achievements of women pilots, including Bessie Coleman, Amelia Earhart, and Anne Morrow Lindbergh. (Rev: BL 5/15/01; HBG 10/01; SLJ 10/01) [629.13]

3231 Warren, Andrea. *We Rode the Orphan Trains* (4–8). Illus. 2001, Houghton $18.00 (0-618-11712-1). 144pp. Eight moving biographical accounts of men and women, now in their 80s and 90s, who traveled to the Midwest to find new homes and families. (Rev: BCCB 11/01; BL 11/1/01; HBG 3/02; SLJ 11/01) [362.73]

3232 Wheeler, Jill C. *America's Leaders* (4–7). Series: War on Terrorism. 2002, ABDO LB $16.95 (1-57765-661-X). 48pp. This book contains brief profiles of important American figures in the war against terrorism such as President Bush, Colin Powell, John Ashcroft, and Rudy Giuliani. (Rev: BL 5/15/02; HBG 10/02) [920]

African Americans

BETHUNE, MARY MCLEOD

3233 McKissack, Patricia, and Fredrick McKissack. *Mary McLeod Bethune: A Great Teacher*. Rev. ed. (2–4). Series: Great African Americans. 2001, Enslow LB $14.95 (0-7660-1680-3). 32pp. An updated biography of the former slave who dedicated her life to the education of African Americans, with new illustrations. (Rev: HBG 3/02; SLJ 5/02) [921]

BROWN, CLARA

3234 Lowery, Linda. *One More Valley, One More Hill: The Story of Aunt Clara Brown* (5–8). Illus. 2002, Random LB $17.99 (0-375-91092-1). 144pp. A biography of the freed slave and pioneer who found success in Colorado. (Rev: BL 2/15/03; HBG 3/03; SLJ 2/03) [978.8]

BUNCHE, RALPH J.

3235 McKissack, Patricia, and Fredrick McKissack. *Ralph J. Bunche: Peacemaker* (2–4). Series: Great African Americans. 2002, Enslow LB $14.95 (0-7660-1701-X). 32pp. The inspiring story of the African American diplomat who was active in UN affairs and won the Nobel Peace Prize in 1950. (Rev: BL 7/02; HBG 10/02) [921]

3236 McNair, Joseph D. *Ralph Bunche: 1904-1971* (4–6). Series: Journey to Freedom: The African American Library. 2001, Child's World LB $17.95 (1-56766-922-0). 40pp. An attractive, readable biography of this black politician and internationalist who was a winner of the Nobel Peace Prize. (Rev: BL 12/15/01; SLJ 1/02) [921]

DOUGLASS, FREDERICK

3237 Becker, Helaine. *Frederick Douglass* (4–7). Series: The Civil War. 2001, Gale LB $19.95 (1-56711-557-8). 104pp. Readers of this biography that covers Douglass's life and work as an abolitionist will be particularly interested in the account of his youth as a slave in Maryland and his escape to freedom. (Rev: HBG 3/02; SLJ 4/02) [921]

3238 Lutz, Norma Jean. *Frederick Douglass: Abolitionist and Author* (3–5). Illus. 2001, Chelsea $18.95 (0-7910-6003-9); paper $8.95 (0-7910-6141-8). This brief introduction to the life of the abolitionist includes material on his youth and education. (Rev: BL 5/1/01) [972.81]

3239 McKissack, Patricia, and Frank McKissack. *Frederick Douglass: Leader Against Slavery*. Rev. ed. (2–4). Illus. Series: Great African Americans. 2002, Enslow LB $14.95 (0-7660-1696-X). 32pp. An updated version of a previously released biography about the slave-turned-abolitionist, which includes archival photographs and Web site information. (Rev: BL 2/15/02; SLJ 5/02) [973.8]

JACKSON, MAHALIA

3240 Orgill, Roxane. *Mahalia: A Life in Gospel Music* (5–9). Illus. 2002, Candlewick $19.99 (0-7636-1011-9). 144pp. An impassioned biography about the life of gospel singer Mahalia Jackson set against the backdrop of social and political events of the times. (Rev: BL 2/15/02; HBG 10/02; SLJ 1/02) [782.25]

KING, CORETTA SCOTT

3241 Mattern, Joanne. *Coretta Scott King: Civil Rights Activist* (1–3). Illus. Series: Women Who Shaped History. 2003, Rosen LB $17.25 (0-8239-6504-X). 24pp. The life of Coretta Scott King, for new readers. (Rev: BL 2/15/03) [323]

KING, HORACE

3242 Gibbons, Faye. *Horace King: Bridges to Freedom* (5–8). Illus. 2002, Crane Hill paper $9.95 (1-57587-199-8). 112pp. The story of a slave who went on to become a builder and later a public servant in the post-Civil War South. (Rev: BL 2/15/03) [328.761]

KING, MARTIN LUTHER, JR.

3243 Adler, David A. *Dr. Martin Luther King, Jr.* (1–3). Illus. by Colin Bootman. Series: Holiday House Reader. 2001, Holiday $14.95 (0-8234-1572-4). 48pp. A brief account of King's life, achievements, and legacy that will also appeal to older children who are having difficulties reading. (Rev: BL 7/01; SLJ 6/01) [323]

3244 Farris, Christine King. *My Brother Martin* (K–3). Illus. by Chris Soentpiet. 2003, Simon & Schuster $17.95 (0-689-84387-9). 40pp. A fond biography of Dr. Martin Luther King, Jr., by his older sister. (Rev: BL 2/15/03; HB 3–4/03; SLJ 2/03) [323]

3245 January, Brendan. *Martin Luther King Jr.: Minister and Civil Rights Activist* (4–8). Series: Ferguson's Career Biographies. 2001, Ferguson LB $16.95 (0-89434-342-4). 127pp. This concise account focuses on King's career as a minister as well as his work as an advocate of civil rights and includes a section on training for the ministry. (Rev: SLJ 4/01) [921]

3246 McKissack, Patricia, and Fredrick McKissack. *Martin Luther King, Jr.: Man of Peace*. Rev. ed. (2–4). Series: Great African Americans. 2001, Enslow LB $14.95 (0-7660-1678-1). 32pp. A newly illustrated edition of this title that includes information on King's early life. (Rev: HBG 3/02; SLJ 5/02) [921]

3247 McLeese, Don. *Martin Luther King, Jr.* (2–5). Series: Equal Rights Leaders. 2002, Rourke LB $19.27 (1-58952-286-9). 24pp. Simple text and well-chosen illustrations tell the story of King's life, with good coverage of his youth and education. (Rev: SLJ 1/03) [323]

3248 Petit, Jane. *Martin Luther King Jr.: A Man with a Dream* (4–6). Series: Book Report Biographies. 2001, Watts LB $22.00 (0-531-11670-0); paper $6.95 (0-531-15553-6). 28pp. A concise, well-researched biography of the great religious and civil rights leader. (Rev: BL 8/1/01) [921]

3249 Rappaport, Doreen. *Martin's Big Words* (PS–4). Illus. by Bryan Collier. 2001, Hyperion LB $15.89 (0-7868-2591-X). 32pp. Clear, brief text and colorful collages celebrate the life and activism of Dr. Martin Luther King, Jr. (Rev: BL 10/1/01; HB 1–2/02*; HBG 3/02; SLJ 10/01) [323]

MALCOLM X

3250 Benson, Michael. *Malcolm X* (5–8). Series: Biography. 2001, Lerner LB $25.56 (0-8225-5025-3). An accessible text and many photographs are used to enliven this biography of the black civil rights leader who was assassinated in 1965. (Rev: BL 4/1/02; HBG 3/02; SLJ 3/02) [921]

3251 Crushshon, Theresa. *Malcolm X: 1925-1965* (4–6). Series: Journey to Freedom: The African American Library. 2001, Child's World LB $17.95 (1-56766-920-4). 40pp. On attractive, oversize volume that introduces the life, achievements, and importance of Malcolm X. (Rev: BL 12/15/01; HBG 3/02; SLJ 1/02) [921]

MALONE, ANNIE TURNBO

3252 Wilkerson, J. L. *Story of Pride, Power and Uplift: Annie T. Malone* (4–8). Illus. 2003, Acorn $9.95 (0-9664470-8-5). 96pp. Malone, a child of slaves, created beauty products for African American women at the turn of the 20th century and became a wealthy woman and philanthropist. (Rev: BL 3/1/03) [646.7]

MARSHALL, THURGOOD

3253 Williams, Carla. *Thurgood Marshall: 1908–1993* (4.6). Series: Journey to Freedom: The African American Library. 2001, Child's World LB $17.95 (1-56766-924-7). 40pp. The story of the noted liberal black Supreme Court justice who was a civil rights advocate particularly in the fight to end school segregation. (Rev: BL 12/15/01; HBG 3/02; SLJ 1/02) [921]

PARKS, ROSA

3254 Klingel, Cynthia, and Robert B. Noyed. *Rosa Parks* (K–2). Series: Wonder Books. 2001, Child's World LB $21.36 (1-56766-951-4). 24pp. A basic introduction for beginning readers that explains complex concepts in simple vocabulary. (Rev: HBG 3/02; SLJ 2/02) [921]

3255 McLeese, Don. *Rosa Parks* (2–5). Series: Equal Rights Leaders. 2002, Rourke LB $19.27 (1-58952-287-7). 24pp. Simple text and well-chosen illustrations tell the story of Parks's life, with good coverage of her youth and education. (Rev: SLJ 1/03) [323]

RICE, CONDOLEEZA

3256 Wade, Mary Dodson. *Condoleezza Rice: Being the Best* (4–7). Illus. 2003, Millbrook LB $23.90 (0-7613-2619-7). 48pp. An interesting profile with a focus on Rice's talented youth and southern upbringing. (Rev: BL 3/1/03) [355]

TERRELL, MARY CHURCH

3257 McKissack, Patricia, and Frank McKissack. *Mary Church Terrell: Leader for Equality*. Rev. ed. (2–4). Illus. Series: Great African Americans. 2002, Enslow LB $14.95 (0-7660-1697-8). 32pp. An updated version of a previously released biography about the 19th-century activist, including archival photographs and Web site information. (Rev: BL 2/15/02; HBG 10/02; SLJ 5/02) [323]

TRUTH, SOJOURNER

3258 Bernard, Catherine. *Sojourner Truth: Abolitionist and Women's Rights Activist* (5–8). Series: Historical American Biographies. 2001, Enslow LB $20.95 (0-7660-1257-3). 112pp. The life story of the freed slave who traveled throughout the North preaching emancipation and women's rights before the Civil War. (Rev: BL 4/15/01; HBG 10/01) [921]

3259 Leebrick, Kristal. *Sojourner Truth* (4–6). Illus. Series: Let Freedom Ring. 2002, Capstone LB $16.95 (0-7368-1090-0). 48pp. An accessible account of Truth's life and influence on others, with sidebar features, maps, reproductions, quotations from primary sources, and a timeline. (Rev: HBG 3/03; SLJ 8/02) [921]

3260 McKissack, Patricia, and Fredrick McKissack. *Sojourner Truth: A Voice for Freedom* (2–4). Series: Great African Americans. 2002, Enslow LB $14.95 (0-7660-1693-5). 32pp. A simple biography of the black American evangelist and reformer who gained fame as a preacher and fighter for women's suffrage. (Rev: BL 7/02) [921]

3261 Mattern, Joanne. *Sojourner Truth: Early Abolitionist* (1–3). Illus. Series: Women Who Shaped History. 2003, Rosen LB $17.25 (0-8239-6502-3). 24pp. The life of Sojourner Truth, for new readers. (Rev: BL 2/15/03) [305.5]

3262 Roop, Peter, and Connie Roop. *Sojourner Truth* (3–5). Illus. Series: In Their Own Words. 2003, Scholastic paper $4.50 (0-439-26323-9). 128pp. A simply written account of the former slave who became an abolitionist, drawing from Truth's own words. (Rev: BL 2/15/03) [305.5]

TUBMAN, HARRIET

3263 Gayle, Sharon. *Harriet Tubman and the Freedom Train* (1–3). Illus. by Felicia Marshall. Series: Ready-to-Read Stories of Famous Americans. 2003, Simon & Schuster LB $11.89 (0-689-85481-1); paper $3.99 (0-689-85480-3). 32pp. A fictionalized account of the former slave's efforts to free others. (Rev: BL 2/15/03; SLJ 3/03) [973.7]

3264 Nielsen, Nancy L. *Harriet Tubman* (4–6). Illus. Series: Let Freedom Ring. 2002, Capstone LB $16.95 (0-7368-1087-0). 48pp. An accessible account of Tubman's life and influence on others, with sidebar features, maps, reproductions, quotations from primary sources, and a timeline. (Rev: HBG 3/03; SLJ 8/02) [921]

3265 Schraff, Anne. *Harriet Tubman: Moses of the Underground Railroad* (4–8). Series: African-American Biographies. 2001, Enslow LB $20.95 (0-7660-1548-3). 128pp. This is an absorbing account of the life of the Underground Railroad leader that covers her work as a nurse, a scout, and a spy. (Rev: HBG 3/02; SLJ 10/01) [921]

3266 Sullivan, George. *Harriet Tubman* (3–5). Series: In Their Own Words. 2002, Scholastic $12.95 (0-439-32667-2); paper $4.50 (0-439-16584-9). 128pp. Using original sources including letters and autobiographical writings, the life of Harriet Tubman and her role in the Underground Railroad are re-created. (Rev: BL 8/02; HBG 10/02; SLJ 11/02) [921]

WASHINGTON, BOOKER T.

3267 McKissack, Patricia, and Fredrick McKissack. *Booker T. Washington: Leader and Educator* (2–4). Illus. Series: Great African Americans. 2001, Enslow LB $14.95 (0-7660-1679-X). 32pp. Updated artwork gives this previously published biography of former slave and educator Booker T. Washington a new look. (Rev: BL 1/1–15/02; HBG 3/02) [370]

WOODSON, CARTER G.

3268 McKissack, Patricia, and Fredrick McKissack. *Carter G. Woodson: The Father of Black History* (2–4). Series: Great African Americans. 2002, Enslow LB $14.95 (0-7660-1698-6). 32pp. A beginning chapter book that covers the life of the black historian who founded the Association for the Study of Negro Life and History in 1915 and began its *Journal of Negro History*. (Rev: BL 7/02) [921]

Hispanic Americans

CHAVEZ, CESAR

3269 Griswold del Castillo, Richard. *César Chávez: The Struggle for Justice / La Lucha por la Justicia* (2–4). Illus. by Anthony Accardo. 2002, Arte Publico $14.95 (1-55885-324-3). 32pp. Bilingual text and full-page paintings bring Mexican American labor leader César Chávez to life. (Rev: BL 12/15/02) [331.88]

3270 McLeese, Don. *Cesar E. Chavez* (2–5). 2002, Rourke LB $19.27 (1-58952-285-0). 24pp. Simple text and well-chosen illustrations tell the story of Chavez's life, with good coverage of his youth, education, and early years working in the fields. (Rev: SLJ 1/03) [331.88]

DE PORTOLA, GASPAR

3271 Whiting, Jim. *Gaspar de Portola* (5–7). Series: Latinos in American History. 2002, Mitchell Lane LB $19.95 (1-58415-148-X). 48pp. The story of the Latino governor of "Las Californias" from 1768 to 1770 who was responsible for expelling Jesuits from the area. (Rev: BL 2/15/03) [921]

DE ZAVALA, LORENZO

3272 Tracy, Kathleen. *Lorenzo de Zavala* (5–7). Series: Latinos in American History. 2002, Mitchell Lane LB $19.95 (1-58415-154-4). 48pp. The biography of the 19th-century Mexican who became vice president of the Republic of Texas and was one of the signers of its constitution. (Rev: BL 2/15/03) [921]

HUERTA, DOLORES

3273 Murcia, Rebecca Thatcher. *Dolores Huerta* (5–7). Series: Latinos in American History. 2002, Mitchell Lane LB $19.95 (1-58415-155-2). 48pp. The story of the gallant woman who worked along with Cesar Chavez to protect the rights of farm workers. (Rev: BL 2/15/03) [921]

IDAR, JOVITA

3274 Gibson, Karen Bush. *Jovita Idar* (5–7). Series: Latinos in American History. 2002, Mitchell Lane LB $19.95 (1-58415-151-X). 48pp. The inspiring story of the Latin American woman who started San Antonio's first free kindergarten and who founded the League of Mexican American women in 1911 to educate poor children. (Rev: BL 2/15/03) [921]

VALLEJO, MARIANO GUADALUPE

3275 Tracy, Kathleen. *Mariano Guadalupe Vallejo* (5–7). Series: Latinos in American History. 2002, Mitchell Lane LB $19.95 (1-58415-152-8). 48pp. The story of the 19th-century military man who supported the U.S. annexation of California and later served in the state's first Senate. (Rev: BL 2/15/03) [921]

Historical Figures and Important Contemporary Americans

BOONE, DANIEL

3276 Armentrout, David, and Patricia Armentrout. *Daniel Boone* (2–4). Series: Discover Someone Who Made a Difference. 2001, Rourke LB $18.60 (1-58952-052-1). As well as a life of this famous outdoorsman, this biography explains how he has influenced our lives today. (Rev: BCCB 3/02; BL 1/1–15/02; SLJ 3/02) [921]

ALLEN, ETHAN

3277 Aronson, Virginia. *Ethan Allen: Revolutionary Hero* (4–6). 2000, Chelsea LB $18.95 (0-7910-5974-X); paper $8.95 (0-7910-6132-9). 80pp. This introduction to the life of Ethan Allen presents both his triumphs and his failings. (Rev: SLJ 7/01) [973.3]

3278 Raabe, Emily. *Ethan Allen: The Green Mountain Boys and Vermont's Path to Statehood* (4–7). Series: Library of American Lives and Times. 2001, Rosen LB $23.95 (0-8239-5722-5). 112pp. Extraordinary illustrations and fine text tell the story of the controversial founder of Vermont who led the Green Mountain Boys in the capture of Fort Ticonderoga and Crown Point. (Rev: BL 10/15/01) [921]

ARNOLD, BENEDICT

3279 Gaines, Ann Graham. *Benedict Arnold: Patriot or Traitor?* (5–8). Series: Historical American Biographies. 2001, Enslow LB $20.95 (0-7660-1393-6). 112pp. Many facets of the character of this controversial American are examined in this well-illustrated volume. (Rev: BL 4/15/01; HBG 10/01; SLJ 6/01) [921]

3280 Gregson, Susan R. *Benedict Arnold* (5–6). Series: Let Freedom Ring. 2001, Capstone LB $16.95 (0-7368-1032-3). 48pp. An introduction to Arnold's life and contributions, with discussion of the reasons why he became a traitor. (Rev: HBG 3/02; SLJ 4/02) [921]

BARNUM, P. T.

3281 Warrick, Karen Clemens. *P. T. Barnum: Genius of the Three-Ring Circus* (5–8). Series: Historical American Biographies. 2001, Enslow LB $20.95 (0-7660-1447-9). 112pp. The story of the showman and creator of "The Greatest Show on Earth" who presented such attractions as General Tom Thumb and Jenny Lind. (Rev: BL 4/15/01; HBG 10/01; SLJ 7/01) [921]

BEZOS, JEFF

3282 Garty, Judy. *Jeff Bezos* (5–8). Illus. Series: Internet Biographies. 2003, Enslow LB $18.95 (0-7660-1972-1). 48pp. A reader-friendly biography of the creator of Amazon.com, with plenty of information on his youth. (Rev: BL 3/15/03) [380.1]

BRADLEY, BILL

3283 Buckley, James, Jr. *Bill Bradley* (5–8). Illus. Series: Basketball Hall of Famers. 2002, Rosen LB $29.25 (0-8239-3479-9). 112pp. An easy-to-read, detailed biography of the former athlete, with plenty of photographs. (Rev: BL 9/1/02) [796.323]

BRADY, MATHEW

3284 Pflueger, Lynda. *Mathew Brady* (5–8). Series: Historical American Biographies. 2001, Enslow LB $20.95 (0-7660-1444-4). A biography of the photographer known primarily for his coverage of the Civil War, illustrated with many of his works. (Rev: BL 1/1–15/02; HBG 10/01; SLJ 9/01) [921]

BROWN, JOHN

3285 Becker, Helaine. *John Brown* (4–7). Series: The Civil War. 2001, Gale LB $19.95 (1-56711-558-6). 104pp. Brown's life is detailed from childhood through his adult achievements, and is carefully placed in the context of the time and his family background. (Rev: HBG 3/02; SLJ 4/02) [921]

3286 Brackett, Virginia. *John Brown: Abolitionist* (3–5). Series: Famous Figures of the Civil War Era. 2001, Chelsea LB $20.85 (0-7910-6408-5). Told with many color illustrations and a vivid text, this is the story of the obsessive abolitionist who was hanged for treason in 1859. (Rev: BL 4/1/02; HBG 10/02; SLJ 5/02) [921]

BURR, AARON

3287 Ingram, W. Scott. *Aaron Burr and the Young Nation* (5–8). Series: Major World Leaders. 2002, Chelsea LB $27.44 (1-56711-250-1). 112pp. The story of the controversial political leader who killed Alexander Hamilton in a duel and later was tried and found guilty of treason. (Rev: BL 1/1–15/03; SLJ 10/02) [921]

CHAPMAN, JOHN

3288 Moses, Will. *Johnny Appleseed: The Story of a Legend* (4–6). Illus. 2001, Putnam $16.99 (0-399-23153-6). 32pp. This account of the life of Johnny Appleseed is enhanced by the author's folk-art paintings. (Rev: BL 9/1/01; HBG 3/02; SLJ 9/01) [634]

3289 Warrick, Karen Clemens. *John Chapman: The Legendary Johnny Appleseed* (5–8). Series: Historical American Biographies. 2001, Enslow LB $20.95 (0-7660-1443-6). 112pp. An engrossing, nicely illustrated portrait of the man who wandered the Midwest promoting apple cultivation. (Rev: BL 4/15/01; HBG 10/01; SLJ 4/01) [921]

CODY, BUFFALO BILL

3290 Shields, Charles J. *Buffalo Bill Cody* (3–6). Series: Famous Figures of the American Frontier. 2001, Chelsea LB $19.75 (0-7910-6497-2); paper $8.95 (0-7910-6498-0). 64pp. An appealing account of Cody's life with black-and-white and full-color illustrations and handy fact boxes. (Rev: SLJ 3/02) [921]

COFFIN, LEVI

3291 Swain, Gwenyth. *President of the Underground Railroad: A Story About Levi Coffin* (3–6). Illus. by Ralph L. Ramstad. Series: Creative Minds Biographies. 2001, Carolrhoda LB $21.27 (1-57505-551-1); paper $5.95 (1-57505-552-X). 64pp. This is a readable account of the life of Levi Coffin, a Quaker from North Carolina who devoted time and money to helping slaves escape to freedom. (Rev: HBG 10/01; SLJ 7/01) [973.7]

DAVIS, JEFFERSON

3292 Frazier, Joey. *Jefferson Davis: Confederate President* (3–5). Illus. 2001, Chelsea $18.95 (0-7910-6006-3); paper $8.95 (0-7910-6144-2). 80pp. A brief biography that covers Davis's life, with information on his education, his rise to become

president of the Confederacy, and the problems of his administration. (Rev: BL 5/1/01; SLJ 9/01) [973.7]

3293 Ingram, W. Scott. *Jefferson Davis* (5–8). Series: Triangle Histories of the Civil War. 2002, Gale LB $23.94 (1-56711-565-9). 104pp. A useful account of Davis's life and career with a sidebar feature on the servant who perhaps was a spy. (Rev: SLJ 1/03) [921]

DIX, DOROTHEA

3294 Herstek, Amy Paulson. *Dorothea Dix* (5–8). Series: Historical American Biographies. 2001, Enslow LB $20.95 (0-7660-1258-1). The life of this militant reformer who fought for more humane treatment of the insane. (Rev: BL 1/1–15/02; HBG 3/02; SLJ 1/02) [921]

DOUGLAS, STEPHEN

3295 Bonner, Mike. *Stephen Douglas: Champion of the Union* (3–5). Series: Famous Figures of the Civil War Era. 2001, Chelsea LB $20.85 (0-7910-6402-6). The story of the American politician named the "Little Giant" who engaged in a famous series of debates with Lincoln but later became his staunch supporter. (Rev: BL 4/1/02; HBG 10/02; SLJ 5/02) [921]

EARP, WYATT

3296 Staeger, Rob. *Wyatt Earp* (3–6). Series: Famous Figures of the American Frontier. 2001, Chelsea LB $19.75 (0-7910-6485-9); paper $8.95 (0-7910-6486-7). 64pp. An appealing biography of the famous gunfighter, with black-and-white and full-color illustrations and handy fact boxes. (Rev: HBG 10/02; SLJ 3/02) [921]

EDWARDS, JONATHAN

3297 Lutz, Norma Jean. *Jonathan Edwards: Colonial Religious Leader* (5–7). Series: Colonial Leaders. 2001, Chelsea LB $16.95 (0-7910-5961-8); paper $8.95 (0-7910-6118-3). 80pp. The life of Edwards, a leader in the Great Awakening spiritual movement and preacher among Native American tribes, is presented here with discussion of his contributions and his failings. (Rev: SLJ 5/01) [921]

FARRAGUT, DAVID

3298 Adelson, Bruce. *David Farragut: Union Admiral* (3–5). Series: Famous Figures of the Civil War Era. 2001, Chelsea LB $20.85 (0-7910-6416-6). The story of the American admiral who served in the War of 1812 and the Mexican War, and gained fame as a blockade runner during the Civil War. (Rev: BL 4/1/02) [921]

3299 Roop, Peter, and Connie Roop. *Take Command, Captain Farragut!* (3–5). Illus. by Michael McCurdy. 2002, Simon & Schuster $16.00 (0-689-83022-X). 48pp. Part fact and part fiction, this is the story of the early life of the great naval hero as revealed in a series of fictitious letters written by him at age 13. (Rev: BCCB 4/02; BL 4/15/02; HBG 10/02; SLJ 4/02) [921]

FRANKLIN, BENJAMIN

3300 Adler, David A. *B. Franklin, Printer* (4–8). Illus. 2001, Holiday $19.95 (0-8234-1675-5). 128pp. Quotations, anecdotes, and wonderful illustrations round out this excellent volume about the life and accomplishments of Benjamin Franklin. (Rev: BCCB 2/02; BL 1/1–15/02; HBG 10/02; SLJ 2/02*) [973.3]

3301 Fradin, Dennis Brindell. *Who Was Ben Franklin?* (3–5). Illus. by John O'Brien. 2002, Putnam paper $4.99 (0-448-42495-9). 112pp. This book traces the fascinating, eclectic life and varied careers of Benjamin Franklin. (Rev: BL 3/1/02; HBG 10/02; SLJ 3/02) [973.3]

3302 Krensky, Stephen. *Ben Franklin and His First Kite* (1–3). Illus. by Bert Dodson. Series: Childhood of Famous Americans. 2002, Simon & Schuster LB $11.89 (0-689-84985-0); paper $3.99 (0-689-84984-2). 31pp. The story of young Franklin's first experiment with a kite is told for beginning readers. (Rev: HBG 3/03; SLJ 10/02) [921]

3303 Schanzer, Rosalyn. *How Ben Franklin Stole the Lightning* (2–4). Illus. by author. 2003, HarperCollins LB $17.89 (0-688-16994-5). A lively account of Franklin's role as an inventor, with a focus on his flying a kite during a rainstorm. (Rev: BCCB 3/03; SLJ 1/03) [530]

3304 Sherrow, Victoria. *Benjamin Franklin* (3–4). Series: History Maker Bios. 2002, Lerner LB $23.93 (0-8225-0198-8). 48pp. The life of this multitalented genius of the colonial period is presented in a simple text with many illustrations. (Rev: BL 6/1–15/02; HBG 3/03) [921]

3305 Streissguth, Tom. *Benjamin Franklin* (5–8). Series: Biography. 2001, Lerner LB $25.26 (0-8225-4997-2). A readable biography of the many-faceted genius of the newly formed United States. (Rev: BL 4/1/02; HBG 10/02) [921]

GIULIANI, RUDOLPH W.

3306 Freemont, Eleanor. *Rudolph W. Giuliani* (4–8). 2002, Simon & Schuster paper $4.99 (0-689-85423-4). 96pp. The story of the man *Time* magazine called "the mayor of the world" including material on his personal life and his rise to prominence with the attacks on September 11, 2001. (Rev: BL 9/1/02; SLJ 9/02) [974.7]

HALE, NATHAN

3307 Krizner, L. J., and Lisa Sita. *Nathan Hale: Patriot and Martyr of the American Revolution* (4–7). Series: Library of American Lives and Times. 2001, Rosen LB $23.95 (0-8239-5724-1). 112pp. Nathan Hale, executed by the British in 1776, represented the life-and-death issues fought for in the Revolution and became a symbol of courage and patriotism. (Rev: BL 10/15/01) [921]

3308 Zemlicka, Shannon. *Nathan Hale: Patriot Spy* (2–4). Illus. by Craig Orback. Series: On My Own Biography. 2002, Carolrhoda LB $22.60 (0-87614-597-7); paper $6.95 (0-87614-905-0). 48pp. For beginning readers, this is an absorbing life of the Revolutionary War hero who was executed for spying. (Rev: HBG 3/03; SLJ 12/02) [973.3]

HAMILTON, ALEXANDER

3309 Kallen, Stuart A. *Alexander Hamilton* (4–6). Series: Founding Fathers. 2001, ABDO LB $16.95 (1-57765-006-9). 64pp. A lively biography of the first secretary of the U.S. Treasury that covers his underprivileged early life and details his importance in the creation of the United States. (Rev: HBG 3/02; SLJ 1/02) [921]

HENRY, PATRICK

3310 Kukla, Amy, and Jon Kukla. *Patrick Henry: Voice of the Revolution* (4–7). Illus. Series: Library of American Lives and Times. 2001, Rosen LB $23.95 (0-8239-5725-X). 112pp. Detailed text, a variety of illustrations, and a timeline give readers a good understanding of Henry's importance. (Rev: BL 10/15/01) [973.3]

HOOVER, J. EDGAR

3311 Streissguth, Tom. *J. Edgar Hoover: Powerful FBI Director* (5–8). Series: Historical American Biographies. 2002, Enslow LB $20.95 (0-7660-1623-4). 128pp. Streissguth looks at Hoover's life from youth, his personality, and his work as head of the FBI, and explores the areas in which his influence was felt, including civil rights and politics. (Rev: HBG 10/02; SLJ 8/02)

JACKSON, STONEWALL

3312 Robertson, James I. *Standing like a Stone Wall: The Life of General Thomas J. Jackson* (5–8). Illus. 2001, Simon & Schuster $22.00 (0-689-82419-X). 192pp. Readers will gain a good understanding of Jackson's early life and career before the Civil War as well as his leadership during the war years. (Rev: BL 5/1/01; HBG 10/01; SLJ 6/01) [973.7]

JAY, JOHN

3313 Kallen, Stuart A. *John Jay* (4–6). Series: Founding Fathers. 2001, ABDO LB $16.95 (1-57765-013-1). 64pp. A lively biography of the first chief justice of the Supreme Court that covers his life and details his importance in the creation of the United States. (Rev: SLJ 1/02) [921]

JOBS, STEVE

3314 Wilson, Suzan. *Steve Jobs: Wizard of Apple Computer* (5–8). Series: People to Know. 2001, Enslow LB $20.95 (0-7660-1536-X). 128pp. An engrossing biography that will attract computer-lovers, in which Jobs's early passion for electronics is shown as paving the way for his success — and failures — at Apple and other companies. (Rev: HBG 3/02; SLJ 3/02) [921]

JOHNSTON, JOSEPH E.

3315 Ditchfield, Christin. *Joseph E. Johnston: Confederate General* (3–5). Series: Famous Figures of the Civil War Era. 2001, Chelsea LB $20.85 (0-7910-6412-3). The story of the Confederate general who commanded forces during the Civil War and later served a term in the U.S. House of Representatives. (Rev: BL 4/1/02) [921]

JONES, JOHN PAUL

3316 Bradford, James C. *John Paul Jones and the American Navy* (4–7). Series: Library of American Lives and Times. 2001, Rosen LB $23.95 (0-8239-5726-8). 112pp. This attractively designed volume combines the life story of the naval hero of the American Revolution with a history of the birth and growth of the American navy. (Rev: BL 10/15/01) [921]

3317 Tibbitts, Alison Davis. *John Paul Jones: Father of the American Navy* (5–8). Series: Historical American Biographies. 2002, Enslow LB $20.95 (0-7660-1448-7). The life of the American naval officer noted for his role in the Revolution and for the statement, "I have not yet begun to fight." (Rev: BL 4/1/02; HBG 10/02; SLJ 5/02) [921]

LIEBERMAN, JOSEPH

3318 Feinberg, Barbara Silberdick. *Joseph Lieberman: Keeping the Faith* (4–6). Illus. 2001, Millbrook LB $22.90 (0-7613-2303-1). 48pp. This profile of the first Jewish candidate for the vice presidency of the United States includes photographs, a timeline, and a bibliography. (Rev: BL 9/15/01; HBG 3/02) [973.929]

MACARTHUR, DOUGLAS

3319 Gaines, Ann Graham. *Douglas MacArthur: Brilliant General, Controversial Leader* (5–8). Series: Historical American Biographies. 2001, Enslow LB $20.95 (0-7660-1445-2). 112pp. Using many black-and-white photographs as illustrations, this account gives a well-rounded, unbiased picture of this controversial general. (Rev: BL 4/15/01; HBG 10/01; SLJ 6/01) [921]

MCCLELLAN, GEORGE

3320 Kelley, Brent. *George McClellan: Union General* (3–5). Series: Famous Figures of the Civil War Era. 2001, Chelsea LB $20.85 (0-7910-6404-2). The life of this important Union army leader, who was removed from his command by Lincoln, is re-created in pictures and text. (Rev: BL 4/1/02; SLJ 5/02) [921]

MARION, FRANCIS

3321 Towles, Louis P. *Francis Marion: The Swamp Fox of the American Revolution* (4–7). Series: Library of American Lives and Times. 2001, Rosen LB $23.95 (0-8239-5728-4). The life of the Revolutionary War hero known as the Swamp Fox because of his stealthy retreats into the swamp lands. (Rev: BL 1/1–15/02) [921]

MEADE, GEORGE GORDON

3322 Adelson, Bruce. *George Gordon Meade: Union General* (3–5). Series: Famous Figures of the Civil War Era. 2001, Chelsea LB $20.85 (0-7910-6410-7). The story of the Civil War general who fought in battles including Bull Run, Antietam, Chancellorsville, and Gettysburg. (Rev: BL 4/1/02; HBG 10/02) [921]

O'CONNOR, SANDRA DAY

3323 Williams, Jean Kinney. *Sandra Day O'Connor: Lawyer and Supreme Court Justice* (4–6). Series: Ferguson's Career Biographies. 2001, Ferguson LB $16.95 (0-89434-355-6). 127pp. The story of O'Connor's life from childhood plus information on the confirmation process for Supreme Court appointees and on how to become a lawyer or judge. (Rev: SLJ 5/01) [921]

OGLETHORPE, JAMES

3324 Lommel, Cookie. *James Oglethorpe: Humanitarian and Soldier* (4–6). Series: Colonial Leaders. 2001, Chelsea LB $16.95 (0-7910-5963-4); paper $8.95 (0-7910-6120-5). 80pp. Oglethorpe, the English founder and first governor of the colony of Georgia, was active in a number of areas including prison reform, the guarantee of religious freedom, and relations with Native Americans. (Rev: HBG 10/01; SLJ 7/01) [975.8]

OSBORN, SHANE

3325 Osborn, Shane, and Malcolm McConnell. *Born to Fly: The Heroic Story of Downed U.S. Navy Pilot Lt. Shane Osborn* (5–8). Adapted by Michael French. 2001, Delacorte LB $17.99 (0-385-90045-7). 183pp. This adaptation of an adult book tells the story of Osborn's training as a pilot and the collision in 2001 that led to tensions between the United States and China, with lots of interesting career information. (Rev: HBG 3/02; SLJ 1/02) [921]

PAINE, THOMAS

3326 McCarthy, Pat. *Thomas Paine: Revolutionary Poet and Writer* (5–8). Series: Historical American Biographies. 2001, Enslow LB $20.95 (0-7660-1446-0). 112pp. A balanced, well-researched biography of the American political theorist and writer who created controversy throughout his lifetime. (Rev: BL 4/15/01; HBG 10/01) [921]

3327 McCartin, Brian. *Thomas Paine: Common Sense and Revolutionary Pamphleteering* (4–7).

Series: Library of American Lives and Times. 2001, Rosen LB $23.95 (0-8239-5729-2). 112pp. The story of the British-born colonialist who heard the cries for liberty around him and whose writings set the stage for the Declaration of Independence. (Rev: BL 10/15/01) [921]

REVERE, PAUL

3328 Klingel, Cynthia, and Robert B. Noyed. *Paul Revere's Ride* (1–3). Series: Wonder Books. 2001, Child's World LB $21.36 (1-56766-960-3). 32pp. Paul Revere's life and importance are presented here with color illustrations and a map. (Rev: HBG 3/02; SLJ 11/01) [921]

3329 Randolph, Ryan P. *Paul Revere and the Minutemen of the American Revolution* (4–7). Series: Library of American Lives and Times. 2001, Rosen LB $23.95 (0-8239-5727-6). 112pp. Fairly large type and many illustrations bring to life Paul Revere, a businessman and family man but also a soldier and spy, and the group of patriots known as the Minutemen. (Rev: BL 10/15/01) [921]

3330 Sutcliffe, Jane. *Paul Revere* (3–4). Series: History Maker Bios. 2002, Lerner LB $23.93 (0-8225-0195-3). 48pp. This basic biography describes the life of this patriot who fought in the Revolutionary War and also worked as a silversmith, dentist, coppersmith, and printer. (Rev: BL 6/1–15/02; HBG 3/03) [921]

ROGERS, ROBERT

3331 Quasha, Jennifer. *Robert Rogers: Rogers' Rangers and the French and Indian War* (4–7). Series: Library of American Lives and Times. 2001, Rosen LB $23.95 (0-8239-5731-4). 112pp. A beautifully illustrated biography of Major Robert Rogers, who recruited companies of soldiers known as Rogers' Rangers to fight for the British in the French and Indian War. (Rev: BL 10/15/01) [921]

ROSS, BETSY

3332 Randolph, Ryan P. *Betsy Ross: The American Flag and Life in a Young America* (4–7). Series: Library of American Lives and Times. 2001, Rosen LB $23.95 (0-8239-5730-6). This contemporary of George Washington was supposedly the seamstress of the American flag. (Rev: BL 1/1–15/02) [921]

SEWARD, WILLIAM HENRY

3333 Burgan, Michael. *William Henry Seward: Senator and Statesman* (3–5). Series: Famous Figures of the Civil War Era. 2001, Chelsea LB $20.85 (0-7910-6418-2). A clear and concise biography of the man who was secretary of state during the Civil War and who later negotiated the purchase of Alaska from Russia. (Rev: BL 4/1/02; HBG 10/02) [921]

SHERIDAN, PHILIP

3334 Balcavage, Dynise. *Philip Sheridan: Union General* (3–5). Series: Famous Figures of the Civil

War Era. 2001, Chelsea LB $20.85 (0-7910-6406-9). About 20 full-color illustrations are used with a simple text to tell the story of the Civil War army commander who forced Lee's surrender at Appomattox. (Rev: BL 4/1/02) [921]

SHERMAN, WILLIAM T.

3335 King, David C. *William T. Sherman* (5–8). Series: Triangle Histories of the Civil War. 2002, Gale LB $23.94 (1-56711-563-2). 104pp. Sherman's march to the sea and relationship with Joseph Johnston, the confederate general, are among the topics covered in this solid introduction. (Rev: SLJ 1/03) [921]

STANTON, EDWIN

3336 Allison, Amy. *Edwin Stanton: Union War Secretary* (3–5). Series: Famous Figures of the Civil War Era. 2001, Chelsea LB $20.85 (0-7910-6420-4). The fascinating story of the lawyer and public official who was secretary of war during the Civil War and whose feud with President Johnson was legendary. (Rev: BL 4/1/02) [921]

STUART, JEB

3337 Greene, Meg. *James Ewell Brown Stuart: Confederate General* (3–5). Series: Famous Figures of the Civil War Era. 2001, Chelsea LB $20.85 (0-7910-6414-X). Known as Jeb Stuart, this distinguished Confederate army leader was killed in 1864 at Spotsylvania Courthouse. (Rev: BL 4/1/02; HBG 10/02) [921]

STUYVESANT, PETER

3338 Krizner, L. J., and Lisa Sita. *Peter Stuyvesant: New Amsterdam, and the Origins of New York* (4–7). Series: Library of American Lives and Times. 2001, Rosen LB $23.95 (0-8239-5732-2). 112pp. The story of New Amsterdam's best-known leader and how the Dutch presence in America influenced our culture for years to come. (Rev: BL 10/15/01; SLJ 7/01*) [921]

TWEED, WILLIAM "BOSS"

3339 Johnson, Suzan. *Boss Tweed and Tammany Hall* (5–8). Series: Major World Leaders. 2002, Chelsea LB $27.44 (1-56711-224-4). 112pp. The amazing life of the corrupt New York politician who defrauded the city of more than $30 million and whose life ended in prison. (Rev: BL 1/1–15/03) [921]

VENTURA, JESSE

3340 Cohen, Daniel. *Jesse Ventura: The Body, the Mouth, the Mind* (5–8). 2001, Twenty-First Century LB $25.40 (0-7613-1905-0). 112pp. A comprehensive profile of Ventura's private life and his stints as Navy Seal, talk-show host, actor, wrestler, and politician. (Rev: BL 10/1/01; HBG 3/02; SLJ 12/01)

187

3341 Uschan, Michael V. *Jesse Ventura* (5–8). Series: People in the News. 2001, Lucent LB $27.45 (1-56006-777-2). From a career in wrestling to a state governorship, this is the story of the amazing Jesse Ventura. (Rev: BL 4/1/02) [921]

WEBSTER, DANIEL

3342 Harvey, Bonnie Carman. *Daniel Webster* (5–8). Series: Historical American Biographies. 2001, Enslow LB $20.95 (0-7660-1392-8). An engrossing biography of the American statesman, lawyer, and orator who fought to save the Union. (Rev: BL 1/1–15/02; HBG 3/02; SLJ 12/01) [921]

Native Americans

COLLECTIVE

3343 Rappaport, Doreen. *We Are the Many: A Picture Book of American Indians* (K–3). Illus. by Cornelius Van Wright and Ying-Hwa Hu. 2002, HarperCollins LB $17.89 (0-06-001139-4). 32pp. A collection of 13 brief biographies of Native Americans from different tribes, including Tisquantum (Squanto), Jim Thorpe, and Maria Tallchief. (Rev: BL 10/15/02; HBG 3/03; SLJ 9/02) [970.004]

CRAZY HORSE, CHIEF

3344 Birchfield, D. L. *Crazy Horse* (3–6). Series: Raintree Biographies. 2003, Raintree Steck-Vaughn LB $25.69 (0-7398-5673-1). 32pp. A simple biography of the Sioux chief's life and achievements, with sidebar features containing primary and background material. (Rev: HBG 3/03; SLJ 3/03) [978]

3345 Brennan, Kristine. *Crazy Horse* (4–7). Series: Famous Figures of the American Frontier. 2001, Chelsea LB $19.75 (0-7910-6493-X); paper $8.95 (0-7910-6494-8). 64pp. Report writers will find this a useful source of information on this Native American leader's adult life and achievements in battle. (Rev: HBG 10/02; SLJ 4/02) [921]

GERONIMO

3346 Thompson, Bill, and Dorcas Thompson. *Geronimo* (4–7). Series: Famous Figures of the American Frontier. 2001, Chelsea LB $19.75 (0-7910-6491-3); paper $8.95 (0-7910-6492-1). 64pp. A balanced biography of the Apache leader that report writers will find a useful resource. (Rev: HBG 10/02; SLJ 4/02) [921]

JOSEPH, CHIEF

3347 Klingel, Cynthia, and Robert B. Noyed. *Chief Joseph: Chief of the Nez Perce* (3–6). Illus. Series: Our People. 2002, Child's World LB $27.07 (1-56766-165-3). 32pp. This is an attractive, brief introduction to the leader of the Nez Perce Indians. (Rev: BL 1/1–15/03; SLJ 2/03) [979.004]

LADUKE, WINONA

3348 Silverstone, Michael. *Winona LaDuke: Restoring Land and Culture in Native America* (5–8). Series: Women Changing the World. 2001, Feminist Pr. $19.95 (1-55861-260-2). 112pp. A candidate for the vice presidency under Ralph Nader in 2000, this professional author and activist lives on a land reservation in Minnesota where she is dedicated to restoring the land and the culture. (Rev: BL 12/15/01; HBG 10/02) [921]

POCAHONTAS

3349 Raatma, Lucia. *Pocahontas* (1–5). 2001, Compass Point LB $19.93 (0-7565-0115-6). 32pp. An accessible and attractive book that is careful to distinguish facts from legends. (Rev: SLJ 1/02) [921]

3350 Sullivan, George. *Pocahontas* (3–5). Series: In Their Own Words. 2002, Scholastic $12.95 (0-439-32668-0); paper $4.50 (0-439-16585-7). 128pp. After explaining the difference between primary and secondary sources, the author re-creates the life of Pocahontas by quoting from original documents. (Rev: BL 8/02; HBG 10/02; SLJ 11/02) [921]

3351 Zemlicka, Shannon. *Pocahontas* (2–3). Illus. by Jeni Reeves. Series: On My Own Biography. 2002, Carolrhoda LB $22.60 (0-87614-598-5); paper $6.95 (0-87614-906-9). 48pp. This biography for beginning readers covers the Powhatan Indian's birth, contacts with English settlers, family life, and death, and points out what information is reliable and where exaggeration may occur. (Rev: SLJ 1/03) [921]

SACAGAWEA

3352 Marcovitz, Hal. *Sacagawea: Guide for the Lewis and Clark Expedition* (4–6). Illus. Series: Explorers of New Worlds. 2000, Chelsea LB $17.95 (0-7910-5959-6); paper $8.95 (0-7910-6169-8). 63pp. In addition to the usual information on Sacagawea's life, this biography discusses why she has remained such an inspiration. (Rev: SLJ 4/01) [921]

3353 Milton, Joyce. *Sacajawea* (1–2). Illus. by Shelly Hehenberger. Series: All Aboard Reading. 2001, Putnam LB $13.89 (0-448-42616-1); paper $3.99 (0-448-42539-4). 48pp. A simple introduction to the life of Sacajawea for beginning readers. (Rev: BL 2/1/02; HBG 3/02; SLJ 2/02) [978.004]

3354 Witteman, Barbara. *Sacagawea* (2–4). Series: Photo-Illustrated Biographies. 2002, Capstone LB $13.95 (0-7368-1112-5). 24pp. A concise exploration of the little that is known about Sacagawea's life and of her contribution to the Lewis and Clark Expedition. (Rev: SLJ 7/02) [921]

SEQUOYAH

3355 Fitterer, C. Ann. *Sequoyah: Native American Scholar* (2–4). Series: Spirit of America: Our People. 2002, Child's World LB $27.07 (1-56766-167-X). 32pp. A concise introduction to the life of the Cherokee Indian who invented an alphabet for their language. (Rev: SLJ 12/02) [921]

SITTING BULL (SIOUX CHIEF)

3356 Davis, Kenneth C. *Don't Know Much About Sitting Bull* (3–7). Illus. by Sergio Martinez. 2003, HarperCollins LB $16.89 (0-06-028818-3); paper $4.99 (0-06-442125-2). 128pp. The life and importance of Sitting Bull are presented in an easy question-and-answer format with featured highlights that will appeal to reluctant readers. (Rev: BL 1/1–15/03) [978.004]

3357 Marcovitz, Hal. *Sitting Bull* (3–6). Series: Famous Figures of the American Frontier. 2001, Chelsea LB $19.75 (0-7910-6487-5); paper $8.95 (0-7910-6488-3). 64pp. The Sioux chief's efforts to improve relations between the Native Americans and the European newcomers are emphasized in this appealing biography. (Rev: SLJ 3/02) [921]

Presidents

ADAMS, JOHN

3358 Feinstein, Stephen. *John Adams* (5–9). 2002, Enslow/MyReportLinks.com LB $19.95 (0-7660-5001-7). 48pp. A well-written and accessible overview of Adams's life and contributions that is extended by a number of recommended Web sites. (Rev: SLJ 6/02) [921]

3359 Harness, Cheryl. *The Revolutionary John Adams* (3–6). Illus. 2002, National Geographic $17.95 (0-7922-6970-5). 48pp. Ample quotes, appealing illustrations, and a timeline enhance this biography of America's somewhat neglected second president. (Rev: BL 12/1/02; HBG 3/03; SLJ 2/03) [973.3]

ADAMS, JOHN QUINCY

3360 Feinstein, Stephen. *John Quincy Adams* (5–9). 2002, Enslow/MyReportLinks.com LB $19.95 (0-7660-5002-5). 48pp. Adams's early and later life are covered in this concise biography that includes several pages of annotated Web site recommendations. (Rev: HBG 10/02; SLJ 10/02) [921]

ARTHUR, CHESTER A.

3361 Young, Jeff C. *Chester A. Arthur* (4–7). Series: Presidents. 2002, Enslow/MyReportLinks.com LB $19.95 (0-7660-5077-7). 48pp. As well as an overview of the life and accomplishments of Chester A. Arthur, this book gives a pre-evaluated listing of Web sites where more material can be found. (Rev: BL 12/15/02) [921]

BUSH, GEORGE W.

3362 Gormley, Beatrice. *President George W. Bush* (4–7). Illus. 2001, Simon & Schuster paper $4.99 (0-689-84123-X). 176pp. An appealing, chronological account of Bush's life that shows him against his family background and looks at his uneven record of achievement. (Rev: BL 5/15/01; SLJ 6/01) [973.931]

3363 Jones, Veda Boyd. *George W. Bush* (5–8). Series: Major World Leaders. 2002, Chelsea LB $23.95 (0-7910-6940-0). 124pp. Using both color and sepia photographs, this account introduces George W. Bush and his family with coverage through the early part of his presidency. (Rev: BL 1/1–15/03; HBG 3/03) [921]

3364 Marquez, Heron. *George W. Bush* (5–8). Series: Biography. 2001, Lerner LB $25.26 (0-8225-4995-6). The life story of our president from birth through the turmoil of his presidential election. (Rev: BL 4/1/02; HBG 10/02) [921]

3365 Ryan, Patrick. *George W. Bush* (1–3). Illus. Series: United States Presidents. 2001, ABDO LB $14.95 (1-57765-302-5). 32pp. Report writers will find the basic information they need on Bush's life, with many clear photographs in both color and black and white. (Rev: HBG 10/01; SLJ 9/01) [921]

3366 Thompson, Bill, and Dorcas Thompson. *George W. Bush* (4–8). Series: Childhoods of the Presidents. 2002, Mason Crest LB $17.95 (1-59084-281-2). 48pp. Information on Bush's privileged childhood, his education, his family life, and his interest in politics will draw readers into the details of his later life. (Rev: SLJ 2/03)

3367 Wheeler, Jill C. *George W. Bush* (4–7). Series: War on Terrorism. 2002, ABDO LB $16.95 (1-57765-662-8). 48pp. A brief profile of President Bush with particular emphasis on his war on terrorism. (Rev: BL 5/15/02; HBG 10/02) [921]

CARTER, JAMES E.

3368 O'Shei, Tim. *Jimmy Carter* (5–9). 2002, Enslow/MyReportLinks.com LB $19.95 (0-7660-5051-3). 48pp. This introduction to Carter's life, including his childhood, and his contributions contains a long list of recommended Web sites that extend the printed material. (Rev: HBG 10/02; SLJ 6/02) [921]

3369 Santella, Andrew. *James Earl Carter Jr.* (4–7). Series: Profiles of the Presidents. 2002, Compass Point LB $23.93 (0-7565-0283-7). 64pp. A straightforward profile that touches on Carter's southern roots, his successes and failures as president, and his subsequent work in the fields of human rights and democracy. (Rev: SLJ 1/03) [921]

CLINTON, BILL

3370 Heinrichs, Ann. *William Jefferson Clinton* (4–8). Series: Profiles of the Presidents. 2002, Compass Point LB $23.93 (0-7565-0207-1). 64pp. This absorbing account of Clinton's life and career covers both the good and bad sides of his presidency and includes a discussion of Hillary's role. (Rev: SLJ 6/02)

3371 Marcovitz, Hal. *Bill Clinton* (4–8). Series: Childhoods of the Presidents. 2002, Mason Crest LB $17.95 (1-59084-273-1). 48pp. Information on Clinton's childhood, his dysfunctional family, and his interest in civil rights and politics at a young age will draw readers into the details of his later life. (Rev: SLJ 2/03) [921]

EISENHOWER, DWIGHT D.

3372 Adler, David A. *A Picture Book of Dwight David Eisenhower* (1–3). Illus. Series: Picture Book Biography. 2002, Holiday $16.95 (0-8234-1702-6). 32pp. Traces the life of the 34th president, Dwight D. Eisenhower, from his childhood in Kansas to his death in 1969. (Rev: BL 10/15/02; HBG 3/03; SLJ 10/02) [973.921]

3373 Raatma, Lucia. *Dwight D. Eisenhower* (4–7). Series: Profiles of the Presidents. 2002, Compass Point LB $23.93 (0-7565-0279-9). 64pp. A straightforward account that focuses on Eisenhower's military career and successes in World War II. (Rev: SLJ 1/03) [921]

FORD, GERALD R.

3374 Francis, Sandra. *Gerald R. Ford: Our Thirty-Eighth President* (3–5). Illus. Series: Spirit of America: Our Presidents. 2001, Child's World LB $27.07 (1-56766-872-0). 48pp. This brief biography of Ford includes photographs, sidebars, a timeline, and lists of additional resources. (Rev: BL 10/15/01) [973.925]

GRANT, ULYSSES S.

3375 Alter, Judy. *Ulysses S. Grant* (5–9). 2002, Enslow/MyReportLinks.com LB $19.95 (0-7660-5014-9). 48pp. Grant's early and later life are covered in this concise and balanced biography that includes several pages of annotated Web site recommendations. (Rev: SLJ 10/02) [921]

HARRISON, WILLIAM HENRY

3376 Gaines, Ann Graham. *William Henry Harrison: Our Ninth President* (4–6). Series: Spirit of America: Our Presidents. 2001, Child's World LB $27.07 (1-56766-848-8). 48pp. A well-illustrated and appealing biography that discusses influences that shaped Harrison's policies and looks at his legacy. (Rev: SLJ 12/01) [920]

JACKSON, ANDREW

3377 Behrman, Carol H. *Andrew Jackson* (5–8). Series: Presidential Leaders. 2002, Lerner LB $26.60 (0-8225-0093-0). 111pp. Jackson's life and character are brought to life in this narrative that points out his failings as well as his achievements. (Rev: HBG 3/03; SLJ 1/03) [921]

3378 Feinstein, Stephen. *Andrew Jackson* (5–9). 2002, Enslow/MyReportLinks.com LB $19.95 (0-7660-5003-3). 48pp. A well-written and accessible overview of Jackson's life and contributions that is extended by a number of recommended Web sites. (Rev: SLJ 6/02) [921]

JEFFERSON, THOMAS

3379 Aldridge, Rebecca. *Thomas Jefferson* (5–6). Series: Let Freedom Ring. 2001, Capstone LB $16.95 (0-7368-1035-8). 48pp. An introduction to the life and work of Jefferson that touches on his attachment to Sally Hemmings. (Rev: HBG 3/02; SLJ 4/02) [921]

3380 Reiter, Chris. *Thomas Jefferson* (4–7). Illus. Series: MyReportLinks.com. 2002, Enslow/MyReportLinks.com $19.95 (0-7660-5071-8). 48pp. A concise biography suitable for students doing reports that provides extensive Web links for further research and uses Web site images among the many illustrations. (Rev: BL 9/1/02; HBG 3/03) [973.4]

3381 Sherrow, Victoria. *Thomas Jefferson* (3–4). Illus. Series: History Maker Bios. 2002, Lerner LB $23.93 (0-8225-0197-X). 48pp. A heavily illustrated story of the multitalented man who was also an important president. (Rev: BL 6/1–15/02) [973.4]

JOHNSON, ANDREW

3382 Alter, Judy. *Andrew Johnson* (5–8). 2002, Enslow/MyReportLinks.com LB $19.95 (0-7660-5007-6). 48pp. This overview of Johnson's life and career contains a listing of about 30 Web sites that will extend the information contained in the book. (Rev: SLJ 6/02) [921]

JOHNSON, LYNDON B.

3383 Colbert, Nancy A. *Great Society: The Story of Lyndon Baines Johnson* (4–8). Illus. 2002, Morgan Reynolds $20.95 (1-883846-84-6). 144pp. A solid, readable life of the hardworking president that presents fairly both his virtues and defects. (Rev: BL 4/15/02; HBG 3/03; SLJ 8/02) [921]

3384 Levy, Debbie. *Lyndon B. Johnson* (5–9). Series: Presidential Leaders. 2003, Lerner LB $26.60 (0-8225-0097-3). 112pp. A look at the fascinating personal and political life of the president known for his support for civil rights and for increasing the U.S. involvement in Vietnam. (Rev: SLJ 2/03) [921]

KENNEDY, JOHN F.

3385 Schultz, Randy. *John F. Kennedy* (4–7). Illus. Series: MyReportLinks.com. 2002, Enslow/MyReportLinks.com $19.95 (0-7660-5012-2). 48pp. A basic, illustrated account of Kennedy's life and accomplishments that provides extensive Web links for students to do further research. (Rev: BL 9/1/02) [973.922]

LINCOLN, ABRAHAM

3386 Cohn, Amy L., and Suzy Schmidt. *Abraham Lincoln* (K–3). Illus. by David A. Johnson. 2002, Scholastic $16.95 (0-590-93566-6). 40pp. A large-format picture book that tells of the heroism and importance of Lincoln through a lively text and memorable illustrations. (Rev: BCCB 2/02; BL 4/1/02; HB 3–4/02; HBG 10/02; SLJ 2/02*) [921]

3387 Fontes, Justine, and Ron Fontes. *Abraham Lincoln: Lawyer, Leader, Legend* (2–4). Illus. Series:

Dorling Kindersley Readers. 2001, DK $12.95 (0-7894-7376-3); paper $3.95 (0-7894-7375-5). 48pp. An accessible introduction to Lincoln's life with many facts, illustrations, and maps. (Rev: BCCB 2/02; HBG 10/01; SLJ 8/01) [921]

3388 Krensky, Stephen. *Abe Lincoln and the Muddy Pig* (1–2). Illus. by Gershom Griffith. Series: Childhood of Famous Americans. 2002, Simon & Schuster LB $11.89 (0-689-84112-4); paper $3.99 (0-689-84103-5). 27pp. An anecdote about a nattily dressed Lincoln rescuing a stuck pig serves to introduce Lincoln's character in this book for beginning readers. (Rev: HBG 10/02; SLJ 7/02) [921]

3389 Mara, Wil. *Abraham Lincoln* (1–2). Illus. Series: Rookie Biographies. 2002, Children's LB $19.00 (0-516-22518-9); paper $4.95 (0-516-27334-5). 31pp. A simple account of Lincoln's life for beginning readers. (Rev: BCCB 2/02; SLJ 1/03) [921]

3390 Schott, Jane A. *Abraham Lincoln* (3–4). Series: History Maker Bios. 2002, Lerner LB $23.93 (0-8225-0196-1). 48pp. Using many true stories, historical photography, and other artwork, this lively biography describes Lincoln's journey from log cabin to the White House. (Rev: BCCB 2/02; BL 6/1–15/02) [921]

3391 Sullivan, George. *Abraham Lincoln* (3–5). Illus. Series: In Their Own Words. 2001, Scholastic $12.95 (0-439-14750-6); paper $4.50 (0-439-09554-9). 128pp. Using speeches, letters, and other primary sources, this is an entertaining, appealing biography of Lincoln. (Rev: BCCB 2/02; BL 4/1/01; HBG 10/01; SLJ 4/01) [921]

3392 Winters, Kay. *Abe Lincoln: The Boy Who Loved Books* (K–2). Illus. by Nancy Carpenter. 2003, Simon & Schuster $16.95 (0-689-82554-4). 40pp. Simple language and detailed illustrations describe Lincoln's childhood and young adult years, with a focus on his love of reading. (Rev: BL 1/1–15/03; SLJ 1/03) [973.7]

NIXON, RICHARD M.

3393 Marquez, Heron. *Richard M. Nixon* (5–9). Series: Presidential Leaders. 2003, Lerner LB $26.60 (0-8225-0098-1). 112pp. The Vietnam War, relations with China, and Watergate all feature prominently in this look at Nixon's private and public life. (Rev: SLJ 2/03) [921]

ROOSEVELT, FRANKLIN D.

3394 Burgan, Michael. *Franklin D. Roosevelt* (4–8). Series: Profiles of the Presidents. 2002, Compass Point LB $23.93 (0-7565-0203-9). 64pp. An absorbing introduction to Roosevelt's life and career, with details of his youth and education and the role that his illness played in shaping his character. (Rev: SLJ 6/02)

3395 Knapp, Ron. *Franklin D. Roosevelt* (5–9). 2002, Enslow/MyReportLinks.com LB $19.95 (0-7660-5009-2). 48pp. A listing of recommended Web sites extends the contents of this introduction

to Roosevelt's life and presidency. (Rev: HBG 10/02; SLJ 6/02) [921]

TAYLOR, ZACHARY

3396 Brunelli, Carol. *Zachary Taylor: Our Twelfth President* (4–6). Series: Spirit of America: Our Presidents. 2001, Child's World $27.07 (1-56766-836-4). 48pp. A well-illustrated and appealing biography that discusses influences that shaped Taylor's policies and looks at his legacy. (Rev: SLJ 12/01) [920]

TRUMAN, HARRY S.

3397 Gaines, Ann Graham. *Harry S. Truman: Our Thirty-Third President* (3–5). Illus. Series: Spirit of America: Our Presidents. 2001, Child's World LB $27.07 (1-56766-867-4). 48pp. This brief biography of the president features photographs, sidebars, a timeline, and lists of additional print and Web resources. (Rev: BL 10/15/01; SLJ 12/01) [973.918]

VAN BUREN, MARTIN

3398 Ferry, Steven. *Martin Van Buren: Our Eighth President* (4–6). Series: Spirit of America: Our Presidents. 2001, Child's World LB $27.07 (1-56766-837-2). 48pp. A well-illustrated and appealing biography that discusses influences that shaped Van Buren's policies and looks at his legacy. (Rev: SLJ 12/01) [920]

WASHINGTON, GEORGE

3399 Chandra, Deborah, and Madeleine Comora. *George Washington's Teeth* (K–3). Illus. by Brock Cole. 2003, Farrar $16.00 (0-374-32534-0). 40pp. George Washington's dental problems are examined in lively, witty verses perfectly paired with sprightly watercolors. (Rev: BCCB 2/03; BL 1/1–15/03; HB 3–4/03*; SLJ 1/03) [973.4]

3400 Davis, Kenneth C. *Don't Know Much About George Washington* (3–7). Illus. by Rob Shepperson. 2003, HarperCollins LB $16.89 (0-06-028817-5); paper $4.99 (0-06-442124-4). 128pp. Readers learn more about George Washington's life and political importance in an easy question-and-answer format with featured highlights that will appeal to reluctant readers. (Rev: BL 1/1–15/03; SLJ 1/03) [973.4]

3401 Mara, Wil. *George Washington* (K–4). Illus. 2002, Children's LB $19.00 (0-516-22519-7); paper $4.95 (0-516-27335-3). 32pp. A simple account of Washington's life for beginning readers. (Rev: SLJ 1/03) [921]

3402 Ransom, Candice F. *George Washington* (3–4). Series: History Maker Bios. 2002, Lerner LB $23.93 (0-8225-0374-3). 48pp. An introductory biography of the man who was chosen to lead the army and then the country during and after the American Revolution. (Rev: BL 6/1–15/02) [921]

First Ladies and Other Women

ADAMS, ABIGAIL

3403 Ching, Jacqueline. *Abigail Adams: A Revolutionary Woman* (4–7). Series: Library of American Lives and Times. 2001, Rosen LB $23.95 (0-8239-5723-3). 112pp. This biography of Abigail Adams stresses the fact that her husband, John Adams, relied heavily on her advice and that her vision of equality and justice inspired the early consideration of women's rights. (Rev: BCCB 4/01; BL 10/15/01) [921]

3404 McCarthy, Pat. *Abigail Adams: First Lady and Patriot* (5–8). Series: Historical American Biographies. 2002, Enslow LB $20.95 (0-7660-1618-8). The life story of the prolific letter-writer who was wife of the second president of the United States, John Adams. (Rev: BCCB 4/01; BL 4/1/02; HBG 10/02; SLJ 7/02) [921]

ADDAMS, JANE

3405 Armentrout, David, and Patricia Armentrout. *Jane Addams* (2–4). Series: Discover Someone Who Made a Difference. 2001, Rourke LB $18.60 (1-58952-054-8). A beginning biography of the famous American social worker who won a Nobel Peace Prize. (Rev: BL 1/1–15/02; SLJ 3/02) [921]

ANTHONY, SUSAN B.

3406 Klingel, Cynthia, and Robert B. Noyed. *Susan B. Anthony: Reformer* (3–6). Illus. 2002, Child's World LB $27.07 (1-56766-171-8). 32pp. An attractive, brief introduction to the life of Susan B. Anthony. (Rev: BL 1/1–15/03) [305.42]

3407 McLeese, Don. *Susan B. Anthony* (2–5). Series: Equal Rights Leaders. 2002, Rourke LB $19.27 (1-58952-284-2). 24pp. Simple text and well-chosen illustrations tell the story of Anthony's life, with good coverage of her youth and education. (Rev: SLJ 1/03) [324.6]

BARTON, CLARA

3408 Francis, Dorothy. *Clara Barton: Founder of the American Red Cross* (4–6). Series: Gateway Greens. 2002, Millbrook LB $23.90 (0-7613-2621-9). 48pp. The story of the Red Cross founder who obtained and distributed supplies for the wounded during the Civil War. (Rev: BL 7/02; HBG 3/03) [921]

BROADWICK, GEORGIA "TINY"

3409 Roberson, Elizabeth Whitley. *Tiny Broadwick: The First Lady of Parachuting* (4–8). Illus. 2001, Pelican paper $9.95 (1-56554-780-2). 112pp. Less than 5 feet tall, "Tiny" Broadwick joined a hot-air balloon act as a teenager and became the first woman to jump with a parachute. (Rev: BL 7/01) [797.5]

BUSH, LAURA WELCH

3410 Gormley, Beatrice. *Laura Bush: America's First Lady* (5–8). Illus. 2003, Simon & Schuster $11.89 (0-689-85628-8); paper $4.99 (0-689-85366-1). 112pp. A chronological account of Laura Bush's life, with information on her childhood as well as her later public life. (Rev: BL 3/1/03) [973.931]

3411 Stone, Tanya Lee. *Laura Welch Bush* (4–6). Illus. 2001, Millbrook LB $22.90 (0-7613-2304-X). 48pp. A biography of President George W. Bush's wife, with photographs and "fun facts." (Rev: BL 9/15/01; HBG 3/02; SLJ 9/01) [973.931]

CATT, CARRIE CHAPMAN

3412 Somervill, Barbara A. *Votes for Women! The Story of Carrie Chapman Catt* (5–8). Illus. 2002, Morgan Reynolds $21.95 (1-883846-96-X). 128pp. This is the story of Carrie Chapman Catt, who devoted her early life to the quest for women's right to vote and later turned her energies to helping Jewish refugees. (Rev: BL 11/15/02; HBG 3/03; SLJ 1/03) [324.6]

CRANDALL, PRUDENCE

3413 Lucas, Eileen. *Prudence Crandall: Teacher for Equal Rights* (1–3). Illus. by Kimanne Smith. 2001, Carolrhoda LB $21.27 (1-57505-480-9). 48pp. A biography for beginning readers of Crandall, a Quaker teacher who struggled to run a school for African American students in the 1830s. (Rev: HBG 3/02; SLJ 1/02) [921]

GRAHAM, KATHARINE

3414 Mattern, Joanne. *Katharine Graham and 20th Century American Journalism* (1–4). Series: Women Who Shaped History. 2003, Rosen LB $17.25 (0-8239-6500-7). 24pp. The story of the woman who ran the *Washington Post* after her husband's death and who helped uncover the Watergate scandal. (Rev: BL 2/15/03) [921]

HOPPER, GRACE

3415 Mattern, Joanne. *Grace Hopper: Computer Pioneer* (1–4). Series: Women Who Shaped History. 2003, Rosen LB $17.25 (0-8239-6505-8). 24pp. The amazing story of the U.S. Navy rear admiral who was a pioneer software engineer and the inventor of the compiler that translates English to the language of the target computer. (Rev: BL 2/15/03) [921]

INGLES, MARY DRAPER

3416 Furbee, Mary R. *Shawnee Captive: The Story of Mary Draper Ingles* (5–8). Illus. 2001, Morgan Reynolds $20.95 (1-883846-69-2). 112pp. The tragic and exciting story of a pioneer woman captured by Shawnee Indians, her daring escape, and her long and difficult journey home. (Rev: BL 5/15/01; HBG 10/01; SLJ 6/01) [975.5]

KELLER, HELEN

3417 Lakin, Patricia. *Helen Keller and the Big Storm* (1–2). Illus. by Diana Magnuson. Series: Childhood of Famous Americans. 2002, Simon & Schuster LB $11.89 (0-689-84025-X); paper $3.99 (0-689-84104-3). 30pp. An anecdote about her teacher rescuing Helen when she is caught in a tree during a storm serves to introduce beginning readers to Helen's character and problems. (Rev: HBG 10/02; SLJ 7/02) [921]

3418 Lawlor, Laurie. *Helen Keller: Rebellious Spirit* (4–8). Illus. 2001, Holiday $22.95 (0-8234-1588-0). 161pp. This account puts Keller's life in the context of her time and looks at the opinions and beliefs that made her a "rebellious spirit," with photographs, quotations, a bibliography, and the manual alphabet. (Rev: BL 9/1/01; HB 9–10/01; HBG 3/02; SLJ 9/01*) [362.4]

3419 Shichtman, Sandra H. *Helen Keller: Out of a Dark and Silent World* (4–6). Series: Gateway Greens. 2002, Millbrook LB $23.90 (0-7613-2550-6). 48pp. The inspiring story of the woman who overcame multiple handicaps to become a role model for others. (Rev: BL 7/02; HBG 3/03) [921]

3420 Sullivan, George. *Helen Keller* (3–5). Illus. 2001, Scholastic $12.95 (0-439-14751-4); paper $4.50 (0-439-59555-7). 128pp. Using excerpts from her biographical works, the author presents an interesting picture of Keller, her problems, and her life. (Rev: BL 4/1/01; HBG 10/01; SLJ check) [921]

3421 Sutcliffe, Jane. *Helen Keller* (2–4). Illus. by Elaine Verstraete. Series: On My Own Biography. 2002, Carolrhoda LB $22.60 (0-87614-600-0); paper $5.95 (0-87614-903-4). 48pp. For beginning readers, this is an appealing introduction to Keller's life. (Rev: HBG 3/03; SLJ 12/02) [921]

MADISON, DOLLEY

3422 Klingel, Cynthia, and Robert B. Noyed. *Dolley Madison: First Lady* (2–4). Illus. Series: Spirit of America: Our People. 2002, Child's World LB $27.07 (1-56766-170-X). 32pp. A solid introduction to the life of Dolley Madison and her skill as a hostess. (Rev: SLJ 1/03) [921]

3423 Patrick, Jean L. S. *Dolley Madison* (3–4). Illus. Series: History Maker Bios. 2002, Lerner LB $23.93 (0-8225-0194-5). 48pp. Using both cartoons and regular illustrations, this is a biography of the brave and gracious first lady who became a famous hostess. (Rev: BL 6/1–15/02; HBG 3/03) [921]

3424 Weatherly, Myra. *Dolley Madison: America's First Lady* (5–8). Illus. Series: Founders of the Republic. 2002, Morgan Reynolds LB $20.95 (1-883846-95-1). 128pp. This portrait of Dolley Madison conveys her popularity and courage, with reproductions of period paintings, prints, and maps. (Rev: BL 11/1/02; HBG 3/03; SLJ 3/03) [973.5]

MARTINI, HELEN DELANEY

3425 Lyon, George Ella. *Mother to Tigers* (K–3). Illus. by Peter Catalanotto. 2003, Simon & Schuster $16.95 (0-689-84221-X). 32pp. A picture-book

biography of the woman who looked after tiger cubs in her own home before she established a nursery at the Bronx Zoo. (Rev: BL 3/1/03; SLJ 3/03) [590]

NATION, CARRY A.

3426 Harvey, Bonnie Carman. *Carry A. Nation: Saloon Smasher and Prohibitionist* (5–8). Series: Historical American Biographies. 2002, Enslow LB $20.95 (0-7660-1907-1). 128pp. A lively and balanced biography of the prohibitionist who fought alcohol with violence. (Rev: HBG 3/03; SLJ 1/03) [921]

PITCHER, MOLLY

3427 Rockwell, Anne. *They Called Her Molly Pitcher* (3–5). Illus. by Cynthia von Buhler. 2002, Knopf $15.95 (0-679-89187-0). 32pp. The story of the gallant Revolutionary War heroine who offered water to soldiers during the Battle of Monmouth and fired her husband's canon after he was shot. (Rev: BCCB 6/02; BL 4/15/02; HB 5–6/02; HBG 10/02; SLJ 6/02) [921]

ROOSEVELT, ELEANOR

3428 Feinberg, Barbara Silberdick. *Eleanor Roosevelt: A Very Special Lady* (3–5). Illus. Series: Gateway. 2003, Millbrook LB $23.90 (0-7613-2623-5). 48pp. A biography of the First Lady, with photographs, a timeline, and a list of relevant Web sites. (Rev: BL 2/1/03) [973.917]

3429 Mattern, Joanne. *Eleanor Roosevelt: More than a First Lady* (1–4). Series: Women Who Shaped History. 2003, Rosen LB $17.25 (0-8239-6501-5). 24pp. Through classic photographs and an accessible text, readers will learn about the amazing woman who changed the role of the first lady and had a great influence on world affairs. (Rev: BL 2/15/03) [921]

ROSS, BETSY

3430 Duden, Jane. *Betsy Ross* (4–6). Illus. Series: Let Freedom Ring. 2001, Capstone LB $22.60 (0-7368-1036-6). 48pp. Ross's early life, her work as an upholsterer, and the famous sewing of the flag are placed in historical context. (Rev: HBG 3/02; SLJ 7/02) [921]

3431 Franchino, Vicky. *Betsy Ross: Patriot* (2–4). Illus. Series: Spirit of America: Our People. 2002, Child's World LB $27.07 (1-56766-169-6). 32pp. A solid introduction to the life of Betsy Ross and her work as a seamstress. (Rev: SLJ 1/03) [921]

SCOTT, BLANCHE STUART

3432 Cummins, Julie. *Tomboy of the Air: Daredevil Pilot Blanche Stuart Scott* (3–6). Illus. 2001, HarperCollins LB $16.89 (0-06-029243-1). 80pp. Scott was a daredevil from childhood, graduating from driving cars to stunt-flying, and was the first American woman flyer. (Rev: BL 5/15/01; HB 5–6/01; HBG 3/02; SLJ 6/01*) [629.13]

SHAW, ANNA HOWARD

3433 Brown, Don. *A Voice from the Wilderness: The Story of Anna Howard Shaw* (1–3). Illus. 2001, Houghton $16.00 (0-618-08362-6). 32pp. This is the story of Anna Howard Shaw, who came to America in the mid-19th century and overcame adversity to become a teacher and champion of women's suffrage. (Rev: BL 9/15/01; HB 11–12/01; HBG 3/02; SLJ 9/01) [324.6]

STANTON, ELIZABETH CADY

3434 Salisbury, Cynthia. *Elizabeth Cady Stanton: Leader of the Fight for Women's Rights* (5–8). Series: Historical American Biographies. 2002, Enslow LB $20.95 (0-7660-1616-1). The life of the fighter for women's suffrage and the organizer of the first women's rights convention. (Rev: BL 4/1/02; HBG 10/02; SLJ 5/02) [921]

STINSON, KATHERINE

3435 Winegarten, Debra L. *Katherine Stinson: The Flying Schoolgirl* (4–7). 2001, Eakin $26.95 (1-57168-459-X). 115pp. An absorbing introduction to Stinson's accomplishments, which include a whole series of "firsts," that interweaves fiction and fact. (Rev: HBG 10/01; SLJ 6/01)

Scientists, Inventors, and Naturalists

Collective

3436 Bankston, John. *Francis Crick and James Watson: Pioneers in DNA Research* (5–7). Series: Unlocking the Secrets of Science. 2002, Mitchell Lane LB $17.95 (1-58415-122-6). 56pp. An accessible account of the discovery of the structure of DNA and the lives of the two scientists involved. (Rev: SLJ 1/03) [576.5]

3437 Carruthers, Margaret W., and Susan Clinton. *Pioneers of Geology: Discovering Earth's Secrets* (5–9). Illus. Series: Lives in Science. 2001, Watts LB $25.00 (0-531-11364-7). 143pp. Chronologically arranged biographies of important geologists give information on the individual's life and work and also on the state of scientific knowledge at the time. (Rev: SLJ 11/01)

3438 French, Laura. *Internet Pioneers: The Cyber Elite* (5–9). Series: Collective Biographies. 2001, Enslow LB $20.95 (0-7660-1540-8). 112pp. French tells the stories of 10 Internet innovators — including Andrew Grove, Bill Gates, Larry Ellison, and Jeff Bezos — detailing their successes and revealing their very different backgrounds. (Rev: HBG 3/02; SLJ 9/01) [920]

3439 Greenberg, Lorna, and Margot F. Horwitz. *Digging into the Past: Pioneers of Archeology* (5–9). Series: Lives in Science. 2001, Watts LB $25.00 (0-531-11857-6). 127pp. Chronologically arranged biographies of important archaeologists including Howard Carter and Kathleen Kenyon give information on the individual's life and work and also on the state of scientific knowledge at the time. (Rev: BL 11/15/01; SLJ 11/01)

3440 Kirsh, Shannon, and Florence Kirsh. *Fabulous Female Physicians* (4–8). 2002, Second Story $7.95 (1-896764-43-6). 100pp. Using short chapters and black-and-white photographs, this account profiles 10 mostly unknown female doctors and their accomplishments. (Rev: BL 6/1–15/02) [921]

3441 Sherman, Josepha. *Jerry Yang and David Filo: Chief Yahoos of Yahoo* (5–8). Series: Techies. 2001, Millbrook LB $22.90 (0-7613-1961-1). This is the story of the creators of Yahoo!, the world's most heavily trafficked Web site. (Rev: BL 4/1/02; HBG 3/02; SLJ 12/01) [921]

3442 Thimmesh, Catherine. *The Sky's the Limit: Stories of Discovery by Women and Girls* (5–7). Illus. by Melissa Sweet. 2002, Houghton $16.00 (0-618-07698-0). 80pp. Details discoveries in the sciences, all made by women and girls. A sequel to *Girls Think of Everything* (2000). (Rev: BL 3/1/02; HB 5–6/02; HBG 10/02; SLJ 5/02) [500]

Individual

ALVAREZ, LUIS

3443 Allison, Amy. *Luis Alvarez and the Development of the Bubble Chamber* (5–8). Series: Unlocking the Secrets of Science. 2002, Mitchell Lane LB $17.95 (1-58415-140-4). 48pp. Alvarez was a scientist of wide-ranging interests who won a Nobel Prize for developing a bubble chamber to track atomic particles. (Rev: HBG 3/03; SLJ 2/03) [921]

ANDREWS, ROY CHAPMAN

3444 Marrin, Albert. *Secrets from the Rocks: Dinosaur Hunting with Roy Chapman Andrews* (4–8). Illus. 2002, Dutton $18.99 (0-525-46743-2). 80pp. This photo-biography of the famous paleontologist concentrates on his Mongolian expeditions in the 1920s and his great dinosaur discoveries. (Rev: BL 4/15/02; HB 7–8/02; HBG 10/02; SLJ 4/02) [921]

ANNING, MARY

3445 Goodhue, Thomas. *Curious Bones: Mary Anning and the Birth of Paleontology* (5–8). Illus. 2002, Morgan Reynolds LB $20.95 (1-883846-93-

5). 112pp. A readable biography of the ground-breaking female paleontologist (1799–1847) that places her achievements in historical context, with a glossary, bibliography, and timeline. (Rev: BL 7/02; HBG 3/03; SLJ 9/02) [560.92]

BANNEKER, BENJAMIN

3446 Blue, Rose, and Corinne J. Naden. *Benjamin Banneker: Mathematician and Stargazer* (4–6). Illus. Series: Gateway Biography. 2001, Millbrook LB $22.90 (0-7613-1805-4). 48pp. An informative introduction to Banneker's life and achievements as America's "first major black man of science." (Rev: HBG 3/02; SLJ 9/01) [921]

BARNARD, CHRISTIAAN

3447 Bankston, John. *Christiaan Barnard and the Story of the First Successful Heart Transplant* (4–5). Series: Unlocking the Secrets of Science. 2002, Mitchell Lane LB $17.95 (1-58415-120-X). 48pp. A concise but complete look with interesting anecdotal information at the life of the courageous doctor who performed the first successful heart transplant. (Rev: BL 8/02; SLJ 10/02) [921]

BELL, ALEXANDER GRAHAM

3448 Gaines, Ann. *Alexander Graham Bell* (2–3). Series: Discover the Life of an Inventor. 2001, Rourke LB $18.60 (1-58952-117-X). 24pp. Besides a life of this great inventor, this book describes the science behind the telephone. (Rev: BL 10/15/01; SLJ 1/02) [921]

3449 Sherrow, Victoria. *Alexander Graham Bell* (1–3). Illus. by Elaine Verstraete. Series: On My Own Biography. 2001, Carolrhoda LB $21.27 (1-57505-460-4); paper $6.95 (1-57505-533-3). 48pp. Bell's early working years and growing interest in inventions are the focus of this biography that will suit reluctant and beginning readers, with an afterword that covers his personal life and later career. (Rev: HBG 3/02; SLJ 1/02) [921]

BERNERS-LEE, TIM

3450 Gaines, Ann. *Tim Berners-Lee and the Development of the World Wide Web* (4–7). Series: Unlocking the Secrets of Science. 2001, Mitchell Lane LB $17.95 (1-58415-096-3). 48pp. A profile of the man who created the user-friendly way of accessing much of the information on the Internet. (Rev: HBG 10/02; SLJ 2/02) [921]

3451 Stewart, Melissa. *Tim Berners-Lee: Inventor of the World Wide Web* (4–7). Series: Ferguson's Career Biographies. 2001, Ferguson LB $16.95 (0-89434-367-X). 127pp. Young readers will be fascinated by the details of Berners-Lee's life and career and the accompanying information on the skills needed to become a computer programmer. (Rev: SLJ 10/01) [921]

CARLSON, CHESTER

3452 Zannos, Susan. *Chester Carlson and the Development of Xerography* (4–5). Series: Unlocking the Secrets of Science. 2002, Mitchell Lane LB $17.95 (1-58415-117-X). 56pp. The story of the man whose determination to simplify the process of copying documents led to the invention of xerography. (Rev: BL 9/15/02; HBG 3/03; SLJ 11/02) [921]

CAROTHERS, WALLACE

3453 Gaines, Ann Graham. *Wallace Carothers and the Story of DuPont Nylon* (4–5). Series: Unlocking the Secrets of Science. 2001, Mitchell Lane LB $17.95 (1-58415-097-1). 56pp. This biography of the inventor of nylon includes information on his suicide. (Rev: BL 10/15/01; SLJ 11/01) [547]

CARVER, GEORGE WASHINGTON

3454 McKissack, Patricia, and Fredrick McKissack. *George Washington Carver: The Peanut Scientist* (2–4). Series: Great African Americans. 2002, Enslow LB $14.95 (0-7660-1700-1). 32pp. Black-and-white photographs and a readable style are highlights of this biography about the famous African American botanist who was the son of slave parents. (Rev: BL 7/02) [921]

CASE, STEVE

3455 Ashby, Ruth. *Steve Case: America Online Pioneer* (5–8). Series: Techies. 2002, Millbrook LB $22.90 (0-7613-2655-3). The story of the Honolulu native who was a leader of AOL and the driving force behind its merger with Time-Warner. (Rev: BL 4/1/02; HBG 10/02) [921]

COPERNICUS

3456 Andronik, Catherine M. *Copernicus: Founder of Modern Astronomy* (4–8). Illus. Series: Great Minds of Science. 2002, Enslow LB $20.95 (0-7660-1755-9). 112pp. This absorbing biography that covers Copernicus's youth and succeeds in explaining necessary scientific concepts also includes activities that reinforce this understanding. (Rev: HBG 10/02; SLJ 6/02)

CURIE, MARIE

3457 Santella, Andrew. *Marie Curie* (3–6). Series: Trailblazers of the Modern World. 2001, World Almanac LB $26.60 (0-8368-5061-0). 48pp. An attractive, chronological biography of Curie's life and devotion to scientific research. (Rev: SLJ 1/02) [921]

DAMADIAN, RAYMOND

3458 Kjelle, Marylou Morano. *Raymond Damadian and the Development of MRI* (5–7). Series: Unlocking the Secrets of Science. 2002, Mitchell Lane LB $17.95 (1-58415-141-2). 48pp. This account focuses on Damadian's scientific accomplishments. (Rev: SLJ 1/03) [921]

DARWIN, CHARLES

3459 Senker, Cath. *Charles Darwin* (4–8). Illus. Series: Scientists Who Made History. 2002, Raintree Steck-Vaughn LB $18.98 (0-7398-4843-7). 48pp. Darwin's life and contributions are presented in clear text and ample illustrations, with historical detail that places the information in context. (Rev: HBG 10/02; SLJ 9/02)

3460 Sproule, Anna. *Charles Darwin: Visionary Behind the Theory of Evolution* (4–7). Illus. Series: Giants of Science. 2003, Gale LB $21.95 (1-56711-655-8). 64pp. Darwin's life and accomplishments are presented in concise text. (Rev: SLJ 1/03) [921]

DOMAGK, GERHARD

3461 Bankston, John. *Gerhard Domagk and the Discovery of Sulfa* (4–5). Series: Unlocking the Secrets of Science. 2002, Mitchell Lane LB $17.95 (1-58415-115-3). 56pp. The story of the man who discovered the antibiotic properties of sulfa but whose accomplishments were overshadowed by other advances in antibiotics. (Rev: BL 9/15/02; SLJ 11/02) [921]

DREW, CHARLES

3462 Whitehurst, Susan. *Dr. Charles Drew: Medical Pioneer* (4–6). Series: Journey to Freedom: The African American Library. 2001, Child's World LB $17.95 (1-56766-926-6). 40pp. An attractive biography of this pioneering American black scientist who was noted for his research in blood plasma and his work in developing the concept of the Blood Bank. (Rev: BL 12/15/01; HBG 3/02; SLJ 1/02) [921]

DYSON, ESTHER

3463 Jablonski, Carla. *Esther Dyson: Web Guru* (5–8). Series: Techies. 2002, Millbrook LB $22.90 (0-7613-2657-X). A leading light in the computer world, Dyson is the owner of EDventure Holdings, and is an active developer of emerging technologies and companies. (Rev: BL 4/1/02; HBG 10/02) [921]

EDISON, THOMAS ALVA

3464 Gaines, Ann. *Thomas Edison* (2–3). Series: Discover the Life of an Inventor. 2001, Rourke LB $18.60 (1-58952-122-6). 24pp. A simple, introductory biography that describes Edison's life, contributions, and struggles. (Rev: BL 10/15/01; SLJ 1/02) [921]

3465 Mason, Paul. *Thomas A. Edison* (4–6). Illus. Series: Scientists Who Made History. 2001, Raintree Steck-Vaughn LB $18.98 (0-7398-4414-8). 48pp. This well-illustrated profile of Edison and his life and work will be useful for report writers. (Rev: HBG 10/02; SLJ 2/02) [921]

EHRLICH, PAUL

3466 Zannos, Susan. *Paul Ehrlich and Modern Drug Development* (4–5). Series: Unlocking the Secrets of Science. 2002, Mitchell Lane LB $17.95 (1-58415-121-8). 56pp. The story of the man often called the "father of modern drug development" and his discovery of a "magic bullet." (Rev: BL 9/15/02; SLJ 3/03) [921]

EINSTEIN, ALBERT

3467 Bankston, John. *Albert Einstein and the Theory of Relativity* (5–8). Series: Unlocking the Secrets of Science. 2002, Mitchell Lane LB $17.95 (1-58415-137-4). 56pp. Einstein's accomplishments and the many challenges he faced are explored in concise text with many black-and-white photographs. (Rev: SLJ 2/03) [921]

3468 Brallier, Jess. *Who Was Albert Einstein?* (3–5). Illus. by Robert Andrew Parker. 2002, Grosset LB $13.89 (0-448-42659-5); paper $4.99 (0-448-42496-7). 105pp. Einstein is portrayed in some depth and with some humor in this biography, with discussion of his early difficulties focusing his energies, his family life, his departure from Germany, his desire to see a peaceful world, and, of course, his key discoveries. (Rev: HBG 10/02; SLJ 6/02) [921]

3469 Heinrichs, Ann. *Albert Einstein* (4–7). Series: Trailblazers of the Modern World. 2002, World Almanac LB $26.60 (0-8368-5069-6). 48pp. The impact of Einstein's work on the scientists of the 20th century is highlighted in this biography describing his life and contributions. (Rev: SLJ 7/02)

3470 MacLeod, Elizabeth. *Albert Einstein: A Life of Genius* (5–7). Illus. 2003, Kids Can $14.95 (1-55337-396-0); paper $6.95 (1-55337-397-9). 32pp. Small photographs and illustrations accompany this attractive chronological introduction to the life of Einstein that focuses on the man rather than his theories. (Rev: BL 3/1/03) [530]

3471 Wishinsky, Frieda. *What's the Matter with Albert? A Story of Albert Einstein* (2–4). Illus. by Jacques Lamontagne. 2002, Maple Tree $19.95 (1-894379-31-4); paper $6.95 (1-894379-32-2). 32pp. Cub reporter Billy is assigned to interview Albert Einstein for his elementary school newspaper in 1954, and Einstein tells Billy about his youth in this informative account that is careful to specify which parts are fiction. (Rev: BL 1/1–15/03; SLJ 11/02) [530]

ELLISON, LARRY

3472 Ehrenhaft, Daniel. *Larry Ellison: Sheer Nerve* (5–8). Series: Techies. 2001, Millbrook LB $22.90 (0-7613-1962-X). The life story of one of the world's richest men and co-founder of Oracle, the world's leading supplier of software for information management. (Rev: BL 4/1/02; HBG 3/02; SLJ 12/01) [921]

FANNING, SHAWN

3473 Mitten, Christopher. *Shawn Fanning: Napster and the Music Revolution* (5–8). Series: Techies. 2002, Millbrook LB $22.90 (0-7613-2656-1). Using many photographs and an interesting text, this is the biography of the creator of Napster, a software package for downloading music from computers. (Rev: BL 4/1/02; HBG 10/02; SLJ 6/02) [921]

FLEMING, ALEXANDER

3474 Bankston, John. *Alexander Fleming and the Story of Penicillin* (5–8). Series: Unlocking the Secrets of Science. 2001, Mitchell Lane LB $17.95 (1-58415-106-4). 56pp. This absorbing biography of the Scottish Nobel Prize winner covers his personal life as well as his scientific career. (Rev: HBG 3/02; SLJ 1/02)

3475 Birch, Beverley. *Alexander Fleming: Pioneer with Antibiotics* (4–7). Illus. Series: Giants of Science. 2003, Gale LB $21.95 (1-56711-656-6). 64pp. Fleming's life, education, research, and discovery of penicillin are presented in concise text. (Rev: SLJ 1/03) [921]

3476 Tocci, Salvatore. *Alexander Fleming: The Man Who Discovered Penicillin* (5–8). Series: Great Minds of Science. 2002, Enslow LB $20.95 (0-7660-1998-5). 128pp. An absorbing account of Fleming's childhood and later life, with solid information on his contributions to medical science and his legacy. (Rev: HBG 10/02; SLJ 9/02) [921]

FORD, HENRY

3477 Gaines, Ann. *Henry Ford* (2–3). Illus. Series: Discover the Life of an Inventor. 2001, Rourke LB $18.60 (1-58952-120-X). 24pp. This biography of Ford concentrates on his influence on the automobile industry. (Rev: BL 10/15/01) [338.7]

3478 McCarthy, Pat. *Henry Ford: Building Cars for Everyone* (5–8). Series: Historical American Biographies. 2002, Enslow LB $20.95 (0-7660-1620-X). 128pp. Ford is shown as an eccentric but successful father, engineer, and businessman, who made the automobile widely available but expected his workers to suffer difficult conditions. (Rev: HBG 3/03; SLJ 1/03)

FOSSEY, DIAN

3479 Blue, Rose, and Corinne J. Naden. *Dian Fossey: At Home with the Giant Gorillas* (4–6). Series: Gateway Greens. 2002, Millbrook LB $23.90 (0-7613-2569-7). 48pp. A brief, nicely illustrated biography of the U.S.-born zoologist who studied the mountain gorilla in its natural habitat in Africa and was killed because of her efforts. (Rev: BL 7/02; HBG 3/03) [921]

3480 Gogerly, Liz. *Dian Fossey* (5–8). Illus. Series: Scientists Who Made History. 2003, Raintree Steck-Vaughn LB $27.12 (0-7368-5225-6). 48pp. A riveting profile of the woman who became an expert on gorillas and the militant stance that may have led to her murder. (Rev: BL 3/1/03) [599.884]

FRANKLIN, ROSALIND

3481 Senker, Cath. *Rosalind Franklin* (5–8). Illus. Series: Scientists Who Made History. 2003, Raintree Steck-Vaughn LB $27.12 (0-7398-5226-4). 48pp. An interesting biography of the woman who never gained credit for her contributions to the discovery of the structure of DNA. (Rev: BL 3/1/03) [572.8]

GALILEO

3482 Goldsmith, Mike. *Galileo Galilei* (4–6). Illus. Series: Scientists Who Made History. 2001, Raintree Steck-Vaughn LB $18.98 (0-7398-4416-4). 48pp. This well-illustrated profile of Galileo and his life and work will be useful for report writers. (Rev: HBG 10/02; SLJ 2/02) [921]

GATES, BILL

3483 Barton-Wood, Sara. *Bill Gates: Computer Legend* (4–6). Illus. Series: Famous Lives. 2001, Raintree Steck-Vaughn LB $18.98 (0-7398-4432-6). 48pp. An introduction to the life and career of Microsoft founder Bill Gates. (Rev: BL 1/1–15/02; HBG 10/02) [338.7]

3484 Peters, Craig. *Bill Gates* (5–8). Illus. Series: Internet Biographies. 2003, Enslow LB $18.95 (0-7660-1969-1). 48pp. A reader-friendly biography of the creator of Microsoft, with information on his youth as well as his successful later life. (Rev: BL 3/15/03) [338.7]

GODDARD, ROBERT

3485 Bankston, John. *Robert Goddard and the Liquid Rocket Engine* (4–7). Series: Unlocking the Secrets of Science. 2001, Mitchell Lane LB $17.95 (1-58415-107-2). 56pp. Bankston combines an introduction to Goddard's commitment to rocketry and his difficulty finding funding with an understandable explanation of the scientific challenges. (Rev: HBG 3/02; SLJ 2/02) [621.43]

GOODALL, JANE

3486 January, Brendan. *Jane Goodall: Animal Behaviorist and Writer* (4–7). Series: Ferguson's Career Biographies. 2001, Ferguson LB $16.95 (0-89434-370-X). 127pp. This easily read biography will appeal in particular to reluctant readers and students seeking quick information for a report. (Rev: SLJ 9/01) [921]

GUTENBERG, JOHANN

3487 Pollard, Michael. *Johann Gutenberg: Master of Modern Printing* (5–7). Series: Giants of Science. 2001, Blackbirch $19.95 (1-56711-335-4). 64pp. Good use of illustrations and an interesting text are highlights of this life of the German printer who first used movable type. (Rev: BL 8/1/01; HBG 3/02) [921]

HARRISON, JOHN

3488 Lasky, Kathryn. *The Man Who Made Time Travel* (3–5). Illus. by Kevin Hawkes. 2003, Farrar $17.00 (0-374-37488-3). 48pp. This oversize book presents the story of John Harrison, who worked for 50 years to perfect a timepiece that would track longitude in shipboard navigation. (Rev: BL 3/1/03*) [526]

HEWLETT, WILLIAM

3489 Tracy, Kathleen. *William Hewlett: Pioneer of the Computer Age* (5–7). Series: Unlocking the Secrets of Science. 2002, Mitchell Lane LB $17.95 (1-58415-142-0). 48pp. This accessible account focuses on Hewlett's scientific accomplishments and career in business. (Rev: SLJ 1/03) [921]

HILL, JULIA BUTTERFLY

3490 Fitzgerald, Dawn. *Julia Butterfly Hill: Saving the Redwoods* (4–6). Series: Gateway Greens. 2002, Millbrook LB $23.90 (0-7613-2654-5). 48pp. This is a handsome biography of the environmental activist who lived in a 200-foot-tall redwood named Luna from December 1997 to December 1999. (Rev: BL 7/02; HBG 3/03) [921]

HOUNSFIELD, GODFREY

3491 Zannos, Susan. *Godfrey Hounsfield and the Invention of CAT Scans* (4–5). Series: Unlocking the Secrets of Science. 2002, Mitchell Lane LB $17.95 (1-58415-119-6). 56pp. The story of the man who realized that X-rays could be manipulated by computers and later invented the amazingly accurate diagnostic device known as the computerized axial tomography or CAT scanner. (Rev: BL 9/15/02; SLJ 1/03) [921]

JARVIK, ROBERT

3492 Bankston, John. *Robert Jarvik and the First Artificial Heart* (4–5). Series: Unlocking the Secrets of Science. 2002, Mitchell Lane LB $17.95 (1-58415-116-1). 48pp. This readable biography with interesting, unexpected facts covers the life and work of the doctor who invented the first artificial heart. (Rev: BL 8/02; HBG 3/03; SLJ 10/02) [921]

KNIGHT, MARGARET

3493 Brill, Marlene Targ. *Margaret Knight: Girl Inventor* (2–5). Illus. by Joanne Friar. 2001, Millbrook $22.90 (0-7613-1756-2). 32pp. Margaret Knight was driven to invent life- and labor-saving devices by her early experiences working in a textile mill. (Rev: BL 9/15/01; HBG 3/02; SLJ 12/01) [609.2]

KOLFF, WILLEM

3494 Tracy, Kathleen. *Willem Kolff and the Invention of the Dialysis Machine* (5–8). Illus. Series: Unlocking the Secrets of Science. 2002, Mitchell Lane LB $17.95 (1-58415-135-8). 48pp. Kolff invented the dialysis machine in 1942 in the Nazi-occupied Netherlands. (Rev: HBG 3/03; SLJ 12/02)

LAMARR, HEDY

3495 Gaines, Ann. *Hedy Lamarr* (2–3). Illus. Series: Discover the Life of an Inventor. 2001, Rourke LB $18.60 (1-58952-119-6). 24pp. The little-known story of the actress Hedy Lamarr and the communications system she devised during World War II, for beginning readers. (Rev: BL 10/15/01; SLJ 1/02) [621.382]

LEOPOLD, ALDO

3496 Yannuzzi, Della. *Aldo Leopold: Protector of the Wild* (4–6). Series: Gateway Greens. 2002, Millbrook LB $23.90 (0-7613-2465-8). 48pp. An attractive biography of the U.S. environmentalist who helped create the first national wildlife area in 1924 and founded the Wilderness Society in 1935. (Rev: BL 7/02; HBG 3/03) [921]

MCCLINTOCK, BARBARA

3497 Tracy, Kathleen. *Barbara McClintock: Pioneering Geneticist* (4–7). Series: Unlocking the Secrets of Science. 2001, Mitchell Lane LB $17.95 (1-58415-111-0). 48pp. An absorbing look at the life and research of this Nobel Prize winner. (Rev: HBG 3/02; SLJ 2/02) [921]

MARCONI, GUGLIELMO

3498 Birch, Beverley. *Guglielmo Marconi: Radio Pioneer* (5–8). Series: Giants of Science. 2001, Gale LB $19.95 (1-56711-337-0). 64pp. This account of Marconi and his accomplishments also looks at how his inventions have evolved. (Rev: HBG 3/02; SLJ 2/02) [921]

MUIR, JOHN

3499 Armentrout, David, and Patricia Armentrout. *John Muir* (2–4). Illus. 2002, Rourke LB $18.60 (1-58952-055-6). 24pp. A simple introduction for younger readers to the life of naturalist John Muir. (Rev: BL 1/1–15/02; SLJ 3/02) [333.7]

MURRAY, JOSEPH E.

3500 Mattern, Joanne. *Joseph E. Murray and the Story of the First Human Kidney Transplant* (5–8). Illus. Series: Unlocking the Secrets of Science. 2002, Mitchell Lane LB $17.95 (1-58415-136-6). 48pp. A look at the work of the surgeon who performed the first successful kidney transplant. (Rev: SLJ 12/02)

NEWTON, ISAAC

3501 Mason, Paul. *Isaac Newton* (4–8). Illus. Series: Scientists Who Made History. 2002, Raintree Steck-Vaughn LB $18.98 (0-7398-4845-3). 48pp. Newton's life and contributions are presented in clear text and ample illustrations, with historical detail that places the information in context. (Rev: HBG 10/02; SLJ 9/02)

OSWALD AVERY

3502 Severs, Vesta-Nadine, and Jim Whiting. *Oswald Avery and the Story of DNA* (4–7). Series: Unlocking the Secrets of Science. 2002, Mitchell Lane LB $17.95 (1-58415-110-2). 48pp. The importance of Avery's early research is reinforced by a description of DNA evidence being used to free wrongly accused prisoners. (Rev: HBG 10/02; SLJ 6/02)

PASTEUR, LOUIS

3503 Armentrout, David, and Patricia Armentrout. *Louis Pasteur* (2–4). Series: Discover Someone Who Made a Difference. 2001, Rourke LB $18.60 (1-58952-056-4). This basic biography describes the life and times of Pasteur and how his accomplishments affect our lives today. (Rev: BL 1/1–15/02; SLJ 3/02) [921]

3504 Birch, Beverley. *Louis Pasteur: Father of Modern Medicine* (5–7). Series: Giants of Science. 2001, Blackbirch $19.95 (1-56711-336-2). 64pp. A readable, well-organized biography of the French chemist whose varied accomplishments include discovery of the process known now as pasteurization. (Rev: BL 8/1/01; HBG 3/02) [921]

ROBERTS, EDWARD

3505 Zannos, Susan. *Edward Roberts and the Story of the Personal Computer* (5–7). Series: Unlocking the Secrets of Science. 2002, Mitchell Lane LB $17.95 (1-58415-118-8). 48pp. This accessible account focuses on Roberts's accomplishments as an electronic engineer. (Rev: SLJ 1/03) [921]

ROENTGEN, WILHELM

3506 Garcia, Kimberly. *Wilhelm Roentgen and the Discovery of X Rays* (4–5). Series: Unlocking the Secrets of Science. 2002, Mitchell Lane LB $17.95 (1-58415-114-5). 48pp. The story of the German physical scientist who stumbled upon X-rays while working on experiments with electricity. (Rev: BL 8/02; HBG 3/03; SLJ 10/02) [921]

SALK, JONAS

3507 Bankston, John. *Jonas Salk and the Polio Vaccine* (4–5). Series: Unlocking the Secrets of Science. 2001, Mitchell Lane LB $17.95 (1-58415-093-9). 56pp. A biography of the famous scientist, with photographs, a glossary, and a list of additional resources. (Rev: BL 10/15/01; SLJ 11/01) [610]

3508 Durrett, Deanne. *Jonas Salk* (2–5). Illus. Series: Inventors and Creators. 2002, Gale LB $23.70 (0-7377-1277-5). 48pp. This brief biography

presents Salk's life from childhood and his determination to persevere to find a cure for polio, with many photographs, a glossary, and a bibliography. (Rev: BL 11/1/02; SLJ 10/02) [610]

3509 McPherson, Stephanie Sammartino. *Jonas Salk: Conquering Polio* (5–8). Series: Lerner Biographies. 2001, Lerner LB $25.26 (0-8225-4964-6). 128pp. An absorbing account of Salk's life and contributions to medicine that discusses his confrontation with Sabin and the early failures of Salk's vaccine. (Rev: HBG 3/02; SLJ 4/02) [921]

TELLER, EDWARD

3510 Bankston, John. *Edward Teller and the Development of the Hydrogen Bomb* (5–8). Series: Unlocking the Secrets of Science. 2001, Mitchell Lane LB $17.95 (1-58415-108-0). 56pp. The life of the scientist born in Hungary who played a key role in the development of the H-bomb. (Rev: HBG 3/02; SLJ 1/02)

TORVALDS, LINUS

3511 Brashares, Ann. *Linus Torvalds: Software Rebel* (5–8). Series: Techies. 2001, Millbrook LB $22.90 (0-7613-1960-3). The story of the computer genius who created the Linux operating system. (Rev: BL 4/1/02; HBG 3/02; SLJ 12/01) [921]

WAKSMAN, SELMAN

3512 Gordon, Karen. *Selman Waksman and the Discovery of Streptomycin* (5–7). Series: Unlocking the Secrets of Science. 2002, Mitchell Lane LB $17.95 (1-58415-138-2). 48pp. An accessible account of Waksman's life and scientific research. (Rev: SLJ 1/03) [921]

WATT, JAMES

3513 Sproule, Anna. *James Watt: Master of the Steam Engine* (5–8). Series: Giants of Science. 2001, Gale LB $19.95 (1-56711-338-9). 64pp. This exploration of Watt's life and accomplishments also looks at how his inventions have evolved. (Rev: HBG 3/02; SLJ 2/02) [921]

WEINBERG, ROBERT A.

3514 Gaines, Ann, and Jim Whiting. *Robert A. Weinberg and the Search for the Cause of Cancer* (4–7). Series: Unlocking the Secrets of Science. 2002, Mitchell Lane LB $17.95 (1-58415-095-5). 48pp. The life and achievements of the scientist who specializes in the genetic causes of disease. (Rev: HBG 10/02; SLJ 6/02)

WHITNEY, ELI

3515 Gaines, Ann. *Eli Whitney* (2–3). Series: Discover the Life of an Inventor. 2001, Rourke LB $18.60 (1-58952-118-8). 24pp. The life of the inventor of the cotton gin is presented simply with material on how this invention works. (Rev: BL 10/15/01) [921]

WOZNIAK, STEPHEN

3516 Riddle, John, and Jim Whiting. *Stephen Wozniak and the Story of Apple Computer* (4–7). Series: Unlocking the Secrets of Science. 2001, Mitchell Lane LB $17.95 (1-58415-109-9). 48pp. A profile of the life and achievements of the co-founder of Apple, who is known for his philanthropy and teaching in elementary schools. (Rev: HBG 10/02; SLJ 2/02) [921]

WRIGHT, WILBUR AND ORVILLE

3517 Busby, Peter. *First to Fly* (3–5). Illus. by David Craig. 2003, Crown $19.95 (0-375-81287-3). 32pp. The obstacles surmounted by the Wright brothers as they took to the sky are handsomely presented in this large, richly illustrated text. (Rev: BL 1/1–15/03; SLJ 3/03) [921]

3518 Collins, Mary. *Airborne: A Photobiography of Wilbur and Orville Wright* (4–8). Illus. 2003, National Geographic $18.95 (0-7922-6957-8). 64pp.

Sixty photographs are only the beginning of this intriguing book packed with information about the brothers and their famous flight. (Rev: BL 2/1/03*; HB 3–4/03; SLJ 3/03) [629.13]

3519 Gaines, Ann. *Orville and Wilbur Wright* (2–3). Series: Discover the Life of an Inventor. 2001, Rourke LB $18.60 (1-58952-121-8). 24pp. A very simple biography of the Wright brothers with material on their struggles and an explanation of how the airplane works. (Rev: BL 10/15/01) [973]

3520 MacLeod, Elizabeth. *The Wright Brothers: A Flying Start* (3–5). Illus. 2002, Kids Can $14.95 (1-55074-933-1). 32pp. Using double-page spreads, with pictures on one and text on the other, this attractive biography is a fine introduction to the Wright brothers and their work. (Rev: BL 4/1/02; HBG 10/02; SLJ 7/02) [921]

3521 Yolen, Jane. *My Brothers' Flying Machine: Wilbur, Orville, and Me* (3–5). Illus. by Jim Burke. 2003, Little, Brown $16.95 (0-316-97159-6). 32pp. The story of the Wright brothers is told in free verse by their sister Katherine, who looked after the brothers while they tended to their dream. (Rev: BL 3/1/03; SLJ 3/03) [629.13]

Sports Figures

Collective

3522 Aaseng, Nathan. *Women Olympic Champions* (5 Up). Series: History Makers. 2000, Lucent LB $19.96 (1-56006-709-8). 112pp. Aaseng profiles famous women Olympic competitors and looks at the history of women's participation. (Rev: SLJ 4/01)

3523 Bryant, Jill. *Amazing Women Athletes* (4–8). Illus. Series: Women's Hall of Fame. 2002, Second Story paper $7.95 (1-896764-44-4). 100pp. This book contains profiles of 10 distinguished women athletes including mountain climber Annie Smith Peck and tennis stars Venus and Serena Williams. (Rev: BL 6/1–15/02; SLJ 8/02) [920]

3524 Sullivan, George. *Power Football: The Greatest Running Backs* (4 Up). 2001, Simon & Schuster $18.00 (0-689-82432-7). 60pp. Profiles eighteen 20th-century running backs, including O. J. Simpson, Terrell Davis, and Emmitt Smith. (Rev: HBG 3/02; SLJ 11/01) [920]

3525 Winter, Jonah. *Beisbol! Latino Baseball Pioneers and Legends* (3–8). Illus. 2001, Lee & Low $16.95 (1-58430-012-4). 32pp. Sports fans will appreciate the format here, with statistics and other facts about 14 Latino baseball players presented in trading-card-style profiles. (Rev: BCCB 10/01; BL 10/1/01; HBG 10/01; SLJ 7/01) [796.357]

Automobile Racing

PETTY FAMILY

3526 Stewart, Mark. *The Pettys: Triumphs and Tragedies of Auto Racing's First Family* (4–8). Illus. 2001, Millbrook LB $24.90 (0-7613-2273-6). 64pp. Photos, quotations, anecdotes, and informative text introduce readers to the famous Petty family and their sometimes tragic involvement in automobile racing. (Rev: BL 9/1/01; HBG 3/02) [796.72]

Baseball

BELL, COOL PAPA

3527 McCormack, Shaun. *Cool Papa Bell* (4–7). Series: Baseball Hall of Famers of the Negro Leagues. 2002, Rosen LB $29.25 (0-8239-3474-8). 112pp. A biography of James Thomas "Cool Papa" Bell of Negro League baseball, who is said to have stolen 175 bases in one season. (Rev: BL 7/02) [921]

GIBSON, JOSH

3528 Twemlow, Nick. *Josh Gibson* (4–7). Series: Baseball Hall of Famers of the Negro Leagues. 2002, Rosen LB $29.25 (0-8239-3475-6). 112pp. In addition to racial prejudice in the world of baseball, Josh Gibson suffered many personal misfortunes as this life story recounts. (Rev: BL 7/02) [921]

IRVIN, MONTE

3529 Haegele, Katie. *Monte Irvin* (4–7). Series: Baseball Hall of Famers of the Negro Leagues. 2002, Rosen LB $29.25 (0-8239-3477-2). 112pp. Though recruited into the Negro leagues when he was 17, Irvin, a very talented player, was past his prime when he finally became a major leaguer. (Rev: BL 7/02) [921]

JOHNSON, JUDY

3530 Billus, Kathleen. *Judy Johnson* (4–7). Illus. Series: Baseball Hall of Famers of the Negro Leagues. 2002, Rosen LB $29.25 (0-8239-3476-4). 112pp. A biography of Johnson covering his years as player, coach, manager, and scout, with black-

and-white photographs, glossary, timeline, and lists of additional resources. (Rev: BL 7/02) [796.357]

JOHNSON, MAMIE "PEANUT"

3531 Green, Michelle Y. *A Strong Right Arm: The Story of Mamie "Peanut" Johnson* (4–7). 2002, Dial $15.99 (0-8037-2661-9). 128pp. The life story of the woman who was one of three to play professional baseball and of her career as pitcher with the Negro Leagues' Indianapolis Clowns. (Rev: BL 6/1–15/02*; HBG 3/03; SLJ 8/02) [921]

LEONARD, BUCK

3532 Payment, Simone. *Buck Leonard* (4–7). Series: Baseball Hall of Famers of the Negro Leagues. 2002, Rosen LB $29.25 (0-8239-3473-X). 112pp. The story of one of the greatest baseball players of all time, who missed worldwide fame because of his color. (Rev: BL 7/02) [921]

PAIGE, SATCHEL

3533 Schmidt, Julie. *Satchel Paige* (4–7). Illus. Series: Baseball Hall of Famers of the Negro Leagues. 2002, Rosen LB $29.25 (0-8239-3478-0). 112pp. A biography of the famous pitcher who became the oldest rookie ever, with black-and-white photographs, glossary, timeline, and lists of additional resources. (Rev: BL 7/02) [796.357]

ROBINSON, JACKIE

3534 De Marco, Tony. *Jackie Robinson: 1919-1972* (4–6). Series: Journey to Freedom: The African American Library. 2001, Child's World LB $17.95 (1-56766-918-2). 40pp. An attractive biography illustrated with sepia-toned photographs that presents the life of this trailblazing baseball great. (Rev: BL 12/15/01; HBG 3/02; SLJ 1/02) [921]

3535 Mara, Wil. *Jackie Robinson* (K–2). Series: Rookie Biographies. 2002, Children's LB $19.00 (0-516-22520-0); paper $4.95 (0-516-27336-1). 32pp. For beginning readers, this is a simple introduction to the legendary baseball player. (Rev: SLJ 12/02) [821]

RODRIGUEZ, ALEX

3536 Macnow, Glen. *Alex Rodriguez* (5–8). Series: Sports Great. 2002, Enslow LB $17.95 (0-7660-1845-8). 64pp. An easy-to-read yet fairly detailed biography of the baseball player, with plenty of statistics and quotes. (Rev: BL 9/1/02; HBG 10/02) [796.357]

SUZUKI, ICHIRO

3537 Stewart, Mark. *Ichiro Suzuki: Best in the West* (4–7). Illus. Series: Sports New Wave. 2002, Millbrook LB $22.90 (0-7613-2616-2). 48pp. A well-constructed biography of the famous Japanese Seattle Mariners player that offers information on the game itself as well as statistics, color photo-

graphs, and quotes that illustrate his achievements. (Rev: BL 9/1/02; HBG 3/03) [796.357]

WEISS, ALTA

3538 Hopkinson, Deborah. *Girl Wonder: A Baseball Story in Nine Innings* (2–4). Illus. by Terry Widener. 2003, Simon & Schuster $16.95 (0-689-83300-8). 40pp. Alta Weiss's inspiring story swings along in lyrical prose, relating her adventures as a teenage baseball phenomenon who pitched for a men's team in 1907 at the age of 17. (Rev: BL 1/1–15/03*; HB 3–4/03; SLJ 3/03)

Basketball

ABDUL-JABBAR, KAREEM

3539 Kneib, Martha. *Kareem Abdul-Jabbar* (5–8). Series: Basketball Hall of Famers. 2002, Rosen LB $29.25 (0-8239-3483-7). 112pp. An in-depth look at this basketball great's life, with highlights from his childhood through his NBA career. (Rev: BL 9/1/02) [921]

BRYANT, KOBE

3540 Kennedy, Nick. *Kobe Bryant: Star Guard* (4–8). Series: Sports Reports. 2002, Enslow $20.95 (0-7660-1828-8). 104pp. An accessible biography of the basketball player, with detailed descriptions of career highlights. (Rev: BL 9/1/02; HBG 3/03) [796.323]

3541 Thornley, Stew. *Super Sports Star Kobe Bryant* (2–5). Illus. Series: Super Sports Stars. 2001, Enslow LB $18.95 (0-7660-1514-9). 48pp. Photographs and statistics accompany text about the famous basketball player, from his childhood to his professional career with the L.A. Lakers. (Rev: BL 10/15/01; HBG 3/02) [796.323]

CARTER, VINCE

3542 Savage, Jeff. *Vince Carter* (5–8). Series: Sports Great. 2002, Enslow LB $17.95 (0-7660-1767-2). 64pp. An accessible biography of the Toronto Raptors basketball player that will be useful for students writing reports. (Rev: BL 9/1/02; HBG 10/02) [796.323]

3543 Thornley, Stew. *Super Sports Star Vince Carter* (2–5). Series: Super Sports Stars. 2002, Enslow LB $18.95 (0-7660-1805-9). 48pp. The life of the Toronto Raptors guard-forward is told in an account that features simple text, large type, and many color photographs. (Rev: BL 9/1/02; HBG 10/02) [921]

DUNCAN, TIM

3544 Torres, John Albert. *Sports Great Tim Duncan* (5–8). Series: Sports Great. 2002, Enslow LB $17.95 (0-7660-1766-4). 64pp. The life of this basketball star is re-created using an easy-reading text and many photographs. (Rev: BL 9/1/02; HBG 10/02) [921]

GARNETT, KEVIN

3545 Bernstein, Ross. *Kevin Garnett: Star Forward* (4–8). Series: Sports Reports. 2002, Enslow LB $20.95 (0-7660-1829-6). 104pp. An in-depth look at the life of this emerging basketball star in a simple account suitable for reluctant readers. (Rev: BL 9/1/02; HBG 3/03) [921]

3546 Stewart, Mark. *Kevin Garnett: Shake Up the Game* (4–7). Series: Sports New Wave. 2002, Millbrook LB $21.90 (0-7613-2615-4). 48pp. A short biography that chronicles the career of the new star of the Minnesota Timberwolves. (Rev: BL 9/1/02; HBG 10/02) [921]

3547 Thornley, Stew. *Super Sports Star Kevin Garnett* (2–5). Series: Super Sports Stars. 2001, Enslow LB $18.95 (0-7660-1515-7). 48pp. Garnett, a small forward for the Minnesota Timberwolves, gets an interesting profile complete with game details and statistics plus plenty of action photographs. (Rev: BL 10/15/01; HBG 3/02) [921]

HARDAWAY, PENNY

3548 Rappoport, Ken. *Super Sports Star Penny Hardaway* (2–5). Illus. Series: Super Sports Stars. 2001, Enslow LB $18.95 (0-7660-1516-5). 48pp. Photographs and statistics accompany text about the famous basketball player, from his childhood to his professional career. (Rev: BL 10/15/01; HBG 3/02) [796.323]

HILL, GRANT

3549 Lowenstein, Felicia. *Grant Hill* (2–5). Series: Super Sports Stars. 2001, Enslow LB $18.95 (0-7660-1517-3). Simple sentences and many color photographs are used in this beginning biography of the Orlando Magic forward. (Rev: BL 4/1/02; HBG 10/02) [921]

JOHNSON, MAGIC

3550 Gottfried, Ted. *Earvin "Magic" Johnson: Champion and Crusader* (4–6). Series: Book Report Biographies. 2001, Watts LB $22.00 (0-531-20386-7); paper $6.95 (0-531-15550-1). 28pp. A well-researched biography of the former Lakers point guard and NBA Hall of Famer who is now a supporter of many community-based causes. (Rev: BL 8/1/01; SLJ check) [921]

KIDD, JASON

3551 Thornley, Stew. *Super Sports Star Jason Kidd* (2–5). Series: Super Sports Stars. 2002, Enslow LB $18.95 (0-7660-1806-7). 48pp. Complete with game statistics and sports action, this is a simple, attractive biography of the star guard of the New Jersey Nets. (Rev: BL 9/1/02; HBG 10/02) [921]

MARBURY, STEPHON

3552 Plum-Ucci, Carol. *Super Sports Star Stephon Marbury* (2–5). Series: Super Sports Stars. 2002, Enslow LB $18.95 (0-7660-1810-5). 48pp. An exciting life story of Marbury, the black basketball player who has established a reputation as point guard for the Phoenix Suns. (Rev: BL 2/15/03; HBG 3/03) [921]

PAYTON, GARY

3553 Mandell, Judith. *Super Sports Star Gary Payton* (2–5). Series: Super Sports Stars. 2001, Enslow LB $1895.00 (0-7660-1519-X). 48pp. With large type and colorful photographs, this is an easily read biography of the black point guard of the Los Angeles Lakers. (Rev: BL 10/15/01; HBG 3/02) [921]

RICE, GLEN

3554 Rappoport, Ken. *Super Sports Star Glen Rice* (2–5). Series: Super Sports Stars. 2002, Enslow LB $18.95 (0-7660-1808-3). 48pp. Large type, colorful photographs, and an appealing format highlight this simple biography of the Houston Rockets star. (Rev: BL 9/1/02; HBG 10/02) [921]

SPREWELL, LATRELL

3555 Pellowski, Michael J. *Super Sports Star Latrell Sprewell* (2–5). Series: Super Sports Stars. 2002, Enslow LB $18.95 (0-7660-1811-3). 48pp. With color photographs on each page plus a simple text, this is an exciting biography of the NBA star who plays guard and forward for the New York Knicks. (Rev: BL 9/1/02; HBG 3/03) [921]

STILES, JACKIE

3556 Stewart, Mark. *Jackie Stiles: Gym Dandy* (4–7). Illus. Series: Sports New Wave. 2002, Millbrook LB $22.90 (0-7613-2614-6). 48pp. A biography of the WNBA star, with information on her childhood and family, statistics, color photographs, and general material on the game itself. (Rev: BL 9/1/02; HBG 3/03) [796.323]

SWOOPES, SHERYL

3557 Rappoport, Ken. *Sheryl Swoopes* (4–8). Illus. Series: Sports Reports. 2002, Enslow $20.95 (0-7660-1827-X). 112pp. An accessible biography of the basketball player, with detailed descriptions of career highlights. (Rev: BL 9/1/02; HBG 3/03) [976.323]

WEBBER, CHRIS

3558 Thornley, Stew. *Chris Webber* (2–5). Series: Super Sports Stars. 2002, Enslow LB $18.95 (0-7660-1807-5). A simple biography with many action photographs of Webber, the NBA power forward of the Sacramento Kings. (Rev: BL 4/1/02; HBG 10/02) [921]

WEST, JERRY

3559 Ramen, Fred. *Jerry West* (5–8). Series: Basketball Hall of Famers. 2002, Rosen LB $29.25 (0-8239-3482-9). 112pp. Facts, stories, and full-color photographs are used to bring alive the story of this basketball great, with material on his NBA career and beyond. (Rev: BL 9/1/02) [921]

Boxing

ALI, MUHAMMAD

3560 Garrett, Leslie. *The Story of Muhammad Ali* (2–4). Illus. 2002, DK $12.95 (0-7894-8516-8); paper $3.95 (0-7894-8517-6). 48pp. A chapter-book biography of Muhammad Ali, from childhood to his battle with Parkinson's disease. (Rev: BL 3/1/02; HBG 10/02; SLJ 4/02) [796.83]

3561 Haskins, Jim. *Champion: The Story of Muhammad Ali* (3–6). Illus. by Eric Velasquez. 2002, Walker $17.95 (0-8027-8784-3). Ali's boyhood, career as Cássius Clay, conversion to Islam, and battle with Parkinson's are among the topics covered in this easy-to-read picture-book biography. (Rev: HB 7–8/02; HBG 10/02; SLJ 7/02) [921]

3562 Shange, Ntozake. *Float Like a Butterfly* (2–4). Illus. by Edel Rodriguez. 2002, Hyperion $15.99 (0-7868-0554-4). 40pp. An appealing picture-book portrait of Muhammad Ali, from his childhood to his heavyweight championships and including material on civil rights, religion, and Vietnam. (Rev: BL 9/1/02; HB 11–12/02; HBG 3/03; SLJ 10/02) [796.83]

Figure Skating

HUGHES, SARAH

3563 Ashby, R. S. *Sarah Hughes: America's Sweetheart* (4–6). Illus. Series: Going for the Gold. 2002, Avon paper $4.99 (0-06-051842-1). 128pp. A profile of the skating star of the 2002 Winter Olympics, with an emphasis on the hard work it takes to become an Olympic athlete and the important role of coaches. (Rev: BL 9/1/02) [796.91]

KWAN, MICHELLE

3564 Stewart, Mark, and Mike Kennedy. *Michelle Kwan: Quest for Gold* (4–6). Illus. 2002, Millbrook LB $24.90 (0-7613-2622-7). 64pp. A chronological biography of Chinese American figure skater Michelle Kwan with color photographs. (Rev: BL 3/1/02; HBG 10/02) [796.91]

Football

BRUNELL, MARK

3565 Steenkamer, Paul. *Mark Brunell: Star Quarterback* (4–8). Series: Sports Reports. 2002, Enslow LB $20.95 (0-7660-1830-X). 104pp. The life story of the Jacksonville Jaguars quarterback, told with detailed summaries of his greatest moments. (Rev: BL 9/1/02; HBG 3/03) [921]

CULPEPPER, DAUNTE

3566 Stewart, Mark. *Daunte Culpepper: Command and Control* (4–7). Series: Sports New Wave. 2002, Millbrook LB $21.90 (0-7613-2613-8). 48pp. This brief biography celebrates the career of the young black footballer and his achievements as quarterback of the Minnesota Vikings. (Rev: BL 9/1/02; HBG 10/02) [921]

3567 Thornley, Stew. *Super Sports Star Daunte Culpepper* (2–5). Series: Super Sports Stars. 2002, Enslow LB $18.95 (0-7660-2051-7). 48pp. The life of Culpepper, the black quarterback of the Minnesota Vikings, is excitingly re-created with colorful photographs and interesting game statistics. (Rev: BL 2/15/03) [921]

FAVRE, BRETT

3568 Thornley, Stew. *Super Sports Star Brett Favre* (2–5). Series: Super Sports Stars. 2002, Enslow LB $18.95 (0-7660-2048-7). 48pp. Using colorful photographs and exciting game details, this is the story of Brett Favre, quarterback of the Green Bay Packers. (Rev: BL 2/15/03) [921]

MANNING, PEYTON

3569 Savage, Jeff. *Peyton Manning: Precision Passer* (4–7). Series: Sports Achievers Biographies. 2001, Lerner LB $22.60 (0-8225-3683-8); paper $5.95 (0-8225-9865-5). Sports statistics, action photographs, and an accessible text highlight this biography of the Indianapolis Colts quarterback. (Rev: BL 4/1/02; HBG 10/02) [921]

MOSS, RANDY

3570 Bernstein, Ross. *Randy Moss: Star Wide Receiver* (4–8). Series: Sports Reports. 2002, Enslow LB $20.95 (0-7660-1503-3). 104pp. A well-illustrated account of the life of this Minnesota Vikings star, told with plenty of sports action. (Rev: BL 9/1/02; HBG 10/02) [921]

3571 Thornley, Stew. *Super Sports Star Randy Moss* (2–5). Series: Super Sports Stars. 2002, Enslow LB $18.95 (0-7660-2049-5). 48pp. An easily read biography of the black wide receiver of the Minnesota Vikings. (Rev: BL 2/15/03) [921]

Tennis

WILLIAMS, VENUS AND SERENA

3572 Morgan, Terri. *Venus and Serena Williams: Grand Slam Sisters* (4–7). Series: Sports Achievers Biographies. 2001, Lerner LB $22.60 (0-8225-3684-6); paper $5.95 (0-8225-9866-3). An action-packed biography of the amazing tennis duo that covers their careers and their family. (Rev: BL 4/1/02; HBG 10/02) [921]

3573 Stout, Glenn. *On the Court with . . . Venus and Serena Williams* (4–6). Illus. Series: Matt Christopher Sports Bio Bookshelf. 2002, Little, Brown paper $4.95 (0-316-13814-2). 128pp. A biography of the tennis greats, with information on their childhoods and family (and the influential role of their father) and details of important matches. (Rev: BL 9/1/02) [796.342]

Track and Field

OWENS, JESSE

3574 McKissack, Patricia, and Fredrick McKissack. *Jesse Owens: Olympic Star.* Rev. ed. (2–5). Series: Great African Americans. 2001, Enslow LB $14.95 (0-7660-1681-1). 32pp. This is an updated version of the 1992 book about the African American athlete whose four medals in the 1936 Olympics displeased Hitler, with factual updates, improved illustrations, and lists of print and Internet resources. (Rev: HBG 10/01; SLJ 8/01) [921]

Miscellaneous Sports

ARMSTRONG, LANCE

3575 Garcia, Kimberly. *Lance Armstrong* (3–4). Series: Real-Life Reader Biographies. 2002, Mitchell Lane LB $15.95 (1-58415-125-0). 32pp. Using a conversational style and black-and-white photographs, this is a biography of the Tour de France-winning cyclist who overcame cancer. (Rev: BL 9/15/02; SLJ 12/02) [921]

LEMIEUX, MARIO

3576 Rossiter, Sean. *Mario Lemieux* (4–8). Illus. Series: Hockey Heroes. 2001, Sterling $12.95 (1-55054-870-0). 64pp. A detailed look at the career of Pittsburgh Penguin Mario Lemieux. (Rev: BL 2/15/02) [796.962]

3577 Stewart, Mark. *Mario Lemieux: Own the Ice* (5–8). Illus. 2002, Millbrook LB $24.90 (0-7613-2555-7); paper $7.95 (0-7613-1687-6). 64pp. A readable biography of the ice hockey star, with photographs, statistics, and information about the athlete's personal life and work ethic. (Rev: BL 9/15/02; HBG 3/03) [796.962]

RIDDLES, LIBBY

3578 Riddles, Libby. *Storm Run: The Story of the First Woman to Win the Iditarod Sled Dog Race* (2–5). Illus. by Shannon Cartwright. 2002, Sasquatch $16.95 (1-57061-298-6). 48pp. Initially published in 1986, this first-person account of training and racing in the Iditarod, written by the first woman ever to win it, is bolstered by fresh illustrations. (Rev: BL 3/1/02; HBG 10/02) [798.8]

THOMPSON, JENNY

3579 Greenberg, Doreen, and Michael Greenberg. *Fast Lane to Victory: The Story of Jenny Thompson* (3–6). Illus. by Phil Velikan. Series: Anything You Can Do . . . New Sports Heroes for Girls. 2001, Wish paper $9.95 (1-930546-38-6). 141pp. Swimmer Jenny Thompson's determination to excel and the highlights of her career are presented here. (Rev: SLJ 8/01) [797.21]

WOODS, TIGER

3580 Roberts, Jeremy. *Tiger Woods* (5–8). Series: Biography. 2002, Lerner LB $25.26 (0-8225-0030-2). The story of the likable wonder boy of golf is told in text and pictures. (Rev: BL 4/1/02; HBG 10/02) [921]

3581 Sirimarco, Elizabeth. *Tiger Woods* (3–6). Series: Sports Heroes. 2000, Capstone LB $21.26 (0-7368-0581-8). 48pp. This brief biography focuses on Woods's athletic development from childhood and the key accomplishments in his career, with plenty of photographs and statistics. (Rev: SLJ 5/01) [921]

World Figures

Collective

3582 Billinghurst, Jane. *Growing Up Royal: Life in the Shadow of the British Throne* (4–7). Illus. 2001, Annick $22.95 (1-55037-623-3); paper $12.95 (1-55037-622-5). 176pp. A look at what it's like to be young and royal, with a focus on the lives of today's British royalty, with color photographs and interesting anecdotes. (Rev: BL 9/1/01; HBG 3/02; SLJ 11/01) [971.082]

3583 Brewster, Hugh, and Laurie Coulter. *To Be a Princess: The Fascinating Lives of Real Princesses* (4–8). Illus. 2001, HarperCollins LB $17.89 (0-06-000159-3). 64pp. Twelve real-life princesses, historical and contemporary, are featured here in chapter-length profiles with timelines, reproductions of museum portraits, and historical details. (Rev: BCCB 12/01; BL 12/1/01; HBG 3/02; SLJ 10/01) [940]

3584 Meltzer, Milton. *Ten Kings and the Worlds They Ruled* (5–8). Illus. by Bethanne Andersen. 2002, Scholastic $21.95 (0-439-31293-0). 144pp. Ten kings from around the world and across the ages are discussed in this attractive book that includes impressive portraits and other illustrations. Also use *Ten Queens* (1998). (Rev: BCCB 9/02; BL 7/02; HBG 10/02; SLJ 10/02) [920.02]

3585 Norris, Kathleen. *The Holy Twins: Benedict and Scholastica* (K–3). Illus. by Tomie dePaola. 2001, Putnam $16.99 (0-399-23424-1). 32pp. The abbot who became Saint Benedict and founded the Benedictine order is much better known than his twin sister Saint Scholastica, but the story of both siblings' lives is told here with illustrations that evoke Italy in the sixth century. (Rev: BCCB 7–8/01; BL 10/1/01; HBG 3/02; SLJ 9/01) [271]

3586 Sanderson, Ruth. *Saints: Lives and Illuminations* (4–6). Illus. 2003, Eerdmans $20.00 (0-8028-5220-3). 40pp. The lives and deaths of 40 saints, accompanied by painted portraits. (Rev: BL 2/1/03) [270]

3587 Sharp, Anne Wallace. *Daring Pirate Women* (5–8). Series: Biography. 2002, Lerner LB $25.26 (0-8225-0031-0). 112pp. Profiles are given of notorious and ruthless female pirates such as Anne Bonny, Mary Read, and Grace O'Malley. (Rev: BL 6/1–15/02; HBG 10/02; SLJ 8/02) [920]

3588 Shaw, Maura D. *Ten Amazing People: And How They Changed the World* (4–7). Illus. 2002, Skylight Paths $17.95 (1-893361-47-0). 48pp. Shaw presents ten well-illustrated biographies of 20th-century religious figures, each with timelines, a quotation, a glossary, and an emphasis on the individual's beliefs. (Rev: BL 10/1/02; HBG 3/03; SLJ 12/02) [200]

Individual

ARAFAT, YASIR

3589 Williams, Colleen Madonna Flood. *Yasir Arafat* (5–8). Illus. 2002, Chelsea House LB $23.95 (0-7910-6941-9); paper $9.95 (0-7910-7186-3). 112pp. The controversial PLO leader is shown as a man of conviction who struggled to balance the desires of his people and of the rest of the world and the resultant terrorism and corruption that plagued his reign. (Rev: BL 1/1–15/03; HBG 3/03; SLJ check) [956.9405]

BEGIN, MENACHEM

3590 Brackett, Virginia. *Menachem Begin* (5–8). Series: Major World Leaders. 2002, Chelsea LB $23.95 (0-7910-6946-X). 104pp. The life of the important Israeli prime minister who was in office when peace was declared between Israel and Egypt. (Rev: BL 1/1–15/03; SLJ 2/03) [921]

BIN LADEN, OSAMA

3591 Louis, Nancy. *Osama bin Laden* (4–7). Series: War on Terrorism. 2002, ABDO LB $16.95 (1-

57765-663-6). 48pp. A brief biography of the terrorist leader told through a matter-of-fact text and many color photographs. (Rev: BL 5/15/02; HBG 10/02) [921]

BLAIR, TONY

3592 Hinman, Bonnie. *Tony Blair* (5–8). Series: Major World Leaders. 2002, Chelsea LB $23.95 (0-7910-6939-7). 110pp. The life of the leader of the British Labour Party who in 1997 became the youngest prime minister in nearly 200 years. (Rev: BL 1/1–15/03) [921]

3593 Wilson, Wayne, and Jim Whiting. *Tony Blair* (3–6). 2002, Mitchell Lane LB $15.95 (1-58415-143-9). 32pp. Blair's colorful youth — as mild rebel and as aspiring rock singer — will draw readers into the story of his later achievements that puts an emphasis on his support of the United States. (Rev: SLJ 12/02) [921]

CABEZA DE VACA, ALVAR NUNEZ

3594 Menard, Valerie. *Alvar Nunez Cabeza de Vaca* (5–7). Series: Latinos in American History. 2002, Mitchell Lane LB $19.95 (1-58415-153-6). 48pp. A biography of the 16th-century Spanish nobleman who lived with Native Americans for eight years and who claimed Florida, Louisiana, and Texas for Spain. (Rev: BL 2/15/03) [921]

CASTRO, FIDEL

3595 Press, Petra. *Fidel Castro: An Unauthorized Biography* (5–7). Series: Heinemann Profiles. 2000, Heinemann LB $24.22 (1-57572-497-9). 56pp. An interesting introduction to the life of Cuba's dictator, with photographs that show urban and rural Cuba. (Rev: SLJ 6/01)

CHURCHILL, SIR WINSTON

3596 Ashworth, Leon. *Winston Churchill* (5–8). Illus. Series: British History Makers. 2002, Cherrytree $17.95 (1-84234-072-7). 32pp. A balanced look at the life and career of the British statesman, with a useful timeline and excellent illustrations. (Rev: SLJ 8/02)

COLUMBA, SAINT

3597 Brown, Don. *Across a Dark and Wild Sea* (K–4). Illus. 2002, Millbrook LB $22.90 (0-7613-2415-1). 32pp. The story of the sixth-century Irish monk and scholar Columcille, or Saint Columba, who founded a monastery on the Scottish island of Iona. (Rev: BCCB 5/02; BL 4/1/02*; HB 5–6/02; HBG 10/02; SLJ 5/02) [921]

CONFUCIUS

3598 Freedman, Russell. *Confucius: The Golden Rule* (4–8). Illus. by Frederic Clement. 2002, Scholastic $15.95 (0-439-13957-0). 48pp. This absorbing account of the life and philosophy of Confucius gives new insight into the character of the man who had so much influence on China. (Rev: BL 10/1/02*; HB 1–2/03; HBG 3/03; SLJ 9/02*) [181]

DALAI LAMA

3599 Gibb, Chris. *The Dalai Lama* (4–6). Series: Famous Lives. 2003, Raintree Steck-Vaughn LB $27.12 (0-7398-5520-4). 48pp. The story of Tibet's exiled political and spiritual leader and of his teachings of peace and civil disobedience. (Rev: BL 2/15/03) [921]

DIANA, PRINCESS OF WALES

3600 Oleksy, Walter. *Princess Diana* (5–8). Series: People in the News. 2001, Lucent LB $27.45 (1-56006-579-6). Using a clear text, many quotes, and good photographs, this is the story of the life and tragic death of Britain's beloved princess. (Rev: BL 4/1/02; HBG 3/01) [921]

ELIZABETH I, QUEEN OF ENGLAND

3601 Havelin, Kate. *Elizabeth I* (5–8). Series: Biography. 2002, Lerner LB $25.26 (0-8225-0029-9). 112pp. The story of one of the most powerful queens in history and how she learned, at an early age, the politics of survival. (Rev: BL 6/1–15/02; HBG 10/02; SLJ 7/02) [921]

ELIZABETH II, QUEEN OF ENGLAND

3602 Barton-Wood, Sara. *Queen Elizabeth II: Monarch of Our Times* (4–6). Illus. Series: Famous Lives. 2001, Raintree Steck-Vaughn LB $18.98 (0-7398-4430-X). 48pp. An affectionate look at the life of Queen Elizabeth II, from childhood through her Golden Jubilee. (Rev: BL 1/1–15/02; HBG 10/02; SLJ 3/02) [941.085]

3603 Malam, John. *Queen Elizabeth II* (2–4). Series: Tell Me About: Kings and Queens. 2002, Evans Brothers LB $13.95 (0-237-52394-9). 22pp. This brief account of the queen's life and reign includes plenty of photographs. (Rev: SLJ 10/02) [921]

FOX, VICENTE

3604 Paprocki, Sherry Beck. *Vicente Fox* (5–8). Series: Major World Leaders. 2002, Chelsea LB $23.95 (0-7910-6944-3). 104pp. The story of the man who became president of Mexico in July 2000, the first opposition candidate to gain presidential office in more than 70 years. (Rev: BL 1/1–15/03) [921]

FRANK, ANNE

3605 Alagna, Magdalena. *Anne Frank: Young Voice of the Holocaust* (5–8). Series: Holocaust Biographies. 2001, Rosen LB $19.95 (0-8239-3373-3). 112pp. This book describes Anne's childhood, her time spent in hiding, her diary, and her life in the concentration camps. (Rev: BL 10/15/01) [921]

3606 Lee, Carol Ann. *Anne Frank's Story: Her Life Retold for Children* (4–6). 2002, Troll paper $4.95 (0-8167-7427-7). 105pp. Anne's brief life is chronicled here in clear text with black-and-white photographs, a letter to a pen pal, and information on memorials around the world. (Rev: SLJ 11/02) [921]

GANDHI, MAHATMA

3607 Claybourne, Anna. *Gandhi* (4–6). Series: Famous Lives. 2003, Raintree Steck-Vaughn LB $27.12 (0-7398-5521-2). 48pp. A brief biography of the Indian leader, his triumphs and hardships, and the story of the nonviolent movement he led. (Rev: BCCB 12/01; BL 2/15/03) [921]

3608 Demi. *Gandhi* (3–6). Illus. 2001, Simon & Schuster $19.95 (0-689-84149-3). 40pp. A moving look at a remarkable man that brings to life his character and the time in which he lived. (Rev: BCCB 12/01; BL 6/1–15/01; HB 9–10/01; HBG 3/02; SLJ 8/01) [954.03]

3609 Heinrichs, Ann. *Mahatma Gandhi* (4–7). Series: Trailblazers of the Modern World. 2001, World Almanac LB $26.60 (0-8368-5064-5). 48pp. A clear and concise biography that focuses on Gandhi's personal life as well as his struggles to free India and belief in nonviolence. (Rev: SLJ 1/02) [921]

HUSSEIN, SADDAM

3610 Shields, Charles J. *Saddam Hussein* (5–8). Illus. Series: Major World Leaders. 2002, Chelsea LB $23.95 (0-7910-6943-5). 112pp. An account of the Iraqi leader's regime, with information on the Iran-Iraq and Persian Gulf wars and on United Nations sanctions and weapons inspections. (Rev: BL 2/1/03; HBG 3/03) [956.7044]

JOAN OF ARC

3611 Tompert, Ann. *Joan of Arc: Heroine of France* (1–4). Illus. by Michael Garland. 2003, Boyds Mills $15.95 (1-59078-009-4). 32pp. This solid account puts the events in Joan's life in clear historical context. (Rev: BL 3/1/03; SLJ 3/03) [944]

JUANA INES DE LA CRUZ, SISTER

3612 Mora, Pat. *A Library for Juana: The World of Sor Juana Ines* (1–3). Illus. by Beatriz Vidal. 2002, Knopf $15.95 (0-375-80643-1). 40pp. This is an absorbing account of the inspiring life of Sor Juana Ines, a child prodigy born in Mexico in the 17th century who became a nun and internationally known scholar and poet. (Rev: BL 11/15/02; HB 11–12/02; HBG 3/03; SLJ 11/02) [861]

KORCZAK, JANUSZ

3613 Adler, David A. *A Hero and the Holocaust: The Story of Janusz Korczak and His Children* (3–5). Illus. by Bill Farnsworth. 2002, Holiday $16.95 (0-8234-1548-1). 32pp. The story of Janusz Korczak's efforts to care for young Jewish children in the Warsaw ghetto and on the trip to the Treblinka death camp, presented in memorable illustrations and a simple text, accompanied by quotes from his diary. (Rev: BL 12/1/02; HBG 3/03; SLJ 3/03) [943.8]

LAFAYETTE, MARQUIS DE

3614 Payan, Gregory. *Marquis de Lafayette: French Hero of the American Revolution* (4–7). Illus. Series: Library of American Lives and Times. 2001, Rosen LB $23.95 (0-8239-5733-0). 112pp. Payan introduces the French general who assisted the American cause, with illustrations, maps, and other aids to understanding his times. (Rev: BL 10/15/01) [944.04]

MANDELA, NELSON

3615 McDonough, Yona Zeldis. *Peaceful Protest: The Life of Nelson Mandela* (2–5). Illus. by Malcah Zeldis. 2002, Walker LB $17.85 (0-8027-8823-8). 40pp. An appealing, readable biography of the anti-apartheid activist that uses folk-art illustrations, including a compelling portrayal of Mandela's cell. (Rev: BL 11/15/02; HBG 3/03; SLJ 10/02) [986.06]

MOHAMMED

3616 Marston, Elsa. *Muhammad of Mecca: Prophet of Islam* (4–6). Series: Book Report Biographies. 2001, Watts LB $22.00 (0-531-15554-4); paper $6.95 (0-531-15554-4). 28pp. A concise, well-researched biography of the seventh-century prophet and founder of one of the world's great religions. (Rev: BL 8/1/01; SLJ 9/01) [921]

NIGHTINGALE, FLORENCE

3617 Armentrout, David, and Patricia Armentrout. *Florence Nightingale* (2–4). Illus. Series: People Who Made a Difference. 200X, Rourke LB $18.60 (1-58952-053-X). 24pp. A simple introduction for younger readers to the life of nursing pioneer Florence Nightingale. (Rev: BL 1/1–15/02; SLJ 3/02) [610.73]

3618 Barnham, Kay. *Florence Nightingale* (4–6). Series: Famous Lives. 2003, Raintree Steck-Vaughn LB $27.12 (0-7398-5523-9). 48pp. The inspirational story of the gallant nurse who treated the wounded soldiers on the front lines during the Crimean War. (Rev: BL 2/15/03) [921]

PAHLAVI, MOHAMMED REZA

3619 Barth, Linda. *Mohammed Reza Pahlavi* (5–8). Series: Major World Leaders. 2002, Chelsea LB $23.95 (0-7910-6948-6). 104pp. An engrossing biography of the last Shah of Iran who ruled during a tumultuous time in the Middle East. (Rev: BL 1/1–15/03) [921]

PUTIN, VLADIMIR

3620 Shields, Charles J. *Vladimir Putin* (5–8). Illus. Series: Major World Leaders. 2002, Chelsea LB $23.95 (0-7910-6945-1). 112pp. Putin's family life, ambitions to be a spy, accession to power, and role today are all covered in this fine biography. (Rev: BL 2/1/03; HBG 3/03; SLJ 3/03) [947.086]

RINGELBLUM, EMMANUEL

3621 Beyer, Mark. *Emmanuel Ringelblum: Historian of the Warsaw Ghetto* (5–8). Illus. Series: Holocaust Biographies. 2001, Rosen LB $26.50 (0-8239-3375-X). 112pp. This true story of a man who recorded events in the Warsaw Ghetto during the Holocaust includes black-and-white photographs. Also use *Mordechai Anielewicz: Hero of the Warsaw Uprising* (2001), about the young man who fought bravely to defend the ghetto against the Nazis. (Rev: BL 10/15/01) [940.53]

SADAT, ANWAR

3622 Kras, Sara Louise. *Anwar Sadat* (5–8). Series: Major World Leaders. 2002, Chelsea LB $23.95 (0-7910-6949-4). 112pp. An absorbing account of the life of the famous Egyptian leader who shared the 1978 Nobel Peace Prize with Israeli Prime Minister Menachem Begin. (Rev: BL 1/1–15/03; HBG 3/03) [921]

SAINT THERESE OF LISIEUX

3623 Driscoll, Chris. *God's Little Flower: The Story of St. Therese of Lisieux* (PS–3). Illus. by Patrick Kelley. 2001, Ambassador $13.95 (1-929039-05-0). 32pp. A simple, illustrated story of the little girl who became a saint. (Rev: BL 10/1/01; HBG 10/01) [270]

SALADIN

3624 Stanley, Diane. *Saladin: Noble Prince of Islam* (5–8). Illus. 2002, HarperCollins LB $18.89 (0-688-17136-2). 48pp. A lavish picture-book biography of a noted Muslim commander during the Crusades that includes good background information on history, geography, and religion. (Rev: BL 9/1/02; HB 1–2/03; HBG 3/03; SLJ 9/02) [956]

SILVA, MARINA

3625 Hildebrant, Ziporah. *Marina Silva: Defending Rainforest Communities in Brazil* (5–8). Series: Women Changing the World. 2001, Feminist Pr. $19.95 (1-55861-292-9). 112pp. Though battling a serious illness, this gallant women, once a leader of the native Amazonians, has become a leading figure in protecting the forests of Brazil. (Rev: BL 12/15/01) [921]

SOYER, ALEXIS

3626 Arnold, Ann. *The Adventurous Chef: Alexis Soyer* (3–6). Illus. 2002, Farrar $17.00 (0-374-31665-1). 40pp. A fascinating, well-illustrated biography that introduces a famous 19th-century chef and innovator who cooked for the rich but also strove to improve nutrition for the poor, the hungry, and the military. (Rev: BL 12/15/02; HB 11–12/02; HBG 3/03; SLJ 10/02) [641.5]

TERESA, MOTHER

3627 Dils, Tracey E. *Mother Teresa* (4–8). Series: Women of Achievement. 2001, Chelsea LB $21.95 (0-7910-5887-5). 112pp. An absorbing account of the humanitarian's life from her childhood in Albania through her early years in India and her international work with the Missionaries of Charity. (Rev: HBG 3/02; SLJ 11/01) [921]

3628 Ransom, Candice F. *Mother Teresa* (1–3). Illus. by Elaine Verstraete. Series: On My Own Biography. 2001, Carolrhoda LB $19.93 (1-57505-441-8). 48pp. Mother Teresa's life from childhood and devotion to charitable work are presented in easy-reading text and full-page, realistic art. (Rev: HBG 10/01; SLJ 7/01) [921]

WILLIAM, PRINCE

3629 Dougherty, Terry. *Prince William* (5–8). Series: People in the News. 2001, Lucent LB $27.45 (1-56006-982-1). Using many quotes, good photographs, and an interesting text, this is a biography of the royal Prince Charming. (Rev: BL 4/1/02) [921]

3630 Landau, Elaine. *Prince William: W.O.W., William of Wales* (4–6). Illus. Series: Gateway Biography. 2002, Millbrook LB $22.90 (0-7613-2120-9). 48pp. A competent biography that explores the life of the very popular prince and his family through text and many color photographs. (Rev: BL 4/15/02; HBG 10/02) [921]

XIAOPING, DENG

3631 Stewart, Whitney. *Deng Xiaoping: Leader in a Changing China* (4–7). Series: Lerner Biographies. 2001, Lerner LB $25.26 (0-8225-4962-X). 128pp. An accessible biography of the most powerful man in China from the 1970s until his death, with details of how his reputation was tarnished by the Tiananmen Square massacre. (Rev: BL 9/15/01; HBG 10/01; SLJ 7/01) [921]

The Arts and Language

Art and Architecture

General and Miscellaneous

3632 Andrews-Goebel, Nancy. *The Pot That Juan Built* (2–4). Illus. by David Diaz. 2002, Lee & Low $16.95 (1-58430-038-8). 32pp. This almost-multimedia introduction to the work of Mexican potter Juan Quezada allows the reader to choose between rhyme, prose, illustration, and photography that all describe facets of the artist's life and work. (Rev: BL 9/15/02; HBG 3/03; SLJ 9/02*) [738]

3633 Burleigh, Robert. *Earth from Above for Young Readers* (4 Up). Photos by Yann Arthus-Bertrand. Illus. by David Giraudon. 2002, Abrams $12.95 (0-8109-3486-8). 77pp. Large aerial views show landscapes around the world, from remote areas of natural beauty to New York's Yankee Stadium. (Rev: HBG 3/03; SLJ 1/03) [779]

3634 Chaplik, Dorothy. *Latin American Arts and Cultures* (5–8). Illus. 2001, Davis $26.95 (0-87192-547-8). 128pp. An encompassing look at Latin American art, architecture, and culture, from pre-Columbian to present-day, complete with pronunciation guide and captioned reproductions or photographs on each page. (Rev: BL 11/1/01) [700.9]

3635 Cressy, Judith. *Can You Find It?* (2–5). Illus. 2002, Abrams $15.95 (0-8109-3279-2). 48pp. Readers are challenged to search for details (bows, cats, flowers, and other items) within artwork from New York City's Metropolitan Museum of Art. (Rev: BL 2/15/03; HBG 3/03; SLJ 1/03) [759]

3636 Fritz, Jean. *Leonardo's Horse* (4–7). Illus. by Hudson Talbott. 2001, Putnam $16.99 (0-399-23576-0). 40pp. The story of a Leonardo da Vinci sculpture that was begun in 1493 and finally completed — thanks to the efforts of Charles Dent — in 1999, along with biographical information about da Vinci and examples of his work. (Rev: BCCB 10/01; BL 10/15/01; HB 9–10/01; HBG 3/02; SLJ 9/01) [730]

3637 Gaff, Jackie. *1920–40: Realism and Surrealism* (4–8). Series: 20th Century Art. 2001, Gareth Stevens LB $22.60 (0-8368-2850-X). 32pp. This appealing overview of art movements — mainly in Europe — offers accessible text, high-quality color reproductions, and black-and-white photographs of important individuals. Also use *1900–10: New Ways of Seeing* and *1910–20: The Birth of Abstract Art* (both 2001). (Rev: HBG 10/01; SLJ 7/01) [708]

3638 Johmann, Carol A. *Skyscrapers!* (3–6). Illus. by Michael Kline. Series: Kaleidoscope Kids. 2001, Williamson paper $10.95 (1-885593-50-3). 96pp. Cartoonlike drawings and black-and-white photographs are including in this appealing and informative look at skyscrapers, their history, and the structural and design challenges they pose, which also includes a number of related activities. (Rev: BL 12/15/01; SLJ 3/02) [720]

3639 Knapp, Ruthie, and Janice Lehmberg. *Modern Art* (5–9). Series: Off the Wall Museum Guides for Kids. 2001, Davis paper $9.95 (0-87192-458-6). 72pp. A lively and colorful survey of 20th-century art including examples from expressionists, cubists, surrealists, and pop artists. (Rev: BL 8/1/01) [709]

3640 MacDonald, Fiona. *Design* (3–5). Illus. Series: Culture Encyclopedia. 2002, Mason Crest LB $18.95 (1-59084-476-9). 40pp. The importance of design in such areas as fashion, food, technology, and architecture is discussed in this introduction to style around the world. (Rev: SLJ 3/03)

3641 Mason, Antony. *Art* (3–5). Illus. Series: Culture Encyclopedia. 2002, Mason Crest LB $18.95 (1-59084-475-0). 40pp. An introduction to art over the centuries that looks at all kinds of drawing, painting, sculpture, photography, commercial art, and so forth. (Rev: SLJ 3/03)

3642 Raczka, Bob. *No One Saw: Ordinary Things Through the Eyes of an Artist* (PS–3). Illus. 2002, Millbrook LB $23.90 (0-7613-2370-8). 32pp. Simple verse introduces young readers to the singular viewpoints of modern artists including Georgia

O'Keefe and Vincent Van Gogh. (Rev: BL 1/1–15/02; HBG 10/02; SLJ 1/02) [759.06]

3643 Rubin, Susan Goldman. *Degas and the Dance: The Painter and the Petits Rats, Perfecting Their Art* (3–5). Illus. 2002, Abrams $17.95 (0-8109-0567-1). 32pp. This volume, with excellent reproductions of preliminary sketches as well as finished works, will attract budding artists and budding ballet dancers; the "petits rats" are young dancers who posed for the painter. (Rev: BL 12/1/02; HBG 3/03; SLJ 12/02) [759.4]

3644 Rubin, Susan Goldman. *There Goes the Neighborhood: Ten Buildings People Loved to Hate* (4–7). 2001, Holiday $18.95 (0-8234-1435-3). 96pp. Many buildings create an uproar from their earliest design but later become nostalgic favorites, among them the Eiffel Tower and Guggenheim Museum, which are profiled here in an absorbing, colorful account that discusses materials and methods of construction. (Rev: BL 8/01; HBG 3/02; SLJ 9/01) [720]

3645 Shuter, Jane. *Ancient Chinese Art* (4–6). Illus. Series: Art in History. 2001, Heinemann LB $23.58 (1-58810-090-1). 32pp. Painting, calligraphy, bronzes, terracotta, and lacquer and jade are among the art forms featured. (Rev: HBG 3/02; SLJ 12/01)

3646 Teitelbaum, Michael. *The Story of Spider-Man* (3–4). Illus. Series: Dorling Kindersley Readers. 2001, DK LB $12.95 (0-7894-7920-6); paper $3.95 (0-7894-7921-4). 48pp. Teitelbaum tells the story of Spider-Man's creation, with sidebar features, photographs, drawings, and reproductions of the comic strips. (Rev: HBG 3/02; SLJ 2/02) [741.5]

3647 Warhola, James. *Uncle Andy's: A Faabbulous Visit with Andy Warhol* (K–3). Illus. 2003, Putnam $16.99 (0-399-23869-7). 32pp. A young boy (the author as a child) enjoys visiting his eccentric artist uncle, Andy Warhol, and is inspired by his work. (Rev: BL 2/15/03; HB 3–4/03) [700]

3648 Wenzel, Angela. *Edgar Degas: Dance Like a Butterfly* (4–6). Trans. from German by Rosie Jackson. Series: Adventures in Art. 2002, Prestel $14.95 (3-7913-2736-4). 28pp. Degas's ballet paintings are presented in a way that encourages readers to appreciate movement, light, and color. (Rev: HBG 3/03; SLJ 11/02)

3649 Wolfe, Gillian. *Look! Zoom in on Art!* (2–5). Illus. 2002, Oxford $19.95 (0-19-521912-0). 40pp. Readers are encouraged to look at a number of paintings in a new way and to make art of their own. (Rev: BL 9/1/02; HBG 3/03) [750]

The Ancient World

3650 Knapp, Ruthie, and Janice Lehmberg. *Greek and Roman Art* (5–9). Series: Off the Wall Museum Guides for Kids. 2001, Davis paper $9.95 (0-87192-549-4). 72pp. Using many photographs, this account highlights a number of art objects, explains relevant terms associated with them, describes their uses, and gives details on Greek and Roman culture. (Rev: BL 8/1/01) [936]

Native American Arts and Crafts

3651 Press, Petra. *Native American Art* (4–6). Illus. Series: Art in History. 2001, Heinemann LB $23.58 (1-58810-092-8). 32pp. Rock art, stone sculpture, sand painting, textiles, and basketry are among the kinds of art featured here. (Rev: HBG 3/02; SLJ 12/01)

3652 Wallace, Mary. *Make Your Own Inuksuk* (2–6). Photos by author. Illus. 2001, Firefly $18.95 (1-894379-09-8); paper $8.95 (1-894379-10-1). 32pp. Directions for making your own stone sculpture in the traditional Inuit fashion. (Rev: HBG 10/01; SLJ 5/01)

United States

3653 Morrison, Taylor. *The Buffalo Nickel* (2–4). Illus. 2002, Houghton $16.00 (0-618-10855-6). 32pp. The story of the artist who designed the buffalo nickel, with information about coin production. (Rev: BL 5/15/02; HBG 10/02; SLJ 4/02) [730]

Communication

General and Miscellaneous

3654 Hauser, Jill Frankel. *Wow! I'm Reading! Fun Activities to Make Reading Happen* (PS–3). Illus. by Stan Jaskiel. Series: A Williamson Little Hands Book. 2000, Williamson paper $12.95 (1-885593-41-4). 141pp. A collection of activities designed to smooth the path to reading, with references to recommended picture books and bright black-and-white cartoons. (Rev: SLJ 4/01) [372.41]

3655 Hegedus, Alannah, and Kaitlin Rainey. *Bleeps and Blips to Rocket Ships: Great Inventions in Communications* (5–9). Illus. by Bill Slavin. 2001, Tundra paper $17.95 (0-88776-452-5). 88pp. This is a fact-packed and appealing look at the field of communications, with information on history and inventors and inventions as well as suggested activities. (Rev: SLJ 8/01) [609.71]

3656 Rovetch, Lissa. *Ook the Book and Other Silly Rhymes* (PS–1). Illus. by Shannon McNeill. 2001, Chronicle $12.95 (0-8118-2660-0). A humorous introduction to vowel sounds and the appearance of letters that will appeal to beginning readers. (Rev: HBG 10/01; SLJ 8/01) [428.1]

Codes and Ciphers

3657 Adams, Simon. *Code Breakers: From Hieroglyphs to Hackers* (4–8). Series: Secret Worlds. 2002, DK $14.95 (0-7894-8529-X); paper $5.95 (0-7894-8530-3). 96pp. A wealth of fascinating information is packed into this book that traces code breaking from the Rosetta Stone to the present world of computers. (Rev: BL 8/02; HBG 10/02) [652]

3658 Dickson, Louise. *Lu and Clancy's Secret Languages* (1–4). Illus. by Pat Cupples. 2001, Kids Can $14.95 (1-55337-025-2); paper $6.95 (1-55074-695-

2). 40pp. Dog detectives Lu and Clancy hone their knowledge of language (Pig Latin, pictograms, invisible ink, and so forth). Also use *Lu and Clancy's Spy Stuff* (2001). (Rev: HBG 10/01; SLJ 8/01) [652.8]

Flags

3659 Ferry, Joseph. *The American Flag* (5–7). Series: American Symbols and Their Meanings. 2002, Mason Crest LB $18.95 (1-59084-026-7). 48pp. Designs that preceded the familiar flag accompany material on Betsy Ross and Francis Scott Key, illustrations of important flag raisings, and discussion of proper use and treatment of the flag, all in a package that will appeal to reluctant readers. (Rev: SLJ 4/02) [929.9]

3660 Smith, Whitney. *Flag Lore of All Nations* (4–6). Illus. 2001, Millbrook $29.90 (0-7613-1753-8). 112pp. One hundred and ninety-one flags are represented in this book. (Rev: BL 9/1/01; SLJ 9/01) [929.9]

Language and Languages

3661 Stojic, Manya. *Hello World! Greetings in 42 Languages Around the Globe!* (K–2). Illus. 2002, Scholastic $14.95 (0-439-36202-4). 40pp. Readers learn how to pronounce 42 words for hello, each introduced by a simple, bold painting of a child from the country and the name of the language concerned. (Rev: BL 12/1/02; HBG 3/03; SLJ 12/02) [413]

3662 Takahashi, Peter X. *Jimi's Book of Japanese: A Motivating Method to Learn Japanese* (3–6). Illus. by Yumie Toka. 2002, PB&J paper $16.95 (0-9723247-0-4). 72pp. A book featuring the Japanese characters (*kana*) and how to write them, for beginning speakers and writers of the language. (Rev: BL 2/15/03) [495.6]

Reading, Speaking, and Writing

Books, Printing, Libraries, and Schools

3663 McElroy, Lisa Tucker, and Abigail Jane Cobb. *Meet My Grandmother: She's a Children's Book Author* (1–4). Photos by Joel Benjamin. 2001, Millbrook LB $22.90 (0-7613-1972-7). 31pp. Vicki Cobb's 9-year-old granddaughter describes her mother's work and how books are created and published. (Rev: HBG 3/02; SLJ 8/01) [509.2]

3664 Wu, Dana Y. *Our Libraries* (2–4). Series: I Know America. 2001, Millbrook LB $22.90 (0-7613-1856-9). 48pp. The Dewey decimal system, the Library of Congress, Banned Books Week, and even MARC records are among the topics covered in this comprehensive overview of libraries. (Rev: HBG 10/01; SLJ 7/01) [027.073]

Signs and Symbols

3665 Bateman, Teresa. *Red, White, Blue and Uncle Who? The Stories Behind Some of America's Patriotic Symbols* (3–6). Illus. by John O'Brien. 2001, Holiday $15.95 (0-8234-1285-7). 64pp. The meaning of patriotic symbols such as Uncle Sam, war memorials, and Mount Rushmore is explained with surprising detail in simple, appealing, and often humorous terms, enhanced by sprightly line drawings. (Rev: BL 12/15/01; HBG 10/02; SLJ 11/01) [929.9]

3666 Mignon, Philippe. *Labyrinths: Can You Escape from the 26 Letters of the Alphabet?* (2–5). Illus. 2002, Firefly $14.95 (1-55297-559-2); paper $9.95 (1-55297-579-7). 64pp. A complex and attractive combination of alphabet book, mazes, poetry, and intriguing tidbits both ancient and modern. (Rev: BL 1/1–15/03; HBG 3/03; SLJ 12/02) [843]

3667 Milich, Zoran. *City Signs* (PS–K). Illus. 2002, Kids Can $15.95 (1-55337-003-1). 32pp. A photographic look at worded signs that will leave preschoolers proud of their "reading" skills. (Rev: BL 10/15/02; HB 1–2/03; HBG 3/03) [659.13]

3668 Votry, Kim, and Curt Waller. *Baby's First Signs* (PS–2). Illus. 2001, Gallaudet Univ. $6.95 (1-56368-114-5). Basic words are introduced in sign language, showing a child signing and clear directions for signing the word yourself. Also use *More Baby's First Signs* (2001). (Rev: SLJ 2/02) [419]

Words and Grammar

3669 Agee, Jon. *Palindromania!* (3–7). Illus. 2002, Farrar $15.51 (0-374-35730-7). 112pp. Hundreds of clever and amusing palindromes are presented

beside black-and-white drawings. (Rev: BL 10/15/02; HB 9–10/02; HBG 3/03; SLJ 11/02) [793.734]

3670 Beinstein, Phoebe. *Dora's Book of Words / Libro de Palabras de Dora* (PS–2). Trans. by Argentina Palacios Ziegler. Illus. by the Thompson Bros. 2003, Simon & Schuster $10.95 (0-689-85626-1). Dora the Explorer looks at some everyday words loved by children in a format that allows the reader to switch from English to Spanish by pulling on a tab. (Rev: SLJ 3/03)

3671 Cleary, Brian P. *Dearly, Nearly, Insincerely: What Is an Adverb?* (2–4). Illus. by Brian Gable. Series: Words Are CATegorical. 2003, Carolrhoda LB $14.95 (0-87614-924-7). Energetic illustrations accompany a bouncy rhyming text that introduces adverbs of all kinds. (Rev: SLJ 3/03)

3672 Cleary, Brian P. *To Root, to Toot, to Parachute: What Is a Verb?* (K–3). Illus. by Jenya Prosmitsky. 2001, Carolrhoda $14.95 (1-57505-403-5). 32pp. A delightful, lively introduction to verbs with action-packed illustrations. (Rev: BL 4/15/01; HBG 10/01; SLJ 7/01) [428.2]

3673 Cleary, Brian P. *Under, Over, By the Clover: What Is a Preposition?* (2–4). Illus. by Brian Gable. 2002, Carolrhoda $14.95 (1-57505-524-4). 32pp. A pack of crazy-colored cartoonlike animals and rhyming text teach younger readers all about prepositions. (Rev: BL 3/1/02; HBG 10/02; SLJ 6/02) [428.2]

3674 Lederer, Richard. *The Circus of Words: Acrobatic Anagrams, Parading Palindromes, Wonderful Words on a Wire, and More Lively Letter Play* (5–8). Illus. by Dave Morice. 2001, Chicago Review paper $12.95 (1-55652-380-7). 143pp. Lovers of words will find lots of entertainment in this selection of challenging exercises. (Rev: SLJ 8/01) [428.1]

3675 Leedy, Loreen, and Pat Street. *There's a Frog in My Throat: 440 Animal Sayings a Little Bird Told Me* (2–5). Illus. by Loreen Leedy. 2003, Holiday $16.95 (0-8234-1774-3). 32pp. An amusing romp through animal-related expressions such as "social butterfly" and "barrel of monkeys." (Rev: BL 3/15/03*) [428.1]

3676 Terban, Marvin. *Building Your Vocabulary* (4–8). Illus. Series: Scholastic Guides. 2002, Scholastic $12.95 (0-439-28561-5). 188pp. In addition to techniques for increasing vocabulary, Terban discusses etymology and how to use a dictionary and thesaurus, giving clear, often entertaining examples throughout. (Rev: SLJ 8/02)

3677 Thomson, Ruth. *A First Thesaurus* (K–3). Illus. 2003, Thameside LB $24.25 (1-931983-08-9). 64pp. Pictures and words are combined to introduce youngsters to the thesaurus; children are encouraged to select alternative words from the illustrated choices provided. Also use *A First Word Bank* (2003). (Rev: BL 12/1/02) [423]

3678 Umstatter, Jack. *Where Words Come From* (4–8). 2002, Watts LB $34.00 (0-531-11902-5). 160pp. Etymology is brought to life through this accessible and often entertaining introduction to a variety of words and their evolution. (Rev: SLJ 7/02)

Writing and Speaking

3679 Englart, Mindi Rose. *Newspapers from Start to Finish* (3–5). Series: Made in the USA. 2001, Blackbirch LB $17.95 (1-56711-484-9). 32pp. The whole manufacturing process — from paper production to the finished edition — is covered in this concise, well-illustrated account. (Rev: BL 3/15/02; HBG 3/02) [070.1]

3680 Fletcher, Ralph. *Poetry Matters: Writing a Poem from the Inside Out* (4–7). 2002, HarperTrophy paper $4.95 (0-380-79703-8). 128pp. A how-to book for young poets, with ideas on how to make images and "music" with words. (Rev: BL 5/15/02; HBG 10/02; SLJ 2/02*) [808.1]

3681 Hambleton, Vicki, and Cathleen Greenwood. *So, You Wanna Be a Writer? How to Write, Get Published, and Maybe Even Make It Big!* (5–9). Illus. by Laura Eldridge and Corey Mistretta. Series: So, You Wanna Be. 2001, Beyond Words paper $8.95 (1-58270-043-5). 160pp. Practical advice is offered in straightforward text with lots of examples, sample letters, interviews with published writers, details of writing contests, and lists of magazines that accept submissions from young writers. (Rev: SLJ 10/01) [808]

3682 Holbrook, Sara. *Wham! It's a Poetry Jam: Discovering Performance Poetry* (2–5). 2002,
Boyds Mills paper $9.95 (1-59078-011-6). 55pp. Holbrook includes some of her poems in this guide to performing poetry — how to move, project your voice, express emotion, and so forth. (Rev: HBG 10/02; SLJ 5/02)

3683 *Kids' Letters to Harry Potter* (3–6). Ed. by Bill Adler. 2001, Carroll & Graf $18.00 (0-7867-0890-5). 200pp. Fans of the Harry Potter novels share thoughts on the books and characters through letters to the boy wizard. (Rev: BL 11/1/01; SLJ 11/01) [826]

3684 Potter, Giselle. *The Year I Didn't Go to School* (1–3). Illus. 2002, Simon & Schuster $16.95 (0-689-84730-0). 40pp. The author remembers the year she was seven, when she toured Italy with her family's puppet theater, using excerpts from the journal she kept at the time and appealing illustrations of typical Italian scenes. (Rev: BCCB 10/02; BL 11/1/02; SLJ 11/02) [818]

3685 Veljkovic, Peggy, and Arthur Schwartz, eds. *Writing from the Heart: Young People Share Their Wisdom* (5 Up). 2001, Templeton Foundation paper $12.95 (1-890151-48-3). 189pp. A collection of the best essays by young people that have been submitted to the Laws of Life program since it began in 1987. (Rev: SLJ 6/01) [170]

3686 Wong, Janet S. *You Have to Write* (2–4). Illus. by Teresa Flavin. 2002, Simon & Schuster $17.00 (0-689-83409-8). 40pp. Wong uses poetic text and a photo album approach to spur young people to think about writing assignments in new ways. (Rev: BL 7/02; HBG 3/03; SLJ 7/02) [811]

Music

General

3687 Barber, Nicola. *Music: An A–Z Guide* (4–8). Illus. 2001, Watts LB $32.50 (0-531-11898-3). 128pp. Basic information on everything from performers and instruments to various forms of music is presented with illustrations and sidebar features. (Rev: SLJ 9/01) [780]

3688 Collins, David R. *Dr. Shinichi Suzuki: Teaching Music from the Heart* (4–8). 2001, Morgan Reynolds LB $20.95 (1-883846-49-8). 112pp. This account covers Suzuki's childhood, his interest in music, and his development of a successful method of teaching music, especially the violin, to young children. (Rev: BL 12/15/01; HBG 3/02; SLJ 4/02) [780]

3689 Ench, Rick, and Jay Cravath. *North American Indian Music* (5–7). Illus. Series: Watts Library — Indians of the Americas. 2002, Watts LB $24.00 (0-531-11772-3); paper $8.95 (0-531-16230-3). 64pp. This title looks at the importance of music in the rituals of North American Indian tribes and describes the forms of beat, rhythm, and melody, with illustrations, a glossary, bibliography, and timeline. (Rev: BL 7/02) [782.62]

3690 Ganeri, Anita, and Nicola Barber. *The Young Person's Guide to the Opera: With Music from the Great Operas on CD* (4–8). 2001, Harcourt $25.00 (0-15-216498-7). 55pp. A bright and friendly introduction to opera that provides historical information and profiles some of the important singers and opera houses, with a companion CD of vocal and instrumental tracks. (Rev: HBG 3/02; SLJ 12/01)

3691 Haskins, James. *One Nation Under a Groove: Rap Music and Its Roots* (4–9). 2000, Hyperion $15.99 (0-7868-0478-5). 166pp. Students seeking information on rap's musical roots will find well-researched details in this volume that includes lyrics and photographs. (Rev: BL 2/15/01; HBG 10/01; SLJ 4/01) [782.421649]

3692 Ingus, Toyomi. *I See the Rhythm* (5–8). Illus. by Michele Wood. 1998, Children's $15.95 (0-892391-51-0). A celebration of African American music of all kinds, in words, pictures, and songs. (Rev: BL 2/15/03)

3693 Kirk, Daniel. *Go!* (PS–3). Illus. 2001, Hyperion $18.99 (0-7868-0305-3). 48pp. This collection of fast-moving poems about motion combines the attraction of various kinds of transport, humor, lively illustration, and a tuneful CD. (Rev: BL 12/15/01; HBG 3/02; SLJ 12/01) [782.42]

3694 Levine, Robert. *The Story of the Orchestra* (5–7). Illus. by Meredith Hamilton. 2001, Black Dog & Leventhal $19.95 (1-57912-148-9). 96pp. Orchestra Bob introduces young readers to orchestra history, famous conductors and their eras, and instruments, in a guided tour that includes amusing cartoons, illustrations, and links to selections on the accompanying CD. (Rev: BL 12/15/01; SLJ 9/01) [784.2]

3695 Morris, Neil. *Music and Dance* (5–8). Illus. by Antonella Pastorelli. Series: Discovering World Cultures. 2001, Crabtree paper $8.06 (0-7787-0249-9). 38pp. A heavily illustrated overview of musical instruments and forms of dance around the world. (Rev: SLJ 5/02) [780]

3696 Rivera, Ursula. *The Supremes* (4–8). Illus. Series: Rock and Roll Hall of Famers. 2002, Rosen LB $29.25 (0-8239-3527-2). 112pp. The Supremes' rise to stardom — and eventual fall from fame without leader Diana Ross — is chronicled here with photographs, glossary, discography, and bibliography. (Rev: BL 10/1/02; SLJ 5/02) [782.421644]

3697 Rodgers, Richard. *Getting to Know You! Rodgers and Hammerstein Favorites* (2–4). Illus. by Rosemary Wells. 2002, HarperCollins $19.99 (0-06-027925-7). 64pp. Children may get their first taste of Rodgers and Hammerstein's music in this collection of 16 songs with child-friendly themes, complete with music and lyrics inside the back cover. (Rev: BL 11/15/02; HBG 3/03; SLJ 11/02) [782.1]

3698 Weatherford, Carole Boston. *The Sound That Jazz Makes* (5–9). Illus. by Eric Velasquez. 2000, Walker LB $17.85 (0-802-78721-5). The history of jazz, tied in with the history of African Americans and told in rhythmic text. (Rev: BL 2/15/03; HBG 9/00; SLJ 7/00)

Ballads and Folk Songs

3699 Hillenbrand, Will. *Fiddle-I-Fee* (2–4). Illus. 2002, Harcourt $16.00 (0-15-201945-6). 40pp. Farm animals form a band to welcome a new baby in this colorful version of the folk song. (Rev: BL 7/02; HB 7–8/02; HBG 10/02; SLJ 3/02) [782.421642]

3700 Margolin, H. Ellen. *Goin' to Boston: An Exuberant Journey in Song* (PS–2). Illus. by Emily Bolam. 2002, Handprint $15.95 (1-929766-45-9). A girl on a bicycle leads a growing parade of people on their way to Boston Common in this new version of an Appalachian folk song. (Rev: HBG 10/02; SLJ 7/02) [782.42164]

3701 Shulman, Lisa. *Old MacDonald Had a Woodshop* (PS–2). Illus. by Ashley Wolff. 2002, Putnam $16.99 (0-399-23596-5). 32pp. Old MacDonald, a female sheep, shares her woodshop with the other farm animals in this entertaining version of the familiar song. (Rev: BL 9/15/02; HB 9–10/02; HBG 3/03; SLJ 9/02*) [784.4]

3702 Trapani, Iza. *Froggie Went A-Courtin'* (PS–3). Illus. by author. 2002, Charlesbridge LB $15.95 (1-58089-028-8). A new, humorous version of the song about Froggie's constant rejections. (Rev: HBG 3/03; SLJ 7/02) [784]

3703 Williams, Suzanne. *Old MacDonald in the City* (PS–1). Illus. by Thor Wickstrom. 2002, Golden Books $14.99 (0-307-10685-3). Old MacDonald has a food cart and a collection of urban animals in this humorous variation of the song that doubles as a counting book. (Rev: HBG 10/02; SLJ 6/02) [784.4]

Holidays

3704 Orozco, Jose-Luis. *Fiestas: A Year of Latin American Songs of Celebration* (2–4). Illus. by Elisa Kleven. 2002, Dutton $17.99 (0-525-45937-5). 56pp. Orozco presents 21 songs in Spanish and English, with music. (Rev: BL 9/15/02; HBG 3/03) [782.42]

Musical Instruments

3705 Dunleavy, Deborah. *The Kids Can Press Jumbo Book of Music* (2–6). Illus. by Louise Phillips. Series: A Kids Can Press Jumbo Book. 2001, Kids Can paper $14.95 (1-55074-723-1). 208pp. Instructions for making a variety of musical instruments from everyday materials are accompanied by suggestions of appropriate music and groupings of instruments. (Rev: SLJ 4/01) [780]

3706 Grace, Kayla. *Percussion Instruments* (1–3). Series: Music Makers. 2002, Child's World LB $22.79 (1-56766-986-7). 24pp. A description of the instruments of the percussion family, the sounds they make, and their importance in music throughout history. Also use *Stringed Instruments* (2002). (Rev: SLJ 12/02) [784]

3707 Hooper, Maureen Brett. *Highlights Fun to Play Recorder Book: Learn with Easy Steps and Familiar Songs* (2–6). Illus. by Judith Hunt. 2001, Boyds Mills $14.95 (1-56397-965-9). 49pp. Basic instructions for playing the recorder are accompanied by suitable songs that increase in difficulty as the reader progresses through the book. (Rev: SLJ 6/01) [784]

3708 Lynch, Wendy. *Brass* (2–4). Series: Musical Instruments. 2001, Heinemann LB $21.36 (1-58810-233-5). A look at the brass family of instruments in words and pictures, with material on the trumpet, tuba, and trombone. (Rev: BL 1/1–15/02; HBG 3/02) [788]

3709 Lynch, Wendy. *Keyboards* (2–4). Illus. Series: Musical Instruments. 2001, Heinemann LB $21.36 (1-58810-234-3). 32pp. Lynch introduces younger readers to keyboard instruments, how they work and how they sound, with back matter that includes a glossary and a bibliography. Also use *Percussion* (2001). (Rev: BL 1/1–15/02; HBG 3/02) [786]

3710 Lynch, Wendy. *Strings* (2–4). Series: Musical Instruments. 2001, Heinemann LB $21.36 (1-58810-236-X). All the stringed instruments of an orchestra are described in text and pictures with an activity based on creating the simulated sound of stringed instruments. (Rev: BL 1/1–15/02; HBG 3/02) [787]

3711 Lynch, Wendy. *Woodwind* (2–4). Series: Musical Instruments. 2001, Heinemann LB $21.36 (1-58810-237-8). All the woodwinds — including the clarinet, bassoon, and saxophone — are pictured and described, and common household objects are used to simulate their sounds. (Rev: BL 1/1–15/02; HBG 3/02) [788]

National Anthems and Patriotic Songs

3712 Berlin, Irving. *God Bless America* (PS). Illus. by Lynn Munsinger. 2002, HarperCollins $15.99 (0-06-009788-4). 32pp. The Irving Berlin classic song set to illustration, depicting a family of bears traveling across America. (Rev: BL 8/02; HBG 3/03) [782.421599]

3713 Johnson, James Weldon. *Lift Every Voice and Sing: A Pictorial Tribute to the Negro National Anthem* (3–6). Illus. 2001, Hyperion $15.99 (0-

7868-0626-5). The famous anthem, accompanied by photographs highlighting the history of African Americans. (Rev: BL 2/15/03; HBG 10/01; SLJ 1/01)

Singing Games and Songs

3714 Bowdish, Lynea. *Francis Scott Key and "The Star Spangled Banner"* (K–3). Illus. by Harry Burman. 2002, Mondo $15.95 (1-59034-195-3). 32pp. A large-format book for younger readers about Francis Scott Key's penning of the national anthem in 1814. (Rev: BL 12/15/02; HBG 3/03) [973.5]

3715 Boynton, Sandra. *Philadelphia Chickens* (PS–5). Illus. by author. 2002, Workman $16.95 (0-7611-2636-8). 64pp. A cast of animal characters bounce through pages of lyrics and musical notations, while the songs are performed on the accompanying CD by celebrities including Meryl Streep and Natasha Richardson. (Rev: SLJ 3/03) [782.1]

3716 Browne, Anthony. *Animal Fair: A Spectacular Pop-Up* (PS–3). Illus. by author. 2002, Candlewick $14.99 (0-7636-1831-4). The big baboon and other animals of the title song star in an illustrated romp that involves many flaps. (Rev: SLJ 12/02)

3717 *Do Your Ears Hang Low?* (PS). Illus. by Caroline Jayne Church. 2002, Scholastic $15.95 (0-439-

12871-4). Two cartoon dogs with long ears cavort to the verses of this popular song. (Rev: HBG 10/02; SLJ 2/02)

3718 Hinojosa, Tish. *Cada Nino/Every Child: A Bilingual Songbook for Kids* (3–6). Illus. by Lucia Angela Perez. 2002, Cinco Puntos $18.95 (0-938317-60-1). 56pp. This is a charming bilingual songbook, with music, presenting 11 traditional and original songs that celebrate the simple things in life. (Rev: BL 6/1–15/02; HBG 10/02) [782.42]

3719 Katz, Alan. *Take Me out of the Bathtub and Other Silly Dilly Songs* (PS–1). Illus. by David Catrow. 2001, Simon & Schuster $15.00 (0-689-82903-5). 32pp. Amusing adaptations of a number of familiar songs are accompanied by equally silly illustrations. (Rev: BL 7/01; HBG 10/01; SLJ 4/01) [782.4216]

3720 Lessac, Frane. *Camp Granada: Sing-Along Camp Songs* (2–5). Illus. 2003, Holt $18.95 (0-8050-6683-7). 48pp. Colorful, humorous illustrations and a brief story about camp activities form a backdrop for the lyrics to 34 camp songs. (Rev: BL 3/1/03) [782.42164]

3721 Newcome, Zita. *Head, Shoulders, Knees, and Toes and Other Action Rhymes* (PS). Illus. 2002, Candlewick $15.99 (0-7636-1899-3). 64pp. Familiar songs and rhymes, with illustrations of children performing movements to accompany them. (Rev: BL 9/15/02; HBG 3/03; SLJ 10/02) [398.8]

Performing Arts

Circuses, Fairs, and Parades

3722 Helfer, Ralph D. *Mosey: The Remarkable Friendship of a Boy and His Elephant* (5–8). 2002, Scholastic $16.95 (0-439-29313-8). 144pp. The adventure-filled story of an enduring friendship between a boy and his elephant, based on actual events in the early 20th century. (Rev: BL 7/02; HBG 3/03; SLJ 7/02) [791.3]

3723 Presnall, Judith Janda. *Circus Animals* (4–7). Series: Animals with Jobs. 2002, Gale LB $18.96 (0-7377-1360-7). 48pp. This colorful book describes the training and performance of such circus animals as elephants, lions, tigers, and horses. (Rev: BL 2/15/03) [791.3]

Dance

3724 Augustyn, Frank, and Shelley Tanaka. *Footnotes: Dancing the World's Best-Loved Ballets* (5–8). Illus. 2001, Millbrook LB $22.90 (0-7613-2323-6). 96pp. A readable account that introduces ballet from a backstage perspective, with material on how it feels to be a dancer in a large ballet company. (Rev: BL 4/15/01; HBG 10/01; SLJ 6/01*) [792.8]

3725 Cooper, Elisha. *Dance!* (2–4). Illus. 2001, Greenwillow $15.95 (0-06-029418-3). 32pp. This is a very visual introduction to the world of dance, with feathery watercolor illustrations and minimal text. (Rev: BL 9/15/01; HB 11–12/01; HBG 3/02; SLJ 9/01) [793.8]

3726 Geras, Adele. *Sleeping Beauty* (3–5). Illus. Series: The Magic of Ballet. 2001, David & Charles $10.95 (1-86233-246-0). 26pp. The story of Sleeping Beauty is told from the perspective of four characters. Also use *Swan Lake* (2001). (Rev: BCCB 1/03; BL 7/01; SLJ 11/01) [823.914]

3727 Hayward, Linda. *A Day in the Life of a Dancer* (PS–K). Series: Dorling Kindersley Readers: Jobs People Do. 2001, DK $12.95 (0-7894-7370-4); paper $3.95 (0-7894-7369-0). 32pp. Using a very limited vocabulary and simple sentences, this beginning reader explores the everyday life of a ballet dancer. (Rev: BL 8/1/01; HBG 10/01) [792.8]

3728 Klingel, Cynthia, and Robert B. Noyed. *Dancers* (K–1). Series: Wonder Books. 2001, Child's World LB $21.36 (1-56766-939-5). 24pp. This book for beginning readers gives basic information about dancers and dancing. (Rev: HBG 3/02; SLJ 2/02)

3729 Pavlova, Anna. *I Dreamed I Was a Ballerina* (3–5). Illus. by Edgar Degas. 2001, Simon & Schuster $16.00 (0-689-84676-2). 32pp. Beautiful Degas illustrations accompany the true story, in her own words, of Pavlova's inspiring first visit to a ballet and her subsequent rise to fame. (Rev: BL 12/1/01; HBG 3/02; SLJ 11/01) [792.8]

3730 Tchaikovsky, Pyotr I. *Swan Lake* (2–4). Trans. by Marianne Martens. Illus. by Lisbeth Zwerger. 2002, North-South LB $16.50 (0-7358-1703-0). 32pp. Hauntingly detailed paintings bring the characters to life in this attractive retelling of the familiar classic that has a happy ending, which is explained in an author's note. (Rev: BCCB 11/02; BL 1/1–15/03; HBG 3/03; SLJ 12/02) [792.8]

Marionettes and Puppets

3731 Bryant, Jill, and Catherine Heard. *Making Shadow Puppets* (4–6). Series: Kids Can Do It. 2002, Kids Can $12.95 (1-55337-028-7); paper $5.95 (1-55337-029-5). 40pp. Two-dimensional puppets that can be created with easily found materials are presented with good step-by-step instructions. (Rev: BL 9/15/02; HBG 3/03; SLJ 12/02) [745.5]

Theater and Play Production

3732 Bany-Winters, Lisa. *Funny Bones: Comedy Games and Activities for Kids* (3–6). Illus. 2002, Chicago Review paper $14.95 (1-55652-444-7). 155pp. In addition to learning games, skits, and songs, readers will find some history of comedy and will gain insight on how to use props, music, make-up, and other techniques to be funny. (Rev: SLJ 12/02) [793]

3733 Friedman, Lise. *Break a Leg! The Kid's Guide to Acting and Stagecraft* (4–7). Illus. by Mary Dowdle. 2002, Workman $24.95 (0-7611-2590-6); paper $14.95 (0-7611-2208-7). 256pp. Some of the topics covered for young would-be actors include analyzing a script, memorizing lines, stage fright, body

language, and monologues. (Rev: BL 5/1/02; HBG 10/02; SLJ check) [292]

3734 McCullough, L. E. *Plays for Learning: Israel Reborn: Legends of the Diaspora and Israel's Modern Rebirth for Grades 4–6* (4–6). Series: Young Actors. 2001, Smith & Kraus paper $15.95 (1-57525-253-8). 204pp. A collection of 12 plays drawn from a variety of sources that portray the Jewish experience from the expulsion from Israel to the creation of the modern state. (Rev: SLJ 6/02)

3735 Siberell, Anne. *Bravo! Brava! A Night at the Opera: Behind the Scenes, with Composers, Cast, and Crew* (3–6). Illus. by author. 2001, Oxford $19.95 (0-19-513966-6). 64pp. An excellent introduction to the many facets of opera, from its history to behind-the-scenes tasks such as makeup and set design. (Rev: BL 2/15/02; HBG 3/02; SLJ 1/02*) [782.1]

History and Geography

History and Geography in General

Miscellaneous

3736 Ajmera, Maya, and John D. Ivanko. *Back to School* (PS–3). Series: It's a Kid's World. 2001, Charlesbridge LB $15.95 (1-57091-383-8); paper $6.95 (1-57091-384-6). This brief look at schooling around the world, with minimal text and color photographs, shows students studying in different situations, unusual methods of getting to school, and various kinds of clothing. (Rev: HBG 3/02; SLJ 6/02)

3737 Arnold, Caroline. *The Geography Book: Activities for Exploring, Mapping, and Enjoying Your World* (4–7). Illus. by Tina Cash-Walsh. 2001, Wiley paper $12.95 (0-471-41236-8). 112pp. An organized introduction to several geography concepts along with step-by-step instructions for projects and experiments. (Rev: BL 2/15/02; SLJ 3/02) [910]

3738 Cunha, Stephen F. *National Geographic Bee Official Study Guide* (4–8). 2002, National Geographic paper $9.95 (0-7922-7850-X). 126pp. Tips on preparing for the geography bee, questions from former bees, and the competition rules and format are all presented in accessible text with plenty of helpful illustrations. (Rev: SLJ 9/02)

3739 Dewey, Jennifer Owings. *Finding Your Way* (4–6). Illus. 2001, Millbrook LB $23.90 (0-7613-0956-X). 64pp. The author relates several tales that involve travel, using one's sense of direction, and becoming lost. (Rev: BL 5/1/01; HBG 10/01; SLJ 7/01) [795.58]

3740 Lewis, J. Patrick. *Earth and You: A Closer View: Nature's Features* (2–4). Illus. by Christopher Canyon. 2001, Dawn $16.95 (1-58469-016-X); paper $7.95 (1-58469-015-1). The author and illustrator present a vivid and lyrical close-up look at natural features of the earth and its plants and animals. (Rev: HBG 10/01; SLJ 4/01) [508]

3741 Rhatigan, Joe, and Heather Smith. *Geography Crafts for Kids: 50 Cool Projects and Activities for Exploring the World* (4–6). Illus. 2002, Sterling $24.95 (1-57990-196-4). 144pp. This collection of projects and activities related to geography is an excellent tool for hands-on learning. (Rev: BL 8/02; HBG 10/02; SLJ 7/02) [372.89]

3742 *Stories from Where We Live: The Great North American Prairie* (4–8). Ed. by Sara St. Antoine. 2001, Milkweed $19.95 (1-57131-630-2). 264pp. A collection of historical and contemporary stories, poems, essays, and journal entries about life on the prairie, with informative appendixes. (Rev: BL 5/15/01) [978]

Maps and Globes

3743 Bredeson, Carmen. *Looking at Maps and Globes* (1–2). Illus. Series: Rookie Read-About Geography. 2001, Children's LB $19.00 (0-516-22351-8). 32pp. An introduction to maps and globes, along with explanations about features such as legends, scale, and the equator. (Rev: BL 11/1/01) [912]

3744 DiSpezio, Michael A. *Map Mania: Discovering Where You Are and Getting to Where You Aren't* (3–5). Illus. by Dave Garbot. 2002, Sterling $19.95 (0-8069-4407-2). 80pp. An entertaining introduction to the usefulness of floor plans, maps, and the ability to navigate. (Rev: HBG 3/03; SLJ 9/02)

3745 Oleksy, Walter. *Mapping the World* (5–7). Series: Watts Library — Geography. 2002, Watts LB $24.00 (0-531-12029-5); paper $8.95 (0-531-16636-8). 64pp. A history of how maps have been made, from the explorers, merchants, and mapmakers of old to the accurate modern products that use new technology. Also use *Mapping the Seas* and *Maps in History* (both 2002). (Rev: BL 10/15/02) [912]

3746 Robson, Pam. *Maps and Plans* (2–4). Illus. by Tony Kenyon. Series: Geography for Fun. 2001, Millbrook LB $22.90 (0-7613-2165-9). 32pp. This combination of maps, charts, games, and activities introduces some basic concepts in an entertaining way. (Rev: HBG 10/01; SLJ 9/01)

Paleontology and Dinosaurs

3747 Agenbroad, Larry D., and Lisa Nelson. *Mammoths: Ice-Age Giants* (5–8). Illus. Series: Discovery! 2002, Lerner LB $26.60 (0-8225-2862-2). 120pp. A detailed look at mammoths, theories on mammoth extinction, and mammoth discoveries, with sidebar features on topics such as human hunters in the Ice Age, and geologic timelines. (Rev: BL 6/1–15/02; HBG 10/02; SLJ 7/02) [569]

3748 Armentrout, David, and Patricia Armentrout. *Dinosaurs* (PS–2). 2002, Rourke LB $26.60 (1-58952-342-3). 32pp. Simple definitions are given for 50 words about dinosaurs, along with a sentence that includes the word. (Rev: SLJ 3/03)

3749 Arnold, Caroline. *Dinosaurs with Feathers: The Ancestors of the Modern Birds* (4–5). Illus. by Laurie Caple. 2001, Clarion $15.00 (0-618-00398-3). 32pp. Arnold presents information on the links between dinosaurs (specifically, theropods) and the birds of today, with illustrations. (Rev: BL 10/1/01; HBG 10/02; SLJ 11/01) [568]

3750 Arnold, Caroline. *When Mammoths Walked the Earth* (3–5). Illus. by Laurie Caple. 2002, Clarion $16.00 (0-618-09633-7). 40pp. An informative, well-illustrated book about key fossil discoveries and the lives of mammoths. (Rev: BL 8/02; HB 11–12/02; HBG 3/03; SLJ 10/02) [569]

3751 Bailey, Jacqui. *The Day of the Dinosaurs* (3–5). Illus. by Matthew Lilly. Series: Cartoon History of the Earth. 2001, Kids Can $16.95 (1-55337-073-2); paper $7.95 (1-55337-082-1). 32pp. A comic-book-style presentation of the age of the dinosaurs. (Rev: BL 10/15/01; HBG 3/02; SLJ 1/02) [567.9]

3752 Barner, Bob. *Dinosaur Bones* (PS–2). Illus. 2001, Chronicle $15.95 (0-8118-3158-2). 36pp. The lively cut-paper collage illustrations are the highlight of this book about dinosaurs and their bones. (Rev: BCCB 9/01; BL 11/1/01; HBG 3/02; SLJ 9/01) [567.9]

3753 Bilgrami, Shaheen. *Amazing Dinosaur Discovery* (PS–3). Illus. by Mike Phillips and Phil Garner. Series: Magic Skeleton. 2002, Sterling $9.95 (0-8069-8591-7). 24pp. A visit to a museum introduces younger readers to dinosaurs and their skeletons in this picture book with an appealing format. (Rev: BL 8/02)

3754 Camper, Cathy. *Bugs Before Time: Prehistoric Insects and Their Relatives* (3–5). Illus. by Steve Kirk. 2002, Simon & Schuster $16.95 (0-689-82092-5). 40pp. An eye-catching introduction to the world of prehistoric insects and arthropods. (Rev: BL 3/15/02; HBG 10/02; SLJ 5/02) [565]

3755 Carr, Karen. *Dinosaur Hunt: Texas — 115 Million Years Ago* (3–6). Illus. by author. 2002, HarperCollins LB $19.89 (0-06-029704-2). Dramatic illustrations are used in this reenactment of a prehistoric battle between two dinosaurs, based on fossil footprints found in Texas. (Rev: HBG 3/03; SLJ 10/02)

3756 Chorlton, Windsor. *Woolly Mammoth: Life, Death, and Rediscovery* (4–6). Illus. 2001, Scholastic $15.95 (0-439-24134-0). 40pp. An exciting presentation of what we know about mammoths and why they disappeared from the earth, spurred by the discovery of a mammoth tusk and remains in Siberia in 1997. (Rev: BL 5/15/01; HBG 10/01; SLJ 8/01) [569]

3757 Chrisp, Peter. *Dinosaur Detectives* (2–4). Illus. Series: Dorling Kindersley Readers. 2001, DK $12.95 (0-7894-7384-4); paper $3.95 (0-7894-7383-6). 48pp. Chrisp interweaves facts about dinosaurs with fictionalized first-person accounts by fossil hunters in a package that makes good browsing for beginning readers. (Rev: HBG 10/01; SLJ 9/01) [560]

3758 Cole, Stephen, adapt. *Allosaurus! The Life and Death of Big Al: The Story of a Dinosaur and the Science Behind the Story* (3–6). Illus. Series: Discovery Kids. 2001, Dutton paper $7.99 (0-525-46773-4). 48pp. The fictionalized story about Big Al is combined with many facts about the discovery of an Allosaurus skeleton, scientists' forensic work, and the behavior of dinosaurs in general. (Rev: SLJ 7/01)

3759 Cutchins, Judy, and Ginny Johnston. *Giant Predators of the Ancient Seas* (4–7). Illus. Series: Southern Fossil Discoveries. 2001, Pineapple $14.95 (1-56164-237-1). 63pp. A look at the reptiles, fish, whales, sharks, and sea snakes that were found in the seas that once covered much of North America, as well as a discussion of the methods scientists used to reconstruct them. (Rev: HBG 3/02; SLJ 12/01) [566]

3760 *Dinosaur* (3–5). Ed. by Samantha Gray and Sarah Walker. Illus. Series: Eye Wonder. 2001, DK LB $17.95 (0-7894-8179-0); paper $9.95 (0-7894-7851-X). 48pp. Model dinosaurs show how the massive beasts moved, hunted, and lived; theories about their demise are also included. (Rev: BL 12/1/01; HBG 3/02) [567.9]

3761 Dixon, Dougal. *Dinosaurs: The Good, the Bad, and the Ugly* (4–8). Series: Secret Worlds. 2001, DK $14.95 (0-7894-7971-0); paper $7.95 (0-7894-7972-9). 96pp. Dramatic color illustrations and a lively text are used to create interest in this introduction to dinosaurs and their world. (Rev: BL 10/15/01; HBG 3/02) [567.9]

3762 Dixon, Dougal. *Herbivores* (4–6). Illus. Series: Dinosaurs. 2001, Gareth Stevens LB $23.93 (0-8368-2916-6). 36pp. This account explores the world of the herbivore dinosaurs during the Mesozoic Era and discusses related modern species. Also use *Carnivores* and *In the Sky* (2001). (Rev: HBG 3/02; SLJ 3/02) [567.9]

3763 Farlow, James O. *Bringing Dinosaur Bones to Life: How Do We Know What Dinosaurs Were Like?* (4–7). Illus. 2001, Watts LB $24.00 (0-531-11403-1). 64pp. An interesting look at the life of dinosaurs and at the methods paleontologists use to learn about the beasts, pointing out that although scientists can reconstruct animals from skeletons and fossil evidence, they must always differentiate between fact and educated guesses. (Rev: BL 12/15/01; SLJ 12/01) [567.9]

3764 Harris, Nicholas. *The Incredible Journey Through the World of the Dinosaurs* (2–5). Illus. by Inklink Firenze. 2002, McGraw-Hill $18.95 (0-87226-671-0). 32pp. An oversize book that looks at the types, structure, and lifestyles of the dinosaurs that lived in what is now the western United States. (Rev: BL 6/1–15/02; HBG 3/02) [567.9]

3765 Hehner, Barbara. *Ice Age Mammoth: Will This Ancient Giant Come Back to Life?* (5–7). Illus. by Mark Hallett. 2001, Crown LB $18.99 (0-375-91327-0). 32pp. Hehner discusses the anatomy, diet, habitat, behavior, and extinction of the mammoth, as well as the discovery of a mammoth in the Siberian permafrost in 1997 and the potential to clone a mammoth using DNA or frozen sperm. (Rev: HBG 3/02; SLJ 12/01)

3766 Keiran, Monique. *Ornithomimus: Pursuing the Bird-Mimic Dinosaur* (4–6). Illus. 2002, Raincoast $26.95 (1-55192-348-3). 64pp. A look at the discovery of a featherless beaked fossil in Canada with discussion of fossils and evolution in general, enhanced by color photographs and paintings. (Rev: BL 12/1/02; SLJ 11/02) [567.914]

3767 Kerley, Barbara. *The Dinosaurs of Waterhouse Hawkins* (3–5). Illus. by Brian Selznick. 2001, Scholastic $16.95 (0-439-11494-2). 48pp. The true story of Waterhouse Hawkins, the 19th-century British artist who built life-sized dinosaur models, with detailed, dramatic illustrations. (Rev: BCCB 10/01; BL 9/1/01; HBG 3/02; SLJ 10/01) [567.9]

3768 Levy, Elizabeth. *Who Are You Calling a Woolly Mammoth? Prehistoric America* (4–6). Illus. by Daniel McFeely. Series: America's Horrible Histories. 2001, Scholastic LB $12.95 (0-439-30348-6); paper $4.99 (0-590-12938-4). 160pp. A humorous history of prehistoric America from 250 million years ago to the evolution of early man. (Rev: BL 2/15/02; HBG 10/02; SLJ 3/02) [560]

3769 Manning, Mick, and Brita Granstrom. *Dinomania: Things to Do with Dinosaurs* (3–5). Illus. 2002, Holiday $15.95 (0-8234-1641-0). 48pp. This book consists of a series of projects related to dinosaurs, such as creating a diorama of habitats and a mobile of flying creatures. (Rev: BL 6/1–15/02; HBG 10/02; SLJ 4/02) [745.5]

3770 Miller, Debbie S. *A Woolly Mammoth Journey* (2–3). Illus. by Jon Van Zyle. 2001, Little, Brown $15.95 (0-316-57212-8). 32pp. Readers follow a fictional woolly mammoth family through a spring, summer, and fall in what is now Alaska. (Rev: BL 5/1/01; HBG 10/01; SLJ 6/01) [569]

3771 Morrison, Taylor. *The Great Unknown* (3–5). Illus. 2001, Houghton $16.00 (0-395-97494-1). 32pp. An account of Peale's discovery of mastodon bones in New York state in 1799 and their assembly into a skeleton. (Rev: BCCB 7–8/01; BL 5/1/01; HBG 10/01; SLJ 5/01) [569]

3772 Nye, Bill, and Ian G. Saunders. *Bill Nye the Science Guy's Great Big Dinosaur Dig* (5–6). Illus. by Michael Koelsch. 2002, Hyperion LB $17.49 (0-7868-2472-7). 48pp. The Science Guy fills us in on dinosaurs, what we learn from their fossils, and the animals' eventual evolution into birds. (Rev: HBG 3/03; SLJ 1/03) [567.9]

3773 O'Brien, Patrick. *Mammoth* (K–3). Illus. 2002, Holt $16.95 (0-8050-6596-2). 40pp. O'Brien interweaves historical information about mammoths with contemporary scenes of scientists excavating and identifying a skeleton, in a well-illustrated, large-format overview of these animals that touches on their modern elephant relatives. (Rev: BL 12/1/02; HBG 3/03; SLJ 11/02) [569]

3774 O'Brien, Patrick. *Megatooth* (PS–3). Illus. by author. 2001, Holt $16.95 (0-8050-6214-9). O'Brien presents the theories scientists have made about the giant beast also known as the megalodon. (Rev: HBG 10/01; SLJ 6/01)

3775 Olien, Becky. *Fossils* (2–4). Series: The Bridgestone Science Library. 2001, Capstone LB $13.95 (0-7368-0951-1). 24pp. Fossils, famous fossil finds, and fuels made from fossils are covered in this slim volume. (Rev: HBG 3/02; SLJ 2/02)

3776 Rey, Luis V. *Extreme Dinosaurs* (3–7). Illus. by author. 2001, Chronicle $16.95 (0-8118-3086-1). 62pp. Bright, lively illustrations accompany a friendly text that provides lots of information about dinosaur evolution, dinosaur species grouped by continent, and fossil discoveries. (Rev: HBG 3/02; SLJ 9/01)

3777 Sloan, Christopher. *Supercroc and the Origin of Crocodiles* (5–8). Illus. 2002, National Geographic $18.95 (0-7922-6691-9). 64pp. A fascinating account of the discovery in Africa of the fossil *Sarcosuchus*, or SuperCroc, with additional information on paleontology and crocodile evolution. (Rev: BCCB 5/02; BL 9/15/02; HBG 10/02; SLJ 7/02*) [567.9]

3778 Taylor, Barbara. *Oxford First Book of Dinosaurs* (K–3). Illus. 2002, Oxford $19.95 (0-19-521847-7). 48pp. An accessible, oversized introduction to dinosaurs that is full of colorful illustrations. (Rev: HBG 10/02; SLJ 5/02)

3779 Zimmerman, Howard. *Beyond the Dinosaurs! Sky Dragons, Sea Monsters, Mega-Mammals, and Other Prehistoric Beasts* (4–6). Illus. 2001, Simon & Schuster $18.00 (0-689-84113-2). 64pp. A large-format and very appealing presentation full of dramatic illustrations and brief, up-to-date text. (Rev: BL 6/1–15/01; HBG 10/01; SLJ 7/01) [567.9]

3780 Zoehfeld, Kathleen Weidner. *Dinosaur Parents, Dinosaur Young: Uncovering the Mystery of Dinosaur Families* (3–6). Illus. Series: Let's-Read-and-Find-Out Science. 2001, Clarion $17.00 (0-395-91338-2). 60pp. This book explains what we know about dinosaur parenting and how paleontologists have arrived at this information. (Rev: BL 4/15/01) [567.9]

3781 Zoehfeld, Kathleen Weidner. *Dinosaurs Big and Small* (PS–1). Illus. by Lucia Washburn. Series: Let's-Read-and-Find-Out Science. 2002, HarperCollins LB $15.89 (0-06-027936-2); paper $4.95 (0-06-445182-8). 40pp. Dinosaurs are compared with buses, elephants, and other items to help children grasp their size. (Rev: BL 7/02; HBG 10/02; SLJ 7/02) [567.9]

Anthropology and Prehistoric Life

3782 Bailey, Jacqui. *The Dawn of Life* (3–5). Illus. by Matthew Lilly. Series: Cartoon History of the Earth. 2001, Kids Can $16.95 (1-55337-072-4); paper $7.95 (1-55337-081-3). 32pp. The beginnings of plant and animal life on Earth, presented in a comic-book format. Also use *The Birth of the Earth*, *The Day of the Dinosaurs*, and *The Stick and Stone Age* (all 2001). (Rev: BL 10/15/01; HBG 3/02; SLJ 1/02) [576.83]

3783 Bailey, Jacqui. *The Stick and Stone Age* (3–5). Illus. by Matthew Lilly. Series: Cartoon History of the Earth. 2001, Kids Can $16.95 (1-55337-074-0); paper $7.95 (1-55337-083-X). 32pp. A comic-book-style presentation of early prehistoric human culture. (Rev: BL 10/15/01; HBG 3/02; SLJ 1/02) [591.3]

3784 Hehner, Barbara. *Ice Age Cave Bear: The Giant Beast That Terrified Ancient Humans* (4–6). Illus. by Mark Hallett. Series: Ice Age Animals. 2002, Crown $16.95 (0-375-81329-2). 32pp. Covers everything about the Ice Age bear, from its diet to its demise, with absorbing text and exciting illustrations. (Rev: BL 10/15/02; HBG 3/03; SLJ 10/02) [569]

3785 Hehner, Barbara. *Ice Age Sabertooth: The Most Ferocious Cat That Ever Lived* (5–9). Illus. by Mark Hallett. Series: Ice Age Animals. 2002, Random LB $18.99 (0-375-91328-9). 32pp. Dramatic illustrations of the fierce sabertooth tiger grab the reader's attention, and the clear text gives details about this and other Ice Age animals and touches on such topics as extinction and evolution. (Rev: BL 12/15/01; HBG 10/02; SLJ 5/02) [569]

3786 Jenkins, Steve. *Life on Earth: The Story of Evolution* (3–6). Illus. 2002, Houghton $16.00 (0-618-16476-6). 40pp. Superb cut-paper illustrations depict the fundamentals of evolution, touching on Darwin, natural selection, and mutation, and ending with an extraordinary timeline. (Rev: BL 12/15/02; HB 9–10/02*; HBG 3/03; SLJ 12/02) [576.8]

3787 Sloan, Christopher. *Bury the Dead: Tombs, Corpses, Mummies, Skeletons, and Rituals* (5–9). Illus. 2002, National Geographic $18.95 (0-7922-7192-0). 64pp. Young readers will be fascinated by this serious account of burial practices throughout the ages, with timelines, color photographs, diagrams, and clear descriptions of rites around the world. (Rev: BL 12/1/02; HBG 3/03; SLJ 10/02) [393]

Archaeology

3788 Greene, Meg. *Buttons, Bones, and the Organ-Grinder's Monkey: Tales of Historical Archaeology* (5–8). Illus. 2001, Linnet $25.00 (0-208-02498-0). 117pp. This introduction to historical archaeology looks at finds at five different sites in the United States. (Rev: BL 10/1/01; HBG 10/02; SLJ 1/02) [973]

3789 Lourie, Peter. *The Mystery of the Maya: Uncovering the Lost City of Palenque* (5–8). Illus. 2001, Boyds Mills $19.95 (1-56397-839-3). 48pp. The author relates his interesting and often exciting experiences at a dig in Mexico and describes the work of the archaeologists and the history of the site. (Rev: BL 9/15/01; HBG 3/02; SLJ 11/01) [972.75]

3790 Panchyk, Richard. *Archaeology for Kids: Uncovering the Mysteries of Our Past with 25 Activities* (5–8). Illus. 2001, Chicago Review paper $14.95 (1-55652-395-5). 160pp. An introduction for older readers to the history and scientific method of archaeology, full of illustrations and with interesting activities. (Rev: BL 1/1–15/02; SLJ 12/01) [930.1]

World History

General

3791 Blackwood, Gary L. *Highwaymen* (5–8). Illus. Series: Bad Guys. 2001, Marshall Cavendish LB $19.95 (0-7614-1017-1). 72pp. Period artwork, photographs, and intriguing tales bring real highway robbers, and the times they lived in, to life. (Rev: BL 1/1–15/02; HBG 3/02; SLJ 1/02) [364.15]

3792 Blackwood, Gary L. *Swindlers* (5–8). Illus. Series: Bad Guys. 2001, Marshall Cavendish LB $19.95 (0-7614-1031-7). 72pp. The author presents famous swindlers and cheats throughout history, providing illustrations, source notes, and recommended Web sites and further reading. (Rev: BL 1/1–15/02; HBG 3/02) [364.16]

3793 Cooper, Paul. *Going to War in the 18th Century* (4–7). Illus. Series: Armies of the Past. 2001, Watts LB $23.00 (0-531-14593-X). 32pp. All about the armies and navies involved in the American Revolution and major conflicts in Europe — forms of recruitment, artillery, cavalry, uniforms, strategies, camp life, and so forth. Also use *Going to War in the 19th Century* (2001). (Rev: SLJ 2/02)

3794 Hart, Avery, and Paul Mantell. *Who Really Discovered America? Unraveling the Mystery and Solving the Puzzle* (5–7). Illus. by Michael Kline. Series: A Kaleidoscope Kids Book. 2001, Williamson paper $10.95 (1-885593-46-5). 96pp. Several theories are presented about the discovery of America, and students are urged to examine them with open minds, using activities that help them to question and explore. (Rev: SLJ 10/01) [970.01]

3795 Harward, Barnaby. *The Best Book of Pirates* (3–5). Illus. Series: The Best Book Of. 2002, Kingfisher $12.95 (0-7534-5449-1). 31pp. Covers pirates through the ages with pirate flags, information on pirate ships and equipment, and a page on contemporary buccaneers. (Rev: HBG 3/03; SLJ 3/03) [910.4]

3796 Haslam, Andrew. *Living History: The Hands-On Approach to History* (3–6). Illus. Series: Make It Work! 2001, Two-Can $29.95 (1-58728-381-6). 256pp. This assemblage of volumes from the Make It Work! series features activities pertaining to daily life in Old Japan, ancient Egypt, ancient Rome, and Native American cultures, such as making togas. (Rev: BL 3/1/02; HBG 3/02) [900]

3797 Kleinman, Joseph, and Eileen Kurtis-Kleinman. *Life on an African Slave Ship* (5 Up). Series: The Way People Live. 2000, Lucent LB $19.96 (1-56006-653-9). 112pp. The author uses quotations from primary sources and many illustrations in this portrayal of life aboard a slave ship bound for America. (Rev: SLJ 5/01) [380.1]

3798 Lauber, Patricia. *What You Never Knew About Tubs, Toilets, and Showers* (2–4). Illus. 2001, Simon & Schuster $16.00 (0-689-82420-3). 40pp. An amusing and informative account of plumbing and personal hygiene through the ages that is bound to entertain young readers. (Rev: BCCB 7–8/01; BL 5/15/01; HB 5–6/01; HBG 10/01; SLJ 6/01*) [391.6]

3799 Levy, Elizabeth. *Awesome Ancient Ancestors! Mound Builders, Maya, and More* (5–8). Illus. by Daniel McFeely. Series: America's Horrible Histories. 2001, Scholastic $12.95 (0-439-30349-4); paper $4.99 (0-590-10795-X). 156pp. A humorous and chatty cockroach introduces the early inhabitants of North America and Mesoamerica. (Rev: HBG 10/02; SLJ 5/02) [970.01]

3800 McGowen, Tom. *Assault from the Sea: Amphibious Invasions in the Twentieth Century* (5–8). Series: Military Might. 2002, Twenty-First Century LB $25.90 (0-7613-1811-9). 64pp. Invasions launched from the sea during World Wars I and II and the Korean War are the subject of this introduction that includes black-and-white photographs and maps. Also use *Assault from the Sky: Airborne Infantry of World War II* (2002). (Rev: HBG 10/02; SLJ 6/02)

3801 Pirotta, Saviour. *Buried Treasure* (3–5). Series: Mysteries of the Past. 2001, Raintree Steck-Vaughn LB $17.98 (0-7398-4336-2). 32pp. Egyptian tombs, burial mounds in England, pirate legends, and Nazi loot are among the topics addressed in this overview of underground lore. (Rev: HBG 3/02; SLJ 2/02)

3802 Rumford, James. *Traveling Man: The Journey of Ibn Battuta, 1325–1354* (3–6). Illus. by author. 2001, Houghton $16.00 (0-618-08366-9). Rumford retells the story of the epic travels across Asia and Africa of the 14th-century explorer and scholar Ibn Battuta, with lyric text that flows through the beautiful illustrations. (Rev: HB 1–2/02; HBG 3/02; SLJ 10/01) [910]

3803 Rutsala, David. *The Sea Route to Asia* (4–7). Series: Exploration and Discovery. 2002, Mason Crest LB $19.95 (1-59084-046-1). 64pp. Rutsala presents Portuguese explorers' efforts to find a route around Africa to Asia, with information on Prince Henry the Navigator, Bartholomeu Dias, and Vasco da Gama. (Rev: SLJ 12/02) [910]

3804 Seibert, Patricia. *We Were Here: A Short History of Time Capsules* (3–6). Illus. 2002, Millbrook LB $22.90 (0-7613-0423-1). 48pp. A history of time capsules, including the Century Safe that was assembled in 1876 and opened in 1976. (Rev: BL 4/1/02; HBG 10/02; SLJ 3/02) [151]

Ancient History

General and Miscellaneous

3805 Altman, Susan, and Susan Lechner. *Ancient Africa* (2–5). Illus. by Donna Perrone. Series: Modern Rhymes About Ancient Times. 2001, Children's LB $28.00 (0-516-21151-X). 48pp. Rhyming text and colorful illustrations introduce young readers to a variety of facts about the cultures and peoples of ancient Africa. (Rev: SLJ 4/02)

3806 Bentley, Diana. *The Seven Wonders of the Ancient World* (4–6). Illus. 2002, Oxford LB $17.95 (0-19-521913-9). 32pp. Each of the wonders is covered in four concise, fact-filled pages that include watercolors, photographs, maps, diagrams, quotations, and comparisons with modern icons. (Rev: HBG 3/03; SLJ 1/03) [930]

3807 Curlee, Lynn. *Seven Wonders of the Ancient World* (3–6). Illus. 2002, Simon & Schuster $17.00 (0-689-83182-X). 40pp. An informative introduction for older readers to the wonders of the ancient world, with precise illustrations and thought-provoking text. (Rev: BCCB 3/02; BL 1/1–15/02; HBG 10/02; SLJ 9/02) [709]

3808 Hook, Jason. *Lost Cities* (3–5). Series: Mysteries of the Past. 2001, Raintree Steck-Vaughn LB $17.98 (0-7398-4337-0). 32pp. Ur, Knossos, Babylon, and Troy are among the cities addressed in this introduction to the mysteries surrounding the sites and the efforts to uncover the truth. (Rev: HBG 3/02; SLJ 2/02)

3809 Nelson, Julie. *West African Kingdoms* (3–5). Series: Ancient Civilizations. 2001, Raintree Steck-Vaughn LB $15.98 (0-7398-3581-5). 48pp. Readers will gain an understanding of the history and culture of the ancient civilizations of Ghana, Mali, and Songhai. (Rev: SLJ 2/02)

3810 Pelta, Kathy. *Rediscovering Easter Island* (5 Up). Series: How History Is Invented. 2001, Lerner LB $23.93 (0-8225-4890-9). 112pp. An assortment of illustrations, maps, and inserts add to this exploration of the mysteries of Easter Island. (Rev: BCCB 7–8/01; HBG 10/01; SLJ 2/02)

3811 Service, Pamela F. *300 B.C.* (5–8). Series: Around the World In. 2002, Benchmark LB $19.95 (0-7614-1080-5). 96pp. The author explores what was going on in Europe, Africa, Asia, and the Americas in the year 300 B.C. Also use *1200* (2002). (Rev: HBG 3/03; SLJ 2/03)

3812 Shuter, Jane. *Ancient West African Kingdoms* (3–5). Illus. Series: History Opens Windows. 2002, Heinemann LB $22.79 (1-4034-0255-8). 32pp. Readers will learn about government, trade, and everyday life in the kingdoms of Ghana, Mali, and Songhai. (Rev: HBG 3/03; SLJ 3/03)

3813 Shuter, Jane. *The Indus Valley* (3–5). Illus. Series: History Opens Windows. 2002, Heinemann LB $22.79 (1-4034-0253-1). 32pp. An overview of government, trade, and everyday life in ancient times in the Indus Valley that is now in Pakistan and western India. (Rev: HBG 3/03; SLJ 3/03)

Egypt and Mesopotamia

3814 Altman, Susan, and Susan Lechner. *Ancient Egypt* (2–5). Illus. by Sandy Appleoff. Series: Modern Rhymes About Ancient Times. 2001, Children's LB $28.00 (0-516-21149-8). 48pp. Rhyming text and colorful illustrations introduce young readers to the culture and peoples of ancient Egypt. (Rev: SLJ 4/02)

3815 Chrisp, Peter. *Ancient Egypt Revealed* (4–8). Illus. 2002, DK $12.99 (0-7894-8883-3). 38pp. This absorbing introduction to ancient Egypt uses a crisp text, a variety of beautiful photographs, computer graphics, and transparent cutaways to reveal the secrets of tombs and temples, and to inform readers about culture, writing methods, myths, and so forth. (Rev: BL 1/1–15/03; HBG 3/03; SLJ 3/03) [932]

3816 Cole, Joanna. *Ms. Frizzle's Adventures: Ancient Egypt* (3–6). Illus. by Bruce Degen. 2001, Scholastic $15.95 (0-590-44680-0). 48pp. Ms. Frizzle (of Magic School Bus fame) leads a tour group back in time to explore ancient Egypt with the usual bright mix of fiction, nonfiction, and humor. (Rev: BL 9/1/01; HB 11–12/01; HBG 3/02; SLJ 9/01*) [932]

3817 Holub, Joan. *Valley of the Golden Mummies* (3–5). Illus. by author. Series: Smart About History. 2002, Grosset LB $14.89 (0-448-42817-2); paper $5.99 (0-448-42661-7). 32pp. Humor and fact are interwoven in this text about mummies and archaeology, presented in the form of a school report. (Rev: HBG 3/03; SLJ 12/02)

3818 Jovinelly, Joann, and Jason Netelkos. *The Crafts and Culture of the Ancient Egyptians* (5–8). Series: Crafts of the Ancient World. 2002, Rosen LB $29.25 (0-8239-3509-4). 48pp. As well as learning about the mysteries of ancient Egypt, readers can engage in such craft projects as designing a pharaoh's headdress and necklace and re-creating an ancient marbles game. (Rev: BL 5/15/02; SLJ 6/02) [932]

3819 Kallen, Stuart A. *Pyramids* (5–8). Illus. Series: The Mystery Library. 2002, Gale LB $27.45 (1-56006-773-X). 112pp. Kallen uses many quotations from Egyptologists in this exploration of the reasons for building the pyramids and the construction techniques used. (Rev: BL 7/02; SLJ 7/02)

3820 Krensky, Stephen. *Egypt* (2–3). Series: Scholastic History Readers. 2002, Scholastic paper $3.99 (0-439-27195-9). 48pp. An appealing introduction to Egypt for beginning readers that emphasizes the importance of the Nile and covers such topics as daily life, the life of a ruler, the calendar, and the writing system. (Rev: SLJ 2/03)

3821 McCall, Henrietta. *Egyptian Mummies* (3–5). Illus. by David Antram. Series: Fast Forward. 2000, Watts LB $26.50 (0-531-11877-0); paper $9.95 (0-531-16443-8). 32pp. A concise look at mummies and embalming that uses split spreads that can be opened to reveal additional information. (Rev: SLJ 6/01) [393.3]

3822 McCall, Henrietta. *Gods and Goddesses: In the Daily Life of the Ancient Egyptians* (4–7). Illus. 2002, McGraw-Hill $18.95 (0-87226-635-4). 48pp. A colorful overview of religion in ancient Egypt in a series of double-page spreads that cover particular gods, religious practices, and various pharaohs. (Rev: BL 5/1/02; HBG 10/02) [200]

3823 Malam, John. *Mummies and the Secrets of Ancient Egypt* (4–8). Series: Secret Worlds. 2001, DK $14.95 (0-7894-7975-3); paper $7.95 (0-7894-7976-1). 96pp. As well as fascinating information on ancient Egypt, its religion, and mummification practices, this book contains a fine Web site listing and an eight-page reference section. (Rev: BL 10/15/01; HBG 3/02) [932]

3824 Manning, Ruth. *Ancient Egyptian Women* (5–8). Illus. Series: People in the Past. 2002, Heinemann LB $25.64 (1-40340-313-9). 48pp. A look at the life of, and options open to, women in ancient Egypt. (Rev: BL 3/1/03) [305.42]

3825 Meltzer, Milton. *In the Days of the Pharaohs: A Look at Ancient Egypt* (4–8). Illus. 2001, Watts LB $32.00 (0-531-11791-X). 159pp. A series of color plates add to the visual appeal of this look at ancient Egypt and how archaeological discoveries have contributed to our knowledge of this intriguing society. (Rev: BL 12/1/01; SLJ 12/01)

3826 Millard, Anne. *Going to War in Ancient Egypt* (5–7). Illus. 2001, Watts LB $23. PLB $23 (0-531-14589-1). 32pp. Soldiers, weapons, and military strategies of ancient Egypt are presented with many illustrations and a timeline. (Rev: SLJ 10/01)

3827 Nardo, Don. *Ancient Egypt* (3–6). Illus. 2002, Gale LB $23.70 (0-7377-0955-3). 48pp. A basic introduction to the people of ancient Egypt, nobility and peasants, and to the importance of their religious beliefs. (Rev: SLJ 9/02)

3828 Nardo, Don. *Ancient Egypt* (5–8). Illus. Series: History of the World. 2001, Gale LB $23.70 (0-7377-0774-7). 48pp. Topics covered in this basic introduction to ancient Egypt include customs of worship and burial, the role of the pharaoh, Egyptian history, and important artifacts. (Rev: BL 4/1/02) [932]

3829 Pemberton, Delia. *Egyptian Mummies: People from the Past* (3–6). Illus. 2001, Harcourt $18.00 (0-15-202600-2). 48pp. The author introduces seven ancient Egyptian mummies and discusses who they were during their lifetimes, as well as presenting readable information on archaeology, museums, and the study of mummies. (Rev: BL 9/15/01; HBG 3/02; SLJ 9/01) [932]

3830 Stewart, David. *You Wouldn't Want to Be an Egyptian Mummy! Disgusting Things You'd Rather Not Know* (4–6). Illus. by David Antram. 2001, Watts LB $25.00 (0-531-14597-2); paper $9.95 (0-531-16206-0). 32pp. The symbolism of elaborate Egyptian burials and the process of mummification are explained with many illustrations and cartoon art. (Rev: SLJ 9/01)

Greece

3831 Bailey, Linda. *Adventures in Ancient Greece* (3–5). Illus. by Bill Slavin. Series: Good Times Travel Agency. 2002, Kids Can $14.95 (1-55074-534-4); paper $7.95 (1-55074-536-0). 48pp. Readers take a trip to ancient Greece and learn about democracy, the Olympics, everyday life, and other aspects in an appealing layout that includes cartoon panels. (Rev: BL 11/1/02; HBG 3/03) [938]

3832 Blacklock, Dyan. *Olympia: Warrior Athletes of Ancient Greece* (5–8). Illus. by David Kennett. 2001, Walker $17.95 (0-8027-8790-8). 48pp. A lavishly illustrated introduction to the ancient Olympic Games. (Rev: BL 9/15/01; HBG 3/02; SLJ 10/01) [796.48]

3833 Jovinelly, Joann, and Jason Netelkos. *The Crafts and Culture of the Ancient Greeks* (5–8). Series: Crafts of the Ancient World. 2002, Rosen LB $29.25 (0-8239-3510-8). 48pp. As well as basic information on ancient Greece, this book outlines many craft projects. (Rev: BL 5/15/02) [938]

3834 MacDonald, Fiona. *You Wouldn't Want to Be a Slave in Ancient Greece! A Life You'd Rather Not Have* (4–6). Illus. by David Antram. Series: You Wouldn't Want To. 2001, Watts LB $25.00 (0-531-14600-6); paper $9.95 (0-531-16203-6). 32pp. The story of a woman who is kidnapped and taken to Greece as a slave serves as a good starting point to prove the premise of this book. (Rev: SLJ 9/01)

3835 Middleton, Haydn. *Ancient Greek Jobs* (4–6). Series: People in the Past. 2002, Heinemann LB $25.64 (1-58810-638-1). 48pp. The tasks of the doctor, banker, farmer, merchant, and other professions are explained and placed in historical context. Also use *Ancient Greek Women* and *Ancient Greek Children*. (Rev: HBG 3/03; SLJ 12/02)

3836 Nardo, Don. *Ancient Athens* (5–8). Illus. Series: A Travel Guide To. 2002, Gale $21.96 (1-

59018-016-X). 112pp. This fact-filled "guidebook" introduces aspiring travelers to everyday life in ancient Athens, in addition to information on climate, geography, important sights, and so forth. (Rev: BL 1/1–15/03; SLJ 2/03) [914.75]

3837 Nardo, Don. *Ancient Greece* (3–5). Illus. Series: Daily Life. 2002, Gale LB $21.54 (0-7377-0956-1). 48pp. Nardo presents material on everyday life in ancient Greece, covering everything from food and dress to politics and the rights of women and slaves in an easy-to-read style. (Rev: BL 12/1/02; SLJ 9/02) [938]

3838 Nardo, Don. *Greek Temples* (5–7). Illus. Series: Famous Structures. 2002, Watts LB $24.00 (0-531-12035-X); paper $8.95 (0-531-16225-7). 64pp. Nardo looks at the construction, elements, use, and importance of ancient Greek temples, with illustrations. (Rev: BL 9/1/02; SLJ 8/02) [726]

3839 Solway, Andrew. *Ancient Greece* (3–6). Illus. by Peter Connolly. Series: Ancient World. 2001, Oxford $18.95 (0-19-910810-2). 64pp. Exceptional artwork and detailed descriptions of life and institutions in ancient Greece. (Rev: BL 3/1/02; HBG 3/02; SLJ 2/02) [938.04]

Rome

3840 Butterfield, Moira. *Going to War in Roman Times* (5–7). Illus. Series: Armies of the Past. 2001, Watts LB $23.00 (0-531-14591-3); paper $6.95 (0-531-16352-0). 32pp. Soldiers, weapons, and military strategies of Roman times are presented with many illustrations and a timeline. (Rev: SLJ 10/01)

3841 Hart, Avery, and Sandra Gallagher. *Ancient Rome! Exploring the Culture, People and Ideas of This Powerful Empire* (4–6). Illus. by Michael Kline. Series: A Kaleidoscope Kids Book. 2002, Williamson paper $10.95 (1-885593-60-0). 96pp. A fact-filled overview that introduces readers to all aspects of ancient Rome — history, legends and myths, government, transportation, wars, key individuals, and so forth — and provides activities such as building a triumphal arch. (Rev: SLJ 3/03)

3842 Jovinelly, Joann, and Jason Netelkos. *The Crafts and Culture of the Romans* (5–8). Series: Crafts of the Ancient World. 2002, Rosen LB $29.25 (0-8239-3513-2). 48pp. The daily life and contributions of the ancient Romans are covered, as well as such craft projects as designing a toga. (Rev: BL 5/15/02; SLJ 6/02) [937]

3843 Malam, John. *Gladiator: Life and Death in Ancient Rome* (4–8). Series: Secret Worlds. 2002, DK $14.95 (0-7894-8531-1); paper $5.95 (0-7894-8532-X). 96pp. The world of the Roman gladiator is presented with fascinating, gory details, and everyday life in ancient Rome is described in a lively text with full-color illustrations. (Rev: BL 8/02; HBG 10/02; SLJ 6/02) [937]

3844 Malam, John. *You Wouldn't Want to Be a Roman Gladiator! Gory Things You'd Rather Not Know* (4–6). Illus. by David Antram. Series: You Wouldn't Want To. 2001, Watts LB $25.00 (0-531-14598-0); paper $9.95 (0-531-16204-4). 32pp. Car-

toon art belies the grimness of the content in this book in which readers will find plenty of hard information on how gladiators were acquired and trained, their rules of battle, and details of other savage forms of entertainment. (Rev: SLJ 9/01)

3845 Nardo, Don. *Ancient Rome* (4–6). Series: Daily Life. 2002, Gale LB $21.54 (0-7377-0612-0). 48pp. In this look at daily life in Rome, Nardo covers home and family life, work and education, public baths, and religion, and looks at the roles of men and women, young and old, rich and poor, and free men and slaves. (Rev: SLJ 7/02)

3846 Nardo, Don. *Roman Amphitheaters* (5–7). Illus. Series: Famous Structures. 2002, Watts LB $24.00 (0-531-12036-8); paper $8.95 (0-531-16224-9). 64pp. A clear overview of the construction, elements, use, and importance of ancient Roman amphitheaters, with illustrations. (Rev: BL 9/1/02; SLJ 8/02) [725]

3847 Nardo, Don. *The Roman Empire* (4–6). Illus. Series: History of the World. 2002, Gale LB $23.70 (0-7377-0775-5). 48pp. A concise overview of the important events and figures of the Roman Empire, with discussion of how archaeological finds have contributed to our knowledge. (Rev: SLJ 5/02)

3848 Solway, Andrew. *Ancient Rome* (3–6). Illus. by Peter Connolly. Series: Ancient World. 2001, Oxford $18.95 (0-19-910809-9). 64pp. Exceptional artwork and detailed descriptions of daily life, culture, religion, and sports in ancient Rome. (Rev: BL 3/1/02; HBG 3/02; SLJ 1/02) [937.6]

3849 Solway, Andrew. *Rome: In Spectacular Cross-Section* (4–7). Illus. by Stephen Biesty. 2003, Scholastic $18.95 (0-439-45546-4). 32pp. An inside look at life in ancient Rome, with views of a private home, the Colosseum, the docks, and a bustling festival. (Rev: BL 2/15/03) [937]

3850 Williams, Brian. *Ancient Roman Women* (5–8). Illus. Series: People in the Past. 2002, Heinemann LB $25.64 (1-58810-632-2). 48pp. A look at the life of, and options open to, women in ancient Rome. (Rev: BL 3/1/03) [305.8]

Middle Ages

3851 Doherty, Katherine M., and Craig A. Doherty. *King Richard the Lionhearted and the Crusades in World History* (5–9). Series: In World History. 2002, Enslow LB $20.95 (0-7660-1459-2). 128pp. This introduction to Richard and his chivalrous yet cruel personality conveys the religious fervor and economic needs that inspired the Crusades. (Rev: BL 4/1/02; HBG 10/02; SLJ 6/02)

3852 Marston, Elsa. *The Byzantine Empire* (5–8). Series: Cultures of the Past. 2002, Marshall Cavendish LB $19.95 (0-7614-1495-9). 80pp. Well-written text and colorful graphics present the history and culture of the surviving eastern part of the Roman Empire. (Rev: BL 1/1–15/03; HBG 3/03; SLJ 2/03) [949.5]

3853 Sherrow, Victoria. *Life in a Medieval Monastery* (5 Up). Series: The Way People Live. 2001, Lucent LB $19.96 (1-56006-791-8). 96pp. An absorbing account of religious life in the Middle Ages, with details of clothing, diet, and hairstyles as well as maps and black-and-white reproductions. (Rev: BL 6/1–15/01; SLJ 8/01) [271]

Renaissance

3854 Barter, James. *Renaissance Florence* (5–8). Illus. Series: A Travel Guide To. 2002, Gale $21.96 (1-59018-145-X). 112pp. Travel back in time to Renaissance Florence with this guidebook that gives period-appropriate historical and sight-seeing information as well as a flavor of everyday life in the city. (Rev: BL 1/1–15/03) [914.4]
3855 Schomp, Virginia. *The Italian Renaissance* (5–8). Series: Cultures of the Past. 2002, Marshall Cavendish LB $19.95 (0-7614-1492-4). 80pp. A handsome volume that gives a balanced, well-organized account of the Italian Renaissance, its history, personalities, art, and artifacts. (Rev: BL 1/1–15/03; HBG 3/03) [940.2]

World War I

3856 George, Linda S. *World War I* (5–8). Series: Letters from the Homefront. 2001, Benchmark LB $19.95 (0-7614-1096-1). 96pp. Life at the front and at home during the First World War is depicted through letters and other first-hand accounts. (Rev: BL 10/15/01; HBG 3/02) [973.9]
3857 Gilbert, Adrian. *Going to War in World War I* (4–6). Illus. Series: Armies of the Past. 2001, Watts LB $23.00 (0-531-14595-6). 32pp. Examines World War I from many perspectives, including strategy, weapons, and its effect on society. (Rev: BL 3/1/02; SLJ 10/01) [355.109041]
3858 Granfield, Linda. *Where Poppies Grow: A World War I Companion* (4–7). 2002, Stoddart $16.95 (0-7737-3319-1). 48pp. The horrors of war in the trenches are portrayed in this scrapbook full of photographs, propaganda, and ephemera that includes accounts of two Canadian soldiers. (Rev: BL 6/1–15/02; HBG 10/02; SLJ 7/02)
3859 Grant, Reg. *World War I: Armistice 1918* (5–8). Series: The World Wars. 2001, Raintree Steck-Vaughn LB $18.98 (0-7398-2753-7). 64pp. The negotiations that ended World War I are detailed here, with discussion of the failure of the League of Nations and the lead-up to World War II. (Rev: SLJ 6/01) [940.3]
3860 Hansen, Ole Steen. *World War I: War in the Trenches* (5–8). Series: The World Wars. 2001, Raintree Steck-Vaughn LB $18.98 (0-7398-2752-9). 64pp. The causes of World War I are introduced, followed by information on the major battles and

descriptions of the misery of life in the trenches, with plenty of photographs, reproductions, maps, sidebars, and excerpts from primary sources. (Rev: SLJ 6/01) [940.3]
3861 Ross, Stewart. *Assassination in Sarajevo: The Trigger for World War I* (4–9). Illus. by Stefan Chabluk. Series: Point of Impact. 2001, Heinemann LB $24.22 (1-58810-074-X). 32pp. The assassination of the Archduke of Austria, a precipitating factor in World War I, is put into context and the alliances among the world's nations at the time are clearly explained. (Rev: HBG 10/01; SLJ 7/01) [940.3]

World War II

3862 Allen, Thomas B. *Remember Pearl Harbor: American and Japanese Survivors Tell Their Stories* (5–9). Illus. 2001, National Geographic $17.95 (0-7922-6690-0). 64pp. First-person accounts by Japanese and American men and women give readers a close-up view of the 1941 Japanese attack on Pearl Harbor, with maps and photographs. (Rev: BL 9/1/01; HBG 3/02; SLJ 9/01*) [940.54]
3863 Butterfield, Moira. *Going to War in World War II* (5–7). Illus. 2001, Watts LB $23.00 (0-531-14596-4). 32pp. Soldiers, weapons, and military strategies of World War II are briefly presented with many illustrations and a timeline. (Rev: SLJ 10/01)
3864 Cooper, Michael L. *Remembering Manzanar: Life in a Japanese Relocation Camp* (4–8). Illus. 2002, Clarion $15.00 (0-618-06778-7). 68pp. This evocative account of life in a Japanese American World War II internment center tells its tale through personal accounts of survivors, quotes from the camp newspaper, and revealing photographs. (Rev: BL 1/1–15/03; SLJ 2/03) [940.54]
3865 George, Linda, and Charles George. *The Tuskegee Airmen* (4–6). Series: Cornerstones of Freedom. 2001, Children's LB $20.50 (0-516-21602-3). 32pp. A well-illustrated account of the 332nd Fighter Group of African American aviators and their exploits during World War II. (Rev: BL 4/15/01) [940.54]
3866 Jones, Steven L. *The Red Tails: World War II-s Tuskegee Airmen* (4–8). Illus. Series: Cover-to-Cover Informational Series. 2002, Perfection Learning $15.95 (0-7569-0251-7); paper $8.95 (0-7891-5487-0). 64pp. The story of the heroic African American squadron of World War II fighter pilots, their successful missions, and the prejudices they faced. (Rev: BL 5/1/02) [940.5404]
3867 Krensky, Stephen. *Pearl Harbor* (2–4). Illus. by Larry Day. Series: Ready-to-Read. 2001, Simon & Schuster $15.00 (0-689-84213-9). 39pp. An introduction for beginning readers to the events of December 7, 1941, with a complete description of the attack and historical background that puts it into context. (Rev: HBG 10/01; SLJ 7/01) [996.9]
3868 Landau, Elaine. *Holocaust Memories: Speaking the Truth* (4–6). Series: In Their Own Voices.

2001, Watts LB $22.50 (0-531-11742-1). 95pp. Landau combines survivors' stories of Kristallnacht, the Warsaw Ghetto rebellion, and concentration camps with background information and black-and-white photographs to present a moving whole that includes a story of her own grandfather. (Rev: BL 9/1/01; SLJ 9/01) [940.53]

3869 Langley, Wanda. *Flying Higher: The Women Airforce Service Pilots of World War II* (5–8). Illus. 2002, Linnet $25.00 (0-208-02506-5). 128pp. The women who flew in World War II gained little glory for performing many vital tasks; this arresting volume focuses on the director of the service, Jacqueline Cochran, and one of the pilots. (Rev: BL 11/1/02; HBG 3/03; SLJ 8/02) [940.54]

3870 Levine, Karen. *Hana's Suitcase* (5–8). Illus. 2003, Albert Whitman $15.95 (0-8075-3148-0). 112pp. A Japanese curator of a Holocaust exhibit traces the owner of a suitcase and learns the story of young Hana, who died in Auschwitz. (Rev: BL 3/15/03) [940.53]

3871 Levy, Pat. *Causes* (5–9). Series: The Holocaust. 2001, Raintree Steck-Vaughn LB $19.98 (0-7398-3257-3). 64pp. Levy discusses the causes of the Holocaust, looking at historical, religious, political, social, and economic factors. Also use *The Death Camps* (2002). (Rev: HBG 10/02; SLJ 2/02)

3872 McGowen, Tom. *The Battle of Midway* (4–6). Series: Cornerstones of Freedom. 2001, Children's LB $21.00 (0-516-22005-5). 32pp. The story of the decisive Pacific-theater battle fought in June 1942 that was an important victory for the United States during World War II. (Rev: BL 12/15/01) [940.54]

3873 McGowen, Tom. *Carrier War: Aircraft Carriers in World War II* (5–7). Series: Military Might. 2001, Twenty-First Century LB $25.90 (0-7613-1808-9). 64pp. An introduction to the importance of aircraft carriers in World War II, with coverage of Pearl Harbor and major battles in the Pacific. (Rev: HBG 10/01; SLJ 6/01) [940.54]

3874 McNeese, Tim. *The Attack on Pearl Harbor* (5–8). Illus. Series: First Battles. 2001, Morgan Reynolds $20.95 (1-883846-78-1). 112pp. This book details the 1941 attack on Pearl Harbor and explains the conditions in Japan that led to the assault. (Rev: BL 10/1/01; HBG 3/02; SLJ 1/02) [940.54]

3875 Panchyk, Richard. *World War II for Kids: A History with 21 Activities* (5–7). Illus. 2002, Chicago Review paper $14.95 (1-55652-455-2). 164pp. Features on such topics as living on rations for a day, growing a victory garden, and tracking a ship's movements depict conditions in America and Europe during the war. (Rev: SLJ 12/02)

3876 Raven, Margot Theis. *Mercedes and the Chocolate Pilot* (2–5). Illus. by Gijsbert van Frankenhuyzen. 2002, Sleeping Bear $17.95 (1-58536-069-4). 48pp. The true story of a friendship between a young German girl and an American pilot

who dropped candy for the children during the Berlin Airlift. (Rev: BL 7/02; SLJ 8/02) [943]

3877 Rogasky, Barbara. *Smoke and Ashes: The Story of the Holocaust*. Rev. ed. (5 Up). 2002, Holiday $27.50 (0-8234-1612-7); paper $14.95 (0-8234-1677-1). 256pp. In this new edition, Rogasky updates information where new facts have come to light and expands the details of resistance efforts. (Rev: BL 10/15/02; HBG 3/03; SLJ 10/02)

3878 Schomp, Virginia. *World War II* (5–8). Illus. Series: Letters from the Homefront. 2001, Marshall Cavendish LB $19.95 (0-7614-1098-8). 96pp. Schomp uses letters written during World War II, accompanied by relevant illustrations, to give readers a real understanding of the difficulties of life on the homefront. (Rev: BL 10/15/01; HBG 3/02) [940.54]

3879 Tanaka, Shelley. *Attack on Pearl Harbor: The True Story of the Day America Entered World War II* (5–8). Illus. Series: I Was There. 2001, Hyperion $19.99 (0-7868-0736-9). 64pp. An absorbing account of Pearl Harbor that presents the real-life, and very different, experiences of four young men who were there. (Rev: BL 8/01; HBG 10/01; SLJ 11/01) [940.54]

3880 Whitman, Sylvia. *Children of the World War II Home Front* (3–6). Series: Picture the American Past. 2001, Carolrhoda LB $22.60 (1-57505-484-1). 48pp. The lifestyle of children in America during World War II is presented through text and historic photographs. (Rev: BL 6/1–15/01; HBG 10/01; SLJ 7/01) [940.54]

3881 Yancy, Diane. *The Internment of the Japanese* (5–8). Series: World History. 2002, Gale LB $27.45 (1-59018-013-5). 112pp. An accessible source of information on the internment during World War II and its aftermath. (Rev: BL 8/02; SLJ 8/02) [940.54]

Modern History

3882 Bjornlund, Britta. *The Cold War* (5–9). Series: World History. 2002, Gale LB $27.45 (1-59018-003-8). 128pp. Bjornlund looks at the origins and development of the Cold War, and details the crises and periods of reduced tension that marked the length of the conflict. (Rev: BL 8/02; SLJ 10/02) [940.55]

3883 Chrisp, Peter. *The Cuban Missile Crisis* (5–8). Illus. Series: Cold War. 2002, World Almanac LB $29.27 (0-8368-5273-7). 4pp. This look at the Cold War crisis focuses on the events leading up to the standoff and the reasons for the deteriorating relationship between Moscow and Washington. Also use *The Causes of the Cold War, The Vietnam War,* and *The End of the Cold War* (all 2002). (Rev: BL 11/15/02; SLJ 7/02) [973.922]

Geographical Regions

Africa

Central and Eastern Africa

3884 Broberg, Catherine. *Kenya in Pictures*. Rev. ed. (4–7). Illus. Series: Visual Geography. 2002, Lerner LB $27.93 (0-8225-1957-7). 80pp. Information on all aspects of life in this African country, including extensive coverage of its history, is accompanied by plenty of photographs and a Web site that offers up-to-date links. (Rev: BL 10/15/02; HBG 3/03; SLJ 12/02)

3885 Giles, Bridget. *Kenya* (4–8). Series: Nations of the World. 2001, Raintree Steck-Vaughn LB $34.26 (0-7398-1290-4). 128pp. From snow-capped mountains to scorching deserts, this geographically and culturally diverse African nation is attractively introduced in this volume. (Rev: BL 12/15/01; HBG 3/02; SLJ 12/01) [967.62]

3886 McNair, Sylvia, and Lynne Mansure. *Kenya* (4–7). Series: Enchantment of the World. 2001, Children's LB $34.00 (0-516-21078-5). A superior introduction to the land and people of Kenya with material on such topics as history, culture, problems, climate, resources, and religion. (Rev: BL 1/1–15/02) [967.62]

3887 McQuail, Lisa. *The Masai of Africa* (4–7). Illus. Series: First Peoples. 2001, Lerner LB $23.93 (0-8225-4855-0). 48pp. McQuail provides information about the Masai people, covering their history, customs, and contemporary daily life, with photographs. (Rev: BL 10/15/01; HBG 3/02; SLJ 3/02) [967.6]

3888 Schemenauer, Elma. *Ethiopia* (3–5). Series: Countries: Faces and Places. 2000, Child's World LB $25.64 (1-56766-713-9). 32pp. Basic facts and background material about Ethiopia are given in a simple text with color illustrations on each page. (Rev: BL 4/15/01; HBG 3/01) [963]

3889 Schemenauer, Elma. *Somalia* (3–5). Series: Faces and Places. 2001, Child's World LB $25.64 (1-56766-911-5). 32pp. Basic facts about Somalia

are given in a simple introduction with large type, many color photographs, and a text that emphasizes the everyday life of the people. (Rev: BL 9/15/01; HBG 3/02; SLJ 12/01) [967.73]

Northern Africa

3890 Barter, James. *The Nile* (5–8). Series: Rivers of the World. 2003, Gale LB $21.96 (1-56006-935-X). 112pp. An appealing and informative description of the Nile's source, tributaries, and path; history from ancient times; and the long-term environmental problems affecting the river and actions that are being taken to preserve the river. (Rev: SLJ 1/03) [962]

3891 Meister, Cari. *Nile River* (3–4). Series: Rivers and Lakes. 2002, ABDO LB $13.95 (1-57765-098-0). 24pp. A solid introduction to the Nile, its tributaries, flora and fauna, and the ways in which it has influenced human development in the area throughout history. (Rev: HBG 10/02; SLJ 7/02) [960]

3892 Merrick, Patrick. *Morocco* (3–5). Series: Countries: Faces and Places. 2000, Child's World LB $25.64 (1-56766-737-6). 32pp. An oversize book filled with color illustrations that describes the history, geography, and people of Morocco. (Rev: BL 4/15/01; HBG 3/01) [964]

3893 Weintraub, Aileen. *The Sahara Desert: The Biggest Desert* (3–5). Illus. Series: Great Record Breakers in Nature. 2001, Rosen $18.75 (0-8239-5640-7). 24pp. Informative text and dramatic full-page photographs introduce the world's biggest desert and its composition, extraordinary range of temperatures, residents, and fossil history. (Rev: BL 12/15/01; SLJ 7/01) [966]

Southern Africa

3894 Green, Jen. *South Africa* (4–8). Series: Nations of the World. 2001, Raintree Steck-Vaughn LB $23.98 (0-7398-1282-3). 128pp. A profile of the strongest industrial nation in Africa, with material on its geography, resources, environment, government, economy, and future. (Rev: BL 6/1–15/01; HBG 10/01) [968]

3895 Parker, Linda J. *The San of Africa* (4–6). Series: First Peoples. 2002, Lerner LB $23.93 (0-8225-4177-7). This account describes the history and culture of this nomadic people of the Kalahari Desert. (Rev: BL 5/15/02; HBG 10/02) [968]

3896 Rogers, Barbara Radcliffe, and Stillman D. Rogers. *Zimbabwe* (4–7). Series: Enchantment of the World. 2002, Children's LB $34.00 (0-516-21113-7). 144pp. This troubled African land is introduced with material on topics including history, geography, people, government, and resources. (Rev: BL 5/15/02; SLJ 7/02) [968.9]

3897 Stotko, Mary-Ann. *South Africa* (4–6). Series: Countries of the World. 2002, Gareth Stevens LB $21.95 (0-8368-2347-8). 96pp. This fine, basic introduction to South Africa covers historical subjects as well as contemporary life and problems. (Rev: BL 6/1–15/02; HBG 10/02; SLJ 8/02) [938]

3898 Wulfsohn, Gisèle. *A Child's Day in a South African City* (K–3). Illus. Series: A Child's Day. 2003, Marshall Cavendish $15.95 (0-7614-1407-X). 32pp. A black South African child's experiences in his integrated school and blended family, with explanations of his country's customs and culture. (Rev: BL 2/15/03; HBG 3/03; SLJ 2/03) [968]

Western Africa

3899 Blauer, Ettagale, and Jason Lauré. *Nigeria* (4–7). Series: Enchantment of the World. 2001, Children's LB $34.00 (0-516-22281-3). An interesting and well-illustrated introduction to the nation that is dominated by the delta of the Niger River. (Rev: BL 1/1–15/02) [966.9]

3900 Heinrichs, Ann. *Niger* (4–7). Series: Enchantment of the World. 2001, Children's LB $34.00 (0-516-21633-3). Niger, a predominately Muslim country that is one of the hottest places in the world, is described in this attractive volume with material on topics such as resources, history, and culture. (Rev: BL 1/1–15/02) [967]

3901 Ismail, Yinka. *Nigeria* (4–6). Series: Countries of the World. 2001, Gareth Stevens LB $21.95 (0-8368-2337-0). 96pp. This general introduction to Nigeria is presented in concise, well-organized text and many colorful illustrations and maps. (Rev: BL 12/15/01; HBG 3/02; SLJ 1/02) [966.9]

3902 Onyefulu, Ifeoma. *Saying Good-Bye: A Special Farewell to Mama Nkwelle* (PS–2). Illus. 2001, Millbrook $21.91 (0-7613-1965-4). 32pp. A young boy describes the two weeks of mourning and the traditional Nigerian village funeral that take place on his great-grandmother's death. (Rev: BL 5/1/01; HB 7–8/01; HBG 10/01; SLJ 7/01) [393.9]

3903 Provencal, Francis, and Catherine McNamara. *A Child's Day in a Ghanaian City* (1–3). Series: A Child's Day. 2001, Benchmark LB $15.95 (0-7614-1223-9). 32pp. A 7-year-old escorts readers through a typical day in this book that ends with brief information on history, geography, people, religion, and language. (Rev: BL 11/15/01; SLJ 3/02) [966.7]

3904 Reef, Catherine. *This Our Dark Country: The American Settlers of Liberia* (5 Up). 2002, Clarion $17.00 (0-618-14785-3). 136pp. This chronological account of Liberia's history makes good use of excerpts from letters and diaries. (Rev: BL 11/15/02; HBG 3/03; SLJ 12/02)

Asia

General

3905 Bramwell, Martyn. *Southern and Eastern Asia* (4–8). Illus. Series: The World in Maps. 2001, Lerner LB $23.93 (0-8225-2916-5). 48pp. For each country in these geographical areas, readers will find a color map, the flag, a box containing important facts, and brief discussions of geography, industry, and economy. Also use *Northern and Western Asia* (2001). (Rev: HBG 10/01; SLJ 7/01) [915]

3906 Dramer, Kim. *The Mekong River* (4–8). Series: Watts Library. 2001, Watts LB $24.00 (0-531-11854-1). 63pp. A fact-filled introduction to the history of the Mekong and to the landscape and industry found along it. (Rev: SLJ 5/01) [959.7]

3907 Lobaido, Anthony C., and Yumi Ng. *The Kurds of Asia* (4–6). Illus. Series: First Peoples. 2002, Lerner LB $23.93 (0-8225-0664-5). 48pp. Traditional and contemporary lifestyles are both included in this presentation of the Kurd people, the territory in which they live, and their history, culture, and economy. (Rev: HBG 3/03; SLJ 2/03)

3908 Major, John S., and Betty J. Belanus. *Caravan to America: Living Arts of the Silk Road* (5–8). Illus. 2002, Cricket $24.95 (0-8126-2666-4); paper $15.95 (0-8126-2677-X). 144pp. The traditions and skills emanating from the ancient trade routes are shown as surviving today in the work of a rug restorer in New York, an artist-monk in Los Angeles, a cook from Iran, and other examples in this fascinating approach to an interesting subject. (Rev: BL 11/1/02; HB 1–2/03; HBG 3/03; SLJ 2/03) [745]

China

3909 Behnke, Alison. *China in Pictures*. Rev. ed. (4–8). Illus. Series: Visual Geography. 2002, Lerner LB $27.93 (0-8225-0370-0). 80pp. An excellent introduction to China that includes material on geography, history, people, economy, and culture with maps, photographs, and illustrations. (Rev: BL 10/15/02; HBG 3/03; SLJ 3/03)

3910 Brown, Don. *Far Beyond the Garden Gate: Alexandra David-Neel's Journey to Lhasa* (PS–2). Illus. 2002, Houghton $16.00 (0-618-08364-2). 32pp. This is the dramatic story of the long, intrepid travels of the first Western woman to visit the holy city of Lhasa (in 1924) and of her intense interest in Buddhism. (Rev: BL 10/1/02; HB 9–10/02; HBG 3/03; SLJ 10/02) [915.1]

3911 Costain, Meredith, and Paul Collins. *Welcome to China* (3–5). Illus. Series: Countries of the

World. 2001, Chelsea LB $16.95 (0-7910-6548-0). 32pp. A very basic overview of the country with information on plants and animals, culture, sports, and schooling. (Rev: HBG 3/02; SLJ 2/02)

3912 Deedrick, Tami. *China* (3–6). Series: Ancient Civilizations. 2001, Raintree Steck-Vaughn LB $15.98 (0-7398-3580-7). 48pp. Deedrick covers the Song, Yuan, and Ming dynasties of the Imperial period, giving good, clear information on history, daily life, culture, and inventions. (Rev: HBG 3/02; SLJ 9/01) [951]

3913 DuTemple, Lesley A. *The Great Wall of China* (4–7). Illus. Series: Great Building Feats. 2003, Lerner LB $27.93 (0-8225-0377-8). 80pp. This absorbing account tells the story of the building and importance of the Great Wall of China, with a good selection of illustrations, sidebar features, and maps. (Rev: BL 1/1–15/03) [931]

3914 Meister, Cari. *Yangtze River* (3–4). Series: Rivers and Lakes. 2002, ABDO LB $13.95 (1-57765-103-0). 24pp. A solid introduction to the Yangtze, its tributaries, flora and fauna, and the ways in which it has influenced human development in the area throughout history. (Rev: HBG 10/02; SLJ 7/02)

3915 O'Connor, Jane. *The Emperor's Silent Army: Terracotta Warriors of Ancient China* (4–6). 2002, Viking $17.99 (0-670-03512-2). 48pp. The beautifully packaged story of the amazing discovery of an army of life-size terracotta soldiers in a field in China in 1974, with information about the emperor who oversaw their construction. (Rev: BL 4/15/02*; HBG 10/02; SLJ 4/02) [931]

3916 So, Sungwan. *In a Chinese City* (2–4). 2001, Benchmark LB $15.95 (0-7614-1224-7). 32pp. A 7-year-old escorts readers through a typical day in this book that ends with brief information on history, geography, people, religion, and language. (Rev: HBG 3/02; SLJ 3/02)

India

3917 Chatterjee, Manini, and Anita Roy. *India* (4–8). Illus. Series: Eyewitness Books. 2002, DK LB $19.99 (0-7894-9029-3). 64pp. An informative and attractive overview of all aspects of India's history and culture. (Rev: HBG 3/03; SLJ 12/02)

3918 Dalal, Anita. *India* (4–8). Series: Nations of the World. 2001, Raintree Steck-Vaughn LB $34.26 (0-7398-1289-0). 128pp. A fine introduction to this vast, populous country with chapters on the land and cities, past and present, the economy, arts and living, and the future. (Rev: BL 12/15/01; HBG 3/02) [954]

3919 Nagda, Ann Whitehead. *Snake Charmer* (2–5). Illus. 2002, Holt $16.95 (0-8050-6499-0). 32pp. Readers of this fascinating photo-essay about young Vishnu and his snake charmer father will learn much about life in rural India. (Rev: BL 7/02; HBG 10/02; SLJ 7/02) [791.8]

3920 Srinivasan, Radhika, and Leslie Jermyn. *India*. 2nd ed. (4–8). Illus. Series: Cultures of the World. 2001, Benchmark LB $24.95 (0-7614-1354-5). 144pp. An updated edition of the 1990 title, cover-

ing the history, geography, politics, people, arts, culture, and environmental concerns of India. (Rev: HBG 3/02; SLJ 3/02) [954]

3921 Swan, Erin Pembrey. *India* (4–7). Series: Enchantment of the World. 2002, Children's LB $34.00 (0-516-21121-8). 144pp. This visually attractive introduction to the past and present of India includes coverage on languages, culture, the people, economy, and government. (Rev: BL 5/15/02) [954]

Japan

3922 Boraas, Tracey. *Japan* (3–6). Illus. Series: Countries and Cultures. 2001, Capstone LB $17.95 (0-7368-0770-5). 64pp. An overview of history, geography, government, economy, and culture that will be useful for students preparing reports. (Rev: HBG 3/02; SLJ 4/02)

3923 Costain, Meredith, and Paul Collins. *Welcome to Japan* (3–5). Illus. Series: Countries of the World. 2001, Chelsea LB $16.95 (0-7910-6541-3). 32pp. A basic overview that covers history, government, culture, transportation, plants and animals, sports, and schooling. (Rev: HBG 3/02; SLJ 2/02) [952]

3924 Green, Jen. *Japan* (4–8). Series: Nations of the World. 2001, Raintree Steck-Vaughn LB $23.98 (0-8172-5783-7). 128pp. An attractive, fact-filled introduction to this island nation, its rich culture, advanced technology, and wealthy economy. (Rev: BL 6/1–15/01; HBG 10/01) [952]

3925 Poisson, Barbara Aoki. *The Ainu of Japan* (4–6). Series: First Peoples. 2002, Lerner LB $23.93 (0-8225-4176-9). The Ainu of Japan have shared their homeland with the Japanese for centuries and continue to retain their independent culture. (Rev: BL 5/15/02; HBG 10/02; SLJ 8/02) [952]

3926 Schomp, Virginia. *Japan in the Days of the Samurai* (5–8). Illus. Series: Cultures of the Past. 2001, Marshall Cavendish LB $19.95 (0-7614-0304-3). 80pp. A well-illustrated look at the history of Japan, including information on such cultural topics as the tea ceremony and samurai women. (Rev: BL 2/15/02; HBG 3/02; SLJ 3/02) [952]

3927 Shelley, Rex, and Teo Chuu Yong. *Japan*. 2nd ed. (4–8). Illus. Series: Cultures of the World. 2001, Benchmark LB $24.95 (0-7614-1356-1). 144pp. An updated edition of the 1996 title, covering the history, geography, politics, people, arts, culture, and environmental concerns of Japan. (Rev: HBG 3/02; SLJ 3/02) [952]

3928 Takabayashi, Mari. *I Live in Tokyo* (1–3). Illus. 2001, Houghton $16.00 (0-618-07702-2). 32pp. Readers learn about the customs, traditions, and everyday activities that are part of a 7-year-old Japanese girl's life. (Rev: BL 9/15/01; HB 11–12/01*; HBG 3/02; SLJ 10/01) [952]

Other Asian Lands

3929 Baker, James Michael, and Junia Marion Baker. *Singapore* (4–6). Series: Countries of the

World. 2002, Gareth Stevens LB $21.95 (0-8368-2346-X). 96pp. An attractive introduction to the people, land, and culture of this prosperous island nation. (Rev: BL 6/1–15/02; HBG 10/02) [959.57]

3930 Boraas, Tracey. *Thailand* (4–6). Series: Countries and Cultures. 2002, Capstone LB $23.93 (0-7368-0940-6). 64pp. The land and people of Thailand are introduced with material on climate, landforms, history, traditions, people, and even a recipe. (Rev: BL 1/1–15/03; HBG 3/03; SLJ 2/03) [959.3]

3931 Condra-Peters, Amy. *Vietnam* (4–6). Series: Countries of the World. 2002, Gareth Stevens LB $21.95 (0-8368-2348-6). 96pp. An introduction to this Asian nation that emphasizes the progress made since the war. (Rev: BL 6/1–15/02; HBG 10/02) [959.7]

3932 Ericson, Alex. *Thailand* (3–5). Series: Faces and Places. 2001, Child's World LB $25.64 (1-56766-913-1). 32pp. This oversize volume presents basic facts on Thailand with an emphasis on the people and how they live. (Rev: BL 9/15/01; HBG 3/02) [959.3]

3933 Green, Robert. *Taiwan* (5–8). Series: Modern Nations of the World. 2001, Lucent LB $19.96 (1-56006-819-1). 112pp. Once known as Formosa, this island nation is introduced with material on its history, geography, climate, people, and economy. (Rev: BL 6/1–15/01) [951.24]

3934 Guruswamy, Krishnan. *Sri Lanka* (4–8). Series: Countries of the World. 2002, Gareth Stevens LB $29.27 (0-8368-2354-0). 96pp. History, geography, government, and people are all covered here, with special sections on such topics as the status of women and relations with the United States. Also use *South Korea* (2002). (Rev: HBG 3/03; SLJ 2/03)

3935 Haque, Jameel. *Pakistan* (4–8). Series: Countries of the World. 2002, Gareth Stevens LB $29.27 (0-8368-2352-4). 96pp. A useful source of the standard information on Pakistan plus a discussion of relations with the United States and some interesting sidebar features on such topics as pollution and cricket. (Rev: HBG 3/03; SLJ 1/03)

3936 Holmes, Jim, and Tom Morgan. *A Child's Day in a Vietnamese City* (K–3). Series: A Child's Day. 2002, Marshall Cavendish LB $15.95 (0-7614-1409-6). 32pp. Present-day Vietnam is introduced through the everyday experiences of a Vietnamese child. (Rev: BL 2/15/03; HBG 3/03) [959.7]

3937 McNair, Sylvia. *Malaysia* (4–7). Series: Enchantment of the World. 2002, Children's LB $34.00 (0-516-21009-2). 144pp. This Southeast Asian nation is presented in text and many color photographs that introduce its history, geography, people, culture, and present status. (Rev: BL 9/15/02) [959.505]

3938 Merrick, Patrick. *Vietnam* (3–5). Series: Countries: Faces and Places. 2000, Child's World LB $25.64 (1-56766-740-6). 32pp. With color pictures on each page, this basic introduction to Vietnam covers geography, history, culture, and everyday life. (Rev: BL 4/15/01; HBG 3/01) [959.7]

3939 Millett, Sandra. *The Hmong of Southeast Asia* (4–6). Series: First Peoples. 2001, Lerner LB $23.93 (0-8225-4852-6). 48pp. This attractive introduction to the Hmong people and their native region and culture also contrasts traditional and modern lifestyles. (Rev: HBG 3/02; SLJ 3/02) [305.895]

3940 Mirpuri, Gouri, and Robert Cooper. *Indonesia.* 2nd ed. (5–8). Illus. Series: Cultures of the World. 2001, Marshall Cavendish LB $24.95 (0-7614-1355-3). 144pp. An encompassing look at the history, culture, society, and geography of Indonesia. (Rev: BL 3/1/02; HBG 3/02; SLJ 4/02) [959.8]

3941 Petersen, David. *Thailand* (3–5). 2001, Children's paper $6.95 (0-516-27361-2). 48pp. A colorful overview of Thailand's geography, government, and customs. (Rev: BL 2/1/02) [959.3]

3942 Thomas, Matt. *Singapore* (3–5). Series: Faces and Places. 2001, Child's World LB $25.64 (1-56766-910-7). 32pp. The prosperous, tiny nation of Singapore is presented in a simple text, oversize format, and many attractive color photographs. (Rev: BL 9/15/01; HBG 3/02; SLJ 1/02) [959.57]

3943 Willis, Terri. *Vietnam* (4–7). Series: Enchantment of the World. 2002, Children's LB $34.00 (0-516-22150-7). 144pp. This attractive volume presents basic material on Vietnam's history, geography, and culture, with an emphasis on progress after the war. (Rev: BL 9/15/02; SLJ 12/02) [959.7]

3944 Yin, Saw Myat. *Myanmar.* Rev. ed. (4–8). Illus. Series: Cultures of the World. 2001, Benchmark LB $24.95 (0-7614-1353-7). 144pp. An introduction to every aspect of Myanmar with useful information on daily life and phonetic pronunciations of many foreign words. Also use *Indonesia* (2001). (Rev: HBG 3/02; SLJ 4/02)

Australia and the Pacific Islands

3945 Bartlett, Anne. *The Aboriginal Peoples of Australia* (4–7). Illus. Series: First Peoples. 2001, Lerner LB $23.93 (0-8225-4854-2). 48pp. An introduction to the indigenous people of Australia, including their history, customs, and daily life, with photographs. (Rev: BL 10/15/01; HBG 3/02; SLJ 3/02) [994]

3946 Darlington, Robert. *Australia* (4–8). Series: Nations of the World. 2001, Raintree Steck-Vaughn LB $23.98 (0-7398-1280-7). 128pp. Australia, the world's largest island, is introduced in this attractive volume that gives material on geography, climate, terrain, history, economy, and lifestyles. (Rev: BL 6/1–15/01; HBG 10/01) [994]

3947 Grabowski, John F. *Australia* (5–8). Series: Modern Nations of the World. 2002, Gale LB $21.96 (1-56006-566-4). 112pp. The continent Down Under is introduced with coverage on history, natural resources, landmarks, economy, and people. (Rev: BL 12/15/02) [994]

3948 Sharp, Anne Wallace. *Australia* (5–9). Series: Indigenous Peoples of the World. 2003, Gale LB $21.96 (1-59018-091-7). 112pp. In addition to discussing the customs and traditions of the aboriginal people of Australia, the author looks at their harsh treatment by the European settlers. (Rev: SLJ 1/03)

3949 Shepard, Donna Walsh. *New Zealand* (4–7). Series: Enchantment of the World. 2002, Children's LB $34.00 (0-516-21099-8). 144pp. Some of the subjects covered in this fine introduction to New Zealand are history, people and languages, economy, government, culture, natural resources, and climate. (Rev: BL 5/15/02; SLJ 10/02) [992]

Europe

Central and Eastern Europe

3950 Ake, Anne. *Austria* (5–8). Series: Modern Nations of the World. 2001, Lucent LB $19.96 (1-56006-758-6). 112pp. As well as general information on the history, geography, and culture of Austria, this volume supplies unusual glimpses of the country through the use of sidebars. (Rev: BL 6/1–15/01) [943.6]

3951 Clemmons, Brad, and Pamela K. Harris. *Switzerland* (3–5). Series: Faces and Places. 2001, Child's World LB $25.64 (1-56766-912-3). 32pp. In a series of short chapters with accompanying large color photographs, basic material on Switzerland is given, including facts on people, their work, the land, food, and everyday life. (Rev: BL 9/15/01; HBG 3/02; SLJ 12/01) [949.4]

3952 Grajnert, Paul. *Poland* (4–6). Series: Countries of the World. 2002, Gareth Stevens LB $21.95 (0-8368-2345-1). 96pp. Along with basic background material, this colorful introduction to Poland covers contemporary life. (Rev: BL 6/1–15/02; HBG 10/02; SLJ 5/02) [943.8]

3953 Harvey, Miles. *Look What Came from Switzerland* (2–4). Series: Look What Came From. 2002, Watts LB $23.00 (0-531-11963-7); paper $6.95 (0-531-16630-9). 32pp. Basic material on Switzerland precedes information on items that originated there, including inventions such as Velcro and contact lenses, foods, and music. (Rev: SLJ 1/03)

3954 Lundrigan, Nicole. *Hungary* (4–6). Series: Countries of the World. 2002, Gareth Stevens LB $21.95 (0-8368-2344-3). 96pp. A well-illustrated introduction to the past and present of Hungary with an emphasis on how people live. (Rev: BL 6/1–15/02; HBG 10/02; SLJ 5/02) [943.9]

3955 Nerman, Kemal, and Selina Kuo. *Turkey* (4–6). Series: Countries of the World. 2001, Gareth Stevens LB $21.95 (0-8368-2341-9). 96pp. A recommended introduction to Turkey that includes material on its people, traditions, geography, history, and current affairs. (Rev: BL 12/15/01; HBG 3/02) [956.1]

3956 Netzley, Patricia D. *Switzerland* (5–8). Series: Modern Nations of the World. 2001, Lucent LB $19.96 (1-56006-821-3). 112pp. Interesting sidebars, a chronology, and excellent photographs supplement informative text introducing this small country. (Rev: BL 6/1–15/01) [949.3]

3957 Rogers, Lura. *Switzerland* (4–7). Series: Enchantment of the World. 2001, Children's LB $34.00 (0-516-21080-7). A highly visual introduction to Switzerland that covers such topics as people and languages, history, natural resources, and climate. (Rev: BL 1/1–15/02) [949.4]

3958 Willis, Terri. *Romania* (4–7). Series: Enchantment of the World. 2001, Children's LB $34.00 (0-516-21635-X). Packed with photographs, original maps, and browser-friendly sidebars, this is a fine introduction to Romania that explores a number of aspects of the past and present of this country. (Rev: BL 1/1–15/02) [949.8]

France

3959 Cooper, Margaret. *Exploring the Ice Age* (5–8). Illus. 2001, Simon & Schuster $19.95 (0-689-82556-0). 96pp. Details the everyday lives, from tools and shelter to clothing and art, of humans living in the last Ice Age in southwestern France. (Rev: BL 11/1/01; HB 1–2/02; HBG 3/02; SLJ 10/01) [936]

3960 Corona, Laurel. *France* (5–8). Series: Modern Nations of the World. 2002, Gale LB $21.96 (1-56006-760-8). 112pp. A comprehensive introduction to the land and people of France with material on history, geography, culture, and lifestyles. (Rev: BL 12/15/02) [944]

3961 Costain, Meredith, and Paul Collins. *Welcome to France* (3–5). Illus. Series: Countries of the World. 2001, Chelsea LB $16.95 (0-7910-6551-0). 32pp. Young Gregoire introduces daily life, schooling, sports, transport, important places, and so forth, with interesting color photographs. (Rev: HBG 3/02; SLJ 10/01) [944]

3962 Plain, Nancy. *Louis XVI, Marie-Antoinette and the French Revolution* (5–8). Series: Rulers and Their Times. 2001, Marshall Cavendish LB $19.95 (0-7614-1029-5). In three well-illustrated parts, this book offers a biography of Marie Antoinette, a history of France and its people during the French Revolution, and a generous selection of original documents of the period. (Rev: BL 1/1–15/02; HBG 3/02; SLJ 3/02) [944]

3963 Stevens, Kathryn. *France* (3–5). Series: Countries: Faces and Places. 2000, Child's World LB $25.64 (1-56766-714-7). 32pp. This basic introduction to France, its history, people, and culture uses simple text, color photographs on each page, and an oversize format. (Rev: BL 4/15/01; HBG 3/01) [944]

Germany

3964 Nickles, Greg, and Niki Walker. *Germany* (4–8). Series: Nations of the World. 2001, Raintree Steck-Vaughn LB $23.98 (0-7398-1283-1). 128pp. A profile of this recently united, highly industrialized, and urbanized country, with material on its past, present, and future. (Rev: BL 6/1–15/01; HBG 10/01) [943]

Great Britain and Ireland

3965 Allan, Tony. *The Irish Famine: The Birth of Irish America* (4–9). Illus. by Stefan Chabluk. Series: Point of Impact. 2001, Heinemann LB $24.22 (1-58810-077-4). 32pp. Allan traces the causes of the crisis that started in Ireland in 1845, the subsequent wave of emigration to the United States, and the ill feelings created between Britain and Ireland. (Rev: HBG 10/01; SLJ 7/01) [941.5081]

3966 Ashby, Ruth. *Victorian England* (5–8). Series: Cultures of the Past. 2002, Marshall Cavendish LB $19.95 (0-7614-1493-2). 80pp. The political, historical, and cultural aspects of life in England during the reign of Victoria are covered in this handsome volume. (Rev: BL 1/1–15/03; HBG 3/03) [942]

3967 Blashfield, Jean F. *Ireland* (4–7). Series: Enchantment of the World. 2002, Children's LB $34.00 (0-516-21127-7). 144pp. Using many visual aids and a lively text, this is an introduction to Ireland — the land, the people, and the culture. (Rev: BL 5/15/02; SLJ 12/02) [941.5]

3968 Boraas, Tracey. *England* (4–6). Series: Countries and Cultures. 2002, Capstone LB $23.93 (0-7368-0937-6). 64pp. Using devices such as timelines, maps, sidebars, and a recipe, English history, geography, and culture are introduced. (Rev: BL 1/1–15/03; HBG 3/03) [942]

3969 Brassey, Richard, and Stewart Ross. *The Story of Ireland* (3–5). Illus. 2002, Trafalgar $19.95 (1-85881-848-6); paper $9.95 (1-85881-849-4). 40pp. Fast-paced narrative and brief biographies tell the history of Ireland from prehistoric times. (Rev: BL 3/1/02) [941.5]

3970 Chrisp, Peter. *Welcome to the Globe! The Story of Shakespeare's Theater* (3–5). Illus. 2000, DK $12.95 (0-7894-6641-4); paper $3.95 (0-7894-6640-6). 48pp. The Globe is presented through the words of a variety of characters, real and fictitious, working there and through detailed illustrations. (Rev: HBG 3/01; SLJ 4/01) [792]

3971 Davis, Kenneth C. *Don't Know Much About the Kings and Queens of England* (4–7). Illus. by S. D. Schindler. Series: Don't Know Much About. 2002, HarperCollins LB $15.89 (0-06-028612-1). 48pp. Humorous questions and answers supply information that browsers will enjoy. (Rev: HBG 10/02; SLJ 7/02)

3972 *Feed the Children First: Irish Memories of the Great Hunger* (4–8). Ed. by Mary E. Lyons. Illus. 2002, Simon & Schuster $17.00 (0-689-84226-0). 48pp. Text, full-color reproductions, and occasional photographs clearly document the suffering of ordinary people during the Irish potato famine. (Rev: BL 12/15/01; HB 3–4/02; HBG 10/02; SLJ 3/02*) [941.5081]

3973 Gottfried, Ted. *Northern Ireland: Peace in Our Time?* (5–8). Series: Headliners. 2002, Millbrook LB $24.90 (0-7613-2252-3). This attractive book gives current and background information on the struggles within Northern Ireland and the causes and possible solutions. (Rev: BL 4/15/02; HBG 10/02; SLJ 3/02) [941]

3974 Greenblatt, Miriam. *Elizabeth I and Tudor England* (5–8). Series: Rulers and Their Times. 2001, Marshall Cavendish LB $19.95 (0-7614-1028-7). After a biography of Elizabeth I, this colorful account traces everyday life in Elizabethan times and supplies a selection of primary documents. (Rev: BL 1/1–15/02; HBG 3/02; SLJ 3/02) [942.1]

3975 Harvey, Miles. *Look What Came from Ireland* (2–4). Series: Look What Came From. 2002, Watts LB $23.00 (0-531-11960-2); paper $6.95 (0-531-16628-7). 32pp. Basic material on Ireland precedes information on items that originated there, including Irish stew. (Rev: SLJ 1/03)

3976 Hestler, Anna. *Wales* (5–9). Illus. Series: Cultures of the World. 2001, Marshall Cavendish LB $24.95 (0-7614-1195-X). 128pp. Geography, history, government, arts and culture, and lifestyle are all covered in this interesting and attractive volume. (Rev: HBG 10/01; SLJ 11/01)

3977 Hull, Lisa. *Scotland* (4–6). Series: Countries of the World. 2001, Gareth Stevens LB $21.95 (0-8368-2339-7). 96pp. The history, geography, people, customs, and present status of Scotland are covered in this well-illustrated introduction. (Rev: BL 12/15/01; HBG 3/02) [941.1]

3978 Innes, Brian. *United Kingdom* (4–8). Series: Nations of the World. 2001, Raintree Steck-Vaughn LB $34.26 (0-7398-1288-1). 128pp. An in-depth look at the nation's geography, climate, terrain, history, government, and lifestyles. (Rev: BL 12/15/01) [941]

3979 O'Sullivan, MaryCate. *Scotland* (3–5). Series: Faces and Places. 2001, Child's World LB $25.64 (1-56766-909-3). 32pp. The land and people of Scotland are introduced using a simple text, large type, and color pictures on each page. (Rev: BL 9/15/01; HBG 3/02) [941.1]

3980 Ross, Michael Elsohn. *Children of Ireland* (4–6). Series: The World's Children. 2001, Carolrhoda LB $23.93 (1-57505-521-X). Outstanding photographs of children are used to introduce this land and the daily lives of its people. (Rev: BL 1/1–15/02; HBG 3/02) [951.5]

3981 Ross, Michael Elsohn. *Children of Northern Ireland* (2–5). Photos by Felix Rigau. Series: The World's Children. 2001, Carolrhoda LB $23.93 (1-57505-433-7). 48pp. This look at the daily lives of children in Northern Ireland introduces the history, geography, and culture of the country, with appealing full-color illustrations, a pronunciation guide, and map. (Rev: HBG 10/01; SLJ 6/01) [941.6]

3982 Schemenauer, Elma. *England* (3–5). Series: Countries: Faces and Places. 2000, Child's World LB $25.64 (1-56766-735-X). 32pp. Basic information about the past and present of England and its people is given in an attractive volume with large type and many color photographs. (Rev: BL 4/15/01; HBG 3/01) [942]

3983 Stein, R. Conrad. *Scotland* (4–7). Series: Enchantment of the World. 2001, Children's LB $34.00 (0-516-21112-9). Numerous pictures, charts, maps, and drawings contribute to a fascinating portrait of Scotland's past and present. (Rev: BL 1/1–15/02) [931]

3984 Toht, Betony, and David Toht. *Daily Life in Ancient and Modern London* (4–8). Illus. by Ray Webb. Series: Cities Through Time. 2001, Runestone LB $25.26 (0-8225-3223-9). 64pp. London's evolution from earliest times to today is presented in double-page spreads, with information on political, social, and religious life. (Rev: BL 4/15/01; HBG 10/01; SLJ 7/01)

Greece and Italy

3985 Behnke, Alison. *Italy in Pictures.* Rev. ed. (4–8). Illus. Series: Visual Geography. 2002, Lerner LB $27.93 (0-8225-0368-9). 80pp. An excellent introduction to Italy that includes material on geography, history, people, economy, and culture with maps, photographs, and illustrations. (Rev: HBG 3/03; SLJ 3/03)

3986 Cassidy, Picot. *Italy* (4–8). Series: Nations of the World. 2001, Raintree Steck-Vaughn LB $34.26 (0-7398-1287-4). 128pp. A fine overall picture of Italy, its past, its land, its people, its culture, and present-day problems. (Rev: BL 12/15/01; HBG 3/02) [945]

3987 Costain, Meredith, and Paul Collins. *Welcome to Greece* (1–4). Illus. Series: Countries of the World. 2001, Chelsea LB $16.95 (0-7910-6545-6). 32pp. An attractive introduction to the land and people of Greece, with a recipe, a craft, a brief page of facts, and many illustrations. (Rev: HBG 3/02; SLJ 12/01)

3988 Heinrichs, Ann. *Greece* (4–7). Series: Enchantment of the World. 2002, Children's LB $34.00 (0-516-22271-6). 144pp. With many color illustrations, this book gives a fascinating portrait of Greece's past and present with coverage of topics including natural resources, culture, climate, and religion. (Rev: BL 9/15/02; SLJ 12/02) [949.5]

3989 Hinds, Kathryn. *Venice and Its Merchant Empire* (5–8). Illus. Series: Cultures of the Past. 2001, Marshall Cavendish LB $19.95 (0-7614-0305-1). 80pp. A well-illustrated overview of the history of Venice with a focus on the city's glory during the Renaissance. (Rev: BL 2/15/02; HBG 3/02) [945]

3990 Kotapish, Dawn. *Daily Life in Ancient and Modern Athens* (5–8). Illus. by Bob Moulder. Series: Cities Through Time. 2000, Runestone LB $25.26 (0-8225-3216-6). 64pp. Kotapish explores everyday life, government, and culture in Athens through the ages. (Rev: HBG 3/01; SLJ 5/01) [949.5]

Low Countries

3991 Davis, Kevin. *Look What Came from the Netherlands* (2–4). Series: Look What Came From. 2002, Watts LB $23.00 (0-531-11961-0); paper $6.95 (0-531-16631-7). 32pp. Basic material on the Netherlands precedes information on items that

originated there, including clogs and bowling. (Rev: SLJ 1/03)

3992 NgCheong-Lum, Roseline. *The Netherlands* (4–6). Series: Countries of the World. 2001, Gareth Stevens LB $21.95 (0-8368-2336-2). 96pp. As well as the people, traditions, and lifestyles, this well-illustrated account provides general material on history and geography. (Rev: BL 12/15/01; HBG 3/02) [949.2]

Russia and the Former Soviet States

3993 Corona, Laurel. *Ukraine* (5–8). Series: Modern Nations of the World. 2001, Lucent LB $19.96 (1-56006-737-3). 112pp. This well-illustrated introduction to the former Soviet republic presents material on the people, culture, economy, history, and physical features. (Rev: BL 6/1–15/01) [947]

3994 Frost, Helen. *A Look at Russia* (K–2). Illus. Series: Our World. 2001, Capstone LB $10.95 (0-7368-0986-4). 24pp. Brief text and full-page color photographs give a basic introduction to Russia's land, people, and animals. (Rev: HBG 3/02; SLJ 12/01)

3995 Greenblatt, Miriam. *Genghis Khan and the Mongol Empire* (5–8). Series: Rulers and Their Times. 2001, Marshall Cavendish LB $19.95 (0-7614-1027-9). This handsomely illustrated book presents, in three parts, a life of Genghis Khan, a section on conditions in Russia during his reign, and a selection of documents of the time. (Rev: BL 1/1–15/02; HBG 3/02; SLJ 2/02) [947]

3996 Ilyin, Andrey. *A Child's Day in a Russian City* (1–3). Illus. Series: A Child's Day. 2001, Marshall Cavendish $15.95 (0-7614-1222-0). 32pp. The events in a typical day for Polina, a 7-year-old Russian girl living in St. Petersburg, with color photographs, sections on history and culture, and other background material. (Rev: BL 11/15/01; HBG 3/02; SLJ 3/02) [947.086]

3997 Kinkade, Sheila. *Children of Slovakia* (2–5). Photos by Elaine Little. Series: The World's Children. 2001, Carolrhoda LB $23.93 (1-57505-446-9). 48pp. The daily lives of children in Slovakia are used to introduce the history, geography, and culture of the country, with appealing full-color illustrations, a pronunciation guide, and map. (Rev: HBG 10/01; SLJ 6/01) [943.7305]

3998 Kummer, Patricia. *Ukraine* (4–7). Series: Enchantment of the World. 2001, Children's LB $34.00 (0-516-21101-3). A fine introduction to the past and present of the Ukraine with well-chosen illustrations and material on such topics as resources, daily life, landmarks, languages, and economy. (Rev: BL 1/1–15/02; SLJ 12/01) [947.7]

3999 Rogers, Stillman D. *Russia* (4–7). Series: Enchantment of the World. 2002, Children's LB $34.00 (0-516-22494-8). 144pp. This portrait of Russia in text and illustrations covers such basic subjects as history, resources, geography, people, problems, economy, and culture. (Rev: BL 9/15/02; SLJ 10/02) [947]

4000 Wilson, Neil. *Russia* (4–8). Series: Nations of the World. 2001, Raintree Steck-Vaughn LB $23.98 (0-7398-1281-5). 128pp. Colorful photographs, charts, and maps enrich chapters on Russia's past and present, land and cities, economy, art and culture, and possible future developments. (Rev: BL 6/1–15/01; HBG 10/01) [947]

Scandinavia, Iceland, Greenland, and Finland

4001 Alatalo, Jaakko. *A Child's Day in a Nordic Village* (K–3). Series: A Child's Day. 2002, Marshall Cavendish LB $15.95 (0-7614-1411-8). 32pp. This book takes a Scandinavian child through a typical day, showing the reader about family, friends, culture, and language. (Rev: BL 2/15/03; HBG 3/03) [948]

4002 Boraas, Tracey. *Sweden* (4–6). Series: Countries and Cultures. 2002, Capstone LB $23.93 (0-7368-0939-2). 64pp. This introduction to the land and people of Sweden explores topics including history, landforms, government, economics, and traditions. (Rev: BL 1/1–15/03; HBG 3/03) [948.5]

4003 Butler, Robbie. *Sweden* (4–8). Series: Nations of the World. 2001, Raintree Steck-Vaughn LB $23.98 (0-8172-5784-5). 128pp. Colorful maps, charts and graphs, and photographs supplement the text in this fine profile of Sweden. (Rev: BL 6/1–15/01; HBG 10/01) [948.5]

4004 Dupre, Kelly. *The Raven's Gift: A True Story from Greenland* (K–3). Illus. 2001, Houghton $15.00 (0-618-01171-4). 32pp. An encounter with a raven inspires two men to continue their journey around Greenland, in this effectively illustrated story of an expedition taken by the author's husband. (Rev: BL 8/01; HBG 3/02; SLJ 9/01) [919.82]

4005 Gravett, Christopher. *Going to War in Viking Times* (4–6). Illus. 2001, Watts LB $23.00 (0-531-14592-1). 32pp. Examines war in Viking times from many perspectives, including strategy, weapons, and the impact on society. (Rev: BL 3/1/02; SLJ 10/01) [355]

4006 Hopkins, Andrea. *Viking Explorers and Settlers* (3–6). Illus. Series: The Viking Library. 2001, Rosen LB $19.50 (0-8239-5816-7). 24pp. Beginning report writers will find basic historical information with illustrations, maps, and documents in this slim volume. Also use *Viking Gods and Legends* and *Vikings: The Norse Discovery of America* (both 2002). (Rev: SLJ 6/02) [938]

4007 Jovinelly, Joann, and Jason Netelkos. *The Crafts and Culture of the Vikings* (5–8). Series: Crafts of the Ancient World. 2002, Rosen LB $29.25 (0-8239-3514-0). 48pp. In addition to giving a tour of ancient Scandinavia, this book outlines such craft projects as designing a battle shield and helmet, minting coins, and playing an ancient board game. (Rev: BL 5/15/02) [948]

4008 Robinson, Deborah B. *The Sami of Northern Europe* (4–6). Series: First Peoples. 2002, Lerner LB $23.93 (0-8225-4175-0). This book describes the life and culture of the Sami, once known as Lapps, who were once primarily reindeer herders. (Rev: BL 5/15/02; HBG 10/02; SLJ 8/02) [948]

4009 Wagner, Michele. *Sweden* (4–6). Series: Countries of the World. 2001, Gareth Stevens LB $21.95 (0-8368-2340-0). 96pp. In an attractive format with many illustrations, this basic account covers general topics such as geography, people, lifestyle, economy, history, and traditions. (Rev: BL 12/15/01; HBG 3/02; SLJ 2/02) [948.5]

Spain and Portugal

4010 Blauer, Ettagale, and Jason Lauré. *Portugal* (4–7). Series: Enchantment of the World. 2002, Children's LB $34.00 (0-516-21109-9). 144pp. This highly visual introduction to Portugal includes accessible information on topics including history, people and language, customs, and economy. (Rev: BL 9/15/02) [946.9]

4011 Davis, Kevin. *Look What Came from Spain* (2–4). Series: Look What Came From. 2002, Watts LB $23.00 (0-531-11962-9); paper $6.95 (0-531-16629-5). 32pp. Basic material on Spain precedes information on items that originated there, including inventions, holidays, animals, foods, sports, and music. (Rev: SLJ 1/03)

4012 Goodman, Joan Elizabeth. *A Long and Uncertain Journey: The 27,000-Mile Voyage of Vasco da Gama* (4–8). Illus. by Tom McNeely. 2001, Mikaya $19.95 (0-9650493-7-X). 48pp. Details of Vasco da Gama's explorations and their historical context are accompanied by biographical information, illustrations, journal entries, a map, and a timeline. (Rev: BL 9/1/01; HBG 10/01; SLJ 6/01*) [910]

4013 Mann, Kenny. *Isabel, Ferdinand and Fifteenth-Century Spain* (5–8). Series: Rulers and Their Times. 2001, Marshall Cavendish LB $19.95 (0-7614-1030-9). Following biographies of these great Spanish rulers, there is a section on the life and culture of their times plus a generous selection of original documents of the period. (Rev: BL 1/1–15/02; HBG 3/02; SLJ 3/02) [946]

4014 Rogers, Lura. *Spain* (4–7). Series: Enchantment of the World. 2001, Children's LB $34.00 (0-516-21123-4). A well-designed book that uses clear text, numerous charts, maps, drawings, and photographs to introduce a number of topics related to Spain and its people. (Rev: BL 1/1–15/02) [946]

The Middle East

General

4015 Campbell, Geoffrey A. *Life of an American Soldier* (5 Up). Series: American War Library: The Persian Gulf War. 2001, Lucent LB $19.96 (1-56006-713-6). 128pp. Interviews with Gulf War veterans bring a personal touch to this volume, which includes many photographs of soldiers and equipment along with a history of the war and discussion of the reasons for the conflict. (Rev: SLJ 8/01) [956.7044]

4016 Losleben, Elizabeth. *The Bedouin of the Middle East* (4–6). Series: First Peoples. 2002, Lerner LB $23.93 (0-8225-0663-7). 48pp. Traditional and contemporary lifestyles are included in this presentation of the Bedouin people, the territory in which they live, and their history, culture, and economy. (Rev: HBG 3/03; SLJ 2/03) [961]

4017 Ruggiero, Adriane. *The Ottoman Empire* (5–8). Series: Cultures of the Past. 2002, Marshall Cavendish LB $19.95 (0-7614-1494-0). 80pp. A handsome account that traces the rise and fall of the great Ottoman Empire from its beginning in the 15th century to its collapse and the formation of modern Turkey after World War I. (Rev: BL 1/1–15/03; HBG 3/03; SLJ 2/03) [956]

Egypt

4018 Barghusen, Joan. *Daily Life in Ancient and Modern Cairo* (4–8). Illus. by Bob Moulder. Series: Cities Through Time. 2001, Runestone LB $25.26 (0-8225-3221-2). 63pp. Cairo's evolution from earliest times to today is presented in double-page spreads with information on political, social, and religious life as well as women's issues, with a timeline and quotations. (Rev: BL 4/15/01; HBG 10/01; SLJ 7/01) [962]

4019 Eldash, Khaled, and Dalia Khattab. *A Child's Day in an Egyptian City* (K–3). Series: A Child's Day. 2002, Marshall Cavendish LB $15.95 (0-7614-1410-X). 32pp. An accessible introduction to present-day Egypt through the daily life of its children. (Rev: BL 2/15/03; HBG 3/03) [962]

4020 Hooper, Meredith. *Who Built the Pyramid?* (3–5). Illus. by Robin Heighway-Bury. 2001, Candlewick $15.99 (0-7636-0786-X). 40pp. A combination of fact and fiction is used to describe the roles of various participants — from the king of Egypt to the designer to the water carrier — in the construction of a pyramid 4,000 years ago. (Rev: BCCB 1/02; BL 1/1–15/02; HB 1–2/02; HBG 3/02; SLJ 1/02) [932.013]

4021 Wilson, Neil. *Egypt* (4–8). Series: Nations of the World. 2001, Raintree Steck-Vaughn LB $23.98 (0-7398-1283-1). 128pp. An excellent introduction to the country that housed one of the world's oldest civilizations and is currently a center of Islamic culture and religion. (Rev: BL 6/1–15/01; HBG 10/01) [962]

4022 Zuehlke, Jeffrey. *Egypt in Pictures*. Rev. ed. (4–8). Illus. Series: Visual Geography. 2002, Lerner LB $27.93 (0-8225-0367-0). 80pp. Covers Egypt's geography, history, people, economy, and culture with maps, photographs, and illustrations. (Rev: SLJ 3/03)

Israel

4023 Boraas, Tracey. *Israel* (4–6). Series: Countries and Cultures. 2002, Capstone LB $23.93 (0-7368-0938-4). 64pp. This introduction to Israel includes

basic material on history, wildlife, government, geography, and economics. (Rev: BL 1/1–15/03; HBG 3/03) [956.54]

4024 Green, Jen. *Israel* (4–8). Series: Nations of the World. 2001, Raintree Steck-Vaughn LB $23.98 (0-7398-1286-6). 128pp. A fine, attractive introduction to the land and people of Israel, the nation that was created as a homeland for the Jewish people after World War II. (Rev: BL 6/1–15/01; HBG 10/01) [956.94]

4025 Grossman, Laurie M. *Children of Israel* (2–5). Photos by author. Series: The World's Children. 2001, Carolrhoda LB $23.93 (1-57505-448-5). 48pp. This look at the daily lives of children in Israel introduces the history, geography, and culture of the country with appealing full-color illustrations, a pronunciation guide, and map. (Rev: HBG 10/01; SLJ 6/01)

4026 Jovinelly, Joann, and Jason Netelkos. *The Crafts and Culture of the Ancient Hebrews* (5–8). Illus. Series: Crafts of the Ancient World. 2002, Rosen LB $29.25 (0-8239-3511-6). 48pp. The crafts of the ancient Hebrews and projects related to them are used to give basic information on their history and how they lived. (Rev: BL 4/1/02) [932]

Other Middle Eastern Lands

4027 Augustin, Byron. *United Arab Emirates* (4–7). Series: Enchantment of the World. 2002, Children's LB $34.00 (0-516-20473-4). 144pp. This important nation is introduced with material on topics including history, natural resources, climate, and people. (Rev: BL 5/15/02; SLJ 9/02) [953]

4028 Balcavage, Dynise. *Saudi Arabia* (4–6). Series: Countries of the World. 2001, Gareth Stevens LB $21.95 (0-8368-2338-9). 96pp. A fine introduction to Saudi Arabia told in a simple, well-organized text with many accompanying color photographs. (Rev: BL 12/15/01; HBG 3/02) [953.8]

4029 Cartlidge, Cherese. *Iran* (5–8). Series: Modern Nations of the World. 2002, Gale LB $21.96 (1-56006-971-6). 112pp. This colorful account gives a comprehensive overview of Iran, including history, geography, and culture. (Rev: BL 12/15/02; SLJ 1/03) [955]

4030 Goodwin, William. *Saudi Arabia* (5–8). Series: Modern Nations of the World. 2001, Lucent LB $19.96 (1-56006-763-2). 112pp. The land ruled by the Saud dynasty is presented with details on history, government, geography, resources, and world importance. (Rev: BL 6/1–15/01) [953.8]

4031 Heinrichs, Ann. *Saudi Arabia* (4–7). Series: Enchantment of the World. 2002, Children's LB $34.00 (0-516-22287-2). 144pp. Topics covered in the highly visual introduction to Saudi Arabia include history, religion, language, economy, and government. (Rev: BL 9/15/02) [953.8]

4032 Reed, Jennifer Bond. *The Saudi Royal Family* (5–8). Illus. Series: Major World Leaders. 2002, Chelsea LB $23.95 (0-7910-7063-8); paper $9.95 (0-7910-7187-1). 112pp. Saudi Arabia's ruling royal family is profiled, detailing its rise to power, its Islamic policies, and the various individual rulers, with a look at the contrast between the family's extravagant lifestyle and its religious beliefs. (Rev: BL 1/1–15/03) [953.8]

4033 Temple, Bob. *Saudi Arabia* (3–5). Series: Countries: Faces and Places. 2000, Child's World LB $25.64 (1-56766-717-1). 32pp. Using a simple text, short chapters, and plenty of color illustrations, basic facts about Saudi Arabia and its present-day status are given. (Rev: BL 4/15/01; HBG 3/01) [953]

4034 Wills, Karen. *Jordan* (5–8). Series: Modern Nations of the World. 2001, Lucent LB $19.96 (1-56006-822-1). 112pp. A good profile of Jordan is presented, with basic background material and information on present conditions and the people today. (Rev: BL 6/1–15/01) [956.95]

North and South America (Excluding the United States)

North and South America

4035 Dalal, Anita. *Myths of Pre-Columbian America* (5–8). Illus. Series: Mythic World. 2002, Raintree Steck-Vaughn LB $18.98 (0-7398-3193-3). 48pp. This volume for older readers separates myth from reality about cultures present in America in pre-Columbian times. (Rev: BL 3/1/02; HBG 3/02; SLJ 12/01) [398.2]

Canada

4036 Bowers, Vivien. *Only in Canada! From the Colossal to the Kooky* (4–8). Illus. by Dianne Eastman. Series: Wow Canada! 2002, Maple Tree $24.95 (1-894379-37-3); paper $14.95 (1-894379-38-1). 96pp. Facts of all kinds about Canada and the Canadians are presented in lively text with a wide range of illustrations plus maps and timelines. (Rev: SLJ 2/03)

4037 Greenwood, Barbara. *Gold Rush Fever: A Story of the Klondike, 1898* (4–7). Illus. by Heather Collins. 2001, Kids Can $18.95 (1-55074-852-1); paper $12.95 (1-55074-850-5). 160pp. Thirteen-year-old Tim and his older brother trek to the Yukon to try to win their fortune in this account that interweaves fact and fiction, with many details about the hardships the miners faced. (Rev: BL 12/15/01; HBG 10/02; SLJ 10/01) [971.91]

4038 Kalman, Bobbie. *Canada: The Culture*. Rev. ed. (4–6). Series: The Lands, Peoples, and Cultures. 2001, Crabtree LB $15.45 (0-7787-9360-5); paper $7.16 (0-7787-9728-7). 32pp. This revised and updated edition includes Native, French, and English perspectives as well as discussion of refugees. Also use *Canada: The Land* and *Canada: The People* (both 2002). (Rev: SLJ 6/02)

4039 Major, Kevin. *Eh? to Zed* (2–4). Illus. 2001, Red Deer $16.95 (0-88995-222-1). 32pp. Canadian

history and diverse culture are presented in an alphabet running from "Arctic, apple, aurora, Anik" to "Zamboni, zipper, zinc, zed." (Rev: BL 6/1–15/01; SLJ 7/01) [421.1]

4040 Robinson, Deborah B. *The Cree of North America* (4–6). Series: First Peoples. 2002, Lerner LB $23.93 (0-8225-4178-5). This book describes the culture and history of the Cree of North America, who are found primarily in subarctic Canada. (Rev: BL 5/15/02; HBG 10/02) [971]

4041 Whitcraft, Melissa. *The Niagara River* (4–8). Series: Watts Libraray. 2001, Watts LB $24.00 (0-531-11903-3). 63pp. This absorbing and readable account with maps and historical and contemporary photographs looks at the river's history, industry, and impact on the surrounding region. (Rev: SLJ 5/01) [971.3]

Mexico

4042 Ancona, George. *The Fiestas* (3–6). Illus. Series: Viva Mexico! 2001, Marshall Cavendish LB $16.95 (0-7614-1327-8). 48pp. One in a series of visually exciting photo-essay books for older readers about Mexican culture and traditions that also includes *The Folk Arts* and *The Foods* (both 2001). (Rev: BL 3/1/02; HBG 3/02; SLJ 2/02) [394.26972]

4043 Hamilton, Janice. *Mexico in Pictures*. Rev. ed. (4–8). Illus. Series: Visual Geography. 2002, Lerner LB $27.93 (0-8225-1960-7). 80pp. An excellent introduction to Mexico that includes material on geography, history, people, economy, and culture with maps, photographs, and illustrations. (Rev: HBG 3/03; SLJ 3/03)

4044 Jovinelly, Joann, and Jason Netelkos. *The Crafts and Culture of the Aztecs* (5–8). Illus. Series: Crafts of the Ancient World. 2002, Rosen LB $29.25 (0-8239-3512-4). 48pp. The culture of the Aztecs is covered through a discussion of their crafts and a variety of easily accomplished projects related to them. (Rev: BL 4/1/02) [972]

4045 MacDonald, Fiona. *You Wouldn't Want to Be an Aztec Sacrifice! Gruesome Things You'd Rather Not Know* (4–6). Illus. by David Antram. Series: You Wouldn't Want To. 2001, Watts LB $25.00 (0-531-14602-2); paper $9.95 (0-531-16209-5). 32pp. The circumstances of human sacrifice — and potential ways of avoiding this fate — are discussed with some black humor. (Rev: SLJ 3/02) [972]

4046 Sanna, Ellyn. *Mexico: Facts and Figures* (5–8). Series: Mexico: Our Southern Neighbor. 2002, Mason Crest LB $19.95 (1-59084-088-7). 64pp. An introduction to Mexico and its states, with material on history, people and culture today, and issues of importance such as poverty. Also use *The Geography of Mexico*, *The Economy of Mexico*, and *The Government of Mexico*. (Rev: SLJ 12/02)

Other Central American Lands

4047 Coulter, Laurie. *Secrets in Stone: All About Maya Hieroglyphs* (3–6). Illus. by Sarah Jane English. 2001, Little, Brown $17.95 (0-316-15883-6). 48pp. Coulter describes the process through which Mayan hieroglyphs were finally deciphered and explains the Mayan number system and calendar, as well as providing a chart of common glyphs, crafts and activities, and a timeline, glossary, and list of resources. (Rev: BL 12/15/01; HBG 3/02; SLJ 4/02) [497]

4048 Freedman, Russell. *In the Days of the Vaqueros: America's First True Cowboys* (5 Up). Illus. 2001, Clarion $18.00 (0-395-96788-0). 70pp. Vivid artwork complements this history of the earliest cowboys, the Central American vaqueros who first rode the range in the late 15th century. (Rev: BL 11/15/01*; HB 1–2/02; HBG 3/02; SLJ 9/01) [636.2]

4049 Grandell, Rachel. *Hands of the Maya: Villagers at Work and Play* (K–3). Illus. 2002, Holt $16.95 (0-8050-6687-X). 32pp. This photo-essay takes readers through a day in a Mayan town and shows typical activities and recreations. (Rev: BL 5/1/02; HB 9–10/02; HBG 3/03; SLJ 8/02) [972.83]

4050 Jermyn, Leslie. *Belize* (5–9). Series: Cultures of the World. 2001, Marshall Cavendish LB $24.95 (0-7614-1190-9). 128pp. Geography, history, government, arts and culture, and lifestyle are all covered in this interesting and attractive volume. (Rev: HBG 10/01; SLJ 11/01)

4051 Mann, Elizabeth. *Tikal: The Center of the Maya World* (4–8). Illus. by Tom McNeely. Series: Wonders of the World. 2002, Mikaya $19.95 (1-931414-05-X). 48pp. Mann provides an overview for older readers of the Mayan city of Tikal, covering the location, the people, the architecture, the culture, and their sometimes bloodthirsty customs. (Rev: BL 12/15/02; HBG 3/03; SLJ 1/03) [972.81]

4052 Merrick, Patrick. *Honduras* (3–5). Series: Countries: Faces and Places. 2000, Child's World LB $25.64 (1-56766-736-8). 32pp. With color photographs on each page, this is a simple introduction to the past and present of Honduras and its people and culture. (Rev: BL 4/15/01; HBG 3/01) [972.8]

4053 Morrison, Marion. *Nicaragua* (4–7). Series: Enchantment of the World. 2002, Children's LB $34.00 (0-516-20963-9). 144pp. Such topics as geography, history, people, language, economy, and government are covered in this introduction to Nicaragua. (Rev: BL 5/15/02) [972.8]

4054 Shields, Charles J. *Belize* (5–7). Illus. Series: Discovering Central America. 2002, Mason Crest LB $19.95 (1-59084-092-5). 64pp. Students needing facts about Belize will find everything here: geography, history, people, and culture, all backed up by maps, photographs, a timeline, and even recipes. (Rev: BL 1/1–15/03) [972.82]

4055 Shields, Charles J. *Central America: Facts and Figures* (5–7). Illus. Series: Discovering Central America. 2002, Mason Crest LB $19.95 (1-59084-099-2). 64pp. This look at Central America as a whole covers history, geography, inhabitants, and cultures. (Rev: BL 1/1–15/03) [972.8]

Puerto Rico and Other Caribbean Islands

4056 Bernier-Grand, Carmen. *Shake It, Morena?* (3–5). Illus. by Lulu Delacre. 2002, Millbrook LB $24.90 (0-7613-1910-7). 48pp. This is a collection of games, songs, riddles, and counting rhymes from Puerto Rico with explanations of origins and cultural backgrounds. (Rev: BL 4/15/02; HBG 10/02) [972.9]

4057 Graves, Kerry A. *Haiti* (4–6). Illus. Series: Countries and Cultures. 2002, Capstone LB $18.60 (0-7368-1078-1). 64pp. An introduction to Haiti's geography, history, and culture, with maps, timelines, and other aids. (Rev: BL 5/15/02; HBG 3/03) [972.94]

4058 Petersen, Christine, and David Petersen. *Cuba* (3–5). Illus. Series: True Books — Geography. 2001, Children's paper $6.95 (0-516-27358-2). 48pp. A colorful overview of Cuba's history and geography, with a positive slant on Castro's influence. (Rev: BL 2/1/02) [972.91]

4059 Ross, Michael Elsohn. *Children of Puerto Rico* (4–6). Series: The World's Children. 2001, Carolrhoda LB $23.93 (1-57505-522-8). This handsome volume filled with color photographs of Puerto Rican children describes the daily life of their island home. (Rev: BL 1/1–15/02; HBG 3/02; SLJ 2/02) [972.95]

4060 Schemenauer, Elma. *Haiti* (3–5). Series: Countries: Faces and Places. 2000, Child's World LB $25.64 (1-56766-715-5). 32pp. Basic material about the troubled island nation of Haiti is given in short chapters, simple text, and outstanding color photographs. (Rev: BL 4/15/01; HBG 3/01) [972.94]

4061 Schreier, Alta. *Cuba* (2–4). Series: A Visit To. 2000, Heinemann LB $21.36 (1-57572-380-8). 32pp. An introductory overview of the island nation today, with information on geography, people and culture, language, schools, and transportation presented in large photographs and simple text. (Rev: HBG 10/01; SLJ 4/01) [972.9]

4062 Stevens, Kathryn. *Cuba* (3–5). Series: Faces and Places. 2001, Child's World LB $25.64 (1-56766-906-9). 32pp. The island of Cuba and its people are introduced in this oversize volume with a simple text, short chapters, and color photographs on each page. (Rev: BL 9/15/01; HBG 3/02) [972.91]

4063 Wagner, Michele. *Haiti* (4–8). 2002, Gareth Stevens LB $29.27 (0-8368-2351-6). 96pp. History, geography, government, and people are all covered here, with special sections on such topics as the status of women and relations with the United States. (Rev: HBG 3/03; SLJ 2/03)

4064 Will, Emily Wade. *Haiti* (5–8). Series: Modern Nations of the World. 2001, Lucent LB $19.96 (1-56006-761-6). 112pp. The history, geography, and culture of this island country are presented with colorful prose and pictures plus unusual facts contained in sidebars. (Rev: BL 6/1–15/01) [972.94]

South America

4065 Augustin, Byron. *Bolivia* (4–7). Series: Enchantment of the World. 2001, Children's LB $34.00 (0-516-21050-5). With each page containing a color illustration, this attractive book introduces the land and people, economy, culture, and natural resources of Bolivia. (Rev: BL 1/1–15/02) [984]

4066 Barter, James. *The Amazon* (5–9). Illus. 2003, Gale $21.96 (1-56006-934-1). 112pp. In addition to covering the river's location and importance, Barter reviews the history of the people's living along the Amazon, early exploration by outsiders, and the environmental problems of the area. (Rev: BL 3/15/03; SLJ 1/03) [981]

4067 Boraas, Tracey. *Colombia* (4–6). Illus. Series: Countries and Cultures. 2002, Capstone LB $18.60 (0-7368-1076-5). 64pp. An introduction to Colombia that covers many topics including geography, history, and culture, with maps, timelines, and other aids. (Rev: BL 5/15/02; HBG 3/03) [986.1]

4068 Corona, Laurel. *Peru* (5–8). Series: Modern Nations of the World. 2001, Lucent LB $19.96 (1-56006-862-0). 112pp. Detailed sidebars, a chronology, and national statistics supplement the general information presented in this colorful introduction to Peru. (Rev: BL 6/1–15/01) [985]

4069 Dalal, Anita. *Argentina* (4–8). Series: Nations of the World. 2001, Raintree Steck-Vaughn LB $23.98 (0-7398-1279-3). 128pp. A colorful, interesting introduction to Argentina that covers its land and cities, history, culture, present economic conditions, and possible future developments. (Rev: BL 6/1–15/01; HBG 10/01) [982]

4070 Dalal, Anita. *Brazil* (4–8). Series: Nations of the World. 2001, Raintree Steck-Vaughn LB $23.98 (0-7398-1284-X). 128pp. A profile of the home of Carnival, the Amazon, and Pele with material attractively presented on its past and present, its people, and its culture. (Rev: BL 6/1–15/01; HBG 10/01) [981]

4071 Daniels, Amy S. *Ecuador* (4–6). Series: Countries of the World. 2002, Gareth Stevens LB $21.95 (0-8368-2343-5). 96pp. Using excellent illustrations and a clear text, this is a fine introduction to the land and people of Ecuador. (Rev: BL 6/1–15/02; HBG 10/02) [986.6]

4072 Eagen, James. *The Aymara of South America* (4–6). Series: First Peoples. 2002, Lerner LB $23.93 (0-8225-4174-2). This volume describes the history and present status of the Aymara, who live in the high plains of Peru and Bolivia, where they are known for domesticating the potato. (Rev: BL 5/15/02; HBG 10/02) [985]

4073 Fajardo, Dara Andrea. *A Child's Day in a Peruvian City* (K–3). Series: A Child's Day. 2002, Marshall Cavendish LB $15.95 (0-7614-1408-8). 32pp. The reader meets a Peruvian child and learns about culture, work, and play in modern Peru. (Rev: BL 2/15/03; HBG 3/03; SLJ 12/02) [985]

4074 Heisey, Janet. *Peru* (5–8). Illus. Series: Countries of the World. 2001, Gareth Stevens LB $19.95 (0-8368-2333-8). 96pp. An informative overview of

Peru's history, geography, government, culture, and relationship with other countries in the Western Hemisphere. (Rev: HBG 10/01; SLJ 4/01) [985]

4075 Lourie, Peter. *Tierra del Fuego: A Journey to the End of the Earth* (2–5). Illus. 2002, Boyds Mills $19.95 (1-56397-973-X). 48pp. A fascinating first-person look at Tierra del Fuego, the southernmost island off the coast of South America, including its discovery and the fate of its native peoples. (Rev: BL 10/15/02; HBG 3/03; SLJ 9/02) [918.276]

4076 O'Sullivan, MaryCate. *Peru* (3–5). Series: Countries: Faces and Places. 2000, Child's World LB $25.64 (1-56766-739-2). 32pp. This oversize, picture-filled book supplies basic information about the land and people of Peru. (Rev: BL 4/15/01; HBG 3/01) [985]

4077 Parker, Edward. *The Amazon* (5–9). Illus. Series: Great Rivers of the World. 2003, World Almanac $19.95 (0-8368-5442-X). 48pp. A comprehensive look at the river, its flora and fauna, its importance to mankind throughout history, and efforts to control outside factors threatening its survival. (Rev: BL 3/15/03) [981]

4078 Stevens, Kathryn. *Argentina* (3–5). Series: Countries: Faces and Places. 2000, Child's World LB $25.64 (1-56766-712-0). 32pp. Simple text, many color photographs, and an oversize format are used to supply basic background material on the land and people of Argentina. (Rev: BL 4/15/01; HBG 3/01) [982]

4079 Tagliaferro, Linda. *Galapagos Islands: Nature's Delicate Balance at Risk* (4–8). Illus. 2001, Lerner $25.26 (0-8225-0648-3). 88pp. This is a detailed but accessible introduction to the history, geology, wildlife, and ecology of the Galapagos Islands, with maps and photographs. (Rev: BL 9/15/01; HBG 3/02; SLJ 11/01) [561.9866]

4080 Tahan, Raya. *The Yanomami of South America* (4–6). Illus. Series: First Peoples. 2001, Lerner $23.93 (0-8225-4851-8). 48pp. This attractive introduction to the Yanomami people and their native region and culture also contrasts traditional and modern lifestyles. (Rev: BL 2/1/02; HBG 3/02; SLJ 3/02) [981.004]

4081 Yip, Dora, and Janet Heisey. *Welcome to Peru* (3–4). Illus. Series: Welcome to My Country. 2002, Gareth Stevens LB $23.93 (0-8368-2533-0). 48pp. An introduction to the geography, culture, and daily life of Peru, with a map, quick facts, and pronunciation guide for Spanish and Quechua words. (Rev: HBG 3/03; SLJ 4/02)

Polar Regions

4082 Bial, Raymond. *The Inuit* (5–8). Series: Lifeways. 2001, Marshall Cavendish LB $22.95 (0-7614-1212-3). Using clear language and many intriguing illustrations, this is a fine introduction to the Inuit that begins with a folk story on the origins of the people and continues with material on a variety of basic topics. (Rev: BL 1/1–15/02; HBG 3/02; SLJ 4/02) [979.8]

4083 Byles, Monica. *Life in the Polar Lands* (2–5). Illus. by Francis Mosley. 2000, Two-Can LB $9.95 (1-58728-557-6); paper $4.95 (1-58728-572-X). 31pp. This is a basic introduction to how plants, animals, and humans manage to survive in the Arctic and Antarctic. (Rev: SLJ 4/01) [508.311]

4084 Conlan, Kathy. *Under the Ice* (4–6). Illus. 2002, Kids Can $16.95 (1-55337-001-5). 56pp. This photo-essay relates the author's exciting experiences doing underwater marine biology research in Antarctica. (Rev: BL 11/1/02; HBG 3/03; SLJ 12/02) [578.77]

4085 Corriveau, Danielle. *The Inuit of Canada* (4–6). Illus. Series: First Peoples. 2001, Lerner $23.93 (0-8225-4850-X). 48pp. This attractive introduction to the Inuit people and their native region and culture also contrasts traditional and modern lifestyles. (Rev: BL 2/1/02; HBG 3/02; SLJ 3/02) [979.8]

4086 Fine, Jil. *The Shackleton Expedition* (5–8). Series: Survivor. 2002, Children's LB $19.00 (0-516-23904-X); paper $6.95 (0-516-23489-7). 48pp. For reluctant readers, this is an accessible and exciting account of how Shackleton's men survived the perils of shipwreck in the ice. (Rev: SLJ 9/02)

4087 Gray, Susan H. *Tundra* (2–5). Series: First Reports. 2000, Compass Point LB $15.95 (0-7565-0024-9). 48pp. An informative introduction to the ecosystem, with material on plants and animals, the conditions there, the importance of the biome to the global environment, and features such as the discovery of a woolly mammoth in the permafrost in Russia. (Rev: SLJ 5/01) [577.5]

4088 Green, Jen. *On the Tundra* (2–5). Illus. Series: Small World. 2002, Crabtree LB $15.96 (0-7787-0139-5); paper $8.06 (0-7787-0153-0). 32pp. This book for younger readers takes a close look at the creatures that are found in the tundra, and how plant and animal life coexist there. (Rev: BL 10/15/02; SLJ 8/02) [577.5]

4089 Levinson, Nancy Smiler. *North Pole South Pole* (1–2). Illus. by Diane D. Hearn. 2002, Holiday $14.95 (0-8234-1737-9). 40pp. Basic facts about the two poles for beginning readers. (Rev: HB 1–2/03; HBG 3/03; SLJ 12/02) [574]

4090 Penner, Lucille Recht. *Ice Wreck* (2–4). Illus. Series: Road to Reading. 2001, Golden Books $11.99 (0-307-46408-3); paper $3.99 (0-307-26408-4). 48pp. An absorbing narrative about Shackleton's disastrous expedition and exciting rescue. (Rev: BL 7/01; HBG 3/02) [919.8]

United States

General History and Geography

4091 Cooper, Jason. *Árboles / Trees* (4–8). Trans. by Blanca Rey. Illus. Series: La Guía de Rourke Para los Símbolos de los Estados/Rourke's Guide to State Symbols. 2002, Rourke LB $29.93 (1-58952-

399-7). 63pp. The 50 state trees are introduced in bilingual text and illustrations. Also use *Aves / Birds, Banderas / Flags*, and *Flores / Flowers*. (Rev: SLJ 3/03) [582]

4092 Costain, Meredith, and Paul Collins. *Welcome to the United States of America* (3–5). Illus. Series: Countries of the World. 2001, Chelsea LB $16.95 (0-7910-6542-1). 32pp. This basic introduction to the land, people, and culture of the United States will be useful in work with new immigrants and ESL students. (Rev: HBG 3/02; SLJ 2/02)

4093 Davis, Kenneth C. *Don't Know Much About the 50 States* (3–5). Illus. by Renee W. Andriani. Series: Don't Know Much About. 2001, Harper-Collins LB $15.89 (0-06-028608-3). 61pp. Each state gets its own page packed with facts, statistics, stories, and cartoon drawings, in addition to the standard fare of map, nickname, date of statehood, capital, and major state symbols. (Rev: HBG 3/02; SLJ 9/01)

4094 Davis, Todd, and Marc Frey. *The New Big Book of America* (3–5). 2002, Running Pr. $9.98 (0-7624-1263-1). 56pp. The 50 states are organized in alphabetical order, giving an overview of history, geography, and culture with a map, a list of basic facts, and topics of particular interest. (Rev: HBG 3/03; SLJ 1/03)

4095 De Capua, Sarah E. *Abolitionists: A Force for Change* (4–7). Series: Journey to Freedom. 2002, Child's World LB $25.64 (1-56766-644-2). 40pp. An overview of the efforts of abolitionists in America from the 17th through 19th centuries. (Rev: SLJ 12/02)

4096 Johnston, Robert D. *The Making of America* (5–8). Illus. 2002, National Geographic $29.95 (0-7922-6944-6). 224pp. An informative and balanced overview of American history, this appealing volume divides American history into eight periods; in addition to the narrative, each period profiles two major figures and examines important issues of the time. (Rev: BL 1/1–15/03; HBG 3/03; SLJ 12/02) [973]

4097 Leacock, Elspeth, and Susan Buckley. *Journeys in Time: A New Atlas of American History* (4–6). Illus. 2001, Houghton $15.00 (0-395-97956-0). 48pp. Twenty dramatic stories of "journeys" drawn from true accounts serve to introduce the history of America in an unusual and effective way. (Rev: BL 6/1–15/01; HB 7–8/01; HBG 10/01; SLJ 6/01) [973]

4098 Leacock, Elspeth, and Susan Buckley. *Places in Time: A New Atlas of American History* (4–6). Illus. 2001, Houghton $15.00 (0-395-97958-7). 48pp. In this companion to *Journeys in Time*, 20 significant sites — towns, battlefields, Ellis Island, even a tract house — are used to convey essential elements of American history. (Rev: BL 6/1–15/01; HB 7–8/01; HBG 10/01; SLJ 6/01) [911]

4099 Littlefield, Holly. *Children of the Orphan Trains* (3–6). Illus. Series: Picture the American Past. 2001, Carolrhoda LB $22.60 (1-57505-466-3). 48pp. A brief, informative text is accompanied by moving photographs that dramatically tell the sad story of orphan children transported West to find work and homes. (Rev: BL 5/15/01; HBG 10/01) [362.73]

4100 Lourie, Peter. *On the Trail of Lewis and Clark: A Journey Up the Missouri River* (3–5). Illus. 2002, Boyds Mills $19.95 (1-56397-936-5). 48pp. Lourie connects his own trip up the Missouri River to the more famous journey that Lewis and Clark took years before. (Rev: BL 4/1/02; HBG 10/02; SLJ 6/02) [917.804]

4101 Prevost, John. *Mississippi River* (3–4). Series: Rivers and Lakes. 2002, ABDO LB $13.95 (1-57765-102-2). 24pp. A solid introduction to the Mississippi, its tributaries, flora and fauna, and the ways in which it has influenced human development in the area throughout history. (Rev: HBG 10/02; SLJ 7/02) [976.81]

4102 Tackach, James. *The Abolition of American Slavery* (5–9). Series: World History. 2002, Gale LB $27.45 (1-59018-002-X). 112pp. A comprehensive survey of slavery and the abolition movement in the United States, with closing information on segregation and the civil rights movement of the 20th century. (Rev: BL 8/02; SLJ 9/02)

Historical Periods

NATIVE AMERICANS

4103 Alter, Judy. *Native Americans* (3–5). Series: Spirit of America: Our Cultural Heritage. 2002, Child's World LB $27.07 (1-56766-152-1). 32pp. This account gives an overview of the history of Native Americans, their problems, and the impact of their cultures on present-day American society. (Rev: BL 10/15/02) [973]

4104 Bial, Raymond. *The Nez Perce* (5–8). Series: Lifeways. 2001, Marshall Cavendish LB $22.95 (0-7614-1210-7). This attractively illustrated account gives basic material on the historical and social aspects of this Native American tribe, including discussion of food, clothing, and culture. (Rev: BL 1/1–15/02; HBG 3/02; SLJ 4/02) [973]

4105 Bial, Raymond. *The Powhatan* (5–8). Series: Lifeways. 2001, Marshall Cavendish LB $22.95 (0-7614-1209-3). The story of the Powhatan tribe of Virginia, whose members included Pocahontas, with material on their history and various aspects of their culture. (Rev: BL 1/1–15/02; HBG 3/02) [973]

4106 Bial, Raymond. *The Shoshone* (5–8). Series: Lifeways. 2001, Marshall Cavendish LB $22.95 (0-7614-1211-5). The story of the Native American tribe of buffalo hunters who lived in the Northwest, with material on their history, culture, language, food, and clothing. (Rev: BL 1/1–15/02; HBG 3/02) [973]

4107 Bruchac, Joseph. *Navajo Long Walk: The Tragic Story of a Proud People's Forced March from Their Homeland* (4–8). Illus. by Shonto Begay. 2002, National Geographic $18.95 (0-7922-7058-4). 34pp. Using revealing words and pictures, this large picture book for older readers re-creates the shameful story of the deadly marches of the Navajo in the

1860s. (Rev: BL 5/1/02; HBG 10/02; SLJ 7/02) [979.1]

4108 Bruchac, Joseph. *Seasons of the Circle: A Native American Year* (2–4). Illus. by Robert F. Goetzl. 2002, Troll $15.95 (0-8167-7467-6). 32pp. An overview of Native American activities, lore, and traditions associated with the different seasons, with effective illustrations, a helpful map, and a chart of Native American names of the months. (Rev: BL 10/1/02; HBG 3/03) [391]

4109 Burgan, Michael. *The Trail of Tears* (3–5). Series: We the People. 2001, Compass Point LB $21.26 (0-7565-0101-6). 48pp. A well-illustrated, concise introduction to the Cherokee people and the events leading up to their removal from their lands in 1838. (Rev: SLJ 6/01) [975]

4110 Carew-Miller, Anna. *Native American Cooking* (4–7). Illus. Series: Native American Life. 2002, Mason Crest LB $19.95 (1-59084-131-X). 64pp. The role of the environment in Native American food choices is emphasized in this overview that is organized by region. Also use *Native American Tools and Weapons* and *What the Native Americans Wore* (both 2002). (Rev: SLJ 2/03)

4111 Dennis, Yvonne Wakim, and Arlene Hirschfelder. *Children of Native America Today* (3–6). Illus. 2003, Charlesbridge $19.95 (1-57091-499-0). 64pp. Photos show contemporary Native American young people wearing traditional as well as modern clothes, with maps, reservation locations, and a resource list. (Rev: BL 3/1/03) [306]

4112 Elish, Dan. *The Trail of Tears: The Story of the Cherokee Removal* (5–9). Series: Great Journeys. 2001, Benchmark LB $21.95 (0-7614-1228-X). 96pp. The economic and social reasons for the Cherokee's forced exile to lands in the west are presented in text, quotations from primary sources, and many illustrations and maps. (Rev: BL 1/1–15/02; HBG 10/02; SLJ 3/02) [973]

4113 *Enduring Wisdom: Sayings from Native Americans* (3–6). Ed. by Virginia Driving Hawk Sneve. Illus. by Synthia Saint James. 2003, Holiday $16.95 (0-8234-1455-8). 32pp. A picture-book collection of sayings from 1647 to the present day that are backed up by helpful endnotes. (Rev: BL 3/15/03) [970]

4114 Gibson, Karen Bush. *The Chickasaw Nation* (2–5). Series: Native Peoples. 2002, Capstone LB $18.60 (0-7368-1365-9). 24pp. A clearly written history of this Native American tribe that lived in the northern Mississippi area. (Rev: BL 3/15/03) [973]

4115 Gibson, Karen Bush. *The Potawatomi* (2–5). Series: Native Peoples. 2002, Capstone LB $18.60 (0-7368-1368-3). 24pp. This history of the noted midwestern Native American group includes material on lifestyle, culture, and present status. (Rev: BL 3/15/03) [973]

4116 Gray-Kanatiiosh, Barbara A. *Hopi* (2–4). Illus. by Charles Chimerica. Series: Native Americans. 2002, ABDO LB $14.95 (1-57765-598-2). 32pp. An attractive and accessible introduction to the Hopi people that covers homeland, culture, family life, mythology, crafts, war, early contact with the Europeans, and contemporary lifestyle. Also use *Inuit* (2002). (Rev: HBG 10/02; SLJ 8/02) [973]

4117 Kirk, Connie Ann. *The Mohawks of North America* (4–7). Series: First Peoples. 2001, Lerner LB $23.93 (0-8225-4853-4). 32pp. This book focuses on the history and cultural practices of the Mohawk people and their present status in America. (Rev: BL 10/15/01; HBG 3/02) [973]

4118 Larson, Timothy. *Anasazi* (4–6). Series: Ancient Civilizations. 2001, Raintree Steck-Vaughn LB $15.98 (0-7398-3575-0). 48pp. The history, culture, and daily life of the Anasazi Indians are introduced, with maps and photographs and discussion of archaeological studies and the architecture. (Rev: HBG 3/02; SLJ 6/01) [979]

4119 Lassieur, Allison. *The Apsaalooke (Crow) Nation* (2–5). Series: Native Peoples. 2002, Bridgestone LB $18.60 (0-7368-1103-6). 24pp. This account describes the history and lifestyle of this Native American people who lived on the plains around the Yellowstone River. (Rev: BL 6/1–15/02; HBG 3/03) [973]

4120 Lassieur, Allison. *The Arapaho Tribe* (2–5). Series: Native Peoples. 2001, Bridgestone LB $18.60 (0-7368-0945-7). 24pp. Covers the history, culture, and lifestyle of this Native American tribe from the Colorado-Wyoming region. (Rev: BL 3/15/02; HBG 3/02) [973]

4121 Lassieur, Allison. *The Blackfeet Nation* (2–5). Series: Native Peoples. 2001, Bridgestone LB $18.60 (0-7368-0946-5). 24pp. A brief, colorful introduction to the past and the present of this midwestern Native American nation whose members dyed their moccasins black. (Rev: BL 3/15/02; HBG 3/02) [973]

4122 Lassieur, Allison. *The Choctaw Nation* (2–5). Illus. Series: Native Peoples. 2001, Capstone $12.95 (0-7368-0832-9). 24pp. History and contemporary lifestyle are among the topics covered in this introduction to the Choctaw Indians, the first tribe forced to leave its homeland. Also use *The Shoshone People* (2001). (Rev: BL 5/15/01; HBG 10/01; SLJ 8/01) [973]

4123 Lassieur, Allison. *The Creek Nation* (2–5). Series: Native Peoples. 2001, Bridgestone LB $18.60 (0-7368-0947-3). 24pp. This short history of the Creek people covers present status and conditions as well as offering informative text and full-color historical photographs and illustrations. (Rev: BL 3/15/02; HBG 3/02) [973]

4124 Lassieur, Allison. *The Delaware People* (2–5). Series: Native Peoples. 2002, Bridgestone LB $18.60 (0-7368-1104-4). 24pp. A description of the Native American people who first lived around the Delaware River, and made a famous treaty with William Penn in 1682. (Rev: BL 6/1–15/02) [921]

4125 Lassieur, Allison. *The Hopi* (2–5). Series: Native Peoples. 2002, Bridgestone LB $18.60 (0-7368-1102-8). 24pp. A brief account with many photographs that describes the past and present of this tribe of Pueblo Indians and gives details on the

richness of the culture they developed. (Rev: BL 6/1–15/02) [973]

4126 Lassieur, Allison. *The Pequot Tribe* (2–5). Series: Native Peoples. 2001, Bridgestone LB $18.60 (0-7368-0948-1). 24pp. The story of this Eastern Woodlands group of Native Americans is covered briefly in a simple text with many color illustrations. (Rev: BL 3/15/02; HBG 3/02) [973]

4127 Lassieur, Allison. *The Utes* (2–5). Series: Native Peoples. 2002, Bridgestone LB $18.60 (0-7368-1105-2). 24pp. The history and cultural development of the Native American people who began as fierce nomadic horsemen in what is now Colorado and Utah. (Rev: BL 6/1–15/02; HBG 3/03) [973]

4128 Littlefield, Holly. *Children of the Indian Boarding Schools* (3–6). Illus. Series: Picture the American Past. 2001, Carolrhoda LB $22.60 (1-57505-467-1). 48pp. A brief, informative text is accompanied by moving photographs that dramatically tell the sad story of Native American children taken from their homes and sent to boarding schools to learn European customs. (Rev: BL 5/15/01; HBG 10/01; SLJ 7/01) [371.829]

4129 Netzley, Patricia D. *Apache Warriors* (3–5). Illus. 2003, Gale LB $18.96 (0-7377-0989-8). 48pp. An absorbing look at the Apache warriors in the mid-19th century — with details of housing, clothing, hunting practices, and equipment — that draws on Geronimo's autobiography. (Rev: SLJ 1/03) [979.004]

4130 Nobleman, Marc Tyler. *The Battle of the Little Bighorn* (4–6). Series: We the People. 2001, Compass Point LB $21.26 (0-7565-0150-4). 48pp. A basic overview of Custer's last stand and the motivations of both sides in the battle. (Rev: SLJ 1/02) [973.8]

4131 Press, Petra. *The Pueblo* (3–6). Series: First Reports. 2001, Compass Point LB $21.26 (0-7565-0082-6). 48pp. An absorbing, well-illustrated account of the Pueblo people that covers religion, society, history, culture, and lifestyle today. (Rev: SLJ 7/01) [978.9]

4132 Riehecky, Janet. *The Cree Tribe* (2–5). Series: Native Peoples. 2002, Capstone LB $18.60 (0-7368-1366-7). 24pp. A brief introduction to these Plains Indians with details on their past and present and an emphasis on their place in today's world. (Rev: BL 3/15/03; HBG 3/03) [973]

4133 Riehecky, Janet. *The Osage* (2–5). Series: Native Peoples. 2002, Capstone LB $18.60 (0-7368-1367-5). 24pp. This introduction to these Plains Indians tells about their history, culture, and how they live today. (Rev: BL 3/15/03; HBG 3/03) [973]

4134 Santella, Andrew. *The Cherokee* (2–3). Series: True Books: American Indians. 2001, Children's LB $22.00 (0-516-22216-3); paper $6.95 (0-516-27315-9). 48pp. This simple, colorful introduction to the Cherokee Indians covers topics such as their homelands, traditions, history, and present status. (Rev: BL 8/1/01) [973]

4135 Santella, Andrew. *The Hopi* (3–5). Illus. Series: True Books — American Indians. 2002,

Children's LB $23.50 (0-516-22501-4); paper $6.95 (0-516-26987-9). 48pp. An overview of the history, culture, and contemporary life of the Hopi Indians, with many color photographs. Also use *The Navajo* (2002). (Rev: BL 11/1/02) [979.1004]

4136 Spradlin, Michael P. *The Legend of Blue Jacket* (3–6). Illus. by Ronald Himler. 2002, Harper-Collins LB $17.89 (0-688-15836-6). 32pp. This book looks at theories about the identity of the Shawnee chief known as Blue Jacket, and whether he might in fact have been the kidnapped son of a pioneer family. (Rev: BL 11/1/02; HBG 3/03; SLJ 11/02) [974.004]

4137 Tayac, Gabrielle. *Meet Naiche: A Native Boy from the Chesapeake Bay Area* (3–6). Photos by John Harrington. Series: My World: Young Native Americans Today. 2002, Beyond Words $15.95 (1-58270-072-9). 48pp. Tayac presents the everyday life of a Native American child of mixed heritage living in rural Maryland today, with descriptions of school and a traditional ceremony. (Rev: SLJ 3/03)

4138 Torr, James D., ed. *Primary Sources* (5–9). Series: Indigenous Peoples of North America. 2002, Gale LB $27.45 (1-59018-010-0). 96pp. An anthology of excerpts from primary documents, with a timeline, that covers Native American history and culture since the arrival of Europeans. (Rev: SLJ 8/02)

4139 Woods, Geraldine. *The Navajo* (5–7). Illus. Series: Watts Library — Indians of the Americas. 2002, Watts LB $24.00 (0-531-13950-6); paper $8.95 (0-531-16227-3). 64pp. This account includes information on history and contemporary issues and covers the Navajo code talkers, land disputes, traditions, housing, and clothing. (Rev: BL 7/02) [979.1]

DISCOVERY AND EXPLORATION

4140 Alter, Judy. *Exploring and Mapping the American West* (4–6). Series: Cornerstones of Freedom. 2001, Children's LB $21.00 (0-516-21599-X). 32pp. Using sidebars, a glossary, a timeline, maps, and an informative text, this account traces the exploration of the West and the mapmakers responsible for recording the findings. (Rev: BL 12/15/01) [917.8]

4141 Faber, Harold. *Lewis and Clark: From Ocean to Ocean* (5–8). Illus. Series: Great Explorations. 2001, Benchmark LB $19.95 (0-7614-1241-7). 80pp. This concise, artfully illustrated volume about the journey of Lewis and Clark includes journal entries, a timeline, and Web site information. (Rev: BL 1/1–15/02; HBG 3/02; SLJ 3/02) [917.804]

4142 Johmann, Carol A. *The Lewis and Clark Expedition: Join the Corps of Discovery to Explore Uncharted Territory* (4–6). Illus. by Michael Kline. Series: Kaleidoscope Kids. 2002, Williamson paper $12.95 (1-885593-73-2). 112pp. This is a wide-ranging and lively history of the expedition, providing profiles of the explorers, excerpts from journals, lists of resources, and activities. (Rev: BL 1/1–15/03; SLJ 3/03) [917.804]

4143 Kimmel, Elizabeth Cody. *As Far as the Eye Can Reach: Lewis and Clark's Westward Quest* (3–6). Illus. 2003, Random $14.95 (0-375-81348-9). 112pp. The expedition is brought to life in this well-written account that covers the planning stages, meetings with Native Americans, and the skills of the explorers, with journal excerpts, and a lengthy list of resources. (Rev: BL 1/1–15/03; SLJ 3/03) [917.804]

4144 Parker, Nancy Winslow. *Land Ho! Fifty Glorious Years in the Age of Exploration* (3–5). Illus. 2001, HarperCollins LB $15.89 (0-06-027760-2). 40pp. Brief overviews of 12 European explorers and their travels to the New World are accompanied by drawings and maps. (Rev: BL 11/1/01; HBG 3/02; SLJ 8/01) [910.92]

4145 Patent, Dorothy Hinshaw. *Animals on the Trail with Lewis and Clark* (4–8). Illus. by William Munoz. 2002, Clarion $18.00 (0-395-91415-9). 118pp. A handsome account of the Lewis and Clark expedition with emphasis on the animals that were discovered during the journey. (Rev: BCCB 5/02; BL 4/15/02*; HB 5–6/02; HBG 10/02; SLJ 4/02) [917.804]

4146 Patent, Dorothy Hinshaw. *The Lewis and Clark Trail: Then and Now* (4–8). Illus. by William Munoz. 2002, Dutton $19.99 (0-525-46912-5). 64pp. The hardships faced by the members of the famous expedition are given a new focus, comparing the conditions and landscapes of today to those Lewis and Clark discovered. (Rev: BL 1/1–15/03; HB 1–2/03; HBG 3/03; SLJ 1/03) [917.804]

4147 Roberts, Russell. *Pedro Menendez de Aviles* (5–7). Illus. Series: Latinos in American History. 2002, Mitchell Lane LB $19.95 (1-58415-150-1). 48pp. This account of explorer Pedro Menendez de Aviles' efforts to procure Florida for Spain uses some fictionalized narrative to illustrate the times. (Rev: BL 10/15/02; HBG 3/03; SLJ 10/02) [975.9]

4148 Whiting, Jim. *Francisco Vasquez de Coronado* (5–7). Illus. Series: Latinos in American History. 2002, Mitchell Lane LB $19.95 (1-58415-146-3). 56pp. This account of Francisco Vasquez de Coronado's search for the lost cities of gold, and his subsequent trial for cruelty to Native Americans, uses some fictionalized narrative. (Rev: BL 10/15/02; HBG 3/03; SLJ 10/02) [979]

4149 Wittmann, Kelly. *The European Rediscovery of America* (4–7). Series: Exploration and Discovery. 2002, Mason Crest LB $19.95 (1-59084-052-6). 64pp. Wittmann looks at the explorers of the 15th and 16th centuries, including Columbus and Cabot. (Rev: SLJ 12/02) [970]

COLONIAL PERIOD

4150 Bjornlund, Lydia J. *Massachusetts* (5–8). Series: The Thirteen Colonies. 2001, Lucent LB $27.45 (1-56006-879-5). 96pp. The story of the colony of Massachusetts with particular emphasis on its role in the Revolution and creation of a new nation. (Rev: BL 3/15/02) [973.2]

4151 Blohm, Craig E. *New Hampshire* (5–8). Series: Thirteen Colonies. 2002, Gale LB $27.45 (1-56006-991-0). 96pp. Clear writing and reproductions of period illustrations are the highlights of this history of the New Hampshire colony. (Rev: BL 9/15/02; SLJ 4/02) [973.2]

4152 Britton, Tamara. *The Georgia Colony* (3–4). Series: The Colonies. 2001, ABDO LB $14.95 (1-57765-583-4). 32pp. The history of the colony is presented here, with information on both the settlers and the Native Americans of the area and on housing, clothing, and the economy. Also use *Roanoke: The Lost Colony* (2001). (Rev: HBG 3/02; SLJ 4/02) [975]

4153 Currie, Stephen. *The Salem Witch Trials* (4–6). 2002, Gale LB $23.70 (0-7377-1038-1). 48pp. A brief introduction to the trials that includes color photographs from the 1996 movie *The Crucible*. (Rev: SLJ 11/02)

4154 Davis, Kenneth C. *Don't Know Much About the Pilgrims* (3–5). Illus. by S. D. Schindler. Series: Don't Know Much About. 2002, HarperCollins LB $17.89 (0-06-028610-5). 48pp. A lively and informative look at the lives of the pilgrims. (Rev: BL 8/02; HBG 3/03; SLJ 10/02) [974.48]

4155 Erickson, Paul. *Daily Life in the Pilgrim Colony 1636* (3–5). Illus. Series: Daily Life. 2001, Clarion $20.00 (0-618-05846-X); paper $9.95 (0-395-98841-1). 48pp. Text, drawings, photographs, and maps describe how the Pilgrims lived at the Plymouth colony in 1636. (Rev: BL 10/1/01; HBG 3/02; SLJ 10/01) [974.4]

4156 Fradin, Dennis Brindell. *The Signers: The 56 Stories Behind the Declaration of Independence* (4–6). Illus. by Michael McCurdy. 2002, Walker $22.95 (0-8027-8849-1). 160pp. Report writers will find plenty of information on the 13 colonies and the important individuals of the time in this lively presentation. (Rev: HB 1–2/03; HBG 3/03; SLJ 11/02)

4157 Girod, Christina M. *Connecticut* (5–8). Illus. Series: Thirteen Colonies. 2001, Lucent LB $27.45 (1-56006-892-2). 96pp. This frank history of the Connecticut area covers the period from 1613 to statehood in 1788, with period illustrations, photographs, a map, source notes, and recommended resources. (Rev: BL 12/1/01) [974.6]

4158 Girod, Christina M. *Georgia* (5–8). Series: The Thirteen Colonies. 2001, Lucent LB $27.45 (1-56006-990-2). 96pp. The story of the last of the Thirteen Colonies to be founded is told in a clear, forthright text with many black-and-white period illustrations. (Rev: BL 3/15/02; SLJ 8/02) [973.2]

4159 Girod, Christina M. *South Carolina* (5–8). Series: Thirteen Colonies. 2002, Gale LB $27.45 (1-56006-994-5). 96pp. A history of the colony of South Carolina and its people from the early settlements to admission into the United States, told in concise prose and numerous black-and-white illustrations. (Rev: BL 9/15/02) [973.2]

4160 Hossel, Karen Price. *Virginia* (5–8). Series: Thirteen Colonies. 2002, Gale LB $27.45 (1-56006-995-3). 96pp. A cogently written history of the early years of Virginia, its people, and their lifestyle, plus sketches of their most famous colonial personalities. (Rev: BL 9/15/02) [973.2]

4161 Italia, Bob. *The New York Colony* (3–5). Illus. Series: The Colonies. 2001, ABDO $14.95 (1-57765-589-3). 32pp. An overview for younger readers of the New York colony, including information on early history, settlements, everyday life, and other topics. Also use *Roanoke* (2001). (Rev: BL 1/1–15/02; HBG 3/02; SLJ 2/02) [974.7]

4162 Kallen, Stuart A. *Delaware* (5–8). Series: Thirteen Colonies. 2002, Gale LB $27.45 (1-56006-989-9). 96pp. This history of colonial Delaware offers a clearly written account plus black-and-white portraits, engravings, paintings, some photographs, and a map of the colonies. (Rev: BL 9/15/02; SLJ 4/02) [973.2]

4163 Kalman, Bobbie. *The Blacksmith* (3–5). Illus. by Barbara Bedell. Series: Colonial People. 2002, Crabtree LB $15.96 (0-7787-0747-4); paper $7.16 (0-7787-0793-8). 32pp. Photographs of reenactments at Williamsburg and Old Salem, North Carolina, add appeal to this description of the work of a colonial blacksmith and the equipment he used. Also use *The Milliner* and *The Woodworker* (2002). (Rev: SLJ 10/02)

4164 Kling, Andrew A. *Rhode Island* (5–8). Series: The Thirteen Colonies. 2001, Lucent LB $27.45 (1-56006-873-6). 112pp. In text and period prints, the story of colonial Rhode Island is told from its beginning to its stormy path to Constitution ratification. (Rev: BL 3/15/02; SLJ 8/02) [973.2]

4165 Lilly, Melinda. *The Boston Tea Party* (K–2). Illus. by Patrick O'Brien. Series: Reading American History. 2002, Rourke LB $19.47 (1-58952-357-1). 24pp. A simple account for beginning readers that introduces the key characters behind the rebellion. (Rev: SLJ 3/03) [973.3]

4166 Miller, Brandon Marie. *Growing Up in a New World* (5–8). Series: Our America. 2002, Lerner LB $26.60 (0-8225-0658-0). 64pp. The thrill of landing in the New World for the first time is re-created through true-life adventures of young people. (Rev: BL 2/15/03; HBG 3/03) [973.2]

4167 *Primary Sources* (5–8). Ed. by Melinda Allman. Series: Thirteen Colonies. 2002, Gale LB $27.45 (1-59018-011-9). 112pp. A fascinating collection of primary source material for the young researcher. (Rev: BL 9/15/02; SLJ 10/02) [873.2]

4168 Sateren, Shelley Swanson. *Going to School in Colonial America* (4–6). Series: Going to School in History. 2001, Capstone LB $16.95 (0-7368-0803-5). 32pp. As well as material on schooling in the colonies, this book describes everyday life and the games, crafts, and activities popular at the time. (Rev: BL 10/15/01; HBG 3/02; SLJ 1/02) [973.2]

4169 Sewall, Marcia. *James Towne: Struggle for Survival* (3–5). Illus. 2001, Simon & Schuster $16.00 (0-689-81814-9). 40pp. An 18-year-old carpenter relates his experiences in the colony of Jamestown, sparing little detail of the hardships the settlers faced. (Rev: BL 6/1–15/01; HB 7–8/01; HBG 10/01; SLJ 6/01) [975.5]

4170 Sherrow, Victoria. *Pennsylvania* (5–8). Series: Thirteen Colonies. 2002, Gale LB $27.45 (1-56006-993-7). 96pp. The history of the colony of Pennsylvania from early settlements to achieving statehood. (Rev: BL 9/15/02) [973.2]

4171 Slavicek, Louise Chipley. *Life Among the Puritans* (4–8). Series: The Way People Live. 2001, Lucent LB $19.96 (1-56006-869-8). 108pp. Slavicek discusses the religious beliefs of the Puritans and how these affected the everyday life and policies of the Plymouth Colony and Massachusetts Bay Colony. (Rev: SLJ 9/01)

4172 Streissguth, Thomas. *New Jersey* (5–8). Series: Thirteen Colonies. 2002, Gale LB $27.45 (1-56006-872-8). 96pp. Using many well-chosen quotes and interesting black-and-white illustrations, this is a solid account of colonial New Jersey and its people. (Rev: BL 9/15/02) [973.2]

4173 Uschan, Michael V. *North Carolina* (5–8). Series: The Thirteen Colonies. 2001, Lucent LB $27.45 (1-56006-885-X). 112pp. A straightforward text is combined with many period illustrations and lists of related media to tell North Carolina's early history. (Rev: BL 3/15/02) [973.2]

4174 Whitehurst, Susan. *Plymouth: Surviving the First Winter* (2–4). Series: The Library of the Pilgrims. 2001, Rosen LB $19.50 (0-8239-5809-4). 24pp. An accessible account of the pilgrims' hard first winter, with details of housing, food, and illness. Also use *William Bradford and Plymouth: A Colony Grows* (2001). (Rev: SLJ 3/02) [974.4]

4175 Woog, Adam. *New York* (5–8). Series: The Thirteen Colonies. 2001, Lucent LB $27.45 (1-56006-992-9). 80pp. Well-chosen quotations as well as black-and-white illustrations and maps help bring to life the story of colonial New York State. (Rev: BL 3/15/02) [973.2]

REVOLUTIONARY PERIOD

4176 Beller, Susan Provost. *The Revolutionary War* (5–8). Series: Letters from the Homefront. 2001, Benchmark LB $19.95 (0-7614-1094-5). 96pp. An attractive volume that brings events and living conditions during the Revolution alive through a collection of letters and other personal documents. (Rev: BL 10/15/01; HBG 3/02) [973.3]

4177 Draper, Allison Stark. *George Washington Elected: How America's First President Was Chosen* (2–4). Illus. Series: Headlines from History. 2001, Rosen LB $19.50 (0-8239-5675-X). 24pp. Newspaper headlines and large type make for easy-reading accounts of significant events leading up to and during Washington's tenure. Also use *The Boston Tea Party: Angry Colonists Dump British Tea* (2001). (Rev: SLJ 8/01) [973.4]

4178 Edwards, Pamela Duncan. *Boston Tea Party* (1–3). Illus. by Henry Cole. 2001, Putnam $15.99 (0-399-23357-1). 32pp. Rhythmic text presents the key events in the lead-up to the Tea Party, enlivened by additional commentary from a crew of mice. (Rev: BCCB 6/01; BL 6/1–15/01; HBG 3/02; SLJ 7/01) [973.3]

4179 Fink, Sam. *The Declaration of Independence: The Words That Made America* (4–8). Illus. 2002, Scholastic $19.95 (0-439-40700-1). 160pp. The Declaration of Independence is broken down and examined phrase by phrase, with illustrations that will attract attention and useful appendixes. (Rev: BCCB 10/02; BL 9/15/02; HBG 3/03; SLJ 10/02) [973.313]

4180 Furgang, Kathy. *The Declaration of Independence and John Adams of Massachusetts* (3–4). Illus. Series: Framers of the Declaration of Independence. 2001, Rosen LB $17.25 (0-8239-5590-7). 24pp. Large print and visual interest make this introductory account suitable for reluctant readers. Also use *The Declaration of Independence and Richard Henry Lee of Virginia* and *The Declaration of Independence and Roger Sherman of Connecticut* (both 2002). (Rev: SLJ 5/02)

4181 Furstinger, Nancy. *The Boston Tea Party* (4–6). Illus. Series: Let Freedom Ring. 2002, Capstone LB $22.60 (0-7368-1093-5). 48pp. Furstinger gives a concise account of the event and places it in a simple historical context that will be useful for report writers. Also use *The Boston Massacre* (2002). (Rev: HBG 3/03; SLJ 6/02)

4182 Herbert, Janis. *The American Revolution for Kids* (5–8). Illus. 2002, Chicago Review paper $14.95 (1-55652-456-0). 160pp. A comprehensive look at the American Revolution from its causes through the early 18th century, with biographical information and interesting features. (Rev: BL 10/1/02; SLJ 11/02) [973.3]

4183 Krensky, Stephen. *Paul Revere's Midnight Ride* (3–5). Illus. by Greg Harlin. 2002, HarperCollins LB $17.89 (0-688-16410-2). 32pp. This beautifully illustrated picture book places Revere's ride in historical context, helped by a clear and attractive map of his route. (Rev: BL 10/1/02; HBG 3/03; SLJ 9/02) [973.3]

4184 Leebrick, Kristal. *The United States Constitution* (3–8). Series: Let Freedom Ring. 2002, Capstone LB $16.95 (0-7368-1094-3). 48pp. James Madison's role in creating the constitution, the Constitutional Convention, and the ratification process are all covered here. Also use *The Declaration of Independence* (2002). (Rev: HBG 3/03; SLJ 7/02) [973.3]

4185 Miller, Brandon Marie. *Growing Up in the Revolution and the New Nation* (4–7). Illus. Series: Our America. 2002, Lerner LB $26.60 (0-8225-0078-7). 64pp. An in-depth examination of the lives of children during and immediately after the American Revolution, including biographical information about real youngsters. (Rev: BL 10/15/02; HBG 3/03; SLJ 12/02) [973.3]

4186 Whitelaw, Nancy. *The Shot Heard Round the World: The Battles of Lexington and Concord* (5–8). Illus. 2001, Morgan Reynolds $20.95 (1-883846-75-7). 112pp. Whitelaw details events from the Boston Massacre in 1770 to the first battles of the Revolution in 1775, with profiles of some of the key players. (Rev: BL 5/15/01; HBG 10/01; SLJ 7/01) [973.3]

THE YOUNG NATION, 1789–1861

4187 Burgan, Michael. *The Alamo* (3–6). Series: We the People. 2001, Compass Point LB $21.26 (0-

7565-0097-4). 48pp. The major figures are profiled in this overview of the battle, along with maps, photographs, and paintings that bring the story to life. (Rev: SLJ 8/01) [976.4]

4188 Burgan, Michael. *The Louisiana Purchase* (5–8). Series: We the People. 2002, Compass Point LB $21.26 (0-7565-0210-1). 48pp. An accessible, well-illustrated account of the purchase that doubled the size of the United States. (Rev: SLJ 7/02)

4189 Chase, John Churchill. *Louisiana Purchase: An American Story*. Rev. ed. (5–8). Illus. 2002, Pelican paper $12.95 (1-58980-084-2). 96pp. The story of the Louisiana Purchase, engagingly told in comic-strip format. (Rev: BL 2/1/03) [973.4]

4190 Diouf, Sylviane A. *Growing Up in Slavery* (5–7). 2001, Millbrook LB $24.90 (0-7613-1763-5). 96pp. A compelling account that dispels any myths about happy slave children and describes the hard life and work of life on the plantation as well as the atrocious conditions on slave ships. (Rev: HBG 10/01; SLJ 6/01) [380.1]

4191 Green, Carl R. *The War of 1812* (4–6). Series: U.S. Wars. 2002, Enslow/MyReportLinks.com LB $19.95 (0-7660-5092-0). 48pp. In addition to a concise discussion of the causes, progress, and resolution of the War of 1812, this book contains a lengthy listing of Web sites where students can find additional material on the subject. (Rev: BL 10/15/02; HBG 3/03) [973.5]

4192 Heinrichs, Ann. *The Underground Railroad* (3–5). Series: We the People. 2001, Compass Point LB $21.26 (0-7565-0102-4). 48pp. Heinrichs gives a clear explanation of the causes for the development of this route to freedom, details how it worked, and profiles key figures. (Rev: SLJ 7/01) [973.7]

4193 Marquette, Scott. *War of 1812* (4–7). Illus. Series: America at War. 2002, Rourke LB $27.93 (1-58952-389-X). 48pp. This book for middle-graders studies the war itself and the events that led up to it. (Rev: BL 10/15/02) [973.5]

4194 Meadows, James. *Slavery: The Struggle for Freedom* (4–6). Series: Journey to Freedom: The African American Library. 2001, Child's World LB $17.95 (1-56766-923-9). 40pp. A brief history of black slavery in this country, told with interesting details and well-chosen illustrations. (Rev: BL 12/15/01; HBG 3/02; SLJ 1/02) [973.7]

4195 Moore, Cathy. *The Daring Escape of Ellen Craft* (1–3). Illus. by Mary O. Young. Series: On My Own History. 2002, Carolrhoda LB $21.27 (0-87614-462-8); paper $6.95 (0-87614-787-2). 48pp. This is the story, based on truth, of two slaves' 1848 journey from Georgia to safety in Philadelphia, the woman disguised as a white slave master. (Rev: HBG 10/02; SLJ 4/02)

4196 Murphy, Jim. *Inside the Alamo* (4–8). Illus. 2003, Delacorte LB $18.99 (0-385-90092-9). 122pp. A gripping narrative combines with solid facts to give readers a good understanding of the events at the Alamo, their causes, and their aftermath. (Rev: BL 3/15/03*) [976.4]

4197 Olson, Kay Melchisedech. *Africans in America: 1619–1865* (4–6). Series: Coming to America. 2002, Capstone LB $22.60 (0-7368-1204-0). 32pp. The story of the forced migrations of Africans to America, their life of slavery, their culture and contributions, and information on famous African Americans. (Rev: BL 1/1–15/03; HBG 3/03) [973]

4198 Riehecky, Janet. *The Siege of the Alamo* (3–6). Illus. Series: Landmark Events in American History. 2002, World Almanac LB $26.60 (0-8368-5342-3). 48pp. The factors leading up to the siege are detailed in this account that distinguishes legend from reality and explains the historical significance. (Rev: SLJ 2/03) [976.4]

4199 Santella, Andrew. *The War of 1812* (4–6). Series: Cornerstones of Freedom. 2001, Children's LB $20.50 (0-516-21597-3). 32pp. A well-illustrated introduction to the War of 1812 and its causes, battles, and outcomes. (Rev: BL 4/15/01) [973.5]

4200 Thro, Ellen, and Andrew K. Frank. *Growing and Dividing* (5–8). Series: The Making of America. 2001, Raintree Steck-Vaughn LB $19.98 (0-8172-5704-7). 96pp. The story of the development of the eastern United States from the early days of the Republic through the clashes that led to the Civil War. (Rev: BL 4/15/01; HBG 10/01) [973.5]

4201 Uschan, Michael V. *The Battle of the Little Bighorn* (3–6). Series: Landmark Events in American History. 2002, World Almanac LB $26.60 (0-8368-5338-5). 48pp. The factors leading up to the battle are detailed in this account that distinguishes legend from reality and explains the historical significance of the event. (Rev: SLJ 2/03)

4202 Williams, Carla. *The Underground Railroad* (4–6). Series: Journey to Freedom: The African American Library. 2001, Child's World LB $17.95 (1-56766-926-3). 40pp. Using full-color and sepia-toned historical illustrations and an accessible text, this is a history of the Underground Railroad movement and the people involved. (Rev: BL 12/15/01; HBG 3/02; SLJ 1/02) [973.7]

PIONEER LIFE AND WESTWARD EXPANSION

4203 Anderson, Dale. *Westward Expansion* (5–8). Series: The Making of America. 2001, Raintree Steck-Vaughn LB $19.98 (0-8172-5705-5). 96pp. An attractive, balanced history of the expansion of the United States to the Pacific with many biographies of pioneers given in sidebars. (Rev: BL 4/15/01; HBG 10/01) [978]

4204 Davis, Lucile. *Medicine in the American West* (4–6). Series: Cornerstones of Freedom. 2001, Children's LB $21.00 (0-516-22004-7). 32pp. Lively text and copious illustrations describe the doctors, caregivers, and treatments during the opening up of the American West. (Rev: BL 12/15/01; SLJ 11/01) [978]

4205 George, Linda, and Charles George. *The Natchez Trace* (4–6). Series: Cornerstones of Freedom. 2001, Children's LB $21.00 (0-516-22006-3). 32pp. A history, told through text and illustrations, of the important road that stretched from Natchez,

Mississippi, to Nashville, Tennessee. (Rev: BL 12/15/01; SLJ 11/01) [978]

4206 Glass, Andrew. *Mountain Men: True Grit and Tall Tales* (4–6). Illus. 2001, Doubleday $15.95 (0-385-32555-X). 40pp. Profiles of seven mountain men — including John Colter, Jim Bridger, Mike Fink, and Kit Carson — interweave legend about their amazing feats with information about the beaver trade, their blazing of new trails, and their way of life. (Rev: BL 8/01; HBG 3/02; SLJ 6/01*) [978]

4207 Goldsmith, Connie. *Lost in Death Valley: The True Story of Four Families in California's Gold Rush* (5–8). Illus. 2001, Twenty-First Century LB $23.90 (0-7613-1915-8). 144pp. Using original sources, the author has re-created the story of an ill-fated pioneer trek and the shortcut that led them into Death Valley. (Rev: BL 4/1/01; HBG 10/01; SLJ 4/01) [979.4]

4208 Graves, Kerry A. *Going to School in Pioneer Times* (4–6). Illus. Series: Going to School in History. 2001, Capstone LB $16.95 (0-7368-0804-3). 32pp. Today's students will enjoy this look at the one-room schoolhouse of pioneer days, introduced by historical context and illustrated with period photographs. (Rev: BL 10/15/01; HBG 3/02; SLJ 1/02) [370.977]

4209 Josephson, Judith Pinkerton. *Growing up in Pioneer America: 1800 to 1890* (4–6). Series: Our America. 2002, Lerner LB $26.60 (0-8225-0659-9). 64pp. The lives of children in this period are described with many quotations and excerpts from diaries, letter, and memoirs. (Rev: HBG 3/03; SLJ 2/03)

4210 Rau, Margaret. *The Wells Fargo Book of the Gold Rush* (4–8). 2001, Simon & Schuster $18.00 (0-689-83019-X). 143pp. This comprehensive account of the California Gold Rush, which includes many period photographs and illustrations from the Wells Fargo archives, looks at the miners themselves, their techniques, daily life, the impact on the environment, and the relations among various ethnic groups. (Rev: BCCB 6/01; BL 7/01; HBG 10/01; SLJ 6/01) [979.4]

4211 Saffer, Barbara. *The California Gold Rush* (5–7). Series: The American West. 2002, Mason Crest LB $19.95 (1-59084-060-7). 64pp. Reluctant readers will be drawn to this attractive account of the hardships of traveling to California and the life in the mining camps. (Rev: SLJ 4/02) [979.4]

4212 Savage, Candace. *Born to Be a Cowgirl: A Spirited Ride Through the Old West* (4–8). 2001, Tricycle Pr. $15.95 (1-58246-019-1); paper $9.95 (1-58246-020-5). 64pp. An appealing package of fascinating text, excerpts from letters and journals, and period illustrations that introduces female cowhands and their lifestyle. (Rev: BL 5/15/01; HB 7–8/01; HBG 10/01; SLJ 6/01) [978]

4213 Werther, Scott P. *The Donner Party* (5–7). Illus. 2002, Children's LB $19.00 (0-516-23901-5). 48pp. The fate of the Donner Party is described against the backdrop of life in America in the 1840s

and the dangers of travel to the West and the Pacific. (Rev: SLJ 10/02) [979.4]

4214 Woog, Adam. *A Cowboy in the Wild West* (3–5). Illus. Series: Daily Life. 2002, Gale LB $21.54 (0-7377-0990-1). 48pp. An information-packed review of a cowboy's daily routine, including material on clothing, trail drives and roundups, and the overall history of cowboys. (Rev: BL 12/1/02; SLJ 8/02) [978]

THE CIVIL WAR

4215 Arnold, James R., and Roberta Wiener. *Divided in Two: The Road to Civil War* (4–7). Series: The Civil War. 2002, Lerner LB $25.26 (0-8225-2312-4). 72pp. A well-designed oversize book that describes the events of 1861 that led to the outbreak of the Civil War. (Rev: BL 10/15/02; HBG 10/02; SLJ 7/02) [973.7]

4216 Arnold, James R., and Roberta Wiener. *Life Goes On: The Civil War at Home* (4–7). Series: The Civil War. 2002, Lerner LB $25.26 (0-8225-2315-9). 72pp. Many easy-to-follow maps and illustrations are used with a simple text to describe life on the home front in both South and North during the Civil War. (Rev: BL 10/15/02; HBG 10/02; SLJ 7/02) [973.7]

4217 Arnold, James R., and Roberta Wiener. *Lost Cause: The End of the Civil War* (4–7). Series: The Civil War. 2002, Lerner LB $25.26 (0-8225-2317-5). 72pp. Beginning with the campaign of 1864, this well-illustrated account traces the Civil War to Appomattox and beyond. (Rev: BL 10/15/02; HBG 10/02; SLJ 6/02) [973.7]

4218 Arnold, James R., and Roberta Wiener. *On to Richmond: The Civil War in the East, 1861–1862* (4–7). Illus. Series: Civil War. 2002, Lerner LB $25.26 (0-8225-2313-2). 72pp. Early battles in the Civil War are the subject of this volume for older readers that includes timelines, notes, and lists of Web sites and battlefields to visit. (Rev: BL 10/15/02; HBG 10/02; SLJ 6/02) [973.7]

4219 Arnold, James R., and Roberta Wiener. *River to Victory: The Civil War in the West* (4–7). Series: The Civil War. 2002, Lerner LB $25.26 (0-8225-2314-0). 72pp. The Civil War in the West from 1861 through 1863 is re-created in text and illustrations with many maps and sidebars on personalities and events. (Rev: BL 10/15/02; HBG 10/02; SLJ 6/02) [973.7]

4220 Arnold, James R., and Roberta Wiener. *This Unhappy Country: The Turn of the Civil War* (4–7). Illus. Series: Civil War. 2002, Lerner LB $25.26 (0-8225-2316-7). 72pp. Maps and other period illustrations flesh out the events of 1863, a pivotal year in the Civil War, in this volume for older readers. (Rev: BL 10/15/02; HBG 10/02; SLJ 7/02) [973.7]

4221 Ashby, Ruth. *Gettysburg* (5–8). Series: Civil War Chronicles. 2002, Smart Apple LB $28.50 (1-58340-186-5). 48pp. The three days of battle are covered in some detail, and the text and photographs convey the horrible conditions. (Rev: HBG 3/03; SLJ 2/03) [973]

4222 Bolotin, Norman. *Civil War A to Z: A Young Reader's Guide to Over 100 People, Places, and Points of Importance* (4–8). Illus. 2002, Dutton $19.99 (0-525-46268-6). 160pp. An encyclopedia-style text on the Civil War, with brief entries on important battles; politicians, generals, and other key figures; and crucial issues of the time, with photographs, a glossary, a timeline, and information on further resources. (Rev: BL 7/02; SLJ 7/02) [973.7]

4223 Damon, Duane. *Growing Up In the Civil War: 1861 to 1865* (5–8). Series: Our America. 2002, Lerner LB $26.60 (0-8225-0656-4). 64pp. The lives of children in this period are described with many quotations and excerpts from diaries, letters, and memoirs. (Rev: BL 2/15/03; HBG 3/03; SLJ 2/03) [973.7]

4224 Friend, Sandra. *Florida in the Civil War: A State in Turmoil* (5–8). Illus. 2001, Millbrook LB $25.90 (0-7613-1973-5). 80pp. An account of Florida's involvement in the Civil War, with maps and photographs. (Rev: BL 10/15/01; HBG 3/02; SLJ 2/02) [973.7]

4225 Graves, Kerry A. *Going to School During the Civil War: The Confederacy* (4–6). Series: Going to School in History. 2001, Capstone LB $16.95 (0-7368-0802-7). 32pp. A look at schools in the South during the Civil War with information on subjects studied, the length of the school year, classroom materials, and typical activities and games. (Rev: BL 10/15/01; HBG 3/02) [973.7]

4226 Graves, Kerry A. *Going to School During the Civil War: The Union* (4–6). Series: Going to School in History. 2001, Capstone LB $16.95 (0-7368-0801-9). 32pp. Details of school life in the northern states include curriculum, teaching methods, and subjects taught plus sidebars on crafts and games. (Rev: BL 10/15/01; HBG 3/03) [973.7]

4227 Heinrichs, Ann. *The Emancipation Proclamation* (5–8). Series: We the People. 2002, Compass Point LB $21.26 (0-7565-0209-8). 48pp. An accessible examination of the proclamation's creation that reveals Lincoln's careful attention to detail. (Rev: SLJ 7/02) [973.7]

4228 Holford, David M. *Lincoln and the Emancipation Proclamation in American History* (5–8). Series: In American History. 2002, Enslow LB $20.95 (0-7660-1456-8). 128pp. A well-researched account that gives background material and traces the significance of this document. (Rev: BL 1/1–15/03; HBG 3/03) [973.7]

4229 Jerome, Kate Boehm. *Civil War Sub: The Mystery of the Hunley* (3–4). Illus. by Frank Sofo. Series: All Aboard Reading. 2002, Grosset LB $13.89 (0-448-42880-6); paper $3.99 (0-448-42597-1). 48pp. The story of the Confederate submarine that disappeared is presented for early readers. (Rev: SLJ 3/03)

4230 McKissack, Patricia, and Fredrick McKissack. *Days of Jubilee: The End of Slavery in the United States* (5–8). Illus. 2003, Scholastic $18.95 (0-439-10764-X). 144pp. A moving book on the Civil War and its effect on slaves, based on first-person

accounts. With photographs, artwork and other graphic elements. (Rev: BL 2/15/03) [973.7]

4231 O'Brien, Patrick. *Duel of the Ironclads: The Monitor vs. the Virginia* (2–6). Illus. 2003, Walker LB $18.85 (0-8027-8843-2). 40pp. A beautifully illustrated account of the battle between two state-of-the-art Civil War ships. (Rev: BL 3/15/03*) [973.7]

4232 Schomp, Virginia. *The Civil War* (5–8). Illus. Series: Letters from the Homefront. 2001, Marshall Cavendish LB $19.95 (0-7614-1095-3). 95pp. After placing the conflict in historical context, Schomp uses excerpts from letters and other accounts that bring the period to life. (Rev: BL 10/15/01; HBG 3/02; SLJ 3/02) [973.7]

4233 Weber, Michael. *Civil War and Reconstruction* (5–8). Series: The Making of America. 2001, Raintree Steck-Vaughn LB $19.98 (0-8172-5707-2). 96pp. Using many illustrations, interesting sidebars, and an accessible text, this is a concise history of the Civil War and its immediate aftermath. (Rev: BL 4/15/01) [973.7]

4234 Wisler, G. Clifton. *When Johnny Went Marching: Young Americans Fight the Civil War* (5–8). Illus. 2001, HarperCollins LB $16.89 (0-06-029242-3). 128pp. Stories of young men and women under the age of 18 who enlisted illegally in the Civil War, with period photographs and diary excerpts. (Rev: BL 11/15/01; HB 9–10/01; HBG 3/02; SLJ 11/01) [973.7]

RECONSTRUCTION TO THE KOREAN WAR, 1865–1950

4235 Bial, Raymond. *Tenement: Immigrant Life on the Lower East Side* (5–8). Illus. 2002, Houghton $16.00 (0-618-13849-8). 48pp. Historic photographs complement the simple, descriptive text about life in New York City tenement housing in the late 1800s and early 1900s. (Rev: BL 10/15/02; HB 11–12/02; HBG 3/03; SLJ 9/02) [307.76]

4236 Brown, Harriet. *Welcome to Kit's World — 1934: Growing Up During America's Great Depression* (3–6). Illus. Series: American Girl. 2002, Pleasant $16.95 (1-58485-359-X). 60pp. Double-page spreads are used in this heavily illustrated volume to describe growing up in 1934 during the Great Depression. (Rev: BL 4/15/02; HBG 10/02; SLJ 7/02) [973.9]

4237 Burgan, Michael. *The Great Depression* (4–6). Series: We the People. 2001, Compass Point LB $21.26 (0-7565-0152-0). 48pp. A basic overview of the causes of the Depression and the programs that were intended to alleviate its impact. (Rev: SLJ 1/02)

4238 Dolan, Edward F. *The Spanish-American War* (5–8). Illus. 2001, Millbrook LB $28.90 (0-7613-1453-9). 112pp. This chronological account of the Spanish-American War includes profiles of military personnel, maps, and historical photographs. (Rev: BL 11/1/01; HBG 3/02; SLJ 11/01) [973.8]

4239 Feinstein, Stephen. *The 1940s: From World War II to Jackie Robinson* (5–8). Illus. Series: Decades of the 20th Century. 2000, Enslow LB

$17.95 (0-7660-1428-2). 64pp. A lively look at events of the 1940s, covering everything from fashion and fads to politics, science, technology, medicine, and sports. Also use *The 1930s: From the Great Depression to the Wizard of Oz* (2001) and *The 1950s: From the Korean War to Elvis* (2000). (Rev: HBG 3/01; SLJ 5/01) [973.9]

4240 Feinstein, Stephen. *The 1910s: From World War I to Ragtime Music* (5–8). Series: Decades of the 20th Century. 2001, Enslow LB $17.95 (0-7660-1611-0). 64pp. The events of the 1910s are covered in chapters on lifestyle and fashion, arts and entertainment, sports, politics, and science, technology, and medicine. Also use *The 1920s: From Prohibition to Charles Lindbergh* (2001). (Rev: HBG 10/02; SLJ 2/02) [973.9]

4241 Graves, Kerry A. *Going to School During the Great Depression* (4–6). Series: Going to School in History. 2001, Capstone LB $16.95 (0-7368-0800-7). 32pp. School life during the 1930s and early '40s is covered with material on subjects studied, school supplies, and typical activities and games of the time. (Rev: BL 10/15/01) [973.9]

4242 Green, Carl R. *The Spanish-American War* (4–6). Series: U.S. Wars. 2002, Enslow/MyReportLinks.com LB $19.95 (0-7660-5091-2). 48pp. Preceding a brief history of the Spanish-American War, there is a lengthy section listing Internet sites that offer students additional material on the subject. (Rev: BL 10/15/02; HBG 3/03) [973.8]

4243 Hoffman, Nancy. *Eleanor Roosevelt and the Arthurdale Experiment* (5–8). Illus. 2001, Linnet $22.50 (0-208-02504-9). 108pp. Hoffman includes quotations and black-and-white photographs in her account of the story of Arthurdale, a government-planned community of the 1930s. (Rev: BL 10/15/01; HBG 3/02; SLJ 12/01) [975.4]

4244 Houle, Michelle M. *Triangle Shirtwaist Factory Fire: Flames of Labor Reform* (4–6). Illus. Series: American Disasters. 2002, Enslow LB $18.95 (0-7660-1785-0). 48pp. A frank portrayal of the tragic 1911 fire and the impact it had on the labor movement. (Rev: HBG 3/03; SLJ 12/02)

4245 Isaacs, Sally Senzell. *Life in the Dust Bowl* (2–4). Illus. Series: Picture the Past. 2001, Heinemann LB $21.36 (1-58810-248-3). 32pp. A gripping introduction to the hardships of life on the plains in the 1930s, with information on society at the time. (Rev: SLJ 3/02)

4246 Josephson, Judith Pinkerton. *Growing Up in a New Century* (5–8). Illus. Series: Our America. 2002, Lerner LB $26.60 (0-8225-0657-2). 64pp. A look at the lives of American children of different backgrounds and situations at the dawn of the 20th century. (Rev: BL 2/1/03; HBG 3/03) [973.91]

4247 Josephson, Judith Pinkerton. *Growing Up in World War II* (5–8). Illus. Series: Our America. 2002, Lerner LB $26.60 (0-8225-0660-2). 64pp. A look at the lives of American children of different backgrounds and situations during World War II. (Rev: BL 2/1/03; HBG 3/03) [940.533]

4248 Martin, Bill, Jr., and Michael Sampson. *I Pledge Allegiance* (K–4). Illus. by Chris Raschka.

2002, Candlewick $15.99 (0-7636-1648-6). 40pp. The Pledge of Allegiance, which was adopted in 1892, is explained to young readers in simple language. (Rev: BCCB 10/02; BL 9/1/02; HBG 3/03; SLJ 12/02) [323.6]

4249 Ruth, Amy. *Growing Up in the Great Depression* (5–8). Series: Our America. 2002, Lerner LB $26.60 (0-8225-0655-6). 64pp. Through the use of many sidebars and quotes from original sources, this narrative re-creates the despair and courage of children growing up during the Great Depression. (Rev: BL 2/15/03; HBG 3/03) [973.9]

4250 Stewart, Dave. *You Wouldn't Want to Sail on the Titanic! One Voyage You'd Rather Not Make* (4–6). Illus. by David Antram. Series: You Wouldn't Want To. 2001, Watts LB $25.00 (0-531-14604-9); paper $9.95 (0-531-16210-9). 32pp. The uncomfortable opportunity to imagine yourself aboard the *Titanic*. (Rev: SLJ 3/02) [910.91]

4251 Stone, Tanya Lee. *The Great Depression and World War II* (5–8). Series: Making of America. 2001, Raintree Steck-Vaughn LB $19.98 (0-8172-5710-1). 96pp. Concise text and attractive illustrations re-create the history of America from 1929 through World War II. (Rev: BL 9/15/01; HBG 10/01) [973.9]

4252 Stone, Tanya Lee. *The Progressive Era and World War I* (5–8). Series: Making of America. 2001, Raintree Steck-Vaughn LB $19.98 (0-8172-5709-8). 96pp. Roughly the first 20 years of the 20th century in American history are retold in this history that also looks at home life, culture, and entertainment. (Rev: BL 9/15/01; HBG 10/01; SLJ 6/01) [973.9]

4253 Wells, Donna. *America Comes of Age* (5–8). Series: The Making of America. 2001, Raintree Steck-Vaughn LB $19.98 (0-8172-5708-X). 96pp. A handsomely illustrated account that traces U.S. history from Reconstruction to the beginning of the 20th century. (Rev: BL 4/15/01; HBG 10/01) [973.8]

4254 Wroble, Lisa A. *The New Deal and the Great Depression in American History* (5–8). Series: In American History. 2002, Enslow LB $20.95 (0-7660-1421-5). 128pp. A timeline, maps, chapter notes, and research topics are found in this well-researched account that concentrates on Roosevelt's economic policies during the 1930s. (Rev: BL 1/1–15/03; HBG 3/03) [973.9]

THE 1950S TO THE PRESENT

4255 Anderson, Dale. *America into a New Millennium* (5–8). Series: Making of America. 2001, Raintree Steck-Vaughn LB $19.98 (0-8172-5712-8). 96pp. This last part of a 12-volume series presents American history from the end of the Cold War to the beginning of the 21st century. (Rev: BL 9/15/01; HBG 10/01; SLJ 6/01) [973.9]

4256 Anderson, Dale. *The Cold War Years* (5–8). Series: Making of America. 2001, Raintree Steck-Vaughn LB $19.98 (0-8172-5711-X). 96pp. A concise, easy-to-understand text tells America's story from the end of World War II to the 1990s. (Rev: BL 9/15/01; HBG 10/01; SLJ 6/01) [973.9]

4257 Feinstein, Stephen. *The 1990s: Fom the Persian Gulf War to Y2K* (5–8). Series: Decades of the 20th Century. 2001, Enslow LB $17.95 (0-7660-1613-7). 64pp. The events of the 1990s are covered in chapters on lifestyle and fashion, arts and entertainment, sports, politics, and science, technology, and medicine. (Rev: HBG 10/02; SLJ 2/02) [973.9]

4258 Hamilton, John. *Operation Enduring Freedom* (4–7). Series: War on Terrorism. 2002, ABDO LB $16.95 (1-57765-665-2). 48pp. Using many color photographs and a matter-of-fact text, this book covers various aspects of the U.S. war against terrorism. (Rev: BL 5/15/02; HBG 10/02) [973.9]

4259 Hamilton, John. *Operation Noble Eagle* (4–7). Series: War on Terrorism. 2002, ABDO LB $16.95 (1-57765-664-4). 48pp. A look at U.S. efforts to police and defend its borders as part of the war on terrorism. (Rev: BL 5/15/02; HBG 10/02) [973.9]

4260 Koestler, Rachel. *Going to School During the Civil Rights Movement* (4–6). Illus. Series: Going to School in History. 2001, Capstone LB $16.95 (0-7368-0799-3). 32pp. Koestler explores the difficulties of attending school during segregation. (Rev: BL 10/15/01; HBG 3/02) [379.2]

4261 Lalley, Patrick. *9.11.01: Terrorists Attack the U.S* (4–7). Illus. 2002, Raintree Steck-Vaughn LB $21.98 (0-7398-6021-6). 48pp. A compact look at the terrorist attacks of September 11, 2001, their causes, the world of Islam, the history of the World Trade Center, and personal stories related to the attacks. (Rev: BL 4/1/02; HBG 10/02; SLJ 5/02) [303.6250]

4262 Levitas, Mitchel, ed. *A Nation Challenged: A Visual History of 9/11 and Its Aftermath: Young Reader's Edition* (4–9). 2002, Scholastic $18.95 (0-439-48803-6). 96pp. This is a selection of material first published in the *New York Times* that has been chosen as suitable for young readers. (Rev: BL 9/1/02; SLJ 9/02)

4263 Louis, Nancy. *Heroes of the Day* (4–7). Series: War on Terrorism. 2002, ABDO LB $16.95 (1-57765-658-X). 48pp. This account of September 11, 2001, describes through pictures and case studies the gallant feats of firefighters, police, and those who fought back on Flight 93. (Rev: BL 5/15/02; HBG 10/02; SLJ 6/02) [973.9]

4264 Poffenberger, Nancy. *September 11th, 2001: A Simple Account for Children* (PS–2). Illus. 2002, Fun paper $8.95 (0-938293-12-5). 16pp. Drawings by schoolchildren illustrate a straightforward presentation of the events of September 11. (Rev: BL 7/02) [973.931]

4265 Santella, Andrew. *September 11, 2001* (4–6). Series: Cornerstones of Freedom, Second Series. 2002, Children's LB $24.00 (0-516-22692-4). 48pp. This presentation gives the basic facts on the attacks and the U.S. response. (Rev: SLJ 11/02)

4266 Schomp, Virginia. *The Vietnam War* (5–8). Series: Letters from the Homefront. 2001, Benchmark LB $19.95 (0-7614-1099-6). 96pp. Conditions on the home front during the Vietnam War are re-

created through primary documents such as letters and period photographs. (Rev: BL 10/15/01; HBG 3/02; SLJ 3/02) [973.9]

4267 Stein, R. Conrad. *The Cold War* (4–6). Series: U.S. Wars. 2002, Enslow/MyReportLinks.com LB $19.95 (0-7660-5095-5). 48pp. In addition to a concise history of the causes and progress of the Cold War, this volume includes a listing of pertinent Web sites where additional material such as maps, documents, and biographies can be found. (Rev: BL 10/15/02; HBG 3/03) [973.9]

4268 Stewart, Gail B. *Terrorism* (4–6). Illus. Series: Understanding Issues. 2002, Gale LB $23.70 (0-7377-1287-2). 48pp. Taking September 11, 2001, as a starting point, this account explores the causes and effects of terrorism and the measures taken to combat it. (Rev: BL 6/1–15/02; SLJ 9/02) [303.6]

4269 Taylor, David. *The Cold War* (5–9). Illus. Series: 20th Century Perspectives. 2001, Heinemann LB $25.64 (1-57572-434-0). 48pp. An easily understood account of the causes of tension between the Soviet Union and the West and the major crises of the "war." Also use *The Vietnam War.* (Rev: HBG 3/02; SLJ 11/01)

4270 Wheeler, Jill C. *September 11, 2001: The Day That Changed America* (3–5). Illus. Series: War on Terrorism. 2002, ABDO $16.95 (1-57765-656-3). 64pp. This introductory volume covers the attacks, the rescue efforts, and the initial American response, with lots of photographs. Also use *Ground Zero* and *Heroes of the Day.* (Rev: BL 5/1/02; HBG 10/02; SLJ 6/02) [973.931]

Regions

MIDWEST

4271 Balcavage, Dynise. *Iowa* (5–8). Illus. Series: From Sea to Shining Sea, Second Series. 2002, Children's LB $29.50 (0-516-22481-6). 80pp. An attractive overview of Iowa's land, history, culture, economy, and people. (Rev: SLJ 3/03)

4272 Bennett, Michelle. *Missouri* (4–8). Series: Celebrate the States. 2001, Benchmark LB $35.64 (0-7614-1063-5). 144pp. A logically organized, thorough introduction to Missouri with material on such topics as history, people, landmarks, and famous natives. (Rev: BL 9/15/01; HBG 10/01) [977.8]

4273 Boekhoff, P. M., and Stuart A. Kallen. *Illinois* (4–7). Illus. Series: Seeds of a Nation. 2002, Gale LB $23.70 (0-7377-0279-6). 48pp. This is a compact history of the territory that would become Illinois, with fine coverage of Native American culture and history. (Rev: BL 4/1/02; SLJ 3/02) [977.3]

4274 Deinard, Jenny. *How to Draw Illinois' Sights and Symbols* (3–6). Illus. Series: Kid's Guide to Drawing America. 2002, Rosen LB $25.25 (0-8239-6069-2). 32pp. An eclectic mix of drawing exercises and basic facts about Illinois history, geography, demographics, and important features. Also use *How to Draw Missouri's Sights and Symbols* (2001). (Rev: BL 2/15/02; SLJ 7/02) [743]

4275 Edge, Laura B. *A Personal Tour of Hull-House* (4–7). Series: How It Was. 2001, Lerner LB $25.26 (0-8225-3583-3). 64pp. A firsthand account of the settlement house founded in Chicago by Jane Addams. (Rev: BL 8/1/01) [977.3]

4276 Hahn, Laura. *Mount Rushmore* (4–8). Illus. Series: American Symbols and Their Meanings. 2002, Mason Crest LB $18.95 (1-59084-027-5). 48pp. Hahn describes Gutzon Borglum's struggle to build his monument, with a helpful timeline and many illustrations. (Rev: SLJ 9/02) [730]

4277 Heinrichs, Ann. *Illinois* (3–6). Series: This Land Is Your Land. 2002, Compass Point LB $22.60 (0-7565-0313-2). 48pp. An overview of the geography, history, government, economy, people, and attractions of Illinois. (Rev: SLJ 2/03)

4278 Ling, Bettina. *Wisconsin* (4–6). Series: From Sea to Shining Sea. 2002, Children's LB $29.50 (0-516-22380-1). The state of Wisconsin is introduced through a lively text, many color photographs, maps, a glossary, a timeline, and other attractive features. (Rev: BL 4/15/02) [977.5]

4279 Martin, Michael A. *Ohio: The Buckeye State* (4–7). Series: World Almanac Library of the States. 2002, World Almanac LB $26.60 (0-8368-5124-2). 48pp. Facts, statistics, a pleasing layout, and color photographs make this a useful choice for report writers. Also use *Iowa: The Hawkeye State* (2002). (Rev: SLJ 9/02)

4280 Pfeffer, Wendy. *The Big Flood* (K–3). Illus. by Vanessa Lubach. 2001, Millbrook LB $23.90 (0-7613-1653-1). 32pp. Young Patti describes the Mississippi flood of 1993 and the way the neighbors worked together to try to avert disaster. (Rev: BL 6/1–15/01; HBG 10/01; SLJ 10/01) [363.34]

4281 Price-Groff, Claire. *Illinois* (3–6). Illus. Series: It's My State! 2002, Benchmark LB $18.95 (0-7614-1422-3). 80pp. The usual state information — geography, history, government, people, and economy — is presented in an appealing layout and with an activity. (Rev: BL 3/1/03; SLJ 2/03)

4282 Somervill, Barbara A. *Illinois* (4–6). Illus. Series: From Sea to Shining Sea. 2001, Children's LB $29.50 (0-516-22320-8). 80pp. A good resource for report writing, this book features historical facts, maps, and information about the governmental structure and the people of Illinois. (Rev: BL 3/15/02) [977.3]

MOUNTAIN STATES

4283 Mann, Elizabeth. *Hoover Dam* (3–6). Illus. by Alan Witschonke. Series: Wonders of the World. 2001, Mikaya $19.95 (1-931414-02-5). 48pp. The exciting story of Hoover Dam is presented in a well-designed package with personal anecdotes and an emphasis on the loss of life. (Rev: BL 12/1/01; HB 3–4/02; HBG 10/02; SLJ 12/01) [627]

4284 Stefoff, Rebecca. *Nevada* (4–8). Series: Celebrate the States. 2001, Benchmark LB $35.64 (0-7614-1073-2). 144pp. This well-organized introduction to Nevada gives general information followed by a timeline and special material on tourist attractions, famous natives of Nevada, and

local festivals. (Rev: BL 9/15/01; HBG 10/01) [979.3]

NORTHEAST

4285 Anderson, Dale. *Arriving at Ellis Island* (3–5). Series: Landmark Events in American History. 2002, World Almanac LB $26.60 (0-8368-5337-7). 48pp. Report writers will find this a concise and useful introduction to Ellis Island and the immigrant experience. (Rev: SLJ 1/03)

4286 Ashabranner, Brent. *On the Mall in Washington, D.C.: A Visit to America's Front Yard* (5–7). Illus. by Jennifer Ashabranner. 2002, Twenty-First Century LB $23.90 (0-7613-2351-1). 64pp. An entertaining and informative tour of the National Mall in Washington, D.C. (Rev: BL 3/15/02; HBG 10/02; SLJ 4/02) [917.5304]

4287 Ashabranner, Brent. *Remembering Korea: The Korean War Veterans Memorial* (4–8). Illus. by Jennifer Ashabranner. Series: Great American Memorials. 2001, Twenty-First Century LB $24.90 (0-7613-2156-X). 64pp. Ashabranner explains who the memorial honors, how much it cost, and what it represents. (Rev: BL 9/15/01; HBG 3/02; SLJ 12/01) [951.904]

4288 Ashabranner, Brent. *The Washington Monument: A Beacon for America* (4–8). Illus. by Jennifer Ashabranner. Series: Great American Memorials. 2002, Millbrook LB $25.90 (0-7613-1524-1). 64pp. Ashabranner presents the story behind the monument, including its planning, design, and construction, with full-color photographs and black-and-white period reproductions. (Rev: BL 9/1/02; HBG 3/03; SLJ 11/02) [975.3]

4289 Barenblat, Rachel. *Massachusetts: The Bay State* (4–7). Series: World Almanac Library of the States. 2002, World Almanac LB $26.60 (0-8368-5123-4). 48pp. History, politics, government, culture, and state symbols are all covered, with charts, maps, photographs, biographical sketches, and a list of important events and attractions. (Rev: SLJ 6/02)

4290 Cotter, Kristin. *New York* (3–5). Illus. Series: From Sea to Shining Sea, Second Series. 2002, Children's LB $29.50 (0-516-22485-9). 80pp. This revision of an earlier title adds information and features that will enhance its appeal to report writers. Also use *Connecticut* and *Delaware* (both 2002). (Rev: SLJ 1/03)

4291 Curlee, Lynn. *Brooklyn Bridge* (3–6). Illus. 2001, Simon & Schuster $18.00 (0-689-83183-8). 40pp. The story of the construction of the Brooklyn Bridge with particular emphasis on the role played by the Roebling family. (Rev: BCCB 6/01; BL 4/15/01; HB 7–8/01; HBG 10/01; SLJ 5/01) [624]

4292 Curlee, Lynn. *Capital* (2–5). Illus. 2003, Simon & Schuster $17.95 (0-689-84947-8). 48pp. Stories of five important Washington, D.C., buildings portray much of American history. (Rev: BCCB 2/03; BL 1/1–15/03; SLJ 1/03) [975.3]

4293 Deinard, Jenny. *How to Draw Massachusetts's Sights and Symbols* (3–6). Series: Kid's Guide to Drawing America. 2001, Rosen LB $25.25 (0-8239-6077-3). As well as basic facts on key sights and symbols of Massachusetts, clear instructions are given on how to draw the state seal, flag, bird, and so forth. (Rev: BL 4/15/02; SLJ 7/02) [974.4]

4294 Dornfeld, Margaret. *Maine* (4–8). Series: Celebrate the States. 2001, Benchmark LB $35.64 (0-7614-1071-6). 144pp. An attractive, fact-filled introduction to the state of Maine with material on history, famous places and people, and current concerns. (Rev: BL 9/15/01; HBG 10/01) [974.1]

4295 Elish, Dan. *New York* (4–7). Illus. Series: My State. 2003, Marshall Cavendish $18.95 (0-7614-1419-3). 80pp. Color photographs accompany information on the state's topography, wildlife, climate, population, government, industries, and resources. (Rev: BL 3/1/03) [974.7]

4296 Graham, Amy. *Maine* (4–7). Illus. Series: States. 2002, Enslow/MyReportLinks.com LB $19.95 (0-7660-5017-3). 48pp. This well-illustrated volume offers report writers basic information on the state's land, climate, economy, government, and history, plus recommendations of Web sites that will extend their knowledge. Also use *New York* (2002). (Rev: SLJ 9/02)

4297 Gray, Susan H. *The White House* (2–4). Series: Our Nation. 2001, Compass Point LB $18.60 (0-7565-0145-8). 24pp. An introduction to the interior of the executive mansion. (Rev: SLJ 1/02) [975.3]

4298 Ingram, Scott. *Pennsylvania: The Keystone State* (4–7). Series: World Almanac Library of the States. 2002, World Almanac LB $26.60 (0-8368-5120-X). 48pp. Facts, statistics, a pleasing layout, and color photographs make this a useful choice for report writers. (Rev: SLJ 9/02)

4299 Leotta, Joan. *Massachusetts* (4–6). Series: From Sea to Shining Sea. 2001, Children's LB $29.50 (0-516-22486-7). As well as basic coverage on Massachusetts, this book includes interesting sidebars. (Rev: BL 4/15/02) [974.4]

4300 Louis, Nancy. *Ground Zero* (4–7). Series: War on Terrorism. 2002, ABDO LB $16.95 (1-57765-675-1). 48pp. This heavily illustrated, factually accurate account describes the search, recovery, and cleanup that took place after September 11, 2001, in New York City. (Rev: BL 5/15/02) [974.7]

4301 Marcovitz, Hal. *The Liberty Bell* (4–8). Illus. Series: American Symbols and Their Meanings. 2002, Mason Crest LB $18.95 (1-59084-025-9). 48pp. The history and condition of the bell are presented through text, illustrations, and a useful timeline. Also use *The White House* (2002). (Rev: SLJ 9/02) [974.8]

4302 Rau, Dana Meachen. *The Statue of Liberty* (2–4). Series: Our Nation. 2001, Compass Point LB $18.60 (0-7565-0143-1). 24pp. An introduction to the statue with information on its history, symbolism, and location. (Rev: SLJ 1/02) [974.7]

4303 Zschock, Martha, and Heather Zschock. *Journey Around New York from A to Z* (1–3). Illus. 2002, Commonwealth $17.95 (1-889833-32-0). 32pp. An alphabetical journey around New York that combines information on tourist attractions, history, neighborhoods, and public celebrations. (Rev: BL 6/1–15/02; SLJ 7/02) [917.47]

PACIFIC STATES

4304 Aykroyd, Clarissa. *Exploration of the California Coast* (4–7). Series: Exploration and Discovery. 2002, Mason Crest LB $19.95 (1-59084-043-7). 64pp. Explorers such as Cortes and Drake are covered in this look at 16th-century California. (Rev: SLJ 12/02)

4305 Boekhoff, P. M., and Stuart A. Kallen. *California* (4–7). Illus. Series: Seeds of a Nation. 2002, Gale LB $23.70 (0-7377-0946-4). 48pp. The history of California before statehood is presented with material on Native Americans, missionaries, settlers, and prospectors. (Rev: BL 4/1/02) [979.4]

4306 Brimner, Larry Dane. *Angel Island* (4–6). Series: Cornerstones of Freedom. 2001, Children's LB $20.50 (0-516-21566-3). 32pp. A well-illustrated account of the historically important island (now a national park) in San Francisco Bay. Also use *The Golden Gate Bridge* (2001). (Rev: BL 4/15/01) [979.4]

4307 Chippendale, Lisa A. *The San Francisco Earthquake of 1906* (5–9). Series: Great Disasters: Reforms and Ramifications. 2000, Chelsea LB $19.95 (0-7910-5270-2). 120pp. An interesting account that focuses on the appropriateness of the responses to the disaster by the various authorities and the lessons learned. (Rev: BL 4/15/01; HBG 10/01; SLJ 6/01)

4308 Green, Carl R. *The Mission Trails in American History* (5–8). Series: In American History. 2001, Enslow LB $20.95 (0-7660-1349-9). 128pp. Green traces the creation of these routes, the reasons for building the missions, and the confrontations between newcomers and the Native Americans. (Rev: BL 12/15/01; HBG 3/02; SLJ 3/02)

4309 Heinrichs, Ann. *California* (2–4). Illus. Series: This Land Is Your Land. 2002, Compass Point LB $22.60 (0-7565-0308-6). 48pp. Simple text with age-appropriate language and good illustrations introduce the history, geography, culture, famous people, and attractions of California. (Rev: SLJ 1/03)

4310 Heinrichs, Ann. *The California Missions* (5–8). Series: We the People. 2002, Compass Point LB $21.26 (0-7565-0208-X). 48pp. An accessible, well-illustrated account of the creation of Spanish missions in California and the impact on the native peoples of the region. (Rev: SLJ 7/02) [979.402]

4311 Isaacs, Sally Senzell. *Life in San Francisco's Chinatown* (2–4). Illus. Series: Picture the Past. 2002, Heinemann LB $22.79 (1-58810-692-6). 32pp. A look at life in San Francisco for Chinese immigrants in the years from the Gold Rush through the early 20th century. (Rev: HBG 3/03; SLJ 3/03) [979.4]

4312 Kennedy, Teresa. *California* (4–6). Series: From Sea to Shining Sea. 2001, Children's LB $29.50 (0-516-22309-7). This attractive, oversize volume includes material on the land, history, people, and lifestyle of California. (Rev: BL 4/15/02) [979.4]

4313 Knapp, Ron. *Oregon* (4–7). Illus. Series: MyReportLinks.com. 2002, Enslow LB $19.95 (0-

7660-5021-1). 48pp. An introduction to the government, geography, and history of the state, with helpful Web sites. (Rev: BL 2/1/03; HBG 3/03) [979.5]

4314 Levinson, Nancy Smiler. *Death Valley: A Day in the Desert* (2–3). Illus. by Diane D. Hearn. 2001, Holiday $14.95 (0-8234-1566-X). 32pp. In this easily read book, Death Valley and its plants and animals are introduced with excellent drawings. (Rev: BL 4/15/01; HBG 10/01; SLJ 4/01) [508.794]

4315 Lourie, Peter. *On the Trail of Sacagawea* (4–6). Illus. 2001, Boyds Mills $18.95 (1-56397-840-7). 48pp. In this handsome pictorial account of a family trip retracing the steps of Lewis and Clark, the author interweaves their contemporary experiences and historical notes. (Rev: BL 5/1/01; HBG 3/02; SLJ 4/01) [978.004]

4316 Quasha, Jennifer. *How to Draw California's Sights and Symbols* (3–6). Illus. Series: Kid's Guide to Drawing America. 2002, Rosen LB $25.25 (0-8239-6059-5). 32pp. An eclectic mix of California history, geography, demographics, and state sights and symbols. (Rev: BL 2/15/02; SLJ 7/02) [743]

4317 Stein, R. Conrad. *Los Angeles* (3–6). Series: Cities of the World. 2001, Children's LB $26.40 (0-516-22242-2); paper $9.95 (0-516-27283-7). 64pp. This volume acts as a tourist guide to Los Angeles with maps, lists of famous landmarks, and a rundown on important personalities linked to the city. (Rev: BL 8/1/01) [979.4]

4318 *Stories from Where We Live: The California Coast* (4–7). Ed. by Sara St. Antoine. Illus. by Trudy Nicholson. 2001, Milkweed $19.95 (1-57131-631-0). 288pp. A compilation of poetry and prose focusing on the California coastal region and its plant and animal life. (Rev: BL 1/1–15/02; HBG 10/02) [979.4]

4319 Whitcraft, Melissa. *Seward's Folly* (3–6). Series: Cornerstones of Freedom, Second Series. 2002, Children's LB $24.00 (0-516-22525-1). 48pp. An attractive account of the purchase of the Alaskan territory. (Rev: SLJ 12/02)

SOUTH

4320 Alex, Nan. *North Carolina* (4–6). Series: From Sea to Shining Sea. 2001, Children's LB $29.50 (0-516-22487-5). An attractive, well-organized volume that introduces the land and people of North Carolina. Also use *Florida*, *Georgia*, *Kentucky*, and *Tennessee* (all 2001). (Rev: BL 4/15/02) [975.6]

4321 Heinrichs, Ann. *Virginia* (2–4). Illus. Series: This Land Is Your Land. 2002, Compass Point LB $22.60 (0-7565-0310-8). 48pp. Simple text and good illustrations introduce the history, geography, culture, famous people, and attractions of Virginia. (Rev: SLJ 1/03)

4322 Kent, Deborah. *Atlanta* (3–6). Series: Cities of the World. 2001, Children's LB $26.40 (0-516-21679-1); paper $9.95 (0-516-27282-9). 64pp. An attractive introduction to Atlanta and its geography, history, tourist attractions, personalities, and reasons for importance. (Rev: BL 8/1/01) [975.8]

4323 La Doux, Rita C. *Louisiana*. Rev. ed. (3–5). Illus. Series: Hello U.S.A. 2001, Lerner LB $25.26

(0-8225-4065-7); paper $6.95 (0-8225-4145-9). 84pp. This revision of the 1993 edition features a more spacious layout and some expanded content. (Rev: SLJ 2/02) [976]

4324 MacAulay, Ellen. *Arkansas* (3–5). Illus. 2002, Children's LB $29.50 (0-516-22296-1). 80pp. This revision of an earlier title adds information and features that will enhance its appeal to report writers. (Rev: SLJ 1/03)

4325 Martin, Michael A. *Alabama: The Heart of Dixie* (4–7). Series: World Almanac Library of the States. 2002, World Almanac LB $26.60 (0-8368-5127-7). 48pp. Full-color photographs and graphic elements this informative introduction to the state. Also use *Virginia* (2002). (Rev: SLJ 2/03)

4326 Munro, Roxie. *The Inside-Outside Book of Texas* (K–3). Illus. Series: Inside-Outside. 2001, North-South LB $16.88 (1-58717-051-5). 48pp. Some of the most famous places and landmarks in Texas are pictured in this attractive book with a minimum of text. (Rev: BL 4/1/01; HB 5–6/01; HBG 10/01; SLJ 6/01) [976.4]

4327 Otfinoski, Steve. *Maryland* (3–6). Illus. Series: It's My State! 2002, Benchmark LB $18.95 (0-7614-1421-5). 80pp. The usual state information — geography, history, government, people, and economy — is presented in an appealing layout. (Rev: SLJ 2/03)

4328 Sanford, William R. *The Natchez Trace Historic Trail in American History* (5–8). Series: In American History. 2001, Enslow LB $20.95 (0-7660-1344-8). 112pp. Sanford looks at the history of this ancient Native American trail, the people who used it, and confrontations between newcomers and the indigenous people. (Rev: BL 12/15/01; HBG 3/02; SLJ 3/02) [976]

4329 Shirley, David. *North Carolina* (4–8). Series: Celebrate the States. 2001, Benchmark LB $35.64 (0-7614-1072-4). 144pp. A fine introduction to the land, history, economy, and people of North Carolina. (Rev: BL 9/15/01; HBG 10/01) [975.6]

4330 Streissguth, Thomas. *Maryland* (5–8). Series: The Thirteen Colonies. 2001, Lucent LB $27.45 (1-56006-871-X). 96pp. Source notes, annotated bibliographies, and lists of Internet resources complement this history of Maryland from its beginnings to statehood. (Rev: BL 3/15/02) [973.2]

4331 Yolen, Jane. *Welcome to the River of Grass* (PS–3). Illus. by Laura Regan. 2001, Putnam $15.99 (0-399-23221-4). 32pp. Yolen examines the animal and plant life of the Everglades — and the perils the area faces — in rhythmic text accompanied by excellent illustrations. (Rev: BCCB 2/02; BL 10/1/01; HBG 3/02; SLJ 11/01) [577.68]

SOUTHWEST

4332 Alter, Judy. *New Mexico* (4–7). Illus. Series: MyReportLinks.com. 2002, Enslow LB $19.95 (0-7660-5098-X). 48pp. An introduction to the government, geography, and history of the state, with helpful Web sites. (Rev: BL 2/1/03) [978.9]

4333 Hanson-Harding, Alexandra. *Texas* (4–6). Illus. Series: From Sea to Shining Sea. 2001, Children's LB $29.50 (0-516-22322-4). 80pp. A good resource for report writing, this book features historical facts, maps, and information about the governmental structure and the people of Texas. (Rev: BL 3/15/02) [976.4]

4334 Heinrichs, Ann. *Texas* (2–4). Illus. Series: This Land Is Your Land. 2002, Compass Point LB $22.60 (0-7565-0312-4). 48pp. Simple text with age-appropriate language and good illustrations introduce the history, geography, culture, famous people, and attractions of Texas. (Rev: SLJ 1/03)

4335 Marcovitz, Hal. *The Alamo* (4–8). Illus. Series: American Symbols and Their Meanings. 2002, Mason Crest LB $18.95 (1-59084-037-2). 48pp. A basic and readable introduction to the history of the Alamo and its importance to Americans, with illu-

minating illustrations and inset features. (Rev: SLJ 9/02) [976]

4336 Pelta, Kathy. *Texas*. Rev. ed. (3–5). Illus. Series: Hello U.S.A. 2001, Lerner LB $25.26 (0-8225-4064-9); paper $6.95 (0-8225-4142-4). 84pp. This revision of a 1993 edition features a more spacious layout and some expanded content. (Rev: HBG 3/02; SLJ 2/02) [976.4]

4337 Weintraub, Aileen. *The Grand Canyon: The Widest Canyon* (3–5). Illus. Series: Great Record Breakers in Nature. 2001, Rosen $18.75 (0-8239-5641-5). 24pp. Jam-packed with facts, this book takes readers on a word and photo tour of the formation, history, and appeal of one of the world's natural wonders. (Rev: BL 12/15/01; SLJ 7/01) [979.1]

Social Institutions and Issues

Business and Economics

General

4338 Downing, David. *Capitalism* (5–8). Series: Political and Economic Systems. 2002, Heinemann LB $27.86 (1-40340-315-5). 64pp. In an attractive format, this book explains the capitalistic economic system, its history, key thinkers, and present status. (Rev: BL 1/1–15/03; HBG 3/03; SLJ 2/03) [330.12]

4339 Downing, David. *Communism* (5–8). Series: Political and Economic Systems. 2002, Heinemann LB $27.86 (1-40340-316-3). 64pp. The theoretical basis of communism is explained with material on its application, history, important thinkers and leaders, and different movements. (Rev: BL 1/1–15/03; HBG 3/03; SLJ 2/03) [335.43]

4340 McGowan, Eileen Nixon, and Nancy Lagow Dumas. *Stock Market Smart* (5–8). Illus. 2002, Millbrook LB $23.90 (0-7613-2113-6). 64pp. An accessible question-and-answer presentation on the stock market and different types of investors, with illustrations, tips on saving, activities, a glossary, and list of resources. (Rev: BL 9/1/02; HBG 3/03; SLJ 10/02) [332.63]

Retail Stores and Other Workplaces

4341 Krull, Kathleen. *Supermarket* (K–3). Illus. by Melanie Hope Greenberg. 2001, Holiday $16.95 (0-8234-1546-5). 32pp. This is a fascinating and stimulating overview of what you'll find in the supermarket and how it gets there, including material on the history of shopping from barter onward and lots of interesting tidbits. (Rev: BL 9/15/01; HBG 3/02; SLJ 10/01) [381]

Ecology and Environment

General

4342 Ansary, Mir Tamim. *Earth Day* (2–3). Illus. Series: Holiday Histories. 2002, Heinemann LB $14.95 (1-58810-220-3). 32pp. The author traces the history of the Earth and its natural resources, man's misappropriation of them, and the founding of Earth Day. (Rev: BL 2/1/02) [333.7]

4343 Burnie, David. *Earthwatch* (5–7). Series: Protecting Our Planet. 2001, DK $16.95 (0-7894-6895-6). 60pp. In this attractive title full of illustrations, sidebars, maps, and diagrams, Burnie examines environmental issues including pollution, global warming, and habitat destruction; presents practical ideas that can make a difference; provides features on scientists and others working in the field; and suggests activities that explore the scientific concepts. (Rev: HBG 10/01; SLJ 6/01) [574.5]

4344 Dalgleish, Sharon. *Protecting Wildlife* (4–6). Illus. Series: Our World: Our Future. 2002, Chelsea LB $18.95 (0-7910-7021-2). 32pp. The role of humans is emphasized in this look at the impact on wildlife of vanishing habitats and changes in the weather, and simple actions that children can take are suggested. Also use *Saving Our Water* (2002). (Rev: HBG 3/03; SLJ 1/03)

4345 *The Disappearing Forests* (5–8). Ed. by Janice Parker. Illus. Series: Understanding Global Issues. 2002, Smart Apple LB $19.95 (1-58340-168-7). 56pp. A great deal of information about forest use, abuse, and conservation is packed into double-paged spreads with color illustrations. (Rev: BL 10/15/02; HBG 3/03; SLJ 12/02) [634.9]

4346 Ditchfield, Christin. *Oil* (2–5). Illus. Series: True Books — Natural Resources. 2002, Children's LB $23.50 (0-516-22343-7); paper $6.95 (0-516-29367-2). 48pp. This book discusses oil, its procurement and processing, and the environmental impact of using oil as fuel, with simple text and excellent photographs. (Rev: BL 10/15/02) [553.2]

4347 Ditchfield, Christin. *Water* (2–5). Illus. Series: True Books — Natural Resources. 2002, Children's LB $23.50 (0-516-22345-3); paper $6.95 (0-516-29369-9). 48pp. Ditchfield discusses water as a natural resource, covering in simple text and excellent photographs the forms of water, the water cycle, and the ways in which we use water. (Rev: BL 10/15/02) [553.7]

4348 *The Energy Dilemma* (5–8). Ed. by Celeste Peters. Illus. Series: Understanding Global Issues. 2002, Smart Apple LB $19.95 (1-58340-169-5). 56pp. The information about energy sources, use, and conservation packed into these double-paged spreads with color illustrations will spark debate. (Rev: BL 10/15/02) [333.79]

4349 Kerley, Barbara. *A Cool Drink of Water* (PS–3). Illus. 2002, National Geographic $16.95 (0-7922-6723-0). 32pp. A series of beautiful photographs with minimal text show how water is collected and carried by people throughout the world. (Rev: BL 3/15/02; HBG 10/02; SLJ 4/02*) [363.6]

4350 Powell, Jillian. *World Wildlife Fund* (3–5). Illus. Series: World Organizations. 2001, Watts LB $23.00 (0-531-14626-X); paper $6.95 (0-531-14816-5). 32pp. This volume for younger readers describes the mission, projects, and problems of the World Wildlife Fund. (Rev: BL 1/1–15/02) [639.9]

4351 Suzuki, David, and Kathy Vanderlinden. *Eco-Fun* (5–8). Illus. 2001, Douglas & McIntyre paper $10.95 (1-55054-823-9). 128pp. The activities in this collection reinforce some basic scientific concepts about air, water, earth, and fire, and encourage young readers to think about environmental issues and avoid pollution. (Rev: BL 6/1–15/01; SLJ 8/01) [577]

4352 Taylor, Barbara. *How to Save the Planet* (3–6). Illus. by Scoular Anderson. Series: How To. 2001,

Watts LB $14.00 (0-531-14640-5); paper $4.95 (0-531-14821-1). 96pp. Experiments back up the concepts introduced in this discussion of global warming, pollution, future energy needs, and other important topics. (Rev: SLJ 4/02) [363.7]

Pollution

4353 Chapman, Matthew, and Rob Bowden. *Air Pollution* (5–8). Series: 21st Century Debates. 2002, Raintree Steck-Vaughn LB $18.98 (0-7398-4874-7). 64pp. The causes of air pollution, the present situation, and possible future solutions are presented in this well-illustrated book that presents various points of view and offers topics for debate. (Rev: BL 6/1–15/02) [363.73]

4354 Pringle, Laurence. *Global Warming: The Threat of Earth's Changing Climate* (4–8). Illus. 2001, North-South $16.95 (1-58717-009-4). 48pp. A straightforward account that covers topics including the causes of global warming, the signs that it is occurring, and possible solutions. (Rev: BL 4/1/01; HBG 10/01; SLJ 6/01) [363.738]

Population

4355 Bowden, Rob. *Food Supply* (5–8). Series: 21st Century Debates. 2002, Raintree Steck-Vaughn LB $18.98 (0-7398-4871-2). 64pp. Trends and issues regarding the food supply, and possible solutions for shortages, are presented in this look at pros and cons. (Rev: BL 6/1–15/02) [338.19]

4356 Bowden, Rob. *An Overcrowded World?* (5–8). Series: 21st Century Debates. 2002, Raintree Steck-Vaughn LB $18.98 (0-7398-4872-0). 64pp. Using a well-organized text, plus sidebars for additional facts and statements of opinion, this colorfully illustrated volume explores the current problems of overpopulation and the dire strain it causes on the earth's supplies. (Rev: BL 6/1–15/02) [304.6]

4357 Smith, David J. *If the World Were a Village* (3–5). Illus. by Shelagh Armstrong. 2002, Kids Can $15.95 (1-55074-779-7). 32pp. By condensing the world's population to a "village" of 100 people, this book makes data and statistics more comprehensible — and more fascinating — for younger readers. (Rev: BL 3/1/02; HB 5–6/02; HBG 10/02; SLJ 5/02) [304.6]

Government and Politics

Courts and the Law

4358 De Capua, Sarah E. *Serving on a Jury* (2–5). Series: True Books — Civics. 2002, Children's LB $23.00 (0-516-22329-1); paper $6.95 (0-516-27364-7). 48pp. Chapters in this simple book on the jury system include material on what is a jury, who can serve, how members are selected, and what they do. (Rev: BL 6/1–15/02; SLJ 10/02) [347.73]

4359 Linz, Kathi. *Chickens May Not Cross the Road and Other Crazy (But True) Laws* (2–4). Illus. by Tony Griego. 2002, Houghton $16.00 (0-618-11257-X). 32pp. A compilation of silly laws ("no tying crocodiles to fire hydrants," "no donkeys in bathtubs") from cities across the United States, each with a cartoon illustration. (Rev: BL 9/1/02; HBG 3/03; SLJ 11/02) [348.73]

United Nations and International Affairs

4360 Downing, David. *Democracy* (5–8). Illus. Series: Political and Economic Systems. 2002, Heinemann LB $27.86 (1-40340-317-1). 64pp. Downing explains the history of democracy and looks at its weaknesses and benefits. Also use *Dictatorship* (2002). (Rev: BL 1/1–15/03; HBG 3/03) [321.8]

4361 Hamilton, John. *Behind the Terror* (4–7). Series: War on Terrorism. 2002, ABDO LB $16.95 (1-57765-679-8). 48pp. Using an accessible text and color photographs, this book reports on various international terrorist organizations, their leaders, and their tactics. (Rev: BL 5/15/02) [909.9]

4362 Louis, Nancy. *United We Stand* (4–7). Series: War on Terrorism. 2002, ABDO LB $16.95 (1-57765-660-1). 48pp. In text and pictures, this account describes the support offered to the victims of the terrorist attacks of September 11, 2001, and

their families. (Rev: BL 5/15/02; HBG 10/02) [909.9]

4363 Melvern, Linda. *United Nations* (3–5). Illus. Series: World Organizations. 2001, Watts LB $23.00 (0-531-14624-3); paper $6.95 (0-531-14814-9). 32pp. An overview of the United Nations, for younger readers, that outlines the organization's history and goals as well as the problems it faces. (Rev: BL 1/1–15/02) [341.23]

4364 Suen, Anastasia. *Doctors Without Borders* (1–2). Series: Helping Organizations. 2002, Rosen LB $16.00 (0-8239-6002-1). 24pp. As well as giving a history of this humanitarian organization, this simple account describes how it works and the good work it accomplishes. (Rev: BL 6/1–15/02; SLJ 4/02) [361.7]

4365 Suen, Anastasia. *The Red Cross* (1–2). Illus. Series: Helping Organizations. 2002, Rosen LB $16.00 (0-8239-6003-X). 24pp. This basic introduction to the Red Cross explains how it was formed and the work it does around the world. (Rev: BL 6/1–15/02) [361.7]

4366 Suen, Anastasia. *UNICEF* (1–2). Illus. 2002, Rosen LB $16.00 (0-8239-6005-6). 24pp. This introduction to UNICEF and its mission also tells how volunteers can help and how youngsters can raise money to aid its programs. (Rev: BL 6/1–15/02; SLJ 3/02) [362.7]

4367 Tames, Richard. *Monarchy* (5–8). Series: Political and Economic Systems. 2002, Heinemann LB $27.86 (1-40340-320-1). 64pp. A description of the concept of monarchy, followed by a history of its application, its current status, and its various forms. (Rev: BL 1/1–15/03; HBG 3/03) [321.8]

United States

Civil Rights

4368 Isler, Claudia. *The Right to Free Speech* (4–6). Series: Individual Rights and Civic Responsibility.

2001, Rosen LB $19.95 (0-8239-3234-6). 128pp. The history of the first amendment is followed by information on sedition, protest, obscenity, symbolic speech, and hate speech. (Rev: SLJ 2/02) [342.0853]

4369 Kendall, Martha E. *Failure Is Impossible: The History of American Women's Rights* (5–8). Illus. Series: People's History. 2001, Lerner LB $22.60 (0-8225-1744-2). 96pp. The status of women in the United States is discussed from the time of the Puritans to the present, including information on life for slaves, Native American women, and mill girls, and on equal pay and equal opportunity. (Rev: BL 5/1/01; HBG 10/01; SLJ 6/01) [305.42]

4370 Seidman, David. *Civil Rights* (4–6). Series: Individual Rights and Civic Responsibility. 2001, Rosen LB $19.95 (0-8239-3231-1). 128pp. Covers civil rights issues involving African Americans, women, Native Americans, immigrants, prisoners, and gays and lesbians. (Rev: BL 3/15/02; SLJ 2/02) [323]

4371 Venable, Rose. *The Civil Rights Movement* (4–6). Series: Journey to Freedom: The African American Library. 2001, Child's World LB $17.95 (1-56766-917-4). 40pp. An oversize, attractive volume that supplies details on the 20th-century civil rights movement in the United States, its leaders, and their accomplishments. (Rev: BL 12/15/01; HBG 3/02; SLJ 1/02) [323]

4372 Welch, Catherine A. *Children of the Civil Rights Era* (3–6). Series: Picture the American Past. 2001, Carolrhoda LB $22.60 (1-57505-481-7). 48pp. Large historical photographs and a simple text are used to describe how young people participated in America's civil rights movement. (Rev: BL 6/1–15/01; HBG 10/01) [323]

Constitution

4373 Burgan, Michael. *The Bill of Rights* (4–6). Series: We the People. 2001, Compass Point LB $21.26 (0-7565-0151-2). 48pp. Burgan discusses the reasons behind the creation of the Bill of Rights, with paintings, maps, and documents. (Rev: SLJ 1/02) [342.73]

4374 Catrow, David. *We the Kids* (PS–3). Illus. 2002, Dial $16.99 (0-8037-2553-1). 32pp. A visually engaging, straightforward interpretation of the constitution for young readers. (Rev: BL 3/15/02; HBG 10/02; SLJ 5/02) [342.73]

4375 Hudson, David L. *The Bill of Rights* (5–8). Illus. Series: The Constitution. 2002, Enslow LB $20.95 (0-7660-1903-9). 128pp. All about the first ten amendments to the Constitution and how they have affected the citizens of the United States. (Rev: BL 2/15/03; HBG 3/03) [342.73]

4376 Hudson, David L. *The Fourteenth Amendment: Equal Protection Under the Law* (5–8). Illus. Series: The Constitution. 2002, Enslow LB $20.95 (0-7660-1904-7). 128pp. What the 14th amendment to the Constitution entails and how it has affected the citizens of the United States. (Rev: BL 2/15/03) [342.73]

4377 Nardo, Don. *The U.S. Constitution* (5–8). Illus. Series: History of the World. 2001, Gale LB $23.70 (0-7377-0776-3). 48pp. A history of the Constitution and the Bill of Rights is given plus a discussion of their importance today. (Rev: BL 4/1/02) [342.73]

4378 Sobel, Syl. *The U.S. Constitution and You* (3–5). Illus. by Denise Gilgannon. 2001, Barron's paper $6.95 (0-7641-1707-6). 48pp. Clear text and pen-and-ink sketches provide a concise look at the importance of the Constitution, with chapters on checks and balances and the rights of the people and of the states. (Rev: SLJ 8/01) [342.73]

4379 Weidner, Daniel. *The Constitution: The Preamble and the Articles* (5–8). Series: The Constitution. 2002, Enslow LB $20.95 (0-7660-1906-3). 112pp. Through personal stories and examples, the history of the U.S. Constitution and its meanings are explored. (Rev: BL 2/15/03; HBG 3/03; SLJ 1/03) [342.73]

4380 Weidner, Daniel. *Creating the Constitution: The People and Events That Formed the Nation* (5–8). Series: The Constitution. 2002, Enslow LB $20.95 (0-7660-1905-5). 112pp. This informative volume describes how the U.S. constitution was written and the debates that preceded its adoption. (Rev: BL 2/15/03; HBG 3/03; SLJ 1/03) [342.73]

Crime and Criminals

4381 Blackwood, Gary L. *Gangsters* (4–7). Series: Bad Guys. 2001, Benchmark LB $19.95 (0-7614-1016-3). 72pp. Al Capone is just one of the evildoers profiled in this volume that gives historical context for each "bad guy." Also use *Outlaws* and *Highwaymen* (both 2001). (Rev: HBG 3/02; SLJ 1/02) [364.106]

4382 Brezina, Thomas. *Tips and Tricks for Junior Detectives* (3–6). Illus. 2001, Sterling paper $5.95 (0-8069-0987-0). 96pp. Basic sleuthing strategies for aspiring young detectives. (Rev: BL 7/01) [363.25]

4383 Draper, Allison Stark. *The Assassination of Malcolm X* (5–8). Series: The Library of Political Assassinations. 2002, Rosen LB $26.50 (0-8239-3542-6). 64pp. A description of the assassination and its aftermath is followed by information on Malcolm X's life and beliefs. Also use *The Assassination of Medgar Evers, The Assassination of Abraham Lincoln, The Assassination of Martin Luther King Jr.*, and *The Assassination of Robert F. Kennedy* (all 2002). (Rev: BL 2/15/02; SLJ 7/02)

4384 Farman, John. *The Short and Bloody History of Spies* (5–8). Illus. 2002, Lerner LB $19.93 (0-8225-0845-1); paper $5.95 (0-8225-0846-X). 96pp. A witty and fascinating account of the intriguing lives of spies, with descriptions of spying techniques and gadgets. (Rev: BL 1/1–15/03; HBG 3/03) [327.12]

4385 Friedlander, Mark P., Jr., and Terry M. Phillips. *When Objects Talk: Solving a Crime with Science* (5–8). Illus. Series: Discovery! 2001, Lerner LB $26.60 (0-8225-0649-1). 120pp. A fictional

271

mystery serves to introduce criminal investigation techniques such as fingerprints and DNA. (Rev: HBG 3/02; SLJ 2/02) [363.25]

4386 Johnson, Julie. *Why Do People Join Gangs?* (5–8). Series: Exploring Tough Issues. 2001, Raintree Steck-Vaughn LB $17.98 (0-7398-3236-0). 48pp. Johnson looks at gangs — who joins them and why, and how to get out of one — in the United States and abroad, and includes a chapter on dealing with bullies. Also use *Why Do People Fight Wars?* and *Why Are People Prejudiced?* (both 2002). (Rev: SLJ 11/01) [364.1]

4387 Marquette, Scott. *America Under Attack* (4–7). Illus. Series: America at War. 2002, Rourke LB $27.93 (1-58952-386-5). 48pp. This book for middle graders explains in simple terms the September 11 attacks and other acts of terrorism against the United States, as well as discussing resulting legislation and changing opinions in America. (Rev: BL 10/15/02) [973.931]

4388 Monroe, Judy. *The Susan B. Anthony Women's Voting Rights Trial: A Headline Court Case* (5–9). Series: Headline Court Cases. 2002, Enslow LB $20.95 (0-7660-1759-1). 112pp. Monroe explores the fight for women's suffrage and the trial of Susan B. Anthony for voting illegally in the 1872 election. (Rev: BL 3/15/03; HBG 3/03; SLJ 12/02)

4389 Standiford, Natalie. *The Stone Giant: A Hoax That Fooled America* (1–3). Illus. by Bob Doucet. 2001, Golden Books LB $11.99 (0-307-46404-0); paper $3.99 (0-307-26404-1). 44pp. An absorbing account of the Cardiff Giant, a hoax perpetrated in New York State in 1869 and then copied by P. T. Barnum. (Rev: HBG 3/02; SLJ 8/01) [974.7]

4390 Woodford, Chris. *Criminal Investigation* (4–8). Illus. Series: Science Fact Files. 2001, Raintree Steck-Vaughn LB $18.98 (0-7398-1016-2). 45pp. A concise introduction to the forensic science with information on the newest equipment and techniques. (Rev: HBG 10/01; SLJ 1/02) [363.2]

Elections and Political Parties

4391 Ansary, Mir Tamim. *Election Day* (2–3). Illus. Series: Holiday Histories. 2002, Heinemann LB $14.95 (1-58810-221-1). 32pp. A brief history and overview of the U.S. presidential election system. (Rev: BL 2/1/02) [324.973]

4392 De Capua, Sarah E. *Running for Public Office* (2–5). Series: True Books — Civics. 2002, Children's LB $23.00 (0-516-22333-X); paper $6.95 (0-516-27368-X). 48pp. A simple, large-type text and many photographs are used to introduce the positions open in public office and the steps in running for these positions, including campaigning and elections. (Rev: BL 6/1–15/02; SLJ 10/02) [324.7]

4393 De Capua, Sarah E. *Voting* (2–5). Series: True Books — Civics. 2002, Children's LB $23.00 (0-516-22330-5); paper $6.95 (0-516-27365-5). 48pp. The election system is introduced in simple, large-type text with plenty of attractive color photographs. (Rev: BL 6/1–15/02) [324]

4394 Gottfried, Ted. *The 2000 Election* (5–8). Illus. 2002, Millbrook LB $24.90 (0-7613-2406-2). 64pp. A well-designed and detailed look at the controversial presidential election of 2000, with background information, sidebars on important people, and an electoral map and other graphics. (Rev: BL 7/02; HBG 10/02; SLJ 4/02) [324.973]

4395 Hewson, Martha S. *The Electoral College* (5–9). 2002, Chelsea LB $20.75 (0-7910-6790-4). 64pp. Covers the history of the Electoral College and details of elections of particular interest, including the 2000 Bush–Gore decision. (Rev: HBG 3/03; SLJ 2/03) [324.6]

4396 Landau, Elaine. *The 2000 Presidential Election* (2–5). Series: Cornerstones of Freedom, Second Series. 2002, Children's LB $24.00 (0-516-22527-8). 48pp. A timeline and informative text help to unravel the events between the 2000 election and Gore's concession speech. (Rev: SLJ 3/03)

4397 Murphy, Patricia. *Election Day* (PS–2). Series: Rookie Read-About Holidays. 2003, Children's LB $19.00 (0-516-22663-0); paper $5.95 (0-516-27488-0). 32pp. In very simple words and pictures, this book describes the activities that occur on the first Tuesday after the first Monday in November. (Rev: BL 3/15/03) [324]

4398 Murphy, Patricia J. *The Presidency* (K–2). Series: Let's See. 2001, Compass Point LB $18.60 (0-7565-0142-3). 24pp. A simple introduction in double-page spreads to the office of the president that includes material on the vice president and first lady. (Rev: SLJ 1/02) [353.03]

4399 Murphy, Patricia J. *Voting and Elections* (K–2). Series: Let's See. 2001, Compass Point LB $18.60 (0-7565-0144-X). 24pp. A simple introduction to the voting process and how you register to vote. (Rev: SLJ 1/02) [324.7]

4400 Santella, Andrew. *U.S. Presidential Inaugurations* (3–6). Series: Cornerstones of Freedom, Second Series. 2002, Children's LB $24.00 (0-516-22533-2). 48pp. Inaugural addresses, inaugural balls, and inaugural weather are the focus of this narrative, which also explains the role of the Electoral College and its part in the Gore-Bush presidential election. (Rev: SLJ 12/02)

4401 Zeinert, Karen. *Women in Politics: In the Running* (5–9). 2002, Twenty-First Century LB $29.90 (0-7613-2253-1). 112pp. From 1774 to the present, the author looks at women who have been elected to office or who have been influential in the political field, and discusses the possibility of a woman president. (Rev: BL 12/1/02; HBG 3/03; SLJ 11/02) [320]

Federal Government and Agencies

4402 De Capua, Sarah E. *Becoming a Citizen* (2–5). Illus. Series: True Books — Civics. 2002, Children's LB $23.00 (0-516-22331-3); paper $6.95 (0-516-27366-3). 48pp. This work describes the requirements for becoming a U.S. citizen and the steps one must take to become naturalized. (Rev: BL 6/1–15/02; SLJ check) [342.73]

4403 De Capua, Sarah E. *Paying Taxes* (2–5). Illus. Series: True Books — Civics. 2002, Children's LB $23.00 (0-516-22332-1); paper $6.95 (0-516-27367-1). 48pp. This account explains the taxes people pay, their history, and what the money is used for. (Rev: BL 6/1–15/02; SLJ check) [336.2]

4404 January, Brendan. *The CIA* (4–6). Illus. Series: Watts Library — U.S. Government and Military. 2002, Watts LB $24.00 (0-531-12034-1); paper $8.95 (0-531-16600-7). 64pp. A brief history and overview of the CIA from its conception to September 11, 2001, including photographs and a timeline. (Rev: BL 10/15/02; SLJ 1/03) [327.1273]

4405 January, Brendan. *The FBI* (4–6). Illus. Series: Watts Library — U.S. Government and Military. 2002, Watts LB $24.00 (0-531-12033-3); paper $8.95 (0-531-16601-5). 64pp. An overview of the FBI and its activities from the agency's conception up to September 11, 2001, including photographs and a timeline. (Rev: BL 10/15/02; SLJ 1/03) [363.25]

4406 Kule, Elaine A. *The U.S. Mail* (2–4). Series: Transportation and Communication. 2002, Enslow LB $18.95 (0-7660-1892-X). 48pp. A history of the U.S. Postal Service from colonial days to the present, with material on how it works, its possible future uses, and people important in its development. (Rev: BL 9/15/02; HBG 3/03) [353]

4407 Stein, R. Conrad. *The National Archives* (4–6). Series: Watts Library — U.S. Government and Military. 2002, Watts LB $24.00 (0-531-13032-5); paper $8.95 (0-531-16602-3). 64pp. This account presents in text and pictures a visit to the National Archives, a treasure trove that holds millions of American documents including the original Declaration of Independence. (Rev: BL 10/15/02) [069]

4408 Suen, Anastasia. *The Peace Corps* (1–2). Series: Helping Organizations. 2002, Rosen LB $16.00 (0-8239-6001-3). 24pp. As well as a brief description of the history and activities of the Peace Corps, this beginning reader tells how youngsters can become involved. (Rev: BL 6/1–15/02) [361.6]

State Government and Agencies

4409 Armentrout, David, and Patricia Armentrout. *State Seals* (3–5). Illus. Series: The Rourke Guide to State Symbols. 2001, Rourke LB $27.93 (1-58952-087-4). 48pp. Brief, large-print text explains the history and design of each state's seal. (Rev: SLJ 5/02) [973]

Social Problems and Solutions

4410 Ancona, George. *Harvest* (4–7). Illus. 2001, Marshall Cavendish $15.95 (0-7614-5086-6). 48pp. This volume examines the difficult lives and work of Mexican migrant workers and the crops they harvest, ending with a look at the contributions of labor leader Cesar Chavez. (Rev: BL 1/1–15/02; HBG 3/02; SLJ 4/02) [331.5]

4411 Gellman, Marc, and Thomas Hartman. *Bad Stuff in the News: A Family Guide to Handling the Headlines* (4–7). 2002, North-South $14.95 (1-58717-132-5). 120pp. A reassuring book about difficult current issues, including terrorism, accidents, school violence, and more. (Rev: BL 5/15/02; HBG 10/02; SLJ 3/02) [302.23]

4412 Heinrichs, Ann. *The Ku Klux Klan: A Hooded Brotherhood* (4–7). Series: Journey to Freedom. 2002, Child's World LB $25.64 (1-56766-646-9). 40pp. This brief introduction to the Klan covers the group's origins and history, and touches on the Internet's role in spreading hate messages. (Rev: SLJ 12/02)

4413 Siegel, Danny. *Mitzvah Magic: What Kids Can Do to Change the World* (3–8). Illus. by Naomi Eisenberger. 2002, Kar-Ben paper $8.95 (1-58013-034-8). 64pp. Siegel has amassed a large number of suggestions for children who want to help others. (Rev: BL 10/1/02) [302]

4414 Stearman, Kaye. *Why Do People Live on the Streets?* (5–7). Series: Exploring Tough Issues. 2001, Raintree Steck-Vaughn LB $17.98 (0-7398-3232-8). 48pp. Among reasons given for homelessness are poverty and discrimination. (Rev: HBG 10/01; SLJ 7/01) [305.569]

4415 Suen, Anastasia. *Habitat for Humanity* (1–2). Series: Helping Organizations. 2002, Rosen LB $16.00 (0-8239-6006-4). 24pp. A beginning reader that describes how this organization provides housing for the poor and tells how such people as President Carter participate in its work. (Rev: BL 6/1–15/02; SLJ 3/02) [361.7]

4416 Ventura, Jesse, and Heron Marquez. *Jesse Ventura Tells It Like It Is: America's Most Outspoken Governor Speaks Out About Government* (5–8). Illus. 2002, Lerner $15.95 (0-8225-0385-9). 64pp. A look at the U.S. government and politicians from the viewpoint of wrestler-turned-Minnesota-governor Jesse Ventura. (Rev: BL 8/02; HBG 3/03; SLJ 9/02) [977.6]

Religion and Holidays

General and Miscellaneous

4417 Baring-Gould, Sabine. *Now the Day Is Over* (PS–2). Illus. by Preston McDaniels. 2001, Morehouse $17.95 (0-8192-1868-5). 32pp. Graceful illustrations of a little boy, animals, and angels accompany the four verses of the song. (Rev: BL 6/1–15/01) [242]

4418 Bedard, Michael. *The Wolf of Gubbio* (2–4). Illus. 2001, Stoddart $15.95 (0-7737-3250-0). 24pp. The story of Saint Francis of Assisi and how his ability to talk to animals saved the city of Gubbio from a hungry wolf is retold through the voice of a young child. (Rev: BCCB 6/01; BL 4/15/01) [398.22]

4419 Bolden, Tonya. *Rock of Ages* (K–4). Illus. by R. Gregory Christie. 2001, Knopf LB $18.99 (0-679-99485-8). 32pp. Rhythmic text and striking art present the importance of religion in African American life, from slavery through the civil rights movement to the present. (Rev: BL 10/1/01; HB 1–2/02; HBG 3/02; SLJ 1/02*) [811.5]

4420 Capek, Michael. *A Personal Tour of a Shaker Village* (4–7). Series: How It Was. 2001, Lerner LB $25.26 (0-8225-3584-X). 64pp. An account of life in a Shaker village, seen through the eyes of people who lived there. (Rev: BL 8/1/01; HBG 10/01; SLJ 8/01) [289.8]

4421 Dineen, Jacqueline. *Births* (3–6). Series: Ceremonies and Celebrations. 2001, Raintree Steck-Vaughn LB $17.98 (0-7398-3267-0). 32pp. Traditions surrounding births are explored in six major religions, covering topics from circumcision, baptism, and naming ceremonies to gifts, clothing, food, and horoscopes. Also use *Weddings* (2001). (Rev: SLJ 9/01) [392.12]

4422 Ganeri, Anita. *Buddhism* (3–6). Series: World of Beliefs. 2001, McGraw-Hill $16.95 (0-87226-685-0). 46pp. With a large-format, short paragraphs, and a copious assortment of illustrations, this book gives a brief introduction to Buddhism and its beliefs. (Rev: BL 12/15/01; HBG 3/02; SLJ 11/01) [294]

4423 Gellman, Marc. *And God Cried, Too: A Kid's Book of Healing and Hope* (2–5). Illus. by Harry Bliss. 2002, HarperCollins LB $17.89 (0-06-009887-2); paper $5.99 (0-06-009886-4). 128pp. A fictional story about a young angel-in-training opens this thought-provoking book that deals with questions that challenge faith. (Rev: BL 10/1/02; SLJ 12/02) [291.2]

4424 Griffith, Linda Hill. *Blessings and Prayers for Little Bears* (PS–K). Illus. 2002, HarperCollins $15.95 (0-06-623689-4). 32pp. Traditional children's prayers are illustrated with full-page paintings of teddy bears involved in everyday activities. (Rev: BL 1/1–15/02; HBG 10/02; SLJ 7/02) [242]

4425 Hodges, Margaret. *The Legend of Saint Christopher* (3–6). Illus. by Richard J. Watson. 2002, Eerdmans $18.00 (0-8028-5077-4). 32pp. Hodges retells the story of how Saint Christopher got the name that means "Christ bearer." (Rev: BCCB 12/02; BL 10/1/02; HBG 3/03; SLJ 11/02) [242]

4426 John Paul II. *Every Child a Light: The Pope's Message to Young People* (4–7). Ed. by Jerome M. Vereb. Illus. 2002, Boyds Mills $16.95 (1-56397-090-2). 48pp. Using photographs and snippets from Pope John Paul II's writings for children and teens, this is an inspirational book of comments and advice for youngsters. (Rev: BL 6/1–15/02; HBG 10/02; SLJ 5/02) [248.8]

4427 Keane, Michael. *What You Will See Inside a Catholic Church* (3–6). Illus. 2002, Skylight Paths $17.95 (1-893361-54-3). 32pp. Readers are introduced to the layout, ceremonies, and rituals of a Roman Catholic church. (Rev: BL 3/15/03) [264]

4428 Khan, Rukhsana. *Muslim Child: Understanding Islam Through Stories and Poems* (4–6). Illus. by Patty Gallinger. 2002, Albert Whitman $14.95 (0-8075-5307-7). 104pp. A series of vignettes told by children about living as a Muslim in various countries around the world. (Rev: BL 2/15/02; HBG 10/02; SLJ 2/02) [297]

4429 *Let There Be Light: Poems and Prayers for Repairing the World* (2–6). Ed. by Jane Breskin Zalben. Illus. 2002, Dutton $16.99 (0-525-46995-8). 32pp. Zalben has chosen a selection of spiritual passages from sources ranging from the Bible and Koran to Native American peoples and Mahatma Gandhi. (Rev: BL 10/1/02*; HBG 3/03; SLJ 11/02) [242.8]

4430 Lutz, Norma Jean. *The History of the Black Church* (5–8). Illus. Series: African American Achievers. 2001, Chelsea $19.95 (0-7910-5822-0); paper $9.95 (0-7910-5823-9). 112pp. Historical and contemporary photographs illustrate this history of African American religious life and institutions. (Rev: BL 10/1/01; HBG 3/02; SLJ 12/01) [277.3]

4431 Mayer, Marianna. *Seeing Jesus in His Own Words* (4–8). Illus. 2002, Penguin Putnam $16.99 (0-8037-2742-9). 32pp. A range of styles of paintings illustrate this collection of sayings of Jesus that are restated in words young people will understand. (Rev: BL 10/1/02; HBG 3/03; SLJ 1/03) [232.9]

4432 Morris, Neil. *Islam* (3–6). Illus. Series: World of Beliefs. 2001, McGraw-Hill $16.95 (0-87226-693-1). 46pp. A large-format introduction to the religion of Islam both in history and today that touches on the role of women, with concise text and lots of photographs and illustrations. (Rev: BL 10/1/01; HBG 3/02; SLJ 11/01) [297]

4433 Rockwell, Anne. *The Prince Who Ran Away: The Story of Gautama Buddha* (4–6). Illus. by Fahimeh Amiri. 2001, Knopf $16.95 (0-679-89188-9). 40pp. Absorbing illustrations highlight the life of Buddha in this picture book for older readers that also explains such concepts as nirvana. (Rev: BL 12/15/01; HBG 3/02; SLJ 12/01) [294.3]

4434 Schwartz, Howard. *Invisible Kingdoms: Jewish Tales of Angels, Spirits, and Demons* (3–5). Illus. by Stephen Fieser. 2002, HarperCollins LB $18.89 (0-06-027856-0). 80pp. Schwartz retells nine varied tales peopled with angels, ghosts, and demons. (Rev: BL 10/1/02; HB 11–12/02; HBG 3/03; SLJ 10/02) [398.2]

4435 Senker, Cath. *Judaism* (3–6). Illus. Series: World of Beliefs. 2001, McGraw-Hill $16.95 (0-87226-684-2). 46pp. Concise text and plentiful photographs and illustrations are used in this introduction to the history and current practice of Judaism that covers the creation of the state of Israel. (Rev: BL 10/1/01; HBG 3/02; SLJ 12/01) [296]

4436 Stauffacher, Sue. *The Angel and Other Stories* (2–6). Illus. by Leonid Gore. 2002, Eerdmans $20.00 (0-8028-5203-3). 80pp. Stauffacher retells 10 stories that reflect on faith and prayer written by authors including Hans Christian Andersen, Fyodor Dostoyevsky, and Oscar Wilde. (Rev: BCCB 11/02; BL 10/1/02; HBG 3/03; SLJ 1/03) [242]

4437 Waldman, Neil. *The Promised Land: The Birth of the Jewish People* (4–7). Illus. 2002, Boyds Mills $21.95 (1-56397-332-4). 40pp. Waldman interweaves information on Jewish religious tradition

and the experiences of the Jewish people over time in this handsome volume. (Rev: BL 10/1/02; HBG 3/03; SLJ 9/02) [909]

4438 Wilkinson, Philip. *Islam* (4–8). Illus. Series: Eyewitness Books. 2002, DK LB $19.99 (0-7894-8871-X). 64pp. This overview of Islam gives readers a good understanding of the history and tenets of Islam as well as the ways in which it is practiced today. (Rev: BL 10/1/02; HBG 3/03; SLJ 1/03) [297]

Bible Stories

4439 Alexander, Pat. *My First Bible* (PS–1). Illus. by Leon Baxter. 2002, Good Books $17.99 (1-56148-360-5). 480pp. A collection of more than 60 stories from the Old and New Testaments, with amusing, cartoon-style illustrations. (Rev: SLJ 12/02)

4440 Chaikin, Miriam. *Angels Sweep the Desert Floor: Bible Legends About Moses in the Wilderness* (4–7). Illus. by Alexander Koshkin. 2002, Clarion $19.00 (0-395-97825-4). 102pp. This collection of stories mixes religious history and rabbinic literature to tell the story of the Israelites' 40 years in the wilderness. (Rev: BL 10/1/02; HB 11–12/02; HBG 3/03; SLJ 9/02) [296.1]

4441 Chancellor, Deborah, retel. *DK Children's Everyday Bible: A Bible Story for Every Day of the Year* (K–4). Illus. by Anna C. Leplar. 2002, DK $19.99 (0-7894-8858-2). 383pp. Retellings of Old and New Testament stories for each day of the year. (Rev: SLJ 12/02)

4442 Gilles-Sebaoun, Elisabeth, retel. *A Young Child's Bible* (PS–3). Trans. from French by Joan Robins. Illus. by Charlotte Roederer. 2001, HarperCollins $12.95 (0-06-029464-7). 87pp. This is a lively, conversational retelling of 30 of the most important stories of both Testaments with rich full-color illustrations. (Rev: HBG 10/01; SLJ 8/01) [224]

4443 Greene, Rhonda Gowler. *The Beautiful World That God Made* (PS–1). Illus. by Anne Wilson. 2002, Eerdmans $16.00 (0-8028-5213-0). 32pp. A creation story in cumulative verse illustrated with colorful collages. (Rev: BL 2/1/02; HBG 10/02; SLJ 9/02) [231.7]

4444 Harik, Ramsay M. *Jesus of Nazareth: Teacher and Prophet* (5–8). Illus. Series: Book Report Biographies. 2001, Watts LB $22.00 (0-531-20370-0); paper $6.95 (0-531-15552-8). 128pp. Harik presents the life and ministry of Jesus. (Rev: BL 8/01) [232.9]

4445 Hoffman, Mary. *Animals of the Bible* (K–3). Illus. by Jackie Morris. 2003, Penguin Putnam $16.99 (0-8037-2842-5). 32pp. Lovely illustrations flow along with Hoffman's retellings of Bible tales including the plague of frogs, Jonah and the whale, and Daniel in the lion's den. (Rev: BL 1/1–15/03) [221.8]

4446 Hoffman, Mary. *Miracles: Wonders Jesus Worked* (K–3). Illus. by Jackie Morris. 2001, Penguin Putnam $16.99 (0-8037-2610-4). 32pp. This companion to *Parables* (2000) looks at nine of Jesus's miracles. (Rev: BL 10/1/01; HBG 3/02; SLJ 10/01) [226.7]

4447 Kimmel, Eric. *Why the Snake Crawls on Its Belly* (K–3). Illus. by Allen Davis. 2001, Pitspopany $14.95 (1-930143-20-6). 32pp. This very readable pourquoi story relates how God punishes the snake for tempting Adam and Eve in the Garden of Eden. (Rev: BL 10/1/01; HBG 3/02; SLJ 12/01)

4448 Kuskin, Karla. *The Animals and the Ark* (PS–3). Illus. by Michael Grejniec. 2002, Simon & Schuster $16.95 (0-689-83095-5). 40pp. A secular version of the story of Noah and the ark. (Rev: BCCB 3/02; BL 1/1–15/02; HB 3–4/02; HBG 10/02; SLJ 4/02) [222]

4449 *The Lord Is My Shepherd* (PS–2). Illus. by Anne Wilson. 2003, Eerdmans $16.00 (0-8028-5250-5). 32pp. The 23rd psalm is accompanied by expressive art. (Rev: BL 2/1/03) [223]

4450 McCarthy, Michael. *The Story of Noah and the Ark* (PS–K). Illus. by Giuliano Ferri. 2001, Barefoot $16.99 (1-84148-361-3). 32pp. Wonderful illustrations show the animals arrayed around the decks, the roiling seas, and the arrival of the dove. (Rev: BL 10/1/01; HBG 3/02; SLJ 11/01) [222]

4451 McGee, Marni. *The Colt and the King* (PS–3). Illus. by John Winch. 2002, Holiday $16.95 (0-8234-1695-X). 32pp. Told from the standpoint of the donkey that carried Jesus into Jerusalem on Palm Sunday, this is a beautifully illustrated retelling of a Bible story. (Rev: BCCB 4/02; BL 4/1/02; HB 3–4/02; HBG 10/02; SLJ 4/02)

4452 Manushkin, Fran. *Daughters of Fire* (4–7). Illus. by Uri Shulevitz. 2001, Harcourt $20.00 (0-15-201869-7). 88pp. Rich, striking illustrations accompany a selection of stories about biblical women. (Rev: BL 12/15/01; HBG 3/02; SLJ 10/01) [221.9]

4453 Pinkney, Jerry. *Noah's Ark* (2–5). Illus. 2002, North-South LB $16.50 (1-58717-202-X). 40pp. Pinkney offers a fresh take on the popular story while keeping his narrative fairly close to the standard version. (Rev: BCCB 1/03; BL 10/1/02; HB 1–2/03; HBG 3/03; SLJ 11/02*) [222]

4454 Rock, Lois. *Everlasting Stories: A Family Bible Treasury* (3–5). Illus. by Christina Balit. 2001, Chronicle $24.95 (0-8118-3258-9). 224pp. One hundred biblical stories told in simple narrative surrounded by vibrant illustrations. (Rev: BL 1/1–15/02; HBG 3/02; SLJ 4/02) [220.9]

4455 Sasso, Sandy Eisenberg. *Cain and Abel: Finding the Fruits of Peace* (K–3). Illus. by Joani Keller Rothenberg. 2001, Jewish Lights $16.95 (1-58023-123-3). 32pp. This retelling of a biblical parable encourages children to think about the harmful consequences of jealousy and anger. (Rev: BL 11/15/01; HBG 10/02; SLJ 2/02) [222.1]

4456 Sasso, Sandy Eisenberg. *Naamah, Noah's Wife* (PS–K). Illus. by Bethanne Andersen. 2002, Jewish Lights $7.95 (1-893361-56-X). 24pp. This board-

book version of *Noah's Wife: The Story of Naamah* (2002) shows Naamah gathering seeds and planting them aboard the ark, and then restocking the earth's plant life after the flood. (Rev: BL 1/1–15/03) [222]

4457 Stickney, Anne Elizabeth. *The Loving Arms of God* (3–6). Illus. 2001, Eerdmans $22.00 (0-8028-5171-1). 164pp. An appealing collection of Bible stories that progresses from the Old to the New Testament. (Rev: BL 6/1–15/01; HBG 3/02; SLJ 8/01) [220.9]

4458 *Stories from the Bible* (5–7). Illus. by Lisbeth Zwerger. 2002, North-South $19.95 (0-7358-1413-9). 160pp. Sophisticated paintings illustrate verbatim excerpts from the King James version of both the Old and New Testaments. (Rev: BCCB 9/02; BL 4/1/02; HB 7–8/02; HBG 10/02; SLJ 5/02) [220.5]

4459 Watts, Murray. *The Bible for Children* (K–4). Illus. by Helen Cann. 2002, Good Books $23.99 (1-56148-362-1). 352pp. Watts vividly retells more than 200 stories from both Old and New Testaments in this handsome volume that includes a map, a glossary, and indexes of people and places. (Rev: BL 10/1/02; HBG 3/03; SLJ 1/03) [220.9]

4460 Wildsmith, Brian. *Mary* (PS–3). Illus. 2002, Eerdmans $20.00 (0-8028-5231-9). 30pp. Using legends and excerpts from the Bible, the noted illustrator re-creates the life of Mary and the role she played in the life of Jesus. (Rev: BL 4/1/02; SLJ 6/02) [232.91]

4461 Wilson, Anne. *Noah's Ark* (PS–3). Illus. 2002, Chronicle $15.95 (0-8118-3563-4). 32pp. Paper-collage illustrations give a fresh look to a retelling that is faithful to the original story. (Rev: BCCB 1/03; BL 10/1/02; HBG 3/03; SLJ 10/02) [222]

Holidays and Holy Days

General and Miscellaneous

4462 Barner, Bob. *Parade Day: Marching Through the Calendar Year* (PS–1). Illus. 2003, Holiday $16.95 (0-8234-1690-9). 32pp. A parade for each month — some for holidays, others (such as a pet parade) just for fun. (Rev: BL 2/15/03)

4463 Bennett, Kelly. *Flag Day* (PS–2). Series: Rookie Read-About Holidays. 2003, Children's LB $19.00 (0-516-22862-5); paper $5.95 (0-516-27755-3). 32pp. An easy-to-read book that introduces the holiday celebrated on June 14, with details on its origin and observances. (Rev: BL 3/15/03) [394]

4464 Gardeski, Christina Mia. *Diwali* (PS–2). Illus. Series: Rookie Read-About Holidays. 2001, Children's LB $19.00 (0-516-22372-0); paper $5.95 (0-516-26311-0). 32pp. A basic introduction to the Hindu festival of Diwali and the way it is celebrated. (Rev: BL 12/1/01) [294.5]

4465 Gnojewski, Carol. *Cinco de Mayo: Celebrating Hispanic Pride* (3–5). Illus. Series: Finding Out About Holidays. 2002, Enslow LB $18.95 (0-7660-1575-0). 48pp. Simple text and colorful photographs cover many aspects of Cinco de Mayo, from its history to the way it is celebrated today. (Rev: BL 12/15/02; HBG 3/03; SLJ 11/02) [394.26972]

4466 Gnojewski, Carol. *Martin Luther King, Jr., Day: Honoring a Man of Peace* (2–4). Series: Finding Out About Holidays. 2002, Enslow LB $18.95 (0-7660-1574-2). 48pp. Information on the holiday and how it is celebrated follows a brief introduction to King's life. (Rev: HBG 3/03; SLJ 12/02)

4467 Hoyt-Goldsmith, Diane. *Celebrating a Quinceañera: A Latina's 15th Birthday Celebration* (3–6). Photos by Lawrence Migdale. 2002, Holiday $16.95 (0-8234-1693-3). 30pp. A detailed description of a young woman's preparations for and celebration of her quinceanera, the ritual coming of age at 15. (Rev: HBG 3/03; SLJ 9/02) [395.24]

4468 Hoyt-Goldsmith, Diane. *Celebrating Ramadan* (2–5). Illus. by Lawrence Migdale. 2001, Holiday $16.95 (0-8234-1581-3). 32pp. This informative picture-book introduction to Islam and the month of Ramadan features a fourth-grade New Jersey boy named Ibraheem. (Rev: BCCB 12/01; BL 10/1/01; HB 1–2/02; HBG 3/02; SLJ 8/01) [297]

4469 Jackson, Ellen. *The Spring Equinox: Celebrating the Greening of the Earth* (3–5). Illus. by Jan Davey Ellis. 2002, Millbrook LB $22.90 (0-7613-1955-7). 32pp. Many of the holidays associated with spring — including Passover, Easter, Earth Day, and Holi — are highlighted in a series of illustrated double-page spreads. (Rev: BL 4/15/02; HBG 10/02; SLJ 6/02) [394.262]

4470 Landau, Elaine. *Columbus Day[EM]Celebrating a Famous Explorer* (3–6). Series: Finding Out About Holidays. 2001, Enslow LB $18.95 (0-7660-1573-4). 48pp. After introducing Christopher Columbus, this account describes the history of the holiday that honors him and tells how it is celebrated. (Rev: BL 9/15/01; HBG 3/02; SLJ 9/01) [394.2]

4471 Landau, Elaine. *Earth Day: Keeping Our Planet Clean* (3–6). Series: Finding Out About Holidays. 2002, Enslow LB $18.95 (0-7660-1778-8). 48pp. A look at the founding of Earth Day in 1970 by Senator Gaylord Nelson and how Earth Day is observed today. (Rev: BL 7/02; HBG 10/02; SLJ 7/02) [333.7]

4472 Landau, Elaine. *Independence Day: Birthday of the United States* (3–6). Series: Finding Out About Holidays. 2001, Enslow LB $18.95 (0-7660-1571-8). 48pp. Short chapters and plenty of color photographs introduce the history of the July 4th holiday and how it is celebrated today. (Rev: BL 9/15/01; HBG 3/02; SLJ 9/01) [394]

4473 Landau, Elaine. *Mardi Gras: Parades, Costumes, and Parties* (3–6). Series: Finding Out About Holidays. 2002, Enslow LB $18.95 (0-7660-1776-1). 48pp. The origins of Mardi Gras are explained, with material on how the holiday is observed in locations including New Orleans. (Rev: BL 7/02; HBG 10/02; SLJ 8/02) [394.2]

4474 Landau, Elaine. *St. Patrick's Day: Parades, Shamrocks, and Leprechauns* (3–6). Series: Finding Out About Holidays. 2002, Enslow LB $18.95 (0-7660-1777-X). 48pp. Saint Patrick is introduced along with material on the symbols connected with this holiday and ways it is observed. (Rev: BL 7/02; HBG 3/03; SLJ 10/02) [394.2]

4475 Landau, Elaine. *Veteran's Day: Remembering Our War Heroes* (3–6). Series: Finding Out About Holidays. 2002, Enslow LB $18.95 (0-7660-1775-3). 48pp. Landau traces the origins of this holiday and details how it is observed across the United States. (Rev: BL 7/02; HBG 10/02) [394.264]

4476 Lankford, Mary D. *Birthdays Around the World* (2–4). Illus. by Karen M. Dugan. 2002, HarperCollins LB $17.89 (0-688-15432-8). 32pp. Presents the customs surrounding birthday celebrations in seven countries, with ideas for an around-the-world birthday party. (Rev: BL 2/1/03; HBG 3/03; SLJ 1/03) [394.2]

4477 Marx, David F. *Chinese New Year* (PS–1). Series: Rookie Read-about Holidays. 2002, Children's LB $19.00 (0-516-22267-8); paper $5.95 (0-516-27375-2). 32pp. An introduction for very young readers to the rituals of the Chinese New Year. Also use *Ramadan*. (Rev: SLJ 9/02) [394.2]

4478 Robinson, Fay. *Chinese New Year: A Time for Parades, Family, and Friends* (3–6). Illus. Series: Finding Out About Holidays. 2001, Enslow LB $18.95 (0-7660-1631-5). 48pp. This detailed account gives the history behind this traditional holiday and explains how Chinese Americans celebrate it. (Rev: BL 9/15/01; HBG 3/02; SLJ 1/02) [394.261]

4479 Roop, Connie, and Peter Roop. *Let's Celebrate Earth Day* (1–3). Illus. by Gwen Connelly. 2001, Millbrook LB $21.90 (0-7613-1812-7). 32pp. Information on the history and purpose of Earth Day is presented in a question-and-answer format. (Rev: BL 5/1/01; HBG 10/01) [363.7]

4480 Saint James, Synthia. *It's Kwanzaa Time! A Lift-the-Flap Story* (PS–2). Illus. by author. 2001, Simon & Schuster paper $5.99 (0-689-84163-9). A simple introduction to the traditions of Kwanzaa that uses flaps to reveal the important principles. (Rev: SLJ 10/01)

4481 San Vicente, Luis. *The Festival of Bones / El Festival de las Calaveras: The Little-Bitty Book for the Day of the Dead* (PS–3). Illus. by author. 2002, Cinco Puntos $14.95 (0-938317-67-9). Dancing skeletons accompany the text describing the Mexican festival known as the Day of the Dead, or el Día de los Muertos. (Rev: HBG 3/03; SLJ 3/03) [394.266]

4482 Schuh, Mari C. *New Year's Day* (K–2). Series: Holidays and Celebrations. 2002, Capstone LB $14.60 (0-7368-1446-9). 24pp. Double-page spreads with bright full-page photographs on the left and a brief text on the right introduce the history, traditions, and celebrations that surround New Year's Day. (Rev: BL 1/1–15/03; HBG 3/03) [394.2]

4483 Schuh, Mari C. *St. Patrick's Day* (K–2). Illus. Series: Holidays and Celebrations. 2002, Capstone $14.60 (0-7368-1447-7). 24pp. This small, square book about Saint Patrick's Day includes discussion of the holiday's symbols and traditions and includes reference sources and a glossary. (Rev: BL 1/1–15/03; HBG 3/03) [296.4]

4484 Simonds, Nina, et al. *Moonbeams, Dumplings and Dragon Boats: A Treasury of Chinese Holiday Tales, Activities and Recipes* (4–6). Illus. by Meilo So. 2002, Harcourt $20.00 (0-15-201983-9). 80pp. This vibrantly illustrated book for older readers examines five Chinese holidays and includes stories, recipes, and crafts related to each. (Rev: BL 10/15/02; HBG 3/03; SLJ 11/02*) [394.26]

4485 Taylor, Charles A. *Juneteenth: A Celebration of Freedom* (5–8). Illus. by author. 2002, Open Hand $19.95 (0-940880-68-7). 32pp. A well-organized account of this holiday, which celebrates emancipation, with a discussion of the history of slavery. (Rev: SLJ 11/02) [394.2]

4486 Verma, Jatinder. *The Story of Divaali* (1–3). Illus. by Nilesh Mistry. 2002, Barefoot $16.99 (1-84148-936-0). 40pp. Verma effectively retells the complex story, based on the Sanskrit *Ramayana*, of the lighting of lamps that started the celebration of the Hindu festival of Diwali. (Rev: BL 1/1–15/03; HBG 3/03; SLJ 11/02) [294.5]

4487 Walsh, Kieran. *Chinese New Year* (2–3). Series: Holiday Celebrations. 2003, Rourke LB $19.27 (1-58952-215-X). 24pp. Provides basic information about how the holiday began and how it is celebrated. Also use *Cinco de Mayo* (2003). (Rev: SLJ 1/03) [394.261]

Christmas

4488 *The Christmas Story: From the Gospel According to St. Luke from the King James Bible* (PS–2). Illus. by James Bernardin. 2002, Harper-Collins $15.99 (0-06-028882-5). 32pp. Realistic paintings help to tell the story of Christmas and give young readers a sense of context and historical background. (Rev: BL 9/1/02; HBG 3/03; SLJ 10/02) [226.4]

4489 Davis, Katherine, et al. *The Little Drummer Boy* (K–3). Illus. by Kristina Rodanas. 2001, Clarion $15.00 (0-395-97015-6). 32pp. An attractive rendering of the traditional Christmas song about the little boy and the value of gifts. (Rev: BL 9/1/01; HBG 3/02; SLJ 10/01) [782.42]

4490 Erlbach, Arlene. *Christmas[EM]Celebrating Life, Giving, and Kindness* (3–6). Series: Finding Out About Holidays. 2001, Enslow LB $18.95 (0-7660-1576-9). 48pp. In a series of short chapters that include many attractive color photographs, this book explores the history of Christmas and tells how it is observed in the United States. (Rev: BL 9/15/01; HBG 3/02; SLJ 10/01) [394.2]

4491 Erlbach, Arlene, and Herb Erlbach. *Merry Christmas, Everywhere!* (K–2). Illus. by Sharon L. Holm. 2002, Millbrook LB $23.90 (0-7613-1699-X); paper $8.95 (0-7613-1699-X). 48pp. Fine illustrations and maps introduce Christmas traditions in countries around the world, accompanied by illustrations, recipes, and crafts. (Rev: BL 9/15/02; HBG 3/03; SLJ 10/02) [394.2663]

4492 Flanagan, Alice K. *Christmas* (2–3). Series: Holidays and Festivals. 2001, Compass Point LB $22.60 (0-7565-0085-0). 32pp. An easy-to-read picture book that describes the origins of Christmas and the many ways in which it is celebrated. (Rev: BL 10/15/01; SLJ 10/01) [394]

4493 French, Fiona. *Bethlehem* (PS–3). Illus. 2001, HarperCollins $15.95 (0-06-029623-2). 32pp. Stained-glass style illustrations illuminate the story of the first Christmas as told in the King James version of the gospels of St. Luke and St. Matthew. (Rev: BL 10/15/01; HBG 3/02; SLJ 10/01) [226]

4494 Mayer, Marianna. *The Real Santa Claus* (3–6). Illus. 2001, Penguin Putnam $17.99 (0-8037-2624-4). 32pp. The poem "A Visit from Saint Nicholas" is followed by the story of the real Saint Nicholas, illustrated with reproductions of Renaissance art. (Rev: BCCB 11/01; BL 10/1/01; HBG 3/02; SLJ 10/01) [394.26]

4495 Ross, Michael Elsohn. *A Mexican Christmas* (K–3). Photos by Felix Rigau. 2002, Carolrhoda LB $23.93 (0-87614-601-9). 40pp. Christmas customs in Oaxaca are described in text and photographs. (Rev: HBG 3/03; SLJ 10/02) [394.2663]

4496 Schuh, Mari C. *Christmas* (PS–2). Series: Holidays and Celebrations. 2002, Capstone LB $14.60 (0-7368-0979-1). 24pp. An overview of holiday traditions in the United States for beginning readers. (Rev: HBG 3/02; SLJ 10/02)

Easter

4497 French, Fiona. *Easter: With Words from the King James Bible* (K–3). Illus. 2002, HarperCollins $15.95 (0-06-623929-X). 32pp. This King James Bible version of the Easter story features rich stained-glass images. (Rev: BCCB 2/02; BL 2/15/02; HBG 10/02; SLJ 1/02) [226]

4498 Schuh, Mari C. *Easter* (K–2). Series: Holidays and Celebrations. 2002, Capstone LB $14.60 (0-7368-1445-0). 24pp. This small, square book uses full-page photographs and a brief text to present the meaning of Easter, its symbols, celebrations, and importance. (Rev: BCCB 2/02; BL 1/1–15/03; HBG 3/03) [394.2]

Halloween

4499 Flanagan, Alice K. *Halloween* (2–3). Series: Holidays and Festivals. 2001, Compass Point LB $22.60 (0-7565-0086-9). 32pp. An attractive picture book that describes the origins of Halloween and how it is celebrated by youngsters today. (Rev: BCCB 10/02; BL 10/15/01; SLJ 1/02) [745.5]

4500 Gibbons, Gail. *Halloween Is . . .* (PS–2). Illus. 2002, Holiday $16.95 (0-8234-1758-1). 32pp. A larger, revised version with new, enhanced illustrations of the 1984 *Halloween*, describing the holiday's history and traditions. (Rev: BL 9/15/02; HBG 3/03) [394.2646]

4501 Parker, Toni Trent. *Sweets and Treats* (PS). Photos by Earl Anderson. 2002, Scholastic $6.95 (0-439-33871-9). Babies, toddlers, and preschoolers are portrayed in full costume, ready to hit Halloween streets. (Rev: HBG 3/03; SLJ 9/02)

4502 Robinson, Fay. *Halloween — Costumes and Treats on All Hallows' Eve* (3–6). Series: Finding Out About Holidays. 2001, Enslow LB $18.95 (0-7660-1632-3). 48pp. The origins of Halloween are described, with material on how this holiday has evolved and how it is currently celebrated in the United States. (Rev: BL 9/15/01; HBG 3/02; SLJ 9/01) [745.5]

Jewish Holy Days and Celebrations

4503 Cooper, Ilene. *Jewish Holidays All Year Round: A Family Treasury* (3–5). Illus. by Elivia Savadier. 2002, Abrams $18.95 (0-8109-0550-7). 80pp. Details of the rituals that take place at home and in the synagogue are given in this overview of the holidays of the Jewish year, with an activity and recipe for each celebration. (Rev: HBG 3/03; SLJ 3/03) [296.4]

4504 Fishman, Cathy Goldberg. *On Shabbat* (K–3). Illus. by Melanie Hall. 2001, Simon & Schuster $16.00 (0-689-83894-8). 40pp. Using a Jewish family as a focus, this account explains the preparations, rituals, and meanings involved with the Friday evening Sabbath services. (Rev: BL 4/1/01; HBG 10/01; SLJ 8/01) [296.4]

4505 Kropf, Latifa Berry. *It's Challah Time!* (PS–1). Illus. by Tod Cohen. 2002, Kar-Ben LB $10.95 (1-58013-036-4). 24pp. Color photographs show happy young children making challah for the Sabbath, singing blessings, and tasting the final product. (Rev: BL 10/1/02; HBG 3/03; SLJ 12/02) [641.5]

4506 Schuh, Mari C. *Passover* (K–2). Illus. Series: Holidays and Celebrations. 2002, Capstone $14.60 (0-7368-1448-5). 24pp. Colorful photographs and simple text explain the meaning, history, and traditions of the Passover celebration in this small, square book. (Rev: BL 1/1–15/03; HBG 3/03) [394.262]

Thanksgiving

4507 Anderson, Laurie Halse. *Thank You, Sarah: The Woman Who Saved Thanksgiving* (K–3). Illus. by Matt Faulkner. 2002, Simon & Schuster $16.95 (0-689-84787-4). 40pp. Humorous illustrations accompany this true tale of a woman who campaigned for almost four decades to make Thanksgiving a national holiday. (Rev: BL 12/15/02; HBG 3/03; SLJ 12/02) [394.2649]

4508 Bartlett, Robert Merrill. *The Story of Thanksgiving* (PS–3). Illus. by Sally Wern Comport. 2001, HarperCollins LB $14.89 (0-06-028779-9). 40pp. A reissue of the author's 1965 *Thanksgiving Day*, with new illustrations and other updates. (Rev: BL 9/15/01; HBG 3/02; SLJ 9/01) [394.2649]

4509 Flanagan, Alice K. *Thanksgiving* (2–4). Illus. by Kathi Kelleher. Series: Holidays and Festivals. 2001, Compass Point LB $22.60 (0-7565-0087-7). 32pp. The history behind Thanksgiving, with infor-

mation about how we celebrate the holiday today. (Rev: BL 10/15/01; SLJ 1/02) [394.2]

4510 Grace, Catherine O'Neill, and Margaret M. Bruchac. *1621: A New Look at Thanksgiving* (K–4). Illus. by Sisse Brimberg and Cotton Coulson. 2001, National Geographic $17.95 (0-7922-7027-4). 48pp. This appealing and informative photo-essay presents the historically correct story of the first Thanksgiving, as reenacted at the Plimoth Plantation. (Rev: BL 9/1/01; HBG 10/02; SLJ 9/01*) [394.2649]

4511 Landau, Elaine. *Thanksgiving Day: A Time to Be Thankful* (3–6). Illus. Series: Finding Out About Holidays. 2001, Enslow LB $18.95 (0-7660-1572-6). 48pp. A general introduction to this traditional American holiday, its history, and how it is celebrated. (Rev: BL 9/15/01; HBG 3/02; SLJ 1/02) [394.2649]

4512 Waters, Kate. *Giving Thanks: The 1621 Harvest Feast* (2–4). Illus. by Russ Kendall. 2001, Scholastic $16.95 (0-439-24395-5). 40pp. The first Thanksgiving from the perspectives of a Wampanoag boy and an English boy, reenacted and photographed at Plimoth Plantation. (Rev: BL 9/15/01; HBG 3/02; SLJ 9/01) [394.2649]

Valentine's Day

4513 Flanagan, Alice K. *Valentine's Day* (2–4). Illus. by Shelley Dieterichs. Series: Holidays and Festivals. 2001, Compass Point LB $22.60 (0-7565-0088-5). 32pp. Flanagan tells readers about the origins of Valentine's Day (as a Roman festival) and details how we celebrate the holiday today. (Rev: BL 10/15/01; SLJ 1/02) [394.2618]

4514 Landau, Elaine. *Valentine's Day: Candy, Love, and Hearts* (3–6). Series: Finding Out About Holidays. 2002, Enslow LB $18.95 (0-7660-1779-6). 48pp. Material on Saint Valentine is included with information on the symbols connected with the holiday and the ways in which it is celebrated. (Rev: BL 7/02; HBG 10/02; SLJ 10/02) [394.2]

Prayers

4515 *Amazing Graces: Prayers and Poems for Children* (PS–1). Ed. by June Cotner. Illus. by Jan Palmer. 2001, HarperCollins LB $12.89 (0-68-815567-7). 64pp. A collection of 43 prayers and poems, some traditional, some funny, and some written by children, with watercolor illustrations. (Rev: BL 10/1/01; HBG 3/02; SLJ 12/01) [242]

4516 Carlstrom, Nancy White. *Glory* (PS–2). Illus. by Debra R. Jenkins. 2001, Eerdmans $17.00 (0-8028-5143-6). 32pp. Animals — and one little girl — joyfully reflect the glory of God in this prayer with bright, bold illustrations. (Rev: BL 10/1/01; HBG 3/02; SLJ 12/01) [811]

4517 Emerson, Ralph Waldo. *Father, We Thank You* (PS–3). Illus. by Mark Graham. 2001, North-South LB $15.88 (1-58717-073-6). 32pp. Based on Emerson's classic poem, this beautiful book is a paean to God for flowers, grass, birds' songs, and other phenomena found in nature. (Rev: BL 4/1/01; HBG 10/01; SLJ 6/01) [811]

4518 Hennessy, B. G. *My Book of Thanks* (PS). Illus. 2002, Candlewick $12.00 (0-7636-1523-4). 32pp. Vivid watercolor illustrations accompany these short, sweet prayers for very young children. (Rev: BL 12/15/02; HBG 3/03) [242]

4519 Lee, Karlynn Keyes, comp. *Children's Prayers for America: Young People of Many Faiths Share Their Hopes for Our Nation* (K–8). Illus. 2001, Ris-

ing Moon paper $9.95 (0-87358-812-6). A collection of brightly illustrated short prayers by children collected after the attacks of September 11, 2001, most in the children's own handwriting. (Rev: SLJ 8/02)

4520 Maccarone, Grace. *A Child's Good Night Prayer* (PS). Illus. by Sam Williams. 2001, Scholastic $10.95 (0-439-23505-7). 32pp. Children of different ethnic backgrounds ask for nighttime blessings for their favorite things in this appealing picture book with rhyming text. (Rev: BL 10/1/01; HBG 10/02; SLJ 10/01) [291.4]

Social Groups

Ethnic Groups

4521 Alter, Judy. *Mexican Americans* (3–5). Series: Spirit of America: Our Cultural Heritage. 2002, Child's World LB $27.07 (1-56766-156-4). 32pp. A useful overview of the history of Mexican Americans, their immigration to the United States, and their contributions to the nation's culture. (Rev: BL 10/15/02; SLJ 12/02) [973]

4522 Bolden, Tonya. *Tell All the Children Our Story: Memories and Mementos of Being Young and Black in America* (4–8). Illus. 2002, Abrams $24.95 (0-8109-4496-0). 128pp. From the first recorded birth of a black child in the United States to the Million Man March, this book describes the African American experience through both personal and historical accounts, using a scrapbook format. (Rev: BL 2/15/02; HB 3–4/02; HBG 10/02; SLJ 3/02**) [973]

4523 De Capua, Sarah E. *Irish Americans* (3–5). Series: Spirit of America: Our Cultural Heritage. 2002, Child's World LB $27.07 (1-56766-155-6). 32pp. De Capua discusses the reasons for Irish migration to the United States and the lasting contributions this group has made. (Rev: BL 10/15/02) [973]

4524 Fitterer, C. Ann. *Arab Americans* (3–5). Illus. Series: Spirit of America: Our Cultural Heritage. 2002, Child's World LB $27.07 (1-56766-150-5). 32pp. An overview of the Arab American experience, including the history of Arab immigration, post 9/11 discrimination, and the contributions of Arab Americans to society as a whole. (Rev: BL 10/15/02; SLJ 2/03) [973]

4525 Fitterer, C. Ann. *German Americans* (3–5). Series: Spirit of America: Our Cultural Heritage. 2002, Child's World LB $27.07 (1-56766-151-3). 32pp. Fitterer discusses German migration to the United States and the contributions of this community. (Rev: BL 10/15/02; SLJ 2/03) [973]

4526 Fitterer, C. Ann. *Russian Americans* (3–5). Series: Spirit of America: Our Cultural Heritage. 2002, Child's World LB $27.07 (1-56766-158-0). 32pp. Russian migration to the United States is discussed in this richly illustrated account that includes material on famous immigrants. (Rev: BL 10/15/02; SLJ 12/02) [973]

4527 Fitterer, C. Ann. *Vietnamese Americans* (3–5). Series: Spirit of America: Our Cultural Heritage. 2002, Child's World LB $27.07 (1-56766-160-2). 32pp. A history of recent migration to the United States by the Vietnamese is accompanied by material on this group's reception, contributions, and assimilation. (Rev: BL 10/15/02; SLJ 12/02) [973]

4528 Franchino, Vicky. *Italian Americans* (3–5). Series: Spirit of America: Our Cultural Heritage. 2002, Child's World LB $27.07 (1-56766-153-X). 32pp. How Italian immigrants changed American life is one of the topics discussed in this simple account of why and how they came to this country, their reception, and a rundown of famous Italian Americans. (Rev: BL 10/15/02) [973]

4529 Frost, Helen. *German Immigrants, 1820–1920* (4–6). Illus. Series: Coming to America. 2001, Capstone LB $16.95 (0-7368-0794-2). 32pp. A look at German immigrants to the United States, including why they migrated, where they settled, and their customs, with historical photographs and features such as maps, crafts, and recipes. Also use *Norwegian, Swedish, and Danish Immigrants, 1820–1920* (2001). (Rev: BL 10/15/01; HBG 3/02) [973.04]

4530 Frost, Helen. *Russian Immigrants: 1860–1915* (4–6). Series: Coming to America. 2002, Capstone LB $22.60 (0-7368-1209-1). 32pp. After a look at why Russians left their country to migrate to the United States, this account covers their destinations, culture, and contributions. (Rev: BL 1/1–15/03; HBG 3/03; SLJ 3/03) [973]

4531 Haberle, Susan E. *Jewish Immigrants: 1880–1924* (4–6). Series: Coming to America. 2002, Capstone LB $22.60 (0-7368-1207-5). 32pp. A brief overview of why Jews left Europe, plus an account of where they settled in America, their cultural contributions, and a list of famous Jewish Americans. (Rev: BL 1/1–15/03; HBG 3/03) [973]

4532 Lingen, Marissa. *The Jewish Americans* (4–7). Illus. Series: We Came to America. 2002, Mason Crest LB $19.95 (1-59084-109-3). 64pp. Lingen traces the history of Jewish migration to the United States and provides a list of Jewish Americans of note. Also use *The Arab Americans* (2002). (Rev: SLJ 9/02) [973.049]

4533 Lock, Donna. *The Polish Americans* (5–8). Illus. Series: We Came to America. 2002, Mason Crest LB $19.95 (1-59084-112-3). 64pp. A look at the customs and contributions of this ethnic group, including information on famous Polish Americans, with a bibliography, glossary, timeline, and resources for tracing ancestors. (Rev: BL 7/02) [305.891]

4534 McDaniel, Melissa. *Japanese Americans* (3–5). Series: Spirit of America: Our Cultural Heritage. 2002, Child's World LB $27.07 (1-56766-154-8). 32pp. The history of Japanese migration to the United States is discussed, with material on the discrimination the new citizens faced and the many ways in which they have changed American culture. (Rev: BL 10/15/02; SLJ 12/02) [973]

4535 Morris, Ann. *Grandma Esther Remembers: A Jewish-American Family Story* (1–3). Series: What Was It Like, Grandma? 2002, Millbrook LB $22.90 (0-7613-2318-X). 32pp. In double-page spreads (with a picture opposite a page of simple text), a Jewish American grandmother describes her life in the old country and her early experiences in the United States. (Rev: BL 9/15/02; HBG 10/02; SLJ 6/02) [973]

4536 Morris, Ann. *Grandma Francisca Remembers: A Mexican-American Family Story* (1–3). Illus. by Peter Linenthal. Series: What Was It Like, Grandma? 2002, Millbrook LB $22.90 (0-7613-2315-5). 32pp. Some Spanish vocabulary, a recipe for stew, and instructions for making a sock doll accompany this account of the activities of a young Mexican American girl and her grandmother. (Rev: BL 2/15/02; HBG 10/02; SLJ 4/02) [973]

4537 Morris, Ann. *Grandma Lai Goon Remembers: A Chinese-American Family Story* (1–3). Series: What Was It Like, Grandma? 2002, Millbrook LB $22.90 (0-7613-2314-7). 32pp. Activities such as making a Chinese doll, making Chinese buns, and playing a Chinese game complement the story of a Chinese American grandmother's life. (Rev: BL 9/15/02; HBG 10/02; SLJ 6/02) [973]

4538 Morris, Ann. *Grandma Lois Remembers: An African-American Family Story* (1–3). Series: What Was It Like, Grandma? 2002, Millbrook LB $22.90 (0-7613-2316-3). 32pp. An African American grandmother tells the family history to her grandson, with appended activities and games. (Rev: BL 9/15/02; HBG 10/02; SLJ 3/02) [976.1]

4539 Morris, Ann. *Grandma Maxine Remembers: A Native-American Family Story* (1–3). Series: What Was It Like, Grandma? 2002, Millbrook LB $22.90

(0-7613-2317-1). 32pp. Native American culture is explored through the memories of a grandmother who tells about her experiences as young girl. An appropriate activity, recipe, and game are appended. (Rev: BL 9/15/02; HBG 10/02; SLJ 10/02) [973]

4540 Morris, Ann. *Grandma Susan Remembers: A British-American Family Story* (1–3). Series: What Was It Like, Grandma? 2002, Millbrook LB $22.90 (0-7613-2319-8). 32pp. A grandmother who was born in Britain recalls her childhood and the culture of the land she left. Activities are appended. (Rev: BL 9/15/02; HBG 10/02; SLJ 6/02) [973]

4541 O'Hara, Megan. *Irish Immigrants: 1840–1920* (4–6). Series: Coming to America. 2001, Capstone LB $16.95 (0-7368-0795-0). 32pp. This account, complete with many reader activities, takes a quick look at Irish history, explains why the migrants left their country, and describes their reception in the United States and their contributions to American life. (Rev: BL 10/15/01; HBG 3/02; SLJ 1/02) [973]

4542 Olson, Kay Melchisedech. *Chinese Immigrants: 1850–1900* (4–6). Series: Coming to America. 2001, Capstone LB $16.95 (0-7368-0793-4). 32pp. Using many sidebars, recipes, and suggested activities, this book tells how and why the Chinese originally came to the United States and the contributions they have made to American culture. (Rev: BL 10/15/01; HBG 3/02) [973]

4543 Olson, Kay Melchisedech. *French Immigrants: 1840–1940* (4–6). Series: Coming to America. 2002, Capstone LB $22.60 (0-7368-1205-9). 32pp. Covers the reasons why French citizens left their country for America and gives details of their struggle to retain their traditions, of their contributions, and the lives of famous immigrants and their descendants. (Rev: BL 1/1–15/03; HBG 3/03) [973]

4544 Perl, Lila. *North Across the Border: The Story of the Mexican Americans* (5–9). Series: Great Journeys. 2001, Benchmark LB $21.95 (0-7614-1226-3). 112pp. The economic and social reasons for Mexican migration to the north through history are presented in text, quotations from primary sources, and many illustrations and maps. (Rev: BL 1/1–15/02; HBG 10/02; SLJ 3/02) [973.0468]

4545 Raatma, Lucia. *Chinese Americans* (3–5). Illus. Series: Spirit of America: Our Cultural Heritage. 2002, Child's World LB $27.07 (1-56766-149-1). 32pp. An overview of the Chinese American experience that includes maps, timelines, and other visuals. (Rev: BL 10/15/02) [973]

4546 Raatma, Lucia. *Polish Americans* (3–5). Series: Spirit of America: Our Cultural Heritage. 2002, Child's World LB $27.07 (1-56766-157-2). 32pp. Provides a history of Polish migration to this country, with emphasis on the many contributions this group has made to American life and culture. (Rev: BL 10/15/02) [973]

4547 Raatma, Lucia. *Swedish Americans* (3–5). Series: Spirit of America: Our Cultural Heritage. 2002, Child's World LB $27.07 (1-56766-159-9). 32pp. Swedish migration to the United States is the topic of this work, with material on the group's native culture, ethnic background, and the impact they have had on present-day American society. (Rev: BL 10/15/02) [973]

4548 Stepanchuk, Carol. *Exploring Chinatown* (4–8). Illus. by Leland Wong. 2002, Pacific View $22.95 (1-881896-25-0). 64pp. This "walk" through San Francisco's Chinatown explores the Chinese culture and customs, and offers historical facts as well as a few hands-on projects. (Rev: BL 8/02; SLJ 9/02) [305.8951073]

4549 Temple, Bob. *The Arab Americans* (5–8). Illus. Series: We Came to America. 2002, Mason Crest LB $19.95 (1-59084-102-6). 64pp. Temple reviews the history of Arab immigration to North America, the group's customs and contributions, and famous Arab Americans, with the aid of photographs, a timeline, and glossary. (Rev: BL 7/02; SLJ 9/02) [305.892]

4550 Todd, Anne M. *Italian Immigrants: 1880–1920* (4–6). Series: Coming to America. 2001, Capstone LB $16.95 (0-7368-0796-9). 32pp. The rich heritage and cultural contributions of Italian Americans are covered in this book that also explores why and how they came to the United States. (Rev: BL 10/15/01; HBG 3/02) [973]

4551 Wallner, Rosemary. *Greek Immigrants: 1890–1920* (4–6). Series: Coming to America. 2002, Capstone LB $22.60 (0-7368-1206-7). 32pp. Using many primary sources, this book traces the causes of Greek immigration and provides information on the Greek immigrants' journeys, culture, integration, and contributions. (Rev: BL 1/1–15/03; HBG 3/03; SLJ 3/03) [973]

4552 Wallner, Rosemary. *Japanese Immigrants: 1850–1950* (4–6). Series: Coming to America. 2001, Capstone LB $16.95 (0-7368-0797-9). 32pp. A century of Japanese migration to the United States is detailed with material on their contributions, cultural heritage, and treatment on arrival. (Rev: BL 10/15/01) [973]

4553 Wallner, Rosemary. *Polish Immigrants: 1890–1920* (4–6). Series: Coming to America. 2002, Capstone LB $22.60 (0-7368-1208-3). 32pp. The exodus from Poland to America is traced through text, timelines, maps, and personal memoirs, with material on such topics as Polish culture, contributions to American life, and famous Polish Americans. (Rev: BL 1/1–15/03; HBG 3/03) [973]

Personal Development

Behavior

General

4554 Barron, T. A. *The Hero's Trail: A Guide for Heroic Life* (4–7). Illus. 2002, Putnam $14.99 (0-399-23860-3). 160pp. This collection of anecdotes about both real and fictional characters aims to define heroism, and explores how one can lead a heroic life. (Rev: BL 10/15/02; HBG 3/03; SLJ 12/02) [170]

4555 Damm, Antje. *Ask Me* (PS–3). Trans. from German by Doris Orgel. Illus. by author. 2003, Millbrook $14.95 (0-7613-1845-3). 220pp. This is a compilation of questions, ranging from the fairly basic to the thought-provoking and accompanied by imaginative illustrations, that can be used to prompt discussion. (Rev: BCCB 3/03; SLJ 3/03) [306.874]

4556 Dee, Catherine, ed. *The Girls' Book of Friendship: Cool Quotes, True Stories, Secrets and More* (5 Up). Illus. by Ali Douglass. 2001, Little, Brown paper $8.95 (0-316-16818-1). 194pp. A well-organized collection of humorous and affecting entries encompassing material from celebrities and everyday teens. (Rev: SLJ 11/01) [177]

4557 Farrell, Juliana, and Beth Mayall. *Middle School: The Real Deal* (5–7). Illus. 2001, Harper-Collins paper $7.95 (0-380-81313-0). 144pp. Advice on coping with school work, teachers, and social life is presented in an appealing format. (Rev: BL 6/1–15/01) [373.18]

4558 Holyoke, Nancy. *A Smart Girl's Guide to Boys: Surviving Crushes, Staying True to Yourself, and Other Love Stuff* (4–6). Illus. 2001, Pleasant $9.95 (1-58485-368-9). 112pp. Age-appropriate advice on dealing with boys, first kisses, and balancing friends and boyfriends is interwoven with magazine-style quizzes and letters from girls. (Rev: BL 8/01; SLJ 9/01) [305.23]

4559 Jackson, Ellen. *Sometimes Bad Things Happen* (PS–2). Photos by Shelley Rotner. 2002, Millbrook LB $22.90 (0-7613-2810-6); paper $7.95 (0-7613-1734-1). Children are reassured that while bad things do happen, there are ways to cope and people who will want to help. (Rev: HBG 3/03; SLJ 2/03)

4560 Klingel, Cynthia, and Robert B. Noyed. *Friendship* (K–3). Series: Wonder Books. 2002, Child's World LB $21.36 (1-56766-088-6). 32pp. A series of vignettes give everyday examples of how to make friends and how to be a friend. Also use *Honesty* and *Respect* (both 2002). (Rev: SLJ 12/02) [177]

4561 Madison, Lynda. *The Feelings Book: The Care and Keeping of Your Emotions* (4–6). Illus. by Norm Bendell. 2002, Pleasant paper $8.95 (1-58485-528-2). 104pp. Madison tackles the topic of the emotional upheavals that many youngsters experience as they near their teens and offers tips on identifying and coping with strong feelings. (Rev: BL 12/1/02; SLJ 10/02) [155.43]

4562 Montanari, Donata. *Children Around the World* (PS–K). Illus. by author. 2001, Kids Can $14.95 (1-55337-064-3). Readers are introduced to children in countries around the world who describe their lives in simple sentences that highlight their similarities and differences. (Rev: HBG 3/02; SLJ 12/01) [390.083]

4563 Murkoff, Heidi. *What to Expect at Preschool* (PS–K). Illus. by Laura Rader. Series: What to Expect. 2001, HarperCollins $7.99 (0-694-01326-9). 32pp. A dog named Angus addresses the concerns of anxious preschoolers in the question-and-answer format of the What to Expect series. (Rev: BL 11/15/01; HBG 3/02; SLJ 12/01) [372.21]

4564 Navarra, Tova. *The Kids' Guidebook: Great Advice to Help Kids Cope*. Rev. ed. (4–6). Illus. by Tom Kerr. 2002, Barron's paper $10.95 (0-7641-2066-2). 128pp. Advice on coping with difficult situations, from power outages and dealing with strangers to the death of a loved one. (Rev: SLJ 3/03)

4565 Raatma, Lucia. *Determination* (2–4). Series: Character Education. 2002, Capstone LB $18.60 (0-7368-1387-X). 24pp. The characteristic is described, with examples of how to show determination and a famous person who exhibits it. Also use *Loyalty* and *Leadership* (both 2002). (Rev: HBG 3/03; SLJ 2/03)

4566 Robinson, Sharon. *Jackie's Nine: Jackie Robinson's Values to Live By* (5–8). Illus. 2001, Scholastic $15.95 (0-439-23764-5). 183pp. A collection of inspirational writings, selected by baseball legend Jackie Robinson's daughter and organized under headings including "Courage" and "Determination," that include material by and about such well-known individuals as Christopher Reeve and Oprah Winfrey. (Rev: BL 7/01; HBG 10/01; SLJ 6/01) [158]

4567 Rotner, Shelley, and Sheila Kelly. *What Can You Do? A Book About Discovering What You Do Well* (PS–1). Photos by Shelley Rotner. Illus. 2001, Millbrook LB $21.90 (0-7613-2119-5). 24pp. With illustrations and text that show a variety of activities and talents, the authors ask readers to determine what they can do best. (Rev: BL 4/15/01; HBG 10/01; SLJ 9/01) [153.9]

4568 Schuette, Sarah L. *I Am Cooperative* (PS–2). Series: Character Values. 2002, Capstone LB $14.60 (0-7368-1439-6). 24pp. Photographs and simple text are used to explain how to be cooperative. Also use *I Am Honest*, *I Am Respectful*, and *I Am Responsible*. (Rev: HBG 3/03; SLJ 3/03)

4569 Sheindlin, Judy. *Judge Judy Sheindlin's You Can't Judge a Book by Its Cover: Cool Rules for School* (2–5). Illus. by Bob Tore. 2001, HarperCollins LB $14.89 (0-06-029484-1). Judge Judy looks at common choices young students have to make, presenting a range of possible decisions, some sensible and some clearly not. (Rev: HBG 10/01; SLJ 7/01) [170]

4570 Sherman, Joanne. *Because It's My Body!* (PS–2). Illus. by John S. Gurney. Series: Keep `em Safe. 2002, S.A.F.E. for Children paper $14.95 (0-9711735-0-8). 30pp. This text presents clear strategies for dealing with unwelcome attention, even from friends and family. (Rev: SLJ 12/02)

4571 Waber, Bernard. *Courage* (K–3). Illus. 2002, Houghton $12.00 (0-618-23855-7). 40pp. Waber introduces the concept of courage with amusing illustrations and examples that younger readers can understand. (Rev: BCCB 2/03; BL 12/15/02; HBG 3/03; SLJ 12/02) [179]

4572 Waters, Jennifer. *Be a Good Friend!* (K–1). Series: Spyglass Books. 2002, Compass Point LB $18.60 (0-7565-0376-0). 24pp. For beginning readers, this book lists the qualities that make a good friend. Also use *Be a Good Sport!* (2002). (Rev: SLJ 1/03)

4573 *Yikes! A Smart Girl's Guide to Surviving Tricky, Sticky, Icky Situations* (4–8). Illus. by Bonnie Timmons. Series: American Girl Library. 2002, Pleasant paper $8.95 (1-58485-530-4). 87pp. Advice on everything from dealing with teachers and friends to coping with embarrassing situations and dangerous incidents. (Rev: SLJ 12/02) [305.23]

Etiquette

4574 Doudna, Kelly. *Excuse Me* (PS–1). Series: Good Manners. 2001, ABDO LB $12.95 (1-57765-574-5). 24pp. Simple text suitable for beginning readers introduces the basic concept, accompanied by illustrations of children in appropriate situations. Also in this series are *Please* and *Thank You*. (Rev: HBG 3/02; SLJ 4/02) [395.1]

4575 Dougherty, Karla. *The Rules to Be Cool: Etiquette and Netiquette* (5 Up). Series: Teen Issues. 2001, Enslow LB $17.95 (0-7660-1607-2). 64pp. Respect and consideration for others are the key elements of Dougherty's rules of behavior, with an emphasis on politeness, kindness, and courtesy, on the Internet as well as at home and at school. (Rev: HBG 3/02; SLJ 10/01) [395]

4576 Levitin, Sonia. *When Kangaroo Goes to School* (PS–1). Illus. by Jeff Seaver. 2001, Rising Moon $15.95 (0-87358-791-X). A guide to correct behavior at school designed to ease the fears of first-time students. (Rev: HBG 3/02; SLJ 12/01)

4577 Raatma, Lucia. *Politeness* (K–2). Series: Character Education. 2002, Capstone LB $18.60 (0-7368-1134-6). 24pp. A how-to guide for the very young that provides a definition of politeness, shows how to display it, and offers some practice ideas. Also use *Self-Respect* and *Sportsmanship* (2002). (Rev: SLJ 6/02) [395.1]

Family Relationships

4578 Jussim, Daniel. *Double Take: The Story of Twins* (5 Up). 2001, Viking $17.99 (0-670-88452-9). 72pp. In addition to information on conception, identical twins, conjoined twins, and multiple births, the author presents stories of twins who have lived together and twins who were separated at birth. (Rev: HBG 10/01; SLJ 5/01) [306.875]

4579 Krohn, Katherine. *You and Your Parents' Divorce* (5–8). Series: Family Matters. 2001, Rosen LB $17.95 (0-8239-3354-7). 48pp. Krohn writes about the practicalities and emotional problems of divorce in a style suitable for reluctant readers. (Rev: SLJ 8/01) [155.44]

4580 MacGregor, Cynthia. *The Divorce Helpbook for Kids* (4–7). 2001, Impact Publishers paper $12.95 (1-886230-39-0). 112pp. In this candid, honest book, a divorced mother gives advice to children about how to survive their parent's divorce. (Rev: BL 2/1/02; SLJ 3/02) [306.89]

4581 Roca, Nuria. *La Familia: Del Pequeño al Mayor / Family: From the Youngest to the Oldest* (K–3). Illus. by Rosa Maria Curto. 2000, Barron's paper $6.95 (0-7641-1688-6). 36pp. The message of this book, originally published in Spain, is that families come in many different forms. (Rev: BL 10/1/01)

4582 Rotner, Shelley, and Sheila Kelly. *Lots of Grandparents* (PS–1). Illus. 2001, Millbrook $23.90 (0-7613-2313-9). 24pp. A collection of color photographs showing grandparents of various ethnicities engaged in many activities. (Rev: BL 9/1/01; HBG 3/02; SLJ 9/01) [306.874]

4583 Wolfman, Ira. *Climbing Your Family Tree: Online and Off-Line Genealogy for Kids*. Rev. ed. (5–9). Illus. by Tim Robinson. 2002, Workman paper $13.95 (0-7611-2539-6). 228pp. A wide-ranging look at genealogy and the ways of tracing fami-

ly names through document research, interviews, and the World Wide Web. (Rev: SLJ 2/03) [929]

Personal Problems and Relationships

4584 Clark, Sondra, and Silvana Clark. *You've Got What It Takes! Sondra's Tips for Making Your Dreams Come True* (4–7). 2002, Revell paper $8.99 (0-8007-5836-6). 121pp. Twelve-year-old Sondra, a spokesperson for Childcare International, gives practical tips on achieving goals. (Rev: SLJ 3/03)

4585 Moehn, Heather. *Everything You Need to Know About Cliques* (5–8). Series: Need to Know Library. 2001, Rosen LB $17.95 (0-8239-3326-1). 64pp. Moehn uses first-person narratives to introduce such topics as making friends, peer pressure, bullies, insecurity, and popularity, with a look at how cliques continue after high school. (Rev: SLJ 12/01) [158.25]

Careers

General and Miscellaneous

4586 Flanagan, Alice K. *Mayors* (1–3). Series: Community Workers. 2001, Compass Point LB $19.93 (0-7565-0064-8). 32pp. This is an easily read introduction to the work of mayors, the skills and training required, and their contributions to the community. Also use *Teachers* (2001). (Rev: SLJ 5/01) [352.23]

4587 Gorman, Jacqueline Laks. *Librarian / El Bibliotecario* (PS–2). Photos by Gregg Andersen. Series: People in My Community/La Gente de Mi Comunidad. 2002, Gareth Stevens LB $18.60 (0-8368-3310-4). 24pp. Full-color photographs and single-sentence descriptions, in English and in Spanish, introduce various aspects of a librarian's job. (Rev: SLJ 3/03)

4588 *History* (4–8). Illus. Series: Discovering Careers for Your Future. 2001, Ferguson LB $15.95 (0-89434-391-2). 92pp. A useful introduction to the career opportunities in this field, with information on the skills required, potential earnings, and job outlook. (Rev: SLJ 11/01)

4589 Liebman, Dan. *I Want to Be a Teacher* (K–2). Series: I Want to Be . . . 2001, Firefly LB $14.95 (1-55209-572-X). 24pp. A teacher's typical working day is described with a color photograph and two or three lines of text on each page in this easily read book. (Rev: BL 12/15/01; HBG 10/01) [371.1]

4590 Manley, Claudia B. *Secret Agents: Life as a Professional Spy* (4–7). Series: Extreme Careers. 2001, Rosen LB $19.95 (0-8239-3369-5). 64pp. A high-interest look at the extensive skills required to become an intelligence agent and the kinds of intelligence that are gathered (strategic, tactical, counterintelligence), with material on the history of espionage and on real-life and fictional spies. (Rev: SLJ 1/02) [327.12]

4591 Meltzer, Milton. *Case Closed: The Real Scoop on Detective Work* (5–9). Illus. 2001, Scholastic $18.95 (0-439-29315-4). 96pp. Meltzer introduces the methods that detectives (both police and private) use to investigate crimes and provides case studies and a look at the history of detective agencies. (Rev: BL 9/15/01; HBG 10/02; SLJ 9/01) [363.25]

4592 Reeves, Diane Lindsey, and Nancy Heubeck. *Career Ideas for Kids Who Like Adventure* (5–8). Illus. by Nancy Bond. Series: Career Ideas for Kids. 2001, Facts on File $23.00 (0-8160-4321-3). 170pp. An attractive introduction to careers such as fire fighting, scuba diving, oil rig work, and piloting, with personal profiles of individuals in the various fields and attractive cartoons. Also use *Career Ideas for Kids Who Like Money* (2001). (Rev: BL 7/01; HBG 3/02; SLJ 8/01) [331.7]

4593 Talbert, Marc. *Holding the Reins: A Ride Through Cowgirl Life* (3–6). Photos by Barbara Van Cleve. Illus. 2003, HarperCollins LB $17.89 (0-06-029256-3). 112pp. Being a cowgirl is both hard work and fun, as readers will discover in this account of four teen ranch girls as they balance school, work, and free time through the seasons. (Rev: BL 1/1–15/03) [978]

Arts and Entertainment

4594 Amara, Philip. *So, You Wanna Be a Comic Book Artist?* (5–8). Illus. by Pop Mhan. 2001, Beyond Words paper $9.95 (1-58270-058-3). 160pp. A comprehensive, engaging look at the world of comic-book illustration, with tips on everything from buying supplies to submitting work to publishers. (Rev: BL 1/1–15/02; SLJ 4/02) [808]

4595 *Art* (4–8). Illus. Series: Discovering Careers for Your Future. 2001, Ferguson LB $15.95 (0-89434-388-2). 92pp. A useful introduction to career opportunities in art, with information on the skills required, potential earnings, and job outlook. (Rev: SLJ 11/01)

4596 Johnson, Marlys H. *Careers in the Movies* (5 Up). Series: Career Resource Library. 2001, Rosen LB $18.95 (0-8239-3186-2). 122pp. Job descriptions and qualifications are clearly laid out in this guide for aspiring filmmakers that also discusses the history of the industry and the basic steps in film production. (Rev: SLJ 8/01) [791.43]

4597 Lehn, Barbara. *What Is an Artist?* (PS–2). Illus. by Carol Krauss. 2002, Millbrook LB $21.90 (0-7613-2259-0). 32pp. An introduction of the concept of "artist," presented in a friendly format for younger readers. (Rev: BL 12/15/02; HBG 3/03) [709]

4598 Marcus, Leonard S. *Side by Side: Five Favorite Picture-Book Teams Go to Work* (4–7). Illus. 2001, Walker LB $23.85 (0-8027-8779-7). 64pp. A look at how members of five well-known collaborative teams work together to create picture books, from concept to finished product. (Rev: BL 11/15/01; HB 1–2/02; HBG 3/02; SLJ 11/01) [070.5]

4599 White, Matt. *Cameras on the Battlefield: Photos of War* (5–7). Series: High Five Reading. 2002, Capstone LB $16.95 (0-7368-4004-4). 64pp. For reluctant readers, this is an appealing look at photographs of war, both those that celebrate war and those that document its horrors. (Rev: SLJ 8/02)

Engineering, Technology, and Trades

4600 *Computers* (4–8). Illus. Series: Discovering Careers for Your Future. 2001, Ferguson LB $15.95 (0-89434-389-0). 92pp. A useful introduction to the career opportunities in this field, with information on the skills required, potential earnings, and job outlook. (Rev: SLJ 11/01)

4601 Hayhurst, Chris. *Astronauts: Life Exploring Outer Space* (4–7). Series: Extreme Careers. 2001, Rosen LB $19.95 (0-8239-3364-4). 64pp. A high-interest look at the extensive skills required to become an astronaut, with brief coverage of space exploration and profiles of astronauts. (Rev: SLJ 1/02) [629]

4602 Hovanec, Erin M. *Careers as a Content Provider for the Web* (5–8). Series: The Library of E-Commerce and Internet Careers. 2001, Rosen LB $19.95 (0-8239-3418-7). 64pp. A basic guide to career opportunities in the high-tech sector, with personal stories, information on skills needed and how to get started, and lists of recommended resources, many of which are on the Web. Also use *E-Tailing: Careers Selling Over the Web* (2001). (Rev: SLJ 4/02) [004]

4603 Maupin, Melissa. *Computer Engineer* (4–6). Series: Career Exploration. 2000, Capstone LB $21.26 (0-7368-0591-5). 48pp. Readers follow the

events of a typical day for a computer engineer and learn the skills and temperament required for such a job, with full-color photographs, charts, and fast facts that include salary ranges and job outlook. Also use *Police Detective* and *Human Services Worker* (both 2000). (Rev: SLJ 5/01) [004]

4604 Willett, Edward. *Careers in Outer Space: New Business Opportunities* (4–9). Series: The Career Resource Library. 2002, Rosen LB $25.25 (0-8239-3358-X). 92pp. An interesting look at opportunities in the fields of science, math, engineering, technology, communication, and, of course, aeronautics, with information on required skills and training and on the pros and cons of working in the public and private sectors. (Rev: SLJ 6/02) [629.4]

Health and Medicine

4605 Gorman, Jacqueline Laks. *Dentist / El Dentista* (PS–2). Photos by Gregg Andersen. Series: People in My Community/La Gente de Mi Comunidad. 2002, Gareth Stevens LB $18.60 (0-8368-3307-4). 24pp. Full-color photographs and single-sentence descriptions, in English and in Spanish, introduce various aspects of a dentist's work. Also use *Doctor / El Medico* (2002). (Rev: HBG 3/03; SLJ 3/03)

4606 Liebman, Dan. *I Want to Be a Nurse* (K–2). Series: I Want to Be . . . 2001, Firefly LB $14.95 (1-55209-568-1). 24pp. With color photographs and two or three lines of simple text on each page, the working day of a nurse is described. (Rev: BL 12/15/01; HBG 10/01) [610]

Police and Fire Fighters

4607 Gorman, Jacqueline Laks. *Firefighter / El Bombero* (PS–2). Photos by Gregg Andersen. Series: People in My Community/La Gente de Mi Comunidad. 2002, Gareth Stevens LB $18.60 (0-8368-3309-0). 24pp. Full-color photographs and single-sentence descriptions, in English and in Spanish, introduce various aspects of a fire fighter's job. Also use *Police Officer / El Policía* (2002). (Rev: SLJ 3/03)

4608 Hayward, Linda. *A Day in the Life of a Firefighter* (PS–K). Series: Dorling Kindersley Readers: Jobs People Do. 2001, DK $12.95 (0-7894-7366-6); paper $3.95 (0-7894-7365-8). 32pp. In this beginning reader that uses a limited vocabulary and simple sentences, the daily life of a fire fighter is portrayed. (Rev: BL 8/1/01; HBG 10/01) [363]

4609 Landau, Elaine. *Smokejumpers* (3–6). Illus. 2002, Millbrook LB $23.90 (0-7613-2324-4). 48pp. An excellent tribute to the life and work of the gallant men and women who jump from planes to fight forest fires. (Rev: BCCB 3/02; BL 6/1–15/02; HBG 10/02; SLJ 7/02) [634.9]

Science

4610 Batten, Mary. *Anthropologist: Scientist of the People* (4–7). Illus. Series: Scientists in the Field. 2001, Houghton $16.00 (0-618-08368-5). 64pp. Striking photographs of a Paraguayan tribe of hunter-gatherers serve as a powerful backdrop to this explanation of the work of anthropologists. (Rev: BL 8/01; HB 1–2/02*; HBG 3/02; SLJ 9/01) [627]

4611 Bottone, Frank G., Jr. *The Science of Life: Projects and Principles for Beginning Biologists* (5–8). Illus. 2001, Chicago Review paper $14.95 (1-55652-382-3). 126pp. Twenty-five projects introduce readers to the basics of biology and the rigors of scientific research. (Rev: SLJ 11/01) [570.78]

4612 Collard, Sneed B., III. *A Firefly Biologist at Work* (4–6). Illus. Series: Wildlife Conservation Society. 2001, Watts LB $22.50 (0-531-11798-7); paper $6.95 (0-531-16568-X). 48pp. Readers learn about the career of a firefly researcher, with information both about fireflies themselves and about the life and interests of a biologist. (Rev: BL 12/1/01; SLJ check) [595.7]

4613 Swinburne, Stephen R. *The Woods Scientist* (4–8). Photos by Susan C. Morse. Illus. Series: Scientists in the Field. 2003, Houghton $16.00 (0-618-04602-X). 48pp. Swinburne describes his fascinating expeditions in the company of a conservationist and ecologist in the woods of Vermont, and provides lots of information on risks to wildlife. (Rev: BCCB 3/03; BL 3/15/03) [591.73]

Transportation

4614 Gorman, Jacqueline Laks. *Bus Driver / El Conductor del Autobús* (PS–2). Photos by Gregg Andersen. Series: People in My Community/La Gente de Mi Comunidad. 2002, Gareth Stevens LB $18.60 (0-8368-3306-6). 24pp. Full-color photographs and single-sentence descriptions, in English and in Spanish, introduce various aspects of a bus driver's job. (Rev: HBG 3/03; SLJ 3/03)

4615 Liebman, Dan. *I Want to Be a Truck Driver* (K–2). Series: I Want to Be . . . 2001, Firefly LB $14.95 (1-55209-576-2). 24pp. The daily life of a truck driver is described using a brief text and color photographs on each page. (Rev: BL 12/15/01; HBG 10/01) [629.24]

Veterinarians

4616 Marino, Betsy. *Emergency Vets* (3–6). Series: Animal Planet. 2001, Dutton $15.99 (0-525-46662-2); paper $5.99 (0-525-46501-4). 153pp. Aspiring veterinarians will enjoy this hybrid of fact and fiction that shows young Megan's summer helping her uncle at a veterinary hospital in Denver. (Rev: BCCB 7–8/01; HBG 3/02; SLJ 7/01) [636.089]

4617 Patrick, Jean L. S. *Cows, Cats, and Kids: A Veterinarian's Family at Work* (3–6). Illus. by Alvis Upitis. 2003, Boyds Mills $17.95 (1-56397-111-9). 48pp. A rural vet's wife describes the family's love of animals and the ways in which her children are able to help their father. (Rev: BL 3/1/03) [636.089]

Health and the Human Body

Aging and Death

4618 Perl, Lila. *Dying to Know . . .: About Death, Funeral Customs, and Final Resting Places* (5–7). Illus. 2001, Twenty-First Century LB $25.90 (0-7613-1564-0). 95pp. Ancient and contemporary funeral and burial practices are covered in this book that ends with a selection of humorous epitaphs. (Rev: BL 12/1/01; HBG 10/02; SLJ 12/01) [393]

4619 Rebman, Renee C. *Euthanasia and the "Right to Die": A Pro/Con Issue* (5–8). Illus. Series: Pro/Con Issues. 2002, Enslow LB $19.95 (0-7660-1816-4). 64pp. An objective examination of both sides of the issue of euthanasia. (Rev: BL 9/1/02; HBG 3/03) [179.7]

4620 Stalfelt, Pernilla. *The Death Book* (2–4). Illus. 2002, Groundwood $15.95 (0-88899-482-6). 32pp. A straightforward yet lighthearted look at death, including the customs surrounding it, what might happen when we die, and an "interview" with a ghost. (Rev: BL 2/1/03; HBG 3/03) [306.9]

4621 Wilson, Antoine. *You and a Death in Your Family* (5–8). Series: Family Matters. 2001, Rosen LB $17.95 (0-8239-3355-5). 48pp. Wilson provides concise, readable advice on coping with the death of a relative or pet and stresses that youngsters should seek help when necessary. (Rev: SLJ 8/01) [155.9]

Alcohol, Drugs, and Smoking

4622 Westcott, Patsy. *Why Do People Take Drugs?* (5–7). Series: Exploring Tough Issues. 2001, Raintree Steck-Vaughn LB $17.98 (0-7398-3231-X). 48pp. Drugs from caffeine to cocaine are explored, with discussion of society's attitudes toward drugs, legal issues, and the reasons some people are more tempted to abuse substances. (Rev: HBG 10/01; SLJ 7/01) [362.29]

Bionics and Transplants

4623 Fullick, Ann. *Rebuilding the Body* (5–8). Illus. Series: Science at the Edge. 2002, Heinemann LB $27.86 (1-58810-700-0). 64pp. An insightful volume about transplant procedures, including a section on how the organs of the body function and a discussion about ethics. (Rev: BL 10/15/02; HBG 3/03) [617.9]

Disabilities, Physical and Mental

4624 Heelan, Jamee Riggio. *Can You Hear a Rainbow? The Story of a Deaf Boy Named Chris* (K–3). Illus. by Nicola Simmonds. 2002, Peachtree $14.95 (1-56145-268-8). Chris tells the reader how sign language and other aids help him to cope with his deafness. (Rev: HBG 10/02; SLJ 9/02) [362.42]

4625 Kennedy, Mike. *Special Olympics* (3–5). Series: True Books — Sports. 2002, Children's LB $23.50 (0-516-22338-0); paper $6.95 (0-516-29375-3). 48pp. From the origins of the Special Olympics in 1963 through today's competitions, this account gives simple, well-illustrated information about these games for the physically handicapped. (Rev: BL 1/1–15/03) [796]

4626 Riggs, Stephanie. *Never Sell Yourself Short* (3–6). Illus. 2001, Albert Whitman $15.95 (0-8075-5563-0). 32pp. Through text and photographs, readers learn how Josh, a 14-year-old dwarf, enjoys his life despite obstacles. (Rev: BCCB 1/02; BL 9/1/01; HBG 3/02; SLJ 11/01) [618.92]

4627 Silverstein, Alvin, et al. *Scoliosis* (3–5). Series: My Health. 2002, Watts LB $24.00 (0-531-12046-5); paper $6.95 (0-531-16639-2). 48pp. The causes of this abnormal curvature of the spine are covered with material on how it affects young people and how it can be treated. (Rev: BL 12/15/02) [616]

4628 Silverstein, Alvin, and Virginia Silverstein. *Attention Deficit Disorder* (3–5). Series: My Health. 2001, Watts LB $23.00 (0-531-11778-2). With many color photographs, this account discusses ADD, its causes, symptoms, and treatment. (Rev: BL 1/1–15/02; SLJ 5/01) [618.92]

4629 Silverstein, Alvin, et al. *Dyslexia* (3–5). Series: My Health. 2001, Watts LB $23.00 (0-531-11862-2). This account describes dyslexia, its symptoms, its diagnosis, and how to get help, and provides material on brain structure and famous dyslexics. (Rev: BL 1/1–15/02; SLJ 10/01) [371.92]

4630 Wiltshire, Paula. *Dyslexia* (5–8). Illus. Series: Health Issues. 2002, Raintree Steck-Vaughn LB $28.54 (0-7398-5221-3). 64pp. Color photographs and straightforward text introduce dyslexia's symptoms and treatment and explain how it affects learning, with tips on how to cope with the disability. (Rev: BL 12/15/02; HBG 3/03; SLJ 3/03) [616.85]

Disease and Illness

4631 Abramovitz, Melissa. *Leukemia* (5–8). Illus. Series: Diseases and Disorders. 2002, Gale LB $21.96 (1-56006-863-9). 112pp. A look at the different types of leukemia, the possible causes, diagnosis, treatment, and the serious nature of the disease. (Rev: SLJ 3/03)

4632 Bridge, Chris. *Andrew's Story: A Book About a Boy Who Beat Cancer* (2–4). Illus. 2001, Lerner LB $21.27 (0-8225-2587-9). 32pp. A straightforward account of a boy's battle with cancer written in a nine-year-old's voice. (Rev: BL 1/1–15/02; HBG 3/02; SLJ 12/01) [362.1]

4633 Carter, Alden R. *I'm Tougher than Diabetes!* (2–4). Illus. 2001, Albert Whitman $14.95 (0-8075-1572-8). 32pp. A first-person account from the perspective of a pre-teen girl about the management of Type 1 diabetes, with color photographs and frequently asked questions. (Rev: BL 1/1–15/02; HBG 3/02; SLJ 5/02) [616.4]

4634 Cefrey, Holly. *Syphilis and Other Sexually Transmitted Diseases* (5–8). Illus. Series: Epidemics. 2001, Rosen LB $26.50 (0-8239-3488-8). 64pp. Cefrey describes historic outbreaks and treatments, as well as the symptoms and cure, of syphilis and other sexually transmitted diseases. (Rev: BL 3/15/02) [616.95]

4635 Cefrey, Holly. *Yellow Fever* (5–8). Series: Epidemics. 2002, Rosen LB $26.50 (0-8239-3489-6). 64pp. Yellow fever, spread by mosquitoes, was the cause of several epidemics in American cities during the 19th century before a cure was found by dedicated doctors who risked their lives. (Rev: BL 8/02) [616]

4636 Donnelly, Karen. *Leprosy (Hansen's Disease)* (5–8). Series: Epidemics. 2002, Rosen LB $26.50 (0-8239-3498-5). 64pp. This is the story of leprosy, the disease that created social outcasts of its victims, and of a man named Hansen who discovered an effective treatment. (Rev: BL 8/02) [616.9]

4637 Draper, Allison Stark. *Ebola* (5–8). Illus. Series: Epidemics. 2002, Rosen LB $26.50 (0-8239-3496-9). 64pp. Discusses the Ebola virus in both scientific and human terms. Also use *Mad Cow Disease* (2002). (Rev: BL 8/02; SLJ 6/02) [616.9]

4638 Fleischman, John. *Phineas Gage: A Gruesome but True Story About Brain Science* (5 Up). Illus. 2002, Houghton $16.00 (0-618-05252-6). 86pp. This riveting story of the amiable man whose personality changed when an iron rod shot through his brain presents lots of information on brain science and medical knowledge in the 19th century. (Rev: BL 3/1/02; HB 5–6/02; HBG 10/02; SLJ 3/02) [362.1]

4639 Gilman, Laura Anne. *Coping with Cerebral Palsy* (5 Up). Series: Coping. 2001, Rosen LB $18.95 (0-8239-3150-1). 92pp. This is a self-help book that looks at ways to deal with school, work, and travel as well as coping with other people and their attitudes. (Rev: SLJ 2/02) [616.836]

4640 Gold, Susan Dudley. *Sickle Cell Disease* (4–7). Illus. Series: Health Watch. 2001, Enslow LB $18.95 (0-7660-1662-5). 48pp. Readers are introduced to the symptoms and treatment of this disease through the true story of a young African American boy called Keone who received a successful stem-cell transplant. (Rev: HBG 3/02; SLJ 12/01) [616.1]

4641 Goldstein, Margaret J. *Everything You Need to Know About Multiple Sclerosis* (5–8). Series: Need to Know Library. 2001, Rosen LB $17.95 (0-8239-3292-3). 64pp. An introduction to multiple sclerosis, its symptoms and treatment, and how it affects the nervous system, along with information on the importance of treating the emotional impact of this disease. (Rev: SLJ 5/01) [616]

4642 Gray, Shirley Wimbish. *Living with Asthma* (3–5). Illus. Series: Living Well. 2002, Child's World LB $25.64 (1-56766-100-9). 32pp. Explains various aspects of asthma, from why attacks occur to treatment of this chronic illness. Other titles in this series include *Living with Diabetes*, *Living with Epilepsy*, and *Living with Cerebral Palsy* (all 2002). (Rev: BL 10/15/02; SLJ 1/03) [618.92]

4643 Gray, Susan H. *Living with Cystic Fibrosis* (3–5). Series: Living Well. 2002, Child's World LB $25.64 (1-56766-105-X). 32pp. The nature of cystic fibrosis is discussed with details on how it affects the body, its causes, and how to live with it, plus anecdotes from people who suffer from the illness. (Rev: BL 10/15/02) [616]

4644 Gray, Susan H. *Living with Juvenile Rheumatoid Arthritis* (3–5). Illus. Series: Living Well. 2002, Child's World LB $25.64 (1-56766-104-1). 32pp. First-hand accounts from children with juvenile rheumatoid arthritis enhance the information on the disease, from diagnosis to treatment. (Rev: BL 10/15/02; SLJ 3/03) [618.92]

4645 Hawkins, Trisha. *Everything You Need to Know About Measles and Rubella* (4–8). Series: Need to Know Library. 2001, Rosen LB $17.95 (0-8239-3322-9). 64pp. Simple text and photographs describe the diseases and methods of prevention and treatment, and discuss public-health issues. Also use

Everything You Need to Know About Chicken Pox and Shingles (2001). (Rev: SLJ 8/01) [616.9]

4646 Hayhurst, Chris. *Cholera* (5–9). Series: Epidemics. 2001, Rosen LB $19.95 (0-8239-3345-8). 64pp. In a readable style, Hayhurst discusses the history of cholera, formerly a deadly disease, and explains how its treatment was developed. Also use *Polio* and *Smallpox* (both 2001). (Rev: SLJ 7/01) [616.9]

4647 Isle, Mick. *Everything You Need to Know About Food Poisoning* (4–8). Illus. Series: Need to Know Library. 2001, Rosen LB $17.95 (0-8239-3396-2). 64pp. Safe ways to prepare food are the main focus of this book, which also describes the symptoms and treatment of food poisoning. (Rev: SLJ 10/01) [615.954]

4648 Lamb, Kirsten. *Cancer* (5–8). Series: Health Issues. 2002, Raintree Steck-Vaughn LB $28.54 (0-7398-5219-1). 64pp. An informative account that covers various kinds of cancer, giving real-life stories, and also deals with issues and choices facing teens today. (Rev: BL 12/15/02; HBG 3/03; SLJ 3/03) [616.99]

4649 Lennard-Brown, Sarah. *Asthma* (5–8). Illus. Series: Health Issues. 2002, Raintree Steck-Vaughn LB $28.54 (0-7398-5218-3). 64pp. Color photographs and straightforward text explain the symptoms, diagnosis, and treatment of asthma. (Rev: BL 12/15/02; HBG 3/03) [616.2]

4650 Marrin, Albert. *Dr. Jenner and the Speckled Monster: The Search for the Smallpox Vaccine* (4–8). Illus. 2002, Dutton $17.99 (0-525-46922-2). 96pp. This highly readable and detailed account describes the impact of smallpox from the time of the Aztecs, major outbreaks over the years, the way the virus works, the work of Jenner in developing a vaccine, and the virus's potential as a weapon of mass destruction. (Rev: BL 11/15/02; HB 11–12/02; HBG 3/03; SLJ 1/03) [614.5]

4651 Monroe, Judy. *Cystic Fibrosis* (5–9). Illus. Series: Perspectives on Disease and Illness. 2001, Capstone LB $17.95 (0-7368-1026-9). 64pp. A straightforward account of the symptoms, diagnosis, and treatment of this disease, with discussion of the impact on the life of the patient and other family members. Also use *Breast Cancer* (2001). (Rev: HBG 3/02; SLJ 3/02) [616.3]

4652 Morgan, Sally. *Germ Killers: Fighting Disease* (5–8). Series: Science at the Edge. 2002, Heinemann LB $27.86 (1-58810-699-3). 64pp. Current advances in fighting disease are outlined with their current applications and future possibilities. (Rev: BL 10/15/02; HBG 3/03) [616]

4653 Nardo, Don. *Germs* (4–5). Illus. Series: KidHaven Science Library. 2002, Gale LB $23.70 (0-7377-0943-X). 48pp. This volume covers a broad spectrum of germs including viruses, bacteria, microscopic fungi, and some algae, with information on their structure and functions. (Rev: BL 5/1/02) [579]

4654 Ramen, Fred. *Sleeping Sickness and Other Parasitic Tropical Diseases* (5–8). Series: Epidemics. 2002, Rosen LB $26.50 (0-8239-3499-3).

64pp. After a history of parasitic diseases around the globe and the role played by bloodsucking killers like the tsetse fly, this account describes the treatments now available. (Rev: BL 8/02; SLJ 7/02) [616]

4655 Ray, Kurt. *Typhoid Fever* (5–8). Illus. Series: Epidemics. 2002, Rosen LB $26.50 (0-8239-3572-8). 64pp. An introduction to the history and treatment of typhoid fever, including coverage of Typhoid Mary. (Rev: BL 3/15/02) [614.5]

4656 Sherrow, Victoria. *Polio Epidemic: Crippling Virus Outbreak* (4–7). Series: American Disasters. 2001, Enslow LB $18.95 (0-7660-1555-6). 48pp. In this readable account, Sherrow looks at the history of polio, its treatment, the epidemic in the United States that started in 1952, and the creation of the polio vaccine. (Rev: HBG 3/02; SLJ 3/02) [362.1]

4657 Silverstein, Alvin, et al. *Asthma* (3–5). Series: My Health. 2002, Watts LB $24.00 (0-531-12048-1); paper $6.95 (0-531-16637-6). 48pp. Using many color photographs and cartoons, this brief account explains asthma's causes, symptoms, effects, and the methods of treatment. Also use *Diabetes* and *What Are Germs?* (Rev: BL 12/15/02) [616.2]

4658 Silverstein, Alvin, and Virginia Silverstein. *Parkinson's Disease* (4–6). Illus. Series: Diseases and People. 2002, Enslow LB $20.95 (0-7660-1593-9). 128pp. Actor Michael J. Fox's diagnosis of Parkinson's serves as an introduction to the history, causes, symptoms, and treatment of this disease. (Rev: HBG 3/03; SLJ 12/02)

4659 Silverstein, Alvin, and Virginia Silverstein. *Vaccinations* (3–5). Series: My Health. 2002, Watts LB $23.00 (0-531-11874-6); paper $6.95 (0-531-15564-1). 48pp. Using many visuals and a clear, simple text, this book describes how vaccinations were developed, how they work, and the various types. (Rev: BL 6/1–15/02; SLJ 8/02) [614.4]

4660 Silverstein, Alvin, et al. *Chickenpox* (3–5). Series: My Health. 2001, Watts LB $23.00 (0-531-11782-0). The disease chickenpox is introduced with discussion of its causes, symptoms, dangers, treatment, and immunization. (Rev: BL 1/1–15/02; SLJ 8/01) [616.9]

4661 Silverstein, Alvin, et al. *Headaches* (3–5). Series: My Health. 2001, Watts LB $23.00 (0-531-11872-X). Different types of headaches are introduced, with their causes, treatment, and prevention. (Rev: BL 1/1–15/02; SLJ 12/01) [616.8]

4662 Silverstein, Alvin, et al. *Lyme Disease* (3–5). Series: My Health. 2001, Watts LB $23.00 (0-531-11638-7). Covers the symptoms, causes, prevention, and treatment of this disease named after Lyme, Connecticut, where it was first identified. (Rev: BL 1/1–15/02; SLJ 12/01) [616]

4663 Spray, Michelle. *Growing up with Scoliosis: A Young Girl's Story* (5 Up). Illus. by author. 2002, Book Shelf paper $12.95 (0-9714160-3-6). 119pp. An autobiographical account of the treatment of scoliosis and the emotional impact on the patient, with clear illustrations. (Rev: SLJ 12/02)

4664 Stewart, Gail B. *Sleep Disorders* (5–8). Illus. Series: Diseases and Disorders. 2002, Gale LB

$21.96 (1-56006-909-0). 112pp. Insomnia, narcolepsy, apnea, and night terrors are among the problems discussed here, with material on treatments, new research, and attitudes toward people who are always tired. (Rev: SLJ 3/03)

4665 Wainwright, Tabitha. *You and an Illness in Your Family* (5–8). Series: Family Matters. 2001, Rosen LB $17.95 (0-8239-3352-0). 48pp. Concise, readable advice is accompanied by full-page photographs of young teens and the recommendation to seek help when necessary. (Rev: SLJ 8/01) [610]

4666 Whelan, Jo. *Diabetes* (5–8). Series: Health Issues. 2002, Raintree Steck-Vaughn LB $28.54 (0-7398-5220-5). 64pp. Case histories of youngsters with diabetes are used to explain the nature of this disease, the problems it produces, and the treatments available. (Rev: BL 12/15/02; HBG 3/03) [616.4]

4667 Zonta, Pat. *Jessica's X-Ray* (2–5). Illus. by Clive Dobson. 2002, Firefly $19.95 (1-52297-578-9); paper $8.95 (1-55297-577-0). 28pp. When Jessica breaks her arm, the doctor orders X-rays and the reader is introduced to the whys and hows of this diagnostic tool. (Rev: BL 5/1/02; HBG 10/02; SLJ check) [616.0750]

Doctors and Medicine

4668 Dowswell, Paul. *Medicine* (5–8). Illus. Series: Great Inventions. 2001, Heinemann LB $24.22 (1-58810-213-0). 48pp. A chronological look at new medical instruments and procedures over the ages, with diagrams and information on the inventors. (Rev: HBG 3/02; SLJ 2/02) [610]

4669 Jefferis, David. *Bio Tech: Frontiers of Medicine* (4–8). Illus. Series: Megatech. 2001, Crabtree LB $15.45 (0-7787-0051-8); paper $8.06 (0-7787-0061-5). 32pp. An eye-catching look at future medical possibilities such as artificial body parts, enhanced use of robots, special foods, and so forth. (Rev: SLJ 6/02)

4670 Manson, Ainslie. *House Calls: The True Story of a Pioneer Doctor* (3–6). Illus. by Mary Jane Gerber. 2001, Groundwood $15.95 (0-88899-446-X). 56pp. Though the narrator of this book is a fictional girl, the story details the real life of an early 19th-century rural Canadian doctor with information on tools and treatment. (Rev: BL 2/1/02; HBG 3/02; SLJ 12/01) [610.92]

4671 Swanson, Diane. *The Doctor and You* (PS–1). Illus. 2001, Annick $19.95 (1-55037-673-X); paper $7.95 (1-55037-672-1). 32pp. Designed to prepare young children for a visit to the doctor, this book features clear photographs and simple text explaining medical equipment and procedures. (Rev: BL 1/1–15/02; HBG 10/01) [610]

Genetics

4672 Allan, Tony. *Understanding DNA: A Breakthrough in Medicine* (5–8). Illus. Series: Point of Impact. 2002, Heinemann LB $16.95 (1-58810-557-1). 32pp. A history of genetics with profiles of the important scientists and discussion of future uses of this knowledge in cloning, medicine, and production of food. (Rev: SLJ 9/02)

4673 Beatty, Richard. *Genetics* (4–8). Illus. Series: Science Fact Files. 2001, Raintree Steck-Vaughn LB $18.98 (0-7398-1015-4). 42pp. Cells, chromosomes, genes, and genetic engineering are covered here, with profiles of key scientists. (Rev: HBG 10/01; SLJ 1/02) [660]

4674 Morgan, Sally. *Body Doubles: Cloning Plants and Animals* (5–8). Illus. Series: Science at the Edge. 2002, Heinemann LB $27.86 (1-58810-698-5). 64pp. A discussion of the scientific and ethical issues of cloning, with excellent diagrams. (Rev: BL 10/15/02; HBG 3/03) [660.6]

4675 Nicolson, Cynthia Pratt. *Baa! The Most Interesting Book You'll Ever Read About Genes and Cloning* (4–6). Illus. by Rose Cowles. Series: Mysterious You. 2001, Kids Can $14.95 (1-55074-856-4); paper $6.95 (1-55074-886-6). 40pp. Nicolson provides succinct definitions and descriptions of genetics and cloning-related issues in an easy-to-read volume. (Rev: BL 1/1–15/02; HBG 3/02) [572.8]

4676 Silverstein, Alvin, et al. *DNA* (4–8). Series: Science Concepts. 2002, Millbrook LB $26.90 (0-7613-2257-4). 64pp. This book examines the structure of DNA and clearly explains its components and functions and includes current topics such as the genome project, genetic engineering, gene therapy, and cloning. (Rev: BL 9/15/02; HBG 3/03; SLJ 11/02) [574.87]

Hospitals

4677 Amos, Janine. *The Hospital* (1–4). Photos by Angela Hampton. Illus. by Gwen Green. Series: Separations. 2002, Gareth Stevens LB $21.26 (0-8368-3091-1). 31pp. Letters, stories, and informational text will help a child to prepare for a visit to a hospital. The same format is used in *Death* and *Divorce* (both 2002). (Rev: HBG 10/02; SLJ 6/02) [362.1]

4678 Murphy, Patricia J. *Everything You Need to Know About Staying in the Hospital* (5–8). Series: Need to Know Library. 2001, Rosen LB $17.95 (0-8239-3325-3). 64pp. This volume explains the basic hospital process from admission to discharge and follows a patient through a typical day. (Rev: SLJ 5/01) [362.1]

The Human Body

General

4679 Davidson, Sue, and Ben Morgan. *Human Body Revealed* (5–8). Illus. 2002, DK $12.99 (0-7894-8882-5). 38pp. Overlays, cutaway photographs, diagrams, and captions are all used effectively to give a picture of what's contained in various parts of the body. (Rev: BL 12/1/02; HBG 3/03) [611]

4680 Ewald, Wendy. *The Best Part of Me: Children Talk About Their Bodies in Pictures and Words* (1–3). Illus. 2001, Little, Brown $16.95 (0-316-70306-0). 32pp. In their own words, youngsters describe what they like best about their bodies. (Rev: BL 9/1/01; HBG 3/02; SLJ 10/01) [810.8]

4681 Klingel, Cynthia, and Robert B. Noyed. *Feet* (PS–1). Photos by Gregg Andersen. Series: Let's Read About Our Bodies. 2002, Gareth Stevens LB $18.60 (0-8368-3064-4). 24pp. Full-page, full-color close-ups and minimal text present toes, feet, and shoes. Also use *Nose* and *Skin* (2002). (Rev: HBG 10/02; SLJ 5/02) [612.98]

4682 Ross, Michael Elsohn. *Body Cycles* (PS–1). Illus. by Gustav Moore. Series: Cycles. 2002, Millbrook LB $22.40 (0-7613-1816-X). Young readers are introduced to the ways in which the body uses oxygen, blood, and nutrients. (Rev: HBG 10/02; SLJ 8/02) [612]

4683 Seuling, Barbara. *From Head to Toe: The Amazing Human Body and How It Works* (3–4). Illus. by Edward Miller. 2002, Holiday $16.95 (0-8234-1699-2). 32pp. An accessible overview of the various body systems, omitting reproduction, with clear illustrations and several experiments. (Rev: SLJ 11/02) [612]

4684 Walker, Richard. *Body: Bones, Muscle, Blood and Other Body Bits* (4–8). Series: Secret Worlds. 2001, DK $14.95 (0-7894-7967-2); paper $7.95 (0-7894-7968-0). 96pp. A lively, unusual introduction to human anatomy that uses attractive layouts and lively text as well as providing a listing of tested Web sites and a special reference section. (Rev: BL 10/15/01; HBG 3/02) [612]

Circulatory System

4685 Frost, Helen. *The Circulatory System* (K–2). Illus. Series: Human Body Systems. 2000, Capstone LB $13.25 (0-7368-0648-2). 24pp. A small-format, basic introduction for beginning readers. (Rev: HBG 10/01; SLJ 4/01) [612.1]

4686 Viegas, Jennifer. *The Heart: Learning How Our Blood Circulates* (5–9). Illus. Series: 3-D Library of the Human Body. 2002, Rosen LB $26.50 (0-8239-3532-9). 48pp. An introduction to the anatomy and function of the human heart and the circulatory system that includes illustrations, diagrams, a glossary, and other aids. (Rev: BL 7/02) [612.1]

Digestive and Excretory Systems

4687 Brynie, Faith Hickman. *101 Questions About Food and Digestion That Have Been Eating at You . . . Until Now* (5–8). Illus. 2002, Millbrook LB $27.90 (0-7613-2309-0). 176pp. A question-and-answer format succeeds in conveying lots of food for thought, with details on digestive functions, digestive disorders, food safety, fat cells, Mad Cow disease, vitamins, and so forth. (Rev: BL 1/1–15/03; HBG 3/03; SLJ 3/03) [612.3]

4688 Frost, Helen. *The Digestive System* (K–2). Illus. Series: Human Body Systems. 2000, Capstone LB $13.25 (0-7368-0649-0). 24pp. This is a simple introduction to the digestive system that includes clearly labeled diagrams and full-color photographs. (Rev: HBG 10/01; SLJ 4/01) [612.3]

4689 Showers, Paul. *What Happens to a Hamburger?* (K–3). Illus. by Edward Miller. Series: Let's-Read-and-Find-Out Science. 2001, HarperCollins LB $15.89 (0-06-027948-6); paper $4.95 (0-06-445183-6). 32pp. A new edition of this interesting easy reader that explains the mysteries of digestion. (Rev: BL 4/15/01; HBG 10/01) [612.3]

4690 Toriello, James. *The Stomach: Learning How We Digest* (5–9). Series: 3-D Library of the Human Body. 2002, Rosen LB $19.95 (0-8239-3536-1). 48pp. Using outstanding diagrams and clear explanations, the digestive system is highlighted with material on each of its parts and their functions. (Rev: BL 7/02; SLJ 7/02) [612.3]

Nervous System

4691 Brynie, Faith Hickman. *The Physical Brain* (5–9). Illus. Series: The Amazing Brain. 2001, Blackbirch LB $21.95 (1-56711-424-5). 64pp. Photographs and absorbing text introduce the physical characteristics of the brain. Also use *Neurological Disorders* (2001). (Rev: BL 10/15/01; HBG 3/02; SLJ 9/01) [612.8]

4692 Degezelle, Terri. *Your Brain* (K–2). Illus. Series: The Bridgestone Science Library. 2002, Capstone LB $13.95 (0-7368-1147-8). 24pp. An attractive, basic overview of the brain with "Fun Facts" and an easy activity. (Rev: SLJ 7/02) [612.8]

4693 Hayhurst, Chris. *The Brain and Spinal Cord: Learning How We Think, Feel, and Move* (5–9). Series: 3-D Library of the Human Body. 2002, Rosen LB $19.95 (0-8239-3528-0). 48pp. Exceptional illustrations and a clear text are used to explain the composition of the brain with explanations of how it works and how emotions influence our thoughts. (Rev: BL 7/02; SLJ 7/02) [612.8]

4694 Walker, Richard. *Brain: Inner Workings of the Gray Matter* (4–8). Series: Secret Worlds. 2002, DK $14.95 (0-7894-8527-3); paper $5.95 (0-7894-8528-1). 96pp. This book contains a wealth of information (some quite detailed) on the structure and functions of the brain, all presented in a pleasing layout with excellent illustrations. (Rev: BL 8/02; HBG 10/02)

Respiratory System

4695 Frost, Helen. *The Respiratory System* (K–2). Illus. Series: Human Body Systems. 2000, Capstone LB $13.25 (0-7368-0652-0). 24pp. Simple, brief text introduces the respiratory system, with clearly labeled diagrams and full-color photographs. (Rev: HBG 10/01; SLJ 4/01) [612]

4696 Furgang, Kathy. *My Lungs* (K–3). Illus. Series: My Body. 2001, Rosen LB $19.50 (0-8239-5575-3). 24pp. A basic overview of the lungs, their anatomy, how they function, and diseases of the lung, with helpful illustrations. (Rev: SLJ 9/01) [612.2]

4697 Hayhurst, Chris. *The Lungs: Learning How We Breathe* (5–9). Series: 3-D Library of the Human Body. 2002, Rosen LB $19.95 (0-8239-3534-5). 48pp. Amazing computer graphics are used to explain the composition of the lungs, how they work, and what keeps them healthy. (Rev: BL 7/02) [612.6]

Senses

4698 Cobb, Vicki. *Open Your Eyes: Discover Your Sense of Sight* (2–5). Illus. by Cynthia C. Lewis. Series: The Five Senses. 2002, Millbrook LB $22.90 (0-7613-1705-8). An appealing look at the eye, the parts of the eye, and how the eye works, with easy experiments and optical illusions. (Rev: HBG 10/02; SLJ 5/02) [612.84]

4699 Cobb, Vicki. *Perk up Your Ears: Discover Your Sense of Hearing* (3–6). Illus. by Cynthia C. Lewis. Series: The Five Senses. 2001, Millbrook LB $22.90 (0-7613-1704-X). An entertaining overview of hearing that encourages children to do lots of experimenting. (Rev: HBG 3/02; SLJ 4/02) [612.8]

4700 Furgang, Kathy. *My Ears* (K–3). Illus. Series: My Body. 2001, Rosen LB $19.50 (0-8239-5572-9). 24pp. A basic overview of the ears, their anatomy, how they function, and diseases of the ear, with helpful illustrations. (Rev: SLJ 9/01) [612.8]

4701 Gordon, Sharon. *Seeing* (1–2). Illus. Series: Rookie Read-About Health. 2001, Children's $19.00 (0-516-22291-0); paper $5.95 (0-516-25990-3). 32pp. Very young readers are encouraged to think about their eyes and their ability to see. Also use *Smelling* (2001). (Rev: BL 12/1/01) [612.8]

4702 Sherman, Josepha. *The Ear: Learning How We Hear* (5–9). Series: 3-D Library of the Human Body. 2002, Rosen LB $19.95 (0-8239-3529-9). 48pp. Using amazing illustrations and clear explanations, Sherman introduces the ear, its anatomy, uses, operation, and problems that can develop. (Rev: BL 7/02) [612.8]

4703 Silverstein, Alvin, and Virginia Silverstein. *Earaches* (3–5). Series: My Health. 2002, Watts LB $23.00 (0-531-11873-8); paper $6.95 (0-531-15562-5). 48pp. This book describes, in a simple text and many pictures, how the ear functions, what can cause earaches, and how to treat them. (Rev: BL 6/1–15/02) [612.8]

4704 Silverstein, Alvin, and Virginia Silverstein. *Smelling and Tasting* (4–6). Illus. by Anne Canevari Green. Series: Senses and Sensors. 2002, Twenty-

First Century LB $25.90 (0-7613-1667-1). 64pp. Human and animal senses of smell and taste are covered in this well-organized and readable volume. Also use *Touching and Feeling* (2002). (Rev: BL 3/15/02; HBG 10/02; SLJ 8/02)

4705 Silverstein, Alvin, et al. *Can You See the Chalkboard?* (3–5). Series: My Health. 2001, Watts LB $23.00 (0-531-11783-9). Problems with vision are discussed with material on the structure of the eye, diagnosis of these problems, and treatments available. (Rev: BL 1/1–15/02; SLJ 8/01) [612.8]

4706 Simon, Seymour. *Eyes and Ears* (5–8). Illus. 2003, HarperCollins LB $16.89 (0-688-15304-6). 32pp. Simon explains in clear, straightforward terms our ability to see and hear. (Rev: BL 3/15/03*) [612.8]

4707 Viegas, Jennifer. *The Eye: Learning How We See* (5–9). Illus. Series: 3-D Library of the Human Body. 2002, Rosen LB $26.50 (0-8239-3530-2). 48pp. This volume on the anatomy and function of the human eye includes illustrations, diagrams, a glossary, and other aids. (Rev: BL 7/02) [612.8]

4708 Viegas, Jennifer. *The Mouth and Nose: Learning How We Taste and Smell* (5–9). Series: 3-D Library of the Human Body. 2002, Rosen LB $19.95 (0-8239-3535-3). 48pp. The mouth and nose are featured in this heavily illustrated account that covers their composition, functions, and how they work together. (Rev: BL 7/02) [612]

4709 Ziefert, Harriet. *You Can't Taste a Pickle with Your Ear* (K–2). Illus. by Amanda Haley. 2002, Blue Apple $15.95 (1-929766-68-8). 40pp. The five senses are explored in humorous style as Ziefert blends facts, goofy rhymes, cartoons, and questions that will spur further investigation. (Rev: BL 1/1–15/03; SLJ 1/03) [612.8]

Skeletal-Muscular System

4710 Degezelle, Terri. *Your Bones* (K–2). Illus. Series: The Bridgestone Science Library. 2002, Capstone LB $13.95 (0-7368-1146-X). 24pp. An attractive, basic overview of bones with "Fun Facts" and an easy activity. (Rev: SLJ 7/02) [612.7]

4711 Frost, Helen. *The Muscular System* (K–2). Illus. Series: Human Body Systems. 2000, Capstone LB $13.25 (0-7368-0650-4). 24pp. Short, simple text introduces the muscular system, accompanied by full-color illustrations. (Rev: HBG 10/01; SLJ 4/01) [612]

4712 Oleksy, Walter. *The Head and Neck: Learning How We Use Our Muscles* (5–9). Series: 3-D Library of the Human Body. 2002, Rosen LB $19.95 (0-8239-3531-0). 48pp. The muscles of the head and neck and their roles in controlling the sense organs, chewing and swallowing, facial expressions, and conveying emotions are explained in this well-illustrated account. (Rev: BL 7/02) [612.7]

4713 Sherman, Josepha. *The Upper Limbs: Learning How We Use Our Arms, Elbows, Forearms, and Hands* (5–9). Series: 3-D Library of the Human Body. 2002, Rosen LB $19.95 (0-8239-3537-X). 48pp. The parts of the arm and hand are examined with illustrated material on how the muscles in these areas function and receive support from the skeletal structure. (Rev: BL 7/02) [612.7]

4714 Silverstein, Alvin, et al. *Broken Bones* (3–5). Series: My Health. 2001, Watts LB $23.00 (0-531-11781-2). This book describes what happens when bones get broken, the causes, treatments available, and how mending takes place. (Rev: BL 1/1–15/02; SLJ 8/01) [612.7]

4715 Viegas, Jennifer. *The Lower Limbs: Learning How We Use Our Thighs, Knees, Legs, and Feet* (5–9). Series: 3-D Library of the Human Body. 2002, Rosen LB $19.95 (0-8239-3533-7). 48pp. The bones and muscles of the legs and feet and their functions are described in a clear text and exceptional illustrations. (Rev: BL 7/02; SLJ 7/02) [612.7]

Skin and Hair

4716 Silverstein, Alvin, and Virginia Silverstein. *Burns and Blisters* (3–5). Series: My Health. 2002, Watts LB $23.00 (0-531-11871-1); paper $6.95 (0-531-15561-7). 48pp. Using photographs, cartoons, and other visuals as well as a lively text, this book explains what happens when the skin becomes burned and blistered. (Rev: BL 6/1–15/02; SLJ 8/02) [612.7]

4717 Swain, Ruth Freeman. *Hairdo! What We Do and Did to Our Hair* (K–2). Illus. by Cat B. Smith. 2002, Holiday $16.95 (0-8234-1522-8). 32pp. Younger readers will enjoy these entertaining facts about hair and hairstyles through the ages. (Rev: BL 12/15/02; HBG 3/03; SLJ 10/02) [391.5]

Teeth

4718 Murkoff, Heidi. *What to Expect When You Go to the Dentist* (1–3). Illus. by Laura Rader. Series: What To Expect Kids. 2002, HarperFestival $7.99 (0-694-01328-5). 32pp. Angus the dog gives good advice and some projects to prepare youngsters for their first visit to a dentist. (Rev: BL 6/1–15/02; HBG 10/02) [617.601]

4719 Swanson, Diane. *The Dentist and You* (2–4). 2002, Annick LB $19.95 (1-55037-729-9); paper $7.95 (1-55037-728-0). 32pp. Cleanings, fillings, X-rays, and impressions are all covered in a reassuring way, with tips for distracting oneself in the dental chair. (Rev: HBG 10/02; SLJ 6/02) [617.6]

Hygiene, Physical Fitness, and Nutrition

4720 Crump, Marguerite. *Don't Sweat It! Every Body's Answers to Questions You Don't Want to Ask: A Guide for Young People* (5–9). Illus. by Chris Sharp. 2002, Free Spirit paper $13.95 (1-57542-114-3). 118pp. Crump tackles potentially embarrassing questions about personal hygiene. (Rev: SLJ 1/03)

4721 De Brunhoff, Laurent. *Babar's Yoga for Elephants* (2–4). Illus. 2002, Abrams $16.95 (0-8109-1021-7). 48pp. The sage elephant Babar re-creates yoga poses, which kids may be tempted to do as well, in this nonfiction book best read with an adult nearby. (Rev: BL 10/15/02; HBG 3/03) [613.7]

4722 Ehrlich, Fred. *Does a Lion Brush?* (PS). Illus. by Emily Bolam. Series: Early Experiences. 2002, Handprint $10.95 (1-929766-64-5). This small-format picture book gives a humorous introduction to tooth brushing. Also use *Does a Pig Flush?* (2002). (Rev: SLJ 3/03)

4723 Feeney, Kathy. *Get Moving: Tips on Exercise* (K–3). Series: Your Health. 2001, Capstone LB $13.95 (0-7368-0973-2). 24pp. The importance of exercise is stressed through simple text and an activity pyramid. (Rev: HBG 3/02; SLJ 4/02) [613.7]

4724 Gedatus, Gus. *Exercise for Weight Management* (4–7). Series: Nutrition and Fitness. 2001, Capstone $16.95 (0-7368-0706-3). 64pp. As well as outlining a simple, practical exercise program, this volume stresses good nutrition and contains some healthy recipes. (Rev: BL 9/15/01; HBG 10/01) [613.7]

4725 Gillies, Judi, and Jennifer Glossop. *The Jumbo Vegetarian Cookbook* (4–8). Illus. 2002, Kids Can $14.95 (1-55074-977-3). 256pp. An introduction to the vegetarian lifestyle, including nutrition and recipes. (Rev: BCCB 7–8/02; BL 3/1/02; SLJ 7/02) [641.5]

4726 Gordon, Sharon. *Exercise* (3–5). Series: Rookie Read-About Health. 2002, Children's LB $19.00 (0-516-22571-5); paper $5.95 (0-516-26950-X). 32pp. This easy-reader explains how exercise builds strong muscles and shows how children can have fun while doing favorite activities. (Rev: BL 12/15/02) [613.7]

4727 Gordon, Sharon. *Keeping Clean* (3–5). Series: Rookie Read-About Health. 2002, Children's LB $19.00 (0-516-22572-3); paper $5.95 (0-516-26951-8). 32pp. From bathing after exercise to washing one's hand before eating, this is a simple guide to personal hygiene and on how to keep germs from spreading. (Rev: BL 12/15/02) [613]

4728 Gordon, Sharon. *You Are What You Eat* (3–5). Series: Rookie Read-About Health. 2002, Children's LB $19.00 (0-516-22573-1); paper $5.95 (0-516-26952-6). 32pp. This book uses simple language to explain such nutritional facts as why breakfast is the most important meal of the day and why an apple is a better snack than potato chips. (Rev: BL 12/15/02) [613]

4729 Manning, Mick, and Brita Granstrom. *Wash, Scrub, Brush* (K–3). Illus. 2001, Albert Whitman $15.95 (0-8075-8668-4). 32pp. Information about hygiene is blended into a story line about a forthcoming party, and lightened by comparisons to animal hygiene. (Rev: BL 5/1/01; HBG 10/01; SLJ 4/01) [613.4]

4730 Schwartz, Ellen. *I'm a Vegetarian: Amazing Facts and Ideas for Healthy Vegetarians* (5–8). Illus. by Farida Zaman. 2002, Tundra paper $9.95 (0-88776-588-2). 112pp. The social aspects of being a vegetarian are handled here with humor and sensitivity. (Rev: BL 7/02; SLJ 9/02) [613.2]

4731 Silverstein, Alvin, and Virginia Silverstein. *Physical Fitness* (3–5). Series: My Health. 2002, Watts LB $23.00 (0-531-11860-6); paper $6.95 (0-531-15563-3). 48pp. Using photographs, cartoons, and other visuals plus a simple text, this book describes the importance of physical fitness and how to maintain it. (Rev: BL 6/1–15/02) [613.7]

4732 Turck, Mary. *Food and Emotions* (4–7). Series: Nutrition and Fitness. 2001, Capstone $16.95 (0-7368-0711-X). 64pp. This book explains the relationship between nutrition and a healthy emotional life and gives many tips and recipes for healthy living. (Rev: BL 9/15/01; HBG 10/01; SLJ 7/01) [613.2]

4733 Turck, Mary. *Healthy Eating for Weight Management* (4–7). Series: Nutrition and Fitness. 2001, Capstone $16.95 (0-7368-0709-8). 64pp. Good nutrition is emphasized as an effective method of controlling one's weight, and readers will find a fitness plan and several tempting recipes. (Rev: BL 9/15/01; HBG 10/01; SLJ 7/01) [613.2]

4734 Turck, Mary. *Healthy Snack and Fast-Food Choices* (4–7). Series: Nutrition and Fitness. 2001, Capstone $16.95 (0-7368-0710-1). 64pp. Making healthy eating decisions is the focus of this guide to good nutrition that contains some delicious recipes. (Rev: BL 9/15/01; HBG 10/01) [613.2]

Safety and Accidents

4735 Gale, Karen Buhler. *The Kids' Guide to First Aid: All About Bruises, Burns, Stings, Sprains and Other Ouches* (4–6). Illus. by Michael Kline. 2002, Williamson paper $12.95 (1-885593-58-9). 128pp. Readers learn to distinguish between situations they can handle and when they need to call for help, and gain useful information on stopping bleeding, applying bandages, and dealing with choking. (Rev: SLJ 4/02) [616.04]

4736 Gordon, Sharon. *Bruises* (1–2). Series: Rookie Read-About Health. 2002, Children's LB $19.00 (0-516-22568-5); paper $5.95 (0-516-26872-4). 31pp. Readers learn why bruises change color and how to treat them, with reminders of the protection that proper clothing can offer. Also use *Cuts and Scrapes* (2001). (Rev: SLJ 8/02) [616.04]

4737 Roberts, Robin. *Sports Injuries: How to Stay Safe and Keep on Playing* (5–8). Series: Get in the Game! With Robin Roberts. 2001, Millbrook LB $21.90 (0-7613-2116-0). 48pp. This general sports book that targets girls as a primary audience discusses safety in a variety of sports and how to cope

with injuries. (Rev: BL 9/15/01; HBG 3/02; SLJ 1/02) [790]

4738 Silverstein, Alvin, et al. *Bites and Stings* (3–5). Series: My Health. 2001, Watts LB $23.00 (0-531-11861-4). Insect and animal bites and stings are discussed with material on why they occur and on their prevention and treatment. (Rev: BL 1/1–15/02; SLJ 10/01) [617.1]

Sleep and Dreams

4739 Feeney, Kathy. *Sleep Well: Why You Need to Rest* (K–3). Series: Your Health. 2001, Capstone LB $13.95 (0-7368-0970-8). 24pp. Simple text and illustrations stress the importance of sleep and discuss sleepwalking and nightmares. (Rev: HBG 3/02; SLJ 4/02) [612.82]

4740 Garfield, Patricia. *The Dream Book: A Young Person's Guide to Understanding Dreams* (5–8). 2002, Tundra paper $9.95 (0-88776-594-7). 124pp. The author, a psychologist, explains the meanings of common (and uncommon) dreams and suggests how to use dreams to good effect. (Rev: BL 9/15/02; SLJ 9/02) [154.6]

4741 Gordon, Sharon. *A Good Night's Sleep* (3–5). Series: Rookie Read-About Health. 2002, Children's LB $19.00 (0-516-22570-7); paper $5.95 (0-516-26874-0). 32pp. After explaining the reasons why sleep is important, this easy-reader gives a few hints on how to fall asleep fast. (Rev: BL 12/15/02) [616.5]

4742 Lobb, Janice. *Counting Sheep! Why Do We Sleep?* (1–3). Series: At Home with Science. 2001, Kingfisher $10.95 (0-7534-5361-4). 32pp. Easily accomplished experiments answer questions involving why sleep is necessary, the important of lights, proper clothing materials, night fears, and bedroom critters. (Rev: BL 12/15/01; HBG 10/02; SLJ 2/02) [616.5]

4743 Mcphee, Andrew T. *Sleep and Dreams* (5–8). Illus. 2001, Watts LB $24.00 (0-531-11735-9). 111pp. Normal sleep patterns, sleep deprivation, and sleep disorders (sleep walking and sleep apnea) are discussed along with the nature and symbolism of dreams. (Rev: BL 6/1–15/01; SLJ 8/01) [616.8]

4744 Romanek, Trudee. *Zzz . . .: The Most Interesting Book You'll Ever Read About Sleep* (3–6). Illus. by Rose Cowles. 2002, Kids Can $14.95 (1-55074-944-7); paper $6.95 (1-55074-946-3). 40pp. With lively, amusing illustrations and an interesting text, this book covers such topics related to sleep as REM sleep, dreams, sleep cycles, snoring, and yawning. (Rev: BL 6/1–15/02; HBG 10/02; SLJ 6/02) [612.8]

Sex Education and Reproduction

Babies

4745 Cole, Joanna. *When You Were Inside Mommy* (PS). Illus. by Maxie Chambliss. 2001, Harper-Collins $5.95 (0-688-17043-9). 32pp. Basic facts about a child's development are presented in this small-format picture book. (Rev: BL 8/01; HBG 3/02; SLJ 12/01) [612.6]

4746 Heiligman, Deborah. *Babies: All You Need to Know* (K–2). Illus. by Laura Freeman. Series: Jump into Science. 2002, National Geographic $16.95 (0-7922-8205-1). 32pp. Young readers learn how babies grow, what they eat, how they learn, and so forth. (Rev: BCCB 10/02; BL 10/1/02; HBG 3/03; SLJ 10/02) [612.6]

4747 Johnson, Kelly. *Look at the Baby* (PS). Photos by author. 2002, Holt $14.95 (0-8050-6522-9). Photographs of multicultural babies look at noses, fingers, toes, and so forth. (Rev: BCCB 1/03; HBG 3/03; SLJ 12/02)

4748 Murkoff, Heidi. *What to Expect When the New Baby Comes Home* (PS–K). Illus. by Laura Rader. 2001, HarperCollins $7.99 (0-694-01327-7). 32pp. Angus the Answer Dog guides readers through answers to such questions as "What do new babies eat?" and "Can I play with the new baby?" (Rev: BL 7/01; HBG 10/01; SLJ 6/01) [305.232]

4749 Sears, William, et al. *Baby on the Way* (K–3). Illus. by Renee W. Andriani. 2001, Little, Brown $12.95 (0-316-78767-1). 32pp. A reassuring, colorfully illustrated book that tells young children about the effects of pregnancy on the mother. (Rev: BL 9/15/01; HBG 3/02; SLJ 10/01) [618.2]

4750 Sears, William, et al. *What Baby Needs* (K–3). Illus. by Renee W. Andriani. 2001, Little, Brown $12.95 (0-316-78828-7). 32pp. A readable look at the changes boys and girls can expect when they become big brothers or sisters. (Rev: BL 9/15/01; HBG 3/02; SLJ 10/01) [649]

Reproduction

4751 Fullick, Ann. *Test Tube Babies: In Vitro Fertilization* (5–8). Series: Science at the Edge. 2002, Heinemann LB $27.86 (1-58810-703-5). 64pp. This attractive book balances hard science with thought-provoking discussion on this controversial topic. (Rev: BL 10/15/02; HBG 3/03) [613.9]

4752 Jackson, Donna M. *Twin Tales: The Magic and Mystery of Multiple Birth* (5–8). Illus. 2001, Little, Brown $16.95 (0-316-45431-1). 48pp. A clear account of current scientific knowledge about multiple births, with anecdotes from children of multiple births and their families. (Rev: BCCB 2/01; BL 5/15/01; HB 3–4/01; HBG 10/01; SLJ 5/01*) [618.2]

Sex Education and Puberty

4753 Madaras, Lynda, and Area Madaras. *The What's Happening to My Body? Book for Boys: A Growing Up Guide for Parents and Sons*. 3rd ed. (4–8). Illus. 2001, Newmarket $22.95 (1-55704-447-3); paper $12.95 (1-55704-443-0). 238pp. This new edition of the classic guide has been recast to suit today's children and their earlier puberty. Also use *The What's Happening to My Body? Book for Girls: A Growing Up Guide for Parents and Daughters* (2001). (Rev: BL 9/1/01) [613.9]

Physical and Applied Sciences

General Science

Miscellaneous

4754 Bridgman, Roger. *1000 Inventions and Discoveries* (5–9). Illus. 2002, DK $24.99 (0-7894-8826-4). 256pp. A heavily illustrated overview of scientific discoveries, arranged chronologically with a timeline of concurrent historical and cultural events. (Rev: SLJ 3/03)

4755 Koss, Amy Goldman. *Where Fish Go in Winter and Other Great Mysteries* (PS–2). Illus. by Laura J. Bryant. Series: Dial Easy-to-Read. 2002, Dial $13.99 (0-8037-2704-6). 32pp. Beginning readers will enjoy these poetic answers to such questions as why onions make people cry and how cats purr. (Rev: BL 1/1–15/03; HBG 3/03; SLJ 1/03) [500]

4756 Kramer, Stephen. *Hidden Worlds: Looking Through a Scientist's Microscope* (4–7). Illus. Series: Scientists in the Field. 2001, Houghton $16.00 (0-618-05546-0). 61pp. Striking photographs, mostly taken with electron microscopes by scientist Dennis Kunkel, serve to illustrate this explanation of how scientists use microscopes in their work. (Rev: BL 8/01; HB 1–2/02; HBG 3/02; SLJ 9/01*) [570]

4757 Masoff, Joy. *Oh, Yuck! The Encyclopedia of Everything Nasty* (4–8). Illus. by Terry Sirrell. 2001, Workman paper $14.95 (0-7611-0771-1). 212pp. This unsavory, fact-filled look at smells, noises, creepy-crawlies, toilets, and other fascinating topics even includes some suitably gross experiments. (Rev: SLJ 5/01) [031.02]

4758 Ripley, Catherine. *Why? The Best Ever Question and Answer Book About Nature, Science and the World Around You* (K–2). Illus. by Scot Ritchie. 2001, Firefly $19.95 (1-894379-25-X). 192pp. Answers to typical children's questions are organized into sections such as supermarket, outdoor, kitchen, and farm animal. (Rev: HBG 3/02; SLJ 12/01) [500]

4759 Robinson, Richard. *Science Magic in the Bedroom: Amazing Tricks with Ordinary Stuff* (4–7). Illus. by Alan Rowe. Series: Science Magic. 2002, Simon & Schuster paper $4.99 (0-689-84335-6). 95pp. Robinson presents tricks that fool the sight, hearing, and touch and explains the underlying science and physiology. (Rev: SLJ 7/02) [507.8]

4760 Ross, Michael Elsohn. *Re-Cycles* (K–2). Illus. by Gustav Moore. 2002, Millbrook LB $22.90 (0-7613-1818-6). 32pp. Readers learn how water and soil are constantly being recycled for reuse, and how humans can contribute to nature's efforts. (Rev: BL 11/1/02; HBG 3/03; SLJ 1/03) [551.3]

4761 Schwartz, David M. *Q Is for Quark: A Science Alphabet Book* (4 Up). Illus. by Kim Doner. 2001, Tricycle Pr. $15.95 (1-58246-021-3). 64pp. An entertaining and informative alphabet book from atom to Zzzzzzzz that doesn't hesitate to tackle difficult topics. (Rev: HBG 3/02; SLJ 11/01) [500]

4762 Swanson, Diane. *Nibbling on Einstein's Brain* (5–8). Illus. by Warren Clark. 2001, Firefly $24.95 (1-55037-687-X); paper $14.95 (1-55037-686-1). 112pp. Swanson looks at "bad" science and examines the difference between sound scientific theory and hype, teaching kids how to ask the right questions when analyzing advertisers' claims. (Rev: BL 2/15/02; HBG 3/02; SLJ 11/01) [507.2]

Experiments and Projects

4763 Cobb, Vicki. *I Get Wet* (PS–2). Illus. by Julia Gorton. Series: Science Play. 2002, HarperCollins LB $17.89 (0-688-17839-1). 40pp. An introduction to the properties of water that includes bright illustrations and simple experiments sure to stimulate the curiosity of younger readers. Also use *I See Myself* (2002), an introduction to the properties of light. (Rev: BL 8/02; HB 11–12/02; HBG 3/03; SLJ 10/02) [546]

4764 Cobb, Vicki. *See for Yourself: More Than 100 Experiments for Science Fairs and Projects* (3–8). Illus. by Dave Klug. 2001, Scholastic $16.95 (0-439-09010-5); paper $7.95 (0-439-09011-3). 192pp. A collection of experiments and activities arranged by topic, with a notation of the level of difficulty. (Rev: HBG 10/02; SLJ 3/02) [507.8]

4765 Graham, John, et al. *Hands-On Science* (4–6). Illus. by David Le Jars. Series: Hands-On. 2002, Kingfisher paper $10.95 (0-7534-5440-8). 160pp. More than 100 easy-to-follow, nicely presented experiments teach students about basic science concepts. (Rev: SLJ 8/02)

4766 Haduch, Bill. *Science Fair Success Secrets: How to Win Prizes, Have Fun, and Think Like a Scientist* (5–8). Illus. by Philip Scheuer. 2002, Dutton paper $10.99 (0-525-46534-0). 128pp. A handy and appealing introduction to how to conduct a science experiment, with examples of award-winning projects, a list of ideas, and metric conversion tables. (Rev: BL 12/1/02; SLJ 3/03) [507]

4767 Levine, Shar, and Leslie Johnstone. *Bathtub Science* (2–6). Photos by Jeff Connery. Illus. by Dave Garbot. 2001, Sterling $19.95 (0-8069-7185-1). 80pp. Thirty-five experiments and activities that involve water — such as learning how a submarine works and making paper flowers that absorb moisture — are accompanied by colorful photographs, cartoons, and advice on safety. (Rev: HBG 10/01; SLJ 8/01) [532]

4768 Maynard, Chris. *Kitchen Science* (3–5). Illus. 2001, DK $12.95 (0-7894-6972-3). 48pp. A humorous and attractive collection of projects that include creating emulsions, observing mold, and making fizzy and bubbly concoctions. Also use *Backyard Science* (2001). (Rev: SLJ 12/01) [507.8]

4769 Ross, Michael Elsohn. *Toy Lab* (4–6). Illus. by Tim Seeley. Series: You Are the Scientist. 2002, Carolrhoda LB $23.93 (0-87614-456-3). 48pp. Toys such as slinkies, silly putty, frisbees, and blocks are all put to good use as readers learn about gravity, flight, motion, and other basic concepts. (Rev: HBG 3/03; SLJ 2/03)

4770 Rybolt, Thomas R., and Leah M. Rybolt. *Science Fair Success with Scents, Aromas, and Smells* (5–8). Series: Science Fair Success. 2002, Enslow LB $20.95 (0-7660-1625-0). 112pp. Several science fair projects using the sense of smell are presented with clear instructions and easy-to-find materials. (Rev: BL 5/15/02; HBG 10/02; SLJ 11/02) [507]

4771 Simon, Seymour, and Nicole Fauteux. *Let's Try It Out in the Air* (PS–4). Illus. by Doug Cushman. 2001, Simon & Schuster LB $15.00 (0-689-82918-3). 32pp. Children are encouraged to perform simple science experiments and consider such questions as why balloons fly or how the scent of cookies travels through the air. Also use *Let's Try It Out in the Water* (2001). (Rev: BL 12/1/01; HBG 3/02; SLJ 12/01) [533]

4772 Tocci, Salvatore. *Using Household Products* (5–8). Series: Science Fair Success. 2002, Enslow LB $20.95 (0-7660-1626-9). This useful volume outlines a number of science fair projects that can be done using materials found around the house. (Rev: BL 4/15/02; HBG 10/02) [509]

4773 Wells, Rosemary. *Discover and Explore* (PS–K). Illus. by Michael Koelsch. Series: Get Set for Kindergarten! 2001, Viking paper $5.99 (0-14-056845-X). 24pp. Wells uses familiar characters from her other books to explore concepts with Mrs. Jenkins and to join in activities that look at topics including buoyancy, the senses, and the seasons. (Rev: SLJ 10/01) [372.3]

Astronomy

General

4774 Bortz, Fred. *Collision Course! Cosmic Impacts and Life on Earth* (4–7). Illus. 2001, Millbrook $23.90 (0-7613-1403-2). 72pp. A straightforward discussion of an intriguing subject that includes material on past collisions and on detecting and perhaps deflecting future "near Earth objects." (Rev: BL 5/1/01; HBG 10/01; SLJ 5/01) [523.44]

4775 Davis, Kenneth C. *Don't Know Much About Space* (3–7). Illus. by Sergio Ruzzier. Series: Don't Know Much About. 2001, HarperCollins LB $19.89 (0-06-028602-4); paper $6.95 (0-06-440835-3). 144pp. An entertaining, informal, question-and-answer introduction to astronomy. (Rev: BL 9/15/01; HBG 3/02; SLJ 8/01) [520]

4776 Gifford, Clive. *The Kingfisher Facts and Records Book of Space: The Ultimate Information Database* (4–6). Illus. 2001, Kingfisher $14.95 (0-7534-5363-0). 64pp. Among the topics covered in this fact-packed volume are the solar system, the Milky Way and other galaxies, astronomical equipment, and man's journeys into space. (Rev: HBG 10/02; SLJ 12/01) [520]

4777 Graun, Ken, and Suzanne Maly. *Our Galaxy and the Universe* (4–6). Illus. Series: 21st Century Astronomy. 2002, Ken Pr. $15.95 (1-928771-08-4). 36pp. Excellent illustrations add to the appeal of this look at the stars. (Rev: SLJ 12/02)

4778 Jackson, Ellen. *Looking for Life in the Universe: The Search for Extraterrestrial Intelligence* (4–7). Illus. by Nic Bishop. 2002, Houghton $16.00 (0-618-12894-8). 64pp. Jackson examines the possibility of life elsewhere and profiles Dr. Jill Tarter, a research astrophysicist, as she searches for traces of an extraterrestrial signal. (Rev: BL 12/1/02; HB 1–2/03; HBG 3/03; SLJ 12/02) [576.8]

4779 Oleksy, Walter. *Mapping the Skies* (5–7). Series: Watts Library — Geography. 2002, Watts LB $24.00 (0-531-12031-7); paper $8.95 (0-531-16635-X). 64pp. From the ancient Greeks and Romans through Galileo to astronomers today, this is a history of how the stars, planets, and space have been mapped. (Rev: BL 10/15/02) [520]

4780 Simon, Seymour. *Destination: Space* (3–5). Illus. Series: Destination. 2002, HarperCollins LB $15.89 (0-688-16290-8). 32pp. An attractive collection of pictures from the Hubble Space Telescope with explanations of what these images from space mean. (Rev: BL 6/1–15/02; HB 9–10/02; HBG 3/03; SLJ 5/02) [520]

4781 Spangenburg, Ray, and Kit Moser. *The Hubble Space Telescope* (5–9). Illus. Series: Out of This World. 2002, Watts LB $32.00 (0-531-11894-0); paper $14.95 (0-531-15565-X). 128pp. A look at the telescope itself, its development and launch, the subsequent problems, and the information it has provided to scientists. (Rev: SLJ 12/02) [522]

4782 Tagholm, Sally. *The Complete Book of the Night* (4–6). Illus. 2001, Kingfisher $18.95 (0-7534-5323-1). 96pp. This eclectic overview looks at sleep and dreams, evening celebrations around the world, nocturnal plants and animals, and fireworks. (Rev: HBG 10/02; SLJ 2/02) [525]

4783 Wills, Susan, and Steven Wills. *Astronomy: Looking at the Stars* (5–8). Illus. Series: Innovators. 2001, Oliver LB $21.95 (1-881508-76-5). 144pp. A good starting point for research into astronomy, with profiles of individuals including Ptolemy, Copernicus, Galileo, and Newton. (Rev: HBG 10/02; SLJ 2/02) [520.922]

Earth

4784 Davis, Kenneth C. *Don't Know Much About Planet Earth* (3–6). Illus. by Tom Bloom. Series: Don't Know Much About. 2001, HarperCollins LB $19.89 (0-06-028600-8); paper $6.95 (0-06-440834-5). 144pp. A question-and-answer format with cartoonlike drawings makes an attractive backdrop for this overview of the earth's physical and environmental features, as well as today's political divisions and a timeline of historical highlights. (Rev: BL 12/15/01; HBG 3/02; SLJ 8/01) [910]

Moon

4785 Cole, Michael D. *The Moon: Earth's Companion in Space* (3–7). Series: Countdown to Space. 2001, Enslow LB $18.95. (0-7660-1510-6). 48pp. Handsomely illustrated with color and black-and-white photographs, this is a good introduction to the moon, its evolution, composition, and exploration. (Rev: BL 6/1–15/01; HBG 10/01) [523.3]

Planets

4786 Branley, Franklyn M. *Mission to Mars* (K–3). Illus. Series: Let's-Read-and-Find-Out Science. 2002, HarperCollins LB $17.89 (0-06-029808-1). 40pp. Readers are invited to travel along to a future Mars, where astronauts rendezvous with unmanned spacecraft, explore the surface, grow food, and drill for water. (Rev: BL 1/1–15/03; HBG 3/03; SLJ 10/02) [629.45]

4787 Gifford, Clive. *How to Live on Mars* (3–6). Illus. by Scoular Anderson. Series: How To. 2001, Watts LB $14.00 (0-531-14647-2); paper $4.95 (0-531-16201-X). 96pp. Experiments back up the concepts introduced in this discussion of the possibilities of traveling to and living on Mars. (Rev: SLJ 4/02) [523.4]

4788 Miller, Ron. *Jupiter* (5–8). Series: Worlds Beyond. 2002, Millbrook LB $25.90 (0-7613-2356-2). 64pp. An excellent oversize volume that explores the largest of the planets with amazing full-page color illustrations and a detailed text. Also use *Venus* (2002). (Rev: BL 8/02; HBG 3/03; SLJ 8/02) [523.4]

4789 Rau, Dana Meachen. *Jupiter* (3–5). Illus. Series: Our Solar System. 2002, Compass Point LB $15.95 (0-7565-0198-9). 32pp. An appealing introduction to the planet, with large photographs. Also use *Mars, Mercury*, and *Venus* (all 2002). (Rev: BL 5/15/02; SLJ 7/02) [523.45]

4790 Simon, Seymour. *Planets Around the Sun* (1–3). Series: See More Readers. 2002, North-South $13.95 (1-58717-145-7); paper $3.95 (1-58717-146-5). 32pp. The plants and the solar system are introduced in this beginning reader. (Rev: BL 7/02; HBG 10/02; SLJ 6/02) [523.2]

Solar System

4791 Davis, Kenneth C. *Don't Know Much About the Solar System* (3–5). Illus. by Pedro Martin. Series: Don't Know Much About. 2001, Harper-Collins LB $15.89 (0-06-028614-8). 47pp. A fact-filled, basic introduction to the parts of the solar system that takes a humorous, question-and-answer approach. (Rev: HBG 3/02; SLJ 11/01) [523.3]

4792 Graun, Ken. *Our Earth and the Solar System* (4–6). Illus. 2001, Ken Pr. $15.95 (1-928771-02-5). 36pp. A large-format, interesting guide to the solar system that also looks at the equipment we use to look at these bodies. (Rev: BL 5/1/01; SLJ 6/01) [523.2]

Stars

4793 Tomecek, Steve. *Stars* (K–3). Illus. by Sachiko Yoshikawa. 2003, National Geographic $16.95 (0-7922-6955-1). 32pp. A boy introduces young readers to the stars in this book that includes a star activity. (Rev: BL 2/1/03) [523.8]

Sun and the Seasons

4794 Branley, Franklyn M. *The Sun: Our Nearest Star*. Rev. ed. (K–2). Illus. by Edward Miller. Series: Let's-Read-and-Find-Out Science. 2002, HarperCollins LB $15.89 (0-06-028535-4); paper $4.95 (0-06-445202-6). 32pp. An updated edition of this standard text full of facts about the sun and about how we benefit from it. (Rev: BL 7/02; HBG 10/02; SLJ 7/02) [523.7]

4795 Dolan, Graham. *The Greenwich Guide to the Seasons* (3–6). Illus. Series: Greenwich Guide To. 2001, Heinemann LB $22.79 (1-58810-044-8). 32pp. Color photographs and clear text introduce the seasons, with a glossary and other aids. (Rev: BL 10/15/01) [525]

4796 Glaser, Linda. *It's Fall!* (2–4). Illus. by Susan Swan. 2001, Millbrook $21.90 (0-7613-1758-9). 32pp. A young boy observes the changes that occur in nature in the fall, with suggested nature activities for the season. (Rev: BL 9/15/01; HBG 3/02; SLJ 10/01)

4797 Jackson, Ellen. *The Summer Solstice* (2–4). Illus. 2001, Millbrook LB $21.90 (0-7613-1623-X). 32pp. An attractive resource that explains the summer solstice, why it is the longest day of the year, and its cultural significance. (Rev: BL 4/1/01; HBG 10/01; SLJ 5/01) [394.263]

4798 Meyer, Mary L. *Spring* (2–3). Series: Seasons. 2002, Smart Apple $21.35 (1-58340-143-1). 24pp. The weather, animals, plants, and activities of spring are presented in concise text with attractive full-color photographs. Also use *Fall* (2002). (Rev: SLJ 2/03)

4799 Miller, Ron. *The Sun* (5–8). Illus. Series: Worlds Beyond. 2002, Millbrook LB $25.90 (0-7613-2355-4). 64pp. Miller explores the nature and structure of the sun and the importance of solar energy. (Rev: BL 4/1/02; HBG 10/02; SLJ 5/02) [523.7]

Biological Sciences

General

4800 Arnold, Katya. *Let's Find It! My First Nature Guide* (PS–1). Illus. 2002, Holiday $16.95 (0-8234-1539-2). 32pp. Young readers search for plants and animals in painted scenes of habitats in this colorful introduction to nature. (Rev: BL 8/02; HBG 3/03; SLJ 10/02) [570]

4801 Batten, Mary. *Aliens from Earth: When Animals and Plants Invade Other Ecosystems* (3–5). Illus. by Beverly J. Doyle. 2003, Peachtree $15.95 (1-56145-236-X). 32pp. A narrative overview of the results of animal and plant migrations to new home ecosystems, with full-page illustrations. (Rev: BL 3/1/03) [577]

4802 Gallant, Roy A. *The Wonders of Biodiversity* (5–8). Illus. Series: The Story of Science. 2002, Benchmark LB $19.95 (0-7614-1427-4). 80pp. Gallant discusses the importance of biodiversity, the plight of species that are affected by loss of habitat and other environmental factors, and species interdependence. (Rev: HBG 3/03; SLJ 2/03)

4803 Gifford, Clive, and Jerry Cadle. *The Kingfisher Young People's Book of Living Worlds* (5–7). Illus. Series: Kingfisher Young People's Book Of. 2002, Kingfisher $21.95 (0-7534-5390-8). 80pp. Habitats and ecosystems are covered in an attractive, fact-filled format that looks at man's impact on nature. (Rev: HBG 3/03; SLJ 12/02)

4804 Green, Jen. *In a Backyard* (2–5). Illus. Series: Small World. 2002, Crabtree LB $15.96 (0-7787-0141-7); paper $8.06 (0-7787-0155-7). 32pp. This book for younger readers takes a close look at the creatures that might be found in a backyard, and how plant and animal life coexist there. (Rev: BL 10/15/02) [591.75]

4805 Jones, Jennifer Berry. *Who Lives in the Snow?* (PS–3). Illus. by Consie Powell. 2001, Court Wayne $15.95 (1-57098-287-2). 32pp. Cutaway illustra-

tions give young readers a glimpse below the surface of a snowy meadow to see what happens to plants, insects, and animals during winter. (Rev: BL 11/15/01) [591.4]

4806 Parker, Steve. *Survival and Change* (4–7). Series: Life Processes. 2001, Heinemann LB $21.36 (1-57572-340-9). 32pp. Parker considers how organisms evolve and looks at how species behave under threat and the origin of new species in this concise book with diagrams, charts, and color photographs. (Rev: HBG 10/01; SLJ 7/01) [578.4]

4807 Quinlan, Susan E. *The Case of the Monkeys That Fell from the Trees: And Other Mysteries in Tropical Nature* (5–8). Illus. 2003, Boyds Mills $15.95 (1-56397-902-0). 171pp. Quinlan introduces plant and animal mysteries in South and Central American tropical forests and shows how scientists approached solving them. (Rev: BL 3/1/03; SLJ 3/03) [508.313]

4808 Richardson, Hazel. *How to Clone a Sheep* (4–8). Illus. by Andy Cooke. 2001, Watts LB $14.00 (0-531-14645-6); paper $4.95 (0-531-16200-1). 92pp. Historical developments in the area of biotechnology are accompanied by scientific explanations and information about the scientists who do this kind of research. (Rev: SLJ 6/02) [174.957]

4809 Ross, Michael Elsohn. *Life Cycles* (2–4). Illus. by Gustav Moore. 2001, Millbrook LB $22.40 (0-7613-1817-8). 32pp. Young readers are introduced to the concept of life cycles through the stories a sunflower, a mushroom, and a grasshopper. (Rev: BL 8/01; HBG 3/02; SLJ 1/02) [571.8]

4810 Wallace, Holly. *Classification* (4–7). Series: Life Processes. 2001, Heinemann LB $21.36 (1-57572-337-9). 32pp. A concise look at the system that we use for classifying plants and animals, with diagrams, charts, and color photographs. Also use *Adaptation* and *Cells and Systems* (both 2001). (Rev: HBG 10/01; SLJ 7/01) [570]

Animal Life

General

4811 Armentrout, David, and Patricia Armentrout. *Animals* (PS–2). Series: 50 Words About. 2002, Rourke LB $26.60 (1-58952-341-5). 32pp. Simple definitions are given for 50 words about animals (camouflage, extinct, and so forth), along with a sentence that includes the word. (Rev: SLJ 3/03) [590]

4812 Arnosky, Jim. *Field Trips: Bug Hunting, Animal Tracking, Bird-Watching, Shore Walking* (3–5). Illus. by author. 2002, HarperCollins LB $15.89 (0-688-15173-6). 96pp. Young people heading on an expedition will find safety measures, guidance on observing and identifying animals, and advice on leaving nature unaltered, all in an appealing format with useful charts and notes. (Rev: HB 7–8/02; HBG 10/02; SLJ 6/02) [508]

4813 Berger, Melvin, and Gilda Berger. *Do Tarantulas Have Teeth? Questions and Answers About Poisonous Creatures* (3–5). Illus. by Jim Effler. Series: Scholastic Question and Answer. 2000, Scholastic $14.95 (0-439-09578-6); paper $5.95 (0-439-14877-4). 48pp. Using a question-and-answer format and bright, realistic illustrations, this title presents information on the methods poisonous animals use to inject their venom, how they hunt and feed, and their physical characteristics. (Rev: HBG 3/01; SLJ 5/01) [591]

4814 Bishop, Nic. *Backyard Detective: Critters Up Close* (1–3). Illus. 2002, Scholastic $16.95 (0-439-17478-3). 48pp. Photographic collages show "life-sized" animals and insects found in backyards across the United States, along with two pages of informational text about each and a section of nature projects. (Rev: BL 10/15/02; HBG 3/03; SLJ 10/02) [591.75]

4815 Doinet, Mymi. *The Meanest: Amazing Facts About Aggressive Animals* (3–5). Series: Faces of Nature. 2002, Random $8.99 (0-375-81407-8). Browsers will enjoy this informative and attractive book. Also use *The Laziest: Amazing Facts About Lazy Animals* (2002). (Rev: HBG 10/02; SLJ 5/02) [591.65]

4816 Donovan, Sandra. *Animals of Rivers, Lakes, and Ponds* (2–4). Series: Animals of the Biomes. 2003, Raintree Steck-Vaughn LB $24.26 (0-7398-5690-1). 48pp. The great blue heron, giant water bugs, raccoons, and snapping turtles are featured in this introduction. Also use *Desert Animals*, which looks at roadrunners, scorpions, camels, and Gila monsters. (Rev: HBG 3/03; SLJ 2/03)

4817 DuQuette, Keith. *They Call Me Woolly: What Animal Names Can Tell You* (K–4). Illus. 2002, Putnam $15.99 (0-399-23445-4). 32pp. Younger readers will discover how animal names — polar bear, zebra butterfly — reflect their traits in this informative and well-illustrated book. (Rev: BL 1/1–15/02; HBG 10/02; SLJ 2/02) [590]

4818 Fredericks, Anthony D. *Fearsome Fangs* (4–6). Illus. Series: Watts Library. 2002, Watts LB $24.00 (0-531-11966-1); paper $8.95 (0-531-16597-3). 63pp. Animals with alarming teeth — including some prehistoric beasts — are profiled here, with information on physical features, behavior, distribution, habitat, prey, and relationship with humans. (Rev: SLJ 1/03) [591.47]

4819 Jenkins, Steve, and Robin Page. *What Do You Do with a Tail Like This?* (PS–2). Illus. 2003, Houghton $15.00 (0-618-25628-8). 32pp. The tails, mouths, and other parts of different animals are rendered in cut paper, illustrating interesting animal facts. (Rev: BCCB 3/03; BL 2/15/03*; SLJ 3/03) [573.8]

4820 Kaner, Etta. *Animals at Work: How Animals Build, Dig, Fish and Trap* (2–4). Illus. by Pat Stephens. 2001, Kids Can $10.95 (1-55074-673-1); paper $5.95 (1-55074-675-8). 40pp. Activities, a game, and a quiz are provided in this basic look at the work various animals have to do to find food, shelter, and mates. (Rev: HBG 3/02; SLJ 10/01) [591.5]

4821 Lewin, Ted. *Tooth and Claw: Animal Adventures in the Wild* (3–6). Illus. 2003, HarperCollins LB $16.89 (0-688-14106-4). 112pp. Author Lewin reports on fascinating, face-to-face encounters with animals ranging from raccoons and a howler monkey to bears and sharks, with maps, notes on each animal, and copious illustrations. (Rev: BL 1/1–15/03; HB 3–4/03) [590]

4822 Martin, James W. R. *In a House* (2–5). Series: Small World. 2002, Crabtree LB $15.96 (0-7787-0140-9); paper $8.06 (0-7787-0154-9). 32pp. From bugs and rodents to insects and worms, this is a run-down of the animal life that can be found inside a house. (Rev: BL 10/15/02) [591]

4823 Maze, Stephanie, ed. *Beautiful Moments in the Wild: Animals and Their Colors* (PS–K). Series: Moments in the Wild. 2002, Moonstone $15.00 (0-9707768-7-X). An attractive picture book showing the diversity of animal colors in full-color shots. (Rev: SLJ 3/03)

4824 Presnall, Judith Janda. *Animal Actors* (4–6). Series: Animals with Jobs. 2002, Gale LB $23.70 (0-7377-0934-0). 48pp. Animals that work in television and movies are profiled here with information on their training and care. Also use *Navy Dolphins* (2002). (Rev: SLJ 3/02) [791.43]

4825 Ruurs, Margriet. *Wild Babies* (PS–2). Illus. by Andrew Kiss. 2003, Tundra $14.95 (0-88776-627-7). 32pp. Young animals and birds found in a North American forest are shown in lush, detailed paintings that provide intriguing hints of the next animal. (Rev: SLJ 2/03)

4826 Shields, Carol Diggory. *Homes* (PS–3). Illus. by Svjetlan Junakovic. Series: Animagicals. 2001, Handprint $9.95 (1-929766-27-0). 32pp. Rhyming riddles give clues about animal homes hidden under the flaps in this tall-format picture book. (Rev: BL 2/1/02; HBG 3/02; SLJ 2/02) [811]

4827 Squire, Ann O. *African Animals* (2–3). Series: True Books — Animals. 2001, Children's LB

$23.00 (0-516-22186-6). 48pp. A compact guide to the most common animals of Africa is presented in a simple text with color photographs on each page. (Rev: BL 12/15/01) [599]

4828 Suen, Anastasia. *ASPCA* (1–2). Series: Helping Organizations. 2002, Rosen LB $16.00 (0-8239-6004-8). 24pp. As well as a history of this organization, this easily read account describes how it works and how young people can get involved. (Rev: BL 6/1–15/02; SLJ 4/02) [179.3]

4829 Wadsworth, Ginger. *River Discoveries* (2–4). Illus. by Paul Kratter. 2002, Charlesbridge $16.95 (1-57091-418-4); paper $6.95 (1-57091-419-2). 32pp. An introduction to the varied wildlife that surrounds and depends on a river, describing the activities of 13 types of animals over a 24-hour period. (Rev: BL 9/15/02; HBG 3/03; SLJ 8/02) [591.76]

Amphibians and Reptiles

GENERAL AND MISCELLANEOUS

4830 Jango-Cohen, Judith. *Desert Iguanas* (PS–2). Series: Pull Ahead Books. 2001, Lerner LB $22.95 (0-8225-3635-8). 32pp. A color photograph and two lines of simple text are found on each page of this attractive basic introduction to these desert reptiles. (Rev: BL 6/1–15/01; HBG 10/01) [597.9]

4831 Llewellyn, Claire. *Question Time: Reptiles* (3–5). Illus. Series: Question Time. 2002, Kingfisher $11.95 (0-7534-5451-3); paper $6.95 (0-7534-5463-7). 32pp. Topics covered in a question-and-answer format include the different types of reptiles, and their characteristics, habitat, and defense mechanisms. (Rev: HBG 3/03; SLJ 2/03)

4832 *Reptiles* (3–5). Ed. by Simon Holland. 2002, DK LB $17.95 (0-7894-8555-9). 48pp. This is a visually stunning introduction to all kinds of reptiles with details on their characteristics, habits, and habitats. (Rev: BL 6/1–15/02; HBG 10/02) [597.96]

4833 Sill, Cathryn. *About Amphibians: A Guide for Children* (PS–2). Illus. by John Sill. 2001, Peachtree $14.95 (1-56145-234-3). 40pp. An introduction for young children that has colorful, realistic paintings facing brief text. (Rev: BL 5/15/01; HBG 10/01; SLJ 6/01) [597.8]

4834 Stewart, Melissa. *Amphibians* (2–3). Series: True Books — Animals. 2001, Children's LB $23.00 (0-516-22037-3). 48pp. In this colorful, simple volume, a variety of amphibians are introduced with material on their appearance, habits, and distinctive characteristics. (Rev: BL 12/15/01) [597.6]

ALLIGATORS AND CROCODILES

4835 Jango-Cohen, Judith. *Crocodiles* (4–6). Series: Animals Animals. 2002, Benchmark LB $15.95 (0-7614-1446-0). 48pp. This is an oversize book filled with excellent photographs and text covering the anatomy, habits, food, and habitats of crocodiles. (Rev: BL 12/15/02; HBG 3/03; SLJ 2/03) [597.98]

4836 Kallen, Stuart A., and P. M. Boekhoff. *Alligators* (4–6). Series: Nature's Predators. 2002, Gale LB $23.70 (0-7377-0642-2). Color photographs are

used with a simple text to describe characteristics of alligators and their habitats, with coverage on how they kill their prey and how they also are hunted. (Rev: BL 1/1–15/02; SLJ 6/02) [597.98]

4837 London, Jonathan. *Crocodile: Disappearing Dragon* (1–3). Illus. by Paul Morin. 2001, Candlewick $15.99 (1-56402-634-5). 32pp. The tale of a mother alligator's encounter with a hunter lays the scene for a thoughtful account of the plight of the nearly extinct species, including facts about its life cycle and habitat. (Rev: BL 12/1/01; HBG 3/02; SLJ 11/01) [596.698]

4838 Noonan, Diana. *The Crocodile* (2–4). Illus. Series: Life Cycles. 2002, Chelsea LB $14.95 (0-7910-6964-8). 32pp. Handsome photographs and simple text describe the life cycle, habitat, appearance, and predators of the crocodile, in a small, square, photo-essay format. (Rev: BL 1/1–15/03; HBG 3/03) [597.98]

FROGS AND TOADS

4839 Arnosky, Jim. *All About Frogs* (2–4). Illus. Series: All About. 2002, Scholastic $15.95 (0-590-48164-9). 32pp. Excellent illustrations accompany the in-depth information about the anatomy and habitats of various species of frogs in this book for younger readers. (Rev: BL 2/1/02; HB 3–4/02; HBG 10/02; SLJ 3/02) [597.8]

4840 Noonan, Diana. *The Frog* (2–4). Series: Life Cycles. 2002, Chelsea LB $14.95 (0-7910-6966-4). 32pp. This account follows the life cycle of this amphibian from egg to tadpole and finally the growth of lungs and legs needed to live on land. (Rev: BL 12/15/02; HBG 3/03) [597.8]

4841 Stone, Tanya. *Toads* (3–5). Series: Wild America. 2002, Gale LB $24.94 (1-56711-646-9). 24pp. A close-up look at these amphibians that gives material on where they live and their physical features, life cycle, and habits. (Rev: BL 10/15/02) [597.8]

4842 Vern, Alex. *Where Do Frogs Come From?* (K–2). 2001, Harcourt paper $3.95 (0-15-216296-8). An easy-reading, lively introduction to the life of a frog. (Rev: HBG 3/02; SLJ 12/01) [597.8]

4843 Wechsler, Doug. *Bullfrogs* (3–6). Series: The Really Wild Life of Frogs. 2002, Rosen LB $18.75 (0-8239-5855-8). 24pp. The bullfrog's physical characteristics, habitat, diet, predators, and so forth are presented with close-up photographs and boxed features. Also use *Leopard Frogs*, *Treefrogs*, and *Wood Frogs* (all 2002). (Rev: SLJ 5/02) [597.89]

LIZARDS

4844 Mattern, Joanne. *Lizards* (3–6). Series: Animals, Animals. 2001, Benchmark LB $15.95 (0-7614-1259-X). 48pp. In addition to describing physical characteristics, behavior, habitat, and so forth of more than two dozen species, Mattern looks at related folklore and at the animals' relationship with humans. (Rev: HBG 10/02; SLJ 6/02) [597.95]

4845 Welsbacher, Anne. *Komodo Dragons* (3–5). Series: Predators in the Wild. 2002, Capstone LB

$21.26 (0-7368-1066-8). 32pp. Basic information about the komodo dragon's life, habitat, diet, and endangered status is presented in a format that will suit both browsers and report writers. (Rev: SLJ 8/02) [597.95]

SNAKES

4846 Behler, Deborah, and John Behler. *Snakes* (5–8). Series: AnimalWays. 2001, Marshall Cavendish LB $19.95 (0-7614-1265-4). 112pp. Brilliant photographs highlight this fine introduction to snakes, their habitats, behavior, species, evolution, and anatomy. (Rev: BL 3/15/02; HBG 10/02) [597.96]

4847 Greenaway, Theresa. *Snakes* (4–7). Series: The Secret World of . . . 2001, Raintree Steck-Vaughn LB $18.98 (0-7368-3510-6). 48pp. A look at the world of snakes with material on their structure, habitats, behavior, food, mating habits, and enemies. (Rev: BL 10/15/01) [597.96]

4848 Ruth, Maria Mudd. *Snakes* (3–6). Series: Animals, Animals. 2001, Benchmark LB $15.95 (0-7614-1262-X). 48pp. In addition to describing physical characteristics, behavior, habitat, locomotion, and so forth of more than a dozen species, Mattern looks at related folklore and at the animals' relationship with humans. (Rev: HBG 10/02; SLJ 6/02) [597.96]

4849 Welsbacher, Anne. *Anacondas* (3–6). Series: Predators in the Wild. 2001, Capstone LB $15.95 (0-7368-0785-3). 32pp. Myths about the anaconda are presented along with facts in this general introduction to the snake's characteristics and habitat. (Rev: HBG 10/01; SLJ 1/02) [597.96]

TURTLES AND TORTOISES

4850 Cooper, Jason. *Loggerhead Turtle* (1–3). Series: Life Cycles. 2002, Rourke LB $23.93 (1-58952-354-7). 24pp. Handsome photographs and simple text describe the life cycle, habitat, appearance, and behavior of these animals. (Rev: SLJ 12/02) [597.92]

4851 Davies, Nicola. *One Tiny Turtle* (PS–4). Illus. by Janet Chapman. 2001, Candlewick $15.99 (0-7636-1549-8). 32pp. An appealing overview of the loggerhead sea turtle, introduced by the story of one turtle's life from hatching to laying her own eggs on the beach of her birth. (Rev: BCCB 11/01; BL 12/1/01; HBG 3/02; SLJ 12/01) [597.92]

4852 Kalman, Bobbie. *The Life Cycle of a Sea Turtle* (2–4). Illus. Series: The Life Cycle. 2001, Crabtree LB $15.45 (0-7787-0652-4); paper $5.36 (0-7787-0682-6). 32pp. After a general description of the sea turtle, the author clearly explains its life cycle and discusses what can be done to curb human encroachment. (Rev: SLJ 6/02) [597.92]

4853 Korman, Susan. *Box Turtle at Silver Pond Lake* (K–3). Illus. by Stephen Marchesi. Series: Smithsonian Backyard. 2001, Smithsonian Institution $15.95 (1-56899-860-0). 32pp. A female box turtle's daily life is presented in simple text with realistic illustrations. (Rev: BL 9/15/01; HBG 10/01; SLJ 8/01)

4854 Noonan, Diana. *The Green Turtle* (2–4). Series: Life Cycles. 2002, Chelsea LB $14.95 (0-7910-6967-2). 32pp. The story of this endangered reptile that lives and mates in the sea is told with material on how the female goes ashore to lay her eggs and what happens when the young hatch. (Rev: BL 12/15/02; HBG 3/03) [597.92]

4855 Theodorou, Rod. *Leatherback Sea Turtle* (2–4). Illus. Series: Animals in Danger. 2001, Heinemann LB $21.36 (1-57572-272-0). 32pp. Basic information about the sea turtle and its endangered status. (Rev: BL 7/01; HBG 10/01) [597.2]

Animal Behavior and Anatomy

GENERAL

4856 Arnold, Caroline. *Did You Hear That? Animals with Super Hearing* (3–5). Illus. by Cathy Trachok. 2001, Charlesbridge $16.95 (1-57091-404-4). 32pp. This book full of color pictures introduces bats' and dolphins' echolocation skills, rhinos' ability to communicate over long distances, and other facts to do with animal hearing. (Rev: BL 12/1/01; HBG 3/02; SLJ 8/01) [591.59]

4857 Aruego, Jose, and Ariane Dewey. *Weird Friends: Unlikely Allies in the Animal Kingdom* (1–3). Illus. 2002, Harcourt $16.00 (0-15-202128-0). 40pp. Fourteen symbiotic relationships among animals are explained and brightly illustrated. (Rev: BL 5/15/02; HBG 10/02; SLJ 4/02) [577.8]

4858 Bonsignore, Joan. *Stick Out Your Tongue! Fantastic Facts, Features, and Functions of Animal and Human Tongues* (2–3). Illus. by John T. Ward. 2001, Peachtree $15.95 (1-56145-230-0). 32pp. A look at how animals of all kinds use their tongues with comparisons to similar human behavior. (Rev: BL 8/01; HBG 3/02; SLJ 11/01) [612.8]

4859 Bredeson, Carmen. *Animals That Migrate* (3–5). Series: Watts Library. 2001, Watts LB $24.00 (0-531-11865-7); paper $8.95 (0-531-16573-6). 63pp. The travels of fish, birds, insects, and other animals are detailed in this well-illustrated volume. Also use *Animals That Hibernate* (2001). (Rev: SLJ 2/02) [591.568]

4860 Collard, Sneed B., III. *Leaving Home* (PS–3). Illus. by Joan Dunning. 2002, Houghton $15.00 (0-618-11454-8). 32pp. This unique book for younger readers explores the various ways in which animals leave their homes upon maturation. (Rev: BL 3/1/02; HBG 10/02; SLJ 4/02) [591.5]

4861 Dolbear, Emily J., and E. Russell Primm. *Kangaroos Have Joeys* (K–2). Series: Animals and Their Young. 2001, Compass Point LB $18.60 (0-7565-0061-3). 24pp. Close-up color photographs accompany information on gestation, birth, and growth, along with a lighthearted "Did You Know?" facts section. Also use *Pandas Have Cubs* (2001). (Rev: SLJ 11/01) [599.2]

4862 Goodman, Susan E. *Claws, Coats, and Camouflage: The Ways Animals Fit into Their World* (2–5). Illus. by Michael Doolittle. 2001, Millbrook

$22.90 (0-7613-1865-8). 48pp. The ways in which animals (and finally, humans) adapt to their worlds are presented in broad categories with brief text and photographs. (Rev: BL 12/1/01; HBG 3/02; SLJ 1/02) [591.4]

4863 Jenkins, Steve, and Robin Page. *Animals in Flight* (PS–3). Illus. by Steve Jenkins. 2001, Houghton $16.00 (0-618-12351-2). 32pp. The wonder of flight is explained in simple prose and sensational cut-paper collages. (Rev: BCCB 12/01; BL 12/15/01; HBG 3/02; SLJ 11/01) [573.7]

4864 Kalman, Bobbie. *How Do Animals Find Food?* (2–4). Illus. Series: The Science of Living Things. 2001, Crabtree LB $14.97 (0-86505-986-1); paper $5.36 (0-86505-963-2). 32pp. Colorful illustrations present details of animals of various kinds and their ways of killing and devouring their prey. (Rev: SLJ 12/01) [591.5]

4865 Myers, Jack. *How Dogs Came from Wolves: And Other Explorations of Science in Action* (3–6). Illus. by John Rice. 2001, Boyds Mills $17.95 (1-56397-411-8). 64pp. A professor of zoology presents 12 fascinating animal abilities and adaptations, such as elephant "speech" and dog domestication. (Rev: BL 9/15/01; HBG 3/02; SLJ 10/01) [590]

4866 Singer, Marilyn. *A Pair of Wings* (2–3). Illus. by Anne Wertheim. 2001, Holiday $16.95 (0-8234-1547-3). 32pp. A fascinating introduction to all the ways in which animals' wings are used in addition to simple flying. (Rev: BL 5/15/01; HBG 10/01; SLJ 6/01) [591.47]

4867 Swanson, Diane. *Animals Can Be So Playful* (K–1). Illus. by Rose Cowles. Series: Animals Can Be So. 2002, Douglas & McIntyre $10.95 (1-55054-900-6). 24pp. Various animals are seen at play in a series of excellent color photographs and an accompanying simple text. (Rev: BL 4/1/02) [591.5]

4868 Swanson, Diane. *Headgear That Hides and Plays* (2–4). Series: Up Close. 2001, Greystone $9.95 (1-55054-819-0). 32pp. This interesting science book starts with the human skin and then describes the outer coverings of different animals, from the armored skin of an African rhino to the poison-packed needles on the back of a red lionfish. (Rev: BL 8/1/01; SLJ 1/02) [591]

4869 Swanson, Diane. *Skin That Slimes and Scares* (2–4). Series: Up Close. 2001, Greystone $9.95 (1-55054-817-4). 32pp. Beginning with the human skull, this book describe the head structure of a number of animals from birds to the musk ox and tells how their heads help them to compete, court, and defend themselves. (Rev: BL 8/1/01; SLJ 1/02) [591]

BABIES

4870 Batten, Mary. *Hey, Daddy! Animal Fathers and Their Babies* (K–3). Illus. by Higgins Bond. 2002, Peachtree $15.95 (1-56145-272-6). 32pp. Detailed illustrations are paired with descriptive text to introduce animal fathers that share in parenting. (Rev: BL 10/1/02; HBG 3/03; SLJ 12/02) [591.56]

4871 Fraser, Mary Ann. *How Animal Babies Stay Safe* (PS–1). Illus. Series: Let's-Read-and-Find-Out

Science. 2002, HarperCollins $15.95 (0-06-028803-5). 40pp. An introduction to the many ways in which nature protects baby animals, from camouflage to parental supervision. (Rev: BL 2/1/02; HBG 10/02; SLJ 2/02) [591.56]

4872 Hickman, Pamela. *Animals and Their Young: How Animals Produce and Care for Their Babies* (3–5). Illus. by Pat Stephens. 2003, Kids Can $10.95 (1-55337-061-9); paper $5.95 (1-55337-062-7). 40pp. This picture-book-format account shows animals' reproductive habits and care of the young. (Rev: BL 3/1/03) [591.56]

4873 Maze, Stephanie, ed. *Tender Moments in the Wild: Animals and Their Babies* (PS–2). 2001, Moonstone $15.00 (0-9707768-0-2). Adult animals caring for their young are shown in attractive spreads with minimal text. (Rev: SLJ 12/01)

4874 Simon, Seymour. *Baby Animals* (1–3). Series: See More Readers. 2002, North-South $13.95 (1-58717-170-8); paper $3.95 (1-58717-171-6). 32pp. Double-page spreads containing a brief text opposite a color photograph introduce a number of different baby animals with material on how they are raised. (Rev: BL 7/02; HBG 3/03; SLJ 10/02) [591.3]

4875 Singer, Marilyn. *Tough Beginnings: How Baby Animals Survive* (2–4). Illus. by Anna Vojtech. 2001, Holt $16.95 (0-8050-6164-9). 32pp. The chances of survival for some animal babies — and the very varied threats — are the subject of this interesting book that combines straightforward text and appealing illustrations. (Rev: BL 8/01; HB 9–10/01; HBG 3/02; SLJ 8/01) [591.3]

4876 Squire, Ann O. *Animal Babies* (2–3). Series: True Books — Animals. 2001, Children's LB $23.00 (0-516-22188-4). 48pp. The young of many species are presented in colorful pictures and simple text. (Rev: BL 12/15/01) [591.3]

CAMOUFLAGE

4877 Kalman, Bobbie. *What Are Camouflage and Mimicry?* (2–4). Illus. Series: The Science of Living Things. 2001, Crabtree LB $14.97 (0-86505-985-3); paper $5.36 (0-86505-962-4). 32pp. Dramatic close-up photographs with informative captions accompany details of animals' efforts to become invisible. (Rev: SLJ 12/01) [591]

4878 Stone, Tanya Lee. *Living in a World of Green: Where Survival Means Blending In* (2–4). Series: Living in a World Of. 2001, Gale LB $17.95 (1-56711-583-7). 24pp. A look at animal camouflage in temperate and tropical areas, with photographs, facts, and clear, spare text. Also use *Living in a World of White: Where Survival Means Blending In* (2001). (Rev: HBG 3/02; SLJ 1/02) [591]

4879 Swanson, Diane. *Animals Can Be So Hard to See* (K–1). Illus. by Rose Cowles. Series: Animals Can Be So. 2002, Douglas & McIntyre $10.95 (1-55054-901-4). 24pp. Using double-page spreads with a color photograph on one side and simple text on the other, the camouflaging abilities of a variety of animals are explored. (Rev: BL 4/1/02; SLJ 8/02) [591.47]

COMMUNICATION

4880 Jenkins, Steve. *Slap, Squeak, and Scatter: How Animals Communicate* (K–3). Illus. 2001, Houghton $16.00 (0-618-03376-9). 48pp. An introduction to the many wonderful ways in which animals communicate with each other. (Rev: BL 5/15/01; HBG 10/01; SLJ 5/01) [591.59]

4881 Kaner, Etta. *Animal Talk: How Animals Communicate Through Sight, Sound and Smell* (2–4). Illus. by Greg Douglas. 2002, Kids Can $10.95 (1-55074-982-X); paper $5.95 (1-55074-984-6). 40pp. Double-page spreads with photographs and original artwork explain how a variety of animals communicate through smell, sound, and body language. (Rev: BL 4/15/02; HBG 10/02; SLJ 7/02) [581.59]

4882 Sayre, April Pulley. *Secrets of Sound: Studying the Calls and Songs of Whales, Elephants, and Birds* (4–7). Illus. 2002, Houghton $16.00 (0-618-01514-0). 64pp. Fascinating profiles of scientists who study animal sounds serve to introduce readers to a number of scientific concepts. (Rev: BL 12/1/02; HB 9–10/02; HBG 3/03; SLJ 10/02) [559.159]

4883 Schlein, Miriam. *Hello, Hello!* (K–2). Illus. by Daniel Kirk. 2002, Simon & Schuster $16.95 (0-689-83435-7). 32pp. This simple picture book shows how different animals greet each other. (Rev: BL 6/1–15/02; HB 7–8/02; HBG 10/02; SLJ 7/02) [591.59]

HOMES

4884 Squire, Ann O. *Animal Homes* (2–3). Series: True Books — Animals. 2001, Children's LB $23.00 (0-516-22189-2). 48pp. Various kinds of animal homes are presented with well-captioned color pictures on each page plus a few lines of accompanying text. (Rev: BL 12/15/01) [591.56]

REPRODUCTION

4885 Gill, Shelley. *The Egg* (K–3). Illus. by Jo-Ellen Bosson. 2001, Charlesbridge $16.95 (1-57091-377-3). 32pp. A fact-filled book about eggs and egg-bearers with attractive illustrations and humorous text. (Rev: BCCB 2/01; BL 11/1/01; HBG 3/02; SLJ 7/01) [591.4]

Animal Species

GENERAL AND MISCELLANEOUS

4886 Berger, Melvin, and Gilda Berger. *Brrr! A Book About Polar Animals* (1–4). 2001, Scholastic paper $3.99 (0-439-20165-9). The wildlife of the Arctic and Antarctic is described with well-chosen illustrations and plenty of simple facts. (Rev: SLJ 9/01) [591.7]

4887 Butler, John. *Whose Baby Am I?* (PS). Illus. 2001, Viking $10.99 (0-670-89683-7). 24pp. Nine animal babies ask "Whose baby am I?" and the answer is found by turning the page. (Rev: BL 6/1–15/01; HBG 10/01; SLJ 7/01) [591.39]

4888 Cole, Melissa. *Rhinos* (3–5). Series: Wild Africa. 2002, Gale LB $19.95 (1-56711-633-7). 24pp. An introduction to the life and habits of this heavy pachyderm that, in spite of its reputation, is a peaceful herbivore now facing extinction in many parts of Asia and Africa. Also use *Hippos, Wildebeest*, and *Zebras* (all 2002). (Rev: BL 10/15/02) [599.72]

4889 Jacobs, Lee. *Raccoon* (3–5). Illus. Series: Wild America. 2002, Gale LB $19.95 (1-56711-644-2). 24pp. Packed with colorful photographs, this volume is filled with information about the life of the raccoon. (Rev: BL 10/15/02; SLJ 2/03) [599.76]

4890 MacKen, JoAnn Early. *Zebras* (K–2). Series: Animals I See at the Zoo. 2002, Gareth Stevens LB $18.60 (0-8368-3277-9). 24pp. Large type and clear pictures make this introduction appealing to beginning readers. (Rev: SLJ 2/03) [599.72]

4891 Markert, Jenny. *Zebras* (2–4). Series: Naturebooks. 2001, Child's World LB $24.21 (1-56766-883-6). 32pp. Double-page spreads (color photograph on one page, simple text on the other) are used to introduce this animal and its habitats. Also use *Rhinos* (2001). (Rev: BL 9/15/01; HBG 10/01) [599.72]

4892 Miller, Sara Swan. *Moles and Hedgehogs: What They Have in Common* (3–5). Series: Animals in Order. 2001, Watts LB $23.00 (0-531-11633-6). 32pp. Using two-page spreads (a color photograph on one side and text on the other), the world of these related mammals is explored. (Rev: BL 6/1–15/01) [599.3]

4893 Nelson, Kristin L. *Spraying Skunks* (2–3). Series: Pull Ahead Books. 2003, Lerner LB $22.60 (0-8225-4670-1); paper $5.95 (0-8225-3598-X). 32pp. An introduction to skunks and their habits that contains many color photographs and a map activity. (Rev: BL 3/15/03) [599.74]

4894 Penny, Malcolm. *Black Rhino* (3–6). Illus. Series: Natural World. 2001, Raintree Steck-Vaughn LB $18.98 (0-7398-4438-5). 48pp. A fine guide to the black rhinoceros with accessible text, memorable photographs, a glossary, and list of Web sites. (Rev: BL 12/15/01; HBG 10/02) [599.66]

4895 Pringle, Laurence. *Strange Animals, New to Science* (4–7). Illus. 2002, Marshall Cavendish $16.95 (0-7614-5083-1). 112pp. The results of scientists' efforts to discover new animal species are presented here, with color photographs and coverage of the reasons behind disappearing habitats. (Rev: BCCB 9/02; BL 7/02; HBG 10/02; SLJ 8/02) [591.68]

4896 Ring, Susan. *Project Hippopotamus* (3–6). Illus. Series: Zoo Life. 2002, Weigl LB $15.95 (1-59036-013-3). 32pp. This volume looks at both the good and bad aspects of raising hippopotamuses in zoos, and discusses their natural habitat, physiology, and so forth, using color photographs and featured sidebars. (Rev: BL 12/15/02; HBG 3/03) [599.63]

4897 Sharth, Sharon. *Wildebeests* (K–3). Series: Naturebooks. 2001, Child's World LB $24.21 (1-56766-882-8). 32pp. Concise text and full-page photographs present basic information on the wildebeest in a friendly, question-and-answer format. (Rev: SLJ 7/01) [599.64]

4898 Souza, D. M. *Skunks Do More Than Stink!* (3–5). Illus. 2002, Millbrook LB $21.90 (0-7613-2503-4). 32pp. This volume is filled with photographs and easily understandable text about the lives of skunks. (Rev: BL 3/1/02; HBG 10/02; SLJ 3/02) [599.76]

4899 Stanley, George Edward. *Wild Horses* (2–4). Illus. by Michael Langham Rowe. Series: Road to Reading. 2001, Golden Books $11.99 (0-307-46409-1); paper $3.99 (0-307-26409-2). 40pp. An introduction to wild horses found around the world today, with information on prehistoric horses and on efforts today to save wild horses. (Rev: BL 8/01; HBG 3/02) [599.665]

4900 Stewart, Melissa. *Hippopotamuses* (2–3). Series: Animals. 2002, Children's LB $23.00 (0-516-22200-7); paper $6.95 (0-516-26991-7). 48pp. The anatomy, life cycle, and habits of the hippopotamus are covered in a simple, large-type text and many color photographs. Also use *Rhinoceroses* and *Zebras* (both 2002). (Rev: BL 8/02) [599.63]

4901 Stone, Tanya. *Skunk* (3–5). Series: Wild America. 2002, Gale LB $24.94 (1-56711-641-8). 24pp. A photo-essay on this much-shunned animal with material on its appearance, unusual abilities, food, and life cycle. (Rev: BL 10/15/02; SLJ 2/03) [599.74]

4902 Swanson, Diane. *Skunks* (2–4). Series: Welcome to the World of Animals. 2002, Gareth Stevens LB $22.60 (0-8368-3317-1). 32pp. A slim volume that provides information on the animal's home, diet, communication, and lifestyle. (Rev: HBG 3/03; SLJ 3/03) [599.74]

4903 Theodorou, Rod. *Black Rhino* (K–2). Illus. Series: Animals in Danger. 2000, Heinemann LB $21.36 (1-57572-262-3). 32pp. The endangered black rhino is introduced, with information on diet, habitat, life cycle, and so on, as well as the reasons why the animal is imperiled. (Rev: HBG 3/01; SLJ 4/01) [599]

APE FAMILY

4904 Goodall, Jane. *The Chimpanzees I Love: Saving Their World and Ours* (5–8). Illus. 2001, Scholastic $17.95 (0-439-21310-X). 80pp. Jane Goodall combines details of her own life researching chimpanzees with fact-filled descriptions of the animals' behavior and a cry for chimpanzee protection. (Rev: BL 12/1/01; HB 1–2/02; HBG 3/02; SLJ 9/01*) [599]

4905 Jango-Cohen, Judith. *Gorillas* (4–6). Series: Animals Animals. 2002, Benchmark LB $15.95 (0-7614-1444-4). 48pp. The world of the giant gorilla is explored in this volume that covers topics including physical characteristics, habitat, care of the young, food, and social life. (Rev: BL 12/15/02; HBG 3/03) [599.884]

4906 Kane, Karen. *Mountain Gorillas* (2–3). Series: Early Bird Nature Books. 2001, Lerner LB $22.60 (0-8255-3040-6). 48pp. An easy-to-read text and numerous color photographs highlight this introduc-

tion to mountain gorillas that covers their life cycle, habits, anatomy, and habitats. (Rev: BL 8/1/01) [599.884]

4907 Platt, Richard. *Apes and Other Hairy Primates* (4–8). Illus. Series: Secret Worlds. 2001, DK $14.95 (0-7894-8003-4); paper $7.95 (0-7894-8019-0). 96pp. An engaging introduction to apes and their cousins (including their diet, habitat, and behavior), with photographs and interesting facts. (Rev: BL 10/15/01; HBG 3/02) [599]

BATS

4908 Greenaway, Theresa. *The Secret Life of Bats* (4–7). Series: The Secret World of . . . 2002, Raintree Steck-Vaughn LB $27.12 (0-7398-4982-4). 48pp. An accessible, attractive volume that begins with little-known facts about bats and continues with information on their structure, habits, food, and habitats. (Rev: BL 8/02) [599.4]

4909 Welsbacher, Anne. *Vampire Bats* (3–6). Series: Predators in the Wild. 2001, Capstone LB $15.95 (0-7368-0787-X). 32pp. Myths about the vampire bat are presented along with facts in this general introduction to the animal's characteristics and habitat. (Rev: HBG 10/01; SLJ 1/02) [599.4]

BEARS

4910 Deady, Kathleen W. *Grizzly Bears* (3–5). Series: Predators in the Wild. 2002, Capstone LB $21.26 (0-7368-1063-3). 32pp. Basic information about grizzly bears' lives, habitat, diet, and endangered status is presented in a format that will suit both browsers and report writers. (Rev: SLJ 8/02) [599.74]

4911 Gibbons, Gail. *Polar Bears* (2–4). Illus. 2001, Holiday $16.95 (0-8234-1593-7). 32pp. An accessible, nicely illustrated introduction to the habitat, behavior, diet, and anatomy of the polar bear. (Rev: BL 9/15/01; HBG 3/02; SLJ 9/01) [599.786]

4912 Hall, Eleanor J. *Grizzly Bears* (4–6). Series: Nature's Predators. 2002, Gale LB $23.70 (0-7377-0941-3). As well as introducing grizzly bears and their anatomy, habits, and habitats, this account explains how they hunt and kill their prey. Also use *Polar Bears* (2001). (Rev: BL 1/1–15/02; SLJ 6/02) [599.74]

4913 Lang, Aubrey. *The Adventures of Baby Bear* (K–2). Illus. by Wayne Lynch. Series: Nature Babies. 2001, Fitzhenry & Whiteside $11.95 (1-55041-670-7). 28pp. Readers accompany two young bear cubs from birth to adolescence, in a photographic presentation with simple text and a page of facts. (Rev: BL 12/15/01; SLJ 2/02) [599.78]

4914 Patent, Dorothy Hinshaw. *A Polar Bear Biologist at Work* (4–6). Series: Wildlife Conservation Society. 2001, Watts LB $22.50 (0-531-11850-9). 48pp. Basic information on polar bears is enlivened by the portrayal of biologist Chuck Jonkel at work and by his comments on bears and the environment. (Rev: SLJ 11/01) [599.786]

4915 Preston-Mafham, Rod. *The Secret Life of Bears* (4–7). Series: The Secret World of . . . 2002,

Raintree Steck-Vaughn LB $27.12 (0-7398-4983-2). 48pp. In this attractive volume readers learn why bears behave as they do, how they feed, communicate, and reproduce, and what dangers face their future. (Rev: BL 8/02) [599.74]

4916 Simon, Seymour. *Wild Bears* (1–3). Series: See More Readers. 2002, North-South $13.95 (1-58717-143-0); paper $3.95 (1-58717-144-9). 32pp. Simple text and stunning color photographs introduce bears, their habits, and habitats in this beginning reader. (Rev: BL 7/02; HBG 10/02; SLJ 4/02) [599.74]

4917 Stefoff, Rebecca. *Bears* (5–8). Series: Animal-Ways. 2001, Marshall Cavendish LB $19.95 (0-7614-1268-9). 112pp. Various species of bears are introduced in text and color photographs with additional material on their location, anatomy, habits, and behavior. (Rev: BL 3/15/02; HBG 10/02) [599.74]

BIG CATS

4918 Aaseng, Nathan. *Cheetahs* (4–6). Series: Nature's Predators. 2002, Gale LB $23.70 (0-7377-0700-3). An attractive introduction to cheetahs, how they hunt and kill prey, and how they, in turn, are hunted. (Rev: BL 1/1–15/02) [599.74]

4919 *Big Cats* (3–5). Ed. by Sarah Walker. Series: Eye Wonder. 2002, DK LB $17.95 (0-7894-8549-4); paper $9.95 (0-7894-8548-6). 48pp. A brilliantly illustrated look at tigers, lions, and other big cats and how and where they live. (Rev: BL 6/1–15/02; HBG 10/02) [599.74]

4920 Greenberg, Dan. *Leopards* (4–6). Series: Animals Animals. 2002, Benchmark LB $15.95 (0-7614-1448-7). 48pp. This simple introduction to leopards examines, in text and photographs, their anatomy, habitats, behavior, and eating habits. (Rev: BL 12/15/02; HBG 3/03) [599.6]

4921 Hewitt, Joan. *A Tiger Cub Grows Up* (1–3). Series: Baby Animals. 2001, Carolrhoda LB $21.27 (1-57505-163-X); paper $6.95 (0-8225-0089-2). 32pp. For beginning readers, this colorful account describes the youth of a tiger cub in a brief, simple text. (Rev: BL 10/15/01; HBG 3/02; SLJ 10/01) [599.74]

4922 Hirschman, Kris. *Lions* (4–6). Series: Nature's Predators. 2002, Gale LB $23.70 (0-7377-0540-X). Members of the lion family are described, with material on how and where they live and how they hunt their prey. Also use *Tigers* (2002). (Rev: BL 1/1–15/02) [599.757]

4923 McDonald, Mary Ann. *Leopards* (2–4). Series: Naturebooks. 2001, Child's World LB $24.21 (1-56766-886-0). 32pp. An attractive introduction to leopards and their lives, which consists of full-page color photographs facing a few lines of text. Also use *Cheetahs* and *Jaguars* (both 2001). (Rev: BL 9/15/01) [599.74]

4924 MacKen, JoAnn Early. *Tigers* (K–2). Series: Animals I See at the Zoo. 2002, Gareth Stevens $18.60 (0-8368-3276-0). 24pp. Large type and clear pictures make this introduction appealing to beginning readers. (Rev: HBG 3/03; SLJ 2/03)

4925 Schafer, Susan. *Tigers* (3–5). Illus. Series: Animals, Animals. 2000, Benchmark LB $15.95 (0-7614-1170-4). 48pp. Color photographs and brief, readable text introduce these big cats and their anatomy, behavior, diet, reproduction, and so on. Also use *Lions* (2000). (Rev: HBG 3/01; SLJ 7/01) [599.756]

4926 Schlaepfer, Gloria G. *Cheetahs* (5–8). Series: AnimalWays. 2001, Marshall Cavendish LB $19.95 (0-7614-1266-2). 112pp. Cheetahs are introduced with material on anatomy, species identification, habitats, behavior, and endangered status. (Rev: BL 3/15/02; HBG 10/02) [599.7]

4927 Sullivan, Jody. *Cheetahs: Spotted Speedsters* (1–3). Illus. Series: Wild World of Animals. 2002, Capstone LB $18.60 (0-7368-1393-4). 24pp. Facts about the fleet-footed cheetah include habitat, reproduction, behavior, and physical characteristics. (Rev: BL 1/1–15/03; HBG 3/03) [599]

4928 Swinburne, Stephen R. *Bobcat: North America's Cat* (3–6). Illus. 2001, Boyds Mills $15.95 (1-56397-843-1). 32pp. Using a first-person narrative, the author describes his encounters with the bobcat and gives many background facts about this animal. (Rev: BL 4/1/01; HBG 10/01; SLJ 8/01) [599.75]

4929 Theodorou, Rod. *Bengal Tiger* (K–2). Illus. Series: Animals in Danger. 2000, Heinemann LB $21.36 (1-57572-267-4). 32pp. A look at the Bengal tiger and its life cycle, habitat, habits, and diet, with a section on its endangered status and efforts to save the species. (Rev: HBG 3/01; SLJ 4/01) [599.756]

COYOTES, FOXES, AND WOLVES

4930 Gentle, Victor, and Janet Perry. *Wolves* (2–4). Series: Wild Dogs. 2002, Gareth Stevens LB $19.93 (0-8368-3099-7). 24pp. A brief introduction to the life of the wolf, with appealing illustrations and plenty of photographs. Also use *Jackals* and *Dingoes* (both 2002). (Rev: HBG 10/02; SLJ 6/02) [599.773]

4931 Greenaway, Theresa. *Wolves, Wild Dogs, and Foxes* (4–7). Illus. Series: Secret World Of. 2001, Raintree Steck-Vaughn LB $18.98 (0-7398-3507-6). 48pp. Report writers will find information here about wolves, wild dogs, and foxes, including their diet, habitat, and behavior, with photographs and interesting facts. (Rev: BL 10/15/01; HBG 3/02; SLJ 1/02) [599.77]

4932 Greenberg, Dan. *Wolves* (4–6). Series: Animals Animals. 2002, Benchmark LB $15.95 (0-7614-1447-9). 48pp. A colorful introduction to wolves, their physical characteristics, social behavior, and hunting strategies. (Rev: BL 12/15/02; HBG 3/03) [599.773]

4933 Harrington, Fred H. *The Ethiopian Wolf* (2–4). Series: The Library of Wolves and Wild Dogs. 2002, Rosen LB $18.75 (0-8239-5767-5). 24pp. Basic information about this wolf is accompanied by full-page photographs. Also use *The Dingo* and *The African Wild Dog* (2002). (Rev: SLJ 6/02)

4934 Kalman, Bobbie, and Amanda Bishop. *The Life Cycle of a Wolf* (2–5). Illus. by Margaret Amy Reiach. Series: The Life Cycle. 2002, Crabtree LB

$15.45 (0-7787-0657-5); paper $5.36 (0-7787-0687-7). 32pp. Report writers and browsers will find value in this easily read account of the life and habits of wolves that includes plenty of illustrations. (Rev: SLJ 10/02)

4935 Lang, Aubrey. *Baby Fox* (1–3). Photos by Wayne Lynch. Series: Nature Babies. 2002, Fitzhenry & Whiteside $11.95 (1-55041-688-X). 36pp. Browsers will enjoy following the story of a female fox finding a mate, giving birth to pups, and rearing them. (Rev: SLJ 12/02)

4936 Markle, Sandra. *Growing Up Wild: Wolves* (2–4). Illus. Series: Growing Up Wild. 2001, Simon & Schuster $16.00 (0-689-81886-6). 32pp. Beginning with a wolf's birth, this account describes the physical features, habits, and food of wolf pups. (Rev: BL 4/1/01; HB 3–4/01; HBG 10/01; SLJ 9/01) [599.773]

4937 Martin, Patricia A. Fink. *Gray Wolves* (2–3). Series: Animals. 2002, Children's LB $23.50 (0-516-22162-0); paper $6.95 (0-516-27472-4). 48pp. An attractive, well-designed beginning chapter book that introduces gray wolves, their social life, habits, homes, and food. (Rev: BL 8/02) [599.773]

4938 Swanson, Diane. *Coyotes* (2–4). Series: Welcome to the World of Animals. 2002, Gareth Stevens LB $22.60 (0-8368-3313-9). 32pp. A slim volume that provides information on the animal's home, diet, communication, and lifestyle. (Rev: HBG 3/03; SLJ 3/03)

DEER FAMILY

4939 Hiscock, Bruce. *The Big Caribou Herd: Life in the Arctic National Wildlife Refuge* (2–5). Illus. 2003, Boyds Mills $16.95 (1-59078-010-8). 32pp. Beautiful watercolor paintings illustrate this account of a caribou herd's migration through Alaska's Arctic National Wildlife Refuge. (Rev: BL 2/1/03; SLJ 3/03) [599.73]

4940 Stewart, Melissa. *Antelope* (2–3). Series: Animals. 2002, Children's LB $23.00 (0-516-22198-1); paper $6.95 (0-516-26989-5). 48pp. An attractively designed beginning chapter book that introduces the antelope, its life cycle, and how and where it lives. (Rev: BL 8/02) [599.73]

4941 Stone, Tanya. *Deer* (3–5). Series: Wild America. 2002, Gale LB $24.94 (1-56711-643-4). 24pp. A photo-essay showing the life cycle and habits of the deer using short chapters and many color photographs. (Rev: BL 10/15/02) [599.65]

4942 Sullivan, Jody. *Deer: Graceful Grazers* (1–3). Series: Wild World of Animals. 2002, Capstone LB $18.60 (0-7368-1394-2). 24pp. Using a simple text, colorful images, and large type, this is a beginner's introduction to the world of the deer. (Rev: BL 1/1–15/03; HBG 3/03) [599.73]

ELEPHANTS

4943 Buckley, Carol. *Travels with Tarra* (3–5). Illus. 2002, Tilbury $16.95 (0-88448-241-3). 40pp. Buckley tells the story of Tarra, the elephant she trained to do circus acts before creating an elephant sanctuary for Tarra's retirement. (Rev: BL 10/1/02; HBG 3/03) [599.67]

4944 Cole, Melissa. *Elephants* (3–5). Series: Wild Africa. 2002, Gale LB $19.95 (1-56711-638-8). 24pp. Lavish color photographs and a brief text introduce the world's largest and heaviest land mammal, with material on its habits and habitats. (Rev: BL 10/15/02) [599.6]

4945 Darling, Kathy. *The Elephant Hospital* (3–5). Illus. by Tara Darling. 2002, Millbrook LB $23.90 (0-7613-1723-6). 40pp. This is the story of a hospital for sick elephants that was founded in Thailand in 1994. (Rev: BCCB 7–8/02; BL 4/15/02; HBG 10/02; SLJ 4/02) [636.9]

4946 Redmond, Ian. *The Elephant Book: For the Elefriends Campaign* (4 Up). 2001, Candlewick $17.99 (0-7636-1634-6). 48pp. An oversized, attractive presentation of elephant facts with a focus on the animal's complex social life and endangered status. (Rev: BCCB 1/02; HBG 3/02; SLJ 11/01*) [599.61]

4947 Ring, Susan. *Project Elephant* (3–6). Illus. Series: Zoo Life. 2002, Weigl LB $15.95 (1-59036-016-8). 32pp. Ring looks at elephants born in captivity and at the good and bad aspects of being raised in a zoo, with information on the animals' natural habitat and physiology. (Rev: BL 12/15/02; HBG 3/03) [599.67]

4948 Schlaepfer, Gloria G. *Elephants* (5–9). Illus. Series: Animalways. 2003, Marshall Cavendish $20.95 (0-7614-1390-1). 112pp. In addition to material on physical characteristics, behavior, habitats, and threats, Schlaepfer touches on the animal's roles in history, mythology, religion, and literature. (Rev: BL 3/15/03; HBG 3/03) [599.67]

4949 Stewart, Melissa. *Elephants* (2–3). Series: Animals. 2002, Children's LB $23.00 (0-516-22199-X); paper $6.95 (0-516-26990-9). 48pp. This beginning chapter book uses attractive color photographs and a simple text to introduce the elephant and explain where and how it lives and raises its family. (Rev: BL 8/02) [599.6]

GIRAFFES

4950 Cole, Melissa. *Giraffes* (3–5). Illus. by Tom Leeson and Pat Leeson. Series: Wild Africa. 2002, Gale LB $19.95 (1-56711-634-5). 24pp. Packed with colorful photographs, this book is filled with information about the life of a giraffe. (Rev: BL 10/15/02) [599.638]

4951 Jango-Cohen, Judith. *Giraffes* (3–5). Illus. Series: Animals, Animals. 2001, Benchmark LB $15.95 (0-7614-1258-1). 48pp. In addition to the usual information on the species, this book discusses the giraffe's discovery and naming, and its relationship with humans. (Rev: HBG 10/02; SLJ 2/02) [599.638]

4952 Leach, Michael. *Giraffe* (3–6). Illus. Series: Natural World. 2001, Raintree Steck-Vaughn LB $18.98 (0-7398-4435-0). 48pp. Fascinating facts about giraffes are expressed in breezy, clear terms, with memorable close-up photographs, a glossary, and a list of Web sites. (Rev: BL 12/15/01; HBG 10/02) [599.638]

4953 Markert, Jenny. *Giraffes* (K–4). Series: Naturebooks. 2001, Child's World LB $24.21 (1-56766-879-8). 32pp. Concise text and full-page photographs present basic information on the giraffe in a friendly, question-and-answer format. (Rev: HBG 10/01; SLJ 8/01) [599.7]

INVERTEBRATES

4954 Blaxland, Beth. *Annelids: Earthworms, Leeches, and Sea Worms* (3–5). Illus. Series: Invertebrates. 2002, Chelsea LB $17.95 (0-7910-6993-1). 32pp. Close-up photographs, straightforward text, and an enticing layout introduce the annelid invertebrates. Also use *Cephalopods: Octopuses, Squids, and Their Relatives* and *Myriapods: Centipedes, Millipedes, and Their Relatives* (2002). (Rev: BL 12/1/02; HBG 3/03) [592]

4955 *Invertebrates* (4–6). Illus. Series: Discovery Channel School Science: The Plant and Animal Kingdoms. 2002, Gareth Stevens LB $22.60 (0-8368-3216-7). 32pp. An attractive, fact-filled yet accessible introduction with many full-color photographs and charts. (Rev: HBG 3/03; SLJ 2/03)

MARSUPIALS

4956 Dennard, Deborah. *Koala Country: The Story of an Australian Eucalyptus Forest* (2–4). Illus. Series: Wild Habitat. 2001, Soundprints $15.95 (1-56899-887-2). 32pp. An appealing look at a day in the life of a koala, covering the animal's diet, habitat, and nocturnal and reproductive activities. (Rev: BL 6/1–15/01; HBG 10/01; SLJ 11/01) [599.1]

4957 Hewett, Joan. *A Kangaroo Joey Grows Up* (1–3). Illus. by Richard Hewett. Series: Baby Animals. 2001, Lerner LB $21.27 (1-57505-165-6); paper $6.95 (0-8225-0091-4). 32pp. Beginning readers will enjoy this basic book about a young kangaroo joey. (Rev: BL 10/15/01; HBG 3/02; SLJ 10/01) [599.2]

4958 Kalman, Bobbie. *The Life Cycle of a Koala* (2–4). Illus. Series: The Life Cycle. 2001, Crabtree LB $15.45 (0-7787-0655-9); paper $5.36 (0-7787-0685-0). 32pp. After a general description of the koala bear, the author clearly explains its life cycle and discusses what can be done to curb human encroachment. (Rev: SLJ 6/02) [599.1]

4959 Noonan, Diana. *The Kangaroo* (2–4). Illus. Series: Life Cycles. 2002, Chelsea LB $14.95 (0-7910-6968-0). 32pp. Handsome images and simple text describe the life cycle, habitat, appearance, and predators of the kangaroo, in a small, square, photo-essay format. (Rev: BL 1/1–15/03; HBG 3/03) [599.2]

4960 Penny, Malcolm. *The Secret Life of Kangaroos* (4–7). Series: The Secret World of . . . 2002, Raintree Steck-Vaughn LB $27.12 (0-7398-4986-7). 48pp. A visually interesting look at the world of the kangaroo with material on behavior, anatomy, reproduction, and how pollution and habitat destruc-

tion have affected these animals. (Rev: BL 8/02) [599.2]

4961 Swan, Erin Pembrey. *Meat-Eating Marsupials* (3–5). Series: Animals in Order. 2002, Watts LB $24.00 (0-531-11628-X). 48pp. After a general introduction to these pouched animals, individual species are featured in descriptive text and striking color photographs. (Rev: BL 3/15/02) [599.1]

4962 Theodorou, Rod. *Koala* (2–4). Illus. Series: Animals in Danger. 2001, Heinemann LB $21.36 (1-57572-271-2). 32pp. Basic information about the koala and its endangered status. (Rev: BL 7/01; HBG 10/01) [599.2]

PANDAS

4963 Gibbons, Gail. *Giant Pandas* (K–3). Illus. 2002, Holiday $16.95 (0-8234-1761-1). 32pp. Simple text and watercolors introduce facts about pandas in the wild and in zoos. (Rev: BL 1/1–15/03; SLJ 12/02) [599.789]

4964 Martin, Patricia A. Fink. *Giant Pandas* (2–3). Series: Animals. 2002, Children's LB $23.50 (0-516-22165-5); paper $6.95 (0-516-27471-6). 48pp. The giant panda, its anatomy, habits, food, and habitats are introduced in a simple text with many color illustrations. (Rev: BL 8/02) [599.74]

4965 Ryder, Joanne. *Little Panda* (K–3). Illus. 2001, Simon & Schuster $16.95 (0-689-84310-0). 32pp. This photo-essay chronicles the birth and early life of Hua Mei, a panda born at the San Diego Zoo. (Rev: BL 4/15/01; HB 5–6/01; HBG 10/01; SLJ 7/01*) [599.789]

RODENTS

4966 Becker, John E. *The North American Beaver* (3–6). Illus. Series: Returning Wildlife. 2002, Gale LB $23.70 (0-7377-1011-X). 48pp. Becker covers historic and contemporary threats to the beaver's survival, with full-color photographs and a glossary and bibliography. (Rev: BL 12/1/02; SLJ 1/03) [599.37]

4967 Conniff, Richard. *Rats! The Good, the Bad, and the Ugly* (3–5). Illus. 2002, Crown $15.95 (0-375-81207-5). 37pp. A volume packed with information, anecdotes, and color photographs covering the biology, mythology, and history of rats. (Rev: BCCB 12/02; BL 12/15/02; HBG 3/03; SLJ 1/03) [599.35]

4968 Hipp, Andrew. *The Life Cycle of a Mouse* (PS–2). Illus. by Dwight Kuhn. Series: Life Cycle Of. 2002, Rosen LB $18.76 (0-8239-5866-3). 24pp. This book for beginning readers follows the life of a mouse from conception to adulthood. (Rev: BL 12/15/02) [599.35]

4969 Holub, Joan. *Why Do Rabbits Hop?* (K–2). Illus. 2003, Dial $13.99 (0-8037-2771-2); paper $6.99 (0-14-230120-5). 48pp. An interesting introduction to rabbits in a question-and-answer format for beginning readers. (Rev: BL 11/15/02; SLJ 2/03) [636.9]

4970 Markle, Sandra. *Outside and Inside Rats and Mice* (2–4). Illus. Series: Outside and Inside. 2001,

Simon & Schuster $16.00 (0-689-82301-0). 40pp. Facts about rats and mice and their "outsides" (diet, habitat, behavior, etc.) and "insides" (anatomy and physiology) are paired with excellent color photographs and questions and answers. (Rev: BL 9/15/01; HB 9–10/01; HBG 3/02; SLJ 11/01) [599.35]

4971 Miller, Sara Swan. *Rabbits, Pikas, and Hares* (3–5). Series: Animals in Order. 2002, Watts LB $24.00 (0-531-11634-4). 48pp. Following a general explanation of animal classification, this attractive volume describes in text and color photographs several species of rabbits and related animals. (Rev: BL 3/15/02) [599.32]

4972 Richardson, Adele D. *Groundhogs: Woodchuck, Marmots, and Whistle Pigs* (1–3). Illus. Series: Wild World of Animals. 2002, Capstone LB $18.60 (0-7368-1397-7). 24pp. A simple introduction to the groundhog's appearance, behavior, and other basic facts, is followed by a glossary and list of resources. Also use *Beavers* (2002). (Rev: BL 1/1–15/03; HBG 3/03) [599]

4973 Stone, Tanya. *Rabbits* (3–5). Series: Wild America. 2002, Gale LB $24.94 (1-56711-645-0). 24pp. Rabbits in the wild are featured in this picture-filled account that describes appearance, life cycle, food, and survival skills. Also use *Squirrels* (2002). (Rev: BL 10/15/02) [599.32]

Birds

GENERAL AND MISCELLANEOUS

4974 Aziz, Laurel. *Hummingbirds: A Beginner's Guide* (5–8). Illus. 2002, Firefly LB $19.95 (1-55209-487-1); paper $9.95 (1-55209-374-7). 64pp. This heavily illustrated book offers a great deal of information about hummingbirds including their bills, metabolism, flight, nesting, and migration. (Rev: BL 6/1–15/02; HBG 10/02; SLJ check) [598.7]

4975 *Birds* (3–5). Ed. by Samantha Gray and Sarah Walker. 2002, DK LB $17.95 (0-7894-8551-6). 48pp. A visually striking introduction to a variety of birds and their anatomies, habitats, and habits. (Rev: BL 6/1–15/02; HBG 10/02) [598]

4976 Carney, Margaret. *Where Does a Tiger-Heron Spend the Night?* (PS–1). Illus. by Melanie Watt. 2002, Kids Can $15.95 (1-55337-022-8). 32pp. Rhyming text, rich acrylic artwork, and a lift-the-flap format combine to present facts about birds for younger readers. (Rev: BCCB 9/02; BL 3/15/02; HBG 10/02; SLJ 5/02) [598]

4977 Collard, Sneed B., III. *Beaks!* (K–3). Illus. by Robin Brickman. 2002, Charlesbridge $16.95 (1-57091-387-0); paper $6.95 (1-57091-388-9). 32pp. Striking artwork and engrossing text about birds and their beaks will fascinate younger readers. (Rev: BL 8/02; HBG 3/03; SLJ 8/02) [573.3]

4978 Haus, Robyn. *Make Your Own Birdhouses and Feeders* (3–6). Illus. Series: Quick Starts for Kids! 2001, Williamson paper $7.95 (1-885593-55-4). 64pp. A detailed guide for younger readers to feeding and providing shelter for wild birds. (Rev: BL 2/15/02; SLJ 12/01) [690]

4979 Herkert, Barbara. *Birds in Your Backyard* (K–3). Illus. by author. Series: A Sharing Nature with Children Book. 2001, Dawn $17.95 (1-58469-026-7); paper $8.95 (1-58469-025-9). 35pp. Tips on attracting birds to your backyard, instructions for building a birdhouse, and advice on binoculars accompany descriptions of a variety of birds and maps showing birds commonly found in North America. (Rev: HBG 3/02; SLJ 5/02) [598]

4980 Hewitt, Joan. *A Flamingo Chick Grows Up* (1–3). Series: Baby Animals. 2001, Carolrhoda LB $21.27 (1-57505-164-8); paper $6.95 (0-8225-0090-6). 32pp. Using excellent photographs, short sentences, large print, and simple vocabulary, this attractive book describes a flamingo chick's growth to adulthood. (Rev: BL 10/15/01; HBG 3/02; SLJ 10/01) [598]

4981 Kittinger, Jo S. *Birds of North America: East* (5–8). Series: Smithsonian Kids' Field Guides. 2001, DK LB $17.95 (0-7894-7898-6); paper $9.95 (0-7894-7899-4). 160pp. This guide to the birds found in the eastern United States groups birds by kind and includes photographs, sidebars about special features, and information on calls and migratory patterns. Also use *Birds of North America: West* (2001). (Rev: BL 10/15/01) [598]

4982 Martin, Patricia A. Fink. *California Condors* (2–3). Series: Animals. 2002, Children's LB $23.50 (0-516-22161-2); paper $6.95 (0-516-27470-8). 48pp. With a color photograph on almost every page and large type throughout, this is a simple but informative introduction to the California condor. (Rev: BL 8/02) [598.9]

4983 Parker, Edward. *Birds* (5–8). Photos by author. Series: Rain Forest. 2003, Raintree Steck-Vaughn LB $27.12 (0-7398-5239-6). 48pp. Birds that are found in rain forests are the topic of this overview that describes the dangers posed by humans through hunting, pollution, and agriculture. (Rev: HBG 3/03; SLJ 1/03)

4984 Pringle, Laurence. *Crows! Strange and Wonderful* (2–4). Illus. by Bob Marstall. 2002, Boyds Mills $15.95 (1-56397-899-7). 32pp. This is an absorbing, well-illustrated account of the life and behavior of the crow, showing the bird's intelligence, adaptability, and amazing ability to communicate. (Rev: BCCB 12/02; BL 11/1/02; HBG 3/03; SLJ 9/02) [598.964]

4985 Rauzon, Mark J. *Parrots Around the World* (3–5). Series: Animals in Order. 2001, Watts LB $23.00 (0-531-11688-3). 32pp. Following a discussion of the parrot family, various species are introduced through color photographs and a brief text that describes anatomy, habits, and habitats. Also use *Pelicans, Cormorants, and Their Kin* (2002). (Rev: BL 6/1–15/01) [598.71]

4986 Sayre, April Pulley. *The Hungry Hummingbird* (K–3). Illus. by Gay W. Holland. 2001, Millbrook LB $22.90 (0-7613-1951-4). 32pp. A hungry little hummingbird searches for food in this beautifully illustrated book. (Rev: BL 11/15/01; HBG 3/02; SLJ 11/01) [598.7]

4987 Wilkes, Angela. *Question Time: Birds* (3–5). Illus. Series: Question Time. 2002, Kingfisher $11.95 (0-7534-5450-5); paper $6.95 (0-7534-5462-9). 32pp. Topics covered in a question-and-answer format include the different types of birds, and their characteristics, habitat, and defense mechanisms. (Rev: HBG 3/03; SLJ 2/03)

BEHAVIOR

4988 Dewey, Jennifer Owings. *Paisano, the Roadrunner* (4–6). Illus. by Wyman Meinzer. 2002, Millbrook LB $23.90 (0-7613-1250-1). 48pp. The author relates — in photographs, diary entries, and narrative — her experiences with a roadrunner she named "Paisano." (Rev: BCCB 9/02; BL 5/15/02; HB 7–8/02; HBG 10/02; SLJ 8/02) [598.7]

4989 Lerner, Carol. *On the Wing: American Birds in Migration* (3–6). Illus. 2001, HarperCollins $16.95 (0-688-16649-0). 48pp. Lerner looks at all aspects of bird migration — the reasons why, how they navigate, and the impact of environmental change — in clear text, attractive paintings, and useful maps. (Rev: BL 6/1–15/01; HB 9–10/01; HBG 3/02; SLJ 9/01*) [598.156]

4990 Winer, Yvonne. *Birds Build Nests* (PS–3). Illus. by Tony Oliver. 2002, Charlesbridge $16.95 (1-57091-500-8); paper $6.95 (1-57091-501-6). 32pp. A lovely book of poetic text and beautiful, realistic illustrations that introduces the nesting habits of various species of birds to younger readers. (Rev: BL 3/1/02; HBG 10/02; SLJ 3/02) [598.156]

DUCKS, GEESE, AND SWANS

4991 Cooper, Jason. *Canada Goose* (1–3). Series: Life Cycles. 2002, Rourke LB $23.93 (1-58952-351-2). 24pp. Handsome photographs and simple text describe the life cycle, habitat, appearance, and behavior of these animals. (Rev: SLJ 12/02)

4992 Hipp, Andrew. *The Life Cycle of a Duck* (PS–2). Illus. by Dwight Kuhn. Series: Life Cycle Of. 2002, Rosen LB $18.76 (0-8239-5868-X). 24pp. This book for beginning readers follows the life of a duck from conception to adulthood. (Rev: BL 12/15/02) [598.4]

4993 McMillan, Bruce. *Days of the Ducklings* (K–3). Illus. 2001, Houghton $16.00 (0-618-04878-2). 32pp. This eye-catching book of photography and spare text records a young Icelandic girl's efforts to reintroduce wild eider ducklings to her island. (Rev: BCCB 12/01; BL 9/15/01; HB 1–2/02; HBG 3/02; SLJ 9/01) [598.4]

4994 Osborn, Elinor. *Project UltraSwan* (3–6). Illus. 2002, Houghton $16.00 (0-618-14528-1). 64pp. This is a fascinating and readable account of how scientists using ultralight aircraft are working to help trumpeter swans to rediscover their migratory routes. (Rev: BCCB 12/02; BL 12/15/02; HB 1–2/03; HBG 3/03) [598.4]

4995 Watts, Barrie. *Duck* (K–3). Illus. 2002, Smart Apple LB $16.95 (1-58340-197-0). 32pp. This easy-to-read book about ducks includes loads of facts and excellent photography. (Rev: BL 10/15/02; HBG 3/03) [598.4]

EAGLES, HAWKS, AND OTHER BIRDS OF PREY

4996 Bailey, Jill. *The Secret Life of Falcons* (4–7). Series: The Secret World of . . . 2002, Raintree Steck-Vaughn LB $27.12 (0-7398-4985-9). 48pp. This book describes the anatomy and habits of the falcon with material on how they feed, communicate, and reproduce. (Rev: BL 8/02) [598.9]

4997 Becker, John E. *The Bald Eagle* (3–6). Illus. Series: Returning Wildlife. 2002, Gale LB $23.70 (0-7377-1279-1). 32pp. Covers the bald eagle's place in American history and new threats to its livelihood, with lots of photographs, a useful bibliography, and a glossary. (Rev: BL 12/1/02) [598.9]

4998 Haugen, Hayley Mitchell. *Eagles* (4–6). Series: Nature's Predators. 2002, Gale LB $23.70 (0-7377-1004-7). 48pp. In four brief chapters, the lives of eagles are explored with material on the food they eat and how they catch it. (Rev: BL 8/02) [598.8]

4999 Laubach, Christyna, et al. *Raptor! A Kid's Guide to Birds of Prey* (4–7). Illus. 2002, Storey $21.95 (1-58017-475-2); paper $14.95 (1-58017-445-0). 128pp. A large-format treasure trove of facts about raptors, with information on individual species, identification, habits, habitat, range maps, and so forth. (Rev: BL 12/1/02; HBG 3/03; SLJ 10/02) [598.9]

5000 Martin-James, Kathleen. *Soaring Bald Eagles* (PS–2). Series: Pull Ahead Books. 2001, Lerner LB $22.95 (0-8225-3636-6). 32pp. A few lines of simple text plus a color photograph on each page present the world of bald eagles to beginning readers. (Rev: BL 6/1–15/01; HBG 10/01) [598.9]

GULLS AND OTHER SEA BIRDS

5001 Miller, Sara Swan. *Wading Birds: From Herons to Hammerheads* (3–5). Series: Animals in Order. 2001, Watts LB $23.00 (0-531-11630-1). 32pp. The traits and behavior of wading birds are discussed with full color photographs of various species and a simple text. (Rev: BL 6/1–15/01) [598.3]

OWLS

5002 Richardson, Adele D. *Owls: Flat-Faced Flyers* (1–3). Series: Wild World of Animals. 2002, Capstone LB $18.60 (0-7368-1396-9). 24pp. For beginning readers, this is an attractive introduction to owls, their appearance, habits, care of young, and habitats. (Rev: BL 1/1–15/03; HBG 3/03) [598.9]

PENGUINS

5003 Guiberson, Brenda Z. *The Emperor Lays an Egg* (K–3). Illus. by Joan Paley. 2001, Holt $16.95

(0-8050-6204-1). 32pp. Colorful text and lovely collages depict a year in the life of a family of emperor penguins, showing the father's incredible care for the egg, the necessary swimming skills, and the struggle to stay warm in the frigid air. (Rev: BL 12/1/01; HB 1–2/02; HBG 3/02; SLJ 12/01*) [598.47]

5004 Jango-Cohen, Judith. *Penguins* (3–5). Illus. Series: Animals, Animals. 2001, Benchmark LB $15.95 (0-7614-1260-3). 48pp. In addition to the usual information on the species, this book discusses the penguin's discovery and naming, and its relationship with humans. (Rev: HBG 10/02; SLJ 2/02) [598.47]

5005 Lang, Aubrey. *Baby Penguin* (K–2). Illus. by Wayne Lynch. Series: Nature Babies. 2001, Fitzhenry & Whiteside $11.95 (1-55041-675-8). 28pp. Excellent photographs and a brief text present young penguins from birth to adolescence. (Rev: BL 12/15/01; SLJ 2/02) [598.47]

5006 Markle, Sandra. *Growing Up Wild: Penguins* (2–4). Illus. 2002, Simon & Schuster $16.00 (0-689-81887-4). 32pp. Vivid, colorful photographs and concise text depict the life of the Adelie penguin, with a focus on the young. (Rev: BL 12/15/01; HB 5–6/02; HBG 10/02; SLJ 3/02) [598.47]

5007 Noonan, Diana. *The Emperor Penguin* (2–4). Series: Life Cycles. 2002, Chelsea LB $14.95 (0-7910-6965-6). 32pp. This account covers the life cycle of the Antarctic emperor penguin and how these animals grow, mate, incubate their eggs, and feed their chicks. (Rev: BL 12/15/02; HBG 3/03) [598.42]

5008 Raatma, Lucia. *Penguins* (2–4). Series: First Reports. 2001, Compass Point LB $21.26 (0-7565-0058-3). 48pp. Young report writers will quickly find basic information on penguins here. (Rev: SLJ 7/01) [598]

5009 Tatham, Betty. *Penguin Chick* (2–3). Illus. by Helen K. Davie. Series: Let's-Read-and-Find-Out Science. 2002, HarperCollins $15.95 (0-06-028594-X); paper $4.95 (0-06-445206-9). 40pp. An account for younger readers of an emperor penguin chick's survival in an often ruthless habitat. (Rev: BL 3/1/02; HB 5–6/02; HBG 10/02; SLJ 3/02) [598.47]

Conservation of Endangered Species

5010 Astorga, Amalia, and Gary Paul Nabhan. *Efrain of the Sonoran Desert: A Lizard's Life Among the Seri People* (2–6). Illus. by Janet K. Miller. 2001, Cinco Puntos $15.95 (0-938317-55-5). 32pp. The fascinating story of how an endangered lizard can flourish within a special community. (Rev: BL 12/15/01; HBG 3/02; SLJ 12/01) [305.8975]

5011 Barnes, Simon. *Planet Zoo* (4–7). Illus. 2001, Orion $29.95 (1-85881-488-X). 264pp. An overview of 100 endangered species that conveys information in a conversational manner. (Rev: BL 8/01; SLJ 8/01) [578.68]

5012 Becker, John E. *The North American Bison* (4–6). Illus. Series: Returning Wildlife. 2003, Gale LB $18.96 (0-7377-1380-1). 48pp. The bison's

recovery from near-extinction and its importance to Native Americans are detailed here. (Rev: BL 1/1–15/03) [599.64]

5013 Few, Roger. *Animal Watch* (5–7). Illus. Series: Protecting Our Planet. 2001, DK $16.95 (0-7894-7766-1). 60pp. Among the topics discussed in this comprehensive overview are shrinking habitats, species endangered by hunting and trade, extinction, and the work of professionals in this field. (Rev: BL 8/01; HBG 3/02) [333.95]

5014 Penny, Malcolm. *Endangered Species* (5–8). Series: 21st Century Debates. 2002, Raintree Steck-Vaughn LB $18.98 (0-7398-4873-9). 64pp. Topics covered in this well-illustrated book include a history of conservation, how species become endangered, methods for protection such as captive breeding, and saving habitats. (Rev: BL 6/1–15/02) [591]

5015 Radley, Gail. *Forests and Jungles* (2–5). Illus. by Jean Sherlock. Series: Vanishing From. 2001, Carolrhoda LB $22.60 (1-57505-405-1); paper $6.95 (1-57505-567-8). 32pp. The plight of endangered species as humans threaten their habitats serves as an introduction to double-page spreads about specific animals. Also use *Grasslands and Deserts* and *The Skies* (both 2001). (Rev: HBG 3/02; SLJ 10/01) [591]

5016 Salmansohn, Pete, and Stephen W. Kress. *Saving Birds: Heroes Around the World* (4–7). Illus. 2003, Tilbury $16.95 (0-88448-237-5). 40pp. Efforts to save endangered bird species are detailed in informative text and arresting, full-color photographs. (Rev: BL 3/15/03) [333.95]

Insects and Arachnids

GENERAL AND MISCELLANEOUS

5017 Allen, Judy. *Are You a Dragonfly?* (PS–1). Series: Backyard Books. 2002, Kingfisher $9.95 (0-7534-5346-0). 32pp. This book describes life from a dragonfly's point-of-view with information on its life cycle and behavior. Also use *Are You a Grasshopper?* (2002). (Rev: BL 2/15/03) [595.7]

5018 *Bugs* (3–5). Ed. by Penelope York. 2002, DK LB $17.95 (0-7894-8553-2). 48pp. A colorful introduction to insects, their characteristics, life cycles, habitats, and varieties. (Rev: BL 6/1–15/02; HBG 10/02) [595.7]

5019 Frost, Helen. *Praying Mantises* (PS–3). Series: Insects. 2001, Capstone LB $9.95 (0-7368-0853-1). 24pp. Spare text and full-page color photographs — often close-up shots — offer basic information on praying mantises. Also use *Walkingsticks* (2001). (Rev: HBG 3/02; SLJ 9/01) [959.7]

5020 Heinrichs, Ann. *Grasshoppers* (2–4). Series: Nature's Friends. 2002, Compass Point LB $21.26 (0-7565-0166-0). 32pp. Grasshoppers, their anatomy and life cycle, and their relationship to humans are covered in simple text and clear close-up photographs. (Rev: SLJ 7/02) [595.7]

5021 *Insects* (4–6). Illus. Series: Discovery Channel School Science: The Plant and Animal Kingdoms. 2002, Gareth Stevens LB $22.60 (0-8368-3215-9).

32pp. An attractive, fact-filled yet accessible introduction with many full-color photographs and charts. (Rev: HBG 3/03; SLJ 2/03)

5022 Jackson, Donna. *The Bug Scientists* (4–7). Illus. Series: Scientists in the Field. 2002, Houghton $16.00 (0-618-10868-8). 48pp. In addition to describing a variety of professional jobs related to insects, this colorful volume presents excellent information about insects and how they live. (Rev: BCCB 6/02; BL 4/1/02; HB 5–6/02; HBG 10/02; SLJ 4/02) [595.7]

5023 Kite, L. Patricia. *Cockroaches* (2–3). Series: Early Bird Nature Books. 2001, Lerner LB $22.60 (0-8225-3046-5). 48pp. Using a simple text and color photographs on each page, this book effectively introduces the life cycle of the cockroach with material on its habits, anatomy, and homes. Also use *Fireflies* (2001). (Rev: BL 8/1/01) [595.7]

5024 Kite, L. Patricia. *Insect: Facts and Folklore* (3–6). Illus. 2001, Millbrook LB $27.90 (0-7613-1822-4). 80pp. Fascinating information (mixing facts, folklore, and interesting anecdotes) about insects, all colorfully presented. (Rev: BL 9/1/01; HBG 3/02; SLJ 10/01) [595.7]

5025 McEvey, Shane F. *Beetles* (3–5). Series: Insects and Spiders. 2001, Chelsea LB $16.95 (0-7910-6600-2). 32pp. Beetle facts of all kinds are amplified by information on how scientists collect and study them and by tips on keeping beetles as pets. Also use *Bugs* (2001). (Rev: HBG 3/02; SLJ 2/02) [595.76]

5026 Maynard, Chris. *Bugs: A Close-up View of the Insect World* (4–8). Series: Secret Worlds. 2001, DK $14.95 (0-7894-7969-9); paper $7.95 (0-7894-7970-2). 96pp. Unusual page layouts and an eight-page reference section are two bonuses of this attractive introduction to insects and their world. (Rev: BL 10/15/01; HBG 3/02) [575.7]

5027 Meister, Cari. *Mosquitoes* (2–4). Illus. Series: Checkerboard Science and Nature Library: Insects. 2001, ABDO LB $13.95 (1-57765-464-1). 24pp. An introduction to mosquitoes and their structure, diet, habitat, and habits. (Rev: BL 10/15/01; HBG 10/01) [595.77]

5028 Miller, Sara Swan. *Grasshoppers and Crickets of North America* (3–5). Series: Animals in Order. 2002, Watts $25.00 (0-531-12170-4). 48pp. This colorful volume explores insect jumpers of the orthopteran order, which includes grasshoppers, crickets, and katydids. (Rev: BL 9/15/02) [595]

5029 Needham, Karen, and Launi Lucas. *Strange Beginnings* (K–2). Illus. by Launi Lucas. 2002, Tradewind paper $6.95 (1-896580-11-4). An attractive introduction to the various insects that emerge from water to spend their often brief adult lives in the air. (Rev: SLJ 9/02) [595.7176]

5030 Pringle, Laurence. *A Dragon in the Sky: The Story of a Green Darner Dragonfly* (3–5). Illus. 2001, Scholastic $18.95 (0-531-30315-2). 64pp. The reader follows a green darner from egg to mating in this attractive, large-format book. (Rev: BL 6/1–15/01; HB 7–8/01; HBG 10/01; SLJ 8/01) [595.7]

5031 Rockwell, Anne. *Bugs Are Insects* (K–3). Illus. by Steve Jenkins. Series: Let's-Read-and-Find-Out Science. 2001, HarperCollins $15.95 (0-06-028568-0); paper $15.89 (0-06-028569-9). 32pp. Rockwell makes clear the distinctions between insects and spiders and the characteristics of bugs and beetles. (Rev: BCCB 7–8/01; BL 5/1/01; HB 9–10/01; HBG 3/02; SLJ 10/01) [595.7]

5032 Sill, Cathryn. *About Arachnids: A Guide for Children* (PS–2). Illus. by John Sill. 2003, Peachtree $15.95 (1-56145-038-8). 40pp. Clear simple sentences and naturalistic paintings present basic information about arachnids. (Rev: BL 3/1/03) [595.4]

5033 Woodward, John. *What Lives in the Garden?* (3–6). Illus. 2002, Barron's paper $7.95 (0-7641-2108-1). 48pp. The many small creatures that are found in gardens — grasshoppers, earwigs, and termites, to name just a few — are profiled in text and interesting sidebars and shown in dramatic close-up photographs. Also use *What Lives Under the Carpet?* (2002). (Rev: SLJ 10/02)

ANTS

5034 Allen, Judy. *Are You an Ant?* (PS–1). Series: Backyard Books. 2002, Kingfisher $9.95 (0-7534-5365-7). 32pp. A young ant faces many challenges on the road to adulthood in this beginning science book. (Rev: BL 6/1–15/02; SLJ 7/02) [595.79]

5035 Fleisher, Paul. *Ants* (5–8). Series: Animal-Ways. 2001, Marshall Cavendish LB $19.95 (0-7614-1269-7). 112pp. This introduction to ants and their habits and habitats also includes fine color images and material on species identification, anatomy, and classification. (Rev: BL 3/15/02; HBG 10/02) [595.79]

5036 Gomel, Luc. *The Ant: Energetic Worker* (3–6). Illus. by Remy Amann and Dominique Stoffell. Series: Face-to-Face. 2001, Charlesbridge $9.95 (1-57091-451-6). 32pp. This is a detailed look at ants and the ant world, with arresting photographs. (Rev: BL 10/15/01; HBG 3/02) [595.79]

5037 Greenaway, Theresa. *Ants* (4–7). Series: The Secret World of . . . 2001, Raintree Steck-Vaughn LB $18.98 (0-7368-3511-4). 48pp. After presenting interesting and unusual facts about ants, this book examines their structure, homes, behavior, and enemies. (Rev: BL 10/15/01) [595.79]

5038 Orr, Tamra B. *Fire Ants* (4–6). Series: Nature's Predators. 2002, Gale LB $18.96 (0-7377-1389-5). 48pp. In four fascinating chapters with numerous illustrations, the life and habits of these insects are introduced. (Rev: BL 2/15/03) [595.78]

5039 Sayre, April Pulley. *Army Ant Parade* (PS–2). Illus. by Rick Chrustowski. 2002, Holt $16.95 (0-8050-6353-6). 32pp. This beautifully illustrated book for younger readers gives a detailed description of an army ant swarm in a Central American jungle. (Rev: BCCB 3/02; BL 3/1/02; HB 9–10/02; HBG 3/03; SLJ 5/02) [595.79]

BEES AND WASPS

5040 Allen, Judy. *Are You a Bee?* (PS–1). Series: Backyard Books. 2002, Kingfisher $9.95 (0-7534-5345-2). 32pp. This simple science book describes life as experienced by a bee and, with interesting color drawings, portrays the bee's life cycle and social life. (Rev: BL 2/15/03) [595.79]

5041 Helligman, Deborah. *Honeybees* (K–3). Illus. by Carla Golembe. Series: Jump into Science. 2002, National Geographic $16.95 (0-7922-6678-1). 32pp. Paintings and lucid text introduce honeybees and their hives, division of labor, life cycle, and behavior. (Rev: BCCB 9/02; BL 5/1/02; HBG 10/02; SLJ 5/02) [595.79]

BEETLES

5042 Miller, Sara Swan. *Beetles: The Most Common Insects* (3–5). Series: Animals in Order. 2001, Watts LB $23.00 (0-531-11629-8). 32pp. After an overview of animal classification, this book describes in text and color photographs a variety of beetles and their anatomy, traits, and behavior. (Rev: BL 6/1–15/01) [595.76]

5043 Posada, Mia. *Ladybugs: Red, Fiery, and Bright* (PS–2). Illus. by author. 2002, Carolrhoda LB $15.95 (0-87614-334-6). A rhythmic look at ladybugs and their life cycle and behavior. (Rev: HBG 10/02; SLJ 5/02) [595.7]

5044 Tracqui, Valerie. *Face-to-Face with the Ladybug* (3–6). Series: Face-to-Face. 2002, Charlesbridge $9.95 (1-57091-453-2). 32pp. The physical characteristics, habits, life cycle, and habitats of the industrious, colorful ladybug are featured in this attractive volume. (Rev: BCCB 10/02; BL 9/15/02; HBG 3/03) [595.76]

CATERPILLARS, BUTTERFLIES, AND MOTHS

5045 Frost, Helen. *Moths* (PS–3). Series: Insects. 2001, Capstone LB $9.95 (0-7368-0852-3). 24pp. Spare text and full-page color photographs — often close-up shots — offer basic information on moths. (Rev: HBG 3/02; SLJ 9/01) [595.78]

5046 Kalman, Bobbie. *The Life Cycle of a Butterfly* (2–4). Illus. Series: The Life Cycle. 2001, Crabtree LB $15.45 (0-7787-0650-8); paper $5.36 (0-7787-0680-X). 32pp. After a general description of the butterfly, the author clearly explains the stages of its life cycle and discusses what can be done to curb human encroachment. (Rev: SLJ 6/02) [595.789]

5047 Lerner, Carol. *Butterflies in the Garden* (2–4). Illus. 2002, HarperCollins LB $16.89 (0-688-17479-5). 32pp. Using beautiful watercolors and simple explanations, the author describes the characteristics of butterflies and their life cycle. (Rev: BL 6/1–15/02; HB 7–8/02; HBG 10/02; SLJ 5/02) [595.78]

5048 List, Ilka Katherine. *Moths and Butterflies of North America* (3–5). Series: Animals in Order. 2002, Watts LB $24.00 (0-531-11597-6). 48pp. After a general discussion of animal classification, this book describes in words and pictures 15 species

of moths and butterflies that live in North America. (Rev: BL 3/15/02) [595.78]

5049 Meister, Cari. *Butterflies* (2–4). Illus. Series: Checkerboard Science and Nature Library: Insects. 2001, ABDO LB $13.95 (1-57765-459-5). 24pp. This is an attractive, basic introduction to butterflies. (Rev: BL 10/15/01; HBG 10/01) [595.78]

5050 Noonan, Diana. *The Butterfly* (2–4). Series: Life Cycles. 2002, Chelsea LB $14.95 (0-7910-6963-X). 32pp. Full-color illustrations show the various stages in the life cycle of the butterfly from egg to caterpillar and pupa to the mature butterfly. (Rev: BL 12/15/02; HBG 3/03) [595.78]

5051 Preston-Mafham, Rod. *The Secret Life of Butterflies and Moths* (4–7). Series: The Secret World of . . . 2002, Raintree Steck-Vaughn LB $27.12 (0-7398-4984-0). 48pp. Beginning with little-known facts about butterflies and moths, this book explores their life cycles, behavior, mating habits, enemies, food, and habitats. (Rev: BL 8/02) [595.78]

5052 Rockwell, Anne. *Becoming Butterflies* (PS–2). Illus. by Megan Halsey. 2002, Walker LB $16.85 (0-8027-8798-3). 32pp. The story of the metamorphosis of monarch butterflies is told in a clear, concise manner for young readers. (Rev: BCCB 5/02; BL 3/15/02; HBG 10/02; SLJ 3/02) [595.78]

SPIDERS AND SCORPIONS

5053 Berger, Melvin, and Gilda Berger. *Do All Spiders Spin Webs? Questions and Answers About Spiders* (3–5). Illus. by Roberto Osti. Series: Scholastic Question and Answer. 2000, Scholastic $14.95 (0-439-09586-7); paper $5.95 (0-439-14881-2). 48pp. The authors give informative answers to such questions as "What happens when an enemy bites off a spider's leg?" Also use *Tarantulas* (2001). (Rev: HBG 3/01; SLJ 5/01) [595.4]

5054 Greenaway, Theresa. *Spiders* (4–7). Series: The Secret World of . . . 2001, Raintree Steck-Vaughn LB $18.98 (0-7368-3509-2). 48pp. An information-crammed text and attractive illustrations introduce spiders, how and where they live, and their behavior. (Rev: BL 10/15/01) [595.4]

5055 Kallen, Stuart A. *Spiders* (4–6). Illus. Series: Nature's Predators. 2001, Gale LB $23.70 (0-7377-0630-9). 48pp. Spiders' methods of hunting, catching, and eating their prey are presented, with illustrations. (Rev: BL 10/15/01) [595.4]

5056 McGinty, Alice B. *The Jumping Spider* (3–6). 2001, Rosen LB $18.75 (0-8239-5568-0). 24pp. Two-page chapters with arresting photographs discuss topics such as the spider's anatomy, behavior, habitat, and relationship to humans. Other titles in this series include *The Black Widow* and *The Tarantula* (both 2001). (Rev: SLJ 3/02) [595.4]

Marine and Freshwater Life

GENERAL AND MISCELLANEOUS

5057 Cerullo, Mary M. *Sea Soup: Zooplankton* (4–7). Illus. by Bill Curtsinger. 2001, Tilbury $16.95 (0-88448-219-7). 48pp. An inviting introduction to the world of tiny drifting animals known as zooplankton that includes intriguing photographs. (Rev: BL 7/01; HBG 10/01; SLJ 8/01) [592.1776.]

5058 Hirschmann, Kris. *Moray Eels* (4–6). Illus. Series: Creatures of the Sea. 2003, Gale LB $18.96 (0-7377-0985-5). 48pp. Introduces the moray eel, with color photographs and readable text. (Rev: SLJ 3/03) [597]

5059 Squire, Ann O. *Animals of the Sea and Shore* (2–3). Series: True Books — Animals. 2001, Children's LB $23.00 (0-516-22190-6). 48pp. A variety of common marine animals are introduced with well-captioned color pictures on each page and a concise text. (Rev: BL 12/15/01) [591.32]

5060 Stone, Lynn M. *The Food Chain* (2–4). Illus. Series: Under the Sea Discovery Library. 2001, Rourke LB $18.60 (1-58952-113-7). 24pp. A look at how food is used to provide energy and at the structure of the food chain found in the underwater world. (Rev: BL 12/15/01; SLJ 3/02) [577.7]

5061 Stone, Lynn M. *Getting Around* (2–3). Series: Under the Sea. 2001, Rourke LB $18.60 (1-58952-110-2). 24pp. Text and full-page color photographs provide a simple introduction to the locomotion of various sea animals. (Rev: BL 3/15/02; SLJ 3/02) [591.7]

5062 Stone, Lynn M. *Life of the Kelp Forest* (2–3). Series: Under the Sea. 2001, Rourke LB $18.60 (1-58952-112-9). 24pp. The vegetation and marine life found in an ocean kelp forest are introduced with simple text and full-page photographs. (Rev: BL 3/15/02; SLJ 2/02) [589.4]

5063 Stone, Lynn M. *Partners* (2–4). Illus. Series: Under the Sea Discovery Library. 2001, Rourke LB $18.60 (1-58952-114-5). 24pp. Underwater partnerships such as parasites and symbiotic relationships are the focus of this slim volume with full-color double-page spreads. (Rev: BL 12/15/01; SLJ 2/02) [591.77]

CORALS AND JELLYFISH

5064 Earle, Sylvia A. *Coral Reefs* (K–2). Illus. by Bonnie Matthews. Series: Jump into Science. 2003, National Geographic $16.95 (0-7922-6953-5). 32pp. A young swimmer describes the passing world of a coral reef, explaining its ecology, plants, and sea life, illustrated by vivid paintings and accompanied by a map and an activity. (Rev: BL 1/1–15/03) [577.7]

5065 Furgang, Kathy. *Let's Take a Field Trip to a Coral Reef* (3–5). Illus. Series: Neighborhoods in Nature. 2000, Rosen LB $18.60 (0-8239-5445-5). 24pp. This book looks at the formation of coral reefs, the types of plants and animals found there, and the impact of human activities. (Rev: SLJ 4/01) [574.9]

5066 Green, Jen. *A Coral Reef* (2–5). Series: Small World. 2002, Crabtree LB $15.96 (0-7787-0138-7); paper $8.06 (0-7787-0152-2). 32pp. The variety of life found in a coral reef is described in a simple text with stunning pictures. (Rev: BL 10/15/02; SLJ 8/02) [574.5]

5067 Martin-James, Kathleen. *Floating Jellyfish* (PS–2). Series: Pull Ahead Books. 2001, Lerner LB $22.95 (0-8225-3766-4). 32pp. Each page contains two lines of simple text and a color photograph in this introduction to jellyfish for beginning readers. (Rev: BL 6/1–15/01; HBG 10/01) [593.5]

5068 Sharth, Sharon. *Sea Jellies: From Corals to Jellyfish* (3–5). Series: Animals in Order. 2002, Watts LB $24.00 (0-531-11867-3). 48pp. An amazing diversity of sea jellies and their individual characteristics and habitats are described in text with color photographs. (Rev: BL 3/15/02; SLJ 7/02) [593.5]

CRUSTACEANS

5069 Blaxland, Beth. *Crustaceans: Crabs, Crayfishes, and Their Relatives* (4–6). Series: Invertebrates. 2002, Chelsea LB $18.95 (0-7910-6994-X). 32pp. Blaxland defines crustaceans and describes their physical characteristics, life cycles, habitats, senses, food, and means of self-defense. (Rev: HBG 3/03; SLJ 1/03)

5070 Greenaway, Theresa. *Crabs* (4–6). Illus. Series: The Secret World Of. 2001, Raintree Steck-Vaughn LB $18.98 (0-7398-3506-8). 48pp. An attractive, well-organized account of the life cycle, anatomy, and habits of the crab, with information on the animal's place in the ecosystem and interesting material on peculiar features or unusual subspecies. (Rev: BL 10/15/01; HBG 3/02; SLJ 1/02) [595.3]

5071 Pascoe, Elaine. *Pill Bugs and Sow Bugs* (4–7). Series: Nature Close-Up. 2001, Blackbirch $18.95 (1-56711-473-3). 32pp. This informative book of facts and easy-to-do projects introduces some small land crustacea found under stones and in other damp places. (Rev: BL 9/15/01; HBG 3/02) [595.3]

DOLPHINS AND PORPOISES

5072 Cole, Melissa. *Dolphins* (4–6). Photos by Brandon Cole. Series: Wild Marine Animals! 2001, Gale LB $17.95 (1-56711-443-1). 24pp. Basic information on dolphins and their distribution in the world's waters is enhanced by many large color photographs. (Rev: HBG 3/02; SLJ 3/02) [599.53]

5073 Davies, Nicola. *Wild About Dolphins* (3–6). Illus. 2001, Candlewick $10.99 (0-7636-1454-8). 56pp. Zoologist Davies' fascination with dolphins from a young age has led her to write a book full of interesting facts and wonderful photographs. (Rev: BCCB 10/01; BL 11/1/01; HBG 3/02; SLJ 10/01) [599.53]

5074 Hirschi, Ron. *Dolphins* (4–6). Series: Animals Animals. 2002, Benchmark LB $15.95 (0-7614-1443-6). 48pp. An oversize book filled with excellent photographs and a simple text that introduces dolphins and their structure, habits, and homes. (Rev: BL 12/15/02; HBG 3/03) [599.5]

5075 Stahl, Dean. *Dolphins* (2–4). Illus. 2001, Child's World LB $24.21 (1-56766-889-5). 32pp. Concise text and full-page photographs present basic information on the dolphin in a friendly, question-and-answer format. (Rev: BL 7/01; HBG 10/01) [599.53]

FISH

5076 Hirschmann, Kris. *Rays* (4–7). Illus. 2003, Gale $18.96 (0-7377-0988-X). 48pp. Hirschmann presents basic information about the ray's anatomy, movement, feeding, defense, reproduction, and man's fascination with this fish. (Rev: BL 3/1/03) [597.3]

5077 Hodge, Deborah. *Salmon* (3–5). Illus. by Nancy Gray Ogle. Series: Wildlife. 2002, Kids Can $10.95 (1-55074-961-7); paper $5.95 (1-55074-963-3). 32pp. Atlantic and Pacific salmon are covered along with subspecies in a flowing text and detailed paintings. (Rev: HBG 10/02; SLJ 7/02) [597.56]

5078 Kurlansky, Mark. *The Cod's Tale* (3–5). Illus. by S. D. Schindler. 2001, Putnam $16.99 (0-399-23476-4). 48pp. Kurlansky looks at the surprisingly fascinating relationship between cod and humans, presenting basic facts about the fish itself (including how to cook it) and exploring its importance throughout history. (Rev: BCCB 10/01; BL 12/1/01; HB 11–12/01; HBG 3/02; SLJ 10/01) [639.2]

5079 LeBox, Annette. *Salmon Creek* (3–6). Illus. by Karen Reczuch. 2002, Douglas & McIntyre $16.95 (0-88899-458-3). 48pp. Readers learn about fish and the environment as they follow Sumi the salmon through her life cycle in lyrical text and vivid watercolors. (Rev: BL 1/1–15/03*; HBG 3/03; SLJ 1/03) [811]

5080 Miller, Sara Swan. *Seahorses, Pipefishes, and Their Kin* (3–5). Series: Animals in Order. 2002, Watts $25.00 (0-531-12171-2). 48pp. The sea horse, banded pipefish, cornetfish, and brook stickleback, all members of the gasterosteiforme order, are described in a simple text and excellent photographs. (Rev: BL 9/15/02; SLJ 10/02) [597]

5081 Sill, Cathryn. *About Fish: A Guide for Children* (PS–1). Illus. by John Sill. 2002, Peachtree $14.95 (1-56145-256-4). 40pp. Watercolor illustrations and simple text describe for preschoolers how fish live and move. Also use *About Amphibians* (2001). (Rev: BL 3/1/02; HBG 10/02; SLJ 6/02) [597]

5082 Stone, Lynn M. *Ocean Hunters* (2–3). Series: Under the Sea. 2001, Rourke LB $18.60 (1-58952-111-0). 24pp. A basic introduction to various sea animals and how they find, kill, and eat their food. (Rev: BL 3/15/02) [597]

5083 Walker, Sally M. *Fossil Fish Found Alive: Discovering the Coelacanth* (5–8). Illus. 2002, Carolrhoda $17.95 (1-57505-536-8). 64pp. An engaging look at the search for and study of coelacanths, a fish believed to be extinct until 1938. (Rev: BL 3/15/02; HB 1–2/03; HBG 3/03; SLJ 5/02*) [597.3]

5084 Walker, Sally M. *Seahorse Reef: A Story of the South Pacific* (1–3). Illus. by Steven J. Petruccio. Series: Smithsonian Oceanic. 2001, Smithsonian Institution $15.95 (1-56899-869-4). 32pp. Information about the sea horse — behavior, habitat, and reproduction — is presented through the story of

one sea horse and his mate. (Rev: BL 9/15/01; HBG 10/01; SLJ 8/01) [597]

MOLLUSKS, SPONGES, AND STARFISH

5085 Blaxland, Beth. *Echinoderms: Sea Stars, Sea Urchins, and Their Relatives* (4–6). Series: Invertebrates. 2002, Chelsea LB $18.95 (0-7910-6996-6). 32pp. Blaxland defines echinoderms and describes their physical characteristics, life cycles, habitats, senses, food, and means of self-defense. (Rev: HBG 3/03; SLJ 1/03)

5086 Hirschmann, Kris. *Sea Stars* (4–6). Illus. Series: Creatures of the Sea. 2003, Gale LB $18.96 (0-7377-1362-3). 48pp. Introduces the marine invertebrate also known as the starfish. (Rev: SLJ 3/03)

5087 Zuchora-Walske, Christine. *Spiny Sea Stars* (PS–2). Series: Pull Ahead Books. 2001, Lerner LB $22.95 (0-8225-3765-6). 32pp. A variety of starfish and their habits and habitats are presented with a simple, basic text and attractive color photographs. (Rev: BL 6/1–15/01; HBG 10/01) [593.9]

OCTOPUS

5088 Trueit, Trudi Strain. *Octopuses, Squids, and Cuttlefish* (3–5). Series: Animals in Order. 2002, Watts $25.00 (0-531-11930-0). 48pp. A look at how these animals change color, camouflage themselves, and display a remarkable intelligence. (Rev: BL 9/15/02; SLJ 10/02) [594]

SEA MAMMALS

5089 Becker, John E. *North American River Otters* (4–6). Illus. Series: Returning Wildlife. 2002, Gale LB $23.70 (0-7377-0755-0). 48pp. The reasons why the otter became endangered are described, followed by a discussion of the animal's habitat and habits, and descriptions of efforts to reintroduce otters to their native environment. (Rev: SLJ 1/03)

5090 Boyle, Doe. *Otter on His Own: The Story of a Sea Otter*. 2nd ed. (K–2). Illus. by Robert Lawson. 2002, Soundprints $15.95 (1-56899-129-0); paper $5.95 (1-931465-53-3). 31pp. A revision of the exciting story of an otter pup's childhood, with plenty of facts about sea otters. (Rev: HBG 3/03; SLJ 11/02) [599.74]

5091 Hewett, Joan. *A Harbor Seal Grows Up* (1–3). Illus. by Richard Hewett. Series: Baby Animals. 2001, Lerner LB $21.27 (1-57505-166-4); paper $6.95 (0-8225-0092-2). 32pp. A book for beginning readers about a baby harbor seal being raised in captivity. (Rev: BL 10/15/01; HBG 3/02; SLJ 10/01) [599.79]

5092 Hirschi, Ron. *Seals* (4–6). Series: Animals Animals. 2002, Benchmark LB $15.95 (0-7614-1445-2). 48pp. Pictures and text present these animals' anatomy, diet, habits, and social interactions. (Rev: BL 12/15/02; HBG 3/03; SLJ 2/03) [599.74]

5093 Martin, Patricia A. Fink. *Manatees* (2–3). Series: Animals. 2002, Children's LB $23.50 (0-516-22163-9); paper $6.95 (0-516-27473-2). 48pp. Color photographs on almost every page and large-type text are used to introduce these endangered sea mammals and explain their life cycle, habits, and habitats. (Rev: BL 8/02) [599.5]

5094 Richardson, Adele D. *Manatees: Peaceful Plant-Eaters* (1–3). Series: Wild World of Animals. 2002, Capstone LB $18.60 (0-7368-1395-0). 24pp. This endangered aquatic mammal is introduced with many color photographs, large type, and simple language. (Rev: BL 1/1–15/03; HBG 3/03) [599.55]

5095 Rotter, Charles. *Seals* (K–3). Series: Naturebooks. 2001, Child's World LB $24.21 (1-56766-891-7). 32pp. Concise text and full-page photographs present basic information on seals in a friendly, question-and-answer format. Also use *Walruses* (2001). (Rev: HBG 10/01; SLJ 7/01) [599.79]

5096 Theodorou, Rod. *Florida Manatee* (K–2). Illus. Series: Animals in Danger. 2000, Heinemann LB $21.36 (1-57572-265-8). 32pp. This is an introductory overview of the manatee, with basic information on the animal, its diet and habitat, and the reasons it is endangered. (Rev: HBG 3/01; SLJ 4/01) [599.5]

SHARKS

5097 Burnham, Brad. *The Hammerhead Shark* (1–4). Illus. Series: Underwater World of Sharks. 2001, Rosen LB $18.75 (0-8239-5584-2). 24pp. A fact-filled, easy-to-read book about the odd-looking hammerhead shark, with full-color photographs and a list of Web sites. (Rev: BL 12/15/01) [597.3]

5098 Clarke, Ginjer. *Sharks!* (1–3). Illus. by Steven J. Petruccio. Series: All Aboard Reading. 2001, Grosset LB $13.89 (0-448-42588-2); paper $3.99 (0-448-42490-8). 32pp. Bright illustrations accompany basic facts about sharks for beginning readers. (Rev: SLJ 10/01) [597.3]

5099 Cole, Melissa. *Sharks* (4–6). Photos by Brandon Cole. Series: Wild Marine Animals! 2001, Gale LB $17.95 (1-56711-442-3). 24pp. Basic information on sharks and their distribution in the world's waters is enhanced by many large color photographs. (Rev: HBG 3/02; SLJ 3/02) [597]

5100 Gentle, Victor, and Janet Perry. *Killer Sharks, Killer People* (2–4). Series: Sharks: An Imagination Library. 2001, Gareth Stevens LB $19.93 (0-8368-2826-7). 24pp. This slim volume presents the many ways in which sharks are useful to people, providing materials that can be used as food, medicine, tools, clothing, even weapons. Other titles in the series include *Baby Sharks, Chasing Sharks*, and *Shark Camouflage and Armour* (all 2001). (Rev: HBG 10/01; SLJ 6/01) [597.3]

5101 Hirschmann, Kris. *Sharks* (4–6). Series: Nature's Predators. 2002, Gale LB $23.70 (0-7377-1005-5). 48pp. The shark is introduced in four brief chapters, with information on how they hunt and kill their prey and on how they, in turn, become prey. (Rev: BL 8/02) [597.31]

5102 MacQuitty, Miranda. *Sharks and Other Scary Creatures* (4–8). Series: Secret Worlds. 2002, DK $14.95 (0-7894-8533-8); paper $5.95 (0-7894-8534-6). 96pp. Full-color photographs, interesting page layouts, and plenty of Web sites highlight this book on sharks and other scary creatures. (Rev: BL 8/02; HBG 10/02) [597.31]

5103 Mallory, Kenneth. *Swimming with Hammerhead Sharks* (3–7). Illus. Series: Scientists in the Field. 2001, Houghton $16.00 (0-618-05543-6). 48pp. Vivid photographs and first-person narrative depict the excitement of swimming with sharks and describe this creature of the deep. (Rev: BL 4/1/01; HB 7–8/01; HBG 10/01; SLJ 7/01*) [597.3]

5104 Pringle, Laurence. *Sharks! Strange and Wonderful* (3–5). Illus. 2001, Boyds Mills $15.95 (1-56397-863-6). 32pp. A picture book for older children that explains the shark's anatomy and habits, and introduces several different species. (Rev: BL 4/15/01; HBG 10/01; SLJ 8/01) [597.3]

5105 Raatma, Lucia. *Sharks* (2–4). Series: First Reports. 2001, Compass Point LB $21.26 (0-7565-0056-7). 48pp. Young report writers will quickly find basic information on sharks here. (Rev: SLJ 7/01) [597.3]

5106 Sharth, Sharon. *Sharks and Rays: Underwater Predators* (3–5). Series: Animals in Order. 2002, Watts LB $24.00 (0-531-11868-1). 48pp. After an introduction to animal classification, a variety of sharks and rays are featured, each with a color photograph and descriptive materials on appearance, habits, and habitats. (Rev: BL 3/15/02) [597]

5107 Sieswerda, Paul L. *Sharks* (5–8). Series: AnimalWays. 2001, Marshall Cavendish LB $19.95 (0-7614-1267-0). 112pp. Photographs, maps, and text introduce many species of sharks, their behavior, anatomy, and habitats. (Rev: BL 3/15/02; HBG 10/02) [597.31]

5108 Troll, Ray. *Sharkabet: A Sea of Sharks from A to Z* (2–4). Illus. 2002, Graphic Arts paper $8.95 (1-55868-519-7). 40pp. From angel sharks to zebra sharks (and including some non-shark species), Troll includes many interesting shark facts in this unusual and beautifully illustrated alphabet book. (Rev: BL 9/1/02; HBG 10/02; SLJ 5/02) [597.3]

SHELLS

5109 Berkes, Marianne. *Seashells by the Seashore* (PS–2). Illus. by Robert Noreika. 2002, Dawn $16.95 (1-58469-035-6); paper $8.95 (1-58469-034-8). 32pp. Using rhyme and lovely illustrations, this picture book combines a lesson in counting with a lesson in seashell identification. (Rev: BL 3/1/02; HBG 10/02; SLJ check) [594.147]

WHALES

5110 Greenaway, Theresa. *Whales* (4–7). Illus. Series: Secret World Of. 2001, Raintree Steck-Vaughn LB $18.98 (0-7398-3508-4). 48pp. A look at whales' diet, habitat, and behavior, with photographs and interesting facts. (Rev: BL 10/15/01; HBG 3/02) [599.5]

5111 Greenberg, Dan. *Whales* (5–9). Illus. Series: Animalways. 2003, Marshall Cavendish $20.95 (0-7614-1389-8). 110pp. In addition to material on physical characteristics, behavior, habitats, and threats, Greenberg touches on the animal's roles in history, mythology, religion, and literature. (Rev: BL 3/15/03; HBG 3/03) [599.5]

5112 Hirschmann, Kris. *Humpback Whales* (4–7). Illus. Series: Creatures of the Sea. 2003, Gale $18.96 (0-7377-0984-7). 48pp. Hirschmann presents basic information about the humpback whale's anatomy, movement, feeding, defense, reproduction, endangered status, and means of communication, with lots of clear photographs. (Rev: BL 3/1/03) [599.5]

5113 Pringle, Laurence. *Whales! Strange and Wonderful* (3–5). Illus. by Meryl Henderson. 2003, Boyds Mills $15.95 (1-56397-439-8). 32pp. Whales and their physical and behavioral characteristics are introduced, with brief information on whaling history and current conservation efforts. (Rev: BL 3/15/03) [599.53]

5114 Simon, Seymour. *Killer Whales* (1–3). Series: See More Readers. 2002, North-South $13.95 (1-58717-141-4); paper $3.95 (1-58717-142-2). 32pp. Stunning photographs placed opposite a few lines of text give basic information about killer whales in this beginning reader. (Rev: BL 7/02; HBG 10/02; SLJ 4/02) [599.5]

5115 Woog, Adam. *Killer Whales* (4–6). Series: Nature's Predators. 2002, Gale LB $23.70 (0-7377-0702-X). Woog presents the life cycle of the killer whale and describes how they hunt and kill their prey, and how, they in turn, become prey. (Rev: BL 1/1–15/02) [599.5]

Microscopes and Microbiology

5116 Silverstein, Alvin, et al. *Cells* (4–8). Series: Science Concepts. 2002, Millbrook LB $26.90 (0-7613-2254-X). 64pp. The functions and components of plant and animal cells are discussed along with such topics as cloning, cell fusion, and stem cell research. (Rev: BL 9/15/02; HBG 3/03) [574.87]

Oceanography

GENERAL

5117 Berger, Melvin, and Gilda Berger. *What Makes an Ocean Wave? Questions and Answers About Oceans and Ocean Life* (3–6). Illus. 2001, Scholastic $14.95 (0-439-09588-3); paper $5.95 (0-439-09588-3). 48pp. In question-and-answer format, this title tackles topics of interest both to browsers and report writers. (Rev: BL 7/01; HBG 10/01) [551.46]

5118 Castaldo, Nancy F. *Oceans: An Activity Guide for Ages 6–9* (3–5). Illus. 2002, Chicago Review paper $14.95 (1-55652-443-9). 134pp. All about the world's oceans, including their plant and animal life, folklore, and currents and tides, with related crafts and experiments. (Rev: BL 5/15/02; SLJ 3/02) [372.3]

5119 Gray, Samantha. *Ocean* (3–5). Illus. Series: Eye Wonder. 2001, DK LB $17.95 (0-7894-8180-4); paper $9.95 (0-7894-7852-8). 48pp. The ocean,

marine animals, and marine research are among the topics tackled in this fact-filled book. (Rev: BL 12/1/01; HBG 3/02) [591.77]

5120 Littlefield, Cindy A. *Awesome Ocean Science!* (3–5). Illus. by Sarah Rakitin. Series: Kids Can. 2003, Williamson paper $12.95 (1-885593-71-6). 120pp. This informative book looks at the water cycle, the oceans and their animal life, and at conservation, and provides simple projects that illustrate or reinforce some of the basic concepts. (Rev: BL 1/1–15/03) [551.46]

UNDERWATER EXPLORATION

5121 Collard, Sneed B., III. *The Deep-Sea Floor* (2–4). Illus. by Gregory Wenzel. 2003, Charlesbridge $16.95 (1-57091-402-8); paper $6.95 (1-57091-403-6). 32pp. A look at the amazing discoveries gleaned from the exploration of the deep-sea floor, including plant and animal life and geologic finds, with watercolor illustrations. (Rev: BL 2/1/03) [591.779]

Pets

GENERAL AND MISCELLANEOUS

5122 Barnes, Julia. *101 Facts About Terrarium Pets* (2–4). Series: 101 Facts About Pets. 2002, Gareth Stevens LB $21.26 (0-8368-3021-0). 32pp. Facts about snakes, lizards, salamanders, and other animals will help readers decide if they will make a suitable pet. (Rev: HBG 10/02; SLJ 8/02)

5123 Hamilton, Lynn. *Caring for Your Bird* (3–5). Illus. 2002, Weigl LB $24.95 (1-59036-037-0). 32pp. A guide to choosing and looking after a feathered pet with information on different avian breeds. (Rev: BL 12/1/02; HBG 3/03) [636.6]

5124 Hernandez-Divers, Sonia. *Geckos* (4–8). Illus. Series: Keeping Unusual Pets. 2003, Heinemann $24.22 (1-40340-282-5). 48pp. An appealing and informative introduction to geckos that provides much practical guidance on actually keeping one as a pet. Also use *Chinchillas, Ferrets, Snakes* (all 2002), and *Rats* (2003). (Rev: BL 3/15/03) [639.3]

5125 Horton-Bussey, Claire. *101 Facts About Ferrets* (2–4). Series: 101 Facts About Pets. 2002, Gareth Stevens LB $21.26 (0-8368-3016-4). 32pp. Readers learn about the history of ferrets and how to care for them and train them. (Rev: HBG 10/02; SLJ 8/02) [636]

5126 Nelson, Robin. *Pet Frog* (PS). Series: Classroom Pets. 2002, Lerner LB $15.93 (0-8225-1271-8). 24pp. With only a few sentences of text and full-page color illustrations, this book introduces the frog as a pet and describes its care and feeding. Also use *Pet Guinea Pig, Pet Hamster*, and *Pet Hermit Crab* (all 2002). (Rev: BL 10/15/02; HBG 3/03; SLJ 10/02) [597.8]

5127 Rockwell, Anne. *My Pet Hamster* (K–2). Illus. by Bernice Lum. Series: Let's-Read-and-Find-Out Science. 2002, HarperCollins LB $17.89 (0-06-028565-6); paper $4.99 (0-06-445205-0). 33pp. Facts about hamsters blend easily with the text about a young girl selecting, looking after, and playing with her pet. (Rev: HBG 3/03; SLJ 12/02) [636]

5128 Ross, Veronica. *My First Hamster* (K–2). Illus. Series: My First Pet. 2002, Thameside LB $16.95 (1-930643-75-6). 32pp. A basic guide to caring for a hamster, with information on diet and hygiene. (Rev: BL 3/1/03) [636.935]

CATS

5129 Mattern, Joanne. *The American Shorthair Cat* (4–7). Illus. Series: Learning About Cats. 2002, Capstone LB $21.26 (0-7368-1300-4). 48pp. Beautiful photographs of frisky felines are accompanied by data about the physical characteristics and personality, with a glossary, bibliography, and lists of addresses and Web sites. Also use *The Manx Cat* (2002). (Rev: BL 12/1/02; HBG 3/03) [636.8]

5130 Ring, Susan. *Caring for Your Cat* (3–5). Illus. 2002, Weigl LB $24.95 (1-59036-032-X). 32pp. A detailed introduction to the various breeds of cat and how to care for one — in more than the strict physical sense — with photographs and a list of relevant Web sites. (Rev: BL 12/1/02; HBG 3/03) [636.8]

5131 Ross, Veronica. *My First Cat* (K–2). Illus. Series: My First Pet. 2002, Thameside LB $16.95 (1-930643-72-1). 32pp. A basic guide to choosing and caring for a cat. (Rev: BL 3/1/03; HBG 3/03) [636.8]

DOGS

5132 Ajmera, Maya, and Alex Fisher. *A Kid's Best Friend* (1–3). Illus. 2002, Charlesbridge $15.95 (1-57091-513-X); paper $6.95 (1-57091-514-8). 32pp. Photographs of children and their dogs show that dogs are friends and helpers everywhere in the world. (Rev: BL 9/1/02; HBG 3/03; SLJ 8/02) [636.7]

5133 Lawrenson, Diana. *Guide Dogs: From Puppies to Partners* (4–6). 2002, Allen & Unwin paper $7.95 (1-86508-246-5). 32pp. The breeding, care, and training of guide dogs are covered in this title from Australia, with profiles of several dogs and their partners and an interesting chart of commands. (Rev: SLJ 10/02)

5134 Meister, Cari. *Basset Hounds* (3–5). Series: Dogs. 2001, ABDO $13.95 (1-57765-478-1). 24pp. A simple colorful introduction to this breed of dog that describes its physical and behavioral characteristics and gives tips on proper care. Other titles in this series include *Boxers, Greyhounds,* and *Saint Bernards* (all 2001). (Rev: BL 12/15/01; HBG 3/02) [636.7]

5135 Meister, Cari. *Bulldogs* (3–5). Series: Dogs. 2001, ABDO $13.95 (1-57765-476-5). 24pp. Attractive color photographs show bulldogs playing, eating, and sleeping, and a simple text describes the breed, its many varieties, and its characteristics. (Rev: BL 12/15/01; HBG 3/02) [636.7]

5136 Presnall, Judith Janda. *Police Dogs* (4–7). Illus. Series: Animals with Jobs. 2002, Gale $23.70 (0-7377-0631-7). 48pp. This well-illustrated account describes the various ways in which dogs are used to fight crime. (Rev: BL 4/1/02) [363.2]

5137 Stone, Lynn M. *Beagles* (K–2). Series: Eye to Eye with Dogs. 2002, Rourke LB $23.93 (1-58952-325-3). 24pp. From puppyhood to adult status, this is an introduction to beagles and their behavior, characteristics, and care. Other titles in this series include *German Shepherds, Golden Retrievers, Labrador Retrievers,* and *Poodles* (all 2002). (Rev: BL 10/15/02) [636.7]

5138 Stone, Lynn M. *Dachshunds* (K–2). Series: Eye to Eye with Dogs. 2002, Rourke LB $23.93 (1-58952-326-1). 24pp. The five short sections in this simple book give information on dachshunds' characteristics, history, appearance, and care, and discuss how dachshunds help people. (Rev: BL 10/15/02) [636.7]

5139 Tracqui, Valerie. *The Dog: Loyal Companion* (2–4). Trans. from French by Lisa Laird. Photos by Marie-Luce Hubert and Jean-Louis Klein. Series: Face-to-Face. 2002, Charlesbridge $9.95 (1-57091-452-4). 32pp. A celebration of dogs' relationship with humans, their ability to follow commands, and their contributions to the lost and handicapped. (Rev: SLJ 8/02) [636.7]

5140 Wood, Ted. *Bear Dogs: Canines with a Mission* (4–6). Illus. Series: Canines with a Mission. 2001, Walker LB $17.85 (0-8027-8759-2). 32pp. These dogs are trained to bark and chase bears, frightening them back to their natural habitats and saving their lives. (Rev: BL 4/1/01; HBG 10/01; SLJ 7/01) [636.7]

FISH

5141 Nelson, Robin. *Pet Fish* (PS–K). Illus. Series: Classroom Pets. 2002, Lerner LB $15.93 (0-8225-1267-X). 24pp. A preschooler's introduction to the care and feeding of classroom fish, with fish facts, a glossary, and an index. (Rev: BL 10/15/02; HBG 3/03) [639.34]

HORSES AND PONIES

5142 Arnosky, Jim. *Wild Ponies* (PS–3). Illus. by author. Series: One Whole Day. 2002, National Geographic $16.95 (0-7922-7121-1). Bright illustrations and simple rhyming text introduce the small ponies of Assateague Island and the other animals that live there. (Rev: HBG 3/03; SLJ 10/02)

5143 Gentle, Victor, and Janet Perry. *Florida Cracker Horses* (3–5). Series: Great American Horses. 2001, Gareth Stevens LB $19.93 (0-8368-2936-0). 24pp. The physical features, history, and primary use of these horses are presented along with illustrations of famous horses of the breed. Also use *Chincoteague Ponies, Miniature Horses, Saddlebreds, Standardbreds,* and *Tennessee Walking Horses.* (Rev: HBG 3/02; SLJ 3/02) [636.1]

5144 Hayden, Kate. *Horse Show* (1–3). Series: Dorling Kindersley Readers. 2001, DK $12.95 (0-7894-7372-0); paper $3.95 (0-7894-7371-2). 32pp. An introduction to gymkhanas and the preparations that horses and riders undergo, for beginning readers. (Rev: HBG 10/01; SLJ 6/01) [798.24]

5145 Hill, Cherry. *Horse Care for Kids* (4–8). Illus. 2002, Storey $23.95 (1-58017-476-0); paper $16.95 (1-58017-407-8). 128pp. A very practical guide for young horse lovers and their parents using clear prose and topnotch illustrations to cover everything from selecting a horse and instructor to proper care and equine psychology. (Rev: BL 12/1/02; HBG 3/03; SLJ 1/03) [636.1]

5146 Holub, Joan. *Why Do Horses Neigh?* (K–2). Illus. Series: Dial Easy-to-Read. 2003, Dial $13.99 (0-8037-2770-4); paper $6.99 (0-14-230119-1). 48pp. Beginning readers will enjoy this introduction to horses that presents interesting material in a question-and-answer format. (Rev: BL 11/15/02; SLJ 2/03) [636.1]

5147 Kelley, Brent. *Horse Breeds of the World* (4–8). Series: Horse Library. 2001, Chelsea LB $19.75 (0-7910-6652-5). 64pp. In addition to basic facts about nearly 40 types of horses around the world, this account looks briefly at the horse's evolutionary history and related species. (Rev: HBG 3/02; SLJ 3/02) [636.1]

5148 Patent, Dorothy Hinshaw. *Horses* (2–3). Series: Early Bird Nature Books. 2001, Lerner LB $22.60 (0-8225-3045-7). 48pp. With color photographs on each page and a simple text, this book introduces the life cycle of the horse with material on its anatomy, habits, and relationship to humans. (Rev: BL 8/1/01; HBG 10/01) [636.1]

5149 Penny, Malcolm. *The Secret Life of Wild Horses* (4–7). Series: The Secret World of . . . 2002, Raintree Steck-Vaughn LB $27.12 (0-7398-4987-5). 48pp. A page of little-known facts about wild horses introduces this book that explores the horse's life, habits, mating, behavior, and threats to its future. (Rev: BL 8/02) [636.1]

5150 Peterson, Chris. *Wild Horses* (3–8). Illus. 2003, Boyds Mills $16.95 (1-56397-745-1). 32pp. Peterson presents photographs of and information about the horses living in the Wild Horse Sanctuary in the Black Hills of South Dakota. (Rev: BL 2/15/03; SLJ 3/03) [599.665]

5151 Presnall, Judith Janda. *Horse Therapists* (4–7). Illus. Series: Animals with Jobs. 2002, Gale $23.70 (0-7377-0615-5). 48pp. Numerous photographs show how horses are used in various therapeutic situations including exercise for people with physical and mental disabilities. (Rev: BL 4/1/02; SLJ 3/02) [636.1]

5152 Ransford, Sandy. *Horse and Pony Care* (4–7). Illus. by Bob Langrish. 2002, Kingfisher $14.95 (0-7534-5439-4). 64pp. A well-illustrated account that gives clear instructions on such topics as washing and clipping a pony, exercise routines, and caring for pastureland. (Rev: BL 5/1/02; SLJ 7/02) [636.1]

5153 Tracqui, Valerie. *The Horse: Faster Than the Wind* (3–6). Illus. by Gilles Delaborde. Series: Face-to-Face. 2001, Charlesbridge $9.95 (1-57091-450-8). 32pp. Clear text and photographs introduce the horse, with information on habitat, behavior, and

reproduction. (Rev: BL 10/15/01; HBG 3/02) [599.665]

Zoos and Marine Aquariums

5154 Ricciuti, Edward R. *A Pelican Swallowed My Head and Other Zoo Stories* (4–8). 2002, Simon & Schuster $17.00 (0-689-82532-3). 222pp. Anecdotes about a variety of animals and their keepers serve as a framework for information on the Bronx Zoo's innovative approach to designing animal-friendly, environmentally appropriate habitats. (Rev: HBG 3/03; SLJ 10/02) [590.74]

Botany

General and Miscellaneous

5155 Patent, Dorothy Hinshaw. *Plants on the Trail with Lewis and Clark.* (5–8). Photos by William Muñoz. 2003, Clarion $18.00 (0-618-06776-0). 102pp. This introduction to the trees and plants seen by Lewis and Clark also discusses Lewis's training as a botanist and his contributions to the field. (Rev: BL 3/1/03) [581.978]

Flowers

5156 Souza, D. M. *Freaky Flowers* (4–7). Series: Watts Library. 2002, Watts LB $24.00 (0-531-11981-5). 64pp. Flowering plants are the main focus in this discussion of basic botany, the ways in which flowers attract pollinators, and the environmental dangers plants are facing. (Rev: SLJ 7/02) [582]

Foods and Farming

GENERAL

5157 Bramwell, Martyn. *Food Watch* (5–7). Illus. Series: Protecting Our Planet. 2001, DK $16.95 (0-7894-7765-3). 60pp. Bramwell explains the agricultural problems we face, the different production techniques, and the kinds of professionals who work in this field. (Rev: BL 8/01; HBG 3/02) [641.7]

5158 Morgan, Sally. *Superfoods: Genetic Modification of Foods* (5–8). Series: Science at the Edge. 2002, Heinemann LB $27.86 (1-58810-702-7). 64pp. A look at the history and genetic alteration of foods, with discussion of the controversy this has created. (Rev: BL 10/15/02; HBG 3/03) [174.957]

5159 Thomas, Ann. *Dairy Products* (K–4). Series: Food. 2002, Chelsea Clubhouse LB $14.95 (0-7910-6980-X). 32pp. A simple introduction to milk (including goat and soy milks), cheese, yogurt, and other dairy products. Also use *Meat and Protein* and *Vegetables* (both 2002). (Rev: HBG 3/03; SLJ 2/03)

FARMS, RANCHES, AND FARM ANIMALS

5160 Bial, Raymond. *The Farms* (4–7). Photos by author. Illus. Series: Building America. 2001,

Benchmark LB $17.95 (0-7614-1332-4). 56pp. An interesting, beautifully illustrated look at the ways in which farms developed in America, with information on their structure and significance to the country as a whole. Also use *The Mills* (2001). (Rev: HBG 3/02; SLJ 2/02*) [630]

5161 Klingel, Cynthia, and Robert B. Noyed. *Farmers* (K–1). Series: Wonder Books. 2001, Child's World LB $21.36 (1-56766-940-9). 24pp. This book for beginning readers gives basic information about farms and farmers. (Rev: HBG 3/02; SLJ 2/02) [630]

5162 Peterson, Chris. *Amazing Grazing* (3–5). Illus. by Alvis Upitis. 2002, Boyds Mills $16.95 (1-56397-942-X). 32pp. Color photographs and a lucid text show how three Montana cattle ranchers are using environment-friendly practices. (Rev: BL 4/1/02; HBG 10/02; SLJ 4/02) [636.0845]

5163 Powell, Jillian. *From Calf to Cow* (PS–3). Series: How Do They Grow? 2001, Raintree Steck-Vaughn LB $17.98 (0-7398-4426-1). 32pp. Brief text and large, full-color photographs follow calves through birth and growth. Also use *From Chick to Chicken* and from *From Piglet to Pig* (both 2001). (Rev: HBG 3/02; SLJ 1/02) [636.2]

5164 Rendon, Marcie, and Cheryl Walsh Bellville. *Farmer's Market: Families Working Together* (4–6). Illus. 2001, Carolrhoda $23.93 (1-57505-462-0). 48pp. A look at truck farming and the sale of the produce at farmers' markets, with profiles of two Midwest families. (Rev: BL 5/1/01; HBG 10/01) [635]

5165 Schuh, Mari C. *Chickens on the Farm* (PS–2). Series: On the Farm. 2001, Capstone LB $10.95 (0-7368-0991-0). 24pp. Spare text and full-color photographs convey simple facts about chickens. Also use *Pigs on the Farm* and *Sheep on the Farm* (both 2001). (Rev: HBG 3/02; SLJ 1/02) [636.5]

5166 Wolfman, Judy. *Life on a Cattle Farm* (4–6). Illus. by David Lorenz Winston. Series: Life on a Farm. 2001, Carolrhoda LB $23.93 (1-57505-516-3). 48pp. A photo-illustrated look at activities on a Pennsylvania cattle farm, told from a teenager's point of view. Also use *Life on a Crop Farm*, *Life on a Goat Farm*, and *Life on a Horse Farm* (all 2001). (Rev: BL 11/15/01; HBG 3/02; SLJ 11/01) [636.2]

FOODS

5167 Burleigh, Robert. *Chocolate: Riches from the Rainforest* (3–6). Illus. 2002, Abrams $16.95 (0-8109-5734-5). 40pp. Traces the rich history of chocolate, from the Aztecs to Hershey's. (Rev: BL 3/1/02; HBG 10/02; SLJ 4/02) [641.3]

5168 Fleisher, Paul. *Ice Cream Treats: The Inside Scoop* (4–6). Photos by David O. Saunders. 2001, Carolrhoda LB $23.93 (1-57505-268-7). 48pp. This is an appealing overview of the history of ice cream,

with a tour of a factory and a few simple recipes. (Rev: HBG 10/01; SLJ 7/01) [641.8]

5169 Jones, Carol. *Cheese* (4–7). Illus. Series: From Farm to You. 2002, Chelsea LB $17.95 (0-7910-7005-0). 32pp. This is an absorbing account of the techniques used in manufacturing cheese and the history of cheese, with an overview of the many varieties and a map of cheese eating around the world. Also use *Pasta and Noodles* (2002). (Rev: BL 11/1/02; HBG 3/03) [641.3]

5170 Landau, Elaine. *Popcorn!* (2–4). Illus. by Brian Lies. 2003, Charlesbridge $16.95 (1-57091-442-7); paper $6.95 (1-57091-443-5). 32pp. An entertaining look at the history of the popular snack, with humorous illustrations. (Rev: BL 2/1/03) [646.6]

5171 Older, Jules. *Ice Cream* (3–6). Illus. by Lyn Severance. 2002, Charlesbridge $16.95 (0-88106-111-5); paper $6.95 (0-88106-112-3). 32pp. A fact-packed, colorful, and lighthearted book about the history of ice cream and important ice cream inventions, such as the cone and the banana split. (Rev: BL 2/15/02; HBG 10/02; SLJ 5/02) [641.8]

5172 Scott, Janine. *Let's Eat: Foods of Our World* (K–2). Series: Spyglass Books. 2002, Compass Point LB $18.60 (0-7565-0365-5). 24pp. A basic look, for beginning readers, at the kinds of foods people eat around the world. (Rev: SLJ 3/03)

FRUITS

5173 Gibbons, Gail. *The Berry Book* (PS–2). Illus. 2002, Holiday $16.95 (0-8234-1697-6). 32pp. A well-illustrated introduction to North American berries, including a few simple recipes. (Rev: BL 3/1/02; HBG 10/02; SLJ 3/02) [634]

5174 Hubbell, Will. *Apples Here!* (PS–1). Illus. 2002, Albert Whitman $15.95 (0-8075-0397-5). 32pp. The life of apples, from buds to blossoms to fruit, is the subject of this informative book. (Rev: BL 10/15/02; HBG 3/03; SLJ 9/02) [634.11]

5175 Klingel, Cynthia, and Robert B. Noyed. *Fruit* (PS–1). Photos by Gregg Andersen. Series: Let's Read About Food. 2002, Gareth Stevens LB $18.60 (0-8368-3057-1). 24pp. The importance of fruit as part of a healthy diet is emphasized in this attractive volume. (Rev: HBG 10/02; SLJ 7/02) [641.34]

5176 Robbins, Ken. *Apples* (2–4). Photos by author. 2002, Simon & Schuster $15.95 (0-689-83024-6). 32pp. An appealing account of apples — how they are grown, harvested, and consumed — with information on apples in history, in literature, and in language. (Rev: BCCB 12/02; HBG 3/03; SLJ 9/02) [634.11]

5177 Weninger, Brigitte. *Little Apple: A Book of Thanks* (PS–1). Illus. by Anne Moller. 2001, North-South LB $13.88 (0-7358-1427-9). 32pp. The life cycle of an apple is told in bold, clear illustrations and a simple text. (Rev: BL 4/1/01; HBG 10/01; SLJ 6/01) [634]

VEGETABLES

5178 Klingel, Cynthia, and Robert B. Noyed. *Vegetables* (PS–1). Photos by Gregg Andersen. Series: Let's Read About Food. 2002, Gareth Stevens LB $18.60 (0-8368-3060-1). 24pp. The importance of vegetables as part of a healthy diet is emphasized in this attractive volume. (Rev: HBG 10/02; SLJ 7/02) [613.262]

5179 Watts, Barrie. *Pumpkin* (K–3). Illus. 2002, Smart Apple LB $16.95 (1-58340-199-7). 32pp. This easy-to-read book about pumpkins includes lots of facts and excellent photography. (Rev: BL 10/15/02; HBG 3/03; SLJ 2/03) [635]

Fungi

5180 Souza, D. M. *What Is a Fungus?* (4–7). Series: Watts Library. 2002, Watts LB $24.00 (0-531-11979-3); paper $8.95 (0-531-16223-0). 63pp. In readable and appealing text, Souza explains what a fungus is and how it lives, eats, and reproduces. (Rev: SLJ 8/02)

Leaves and Trees

5181 Bulla, Clyde Robert. *A Tree Is a Plant* (PS–1). Illus. by Stacey Schuett. Series: Let's-Read-and-Find-Out Science. 2001, HarperCollins LB $4.95 (0-06-445196-8); paper $15.89 (0-06-028172-3). 34pp. Vivid paintings grace this new version of the book first published in 1960 that portrays the life cycle of an apple tree and discusses how the different parts of a tree work. (Rev: BL 12/15/01; HBG 10/02; SLJ 11/01) [583]

5182 Fowler, Allan. *Maple Trees* (1–2). Series: Rookie Read-About Science. 2001, Children's LB $19.00 (0-516-21684-8). 32pp. For beginning readers, a simple text with color illustrations introduces trees, their varieties, parts, and growth cycles. (Rev: BL 1/1–15/02) [582.16]

5183 Gibbons, Gail. *Tell Me, Tree: All About Trees for Kids* (PS–3). Illus. 2002, Little, Brown $15.95 (0-316-30903-6). 32pp. An oversize basic guide that introduces different kinds of trees, and explains their parts and how each operates. (Rev: BL 4/1/02; HB 7–8/02; HBG 10/02; SLJ 3/02) [582.16]

5184 Miller, Debbie S. *Are Trees Alive?* (K–3). Illus. by Stacey Schuett. 2002, Walker LB $17.85 (0-8027-8802-5). 32pp. This colorful picture book explains how trees live and survive in different environments. (Rev: BL 6/1–15/02; HBG 10/02; SLJ 5/02) [582.16]

5185 Pascoe, Elaine. *Leaves and Trees* (4–7). Series: Nature Close-Up. 2001, Blackbirch $18.95 (1-56711-474-1). 32pp. Easy projects and a simple text are used to introduce the nature of trees and leaves and the living processes involved. (Rev: BL 9/15/01; HBG 3/02) [582.16]

Plants

5186 Fowler, Allan. *Ferns* (1–2). Series: Rookie Read-About Science. 2001, Children's LB $19.00 (0-516-25984-9). 32pp. In this beginning science reader, different ferns are introduced in color photographs and a simple text. (Rev: BL 1/1–15/02) [587]

5187 Goodman, Susan E. *Seeds, Stems, and Stamens: The Ways Plants Fit into Their World* (2–4). Illus. by Michael Doolittle. 2001, Millbrook LB $22.90 (0-7613-1874-7). 48pp. A clear look at how plants adapt to their environments, with stunning photographs and questions to stimulate investigation. (Rev: BL 9/15/01; HBG 3/02; SLJ 11/01) [581.4]

5188 Griswell, Kim T. *Carnivorous Plants* (4–6). Series: Nature's Predators. 2002, Gale LB $18.96 (0-7377-1387-9). 48pp. An introduction to many kinds of carnivorous plants with material on how they trap, kill, and eat their prey. (Rev: BL 2/15/03) [581.5]

Seeds

5189 Richards, Jean. *A Fruit Is a Suitcase for Seeds* (PS–2). Illus. by Anca Hariton. 2002, Millbrook LB $21.90 (0-7613-1622-1). An accessible and very visual introduction to seeds and how they are dispersed. (Rev: HBG 10/02; SLJ 5/02) [581.467]

Chemistry

5190 Farndon, John. *Chemicals* (3–6). Series: Science Experiments. 2002, Marshall Cavendish LB $16.95 (0-7614-1466-5). 32pp. Simple experiments with easy-to-follow instructions explore the nature and properties of chemicals. (Rev: BL 12/15/02; HBG 3/03) [540]

5191 O'Daly, Anne. *Sodium* (4–8). Series: The Elements. 2001, Marshall Cavendish LB $15.95 (0-7614-1271-9). 32pp. Diagrams and full-color illustrations are used to introduce sodium and its characteristics and importance in everyday life. (Rev: BL 3/15/02; HBG 3/02) [546]

5192 Thomas, Jens. *Silicon* (4–8). Series: The Elements. 2001, Marshall Cavendish LB $15.95 (0-7614-1274-3). 32pp. Thomas introduces this

important element and its origins, discovery, and many uses. (Rev: BL 3/15/02; HBG 3/02) [546]

5193 Watt, Susan. *Chlorine* (4–8). Series: The Elements. 2001, Marshall Cavendish LB $15.95 (0-7614-1272-7). 32pp. Using diagrams, photographs, and a concise text, this book introduces this active, nonmetallic element with material on its composition, characteristics, and many uses — including as a disinfectant and in water purification. (Rev: BL 3/15/02; HBG 3/02) [546]

5194 Watt, Susan. *Lead* (4–8). Series: The Elements. 2001, Marshall Cavendish LB $15.95 (0-7614-1273-5). 32pp. Explores the history, origins, discovery, characteristics, and uses of this heavy metallic element in everyday life. (Rev: BL 3/15/02; HBG 3/02) [546]

Geology and Geography

Earth and Geology

5195 Bailey, Jacqui. *The Birth of the Earth* (3–5). Illus. by Matthew Lilly. Series: Cartoon History of the Earth. 2001, Kids Can $16.95 (1-55337-071-6); paper $7.95 (1-55337-080-5). 32pp. A comic-book-style presentation of the origin of the planet. (Rev: BL 10/15/01; HBG 3/02; SLJ 1/02) [523.1]

5196 Redmond, Jim, and Ronda Redmond. *Landslides and Avalanches* (3–5). Illus. Series: Nature on the Rampage. 2001, Raintree Steck-Vaughn LB $15.98 (0-7398-4704-X). 32pp. The authors look at our knowledge of landslides and avalanches and their causes, and discuss the ways in which we can protect ourselves from danger. (Rev: HBG 3/02; SLJ 2/02) [551.3]

5197 Robson, Pam. *Mountains and Our Moving Earth* (2–4). Illus. by Tony Kenyon. Series: Geography for Fun. 2001, Millbrook LB $22.90 (0-7613-2166-7). 32pp. Step-by-step instructions for projects that reinforce the information given here on geology, weather and erosion, and earthquakes and volcanoes. (Rev: HBG 10/01; SLJ 9/01) [551.43]

5198 Williams, Brian. *Earth Time* (4–6). Series: About Time. 2002, Smart Apple LB $24.25 (1-58340-210-1). 32pp. An exploration of geologic and evolutionary time that looks at the forms of life appearing in each era. (Rev: HBG 3/03; SLJ 12/02)

Earthquakes and Volcanoes

5199 Harrison, David L. *Volcanoes: Nature's Incredible Fireworks* (1–3). Illus. by Cheryl Nathan. Series: Earthworks. 2002, Boyds Mills $15.95 (1-56397-996-9). 32pp. The forces underlying volcanic eruptions are discussed here, with rich and informative illustrations. (Rev: BL 7/02; HBG 3/03; SLJ 9/02) [551.21]

5200 Nicholson, Cynthia Pratt. *Volcano!* (2–5). Illus. Series: Disaster. 2001, Kids Can $14.95 (1-55074-908-0); paper $6.95 (1-55074-966-8). 32pp. A tabloid-style format with sensational headlines draws attention to this survey of volcanoes, famous volcanic eruptions, and the work of volcanologists. (Rev: BL 12/1/01; HBG 3/02) [551.21]

5201 Nicolson, Cynthia Pratt. *Earthquake!* (3–6). Illus. 2002, Kids Can $14.95 (1-55074-949-8); paper $6.95 (1-55074-968-4). 32pp. Using double-page spreads that contain concise text and dramatic photographs, various aspects of earthquakes and their causes and effects are covered. (Rev: BL 5/1/02; HBG 10/02; SLJ 5/02) [551.22]

5202 Prager, Ellen. *Earthquakes* (K–3). Illus. by Susan Greenstein. Series: Jump into Science. 2002, National Geographic $16.95 (0-7922-8202-7). 32pp. This is a colorful book that explains simply what earthquakes are, where and why they occur, and their effects. (Rev: BL 6/1–15/02; HBG 10/02) [551.22]

5203 Simon, Seymour. *Danger! Earthquakes* (1–3). Illus. Series: SeeMore Readers. 2002, North-South LB $13.95 (1-58717-139-2); paper $3.95 (1-58717-140-6). 32pp. Double-page spreads that use color photographs and diagrams explain the causes and impact of earthquakes. (Rev: BL 4/15/02; HBG 10/02; SLJ 3/02) [551.22]

5204 Simon, Seymour. *Danger! Volcanoes* (1–3). Series: See More Readers. 2002, North-South $13.95 (1-58717-181-3); paper $3.95 (1-58717-182-1). 32pp. Outstanding pictures and a brief, simple text are the highlights in this first reader that explores the world of volcanoes. (Rev: BL 7/02; HBG 3/03; SLJ 8/02) [551.2]

Physical Geography

General and Miscellaneous

5205 Harrison, David L. *Caves: Mysteries Beneath Our Feet* (1–3). Illus. by Cheryl Nathan. 2001, Boyds Mills $15.95 (1-56397-915-2). 32pp. A general discussion of caves follows the story of the discovery of New York's Howe Caverns in 1842. (Rev: BL 9/15/01; HBG 3/02; SLJ 10/01) [551.447]

5206 Jennings, Terry. *Coasts and Islands* (3–6). Illus. Series: Restless Earth. 2003, Thameside LB $24.25 (1-931983-18-6). 32pp. Diagrams, photographs, and paintings combine with the text to illustrate how islands, coral reefs, and atolls are created and how water and earth interact. (Rev: BL 12/1/02; HBG 3/03) [551.457]

5207 Sayres, Meghan Nuttall. *The Shape of Betts Meadow: A Wetlands Story* (K–3). Illus. by Joanne Friar. 2002, Millbrook LB $22.90 (0-7613-2115-3). 32pp. A stunning picture book set in Washington State that shows how a local doctor purchased a dry meadow and restored it to its original condition as a wetland. (Rev: BL 6/1–15/02; HBG 10/02; SLJ 4/02) [333.91]

Deserts

5208 Lazaroff, David. *Correctamundo! Prickly Pete's Guide to Desert Facts and Cactifracts* (K–3). Illus. by Preston Neel. 2001, Arizona-Sonora Desert Museum paper $9.95 (1-886679-17-7). A bright, lively question-and-answer introduction to desert plants and animals, conducted by a packrat named Prickly Pete. (Rev: SLJ 8/01) [574.5]

5209 Le Rochais, Marie-Ange. *Desert Trek: An Eye-Opening Journey Through the World's Driest Places* (3–5). Trans. by George L. Newman. Illus. 2001, Walker LB $18.85 (0-8027-8766-5). 40pp. Dramatic spreads and brief text show the diversity of desert landscapes around the world, with features ranging from plants, animals, and oases to people hunting and working. (Rev: BL 6/1–15/01; HBG 10/01; SLJ 9/01) [577.54]

5210 Pratt-Serafini, Kristin Joy. *Saguaro Moon: A Desert Journal* (3–6). Illus. 2002, Dawn $16.95 (1-58469-037-2); paper $7.95 (1-58469-036-4). 32pp. In this hybrid, factual information about desert plant and animal life is presented in the form of a nature journal written by a girl named Megan, who has recently moved to Arizona. (Rev: BL 10/15/02; HBG 3/03; SLJ 9/02) [508.3154]

5211 Salzmann, Mary Elizabeth. *In the Desert* (K–1). Illus. Series: What Do You See? 2001, ABDO LB $12.95 (1-57765-564-8). 24pp. Colorful double-page spreads introduce the desert in simple language for beginning readers. (Rev: HBG 3/02; SLJ 3/02) [577.54]

Forests and Rain Forests

5212 Knight, Tim. *Journey into the Rainforest* (3–5). Illus. by Juan Pablo Moreiras and Tim Knight. 2001, Oxford $18.95 (0-19-521751-9). 48pp. Readers take a colorful tour through a rain forest, observing the vegetation and wildlife as they go and learning about the ecosystem's intricacies and endangered status. (Rev: BL 9/15/01; HBG 3/02; SLJ 10/01) [577.34]

5213 Montgomery, Sy. *Encantado: Pink Dolphin of the Amazon* (5–8). Illus. by Diane Taylor-Snow. 2002, Houghton $18.00 (0-618-13103-5). 80pp. The author describes the flora and fauna of the South American rainforest in her unsuccessful journey to locate the encantado, the elusive pink dolphin. (Rev: BL 4/1/02; HB 7–8/02; HBG 10/02; SLJ 5/02*) [599.53]

5214 Parker, Edward. *People* (5–8). Photos by author. Series: Rain Forest. 2003, Raintree Steck-Vaughn LB $27.12 (0-7398-5242-6). 48pp. An introduction to the various peoples of the rain forest. (Rev: HBG 3/03; SLJ 1/03) [304.2]

5215 Parker, Edward. *Rain Forest Mammals* (5–9). Illus. Series: Rain Forest. 2002, Raintree Steck-Vaughn LB $27.12 (0-7398-5241-8). 48pp. Mammals of the rain forest and the importance of preserving their habitat are introduced in close-up color photographs and a catchy layout, with a glossary, bibliography, and list of related organizations. Also use *Rain Forest Reptiles and Amphibians* (2002). (Rev: BL 12/1/02; HBG 3/03) [599]

5216 Rapp, Valerie. *Life in an Old Growth Forest* (5–8). Series: Ecosystems in Action. 2002, Lerner LB $26.60 (0-8225-2135-0). 72pp. In pictures and text, this book introduces life in an established forest with material on the interdependence of organisms there, and how human intervention has changed this ecosystem. (Rev: BL 12/15/02; HBG 3/03; SLJ 2/03) [574.5]

Mountains

5217 Jennings, Terry. *Mountains* (3–6). Illus. 2003, Thameside LB $24.25 (1-931983-19-4). 32pp. Vivid photographs help to explain how mountains are formed and eroded, their importance in our climate, and the kind of life there. (Rev: BL 12/1/02; HBG 3/03) [551.432]

5218 Locker, Thomas. *Mountain Dance* (K–4). Illus. by author. 2001, Harcourt $16.00 (0-15-202622-3). Verse and oil paintings describe various kinds of mountains and how they were formed, in an informative combination that appends additional details. (Rev: BCCB 2/02; HBG 3/02; SLJ 10/01) [551.4]

5219 Rotter, Charles. *Mountains: The Towering Sentinels* (4–6). Series: Lifeviews. 2002, Creative Editions LB $24.25 (1-58341-123-2). 32pp. The various types of mountains are detailed, with information on climate, ecosystems, and environmental concerns. (Rev: HBG 3/03; SLJ 1/03)

Ponds, Rivers, and Lakes

5220 Harrison, David L. *Rivers: Nature's Wondrous Waterways* (K–3). Illus. by Cheryl Nathan. 2002, Boyds Mills $15.95 (1-56397-968-3). 32pp. Using verse and color illustrations, this basic science book explains how rivers are formed, how they support life, and their importance in conservation and pollution. (Rev: BL 4/1/02; HBG 10/02; SLJ 5/02) [551.48]

5221 Morrison, Gordon. *Pond* (3–6). Illus. 2002, Houghton $16.00 (0-618-10271-X). 32pp. Wonderful watercolors, descriptive text, and detailed insets show life in and around a pond through the seasons of the year. (Rev: BL 1/1–15/03; HBG 3/03; SLJ 10/02) [577.63]

5222 Rapp, Valerie. *Life in a River* (5–8). Illus. Series: Ecosystems in Action. 2002, Lerner LB $26.60 (0-8225-2136-9). 72pp. The first title in a new series about ecosystems, this volume uses the example of the Columbia River to explain the concept and the interrelationship of rivers, animals, and humans. (Rev: BL 10/15/02; HBG 3/03; SLJ 1/03) [577.6]

5223 Stewart, Melissa. *Life in a Lake* (5–8). Series: Ecosystems in Action. 2002, Lerner LB $26.60 (0-8225-2138-5). 72pp. The diversity and interdependence of life in a typical lake is introduced with material on how this ecosystem works and how man's interference has changed the balance of nature. (Rev: BL 12/15/02; HBG 3/03) [551.48]

5224 Walker, Sally M. *Life in an Estuary* (5–8). Series: Ecosystems in Action. 2002, Lerner LB $26.60 (0-8225-2137-7). 72pp. Life at the tidal mouths of rivers is introduced with material on the diversity of life here, its interdependence, the balance of nature, and how human interaction has changed this ecosystem. (Rev: BL 12/15/02; HBG 3/03; SLJ 2/03) [574]

Prairies and Grasslands

5225 Bannatyne-Cugnet, Jo. *Heartland: A Prairie Sampler* (3–5). Illus. by Yvette Moore. 2002, Tundra $18.95 (0-88776-567-X). 40pp. Life on the prairie — weather, geography, nature, people, economy, and even cuisine — is detailed in bright, realistic paintings and informative text. (Rev: BL 1/1–15/03) [971.2]

5226 Patent, Dorothy Hinshaw. *Life in a Grassland* (5–8). Series: Ecosystems in Action. 2002, Lerner LB $26.60 (0-8225-2139-3). 72pp. Using excellent pictures and a clear text, this volume explores the flora and fauna of different kinds of grasslands, with material on conservation. (Rev: BL 12/15/02; HBG 3/03) [574.5]

Rocks, Minerals, and Soil

5227 Ditchfield, Christin. *Soil* (2–5). Series: True Books — Natural Resources. 2002, Children's LB $23.50 (0-516-22344-5); paper $6.95 (0-516-29368-0). 48pp. This book covers such topics as how soil is formed, what it is made of, what it's used for, and how we can protect this important resource. (Rev: BL 10/15/02) [631.5]

5228 Farndon, John. *Rocks and Minerals* (3–6). Series: Science Experiments. 2002, Marshall Cavendish LB $16.95 (0-7614-1468-1). 32pp. Clear illustrations and good step-by-step instructions are used to present a series of experiments that reveal the nature and properties of rocks and minerals. (Rev: BL 12/15/02; HBG 3/03) [552]

5229 Friend, Sandra. *Sinkholes* (4–7). Illus. 2002, Pineapple $18.95 (1-56164-258-4). 96pp. This volume uncovers the geological and ecological causes of sinkholes, holes in the earth's surface that occur naturally, sometimes with devastating consequences. (Rev: BL 8/02; HBG 10/02) [551.44]

5230 Oxlade, Chris. *Rock* (2–3). Series: Materials, Materials, Materials. 2002, Heinemann LB $21.36 (1-58810-585-7). 32pp. Using a few lines of text and a color picture on each page, this is a simple introduction to rocks, their composition, structure, and uses. (Rev: BL 6/1–15/02) [552]

5231 Oxlade, Chris. *Soil* (2–3). Series: Materials, Materials, Materials. 2002, Heinemann LB $21.36 (1-58810-587-3). 32pp. The composition of soil and its properties, uses, and formation are topics covered in this easily-read beginning science book. (Rev: BL 6/1–15/02) [631.5]

5232 Richardson, Adele D. *Rocks* (2–4). Illus. Series: The Bridgestone Science Library. 2001, Capstone LB $13.95 (0-7368-0953-8). 24pp. Rock types, rock formation, and the Mohs scale of hardness are covered in this slim volume. (Rev: HBG 3/02; SLJ 2/02) [552]

5233 Tomecek, Steve. *Dirt* (1–3). Illus. by Nancy Woodman. Series: Jump into Science. 2002, National Geographic $16.95 (0-7922-8204-3). 31pp. This discussion of soil's composition, inhabitants, and uses combines scientific fact with appealing humor. (Rev: BCCB 11/02; HBG 3/03; SLJ 10/02) [631.5]

Mathematics

General

5234 Bruce, Sheila. *Everybody Wins!* (2–3). Illus. by Paige Billin-Frye. Series: Math Matters. 2001, Kane paper $4.95 (1-57565-101-7). 32pp. Readers learn the usefulness of math skills as they see friends agreeing to share. Also use *Keep Your Distance*. (Rev: SLJ 12/01) [513]

5235 Caron, Lucille, and Philip M. St. Jacques. *Fractions and Decimals* (4–8). Illus. Series: Math Success. 2000, Enslow LB $17.95 (0-7660-1430-4). 64pp. Many examples accompany explanations of how to add, subtract, multiply, and divide fractions and decimals. Also use *Addition and Subtraction* (2001). (Rev: HBG 3/01; SLJ 7/01) [513.2]

5236 Daniels, Teri. *Math Man* (1–3). Illus. by Timothy Bush. 2001, Scholastic $16.95 (0-439-29308-1). 32pp. Marnie's class takes a trip to the supermarket where they meet a math whiz stock boy, who takes them on a "math-in-action" tour. (Rev: BL 11/1/01; HBG 3/02; SLJ 1/02)

5237 Ho, Oliver. *Amazing Math Magic* (3–6). Illus. 2001, Sterling $14.95 (0-8069-6017-5). 96pp. Card, coin, and number tricks abound in this guide for mathematically inclined young magicians. (Rev: BL 7/01; HBG 3/02) [793.8]

5238 Littlefield, Cindy A. *Real-World Math for Hands-On Fun!* (3–5). Illus. by Michael Kline. Series: A Williamson Kids Can! Book. 2001, Williamson paper $12.95 (1-885593-51-1). 128pp. Numbers, shapes, measurements, time, probability, and money are all discussed here, with puzzles, activities, and experiments that include a water clock, a pyramid of clay, and a pendulum made from a plastic bottle. (Rev: SLJ 3/02) [510]

5239 Long, Lynette. *Fabulous Fractions: Games and Activities that Make Math Easy and Fun* (2–6). Illus. 2001, Wiley $12.95 (0-471-36981-0). 128pp. Games and projects are used to teach youngsters the nature of fractions and how they can be manipulated. (Rev: BL 4/1/01; SLJ 7/01) [513.2]

5240 Murphy, Stuart J. *Bigger, Better, Best!* (K–3). Illus. by Marsha Winborn. Series: MathStart. 2002, HarperCollins LB $17.89 (0-06-028919-8); paper $4.99 (0-06-446247-1). 33pp. A story of siblings choosing rooms in a new house is a backdrop for math instruction. (Rev: HBG 3/03; SLJ 1/03)

5241 Murphy, Stuart J. *Captain Invincible and the Space Shapes* (1–4). Illus. by Remy Simard. Series: MathStart. 2001, HarperCollins LB $15.89 (0-06-028023-9); paper $4.95 (0-06-446731-7). 40pp. Astronaut Captain Invincible and his dog Comet introduce three-dimensional shapes as they travel through space in this Mathstart series book featuring bright, attractive cartoons. (Rev: BL 11/15/01; HBG 3/02; SLJ 10/01) [516]

5242 Murphy, Stuart J. *Dinosaur Deals* (2–4). Illus. by Kevin O'Malley. Series: MathStart. 2001, HarperCollins LB $15.89 (0-06-028927-9); paper $4.95 (0-06-446251-X). 30pp. Math concepts and dinosaur facts are interwoven in this story of the search for a Tyrannosaurus rex trading card. (Rev: HBG 3/02; SLJ 1/02)

5243 Murphy, Stuart J. *Safari Park* (1–4). Illus. by Steve Bjorkman. Series: MathStart. 2002, HarperCollins LB $4.95 (0-06-446245-5); paper $15.89 (0-06-028915-5). 40pp. On a visit to an amusement park, children must figure out how many tickets they need for each activity. (Rev: BL 2/1/02; HBG 10/02; SLJ 8/02) [512.9]

5244 Murphy, Stuart J. *Seaweed Soup* (PS–K). Illus. by Frank Remkiewicz. Series: MathStart. 2001, HarperCollins LB $15.89 (0-06-028033-6); paper $4.95 (0-06-446736-8). 40pp. An amusing story about a turtle serving lunch serves as an introduction to the concepts of sets and counting. (Rev: BL 9/15/01; HBG 3/02; SLJ 1/02) [511.3]

5245 Murphy, Stuart J. *Sluggers' Car Wash* (1–3). Illus. by Barney Saltzberg. 2002, HarperCollins LB $17.89 (0-06-028921-X); paper $4.99 (0-06-

446248-X). 40pp. A car wash fund-raiser serves as a lesson in making change and other math concepts. (Rev: BL 2/1/03; HBG 3/03; SLJ 1/03) [513.12]

5246 Murphy, Stuart J. *The Sundae Scoop* (1–3). Illus. by Cynthia Jabar. 2003, HarperCollins LB $16.89 (0-06-028925-2); paper $4.99 (0-06-446250-1). 40pp. A story of the various flavor combinations available at an ice-cream booth illustrates a basic math concept in a way sure to appeal. (Rev: BL 1/1–15/03) [511]

5247 Neuschwander, Cindy. *Sir Cumference and the Great Knight of Angleland: A Math Adventure* (1–4). Illus. by Wayne Geehan. 2001, Charlesbridge LB $16.95 (1-57091-170-3); paper $7.95 (1-57091-169-X). 32pp. The pun-full exploits of Radius, son of Sir Cumference and Lady Di of Ameter, involve the mastery of angles, squares, circles, and so forth, in this story that can be read on several levels. (Rev: HBG 3/02; SLJ 2/02) [516]

5248 Pistoia, Sara. *Counting* (1–3). Illus. Series: Mighty Math. 2002, Child's World LB $24.21 (1-56766-114-9). 24pp. Counting by fives and tens is shown with clear examples and advice from cartoon character Math Mutt. Also use *Money*, which discusses counting change. (Rev: SLJ 3/03)

5249 Skinner, Daphne. *Tightwad Tod* (1–3). Illus. by John Nez. Series: Math Matters. 2001, Kane paper $4.95 (1-57565-109-2). 32pp. Tod has $20 to spend, and the story follows his purchases and deducts the amounts spent, in this book that includes three math problems. (Rev: SLJ 1/02) [512.9]

5250 Tang, Greg. *The Best of Times: Math Strategies That Multiply* (2–3). Illus. by Harry Briggs. 2002, Scholastic $16.95 (0-439-21044-5). 32pp. A rhyming approach to remembering the multiplication tables from one to ten. (Rev: BL 11/1/02; HBG 3/03; SLJ 9/02) [513.2]

5251 Wells, Rosemary. *Adding It Up* (PS–K). Illus. by Michael Koelsch. Series: Get Set for Kindergarten! 2001, Viking paper $5.99 (0-14-230040-3). 24pp. Familiar characters tackle basic math skills — adding, subtracting, counting, sorting, and graphs. (Rev: HBG 3/02; SLJ 3/02) [513.211]

5252 Zaslavsky, Claudia. *Number Sense and Nonsense: Building Math Creativity and Confidence Through Number Play* (3–6). Illus. 2001, Chicago Review paper $14.95 (1-55652-378-5). 120pp. Readers are encouraged to develop "number sense" rather than learning by rote, in chapters that introduce mathematical concepts, look at money and measurement, and provide puzzles, games, and some history. (Rev: SLJ 7/01) [510]

Mathematical Puzzles

5253 Barber, Patti. *First Number Book* (PS–1). Illus. by Mandy Stanley. 2001, Kingfisher $12.95 (0-7534-5338-X). 48pp. More than a counting book, this brightly illustrated guide also looks at shapes

and sizes and addition and subtraction and includes beginning mathematical puzzles and exercises. (Rev: BL 10/1/01; SLJ 7/01) [513.2]

5254 Blum, Raymond. *Mathemania* (3–6). Illus. by Jeff Sinclair. 2001, Sterling $14.95 (0-8069-2399-7). 96pp. Thirty-four math-based tricks are shown with clear directions and explanations of why the trick works. (Rev: HBG 3/02; SLJ 3/02) [793.74]

5255 Hemme, Heinrich. *Math Mind Games* (5 Up). Illus. by Matthias Schwoerer. 2002, Sterling paper $12.95 (0-8069-7691-8). 128pp. Challenging text-based puzzles are accompanied by enlightening illustrations and an answer section that is clear and attractive. (Rev: SLJ 9/02) [793.7]

5256 Lewis, J. Patrick. *Arithme-Tickle: An Even Number of Odd Riddle-Rhymes* (2–4). Illus. by Frank Remkiewicz. 2002, Harcourt $16.00 (0-15-216418-9). 32pp. A book of puzzles and problems that entertain while testing elementary mathematics skills, with illustrations. (Rev: BL 5/15/02; HBG 10/02; SLJ 4/02) [513]

5257 Tang, Greg. *Math Appeal: Mind-Stretching Math Riddles* (2–4). Illus. by Harry Briggs. 2003, Scholastic $16.95 (0-439-21046-1). 40pp. Counting and adding puzzles encourage children to find answers in creative ways. (Rev: BL 2/15/03; SLJ 2/03) [510]

5258 Tang, Greg. *Math for All Seasons: Mind-Stretching Math Riddles* (1–3). Illus. by Harry Briggs. 2002, Scholastic $16.95 (0-439-21042-9). 40pp. Each spread of this book for younger readers features a different math riddle, as well as clues to counting in different ways. (Rev: BL 2/1/02; HBG 10/02; SLJ 3/02) [513]

5259 Wise, Bill. *Whodunit Math Puzzles* (5–8). Illus. 2001, Sterling $14.95 (0-8069-5896-0). 96pp. Cal Q. Leiter tests his wit in a number of pesky puzzles. (Rev: BL 6/1–15/01; HBG 10/01) [793.7]

Time, Clocks, and Calendars

5260 Dolan, Graham. *The Greenwich Guide to Day and Night* (3–6). Illus. Series: Greenwich Guide To. 2001, Heinemann LB $22.79 (1-58810-042-1). 32pp. Dolan explains how day becomes night, with photographs, a glossary, and other aids. Also use *The Greenwich Guide to Measuring Time* (2001). (Rev: BL 10/15/01) [525]

5261 Farndon, John. *Time* (3–6). Series: Science Experiments. 2002, Marshall Cavendish LB $16.95 (0-7614-1470-3). 32pp. Through simple experiments using common household objects, the nature and properties of time are explored. (Rev: BL 12/15/02; HBG 3/03) [529]

5262 Nagda, Ann Whitehead, and Cindy Bickel. *Chimp Math: Learning About Time from a Baby Chimpanzee* (2–5). Illus. 2002, Holt $16.95 (0-8050-6674-8). 32pp. This is a delightful and effective combination, presenting both the story of young chimp Jiggs being raised by humans and the various methods of timekeeping — clocks, calendars, time-lines, charts — that recorded his growth and development. (Rev: BL 11/1/02; HB 9–10/02; HBG 3/03; SLJ 9/02) [529]

5263 Wells, Robert E. *How Do You Know What Time It Is?* (2–5). Illus. 2002, Albert Whitman $14.95 (0-8075-7939-4); paper $6.95 (0-8075-7940-8). 32pp. In picture-book format, the author traces the history of timekeeping — from sundials to quartz crystals, from lunar and solar calendars to the one we know today. (Rev: BL 12/1/02; HBG 3/03; SLJ 1/03) [529]

5264 Williams, Brian. *Calendars* (4–6). Series: About Time. 2002, Smart Apple LB $24.25 (1-58340-207-1). 32pp. The need for keeping time and the various methods used over the centuries are explained in text and illustrations. (Rev: HBG 3/03; SLJ 12/02) [909.83]

Weights and Measures

5265 Long, Lynette. *Measurement Mania: Games and Activities that Make Math Easy and Fun* (2–6). Illus. 2001, Wiley $12.95 (0-471-36980-2). 128pp. Forty activities are outlined, such as measuring the length of a smile, in this entertaining book that teaches the rudiments of measurement. (Rev: BL 4/1/01; SLJ 7/01) [513.2]

5266 Schwartz, David M. *Millions to Measure* (1–4). Illus. by Steven Kellogg. 2003, HarperCollins LB $17.89 (0-06-623784-X). 40pp. Marvelosissimo the Mathematical Magician explains the history of measures and measurement (with an appendix on the metric system) in this informative and entertaining book. (Rev: BL 2/1/03*; HB 3–4/03; SLJ 3/03) [530.8]

Meteorology

Air

5267 Friend, Sandra. *Earth's Wild Winds* (5–8). Illus. Series: Exploring Planet Earth. 2002, Twenty-First Century LB $24.90 (0-7613-2673-1). 63pp. Report writers will find good material in this attractively presented coverage of all kinds of winds that also looks at the ways in which humans have attempted to harness wind power. (Rev: HBG 3/03; SLJ 10/02)

5268 Gallant, Roy A. *Atmosphere: Sea of Air* (4–8). Illus. Series: Earthworks. 2003, Marshall Cavendish $19.95 (0-7614-1366-9). 80pp. An intriguing and well-presented look at how changes in the atmosphere affect us — from storms to beautiful rainbows and sunsets — and how we affect the atmosphere. (Rev: BL 3/15/03; HBG 3/03) [551.51]

Storms

5269 Allaby, Michael. *Tornadoes and Other Dramatic Weather Systems* (4–8). Series: Secret Worlds. 2001, DK $14.95 (0-7894-7979-6); paper $7.95 (0-7894-7980-X). 96pp. Unusual page design and attractive illustrations are found in this book on violent weather systems with an emphasis on tornadoes, how they are formed and tracked, and their effects when they strike. (Rev: BL 10/15/01; HBG 3/02) [551.5]

5270 De Hahn, Tracee. *The Blizzard of 1888* (5–9). Series: Great Disasters: Reforms and Ramifications. 2000, Chelsea LB $19.95 (0-7910-5787-9). 104pp. De Hahn looks at the impact of this famous blizzard and at the changes in infrastructure and services that resulted from it. (Rev: BL 4/15/01; HBG 10/01; SLJ 6/01) [974.7]

5271 Nicolson, Cynthia Pratt. *Hurricane!* (4–8). Illus. Series: Disaster. 2002, Kids Can $14.95 (1-55074-906-4); paper $6.95 (1-55074-970-6). 32pp. An accessible text and many photographs provide information on hurricane formation and intensity, on the preparations for major hurricanes, and on famous storms of the past. (Rev: HBG 3/03; SLJ 12/02)

5272 Rotter, Charles. *Hurricanes: Storms of the Sea* (4–6). Series: Lifeviews. 2002, Creative Editions LB $24.25 (1-58341-020-1). 32pp. A revised edition with updated text and new photographs that describes hurricanes and their causes and includes two projects. (Rev: HBG 3/03; SLJ 1/03) [551.5]

5273 Simon, Seymour. *Super Storms* (1–3). Series: See More Readers. 2002, North-South $13.95 (1-58717-137-6); paper $3.95 (1-58717-138-4). 32pp. Violent storms and their causes are covered in this beginning reader that uses double-page spreads consisting each of a large color picture opposite a few lines of text. (Rev: BL 7/02; HBG 10/02) [551.5]

5274 Steele, Christy. *Tsunamis* (3–5). Illus. 2001, Raintree Steck-Vaughn LB $15.98 (0-7398-4706-6). 32pp. The authors look at our knowledge of tidal waves and their causes, and discuss the ways in which we can protect ourselves from danger. (Rev: HBG 3/02; SLJ 2/02) [551.55]

5275 Wade, Mary Dodson. *Tsunami: Monster Waves* (4–8). Series: American Disasters. 2002, Enslow LB $18.95 (0-7660-1786-9). 48pp. This book explains in photographs and text how these giant sea swells are created, how they are tracked, and their effects. (Rev: BL 6/1–15/02; HBG 10/02; SLJ 10/02) [551.55]

Water

5276 Gallant, Roy A. *Water: Our Precious Resource* (4–8). Illus. Series: Earthworks. 2003, Marshall Cavendish $19.95 (0-7614-1365-0). 80pp. A thought-provoking and well-presented overview of the sources of water; the ways in which we use, misuse, and recycle water; and efforts to preserve this vital natural resource. (Rev: BL 3/15/03; HBG 3/03; SLJ 2/03) [553.7]

5277 Hamilton, Kersten. *This Is the Ocean* (PS–2). Illus. by Lorianne Siomades. 2001, Boyds Mills $15.95 (1-56397-890-3). 32pp. Using rhyming couplets and lovely three-dimensional collages, this book presents the water cycle to a young audience. (Rev: BL 4/15/01; HBG 10/01; SLJ 6/01) [551.46]

5278 Neye, Emily. *Water* (K–3). Illus. by Cindy Revell. Series: All Aboard Science Reader. 2002, Grosset LB $13.89 (0-448-42878-4); paper $3.99 (0-448-42847-4). 32pp. The sources, properties, and uses of water are presented in simple text and picture clues that make an appealing package. (Rev: SLJ 3/03)

5279 Oxlade, Chris. *Water* (2–3). Series: Materials, Materials, Materials. 2002, Heinemann LB $21.36 (1-58810-588-1). 32pp. Color photographs and an easy text are used to introduce water, its properties, and its uses. (Rev: BL 6/1–15/02) [533.7]

5280 Schaefer, Lola M. *This Is the Rain* (PS–1). Illus. by Jane Wattenberg. 2001, Greenwillow LB $15.89 (0-688-17040-4). 32pp. Simple, rhythmic text echoes the movement of water through its cycle from sea to sky to streams in this book with inventive illustrations. (Rev: BCCB 10/01; BL 12/15/01; HBG 3/02; SLJ 9/01) [551]

Weather

5281 Armentrout, David, and Patricia Armentrout. *Weather* (PS–2). Illus. 2002, Rourke LB $26.60 (1-58952-346-6). 32pp. Simple definitions are given for 50 words about weather (arid, breeze, and so forth), along with a sentence that includes the word. (Rev: SLJ 3/03)

5282 Bredeson, Carmen. *El Nino and La Nina: Deadly Weather* (4–8). Series: American Disasters.

2002, Enslow LB $18.95 (0-7660-1551-3). 48pp. A well-researched account of these two weather phenomena, their effects, and how they can be traced. (Rev: BL 6/1–15/02; HBG 10/02; SLJ 6/02) [551.6]

5283 DiSpezio, Michael A. *Weather Mania: Discovering What's Up and What's Coming Down* (3–5). Illus. by Dave Garbot. 2003, Sterling $19.95 (0-8069-7745-0). 80pp. An introduction to basic weather facts and concepts that includes activities using everyday materials. (Rev: BL 3/15/03) [551.5]

5284 Nelson, Robin. *A Rainy Day* (PS–1). Illus. Series: Weather. 2001, Lerner LB $15.93 (0-8225-0173-2); paper $3.95 (0-8225-1962-3). 23pp. In a small format for beginning readers, some simple facts about rainy days are accompanied by bold illustrations. Also use *A Snowy Day* and *A Sunny Day* (both 2001). (Rev: HBG 3/02; SLJ 4/02) [551.57]

5285 Stein, Paul. *Forecasting the Climate of the Future* (5–7). Series: The Library of Future Weather and Climate. 2001, Rosen LB $19.95 (0-8239-3413-6). 64pp. A fascinating, well-organized account that looks at long-range weather predictions and at the use and accuracy of computer models in forecasting future weather patterns, especially with regard to global warming. Also use *Storms of the Future* (2001), which looks at whether global warming might cause stronger storms. (Rev: SLJ 4/02) [551.5]

5286 Stein, Paul. *Ice Ages of the Future* (5–7). Series: The Library of Future Weather and Climate. 2001, Rosen LB $19.95 (0-8239-3415-2). 64pp. A look at the possibility that the greenhouse effect and other factors could in fact cause a wave of colder rather than warmer air. (Rev: SLJ 11/01) [551.6]

5287 Vogel, Carole Garbuny. *Weather Legends: Native American Lore and the Science of Weather* (4–8). Illus. 2001, Millbrook LB $27.90 (0-7613-1900-X). 80pp. Native American weather myths are paired with scientific information about actual weather phenomena. (Rev: BL 9/1/01; HBG 3/02; SLJ 10/01) [398.2]

Physics

General

5288 Bradley, Kimberly Brubaker. *Pop! A Book About Bubbles* (PS–1). Illus. by Margaret Miller. Series: Let's-Read-and-Find-Out Science. 2001, HarperCollins LB $15.89 (0-06-028701-2). 40pp. This overview of bubbles doesn't attempt to answer all questions that may arise, but presents basic concepts and invites readers to try the experiments at the end. (Rev: BCCB 9/01; BL 8/01; HBG 3/02; SLJ 10/01) [530.4]

5289 Farndon, John. *Buoyancy* (3–6). Series: Science Experiments. 2002, Marshall Cavendish LB $16.95 (0-7614-1467-3). 32pp. The nature of buoyancy is explained through a simple text, color photographs, and an explanatory experiment in each chapter. (Rev: BL 12/15/02; HBG 3/03) [530]

5290 Goodstein, Madeline. *Fish Tank Physics Projects* (5–8). Series: Science Fair Success. 2002, Enslow LB $20.95 (0-7660-1624-2). 112pp. Using a common fish tank and its contents, various aspects of laws of physics are presented in the form of science fair projects. (Rev: BL 5/15/02; HBG 10/02; SLJ 11/02) [621.9]

5291 Parker, Barry. *The Mystery of Gravity* (5–8). Illus. Series: The Story of Science. 2002, Benchmark LB $19.95 (0-7614-1428-2). 78pp. Parker traces our understanding of gravity from the early Greek philosophers through Einstein and Hubble, with discussion of the Big Bang theory and black holes. (Rev: HBG 3/03; SLJ 2/03) [531]

5292 Tiner, John Hudson. *Gravity* (4–7). Series: Understanding Science. 2002, Smart Apple LB $24.25 (1-58340-157-1). 32pp. Through a number of simple projects, colorful illustrations, and a clear text, the fundamentals of gravity are explored. (Rev: BL 3/15/03; HBG 3/03) [531]

Energy and Motion

General

5293 Bradley, Kimberly Brubaker. *Energy Makes Things Happen* (1–3). Illus. by Paul Meisel. Series: Let's-Read-and-Find-Out Science. 2003, HarperCollins LB $16.89 (0-06-028909-0); paper $4.99 (0-06-445213-1). 40pp. An entertaining introduction to energy and its sources and uses, for young readers. (Rev: BL 2/1/03; SLJ 1/03) [531]

5294 Cobb, Vicki. *Whirlers and Twirlers: Science Fun with Spinning* (3–5). Illus. by Steve Haefele. 2001, Millbrook LB $23.40 (0-7613-1573-X). 64pp. A lighthearted introduction to the physics involved in the motion of spinning, with experiments with tops, pinwheels, and other objects. (Rev: BL 10/15/01; HBG 3/02; SLJ 1/02) [531]

5295 Farndon, John. *Energy* (3–6). Series: Science Experiments. 2002, Marshall Cavendish LB $16.95 (0-7614-1469-X). 32pp. The nature and forms of energy are introduced through a series of easy-to-follow experiments and a simple explanatory text with many color photographs and diagrams. (Rev: BL 12/15/02; HBG 3/03) [531.6]

5296 Farndon, John. *Motion* (3–6). Series: Science Experiments. 2002, Marshall Cavendish LB $16.95 (0-7614-1471-1). 32pp. The properties of motion are revealed to the young scientist through several easy-to-follow activities using common household materials. (Rev: BL 12/15/02; HBG 3/03) [531]

Coal, Gas, and Oil

5297 Ditchfield, Christin. *Coal* (2–5). Series: True Books — Natural Resources. , Children's LB $23.50 (0-516-22342-9); paper $6.95 (0-516-29366-4). 48pp. This simple introduction to coal explains how it is formed, where it is found, how it is used, and how it affects our environment. (Rev: BL 10/15/02) [622]

Nuclear Energy

5298 Cole, Michael D. *Three Mile Island: Nuclear Disaster* (4–8). Series: American Disasters. 2002, Enslow LB $18.95 (0-7660-1556-4). 48pp. An informative, well-researched account of the disaster that affected the development of nuclear power plants in this country. (Rev: BL 6/1–15/02; HBG 10/02; SLJ 6/02) [621.48]

Light and Color

5299 Boekhoff, P. M., and Stuart A. Kallen. *Lasers* (4–5). Illus. Series: KidHaven Science Library. 2002, Gale LB $23.70 (0-7377-0944-8). 48pp. A discussion of the discovery of lasers and of their uses today in such fields as industry, medicine, recreation, and the armed forces. (Rev: BL 5/1/02; SLJ 9/02) [621.36]

5300 Lobb, Janice. *Color and Noise! Let's Play with Toys!* (1–3). Series: At Home with Science. 2001, Kingfisher $10.95 (0-7534-5362-2). 32pp. Easily accomplished experiments, attractive diagrams, and large simple text are used to answer basic questions about color. (Rev: BL 12/15/01; HBG 10/02; SLJ 2/02) [536]

Magnetism and Electricity

5301 Bartholomew, Alan. *Electric Mischief* (4–7). Series: Kids Can Do It. 2002, Kids Can $12.95 (1-55074-923-4); paper $5.95 (1-55074-925-0). 48pp. An activity book that outlines simple, safe experiments with electricity. (Rev: BL 3/15/03; HBG 3/03; SLJ 12/02) [537]

5302 Tiner, John Hudson. *Magnetism* (4–7). Series: Understanding Science. 2002, Smart Apple LB $24.25 (1-58340-158-X). 32pp. Using clear explanations, simple projects, and good illustrations, the concept of magnetism is introduced. (Rev: BL 3/15/03; HBG 3/03) [538.4]

Optical Illusions

5303 DiSpezio, Michael A. *Eye-Popping Optical Illusions* (3–6). Illus. 2001, Sterling $17.95 (0-8069-6641-6). 80pp. A bright and absorbing look at illusions found in geometric patterns, 3-D photography, shading and light, and other tricks that fool the eye, with scientific explanations and a few projects. (Rev: BL 8/01; HBG 10/01; SLJ 7/01) [152.14]

5304 DiSpezio, Michael A. *Simple Optical Illusion Experiments with Everyday Materials* (3–6). Illus. 2001, Sterling $14.95 (0-8069-6635-1). 128pp. A collection of optical tricks that range from the simple to the complex, with full explanations of the underlying science. (Rev: BL 7/01; HBG 10/01; SLJ 8/01) [152.14]

5305 Wenzel, Angela. *Do You See What I See? The Art of Illusion* (5–8). Trans. from German by Rosie Jackson. 2001, Prestel $14.95 (3-7913-2488-8). 29pp. Tricks with perspective and color, coded messages, and hidden images are all presented in this attractive volume that makes for excellent browsing. (Rev: HBG 3/02; SLJ 2/02) [152]

Simple Machines

5306 Armentrout, David, and Patricia Armentrout. *An Inclined Plane* (1–3). Illus. Series: How Can I Experiment With . . . ? 2002, Rourke LB $26.60 (1-58952-333-4). 32pp. This volume teaches younger readers, through illustration, narrative, and experimentation, about inclined planes. Other titles in this series include *A Lever*, *A Screw*, *A Wedge*, and *A Wheel* (all 2002). (Rev: BL 10/15/02; SLJ 3/03) [621.8]

5307 Fowler, Allan. *Simple Machines* (1–2). Illus. Series: Rookie Read-About Science. 2001, Children's $19.00 (0-516-21680-5). 32pp. A basic introduction to the lever, inclined plane, pulley, and wheel and axle. (Rev: BL 7/01) [621.8]

5308 Royston, Angela. *Screws* (2–4). Illus. Series: Machines in Action. 2000, Heinemann LB $21.36 (1-57572-322-0). 32pp. An easy-to-read introduction to how screws work and the different kinds of screws we find in objects all around us. Also use *Springs* (2000). (Rev: HBG 3/01; SLJ 4/01) [621.8]

5309 Walker, Sally M., and Roseann Feldmann. *Inclined Planes and Wedges* (2–4). Photos by Andy King. 2001, Lerner LB $23.93 (0-8225-2221-7). 47pp. A concise explanation of these simple machines, that increases in complexity as the reader progresses through the book, with simple experiments and clear illustrations. Also use *Pulleys* and *Wheels and Axles* (both 2001). (Rev: HBG 3/02; SLJ 2/02) [621.8]

Space Exploration

5310 Berger, Melvin, and Gilda Berger. *Can You Hear a Shout in Space? Questions and Answers About Space Exploration* (3–6). Illus. 2001, Scholastic $14.95 (0-439-09582-4); paper $5.95 (0-439-14879-0). 48pp. In question-and-answer format, this title tackles topics of interest both to browsers and report writers. (Rev: BL 7/01; HBG 10/01) [629.4]

5311 Beyer, Mark. *Crisis in Space: Apollo 13* (3–4). Illus. Series: Survivor. 2002, Children's LB $19.00 (0-516-23903-1); paper $6.95 (0-516-23485-4). 48pp. A suspenseful account of the problems encountered on the *Apollo 13* mission and the dangers the astronauts faced. (Rev: SLJ 6/02) [629.45]

5312 Goodman, Susan E. *Ultimate Field Trip 5: Blasting Off to Space Academy* (3–5). Illus. Series: Ultimate Field Trip. 2001, Simon & Schuster $17.00 (0-689-83044-0). 48pp. This book follows 16 young people through a week-long training session at the U.S. Space Academy and includes the children's own comments and some space facts. (Rev: BL 5/1/01; HBG 10/01; SLJ 6/01) [629.45]

5313 Mason, Paul. *Space Race* (3–5). Series: Space Busters. 2002, Raintree Steck-Vaughn LB $17.98 (0-7398-4851-8). 32pp. The Apollo Program is the major focus of this look at efforts to win the space competition. (Rev: HBG 10/02; SLJ 4/02) [629.45]

5314 Spangenburg, Ray, and Kit Moser. *Life on Other Worlds* (5–9). Illus. Series: Out of This World. 2002, Watts LB $32.00 (0-531-11895-9); paper $14.95 (0-531-15566-8). 112pp. The possibilities of extraterrestrial life and the efforts to intercept any communications are discussed in this narrative, along with the origins of the solar system and the composition of the planet Mars. (Rev: SLJ 12/02) [001.9]

5315 Spangenburg, Ray, and Kit Moser. *Onboard the Space Shuttle* (5–9). Illus. Series: Out of This World. 2002, Watts LB $32.00 (0-531-11896-7); paper $14.95 (0-531-15568-4). 112pp. The problems of living and working in space are presented, plus the history of the shuttle program, information on individual astronauts, statistics, and lots of photographs. (Rev: SLJ 9/02) [629.441]

5316 Vogt, Gregory L. *Disasters in Space Exploration* (5–8). Illus. 2001, Millbrook $23.90 (0-7613-1920-4). 72pp. Accidents and failures that have marred the success rates of the American and Soviet space programs are covered in interesting detail with many photographs. (Rev: BL 10/1/01; HBG 3/02; SLJ 8/01*) [363.12]

5317 Woodford, Chris. *Space Dramas* (3–5). Illus. Series: Space Busters. 2002, Raintree Steck-Vaughn LB $17.98 (0-7398-4850-X). 32pp. Natural space events such as comet collisions are described along with disasters that have hit manned and unmanned missions outside our atmosphere. (Rev: HBG 10/02; SLJ 4/02) [629.45]

Technology, Engineering, and Industry

General and Miscellaneous Industries and Inventions

5318 Baker, Christopher W. *A New World of Simulators: Training with Technology* (5–8). Illus. 2001, Millbrook $22.90 (0-7613-1352-4). 48pp. An introduction to the uses of simulators and their importance in training workers who operate complex technologies like those found in airplanes, ships, and nuclear power plants. (Rev: BL 8/01; HBG 3/02; SLJ 8/01) [003]

5319 Cooper, Elisha. *Ice Cream* (1–3). Illus. 2002, HarperCollins LB $15.89 (0-06-001424-5). 40pp. An entertaining look at the production of ice cream, tracing its way from cow to consumer. (Rev: BL 5/15/02; HB 5–6/02; HBG 10/02; SLJ 5/02) [637.4]

5320 Ditchfield, Christin. *Wood* (2–5). Series: True Books — Natural Resources. 2002, Children's LB $23.50 (0-516-22346-1); paper $6.95 (0-516-29370-2). 48pp. This simple account shows the importance of wood in such industries as building and papermaking, and tells how we can protect this resouce from forest fires and pollution. (Rev: BL 10/15/02) [674]

5321 Englart, Mindi Rose. *Pens* (3–5). Series: Made in the USA. 2002, Gale LB $21.54 (1-56711-487-3). 32pp. The evolution of writing pens is described along with a detailed view of how they are made today. (Rev: BL 9/15/02) [681]

5322 Harper, Charise Mericle. *Imaginative Inventions* (2–4). Illus. 2001, Little, Brown $14.95 (0-316-34725-6). 32pp. An imaginative look at the origins of products ranging from chewing gum and doughnuts to roller skates and high-heeled shoes. (Rev: BL 12/15/01; HBG 3/02; SLJ 10/01) [609]

5323 Lockie, Mark. *Biometric Technology* (5–8). Series: Science at the Edge. 2002, Heinemann LB $27.86 (1-58810-701-9). 64pp. Lockie explores the study of biometry and its applications in such areas

as voice-speaker identification and facial recognition. (Rev: BL 10/15/02; HBG 3/03) [609]

5324 Oxlade, Chris. *Glass* (2–3). Series: Materials, Materials, Materials. 2001, Heinemann LB $21.36 (1-58810-154-1). 32pp. Though in a compact format, this book contains lots of information about how glass is manufactured, its history, forms, and uses. (Rev: BL 10/15/01) [666]

5325 Oxlade, Chris. *Paper* (2–3). Series: Materials, Materials, Materials. 2001, Heinemann LB $21.36 (1-58810-156-8). 32pp. An attractive, introductory look at paper, how it is produced, its uses, and its recycling and conservation. (Rev: BL 10/15/01) [676]

5326 Oxlade, Chris. *Plastic* (2–3). Series: Materials, Materials, Materials. 2001, Heinemann LB $21.36 (1-58810-157-6). 32pp. Using a compact format with a color illustration and text on each page, this introductory work explains what plastics are, how they are made, their uses, and their role in conservation. (Rev: BL 10/15/01) [547.7]

5327 Oxlade, Chris. *Rubber* (2–3). Series: Materials, Materials, Materials. 2002, Heinemann LB $21.36 (1-58810-586-5). 32pp. This book provides a simple, clear introduction to rubber, its properties, where it comes from, and its uses in everyday life. (Rev: BL 6/1–15/02) [633.8]

5328 Oxlade, Chris. *Wood* (2–3). Illus. Series: Materials, Materials, Materials. 2001, Heinemann LB $21.36 (1-58810-158-4). 32pp. A discussion of where wood comes from and how it is made into products we use, with photographs. (Rev: BL 10/15/01) [674]

5329 Romanek, Trudee, and Pat Cupples. *The Technology Book for Girls: And Other Advanced Beings* (3–6). 2001, Kids Can $14.95 (1-55074-936-6); paper $8.95 (1-55074-619-7). 56pp. The workings of a variety of everyday items — remote controls, smoke detectors, lasers, and so forth — are detailed in this lighthearted book that also profiles women with science-based careers. (Rev: HBG 10/01; SLJ 6/01) [604.83]

5330 St. George, Judith. *So You Want to Be an Inventor?* (3–5). Illus. by David Small. 2002, Putnam $16.99 (0-399-23593-0). 56pp. A spirited and informative look at inventors and their inventions with eye-catching and amusing illustrations. (Rev: BCCB 10/02; BL 8/02; HB 9–10/02; HBG 3/03; SLJ 9/02) [608]

5331 Stone, Tanya Lee. *Toothpaste: From Start to Finish* (3–5). Series: Made in the USA. 2001, Blackbirch $16.95 (1-56711-481-4). 32pp. A behind-the-scenes look at a factory where toothpaste is made, with information on the entire manufacturing process from raw materials to finished product. (Rev: BL 8/1/01; HBG 3/02) [668]

5332 Wulffson, Don L. *The Kid Who Invented the Trampoline* (3–6). Illus. 2001, Dutton $15.99 (0-525-46654-1). 128pp. Fifty inventions, arranged alphabetically, range from disposable diapers and Post-It Notes to parking meters and trampolines. (Rev: BL 7/01; HBG 3/02; SLJ 10/01) [609]

Aeronautics and Airplanes

5333 Gaffney, Timothy R. *Hurricane Hunters* (4–7). Series: Aircraft. 2001, Enslow LB $18.95 (0-7660-1569-6). 48pp. Information on the planes that investigate hurricanes is accompanied by quotes from the pilots and scientists who fly in them. (Rev: HBG 3/02; SLJ 2/02) [551.55]

5334 Iversen, Eve. *Animal Aviators: Masters of Flight* (4–7). Illus. 2001, Watts $24.00 (0-531-11749-9). 128pp. An intriguing account that looks at animals' ability to fly and glide and at human attempts to duplicate this talent. (Rev: BL 7/01) [573.7]

5335 Old, Wendie. *To Fly: The Story of the Wright Brothers* (3–5). Illus. by Robert Andrew Parker. 2002, Clarion $16.00 (0-618-13347-X). 48pp. An attractive, large-format introduction to the brothers and their accomplishments with good coverage of the basic principles of flight. (Rev: BL 10/1/02; HB 11–12/02; HBG 3/03; SLJ 10/02) [629.13]

5336 Oxlade, Chris. *Plane* (4–6). Series: Take It Apart. 2002, Thameside $16.95 (1-930643-95-0). 32pp. Readers get an inside look at the various parts of a plane with cutaway illustrations, in-depth diagrams, and fact boxes. (Rev: BL 1/1–15/03; HBG 3/03) [629.133]

5337 Rinard, Judith E. *Book of Flight* (4–8). Illus. 2001, Firefly $24.95 (1-55209-619-X); paper $14.95 (1-55209-599-1). 128pp. Significant moments in man's quest for flight each cover a two-page spread in this book based on the Smithsonian's Air and Space Museum collection. (Rev: BL 11/1/01; HBG 3/02; SLJ 12/01) [629.1309]

5338 Rinard, Judith E. *The Story of Flight* (3–6). Illus. 2002, Firefly $16.95 (1-55297-642-4); paper $8.95 (1-55297-694-7). 64pp. From balloon travel to possible manned space flights to Mars, this well-illustrated overview of the history of flight was published in cooperation with the National Air and Space Museum. (Rev: BL 12/15/02; HBG 3/03; SLJ 12/02) [629.1]

5339 Rogers, Hal. *Airplanes* (PS–1). Series: Machines at Work. 2001, Child's World LB $21.36 (1-56766-962-X). 32pp. A beginning reader that uses a simple text and many color photographs to introduce the world of airplanes. (Rev: BL 6/1–15/01; HBG 10/01) [629.133]

5340 Santella, Andrew. *Air Force One* (4–7). Illus. 2003, Millbrook LB $24.90 (0-7613-2617-0). 48pp. An overview of the aircraft that have transported United States presidents, with an inside look at today's Air Force One. (Rev: BL 2/15/03) [387.7]

5341 Sherrow, Victoria. *The Hindenburg Disaster: Doomed Airship* (4–8). Series: American Disasters. 2002, Enslow LB $18.95 (0-7660-1554-8). 48pp. Excellent illustrations and a clear text are used to tell the story of the destruction of the mighty German dirigible. (Rev: BL 6/1–15/02; HBG 10/02; SLJ 6/02) [629.133]

5342 Simon, Seymour. *Amazing Aircraft* (1–3). Illus. Series: See More Readers. 2002, North-South $13.95 (1-58717-179-1); paper $3.95 (1-58717-180-5). 32pp. Simon uses concise text and colorful photographs to present information about different types of aircraft from the earliest to Concorde and the Stealth fighter. (Rev: BL 7/02; HBG 3/03; SLJ 8/02) [629.133]

5343 Suen, Anastasia. *Air Show* (PS–1). Illus. by Cecco Mariniello. 2001, Holt $15.95 (0-8050-4952-5). 32pp. Young airplane fans will love this almost wordless introduction to air shows and to vintage planes, with detailed drawings, specifications, and a timeline of flight firsts. (Rev: BCCB 5/01; BL 6/1–15/01; HBG 10/01) [629.1]

5344 Weitzman, David. *Jenny: The Airplane That Taught America to Fly* (2–4). Illus. 2002, Millbrook LB $22.90 (0-7613-2565-4). 40pp. Weitzman uses the story of a former pilot telling her grandchildren about their great-grandmother's adventures as a flyer to introduce detailed information about her early plane and how it was constructed. (Rev: BL 12/1/02; HBG 3/03; SLJ 2/03) [629.133]

5345 Zaunders, Bo. *Feathers, Flaps, and Flops: Fabulous Early Fliers* (3–5). Illus. by Roxie Munro. 2001, Dutton $17.99 (0-525-46466-2). 48pp. After a fascinating introductory chapter that starts with very early and fanciful attempts at flight and ends with the lunar landing, the author profiles lesser-known pioneers including the Montgolfier brothers, Alberto Santos-Dumont, and Jimmy Doolittle. (Rev: BL 8/01; HB 7–8/01; HBG 10/01; SLJ 7/01*) [629.13]

Building and Construction

General

5346 Adkins, Jan. *Bridges: From My Side to Yours* (4–8). Illus. 2002, Millbrook LB $25.90 (0-7613-2510-7). 96pp. An illustrated and very readable history of bridge building — from the Stone Age to the modern age — with information on materials and techniques used and with detailed sketches. (Rev: BL 7/02; HB 7–8/02; HBG 10/02; SLJ 7/02) [624]

5347 Ardagh, Philip. *A Hole in the Road* (PS–K). Illus. by Tig Sutton. Series: British Mighty Machines. 2003, Thameside LB $24.25 (1-931983-02-X). 32pp. A burst water pipe causes a hole in the road and a great deal of digging, earth moving, and paving involving a variety of large machines. (Rev: BL 12/1/02; HBG 3/03) [621.8]

5348 Farbman, Melinda. *Bridges* (2–4). Series: Transportation and Communication. 2001, Enslow LB $18.95 (0-7660-1647-1). 48pp. Basic facts are given on the history of bridges and their present-day construction in this heavily illustrated volume. (Rev: BL 3/15/02; HBG 3/02) [624]

5349 Kent, Peter. *Great Building Stories of the Past* (4–7). Illus. 2002, Oxford $18.95 (0-19-521846-9). 48pp. Provides information on famous architectural marvels (the Great Pyramid, the Great Wall of China, Beauvais Cathedral, the Panama Canal, and others) and how they were built. (Rev: BL 5/15/02; HBG 10/02; SLJ 10/02) [720]

5350 Owens, Thomas S. *Football Stadiums* (5–8). Illus. Series: Sports Palaces. 2001, Millbrook LB $25.90 (0-7613-1764-3). 64pp. Rather than highlighting individual stadiums, this book covers general topics such as their design, replacement, funding, amenities, and history. (Rev: BL 4/1/01; HBG 10/01; SLJ 4/01) [796.332]

5351 Stone, Lynn M. *Bridges* (3–5). Illus. Series: How Are They Built? 2001, Rourke LB $26.60 (1-58952-135-8). 48pp. How, why, and where bridges are built, with photographs, a glossary, and other features. Also use *Dams* (2001). (Rev: BL 10/15/01) [624]

5352 Stone, Lynn M. *Roads and Highways* (3–5). Series: How Are They Built? 2001, Rourke LB $19.95 (1-58952-138-2). 48pp. Following information on the history of roads, this book gives details on highway construction today, the materials used, and the techniques employed. (Rev: BL 10/15/01) [625.7]

5353 Stone, Lynn M. *Skyscrapers* (3–5). Series: How Are They Built? 2001, Rourke LB $19.95 (1-58952-139-0). 48pp. Background material on skyscrapers is followed by coverage of how they are built, their design, materials used, and present-day practices and concerns. (Rev: BL 10/15/01) [720]

Houses

5354 Bial, Raymond. *The Houses* (4–8). Illus. Series: Building America. 2001, Marshall Cavendish LB $17.95 (0-7614-1335-9). 56pp. A history of different types of housing in the United States that includes excellent photographs and drawings. (Rev: BL 3/1/02; HBG 3/02) [392.3]

5355 Stone, Lynn M. *Houses* (3–5). Series: How Are They Built? 2001, Rourke LB $19.95 (1-58952-137-5). 48pp. After some historical material, this book describes how houses are built today and the materials used. (Rev: BL 10/15/01) [690]

Clothing, Textiles, and Jewelry

5356 Carlson, Laurie. *Queen of Inventions: How the Sewing Machine Changed the World* (3–5). Illus. 2003, Millbrook LB $22.90 (0-7613-2706-1). 32pp. The history of the sewing machine and its impact on home and commercial garment-making, with illustrations and photographs. (Rev: BL 2/15/03) [681]

5357 MacDonald, Fiona. *Clothing and Jewelry* (5–8). Illus. Series: Discovering World Cultures. 2001, Crabtree paper $8.06 (0-7787-0246-4). 38pp. Readers will enjoy browsing through this heavily illustrated guide that includes fashion, religious garb, and jewelry from around the world. (Rev: SLJ 5/02) [391]

5358 Oxlade, Chris. *Cotton* (2–3). Series: Materials, Materials, Materials. 2002, Heinemann LB $21.36 (1-58810-584-9). 32pp. With a color picture and brief text on each page, this is a basic introduction to cotton and how it is grown, processed, and made into other things. (Rev: BL 6/1–15/02) [633.5]

5359 Oxlade, Chris. *Wool* (2–3). Illus. Series: Materials, Materials, Materials. 2001, Heinemann LB $21.36 (1-58810-159-2). 32pp. Photographs accompany detailed information about where wool comes from and how it is made into products we use. (Rev: BL 10/15/01) [677]

5360 Scott, Janine. *Let's Get Dressed: What People Wear* (K–2). Series: Spyglass Books. 2002, Compass Point LB $18.60 (0-7565-0366-3). 24pp. A basic look, for beginning readers, at clothing around the world with information on customs such as wearing black at funerals. (Rev: SLJ 3/03) [745]

5361 Whitty, Helen. *Protective Clothing* (3–8). Illus. Series: Clothing. 2001, Chelsea LB $17.95 (0-7910-6574-X). 32pp. An interesting look at apparel that includes aprons, armor, firefighting suits, and space suits. Also use *You Are What You Wear* and *Underwear* (both 2001). (Rev: HBG 3/02; SLJ 12/01) [745]

5362 Woods, Samuel G. *Kids' Clothes from Start to Finish* (3–5). Series: Made in the USA. 2001, Blackbirch LB $17.95 (1-56711-483-0). 32pp. The steps in the manufacture of children's clothing from design to finished product are discussed in this colorful, easily read account. (Rev: BL 3/15/02; HBG 3/02) [687]

Computers and Automation

5363 Baker, Christopher W. *Robots Among Us: The Challenges and Promises of Robotics* (5–8). Illus. Series: New Century Technology. 2002, Millbrook LB $22.90 (0-7613-1969-7). 48pp. A lavishly illustrated account that describes the science of robotics, current developments, and what might be expected in the future. (Rev: BL 6/1–15/02; HBG 10/02; SLJ 9/02) [629.8]

5364 Chorlton, Windsor. *The Invention of the Silicon Chip: A Revolution in Daily Life* (5–8). Series: Point of Impact. 2002, Heinemann LB $16.95 (1-58810-554-7). 32pp. Chorlton explores computers before and after the invention of the chip, introduces key players in the field, and discusses the impact of this new technology on society. (Rev: SLJ 9/02) [621.3815]

5365 Douglas, Julie. *The Internet* (2–4). Series: Transportation and Communication. 2002, Enslow LB $18.95 (0-7660-1889-X). 48pp. A basic introduction to the Internet that supplies material on what it is, its history, people behind it, safety while online, and possible future developments. (Rev: BL 9/15/02; HBG 3/03) [004]

5366 Gifford, Clive. *How to Build a Robot* (4–8). Illus. by Tim Benton. Series: How To. 2001, Watts LB $14.00 (0-531-14649-9); paper $4.95 (0-531-13997-2). 96pp. Robots past, present, and future are presented, with discussion of their suitability for use in high-tech environments and in conditions that make work by humans difficult or dangerous. (Rev: SLJ 6/02) [629.892]

5367 Jefferis, David. *Internet: Electronic Global Village* (4–8). Illus. Series: Megatech. 2001, Crabtree LB $15.45 (0-7787-0052-6); paper $8.06 (0-7787-0062-3). 32pp. An eye-catching look at the development of the Internet and the World Wide Web and their uses in communication and commerce. (Rev: SLJ 6/02) [4.678]

5368 Lindsay, Dave. *Dave's Quick 'n' Easy Web Pages: An Introductory Guide to Creating Web Sites*. 2nd ed. (4–8). Illus. by Sean Lindsay. 2001, Erin paper $11.95 (0-9690609-8-X). 116pp. Fourteen-year-old Dave, with the help of his brother and father, gives good, basic information on HTML coding and Web page design. (Rev: SLJ 8/01) [005.7]

5369 Macdonald, Joan Vos. *Cybersafety: Surfing Safely Online* (5–7). Illus. Series: Teen issues. 2001, Enslow LB $17.95 (0-7660-1580-7). 64pp. Various dangers of venturing online are covered, from viruses and other problems that can infect your computer to activities such as hacking, cyberstalking, and copying software illegally. (Rev: HBG 3/02; SLJ 12/01) [004.6]

5370 Menhard, Francha Roff. *Internet Issues: Pirates, Censors, and Cybersquatters* (5–8). Series: Issues in Focus. 2001, Enslow LB $20.95 (0-7660-1687-0). 128pp. Menhard's overview of problems with filtering, copyright, privacy, and piracy will serve as a good starting point for students, who may need to turn to the Web for the most recent information. (Rev: BL 2/1/02; HBG 10/02; SLJ 2/02) [384.33]

5371 Rooney, Anne. *Chilling Out: How to Use the Internet to Make the Most of Your Free Time* (3–6). Illus. by Debi Ani. Series: Internet @ction. 2001, Big Fish $9.95 (0-8069-4149-9). 48pp. Both beginners and advanced users will find material of interest here. Also use *Homework Busters: How to Use the Internet for A+ Grades*. (Rev: SLJ 1/02) [004]

5372 Spangenburg, Ray, and Kit Moser. *Savvy Surfing on the Internet: Searching and Evaluating Web Sites* (5–8). Illus. Series: Issues in Focus. 2001, Enslow LB $20.95 (0-7660-1590-4). 112pp. Readers are encouraged to view much of the information on the Internet with healthy suspicion and are given advice on efficient searching for and assessment of Web sites. (Rev: HBG 3/02; SLJ 12/01) [004.6]

5373 Williams, Brian. *Computers* (5–8). Illus. Series: Great Inventions. 2001, Heinemann LB $24.22 (1-58810-210-6). 48pp. A chronological look at computers and their predecessors, from the abacus onward, with diagrams and information on the inventors. (Rev: HBG 3/02; SLJ 2/02) [004]

5374 Wolinsky, Art. *Internet Power Research Using the Big6 Approach* (4–8). Illus. Series: The Internet Library. 2002, Enslow LB $17.95 (0-7660-2094-0). 64pp. Readers accompany young researchers as they conduct searches using the Big6 method. (Rev: HBG 3/03; SLJ 12/02) [025.04]

Machinery

5375 Simon, Seymour. *Giant Machines* (1–3). Series: See More Readers. 2002, North-South $13.95 (1-58717-126-0); paper $3.95 (1-58717-127-9). 32pp. A beginning reader that uses double-page spreads to give basic information about large machinery. (Rev: BL 7/02; HBG 10/02; SLJ 3/02) [623.6]

Metals

5376 Oxlade, Chris. *Metal* (2–3). Series: Materials, Materials, Materials. 2001, Heinemann LB $21.36 (1-58810-155-X). 32pp. With color photographs and brief text on each page, the story of what metals are is covered plus where they are found and extracted, and their uses in everyday life. (Rev: BL 10/15/01) [669]

Telegraph, Telephone, and Telecommunications

5377 Mattern, Joanne. *From Radio to the Wireless Web* (2–4). Series: Transportation and Communication. 2002, Enslow LB $18.95 (0-7660-1893-8). 48pp. This book explains the development of telecommunications, present uses, possible future developments, and people involved in its history. (Rev: BL 9/15/02; HBG 10/02) [384]

5378 Mattern, Joanne. *Telephones* (2–4). Series: Transportation and Communication. 2002, Enslow LB $18.95 (0-7660-1888-1). 48pp. From Alexander Graham Bell to the cell phones of today, this is the history of the telephone with material on how it works and possible future developments. (Rev: BL 9/15/02; HBG 10/02) [384.6]

Television, Motion Pictures, Radio, and Recording

5379 Englart, Mindi Rose. *Music CDs from Start to Finish* (3–5). Series: Made in the USA. 2001, Blackbirch LB $17.95 (1-56711-485-7). 32pp. From raw material to finished product, this is a behind-the-scenes look at how music compact discs are made. (Rev: BL 3/15/02; HBG 3/02; SLJ 3/02) [321.389]

5380 Feeney, Kathy. *Television* (2–4). Series: Transportation and Communication. 2001, Enslow LB $18.95 (0-7660-1644-7). 48pp. A simple, well-illustrated volume on the history of television, its development, and its many uses. (Rev: BL 3/15/02; HBG 3/02) [384.55]

Transportation

General

5381 Bial, Raymond. *The Canals* (4–8). Illus. Series: Building America. 2001, Marshall Cavendish LB $17.95 (0-7614-1336-7). 56pp. This history of the U.S. canal system and how it works includes excellent photographs and illustrations that help to explain the technical aspects of canals. (Rev: BL 3/1/02; HBG 3/02; SLJ 2/02*) [386]

5382 DuTemple, Lesley A. *New York Subways* (4–7). Illus. Series: Great Building Feats. 2003, Lerner LB $27.93 (0-8225-0378-6). 80pp. DuTemple presents the history of the subway system with details of its difficult construction, continuing financial problems, and the damage caused in the destruction of the World Trade Center. (Rev: BL 1/1–15/03) [388.4]

5383 Francis, Dorothy. *Our Transportation System* (3–4). Illus. Series: I Know America. 2002, Millbrook LB $23.90 (0-7613-2366-X). 48pp. A historical look at transportation in the United States, from roads to rail, water, and air. (Rev: BL 2/1/02; HBG 10/02) [388]

5384 Kent, Peter. *Hidden Under the Sea: The World Beneath the Waves* (2–4). Illus. by author. 2001, Dutton $17.99 (0-525-46772-6). 33pp. Submarines, dredgers, shipwrecks, undersea construction, and underwater legends all figure in this volume full of illustrations of equipment. (Rev: HBG 3/02; SLJ 10/01) [551.46]

5385 Mayo, Margaret. *Dig Dig Digging* (PS). Illus. by Alex Ayliffe. 2002, Holt $14.95 (0-8050-6840-6). 32pp. A rhyming book, with illustrations, about tractors, fire engines, helicopters, and other favorite vehicles. (Rev: BL 5/15/02; HBG 10/02; SLJ 5/02) [629.225]

5386 Vandewarker, Paul. *The Big Dig: Reshaping an American City* (5–8). Illus. 2001, Little, Brown $17.95 (0-316-60598-0). 56pp. This is a fascinating and informative account of Boston's massive effort to overhaul its transportation infrastructure. (Rev: BL 10/1/01; HB 1–2/02; HBG 3/02; SLJ 12/01) [624]

Automobiles and Trucks

5387 Anderson, Jenna. *How It Happens at the Truck Plant* (1–3). Photos by Bob Wolfe and Diane Wolfe. Series: How It Happens. 2002, Oliver LB $19.95 (1-881508-93-5). 32pp. How trucks are manufactured is described in text and photographs. (Rev: HBG 10/02; SLJ 12/02) [629]

5388 Burgan, Michael. *The World's Fastest Cars* (3–8). Illus. Series: Built for Speed. 2000, Capstone LB $21.26 (0-7368-0570-2). 48pp. Dragsters, Indie 500 race cars, and other fast automobiles are covered in this visually appealing account that will be attractive to reluctant readers. (Rev: HBG 10/01; SLJ 6/01) [629.228]

5389 Flammang, James M. *Cars* (2–4). Illus. Series: Transportation and Communication. 2001, Enslow LB $18.95 (0-7660-1646-3). 48pp. Car lovers will enjoy this easy-reading look at automobiles past and present with black-and-white and color photographs, a timeline, a glossary, and lists of further resources. (Rev: BL 10/15/01; HBG 3/02) [629.222]

5390 Jango-Cohen, Judith. *Dump Trucks* (2–3). Series: Pull Ahead Books. 2002, Lerner LB $22.60 (0-8225-0688-2); paper $5.95 (0-8225-0602-5). 32pp. This colorful account introduces dump trucks, explains their parts, tells how they work, and describes their functions. (Rev: BL 8/02; HBG 3/03) [629.224]

5391 Jango-Cohen, Judith. *Fire Trucks* (2–3). Series: Pull Ahead Books. 2002, Lerner LB $22.60 (0-8225-0077-9); paper $5.95 (0-8225-0604-1). 32pp. After describing the parts of a fire truck in text and pictures, this book explains how they work and the jobs they do. (Rev: BL 8/02; HBG 3/03) [629.255]

5392 Johnstone, Mike. *Monster Trucks* (5–8). Series: Need for Speed. 2002, Lerner LB $23.95 (0-8225-0388-3). 32pp. In stunning action-filled text and pictures, this book highlights huge trucks that weigh thousands of pounds and stand more than 10 feet high. (Rev: BL 8/02; HBG 10/02; SLJ 7/02) [629.225]

5393 McKenna, A. T. *Lamborghini* (4–7). Series: Ultimate Cars. 2000, ABDO LB $15.95 (1-57765-125-1). 32pp. Car lovers and reluctant readers will enjoy the gleaming photographs of vintage and contemporary Lamborghini and the information on the car's design, engine, and performance. Also use *Porsche* (2000). (Rev: BL 1/01; HBG 10/01; SLJ 5/01) [629.222]

5394 Molzahn, Arlene Bourgeois. *Fire Engines* (2–4). Illus. Series: Transportation and Communication. 2001, Enslow LB $18.95 (0-7660-1643-9). 48pp. The ever-popular fire engine is featured here, with photographs of vehicles past and present, a timeline, a glossary, and lists of further resources. (Rev: BL 10/15/01; HBG 3/02) [628.9]

5395 Molzahn, Arlene Bourgeois. *Highways and Freeways* (2–4). Series: Transportation and Communication. 2002, Enslow LB $18.95 (0-7660-1891-1). 48pp. This book traces the development of road transportation, how networks developed, their importance, and possible future developments. (Rev: BL 9/15/02; HBG 3/03) [388.11]

5396 Molzahn, Arlene Bourgeois. *Police and Emergency Vehicles* (2–4). Series: Transportation and Communication. 2002, Enslow LB $18.95 (0-7660-1890-3). 48pp. Various kinds of emergency vehicles are presented with background history, details of people who were important in their development, and potential future improvements. (Rev: BL 9/15/02; HBG 3/03) [629.04]

5397 Nelson, Kristin L. *Farm Tractors* (2–3). Series: Pull Ahead Books. 2002, Lerner LB $22.60 (0-8225-0690-4); paper $5.95 (0-8225-0607-6). 32pp. Farm tractors are introduced with many photographs and large-type text and coverage is given on the jobs they do like towing a plow, seed drill, or a mower. (Rev: BL 8/02; HBG 3/03; SLJ 10/02) [621.8]

5398 Nelson, Kristin L. *Monster Trucks* (2–3). Series: Pull Ahead Books. 2002, Lerner LB $22.60 (0-8225-0691-2); paper $5.95 (0-8225-0605-X). 32pp. The world of monster trucks is introduced in color photographs and a simple text with material on their structure and functions such as heavy towing. (Rev: BL 8/02; HBG 3/03) [629.225]

5399 Oxlade, Chris. *Car* (4–6). Illus. Series: Take It Apart. 2002, Thameside $16.95 (1-930643-94-2). 32pp. The mechanically minded will particularly enjoy this look at cars that uses cutaways and detailed diagrams to show its major parts. (Rev: BL 1/1–15/03; HBG 3/03) [629.222]

5400 Rogers, Hal. *Buses* (PS–1). Series: Machines at Work. 2001, Child's World LB $21.36 (1-56766-963-8). 32pp. Large type and many full-color illustrations are used in this beginning reader to present different kinds of buses, their structures, and their uses. (Rev: BL 6/1–15/01; HBG 10/01) [629]

5401 Rogers, Hal. *Cars* (PS–1). Series: Machines at Work. 2001, Child's World LB $21.36 (1-56766-964-6). 32pp. An oversize volume that presents different cars and their parts through a simple text, large type, and many attractive photographs. (Rev: BL 6/1–15/01; HBG 10/01) [629]

5402 Stickland, Paul. *Big Dig: A Pop-Up Construction!* (PS–K). Illus. 2002, Ragged Bear $17.95 (1-929927-41-X). 16pp. This pop-up picture book presents construction trucks readying a site for a new building. (Rev: BL 8/02)

5403 Stille, Darlene R. *Race Cars* (K–2). Illus. Series: Transportation. 2001, Compass Point LB $19.93 (0-7565-0149-0). 32pp. Children's go-karts and adult racing cars zoom past in this overview that includes vivid photographs, basic information, and a glossary. (Rev: BL 12/15/01) [629.228]

5404 Weitzman, David. *Model T: How Henry Ford Built a Legend* (3–5). Illus. by author. 2002, Crown LB $18.99 (0-375-91107-3). Details of the design and innovative assembly of the Model T are accompanied by statistics and tidbits that will be of interest from both a historical and automotive perspective. (Rev: HBG 3/03; SLJ 12/02) [629.222]

5405 Wright, David K. *The Story of Chevy Corvettes* (1–3). Series: Classic Cars. 2002, Gareth Stevens LB $19.93 (0-8368-3189-6). 24pp. The Chevrolet Corvette is introduced in color photographs and a simple text that describes its history and design. (Rev: BL 10/15/02; HBG 3/03) [629]

5406 Wright, David K. *The Story of Chevy Impalas* (1–3). Illus. Series: Classic Cars. 2002, Gareth Stevens LB $19.93 (0-8368-3190-X). 24pp. Young automobile enthusiasts will enjoy seeing how the Impala has changed over the years. (Rev: BL 10/15/02; HBG 3/03) [629.222]

5407 Wright, David K. *The Story of Ford Thunderbirds* (1–3). Series: Classic Cars. 2002, Gareth Stevens LB $19.93 (0-8368-3191-8). 24pp. The history of the legendary Ford Thunderbird is told with bright full-page photographs and a simple text. (Rev: BL 10/15/02; HBG 3/03) [629]

5408 Wright, David K. *The Story of Model T Fords* (1–3). Series: Classic Cars. 2002, Gareth Stevens LB $19.93 (0-8368-3192-6). 24pp. The Model T Ford holds a unique position in the history of the automobile. Its story is told here in beginning text and many pictures. (Rev: BL 10/15/02; HBG 3/03) [639]

5409 Wright, David K. *The Story of Porsches* (1–3). Series: Classic Cars. 2002, Gareth Stevens LB $19.93 (0-8368-3193-4). 24pp. The story of this pioneering European automobile is told in full-page color pictures and a beginning-reader text. (Rev: BL 10/15/02; HBG 3/03) [629]

5410 Wright, David K. *The Story of Volkswagen Beetles* (1–3). Illus. Series: Classic Cars. 2002, Gareth Stevens LB $19.93 (0-8368-3194-2). 24pp. Traces the history of the Volkswagen Beetle, from its inception in the 1930s to its revival in the 1990s. (Rev: BL 10/15/02; HBG 3/03) [629.222]

Railroads

5411 Cefrey, Holly. *High Speed Trains* (4–7). Illus. Series: Built for Speed. 2001, Children's LB $19.00 (0-516-23157-X); paper $6.95 (0-516-23260-6). 48pp. Train fans will enjoy this attractive overview of high-speed rail in various countries, with information on history, design, and future trends. (Rev: BL 12/1/01) [385]

5412 Maynard, Chris. *High-Speed Trains* (5–8). Series: Need for Speed. 2002, Lerner LB $23.95 (0-8225-0387-5). 32pp. This action-packed book looks at fast trains from around the world, propelled by steam, oil, magnets, and electricity. (Rev: BL 8/02; HBG 10/02) [625.1]

5413 Perry, Phyllis. *Trains* (2–4). Series: Transportation and Communication. 2001, Enslow LB $18.95 (0-7660-1645-5). 32pp. In an attractive format, this book supplies information on the history, development, and use of trains in North America. (Rev: BL 10/15/01; HBG 3/02) [625.1]

5414 Rogers, Hal. *Trains* (PS–1). Series: Machines at Work. 2001, Child's World LB $21.36 (1-56766-965-4). 32pp. Trains, their types, parts and uses, are concisely presented in a beginning-reader text and many color photographs. (Rev: BL 6/1–15/01; HBG 10/01) [625.1]

5415 Simon, Seymour. *Seymour Simon's Book of Trains* (PS–3). Illus. 2002, HarperCollins LB $16.89 (0-06-028476-5). 40pp. An oversized volume with striking photographs of trains coupled with simple but fascinating information ranging from early steam locomotives to today's high-speed trains. (Rev: BCCB 3/02; BL 2/15/02; HB 5–6/02; HBG 10/02; SLJ 5/02) [385]

5416 Stille, Darlene R. *Freight Trains* (K–2). Illus. Series: Transportation. 2001, Compass Point LB $19.93 (0-7565-0148-2). 32pp. Simple descriptions and an attractive layout will appeal to young train fans. (Rev: BL 12/15/01) [625.1]

Ships, Boats, and Lighthouses

5417 Ardagh, Philip. *All at Sea* (PS–K). Illus. by Tig Sutton. Series: British Mighty Machines. 2003, Thameside LB $24.25 (1-931983-04-6). 32pp. Young boat lovers will enjoy the parade of yachts, submarines, aircraft carrier, hovercraft, ferry, and other vessels portrayed here in bright illustrations and simple words. (Rev: BL 12/1/02; HBG 3/03) [387.2]

5418 Cook, Nick. *The World's Fastest Boats* (3–8). Illus. Series: Built for Speed. 2000, Capstone LB $21.26 (0-7368-0569-9). 48pp. Catamarans, hydrofoils, and jetboats are all included in this visually appealing account that will be attractive to reluctant readers. (Rev: HBG 10/01; SLJ 6/01) [623.8]

5419 Frederick, Dawn. *How It Happens at the Boat Factory* (1–3). Photos by Bob Wolfe and Diane Wolfe. Series: How It Happens. 2002, Oliver LB $19.95 (1-881508-90-0). 32pp. How boats are manufactured is described in text and photographs. (Rev: HBG 10/02; SLJ 12/02)

5420 Kalman, Maira. *Fireboat: The Heroic Adventures of the John J. Harvey* (2–6). Illus. 2002, Putnam $16.99 (0-399-23953-7). 48pp. A beautifully and sensitively presented account of the work of the *John J. Harvey* fireboat, from its launch in 1931 through its restoration in the 1990s and its role in fighting fires in New York City on September 11, 2001. (Rev: BL 9/1/02; HB 9–10/02*; HBG 3/03; SLJ 9/02*) [974.71044]

5421 Kently, Eric. *The Story of the Titanic* (4–8). Illus. by Steve Noon. 2001, DK $17.95 (0-7894-7943-5). 32pp. Details of life aboard ship, double-page spreads, cutaways and cross-sections, facts and trivia, and a well-designed layout, are just a few of the features of this beautifully designed large-format book. (Rev: BL 12/15/01; HBG 3/02; SLJ 12/01) [363.1]

5422 O'Brien, Patrick. *The Great Ships* (3–6). Illus. 2001, Walker LB $17.85 (0-8027-8775-4). 40pp. From an ancient Viking ship to the doomed *Titanic* and beyond, this volume introduces 17 historically significant vessels in gorgeous double-page spreads. (Rev: BCCB 2/02; BL 1/1–15/02; HBG 3/02; SLJ 9/01) [387.2]

Weapons, Submarines, and the Armed Forces

5423 Aaseng, Nathan. *The Marine Corps in Action* (4–8). Series: U.S. Military Branches and Careers. 2001, Enslow LB $20.95 (0-7660-1637-4). 128pp. This attractive introduction to all aspects of the Marine Corps also looks at the future of this military branch and the number of women and minorities included. (Rev: HBG 3/02; SLJ 4/02) [359.9]

5424 Hamilton, John. *Armed Forces* (4–7). Illus. Series: War on Terrorism. 2002, ABDO $16.95 (1-57765-674-1). 48pp. An introduction to the U.S. military and the roles these services play in protecting the country, with color photographs, a glossary, and list of Web sites. (Rev: BL 8/02; HBG 10/02) [355]

5425 Hamilton, John. *Weapons of War* (4–7). Illus. Series: War on Terrorism. 2002, ABDO LB $16.95 (1-57765-673-3). 48pp. This account describes the weapons currently available to U.S. military personnel, including fighter planes, bombers, helicopters, bombs, missiles, and ships. (Rev: BL 5/1/02; HBG 10/02) [623.4]

Recreation

Crafts

General and Miscellaneous

5426 Baker, Diane. *Make Your Own Hairwear: Beaded Barrettes, Clips, Dangles and Headbands* (4–8). Illus. by Alexandra Michaels. 2001, Williamson paper $7.95 (1-885593-63-5). 63pp. Easy instructions guide readers through the steps of making hair accessories using beads, shells, rhinestones, and other materials. (Rev: SLJ 4/02) [745.58]

5427 Blakey, Nancy. *Go Outside! Activities for Outdoor Adventures* (3–7). Photos by Dana Dean Doering. 2002, Tricycle Pr. paper $13.95 (1-58246-064-7). 144pp. Double-page spreads suggest outdoor activities for each of the seasons, some for learning and some for pure fun. (Rev: BL 4/15/02; SLJ 9/02) [796]

5428 Blanchette, Peg, and Terri Thibault. *Really Cool Felt Crafts* (3–5). Illus. Series: Quick Starts for Kids! 2002, Williamson paper $7.95 (1-885593-80-5). 64pp. This book of easy-to-make felt projects includes instructions accompanied by drawings, and a section of full-sized templates. (Rev: BL 12/15/02; SLJ 1/03) [746]

5429 Castaldo, Nancy F. *Winter Day Play! Activities, Crafts, and Games for Indoors and Out* (PS–3). Illus. 2001, Chicago Review paper $13.95 (1-55652-381-5). 161pp. The more than 70 suggested activities range from scientific projects and artistic endeavors to parties and cooking. (Rev: SLJ 12/01) [790]

5430 Drake, Jane, and Ann Love. *The Kids Winter Handbook* (3–5). Illus. by Heather Collins. 2001, Kids Can $18.95 (1-55337-033-3); paper $12.95 (1-55074-969-2). 127pp. Crafts, recipes, games, and other activities are geared to indoor and outdoor winter entertainment. (Rev: HBG 3/02; SLJ 11/01) [790.1]

5431 Freedman, Claire. *An Ark Full of Activities* (3–6). Illus. 2001, HarperCollins paper $13.95 (0-551-03242-1). 64pp. Projects that will extend Bible study include making a scroll and a T-shirt of many colors. (Rev: BL 5/1/01) [745]

5432 Furstinger, Nancy. *Creative Crafts for Critters* (2–4). Illus. by Philippe Beha. 2001, Stoddart paper $8.95 (0-7737-6135-7). 48pp. Pet lovers will find lots of craft ideas for animal toys, clothing, and nutrition. (Rev: SLJ 1/02) [745.5]

5433 Gessat, Audrey. *Crafts from Salt Dough* (2–4). Trans. from French by Cheryl L. Smith. Series: Step by Step. 2002, Capstone LB $22.60 (0-7368-1475-2). 32pp. Tips on working with dough accompany instructions for making items including a candle-holder and a clown pencil. Also use *Crafts from Felt* and *Crafts from Modeling Clay* (both 2002). (Rev: HBG 3/03; SLJ 2/03)

5434 Goodman, Polly. *Space and Art Activities* (2–4). Illus. Series: Arty Facts. 2002, Crabtree LB $17.95 (0-7787-1112-9); paper $8.06 (0-7787-1140-4). 48pp. Double-page spreads give factual information on the left and creative ideas on the right. Also use *Structures, Materials and Art Activities* (2002). (Rev: SLJ 9/02) [745.5]

5435 Halls, Kelly Milner, ed. *Look What You Can Make with Craft Sticks: Over 80 Pictured Crafts and Dozens of Other Ideas* (2–4). Photos by Hank Schneider. 2002, Boyds Mills paper $5.95 (1-56397-997-7). 48pp. Younger children may need help with some of the projects here, which use everyday materials to make a wide variety of items. Also use *Look What You Can Make with Plastic Bottles and Tubs: Over 80 Pictured Crafts and Dozens of Other Ideas* (2002). (Rev: SLJ 4/02) [745.5]

5436 Halls, Kelly Milner, ed. *Look What You Can Make with Plastic-Foam Trays: Over 90 Pictured Crafts and Dozens of Other Ideas* (K–3). Illus. 2003, Boyds Mills paper $5.95 (1-59078-078-7). 48pp. Child-friendly ideas for using plastic-foam trays in a variety of inventive ways. (Rev: SLJ 2/03)

5437 Hendry, Linda. *Cat Crafts* (4–6). Illus. Series: Kids Can Do It. 2002, Kids Can $12.95 (1-55074-964-1); paper $5.95 (1-55074-921-8). 40pp. Using double-page spreads, this book outlines 17 cat-related projects. (Rev: BL 4/1/02; HBG 10/02; SLJ 6/02) [745.5]

5438 Hendry, Linda. *Dog Crafts* (4–6). Illus. Series: Kids Can Do It. 2002, Kids Can $12.95 (1-55074-960-9); paper $5.95 (1-55074-962-5). 40pp. Seventeen projects, such as making jewelry and toys, and all related to dogs, are presented in double-page spreads with easy-to-follow instructions. (Rev: BL 4/1/02; HBG 10/02; SLJ 6/02) [745.5]

5439 Hunter, Dette. *38 Ways to Entertain Your Grandparents* (K–2). Illus. by Deirdre Betteridge. 2002, Annick LB $19.95 (1-55037-749-3); paper $9.95 (1-55037-748-5). 48pp. Hunter deftly interweaves Sarah's story of all the entertaining things she does with her grandparents with instructions for young readers to do likewise, including rules for games, recipes, and craft projects. (Rev: BL 12/1/02; HBG 3/03) [793]

5440 Irvin, Christine M. *Egg Carton Mania* (2–4). Illus. Series: Craft Mania. 2002, Children's LB $22.00 (0-516-22277-5); paper $6.95 (0-516-27758-8). 32pp. Projects using egg cartons range from finger puppets to a double-decker bus. (Rev: BL 1/1–15/03; SLJ check) [745.5]

5441 Johnson, Ginger. *Make Your Own Christmas Ornaments* (3–5). Illus. by Norma Jean Martin-Jordenais. Series: Quick Starts for Kids! 2002, Williamson paper $7.95 (1-885593-79-1). 64pp. A collection of 25 ornaments with clear instructions and photographs of finished products. (Rev: BL 12/15/02; SLJ 10/02)

5442 Kilby, Janice Eaton, and Deborah Morgenthal. *The Book of Wizard Craft: In Which the Apprentice Finds Spells, Potions, Fantastic Tales and 50 Enchanting Things to Make* (4–6). Illus. by Lindy Burnett. 2001, Sterling $19.95 (1-57990-206-5). 144pp. An ancient wizard reveals the recipes for potions and instructions for crafts and skills (making a wizard's robe, reading tea leaves), some of which will require help from an adult. (Rev: HBG 10/01; SLJ 6/01) [745.5]

5443 Kimble-Ellis, Sonya. *Traditional African American Arts and Activities* (3–7). Illus. Series: Celebrating Our Heritage. 2002, Wiley paper $12.95 (0-471-41046-2). 120pp. The projects featured in this title will teach students something about traditional culture, foods, holidays, crafts, and games. (Rev: SLJ 8/02)

5444 *Kit's Friendship Fun* (3–5). Illus. 2002, Pleasant paper $12.95 (1-58485-415-4). 96pp. After a discussion of family life during the Depression, recipes, crafts, and games typical of the era are introduced. (Rev: SLJ 2/03)

5445 Levine, Shar, and Michael Ouchi. *The Ultimate Balloon Book* (5–8). Illus. 2001, Sterling $9.95 (0-8069-2959-6). 96pp. A guide to balloon creations that progresses from the simple (dachshunds) to the advanced. (Rev: BL 8/01; SLJ 10/01) [745.594]

5446 *Look What You Can Make with Dozens of Household Items!* (4–6). Ed. by Kathy Ross. Photos by Hank Schneider. Series: Look What You Can Make With. 2003, Boyds Mills $24.99 (1-59078-058-2). 384pp. Common household items are used to create a wide range of crafts. (Rev: BL 12/15/02) [745]

5447 MacLeod, Elizabeth. *Gifts to Make and Eat* (4–7). Illus. by June Bradford. Series: Kids Can Do It. 2001, Kids Can $12.95 (1-55074-956-0); paper $5.95 (1-55074-958-7). 40pp. Kids learn through step-by-step instructions how to make an array of edible and craft gifts. (Rev: BL 11/1/01; HBG 3/02; SLJ 2/02) [641.5]

5448 Merrill, Yvonne Y. *Hands-On America: Art Activities About Vikings, Woodland Indians and Early Colonists*, vol. 1 (4–7). Illus. Series: Hands-On America. 2001, Kits paper $20.00 (0-9643177-6-1). 92pp. Varied and relatively easy activities focusing on early America will entertain at the same time as enhancing students' knowledge of historical events and concepts. (Rev: SLJ 3/02) [745.5]

5449 Monaghan, Kathleen, and Hermon Joyner. *You Can Weave! Projects for Young Weavers* (4–7). Illus. 2001, Sterling $19.95 (0-87192-493-5). 104pp. Step-by-step instructions and photographs guide young crafters through weaving projects of varying complexity. (Rev: BL 11/1/01) [746.41]

5450 Mueller, Stephanie R., and Ann E. Wheeler. *101 Great Gifts from Kids: Fabulous Gifts Every Child Can Make* (PS–3). Illus. 2002, Gryphon House paper $14.95 (0-87659-279-5). 174pp. Gift ideas that vary in difficulty and may require some adult help are accompanied by line drawings of the process involved and the end product. (Rev: SLJ 9/02) [745.5]

5451 O'Sullivan, Joanne. *Girls' World: Making Cool Stuff for Your Room, Your Friends and You* (3–6). Illus. 2002, Sterling paper $12.95 (1-57990-291-X). 112pp. Items to make range from gifts for friends and animals to room decorations and school supplies, all with clear instructions and lists of materials that are available in craft and fabric stores. (Rev: SLJ 7/02) [745.5]

5452 Otten, Jack. *Watch Me Make a Bird Feeder* (PS–2). Series: Making Things. 2002, Children's LB $13.50 (0-516-23943-0); paper $4.95 (0-516-23497-8). 24pp. The process of making a bird feeder is simply explained in language that will suit challenged early readers. Also use *Watch Me Plant a Garden* (2002). (Rev: SLJ 6/02) [690.89]

5453 Phillips, Matt. *Make Your Own Fun Frames!* (3–6). Illus. by Stan Jaskiel. 2001, Williamson paper $7.95 (1-885593-64-3). 63pp. Basic instructions for making frames and matting, cropping photographs, and hanging frames are accompanied by design suggestions using a variety of everyday materials. (Rev: SLJ 6/02) [749.7]

5454 Powell, Michelle. *Beadwork* (3–5). Illus. Series: Step-by-Step. 2002, Heinemann LB $24.22 (1-4034-0696-0). 32pp. Color photographs show each step in creating beadwork projects. (Rev: BL 12/15/02; HBG 3/03) [745.58]

5455 Powell, Michelle. *Mosaics* (4–7). Series: Step-by-Step. 2001, Heinemann $24.22 (1-57572-332-8). 32pp. A number of fascinating projects creating mosaics are described with step-by-step instructions and many colorful illustrations. (Rev: BL 8/1/01; HBG 10/01; SLJ 10/01) [745]

5456 Press, Judy. *All Around Town: Exploring Your Community Through Craft Fun* (PS–3). Illus. Series: Little Hands. 2002, Williamson paper $12.95 (1-885593-68-6). 128pp. Projects using everyday materials that will introduce youngsters to community institutions such as schools, libraries, and gas stations are shown with instructions and illustrations. (Rev: BL 1/1–15/03) [307]

5457 Press, Judy. *Around-the-World Art and Activities: Visiting the 7 Continents Through Craft Fun* (PS–2). Illus. by Betsy Day. Series: Little Hands. 2001, Williamson paper $12.95 (1-885593-45-7). 128pp. Activities, which are coded by level of difficulty, include making travel-related items such as a passport and suitcase, and cultural items such as totem poles, leis, nesting Russian dolls, gaucho belts, and Korean drums. (Rev: SLJ 5/01) [745]

5458 Press, Judy. *At the Zoo: Explore the Animal World with Craft Fun* (PS–3). Illus. by Jenny Campbell. Series: A Little Hands Book. 2002, Williamson paper $12.95 (1-885593-61-9). 126pp. Crafts using widely available materials are grouped in broad categories such as "African Safari" and "Tropical Forest" that are introduced by a map and brief general information, followed by individual animal projects. (Rev: SLJ 8/02)

5459 Ross, Kathy. *All New Crafts for Valentine's Day* (1–3). Illus. by Barbara Leonard. 2002, Millbrook LB $23.90 (0-7613-2553-0); paper $7.95 (0-7613-1576-4). 48pp. Easy crafts are accompanied by step-by-step instructions and bright watercolor paintings. (Rev: HBG 3/03; SLJ 11/02) [745.594]

5460 Ross, Kathy. *Christmas Presents Kids Can Make* (4–6). Illus. by Sharon L. Holm. 2001, Millbrook LB $24.40 (0-7613-1754-6). 64pp. The author provides new ideas for 29 creative Christmas gifts using everyday items. (Rev: BL 9/15/01; HBG 3/02; SLJ 10/01) [745.5]

5461 Ross, Kathy. *Crafts from Your Favorite Children's Songs* (PS–2). Illus. by Vicky Enright. 2001, Millbrook LB $24.40 (0-7613-1912-3). 47pp. Crafts designed to accompany familiar songs are presented with simple instructions. (Rev: HBG 10/01; SLJ 5/01) [745.5]

5462 Ross, Kathy. *Crafts from Your Favorite Children's Stories* (1–4). Illus. by Elaine Garvin. 2001, Millbrook LB $24.40 (0-7613-1772-4). 47pp. Young children may need help with some of these projects, which include a "Bear Hug Puppet," a spinning Dorothy house on its way to Oz, and a Sourdough Sam. (Rev: HBG 3/02; SLJ 9/01) [745.5]

5463 Ross, Kathy. *Crafts from Your Favorite Nursery Rhymes* (3–5). Illus. by Elaine Garvin. 2002, Millbrook LB $24.90 (0-7613-2523-9); paper $8.95 (0-7613-1589-6). 48pp. Simple directions and clear illustrations accompany projects of varying difficulty; young children will need some help with these activities related to popular rhymes. (Rev: BL 1/1–15/03; HBG 3/03; SLJ 12/02) [745.5]

5464 Ross, Kathy. *Kathy Ross Crafts Triangles, Rectangles, Circles, and Squares* (PS–1). Illus. by Jan Barger. Series: Learning Is Fun! 2002, Millbrook LB $23.90 (0-7613-2104-7); paper $7.95 (0-7613-1696-5). 48pp. Projects that introduce basic geometric shapes include puppets, jewelry, games, and hanging objects. (Rev: HBG 3/03; SLJ 1/03)

5465 Ross, Kathy. *Play-Doh Animal Fun* (K–4). Illus. by Sharon Hawkins Vargo. 2002, Millbrook LB $24.40 (0-7613-2506-9). 48pp. Twenty animals to make with play-doh range from simple clams to a rattlesnake with a rattle. Also use *Play-Doh Art Projects* (2002). (Rev: HBG 10/02; SLJ 5/02) [745.5]

5466 Sadler, Judy Ann. *Jumbo Book of Easy Crafts* (3–5). Illus. 2001, Kids Can $14.95 (1-55074-811-4). 208pp. Crafts using everyday items — paper plates, popsicle sticks, aluminum foil, beans, beads, and so forth — are arranged by type of material. (Rev: BL 6/1–15/01; SLJ 7/01) [745.5]

5467 Schwarz, Renée. *Funky Junk* (4–7). Series: Kids Can Do It. 2002, Kids Can $12.95 (1-55337-387-1); paper $5.95 (1-55337-388-X). 48pp. Using easily found materials, this craft book supplies details on how to make unusual conversation pieces. (Rev: BL 3/15/03) [745.5]

5468 Senisi, Ellen B. *Berry Smudges and Leaf Prints* (4–6). Illus. 2001, Dutton $16.99 (0-525-46139-6). 40pp. Projects using natural dyes include printing with potatoes and other plant materials, pressing flowers, creating collages, and so forth. (Rev: BL 6/1–15/01; HBG 10/01; SLJ 5/01*) [745.2]

5469 Smith, Heather, and Joe Rhatigan. *Earth-Friendly Crafts for Kids* (3–6). Illus. 2002, Sterling $24.95 (1-57990-340-1). 144pp. Instructions for crafts made from recyclable materials, with further "Earth-friendly" ideas. (Rev: BL 2/15/03; HBG 3/03; SLJ 1/03) [745.5]

5470 Souter, Gillian. *Holiday Handiworks* (3–6). Illus. Series: Handy Crafts. 2002, Gareth Stevens LB $23.93 (0-8368-3050-4). 48pp. A well-organized collection of crafts with clear instructions, aimed at holidays including Easter, Passover, Kwanzaa, and Chinese New Year. Also use *Rainy Day Fun* and *Terrific Toys* (both 2002). (Rev: HBG 10/02; SLJ 6/02) [745.5]

5471 Souter, Gillian. *Perfect Parties* (2–5). Photos by Andre Martin. Illus. by Clare Watson. Series: Handy Crafts. 2001, Gareth Stevens LB $22.60 (0-8368-2822-4). 48pp. A useful party checklist precedes discussion of each important consideration and step-by-step instructions for creating a wide selection of decorations and games and some foods. Also use *Great Gifts* and *Beads 'n' Bangles* (both 2001). (Rev: HBG 10/01; SLJ 7/01) [793.2]

5472 Stetson, Emily, and Vicky Congdon. *Little Hands Fingerplays and Action Songs: Seasonal Rhymes and Creative Play for 2- to 6-Year-Olds* (PS–1). Illus. by Betsy Day. Series: Little Hands. 2001, Williamson paper $12.95 (1-885593-53-8). 128pp. Suggestions for songs, games, and crafts are organized by season and accompanied by brief facts and short reading lists. (Rev: SLJ 11/01) [793.4]

5473 Temko, Florence. *Traditional Crafts from Japan* (3–5). Illus. by Randall Gooch. Series: Culture Crafts. 2001, Lerner LB $23.93 (0-8225-2938-6). 64pp. Eight traditional Japanese handicrafts are presented with instructions for making them and explanations of their significance in Japanese culture. (Rev: HBG 10/01; SLJ 4/01) [745]

5474 Wallace, Mary. *I Can Make That! Fantastic Crafts for Kids* (K–5). Illus. Series: I Can Make That. 2002, Maple Tree $19.95 (1-894379-41-1). 160pp. This compilation of five earlier I Can Make That! books contains step-by-step instructions and photographs to help children create their own toys, games, and other crafts. (Rev: BL 10/15/02; SLJ 11/02) [745.5]

5475 White, Linda. *Haunting on a Halloween* (5–7). Illus. by Fran Lee. 2002, Gibbs Smith paper $9.95 (1-58685-112-8). 64pp. Everything young party planners need to host a Halloween get-together, with instructions for crafts, food, decorations, and costumes. (Rev: BL 9/15/02) [745.594]

5476 Williams, Joy. *Nature Crafts* (4–6). Photos by Christine Polomsky. Series: Creative Kids. 2002, North Light paper $12.99 (1-58180-292-7). 64pp. A guide to making a variety of crafts using natural materials whenever possible. (Rev: SLJ 9/02) [745.5]

5477 Zakarin, Debra Mostow. *Happening Hanukkah: Creative Ways to Celebrate* (4–6). Illus. by Amanda Haley. 2002, Grosset paper $5.99 (0-448-42869-5). 64pp. A treasure trove of Hanukkah gift ideas plus suggestions for parties, food, and games. (Rev: SLJ 10/02)

Clay and Other Modeling Crafts

5478 Ellis, Mary. *Ceramics for Kids: Creative Clay Projects to Pinch, Roll, Coil, Slam and Twist* (3–6). Illus. 2002, Sterling $24.95 (1-57990-198-0). 144pp. Ceramics projects for older readers, organized by the skill required and growing in complexity as readers progress through the book, are outlined step-by-step. (Rev: BL 12/15/02; HBG 3/03; SLJ 1/03) [738.1]

Costume and Jewelry Making

5479 Baker, Diane. *Jazzy Jewelry: Power Beads, Crystals, Chokers, and Illusion and Tattoo Styles* (5–9). Illus. by Alexandra Michaels. 2001, Williamson paper $12.95 (1-885593-47-3). 144pp. Jewelry projects for bead lovers include chokers, headbands, and bobby pins, all presented with black-and-white line drawings and guidance on color choice, clasps and knots, and proper storage. (Rev: SLJ 7/01) [745.594]

Drawing and Painting

5480 Artell, Mike. *Cartooning for Kids* (4–6). Illus. by author. 2001, Sterling paper $17.95 (0-8069-4814-0). 128pp. Instructions for drawing animals and people show how to portray movement and emotions. (Rev: SLJ 1/02) [741.5]

5481 Balchin, Judy. *Creative Lettering* (4–7). Series: Step-by-Step. 2001, Heinemann $24.22 (1-57572-331-X). 32pp. Using easy-to-find materials, this craft book gives clear directions for several fascinating lettering projects. (Rev: BL 8/1/01; HBG 10/01) [745.6]

5482 Balchin, Judy. *Decorative Painting* (4–7). Series: Step-by-Step. 2001, Heinemann $24.22 (1-57572-330-1). 32pp. With easy-to-follow directions and illustrations that describe each step, this colorful book contains a number of simple projects on how to decorate with paints. (Rev: BL 8/1/01; HBG 10/01; SLJ 10/01) [745]

5483 Barr, Steve. *1-2-3 Draw Cartoon Animals* (2–5). Illus. 2002, Peel paper $8.99 (0-939217-48-1). 64pp. Easy, step-by-step directions guide budding young artists to draw a variety of animals using a cartoon style. Also use *1-2-3 Draw Cartoon Faces* and *1-2-3 Draw Cartoon People* (both 2002). (Rev: BL 1/1–15/03) [741.5]

5484 *Cartoon Magic* (2–6). Illus. 2001, North Light paper $12.99 (1-58180-229-3). 64pp. Readers will learn to draw people and animals, to show movement and use perspective, and to use color and word balloons to best effect. Also use *Drawing Magic* (2001). (Rev: SLJ 11/01) [741.2]

5485 Emberley, Ed. *Ed Emberley's Drawing Book of Trucks and Trains* (1–3). Illus. 2002, Little, Brown $15.95 (0-316-23898-8); paper $6.95 (0-316-23786-8). 32pp. Step-by-step instructions are given for drawing such vehicles as locomotives, baggage carts, and pickup trucks. (Rev: BL 5/1/02; HBG 10/02; SLJ 7/02) [741.2]

5486 Emberley, Ed. *Ed Emberley's Drawing Book of Weirdos* (1–4). Illus. by author. 2002, Little, Brown paper $7.95 (0-316-23314-5). Werewolves, skeletons, ghosts, vampires, goblins, and witches are all here with step-by-step instructions. (Rev: HBG 3/03; SLJ 1/03) [741.2]

5487 Emberley, Ed. *Ed Emberley's Fingerprint Drawing Book* (1–3). Illus. 2001, Little, Brown $15.95 (0-316-23638-1); paper $6.95 (0-316-23319-6). 48pp. Emberley gives step-by-step instructions for making fingerprint images, progressing from the most basic to advanced complete pictures. (Rev: BL 6/1–15/01; HBG 3/02; SLJ 7/01) [741.2]

5488 Hart, Christopher. *Kids Draw Anime* (4–8). Illus. 2002, Watson-Guptill $10.95 (0-8230-2690-6). 128pp. Instructions on how to draw anime (Japanese cartoons) characters, with many colorful examples. (Rev: BL 2/1/03; SLJ 11/02) [741.5]

5489 Hart, Christopher. *Kids Draw Funny and Spooky Holiday Characters* (3–6). Illus. by author. 2001, Watson-Guptill paper $10.95 (0-8230-2626-4). 64pp. Cartoon drawing for Halloween and

Christmas are the focus of this guide that covers the basic principles of showing movement and good positioning of characters. (Rev: SLJ 9/01) [741.5]

5490 Hart, Christopher. *Manga Mania: How to Draw Japanese Comics* (5 Up). Illus. 2001, Watson-Guptill paper $19.95 (0-8230-3035-0). 144pp. Hart looks at the techniques for drawing typical Japanese comic characters and animals, providing examples of published manga along with an introduction to the various genres of manga and an interview with a manga publisher. (Rev: BL 7/01; SLJ 7/01) [741.5]

5491 Hart, Christopher. *Mecha Mania: How to Draw the Battling Robots, Cool Spaceships, and Military Vehicles of Japanese Comics* (4–8). Illus. 2002, Watson-Guptill paper $19.95 (0-8230-3056-3). 128pp. Instructions on how to draw the high-tech, scary, fanciful machines and weapons that fill the pages of Japanese comic books. (Rev: BL 2/1/03) [741.5]

5492 Leroux-Hugon, Helene. *I Can Draw Polar Animals* (3–5). Trans. from French by Valerie J. Weber. Illus. by author. Series: I Can Draw Animals! 2001, Gareth Stevens LB $21.27 (0-8368-2840-2). 40pp. Three-step instructions for a line drawing of an animal are paired with a completed, color illustration of the animal and simple facts about it, all preceded by encouragement to be observant and to practice drawing. Also use *I Can Draw Wild Animals* (2001). (Rev: HBG 10/01; SLJ 9/01) [743.6]

5493 Levin, Freddie. *1-2-3 Draw: Cars, Trucks, and Other Vehicles* (3–5). Illus. 2002, Peel paper $8.99 (0-939217-43-0). 64pp. A large-format paperback that shows how to draw 24 vehicles including a race car, cement truck, and a school bus. (Rev: BL 4/15/02; SLJ 7/02) [743]

5494 McGillian, Jamie Kyle. *Sidewalk Chalk: Outdoor Fun and Games* (1–6). Illus. by Blanche Sims. 2002, Sterling $17.95 (0-8069-7905-4). 80pp. Plenty of inventive ideas for the sidewalk set, including making your own chalk. (Rev: HBG 10/02; SLJ 12/02)

5495 Mayne, Don. *Draw Your Own Cartoons* (3–8). Illus. by author. 2001, Williamson paper $7.95 (1-885593-76-7). 64pp. A cartoon-like atmosphere prevails in this guide that teaches readers to draw characters. (Rev: SLJ 6/01) [741.5]

5496 Murawski, Laura. *How to Draw Cats* (2–5). Illus. by author. Series: A Kid's Guide to Drawing. 2001, Rosen LB $21.25 (0-8239-5549-4). 24pp. Information about each breed precedes instructions on how to draw it in stages that begin with basic shapes and proceed to add details. Also use *How to Draw Dogs* (2001). (Rev: SLJ 8/01) [741]

5497 Souter, Gillian. *Paints Plus* (2–5). Photos by Andre Martin. Illus. by Clare Watson. Series: Handy Crafts. 2001, Gareth Stevens LB $22.60 (0-8368-2821-6). 48pp. Lively spreads full of color and practical directions introduce painting equipment and ways to decorate a variety of everyday materials. (Rev: HBG 10/01; SLJ 7/01) [745.7]

5498 Wellford, Lin. *Painting on Rocks for Kids* (K–3). Illus. 2002, North Light paper $12.99 (1-

58180-255-2). 64pp. Step-by-step instructions and tips on technique accompany ideas for making cars, flowers, dinosaurs, fish, food, and other items from painted stones and rocks. (Rev: SLJ 1/03) [745.7]

Masks and Mask Making

5499 Schwarz, Renée. *Making Masks* (4–6). Series: Kids Can Do It. 2002, Kids Can $12.95 (1-55074-929-3); paper $5.95 (1-55074-931-5). 40pp. A basic volume on making masks from a various of easily obtained materials. (Rev: BL 9/15/02; HBG 3/03; SLJ 12/02) [731.785]

Paper Crafts

5500 Boursin, Didier. *Origami Paper Airplanes* (4–7). Illus. 2001, Firefly LB $19.95 (1-55209-626-2); paper $9.95 (1-55209-616-5). 64pp. Paper airplane devotees will love the origami models offered here, which are categorized by difficulty of construction. (Rev: BCCB 12/01; BL 1/1–15/02; HBG 3/02; SLJ 12/01) [745.592]

5501 Carter, Tamsin. *Handmade Cards* (3–5). Illus. Series: Step-by-Step. 2002, Heinemann LB $24.22 (1-4034-0698-7). 32pp. This volume provides simple instructions, explained one step at a time, for creating and decorating greeting cards. (Rev: BL 12/15/02; HBG 3/03) [745.594]

5502 Check, Laura. *The Kids' Guide to Making Scrapbooks and Photo Albums! How to Collect, Design, Assemble, Decorate* (4–6). Illus. by Betsy Day. 2002, Williamson paper $12.95 (1-885593-59-7). 128pp. Check discusses the best ways to use images to tell stories as well as giving practical instructions for creating scrapbooks and albums. (Rev: SLJ 7/02) [745.593]

5503 Irvin, Christine M. *Paper Plate Mania* (K–2). Illus. Series: Craft Mania. 2002, Children's LB $22.00 (0-516-21675-9); paper $6.95 (0-516-27761-8). 32pp. Masks and sun catchers are among the many inventive uses for paper plates suggested in this book that emphasizes the importance of recycling. Also use *Paper Cup Mania* (2002). (Rev: SLJ 9/02) [745.54]

5504 Johnson, Ginger. *Paper-Folding Fun! 50 Awesome Crafts to Weave, Twist and Curl* (3–5). Illus. Series: Kids Can. 2002, Williamson paper $12.95 (1-885593-67-8). 128pp. Step-by-step directions accompany each idea for making objects from paper, including jewelry, mobiles, and books. (Rev: BL 11/1/02) [745.54]

5505 Lafosse, Michael G. *Making Origami Christmas Decorations Step by Step* (2–4). Illus. by author. Series: Kid's Guide to Origami. 2002, Rosen LB $21.25 (0-8239-5874-4). 24pp. Nine projects related to Christmas are suitable for beginning folders. (Rev: SLJ 10/02)

5506 Lewis, Amanda. *The Jumbo Book of Paper Crafts* (3–6). Illus. by Jane Kurisu. 2002, Kids Can paper $14.95 (1-55074-940-4). 160pp. Easy, illustrated techniques and instructions teach older children how to create a multitude of crafts with paper and cardboard. (Rev: BL 12/15/02; SLJ 12/02) [745]

5507 Nguyen, Duy. *Fantasy Origami* (5–7). Illus. by author. 2002, Sterling $19.95 (0-8069-8007-9). 96pp. These 16 origami designs, which are not for beginners, do call for the use of scissors and glue. (Rev: BL 1/1–15/02; SLJ 6/02) [736.982]

5508 Ross, Kathy, ed. *Look What You Can Make with Newspapers, Magazines, and Greeting Cards: Over 80 Pictured Crafts and Dozens of Other Ideas* (2–4). Photos by Hank Schneider. 2002, Boyds Mills paper $5.95 (1-56397-566-1). 48pp. Final products include dolls with clothes, boxes, banks, signs and cards, and mobiles; the illustrations enhance the written instructions. (Rev: SLJ 4/02) [745.54]

5509 Schmidt, Norman. *Incredible Paper Flying Machines* (5–8). Illus. 2001, Sterling $19.95 (1-895569-37-0). 96pp. Young model builders with some experience will enjoy these intricate models of historical aircraft that are glued and laminated. (Rev: HBG 10/02; SLJ 2/02) [745.592]

5510 Stevens, Clive. *Paperfolding* (4–7). Series: Step-by-Step. 2001, Heinemann $24.22 (1-57572-333-6). 32pp. Easy-to-find materials are used in a number of exciting paper folding projects, each of which is described in clear, detailed directions with step-by-step illustrations. (Rev: BL 8/1/01; HBG 10/01; SLJ 10/01) [745.5]

5511 Williams, Joy. *Paper Creations* (3–6). Illus. Series: Creative Kids. 2002, North Light paper $12.99 (1-58180-290-0). 64pp. Using everyday materials, the reader can learn to make projects including jewelry, gifts, and decorations. (Rev: SLJ 1/03)

Sewing and Needle Crafts

5512 Kinsler, Gwen Blakley, and Jackie Young. *Crocheting* (4–7). Series: Kids Can Do It. 2003, Kids Can $12.95 (1-55337-176-3); paper $5.95 (1-55337-177-1). 48pp. A simple introduction to crocheting with many easily followed diagrams and clear directions. (Rev: BL 3/15/03) [745.5]

5513 Mahren, Sue. *Make Your Own Teddy Bears and Bear Clothes* (3–6). Illus. by Stan Jaskiel. Series: Quick Starts for Kids! 2001, Williamson paper $7.95 (1-885593-75-9). 64pp. Patterns for two teddy bears are followed by patterns for clothing that are clear and easy to follow using only scissors, needle, and thread. Also use *Kids' Easy Knitting Projects* and *Kids' Easy Quilting Projects* (both 2001). (Rev: SLJ 7/01) [745.592]

5514 Sadler, Judy Ann. *Knitting* (4–6). Series: Kids Can Do It. 2002, Kids Can $12.95 (1-55337-050-3); paper $5.95 (1-55337-051-1). 40pp. The basic stitches in knitting are described in text and color illustrations, followed by a series of easily accomplished knitting projects. (Rev: BL 9/15/02; HBG 3/03; SLJ 11/02) [746.43]

5515 Storms, Biz. *Quilting* (4–7). Illus. by June Bradford. Series: Kids Can Do It. 2001, Kids Can $12.95 (1-55074-967-6); paper $5.95 (1-55074-805-X). 40pp. Easy-to-follow, step-by-step instructions take kids through quilting projects of varying difficulty. (Rev: BL 11/1/01; HBG 3/02; SLJ 2/02) [746.46]

Toys and Dolls

5516 Coleman, Janet Wyman. *Famous Bears and Friends: One Hundred Years of Teddy Bear Stories, Poems, Songs, and Heroics* (3–5). Illus. 2002, Dutton $19.99 (0-525-46925-7). 64pp. The history of the teddy bear — beginning with the famous Teddy Roosevelt story and including well-known bears such as Winnie-the-Pooh and Paddington — with charming photographs and illustrations. (Rev: BL 2/15/03; SLJ 2/03) [808.8]

5517 Hall, Patricia. *The Real-for-Sure Story of Raggedy Ann* (PS–3). Illus. by Joni Gruelle Wannamaker. 2001, Pelican $14.95 (1-56554-763-2). A story about the origins of the doll, portraying the details of her clothes and the way the first dolls were made. (Rev: HBG 10/01; SLJ 11/01) [688.7]

5518 Polacco, Patricia. *Betty Doll* (3–5). Illus. 2001, Putnam $16.99 (0-399-23638-4). 32pp. In this picture book for older children, Polacco tells the story of her mother's precious Betty Doll, which accompanied her mother on many journeys until her death, when the doll was passed on to her daughter. (Rev: BL 8/01; HBG 10/01; SLJ 4/01) [973.4]

Hobbies

General and Miscellaneous

5519 Burgess, Ron. *Be a Clown! Techniques from a Real Clown* (K–3). Illus. by Heather Barberie. 2001, Williamson paper $7.95 (1-885593-57-0). 63pp. Aspiring clowns will appreciate this guide to clown costumes and makeup, actions and gags, and magic tricks, along with some historical information about traditional clowns and clowning. (Rev: SLJ 10/01) [791.3]

5520 Stetson, Emily. *Knots to Know: 40 Hitches, Loops, Bends and Bindings* (3–6). Illus. by Marc Nadel and Sarah Rakitin. 2002, Williamson paper $7.95 (1-885593-70-8). 64pp. A simple guide to the types and uses of knots, with step-by-step instructions on how to tie them. (Rev: BL 8/02; SLJ 9/02) [623.88]

Cooking

5521 Bisignano, Alphonse. *Cooking the Italian Way*. Rev. ed. (5–9). Series: Easy Menu Ethnic Cookbooks. 2001, Lerner LB $25.26 (0-8225-4113-0); paper $7.95 (0-8225-4161-0). 72pp. A revised edition that now includes vegetarian and low-fat recipes as well as an expanded introductory section on the country, the people, and the culture. (Rev: HBG 3/02; SLJ 9/01) [641]

5522 Coronado, Rosa. *Cooking the Mexican Way*. Rev. ed. (5–8). Series: Easy Menu Ethnic Cookbooks. 2001, Lerner LB $25.26 (0-8225-4117-3). 72pp. Recipes organized by type of meal are preceded by a section that covers the geography, culture, and festivals and by information on equipment, ingredients, and eating customs. Other titles in this series include *Cooking the East African Way*, *Cooking the Spanish Way*, and *Cooking the French Way* (all 2001). (Rev: HBG 3/02; SLJ 2/02) [641]

5523 Dahl, Roald, and Felicity Dahl. *Roald Dahl's Even More Revolting Recipes* (4–6). Illus. by Quentin Blake. 2001, Viking $17.99 (0-670-03515-7). 64pp. A follow-up to *Revolting Recipes* (1994), this volume includes 31 new recipes inspired by Dahl's books. (Rev: BL 2/1/02; HBG 3/02; SLJ 11/01) [641.5]

5524 Duden, Jane. *Vegetarianism for Teens* (4–7). Illus. Series: Nutrition and Fitness. 2001, Capstone $16.95 (0-7368-0712-8). 32pp. An overview of vegetarian diets that includes a checklist and tips on coping with people who discount the appeal of a meatless life. (Rev: BL 7/01; HBG 10/01; SLJ 7/01) [613.2]

5525 Gioffre, Rosalba. *The Young Chef's French Cookbook* (4–7). Series: I'm the Chef! 2001, Crabtree LB $22.60 (0-7787-0282-0); paper $8.95 (0-7787-0296-0). 32pp. This oversize book uses double-page spreads to present 15 appetizing French recipes along with good background material, clear directions, and excellent illustrations. (Rev: BL 10/15/01) [641]

5526 Gioffre, Rosalba. *The Young Chef's Italian Cookbook* (4–7). Series: I'm the Chef! 2001, Crabtree LB $22.60 (0-7787-0279-0); paper $8.95 (0-7787-0293-6). 32pp. Along with good background material, recipes, and clear instructions are presented for 15 Italian dishes in this well-illustrated, oversize book. (Rev: BL 10/15/01; SLJ 11/01) [641]

5527 Hill, Mary. *Let's Make Pizza* (PS–1). Series: In the Kitchen. 2002, Children's LB $14.50 (0-516-23959-7); paper $4.95 (0-516-24020-X). 24pp. For beginning readers, this is a simple introduction to the ingredients of a pizza and the technique for making one. Also use *Let's Make Tacos* (2002). (Rev: SLJ 2/03)

5528 Hopkinson, Deborah. *Fannie in the Kitchen: The Whole Story from Soup to Nuts of How Fannie Farmer Invented Recipes with Precise Measurements* (K–3). Illus. by Nancy Carpenter. 2001, Simon & Schuster $16.00 (0-689-81965-X). 40pp. Fannie Farmer teaches a young girl to cook in this fictionalized account that is interspersed with excerpts from Farmer's cookbook. (Rev: BCCB 6/01; BL 5/15/01*; HB 5–6/01; HBG 10/01; SLJ 5/01*) [641.5]

5529 Lagasse, Emeril. *Emeril's There's a Chef in My Soup: Recipes for the Kid in Everyone* (5–8). Illus. by Charles Yuen. 2002, HarperCollins $22.99 (0-688-17706-9). 256pp. The famed TV chef presents a series of simple recipes for main dishes, pasta, desserts, breakfast and lunch items, and salads. (Rev: BL 5/1/02; HBG 10/02) [641.5]

5530 Lee, Frances. *The Young Chef's Chinese Cookbook* (4–7). Illus. Series: I'm the Chef! 2001, Crabtree LB $22.60 (0-7787-0280-4); paper $8.95 (0-7787-0294-4). 40pp. Fifteen child-friendly recipes for Chinese dishes are presented with step-by-step directions and photographs. Also use *The Young Chef's Mexican Cookbook* (2001). (Rev: BL 10/15/01; SLJ 11/01) [641.5951]

5531 McCulloch, Julie. *The Caribbean* (3–6). Illus. Series: World of Recipes. 2001, Heinemann LB $24.22 (1-58810-153-3). 48pp. Recipes, arranged by difficulty, follow information on the region and typical food choices. (Rev: BL 8/01; HBG 10/01) [641.59]

5532 McCulloch, Julie. *China* (3–6). Illus. Series: World of Recipes. 2001, Heinemann LB $24.22 (1-58810-152-5). 48pp. Recipes, arranged by difficulty, follow information on China and the kinds of foods eaten there. (Rev: BL 8/01; HBG 10/01; SLJ 10/01) [641.5951]

5533 McCulloch, Julie. *India* (4–6). Illus. Series: A World of Recipes. 2001, Heinemann LB $24.22 (1-58810-085-5). 48pp. A discussion of the history and traditions of Indian food is accompanied by a selection of typical recipes, most of which require adult participation. Also use *Mexico*. (Rev: HBG 10/01; SLJ 12/01) [641.5954]

5534 McCulloch, Julie. *Japan* (4–6). Illus. by Nicholas Beresford-Davies. Series: A World of Recipes. 2001, Heinemann LB $24.22 (1-58810-087-1). 48pp. Step-by-step instructions clearly show how to make dishes that are typical of Japanese cuisine, accompanied by advice on handling chopsticks. Also use *China* (2001). (Rev: HBG 10/01; SLJ 10/01) [641.5952]

5535 MacLeod, Elizabeth. *Bake and Make Amazing Cakes* (4–6). Illus. by June Bradford. Series: Kids Can Do It. 2001, Kids Can $12.95 (1-55074-849-1); paper $5.95 (1-55074-848-3). 40pp. A collection of child-friendly cake recipes with easy-to-follow instructions. (Rev: SLJ 6/01) [641.8653]

5536 Marchant, Kerena. *Hindu Cookbook* (3–5). Photos by Zul Mukhida. Series: Holiday Cookbooks from Around the World. 2001, Raintree Steck-Vaughn LB $17.98 (0-7398-3264-6). 32pp. Marchant looks at three Hindu holidays (Holi, Divali, and Ganesh Chaturthi), describes how they are celebrated, and provides appropriate recipes, with appealing photographs. Also use *Chinese Cookbook* (2001). (Rev: SLJ 8/01) [641.5]

5537 Montgomery, Bertha Vining, and Constance Nabwire. *Cooking the West African Way*. Rev. ed.

(5–8). Series: Easy Menu Ethnic Cookbooks. 2002, Lerner LB $25.26 (0-8225-4163-7). 72pp. An appealing introduction to West African cuisine, with information on the land, people, and culture, and several low-fat and vegetarian recipes. Also use *Holiday Cooking Around the World* (2002). (Rev: HBG 10/02; SLJ 5/02) [641.5966]

5538 Munsen, Sylvia. *Cooking the Norwegian Way*. Rev. ed. (5–8). Series: Easy Menu Ethnic Cookbooks. 2002, Lerner LB $25.26 (0-8225-4118-1). 72pp. A revised edition of an earlier publication that gives information on the country and culture in addition to a selection of typical recipes. Also use *Cooking the Greek Way* and *Cooking the Vietnamese Way* (both 2002). (Rev: BL 7/02; SLJ 9/02) [641.59]

5539 Napier, Tanya. *The Totally Tea-rific Tea Party Book: Teas to Taste, Treats to Bake, and Crafts to Make from Around the World and Beyond* (1–6). Photos by Julie Brown. Illus. by Annie Galvin. 2002, Barron's $13.95 (0-7641-5493-1). 79pp. Tea party suggestions from the traditional to the inventive (with a golf theme) come with tips on decor, a recipe, and an activity or craft. (Rev: HBG 3/03; SLJ 7/02) [641.53]

5540 Raabe, Emily. *An Easter Holiday Cookbook* (2–5). Series: Festive Foods for the Holidays. 2001, Rosen LB $19.50 (0-8239-5624-5). 24pp. Spring holidays and their foods are presented with large print and colorful illustrations. Also use *A Passover Holiday Cookbook* (2001). (Rev: SLJ 2/02) [641.568]

5541 Williamson, Sarah A. *Bake the Best-Ever Cookies!* (3–6). Illus. by Tom Ernst. Series: Quick Starts for Kids! 2001, Williamson paper $7.95 (1-885593-56-2). 64pp. Simple recipes follow basic information on equipment and ingredients and a number of frequently asked questions. (Rev: SLJ 11/01) [641.8654]

Gardening

5542 Nichol, Barbara. *One Small Garden* (3–6). Illus. by Barry Moser. 2001, Tundra $17.95 (0-88776-475-4). 56pp. A Toronto garden is the focus of this lyrical narrative describing plants, animals, and even the people who have enjoyed it. (Rev: BL 12/15/01; HBG 3/02; SLJ 12/01) [635]

Magic

5543 Colbert, David. *The Magical Worlds of Harry Potter: A Treasury of Myths, Legends, and Fascinating Facts* (5 Up). Illus. 2001, Lumina paper $14.95 (0-9708442-0-4). 223pp. Information on more than 50 topics in Harry's universe — such as alchemy, Grindylows, and Voldemort — is arranged in alphabetical order. (Rev: SLJ 2/02) [823]

5544 Jones, Richard. *That's Magic! 40 Foolproof Tricks to Delight, Amaze and Entertain* (5–8). Illus. 2001, New Holland $19.95 (1-85974-668-3). 112pp. Simple instructions and photographs teach the beginning magician a few tricks. (Rev: BL 1/1–15/02; SLJ 1/02) [793.8]

5545 Kronzek, Allan Zola, and Elizabeth Kronzek. *The Sorcerer's Companion: A Guide to the Magical World of Harry Potter* (4 Up). Illus. 2001, Broadway paper $15.00 (0-7679-0847-3). 286pp. Young readers may be amazed to learn how much of Harry's magic is standard fare when they read the references here to magical items and concepts in literature, legend, mythology, and religion. (Rev: SLJ 12/01) [823]

Photography and Filmmaking

5546 Friedman, Debra. *Picture This: Fun Photography and Crafts* (4–7). Series: Kids Can Do It. 2003, Kids Can $12.95 (1-55337-046-5); paper $5.95 (1-55337-047-3). 48pp. An easy-to-follow project book that combines the use of photographs and craft work. (Rev: BL 3/15/03) [770]

5547 Johnson, Neil. *National Geographic Photography Guide for Kids* (4–7). Illus. 2001, National Geographic $18.95 (0-7922-6371-5). 80pp. A comprehensive and easily understood introduction to cameras, lenses, and films, with tips from National Geographic photographers and clear information on techniques of composition and photography of people, sports, animals, landscapes, and so forth. (Rev: HBG 3/02; SLJ 9/01*) [770]

Stamp, Coin, and Other Types of Collecting

5548 Hubley, Dan, and Mary Hubley. *Kids Collect: Amazing Collections for Fun, Crafts, and Science Fair Projects* (3–6). Illus. 2002, Bluefish Bay paper $13.95 (0-9707-2671-6). 176pp. Provides tips on the selection of an item to collect; the development of the collection itself through buying, trading, and selling; and using the collection as part of a science fair or other school project. (Rev: SLJ 3/03)

5549 Owens, Thomas S. *Collecting Baseball Cards: 21st Century Edition*. Rev. ed. (4–8). 2001, Millbrook LB $24.90 (0-7613-1708-2). 80pp. An entertaining introduction to collecting baseball cards, with information on the history of the industry, on how to determine the condition of cards, and how to use the Internet to buy and sell. (Rev: HBG 10/01; SLJ 7/01) [796]

5550 Owens, Thomas S. *Collecting Stock Car Racing Memorabilia* (4–8). Illus. 2001, Millbrook LB $25.90 (0-7613-1853-4). 80pp. NASCAR fans in particular will appreciate this practical and detailed guide to collecting, which includes extensive lists of useful addresses. (Rev: BL 12/15/01; HBG 3/02; SLJ 11/01) [796.72]

Jokes, Puzzles, Riddles, Word Games

Jokes and Riddles

5551 Downs, Mike. *Pig Giggles and Rabbit Rhymes: A Book of Animal Riddles* (K–3). Illus. by David Sheldon. 2002, Chronicle $13.95 (0-8118-3114-0). 32pp. Riddles are presented on righthand pages with rhyming answers overleaf, accompanied by funny illustrations that contain clues. (Rev: BL 9/15/02; HBG 10/02; SLJ 7/02) [398.6]

5552 Hall, Katy, and Lisa Eisenberg. *Dino Riddles* (K–2). Illus. by Nicole Rubel. 2002, Dial $13.99 (0-8037-2239-7). 40pp. A collection of easy-reading riddles for the dinosaur gang. (Rev: BCCB 3/02; HBG 10/02; SLJ 2/02) [793.735]

5553 Hall, Katy, and Lisa Eisenberg. *Turkey Riddles* (1–3). Illus. by Kristin Sorra. 2002, Dial $13.99 (0-8037-2530-2). 40pp. A collection of silly, attractively illustrated riddles about turkeys, just right for Thanksgiving. (Rev: BL 9/1/02; HBG 3/03) [793.735]

5554 Rosenbloom, Joseph. *Giggle Fit: Silly Knock-Knocks* (PS–2). Illus. by Steve Harpster. 2001, Sterling $12.95 (0-8069-8015-X). 48pp. An A to Z of knock-knock nonsense answers of the "Olivia me alone" variety. (Rev: BL 12/15/01; HBG 3/02) [793.73]

5555 Shields, Carol Diggory. *Sports* (PS–3). Illus. by Svjetlan Junakovic. Series: Animagicals. 2001, Handprint $9.95 (1-929766-28-9). 32pp. Rhyming riddles give clues about animals hidden under the flaps in this tall-format picture book. (Rev: BL 2/1/02; HBG 3/02; SLJ 2/02) [811]

5556 Thomas, Lyn. *Ha! Ha! Ha! 1000+ Jokes, Riddles, Facts, and More* (3–8). Illus. by Dianne Eastman. 2001, Firefly $19.95 (1-894379-15-2); paper $9.95 (1-894379-16-0). 128pp. Laughs abound in this compendium that includes computer jokes, puns, and optical illusions. (Rev: HBG 10/01; SLJ 5/01) [793.73]

Puzzles

5557 Burnard, Damon. *I Spy in the Jungle* (PS–K). Illus. by Julia Cairns. 2001, Chronicle $6.95 (0-8118-2987-1). Die-cut circles give young readers a glimpse of the animal that is revealed when the page is turned. Also use *I Spy in the Ocean* (2001). (Rev: SLJ 11/01) [793.73]

5558 Marzollo, Jean. *I Spy Year-Round Challenger! A Book of Picture Riddles* (PS–2). Illus. by Walter Wick. 2001, Scholastic $13.95 (0-439-31634-0). 40pp. A book of double-page picture puzzles with holiday themes, one for each of the 12 months. (Rev: BL 2/1/02; HBG 10/02; SLJ 4/02) [793.73]

5559 Munro, Roxie. *Mazescapes* (1–4). Illus. by Roxie Hmunro. 2001, North-South $16.95 (1-58717-060-4). 36pp. Bright, detailed paintings show aerial views of rural and urban landscapes through which punch-out cars can be moved, with additional puzzles and games that will hold attention on long car trips. (Rev: HB 9–10/01; HBG 3/02; SLJ 8/01*) [793.73]

5560 Riedler, Isabella. *Tricky Puzzles for Clever Kids* (2–5). Illus. 2001, Sterling paper $5.95 (0-8069-6753-6). 128pp. A collection of challenging visual puzzles illustrated in black and white. (Rev: BL 2/15/02) [793.73]

5561 White, Graham. *Secrets of the Pyramids: A Maze Adventure* (3–6). Illus. 2002, National Geographic paper $8.95 (0-7922-6938-1). 32pp. Fans of mazes will enjoy helping 12-year-old Hemon look for his father in the pyramid, and will learn about ancient Egypt in the process. (Rev: SLJ 11/02) [793.7]

5562 Wick, Walter. *Can You See What I See? Picture Puzzles to Search and Solve* (K–3). Illus. 2002, Scholastic $13.95 (0-429-16391-9). 40pp. A collection of clever picture puzzles that test the visual perception of young readers. (Rev: BL 4/15/02; HBG 10/02; SLJ 3/02) [792.73]

Word Games

5563 Gardner, Martin. *Mind-Boggling Word Puzzles* (4–8). Illus. 2001, Sterling $14.95 (0-8069-7186-X). 96pp. Entertaining word games, many illustrated, will challenge students in fourth through eighth grades. (Rev: BL 9/1/01; HBG 3/02) [793.73]

5564 McCall, Francis, and Patricia Keeler. *A Huge Hog Is a Big Pig: A Rhyming Word Game* (K–3). Illus. 2002, HarperCollins LB $15.89 (0-06-029766-2). 32pp. "A wet hound is . . . a soggy doggy!" and other wondrous rhymes are accompanied by photographs of children from a mix of races and of the appropriate animals. (Rev: BL 12/15/01; HBG 10/02; SLJ 2/02)

Mysteries, Monsters, Curiosities, and Trivia

5565 Ash, Russell. *The Top 10 of Everything 2002* (4 Up). 2001, DK $26.95 (0-7894-8042-5); paper $17.95 (0-7894-8043-3). 288pp. A useful and attractive source of facts on a wide range of topics. (Rev: SLJ 1/02) [031.02]

5566 Aslan, Madalyn. *What's Your Sign? A Cosmic Guide for Young Astrologers* (5–9). Illus. by Jennifer Kalis. 2002, Grosset $12.99 (0-448-42693-5). A lively, spiral-bound guide to the 12 signs of the zodiac and the personality traits they represent, with information on the underlying mythology and lists of famous people born under each sign. (Rev: SLJ 9/02) [133.5]

5567 Cohen, Daniel, and Susan Cohen. *Hauntings and Horrors: The Ultimate Guide to Spooky America* (4–6). Illus. 2002, Dutton $9.99 (0-525-46900-1). 144pp. This travel guide to the haunted and supernatural features such sites as Houdini's grave and Roswell, New Mexico. (Rev: BL 8/02) [133.1]

5568 Delrio, Martin. *The Loch Ness Monster* (3–5). Series: Unsolved Mysteries. 2002, Rosen LB $25.25 (0-8239-3564-7). 48pp. Here is a rundown on the many sightings and stories surrounding the Lock Ness monster, including the expeditions that tried and failed to find the truth. (Rev: BL 10/15/02) [001.9]

5569 Farman, John. *The Short and Bloody History of Ghosts* (4–6). Illus. by author. Series: Short and Bloody Histories. 2002, Lerner LB $19.93 (0-8225-0837-0); paper $5.95 (0-8225-0838-9). 96pp. Ghosts and other supernatural beings are the focus of this overview of sightings around the world today and in the past, with most of the events occurring in Britain. (Rev: HBG 3/03; SLJ 2/03)

5570 Gilman, Laura Anne. *Yeti, the Abominable Snowman* (3–5). Illus. Series: Unsolved Mysteries. 2002, Rosen LB $25.25 (0-8239-3565-5). 48pp. The author presents historical accounts of the elusive yeti of the Himalayas. (Rev: BL 10/15/02) [001.944]

5571 Gorman, Jacqueline Laks. *The Bermuda Triangle* (3–5). Illus. Series: X Science: An Imagination Library. 2002, Gareth Stevens LB $19.93 (0-8368-3196-9). 24pp. An introduction to the mysterious Bermuda Triangle, with discussion of theories, evidence, and research. Also use *Bigfoot* and *The Loch Ness Monster* (both 2002). (Rev: HBG 3/03; SLJ 2/03) [001.9]

5572 Roleff, Tamara L., ed. *Black Magic and Witches* (5–8). Series: Fact or Fiction? 2003, Gale LB $21.96 (0-7377-1318-6); paper $14.96 (0-7377-1319-4). 127pp. A good starting point for debate over witchcraft, with essays for and against witches, magic, and Harry Potter, and some history of persecution of witches. (Rev: SLJ 3/03)

5573 Scott, Janine. *Cool Customs* (K–2). Series: Spyglass Books. 2002, Compass Point LB $18.60 (0-7565-0364-7). 24pp. A basic look, for beginning readers, at customs and traditions around the world. (Rev: SLJ 3/03) [394.2]

5574 Stirling, Janet. *UFOs* (3–5). Illus. Series: Unsolved Mysteries. 2002, Rosen LB $25.25 (0-8239-3566-3). 48pp. An account of UFO sightings over time, from early glimpses of Army blimps to the continuing flying saucer reports. (Rev: BL 10/15/02) [001.942]

5575 Watkins, Graham. *Ghosts and Poltergeists* (3–5). Series: Unsolved Mysteries. 2002, Rosen LB $25.25 (0-8239-3563-9). 48pp. This book explores actual case histories of hauntings and poltergeist activity, as well as a look into the way a real ghost hunter works. (Rev: BL 10/15/02) [133.1]

Sports and Games

General and Miscellaneous

5576 Ajmera, Maya, and John D. Ivanko. *Come Out and Play* (PS–2). Series: It's a Kid's World. 2001, Charlesbridge LB $15.95 (1-57091-385-4); paper $6.95 (1-57091-386-2). Photographs and simple text show the differences and similarities in children's play around the world. (Rev: HBG 10/01; SLJ 8/01) [790]

5577 Burgess, Ron. *Yo-Yo! Tips and Tricks from a Pro* (3–6). Illus. by author. 2001, Williamson paper $7.95 (1-885593-54-6). 64pp. Burgess shows simple and complex yo-yo techniques in easy-to-follow line drawings. (Rev: SLJ 1/02) [796.2]

5578 Case, Jeremy. *Scooters: The Ultimate Guide to the Coolest Ride!* (3–8). Illus. by Zac Sandler. 2001, Simon & Schuster paper $3.99 (0-689-84529-4). 92pp. Scooter fans will enjoy this chatty guide that gives advice on tricks, stunts, and safety, as well as exploring the history and potential future of this mode of transport, and the specs of various models. (Rev: SLJ 9/01) [796.6]

5579 Chambers, Veronica. *Double Dutch: A Celebration of Jump Rope, Rhyme, and Sisterhood* (4–8). Illus. 2002, Hyperion $16.99 (0-7868-0512-9). 72pp. An exuberant look at Double Dutch jump roping, including its history, rhymes, and exciting photographs. (Rev: BCCB 10/02; BL 10/15/02; HBG 3/03; SLJ 12/02) [796.2]

5580 Chapman, Garry. *Air* (3–5). Series: Extreme Sports. 2001, Chelsea LB $16.95 (0-7910-6609-6). 32pp. Sky diving, bungee jumping, sky surfing, and other aerial sports are covered in this attractively illustrated volume. (Rev: BL 10/15/01; HBG 3/02) [796]

5581 Chapman, Garry. *Mountains* (3–5). Series: Extreme Sports. 2001, Chelsea LB $16.95 (0-7910-6610-X). 32pp. Mountain climbing, adventure racing, mountain biking, and extreme hiking are highlighted in this book that also covers weather conditions, safety precautions, and competitions. (Rev: BL 10/15/01; HBG 3/02; SLJ 12/01) [796.5]

5582 Chapman, Garry. *Rivers* (3–5). Illus. Series: Extreme Sports. 2001, Chelsea LB $16.95 (0-7910-6608-8). 32pp. This account looks at "extreme" water sports (such as white-water kayaking and riverboarding), with information on required gear, terminology, and stunts, accompanied by photographs. (Rev: BL 10/15/01; HBG 3/02; SLJ 12/01) [797.1]

5583 Chapman, Garry. *Snow* (3–5). Series: Extreme Sports. 2001, Chelsea LB $16.95 (0-7910-6606-X). 32pp. A variety of snow sports such as skiing and sledding are presented, with descriptions of unique winter environments. (Rev: BL 10/15/01) [796.95]

5584 Chapman, Garry. *Streets* (3–5). Illus. Series: Extreme Sports. 2001, Chelsea LB $16.95 (0-7910-6612-6). 32pp. "Extreme" sports such as BMX riding, luge racing, and inline skating that can be practiced on the street are covered here, with information on required gear, terminology, and stunts, accompanied by photographs. (Rev: BL 10/15/01; HBG 3/02) [796.2]

5585 Chester, Jonathan. *The Young Adventurer's Guide to Everest: From Avalanche to Zopkio* (5–8). Illus. 2002, Tricycle Pr. $15.95 (1-58246-069-8). 48pp. A book about Mount Everest and those who have climbed it, in an alphabetical format with photographs. (Rev: BL 5/15/02; HBG 10/02; SLJ 4/02) [796.52]

5586 Corbett, Doris, and John Cheffers, eds. *Unique Games and Sports Around the World: A Reference Guide* (4 Up). Illus. 2001, Greenwood $59.95 (0-313-29778-9). 407pp. More than 300 games and sports are organized by continent and then by country, with details of the number of players, equipment, rules, and so forth, and indications of whether this is a suitable game for the classroom or playground. (Rev: SLJ 8/01) [790.1]

5587 Crossingham, John. *In-Line Skating in Action* (4–7). Series: Sports in Action. 2002, Crabtree LB $21.28 (0-7787-0328-2); paper $6.95 (0-7737-0348-7). 32pp. A fine introduction to this fast-growing sport with easy-to-follow descriptions of moves and techniques. (Rev: BL 1/1–15/03) [796.9]

5588 Crossingham, John. *Lacrosse in Action* (4–7). Series: Sports in Action. 2002, Crabtree LB $21.28 (0-7787-0329-0); paper $6.95 (0-7737-0349-5). 32pp. A clear, concise introduction to lacrosse that discusses techniques, equipment, rules, and safety precautions. (Rev: BL 1/1–15/03) [796.34]

5589 Donkin, Andrew. *Danger on the Mountain: Scaling the World's Highest Peaks* (2–4). Illus. Series: Dorling Kindersley Readers. 2001, DK $12.95 (0-7894-7386-0); paper $3.95 (0-7894-7385-2). 48pp. Donkin presents details of some famous expeditions as well as discussing the hazards involved and the way climbing equipment has changed over the years. (Rev: HBG 10/01; SLJ 11/01) [796.52]

5590 Eckart, Edana. *I Can Bowl* (K–2). Series: Sports. 2002, Children's LB $14.50 (0-516-23972-4); paper $4.95 (0-516-24028-5). 24pp. This slim volume for beginning readers shows Emma bowling with her father and discusses equipment and safety. Also use *I Can Swim*, *I Can Play Soccer*, and *I Can Ride a Bike* (all 2002). (Rev: SLJ 9/02) [794.6]

5591 Gedatus, Gus. *In-Line Skating for Fitness* (4–7). Series: Nutrition and Fitness. 2001, Capstone $16.95 (0-7368-0707-1). 64pp. Inline skating is introduced with emphasis on fitness benefits and the necessity of a healthy diet. (Rev: BL 9/15/01; HBG 10/01) [796]

5592 Gedatus, Gus. *Weight Training* (4–7). Illus. Series: Nutrition and Fitness. 2001, Capstone $16.95 (0-7368-0708-X). 32pp. Weight training equipment, proper form, and sample workouts are presented, as well as advice on diet and supplements. (Rev: BL 7/01; HBG 10/01) [613.7]

5593 Gordon, John. *The Kids Book of Golf* (3–6). Illus. 2001, Kids Can $14.95 (1-55337-017-1); paper $7.95 (1-55074-617-0). 48pp. History, equipment, technique, rules, competitions, and humorous anecdotes are all included here, along with diagrams and full-color photographs showing children and famous golfers. (Rev: HBG 10/01; SLJ 7/01) [796.352]

5594 Griffin, Margot. *The Sleepover Book* (2–7). Illus. by Jane Kurisu. 2001, Kids Can paper $14.95 (1-55074-522-0). 144pp. These sleepover activities range from making a music video, cooking midnight snacks, treasure hunts, games and crafts, and, of course, telling scary stories. (Rev: SLJ 6/01) [793.21]

5595 Howes, Chris. *Caving* (4–8). Series: Radical Sports. 2003, Heinemann LB $24.22 (1-58810-626-8). 32pp. Technique, safety, gear, and other vital aspects are covered in this introduction to the sport. (Rev: BL 2/15/03; HBG 3/03) [796.52]

5596 Jaffe, Elizabeth Dana. *Dominoes* (1–4). Illus. Series: Games Around the World. 2001, Compass Point LB $21.26 (0-7565-0132-6). 32pp. Variations of dominoes games are presented with instructions and diagrams, along with a section on using them to create a domino effect. (Rev: SLJ 10/01) [795.3]

5597 Jaffe, Elizabeth Dana. *Hopscotch* (3–5). Illus. Series: Games Around the World. 2001, Compass Point LB $21.26 (0-7565-0133-4). 32pp. All about the favorite game of hopscotch — its rules, variations, and history. Also use *Marbles* and *Jacks* (both 2001). (Rev: BL 12/1/01; SLJ 10/01) [796.2]

5598 Jaffe, Elizabeth Dana. *Juggling* (3–5). Series: Games Around the World. 2002, Compass Point LB $21.26 (0-7565-0191-1). 32pp. This work contains a history of juggling and describes equipment and basic techniques, using colorful illustrations. (Rev: BL 5/15/02; SLJ 7/02) [793.8]

5599 Klingel, Cynthia, and Robert B. Noyed. *Yo-Yo Tricks* (3–5). Series: Games Around the World. 2002, Compass Point LB $21.26 (0-7565-0193-8). 32pp. The development of the yo-yo is covered in this volume, along with colorful illustrations and diagrams that describe techniques and moves. (Rev: BL 5/15/02; SLJ 7/02) [796]

5600 Lehn, Barbara. *What Is an Athlete?* (PS–2). Illus. by Carol Krauss. 2002, Millbrook LB $21.90 (0-7613-2258-2). 32pp. An introduction of the concept of "athlete," presented in a friendly format for younger readers. (Rev: BL 12/15/02; HBG 3/03) [796]

5601 Manley, Claudia B. *Competitive Volleyball for Girls* (4–7). Illus. Series: Sportsgirl. 2001, Rosen LB $19.95 (0-8239-3404-7). 64pp. An introduction to the rules of volleyball, the training necessary, and the special opportunities for girls, with material on nutrition and the dangers of overtraining. (Rev: SLJ 3/02) [796.325]

5602 Masoff, Joy. *Everest: Reaching for the Sky* (2–4). Series: Scholastic History Readers. 2002, Scholastic paper $3.99 (0-439-26707-2). 48pp. For beginning readers, this is an appealing and informative account of Edmund Hillary and Tenzing Norgay's ascent in 1953. (Rev: SLJ 2/03) [796.5]

5603 Mason, Paul. *Skiing* (4–8). Illus. 2003, Heinemann LB $24.22 (1-58810-628-4). 32pp. Technique, safety, gear, and profiles of famous skiers are all covered in this introduction to the sport. (Rev: BL 2/15/03; HBG 3/03) [796.93]

5604 Miller, Debbie S. *The Great Serum Race: Blazing the Iditarod Trail* (2–4). Illus. by Jon Van Zyle. 2002, Walker LB $17.85 (0-8027-8812-2). 32pp. This absorbing picture book for older children gives all the details of the famous race, with effective illustrations that convey the icy cold. (Rev: BL 1/1–15/03; HBG 3/03; SLJ 11/02) [798.8]

5605 Roberts, Robin. *Which Sport Is Right for You?* (5–8). Series: Get in the Game! With Robin Roberts. 2001, Millbrook LB $21.90 (0-7613-2117-9). 48pp. Written with girls in mind, this short book explores how to choose a sport that is right for one's capabilities and interests. (Rev: BL 9/15/01; HBG 3/02; SLJ 1/02) [796]

5606 Roper, Ingrid. *Yo-Yos: Tricks to Amaze Your Friends* (3–6). 2001, HarperCollins $15.95 (0-688-14663-5); paper $7.95 (0-688-14665-1). 64pp. A guide to different kinds of yo-yos and yo-yo technique that starts with the basic and progresses to the more advanced. (Rev: BL 5/15/01; HBG 10/01; SLJ 8/01) [796.2]

5607 Skreslet, Laurie, and Elizabeth MacLeod. *To the Top of Everest* (5–9). Illus. 2001, Kids Can

$16.95 (1-55074-721-5). 56pp. Skreslet relates his lifelong ambition to climb Everest and his actual experiences doing so, with many facts about the mountain and the dangers involved and stunning photographs of his adventure. (Rev: BCCB 10/01; BL 9/15/01; HBG 3/02; SLJ 9/01*) [796.52]

5608 Smith, Graham. *Karting* (4–8). Series: Radical Sports. 2002, Heinemann LB $24.22 (1-58810-624-1). 32pp. The sport of karting is introduced with discussion of equipment selection, basic skills, fitness and training, and safety. (Rev: BL 2/15/03; HBG 3/03) [796.7]

5609 Takeda, Pete. *Climb! Your Guide to Bouldering, Sport Climbing, Trad Climbing, Ice Climbing, Alpinism, and More* (4–9). Illus. Series: Extreme Sports. 2002, National Geographic paper $8.95 (0-7922-6744-3). 64pp. An attractive guide to climbing of all types — sport, wall, ice, alpine, and so forth — and to the equipment, techniques, and dangers. (Rev: SLJ 1/03)

5610 Teitelbaum, Michael. *Great Moments in Women's Sports* (4–7). Series: Great Moments in Sports. 2002, World Almanac LB $26.60 (0-8368-5349-0). 48pp. A timeline running from 1904 to 2001 provides a backdrop for information on athletes who participated in the Olympic Games and achieved other significant milestones. (Rev: SLJ 3/03)

5611 U.S. Olympic Committee. *A Basic Guide to Decathlon* (4–8). Series: Olympic Guides. 2001, Gareth Stevens LB $22.60 (0-8368-2796-1). 152pp. This is an attractive introduction to the sport of decathlon, with information about equipment, training, and famous athletes. (Rev: HBG 10/01; SLJ 7/01) [796.42]

5612 Uschan, Michael V. *Golf* (4–8). Series: History of Sports. 2001, Lucent LB $19.96 (1-56006-744-6). 112pp. An absorbing exploration of the history of golf, with information on etiquette, famous players, tours, and famous courses, with many photographs and reproductions. (Rev: SLJ 7/01) [796.352]

5613 Van Steenwyk, Elizabeth. *Let's Go to the Beach: A History of Sun and Fun by the Sea* (5–7). 2001, Holt $18.95 (0-8050-6235-1). 144pp. This fascinating exploration of beach-going over the centuries looks at everything from social changes and fashion to sand castle competitions, surfing, music, and beach food. (Rev: BL 5/1/01; HBG 10/01; SLJ 8/01) [797]

5614 Warshaw, Hallie, and Jake Miller. *Get Out! Outdoor Activities Kids Can Enjoy Anywhere (Except Indoors)* (3–6). Illus. 2001, Sterling $19.95 (0-8069-9091-0). 128pp. This well-designed, colorful volume suggests all kinds of games and activities kids can do outdoors, from crafts to community service. (Rev: BL 1/1–15/02; SLJ 4/02) [796]

5615 Warshaw, Hallie, and Mark Shulman. *Zany Rainy Days: Indoor Ideas for Active Kids* (2–5). Photos by Morten Kettel. Illus. 2001, Sterling $19.95 (0-8069-6623-8). 128pp. Games, crafts, projects, and recipes — from scavenger hunts and storytelling to making forts and dog biscuits — are presented in lively text with photographs and clear instructions, as well as icons that denote the difficulty of the undertaking and the length of time required. (Rev: SLJ 8/01) [793]

Automobile Racing

5616 Dooling, Michael. *The Great Horse-less Carriage Race* (2–4). Illus. 2002, Holiday $16.95 (0-8234-1640-2). 32pp. Car lovers will particularly appreciate this lively picture-book presentation of the country's first car race, which took place in Chicago in 1895, with competitors reaching the heady average speed of 7 mph. (Rev: BCCB 2/03; BL 11/15/02; HBG 3/03; SLJ 12/02) [796.72]

5617 Johnstone, Mike. *NASCAR* (5–8). Series: Need for Speed. 2002, Lerner LB $23.95 (0-8225-0389-1). 32pp. This book highlights the fast-growing sport of NASCAR auto racing, with detailed descriptions of the drivers, their cars, and the circuits. (Rev: BL 8/02; HBG 10/02; SLJ 7/02) [796.7]

5618 Parr, Danny. *Lowriders* (4–7). Illus. Series: Wild Rides! 2001, Capstone LB $15.95 (0-7368-0928-7). 32pp. This volume on "lowrider" cars discusses the types of vehicles that are popular, the history of this trend, and the competitions that are held. (Rev: BL 10/15/01; HBG 3/02) [628.28]

5619 Pitt, Matthew. *Drag Racer* (4–7). Illus. Series: Built for Speed. 2001, Children's LB $19.00 (0-516-23159-6); paper $6.95 (0-516-23262-2). 48pp. The cars, the driving techniques, the race regulations, and other information important to this activity are all covered in this attractive book. (Rev: BL 12/1/01) [796.72]

Baseball

5620 Buckley, James, Jr. *Play Ball! The Official Major League Baseball Guide for Young Players* (3–7). Illus. by Mike Eliason. 2002, DK $12.95 (0-7894-8509-5). 48pp. A colorful guide to the game of baseball, with tips from the pros, pointers on important skills, trivia, and more, including photographs of both boy and girl players. (Rev: BL 5/15/02; HBG 10/02; SLJ 7/02) [796.357]

5621 Driscoll, Laura. *Negro Leagues: All-Black Baseball* (3–5). Illus. by Tracy Mitchell. Series: Smart About History. 2002, Grosset LB $14.89 (0-448-42821-0); paper $5.99 (0-448-42684-6). 32pp. Through Emily's report on her visit to the National Baseball Hall of Fame, readers learn about the history of the Negro Leagues and the famous African American players. (Rev: BL 9/1/02; HBG 3/03; SLJ 12/02) [796.35764]

5622 Fuerst, Jeffrey B. *The Kids' Baseball Workout: A Fun Way to Get in Shape and Improve Your Game* (5–8). Illus. by Anne Canevari Green. 2002, Millbrook LB $24.90 (0-7613-2307-4). 80pp. This book offers exercises, stretches, and skills that will help young baseball players improve their game. (Rev: BL 9/1/02; HBG 10/02; SLJ 7/02) [796.357]

5623 Grabowski, John. *The Boston Red Sox Baseball Team* (4–6). Series: Great Sports Teams. 2001, Enslow $18.95 (0-7660-1488-6). 48pp. This introduction to the Boston Red Sox gives lively information on the team's past, present, and future prospects. (Rev: BL 9/15/01; HBG 10/01) [796.357]

5624 Kennedy, Mike. *Baseball* (2–4). Series: True Books — Sports. 2002, Children's LB $23.50 (0-516-22334-8); paper $6.95 (0-516-29371-0). 48pp. Using large type and many color photographs, this is a simple introduction to baseball, its history, and how it is played. (Rev: BL 9/1/02; SLJ check) [796.357]

5625 Krasner, Steven. *Play Ball Like the Pros: Tips for Kids from 20 Big League Stars* (5–9). Illus. 2002, Peachtree paper $12.95 (1-56145-261-0). 160pp. Each chapter features a professional player talking about the position he plays and giving tips to the young athlete. (Rev: BL 5/1/02; SLJ 6/02) [796.357]

5626 *My Baseball Book* (PS). Illus. 2002, DK $7.95 (0-7894-8508-7). 16pp. A preschooler's introduction to baseball, with descriptions of each position on the field and bright, colorful photographs of players in action. (Rev: BL 3/1/02) [796.357]

5627 Pietrusza, David. *The Cleveland Indians Baseball Team* (4–6). Series: Great Sports Teams. 2001, Enslow $18.95 (0-7660-1491-6). 48pp. Using fast-paced writing and many photographs, Pietrusza supplies a good thumbnail sketch of the team, its famous players, and outstanding games. (Rev: BL 9/15/01; HBG 3/02) [796.357]

5628 Pietrusza, David. *The St. Louis Cardinals Baseball Team* (4–6). Series: Great Sports Teams. 2001, Enslow $18.95 (0-7660-1490-8). 48pp. An exciting introduction to the team with material on its history, key players, exciting seasons, and present status. (Rev: BL 9/15/01; HBG 3/02) [7.9.6.3.5.7]

5629 Suen, Anastasia. *The Story of Baseball* (1–3). Illus. Series: Sports History. 2002, Rosen LB $16.00 (0-8239-6000-5). 24pp. A basic, easy-to-read introduction to the sport. (Rev: BL 5/15/02) [796.357]

Basketball

5630 Aretha, David. *The Detroit Pistons Basketball Team* (4–6). Series: Great Sports Teams. 2001, Enslow LB $18.95 (0-7660-1487-8). 48pp. In narrative and pictures, this volume highlights the history and achievements of the Detroit Pistons with material on their key players and important seasons, past and present. (Rev: BL 12/15/01; HBG 3/02) [796.323]

5631 Burgan, Michael. *Great Moments in Basketball* (4–7). Series: Great Moments in Sports. 2002, World Almanac LB $26.60 (0-8368-5345-8). 48pp. Great basketball achievements of the years from 1962 to 2002 are detailed here, with a timeline that starts in 1891 and comments from coaches and players. (Rev: SLJ 3/03)

5632 Kennedy, Mike. *Basketball* (3–5). Series: True Books — Sports. 2002, Children's LB $23.50 (0-516-22335-6); paper $6.95 (0-516-29372-9). 48pp. Covers the basic elements of basketball, its history, and superstars, with color photographs on each page plus large type and simple text. (Rev: BL 1/1–15/03) [796.323]

5633 Kuklin, Susan, and Sheryl Swoopes. *Hoops with Swoopes* (1–3). Illus. 2001, Hyperion $15.99 (0-7868-0551-X). 32pp. Basketball star Swoopes introduces the basics of the game in simple text and energetic illustrations. (Rev: BCCB 11/01; BL 6/1–15/01; HB 5–6/01; HBG 3/02; SLJ 8/01) [796.323]

5634 Owens, Thomas S. *Basketball Arenas* (5–8). Illus. Series: Sports Palaces. 2002, Millbrook LB $25.90 (0-7613-1766-X). 64pp. Lots of basketball lore and history are included in a visit to the Boston Garden, Chicago Stadium, and the old Madison Square Garden. (Rev: BL 6/1–15/02; HBG 10/02) [796.323]

Bicycles

5635 Crossingham, John. *Cycling in Action* (4–7). Illus. by Bonna Rouse. Series: Sports in Action. 2002, Crabtree LB $19.96 (0-7787-0118-2); paper $5.95 (0-7787-0124-7). 32pp. Photographs and drawings illustrate important concepts in this introduction to the sport of cycling that covers equipment and technique. (Rev: BL 9/1/02) [796.4]

5636 Deady, Kathleen W. *BMX Bikes* (4–7). Illus. Series: Wild Rides! 2001, Capstone LB $15.95 (0-7368-0925-2). 32pp. Bicycle motocross fans will enjoy the color photographs and concise text that explains the equipment and skills needed for BMX racing. (Rev: BL 10/15/01; HBG 3/02) [629.22]

5637 Dick, Scott. *BMX* (4–8). Series: Radical Sports. 2002, Heinemann LB $24.22 (1-58810-623-3). 32pp. This introduction to BMX (bicycle motocross) gives material on equipment, skills, training, and safety. (Rev: BL 2/15/03; HBG 3/03) [796.6]

5638 Englart, Mindi Rose. *Bikes* (3–5). Series: Made in the USA. 2002, Gale LB $21.54 (1-56711-486-5). 32pp. A behind-the-scenes look at how bicycles are made, starting with the raw materials and continuing through the finished product. (Rev: BL 9/15/02) [629]

5639 Gedatus, Gus. *Bicycling for Fitness* (4–7). Series: Nutrition and Fitness. 2001, Capstone $16.95 (0-7368-0705-5). 64pp. This book explains the benefits of bicycling in promoting good health and outlines a fitness plan, nutrition program, and delicious recipes. (Rev: BL 9/15/01; HBG 10/01) [796.6]

5640 Maurer, Tracy Nelson. *BMX Freestyle* (3–6). Series: Radsports. 2001, Rourke LB $27.93 (1-58952-102-1). 48pp. Safety is emphasized in this account of BMX history, equipment, and techniques. (Rev: SLJ 5/02) [796.62]

Bowling

5641 Nace, Don. *Bowling for Beginners: Simple Steps to Strikes and Spares* (5 Up). Photos by Bruce Curtis. 2001, Sterling $19.95 (0-8069-4968-6). 96pp. Equipment, technique, scoring, competition play, and etiquette are all discussed here, with excellent diagrams and color photographs. (Rev: BL 6/1–15/01; SLJ 7/01) [794.6]

Chess

5642 Basman, Michael. *Chess for Kids* (4–8). Illus. 2001, DK $12.95 (0-7894-6540-X). 44pp. A guide to the game of chess that includes everything from the basic moves and important strategies to information on the game's origins and the roles the game has played in arenas ranging from literature to history. (Rev: BL 7/01; HBG 10/01) [794.1]

Fishing

5643 Bailey, John. *Fishing* (5–8). Illus. 2001, DK $9.95 (0-7894-7389-5). 48pp. An appealing introduction to fish and fishing, with details of equipment, technique, and proper respect for the environment. (Rev: BL 6/1–15/01; HBG 10/01) [799.1]

Football

5644 Aretha, David. *The Notre Dame Fighting Irish Football Team* (4–6). Series: Great Sports Teams. 2001, Enslow LB $18.95 (0-7660-1486-X). 48pp. Fast-paced writing and many action photographs feature in this account of the Fighting Irish team, its most exciting seasons, star players, and present status. (Rev: BL 12/15/01; HBG 3/02) [796.48]

5645 Kennedy, Mike. *Football* (3–5). Series: True Books — Sports. 2002, Children's LB $23.50 (0-516-22336-4); paper $6.95 (0-516-29373-7). 48pp. Large type and a simple text plus plenty of well-captioned color photographs are highlights of this basic introduction to football, its history, rules, and key players. (Rev: BL 1/1–15/03) [796.332]

5646 Macnow, Glen. *The Denver Broncos Football Team* (4–6). Series: Great Sports Teams. 2001, Enslow $18.95 (0-7660-1489-4). 48pp. A simple account that gives information on the history of the team, its star players, and most exciting seasons. (Rev: BL 9/15/01; HBG 3/02) [796.332]

5647 O'Shei, Tim. *The Chicago Bears Football Team* (4–6). Series: Great Sports Teams. 2001, Enslow LB $18.95 (0-7660-1285-9). 48pp. The history of the Chicago Bears is given in text and pic-

tures with coverage of key seasons, important players, and future outlook. (Rev: BL 12/15/01; HBG 3/02) [796.48]

Gymnastics

5648 Kalman, Bobbie, and John Crossingham. *Gymnastics in Action* (4–7). Series: Sports in Action. 2002, Crabtree LB $21.28 (0-7787-0330-4); paper $6.95 (0-7737-0350-9). 32pp. Various branches of gymnastics are introduced in text and pictures with coverage of techniques, equipment, and basic movements. (Rev: BL 1/1–15/03) [796.44]

5649 Schlegel, Elfi, and Claire Ross Dunn. *The Gymnastics Book: The Young Performer's Guide to Gymnastics* (4–6). Illus. 2001, Firefly $24.95 (1-55209-414-6); paper $15.95 (1-55209-416-2). 128pp. An informative and appealing overview written by an expert gymnast. (Rev: BL 5/1/01; HBG 10/01; SLJ 4/01*) [796.44]

Horsemanship

5650 Bolt, Betty. *Jumping* (4–8). Series: Horse Library. 2001, Chelsea LB $19.75 (0-7910-6657-6). 64pp. Show jumping, eventing, and steeplechase riding are all covered in detail here. Also use *Western Riding*. (Rev: HBG 3/02; SLJ 3/02) [798.4]

5651 Ransford, Sandy. *First Riding Lessons* (3–7). Illus. 2002, Kingfisher $14.95 (0-7534-5454-8). 64pp. This no-nonsense book takes young horse fans through choosing a riding instructor, learning about different types of mounts, basic lessons and exercises, and a brief view of equine competitions. (Rev: BL 1/1–15/03; HBG 3/03; SLJ 12/02) [798.2]

5652 U.S. Olympic Committee. *A Basic Guide to Equestrian* (4–8). Illus. 2001, Gareth Stevens LB $22.60 (0-8368-2797-X). 150pp. An informative guide to Olympic equestrian competitions with material on choosing and looking after a horse and learning to ride. (Rev: HBG 10/01; SLJ 7/01) [798.2]

Ice Hockey

5653 Carson, Paul, and Sean Rossiter. *Hockey the NHL Way: Tips from the Pros* (4–6). Illus. 2001, Sterling paper $9.95 (1-55054-864-6). 64pp. Excellent photographs accompany advice on skills and sportsmanship for young hockey fans from professional players and coaches. (Rev: BL 2/1/02) [796.962]

5654 McFarlane, Brian. *Real Stories from the Rink* (5–8). Illus. by Steve Nease. 2002, Tundra paper $14.96 (0-88776-604-8). 96pp. Entertaining true stories give insight into ice hockey's history, rules, and players. (Rev: BL 2/15/03) [796.962]

5655 Thomas, Keltie. *How Hockey Works* (4–7). Illus. 2002, Maple Tree $19.95 (1-894379-35-7); paper $9.95 (1-894379-36-5). 64pp. A volume focusing on the game of ice hockey that presents everything from important skills and equipment to common superstitions, with an appealing layout. (Rev: BL 9/1/02) [796.962]

Ice Skating

5656 Feldman, Jane. *I Am a Skater* (2–6). Photos by author. Series: Young Dreamers. 2002, Random LB $16.99 (0-375-90256-2). Color and black-and-white photographs show 12-year-old Emily Hughes on the ice, meeting famous skaters, choosing costumes, and demonstrating moves. (Rev: HBG 10/02; SLJ 6/02) [796.91]

Indoor Games

5657 Bruder, Mikyla. *The Star Wars Party Book: Recipes and Ideas for Galactic Occasions* (3–5). Photos by Frankie Frankeny. Illus. 2002, Chronicle $17.95 (0-8118-3491-3). 62pp. Six themed parties are suggested here, with recipes, crafts, games, and other activities. (Rev: SLJ 11/02) [642.4]

5658 Kilby, Janice Eaton, and Terry Taylor. *Book of Wizard Parties: In Which the Wizard Shares the Secrets of Creating Enchanted Gatherings* (4–6). Illus. by Marla Baggetta. 2002, Sterling $19.95 (1-57990-292-8). 144pp. Tips on how to throw the ultimate wizard-themed parties, including crafts, food, and magical motifs. (Rev: BL 8/02; HBG 10/02; SLJ 9/02) [793.2]

5659 Klingel, Cynthia, and Robert B. Noyed. *Card Tricks* (3–5). Series: Games Around the World. 2002, Compass Point LB $21.26 (0-7565-0190-3). 32pp. After background material on playing cards, this illustrated book highlights several baffling card tricks and shows how to perform them. (Rev: BL 5/15/02; SLJ 7/02) [795.4]

5660 Street, Michael. *Lucky 13: Solitaire Games for Kids* (3–7). Illus. 2001, North-South $14.95 (1-58717-013-2); paper $6.95 (1-58717-014-0). 128pp. After introducing playing cards, this account gives instructions on how to play 65 games of solitaire ranging from the simplest to the more complex. (Rev: BL 4/15/01; HBG 10/01; SLJ 4/01) [795.4]

Motor Bikes and Motorcycles

5661 Freeman, Gary. *Motocross* (4–8). Series: Radical Sports. 2002, Heinemann LB $24.22 (1-58810-627-6). 32pp. The sport of cross country racing on

motorcycles is introduced, with an emphasis on safety and skill development. (Rev: BL 2/15/03; HBG 3/03) [796.7]

5662 Maurer, Tracy Nelson. *ATV Riding* (4–6). Illus. Series: Radsports. 2002, Rourke LB $27.93 (1-58952-276-1). 48pp. A jargon- and action-filled introduction to a "radical" sport, with photographs and Web sites. (Rev: BL 2/15/03) [796.7]

5663 Stuart, Dee. *Motorcycles* (2–4). Series: Transportation and Communication. 2001, Enslow LB $18.95 (0-7660-1648-X). 48pp. Using simple language and many illustrations, this short book describes the history and present developments related to motorcycles and their uses. (Rev: BL 3/15/02; HBG 3/02) [7796.7]

Olympic Games

5664 U.S. Olympic Committee. *Olympism: A Basic Guide to the History, Ideals, and Sports of the Olympic Movement* (4–8). Illus. Series: Olympic Guides. 2001, Gareth Stevens LB $22.60 (0-8368-2800-3). 152pp. This is an attractive and authoritative overview of the Olympics' history and of the games' importance. (Rev: HBG 10/01; SLJ 7/01) [796.48]

5665 Wukovits, John. *The Encyclopedia of the Winter Olympics* (5–8). Illus. 2001, Watts LB $36.00 (0-531-11885-1). 160pp. A fact-filled but lively volume with quotes from athletes, action highlights, and coverage of political controversies. (Rev: SLJ 11/01) [796.48]

Skateboarding

5666 Crossingham, John. *Skateboarding in Action* (4–7). Series: Sports in Action. 2002, Crabtree LB $19.96 (0-7787-0117-4); paper $5.95 (0-7787-0123-9). 32pp. A well-illustrated introduction to skateboarding with good material on equipment and injury prevention. (Rev: BL 9/1/02; SLJ 11/02) [795.2]

5667 Freimuth, Jeri. *Extreme Skateboarding Moves* (4–7). Illus. Series: Behind the Moves. 2001, Capstone $15.95 (0-7368-0783-7). 32pp. Skateboard slang is just one appealing part of this account of proper equipment and technique, with safety tips and some tricks. (Rev: BL 6/1–15/01; HBG 10/01; SLJ 9/01) [796.22]

5668 Horsley, Andy. *Skateboarding* (4–7). Illus. Series: To the Limit. 2001, Raintree Steck-Vaughn $17.98 (0-7398-3163-1). 32pp. A brief history of skateboarding is included here along with material on equipment, moves, and some advice on turning pro. (Rev: BL 6/1–15/01) [796.22]

5669 Loizos, Constance. *Skateboard! Your Guide to Street, Vert, Downhill, and More* (4–9). Illus. Series: Extreme Sports. 2002, National Geographic paper $8.95 (0-7922-8229-9). 64pp. An attractive guide to skateboarding equipment, technique, rules, etiquette, jargon, and safety. (Rev: SLJ 1/03)

5670 Maurer, Tracy Nelson. *Skateboarding* (3–6). Series: Radsports. 2001, Rourke LB $27.93 (1-58952-104-8). 48pp. Safety is emphasized in this account of skateboarding's history, equipment, and techniques that includes "Pro Spotlights." (Rev: SLJ 5/02) [796.22]

Snowboarding

5671 Crossingham, John. *Snowboarding in Action* (4–7). Illus. by Bonna Rouse. Series: Sports in Action. 2002, Crabtree LB $19.96 (0-7787-0119-0); paper $5.95 (0-7787-0125-5). 32pp. Aspiring snowboarders will find much of interest here, including basic techniques to get going — and stopping. (Rev: BL 9/1/02; SLJ 11/02) [796.9]

Soccer

5672 Kennedy, Mike. *Soccer* (3–5). Series: True Books — Sports. 2002, Children's LB $23.50 (0-516-22337-2); paper $6.95 (0-516-29374-5). 48pp. In addition to a short history of soccer, this account describes the different positions, moves, competitions, and famous players. (Rev: BL 1/1–15/03) [796.334]

5673 Mackin, Bob. *Soccer the Winning Way: Play Like the Pros* (4–7). Illus. 2002, Douglas & McIntyre paper $10.95 (1-55054-825-5). 62pp. A guide to mastering crucial soccer skills, with photographs and words of wisdom from the pros. (Rev: BL 5/15/02) [796]

5674 Otten, Jack. *Soccer* (1–6). Series: Sports Training. 2002, Rosen LB $16.00 (0-8239-5972-4). 24pp. A brief and basic introduction to the sport that will be useful for reluctant readers and ESL students. (Rev: SLJ 3/02) [796.334]

5675 Sherman, Josepha. *Competitive Soccer for Girls* (4–7). Series: Sportsgirl. 2001, Rosen LB $19.95 (0-8239-3405-5). 64pp. An introduction to the rules of soccer, the training necessary, and the special opportunities for girls, with material on nutrition and the dangers of overtraining. (Rev: SLJ 3/02) [796.334]

5676 Suen, Anastasia. *The Story of Soccer* (1–3). Illus. Series: Sports History. 2002, Rosen LB $16.00 (0-8239-5998-8). 24pp. A basic, easy-to-read introduction to the sport. (Rev: BL 5/15/02; SLJ 3/02) [796.334]

5677 Sullivan, George. *All About Soccer* (4–8). Illus. 2001, Putnam $15.99 (0-399-23481-0). 176pp.

Observers and players alike will find much of interest in this comprehensive look at the internationally popular game. (Rev: BL 6/1–15/01; HBG 10/01; SLJ 5/01) [796.334]

Surfing

5678 Chapman, Garry. *Surf* (3–5). Series: Extreme Sports. 2001, Chelsea LB $16.95 (0-7910-6611-8). 32pp. This book covers the history of surfing, safety in the surf, and the extreme sports that began as spin-offs of traditional surfing. (Rev: BL 10/15/01; HBG 3/02; SLJ 12/01) [797.2]

5679 Maurer, Tracy Nelson. *Surfing* (4–6). Illus. Series: Radsports. 2002, Rourke LB $27.93 (1-58952-280-X). 48pp. A jargon- and action-filled introduction to a "radical" sport, with photographs and Web sites. (Rev: BL 2/15/03) [797.3]

Swimming and Diving

5680 Crossingham, John, and Niki Walker. *Swimming in Action* (4–7). Series: Sports in Action. 2002, Crabtree LB $21.28 (0-7787-0331-2); paper $6.95 (0-7737-0351-7). 32pp. Color photographs and many diagrams are used with a clear text to describe swimming basics, with tips on various strokes and safety. (Rev: BL 1/1–15/03) [977.2]

Tennis

5681 Crossingham, John. *Tennis in Action* (4–7). Series: Sports in Action. 2002, Crabtree LB $19.96 (0-7787-0116-6); paper $5.95 (0-7787-0122-0). 32pp. A fine introduction to tennis told through a concise text with easy-to-follow descriptions and material on equipment, rules, and techniques. (Rev: BL 9/1/02; SLJ 11/02) [796.342]

Track and Field

5682 Manley, Claudia B. *Competitive Track and Field for Girls* (4–7). Illus. Series: Sportsgirl. 2001, Rosen LB $19.95 (0-8239-3408-X). 64pp. An introduction to the rules of track and field competitions, the training necessary, and the special opportunities for girls, with material on nutrition and the dangers of overtraining. (Rev: SLJ 3/02) [796.42]

Author and Illustrator Index

Authors and illustrators are arranged alphabetically by last name, followed by book titles — which are also arranged alphabetically — and the text entry number. Book titles may refer to those that appear as a main entry or as an internal entry mentioned in the annotation. Fiction titles are indicated by (F) following the entry number.

Aaseng, Nathan. *Business Builders in Fast Food*, 3214
  Cheetahs, 4918
  The Marine Corps in Action, 5423
  Women Olympic Champions, 3522
Abboreno, Joseph F. *Ho Yi the Archer and Other Classic Chinese Tales*, 2786
Abbott, Tony. *Trapped in Transylvania*, 2070(F)
Aber, Linda Williams. *Carrie Measures Up*, 84(F)
  Grandma's Button Box, 36(F)
Abercrombie, Barbara. *Bad Dog, Dodger!* 1396(F)
Abley, Mark. *Ghost Cat*, 1397(F)
Abramovitz, Melissa. *Leukemia*, 4631
Accardo, Anthony. *César Chávez*, 3269
  The Last Doll / La Ultima Muneca, 1583(F)
Ackerman, Diane. *Animal Sense*, 2996
Ada, Alma Flor. *Daniel's Mystery Egg*, 1728(F)
  I Love Saturdays y Domingos, 1028(F)
  With Love, Little Red Hen, 215(F)
Adams, Eric J. *On the Day His Daddy Left*, 1363(F)
Adams, Georgie. *The Three Little Witches Storybook*, 1666(F)
Adams, Kathleen (jt. author). *On the Day His Daddy Left*, 1363(F)
Adams, Lynn. *Chickens on the Move*, 89(F)
  Kitten Castle, 1437(F)
  What's That Sound? 946(F)
Adams, Simon. *Code Breakers*, 3657
  The Presidents of the United States, 3215
Adams, W. Royce. *Me and Jay*, 1906(F)
Addy, Sharon Hart. *When Wishes Were Horses*, 1166(F)
Adelson, Bruce. *David Farragut*, 3298
  George Gordon Meade, 3322
Adinolfi, JoAnn. *Fred's Bed*, 1002(F)
  This Book Is Haunted, 1847(F)
Adkins, Jan. *Bridges*, 5346
Adler, C. S. *The No Place Cat*, 2266(F)
Adler, David A. *Andy Russell, NOT Wanted by the Police*, 1907(F)
  B. Franklin, Printer, 3300
  Cam Jansen and the First Day of School Mystery, 1908(F)
  Cam Jansen and the School Play Mystery, 1909(F)
  Dr. Martin Luther King, Jr., 3243
  A Hero and the Holocaust, 3613
  A Picture Book of Dwight David Eisenhower, 3372

A Picture Book of Lewis and Clark, 3082
  Young Cam Jansen and the Double Beach Mystery, 1729(F)
  Young Cam Jansen and the Library Mystery, 1730(F)
Adler, Naomi. *The Barefoot Book of Animal Tales*, 2742
Adoff, Arnold. *Black Is Brown Is Tan*, 1029(F)
  Daring Dog and Captain Cat, 421(F)
Agee, Jon. *Milo's Hat Trick*, 422(F)
  Palindromania! 3669
  Potch and Polly, 1224(F)
Agenbroad, Larry D. *Mammoths*, 3747
Ahlberg, Allan. *The Adventures of Bert*, 1167(F)
  A Bit More Bert, 1168(F)
  The Man Who Wore All His Clothes, 2587(F)
  Treasure Hunt, 136(F)
  The Woman Who Won Things, 2597(F)
Ahvander, Ingmarie. *Pancake Dreams*, 1264(F)
Aiken, Joan. *A Necklace of Raindrops*, 2071(F)
  Snow White and the Seven Dwarfs, 2811
Ajhar, Brian. *Rover Saves Christmas*, 2109(F)
Ajmera, Maya. *Back to School*, 3736
  Come Out and Play, 5576
  A Kid's Best Friend, 5132
Ake, Anne. *Austria*, 3950
Alagna, Magdalena. *Anne Frank*, 3605
Alakija, Polly. *Catch That Goat!* 1265(F)
Alarcon, Francisco X. *Iguanas in the Snow and Other Winter Poems / Iguanas en la Nieve y Otros Poemas de Invierno*, 3037
Alatalo, Jaakko. *A Child's Day in a Nordic Village*, 4001
Alborough, Jez. *Fix-It Duck*, 423(F)
Alcorn, Stephen. *Broken Feather*, 3034
  Home to Me, 2943
  Hoofbeats, Claws and Rippled Fins, 3001
Aldridge, Rebecca. *Thomas Jefferson*, 3379
Alex, Nan. *North Carolina*, 4320
Alexander, Lloyd. *The Gawgon and the Boy*, 2499(F)
  The Rope Trick, 2072(F)
Alexander, Martha. *We're in Big Trouble, Blackboard Bear*, 424(F)
Alexander, Pat. *My First Bible*, 4439
Aliki. *One Little Spoonful*, 876(F)
Allaby, Michael. *Tornadoes and Other Dramatic Weather Systems*, 5269
Allan, Tony. *The Irish Famine*, 3965

Gay, Marie-Louise. *Didi and Daddy on the Promenade*, 1129(F)
Good Morning, Sam, 1065(F)
Stella, Fairy of the Forest, 916(F)
Gay-Kassel, Doreen. *Food Fight!* 376(F)
Gayle, Sharon. *Harriet Tubman and the Freedom Train*, 3263
Gedatus, Gus. *Bicycling for Fitness*, 5639
Exercise for Weight Management, 4724
In-Line Skating for Fitness, 5591
Weight Training, 5592
Geehan, Wayne. *Sir Cumference and the Great Knight of Angleland*, 5247
Geis, Alissa Imre. *Winnie Dancing on Her Own*, 1789(F)
Geisert, Arthur. *The Giant Ball of String*, 569(F)
Nursery Crimes, 1713(F)
Prairie Summer, 2567(F)
Geisert, Bonnie. *Prairie Summer*, 2567(F)
Gellety, LeeAnne. *Harriet Beecher Stowe*, 3206
Gellman, Marc. *And God Cried, Too*, 4423
Bad Stuff in the News, 4411
Gentle, Victor. *Florida Cracker Horses*, 5143
Killer Sharks, Killer People, 5100
Wolves, 4930
Genzo, John Paul. *Islands of Ice*, 1455(F)
Geoghegan, Adrienne. *All Your Own Teeth*, 1189(F)
George, Charles (jt. author). *The Natchez Trace*, 4205
The Tuskegee Airmen, 3865
George, Jean Craighead. *Cliff Hanger*, 873(F)
Frightful's Daughter, 1439(F)
Nutik and Amaroq Play Ball, 1288(F)
Tree Castle Island, 1926(F)
George, Kristine O'Connell. *Book!* 917
Little Dog and Duncan, 3000
Swimming Upstream, 2935
Toasting Marshmallows, 2936
George, Linda. *The Natchez Trace*, 4205
The Tuskegee Airmen, 3865
George, Linda S. *World War I*, 3856
Geraghty, Paul. *Tortuga*, 1440(F)
Geras, Adele. *The Cats of Cuckoo Square*, 570(F)
My Wishes for You, 571(F)
Sleep Tight, Ginger Kitten, 1441(F)
Sleeping Beauty, 3726
Gerber, Carole. *Blizzard*, 918(F)
Gerber, Mary Jane. *House Calls*, 4670
Gershator, David. *Moon Rooster*, 572(F)
Gershator, Phillis (jt. author). *Moon Rooster*, 572(F)
Gerson, Mary-Joan. *Fiesta Feminina*, 2891
Gerstein, Mordicai. *A Hare-Raising Tail*, 1805(F)
The Principal's on the Roof, 2175(F)
What Charlie Heard, 3134
Gessat, Audrey. *Crafts from Salt Dough*, 5433
Ghiuselev, Iassen. *The Adventures of Pinocchio*, 2093(F)
Giarrusso, Veronique . *The Blue Pearls*, 2235(F)
Gibala-Broxholm, Scott. *Scary Fright, Are You All Right?* 1768(F)
Gibb, Chris. *The Dalai Lama*, 3599
Gibbon, Rebecca. *Outside the Lines*, 3047
Gibbons, Faye. *The Day the Picture Man Came*, 1190(F)
Emma Jo's Song, 1191(F)
Full Steam Ahead, 1565(F)
Hernando de Soto, 3071
Horace King, 3242
Gibbons, Gail. *Behold . . . the Unicorns!* 2901
The Berry Book, 5173
Giant Pandas, 4963

Halloween Is . . ., 4500
Polar Bears, 4911
Tell Me, Tree, 5183
Gibson, Karen Bush. *The Chickasaw Nation*, 4114
Jovita Idar, 3274
The Potawatomi, 4115
Giff, Patricia Reilly. *All the Way Home*, 2316(F)
Pictures of Hollis Woods, 2282(F)
Gifford, Clive. *How to Build a Robot*, 5366
How to Live on Mars, 4787
The Kingfisher Facts and Records Book of Space, 4776
The Kingfisher Young People's Book of Living Worlds, 4803
Gilbert, Adrian. *Going to War in World War I*, 3857
Gilchrist, Jan S. *Honey, I Love*, 2989
How They Got Over, 3223
Giles, Bridget. *Kenya*, 3885
Gilgannon, Denise. *The U.S. Constitution and You*, 4378
Gill, Shelley. *The Egg*, 4885
Gill-Brown, Vanessa. *Rufferella*, 1192(F)
Gilles, Almira Astudillo. *Willie Wins*, 1066(F)
Gilles-Sebaoun, Elisabeth. *A Young Child's Bible*, 4442
Gillies, Judi. *The Jumbo Vegetarian Cookbook*, 4725
Gilman, Laura Anne. *Coping with Cerebral Palsy*, 4639
Yeti, the Abominable Snowman, 5570
Gilmore, Rachna. *A Gift for Gita*, 1067(F)
Gilson, Jamie. *Stink Alley*, 2387(F)
Ginsburg, Max. *Lisette's Angel*, 2572(F)
Gioffre, Rosalba. *The Young Chef's French Cookbook*, 5525
The Young Chef's Italian Cookbook, 5526
Giraudon, David. *Earth from Above for Young Readers*, 3633
Girnis, Meg. *1, 2, 3 for You and Me*, 106(F)
Girod, Christina M. *Connecticut*, 4157
Georgia, 4158
South Carolina, 4159
Glaser, Linda. *It's Fall!* 4796(F)
It's Spring, 1245(F)
Glass, Andrew. *The Bourbon Street Musicians*, 2819
The Erie Canal Pirates, 306(F)
Mountain Men, 4206
Glasser, Robin P. *Taking Care of Trouble*, 1883(F)
Glassman, Miriam. *Halloweena*, 1672(F)
Gliori, Debi. *Can I Have a Hug?* 573(F)
Debi Gliori's Bedtime Stories, 165
The Dorling Kindersley Book of Nursery Rhymes, 196
Flora's Blanket, 574(F)
Flora's Surprise! 575(F)
Penguin Post, 576(F)
Polar Bolero, 166(F)
Pure Dead Magic, 2120(F)
Pure Dead Wicked, 2121(F)
Tell Me What It's Like to Be Big, 536(F)
Glossop, Jennifer (jt. author). *The Jumbo Vegetarian Cookbook*, 4725
Gnojewski, Carol. *Cinco de Mayo*, 4465
Martin Luther King, Jr., Day, 4466
Goble, Paul. *Storm Maker's Tipi*, 2878
Goddell, Jon. *The Alley Cat's Meow*, 431(F)
Godkin, Celia. *Jack*, 2001(F)
When the Giant Stirred, 1246(F)
Godon, Ingrid. *One Beautiful Baby*, 121(F)
Godwin, Laura. *The Best Fall of All*, 577(F)
Central Park Serenade, 919(F)
Happy Christmas, Honey! 1609(F)
What the Baby Hears, 1442(F)

Title Index

This index contains both main entry and internal titles cited in the entries. References are to entry numbers, not page numbers. Fiction titles are indicated by (F) following the entry number.

Subject/Grade Level Index

All entries are listed by subject and then according to grade level suitability (see the key at the foot of pages for grade level designations). Subjects are arranged alphabetically and subject heads may be subdivided into nonfiction (e.g., "Trucks") and fiction (e.g., "Trucks — Fiction"). References to entries are by entry number, not page number.

A

Aardvarks — Fiction
P: 1646

Abdul-Jabbar, Kareem
IJ: 3539

Abilities
P: 4567

Abolitionists — Biography
I: 3286

Abolitionists — Fiction
PI: 2473 I: 2472

Aborigines (Australia)
IJ: 3945, 3948

Aborigines (Australia) — Fiction
P: 1314

Acadia — Fiction
I: 2423

Accidents
P: 4736 I: 4735

Accidents — Fiction
P: 1001, 1116 I: 2349
IJ: 2273

Acting
IJ: 3733

Acting — Fiction
PI: 1751

Activism — Fiction
I: 2002

Actors and actresses — Biography
PI: 3161 IJ: 3135,
3142–43, 3146, 3156, 3199

Actors and actresses — Fiction
IJ: 1878

Adams, Abigail
IJ: 3403–4

Adams, John
PI: 4180 I: 3359 IJ: 3358

Adams, John Quincy
IJ: 3360

Adams, John Quincy — Fiction
I: 2446

Addams, Jane
PI: 3405 IJ: 4275

Addition
IJ: 5235

Adoption — Fiction
P: 526, 705, 1054, 1080,
1111, 1124, 1145 PI: 1047
I: 2269, 2297 IJ: 2041,
2308

Adventure stories
See also Mystery stories;
Survival stories
P: 872–74, 1289, 1748
PI: 1408 I: 1921, 1932,
1950–51, 1953–55, 2203,
2383, 2429, 2442, 3739
IJ: 1906, 1911–12, 1919,
1923, 1926, 1929–30,
1933–34, 1937, 1940, 1942,
1944, 1957–58, 1968, 2074,
2148, 2242, 2361, 2405,
2408, 2431–32, 2444, 2453,
2461, 2470, 2479, 2481,
2488, 2515, 2538, 2541–42,
2551, 2563, 2629

Adventurers and explorers
I: 3802, 4206 IJ: 3803,
4012, 4149, 4304

Adventurers and explorers — Biography
PI: 3076, 3082 I: 3058,
3060–61, 3065, 3067, 3071,
3075, 3083, 3087, 3089–90,
4144 IJ: 3054, 3057, 3059,
3064, 3073, 3078, 3080,
3084–86, 4147–48

Advertising
IJ: 4762

Aerial sports
I: 5580

Aeronautics
See also Airplanes
IJ: 5334

Aeronautics — History
I: 5345

Afghanistan — Fiction
IJ: 2371

Africa — Animals
P: 4827

Africa — Cookbooks
IJ: 5537

Africa — Fiction
P: 1251, 1316, 2364
PI: 2367 IJ: 1937

Africa — Folklore
P: 2770–73, 2779 PI: 2778
IJ: 2768

Africa — History
PI: 3805 I: 3812

Africa — Peoples
IJ: 3887

Africa, West — Fiction
P: 903 IJ: 2365

Africa, West — History
I: 3809

African Americans
See also Africa; Civil
rights; Civil War (U.S.);
Kwanzaa; Slavery; and
names of individuals,
e.g., Robinson, Jackie
P: 937, 4538 IJ: 2417,
4230, 4522

African Americans — Armed forces
IJ: 3219

African Americans — Biography
P: 3137, 3139, 3144, 3241,
3243–44, 3254, 3261, 3535
PI: 3062, 3079, 3161,
3181–83, 3212, 3233, 3235,
3239, 3246–47, 3255, 3257,
3260, 3267, 3454, 3543,
3547, 3549, 3552–55, 3558,
3567, 3571, 3574 I: 3133,
3136, 3138, 3145, 3175,
3187–89, 3206, 3211, 3223,
3236, 3238, 3248, 3251,
3253, 3259, 3262, 3264,
3266, 3268, 3446, 3462,
3534, 3550, 3561 IJ: 3063,
3094, 3109, 3151–52, 3169,
3199, 3216, 3219, 3224,
3228, 3234, 3237, 3240,
3242, 3245, 3250, 3252,
3256, 3258, 3265, 3285,
3527–29, 3531–32, 3539,
3545–46, 3566, 3570, 3572

African Americans — Fiction
P: 896, 930, 932, 964, 1009,
1053, 1081, 1083, 1295–96,
1334, 1346, 1352, 1358,
1376, 1582, 1740, 1830,
1868–69 PI: 2210, 2574,
2642 I: 1902, 2441, 2566
IJ: 2027, 2295, 2301, 2544,
2585

African Americans — Folklore
PI: 2778

African Americans — History
PI: 4419 I: 3865, 4197,
4371–72 IJ: 3698, 3866,
4430

P = Primary; PI = Primary-Intermediate; I = Intermediate; IJ = Intermediate-Junior High

P = Primary; PI = Primary-Intermediate; I = Intermediate; IJ = Intermediate-Junior High

P = Primary; PI = Primary-Intermediate; I = Intermediate; IJ = Intermediate-Junior High

P = Primary; PI = Primary-Intermediate; I = Intermediate; IJ = Intermediate-Junior High

P = Primary; PI = Primary-Intermediate; I = Intermediate; IJ = Intermediate-Junior High

P = Primary; PI = Primary-Intermediate; I = Intermediate; IJ = Intermediate-Junior High

P = Primary; PI = Primary-Intermediate; I = Intermediate; IJ = Intermediate-Junior High

P = Primary; PI = Primary-Intermediate; I = Intermediate; IJ = Intermediate-Junior High

P = Primary; PI = Primary-Intermediate; I = Intermediate; IJ = Intermediate-Junior High

P = Primary; PI = Primary-Intermediate; I = Intermediate; IJ = Intermediate-Junior High

P = Primary; PI = Primary-Intermediate; I = Intermediate; IJ = Intermediate-Junior High

Flag Day
P: 4463

Flags
I: 3660 IJ: 4091

Flags (U.S.)
IJ: 3659

Flags (U.S.) — Biography
PI: 3431

Flamingos
P: 4980

Flatulence — Fiction
P: 1463

Fleming, Alexander
IJ: 3474–76

Flight
I: 5338

Flight — History
IJ: 5337

Floods
P: 4280

Floods — Fiction
I: 1902

Floods — Folklore
P: 2897

Florence, Italy
IJ: 3854

Florida
I: 4320 IJ: 4224

Florida — History
IJ: 4147

Flowers
IJ: 4091, 5156

Flowers — Folklore
P: 2755

Folk songs
P: 3701 PI: 3699

Folk songs — Fiction
P: 1199

Folklore
See also specific countries
and regions, e.g.,
Germany — Folklore;
and specific topics, e.g.,
Cats — Folklore
P: 2745, 2749, 2753,
2755–56, 2761–62,
2765–66, 2769–73,
2775–77, 2779–81,
2783–84, 2790, 2793–96,
2798–99, 2801, 2804,
2806–9, 2812–14, 2816–18,
2820–21, 2823, 2825–28,
2830–33, 2835–36, 2841,
2844, 2849–53, 2855–62,
2865, 2867–68, 2870–71,
2875–76, 2879–80,
2887–88, 2890, 2892–94,
2896–98 PI: 2742–43,
2752, 2767, 2778, 2788,
2791, 2797, 2810, 2815,
2829, 2842, 2846, 2869,
2873, 2884–86, 2889, 2895
I: 2744, 2746–48, 2757–58,

2763, 2782, 2785, 2787,
2789, 2792, 2800, 2802,
2805, 2819, 2822, 2824,
2837–38, 2847–48, 2863,
2866, 2874, 2877, 2883,
4056 IJ: 2754, 2764, 2768,
2774, 2786, 2840, 2864,
2872, 2881–82, 2891

Folklore — Anthologies
P: 2750, 2759 I: 2760
IJ: 2751, 2803

Food
P: 5172 PI: 5159
IJ: 4647, 5157–58

Food — Fiction
P: 418, 982, 1275, 1351,
2663 I: 2047

Food — Poetry
P: 3020

Food chains
PI: 5060

Food supply
IJ: 4355

Football
I: 5644–47 IJ: 5350

Football — Biography
PI: 3567–68, 3571
IJ: 3524, 3565–66, 3569–70

Football — Fiction
P: 1206

Ford, Gerald R.
I: 3374

Ford, Henry
P: 3477 IJ: 3478

Forensics
IJ: 4385, 4390, 4591

Forest fires
I: 4609

Forests
See also Rain forests
IJ: 4345, 5216

Fortune telling — Fiction
I: 1894

Fossey, Dian
I: 3479 IJ: 3480

Fossils
See also Paleontology
PI: 3757, 3775 I: 3750,
3762, 3766 IJ: 3759, 3763

Fossils — Fiction
IJ: 1889

Foster care — Fiction
P: 1395 IJ: 2052, 2282,
2298

Foster homes — Fiction
I: 2506 IJ: 2018, 2043

Fox, Vicente
IJ: 3604

Foxes
P: 4935 IJ: 4931

Foxes — Fiction
I: 1992

Fractions
IJ: 5235

Frames
I: 5453

France
I: 3961, 3963 IJ: 3960

France — Cookbooks
IJ: 5525

France — Fiction
I: 2318 IJ: 2244, 2382,
2385, 2391

France — Folklore
P: 2711, 2806–9 PI: 2810

France — History
P: 3611

**France — History —
Fiction**
PI: 2572

**Francis of Assisi, Saint —
Fiction**
PI: 4418

Frank, Anne
I: 3606 IJ: 3605

Franklin, Benjamin
P: 3302 PI: 3303–4
I: 3301 IJ: 3300, 3305

**Franklin, Benjamin —
Fiction**
P: 1828 IJ: 2130

Franklin, Rosalind
IJ: 3481

Fraser, James Earle
PI: 3653

Freedom of speech
I: 4368

French Americans
I: 4543

**French and Indian War
— Biography**
IJ: 3331

**French and Indian War
— Fiction**
IJ: 2351, 2421

**French language —
Fiction**
P: 1511

French Revolution
IJ: 3962

Friendship
P: 4560, 4572 IJ: 4556

**Friendship stories —
Fiction**
P: 479, 531, 537, 547, 594,
638, 657, 755, 799, 802,
846, 1147–50, 1152–55,
1157–62, 1165, 1391, 1430,
1473, 1534, 1739, 1755,
1789, 1814, 1839, 2252
PI: 1156, 1390, 1559, 1717,
1771, 1786, 1791, 2013,

2243, 2247, 2250, 2257,
2701 I: 1892, 2019, 2057,
2144, 2245–46, 2253,
2255–56, 2259, 2265, 2316,
2331, 2343–44, 2559, 2566,
2657 IJ: 1888, 2058, 2242,
2244, 2248–49, 2254, 2258,
2260–61, 2263–64, 2274,
2329, 2339, 2505, 2546,
2580, 2652

**Friendship stories —
Poetry**
P: 2990

Frogs and toads
P: 4842, 5126 PI: 4839–40
I: 4841, 4843

Frogs and toads — Fiction
P: 1423, 1494, 1794
PI: 1425

Frontier life (U.S.)
I: 4204–6, 4208–9, 4214
IJ: 4203, 4207, 4212–13

**Frontier life (U.S.) —
Biography**
PI: 3068–69, 3276 I: 3058
IJ: 3057, 3416

**Frontier life (U.S.) —
Fiction**
P: 1297, 1302, 1657
PI: 2460, 2471, 2473
I: 2468, 2472, 2475–77,
2487, 2533 IJ: 2461, 2464,
2469–70, 2481, 2486

Fruit
P: 5173, 5175

Funerals — Fiction
I: 2601

Fungi
IJ: 5180

G

Galapagos Islands
IJ: 4079

Galileo
I: 3482

Games
See also Picture puzzles;
Puzzles; Sports; Word
games and puzzles
P: 5472, 5596 PI: 5615
I: 5430, 5444, 5594, 5597
IJ: 5586

Games — Fiction
P: 397, 935

Games — Outdoor
I: 5614

Gandhi, Mahatma
I: 3607–8 IJ: 3609

Gangs
IJ: 4386

P = Primary; PI = Primary-Intermediate; I = Intermediate; IJ = Intermediate-Junior High

P = Primary; PI = Primary-Intermediate; I = Intermediate; IJ = Intermediate-Junior High

P = Primary; PI = Primary-Intermediate; I = Intermediate; IJ = Intermediate-Junior High

P = Primary; PI = Primary-Intermediate; I = Intermediate; IJ = Intermediate-Junior High

India — Folklore
P: 2793 PI: 2791 I: 2792

India — History
I: 3813

India — History — Fiction
IJ: 2370

India — Holidays
P: 4464

Indian Americans — Fiction
P: 1067

Indians of Central America — History
IJ: 3799

Indonesia
IJ: 3940, 3944

Indus Valley
I: 3813

Influenza epidemic, 1918 — Fiction
P: 1335

Ingles, Mary Draper
IJ: 3416

Inline skating
I: 5584 IJ: 5587, 5591

Insects
See also names of specific insects, e.g., Butterflies
P: 4814, 5017, 5023, 5029, 5031, 5034, 5040–41
PI: 5020, 5047, 5050
I: 3754, 5018, 5021, 5024–25, 5028, 5030, 5033, 5038, 5042, 5044 IJ: 5022, 5026, 5037, 5051

Insects — Fiction
P: 1410, 1475, 1783

Integration — Fiction
P: 1346

Interactive books
P: 63, 212, 355, 377, 506, 608, 778, 885, 1017, 1644, 1696

Interactive books — Fiction
P: 380, 483, 658

Internet (computers)
PI: 5365 I: 5371 IJ: 3450, 5367, 5369–70, 5372, 5374

Interracial families — Fiction
P: 1029

Inuit
See also Alaska; Arctic; Polar regions
I: 4085 IJ: 4082

Inuit — Crafts
PI: 3652

Inuit — Fiction
P: 1288 I: 2415, 2525

Inuit — Folklore
P: 2871 IJ: 2872

Inventors and inventions
See also Scientists; and specific inventions, e.g., Telephones
PI: 5322 I: 2971, 5330, 5332 IJ: 4668, 4754, 5364, 5373

Inventors and inventions — Biography
P: 3448–49, 3464, 3477, 3495, 3515, 3519 PI: 3303, 3493 I: 3453, 3488, 3517, 3520–21 IJ: 3101, 3478, 3518

Inventors and inventions — Fiction
P: 746

Invertebrates
See also Animals; Insects; etc.
I: 4954–55, 5069, 5085

Investing (business)
IJ: 4340

Iowa
IJ: 4271, 4279

Iran
See also Persia
IJ: 4029

Iran — Biography
IJ: 3619

Iraq — Biography
IJ: 3610

Ireland
PI: 3975 I: 3969, 3980 IJ: 3967

Ireland — Fiction
P: 1292 I: 2403 IJ: 2178

Ireland — Folklore
P: 1429, 2828, 2834–35, 2839 I: 2824, 2838

Ireland — History
IJ: 3965, 3972

Ireland, Northern
PI: 3981 IJ: 3973

Irish Americans
I: 4523, 4541

Irish Americans — Fiction
PI: 1578 IJ: 2452

Irvin, Monte
IJ: 3529

Islam
I: 4428, 4432 IJ: 4438

Islam — Biography
I: 3616

Islam — Folklore
P: 2867

Islam — History
IJ: 3624

Islands
See also Caribbean Islands; and specific islands, e.g., Cuba
I: 5206

Islands — Fiction
I: 2003

Israel
PI: 4025 I: 4023 IJ: 4024

Israel — Biography
IJ: 3590

Italian Americans
I: 4528, 4550

Italian Americans — Fiction
PI: 1541 IJ: 2522

Italian Americans — Poetry
IJ: 2978

Italy
P: 3684 IJ: 3854, 3985–86

Italy — Cookbooks
IJ: 5521, 5526

Italy — Fiction
IJ: 2115

Italy — History
IJ: 3636, 3855

Ives, Charles
I: 3134

J

Jackals
PI: 4930

Jacks (game)
I: 5597

Jackson, Andrew
IJ: 3377–78

Jackson, Joe ("Shoeless") — Fiction
PI: 1268

Jackson, Mahalia
IJ: 3240

Jackson, Michael
IJ: 3151

Jackson, Stonewall
IJ: 3312

Jaguars
PI: 4923

Jamaica — Fiction
IJ: 2029

Jamestown Colony
I: 4169

Jamestown Colony — Fiction
I: 2424 IJ: 2426

Japan
P: 3928 I: 3922–23, 3925, 5534 IJ: 3924, 3927

Japan — Crafts
I: 5473

Japan — Fiction
P: 345, 1267, 1300 IJ: 2374

Japan — Folklore
P: 2794–96

Japan — History
I: 3796 IJ: 3926

Japan — Mythology
IJ: 2902

Japanese Americans
I: 4534, 4552 IJ: 3881

Japanese Americans — Fiction
P: 842, 1322 I: 2002

Japanese Americans — History
IJ: 3864

Japanese language
I: 3662

Japanese language — Fiction
P: 485

Jarvik, Robert
I: 3492

Jay, John
I: 3313

Jazz — Biography
P: 3139, 3144 I: 3133, 3138

Jazz — Fiction
P: 31, 431, 993, 1021, 1051, 1286, 1301, 1320 PI: 1272

Jazz — History
IJ: 3698

Jefferson, Thomas
PI: 3381 I: 3379 IJ: 3380

Jefferson, Thomas — Fiction
IJ: 2436

Jellyfish
P: 5067 I: 5068

Jemison, Mae
PI: 3079

Jerusalem — Fiction
P: 1276

Jesus Christ
IJ: 4431, 4444

Jewelry
IJ: 5357

Jewelry making
PI: 5471 IJ: 5479

Jewish Americans
P: 4535 I: 4531 IJ: 4532

Jewish Americans — Fiction
PI: 1109 I: 2526

P = Primary; PI = Primary-Intermediate; I = Intermediate; IJ = Intermediate-Junior High

Jewish holy days
See also specific holy days, e.g., Hanukkah
I: 4503

Jewish holy days — Fiction
P: 1694, 1698, 1700, 1705, 1707

Jews — Fiction
P: 1126, 1276 **I:** 2389, 2594 **IJ:** 2043, 2409, 2495

Jews — Folklore
P: 2861–62, 2865 **I:** 2863

Jews — History
See also Holocaust; Immigration (U.S.); World War II
IJ: 4026, 4026, 4437, 4440

Jews — History — Fiction
I: 2589

Jews — Plays
I: 3734

Joan of Arc
P: 3611

Jobs, Steve
IJ: 3314

John J. Harvey (fireboat)
PI: 5420

John Paul II, Pope
IJ: 4426

Johnson, Andrew
IJ: 3382

Johnson, Judy
IJ: 3530

Johnson, Lyndon B.
IJ: 3383–84

Johnson, Magic
I: 3550

Johnson, Mamie "Peanut"
IJ: 3531

Johnston, Joseph E.
I: 3315

Jokes and riddles
P: 6, 1611, 1697, 1772, 5551–52, 5554 **PI:** 2928 **IJ:** 5556

Jones, John Paul
IJ: 3316–17

Jordan (country)
IJ: 4034

Joseph, Chief
I: 3347

Journals
See also Diaries
P: 3684

Journals — Fiction
I: 1882, 2468

Juana Ines de la Cruz, Sister
P: 3612

Judaism
See also Jews; Jews — History; Religion
I: 4435 **IJ:** 4437

Juggling
I: 5598

July Fourth
I: 4472

July Fourth — Fiction
P: 1574, 1581 **PI:** 1580

Juneteenth
IJ: 4485

Jungles — Fiction
PI: 2412

Junkyards — Fiction
P: 403

Jupiter (planet)
I: 4789 **IJ:** 4788

Jury system
PI: 4358

Justice — Fiction
IJ: 1939 **I:** 3107

K

Kahlo, Frida
P: 3106 **I:** 3107

Kaiulani, Princess of Hawaii — Fiction
IJ: 2555

Kalahari Desert
I: 3895

Kangaroos
P: 4861, 4957 **PI:** 4959 **IJ:** 4960

Kansas — Fiction
PI: 2473, 2482 **I:** 2472 **IJ:** 2498

Kansas — History
I: 2476

Karts and karting
IJ: 5608

Katydids
I: 5028

Kehret, Peg
IJ: 3184

Keller, Helen
P: 3417 **PI:** 3421 **I:** 3419–20 **IJ:** 3418

Kelp forests
P: 5062

Kennedy, John F.
IJ: 3385

Kennedy, Robert F.
IJ: 4383

Kentucky
I: 4320

Kentucky — Fiction
IJ: 2438, 2561

Kenya
IJ: 3884–86

Key, Francis Scott
P: 3714

Kidd, Jason
PI: 3551

Kidnapping — Fiction
I: 1945

Killer whales
P: 5114 **I:** 5115

Kindergarten — Fiction
P: 563, 1538, 1551

King, Coretta Scott
P: 3241

King, Horace
IJ: 3242

King, Martin Luther, Jr.
P: 3243–44 **PI:** 3246–47, 3249 **I:** 3248 **IJ:** 3245, 4383
See also Martin Luther King Day

King Richard I
IJ: 3851

Kings — Biography
IJ: 3584

Kings — Fiction
IJ: 2365

Kisses — Fiction
P: 497, 675

Kites — Fiction
P: 416, 1099, 1287

Klee, Paul
IJ: 3108

Knight, Margaret
PI: 3493

Knights — Folklore
IJ: 2751

Knitting
I: 5514

Knot tying
I: 5520

Koalas
PI: 4956, 4958, 4962

Kolff, Willem
IJ: 3494

Komodo dragons
I: 4845

Korczak, Janusz
I: 3613

Korea — Fiction
P: 1328–29 **I:** 2373 **IJ:** 2376–77

Korea — Folklore
P: 2783–84

Korea — History — Fiction
P: 1284

Korean Americans — Fiction
P: 1328, 1521

Korean War
IJ: 3800

Korean War Veterans Memorial
IJ: 4287

Ku Klux Klan
IJ: 4412

Ku Klux Klan — Fiction
IJ: 2524

Kurds
I: 3907

Kwan, Michelle
I: 3564

Kwanzaa
P: 4480

L

Labor movements — Fiction
P: 894

Labor unions — Fiction
I: 2540

Labrador — Fiction
P: 1097

Lacrosse
IJ: 5588

LaDuke, Winona
IJ: 3348

Ladybugs
P: 5043 **I:** 5044

Lafayette, Marquis de
IJ: 3614

Laffite, Jean — Fiction
P: 269

Lakes
IJ: 5223

Lamarr, Hedy
P: 3495

Lambs — Fiction
I: 1991

Landslides
I: 5196

Language and languages
See also Dictionaries; Spanish language — Fiction; Word books
P: 3661

Language and languages — Fiction
PI: 1109

La NiÒa (weather)
IJ: 5282

Laos — Folklore
PI: 2797

P = Primary; PI = Primary-Intermediate; I = Intermediate; IJ = Intermediate-Junior High

P = Primary; PI = Primary-Intermediate; I = Intermediate; IJ = Intermediate-Junior High

P = Primary; PI = Primary-Intermediate; I = Intermediate; IJ = Intermediate-Junior High

N

P = Primary; PI = Primary-Intermediate; I = Intermediate; IJ = Intermediate-Junior High

P = Primary; PI = Primary-Intermediate; I = Intermediate; IJ = Intermediate-Junior High

P = Primary; PI = Primary-Intermediate; I = Intermediate; IJ = Intermediate-Junior High

P = Primary; PI = Primary-Intermediate; I = Intermediate; IJ = Intermediate-Junior High

P = Primary; PI = Primary-Intermediate; I = Intermediate; IJ = Intermediate-Junior High

P = Primary; PI = Primary-Intermediate; I = Intermediate; IJ = Intermediate-Junior High

P = Primary; PI = Primary-Intermediate; I = Intermediate; IJ = Intermediate-Junior High

P = Primary; PI = Primary-Intermediate; I = Intermediate; IJ = Intermediate-Junior High

P = Primary; PI = Primary-Intermediate; I = Intermediate; IJ = Intermediate-Junior High

P = Primary; PI = Primary-Intermediate; I = Intermediate; IJ = Intermediate-Junior High

P = Primary; PI = Primary-Intermediate; I = Intermediate; IJ = Intermediate-Junior High

P = Primary; PI = Primary-Intermediate; I = Intermediate; IJ = Intermediate-Junior High

Women — Sports
IJ: 5601, 5610, 5675, 5682

Women's rights
I: 3406 IJ: 3412, 4369

Women's rights — Biography
P: 3433 PI: 3407 IJ: 3434

Women's rights — Fiction
IJ: 2519

Wood and wood products
P: 5328 PI: 5320

Wood carving — Fiction
I: 2410

Woods, Tiger
I: 3581 IJ: 3580

Woodson, Carter G.
PI: 3268

Woodwinds (musical instrument)
PI: 3711

Wool
P: 5359

Woolly mammoths
P: 3770 I: 3756

Word books
P: 24, 43, 400, 736, 3670, 3677, 3748, 4811, 5281 PI: 3675 IJ: 3674

Word books — Fiction
P: 1337

Word games and puzzles
P: 5564 IJ: 3674, 5556, 5563

Words
IJ: 3676, 3678

Words — Fiction
P: 879

Work — Fiction
PI: 2021

World history
IJ: 3811

World Trade Center
See September 11, 2001

World War I
I: 3857 IJ: 3800, 3856, 3858–61, 4252

World War I — Fiction
PI: 2384, 2529 IJ: 2390, 2406

World War II
See also specific topics, e.g., Holocaust
P: 3495 PI: 3867 I: 3865, 3872, 3880 IJ: 2560, 3800, 3862–64, 3866, 3869, 3873–75, 3878, 3881, 4247, 4251

World War II — Biography
IJ: 3219, 3319, 3605

World War II — Fiction
P: 1295, 1322 PI: 2572 I: 2357, 2381, 2389, 2570–71 IJ: 2558, 2564, 2568–69, 2576, 2582

World Wide Web
IJ: 3450, 5367–68, 5374

World Wide Web — Fiction
IJ: 2161

World Wildlife Fund
I: 4350

World's Columbian Exposition — Fiction
I: 2532

Wozniak, Stephen
IJ: 3516

Wrestling — Biography
IJ: 3340–41

Wright, Frank Lloyd
IJ: 3129

Wright, Wilbur and Orville
P: 3519 I: 3051, 3517, 3520–21, 5335 IJ: 3518

Wright, Wilbur and Orville — Fiction
IJ: 2507

Writers — Biography
P: 3197, 3204, 3209 PI: 3173, 3177, 3181–83, 3194, 3205, 3207, 3212–13 I: 3175, 3186–89, 3191, 3198, 3200, 3206 IJ: 3170–71, 3174, 3176, 3180, 3190, 3192, 3195–96, 3201–2, 3208, 3210, 3348, 3326

Writers — Children's literature
IJ: 3184

Writing
P: 3663 IJ: 3681, 3685

Writing — Fiction
I: 2141 IJ: 1880, 2254

X

X-rays
PI: 4667

X-rays — Biography
I: 3506

Xerography — Biography
I: 3452

Xiaoping, Deng
IJ: 3631

Y

Yahoo! (computers) — Biography
IJ: 3441

Yang, Jerry
IJ: 3441

Yangtze River
PI: 3914

Yanomami
I: 4080

Yao (African people) — Fiction
PI: 2367

Yellow fever
IJ: 4635

Yeti
See also Big Foot
I: 5570

Yo-yos
I: 5577, 5599, 5606

Yoga
PI: 4721

Yolen, Jane
PI: 3213

Yukon — Fiction
P: 1226

Z

Zambia — Folklore
P: 2765

Zebras
P: 4890, 4900 PI: 4891 I: 4888

Zimbabwe
IJ: 3896

Zoos
IJ: 5154

Zoos — Fiction
P: 1589 IJ: 2274

P = Primary; PI = Primary-Intermediate; I = Intermediate; IJ = Intermediate-Junior High

About the Authors

JOHN T. GILLESPIE, renowned authority in children's literature, is the author of more than 30 books on collection development. In addition to the previous editions of *Best Books for Children*, other volumes include *Best Books for Young Teen Readers*, *Best Books for Junior High Readers*, and *Best Books for Senior High Readers*. He is also the author of the Middlelots, Juniorplots, Teenplots, and Seniorplots Book Talk Guides as well as *The Newbery Companion: Booktalk and Related Materials for Newbery Medal and Honor Books*.

CATHERINE BARR is the coauthor of *High/Low Handbook: Best Books and Web Sites for Reluctant Teen Readers, 4th Edition,* and editor of *From Biography to History: Best Books for Children's Education and Entertainment* and *Reading in Series: A Selection Guide to Books for Children*.